DEDICATION

W9-AYQ-461

In honor of the past:

Georgetta and Raymond Ojanen; Anthony N. Bernardo

In gratitude of the present:

The dedicated nurses we work with every day, Bruce M. Thomas;
C. Richard Packer

In hope for the future:

Kseniya, Billy and Danny Thomas; Rachael and Kailey Brady; Kalen, Tara
and Samantha Bailey

Core Curriculum for Pediatric Emergency Nursing

Second edition

EMERGENCY NURSES ASSOCIATION
SAFE PRACTICE, SAFE CARE

Printed in the United States of America

ISBN 0-9798307-3-7

ISBN 13 978-0-9798307-3-0

Copyright © 2009 by the Emergency Nurses Association (ENA)

Web site: www.ena.org
E-mail: education@ena.org

PREFACE

Children and adolescents use emergency services for a variety of injury and illness related complaints. Pediatric patients represent more than one third of all ED visits. With a lack of access to affordable health care, coupled with decreasing health care reimbursement and a sagging economy, children arriving in the emergency department have higher levels of acuity and more complex health care needs. Furthermore, children with congenital or acquired chronic health conditions are living longer, requiring technology for everyday living. Therefore, emergency nurses must have a core knowledge base of the psychosocial and physiologic considerations in pediatric emergency care to guide their practice.

The *Core Curriculum for Pediatric Emergency Nursing* (second edition) is a supplement for those nurses who desire comprehensive content on pediatric emergency nursing. The curriculum represents another landmark in the evolution of pediatric emergency nursing as a specialty within the Emergency Nurses Association (ENA). In 1991, the ENA convened the first pediatric committee, which was charged with charting a course for the development of pediatric-related projects within the organization. This group was the impetus for other projects, such as the EMSC/ENA Collaborative Curriculum

The need for pediatric-specific knowledge intensified, and subsequently the Pediatric Committee was acknowledged as a standing committee. In 1993, the *Emergency Nursing Pediatric Course* (ENPC) was developed and tested; it is now in its third edition. This course is offered nationally and internationally. Over the years, numerous pediatric-specific resolutions, policy statements and guidelines have been created and disseminated. Pediatric-specific content was strengthened in existing ENA-created courses and authored texts. Additional texts, such as the Comprehensive Care of the Pediatric Patient, demonstrated the ENA's leadership in the care of children throughout the continuum of health care.

This Core Curriculum evolved from a resolution approved 13 years ago, at the 1996 General Assembly, which charged the ENA with developing a pediatric certification in emergency nursing examination. In 2008, the Certified Pediatric Emergency Nurse (CPEN) credential became a reality. A core curriculum provides the necessary theoretical and practical knowledge required for creating and administering such an examination. This book represents the continued dedication to the emergency nursing care of children as professed by the ENA.

The second edition of the Core Curriculum is based on the best evidence available in pediatric emergency care. Current references from the literature, governmental databases and professional websites underscore the importance of integrating theory and practice when developing such a text. This Core Curriculum was written to serve as a timely reference for emergency nurses as they care for ill and injured infants, children and adolescents. Emergency nurses should follow their state's Nurse Practice Act, as well as their emergency department's policies and procedures, when utilizing the resources in this book.

Acknowledgements

To the Emergency Nurses Association for their leadership, vision and endless support:

David Westman
Executive Director

Donna Massey, RN, MSN
Nursing Profession Advancement Officer

Dawn Freiberg, RN, BSN, MBA, CEN
Senior Nursing Editor

Michele Konnick, RN, MS, CEN, CCRN
Nursing Editor

Jennifer Lucas
Editorial Project Coordinator

Lynn Romey
Developmental Editor

Beth Bernardi
Marketing Officer

Lauri Grzelak
Cover Designer & Senior Graphic Designer

Kevin Campbell
Indexer

Editors

Lisa Marie Bernardo, PhD, MPH, RN
Associate Professor
University of Pittsburgh School of Nursing
Pittsburg, PA

Donna Ojanen Thomas, RN, MSN
Director, Emergency Department and Rapid Treatment Unit
Primary Children's Medical Center
Salt Lake City, UT

Contributors

Susan Barbarossa, CRNP
Neonatal Nurse Practitioner
Western Pennsylvania Hospital
Pittsburgh, PA

Michael Beach, DNP, ACNP-BC, PNP
Assistant Professor
University of Pittsburgh School of Nursing
Pittsburgh, PA

Lisa Marie Bernardo, PhD, MPH, RN
Associate Professor
University of Pittsburgh School of Nursing
Pittsburg, PA

Sue M. Cadwell, RN, MSN, CNA-BC
Director, ED Initiative
HCA
Nashville, TN

Kathleen Campbell, RN, MSN, CRNP, NNP-BC
Neonatal Nurse Practitioner
Western Pennsylvania Hospital
Pittsburgh, PA

Catherine E. Campese, RN, MSN, CRNP
Nurse Practitioner
Children's Hospital of Pittsburgh of the
University of Pittsburgh Medical Center
Pittsburgh, PA

Christine B. Cassesse, MSN, FNP-BC, FPMHNP-BC
Faculty
University of Pittsburgh School of Nursing
Pittsburgh, PA

Mary Jo Cerepani, RN, MSN, CRNP, CEN
Emergency Nurse Practitioner
University of Pittsburgh Medical Center
Emergency Resource Management, Inc.
Pittsburgh, PA

Alice E. Conway, PhD, CRNP, FNP-BC
Professor
Edinboro University of Pennsylvania
Edinboro, PA

Steven J. Dasta, RN, BSN
Registered Nurse
Women & Children's Hospital of Buffalo
Buffalo, NY

Nancy J. Denke, RN, MSN, FNP-C, CCRN
Trauma Nurse Practitioner
Scottsdale Healthcare-Osborn
Scottsdale, AZ

Phyllis Maria Flavin, RN, BSN
IV Team RN
University of Pittsburgh Medical Center/Jefferson Regional Home Health, LP
Graduate Student, University of Pittsburgh School of Nursing
Pittsburgh, PA

Kathryn J. Haley, RN, BSN
Trauma Program Director
Nationwide Children's Hospital
Columbus, OH

Margaret S. Hannan, PhD, RN, CPNP-BC
Assistant Professor
University of Pittsburgh School of Nursing
Pittsburgh, PA

Shauna Hansen, APRN
Trauma Charge Nurse
Primary Children's Medical Center
Salt Lake City, UT

Susan McDaniel Hohenhaus, RN, MA, FAEN
President
Hohenhaus & Associates, Inc.
Wellsboro, PA

Reneé Semonin Holleran, RN, PhD, CEN, CCRN, CFRN, CTRN, FAEN
Staff Nurse Emergency Department
Intermountain Medical Center
Salt Lake City, UT

Judith A. Kaufmann, DrPH, FNP-C
Director, Doctor of Nursing Practice Program
Robert Morris University
Moon Township, PA

Susan J. Kelley, PhD, RN, FAAN
Dean and Professor
College of Health and Human Sciences
Atlanta, GA

Merry L. Kruger, BA Nursing, NNP-BC
Neonatal Nurse Practitioner
Western Pennsylvania Hospital
Pittsburgh, PA

Gail Pisarcik Lenehan, RN, MSN, EdD, FAEN, FAAN
Nurse Clinical Specialist, Emergency Department
Massachusetts General Hospital
Boston, MA

Deborah Lesniak, RN, MS
Clinical Director of Emergency & Acute Care Services
Children's Hospital of Pittsburgh of the
University of Pittsburgh Medical Center
Pittsburgh, PA

Sarah A. Martin, RN, MS, CPNP-PC/AC, CCRN
Advanced Practice Nurse
Division of Pediatric Surgery
Children's Memorial Hospital
Chicago, IL

Nancy Mecham, APRN, FNP-BC, CEN
Clinical Nurse Specialist, Emergency Department/Rapid Treatment Unit
Primary Children's Medical Center
Salt Lake City, UT

Julie Ann Melini, RN, MS, FNP-C, SANE-A, SANE-P
Pediatric Emergency Department Nurse Practitioner
Primary Children's Medical Center
Salt Lake City, UT

Kathleen Merkley, RN, MS, FNP
ED Nurse Practitioner
Primary Children's Medical Center
Salt Lake City, UT

Christine Nelson-Tuttle, DNS, RNC, PNP
Associate Professor
St. John Fisher College/Wegmans School of Nursing
Rochester, NY
Nurse Practitioner
Division of Emergency Medicine
Kaleida Women and Children's Hospital of Buffalo
Buffalo, NY

Dana L. Noffsinger, RN, CPNP
Pediatric Nurse Practitioner, Pediatric Surgery/Trauma
Nationwide Children's Hospital
Columbus, OH

Regina M. O'Leary, RN, MSN, CRNP
Neonatal Nurse Practitioner
The Western Pennsylvania Hospital
Pittsburgh, PA

Tracy Ann Pasek, RN, MSN, CCRN, CIMI
Advanced Practice Nurse, Pain
Pediatric Intensive Care Unit
Children's Hospital of Pittsburgh of the
University of Pittsburgh Medical Center
Pittsburgh, PA

Amy M. Pasmann, RN, BSN
ED Nurse Manager
Primary Children's Medical Center
Salt Lake City, UT

Kathryn Puskar, RN, DrPH, FAAN
Professor
University of Pittsburgh School of Nursing
Pittsburgh, PA

Ramona F. Randolph, RN, BSN
Primary Children's Medical Center Clinical Educator for the Emergency Department and Rapid Treatment Unit
Primary Children's Medical Center
Salt Lake City, UT

Rebecca Roloff, RN, MSN, SANE-A, SANE-P
Clinical Educator
Women & Children's Hospital of Buffalo
Buffalo, NY

Kathleen Schenkel, RN, MSN, CEN
Advanced Practice Nurse
Emergency Department
Children's Hospital of Pittsburgh of the University of Pittsburgh Medical Center
Pittsburgh, PA

Lynn Coletta Simko, PhD, RN, CCRN
Associate Professor
Duquesne University
Pittsburgh, PA

Rose Ann Gould Soloway, RN, BSN, MSEd, DABAT
Clinical Toxicologist
National Capital Poison Center
Washington, DC

Kathleen A. Sullivan, RN, PhD
Professor
La Roche College
Pittsburgh, PA

Donna Ojanen Thomas, RN, MSN
Director, Emergency Department and Rapid Treatment Unit
Primary Children's Medical Center
Salt Lake City, UT

Anne Cassels Turner, RN, CEN
Clinical Nurse, Emergency Department
Massachusetts General Hospital
Boston, MA

Elizabeth M. Wertz Evans, RN, BSN, MPM, EMT-P, PHRN, FACMPE
President and CEO
PANDA & Associates, LLC.
Pittsburgh, PA

Erin K. Wright, RN, BSN
Staff Nurse
Children's Hospital of Pittsburgh of UPMC
Pittsburgh, PA

Reviewers

Paul Boackle, RN, BSN, CCRN, CEN, CFRN, CPEN, CTRN
Flight Nurse - UMC AirCare
University of Mississippi Health Care
Jackson, MS

Beth Nachtsheim Bolick, RN, DNP, PNP-BC, CPNP-AC, CCRN
Assistant Professor/Nurse Practitioner
Coordinator Acute/Chronic Care Pediatric Nurse Practitioner Program
Rush University College of Nursing
Women's and Children's Health Nursing
Chicago, IL

Camilia Brandt, RN, MS, CEN, CPEN, CPN
Educator, Emergency Services
Cook Children's Health Care System
Fort Worth, TX

Brenda Braun, RN, BSN, CEN
Clinical Educator, Emergency Department
Shore Memorial Hospital
Somers Point, NJ

Liesel M. Caten, RN, BSN
Emergency Department Staff Nurse
City Hospital-West Virginia University Hospital East
Adjunct Nursing Faculty
Mountain State University
Martinsburg, WV

Christy L. Cooper, RN, MSN, CEN, NREMT-P
Emergency Department Nurse Manager
East Tennessee Children's Hospital
Knoxville, TN

Denise L. Garee, RN, MSN, CEN
President
4N6 Nurse Consulting, LLC
Wilmington, NC

Lisa Gilmore, RN, MSN/Ed., CEN, CPEN, EMT-P
ETC Education Coordinator
St. John's Hospital
Springfield, MO

Harriet S. Hawkins, RN, CCRN, FAEN
Resuscitation Education Coordinator
Children's Memorial Hospital
Chicago, IL

Jennifer Kingsnorth, RN, MSN
EMTC Clinical Manager Staff Development, PI & Research
Children's National Medical Center
Washington, DC

Christine L Marshall, RN, MSN, CEN, CPEN
Clinical Nurse IV
St Joseph/CHOC Emergency Department
Orange, CA

Mary Otting, RN, CEN
EMS Coordinator
Children's Memorial Hospital
Chicago, IL

AnnMarie Papa, RN, MSN, CEN, NE-BC, FAEN
Director, Emergency Services
Doylestown Hospital
Doylestown, PA

Joan M. Rembacz, RN, MS, CCRN, CCNS, CEN, TNS
Clinical Nurse Specialist, Emergency Services
Centegra Health System
McHenry, IL

Nancy Stevens, RN, MS, MSN, FNP-BC, CEN, FAEN
Clinical Nurse Specialist
Erlanger Health System
Chattanooga, TN

Joni Thornton, RN, CPN
Pediatric Medical Education Liaison
Blank Children's Hospital
Des Moines, IA

Michael Vicioso, RN, MSN, CCRN, CPEN
Pediatric Nurse Manager
CHOC Children's/St. Joseph's Emergency Department
Orange, CA

Barbara Weintraub, RN, MSN, MPH, PNP-AC, CEN, FAEN
Director, Emergency Services
Northwest Community Hospital
Arlington Heights, IL

First Edition Contributors

Pam Baker, RN, BSN, CEN, CCRN

Lisa Marie Bernardo, RN, PhD, MPH

Carol Bolinger, RN, MSN, CPNP, CPON

Julie K. Briggs, RN, BSN, MHA

Laurel Campbell, RN, MSN, CEN

Mary Jo Cerepani, MSN, CRNP, CEN

Beth Cohen, RN, MSN, CRNP

Yvette Conley, PhD

Alice Conway, PhD, CRNP

Nancy Eckle, RN, MSN

Laurie Flaherty, RN, MS

Valerie G. A. Grossman, BSN, CEN

Kathy Haley, RN, BSN

Bruce Herman, MD

Reneé S. Holleran, RN, PhD, CEN, CCRN, CFRN

Jackie Jardine, RN

Marilyn K. Johnson, RN

Tracy B. Karp, RNC, MS, NNP

Roger K. Keddington, APRN, MSN, CEN, CCRN

Susan J. Kelly, RN, PhD, FAAN

David C. LaCovey, NREMT-P

Deborah Lesniak, RN, MS

Robin Long, RN, MSN, PNP

Sarah A. Martin, RN, MS, PCCNP, CPNP, CCRN

Nancy L. Mecham, APRN, FNP

Michelle R. Morfin, MS, RN, CNP, CS, CCRN

Christine Nelson, RNC, MS, PNP

Nancy A. Noonan, MS, APRN

Joan O'Connor, RN, MSN, CRNP

Kathryn Puskar, RN, DrPH, CS, FAAN

Cherie Jordan Revere, RN, MSN, CEN, CRNP

Cydne Rivers, RN, MN, CEN

Rachel Rosenfield, RN, BSN

Kathleen Schenkel, RN, BSN, CEN

Rose Ann Soloway, RN, BSN, MSEd, DABAT

Treesa E. Soud, RN, BSN

Kathleen Sullivan, RN, PhD

Donna Ojanen Thomas, RN, MSN

Jeanette H. Walker, RN, BSN

Elizabeth M. Wertz, RN, FACMPE

CONTENTS

SECTION THREE
Specific Pediatric Population Problems

SECTION FOUR
Resuscitation

SECTION FIVE
Clinical Emergencies

SECTION SEVEN
Environmental-Related Emergencies

SECTION EIGHT
Psychosocial Emergencies

SECTION ONE
Clinical Foundations

ONE

Management Issues

Donna Ojanen Thomas, RN, MSN
Lisa Marie Bernardo, RN, PhD, MPH

Introduction

Pediatric patients are seen in all emergency department (ED) settings, from general emergency departments dealing with patients of all ages, to pediatric emergency departments that exist within a pediatric specialty hospital. Since pediatric hospitals represent only 5% of hospitals, the vast majority of pediatric ED visits are made to general hospitals that treat both adults and children in the same department.[1] In 2004, children under 15 years of age represented 20.8% (or 37.8 per 100 visits) of all ED visits. Infants less than one year of age comprised 3.5% of ED visits, 7.5% were 1 to 4 years of age, and 9.7% were 5 to 14 years of age.[2] Data for 2005 shows that children comprised over a quarter of the 115.3 million visits to hospital-affiliated emergency departments. The majority of ED visits by children is and continues to be for "treat and release" conditions.[3] Four of the 10 most common conditions for which children are admitted to the emergency department are respiratory related: pneumonia, asthma, acute bronchitis, and upper respiratory conditions.

Increasingly, it is being acknowledged that children require special considerations not only for staffing, education, medications and equipment, but also in the design of the emergency department. In 2007, the Institute of Medicine (IOM) conducted a study on the future of emergency care. This study outlined the growing use of the emergency department as a primary source of care, problems associated with overcrowding, and recommendations to rectify identified problems. Emergency care for Children—Growing pains, a section of the IOM study, examined the current conditions of pediatric emergency care in the United States and made recommendations for improving pediatric care. Some of the findings are listed below.[1]

❑ Only 6% of all hospitals have all the supplies deemed essential by the American College of Emergency Physicians (ACEP) and the American Academy of Pediatrics (AAP). Half of the hospitals have at least 85% of needed supplies.

❑ Only half of the hospitals that have separate pediatric inpatient units have written transfer agreements with other hospitals. Transfer agreements are necessary when a critically ill or injured child arrives at a hospital without pediatric expertise.

❑ Pediatric continuing education is not required or is extremely limited for many prehospital providers.

❑ Many medications prescribed and administered to children in the emergency department are "off label" meaning that they are not adequately tested or approved for use in children by the Food and Drug Administration (FDA).

❑ Disaster preparedness plans largely overlook the needs of children even though children's needs in a disaster differ from those of adults.

Based on these findings, the IOM made specific recommendations for improving pediatric emergency care. These recommendations are listed in Table 1.1.

The purpose of this chapter is to discuss management issues associated with treating children in the emergency department, including special considerations; staffing, orientation, continuing education, resources, research, equipment, policies and procedures, quality management issues, and safety.

Special Considerations for Caring for Children in the Emergency Department

The following are general considerations for caring for children in the emergency department; specific considerations are discussed in further detail throughout the book.

Adult Considerations

❑ Children are dependent on adults for their care and medical decisions. When caring for children the emergency nurse should be aware they may interact with and provide explanations to a potentially large number of adults about the child's treatment and medical care. Once the family agrees on the plan of care, the child then must be convinced to cooperate with the plan.

❑ Dealing with parents may be more challenging then dealing with the child. Parents who are worried about their child can become emotional, angry and/or confrontational. Staff needs to understand that a

Table 1.1:   A Summary of the Institute of Medicine Recommendations for Improving Pediatric Emergency Care

Improving the Emergency Care System

Evidence-based categorization systems should be developed for emergency medical services, emergency departments, and trauma centers based on adult and pediatric service capabilities.

Prehospital care protocols for the treatment, triage, and transport of patients including children should be created.

Evidence-based indicators of emergency and trauma care system performance, including the performance of pediatric emergency care, should be developed.

A demonstration program should be developed to promote coordinated, regionalized, and accountable emergency care systems throughout the country.

A lead agency for trauma and emergency care should be established. This agency would have primary programmatic responsibility for the trauma care for adults and children.

Congress should appropriate $37.5 million per year for the next 5 years to the EMSC program.

Arming the Emergency Care Workforce with Pediatric Knowledge and Skills

All pediatric- and emergency care-related health professional credentialing and certification bodies should define pediatric emergency care competencies and require practitioners to receive the level of initial and continuing education necessary to achieve and maintain those competencies.

A panel of individuals with multidisciplinary expertise should be convened to develop, evaluate, and update clinical practice guidelines and standards of care for pediatric emergency care.

Hospitals and emergency medical services agencies should appoint a pediatric emergency coordinator to provide pediatric leadership for the organization.

Improving the Quality of Pediatric Emergency Care

Studies should be funded of the efficacy, safety, and health outcomes of medications used for infants, children, and adolescents in emergency care settings in order to improve patient safety.

Medication dosage guidelines, formulations, labeling guidelines, and administration techniques for the emergency care setting should be developed to maximize effectiveness and safety for infants, children, and adolescents. Emergency medical services and hospitals should incorporate these into practice.

Hospitals and emergency medical services agencies should implement evidence-based approaches to reducing errors in emergency and trauma care for children.

Federal agencies and private industry should fund research on pediatric-specific technologies and equipment for use by emergency and trauma care personnel.

Emergency Medical Services agencies and hospitals should integrate family centered care into emergency care practice.

Improving Emergency Preparedness and Response for Children Involved in disasters

Strategies should be developed to address pediatric needs in a disaster. These should include:

- Minimizing parent-child separation and improving methods for reuniting separated children with their families.
- Improving the level of pediatric expertise on Disaster Medical Assist Teams (DMAT) and other organized disaster response teams.
- Assessing pediatric surge capacity for both injured and non-injured children in disaster plans.
- Developing and improving access to specific medical mental health therapies as well as social services, for children in a disaster.
- Developing policies that ensure disaster drills include a pediatric mass casualty incident at least once every two years.

Table 1.1: A Summary of the Institute of Medicine Recommendations for Improving Pediatric Emergency Care

Building the Evidence Base for Pediatric Emergency Care

The gaps and opportunities in emergency care research, including pediatric emergency care, should be examined.

Administrators of state and national trauma registries should include standard pediatric-specific data elements and provide the data to the National Trauma Data Bank. The American College of Surgeons (ACS) should establish a multidisciplinary pediatric specialty committee to continuously evaluate pediatric-specific data elements for the National Trauma Data Bank and identify areas for pediatric research.

Data from: Institute of Medicine, Committee on the Future of Emergency Care in the U.S. Health System. (2007). *Emergency Care for Children: Growing pains.* Washington, DC: National Academy Press.

parent's main concern is for their child. Staff should be taught how to deal with "difficult" families and help them without becoming defensive. Some tips on dealing with families in the emergency department include:

- Keep the family informed about the reasons for delays, and on the plan of care for their child.
- Listen to the parents. They know their child better than anyone else. Listening to the parent's concerns also can prevent errors from being made in the care.
- Provide reassurance about the child's condition.
- When leaving the room always ask "Is there anything else I can do for your child right now?

Child Considerations

☐ Preparing a child for a procedure and performing each step of the procedure takes more time because a child generally will not be cooperative if something is perceived to be unpleasant, invasive, or confusing. Many facilities have added child life professionals to the ED team to help assist the child and family during the ED visit.

☐ Children cannot communicate as effectively as adults, and often the effects of treatment are not readily apparent. Nurses need astute pediatric assessment skills and knowledge of growth and developmental stages in order to notice subtle changes in the child's condition. The nurse must establish a relationship with the caregivers and the child in a short time to develop their trust.

☐ Child abuse has been on the increase over the years. Dealing with specific child abuse issues are discussed in Chapter 44.

Environmental Considerations

☐ Specialized equipment, such as airway management equipment, blood pressure cuffs, medications, and cribs (if patients are to be in the emergency depart-

ment for extended times), are necessary to provide quality care to pediatric patients. This specialized equipment requires training of staff. ED managers should consider adding to their operating and capital budgets any necessary equipment, as this equipment can be expensive.

☐ Specialized training regarding pediatric patients is required, and must be reviewed at least annually. Review more frequently depending on the volume of pediatric patients seen in the emergency department.

☐ A specialized area is preferable to care for the child. Many general emergency departments have designated a pediatric area within the department, which may include a separate resuscitation area. This area usually has equipment and decor suitable for the child. Safety of the child needs to be considered, and the area should be "child proofed."

☐ Family-centered care is an approach to the planning, delivery, and evaluation of health care that is grounded in mutually beneficial partnership among patients, families and health care professionals.[4] Family-centered care is discussed in more detail in Chapter 3.

Staff Considerations

☐ The serious illness, injury, or death of a child is very difficult for staff—even for those who routinely work with children, especially if the injury or death was intentional. Often the hardest part of a pediatric resuscitation is to see the grief of the families. Staff need ways to cope with their feelings and provide support to the families. Some methods for helping staff deal with their feelings and provide care to families who are experiencing a crisis situation are discussed in Chapter 26.

Staffing and Resources

Caring for pediatric patients consumes more resources. Acuity-based billing systems that work for an adult patient will not be applicable to the pediatric patient, and consideration must be given for the amount of time needed to care for children. The Emergency Nurses Association (ENA) believes staffing for individual institutions must be consistent with the percentage and acuity of pediatric patients treated.[5]

To assist with the prediction of staffing needs, the following data have to be evaluated:

❑ Volume of pediatric patients. The number of pediatric visits per year must be divided into appropriate age categories, such as infants younger than 1 year of age, preschool-aged child (younger than 5 years), school-aged child (5 to 12 years), and the adolescent patient. The younger age groups generally are more dependent and take more nursing time. For example, procedures such as catheterizations and intravenous insertions on a toddler require two nurses, whereas in a cooperative, awake adult or adolescent, only one nurse is generally needed. The younger age groups also represent the largest volume of pediatric patients seen in the emergency department.

❑ Distribution of volume. The times of visits throughout the day and during specific times of year can be evaluated. For example, many emergency departments see more children during the evening hours, when doctors' offices are closed and parents are home from work. Lacerations, fractures, and other trauma are more common in the summer months, when school is out and there are more daylight hours. In the winter months, respiratory complaints and influenza may be more common and can overwhelm the emergency department, both in adult and pediatric volumes. If volume distribution and seasonal trends are known, staffing can be planned based around this information.

❑ Types of illnesses and injuries seen in the pediatric population. These may vary according to the geographic location of the hospital. Injuries and severity of injuries differ in the general and pediatric emergency departments. The general emergency department treats a wide variety of pediatric patients but has a larger volume of minor trauma than does the pediatric one.[6]

A core group of nurses who are specially trained in pediatric care could be developed so that at least one such nurse is on staff for each shift. Ideally, all nurses should be trained in pediatric emergency care. The IOM recommends that all general emergency departments have two pediatric liaison staff, one of which should be a physician.[1] The AAP recommends that there be a physician and nurse coordinator for pediatric emergency department care.[8] The responsibilities of these coordinators include:[8]

❑ Coordinating pediatric quality and process improvement and clinical care protocols.

❑ Serving as a liaison to appropriate in-hospital and out-of-hospital pediatric care committees.

❑ Ensuring adequate skills and knowledge of all physicians and nurses in emergency care and resuscitation of infants and children.

❑ Facilitating ED nursing continuing education in pediatrics and providing orientation for new staff nurses.

❑ Assisting in development and periodic review of policies and procedures for pediatric care.

The physician and nurse coordinator should have special interest, knowledge, and skill in emergency medical care of children as demonstrated by training, clinical experience, or focused continuing medical and nursing education.

Emergency Medical Services for Children

An important resource is the Emergency Medical Services for Children (EMSC) model. Emergency Medical Services for Children (EMSC) is specialized care for infants, children, and adolescents who have sustained a serious injury or illness. It is a comprehensive model that includes injury prevention strategies, emergency assessment and treatment, provider training, transportation, facilities, rehabilitation services, and contact with primary care physicians.

The Federal EMSC Program is designed to ensure that all children and adolescents, no matter where they live, attend school, or travel, receive appropriate care in a health emergency. Federal EMSC legislation was sponsored in 1984 and passed (Publ #98-555). The Federal EMSC program is administered by the Maternal and Child Health Bureau of the Health Resources and Services Administration within the Department of Health and Human Services. Since its establishment, the EMSC Program has provided grant funding to all 50 states, the District of Columbia, and five U.S. territories. Many states have enacted EMSC laws, and others have created state offices or resource centers. The Federal EMSC Program supports two resource centers: EMSC National Resource Center (NRC) in Washington, DC, and the National EMSC Data Analysis Resource Center (NEDARC) in Salt Lake City, UT. Educational products have been developed by many of the states and are available free of charge through the EMSC website at http://bolivia.hrsa.gov/emsc/index.aspx

Orientation and Continuing Education

Orientation and continuing education programs should include:

❏ Developmental and psychosocial considerations (Chapter 3). The Joint Commission requires that staff receive training in age-related competencies. Competencies in pediatric assessment, skills and growth and development are important elements of an ED orientation program. These elements are covered in the Emergency Nursing Pediatric Course (ENPC).

❏ Pediatric assessment. The ENA has developed ENPC, encompassing all aspects of pediatric emergency nursing. Nurses working with children should be required to take this course within one-two years of hire.

❏ Pediatric triage. Triage of symptoms can be different for the pediatric patient. For example, fever may be a nonurgent complaint in an adult; however, in a child younger than 2 months of age, fever is an urgent condition. The ENA recommends the use of a standardized 5 level triage system. The Emergency Severity Index is currently being validated for pediatric patients. Further information can be found in Chapter 6.

❏ Resuscitation and trauma. The Trauma Nursing Core Course (TNCC) includes content on pediatric trauma. Nurses who care for children should take an approved course in pediatric advanced life support. A plan for pediatric trauma should be developed, and agreements with pediatric tertiary care centers for the transfer of critically ill or injured children should be established (Chapter 8).

Equipment

The AAP and ACEP have developed guidelines for pediatric equipment and supplies for emergency departments.[8] The guidelines contain lists of equipment that should be available at a minimum, and the committee recommends that this list be modified to meet the severity level of the patient population. These guidelines can be found at the American Academy of Pediatric Web site (http://www.aap.org) or the American College of Emergency Physicians Web site (http://www.acep.org).

The Committee also has made the following recommendations:[8]

❏ Each hospital must develop a method for storage and provide accessibility of medications and equipment for children. The method used must ensure that the health care practitioner can easily identify appropriate dosages of medication based on the patient's weight and choose appropriately sized equipment. Length-based systems or precalculated drug systems should be used to avoid calculation errors of medications delivered.

❏ All equipment and supplies should include age-appropriate and size-appropriate equipment for use for children of all ages and sizes from premature infants through adolescents.

❏ Regular periodic review of drugs and equipment, monitoring of expiration dates of items, and replacement of used items should be done.

Other suggestions for maintaining pediatric supplies include:

❏ When supplies and equipment are purchased, consideration should be given to the growing problem of latex sensitization of both patients and health care workers.

❏ Emergency department staff members should be trained in the use of all equipment and supplies that are available for pediatric emergency care.

❏ Mock codes should be practiced to allow staff to find and use pediatric equipment.

Small rural hospitals should consider forming buying cooperatives or even raise money through donations to purchase needed equipment. In some areas, pediatric hospitals may offer some supplies to hospital emergency departments that cannot purchase their own.

Policies and Procedures

Policies and procedures that apply to the adult patient do not always apply to the pediatric patient. Policies specific to pediatric patients must be developed for the following issues:

❏ Pediatric triage (Chapter 6)

❏ Frequency of vital signs and assessment

❏ Administration of medications and the use of sedation (Chapter 11)

❏ Parental presence during procedures (Chapter 26)

❏ Child abuse and sexual assault protocols (Chapters 44 and 45)

❏ Follow-up visits and callbacks

❏ Use of restraints

❏ Consent including situations when a parent is not available (Chapter 2)

❏ Communication with the pediatric patient's primary health care provider

❏ Transfer procedures and agreements (Chapter 8)

❏ Evidence based clinical guidelines

❏ Disaster management and special considerations for children

Polices should be updated regularly and monitored for compliance. There are many resources to assist with the development of policies, educational material and guidelines, including the following Internet resources:

❏ Emergency Medical Services for Children: http://www.bolivia.hrsa.gov/emsc

❏ Pediatric Emergency Care Applied Research Network: http://www.pecarn.org

❏ American Academy of Pediatrics: http://www.aap.org

❏ National Association of Children's Hospitals and Related Institutions: http://www.childrenshospitals.net

❏ National Guideline Clearinghouse: http://www.guideline.gov

Research

ENA believes that research in the field of pediatrics is crucial in developing and refining clinical practice to children in the emergency department.[5] Nurses should be supported to participate and collaborate in research projects related to pediatric emergency care. These research projects can build upon evidence gained through systematic literature reviews or outcomes from evidence-based practice initiatives. Ways that emergency nurses can become involved in research include:

❏ Working with an established physician or nurse researcher to learn about the research process, from writing a proposal to applying research findings into practice.

❏ Identifying problems or concerns. All research projects start with a simple question. It is important to ask a question that deserves an answer. Such questions may be epidemiologic ("How many newborns are being admitted for jaundice because of early hospital discharge?") or clinical ("Which topical analgesic is more effective in relieving pain during wound repair?"). Interdisciplinary support should be garnered when identifying the research question.

❏ Reading and reviewing the literature to learn more about the question. Other nurses or physicians may have answered the question or at least published a preliminary report. Textbooks, articles, and Internet resources are helpful in acquiring knowledge. Using the systematic review format for evidence-based practice is a helpful strategy for evaluating the published literature.

❏ Developing a plan for answering the question. It is helpful to collaborate with an established researcher, such as an ED clinical nurse specialist or physician or school of nursing faculty, to develop the research plan. This plan includes the methodology (e.g., randomized clinical trial or retrospective descriptive study), study protocol and data analysis.

❏ Writing the research plan in accordance with the hospital's institutional review board (IRB) guidelines (Chapter 2). Other nurses and physicians should be invited to read and critique the proposal. All study investigators must complete human subjects protection training as required by their hospital's IRB.

❏ Revising the plan, as needed, and submitting it for IRB approval. The nurse should consider submitting the project to the ENA for funding.

❏ Moving forward with the research project once the proposal is approved. The researcher should expect delays and setbacks but must stay on track.

❏ Completing the study and writing up the results. The author should consider submitting the completed research project for publication in the *Journal of Emergency Nursing* and for presentation at ENA's Annual Conference or Leadership Conference.

❏ Many questions about clinical practice and ED use by the pediatric population are raised, but few answers are offered. Emergency nurses are capable of becoming researchers through mentoring, a desire to seek new knowledge, and the search for answers to questions that will improve ED practice. Participation in interdisciplinary research allows health professionals to identify and study common issues in pediatric emergency care. This approach fosters communication and mutual respect, enhances collaborative practice, and adds to the knowledge of emergency care.[9]

Evidence-Based Practice

Evidence-based practice (EBP) is an approach that enables nurses and health care professionals to provide the highest quality care to meet the needs of patients and families.[10] While the term evidence-based nursing was created about 10 years ago, its usage is central to the practice of nursing both nationally and internationally.[11] Practicing from an evidence-base is one of the 10 guiding principles in patient-clinician relationships recommended by the Institute of Medicine.[12] As a problem-solving approach, evidence-based practice (EBP) incorporates the search for empirical literature, appraisal of that literature, one's own nursing expertise, and patient values and preferences.[10] Evidence-based practice is complementary to the research process, but practicing the art and science of emergency nursing from an evidence-base extends beyond the application of research findings into practice.[13] Applying research findings into practice may not include children's and families' preferences and values. Relying on the replication of study findings to change practice may not reflect the entire body of evidence relevant to that practice change. The strength, or hierarchy of that evidence, also must be considered when deciding upon its appropriateness for use in the care of children in the emergency department. Thus, practicing from an evidence-base is comprehensive in its scope of balancing the strength of an extant body of knowledge with clinician expertise and patient preferences.[13] Emergency nurses can, however, practice in an environment that supports both research and EBP.[14]

There are five steps of evidence-based practice:[10]

1. Ask the burning clinical question. A clinical question is put into the PICO format—**P**atient population, **I**ntervention of interest, **C**omparison intervention or status, and **O**utcome. Asking the right question is key to obtaining information necessary to improve clinical practice; a carefully formulated question will increase the likelihood that pertinent information can be elicited and subsequently applied in practice.[15] Emergency nurses need time and ability to critically consider and reflect on their practice to develop a clinical question.[16] Reflection provides emergency nurses with the opportunity to synthesize research findings, personal experience, daily practice, and patients' needs as a means of improving nursing practice and patient care; when properly developed, reflection can serve as the foundation for effective questioning in EBP.[16]

2. Collect the best evidence. Electronic data bases, such as PubMed (www.pubmed.gov), CINAHL (http://www.ebscohost.com/cinahl/), and The Cochrane Collaboration (www.cochrane.org) archive published articles on a myriad of topics relevant to the care of children and families in the emergency department. Searching these databases for current evidence requires creativity in the proper use of keywords and subject headings. Klem and Northcutt[17] provide guidance in the basics of literature searching, while Bernardo[18] suggests strategies for reading and abstracting the literature. The evidence gleaned from a successful literature search is graded in terms of its strength. The strongest evidence within the hierarchy is randomized, controlled trials, and weakest evidence is from clinical observation and patient preference.[19]

3. Critically appraise the evidence. Critical appraisal of the obtained evidence is a process whereby a determination is made of the information's validity and reliability. This process occurs in group discussions or through the tabulation and compilation of study information using a standardized approach. Both Melnyk and Fineout-Overholt[10] and DiCenso, et al[11] offer detailed guidelines of how to appraise the literature based on the evidence hierarchy. Using social networking web sites to share appraised evidence can be a useful communication strategy among emergency nurses.[20]

4. Integrate the evidence with one's clinical expertise, patient preferences, and values to change nursing practice. Changing practice occurs over time and includes changing knowledge, beliefs, and values, in addition to hospital policies and procedures. Many hospitals utilize EBP councils that evaluate evidence and incorporate that evidence into policies and procedures. Always keep within established hospital policies and procedures and state nurse practice acts when performing patient care and integrating evidence into practice. Emergency nurses may consider inviting patients and families to participate in aspects of the EBP council to obtain their perspective on the delivery of pediatric emergency care.

5. Evaluate the practice change. The expected outcomes of changes in patients' health, delivery of nursing care or other indicators should be delineated in advance. A stipulated time period to measure changes in practice should be determined in advance and should reflect similar time frames to those found in the literature. Changes can be measured through patient surveys, focus groups, usage of supplies, or other pre-established indicators.

The ENA is committed to incorporating current evidence into emergency nursing practice. The *Journal of Emergency Nursing* hosts a dedicated column on EBP which may be helpful to emergency nurses as they evolve in supporting the practice of pediatric emergency nursing from an evidence base.

Quality Management

The AAP recommends that a pediatric patient review process is integrated into the emergency department Quality Improvement (QI) plan according to the following guidelines:[8]

❏ Components of the process interface with out-of-hospital, emergency department, trauma, inpatient pediatrics, pediatric critical care, and hospital-wide quality improvement or process improvement (PI) activities.

❏ Minimum components of the process should include:
  ▪ Identification of quality indicators
  ▪ Collecting and analyzing data to discover variances

- Defining a plan for improvement, and evaluating or measuring the success of the QI or PI process
- A clearly measured mechanism to monitor professional education and staffing

The development of indicators can be guided by the high-risk, problem-prone diagnoses seen in the pediatric population in a given area. Some examples of indicators are listed below:

❑ Deaths occurring in the emergency department

❑ Discrepancy between the radiologist and ED physician's interpretation of radiologic results

❑ Cardiopulmonary resuscitation performed in the emergency department

❑ The patient returned to the emergency department within 48 hours for the same complaint

❑ The patient and caregiver left without being seen or before care was completed

❑ Lack of appropriate vital sign documentation

❑ Missed diagnosis

❑ Medication errors

❑ Parent complaints

Handling parent complaints regarding their child's care should be part of the quality process in the emergency department. Some strategies for dealing with complaints include:

❑ Call the complainant as soon as possible after the complaint is received.

❑ Listen to the complaint without judgment.

❑ Apologize and let the person calling know that you will follow up with the staff involved to get their side of the story.

❑ Review the complaints at departmental quality meetings and evaluate trends.

❑ Discuss immediately with staff involved.

Some hospitals have a parent liaison that helps to resolve complaints and investigate to determine any action that needs to be taken. The best way to deal with parent complaints is to prevent them by listening to the parents and keeping them involved and updated in the care in the emergency department, and to provide good follow up instructions.

One intervention for improvement of pediatric care in the emergency department is the establishment of a Life Saving Interventions for Little Youth (LILY) Team.[21] This team could include pediatricians, nurses, respiratory care practitioners, pharmacists, other pediatric clinicians, and emergency medicine staff. The LILY team evaluates and improves the capability of an emergency department to

care for children by using evidence-based approaches to reduce errors and in emergency and trauma care for children.

Pediatric Safety

Safety is a consideration in all aspects of pediatric care as well as in adult care. Safety should be considered in all areas including policy development, medication administration, equipment, design, and quality management.

Some strategies for maximizing pediatric safety in the emergency department include:[21]

❑ Keep all room supplies out of reach of small patients and their siblings, including hanging cables.

❑ Implement an infant/child abduction prevention plan.

❑ Have a performance improvement plan with measures that are specific to pediatric safety.

Additional safety considerations are discussed in Chapter 4. Emergency department leadership must be actively involved in the process and commit to improving the quality and safety of pediatric care in the emergency department and willing to support necessary changes in policies and procedures. Nursing leadership also can support and promote pediatric safety by insuring good processes for clinician handoffs, shift to shift and emergency department to inpatient unit report. Organizations seeking to assess their ability to provide pediatric care and improve that care should consider the following issues:[21]

❑ Infrastructure to give sufficient voice to pediatric issues

❑ Staff training and education

❑ System designed to support safety

- Use of a standardized format for the medication process that specifies that all children must be weighed in kilograms.
- All orders must be double-checked.
- The use of preprinted forms for prescriptions has been shown to decrease errors.

❑ Policy development

Conclusion

The majority of children are cared for in general emergency departments. As more and more families find themselves without health insurance, emergency departments will likely continue to see increases in volumes and until there is an answer to our nation's health care issues, many children will use the emergency department as their main source of care. Caring for children in the emergency department takes time, resources, and planning. Many resources are available including the ENA, and other professional nursing and medical organizations.

The IOM report on emergency care has done much to highlight the problems in overcrowding in general and the problems of pediatric emergency care specifically. Recommendations to improve emergency care for children have been made and while some progress has been seen, there is still more to be accomplished to ensure safe care to pediatric patients. General emergency departments must evaluate their pediatric populations and develop ways to educate staff to care for children. Additional staff may be necessary to meet the needs of the child. Having appropriate numbers of properly trained staff and the right equipment will improve both the comfort level of the staff caring for children and the quality of care that is given.

References

1. Institute of Medicine, Committee on the Future of Emergency Care in the U.S. Health System. (2007). *Emergency care for children: Growing pains.* Washington, DC: National Academy Press.

2. McCaig, L. F., & Nawar, E. W. (2006). *National hospital ambulatory medical care survey: 2004 emergency department summary.* Hyattsville, MD: National Center for Health Statistics.

3. Merrill, C. T., Owens, P. L., & Stocks, C. (2008). *Pediatric emergency department visits in community hospitals from selected states, 2005.* Retrieved April 2, 2009, from http://www.hcup-us.ahrq.gov/reports/statbriefs/sb52.pdf

4. O'Malley, P. J., Brown, K., Krug, S. E., & the Committee on Pediatric Emergency Medicine (2008). Patient and family-centered care of children in the emergency department. *Pediatrics, 122*(2), e511–e521.

5. Emergency Nurses Association. (2007). *Position statement: Pediatric care in the emergency setting.* Retrieved April 5, 2009, from http://ena.org/about/position/position/Pediatric_Patient_in_the_Emergency_Setting_-_ENA_PS.pdf

6. Nelson, D. S., Walsh, K., & Fleisher, G. R. (1992). Spectrum and frequency of pediatric illness presenting to a general community hospital emergency department. *Pediatrics, 90*(1), 5–10.

7. Christian, B., & Thomas, D. (1998). A child life program in one pediatric emergency department. *Journal of Emergency Nursing, 24*(4), 359–361.

8. American Academy of Pediatrics, Committee on Pediatric Emergency Medicine and American College of Emergency Physicians, Pediatric Committee. (2001). Care of children in the emergency department: Guidelines for preparedness. *Pediatrics, 107*(4), 777–781.

9. Emergency Nurses Association. (2006). *Position Statement: Research: Collaborative and interdisciplinary.* Retrieved April 5, 2009, from http://ena.org/about/position/position/Research_Collaborative_and_Interdisciplinary_-_ENA_PS.pdf

10. Melnyk, B., & Fineout-Overholt, E. (2005). *Evidence-based practice in nursing and healthcare: A guide to best practice* (pp. 3–37). Philadelphia: Lippincott Williams & Wilkins.

11. DiCenso, A., Guyatt, G., & Ciliska, D. (2005). *Evidence-based nursing: A guide to clinical practice* (pp. xxv–xxvi). St. Louis, MO: Mosby.

12. Institute of Medicine. (2001). *Crossing the quality chasm: A new health system for the 21st century.* Washington, DC: Author.

13. Bernardo, L. (2007). Evidence-based emergency nursing practice: The journey begins. *Journal of Emergency Nursing, 33*(4), 375–376.

14. Holzhauser, K., Cooke, M., Winch, S., Finucane, J., & Davis, C. (2008). Developing a research-active clinical environment within the emergency department: A case study. *Journal of Professional Nursing, 24*(1), 36–41.

15. Engberg, S., & Schlenk, E. (2007). Evidence-based practice: Asking the right question. *Journal of Emergency Nursing, 33*(6), 571–573.

16. Thompson, D., & Burns, H. (2008). Reflection: An essential element of evidence-based practice. *Journal of Emergency Nursing, 34*(3), 246–248.

17. Klem, M., & Northcutt, T. (2008). Finding the best evidence, part 2: The basics of literature searches. *Journal of Emergency Nursing, 34*(2), 151–153.

18. Bernardo, L. (2008). Reading and abstracting the literature. *Journal of Emergency Nursing, 34*(5), 464–465.

19. Matthews, J., & Bernardo, L. (2008). Triaging the evidence. *Journal of Emergency Nursing, 34*(4), 361–362.

References (continued)

20. Donovan, S., & Bernardo, L. (2009). Social networking to enhance evidence based practice. *Journal of Emergency Nursing, 35*(2), 149-150

21. Nadzam, D., & Westergaard, F. (2008). Pediatric safety in the emergency department. Identifying risks and preparing to care for child and family. *Journal of Nursing Care Quality 23*(3), 189–194.

TWO

Ethical and Legal Issues

Lisa Marie Bernardo, RN, PhD, MPH
Deborah Lesniak, RN, MS

Introduction

Emergency nurses face ethical and legal issues when caring for infants, children, and adolescents. These issues relate to assent and consent for treatment or research protocols, as well as legal requirements for transferring and transporting patients from the emergency department (ED). Ethical and legal considerations regarding child maltreatment and child sexual abuse are discussed in Chapters 44 and 45. The purpose of this chapter is to highlight pertinent ethical and legal issues and to describe factors that nurses should consider when faced with such issues.

An emergency exists when immediate treatment is necessary to preserve life, prevent permanent disability, or alleviate pain and suffering. Federal law supports physicians and patient care providers initiating emergency care for children without the consent of a parent or guardian. This is stipulated under the Emergency Medical Treatment and Active Labor Act (EMTALA). EMTALA mandates that treatment shall not be delayed to obtain consent.[1] Therefore, any pediatric patient presenting to the emergency department for treatment is triaged and evaluated to determine whether an emergency exists. There are many other situations for which minors present to the emergency department without parental consent, such as testing and treatment for sexually transmitted diseases, birth control, drug and alcohol abuse, and mental health evaluation[2]; parental consent requirements vary according to state law with respect to provisions of confidentiality. Specific consent regulations for all 50 states can be found in the 2003 Guttmacher Report on Public Policy.[3]

Ethical Issues

Consent for Treatment

Consent is an individual's approval of or compliance with a proposed plan of action. Only patients who have appropriate decisional capacity and legal empowerment can give their informed consent to medical care. In all other situations, parents or other surrogates provide informed permission (Table 2.1) for diagnosis and treatment of children, with the assent of the child whenever appropriate.[4] In particular,

❏ Infants and young children cannot provide consent for proposed treatment.

❏ School-aged children can give assent for treatment, along with their parents' informed permission.

❏ Adolescents can give consent for treatment if they are emancipated or mature minors (Table 2.2).

TABLE 2.1 Elements of Informed Permission
Information and explanations appropriate to the parents' level of understanding regarding the nature of their child's health condition.
The proposed diagnostic and treatment plans and their probability for success.
The potential risks and benefits of the proposed treatment.
The existence, benefits, and risks of alternative treatments, including no treatment.
An assessment of the parents' understanding of the above information.
An assessment of the parents' ability to make an informed decision/give informed permission.
An assurance that the decision is made without coercion or manipulation.

American Academy of Pediatrics. Committee on Drugs. (1995). Guidelines for the ethical conduct of studies to evaluate drugs in pediatric populations. *Pediatrics, 95,* 286–294.

Assent for Treatment

Assent is a child's agreement to receive care. Assent is obtained from the child seven years of age and older to help the child achieve a developmentally appropriate awareness of the health condition. Assent includes:[4]

TABLE 2.2 Consent Situations with Families and Minors

Legal Exception to Informed Consent Requirement	Treatment Setting
Emergency exception	Minor seeks emergency care.
Emancipated minor exception	Minor is self-reliant or independent (married, serving in the military, emancipated by court ruling, financially independent and living apart from parents. Can be college students, runaways, pregnant minor, or minor mothers)
Mature minor exception (age range of 14–18 years, which varies among the states)	Minor is capable of giving informed consent for treatment. Is sufficiently mature and has the intelligence to make an informed decision.
Exceptions based on specific health conditions	Minor seeks health care for mental health services; pregnancy/contraception; testing for HIV or AIDS; STD testing or treatment; drug or alcohol counseling or treatment; care for a crime-related injury.

Note: AIDS = acquired immune deficiency syndrome; HIV = human immunodeficiency virus; STD = sexually transmitted disease.
American Academy of Pediatrics, Committee on Pediatric Emergency Medicine. (2003). Consent for emergency medical services for children and adolescents. Pediatrics, 111(3), 703–706.

❏ Telling the child what to expect during the proposed tests and procedures

❏ Assessing the child's understanding of the situation, as well as any circumstances that may be influencing the child's response

❏ Soliciting the child's willingness to participate in the proposed care

In certain situations, the child's agreement to participate in the treatment plan is not obtained because of the severity of the situation or because of developmental ability to understand what is in the best interest of the child (e.g., a 4-year-old, afraid of "shots," refuses an intravenous infusion for dehydration). The emergency care team still involves the child in discussions about his or her health care by offering the child choices ("In which hand do you want your IV?"), which may foster the child's trust of health care professionals.[4] A child's participation in his or her health care decision making should be increased according to age and ability to understand cause and effect.

Nursing Considerations in Consent and Assent for Treatment

Because emergency treatment is never withheld until parental consent is obtained, interventions to save a child's life or to alleviate pain and suffering are initiated immediately.

❏ Document all attempts to contact a family member to obtain consent for treatment.

❏ Appropriate medical care for the pediatric patient with an urgent or emergent condition should never be withheld or delayed because of issues with obtaining consent.[5]

❏ All emergency departments should develop policies and procedures to comply with state and federal laws regarding consent of minors, including specific guidelines pertaining to confidentiality, billing, and parental notification for the unaccompanied minor.[5] Consultation with the hospital's legal counsel is recommended as policies are developed.

❏ The ED staff should document on the patient's medical record any issues and discussions concerning consent for treatment. The nurse should always seek consent and/or assent for care from the pediatric patient as appropriate for the patient's level of development and understanding.

❏ Emergency nurses should consult with their hospital's legal counsel to determine what their state's laws or legislation deems to be an emergency.

Parents should be encouraged to provide a written consent statement for nonelective health care for the child when the parents may not be available, such as when the child is in a child care setting, at camp, or with noncustodial relatives.[5] They also should be encouraged to complete the emergency information cards provided by schools and camps. Necessary information includes the parents' home and work telephone numbers, immunizations, allergies, chronic health problems, and the primary health care provider's name and telephone number.[5] Electronic mail (e-mail) addresses and cellular phone numbers should be included when available.

Children should be taught their home addresses, telephone numbers, and the names of their parents' workplaces in the event of an unexpected visit to the emergency department.[5]

Refusal of Treatment, Leaving Without Being Seen, Elopement, Leaving Against Medical Advice

Children are not considered cognitively or legally capable of refusing emergency care because they cannot fully understand the long-term consequences of such a refusal. However, the child's reluctance or refusal to participate should be respected when the proposed procedure is not essential to the child's welfare and/or can be deferred without a substantial risk to the child's health.[4] Adolescents may refuse care if they are:

❏ Emancipated (Table 2.2)

❏ A mature minor (Table 2.2)

❏ Meet one of the minor treatment statutes

Over the last few decades, decision making about treatment and end-of-life care has become an increasing ethical and legal dilemma for young children who are very knowledgeable about their medical diagnosis and treatment, but legally cannot make decisions about their care. A broad consensus representing pediatric health professionals and legal representatives has emerged supporting the competency of adolescents (approximately 14 years of age) to make binding medical decisions for themselves[6] (Table 2.3). "Abraham's Law," in particular, gives some adolescents aged 14 years and older the right to refuse recommended therapies, including lifesaving treatment.[7] Of course, there are many other circumstances that enter into the decision making, such as developmental and legal considerations, particularly in emergency treatment.

Emergency professionals may encounter situations in which the parents refuse emergency treatment for their child, for any number of reasons. Religious beliefs are a common example. In a life-threatening situation, overriding parental wishes may be necessary. Such action may involve seeking legal assistance or independent physician action.[7]

Nursing Considerations in Refusal-of-Treatment Issues

Children demonstrate their refusal of treatment through physical means (kicking or screaming) or by attempting to leave the emergency department. Efforts to calm the child and to ascertain the reasons for the refusal should ensue. The child may have a misunderstanding about the treatment plan, or the plan may not have been explained properly. It is inadvisable to proceed against the child's wishes until such time that all explanations have been exhausted. If the treatment must ensue despite the child's refusal, the child should be informed of that fact.[5] Therefore, collaboration to promote excellent communication should be developed early in the patient/health care team relationship to establish trust and to assist in decision making. Such approaches should be combined with appropriate support in absence of personal judgment.[6] Adolescents' refusal of treatment, if not reconciled through mediation with an ethics consultant, social worker, or other health care professional, should be respected. In a busy emergency department with a time-sensitive diagnosis and treatment, such actions should be attempted to the best of the hospital's ability and in accordance with hospital policy.

Parents, too, may need extra time to fully understand the proposed treatment plan for their child. Including a social worker or patient advocate in the discussion may help parents understand the gravity of the situation. Contacting the family health care provider may also be beneficial. If parents leave before their child has been seen, the nurse's documentation should be reviewed to determine the urgency of the child's health condition. If the illness or injury is deemed serious, an attempt should be made to contact the family by telephone. Emergency nurses should be familiar with their state regulations regarding the reporting of patients that leave the emergency department. Many states require reporting of patients that leave the emergency department to the state within 24 hours. The required reporting is based on where the patient was in the treatment process (i.e., screening versus hospital admission). When adolescents or parents choose to leave against medical advice, the emergency department should have a specific form for the adolescent or parent to sign that demonstrates their understanding of the child's health condition and the consequences of refusing proper treatment. If the ED staff believes that it is not in the child's best interest to leave the emergency department, a court order may be obtained to prevent the parents from removing the child from the hospital. For patients who elope, depending on their health condition, hospital police or other legal officers may have to become involved to bring the child and family back to the emergency department. Emergency professionals and parents should understand that although parental authority is acknowledged, it does not carry as much weight as patient autonomy.[7] Emergency professionals and parents should respect children's rights to emergency care; our obligation to provide such care; and, on rare occasions, the potential need to outweigh parents' rights to decide what is best for their child.[7] Emergency departments should have policies and procedures in place for parents and adolescents who refuse ED treatment (Table 2.4).

TABLE 2.3 Consent Considerations with Minors

Situation	*Consent Considerations*
Emancipated minors—minors who are self-supporting, not subject to parental control, not living at home, married, pregnant or a parent, or in the military[4]	Able to give consent for medical treatment. Initiate ED medical screening and treatment.
Mature minors (age range of 14–18 years, which varies among the states), unemancipated minors who understand the nature and risks of treatment, if the treatment is for their benefit, serious risk is not involved, and the ED physician believes the minor can make an informed decision[4]	Able to seek or refuse emergency and nonemergency treatment. Statutes on treatment of minors vary among the states. These statutes allow minors to consent for treatment without parental involvement for such health conditions as sexually transmitted diseases, pregnancy, drug or alcohol abuse, and psychiatric problems.[4] Initiate ED medical screening and treatment.
Divorced or separated parents—parent with custodial authority	The custodial parent has the duty to obtain treatment and give consent/permission; permission does not need to be obtained from the noncustodial parent. Initiate ED medical screening and treatment.
Divorced parents—parent without custodial authority	Assume that the accompanying parent has authority to give consent/permission for treatment; although the parent may not retain the right or duty to provide treatment, the emergency care is provided as necessary. Initiate ED medical screening and treatment.
Divorced parents—joint custody	Assume parental authority to give consent/permission for treatment. Initiate ED medical screening and treatment.
Minors with a nonparental adult (guardianship or legal custody in loco parentis)	Other care can be initiated if the adult has guardianship or legal custody for the minor's health needs. Document the situation in the medical record, including attempts to contact the parents.[5] Initiate ED medical screening and treatment.
Minors residing in foster care	Some states may allow for the individual or institution with custody to give consent/permission for treatment. For high-risk or elective procedures, parental consent/permission may need to be obtained.[5] Initiate ED medical screening and treatment.
Minors in detention facilities	Parental consent/permission for routine health care is not needed. For high-risk or elective procedures, parental consent/permission may need to be obtained. Parental consent for low-risk emergency treatment may not be needed. Initiate ED medical screening and treatment.
Minors in camp, boarding school, and other locations	Parents usually sign a notarized, blanket consent (in loco parentis) for camp or school officials to consent for routine medical care. Parents must give consent/permission for high-risk or elective treatment. Initiate ED medical screening and treatment.
Runaway minors	Attempt to contact parents. If the minor refuses to identify the parents and the health care is routine, initiate the care. Contact legal counsel for high-risk or elective treatments. Initiate ED medical screening and treatment.

Consent for Research

Human subject research that is supported by federal funding is governed by rules and regulations from the U.S. Department of Health and Human Services Code of Federal Regulations (45 CFR 46) and the National Institutes of Health (NIH).[8] Children were added to the Code of Federal Regulations in 1983 (45 CFR 46.402[a]), where children are defined as "persons who have not attained the legal age for consent to treatments or procedures involved

TABLE 2.4 Comparison of Treatment Refusals

Refusal	Description
Leaving without being seen by a physician (LWOT)	The child and family arrive in the emergency department, are evaluated by the triage nurse, and then leave before a physician evaluation. Often they tell no one of their intentions; their absence is detected when they are called to enter an examination room.
Leaving against medical advice (LAMA)	The child and family arrive in the emergency department and receive an examination from the ED physician. The physician recommends a specific treatment that the parent chooses not to accept, such as a diagnostic procedure or hospital admission.
Elopement	The child and family arrive in the emergency department and receive an examination from the ED physician. While the course of treatment is planned, or after the treatment has been decided, the child and family are missing, presumably having left the emergency department. No further treatment can be made.

in the research, under the applicable law of the jurisdiction in which the research will be conducted." The NIH states that "children (individuals < 21 years of age) must be included in all human subjects research conducted or supported by the NIH unless there are scientific and ethical reasons not to include them."[8] Reasons for not including children in human subjects research are:[8]

❐ The research topic is irrelevant to children.

❐ Existing laws or regulations bar the inclusion of children in the research, such as projects that would require a higher level of risk.

❐ The knowledge to be gained from having children participate in the study is available, and an additional study would be redundant.

❐ A separate age-specific study is warranted.

❐ Insufficient data from adult subjects are available to judge the benefits and risks of the proposed intervention in children.

❐ The study involves a longitudinal design that collects data on preenrolled adult subjects.

❐ Other special cases not outlined above are described by the NIH.[8]

All research activities, including those conducted in emergency departments, are required to receive approval from an institutional review board (IRB). The purpose of IRB review and approval is to assure that any risks to the research participants are minimized, the benefit-to-risk ratio is optimized, valid informed consent is obtained, and research participants are treated ethically in accordance with existing regulations governing human subjects research.

Children are considered a vulnerable population because of their limited decision-making capacity.[9] As such, their participation as research subjects is justified only when

the level of risk is very low or if there is the potential for direct benefit through participating in the research.[10] Decision-making capacity requires that:[9]

❐ The child's choice is voluntary.

❐ The child's choice is both reasonable and rational.

❐ The child understands the information relevant to his or her choice.

Before their children's participation in research, parents are required to give their informed consent (permission). Elements of informed consent for research, as outlined by the Department of Health and Human Services Regulations for the Protection of Human Research Subjects, are found in Table 2.5. These elements must be detailed in a consent form that is signed by the parent and researcher. The reading level of consent forms is suggested to be at a seventh grade level to increase the likelihood that research participants will understand what is expected of them. Using plain language helps the research participant understand the medical jargon and enhances the ethical process for obtaining informed consent.[11] For example, in plain language, "venipuncture" is explained as "obtaining a blood sample."

Children are required to give their assent to participate in research. "Assent," as defined by the Code of Federal Regulations, is "a child's affirmative agreement to participate in research."[12] These regulations mean that children are active participants in their decision to participate in research.[13] The IRB determines when children are capable of providing assent on the basis of age, maturity, and psychological state of the potential research participant.[10,14] Federal regulations do not set a specific age limit regarding assent, leaving this decision to the IRB.[9] Usually, the age of seven years is used as the age when assent is obtained, although in some cases younger ages can be included in the assent process.

TABLE 2.5 Elements of Informed Consent for Research
An explanation of the research study's purpose
The expected length of participation
A description of the study protocol or procedures
The identification of experimental procedures
An explanation of the potential risks or discomfort and measures to modify the risks
A description of benefits to the subject or to others
An explanation of any alternative treatments or procedures that might be advantageous
A description of confidentiality and/or anonymity methods for protecting the subjects and notice that the U.S. Food and Drug Administration may inspect the research records (in drug research)
An explanation of compensation for treatment should injury occur and where further information could be obtained
The name of a person to contact for answers to pertinent research-related questions, a description of the subject's research-related rights, and the name of a person to contact if a research-related injury is sustained
A statement that the consent is voluntary and that refusal or withdrawal involves no penalty or loss of entitled benefits

American Academy of Pediatrics. Committee on Drugs. (1995). Guidelines for the ethical conduct of studies to evaluate drugs in pediatric populations. *Pediatrics, 95,* 286–294.

How a child's assent is obtained is determined by the IRB. The child can sign an assent form, or the researcher can sign a consent form attesting that the child's assent was obtained. Both cases are ethically important for meaningful assent so long as the child truly understands what he or she is being asked to do in the research. The child should understand what procedures will be completed, the potential risks and discomforts, and the voluntary nature of the research participation and that such assent was obtained without undue influence or coercion.[13] In obtaining assent, the researcher uses age-appropriate language and answers any questions with plain language information that the child can understand. Including children in the assent process is important to help children learn how to share responsibility in decision making regarding their health, while appreciating that children deserve respect and dignity throughout the research process.[10] In a study of healthy children that involved venipuncture, the majority of children understood why the blood sample was being obtained; the majority of children and their parents

believed that parents should make the final decision about study participation.[15] This finding demonstrates the need for informed consent and assent requirements that respect children's autonomy and understanding of their research participation, as well as the parents' role in providing consent.

Dissent is children's refusal to participate in a research study. When an IRB requires assent, and the child declines to participate, parents may overrule the child's dissent if participation provides direct benefit to the health and well-being of the child. Otherwise, that dissention is binding.[10] Exploring children's fears and concerns about the research may help them understand their participation in the study. However, researchers must be careful not to coerce the child's participation. Because children are taught to obey and respect those in authority, they may submit to the researcher's or parents' desires to participate, even if they do not wish to participate. Declining participation in research does not affect the child's and parents' current or future health care or emergency care, and this caveat should be reinforced. There may be times when a child's dissent may be overruled by parental consent, or when assent is not required at all. These situations are considered in the context in which they occur, and assistance from a patient/family representative, IRB member, ethics committee member, or other advocate may be needed. If children's dissent is overruled, the surrounding circumstances are recorded and explained to the children and families.[4]

Nursing Considerations in Research Consent and Assent

Children and parents should be given enough time to consider their participation in a research study and to make informed decisions about that participation, which may not always be possible in the emergency department. When such a limited therapeutic window exists, there may be no way to obtain meaningful, informed consent or assent; in such circumstances, there should be an adapted way to obtain full informed consent while complying with ethical principles and federal guidelines.[2] Such time limitations are considered during the IRB approval process to avoid the potential for coercion or undue influence during participant recruitment and enrollment. The Emergency Nurses Association (ENA) supports all governmental regulations for the protection of human research subjects and advocates for the inclusion of nurses on IRBs.[16]

Exception from Informed Consent

Conducting research in children and adolescents, as well as adults, who require resuscitation (e.g., trauma arrest) is unique because all potential research subjects are considered vulnerable because of their lack of capacity to understand or to communicate their wishes (assent, consent, dissent) regarding their research participation.[2] The emergency exception from informed consent (EFIC) rule (21 CFR. 50.24 and 45 CFR. 46.101[i]) addresses this situation. In resuscitation research, parents may not be available to give their consent or permission because they may be unavailable, delayed, or involved in the trauma themselves. This population becomes even more vulnerable because they may be routinely excluded from research, and thus new advances to save their lives cannot move forward. To assure proper protection of human subjects under the EFIC rule, certain safeguards must be in place (Table 2.6).

TABLE 2.6 Guidelines for Research Using an Exception from Informed Consent
The health condition must be life-threatening; available treatments are unproved or unsatisfactory; scientific evidence must be obtained to test the safety and effectiveness of the study intervention.
Participating in the research holds the prospect of direct benefit.
It is not feasible to obtain informed consent from the patient or the patient's family.
The proposed research cannot be practically conducted without the exception.
The proposed research defines the therapeutic window and when the consent will be obtained.
The IRB has approved the research and the consent procedures, which are consistent with the Common Rule. Community consultation and public disclosure regarding the research have occurred.
An independent data safety monitoring board is in place.

McRae, A., & Weijer, C. (2008). U.S. federal regulations for emergency research: A practical guide and commentary. *Academic Emergency Medicine, 15,* 88–97.

Nursing Considerations with Exception from Informed Consent

Emergency nurses can serve as members of their hospital's IRB to advocate for children and families involved in research. Becoming involved in their hospital's ethics committee and being acquainted with the hospital's legal counsel are ways in which emergency nurses can serve as patient advocates.

Pharmaceutical Research

Drugs must be studied in children to determine their

safety and efficacy because growth and maturation can alter the kinetics, organ responses, and toxicities of drugs in neonates, infants, children, and adolescents.[17] Generally, drug studies in children are undertaken once initial adult clinical trials have been completed. There are four phases of drug studies: phase I—clinical pharmacology (initial introduction into the human population), phase II—clinical investigation (demonstration of drug effectiveness and safety), phase III—clinical trials (effectiveness and drug-related adverse effects), and phase IV—postmarketing clinical trials (larger-scale trials). Drug studies must include measures to protect children's rights, as in other clinical investigations, and must follow the same procedures for informed consent and assent. Numerous safeguards must be in place for vulnerable pediatric patients, such as children with disabilities, children living in institutions, those requiring emergency care, dying children, children with chronically progressive or potentially fatal disease, and the newly dead (e.g., brain death).[17]

Nursing Considerations in Pharmaceutical Research

Emergency nurses may care for patients who are enrolled in drug studies involving chemotherapeutic agents, vaccine combinations, or other adjunctive therapies. The emergency physician will need to contact the researcher during ED treatment to inform the researcher about the patient's condition. Generally, in double-blinded randomized clinical trials, the blinding will not need to be broken. The researcher will have to decide whether the patient's ED visit is related to the study treatment, which would be considered a serious adverse event. The researcher will follow up with the patient after ED treatment.

Emergency nurses may be asked to administer drugs to patients enrolled in pharmaceutical research. Because this research often involves randomized clinical trials, nurses will be blinded to the study drugs. Emergency nurses should share any concerns about their participation in randomized clinical trials with the study's investigators. Nurses' and investigators' financial relationships with the sponsoring drug company must be disclosed to avoid a conflict of interest. Nurses may receive a "bonus" for enrolling study patients; any rewards must be commensurate with the investigator's efforts to avoid bias or undue influence on reported results.[17]

Legal Issues

Numerous legal considerations confront emergency nurses as they care for children and families. These legal issues range from appropriate screening and assessment to end-of-life decisions. This section outlines the basic legal ramifications faced by emergency nurses as they care for children and families.

Emergency Medical Treatment and Active Labor Act

EMTALA was enacted in 1986 under the umbrella of the Consolidated Omnibus Reconciliation Act (COBRA) (42 USC. 1395dd) to prevent the inappropriate transfer of patients based on their inability to pay for treatment.[18] This law applies only to hospitals that have a provider agreement with Medicare and Medicaid, but all patients are covered under this law regardless of their insurance coverage. EMTALA is a federal law but is regulated by individual states.

Hospitals must state in their institutional bylaws that a medical screening examination will be conducted in all patients presenting to the emergency department for treatment. These bylaws specify that:

❑ An examination must be provided within the capability of the hospital's emergency department to determine whether or not an emergency medical condition exists.

❑ An appropriate medical screening must be performed by a physician or "qualified medical personnel" (QMP). Qualified medical personnel is a coined term only in the context of EMTALA and refers to a practitioner who has been approved by medical staff and is endorsed according to the Medical Staff Bylaws or the Medical Staff Rules and Regulations.[19]

A medical screening examination is defined by the institution as it deems appropriate. One recommendation for the medical screening examination is:[20]

❑ Log entry including disposition
❑ Triage record
❑ Ongoing record of vital signs
❑ History and physical examination
❑ Use of on-call physician as necessary
❑ Discharge/transfer vital signs
❑ Clear documentation of all of the above

Medical screening is not equivalent to triage.[21] The Health Care Financing Administration posits that patients presenting to the emergency department must receive a medical screening examination beyond triage; the hospital must provide the appropriate medical screening examination within its capability, including the use of ancillary services routinely available to the emergency department.[1] The medical screening is documented, and the documentation is placed in the patient's medical record. Triage only designates the order in which the patients are taken for the medical screening examination; triage is not a substitute for the medical screening examination. Therefore, medical screening examinations must be more comprehensive than a triage assessment that determines acuity and must be able to rule out the possibility of a legally defined emergency health care condition.[22]

❑ After the medical screening, the disposition will be one of the following:
  ▪ Remain in the emergency department for treatment
  ▪ Transfer to another area of the hospital
  ▪ Transfer to a different health care facility

❑ Common violations of EMTALA by hospitals include:[23]
  ▪ Referring patients to the proper provider without a medical screening examination
  ▪ Referring patients to the gatekeeper physician
  ▪ Forcing patients to call their insurance provider or gatekeeper for preauthorization
  ▪ Sending patients away on the basis of a managed-care or insurance denial of coverage for a visit

Penalties for EMTALA violations can be severe; the institution could have its Medicare provider agreement terminated, and both the hospital and physician could be fined up to $50,000.[20]

Nursing Considerations Under EMTALA

Emergency nurses should work closely with their hospital legal department to create meaningful policies that meet EMTALA requirements. It is important to avoid asking children and families about their insurance status before their medical screening because the families may believe that their treatment is being based on their ability to pay. This questioning is in violation of EMTALA. If families believe their treatment was in violation of EMTALA requirements, they can register a complaint with the government, and the hospital will be investigated. The caveat to asking patients about their insurance is if there is a delay in initially being seen by the triage nurse, the information can be obtained. In essence, insurance information can be obtained if it does not slow the process of the patient receiving a medical screening.

As access to care becomes increasingly more difficult. The monitoring of EMTALA issues has increased. The Centers for Medicare & Medicaid Services (CMS) provide interpretive guidelines. It is important to be current with EMTALA guidelines. The following are rules under EMTALA that impact emergency departments:

❑ The 250-yard rule: In 2000, CMS issued new amendments to the rules under CFR 489.[24] This amendment stated that an emergency department must respond to any "presentation" on the hospital campus or at any provider-based off-campus facility of the hospital. Under the 2000 rule, the emergency department would be responsible for areas adjacent to the main building and within 250 yards, for example, a local restaurant. In 2003, the revision provides that "the 250-yard zone will continue to apply when defining the 'hospital campus.'" Now, however, that sphere does not include non-medical businesses (shops and restaurants located close to the hospital), nor does it include physicians' offices or other medical entities that have a separate Medicare identity.[24]

❑ Parking: This refers to hospitals that deliberately delay moving a patient from an EMS stretcher to an ED bed in order not to begin their EMTALA obligation. Even if a hospital cannot immediately complete a medical screening, it still must assess the individual's condition on arrival to ensure that the individual is appropriately triaged.[22]

Every employee, from the registration clerk to the nurse and physician, needs to be educated about EMTALA requirements. Each employee has the potential to violate EMTALA in the absence of formal education.

Emergency nurses must initiate a departmental competency program in which nurses can identify core competencies and develop performance objectives. Included in these core competencies should be scenarios related to how hospital employees respond to individuals seeking medical care. All individuals must be offered a medical screening. Any reference of "being too busy" or indicating the possibility of a very long wait may be viewed as an EMTALA violation. Also included is the failure of an on-call physician to come to the hospital to see a patient after being requested by an ED physician; in this circumstance, the on-call physician may be subject to sanctions for violation of EMTALA.[22, 25]

Other requirements under EMTALA include:[26]

❑ Posting of EMTALA signs that alert patients and families of their rights to a screening examination

❑ Reporting of inappropriate transfers from hospitals

❑ Maintaining records of transfers to or from other departments for five years

❑ Maintaining a central log of patients seeking assistance at the department and outcome of each

❑ Maintaining a central call list of on-call physicians

❑ Establishing protocols for the handling of individuals with potential emergency medical conditions at off-campus departments

Stabilization of the patient's emergency health condition requires that the hospital provide staff and facilities for further evaluation and treatment needed to stabilize the patient's condition.

Transfer to another facility occurs after the patient's condition has been stabilized to the best of that facility's ability. The emergency department is not permitted to discharge or transfer the patient without stabilization unless the patient requests transfer in writing and the physician signs a certificate that the benefits of transfer outweigh the transfer risk. The transfer must include assurances that:

❑ Treatment provided by the transferring hospital minimizes the risk of transfer

❑ The receiving facility has the space, qualified personnel, and agreement to accept and treat the patient

❑ The transferring hospital will send the patient's records and informed consent for transfer

❑ Transfer will be facilitated with qualified personnel and equipment

❑ The above stipulations under EMTALA will not be enforced during a declared disaster, and disaster plans for transferring patients will supersede EMTALA restrictions. This does not mean that institutions can refuse patients at will, but they must be in compliance with their disaster preparedness plan.[25]

A hospital's EMTALA obligation ends when a physician or QMP has made a decision that:

❑ No emergency exists

❑ An emergency exists that requires transfer to another facility, or the patient requests transfer to another facility (the EMTALA obligation rests with the transferring hospital until arrival at the receiving hospital)

❑ An emergency exists, and the patient is admitted to the hospital for further stabilizing treatment

Once a patient is admitted, the EMTALA laws no longer apply, as EMTALA laws do not apply to inpatients. If an employee or guest in the hospital is injured or becomes ill on hospital premises, however, this circumstance is covered under EMTALA regulations.[27]

In addition to working with the hospital's legal department to develop medical screening guidelines, emergency nurses should work with the hospital to develop guidelines for transport and transfer (Chapter 8). Transfer agreements should be in place among hospitals to facilitate the transfer and transport of pediatric patients requiring specialized treatment, such as burn care, intensive care, psychiatric care, or obstetric care. Examples of EMTALA-related Web sites include http://www.emtala.com, http://www.medlaw.com, and http://www.acep.org.

Guidelines for Persons with Language Barriers

The Department of Health and Human Services, Office of Civil Rights, recently issued guidelines to assist health care providers in ensuring that persons with limited English proficiency (LEP) or skills can effectively access needed health services. These guidelines apply to all state-administered private and nonprofit facilities, including prehospital and emergency care services that receive Medicare and Medicaid payments. A copy of the guidelines can be downloaded at http://www.hhs.gov/ocr. Emergency departments can enhance their compliance with these guidelines by taking the following steps:[28]

❒ Having policies and procedures for identifying and assessing the language needs of patients and families

❒ Posting notices to persons with LEP of their right to free language assistance

❒ Holding staff training sessions and monitoring programs

❒ Having available a range of oral language assistance options pertinent to each ED's population

❒ Providing written materials in languages other than English when a significant proportion of the ED population requires services or information in another language to effectively communicate

Nursing Considerations in Persons with Language Barriers

The initial patient/family encounter must establish trust and good communication. It is recommended that a professional interpretation services be used at all times. If a family member or friend is used for interpretation, they have a personal role in the information and may possibly misinterpret the translation on the basis of their own feelings and concerns. Sometimes institutions rely on bilingual nurses or other hospital personnel, which could lead to liability issues if there is perceived misinterpretation of the information being offered.[29]

Reportable Health Conditions

Reportable pediatric health conditions in general include:

❒ Infectious diseases

❒ Communicable diseases

❒ Trauma-related injuries of a specific nature (e.g., fireworks injuries or gunshot wounds)

❒ Suspected or documented domestic violence and child maltreatment

Health conditions that must be reported to the local or state health department vary among the states. The reporting of these conditions serves the purpose of determining incidence (number of new cases of a disease within a population for a given time period) and prevalence (number of current or ongoing cases of a disease within a population for a given time period). Accuracy in reporting allows for the calculation of endemic (normal occurrence within the population) disease rates for the population. Failure to report these health conditions may lead to underestimation of the health condition. Local jurisdictions may require the reporting of additional conditions.

Nursing Considerations in Reportable Health Conditions

Emergency nurses should be educated about and maintain a policy and procedure on reportable health conditions. Specific reporting forms should be readily accessible. Reporting is done through hospital protocols that may vary by department (i.e., Infectious Disease, Quality Department, Emergency Department). Inviting local health department officials to the emergency department to review data concerning reportable health conditions is helpful and enhances the transparency of the reporting process.

Patient Self-Determination Act

The Patient Self-Determination Act (advance directives) was passed by Congress in 1990 and was put into effect in 1991. This act requires health maintenance organizations, home health agencies, and others who receive Medicare reimbursement to inform patients about their right to direct decisions about their health care treatment (including cardiopulmonary resuscitation, ventilatory assistance, artificial feeding, and hydration) when they might become terminally ill or permanently unconscious and unable to communicate. These agencies are required by law to:

❒ Inform patients about advance directives

❒ Ask patients if they have advance directives

❒ Educate the community (including employees) about advance directives

Advance directives are written instructions that inform health care (including emergency care) personnel about an individual patient's choices of life-sustaining treatment in the event that the individual could not speak or decide for himself or herself. Two types of advance directives are:

▪ Living will—a written document that describes those health care treatments a person would accept or refuse when that person is no longer capable of making those decisions or is in a permanently unconscious state.

- Durable power of attorney—a legal document that specifies the appointment of another person to make health care decisions for an individual when that individual is no longer able to make those decisions. The living will and durable power of attorney complement each other.

Advance directives pertain to adults; the definition of adult may vary from state to state but generally includes individuals who are 18 years of age or older, are married or have been previously married, and/or have graduated from high school.

Advance directives should be created before a crisis situation occurs. They are designed to encourage open dialogue among family members to prevent family, friends, and health care providers from having to make difficult decisions without the benefit of knowing the patient's wishes. The advance directives may be written on a declaration form available from the hospital. The form requires the signature of two witnesses, is simple to complete, and does not require notarization (although, it is often recommended). Patients wanting to complete a declaration form should discuss the decisions with their physicians and families and should provide copies of the declaration to health care providers, including emergency personnel, when necessary.

The enactment of advance directives in the emergency department is very difficult because the ED staff may have no prior relationship with the family who is forced to make end-of-life decisions. Although it is difficult to enact or ask families about advance directives, such difficulty does not diminish the emergency team's responsibilities to uphold the Patient Self-Determination Act.

Nursing Considerations in Advance Directives

Emergency nurses should work with the hospital legal department to identify methods for incorporating advance directives into ED care. For example, a process should be identified where every eligible patient is queried as to the presence of advance directives. Under the Self-Determination Act, only patients of legal age are required to be informed and asked about living wills. This inquiry could occur at triage, at the registration desk, or on initial treatment. Reassuring patients that the advance directives come into effect only when they are unable to express their wishes about their health care or are in a permanent unconscious state offers them confidence that their advance directives do not affect the course of their ED treatment.

Withdrawing and Withholding Treatment

Withdrawing treatment is the cessation of treatment once it has been initiated. Hospital emergency departments generally establish guidelines for such treatment, such as a specified time or specified number of medication "rounds" administered during cardiopulmonary resuscitation. Such guidelines may evolve from current evidence or research literature.

Withholding treatment is when treatment was never initiated. For example, a patient with a terminal illness may not receive cardiopulmonary resuscitation measures on ED presentation.

Nursing Considerations in Withdrawing and Withholding Treatment

When in doubt about withholding or withdrawing treatment, the ED staff should initiate measures until a legal guardian or representative speaks on behalf of the patient. Contacting the patient's primary care provider and discussing the situation with the provider is essential. Emergency nurses should participate in the development of protocols and policies for withdrawing and withholding life support.[30]

Do Not Resuscitate Orders

Do not resuscitate (DNR) orders are found in children with terminal illnesses. In some states, children with DNR orders attend school and other activities. Generally, these children wear a bracelet that must be updated and signed on a regular interval by the physician. School nurses, prehospital providers, and hospital personnel should uphold the DNR order. On presentation to the emergency department, the emergency personnel should follow the DNR order while providing comfort measures in conjunction with family wishes.

The DNR order can be overridden by the family members who bring the child to the emergency department and "want everything done" to prolong their child's life. In this circumstance, initiation of resuscitation would begin while working with the child's physician and other persons to support the family.

Nursing Considerations with DNR Orders

Emergency nurses should be prepared for the treatment of children in the emergency department with DNR orders by having policies and procedures in place that outline the steps emergency care providers should take when such a situation arises. The parents should be queried as to the enactment of the DNR order; that is, parents may want to resuscitate the child and void the original order.

Parents should bring a copy of the DNR order with them to the emergency department. The emergency staff should contact the child's primary care physician for confirmation of the DNR order; the emergency team can collaborate with the physician and parents on how to proceed. At the time of impending death, the family will require support and understanding as they begin the grieving process. This is very difficult for the emergency nurse who usually does not know the family and their stage in the grieving process. Providing a sense of closure for families is very important.

Organ Donation

Hospitals are required under law to have written policies and procedures to address organ procurement. Each institution must have a written agreement with the specific organ procurement organization in their individual area. The procurement organization under law must be notified of every death or imminent death in the hospital. Previously, the physician caring for the patient was the health care professional who approached the family about organ donation; however, the physician's involvement was often perceived as a conflict of interest. As an improvement to organ procurement, only an organ procurement representative or a designated requestor can approach a family about organ donation. Any individual involved in a request for organ, tissue, and eye donation must be formally trained in the donation request process. Ideally, the organ procurement representative and the designated requestor should decide together who will approach the patient.

Nursing Considerations in Organ Donation

All patient care staff must be trained on organ donation under the law (A0376 482.54[A][S]). This education should be part of all new employee orientation. In each ED procedure, it should be designated who informs the procurement center of an impending death, as the procurement team must be notified of all deaths of any type. Caregivers should be educated in the cultural, religious, and social issues affecting the donation process to support families in times of crisis. Individual beliefs and values of caregivers should not influence patients' and families' decision making. Also under the law, every family must be asked and informed about organ donation in a manner that is respectful. The caregiver's perception that a family is too grief-stricken or that their specific religious beliefs or socioeconomic background would prevent them from donating cannot be used as a reason not to approach a family.

Health Insurance Portability and Accountability Act of 1996 (HIPAA) Privacy Rule

The HIPAA Privacy Rule provides Federal protection for individually identifiable health information held by covered entities, such as hospitals, health care providers and health insurance companies. The HIPAA Privacy Rule gives patients an array of rights with respect to that information. The Rule also permits the disclosure of personal health information needed for patient care and other important purposes.

"Individually identifiable health information" is information, including demographic data, that relates to:[31]

❑ the individual's past, present or future physical or mental health or condition

❑ the provision of health care to the individual, or

❑ the past, present, or future payment for the provision of health care to the individual, and that identifies the individual or for which there is a reasonable basis to believe can be used to identify the individual.[13] Individually identifiable health information includes many common identifiers (e.g., name, address, birth date, Social Security Number).

HIPAA stipulates that the determination of the release of a minor's health record is contingent upon who consented to the treatment. If by state statue a minor is permitted to consent for treatment, then the minor is the only person who can authorize the release of his or her health care record. Individual states have developed acts and codes that determine the conditions under which:

❑ parents can access their minor child's health record.

❑ physicians may restrict parental access to their minor child's health record.

❑ other entities can access a minor's health record.

Nursing Considerations with the HIPAA Privacy Rule

Emergency Department nurses should be aware of their state's acts and codes specific to HIPAA when delivering patient care. All ED staff must comply with the HIPAA Privacy Rule, in accordance with hospital policy, while delivering patient care. This includes:

❑ not talking about patients and families in public areas.

❑ assessing infants and pre-verbal patients in public areas (includes disrobing, changing diapers).

❑ not permitting unauthorized hospital staff to read the charts of or examine vulnerable patients, such as those with malformations, syndromes and special health care needs.

Conclusion

Ethical and legal issues arise in the emergency nursing care of children. Emergency nurses should be prepared to work through these issues by having policies and procedures in place for guidance. Having access to the hospital's ethics committee and IRBs is helpful as well.

References

1. Emergency Medical Treatment & Labor Act, 42 USC 1395 dd. (1986).

2. Baren, J. M. (2006). Ethical dilemma in the care of minors in the emergency department. *Emergency Medical Clinics of North America, 24,* 619–631.

3. Boonstra, H., & Nash, E. (2000). Minors and the right to consent to health care. *The Guttmacher Report on Public Policy, 3*(4), 4–8.

4. American Academy of Pediatrics Committee on Bioethics. (1995). Informed consent, parental permission, and assent in pediatric practice. *Pediatrics, 95,* 314–317.

5. American Academy of Pediatrics, Committee on Pediatric Emergency Medicine. (2003). Consent for emergency medical services for children and adolescents. *Pediatrics, 111*(3), 703–706.

6. Freyer, D. R. (2004). Care of the dying adolescent: Special considerations. *Pediatrics, 111*(2), 381–388.

7. Mercurio, M. (2008). Adolescent's refusal of treatment: Principles in conflict. *Journal of Pediatric Endocrinology & Metabolism, 21,* 3–6.

8. National Institutes of Health. (1998). *NIH policy and guidelines on the inclusion of children as participants in research involving human subjects.* Bethesda, MD: Author.

9. Unguru, Y., Coppes, M., & Kamani, N. (2008). Rethinking pediatric assent: From requirement to ideal. *Pediatric Clinics of North America, 55,* 211–222.

10. Diekema, D. (2006). Conducting ethical research in pediatrics: A brief historical overview and review of pediatric regulations. *Journal of Pediatrics, 149,* S3–S11.

11. Green, J., Duncan, R., Barnes, G., & Oberklaid, F. (2003). Putting the 'informed' into 'consent': A matter of plain language. *Journal of Paediatrics and Child Health, 39,* 700–703.

12. Department of Health and Human Services. Food and Drug Administration protection of human subjects; informed consent, 61(192) *Fed. Reg.* 51,498–51,524 (Oct. 2, 1996). 21 CFR 34, 50, 312, 601, 812, 814.

13. Ungar, D., Joffe, S., & Kodish, E. (2006). Children are not small adults: Documentation of assent for research involving children. *Journal of Pediatrics, 149,* S31–S33.

14. McRae, A., & Weijer, C. (2008). U.S. federal regulations for emergency research: A practical guide and commentary. *Academic Emergency Medicine, 15,* 88–97.

15. John, T., Hope, T., Savulescu, J., Stein, A., & Pollard, A. (2008). Children's consent and paediatric research: Is it appropriate for healthy children to be the decision-makers in clinical research? *Archives of Disease in Childhood, 93*(5), 379–383.

16. Emergency Nurses Association. (2003). *Protection of human subjects' rights.* Des Plaines, IL: Author.

17. American Academy of Pediatrics. Committee on Drugs. (1995). Guidelines for the ethical conduct of studies to evaluate drugs in pediatric populations. *Pediatrics, 95,* 286–294.

18. EMTALA Statute: 42 USC 1395dd. *EMTALA online—Health Law Resource Center.* Retrieved October 30, 2008, from http://www.medlaw.com/statute.htm

19. Teshome, G., & Closson, F. T. (2006). Emergency Medical Treatment and Labor Act: The basics and other medicolegal concerns. *Pediatric Clinics of North America, 53*(1), 139–155.

20. Maha, R. J. (n.d.). *EMTALA.* Emergency Resource Management, Inc. [Powerpoint lecture].

21. Bond, P. G. (2008). Implications of EMTALA on nursing triage and ED staff education. *Journal of Emergency Nursing, 34,* 205–206.

22. Ream, K. (2008). Washington Watch. CMS Updates. EMTALA interpretative guidelines. *American Academy of Emergency Medicine, 15*(1), 10,13–14.

References (continued)

23. Frew Consulting Group. (1996, Spring). Managed care leads COBRA risk list. *Risk Manager.*

24. EMTALA.com. (n.d.). *Special note—What is the 250-yard rule and how does it affect these issues?* Retrieved September 12, 2008, from http://www. emtala.com/250yard.htm

25. Emergency Nurses Association. (n.d.). *EMTALA information.* Retrieved October 30, 2008, from http:// www.ena.org/government/emtala

26. Frank, G. (2000). I was born a rambling law. Complying with EMTALA when coming to the emergency department may not actually mean "coming to the emergency department." *Journal of Emergency Nursing, 26*(4), 360–362.

27. Frank, G. (2002). CMS clarifies application of EMTALA to off-site outpatient departments and to hospital campuses. *Journal of Emergency Nursing, 28*(1), 57–59.

28. U.S. Department of Health and Human Services. (2000). Facilities accepting Medicare, Medicaid get new guidelines for helping persons with limited English skills. *EMSC News, 13*(4), 5.

29. Lehna, C. (2005). Interpreter services in pediatric nursing. *Pediatric Nursing, 31*(4), 293–296.

30. Emergency Nurses Association. (1998). *Resuscitative decisions.* Des Plaines, IL: Author.

31. U.S. Department of Health and Human Services, Office for Civil Rights. (2003). *Summary of the HIPAA Privacy Rule.* Retrieved February 25, 2009, from http://www.hhs.gov/ocr/privacy/hipaa

SECTION TWO
Developmental Aspects of Pediatric Emergency Nursing

THREE

Developmental and Psychosocial Considerations

Alice E. Conway, PhD, FNP-BC

Introduction

To the child of any age, a visit to the emergency department (ED) can be, at best, a frightening event and, at worst, a traumatizing experience. In a brief amount of time, under stressful circumstances, emergency nurses must create and establish a trusting relationship with the child and family (Table 3.1).

Emergency nurses use principles of psychosocial development to facilitate family-centered care and coping among infants, children, and adolescents before, during, and after ED treatment. A working knowledge of these developmental stages allows the emergency nurse to anticipate the child's stage of psychosocial development and expected reactions to emergency care. Emergency nurses recognize that each child develops at his or her own pace (Table 3.2) and is influenced by many factors, including temperament, family relations, culture, experience, and perception of the current situation.

This chapter will demonstrate the integration of psychosocial principles into emergency nursing care and the implementation of approaches to family-centered care. This integration supports The Joint Commission's recommendation for age-specific competencies in the provision of emergency care. The following chapter with its age-specific tables of psychosocial considerations with specific interventions to facilitate coping and development can be used by emergency departments to develop their own guidelines to meet The Joint Commission's recommendations. Children's hospitals that have developed detailed competencies may be willing to share their expertise with community hospitals to further promote pediatric nursing care.

Cultural Influences

Health care decisions are affected by a family's degree of acculturation, language barriers, educational opportunities, economic barriers to care, experiences of prejudice in the larger society and in the health care setting, and child-rearing practices.[1] In an increasingly culturally diverse society, emergency nurses must appreciate each child's and family's sociocultural background. It is too easy to inadvertently insult a child and caregiver when "nurses act only on what they feel is correct, which is usually based only on their own values and education."[2]

Cultural competence is the ability to communicate among cultures and demonstrate cultural skill outside of one's culture of origin.[3] Culturally competent providers work with families to increase mutual understanding, share information and knowledge, and assist families to achieve healthy decisions.[4] Education of health care professionals in dealing with families of different origins can reduce differences in their satisfaction with ED services.[5] Although it is impossible for the emergency nurse to be an expert about all cultures and ethnic groups who present to the emergency department, emergency nurses can:

❐ Have access to a cultural handbook for reference and clarification (see reference list)

❐ Attend educational offerings on specific cultural and ethnic groups to enhance the nurse's sensitivity to specific cultural and ethnic beliefs and concerns

❐ Invite representatives of local cultural and ethnic groups to the emergency department to share their experiences and collaborate with emergency nurses on how to provide culturally sensitive nursing care

❐ Know which cultures and ethnic groups are prevalent in the emergency department's service area

❐ Learn another language

❐ Have an interpreter available if needed[6]

❐ Become familiar with a culture's central issues related to health and illness

❐ Attend local cultural and ethnic events

❐ Review Web site opportunities pertaining to cultural perspectives

  ▪ National Network of Libraries of Medicine: Cultural Competency Resources, http://www.nnlm.gov/mcr/resources/community/competency.html

TABLE 3.1 General Guidelines to Create a Trusting Relationship with the Child and Family During Emergency Department Treatment

Avoid using the words good or bad to denote a child's health status.	Children perceive these words as descriptions of themselves, not as general comments. These words can also reinforce their misconceptions about the cause of the problem.[32]
Provide feedback and reassurance.	Children appreciate reassurance; rewards such as a sticker and praise are especially valued and remembered after a painful procedure. All children do their best to cooperate with the emergency staff.
Provides specialized care to the child.	
Consult other health care professionals, such as child life specialists, social workers, and spiritual counselors.	A calm, soft voice, gentle assertiveness, and confidence help the nurse to maintain control of a difficult situation.
Stay confident and calm.	

- University of California, San Francisco, The Network for Multicultural Health, The Center for Health Professions, http://www.futurehealth.ucsf.edu/TheNetwork/
- National Center for Cultural Competence, http://www11.georgetown.edu/research/gucchd/nccc/

Culturally Sensitive Nursing Assessment

Although a thorough cultural assessment in the emergency department is not feasible or practical, an abbreviated assessment is warranted to provide culturally sensitive care.[7] This assessment is incorporated in the health history and physical assessment (Chapter 5) and includes the following information:

- ❑ Country of origin
- ❑ Length of time the family has resided in the United States, if the child and family are immigrants
- ❑ Child's and family's first and second languages
- ❑ Information the family would like to share about themselves that would facilitate their ED care
- ❑ Information on the use of home remedies or home prescriptions or treatments (type of remedy, when it was last used, for how long it was used, why it was used)
- ❑ Available social and economic resources

Culturally Sensitive Nursing Interventions

Selected culturally sensitive nursing interventions that emergency nurses can incorporate into their practice include:

- ❑ Focusing on the family's attitudes and values while initiating emergency nursing interventions. Asking

about the family's health care practices acknowledges the heterogeneity of such practices within cultural groups.[8] Any generalizations about the family's ethnic group may not apply to certain groups or individuals. However, in general, families of Hispanic origin are insulted if the nurse does not touch the head of a young child. Conversely, it is considered a major insult if a person touches an Asian child's head without permission.[7]

- ❑ Avoiding criticism of the family's cultural beliefs and related health practices. Such attacks may lead the family to mistrust the ED staff and may affect their compliance with treatment regimens.
- ❑ Collaborating with the family to blend traditional and cultural approaches to health care. This approach recognizes the family's values and provides an opportunity for teaching about traditional health care (e.g., the importance of childhood immunizations).
- ❑ Identifying the family's key members, such as a family elder. Failure to include these significant individuals in teaching and decision making can seriously hinder adherence to the plan of care.[9]

Psychosocial Considerations by Age Group

Infants Born Early

More high-risk infants are discharged from neonatal intensive care units to home because of increased sophisticated prenatal and postnatal care. On presentation to the emergency department for treatment, this population requires special considerations (Chapter 9). The major developmental task of infants born early is to become physiologically stable and grow and develop appropriately.

TABLE 3.2 Summary of Psychosocial, Cognitive, Moral, and Spiritual Development Theories

Developmental Theory/Age	Infancy Birth–1 year	Toddlerhood 1–3 years	Preschool 4–6 years	School Age 7–12 years	Adolescence 13–18 years
Psychosocial development[10]	Trust vs. mistrust "I am what I am given."	Autonomy vs. shame and doubt "I am what I will."	Initiative vs. guilt "I am what I can imagine I will be."	Industry vs. inferiority "I am what I learn."	Identity vs. role confusion "I am who I decide to be."
Positive outcome	Hope; can delay gratification	Will, positive self-esteem	Purposeful, self-starter	Competence, perseverance	Fidelity, optimism
Negative outcome	Suspicion, withdrawal	Compulsion, impulsivity	Inhibition	Inadequacy, gives up easily	Defiance, diffidence
Cognitive development[12]	Sensorimotor (birth to 2 years)	Preoperational thought (transducive reasoning, 2 to 4 years of age)	Preoperational thought (intuitive phase, 4 to 7 years of age)	Concrete operations (inductive reasoning and beginning logic)	Formal operations (deductive and abstract reasoning)
Theme	Object permanence	Egocentrism—cannot understand another person's point of view	Two events occur together	Conservation reversibility	Logical conclusions
Moral development[33,34]	N/A	Preconventional (premoral) level	Preconventional (premoral) level	Conventional level	Postconventional level
Theme	N/A	Punishment and obedience orientation	Naive instrumental orientation; child follows rules as he or she desires	Social system and conscience "Good boy/nice girl" orientation Law and order orientation	Social-contract orientation Universal ethical principle
Spiritual development[35]	Undifferentiated	Initiative-projective Imitate behavior of others	Initiative-projective Follow parental values and beliefs, especially about good and bad	Mythical-literal Strong interest in religion; existence of deity usually accepted	Synthetic-convention Early adolescence—begin to question beliefs Individuating—reflective, searching, and accepts uncertainty

They cannot handle stress without serious physiologic changes. Their parents are often more nervous and unsure and need support from professionals in caring for their young infants. Specific interventions to facilitate high-risk infant coping and promote development are outlined in Table 3.3.

TABLE 3.3	Specific Interventions to Facilitate High-Risk Infant Coping and Promote Development	
Interventions	**Rationale**
Keep infant as warm as possible. Swaddle when medically stable.	Maintaining a body temperature is a difficult task for high-risk infants and consumes calories needed for growth.
Facilitate flexion of extremities and midline orientation. Minimize extension positions. Avoid unsupported supine position. Position arms and legs close to body.	Flexion is the preferred position of young infants and helps them maintain physiologic stability.
Offer pacifier for self-calming.	Sucking on a pacifier provides a method for infants to block noxious stimuli.
Keep room warm and quiet, and speak softly.	Decreases stress for infant[36]

Infants Born at Term

The major developmental task of infancy is the attainment of trust.[10] Trust is established gradually and is facilitated when needs (feeding, comfort, and social interaction) are met in a consistent manner by a primary caregiver. If given inconsistent care, infants develop a sense of mistrust because they are not sure that their needs will be met. The following are key characteristics of infants:

❏ Infants pick up their emotional cues from the caregiver and become anxious if the caregiver is anxious.

❏ As infants grow, their motor skills increase and they use active withdrawal as a coping mechanism.

❏ Crying is the infant's major form of communicating distress, and the infant's cry is very stressful to the caregiver.

❏ Infants feel pain and need appropriate analgesia (Chapter 11).

❏ Stranger anxiety and separation anxiety are major cognitive accomplishments in infancy, beginning around 7 or 8 months and peaking at 12 to 18 months.[11]

Specific interventions to facilitate infant coping and promote development are outlined in Table 3.4.

Toddlers

Upright locomotion and increasing language skills allow toddlers to be active explorers of self, others, and the environment. The toddler's developing sense of autonomy leads to a need for control ("Me do it.") and a differentiation of self from others ("No."). Failure to achieve autonomy can produce shame and doubt; the toddler may withdraw and be unable to test limits and learn about the environment.[10] The following are key characteristics of toddlers:

❏ Separation is necessary for autonomy, but this separation causes fears. Methods of coping with these fears include behaviors such as withdrawing, clinging, being aggressive, regressing, and using a transitional object (security blanket).

❏ Toddlers only understand time in terms of a daily schedule ("We'll see daddy after dinner.").

❏ Between 18 and 24 months, toddlers are capable of determining a cause after observing an effect, but only within the limits of their prior experiences[12, 13] (e.g., a visit to the emergency department may mean a hurtful injection).

❏ Toddlers have limited expressive language skills, understanding more than they can verbalize. Toddlers focus their attention for a short time period.

❏ As toddlers learn to control their bodies, they also become fearful of being hurt and will use motor activities (e.g., hitting, kicking, or biting) when hurt.

❏ Toddlers can tell you where they hurt ("arm hurts") but cannot describe the pain.[14]

❏ Toddlers are developing a body image and perceive body boundaries but have fears about bodily injury.

❏ Regressive behaviors, such as temper tantrums and refusal to obey, are often seen as a response to crisis situations and are adaptive.[13]

❏ Specific interventions to facilitate toddler coping and promote development are outlined in Table 3.5.

Preschoolers

During the preschool period, the child believes, "I am what I can imagine I will be."[15] This is a period of initiative where children are ready to try new activities and experiences. Preschoolers have very active imaginations

TABLE 3.4 Specific Interventions to Facilitate Infant Coping and Promote Development

Interventions	Rationale
Offer self-comforting measures, such as the use of pacifiers.	Sucking provides oral comfort.
When possible, secure intravenous access in the non-preferred arm.	This allows the infant access to the preferred hand for sucking.
Keep the young infant, when possible, in a flexed position, with knees to chest and arms midline.	This position helps the infant to retain or regain physiologic and behavioral functioning.[13]
Allow rest periods between procedures and treatments.	Helps the infant to restore energy. Overwhelmed infants will withdraw into sleep. They may also become hypothermic or hypoxic.
Help caregiver to stay calm when comforting the infant.	Infants are able to sense their caregiver's distress cognitively, even though they are not able to understand cause and effect.
Rock, swaddle, and sing softly to the infant.	Provides comfort to a stressed infant.
Reunite the infant and caregiver as soon as possible in security and comfort.	Allowing the caregiver to comfort and hold the infant fosters the infant's body image, which is at a feeling level.
Keep the parent in the infant's sight as much as possible.[37]	Visual contact with the mother promotes maternal following treatments or procedures.
Release the infant from a restrained or held position as soon as possible after a procedure or treatment.	Infants diffuse stress and frustration through motor activity[38]; promotes coping.
Provide pharmacologic and nonpharmacologic pain control as needed (Chapter 11).	Newborns and infants have all of the physiologic mechanisms necessary to perceive pain.[14]
Use warm hands, equipment, and room when caring for the infant.	Infants have a large body surface-to- weight area, and they quickly lose body heat; promotes comfort.
Maintain a safe environment.	Infants easily roll from tables, and older infants put objects into their mouths as they explore their environment.
Distract infants with brightly colored toys, hand puppets, or a human face talking to them.	Provides a diversion or distraction from the task at hand.

that work to their benefit when fantasy is used as a distraction technique. Their imaginations can also increase their fears, and what they imagine is often worse than reality. The development of a sense of guilt is possible because so much of what they would like to do is either forbidden or beyond their psychomotor capabilities. During this period, the child is very active, progressing rapidly in motor abilities, cognitive function, and language development. The following are key characteristics of preschoolers:

❏ Due to their increased language skills they are able to communicate their hurts and fears.

❏ Although preschoolers have a separate identity from that of their parents, they need their parents to reassure, to set limits, and to prevent loss of control.

❏ Because of their rich imaginations and the beginnings of conscience and preoperational cognition,

preschoolers often interpret injury or illness as a result of something they did wrong.

❏ Preschoolers are egocentric and need to have procedures explained in terms of what they will feel, smell, and taste. They also believe that everyone sees the world the way they do.

❏ By 4 years of age, children have a well-defined concept of their external bodies and the relationships among their body parts; however, their concept of the inner body is primitive.[16]

❏ Sex-typing and sex-role identification are major tasks; preschoolers need to know that even brave boys and girls cry.

❏ Preschoolers possess an enhanced repertoire of coping skills. Although they continue to use language and

TABLE 3.5 Specific Interventions to Facilitate Toddler Coping and Promote Development

Interventions	Rationale
Approach the toddler slowly; talk with the caregiver while the child becomes accustomed to the nurse's presence.	Minimizes fear and decreases stranger anxiety. If the caregiver trusts the nurse, then the child will trust as well.
Keep on the child's level—sit down or bend. Be alert to how the ED environment looks from the child's vantage point.	A new environment reminds children of their own small-ness and lack of control.[39]
Encourage the child to examine equipment and perform a procedure on a doll or caregiver. For example, allow the toddler to listen to the nurse's heart first.	Rehearsal helps the child feel a sense of control.
Give choices whenever possible (e.g., "Do you want your mom or dad to hold you while I listen to your heart?").	Gives the child some control and makes the child feel less threatened.
Use simple, concrete terms when explaining to the toddler what the toddler will feel during the procedure immediately before the procedure occurs.	Avoids undue fear or anxiety because the toddler's concept of time is not well developed.
Tolerate a moderate amount of verbal and motor protesting.	Mobility is the child's best avenue for expressing anger[15]; helps the child safely release energy through motor activity.[38]
Give the child something to do (e.g., hold a bandage).	Provides the child with a sense of control, autonomy, and self-respect.[17]
Tell the child, "I will help you to hold still."	Helps the child to gain control; accepting help is a means of coping.[40]
Have the caregiver involve the child in an interactive story (e.g., "We're going on a trip. Where shall we go? Who should we take with us? What should we bring along?").	Becomes an excellent distraction technique for both child and caregiver.[41]
If separation for a treatment or procedure is necessary, allow the toddler to bring a security object (blanket, toy, or stuffed animal) or a parent's personal possession (scarf or hat).	Provides comfort for the child and decreases the child's sense of separation.[42]
If a cast or large bandage is applied, reassure the toddler that the covered body part remains intact.	Promotes a positive body image because toddlers perceive body boundaries as indefinite.[38]
Provide pharmacologic and nonpharmacologic pain control as needed (Chapter 11).	Decreases pain and anxiety.
Praise and reward the child frequently with a sticker or drink of juice; avoid implying that the child was bad.	Praise enhances the child's self-esteem and minimizes the older toddler's tendency to perceive pain as punishment for wrongdoing.[17]
Release any restraint as quickly as possible.	Avoids prolonged anxiety.
Reunite the toddler and the caregiver as soon as possible.	Decreases anxiety resulting from separation; promotes comfort.

TABLE 3.6 Specific Interventions to Facilitate Preschooler Coping and Promote Development

Interventions	*Rationale*
Encourage verbal expression of fears. Ask about any previous hospital experiences.	Permits the nurse to clarify any misconceptions. Egocentric thinking leads the child to believe he or she is being punished for a real or imagined wrongdoing.[44] The preschool child believes that events closely following one another have a cause-effect relationship.[45] Guilt combined with fantasy creates erroneous impressions and causes generalized fears.[10]
Allow the preschooler to explore or use equipment. Demonstrate how the equipment works. Role play with the child. Use puppets for teaching and communication.	Facilitates communication and decreases fear and anxiety. Decreases the child's reported fantasies; direct action is a means of coping.[40]
Use nonthreatening language such as repair, make better, uncomfortable, or sore.	Minimizes children's fear of invasive procedures. These words are descriptive and arouse more manageable feelings than such words as cut or opening.[44]
Explain in simple, concrete words the need for the procedure or treatment; include sensations that the child may experience, such as cold, wet, pinch.[17]	Minimizes the child's fears. Avoids any unexpected sensations that might otherwise increase anxiety and cause the child to lose trust. When the child is told what sensations he or she may feel, the amount of distress associated with pain decreases.[17]
Acknowledge the child's feelings, and reassure the child that it is okay to be scared. Give the child suggestions to help master these feelings, such as, "Hold my hand," "Say ouch," "Take deep breaths," "Let's tell a story together," "Tell me about your favorite place." Have the child blow on a party blower or pinwheel; use soap bubbles as well.	These techniques increase the child's control and promote a sense of mastery; decreases the child's sense of guilt.
Encourage the child to participate in treatments or procedures by holding a bandage or tape.	Promotes cooperation, a sense of control, and self-respect.
Offer choices whenever possible.	Helps the child to feel less threatened.
Use pharmacologic and nonpharmacologic measures for pain control and relief. Use a pain rating scale (Chapter 11).	Pain rating scales provide a subjective measure of pain.
Reinforce the child's coping behaviors ("You're such a big help.").	Avoids instilling a sense of failure in the child and promotes the child's emotional growth.
Actively involve the child with how the child can help during a treatment or procedure; use storytelling that involves the child.	Minimizes stalling techniques.[46]
Observe for stalling techniques that would delay the onset of a procedure or treatment, such as crying, clinging, fighting, making excuses, and bargaining.	Stalling techniques are direct coping mechanisms used by preschool children.[40]
Allow a minimal time lag (1 to 2 minutes) between explaining a procedure and performing the procedure.	Longer time lags cause preschoolers to frighten themselves with imagined horrors.[44]
Use analogies when describing how the body works (e.g., the brain acts like the "boss" of the body and the heart keeps the body running like a car "motor").[43]	Preschoolers understand explanations if familiar words are used. Young children tend to be quite literal in their interpretation of information.
Reward the child frequently with praise, juice, or stickers.	Allows for mastery.

TABLE 3.6 Specific Interventions to Facilitate Preschooler Coping and Promote Development	
Interventions	*Rationale*
Reunite the child with the caregivers as soon as possible.	Avoids prolonged anxiety.
Use bandages liberally; use draping and gowns during examination and treatment.	Recognizes the child's concern for body intactness and vulnerability. Respects the child's modesty.[15]
Use rehearsal to prepare children for an ED visit.	Invite children 4 to 7 years of age to the emergency department for a field trip experience. Have them bring a stuffed animal or doll and describe symptoms as they act as the caregivers. This activity decreases their fear of the emergency department and allows them to perceive the emergency nurses as helpful and the emergency department as less frightening. Those children who participated in such a visit were found to be cooperative during an actual ED encounter.[47]

motor activity as coping strategies, they also can use distraction, storytelling, and simple information to cope with a stressful event.

❑ Body intrusions, such as rectal temperature measurement, otoscopic examinations, and sutures, are major fears. Separation anxiety remains a concern.

❑ Preschool children want to cooperate and please adults.

❑ Preschoolers believe that pain is punishment for "bad" or angry thoughts or actions. Thus, the preschooler whose inquisitiveness led to an injury and ED visit believes that he or she is being punished for this inquisitiveness.

Specific interventions to facilitate preschooler coping and promote development are outlined in Table 3.6.

School-Aged Children

During this age span, children expand their world as they move into school and the world of teachers and peers. They enter the psychosocial stage of industry ("I am what I learn and do.") and eagerly engage in tasks that will win approval.[15] If they experience repeated rejection and failure, a sense of inferiority develops; this can stunt further psychosocial growth. They understand the "rules" of health behavior but also need fairly concrete rewards for following the rules. The following are key characteristics of school-aged children:

❑ Children younger than 7 years of age are able to reason on the basis of only one characteristic at a time. They can recognize the relationships between cause of illness (e.g., virus) and getting sick.[13]

❑ Between 7 and 11 years of age, children can take note

of several features and their interrelationship. They now can understand the reversible nature of cause and effect. Prevention of illness and injury is understood ("Playing with matches can cause fire. Fire can be prevented by not playing with matches.").

❑ School-aged children have an expanding vocabulary. Although they understand the concept of internal organs, they become confused about their function, especially when ill.

❑ Young school-aged children may consider illness as punishment for their actions.

❑ Bodily injury, loss of bodily function, loss of control, and loss of status are major worries and fears of this age group.[17] They need to have their modesty maintained and their questions answered honestly.

❑ School-aged children have increasing coping strategies and want information, but may need prompting to ask questions.[18]

❑ School-aged children shift from a family-oriented environment to a peer-dominated society.[19] Older children may wish to cope without their parents present; however, if stressed, these children may need to have their parents available. When feeling threatened, as in an emergency situation, school-aged children may withdraw and become reserved instead of seeking information.

Specific interventions used to facilitate coping in school-aged children and promote psychosocial development are outlined in Table 3.7.

TABLE 3.7   Specific Interventions Used to Facilitate School-Aged Children's Coping and Promote Development

Interventions	Rationale
Use anatomic models and equipment to explain the child's health condition and the treatment that will ensue.	Takes advantage of the child's concrete thinking abilities by making body organs and processes "real".[50]
Use a Gellert model; have the child draw and label the internal body organs.	Helps to clarify any misconceptions; provides a basis for teaching about the child's health condition and ED treatment.
Prepare for ED procedures with enough time for the child to think of questions and for the nurse to answer them.	Allows time for cognitive processing and mental preparation. Because school-aged children have a concept of time, the approximate length of time for the procedure may be offered, if it is known. Asking questions is a means of coping.[40]
Provide specific instructions about the child's behavior (e.g., "You may make as much noise as you want if you hold your hand still.").[30]	Gives the child a sense of control; sets limits for acceptable behavior.
Offer an open-ended statement to draw out the concerns of the child who appears to be anxious but does not ask questions. For example, "Some children want to know about getting stitches. Would you like to know about getting stitches, too?"	Allows the child to know that his or her questions or fears are normal and that other children have had similar experiences. Provides a means for the child to turn an inhibition-or-action mechanism into a direct-action mechanism, thereby increasing his or her ability to cope.[40]
State the approximate length of the treatment or procedure, but be as accurate as possible. "Five more minutes" should not turn into 15 minutes.	School-aged children have a concept of past, present, and future.[17]
Offer specific choices during treatment, if possible.	Helps the child to feel in control.
Encourage the child to participate in care, as feasible.	Conveys a sense of control and decreases the child's feelings of dependence on others.
Ask the child and family about specific techniques that helped the child cope with a previous stressful event[48]; allow time for the child and family to practice that technique. If no successful techniques are identified, offer concrete examples of coping strategies (e.g., deep breathing, relaxation techniques, self-talk, storytelling, describing a favorite place or event).[49] Practice the techniques, if possible.	Helps the child to feel in control; helps the child to master the situation. Enhances the child's emotional and developmental growth (sense of industry). Direct-action techniques minimize passive resistance, such as clenched fists or teeth and body rigidity.[48]
Use pharmacologic and nonpharmacologic interventions for pain relief; assess for pain with pain rating scales (Chapter 11).	Provides for adequate analgesia. School-aged children can use visual analog scales because they understand the concept of numbering.
Praise the child's efforts to maintain control; offer suggestions and minimize attention to loss of control.	School-aged children's locus of control is becoming more internal than external. They have overly high and sometimes unrealistic expectations of themselves.[19]
Use draping and gowns during examinations and treatment.	Respects the child's modesty.
Allow caregiver to be with the child if the child wants this support; permit siblings or friends to visit, if appropriate.	Gives the child a sense of control in having a support person present.
Maintain a positive manner regardless of the child's reaction; project a positive outcome of ED treatment.	Prevents feelings of inferiority and decreased self-esteem. Minimizes school-aged children's fears of disfigurement and responds to their incomplete understanding of death.[51]

TABLE 3.7	Specific Interventions Used to Facilitate School-Aged Children's Coping and Promote Development	

Interventions	Rationale
Encourage the child to talk about the ED experience.	The child's verbalization of thoughts and feelings allows the nurse to clarify any misconceptions.
Include older children in conversations regarding treatment and discharge instructions.	Allows the child to be involved with the decision-making process and treatment plan, which may increase compliance; increases the child's self-esteem.

Adolescents

Adolescence is a period of rapid growth, characterized by a myriad of interacting biologic, emotional, and social challenges. Early adolescents are still in the world of children, while later adolescents join the adult world. The adolescent experiences conflicts associated with a search for personal identity, separation from the family, peer-group relationships, management of sexual changes and feelings, and future career choices.[20] Principal to these experiences is the effort to develop a personal identity that the adolescent carries into adulthood.[10] If a personal identity is not achieved, role confusion or diffusion occurs, leading to an excessive identification with and persistent dependence on others and a lack of self-confidence. The following are key characteristics of adolescents:

❑ Adolescents are able to take into account all variables within a situation because they are now capable of abstract thought.

❑ Adolescents understand causes of health and illness in physiologic terms. They are able to understand risks and consequences associated with certain behavior, but they generally believe that nothing will happen to them. Some of these risk-taking behaviors, such as active experimentation with alcohol and other drugs, may impair the adolescent's ability to make wise choices about his or her health.[20] Respect for the adolescent's independence and values will increase chances of cooperation.

❑ Peers are important, and emancipation from parents is critical. However, when injured or ill, adolescents will often want a caregiver present; this is an individualized choice.

❑ Ill or injured adolescents fear loss of autonomy and privacy, being "different" from their peers, death, loss of peer acceptance, and disfigurement.

❑ Adolescents become idealistic and are egocentric when considering their ideals in relation to those of others in the world.[21] Because of this idealism and their introspection, they are very critical of their own appearance and behavior, and they think that others are equally focused on them.

❑ Because of their rapidly changing bodies, they are very focused on their bodies and need reassurance that they are normal.

❑ Adolescents have many coping strategies and may need help in asking questions and in making choices to gain a sense of control.

❑ Adolescents can have rapid mood swings.

Specific interventions to facilitate adolescent coping and promote development are outlined in Table 3.8.

Psychosocial Considerations of the Family

Families today are diverse, complex, and self-defined. All family configurations, such as single families, stepfamilies, blended families, intergenerational families, foster families, or adopted families, have common concerns and needs when their child receives emergency treatment, including:[22]

❑ Accurate, timely, frequent, and truthful information about their child's condition, treatment, and prognosis.

❑ Assurance that all treatment is appropriate.

❑ Assurance that treatment is rendered in a competent, caring manner.

❑ The ability to trust their child's caregivers.

❑ The ability to be with their child.

Family-centered care is "an approach to care characterized by mutually beneficial collaboration between patient, family, and health care professional." This approach is a direct reflection "of the expectation that consumers will be involved in their own care [and] in the design and modification of health care systems."[23] Even in the ED setting, family-centered care involves respecting and supporting families during resuscitation, episodic, and acute care.

TABLE 3.8 Specific Interventions to Facilitate Adolescent Coping and Promote Development

Interventions	Rationale
Talk with the adolescent first before talking with the parents.	Demonstrates respect for the adolescent as an individual with a developing sense of self-identity. Also, adolescents want to be part of the decision making about their own bodies and health care.
Ensure and maintain privacy during treatment; use gowns and drapes during examinations and treatments.	Promotes modesty. Recognizes that body image concerns are heightened during adolescence because of increased hormonal, physical, and emotional changes, resulting in increased sensitivity about personal appearance. Respecting physical modesty and autonomy and allowing choices and control facilitate cooperation.[20]
Explain to the adolescent what to expect before touching him or her.	Demonstrates respect for the adolescent as an individual; allows the adolescent to prepare for the treatment.
Allow the adolescent to choose a support person for examinations and treatment.	Promotes autonomy.
Incorporate the adolescent in decision making.	Decreases the adolescent's loss of autonomy; increases the chances for compliance with the treatment regimen.
Allow for the verbalization of fear and anger, but provide coping strategies such as use of music, deep breathing, or guided imagery.	Acknowledges the adolescent's feelings and provides alternative means of expression.
Use pharmacologic and nonpharmacologic interventions for pain relief; use pain rating scales; observe for signs of masked pain behavior (Chapter 11).	Provides for adequate analgesia.
Give realistic and truthful explanations.	Promotes trust. Recognizes that adolescents can use reason and logical thinking and that information seeking is a major way of coping.[40] Shows sensitivity to the adolescent's more advanced understanding of bodily functions and ability to use abstract thought.[17] Acknowledges that adolescents are curious about anything that affects them and that they need reassurance that they are normal.[52]
Use diagrams of the human body or models to explain procedures; use correct terminology.	Shows sensitivity to the adolescent's more advanced understanding of bodily functions and ability to use abstract thought.
Encourage the adolescent to participate in care.	Demonstrates to the adolescent a sense of responsibility for his or her health.
Allow for privacy with the emergency nurse.	Gives the adolescent an opportunity to ask questions and discuss concerns.
Stress normalcy whenever possible.	Body image and concerns are heightened during adolescence, and personal appearance is of critical importance.
Reunite the adolescent with the support person as soon as possible; answer any questions.	Provides support to the adolescent.
Be honest about possible outcomes, but reassure the adolescent that he or she will get better, as appropriate.	Builds trust between the adolescent and the ED staff.

TABLE 3.9 Specific Interventions to Facilitate Family Coping

Interventions	Rationale
Maintain a calm, nonjudgmental approach.	Instills the family with a sense of trust and acceptance; enhances the family's confidence in the ED staff.
Prepare family for the child's appearance (e.g., bandages, casts).	Parents may feel anxious and shocked by their child's appearance; preparation can lessen this shock.[26]
Ask the family about child's previous health care experiences and how child responded, including successful coping strategies.	Demonstrates respect for the child's individual needs.
Reunite the child and the family as soon as possible after examinations and treatment.	Family's fantasies and fears seldom match reality; decreases the child's and the family's anxiety and provides reassurance and comfort.
Provide specific instructions as to how the parent can assist the child (e.g., "I want you to sit by your child's head, stroke your child's forehead, and softly sing your child's favorite song, or talk quietly to your child.").	Parents want to help their child and need to know how to participate. Caring for an ill or injured child may be a new role for the family.
Provide factual information simply and clearly.	In crisis situations, families have a reduced ability to comprehend information and to initiate problem solving.
Have the family identify a support person for themselves or provide one for them, if possible.	Assists the family to maintain emotional stability.
Have a family member give a personal object for the child to hold if the family member cannot or does not want to be with the child during a procedure or treatment.	Respects the family's wishes; gives the child a sense of trust that the family will not desert the child.
Tell the parents, before their participation in a treatment or procedure, that they may be asked to leave depending on how the child is responding or how they themselves are responding.	Establishes an honest relationship and informs the parents that their child's best interest is the priority.
Describe to the family what they can do to support their child during a treatment or procedure, if the parent wants to be present during a procedure. If a family member has difficulty coping during the procedure, the nurse should have the family member take a short break.	Children sense the family's anxiety, which heightens their own anxiety, which in turn increases the family's anxiety (emotional contagion theory). Taking a short break restores the family member's psychosocial strength.
If the parents make statements that seem to demonstrate unrealistic expectations of the child, provide a realistic explanation of what a child of that age might be expected to do. Suggest to parents some positive approaches to assisting the child; serve as a role model.	Provides appropriate information about child development and about how children may respond to stressful events. Prevents censure of the child. Actively incorporating parents in the care of their child helps them to maintain their parenting role and focuses the parents' energies on their strengths and maximizes their positive adaptation to the situation.
Offer respite care to the family member during lengthy procedures or treatments; have another family member or staff member serve as the child's support person.	Respects the family's need for self-care.
Collaborate and consult with additional health care professionals as needed (e.g., social worker, spiritual advisor, translator, or child life specialist).	Recognizes the family's unique needs.

TABLE 3.9 Specific Interventions to Facilitate Family Coping

Interventions	Rationale
Keep the family informed about their child's condition and the course of treatment. Acknowledge the difficulty in waiting. Suggest a short walk or a visit to the cafeteria, or offer a telephone.	Families in stressful situations often neglect themselves.
Respect the family's decisions and acknowledge their contributions to caring for and comforting their child.	Acknowledges the family's contribution to the child's treatment; recognizes the family as the child's source of support.[29]
Provide follow-up as needed. In addition to specific treatment regimens, discuss possible postdischarge behaviors the child might exhibit, such as temporary sleeping and feeding difficulties; clinging behavior; temporary loss of recently acquired developmental milestones, such as staying dry at night or talking in sentences; and rebellious behavior in older children.[53] The child may also play out his or her emergency experience. Tell parents to remain calm, reassure the child, and discuss the emergency experience in simple, honest terms to clarify the child's misconceptions.[54]	Prepares family for adequate health care follow-up. Allows family to anticipate their children's behavior. Children use play to master stressful experiences; role playing the emergency treatment with dolls or siblings helps the child to understand what happened and allows the child to incorporate the experience into his or her development. These behaviors are generally temporary and short-lived. If the behaviors continue, the parents should discuss them with their primary health care professional.[55]

Selected concepts related to family-centered care include:[23]

☐ Respecting each family's human dignity, expertise, values, and culture.

☐ Sharing information that allows families to make informed decisions about their child's emergency care. Such sharing is communicated via methods appropriate to that family, including the use of translators and sign language interpreters.

☐ Collaborating with families in the enactment of an emergency treatment plan. Caregivers know their child best, because they care for their child on a daily basis. Therefore, collaborating with families early in the treatment process helps to assure compliance with subsequent home care or follow-up regimens. Effective communication also increases the families' satisfaction with care provided in the emergency department.[24]

Family-centered care and family presence during invasive procedures are advocated by many professional organizations, including the Emergency Nurses Association. This participation is guided by a number of factors, including:[25]

☐ The urgency of the situation
☐ The invasiveness of the procedure
☐ The staff's comfort in performing the procedure or treatment in the family's presence

☐ The availability of a health care professional to stay with the family exclusively during the procedure or treatment

☐ The availability of written hospital policies, procedures, or standards of care addressing parental participation

☐ The family's ability to support and comfort the child during the procedure or treatment

☐ The staff availability to help parents support their child[26]

Siblings are important family members and should be included as much as is desired, feasible, and practical, on the basis of:[25]

☐ The siblings' ages and developmental abilities
☐ The urgency of the situation
☐ The invasiveness of the procedure or treatment
☐ The staff's comfort in performing the treatment or procedure in the siblings' presence
☐ The availability of a health care professional and family member to stay with the sibling exclusively during the treatment or procedure
☐ The availability of written hospital policies, procedures, or standards of care addressing sibling participation

Specific interventions to facilitate family coping are outlined in Table 3.9.

Conclusion

Emergency nurses treat each child and family as unique individuals, taking into consideration their developmental, ethnic, cultural, and racial diversity.[27] The application of developmental principles and the initiation of family-centered care are the crux of pediatric emergency nursing. Emergency nurses should consider including parents and older children on their ED teams for system design, communications development, and community outreach.[23] Johnson et al[23] includes self-assessment inventories to help emergency medical services and emergency departments to determine their readiness to enact family-centered care. The text can be obtained from the Emergency Medical Services for Children National Resource Center (http://www.childrensnational.org/EMSC/).

References

1. Munoz, C., & Luckman, J. (2005). *Transcultural communication in nursing* (2nd ed.). Clifton Park, NY: Thomson Delmar Learning.

2. Lipson, J., & Dibble, S. (Eds.). (2005). *Culture and clinical care.* San Francisco: UCSF Nursing Press.

3. Dunn, A. M. (2002). Cultural competence and the primary care provider. *Journal of Pediatric Health Care, 16,* 105–111.

4. Camphina-Bacote, J. (2002). The process of cultural competence in the delivery of health care services: A model of care. *Journal of Transcultural Nursing, 13,* 181–184.

5. Mygind, A., Norredam, M., Nielson, A., Bagger, J., & Krasnik, A. (2008). The effect of patient origin and relevance of contact on patient and caregiver satisfaction in the emergency room. *Scandinavian Journal of Public Health, 36,* 76–83.

6. Lehna, C. (2005). Interpreter services in pediatric nursing. *Pediatric Nursing, 31,* 292–296.

7. Spector, R. (2004). *Cultural diversity in health and illness* (6th ed.). Upper Saddle River, NJ: Pearson Prentice Hall.

8. Dunn, A. M. (2008). Cultural perspectives for pediatric primary care. In C. Burns, A. Dunn, M. Brady, N. Starr, & C. Blosser, *Pediatric primary care* (4th ed., pp. 41–50). Philadelphia: Saunders.

9. Ahmann, E. (1994). "Chunky stew:" Appreciating cultural diversity while providing health care for children. *Pediatric Nursing, 20,* 320–324.

10. Erikson, E. (1963). *Childhood and society* (2nd ed.). New York: Norton.

11. Santrock, J. (2004). *Life-span development* (9th ed.). Madison, WI: Brown & Benchmark.

12. Piaget, J., & Helder, S. (1969). *The psychology of the child.* New York: Basic Books.

13. Dixon, S., & Stein, M. (2005). *Encounters with children: Pediatric behavior and development* (4th ed.). St. Louis, MO: Mosby.

14. Frank, L., Greenberg, C., & Stevens, B. (2000). Pain assessment in infants and children. *Pediatric Clinics of North America, 47,* 487–511.

15. Erikson, E. (1967, January). Identity and the life cycle: Selected papers. *Psychological Issues Monograph.*

16. Vessey, J., Braithwaite, K., & Wiedmann, M. (1990). Teaching children about their internal body. *Pediatric Nursing, 16,* 29–33.

17. Pridham, K., Adelson, F., & Hanson, M. (1987). Helping children deal with procedures in a clinic setting: A developmental approach. *Journal of Pediatric Nursing, 2,* 15–21.

18. Salter, E., & Stallard, P. (2004). Young people's experiences of medical services as road traffic accident victims: A pilot qualitative study. *Journal of Child Health, 8*(4), 301–311.

19. Gance-Cleveland, B., & Yousey, Y. (2008). Developmental management of school-age children. In C. Burns, A. Dunn, M. Brady, N. Starr, & C. Blosser, *Pediatric primary care* (4th ed., pp. 109–131). Philadelphia: Saunders.

20. Dunn, A. M. (2008). Developmental management of adolescents. In C. Burns, A. Dunn, M. Brady, N. Starr, & C. Blosser. Pediatric primary care (4th ed., pp. 132–152). Philadelphia: Saunders Elsevier.

21. Maier, H. (1978). Three theories of child development. New York: Harper & Row.

22. Colizza, D., Prior, M., & Green, P. (1996). The ED experience: The development and psychosocial needs of children. *Topics in Emergency Medicine, 18*(3), 27–40.

23. Johnson, B., Thomas, J., & Williams, K. (1997). *Working with families to enhance emergency medical services for children.* Washington, DC: Emergency Medical Services for Children National Resource Center.

References (continued)

24. Cramm, K. J., & Dowd, M. D. (2008). What are you waiting for? A study of resident physician–parent communication in a pediatric emergency department. *Annals of Emergency Medicine, 51*(4), 361–366.

25. Conway, A. (1993). Psychosocial considerations for the child and family. In L. Bernardo & M. Bove (Eds.), *Pediatric emergency nursing procedures* (pp. 11–27). Boston: Jones & Bartlett.

26. Broome, M. E. (2000). Helping parents support their child in pain. *Pediatric Nursing, 26*(3), 315–317.

27. Bernardo, L., & Schenkel, K. (1995). Pediatric medical emergencies. In S. Kitt, J. Selfridge-Thomas, J. Proehl, & J. Kaiser (Eds.), *Emergency nursing: A physiologic and clinical perspective* (2nd ed., pp. 407–427). Philadelphia: Saunders.

28. Lamontagne, L., Hepworth, J., Byington, K., & Chang, C. (1997). Child and parent responses during hospitalization for orthopedic surgery. *Maternal Child Nursing, 22,* 299–303.

29. Newton, M. (2000). Family-centered care: Current realities in parent participation. *Pediatric Nursing, 26,* 164–168.

30. Seidel, J., & Henderson, D. (1997). Approach to the pediatric patient in the ED. In R. Barkin (Ed.), *Pediatric emergency medicine* (pp. 4–10). St. Louis, MO: Mosby-Year Book.

31. Melnyk, B. (2000). Intervention studies involving parents of hospitalized young children. An analysis of the past and future recommendations. *Journal of Pediatric Nursing, 15*(1), 4–13.

32. Stanford, G. (1991). Beyond honesty: Choosing language for talking to children about pain and procedure. *Children's Health Care, 20,* 261–262.

33. Kohlberg, L. (1969). *Stages in the development of moral thought and action.* New York: Holt, Rinehart & Winston.

34. Coles, R. (1997). *The moral intelligence of children.* New York: Random House.

35. Coles, R. (1991). *The spiritual life of children.* New York: Random House.

36. Kenner, C., & McGrath, J. (2004). *Developmental care of newborns and infants: A guide for health professionals.* St. Louis: Mosby.

37. Deloian, B., & Berry, A. (2008). Developmental management of infants. In C. Burns, A. Dunn, M. Brady, N. Starr, & C. Blosser, *Pediatric primary care* (4th ed., pp. 71–90). Philadelphia: Saunders.

38. Bernardo, L., Conway, A., & Bove, M. (1990). The ABC method of emotional assessment and intervention: A new approach in pediatric emergency care. *Journal of Emergency Nursing, 16*(2), 70–76.

39. Murphy, M., & Berry, A. (2008). Developmental management of toddlers and preschoolers. In C. Burns, A. Dunn, M. Brady, N. Starr, & C. Blosser, *Pediatric primary care* (4th ed., pp. 96–108). Philadelphia: Saunders.

40. Ritchie, J., Caty, S., & Ellerton, M. (1988). Coping behaviors of hospitalized preschool children. *Maternal Child Nursing Journal, 17,* 153–172.

41. Zelter, L., Bush, J., & Chen, E. (1997). A psychobiologic approach to pediatric pain: Part II: Prevention and treatment. *Current Problems in Pediatrics, 27,* 264–284.

42. Wear, R. (1974). Separation anxiety reconsidered: Nursing complications. *Maternal and Child Health Nursing Journal, 3,* 14–18.

43. Burke, P. (1995). Developmental considerations. In S. Kelley (Ed.), *Pediatric emergency nursing* (2nd ed., pp. 39–51). Norwalk, CT: Appleton & Lange.

44. Goldberger, J., Gaynard, L., & Wolfer, J. (1990). Helping children cope with healthcare procedures. *Contemporary Pediatrics, 7,* 141–162.

45. Bibace, R., & Walsh, M. (1980). Children's conceptions of illness. In R. Bibace & M. Walsh (Eds.), *Children's conceptions of health, illness, and bodily functions* (pp. 31–48). San Francisco: Jossey-Bass.

46. Ott, M. (1996). Imagine the possibilities! Guided imagery with toddlers and preschoolers. *Pediatric Nursing, 22,* 34–38.

47. Zimmerman, P., & Santen, L. (1997). Teddy says "Hi!": Teddy bear clinics revisited. *Journal of Emergency Nursing, 23,* 41–44.

48. Lutz, W. (1986). Helping hospitalized children and their parents cope with painful procedures. *Journal of Pediatric Nursing, 1,* 25–26, 28.

49. Brennan, A. (1994). Caring for children during procedures: A review of the literature. *Pediatric Nursing, 20,* 451–458.

50. Pidgeon, V. (1977). Characteristics of children's thinking and implications for health teaching. *Maternal Child Nursing Journal, 6*(1), 1–8.

51. Selbst, S., & Henretig, F. (1989). The treatment of pain in the ED. *Pediatric Clinics of North America, 36,* 968–969.

References (continued)

52. Manning, M. (1990). Health assessment of the early adolescent. *Nursing Clinics of North America, 25,* 827–829.

53. Fletcher, B. (1981). Psychological upset in posthospitalized children: A review of the literature. *Maternal Child Nursing Journal,* 10, 185–195.

54. Association for the Care of Children's Health. (1989). *Caring for your child in the emergency room.* Washington, DC: Author.

55. Berkowitz, C. D. (2008). *Pediatrics: A primary care approach.* Elk Grove Village, IL: American Academy of Pediatrics.

FOUR

Health Promotion and Prevention of Illness and Injury

Susan M. Hohenhaus, RN, MA, FAEN

Introduction

There are an estimated 30 million pediatric (younger than age 18 years) emergency department (ED) visits in U.S. hospitals each year, accounting for one fourth of all ED visits.[1] Fortunately, over the past several years much progress has been made in managing and preventing many previously common childhood illnesses and injuries. Because of the increased numbers and types of immunizations developed and their widespread adoption and vaccination, the number of common childhood illnesses has decreased. Improvements in antibiotics and chemotherapeutic agents have also improved the survival rates of children with immunodeficiency disorders and malignancies. Recent public health prevention initiatives include screening for common childhood problems such as lead exposure, and also now for the rising numbers of childhood illnesses that were previously common only in the adult population such as elevated cholesterol and lipids, hypertension, and diabetes. Continued advances in genomics have promised even more progress in the fight against childhood disease. Despite all of the advances made, trauma remains the number one cause of morbidity and mortality in children and youth.[1] Injury prevention efforts, often spearheaded by emergency nurses, have made an tremendous impact in bringing to light safety issues and prevention.

As child advocates, emergency nurses have a professional and community obligation to help reduce the number of childhood illnesses and injuries through education, advocacy, policy, and research. This chapter will describe the challenges of childhood illness and injury and discuss successful approaches to injury prevention programs.

Children And Communicable Disease

Emergency nurses have both opportunity and obligation to address the well-being of the community through screening, counseling, and actively preventing communicable diseases. A communicable disease means any bacterial, viral, or parasitic infection in the body that can be spread from one individual to another, and varies from the common cold and influenza to more uncommon diseases such as meningitis. The precautions necessary to prevent the spread of one disease are the same, regardless of whether the disease is life threatening. Role modeling good hygiene habits for patients is essential. Routinely using universal precautions and visibly practicing the message that *the single most important way to prevent infection is frequent hand washing* is probably the most important illness prevention lesson emergency nurses can share with their patients.

Immunizations have eliminated smallpox infection worldwide, limited the outbreak of polio to countries outside North America, and made formerly common infections such as diphtheria, tetanus, measles, and *Haemophilus influenzae* infections quite rare. One report states that pediatric immunizations are responsible for preventing three million deaths in children each year worldwide.[2] Despite this success there are still outbreaks of various diseases no longer commonly seen in the emergency department. For example, the number of pertussis cases has increased steadily in the United States over the past 20 years.[2]

The Centers for Disease Control and Prevention (CDC) promotes evidence-based guidelines that recommend routine immunization for several childhood illnesses. However, these guidelines and recommendations may be confusing for emergency nurses who may have limited knowledge of or familiarity with them. The introduction of vaccines for newly preventable diseases such as rotavirus and human papillomavirus (HPV) also create additional challenges in an already complex immunization schedule. For example, to complete the 1999 Recommended Childhood Immunization Schedule in the United States, a minimum of 13 separate injections are needed to immunize a child from birth to age 6 years.[3]

Controversy continues over whether the emergency department is the "appropriate" place for routine immunizations. The American College of Emergency Physicians (ACEP) recognizes that the emergency department may represent additional opportunities for providing immunizations to children.[4] Identification of under-vaccination of infants and children may help to prevent disease, assuring that that children receive appropriate, timely immunizations.

Most emergency nurses are familiar with the more "routine" immunizations that have been commonly screened for in the emergency department, including measles-mumps-rubella vaccine, varicella (chickenpox) vaccine, pneumococcal conjugate vaccine, hepatitis B vaccine, diphtheria and tetanus toxoids, and pertussis vaccines. The CDC has an enormous amount of material available to assist the emergency nurse in learning more about current practices and information regarding appropriate child and youth immunization. Vaccine schedules can be downloaded from the CDC Web site.[5] Although it may be helpful for nurses, especially triage nurses, to have access to immunization recommendation schedules, they should be cautious about posting these schedules as they change constantly. Emergency nurses, especially those in leadership roles, should monitor any items such as the CDC immunization guidelines and schedules for currency and provide updates as available.

In the past few years, newer vaccines have been added to the list of CDC recommendations. These vaccines include HPV and meningitis vaccines, as well as influenza and rotavirus vaccines.

Genital Human Papillomavirus

Genital human papillomavirus (HPV) is the most common sexually transmitted infection. A vaccine can now protect females from the four types of HPV that cause most cervical cancers and genital warts. The vaccine is recommended for 11- and 12-year-old girls. It is also recommended for girls and women aged 13 through 26 years who have not yet been vaccinated or completed the vaccine series.

Additional Prevention Recommendations

When counseling a young patient who is sexually active about the risks of HPV, a discussion about condoms may be appropriate. The use of condoms lowers the risk of HPV, if used all the time. Condoms may also lower the risk of development of HPV-related diseases, such as genital warts and cervical cancer. However, it is also important to let the patient know that HPV can infect areas that are not covered by a condom, so condoms may not completely protect against HPV. Counseling about HPV should include that the only sure way to prevent HPV is to avoid all sexual activity.

Influenza

Influenza viruses cause disease among all age groups. According to the CDC, rates of infection are highest among children, with rates of serious illness and death striking children aged less than 2 years, and children of any age who have medical conditions that place them at increased risk for complications from influenza.[6]

The typical incubation period for influenza is 1 to 4 days, with an average of 2 days. Children can be infectious for more than 10 days, and young children can shed virus for several days before the onset of the illness. Uncomplicated influenza illness in children is characterized by fever, myalgia, headache, malaise, nonproductive cough, sore throat, and rhinitis. In young children, otitis media, nausea, and vomiting are also commonly reported with influenza illness. Complications can include pneumonia, dehydration, encephalopathy and sinus problems, ear infections, and exacerbation of chronic medical problems such as heart disease or asthma.

Influenza illness typically resolves after 3 to 7 days for the majority of children, although cough and malaise can persist for more than 2 weeks. Young children with influenza infection can have initial symptoms mimicking bacterial sepsis with high fevers. Deaths from influenza are uncommon among children both with and without high-risk conditions, but they do occur. One study that modeled influenza-related deaths estimated that an average of 92 deaths occurred among children aged less than 5 years annually during the 1990s, compared with 32,651 deaths among adults older than 65 years of age. Reports of 153 laboratory-confirmed influenza-related pediatric deaths from 40 states during the 2003–2004 influenza season indicated that 61 (40%) were less than 2 years of age and, of 92 children aged 2 to 17 years, 64 (70%) did not have an underlying medical condition traditionally considered to place a person at risk for influenza-related complications.[6]

Prevention Recommendations

The CDC recommends that children 6 months to 23 months of age get the flu vaccine. Children and teenagers (2 to 18 years of age) should get the flu vaccine if they are taking long-term aspirin treatment because they may be at risk for the development of Reye's syndrome after a flu infection. They should also get the flu vaccine if they live in a household with someone in the above groups.

Three antiviral medicines for prevention of flu are available by prescription. Oseltamivir is for use in adults and teenagers 13 years and older.[7] Rimantadine and Amantadine may be used by adults and children who are 1 year of age and older.[7]

Addressing the spread of influenza disease in children is essential to the health of families and can have great impact on all others in the nation. As with other prevention efforts, emergency nurses can help prevent the spread of flu in homes, schools, and daycare settings by encouraging children to practice healthy habits. Through prevention efforts, children miss fewer days of school, parents and caregivers miss fewer days of work, and the disease is less likely to spread to others. Encourage children to cover coughs and sneezes, wash hands frequently, and keep hands away from eyes, nose, and mouth. In addition, a sick child is advised to stay at home during the first days of illness when symptoms are most severe and the infection is most contagious. Emergency nurses can advocate for policies for family "sick days" so that parents and other caregivers have an opportunity to care for their sick child.

Adolescents and Meningitis

Meningococcal disease is a serious illness, caused by the bacterium *Neisseria meningitides*. It can be spread between members of the same household or anyone with direct contact with a patient's oral secretions. This places adolescents at particular risk as they interact closely with each other, especially if kissing. Immunization with meningococcal conjugate vaccine is recommended for all children at their routine preadolescent visit (11 to 12 years of age), and, for those who have never been vaccinated previously, a dose is recommended at high school entry.[8]

Rotavirus

Rotavirus is a major cause of acute gastroenteritis in the United States, infecting almost all children in the first 3 to 5 years of life, with severe, dehydrating gastroenteritis occurring primarily among children 3 to 35 months of age. In the first 5 years of life, 1 in 7 will require a clinic or ED visit, 1 in 70 will be hospitalized, and 1 in 200,000 will die of this disease.[9]

In the United States, a high level of rotavirus morbidity continues to occur despite the widespread recommendation by experts, including the American Academy of Pediatrics (AAP) and CDC, for the use of oral rehydration solutions in the treatment of dehydrating gastroenteritis.[10]

Recommendations for prevention of rotavirus include routine vaccination of U.S. infants with three doses of rotavirus vaccine administered orally at ages 2, 4, and 6 months. All three doses of vaccine should be administered by age 32 weeks because of insufficient data on the safety and efficacy of rotavirus vaccine in infants after this age. Pentavalent rotavirus vaccine can be administered together with other vaccines.[11]

The Childhood Obesity "Epidemic"

The increasing number of obese children and youth throughout the United States is a critical public health threat. Since the 1970s, the prevalence (or percentage) of obesity has more than doubled for preschool children aged 2 to 5 years and adolescents aged 12 to 19 years, and it has more than tripled for children aged 6 to 11 years. As defined by the Institute of Medicine, approximately 9 million children over 6 years of age are obese. These children and youths between the ages of 2 and 18 years have body mass indexes (BMIs) equal to or greater than the 95th percentile of the age- and gender-specific BMI charts developed by the CDC.[12] These young people are at risk for the development of serious psychosocial burdens related to being obese in a society that stigmatizes this condition, often fostering shame, self-blame, and low self-esteem that may impair academic and social functioning and carry into adulthood. In a population-based sample, approximately 60% of obese children aged 5 to 10 years had at least one cardiovascular disease risk factor, such as elevated total cholesterol, triglycerides, insulin requirements, or blood pressure, and 25% had two or more cardiovascular disease risk factors.[12] Obesity can also lead to metabolic syndrome, arthritis, and even cancer.[12]

In addition to short-term risks, longer-term risks to good health are being identified. Type 2 diabetes is rapidly becoming a disease of children and adolescents.

Childhood obesity may reduce overall adult life expectancy. The disease prevention efforts of previous decades that allow children to live longer, fuller adult lives may be at risk by this serious childhood health risk.

Prevention Recommendations

Preventing obesity involves promoting healthful eating behaviors and regular physical activity. Emergency nurses can assist in tracking a child's weight and health risks by measuring and recording the BMI in children and youth. Offering relevant evidence-based materials and guidance about childhood obesity and partnering with other health care providers working with professional organizations, insurance companies, and regulatory groups to support prevention efforts are all ways to be involved.

Children and Motor Vehicle Injury

Motor vehicle crashes are the leading cause of death for ages 3 to 6 and 8 to 14 years.[13] Every day in the United States, an average of five children aged 14 years and younger were killed and 548 were injured in motor vehicle crashes during 2007.[13] Research has shown that lap/shoulder seat belts, when used, reduce the risk of fatal injury to front seat occupants (aged 5 years and older) of passenger cars by 45% and the risk of moderate-to-critical injury by 50%. For light-truck occupants, seat belts reduce the risk of fatal injury by 60% and the risk of moderate-to-critical injury by 65%. During 2007, 6,532 passenger vehicle occupants aged 14 years and younger were involved in fatal crashes. For those children where restraint use was known, 25% were unrestrained; among those who were fatally injured, 45% were unrestrained.[13]

Research on the effectiveness of child safety seats has found them to reduce fatal injury by 71% for infants (younger than 1 year old) and by 54% for toddlers (1 to 4 years old) in passenger cars. For infants and toddlers in light trucks, the corresponding reductions are 58% and 59%, respectively. In 2007, there were 385 passenger vehicle occupant fatalities among children aged 4 years and younger. Of those 385 fatalities, where restraint use was known (363), 109 (30%) were totally unrestrained.[13]

Emergency Nurses Association and Child Passenger Safety Injury Prevention Efforts

Prevention of mortality and morbidity due to motor vehicle crashes has long been a priority of emergency nurses. Many injury prevention programs, including promotion of child safety seat use, correct placement of children in restraint systems, and counseling of children and families on the use of passenger restraint systems, have been major emergency nursing initiatives. The Emergency Nurses Association (ENA) has been a leader in the support of policy and educational programs that relate to child passenger safety. The ENA Injury Prevention Institute has focused policy and programs on making right decisions when driving or riding in a motor vehicle, both key issues to consider when caring for children and teens.

Child Passenger Safety Principles

Understanding a few basic principles about child restraint system usage and knowing when and where to refer families for additional information can help emergency nurses provide parents and caregivers with the information they need to promote effective restraint of children in motor vehicles.

According to Safe Kids Worldwide,[14] the following are some key issues to consider when implementing child passenger safety efforts:

❑ Every person riding in a car or truck needs his or her own seat belt. Do not let passengers ride in storage areas or on other people's laps.

❑ Children always ride restrained with a car seat or seat belt and in the back seat.

❑ Infants should ride in rear-facing car seats until at least 20 lbs (9 kg) and at least 1 year old. Do not put a rear-facing car seat in the front seat of a vehicle with an active passenger air bag.

❑ Children over 1 year old and between 20 lb. (9 kg) and 40 lb (18 kg) should ride in forward-facing car seats.

❑ Children aged 4 to 8 years between 40 lb (18 kg) and 80 lb (36 kg) should ride in booster seats restrained with lap and shoulder belts.

❑ Children and adults over 80 lb (36 kg) should use a seat belt for every ride.

In addition, emergency nurses should *be consistent role models*. They should always buckle up on every trip, every time, and make sure that their own children do too.

When to Replace a Child Safety Seat after a Crash

One area that has frustrated many child passenger safety advocates, including emergency nurses, has been the issue of when to replace a child safety seat after a crash. According to the most current recommendations from the National Highway Traffic Safety Administration (NHTSA):

❑ Child safety seats should be replaced after a moderate or severe crash to ensure a continued high level of crash protection for child passengers.

❑ Child safety seats do not automatically need to be replaced after a minor crash.

❑ Minor crashes are those that meet all of the following criteria:

▪ The vehicle was able to be driven away from the crash site.

▪ The vehicle door nearest the safety seat was undamaged.

▪ There were no injuries to any of the vehicle occupants.

▪ The air bags (if present) did not deploy.

▪ There is no visible damage to the safety seat.

According to NHTSA, clarifying the need for child seat replacement will reduce the number of children unnecessarily riding without a child safety seat while a replacement seat is being acquired and the number of children who would have to ride without a child seat if a seat were discarded and not replaced. The clarification will also reduce the financial burden of unnecessary replacement.[15]

Helmets and Injury Prevention

An estimated 75% to 90% of the 1.4 million traumatic brain injury–related deaths, hospitalizations, and ED visits that occur each year are concussions or mild traumatic brain injuries.[16]

Prevention Recommendations

Emergency nurses should encourage all patients, both children and adults, to wear a helmet when:

- ❏ Riding a bike, motorcycle, snowmobile, scooter, or all-terrain vehicle
- ❏ Playing a contact sport, such as football, ice hockey, or boxing
- ❏ Using in-line skates or riding a skateboard
- ❏ Batting and running bases in baseball or softball
- ❏ Riding a horse
- ❏ Skiing or snowboarding

Other Injury Prevention Efforts for Children

Drowning

Drowning is the second leading cause of injury-related death in children and usually occurs when infants and toddlers are left unattended in the bathtub or near an open body of water. More than one in four fatal drowning victims are children 14 years and younger, and, for every child who dies of drowning, another four received ED care for nonfatal submersion injuries.[17] Every year, toddlers die after falling into a bucket of water or falling into a backyard swimming pool with a large group of people around, such as at a birthday party. If no one is directly supervising the young child, he or she may not be missed until the submersion injury is nonreversible.

Prevention Recommendations

Emergency nurses can provide information for parents and other caregivers to prevent drowning injury. For example, a responsible adult should be designated to watch young children while in the bath and all children swimming or playing in or around water. The adult should not be distracted or impaired by any other activity. Constant, careful supervision and barriers such as pool fencing are necessary even when children have completed swimming classes. Emergency nurses can promote and teach cardiopulmonary resuscitation (CPR). Cardiopulmonary resuscitation performed by bystanders has been shown to improve outcomes in drowning victims.

Poisoning

Children, especially those under 6 years of age, are more likely to have unintentional poisonings than older children and adults. Adolescents are also at risk for poisonings, both intentional and unintentional.[17]

Prevention Recommendations

The Injury Prevention Program (TIPP) of the American Academy of Pediatrics recommends these "safety rules" for teaching parents and caregivers about poisonings and children:[18]

- ❏ Keep harmful products locked up and out of your child's sight and reach.
- ❏ Use safety latches or locks on drawers and cabinets where you keep dangerous items.
- ❏ Take extra care during stressful times.
- ❏ Call medicine by its correct name. You do not want to confuse the child by calling medicine "candy."
- ❏ Always replace the safety caps immediately after use.
- ❏ Never leave alcohol within a child's reach.
- ❏ Seek help if your child swallows a substance that is not food.
- ❏ Call the Poison Help Line at 800-222-1222 or your doctor. Don't make your child vomit.

Fire and Burn Injuries

Deaths from fires and burns are the fifth most common cause of unintentional injury deaths in the United States[19] and the third leading cause of fatal home injury.[20] Children aged 4 years and under are one of the groups at increased risk of fire-related injuries and deaths.[21]

Prevention Recommendations

Risk of fire injury and death increases in winter months and often occurs in homes without smoke detectors. Emergency nurses can partner with local fire departments and civic groups to educate the public in preparation for winter, as well as encouraging installation and maintenance of proper smoke detectors. (Chapter 27 details burn injury prevention activities.) The following recommendations offer emergency nurses additional prevention information they can share with families:[22]

- ❏ Do not leave children alone around open flames, stoves, or candles.
- ❏ Keep matches, gasoline, lighters, and other flammable materials out of children's reach.
- ❏ Teach children a plan for escaping your home in a fire and practice it.

❏ Install smoke alarms in your home on every level and in every sleeping area.

- Test once a month.

- Replace batteries once a year.

- Replace alarms every 10 years.

❏ Before bathing children in heated water, always run your open hand through the water to check its temperature.

❏ Keep hot foods and liquids away from table and counter edges. Never carry children and hot foods or liquids at the same time.

❏ Keep things that easily catch fire (such as papers) away from heat sources such as stoves, heaters, and fireplaces.

Fall Injuries

Falls are the leading cause of unintentional home injury and death in the United States. Children younger than 5 years of age have one of the highest rates of falls.[23]

Prevention Recommendations

Window guards have been shown to be effective at preventing falls. For example, New York City passed a regulation in conjunction with an education and window guard distribution program that resulted in a 50% reduction in window-related falls and a 35% reduction in window-related fatalities.[24]

Data show that protective surfaces (versus cement or asphalt) under play equipment can prevent the incidence and reduce the severity of fall-related injuries.[25]

Safety standards for baby walkers went into effect in 1997. These standards include having walkers be too wide to fit through a standard doorway and features that stop the walker at the edge of a step.[26]

Youth Violence

The violence that some of the nation's children endure, and occasionally perpetrate, may make emergency nurses frustrated, sad, or angry; unfortunately, one emotion that they likely do not feel is surprise. In emergency departments, nurses are brought face to face with both the victims and perpetrators of youth violence. According to the CDC in 2004, more than 750,000 young people aged 10 to 24 years were treated in emergency departments for injuries sustained because of violence.[27] Among this group, homicide is the leading cause of death for African Americans, the second leading cause of death for Hispanics, and the third leading cause of death for American Indians, Alaska Natives, and Asian/Pacific Islanders, and

of the 5,570 homicides reported in 2003, 86% were males and 14% were females.[27]

Certain risk factors increase the likelihood that a young person may become violent. These include a history of violent victimization or involvement; attention deficits, hyperactivity, or learning disorders; involvement with drugs, alcohol, or tobacco; signs of gang involvement; poor behavioral control; high emotional distress; and a history of treatment for emotional problems.[27] Although these risk factors do not cause violence, they may contribute to the problem.

Emergency nurses should also be aware that the risk of violence is not limited to outside of the ED walls. Protecting the patients and staff is a critical component of providing safe care in the emergency department. To that end, emergency nurses must believe that children can become violent and prepare accordingly.

The importance of identifying risk factors in the emergency department may assist in providing resources and support to children and families who are impacted by youth violence. To address the problem, the risk in communities needs to be identified and emergency nurses need to select appropriate interventions and evaluate progress.

Prevention Recommendations

In addition to identification of risk factors, specific prevention efforts to reduce firearms injury include:[28]

❏ Children should not have access to firearms. A gun in the home can be a danger to children. Parents should seriously weigh the risks of keeping a gun in the home.

❏ Gun owners should always store firearms (including BB or pellet guns) unloaded and locked up, out of reach of children. Ammunition should be locked in a separate location, also out of reach of children. Quality safety devices such as gun locks, lock boxes, or gun safes should be used for every gun kept in the home. Gun storage keys and lock combinations should be kept hidden in a separate location.

❏ Parents should talk to children about the dangers of guns, teach children never to touch or play with guns, and teach them to tell an adult if they find a gun.

❏ Parents should check with neighbors, friends, relatives, or adults in any other homes where children may visit to ensure they follow safe storage practices if firearms are in their homes.

Preventing Harm from Mental Health Disorders

Studies show that at least one in five children and adolescents have a mental health disorder and one in 10 have a serious emotional disturbance.[29] When *Diagnostic and Statistical Manual* criteria were used, the most common disorders were substance-related disorders, anxiety disorders, and attention deficit and disruptive disorders.[30]

Because of high levels of unmet need for community-based children's mental health services, child mental health-related visits to emergency departments have significantly increased in the past several years. The AAP and American College of Emergency Physicians (ACEP) have developed a position statement that addresses the needs of the pediatric patient with mental health issues.[31] Recognition of and screening for mental health disorders are a first step in preventing further harm to a child experiencing these challenges.

Prevention Recommendations

There is a need for the development of mechanisms for the emergency department to deal with unique pediatric mental health issues, including violence in the community, physical trauma, domestic violence, child maltreatment, mass casualty incidents and disasters, suicides and suicide attempts, and the death of a child in the emergency department. There is also a lack of accurate, validated pediatric mental health screening tools for use in the ED setting. Emergency nurses can advocate for additional research funding dedicated to pediatric emergency mental health issues.

Child Maltreatment

In 2006, 1,530 children died in the United States of abuse and neglect and 905,000 children were victims of maltreatment.[32] Child maltreatment has a negative effect on the health of children and on society. Abused children often suffer physical injuries including cuts, bruises, burns, and broken bones. In addition, maltreatment causes stress that can disrupt early brain development. Extreme stress can harm the development of the nervous and immune systems.[33] As a result, children who are abused or neglected are at higher risk for health problems as adults. These problems include alcoholism, depression, drug abuse, eating disorders, obesity, sexual promiscuity, smoking, suicide, and certain chronic diseases.[34]

Prevention Recommendations

Remember "Sue's Rules" with the "SPICER" acronym.[35]

❑ *S*uspect that child abuse occurs. Believe the child.

❑ *P*rotect the child. Report suspicions of child maltreatment to child protective services. Partner with other professionals who care or advocate for abused and neglected children.

❑ *I*nspect the child. A complete history and physical examination may uncover hidden areas of abuse otherwise missed.

❑ *C*ollect evidence. Encourage the development of specifically trained emergency nurses who care for children who have been abused or neglected.

❑ *E*xpect the unexpected. Just when a nurse thinks she or he has "heard it all," a surprise occurs.

❑ *R*espect the child and family. Though nurses may be angry at times, addressing the problem professionally and objectively is important.

Preventing Harm to Children in the Emergency Department

The threat or occurrence of medical harm to pediatric patients is well described in the literature, sometimes making front-page news headlines. Emergency nurses are aware that there is a need to address the recent recommendations by the Institute of Medicine (Chapter 1) and others that all emergency care providers develop strategies to reduce harm to children and their families and that there must be an understanding of the importance of front-line (bedside) staff. For emergency nurses to continue to act as a pediatric "safety net" there is a need for both knowledge and resources that identify, prioritize, and respond to pediatric patient safety risks within their areas of responsibility.[36]

One strategy that can facilitate an increased awareness of pediatric patient safety in the emergency department is the development and implementation of a unit-based safety team. This team, which should consist of front-line, bedside clinical staff, should meet regularly for the primary purpose of identifying and prioritizing risks and safety concerns to pediatric patients in the emergency department and to develop and implement strategies that decrease the risk of harm. This safety team should be given the authority to recommend and implement reasonable changes. Meetings should follow guidelines similar to other injury prevention efforts: Gather data, make immediate short-term changes, report risks identified, and make recommendations to leadership teams to resolve issues that are beyond the scope of what can be addressed at the local level. Consider rotating team members at prescribed intervals, such as every 6 months, so that observations are varied and include more than one opinion. This keeps all members of the health care team involved and helps to ensure that no one person is overburdened by meetings or task follow-up.

Prevention Recommendations

To enhance the safety of pediatric patients who require emergency care:

❏ Continue to place the child at the center of departmental discussions.

❏ Ask the question, "If this were my family member, what would I expect?"

❏ Ensure that the emergency department has the correct-sized equipment and medications for children.

❏ Promote and facilitate pediatric emergency care education such as ENA's Emergency Nursing Pediatric Course (ENPC).

❏ Lead routine "practice" sessions/mock resuscitations to rehearse pediatric emergency care *before* it occurs to identify systems issues and needs.

❏ Remember that "fixing" one part of the system often complicates another; it may be helpful to partner with other unit-based safety teams who care for children.

❏ Insist on systems involvement; there should be no pediatric emergency care decisions made without the direct input of bedside clinicians.

❏ Bring pediatric safety initiatives to the table of each chapter, state, and national ENA meeting.

Pediatric Medication Safety

Children are at greater risk of experiencing medication errors or adverse drug reactions because of unique characteristics associated with their drug therapy. Risks include that many children cannot evaluate and express their own response to medications; drugs may be approved for marketing without any clinical trials in children, even though the drug may be used in children; pediatric dosage forms may not be available, and there is no standard compounding approach; the medication prescribing and administration process is more labor intensive and detailed for children than for adults; and the process requires increased medication handling, preparation, double-checking, and dosage calculations, increasing the chance for drug-related errors.[37]

Prevention Recommendations

High anxiety, distractions, and complexity have an impact on medication accuracy and safety when caring for a critically ill or injured child. To safely and effectively dose emergency pediatric medications:

❏ Standardized preestablished, precalculated, evidence-based standardized medication dosing tools should be

available.[38]

❏ Standardized education and practice with pediatric medication dosing should be developed.[38]

❏ Emergency nurses should be intimately involved in human factors analysis of the pediatric medication process including but not limited to the creation of national standards for concentrations and reconstitution of drugs, the review and elimination of the presence of look-alike and sound-alike drugs,[38] and reporting of medication error or near misses.[39]

Conclusion

No one can predict every move a child can make, or every object that might be dangerous. Some parents, and even emergency nurses, complain that nurses are "hovering" excessively, worried about the children at every moment. Perhaps the most important message emergency nurses can share with their patients and families is to realize that children, especially young children, need supervision. The goal of prevention efforts is not to frighten or intimidate but to offer greater awareness of potential dangers. Injury and illness prevention efforts including offering information about precautions in those "teachable moments" are obligations of the profession of emergency nursing. Promoting research and awareness of the injury and illness patterns and risks in communities can assist in prioritizing injury and illness prevention efforts.

Emergency nurses have been enthusiastically involved in injury and illness prevention efforts. Yet, there is more to be done. Research efforts over the past decade have led to a better understanding of the problem of injury and illness and have helped to define a successful approach to prevention efforts. Successful injury prevention programs are multifaceted and include three main components: education, modification of the environment, and advocacy leading to policy and/or regulatory changes.

Emergency nurses continue to lead pediatric illness and injury prevention efforts at the local, state, regional, and national levels, facilitating change in attitudes, behaviors, laws, and the environment to prevent childhood injury. In the United States, emergency nurses have contributed to a reduction in the child fatality rate from accidental injury, saving children's lives. It should be the promise of emergency nurses to continue to make injury prevention visible, to role model positive behaviors, and to continue to develop ENA's infrastructure to provide ongoing injury and illness prevention information to their patients and their families, legislators, and the media to meet the goal of protecting the future of the world through their children.

References

1. Middleton, K. R., & Burt, C. W. (2006). Availability of pediatric services and equipment in emergency departments: United States, 2002-03. *Advance Data, 28*(367), 1.

2. Bonanni, P. (1999). Demographic impact of vaccination: a review. *Vaccine, 17*(Suppl. 3), S120–S125.

3. Centers for Disease Control and Prevention. (1999). Recommended childhood immunization schedule—United States, 1999. MMWR. *Morbidity and Mortality Weekly Report, 48,* 12–16.

4. American College of Emergency Physicians. (2008, January). *Policy Statement: Immunization of adults and children in the emergency department.* Retrieved March 13, 2009, from http://www.acep.org/practices

5. Centers for Disease Control and Prevention. *2009 child and adolescent immunization schedule.* Retrieved January 22, 2009, from http://www.cdc.gov/vaccines/recs/schedules/child-schedule.htm

6. Centers for Disease Control and Prevention, National Center for Infectious Diseases. (2005). *Unpublished data.* Retrieved January 22, 2009, from www.cdc.gov

7. Centers for Disease Control and Prevention. (2008). *Children and antiviral drugs.* Retrieved January 22, 2009, from http://www.cdc.gov/flu/children/antiviral.htm

8. Centers for Disease Control and Prevention, National Center for Immunization and Respiratory Diseases, Division of Bacterial Diseases. (2008, May). *Meningococcal diseases: Technical and clinical information.* Retrieved March 11, 2009, from http://www.cdc.gov/meningitis/tech-clinical.htm

9. Glass, R. I., Kilgore, P. E., Holman, R. C., Jin, S., Smith, J. C., Woods, P. A., et al. (1996). The epidemiology of rotavirus diarrhea in the United States: Surveillance and estimates of disease burden. *Journal of Infectious Diseases, 174*(Suppl. 1), S5–S11.

10. Centers for Disease Control and Prevention. (2003). Managing acute gastroenteritis among children: Oral rehydration, maintenance, and nutritional therapy. MMWR. *Recommendations and Reports, 52*(RR-16), 1–16.

11. Rotavirus vaccine for the prevention of rotavirus gastroenteritis among children: recommendations of the Advisory Committee on Immunization Practices (ACIP). (1999). MMWR. *Morbidity and Mortality Weekly Report, 48*(No. RR-2).

12. Koplan, J. P., Liverman, C. T., & Kraak, V. I. (2004). *Preventing childhood obesity: Health in the balance.* Washington, DC: Institute of Medicine, National Academy of Sciences.

13. National Highway Traffic Safety Administration, National Center for Statistics & Analysis. (2007). *Traffic safety facts 2007: Children.* Washington, DC: Author.

14. Safe Kids Worldwide. Retrieved January 22, 2009, from http://www.safekids.org

15. National Highway Traffic Safety Administration. (n.d.). *Child restraint re-use after minor crashes.* Retrieved January 22, 2009, from http://www.nhtsa.dot.gov/people/injury/childps/ChildRestraints/ReUse/RestraintReUse.htm

16. Centers for Disease Control and Prevention, National Center for Injury Prevention and Control. (2003). *Report to Congress on mild traumatic brain injury in the United States: Steps to prevent a serious public health problem.* Atlanta, GA: Centers for Disease Control and Prevention.

17. Centers for Disease Control and Prevention, National Center for Injury Prevention and Control. (2008). *Web-based Injury Statistics Query and Reporting System (WISQARS) [online].* Retrieved January 22, 2009, from http://www.cdc.gov/ncipc/wisqars

18. American Academy of Pediatrics, The Injury Prevention Program. (2009). *Protect your child...prevent poisoning.* Retrieved January 22, 2009, from http://www.aap.org/family/poistipp.htm

19. Centers for Disease Control and Prevention, National Center for Injury Prevention and Control. (2005). *Web-based Injury Statistics Query and Reporting System (WISQARS) [online].* Retrieved January 22, 2009, from http://www.cdc.gov/ncipc/wisqars

20. Runyan, S. W., & Casteel, C. (Eds.). (2004). *The state of home safety in America: Facts about unintentional injuries in the home* (2nd ed.). Washington, DC: Home Safety Council.

21. Centers for Disease Control and Prevention, National Center for Health Statistics. (1998). *National vital statistics system.* Hyattsville, MD: U.S. Department of Health and Human Services.

22. Safe Kids Worldwide. (2009). *Safety tips: Fire and burn safety.* Retrieved March 11, 2009, from http://www.safekids.org/tips/tips_fire.htm

References (continued)

23. Runyan, C., & Casteel, C. (Eds.). (2004). *The state of home safety in America: Facts about unintentional injuries in the home* (2nd ed.). Washington, DC: Home Safety Council.

24. American Academy of Pediatrics. (2001). Falls from heights: Windows, roofs, and balconies (RE9951). *Pediatrics, 107,* 1053–1056.

25. Chalmers, D., Marshall, S., & Langley, J. (1996). Height and surfacing as risk factors for injury in falls from playground equipment: A case-control study. *Injury Prevention, 2,* 98–104.

26. American Academy of Pediatrics. (2001). Injuries associated with infant walkers. *Pediatrics, 108,* 790–792.

27. Centers for Disease Control and Prevention, National Center for Injury Prevention and Control. (2006). *Web-based Injury Statistics Query and Reporting System (WISQARS) [online].* Retrieved January 22, 2009, from http://www.cdc.gov/ncipc/wisqars

28. Safe Kids USA.(2004). *Injury facts: Firearm injury (unintentional).* Retrieved January 22, 2009, from http://www.usa.safekids.org/tier3_cd.cfm?folder_id=540&content_item_id=1131

29. U.S. Department of Health and Human Services. (1999). *Mental health: A report of the Surgeon General.* Rockville, MD: U.S. Department of Health and Human Services.

30. Sills, M. R., & Bland, S. D. (2002). Summary statistics for pediatric psychiatric visits to US emergency departments, 1993–1999. *Pediatrics, 110*(4), e40.

31. American College of Emergency Physicians. (2006, April). *Policy statement: Pediatric mental health emergencies in the emergency medical services system.* Retrieved March 13, 2009, from http://www.acep.org/practices

32. U.S. Department of Health and Human Services, Administration on Children, Youth, and Families. (2006). *Child maltreatment 2006.* Retrieved January 22, 2009, from http://www.acf.hhs.gov

33. National Scientific Council on the Developing Child. (2005). *Excessive stress disrupts the architecture of the developing brain, Working Paper No. 3.* Retrieved January 22, 2009, from http://www.developingchild.net

34. Runyan, D., Wattam, C., Ikeda, R., Hassan, F., & Ramiro, L. (2002). Child abuse and neglect by parents and caregivers. In: E. Krug, L. L. Dahlberg, J. A. Mercy, A. B. Zwi, & R. Lozano (Eds.), *World report on violence and health* (pp. 59–86). Geneva, Switzerland: World Health Organization.

35. Hohenhaus, S. (n.d.).*EMS-C Child Abuse Recognition Education (C.A.R.E.), North Carolina Office of EMS.* Retrieved January 22, 2009, from http://www.ncems.org/files/C.A.R.E.%20slide%20program.ppt

36. Hohenhaus, S., & Frush, K. (2005). Revolutionizing healthcare in the emergency department: Enhancing patient safety in the safety net. *Topics in Emergency Medicine, 27*(3), 206–212.

37. Institute for Safe Medication Practices. (2002, June 2). *Pediatric pharmacy medication safety guidelines seen as important step in reducing medication errors.* Retrieved January 26, 2009, from http://ismp.org/pressroom/PR20020606.pdf

38. Hohenhaus, S. M., Cadwell, S. M., Stone-Griffith, S., Sears-Russell, N., Baxter, T., Hicks, W., et al. (2008). Assessment of emergency nursing practice during critical pediatric medication administration in a simulated resuscitation using the Color Coding Kids Hospital System: A multisite trial. *Advanced Emergency Nursing Journal, 30*(3), 233–241.

39. Hohenhaus, S. M. (2008). Emergency nursing and medical error—a survey of two states. *Journal of Emergency Nursing, 34*(1), 20–25.

FIVE

Health History and Physical Assessment

Judith A. Kaufmann, DrPH, FNP-C

Introduction

Obtaining a health history and performing a physical assessment of infants, children, and adolescents can be a challenge. In a busy emergency department (ED), where time is of the essence, the therapeutic relationship among the patient, parent, and nurse must develop quickly. This relationship affects the quality and progress of the history taking and physical assessment process. Trust is an essential element throughout this process; if the parent and patient develop trust with the emergency nurse, their participation in the assessment may be enhanced, and the data obtained by the nurse will be both timely and accurate.

The purpose of this chapter is to describe a history-taking and physical assessment process that emergency nurses can use with pediatric patients. Focused physical assessments of specific body systems are provided in their respective chapters. The history-taking and physical assessment process discussed in this chapter is applied throughout this core curriculum.

Health History

The health history provides 85% of the information leading to a diagnosis.[1] There are a number of barriers to obtaining a high-quality history in the ED setting:

❐ The high acuity and high census levels are associated with the need to obtain a focused history in lieu of a comprehensive developmental, psychosocial, physical, and cognitive history that would potentially delay emergent attention to the acute concern.

❐ The obvious lack of continuity in patient care prevents the development of a therapeutic relationship between the patient/family and the nurse.

❐ The heterogeneity of the ED patient population places additional demand on the nurse to be familiar with numerous cultural and social needs of families and to approach the history and physical in a culturally sensitive manner.[2]

Despite the immediacy of problems that present in the emergency department, care must be taken to minimize physical and psychological distress for children and their families. Providing care is based on three principles:

1. Identifying stressors for both the pediatric patient and the family.

2. Minimizing separation of the pediatric patient from the family.

3. Controlling pain.[3]

General precepts that the emergency nurse must consider when completing the pediatric health history include the following:

❐ Gain the parents' trust. Address the parent by name to demonstrate the concern for the parent as an individual. Allow the caregivers to be involved, and acknowledge their need for appropriate reassurance and support in the emergent situation. Children sense parents' distrust and fear and will reflect these qualities themselves. Engagement of the parent is an important key to a successful assessment.

❐ Elicit a meaningful health history within the framework of the chief presenting complaint. Allow time for the parent to reveal the child's health problem; rushing into a history without listening to the parent or failing to clarify and validate statements made in haste may result in misinterpretation, inaccurate data, or missing information that may be crucial to planning appropriate care.

❏ Maintain the parent's and child's privacy. Elicit the health history in a private area away from crowded waiting areas or busy hallways, which may contribute to a feeling of vulnerability.

❏ Prepare both the parent and the child for a procedure. Attempt to explain each step in the process, using age-appropriate terms when possible. Assess the parent's level of understanding, and rephrase explanations as necessary.

❏ Integrate essential assessment and interventions with explanations of physical findings, and incorporate health promotion and anticipatory guidance when appropriate. Many children lack ongoing primary care and are seen in emergency departments in lieu of routine well-child care. This is particularly true for nonwhite, low-income children and older children.[4]

Approach to the Health History

The health history should begin with a clear statement regarding the reason for the visit as reported by the child or the parent/caregiver. CIAMPEDS is the format endorsed by the Emergency Nurses Association (ENA) (Table 5.1). Another format for eliciting a history focuses on the events preceding the onset of symptoms and follows an "OLD CART" algorithm:

O—onset of symptoms (did the symptoms begin and end and what happened in between? The patient's "story" of the episode? Reconstruction of exact sequence of events? Was it related to trauma or did it arise without a specific event?)

L—location of the complaint (e.g., abdominal, back/flank, chest, head, localized or generalized?)

D—duration of the symptoms (minutes, hours, days, weeks?)

C—characteristics and chronology (burning, deep, dull? Increasing in intensity, stable, decreasing in intensity over a specific timeframe?)

A—associated symptoms (headache with vomiting? Abdominal pain with constipation/diarrhea? Associated fevers? Anorexia?)/A—*aggravating* factors (worsens with lying flat, worsens with eating?)

R—relieving factors (improved with medications, heat? Ice?)

T—timing (did symptoms begin acutely or have they slowly progressed? Under what circumstances did it take place? Where was the patient when symptoms began? What treatment was administered at home or by another health care provider?)

Once a complete picture of the chief complaint has been elicited, a brief review of pertinent aspects of the following is important information that may have an impact on the child's care and in planning nursing interventions:

1. Past medical history—should include the birth history for children < 2 years of age and children with disabilities, history of accidents, injuries, ingestions, immunizations, major developmental milestones, previous illnesses, hospitalizations and surgeries, known allergies.

2. Family medical history—should be brief and focused on problems related to anesthesia, allergies to medications, significant diseases, disabilities, and genetic disorders.

3. Social history—should ascertain the primary caretaker, siblings, living arrangements, school/day care attendance, extended family support systems and caretakers, education/employment status of parents, need for social services.

Although emergent situations may preclude comprehensive inquiry into the child's habits, preferences, and routines, if time and acuity of the child's situation permits, the emergency nurse should attempt to obtain information on the child's diet and elimination patterns, dental history, indications of risky behaviors, and previous coping patterns (intensity of responses to pain, new situations, baseline personality characteristics).

Use or modification of standardized child health records is encouraged, and a number of health history templates can be accessed through state and national Web sites:

http://www.state.nj.us/health/forms/ch-14.pdf

http://www.dpw.state.pa.us/Resources/Documents/Pdf/FillInForms/ChildrenYouth/CY51.pdf

http://www.pamf.org/forms/143453_Ped_Health_Hx.pdf

Physical Assessment

Ordinarily, the physical examination follows a cephalocaudal sequence, but this sequence is often altered in pediatric emergency patients to accommodate both the child's developmental stage and the acuity of the immediate condition. All physical assessment should begin with a general observation of the child's overall condition. Is the child compromised in any way? Are there signs of excessive pain? Is the child in respiratory distress? Are signs and symptoms indicative of blood loss and impending shock? Is the child crying inconsolably? If the child's condition appears to be stable, then the ED nurse should proceed methodically and use nursing interventions that are focused on the following goals:[5]

TABLE 5.1 CIAMPEDS Format for Obtaining a Health History

Historical Information	*Components and Rationale*
Chief complaint	Focus on the reason for the current ED visit. Identify the primary health problem and its duration.
Immunizations	Determine the child's immunization status and/or potential need for further immunization (e.g., tetanus booster). This helps to determine whether the child's current health problem may be related to inadequate immunization (e.g., respiratory illness in the young infant prior to the initial pertussis immunization).
Isolation	Identify recent exposure to a communicable disease (e.g., varicella) and correlate with assessment findings suggestive of that disease may require isolation from other ED patients. Isolate children who are immunosuppressed from chemotherapy or anti-rejection medications to prevent their exposure to other diseases.
Allergies	Document medication, food, and environmental allergies, including latex allergies. Note reactions to the allergens.
Medications	Elicit prescribed and over-the-counter medications and herbal and dietary supplements that the child is taking to prevent duplication of medication administration and to determine the effectiveness of current medications. Note the medication's name, dosage, route, frequency, duration, effectiveness and most recent dose. Ask for a list of medications for medication reconciliation purposes.
Past health history	Include birth history (maternal age, birth weight, discharge weight, gestational length, complications, and medications) for children younger than 2 years of age and children with disabilities. For all children, the health history should include prior hospitalizations or illnesses, ongoing chronic illnesses or conditions (e.g., asthma, congenital heart disease), physical growth, attainment of developmental milestones, and family health patterns. For sexually active patients, include the use of birth control measures, gravida and para status and any treatment for sexually transmitted diseases.
Parent's impression of the child's health condition	Elicit from the parent perceived changes in the child's health status that prompted the ED visit. The parent is best able to judge improvement or worsening in the child's health condition. Include information about sleep, appetite, and play patterns. Consider cultural differences that may influence parent/child responses.
Events surrounding the illness or injury	Obtain information about the onset (rapid or protracted), duration, and progression of symptoms. Describe involvement of other family members. Inquire about recent travel to another state or a foreign country. Obtain information about the time of the injury, the mechanism of injury, and witnesses to the event. Include administered first aid or treatments.
Diet	Determine the child's normal eating patterns and how they are different with the onset of illness or injury. Elicit the time of the child's last oral intake in the event that surgery or a procedure is indicated.
Diapers	Determine the child's normal urine and bowel elimination patterns. Elicit the time of the child's last urination and bowel movement and changes from the normal patterns.
Symptoms associated with the illness or injury	Symptomatology, supported by the physical assessment, allows for the accurate diagnosis of the child's health condition. Include a description of the symptoms, the time of their onset, and interventions that alleviated or worsened the symptoms.

Emergency Nurses Association. (2004). Emergency nursing pediatric course (ENPC) provider manual (3rd ed.). Des Plaines, IL: Author.

❏ Minimize stress and anxiety associated with the physical assessment. For the child in stable condition, begin the assessment with those activities that can be presented as games and end with more traumatic procedures. A calm, unhurried approach engages even the most taciturn child.

Foster trust among the child, parent, and emergency nurse. Address the child by name. Show a genuine interest in the child; ask about hobbies, likes, dislikes, and pets. Listen to the child. When examining the child focus on the healthy body areas first, then move to the affected areas (i.e., painful or injured) of the body to minimize distress. Respect the need for privacy among children of all ages. Keep in mind that the child may perceive even the most innocuous procedures as threatening (e.g., use of blood pressure arm cuff, speculum examination of the ears or nose, use of a tongue depressor). Use of small toys or decorated instruments can increase the child's readiness to cooperate. Take cues from the child to assess readiness to cooperate (eye contact, body language, responds to questions).

Prepare the child as much as possible for the physical assessment. Explain to the child and parent what the assessment entails and what to expect. Allow some time for the child to adjust to the ED environment before proceeding with the physical assessment. Some children will protest throughout the assessment despite the aforementioned interventions. With these children, proceed calmly and confidently, but in a firm, direct manner.

Maximize the accuracy and reliability of the physical assessment findings. Position the child as needed if he or she exhibits physical distress or anxiety, thus enabling completion of the assessment. Table 5.2 describes age-specific approaches for the pediatric physical assessment.

There are numerous examples of pediatric physical assessment techniques in the literature.[6,7] The ENA[8] recommends the A to I approach for this assessment process in the emergency department:

- Airway
- Breathing
- Circulation
- Disability
- Exposure and environmental control
- Full set of vital signs
- Family presence
- Give comfort measures
- Head-to-toe assessment
- Inspect posterior surfaces

Airway

- Observe for airway patency.
- Listen for sounds of airway obstruction (stridor).

- Observe the child's position for air entry (tripod, neck extended, or lowered jaw).
- Observe for airway obstruction (blood, mucus, oral edema, foreign body, secretions, carbonaceous sputum, or singed nasal hair).
- Note breath odor (e.g., ketones or alcohol).

Breathing

- Observe the child's work of breathing.
  - Nasal flaring, grunting
  - Use of accessory muscles
- Listen for audible adventitious sounds (wheezing).
- Observe the child's breathing pattern.
  - Regular versus irregular
  - Rapid (tachypneic) versus age-appropriate rate
- Observe the depth of respirations.

Circulation

- Observe the color of the skin.
- Measure capillary refill.
  - Theoretically, normal refill time is a measure of adequate peripheral perfusion and thus normal cardiac output and peripheral vascular resistance. In healthy, warm children, a normal capillary refill value is < 3 seconds and > 1 second.
  - A low ambient temperature has a significant effect on capillary refill in both healthy and ill or injured children; thus, it is not used as a sole indicator for shock.
- Palpate the central and peripheral pulses for strength and equality.
- Palpate the skin with the back of the hand to determine skin temperature; compare the temperature of the upper and lower extremities.

Disability

- Observe the child's activity level.
- Note the child's level of consciousness; observe the child's ability to follow directions, respond to questions, and with the caregiver.
- Observe the child's response to the ED environment; note the child's level of consolability.
- Obtain a Glasgow Coma Scale score (Chapter 16) or AVPU assessment:
  - A = Alert
  - V = Responds to verbal stimuli
  - P = Responds to painful stimuli

TABLE 5.2 Age-Specific Approaches to Pediatric Physical Assessment

Age	Position	Sequence	Preparation
Young infant	Infant too young to sit unsupported: Seat the infant on the parent's lap or against the parent's shoulder.	If the infant is quiet or sleeping, auscultate heart, lungs, and abdomen, then palpate these areas as needed.	Undress to diaper but keep wrapped in a blanket. Use distraction techniques (bright objects, rattles, soft talking) to gain cooperation (Chapter 3). Smile; use a soft, gentle voice.
	Infant aged 4–6 months: Place the infant on the parent's lap or examination table.	Proceed using a systematic method: Assess skin, cardiovascular system, thorax, and lungs, proceed with abdomen, genitalia, lower extremities, and finish with the head. Elicit Moro (startle) reflex last.	Pacify with a feeding (if permitted) or a pacifier. Ask the parent to assist with assessment if he or she is able to do so. For example, have the parent palpate the affected area or perform passive range-of-motion exercises to elicit tenderness.
Older infant	Infant able to sit unsupported: Place the infant on the parent's lap whenever possible; if the infant is positioned on the examination table, keep parents in full view.	Perform the most intrusive aspects of the assessment last. Elicit reflexes as the body part is examined.	Avoid quick movements or prolonged eye contact (older infants) to prevent surprises and promote trust.
Toddler	Position sitting or standing on or by parent or sitting upright on parent's lap.	Inspect body areas through play (count fingers, tickle toes). Use minimal contact initially. Introduce equipment slowly. Discuss the child's fears with the parent and order the examination sequence accordingly. Auscultate, percuss, and palpate when the child is quiet. Perform the most intrusive aspects of the assessment last.	Have the parent remove outer clothing; remove the underpants when that body area is examined. Encourage inspection of equipment. Allow the child to hold a transitional object or toy during the assessment. Demonstrate the assessment on a toy, the parent, or self; create a story about the assessment. Speak to the child in terms that a toddler can understand. Keep the parent's face in the child's view. Perform the assessment quickly and efficiently if the child is uncooperative. Praise and reward cooperative behavior. Elicit the parent's assistance if he or she is able to do so, as described in the infant section.

TABLE 5.2 Age-Specific Approaches to Pediatric Physical Assessment

Age	Position	Sequence	Preparation

Preschooler	Position sitting, lying, or standing.
	
	May cooperate when prone or supine.
	
	Prefers parents nearby.
		If cooperative:
		  Proceed in head-to-toe fashion.
		If uncooperative:
		  Proceed as with toddler.
		  Perform the most intrusive aspects of the assessment last.
			Request self-undressing.
			
			Permit underpants to be worn and assure privacy.
			
			Offer equipment for inspection; demonstrate on the parent or a doll.
			
			Create a story about the procedure ("Let's see how strong your muscles are.").
			
			Offer choices when appropriate.
			
			Expect cooperation; elicit the child's help whenever possible ("Point to where it hurts.").
			
			Educate the child about his or her body ("I am going to listen to your heart; can you point to your heart?").

School-aged	Prefers sitting. Cooperates when placed in most positions. Younger school-aged child usually prefers parental presence; older school-aged child may want privacy.	Proceed head-to-toe. Examine genitalia last (may be deferred).	Request self-undressing. Allow to wear underpants and assure privacy. Explain purpose of equipment and significance of procedure in terms the child can understand. Teach about body functioning and healthy habits. Tell the child it is permissible to cry. Offer choices when appropriate.
Adolescent	Prefers sitting. Offer parental or peer presence for support. Speak with the adolescent first before talking with the parent.	Proceed head-to-toe. Examine genitalia last (usually deferred).	Maintain a sense of control and privacy by permitting adolescents to undress unattended. Expose only the body area to be examined. Explain assessment findings. Maintain objectivity and professional demeanor when addressing sexual development and sexual history; emphasize normalcy. Examine genitalia if warranted; approach exam as any other body part; may leave until the end. Consider using a mirror during the genital examination to allow the adolescent to view the genital area.

Hockenberry, M. (2005). *Wong's essentials of pediatric nursing* (7th ed.). St. Louis, MO: Mosby.

Wong, D. (1999). Physical and developmental assessment of the child. In D. Wong (Ed.), *Whaley and Wong's nursing care of infants and children* (6th ed., pp. 217–283). St. Louis, MO: Mosby-Year Book.

- U = Unresponsive
☐ Measure the pupillary equality and response.

Exposure and Environmental Control

☐ Remove the child's clothing as needed to continue the assessment.
☐ Initiate measures to maintain a normothermic state or to warm the child.

Full Set of Vital Signs

☐ Measure the respiratory rate.
  - Count the respiratory rate by auscultation for one full minute in children of all ages.
☐ Measure the heart/pulse rate.
  - Count the apical pulse for one full minute for greatest accuracy in children of all ages; an alternative is to count the brachial pulse.
  - Count the radial pulse in children older than 2 years.
  - Grade the pulse amplitude (Table 5.3).

TABLE 5.3 Pulse Grading

Grade	Description
0	Not palpable
+1	Difficult to palpate, thready; easily obliterated with pressure
+2	Difficult to palpate; may obliterate with pressure
+3	Easy to palpate; not easily obliterated (normal)
+4	Strong, bounding; not obliterated with pressure

☐ Measure the blood pressure.
  - Measure the blood pressure with a sphygmomanometer using a size-appropriate cuff. When using an electronic blood pressure device, recheck abnormal readings with a sphygmomanometer.
☐ Measure the temperature.
  - Select a route for temperature measurement. Table 5.4 compares the advantages and disadvantages of commonly used measurement routes (oral, rectal, axillary, and tympanic).
  - Hyperthermia: > 101.3 °F, (38.5 °C) versus Hypothermia: < 93.2 °F (34.0 °C)
☐ Obtain the child's weight with the appropriate-sized scale.
  - Compare these findings on the male or female growth chart.

- Measure the child's weight to the nearest 10 g or 0.50 oz for infants and 100 g or 0.25 lb for older children.
  - A child whose weight falls below the 5th percentile is underweight.
  - A child whose weight falls above the 95th percentile is overweight.
- When weighing infants, note whether the weight was measured with or without clothes; for infants and young children with questionable dehydration, measure with diaper or underclothes only.
- Always weigh infants and children in kilograms to prevent errors in medication dosing. Medications are generally calculated in milligram per kilogram doses.

Family Presence

☐ Assess needs of family, taking into consideration cultural variables.
☐ Support family's involvement of the child's care.
☐ Assign a health care professional to provide explanations to the family.
☐ Assign a staff member to provide support.

Give Comfort Measures

☐ Base comfort measures on the chief complaint or obvious injury.
☐ Evaluate presence and level of pain (Chapter 11).
☐ Stabilize suspected fractures.

Head-to-Toe Assessment

The head-to-toe assessment is conducted by using *observation, inspection, auscultation, palpation,* and *percussion.*[6,7]

☐ General state of health
  - Posture
  - Gait
  - Fine and gross motor activity
  - Dress, grooming, and hygiene
  - Body piercings
  - Tattoos
  - Dyed hair
  - Odors
  - Facial expressions
  - Speech, state of awareness, and interaction among child, parent, and siblings

TABLE 5.4 Routes for Temperature Measurement		
Route	*Indications*	*Method*
Oral	Useful in children who can follow directions and who can keep the thermometer probe under the tongue without biting (usually 5 years of age, maybe younger).	Insert the thermometer probe into the right or left posterior sublingual pocket; leave in place for approximately 2 to 3 minutes (depending on the model of thermometer used).
Axillary	Useful in children who will not tolerate a rectal temperature measurement and who are too young to keep the oral thermometer in place, such as toddlers; also used in neonates.	Place the thermometer probe in the axillary space, held firmly between the arm and the axilla; leave in place for approximately 5 minutes (depending on the model of thermometer used). Usually, this temperature measurement is 1° lower than an oral temperature measurement.
Tympanic	Useful in children of all ages, although use in infants may depend on the manufacturer's recommendations.	Position the thermometer in the external auditory canal and depress the thermometer "trigger." The temperature measurement requires a few seconds to obtain.
Rectal	Useful in infants and young children; considered to be the "gold standard" in temperature measurement in ill or injured infants and children. Rectal temperatures are contraindicated in children with immune disorders, bleeding disorders, and rectal abnormalities or trauma.	Insert the lubricated thermometer probe no more than 2.5 centimeters or 1 inch into the rectum; leave in place for approximately 3 minutes (depending on the model of thermometer used). The temperature measurement is usually considered 1° higher than an oral temperature measurement.

❐ Head
  ▪ Observe and inspect the shape, symmetry, and hair distribution of the infant's and young toddler's head.
  ▪ Palpate the suture lines in the infant's and young toddler's head. The suture lines may overlap in the newborn, but they usually flatten out by age 6 months.
  ▪ Palpate the anterior and posterior fontanelles while the infant is in a sitting position; note bulging (indicative of increased intracranial pressure) and depressed (indicative of dehydration) fontanelles. Fontanelles are assessed up until about 2 years of age.
  ▪ Observe and inspect the shape, symmetry, and hair distribution of the head of older children.
❐ Ears and eyes
  ▪ Observe and inspect the ears for normal external aural characteristics—ear alignment, size, and position. Observe for piercing or scars.
  ▪ Inspect ear canals for presence of blood or discharge in head injuries.
  ▪ Test for gross hearing by talking with the child and listening to the responses; for the infant, ring a bell or shake a rattle near the infant's ear and observe the infant turn toward the noise.
  ▪ Observe and inspect the pupils for size, equality, and response to light.
  ▪ Test for gross vision by having the child point to an object or having an infant visually follow an object. The six cardinal gazes are assessed beginning at 5 to 6 months of age. Steady fixation and following an object are assessed beginning at 3 months of age. 20/30 vision is not generally noted in a child until approximately 4 years of age.
  ▪ Note strabismus (abnormal alignment of eyes).
❐ Face
  ▪ Observe and inspect the face for symmetric features that are proportioned. Note abnormal facies.
  ▪ Palpate the face to detect contours, pain, or tenderness.
  ▪ Observe and inspect the external nares for discharge, excoriation, and odor.
  ▪ Observe and inspect the oral cavity and pharynx (tongue, lips, and tonsils) for a pink color and moist, intact mucous membranes. Inspect for primary and secondary dentition. By 24 months of age, all deciduous teeth have erupted. Beginning at age 5 to 6 years, deciduous teeth are lost. By age 12, all 32 teeth are in place.

- Mouth
  - Avoid use of tongue blade unless imperative that the posterior pharynx is fully visualized.
  - Note dentition, presence of caries, malocclusions or signs of dental trauma, halitosis, quality of voice and phonation.
- Neck
  - Observe and inspect the neck for surface trauma or scars.
  - Evaluate for presence of nuchal rigidity—resistance to head movement in any direction
  - Palpate lymph glands for enlargement; note their color, size, consistency, location, temperature, and tenderness. Lymphadenopathy is rare in infancy, and the size of the lymph nodes peaks between ages 8 and 16. The majority of enlarged lymph nodes in children are due to viral or bacterial infections. Enlarged supraclavicular nodes are never considered normal and may raise suspicion of malignancy.
- Chest
  - Inspect and observe the chest's anterior-posterior diameter. Observe for symmetric chest expansion on inspiration. Observe for abdominal breathing in children younger than 7 years of age and thoracic breathing in children older than 7 years of age.
  - Auscultate breath sounds in all lung lobes, from the apex to the base as the child breathes normally. Asking the child to take deep breaths may precipitate inaccurate findings.
  - Auscultate for the presence and location of adventitious sounds (Table 5.5).
- Heart and vascular system
  - Observe the anterior chest for symmetry of chest movement, pulsations, and lifts or heaves.
  - Auscultate the heart at the apex and the lower sternal border with the bell of the stethoscope; listen at each auscultatory area with the diaphragm of the stethoscope.
  - In children younger than 7 years of age, the point of maximum intensity is lateral to the left midclavicular line and fourth intercostal space.
  - In children older than 7 years of age, the point of maximum intensity is at the midclavicular line and fifth intercostal space. Heart sounds should be clear, distinct, and synchronous with the radial pulse (Table 5.6).
- Abnormal heart sounds (auscultate for)
  - Clicks
  - Murmurs (Table 5.7)
  - Precordial friction rubs—high-pitched, grating sounds that stop with breath holding
- Peripheral pulses
  - Palpate the peripheral pulses in both extremities.

TABLE 5.5 Significance of Adventitious Sounds

Breath Sound	Characteristics	Underlying Cause
Rales		
Fine	Intermittent, high-pitched; heard during inspiration	Indicates alveolar fluid; pneumonia; congestive heart failure
Medium	Intermittent, wet, loud; heard during inspiration; clear with coughing	Indicates fluid in bronchioles and bronchi; pulmonary edema
Coarse	Loud, bubbling; heard during expiration; clear with coughing	Indicates fluid in bronchioles and bronchi; resolving pneumonia; bronchitis
Rhonchi		
Sonorous	Continuous, snoring, low pitched; heard during inspiration and expiration	Indicates involvement of large bronchi and trachea; bronchitis
Sibilant	Continuous, musical, high pitched; heard during expiration	Indicates edema and small airway obstruction; asthma
Wheezes		
Inspiratory	Sonorous, musical	Upper airway obstruction
Expiratory	Whistling, sighing	Lower airway obstruction

Engel, J. (2006). *Pocket guide to pediatric assessment.* (5th ed.). St. Louis, MO: Mosby-Year Book.

TABLE 5.6 Auscultation of Heart Sounds

Heart Sound	Anatomic Location for Auscultation	Significance of the Heart Sound
S_1	Loudest in the mitral and tricuspid areas; "lubb" from atrioventricular valve closure	Intensified with fever, exercise and anemia; may indicate mitral stenosis; variability in intensity may indicate dysrhythmia
S_2	Base of heart (aortic and pulmonic areas); loudest in these areas; "dupp" from aortic and pulmonic valve closure	Split S_1 or S_2: Occurs because left-sided valves close slightly before right-sided valves
S_3	Lying on left side	Rapid ventricular filling ("Ken-tuc-ky"); normal in children and young adults
S_4	Lying on left side	Atrial contraction at the end of diastole ("Ten-nes-see"); abnormal in most persons

TABLE 5.7 Comparison of Innocent and Organic Heart Murmurs

Characteristic	Innocent Heart Murmur*	Organic Heart Murmur†
Child's growth	Does not increase over time and does not affect the child's growth	May worsen over time; may affect the child's growth
Sound	Systolic; low-pitched; musical heard at the second and third left intercostal spaces	Variable, depending on its associated lesion (harsh, rumbling, or blowing)
Presence	May disappear with a position change	Always present

*Nonpathologic.
†Occurring before age three related to congenital defects; occurring after age three related to rheumatic heart disease

Compare pulse symmetry and quality; note pallor, turgor, or edema of the extremities.

❑ Abdomen

- Inspect and observe the abdomen's contour; observe for protuberance (normal in toddlers; otherwise may indicate fluid retention, tumor, organomegaly, or ascites) and depression (dehydration or high abdominal obstruction).

- Inspect the skin for scars (surgery, child maltreatment), trauma, color (yellowness may indicate jaundice), striae (obesity or fluid retention), and dilated vessels.

- Observe for movement in the abdomen, such as visible peristaltic waves (obstruction or pyloric stenosis).

- Inspect the umbilicus for its color, presence of discharge, inflammation, and herniation.

- Observe the child's reaction to positioning during the assessment, such as splinting or guarding (peritoneal signs).

- Auscultate for bowel sounds in all four quadrants using the diaphragm of the stethoscope. Ideally, bowel sounds should be auscultated for one full minute in each quadrant; auscultate for a minimum of five minutes to determine whether bowel sounds are absent.

- Palpate (lightly and then deeply, moving to the painful area at the end of palpation) and percuss the abdomen in the absence of surgical disease. If the child is in pain or discomfort, defer palpation.

❑ Genitalia and anus (usually deferred)

- Note Tanner stage.

- Inspect the female genitalia and anus for signs of trauma, irritation, or discharge.

- Inspect the male genitalia (penis and scrotum) and anus for signs of trauma, irritation, and discharge.

- Inspect the anal area for irritation, prolapse, or signs of itching (pinworms).

- Palpate the lymph glands in the groin for enlargement; note their color, size, consistency, location, temperature, and tenderness.

❑ Neuromuscular system

- Inspect and observe the upper and lower extremities for signs of trauma, deformities, swelling, and joint effusions.

- Palpate the joints in upper and lower extremities for pain.
- Assess active and passive range of motion.
  - Hyperextension of neck and spine (opisthotonos) and pain with head flexion require immediate medical evaluation.
☐ Test for upper-extremity strength by having the child squeeze the nurse's fingers.
☐ Test for lower-extremity strength by having the child push against the nurse's hands with the soles of the feet.
☐ Assess for congenital hip dislocation in children up to 2 years of age (perform the Ortolani and Barlow maneuvers [adducting the hip while pushing the thigh posteriorly]), and note presence or absence of the Galeazzi sign (shortening of the flexed femur and hip dislocation).

Inspect Posterior Surfaces

☐ Inspect the back for surface trauma and vertebral alignment.
- Observe for the spinal curves (scoliosis).
- Observe for symmetric hip and shoulder alignment.
☐ Observe muscle tone and coordination.
☐ Assess the cranial nerves (may be deferred; Chapter 16).
☐ Skin
- Observe and inspect the skin for odor, abnormal bruising, scars, rashes, or atypical lesions.
- Observe moistness of the exposed skin areas and mucous membranes; dryness indicates dehydration.
- Observe color and pigmentation on basis of cultural and ethnic variations (Table 5.8).
☐ Lesions (Chapter 20)
- Location
- Distribution
- Arrangement
- Type
- Color
☐ Inspect the hair for distribution, color, texture, amount, and quality.
☐ Inspect the nails; note their characteristics—smooth, convex, pink, well-groomed.
☐ Palpate the skin's texture; observe for scars, keloids, or hypertrophic scarring.
☐ Palpate for skin turgor and mobility. (Grasp a fold of skin on the upper arm or abdomen and quickly release it; note time for skin to return to its normal position with residual marks.)
☐ Palpate for edema; compress a thumb into an area that appears to be swollen.

TABLE 5.8 Comparison of Skin Color		
Color	*Suggestive Health Condition*	*Best Location to Detect*
Blue (cyanosis)	Peripheral—anxiety or cold; central—decrease in the blood's oxygen-carrying capacity	Lips, mouth, and trunk
Jaundice	Liver disease, biliary obstruction, severe infection in infants	Sclerae, mucous membranes, and abdomen
Yellow	Carotenemia	Palms, soles, and face (mucous membranes and sclerae not involved)
Yellow	Chronic renal disease	Exposed skin (mucous membranes and sclerae not involved)
Pallor (lack of pink skin tones in whites; ash-gray color in African Americans	Syncope, fever, shock, anemia	Face, mouth, conjunctivae, and nails

Engel, J. (2006). *Pocket guide to pediatric assessment.* (5th ed.). St. Louis, MO: Mosby-Year Book.

TABLE 5.9 Summary of Normal and Abnormal Pediatric Physical Assessment Findings and Nursing Interventions

Assessment Parameter	Normal Findings	Abnormal Findings	Interventions
Airway	Patent Clear Odor-free breath	Inability to maintain own airway Signs of airway obstruction Malodorous breath	Maintain child in position of comfort. Position airway (jaw thrust/chin lift). Insert airway adjunct. Prepare for endotracheal intubation.
Breathing	Respiratory rate within age-appropriate limits Regular breathing pattern Absence of audible adventitious sounds or use of accessory muscles	Bradypnea Tachypnea Nasal flaring Abnormal breath sounds Accessory muscle use Abnormal breathing pattern	Administer supplemental oxygen. Initiate bag-mask ventilation if spontaneous respirations absent or ineffective. Prepare for mechanical ventilation.
Circulation	Heart rate within age-appropriate limits Pink, warm, and dry skin Strong and regular peripheral pulses Capillary refill < 3 seconds and > 1 second	Bradycardia Tachycardia Mottled, pale, cool, or moist skin Weak peripheral pulses Capillary refill > 3 second Capillary refill < 1 second	Initiate chest compressions if cardiac function absent or ineffective. Obtain vascular access. Initiate fluid volume replacement and/or medication therapy. Initiate cardiorespiratory and oxygen saturation monitoring. Prepare for cardiac defibrillation or synchronized cardioversion.
Disability	Awake, alert, active Round, equal pupils reactive to light and accommodation	Altered level of consciousness Unequal, nonreactive pupils or sluggish pupillary responses	Treat the underlying cause. Monitor closely.
Exposure/ environmental control	Intact skin surfaces	Surface trauma indicative of child maltreatment or child sexual abuse (Chapters 44 and 45) Hyperthermia Hypothermia	Notify child protective services. Prepare for interview and examination (Chapters 44 and 45). Employ supplemental warming or cooling measures. Maintain normothermic environment.

TABLE 5.9 Summary of Normal and Abnormal Pediatric Physical Assessment Findings and Nursing Interventions (continued)

Assessment Parameter	Normal Findings	Abnormal Findings	Interventions
Get full set of vital signs.	Vital signs and weight within age-appropriate limits	Fever (infection or poisoning) Hypothermia (sepsis, shock, or exposure) Bradycardia (hypoxia) Tachycardia (early sign of shock) Tachypnea ("quiet tachypnea"—ketoacidosis, dehydration, poisoning, fever, respiratory distress, congestive heart failure) Bradypnea (respiratory failure, shock, acidosis, hypothermia) Hypertension (increased intracranial pressure, renal disease, coarctation of the aorta, or ventriculoperitoneal shunt malfunction) Hypotension (late sign of shock or poisoning)	Monitor vital signs in response to treatment.
Head-to-toe assessment			
General appearance	Clean and age-appropriate physical appearance Well nourished Behavior appropriate for age and level of development Healthy family interaction patterns	Unkempt appearance Unseasonal clothing Malnourished Behavior not usual for the child Unhealthy family interaction patterns	Elicit further family social information; prepare to consult social services. Monitor child's behavior and responses. Observe family dynamics; offer support for parenting.
Head	Well-proportioned size Symmetric features Flat fontanelles in infants and young toddlers Normal hair distribution	Bulging fontanelles (indicative of intracranial pressure). Depressed fontanelles (indicative of dehydration) Asymmetry Occipital bald spots in infants; bald spots in young toddlers Bruises (indicative of child neglect or maltreatment; (Chapters 44 and 45)	Monitor closely for changes in neurologic functioning.

TABLE 5.9 Summary of Normal and Abnormal Pediatric Physical Assessment Findings and Nursing Interventions (continued)

Assessment Parameter	Normal Findings	Abnormal Findings	Interventions
Eyes	External structures within normal limits (lids, lashes, and lacrimal ducts) Equal pupils reactive to light and accommodation Intact extraocular movements Visual acuity within normal limits or corrected with eyeglasses or contacts Pink conjunctiva	Ptosis Sty Irregular pupil size Nonreactive pupils or sluggish reaction to light Strabismus Scleral jaundice Conjunctival injection or discharge	Monitor for pupillary changes. Document noted abnormalities.
Ears	Gross hearing within normal limits or corrected with hearing aid devices Ear size, alignment, and position within normal limit	Hearing loss Red external ear canal Pain or pulling at ears Ear drainage Mastoid tenderness Tragus tenderness Edema or trauma	Note abnormalities. Prepare for otoscopic examination.
Face	Symmetric, well-proportioned features Absence of pain, tenderness, or edema Absence of nasal discharge Pink, moist, and intact oral cavity and pharynx Uvula midline Healthy dentition	Low-set ears Edema Trauma Pain or tenderness on palpation of the frontal and maxillary sinuses Pain or tenderness on palpation of the temporomandibular joint, maxilla, or mandible Nasal discharge and odor Dental caries Missing teeth Malocclusion Enlarged tonsils with exudate Oral lesions or ulcerations Erythema or petechiae on the anterior or posterior pharynx	Note abnormalities. Prepare for diagnostic tests. Prepare for medication administration.
Neck	Absence of surface trauma Nonpalpable lymph glands Flat neck veins Trachea midline	Trauma Palpable lymph glands Distended neck veins Tracheal deviation	Prepare for diagnostic or therapeutic interventions.

TABLE 5.9	Summary of Normal and Abnormal Pediatric Physical Assessment Findings and Nursing Interventions (continued)		
Assessment Parameter	**Normal Findings**	**Abnormal Findings**	**Interventions**
Chest	Age-appropriate anterior-posterior diameter Symmetric expansion Vesicular, bronchovesicular, and bronchotubular breath sounds within normal limits in all lung fields	Thoracic deformity Adventitious sounds Retractions Chest pain Cough Bradypnea Tachypnea Enlarged axillary lymph nodes	Administer oxygen. Monitor cardiorespiratory and oxygen saturation. Administer medications.
Heart and vascular system	Absence of pulsations, lifts, or heaves Absence of abnormal heart sounds Heart rate within normal limit for age Peripheral pulses equal in rate and rhythm Pink, warm, and dry skin	Murmurs Tachycardia Bradycardia Diminished or unequal peripheral pulses Mottled, cool, or clammy skin	Initiate cardiorespiratory and oxygen saturation monitoring. Obtain venous access. Prepare to administer intravenous fluids and/or medications. Prepare to initiate cardiorespiratory resuscitation measures.
Abdomen	Age-appropriate contour Bowel sounds within normal limits Clean and intact umbilicus Absence of pain or tenderness	Enlarged abdominal organs Enlarged inguinal node Abdominal distention Splinting, guarding or tenderness Dilated vessels Umbilical, inguinal, or femoral hernia	Prepare for diagnostic testing. Prepare for medication administration.
Genitalia and anus	Age-appropriate sexual development Secondary sex characteristics: Male Presence or absence of foreskin Meatus/scrotum within normal limits Testes descended Secondary sex characteristics: Female External structures within normal limits Onset of menses Absence of anal trauma or irritation	Anal redness or itching Undescended testes Vaginal or penile irritation or discharge Signs of child sexual abuse (Chapters 44 and 45) Enlarged lymph nodes	Prepare for diagnostic tests. Prepare for sexual abuse/assault examination (Chapters 44 and 45).

Interpretation of Assessment Findings

At the completion of the physical assessment, the normal and abnormal findings are noted and documented in the patient's chart. Normal and abnormal findings are interpreted in the context of the child's health history, triage findings, and the nurse's observations of the child and parent during the assessment (Table 5.9). Red flags that may indicate acute, serious medical conditions that require immediate intervention should be reported to the staff physician or advanced practice nurse.

Conclusion

The history and physical assessment provide a beginning understanding of the child's health condition on presentation to the emergency department and form the basis for the development of nursing diagnoses and a plan of care. Because health is a dynamic state, reassessment should occur at regular intervals, in accordance with the child's health condition, changes in status, and hospital policy. Assessment findings should be documented at regular intervals to reflect stabilization or changes in the child's health condition and modification of the treatment plan. The prepared emergency nurse who has learned the nuances of physical assessment likely will have a successful outcome—a calm, trusting child whose condition is managed in a timely, professional, and holistic manner.

References

1. Gundy, J. (1997). The pediatric physical examination. In R. A. Hoekelman, S. B. Friedman, N. M. Nelson, H. M. Seidel, & M. L. Weitzman (Eds.), *Primary pediatric care* (3rd ed., pp. 55–97). St. Louis, MO: Mosby–Year Book.

2. O'Malley, P. J., Brown, K., Krug, S. E., & Committee on Pediatric Emergency Medicine. (2008). *Patient- and family-centered care of children in the emergency department.* Retrieved September 15, 2008, from http://pediatrics.aappublications.org/cgi/reprint/peds.2008-1569v1

3. Furdon, S., Pfell, V., & Snow, K. (1998). Operationalizing Donna Wong's principle of traumatic care: Pain management protocol in the NICU. *Pediatric Nursing, 24*(4), 336–342.

4. Bloom, B., Tonthat, C., & Centers for Disease Control and Prevention, National Center for Health Statistics. (2002). Summary health statistics for U.S. children: National Health Interview Survey, 1997. *Vital and Health Statistics, 10,* 1–96.

5. Hockenberry, M. (2005). *Wong's essentials of pediatric nursing* (7th ed.). St. Louis, MO: Mosby.

6. Bates, B. (2007). *Bates' guide to physical examination and history taking* (9th ed.). Philadelphia: Lippincott Williams & Wilkins.

7. Engel, J. (2006). *Pocket guide to pediatric assessment.* (5th ed.). St. Louis, MO: Mosby-Year Book.

8. Emergency Nurses Association. (2004). *Emergency nursing pediatric course (ENPC) provider manual* (3rd ed.). Des Plaines, IL: Author.

9. Wong, D. (1999). Physical and developmental assessment of the child. In D. Wong (Ed.), *Whaley and Wong's nursing care of infants and children* (6th ed., pp. 217–283). St. Louis, MO: Mosby-Year Book.

SIX

Triage

Nancy Mecham, APRN, FNP, CEN

Introduction

The word "triage" is derived from the French word that means "to sort." In the emergency department (ED), triage is a process that encompasses the assignment of a priority for treatment, including the use of appropriate personnel and supplies. Triage is unique and an exciting part of being an ED nurse. It is a skill that takes time and practice to master, but triage sets the tone for the care and treatment of every patient who enters the emergency department. The triage process for children can be challenging. But by using a specific triage process, the sorting and recognition of sick children becomes easier with experience. Comprehensive triage education, which includes pediatric triage specifics, is imperative before assigning a nurse to the triage area.[1] Another essential component of any triage education must include some training to help the nurse avoid "empathy burnout."[2] Having empathy or compassion for patients and families during their time of stress is fundamental when working in the emergency department. These behaviors are put to the test every day, especially when a nurse is assigned to a busy triage area for a shift. The constant bombardment from anxious and angry families and patients can take its toll. Teaching a nurse the skills to act appropriately in these situations and to care for his or her own needs can bring long-term benefits. This not only will improve customer service at triage but will play a role in patient safety and patient satisfaction.[2]

The assignment of a triage acuity to pediatric patients can be done by using different types of triage classification systems. Three-level, four-level, and five-level systems are used in the United States and around the world. It was the recommendation of a joint task force made up of representatives from the Emergency Nurses Association (ENA) and American College of Emergency Physicians (ACEP) in 2005 that the "quality of patient care would benefit from implementation of a standardized ED triage scale and acuity categorization process," and on the basis of consensus of currently available evidence they support adoption of a reliable and valid five-level triage scale.[3]

In busy, crowded emergency departments, many patients, including pediatric patients, can wait for long periods of time in the waiting area after triage. The ability of the triage nurse to implement triage guidelines and specific interventions to those patients in the waiting area can be a vital component of care. Thorough, accurate, and timely triage documentation is another important function of the triage nurse that needs consideration when triaging pediatric patients.

Pediatric triage may also include a decision as to whether the patient can be cared for in a facility that sees both children and adults or requires one that specializes in the care of ill or injured children.

Familiarity with Emergency Medical Treatment and Active Labor Act (EMTALA) guideline specifics that affect triage is crucial. The medical screening examination, documenting and transferring care of the patient to another facility, and the patient's/families' rejection of treatment are all regulations that can come up on a regular basis at triage. Chapter 2 discusses the EMTALA guidelines in more detail.

It should be mentioned that triage is a process, not a place. Many emergency departments do in-room registration to get the patient out of the waiting room and to expedite care. The process of triage still needs to be completed no matter where care begins.

Pediatric Triage Assessment Process

Components of Pediatric Triage

Four components of triage include (1) The Pediatric Assessment Triangle, (2) initial primary assessment, (3) pediatric triage history, and (4) triage decision or acuity.[4,5]

❏ *The Pediatric Assessment Triangle*

The Pediatric Assessment Triangle (PAT) is an "across-the-room assessment" or a first-look assessment that is done as soon as the child enters the emergency department or the triage area. The PAT looks at the general appearance of the child, work of breathing, and circulation to the skin.[4]

❏ *Initial Assessment*

In the triage setting, the initial assessment starts with a rapid primary assessment (Chapter 5). Generally, the assessment is focused on the chief complaint. Life-threatening problems identified during the initial assessment may require that the child be taken immediately to a treatment area. After the rapid primary assessment, the secondary assessment is completed. Modifications of this assessment may be necessary because of space and privacy, and many components of the secondary assessment will have to be completed after the child is taken to a room. The following signs and symptoms may be "red flags" or warnings of a serious illness or injury:[4-6]

- Airway
  - Apnea
  - Choking
  - Drooling
  - Audible airway sounds
- Breathing
  - Grunting
  - Retractions, increased work of breathing
  - Increased or decreased respiratory rate
  - Changes in skin color
- Circulation
  - Increased or decreased heart rate
  - Hypotension
  - Decreased or bounding peripheral pulses
  - Uncontrolled bleeding
  - Capillary refill time > 3 seconds or < 1 second "flash"
- Disability
  - Altered level of consciousness
  - Inconsolability
- Exposure
  - Petechiae
  - Purpura
  - Signs and symptoms of abuse
- Vital signs
  - Hypothermia
  - Temperature > 100.4 °F (38 °C) in the infant younger than 90 days of age
  - Temperature > 104 °F to 105.1 °F (40.0 °C to 40.6 °C) at any age
- Comfort
  - Severe pain, assessed on an appropriate pediatric pain scale (Chapter 11)
- History
  - History of chronic disease

- History of immunosuppression
- History of family crisis
- Fever in neonate (younger than 30 days of age)
- Actual or potential threat to self and others (for suicidal patients) (Chapter 25)
- Return visit to emergency department within 24 hours

Pediatric triage assessment can be challenging, especially to nurses who do not triage large numbers of infants and children on a regular basis. Education and periodic education updates about pediatric assessment differences are even more important for those nurses.[7]

❑ *Pediatric Triage History*

The CIAMPEDS mnemonic is a systematic way of obtaining important components of the triage history:[5,8]

C = Chief Complaint

I = Immunizations or Isolation (exposure to communicable disease)

A = Allergies to food or medications

M = Medications

P = Past medical history

E = Events surrounding the illness or injury

D = Diet or Diapers (bladder and bowel habits)

S = Symptoms associated with the illness or injury

Chapter 5 further details the CIAMPEDS mnemonic.

The history at triage should be brief but should allow enough information to make an accurate triage decision and to permit the patient care nurse to build on the information to care for the child.[8] However, the history offered by the parent may be the only evidence that the triage nurse has about the chief complaint in the nonverbal infant or child. Paying special attention to subtle symptoms, particularly in the neonate (younger than 30 days of age), such as poor feeding, changes in sleeping habits, or increased fussiness are important things to remember when triaging neonates. History offered by the parent in regard to the child's sleeping habits and amount of crying in the older infant is important information for the triage nurse to take into consideration as well. Although crying and sleeping are normal behaviors for all children, changes from normal patterns can be significant. "Crying" or "sleeping" are not suitable to document as a level of consciousness. The child needs to be consoled, attempted to be consoled, or wakened or attempted to be awakened to accurately assess neurologic states.

Pain assessment should begin at triage.[9] Scoring guidelines that accompany pain assessment scales are helpful to the emergency nurse in assessing pain intensity. Remember that pain intensity will guide triage decisions.

Pain assessment score documentation is suboptimal in the pediatric population and is likely to be an important contributor to the poor pain management for children in the emergency department.[9,10] Of all pediatric patients, infants are at highest risk for not having their pain score documented.[10] Nurses may consider pain score documentation as merely a regulatory mandate, or they may view a pain score as clinically irrelevant outside the research arena. Conditions that are diagnostic challenges (e.g., pelvic pain) are more likely to have a pain score documented than diagnoses that are commonly considered painful (e.g., ear pain).[10] Because there is a significant association between pain score documentation and the use of any analgesic—particularly opioids—pain score documentation is crucial across all ages and diagnoses.[10] Finally, pain assessment scores, in combination with other pain history components at triage, can help predict the future pain medication needs of the ED patient.[9]

❏ *Triage Decision or Acuity*

The triage decision is made at the completion of the triage process. The triage decision determines the priority for care on the basis of the results of the child's assessment and the chief complaint. The acuity is assigned on the basis of the triage classification system used in each particular emergency department (see later section).

Triage Classification Systems

In the United States, three-level, four-level, and five-level triage classification systems are in use.[5] In a survey, done by ENA in 2001, emergency departments were asked about their triage system. A three-level system was found to be used in the majority of emergency departments reporting (69.4%).[11] A four-level system was used by 11.6%, and five-level used by only 3%. Interestingly enough, 11.7% of emergency departments used no system at all.

Outside of the United States, specifically in Canada, Australia, and Great Britain, five-level systems have been in use since the 1990s.[3,12] The presence of National Health Systems in Canada and Australia explains why mandating a national five-level system is possible compared with the United States.

When considering any triage system, the reliability and the validity of the system are the standard measures most commonly used. Reliability is the consistency of the system to measure what it is supposed to measure when used by different users or nurses. Validity refers to whether the system is measuring what it is supposed to be measuring.[3,12,13]

The five-level system showed greater discrimination, better reliability, and improved sensitivity and specificity when compared with the three-level system.[13]

Two five-level systems are used most commonly in the United States: the Emergency Severity Index (ESI) and the Canadian Severity Index (CTAS).

The Emergency Severity Index

The Emergency Severity Index (ESI) was developed in the United States in the 1990s by a group of emergency physicians and nurses.[3,12] The ESI incorporates the clinical condition of the patient for the highest acuity levels (levels 1 and 2), but also considers the number of resources that will be needed by the emergency department to get the patient through to disposition in the lower acuity levels (levels 3, 4, and 5).[14]

The Canadian Triage and Acuity Scale

Physicians in New Brunswick developed the Canadian Triage and Acuity Scale (CTAS) in the mid-1990s. It is based on the Australian Triage Scale.[3] Trained registered nurses triage all patients and determine the triage category by asking the question, "This patient needs a medical assessment and treatment in no longer than ____minutes." Each triage category has recommended maximum times to treatment and to reassessment as well.[12,15]

Both the ESI and CTAS have had the highest reported reliability consistently in study after study.[3,13,15,16] Validity studies done on CTAS are limited.[17] Validity studies on ESI have shown the ability to predict hospital admission, resource use, and hospital charges.[3]

Pediatric Specifics

The CTAS has published pediatric criteria, and the ESI has integrated pediatric vital sign criteria in its version 4 algorithm.[14,18] The CTAS made revisions to its 2001 Paediatric Guidelines in May 2008.[17] It is important to note that there are still many pediatric triage research questions that require study in regard to these five-level systems. This is an area of future research study.

Triage Education

A comprehensive formal triage education program, which includes pediatric triage specifics, is crucial to the success of the triage nurse.[1] It has long been the recommendation that before nurses are assigned to triage they have at least six months' experience in the emergency department. The reason for this is evident to any nurse who has spent time working in the emergency department. It is essential that the triage nurse have an idea of what will happen to the patient with a particular complaint in the patient care area, as well as having had the experience of seeing and caring for sick and not so sick patients. Development of critical thinking skills and strong prioritization skills are paramount before being assigned to a busy triage area. The comprehensive formal triage education should incorporate not only the process of triage, which includes the importance of using and developing keen assessment skills to quickly recognize the sick patient, but also education to assist nurses in maintaining their "caring ethic" to avoid "empathy burnout."[2] Some suggestions for this could include:[2]

❐ Recognize that verbal attacks of patients and families should not be taken personally and retaliated.

❐ Ask for a break from triage when needed. This represents self-care and not weakness.

❐ Recognize types of patients that may set off inappropriate verbal or nonverbal responses and treat those patient with compassion.

In a recent review of the emergency education literature on pediatric triage, it was found that there is a "need to develop a comprehensive education process specific to pediatric triage in the emergency department."[1] Some of the specific recommendations from that review are the need to have:

1. Evidence-based recommendations on pediatric vital sign parameters.

2. Standardized interdisciplinary approach to pediatric assessment and history taking.

3. Pediatric-specific case scenarios for teaching created and evaluated.

4. Interdisciplinary, comprehensive pediatric emergency educational resource.

No matter what type of triage classification system is in place in a facility, part of the triage education should also focus on the specifics of that system. Staff needs to be aware and clear on what is expected when using a particular triage classification system. For a system to remain reliable and valid, it needs to be used and implemented with consistency. This will decrease mistriage and increase objective understanding between caregivers on the acuity of the patient at time of triage.

The ESI and CTAS five-level systems recommend triage education before triaging patients with their system. They recommend specific education to their triage system of acuity as well. Both systems provide materials to teach their specific triage system, and they both also recommend

that the training be given only to the experienced ED nurse.[1,14,15,17,18]

Triage Interventions

Common interventions that may be initiated in the triage area include the following:

❐ Isolate the child if an infectious disease is suspected or if the child is immunosuppressed.

❐ Initiate individual hospital disease-specific clinical care guidelines or care process models with specific patient inclusion and exclusion criteria.

- Diabetic ketoacidosis
- Pediatric sepsis and shock
- Bronchiolitis
- Asthma
- Febrile infant
- Pain

❐ Assign and explain nothing-by-mouth (NPO) status to patients and family if the child may require surgical consultation or sedation during his or her ED visit.

❐ Administer antipyretics to patients with fever on the basis of individual hospital guidelines.

❐ Obtain orders for radiographic studies according to individual hospital guidelines.

❐ Obtain pulse oximetry reading in patients with respiratory and/or cardiac complaints.

❐ Begin initial health education and/or preventive education (such as immunization schedules and wearing helmets, seat belts, and other protective gear) when appropriate.

Documentation

Documentation of the triage assessment, interventions, and triage acuity is completed before the child leaves the triage area. Reassessments of patients should be done for those patients who are waiting in the waiting area after triage.[7]

Whatever charting format is used, the following must be documented:

❐ Chief complaint

❐ Assessment—may include vital signs

❐ Triage acuity classification

❐ Any treatment or care guidelines initiated

Conclusion

Triage is defined as the process "to sort" patients to determine priority for care in the emergency department. Using the triage process the nurse can decide who needs immediate treatment and who can wait. This triage process includes the skills to perform a rapid "across the room" assessment by using the PAT, then a rapid focused initial assessment or primary assessment of the child's airway, breathing, circulation, and level of consciousness and to collect a focused patient history. On the basis of this initial examination, the triage nurse decides the child's triage acuity using the specific triage classification system in place at that facility.

Five-level triage classification systems are not only the national recommendation but have also been shown in research to be more reliable (consistent among those using the system) and valid (accurate in measuring what they are supposed to measure) than three-level systems. However, no matter what triage classification system is in place in a facility, the triage nurse needs to be familiar with and educated to its use and meaning.

To perform triage effectively, the emergency nurse also needs clinical ED experience and a comprehensive formal triage education, which includes pediatric triage specifics and documentation. Triage is a crucial component in the emergency care of the pediatric patient and should not be underestimated.

References

1. Hohenhaus, S., Travers, D., & Mecham, N. (2008). Pediatric triage: A review of the emergency education literature. *Journal of Emergency Nursing, 34*(4), 308–313.

2. McNair, R. (2005). It takes more than string to fly a kite: 5-Level acuity scales are more effective, but education, clinical experience, and compassion are still essential. *Journal of Emergency Nursing, 31*(6), 600–603.

3. Fernandes, C., Tanabe, P., Bonalumi, N., Gilboy, N., Johnson, L., McNair, R., et al. (2005). Five-level triage; a report from the ACEP/ENA five-level task force. *Journal of Emergency Nursing, 31*(1), 39–50.

4. Ralston, M., Hazinski, M., Zaritsky, A., Schexnayder, S., & Kleinman, M. (2006). *Textbook of pediatric advanced life support.* Chicago: American Academy of Pediatrics and American Heart Association.

5. Emergency Nurses Association (2004). *Emergency nursing pediatric course.* (3rd ed.). Des Plaines, IL: Author.

6. Carcillo, J., & Fields, A. (2002). Clinical practice guidelines for hemodynamic support of pediatric and neonatal patients in septic shock. *Critical Care Medicine, 30*(6), 1365–1378.

7. Hoenhaus, S. (2006). Someone watching over me: Observations in pediatric triage. *Journal of Emergency Nursing, 32*(5), 398–403.

8. Thomas, D. (2002). Special considerations for pediatric triage in the emergency department. *Nursing Clinics of North America, 37*(1), 145–159.

9. Zempsky, W. T., Cravero, J. P., & Committee on Pediatric Emergency Medicine, Section on Anesthesiology and Pain Medicine. (2004). Relief of pain and anxiety in pediatric patients in emergency medical systems. *Pediatrics, 114*(5), 1348–1356.

10. Drendel, A. L., Brousseau, D. C., & Gorelick, M. H. (2006). Pain assessment for pediatric patients in the emergency department. *Pediatrics, 117*(5), 1511–1518.

11. MacLean, S. (2002). *2001 ENA national benchmark guide: Emergency departments.* Des Plaines, IL: Emergency Nurses Association.

12. McMahon, M. (2003). ED triage: Is a five-level triage system best? *American Journal of Nursing, 103*(3), 61–63.

13. Travers, D., Waller, A., Bowling, J., Flowers, D., & Tintinali, J. (2002). Five-level triage system more effective than three-level in tertiary emergency department. *Journal of Emergency Nursing, 28*(5), 395–400.

14. Gilboy, N., Tanabe, P., Travers, D., Rosenau, A., & Eitel, D. (2005). *Emergency severity index version 4; implementation handbook.* Rockville, MD: Agency for Healthcare Research and Quality.

15. Murray, M., Bullard, M., & Grafstein, E. (2004). Revisions to the Canadian Emergency Department Triage and Acuity Scale implementation guidelines. *Canadian Journal of Emergency Medicine, 6*(6), 421–427.

16. Worster, A., Gilboy, N., Fernandez C., Eitel, D., Eva, K., Geisler, R., et al. (2004). Assessment of inter-rater reliability of two five-level triage and acuity scales: A randomized controlled trail. *Canadian Journal of Emergency Medicine, 6*(4), 240–245.

References (continued)

17. Warren, D., Jarvis, A., LeBlanc, L., Gravel, J., & the CTAS working group. (2008). Revisions to the Canadian Triage and Acuity Scale paediatric guidelines (PaedCTAS). *Canadian Journal of Emergency Medicine, 10*(3), 224–231.

18. Canadian Paediatric Triage and Acuity Scales. (2001). *Implementation guidelines for emergency departments.* Retrieved December 27, 2008, from http://www.caep.ca/template.asp?id=B795164082374289BBD9C2BF4B8D32

SEVEN

Children and Youth with Special Health Care Needs

Elizabeth Wertz Evans, RN, BSN, MPM, FACMPE

Introduction

As a result of the vast improvements in health care delivery and technology, children with congenital conditions or life-threatening illnesses and injuries survive to adulthood. These children are valuable members of their communities, but their health conditions pose lifelong challenges that interfere with their growth and development.

Children with special health care needs are those who have or are at increased risk for a chronic physical, developmental, or emotional condition and who also require health and related services of a type or amount beyond that generally required by children.[1] These conditions include mental disabilities, physical disabilities, the need for technologic support, and chronic illnesses[2] (Table 7.1). Although most of these conditions and disabilities are rare, others, such as asthma, respiratory ailments, and allergic reactions, are prevalent in the pediatric population. It is estimated that in the United States, almost 13% of all children have some type of special health care need.[3] In addition, at least one child has a special health care need in 20% of families with children in the United States.[3]

In its 2001 National Survey of Children with Special Health Care Needs, the Maternal and Child Health Bureau reported that 9.3 million children under the age of 18 were children with special health care needs.[4] Of this group, children living in poverty, those over 5 years of age, boys, and non-Hispanics had a greater likelihood of having a special health care need.[4]

Children and youth with special health care needs present to the emergency department (ED) for treatment related to their underlying health condition, as well as for the usual childhood illnesses and injuries. The purposes of this chapter are to familiarize emergency nurses with the care of children and youth with special health care needs and to recommend modifications in emergency nursing care for this patient population.

History

The history is obtained from the patient and parent as outlined in Chapter 5. Additional information is obtained related to the child's special health care needs:[5]

❐ Ask the parent, "What is special about your child?" to promote trust and understanding. The question, "What is wrong with your child?" may create parental anger and resentment.

❐ Ascertain the child's communication patterns. Determine whether the child uses eye blinks, a communication board, sign language, or other nonverbal forms of communication. Learn and use the child's words for descriptions of pain, cold, and so forth.

❐ Ask the parent about the child's comprehension ability and what the child is able to do. This inquiry promotes self-esteem and a healthy self-image. Always assume that the child understands what is being said.

❐ Inquire as to dietary considerations that must be followed. For example, children on the ketogenic diet for intractable seizures should receive intravenous fluid containing normal saline. Administration of dextrose will negate the ketosis and may potentiate breakthrough seizures.

❐ Ask the parent if he or she presented a list of medications at triage. That list will be helpful for medication reconciliation. If not, encourage the parent to explain the child's medication regimen, because some of the medications and their dosages may be unfamiliar to emergency nurses. For example, children with cancer pain may receive very high doses of narcotics, and children with seizures may receive what appear to be inordinate doses of anticonvulsants.

❐ Elicit the child's and parent's assistance in explaining any technologic devices that accompany the child, such as a ventilator, gastrostomy tube, cardiopulmonary monitor, or central venous access device with "cycling" of total parenteral nutrition and lipids. Ask what size suction catheters are usually used or what length of Huber needle works best.

TABLE 7.1 Descriptions of Selected Special Health Care Conditions

Body System	Description
Respiratory	*Congenital:* Laryngeal malacia; underdeveloped lungs; cystic fibrosis
	Acquired: Pulmonary neoplasms; asthma; chronic bronchitis; bronchopulmonary dysplasia
Cardiovascular	*Congenital:* Heart disease (Chapter 15)
	Acquired: Heart disease (Chapter 15)
Neurologic	*Congenital:* Spina bifida; Arnold-Chiari malformation; chromosomal anomalies; Dandy-Walker malformation; hydrocephalus
	Perinatal: Infections; anoxic encephalopathy; birth trauma; cerebral palsy
	Postnatal: Head and spinal cord trauma; neoplasms
	Seizure disorders: Infantile spasms; Lennox-Gastaut syndrome; epilepsy
Immunologic	*Congenital:* Immune disorders
	Acquired: Human immunodeficiency virus; hepatitis; carcinomas
	Induced: Immunosuppression following solid organ or bone marrow transplants and chemotherapy for cancer treatment
Mental retardation	*Physical appearance:* Well-proportioned physical features or characteristic features such as low-set ears, soft neurologic signs (e.g., microcephaly), poor fine and/or gross motor coordination
	Cognitive function: Educable or needing assistance or total care
Other	*Physical:* Limb deformities; craniofacial malformations; paralysis
	Sensory: Alterations in hearing, vision, or tactile perceptibilities
	Cognitive: Alterations in thinking abilities

Adapted with permission from Wertz, E. (2001). *The patient with special needs.* In N. E. McSwain, Jr., & J. L. Paturas, *The basic EMT: Comprehensive prehospital patient care* (2nd ed., p. 770). St. Louis, MO: Mosby.

Assessment

Physical Assessment

The physical assessment of the child with special health care needs follows the same priorities as for all pediatric patients (Chapter 5), with a few exceptions. The neurologic (disability) assessment still refers to the child's neurologic status and not to the child's special needs or disabling condition.

❑ Determine the preexisting level of deficit before the ED visit: "Is this your child's usual behavior (or posture, color, etc.)?" This inquiry implies acceptance of the child's health condition and avoids the normal-abnormal dichotomy. Furthermore, by focusing on the child's abilities and not the disabilities, the question helps to establish trust between the emergency nurse and parent or child.

❑ Seek parental assistance when removing braces or other adaptive devices while performing the physical assessment. Protect the devices carefully, because they usually are customized for the child and can be quite expensive. If the devices are removed, ensure that they leave the emergency department with the child and parent.

❑ Incorporate information about the technologic aid or device into the physical assessment. For example, state the condition of the tracheostomy site and the current ventilator settings.

❑ Note the presence of identifying jewelry, such as a MedicAlert® bracelet or necklace. Older children may resist this identification, because they do not want to draw attention to their differences. Although the absence of such identification does not rule out a disability or chronic condition, its presence can be helpful during the physical assessment and subsequent treatment.

Psychosocial Assessment

The child's and family's coping strategies are assessed. Most families have positive coping strategies and have the emotional fortitude to care for their child. However, in cases where the child is in serious jeopardy or death is imminent, usual coping strategies may not be effective. The following psychosocial considerations should be entertained.[6]

❒ Parents may experience an acute sense of anxiety during the ED visit.

❒ Parents may feel a loss of parental control. These families are familiar with their child's care and routines and may be at a loss in the emergency department when the staff intervenes to treat the child. They may be concerned about staff being too assertive, which they may believe will adversely affect their child's ED treatment.

❒ Parents may perceive their child to be "vulnerable" and may overprotect the child.

❒ Family members may have an unrealistic perception or may fantasize about the child's health condition; they may have signs of grieving or chronic sorrow.

❒ Siblings of these children have psychosocial needs as well. Assessment of their roles and participation in family-centered care is important and should be done early in the treatment process.

Triage Considerations

Triage decisions for children and youth with special health care needs should take into account the underlying condition because these children may be at a higher risk for development of complications than are children without these health concerns. Also consider the possible need for isolation or reverse isolation if the child has a situation in which protection is needed.

Nursing Interventions

Nursing interventions to promote comfort and security, such as addressing the child by name and offering praise and rewards, (Chapter 3) are applied to children and youth with special health care needs. Some nursing interventions may be modified on the basis of the child's underlying health condition:

1. Anticipate modifications in treatment based on the child's health condition. For example, the child with cerebral palsy typically may have profuse oral secretions that can interfere with airway maneuvers. Suction and high-concentration oxygen administration may be needed.

2. Avoid cervical hyperextension in the child with Arnold-Chiari malformation because undue pressure may be placed on the brain stem and result in complications such as respiratory distress or arrest.

3. Adapt equipment to meet the child's needs. For example, the child with cerebral palsy who has severe spinal curvatures may not be able to lie flat on a long backboard. Immobilization may be supplemented with padding from towel rolls or pillows. The child with physical disabilities, such as contractures or rigid body parts, may not be able to remain in a fixed position for procedures or treatments. The contractured limbs should never be forced into a particular position. Frequent rest periods may be necessary during lengthy procedures.

4. If the child has unfamiliar hardware in place or uses equipment that is not easy to understand, contact the subspecialist that has been treating the child for additional information.

5. Use latex-free gloves and equipment. Research has demonstrated that as many as 73% of children and adolescents with spina bifida also have a sensitivity to latex.[7] Because not every child's latex allergy status is known, it is best to have latex-free gloves, at a minimum, in the emergency department.

6. Limit exposure of the child's body by using gowns and drapes as necessary. Emergency Department physicians and nurses may be tempted to show the child's disability to other staff members as a "learning experience." The child's modesty must be respected, and exposure or discussion of the child's disability should be limited to the rendered treatment, in accordance with HIPPA guidelines.

7. Ask the parent whether he or she feels comfortable with performing procedures, such as tracheal suctioning, or whether the emergency nurse can perform the procedures. At times, a home care nurse or aide may accompany the child and family to the emergency department. Policies should be in place for determining the role of these nonhospital health care providers in the child's ED treatment.

8. Initiate consultations with other health care professionals, such as pediatric emergency physicians and nurses, clinical nurse specialists, social services personnel, hospice workers, child life specialists, physical and occupational therapists, and nutritionists. Community organizations also can provide family support. Families may be too proud to ask for assistance or may believe that they are not entitled to or cannot afford to use specialty services. Social services and community organizations can arrange for follow-up contacts and plans before discharge from the emergency department.

Home Care and Prevention

Children and youth with special health care needs and their families should develop a written emergency care plan that is kept in easily accessible places in the children's home or other location where they frequently spend time.[8] This emergency care plan should document any special training needed by emergency personnel, family members, and others who may be called on to provide emergency care to these children. Individuals and groups who should know about the emergency care plans are:

- ❏ Dispatchers for 911
- ❏ Local EMS agencies and fire departments
- ❏ Family members
- ❏ Child care providers
- ❏ Education and health services of the children's school
- ❏ ED, specialty, and primary care physicians

To facilitate the emergency care of these children, it is recommended that a mechanism be available to identify the child or youth with special health care needs when that child presents to the emergency department.[9] The child's special health care needs should be recorded, and this record should be accessible and usable.[10] A standardized information form is available to prepare caregivers and health care professionals for emergencies involving children and youth with special health care needs. It can be downloaded from http://www.aap.org/advocacy/eif.doc.

Additionally, a discharge-planning guide that begins with the initial ED visit is available to assist in planning for children and youth with special health care needs.[10] These guidelines are available from the Emergency Medical Services for Children National Resource Center at http://www.childrensnational.org/EMSC.

Conclusion

Emergency nurses are likely to encounter children and youth with special health care needs. Therefore, it is imperative that there are written policies and procedures in place to facilitate their care. Table 7.2 offers guidelines for disability awareness. Collaboration with the child, family, and specialists throughout the ED treatment promotes family-centered care and expedites the child's return to the home environment.

TABLE 7.2 Guidelines for Disability Awareness
Use the word *disability* instead of the word *handicap*.
Refer first to the person and then to the particular disability.
Avoid calling a person *wheelchair bound* or saying that the person is *confined to a wheelchair*. In reality, people with disabilities are made more mobile by using a wheelchair.
Avoid using negative descriptions of people with disabilities, such as *invalid, mongoloid, epileptic, suffers from*, and *afflicted with*. Avoid referring to seizures as fits.
Do not use the "N" word—*normal*—when describing people without disabilities. Instead, use *typical* or *people without disabilities*.
Avoid making reference to a person's disability unless it is relevant.

Data from Coalition for Tennesseans with Disabilities. (1993). *Talking about disability: A guide to using appropriate language.* Nashville, TN: Author.

References

1. McPherson, M. (1998). A new definition of children with special healthcare needs. *Pediatrics, 102*(1), 137–139.

2. Wallace, H., Biehl, R., MacQueen, J., & Blackman, J. (1997). *Mosby's resource guide to children with disabilities and chronic illness.* St. Louis, MO: Mosby-Year Book.

3. Huang, Z. J., Kogan, M. D., Yu, S. M., & Strickland, S. (2005). Delayed or forgone care among children with special health care needs: An analysis of the 2001 national survey of children with special health care needs. *Ambulatory Pediatrics, 5*(1), 60–68.

4. Rosenberg, D., Onufer, C., Clark, G., Wilkin, T., Rankin, K., & Gupta, K. (2005). The need for care coordination among children with special health care needs in Illinois. *Maternal and Child Health Journal 9S*(2), S41–S47.

5. Wertz, E. (2001). *Emergency care for children.* Albany, NY: Delmar Thomson Publishing.

6. Schultz, A., & Chalanick, K. (1998). Children with special needs. In T. Soud & J. Rogers (Eds.), *Manual of pediatric emergency nursing* (pp. 712–726). St. Louis, MO: Mosby-Year Book.

7. Spina Bifida Association. (2008). Latex (natural rubber) allergy in spina bifida. Retrieved February 18, 2009, from http://www.spinabifidaassociation. org/site/c.liKWL7PLLrF/b.2664425/apps/s/content. asp?ct=3822569

8. Emergency Medical Services for Children. (2008). Common emergencies affecting children and youth with special health care needs fact sheet. Retrieved February 18, 2009, from http://bolivia.hrsa.gov/emsc/ Downloads/CommonEmergenciesCSHCN/CommonE-mergenciesforCSHCN.htm

9. American Academy of Pediatrics. (1999). Policy statement: Emergency preparedness for children with special health care needs. Committee on Pediatric Emergency Medicine. American Academy of Pediatrics. *Pediatrics, 104*(4), e53; reaffirmed in *Pediatrics,* 2008, 122, 450.

10. Rushton, D., & Witte, M. (1998). Children with special healthcare needs—Technology-assisted children. Salt Lake City, UT: Utah Department of Health, Bureau of Emergency Medical Services, Primary Children's Medical Center.

EIGHT

Pediatric Transport

Reneé Semonin Holleran,
RN, PhD, CEN, CCRN, CFRN, CTRN, FAEN

Introduction

The care of the ill or injured pediatric patient requires specialized skills and equipment. This care often extends beyond the emergency department (ED) to the operating room, critical care unit, and other inpatient units. When the personnel and technology needed to care for the pediatric patient with the best care possible are not available, transfer to another facility may be required.

Transfer of the pediatric patient began at the turn of the 20th century, but much of the development of neonatal and pediatric transport did not occur until the 1960s. Today, what is the best composition suited to the transfer of the critically ill or injured pediatric patient is still a topic of debate and research.[1-4]

The Emergency Nurses Association (ENA) has developed a position statement addressing the care of the pediatric patient in the emergency department and the care of any patient who requires transfer and transport.[5,6] ENA believes that:

❏ The goal of pediatric interfacility transfer is to decrease morbidity and mortality and improve pediatric patient outcomes. Emergency departments with limited resources and expertise need to develop clear protocols for transfer and initiate transfer agreements with hospitals capable of providing ongoing critical care to pediatric patients.

❏ The composition of the transfer team and the mode of transport must be based on patient acuity, established and anticipated treatment needs, and special patient circumstances.

❏ Persons involved in the transport of the pediatric patient must have the knowledge and expertise to deliver the appropriate level of care to patients with a variety of illnesses and injuries. The configuration of the team caring for the critically ill or injured child must include a registered professional nurse with pediatric emergency or pediatric critical care expertise.

❏ The transfer team involved in the transport of the critical pediatric patient must complete annual continuing education, pediatric emergency and/or critical care, age-specific competency updates, and maintain verification in the Emergency Nursing Pediatric Course.

❏ The appropriate equipment must be available to accommodate all pediatric patients regardless of age, weight, size, and acuity level.

The purpose of this chapter is to discuss the personnel, skills, and equipment needed to transfer the pediatric patient, as well as to review the indications for transport.

Indications for Transport

The indications for pediatric transport have been developed by consensus from pediatric experts and from other transport and critical care associations, such as the American College of Surgeons and the National Association of Emergency Medical Services.[4,7] These indicators include:

❏ Serious injury to more than one system
❏ Head injury involving the following:
  ▪ Cerebrospinal fluid leak
  ▪ Altered mental status
  ▪ Deteriorating neurologic status
  ▪ Signs and symptoms of increasing intracranial pressure
❏ Hypovolemic shock:
  ▪ Requiring more than one transfusion
  ▪ Requiring operative management to stop the hemorrhage
❏ Spinal cord injuries
❏ Blunt abdominal trauma with hemodynamic instability
❏ Thoracic injuries requiring advanced ventilatory support
❏ Orthopedic injuries involving:
  ▪ Two or more long-bone fractures
  ▪ Fractures of the thoracic cage
  ▪ Compromised neurovascular status
  ▪ Fracture of the axial skeleton
  ▪ Fractures that may require extensive rehabilitation

- Extremity reimplantation
- Respiratory distress:
  - Airway obstruction
  - Respiratory failure
  - Foreign-body aspiration
- Septic shock
- Status epilepticus
- Multiple-organ failure
- Near-drowning
- Arrhythmia/dysrhythmia with impending hemodynamic implications
- Burns
- Specialty referrals:
  - Cardiology: Congenital anomalies requiring surgery
  - Hematology: Need for a bone marrow transplant
  - Oncology: Need for a pediatric oncologist
  - Nephrology: Need for consultation for renal injury or disease
  - Pulmonology: Need for specialized ventilation
  - Specialized surgical procedures: Transplantation, neonatal patient for specialty care
  - Reverse (back or return) transport of a child or neonate to the referring hospital when clinically appropriate

Legal Implications

Comprehensive Omnibus Reconciliation Act (COBRA) and Emergency Medical Treatment and Active Labor Act (EMTALA)[7–9]

- Hospitals must examine all children who present to the ED and provide the necessary care for stabilization before transfer.
- The benefit of the transfer should outweigh the risks related to the transfer of the patient.
- Patients are not to be transferred until they have been assessed and stabilized.
- Patients should be transferred in a vehicle and with personnel comparable to the level of care that they require. Pediatric patients should be transported with personnel trained in the care of the ill or injured pediatric patient.

State and Local Regulations

- Regulations will vary among states and local areas.
- The referring facility and the transport team must be aware of regulations in different areas and adhere to these regulations.

The Centers for Medicare and Medicaid Services (CMS) allow for deviations from policies and procedures during a disaster. An important concept that has been added by CMS to patient transfer is that during disasters communities and hospitals may develop alternative policies and procedures related to transferring and accepting patients. (Chapter 43).

Consent

- Parental consent should be sought before the child is transported if possible.
- The name of the receiving facility and the person accepting for the facility, the method of transport, and the name of the team providing transport must be included on the consent form.
- A written order for the transport must be obtained from the physician.

Licensure

- Transport team members must be appropriately licensed and certified for their area of practice.
- Most transport team members are functioning members of the hospital in which they are based.
- State licensing may not be required, particularly because there are no federal regulations (other than for ambulances, but not specific to critical care or pediatric transport). The Commission on Accreditation of Medical Transport Systems (CAMTS) provides standards related to critical care transport by both air and ground for pediatric and neonatal transport. Information can be found at http://www.camts.org.

Transfer Agreements

- Transfer agreements between facilities should be developed and updated annually.
- Agreements should reflect the levels of responsibility during the transport process.
- Agreements should reflect the local and state regulations that govern the transport process.

Specifications for Pediatric Transport

The transport team may be composed of many types of members. The composition depends on the age of the child and resources needed to monitor and treat the child's condition.

Team Composition

- ❏ Registered nurse
- ❏ Neonatal nurse practitioner
- ❏ Neonatologist
- ❏ Pediatrician
- ❏ Respiratory therapist

Essential Training for Transport[7,10]

Transport team members should receive the following training:

- ❏ How a transport is initiated, including legal implications, transfer agreements, and receiving institutions
- ❏ Communication skills, team interactions, referring-receiving facility personnel interactions
- ❏ Communication equipment use (e.g., radios, cellular telephones)
- ❏ Public relations skills
- ❏ Transport equipment and medications
- ❏ Transport safety
- ❏ Transport regulations
- ❏ Patient care issues in the transport environment
- ❏ Altitude physiology
- ❏ Management of motion sickness:
  - Medications
  - Patient and crew positioning within the transport vehicle
- ❏ Pediatric transport medicine
- ❏ Advanced pediatric management skills including airway, breathing, circulation, and neurologic interventions

Some teams require additional courses such as:

- ❏ Pediatric Advanced Life Support (PALS)
- ❏ Emergency Nursing Pediatric Course (ENPC)
- ❏ Advanced Pediatric Life Support Course (APLS)

Equipment for Pediatric Transport

See Table 8.1 for a summary of the recommended equipment necessary for pediatric transport.

Preparation for Transfer and Transport

- ❏ Identify the need for transport as listed in the section on indications, based on:
  - The child's illness or injury
  - The need for additional interventions
  - The request of the family
- ❏ Contact the referring facility.
  - Determine bed availability.
  - Evaluate whether the necessary equipment and staff are available to care for the patient.
  - Identify the receiving physician and the person accepting the patient on behalf of the hospital (e.g., nursing supervisor).
- ❏ Designate the mode of transportation to be used for transport, based on:
  - The condition of the child and time needed to reach definitive care
  - The distance of the transport
  - The weather and road conditions
  - Resources available within the transfer area
  - Education and preparation of the members of the transport service
- ❏ Provide the initial care for the child, based on the referring facility's abilities to:
  - manage the child's airway, breathing, and circulation.
  - obtain requested laboratory or other diagnostic tests.
  - administer medications as indicated by the child's illness or injury.
  - perform interventions to prevent further injury.
- ❏ Notify the child's family. The family needs the following information:[4,11–13]
  - Why the child has to be transported
  - The mode of transportation and estimated time for transport
  - Who will care for the child during transport
  - Policy on who can accompany the child during transport. Allow the family to see the child before transfer, if possible, especially if the family will not be permitted to accompany the child during transport.
  - Reassurance of the safety of transport. Never promise the family that they may accompany the child during transport.
  - Directions to the referring hospital
  - Where the child will be in the referring hospital and who will be caring for the child
  - Insurance information

TABLE 8.1 Equipment for Pediatric Transport

Airway and ventilation equipment

Bag-mask (infant, child, and adult). (Include appropriate-sized masks for each age group.)

Anesthesia bag

Oxygen masks in various sizes

Nasal cannula (infant and adult)

Intubation equipment for infant, child, and adult

Endotracheal tubes
- Uncuffed: 2.5 to 6.5
- Cuffed: 6.0 to 8.0

Magill forceps (pediatric and adult)

Stylets

Tonsil suction

Suction catheters (sizes 5, 6, 8, 10, and 14)

Oral airways

Laryngeal mask airway (various sizes)

Air-oxygen blender capable of delivering FiO_2 0.21 to 1.0 with flowmeter up to 15 L

Nitric oxide administration equipment

Cricothyrotomy trays

Tracheostomy tubes

Portable suction unit

Pulse oximeter with appropriate-sized probes

CO2 monitor (battery operated and colorimetric)

Benzoin, adhesive tape, and tracheostomy tape

Medications for intubation:
- Sedation agents
- Neuromuscular blocking agents
- Lidocaine
- Atropine

Induction medications such as etomidate or propofol

Transport ventilator

Needle/chest decompression equipment, including chest tubes:
- Heimlich valves
- 10 to 40 French chest tubes

Circulatory equipment

Cardiac monitor

Defibrillator (pediatric paddles, pads)

Transcutaneous pacer

Thoracostomy tray

Blood pressure monitor (various-sized cuffs)

Umbilical catheters (3.5 and 5.0 French)

Gastric tubes

Feeding tubes (5 to 8 French)

Salem sumps (10 to 18 French)

Syringes

Intravenous equipment and medications

Intravenous catheters, various sizes

Conversion kits (7 French)

Blood administration tubing

Stopcocks

Syringes

Intraosseous needles

Extension tubing

Intravenous pumps and monitors

Pressure bags

O-negative blood

Blood cooler

Blood tubes

Intravenous starter packs

Advance Cardiac Life Support/PALS medications

Vasopressor agents per protocols

Mannitol

Other medications as directed by protocols

Additional equipment

Transport incubator

Intracranial pressure monitor

Personal protective equipment

Survival pack

Camera and ability to leave pictures

Directions to the receiving facility

Measuring tapes

Drug and equipment calculation card

Car seat

Pediatric transport board

Cervical collars

Soft restraints

Warming equipment

Preparation of the Child for Transport

- ❒ Explain to the child what is happening and where he or she will be going.
- ❒ Secure any lines, tubes, or dressings after ensuring that they are patent.
- ❒ Remove any wet clothing and cover the patient with dry, warm blankets.
- ❒ Immobilize as indicated by the child's condition.
- ❒ Maintain cervical spine protection during transport of the injured child.
- ❒ Consider the use of restraints for safety. The smaller child may be secured on a papoose board.
- ❒ Consider sedation if the child's neurologic status is intact.
- ❒ Allow the child to keep security objects, such as a stuffed animal, pacifier, or blanket.

Care During Transport

- ❒ Ensure safety of patient and transport team
  - Secure the child in the age-appropriate transport device.
  - Appropriately restrain all equipment and personnel on the basis of the type of transport vehicle that is being used.
  - Position the transport team members for optimal safe patient care.
  - Maintain universal precautions.
- ❒ Provide continuous assessment and management of the child's airway, breathing, and circulation
  - Monitor vital signs.
  - Monitor effectiveness of ventilation.
  - Monitor patency of intravenous lines.
  - Administer medications as indicated by the child's illness or injury.
  - Assess security of tubes and patient equipment.
- ❒ Provide medication for sedation and pain management (Chapter 11).
- ❒ Keep the child warm
  - Wrap the child in a transfer blanket.
  - Turn on vehicle heat.
  - Wrap the child's head for heat conservation, if appropriate.
- ❒ Establish communication
  - Bring all transfer documents with the child.
  - Request that the referring facility provide a report to the receiving facility.
  - Provide an adequate report to the receiving facility on arrival.

Conclusion

The transfer and transport of the ill or injured child requires that the appropriate personnel and vehicle be used. Personnel should be competent in providing care for any emergency they may encounter during transport. The transport vehicle has to be prepared with equipment that is essential to the care of the ill or injured pediatric patient, including equipment to maintain airway, breathing, and circulation.

The family is an important part of the care of the pediatric patient and should be included in the transport process when possible or, at a minimum, be provided with information to make their journey to the receiving facility as easy as possible. Transfer and transport of the pediatric patient should be a lifesaving, not a life-threatening process.

References

1. Horowitz, R., & Rozenfeld, R. (2007). Pediatric critical care interfacility transport. *Clinical Pediatric Emergency Medicine, 8,* 190–202.

2. Belway, D., Henderson, W., Keenan, S., & Levy, A. (2006). Do specialist transport personnel improve hospital outcome in critically ill patients transferred to higher centers? A systematic review. *Journal of Critical Care, 21,* 8–18.

3. Rowney, D., & Simpson, D. (2006). Stabilization and transport of critically ill children. *Anaesthesia and Intensive Care Medicine, 7*(1), 16–21.

4. Holleran, R. S., & Linsler, R. (2006). Pediatric transport team: Intermountain Life Flight. *Pediatric Emergency Care, 22*(5), 374–8.

5. Emergency Nurses Association. (2002). *Position statement: Care of the critically ill or injured patient during intrafacility transfer.* Des Plaines, IL: Author.

6. Emergency Nurses Association. (2007). *Position statement: Care of the pediatric patient in the emergency setting.* Des Plaines, IL: Author.

7. American Academy of Pediatrics. (2007). *Guidelines for air and ground transport of neonatal and pediatric patients.* Elk Grove Village, IL: Author.

8. Williams, M., & Johnson, K. (1995). Transport regulations. In K. McCloskey & R. Orr (Eds.), *Pediatric transport medicine* (pp. 15–32). St. Louis: Mosby-Year Book.

9. McCleary, N. (1997). Air medical transfers: Are you COBRA compliant? *Air Medical Journal, 16*(4), 113–116.

10. Commission on Accreditation of Medical Transport Systems. (2006). *Guidelines for air medical transport systems.* Anderson, SC: Author.

11. Fultz, J., McKee, J., Zalaznik, F., & Kidd, P. (1993). Air medical transport: What the family wants to know. *Air Medical Journal, 12,* 431–435.

12. Lewis, M., Holditch-Davis, D., & Brunssen, S. (1997). Parents as passengers during pediatric transport. *Air Medical Journal, 16*(2), 38–43.

13. Fultz, J. (1999). Tips for helping families of patients transported by helicopter. *Journal of Emergency Nursing, 25*(2), 132–134.

SECTION THREE
Specific Pediatric Population Problems

CHAPTER

NINE

Neonatal Emergencies

Regina O'Leary, RN, MSN, CRNP
Kathleen Campbell, RN, MSN, CRNP, NNP-BC
Merry Kruger, BA Nursing, NNP-BC
Susan Barbarossa, CRNP

Introduction

With the typical hospital discharge of newborns occurring between 48 and 72 hours from birth, and advances in neonatal care resulting in complicated patients being discharged to home, infants are presenting to the emergency department (ED) in the neonatal period. The neonatal period is from birth to 28 days. Neonates may be premature and have a postnatal age greater than 28 days with a corrected gestation age (time post delivery added to birth gestation) of less than 1 month. Risk factors for being ill at birth or in the neonatal period include:

❏ Being preterm or postterm

❏ Having a birth weight of less than 2 kg or greater than 4 kg

❏ Needing cardiopulmonary resuscitation at birth

❏ Being exposed to maternal infection, lack of prenatal care, drug use, or social issues

❏ Having an infection or illness

❏ Being a product of a multiple gestation

❏ Having an obstetric complication requiring cesarean birth

❏ Having one or more congenital malformations or genetic abnormalities

❏ Having a history of fetal problems

❏ Being born to a mother aged < 15 years or > 40 years

The emergency nurse needs to be aware of physiologic differences and potential emergencies associated with this population. Chapter 10 outlines nonemergent neonatal conditions. Table 9.1 lists the equipment required for neonatal care in the emergency department. The purpose of this chapter is to discuss the assessment and treatment of selected neonatal conditions.

TABLE 9.1 Equipment for Neonatal Care

Suction equipment
- Bulb syringe
- Mechanical suction
- Suction catheters 5–12 French

Bag and mask equipment
- Infant Ambu bag with manometer
- Facemasks both newborn and preterm size
- Oxygen source with flowmeter
- Intubation equipment
- Endotracheal tubes size 2.0 to 4.0 internal diameter
- Laryngoscope blades size 0 and 1
- Stylette
- Cloth adhesive tape
- Scissors
- Skin prep
- CO_2 detector

Medications
- Epinephrine 1:10,000
- Normal saline solution for volume expansion
- Sodium bicarbonate 4.2%
- Naloxone hydrochloride 0.4 mg/mL
- 10% dextrose
- Normal saline flushes

Umbilical catheterization supplies
- Sterile drapes and gloves
- Scalpel or scissors
- Antiseptic prep solution
- Umbilical cord tie
- Umbilical catheters size 3.5 and 5 French
- Three-way stopcock
- 4.0 Silk suture
- Syringes 1, 3, 5, 10, 20, 50 mL
- Needles 18, 21, and 25 gauge

Chemically activated warming pad

Pulse oximeter and oximeter probe

Transport incubator or overhead warming bed

Bilirubin lights/phototherapy equipment (available as needed

Physiologic Transitions

From conception to birth, dramatic developmental and physiologic changes take place in the fetus and neonate. These changes must be successful to allow a complete transition from intrauterine to extrauterine life. If this transition is not effective, a cascade of events occurs that leads to the need for neonatal resuscitation (Chapter 12).

Respiratory Transition

The respiratory system is the key component of transition.

❑ The organ of respiration changes from the placenta to the lung.

❑ Effective respirations must be established.

❑ Lung fluid must be reabsorbed and replaced by air.

❑ Surfactant, a combination of phospholipids and proteins that lower surface tension, must be present in sufficient quantities to allow for sustained inflation of the air sacs.

Circulatory Transition

Circulation must convert from the fetal pathways to the postnatal pathways.

❑ After the initial respiration, pulmonary blood flow increases because of the rapid drop in pulmonary vascular resistance.

❑ Systemic vascular resistance dramatically increases with the loss of the low-resistance placenta.

❑ The fetal shunts of the ductus venosus, ductus arteriosus, and foramen ovale functionally close, converting blood flow across these shunts from right to left to none or left to right.

❑ Cardiac output goes from right ventricular predominance to equal output. The neonatal heart responds to stress predominantly by increasing the heart rate.

Thermoregulatory Transition

The neonate transitions from a temperature-controlled environment of the womb to a cooler fluctuating external environment. Maintaining a stable environmental temperature is important for successful transition.

Nutritional Transition

Before birth, the infant's nutritional needs are met through a carefully stabilized fluid and nutritional intake; after birth, the neonate depends on others for sustenance.

Anatomic and Physiologic Differences

Children are not small adults, just as neonates are not small children. There are physiologic and anatomic differences in body systems, requirements, and needs that have an impact on emergency nursing care.

Respiratory System

The infant has one tenth the number of alveoli of an adult. When oxygen needs increase, the neonate has limited ability to alter gas exchange to compensate. Hypoxia can rapidly ensue.[1]

Cardiovascular System

The neonate has limited ability to increase stroke volume during cardiac compromise. To maintain cardiac output, the neonate will rely on increasing the heart rate. Bradycardia is an emergent event because it indicates that the infant is unable to compensate for physiologic changes affecting the cardiovascular system.

Fluids and Nutrition

The neonate has more total body water and extracellular fluid than adults do. The total body water is approximately 75% in the neonate and 60% in the adult. Extracellular fluid is about 40% of the total body water in the newborn but 20% in the adult.[1] Neonates can lose bodily fluids rapidly through normal processes, insensible losses, vomiting, diarrhea, and renal losses. The infant has limited glucose stores and therefore easily may become hypoglycemic during times of illness or stress.

Thermoregulatory System

Neonates have a limited ability to produce and conserve heat, which places them at risk for cold stress.[1] Keeping the infant warm without overheating is a priority in any situation. Heat loss is increased by the neonate's high surface-to-mass ratio and inability to regulate skin blood flow. The head is the leading source of heat loss. A neonate responds to cold by burning brown fat to generate heat. If hypothermic, the infant releases norepinephrine, increasing the metabolic rate and increasing the susceptibility to hypoxia, hypoglycemia, and metabolic acidosis.

Immune System

The neonate has an immature immune system. Physical barriers, such as the skin, are thinner, and mucous membranes are permeable. Chemical barriers, such as tears, are not produced in sufficient quantities to fight infection. Immunoglobulins are inefficient and/or unavailable in sufficient quantities to effectively fight infection. The neonate is unable to localize infection and therefore exhibits few signs and symptoms of infection, making assessment and diagnosis difficult. Although many components of the fetal immune system are present early in gestation, neonates have decreased antibody levels, decreased number of neutrophils, and abnormal neutrophil function (Chapter 24).

Gastrointestinal System

Prenatally, metabolic functions are performed by the placenta. The neonatal liver is immature and cannot effectively conjugate bilirubin. Jaundice can develop in the newborn during the first several days of life because the liver becomes overwhelmed and cannot excrete bilirubin, leading to physiologic jaundice. Because of a relaxed lower esophageal sphincter, neonates frequently spit up. Stool patterns are different for each infant, although most newborns pass their first meconium stool by 24 hours of life.

Pain Response

The recognition of and assessment for pain requires special measurements and techniques (Chapter 11). The Neonatal Pain, Agitation, and Sedation Scale (N-PASS) is a valid and reliable tool useful in measuring the neonate's pain (Chapter 11).

Vital Signs

Because neonates can have infection without fever, the resting heart rate and resting respiratory heart rate are most informative. The temperature should be measured rectally unless there is a contraindication such as imperforate anus or immunocompromise.

Blood pressures should be obtained with the proper size cuff. An important factor to remember is that low blood pressure is a late sign of neonatal cardiopulmonary compromise. Normal ranges for vital signs in the neonate are:

- ❑ Respiratory rate: 40 to 60 breaths per minute
- ❑ Heart rate: 100 to 160 beats per minute
- ❑ Blood pressure: A systolic range of 70 to 50 mm Hg and a diastolic range of 45 to 30 mmHg[2]
- ❑ Rectal temperature: 97.7 °F to 99.5 °F (36.5 °C to 37.5 °C)

Focused History

Maternal History

- ❑ Gravida/para status
- ❑ Birth complications
- ❑ Multiple birth or single birth

Patient Physical History

- ❑ Apgar score, if known
- ❑ Gestational age
- ❑ Congenital anomalies, illness, or surgeries
- ❑ Gestational age. Although there are numerous ways to determine gestational age, this determination usually is not conducted in the emergency department. Generally, the following calculations are made:
  - ▪ Preterm: Less than 37 weeks completed gestation
  - ▪ Term: 38 to 42 weeks
  - ▪ Postterm: Greater than 42 weeks

Patient Behavioral History

- ❑ Changes in feeding behavior
- ❑ Changes in bowel or bladder patterns
- ❑ Change in activity, such as lethargy, irritability, or both

Sibling History

- ❑ Fetal or neonatal death
- ❑ History of inherited disorders
- ❑ History of maternal or paternal inherited disorders, syndromes, or anomalies

Focused Assessment

Physical Assessment

- ❑ Assess the airway for patency.
- ❑ Assess the respiratory system.
  - ▪ Auscultate the chest for:
    - • Respiratory rate
    - • Adventitious sounds
    - • Presence and equality
  - ▪ Assess the chest wall for:
    - • Movement
    - • Rate
    - • Pattern

- Observe for signs of respiratory distress or insufficiency (Chapter 12).
  - Respiratory insufficiency may yield an inadequate heart rate; therefore, the heart rate should be evaluated immediately after the respiratory assessment.
- ☐ Assess the cardiovascular system.
  - Auscultate the heart for:
    - Rate
    - Rhythm
    - Murmurs
  - Palpate the peripheral pulses for:
    - Rate
    - Equality
    - Quality
  - Measure capillary refill.
  - Measure the blood pressure.
  - Measure skin and rectal temperature.
    - Inspect skin color.
    - Cyanosis and pallor may indicate sepsis, anemia, hyaline membrane disease, or a cardiac anomaly.
    - Assess skin turgor.
- ☐ Assess the neurologic system.
  - Assess the neonate's level of consciousness with the AVPU method (*A*lert, responds to *V*erbal stimuli, responds to *P*ain, *U*nresponsive) or Glasgow Coma Scale.
    - Assess for pain (Chapter 11).
  - Assess the neonate's motor patterns.
    - Activity
    - Muscle tone
    - Movement of the extremities
  - Assess the pupillary responses.
  - Assess the basic reflexes:[3]
    - Sucking reflex in response to a nipple or the examiner's finger in the mouth
    - Rooting reflex: Head turns to the side of a facial stimulus.
    - Traction response: When pulled by the arms to a sitting position, the infant's head initially lags, and then with active flexion comes to the midline briefly before falling forward.
    - Palmar grasp with placement of the examiner's finger in the palm
    - Babinski reflex: Toes fan out when the sole of the foot is stroked.

- Deep tendon reflexes
- Placing reflex: Knee flexion and foot dorsiflexion when the foot dorsum is rubbed. Rub the dorsum of one foot on the underside of a surface. The neonate will flex the knee and bring foot up.
- Moro (startle) reflex
- Tonic neck reflexes

- ☐ Assess the abdomen:
  - Auscultate for bowel sounds.
    - Palpate the abdomen for
      - Organ enlargement
      - Pain and tenderness
- ☐ Assess the genitourinary system:
  - Assess urinary output.
  - Assess stool patterns.
    - Color
    - Frequency
    - Amount
    - Breast versus bottle-fed stools
- ☐ Assess the integumentary system:
  - Observe the skin for
    - Rashes
    - Petechiae
    - Color
    - Hydration

Psychosocial Assessment

- ☐ Assess the family's social support system.
- ☐ Assess the attachment behaviors among the parent, neonate, and family members.
- ☐ Note prior need for Social Services and Child Services.

Nursing Interventions

1. Assess and maintain airway, breathing, and circulation.
   - Initiate maneuvers to maintain airway patency, such as positioning and suctioning.
   - Administer 100% oxygen through a nonrebreather mask.
   - Initiate assisted ventilation in the neonate in whom adequate respiratory effort is not being maintained.
     - Prepare for endotracheal intubation in the neonate with cardiopulmonary compromise

2. Initiate cardiorespiratory and continuous oxygen saturation monitoring.

3. Obtain venous access and initiate an intravenous infusion at the prescribed rate.
   - Obtain blood and urine specimens for laboratory analysis.
   - Prepare to administer medications, as prescribed.

4. Reassess neurologic status and cardiopulmonary status.

5. Promote comfort.
   - Maintain a normothermic environment. Maintaining temperature in a neonate is so important and they can lose heat easily.
   - Offer comfort measures (swaddling, holding, nonnutritive sucking [pacifier]) during and after ED treatment.
   - Offer nutritive sucking (breast-feeding or bottle-feeding) if neonate is permitted to eat.

6. Measure intake and output.

7. Prepare for diagnostic tests, as needed.

8. Inform the family frequently about the neonate's condition; provide emotional support to the child and family.

9. Initiate consultations with specialists (e.g., neonatologists, neonatal team).

10. Prepare for transfer and transport to a tertiary care facility as needed (Chapter 8); prepare for hospitalization as indicated.

Specific Neonatal Emergencies

Infection in the Neonate

Despite the development of newer, more potent antimicrobial agents, infections are still important causes of neonatal morbidity and mortality.[4] The common sites of neonatal infection are the blood, cerebrospinal fluid, and lungs. Identifying the newborn with a systemic infection can be one of the greatest challenges in nursing.[5] Nurses are one of the first health care professionals to recognize the symptoms of infection in an infant.

Neonatal Sepsis

Neonatal sepsis is a clinical syndrome of systemic illness accompanied by bacteremia occurring in the first month of life.[4] The incidence of primary sepsis in the neonate is 1 to 8 per 100 live births with a mortality rate of 5% to 25%.[4] Neonatal sepsis results from a complex interaction between pathogens and the human host.[6]

Regardless of the initiating organism, the response is the triggering of the sepsis cascade of inflammation leading to coagulation dysfunction and resulting in impaired fibrinolysis. The clinical result of the sepsis cascade is capillary leak and vasodilatation, which may progress to end organ dysfunction and shock.[6]

Neonatal sepsis is categorized into distinct illnesses based on the postnatal age at onset.

❒ Early onset sepsis:[4]
   - Occurs in the first 7 days of life
   - Is usually associated with fulminant, multisystem involvement
   - Is transmitted from the mother
   - Has a high mortality rate of 5% to 20%
   - Most often occurs from group *ß-hemolytic streptococcus, Escherichia coli (E-coli),* and *Streptococcus viridans*[7]

❒ Late onset sepsis:
   - Occurs in 7 to 90 days of life
   - Is usually consistent with focal infections, such as meningitis, pneumonia, urinary tract infection, and osteomyelitis[8]
   - Is acquired from the caregiving environment
   - Has a mortality rate of approximately 5%[8]
   - Most often occurs from coagulase-negative staphylococcus, *Staphylococcus aureus,* Candida, *E. coli,* Klebsiella, and group *ß-hemolytic streptococcus*[5]

Focused History

❒ Maternal history
   - Group *ß-hemolytic streptococcus* colonization/infection
   - Chorioamnionitis
   - Vaginal infections
   - Premature/prolonged rupture of membranes
   - Herpes simplex infection/history

❒ Neonate history
   - Timing onset of symptoms
   - Prematurity
   - Birth asphyxia
   - Admission to neonatal intensive care unit (NICU)
   - Poor nutrition
   - Exposure to viruses
   - Congenital anomalies (abdominal wall defects, spinal defects)[6,9]

Focused Assessment[6,9]

☐ Assess the respiratory system.

- Respiratory distress. Apnea, grunting, and tachypnea may be present.

☐ Assess the cardiovascular system.

- Heart rate. Tachycardia may be present.
- Blood pressure. Hypertension/hypotension may be present.
- Temperature instability ($< 96.8 \,°F$ or $> 100.4 \,°F$; $< 36 \,°C$ or $> 38 \,°C$)
- Skin temperature. Cold, clammy skin may be noted.

☐ Assess the neurologic system.

- Signs of meningeal irritation. Lethargy, irritability, jitteriness, seizures, high-pitched cry may be present.
- Pain (Chapter 11)

☐ Assess the gastrointestinal system.

- Poor feeding
- Vomiting/diarrhea
- Abdominal distention

☐ Assess the integumentary system.

- Rashes
- Petechiae

Nursing Interventions

1. Assess and maintain airway, breathing, and circulation.

- Initiate maneuvers to maintain airway patency, such as positioning and suctioning.
- Administer 100% oxygen through a nonrebreather mask; initiate assisted ventilation in the neonate who is not maintaining adequate respiratory effort.
  - Prepare for endotracheal intubation for the neonate in whom airway patency cannot be maintained.
- Initiate cardiorespiratory monitoring; measure continuous oxygen saturation.

2. Obtain venous access and initiate an intravenous infusion.

- Initiate a fluid bolus of 10 mL/kg of a isotonic solution if shock is present.
- Initiate hydration at a maintenance rate.
- Administer inotropic agents as indicated.
- Obtain blood specimens.
  - Serum blood cultures, complete blood cell count, C-reactive protein, electrolytes, arterial blood gas

- Viral cultures, wound cultures, urine culture and analysis
  - Administer antimicrobial/antiviral therapy.
  - Maintain a normothermic environment.

3. Monitor neurologic status.

- Assess for changes in level of consciousness and response to stimuli.
- Prepare for a lumbar puncture, if indicated.
- Send cerebrospinal fluid for culture, sensitivity, cell count, protein, and glucose testing.

4. Measure urinary output.

5. Provide psychosocial support to the patient and family.

6. Initiate isolation procedures, if indicated

7. Prepare for transfer and transport to a tertiary care facility (Chapter 8).

Home Care and Prevention

The prevention of neonatal sepsis begins in utero. Mothers who have positive cultures for group B streptococcus should be treated before delivery according to the Centers for Disease Control and Prevention guidelines for group B streptococcus disease.[10] Before delivery, culture and sensitivity testing in mothers with active primary herpes simplex virus lesions should be considered. In the neonatal period, crowds should be avoided to prevent exposing the neonate to illnesses. Frequent hand washing before and after caring for the neonate helps to prevent the spread of disease.

Meningitis

Neonatal meningitis is the infection of the meninges and the central nervous system (CNS) in the first month of life. This is the most common time of life for meningitis to occur.[5] The incidence of meningitis is approximately 1 in 2500 live births. The mortality rate is 20% to 50%, and there is a high incidence ($> 50\%$) of neurodevelopmental sequelae such as motor and mental disabilities, hearing loss, blindness, and convulsions.[4]

Most cases of neonatal meningitis occur because of a primary bacteremia that travels to the meninges and CNS. Although the primary causative organisms are usually bacterial, such as *group B streptococcus* and *E. coli,* viruses and fungi are common agents.

Focused History

☐ CNS defects

☐ Presence of a ventriculoperitoneal (VP) shunt

☐ Prematurity

❐ Maternal infection

❐ Prolonged rupture of membranes

Focused Assessment

❐ Assess the respiratory system for:

- Rate

- Effort

❐ Assess the cardiopulmonary system for:

- Heart rate

- Blood pressure

- Skin color

- Skin temperature. Temperature instability may be present.

❐ Assess the neurologic system for:

- Early signs of meningeal irritation

- Irritability

- Poor muscle tone

- Seizure activity

- Poor feeding

- Late signs of meningeal irritation

- Bulging fontanelle

- Nuchal rigidity

Nursing Interventions[11]

1. Provide cardiorespiratory support.

2. Obtain vascular access.

- Obtain specimens for cultures.

3. Assist in performing a lumbar puncture in the absence of increased intracranial pressure.

- Obtain specimens for culture, sensitivity, cell count, protein, and glucose testing.

4. Administer medications as ordered.

- Initiate intravenous antibiotic therapy.

- Initiate intravenous rehydration therapy if needed.

5. Initiate isolation procedures, if indicated.

6. Prepare for hospital admission or transfer and transport to a tertiary care facility (Chapter 8).

Home Care and Prevention

Crowds should be avoided to prevent exposing the neonate to illnesses. Frequent hand washing before and after caring for the neonate helps to prevent the spread of disease.

Pneumonia/Respiratory Syncytial Virus

Respiratory syncytial virus (RSV) is now recognized to be the most common respiratory pathogen in infants and children (Chapter 14). The most serious illness from RSV generally occurs during the first year of life, particularly in infants with chronic lung disease, congenital heart defects, or prematurity. RSV infects nearly all children by 2 to 3 years of age.[5] RSV is a paramyxovirus that is divided into types A (higher disease severity) and B. Both types may present during epidemics. Humans are the only source of infection. Transmission is by direct or close contact with infected secretions from hand to nose and eye, but large aerosol droplets have been implicated.[12] Viral shedding usually occurs over a period of 3 to 8 days. The incubation period is from 2 to 8 days, but may last up to 4 weeks. RSV can survive for several hours on nonporous surfaces and for up to 30 minutes on the hands.[13] The resultant pneumonia may be bacterial, viral, or of other infectious origins such as Chlamydia. RSV usually occurs in annual epidemics during winter and early spring in temperate climates.

Focused History

❐ Prematurity

❐ < 12 Months of age

❐ Preexisting heart or lung disease

❐ School-age siblings

❐ Attendance in daycare

❐ Lack of breast-feeding

❐ Passive smoke exposure

❐ Winter or early spring season

Focused Assessment

❐ Assess the respiratory system for:

- Rate. Apnea (occurs in 20% of neonates)[11]

- Effort. Cough and respiratory distress may be present.

- Adventitious sounds. Wheezing may be heard.

- Nasal discharge (can be copious)

❐ Assess the cardiovascular system for:

- Heart rate

- Blood pressure

- Temperature. Fever may or may not be present.

Nursing Interventions[5,9]

1. Assess and maintain airway, breathing, and circulation.

- Administer oxygen.

- Administer bronchodilators.
2. Provide cardiovascular support.
   - Obtain venous access.
   - Administer intravenous hydration.
3. Initiate isolation procedures, if needed.
4. Obtain specimens for diagnostic testing.
   - Obtain a nasal pharyngeal aspirate for rapid viral antigen detection.
5. Prepare for hospital admission, if indicated.

Home Care and Prevention

All family members should perform frequent, vigorous hand washing before and after caring for the neonate. Families should avoid high-risk settings, such as crowded, enclosed spaces, especially during RSV season. The American Academy of Pediatrics recommends the administration of palivizumab (Synagis®) (monoclonal antibody) monthly,[12] which is administered in the primary care setting. Daycare centers should practice scrupulous hygiene to prevent transmission among siblings who can then infect the neonate in the home setting.

Congestive Heart Failure

Congestive heart failure (CHF) is a clinical syndrome in which the heart is unable to pump enough blood to the body to meet oxygen demand or to provide adequate venous return (Chapter 15). The signs and symptoms of CHF are manifested by pulmonary or systemic venous congestion and impaired myocardial function. Left ventricular failure results in pulmonary congestion. Right ventricular failure causes systemic venous congestion. Marked failure of either ventricle, however, can affect the function of the other, leading to systemic and pulmonary venous congestion. Later stages of CHF are characterized by signs and symptoms of low cardiac output.[14]

Many classes of disorders can result in increased cardiac demand or impaired cardiac function. Cardiac causes of CHF include dysrhythmias (tachycardia or bradycardia), structural heart disease, and myocardial dysfunction. Noncardiac causes of CHF include processes that (1) increase the preload as in volume overload, (2) increase afterload as in hypertension, (3) reduce oxygen-carrying capacity of the blood as in anemia, or (4) increase demand as in sepsis.[14]

Neonates and infants younger than 2 months are the most likely group to present with CHF related to structural heart disease, primarily acyanotic heart lesions (ductal-dependent lesions).[14] CHF as a complication of congenital heart disease often occurs by 6 months of age in response to a decreased cardiac output in the presence of increased metabolic demand. Volume overload is a common precursor in the child or infant with congenital defects. In addition to poor heart function, renal perfusion is often impaired by the decreased cardiac output.[15]

Focused History

❑ Feeding behavior
   - Increased time to feed
   - Tachypnea and/or diaphoresis during feeding
❑ Poor weight gain
   - Postnatal age at time of symptom presentation
   - Sudden deterioration in health, especially soon after birth, may be caused by closing of a patent ductus arteriosus in the infant with a ductal-dependent lesion.
   - Congestive heart failure from pulmonary overperfusion (left-to-right shunting) usually occurs later in the neonatal period.
❑ Recurrent respiratory infections

Focused Assessment

❑ Assess the respiratory system for:
   - Rate. Tachypnea (respiratory rate consistently > 60 breaths per minute) may be noted, as well as periods of apnea.
   - Increased work of breathing. Retractions, nasal flaring, or grunting may be present.
   - Adventitious sounds. Rales may be auscultated.
❑ Assess the cardiovascular system for:
   - Rate. Tachycardia may be present.
   - Heart sounds. Murmur and active precordium may be heard.
   - Peripheral pulses. Decreased peripheral pulses, mottling of extremities may be present. Femoral pulses may be absent.
   - Skin color. Central or peripheral cyanosis may be noted; pallor and poor perfusion may be present.
   - Skin temperature. Skin may be cool because of decreased perfusion.
   - Capillary refill. Capillary refill may be > 3 seconds.
   - Turgor. Periorbital edema may be present.
   - Workload. Fatigue with feeding, decreased oral intake and excessive diaphoresis, especially during feedings, may be noted.
❑ Palpate the abdomen for:
   - Enlarged organs. Hepatomegaly may be present.

☐ Assess length and weight.

- Poor growth may be noted.

Nursing Interventions

1. Initiate measures to stabilize airway, breathing, and circulation.

   - Initiate oxygen saturation monitoring.
   - Measure blood pressure in all four extremities.

2. Obtain intravenous access.

3. Perform laboratory testing.

   - Oxygen saturation
   - Complete blood cell count and blood culture to assess for sepsis
   - Hemoglobin concentration to evaluate for anemia
   - Electrolyte levels including calcium
   - Blood urea nitrogen and creatinine
   - Liver enzymes
   - Blood gas analysis

4. Prepare for diagnostic testing.

   - Chest radiograph to evaluate for cardiomegaly, pulmonary edema
   - 12-Lead electrocardiogram
   - Echocardiography

5. Administer medications as ordered.

   - Antibiotic therapy
   - Agents to promote cardiovascular functioning:
   - Alprostadil (prostaglandin E1) when ductal-dependent cardiac lesions are diagnosed or when they cannot be ruled out
   - Diuretics (reduce preload)
   - Inotropic agents, such as dopamine
   - Synthetic catecholamines, such as dobutamine
   - Cardiac glycosides, such as digoxin (increase cardiac output and myocardial contractility)
   - Adenosine (treats supraventricular tachycardia)
   - Fluid bolus or bicarbonate to correct acidosis
   - Blood products, typically red cell transfusions to correct anemia

6. Prepare for hospital admission or transfer and transport to a tertiary care facility (Chapter 8).

Home Care and Prevention

Early recognition of congenital heart defects is the best means of preventing CHF in neonates. Emergency nurses must be able to recognize signs and symptoms of CHF to prevent deterioration of the neonate's condition. The success of therapy for correcting CHF is judged according to the infant's growth. A failure to thrive is an indication for increased medical management or, when the option exists, surgical repair of structural heart disease.[14]

Apnea

Apnea is defined as the cessation of breathing for longer than 20 seconds, or a shorter duration in the presence of pallor, cyanosis, or bradycardia. There are multiple possible etiologic factors leading to symptomatic apnea in the preterm and term infant.[16] Most apneic events in term infants have an underlying medical cause. In preterm infants less than 1500 g at birth, approximately 70% will have an apneic episode while in the NICU.[16] The majority of these infants will not have an underlying medical condition and by exclusion are given the diagnosis of apnea of prematurity.

Apnea in a newborn is classified as central, obstructive, or mixed. Most apnea of prematurity is classified as central apnea, in which there is complete absence of respiratory effort. Obstructive apnea occurs when an infant makes a respiratory effort but no airflow is present because of the presence of obstruction. Mixed apnea is a combination of central and obstructive apnea.[17] Regardless, apnea is a sign of significant illness or immaturity of the respiratory control system. The principal goals of treating neonatal apnea are to address its cause and to provide appropriate medical management.[18]

Health conditions that may present with apnea include:[18]

☐ Hypoxemia caused by respiratory distress, anemia, or airway obstruction

☐ Infection

- RSV
- Meningitis
- Encephalitis
- Pertussis
- Pneumonia

☐ Severe congestive heart failure

☐ Inborn errors of metabolism

☐ Electrolyte/metabolic abnormalities

- Hypocalcemia
- Hyponatremia
- Hypoglycemia
- Acidosis
- Hyperammonemia

- ❑ Ingestion of narcotics/other drugs
  - ▪ Direct (intentional or accidental), (e.g. anticonvulsants)
  - ▪ Indirect via breast milk, that is, methadone
- ❑ Gastroesophageal reflux disease
- ❑ Seizures
- ❑ Child maltreatment (Chapter 44)
- ❑ Exposure to general anesthesia
- ❑ Hypothermia
- ❑ Dysrhythmias
- ❑ CNS pathology
- ❑ Intracranial hemorrhage
- ❑ Trauma
- ❑ Tumors
- ❑ Anoxia/or ischemia
- ❑ Stroke
- ❑ Posthemorrhagic hydrocephalus

Apnea is a diagnosis of exclusion and can be the result of respiratory immaturity. Breathing control, both centrally and peripherally, is immature at birth but develops rapidly over the first year of life. Neonates may respond to hypoxemia with a brief increase in respiratory rate, followed by apnea. Hypoxemia also decreases the response to arterial carbon dioxide tension and further depresses the respiratory drive. The infant is more vulnerable during sleep because of the decrease in oxygen tension. Apnea can be potentiated by exposure to anesthesia in premature infants up to 52 weeks postconceptual age, or by systemic illness in postterm infants, especially those with apnea at discharge from the hospital.[18]

The terms apnea and apparent life-threatening event, or ALTE, are often used interchangeably in conversation but have different definitions. An ALTE is defined as a sudden, unexpected change in an infant that is frightening to the caregiver but does not lead to death or persistent collapse.[19] Most patients are younger than 12 months and generally younger than 6 months of age. Episodes are characterized by some combination of apnea, color change, change in muscle tone, choking, and gagging.[16] Emergency department management will depend on the historical information provided by observers and by the physical examination results. Hospitalization may be appropriate for observation and monitoring.[20]

Focused History

- ❑ Gestational age and birth history
- ❑ Previous apnea spells and treatment given
- ❑ Current family illnesses (viral, history of inborn errors

of metabolism)
- ❑ Feeding difficulties
- ❑ Use of home apnea monitor
- ❑ Immunizations (apnea can worsen or reappear within 24 hours after immunizations)[18]

Focused Assessment

- ❑ Assess the respiratory system.
  - ▪ Observe for congenital malformations, especially those involving the airway.
  - ▪ Observe for signs of respiratory distress.
- ❑ Assess the cardiovascular system.
  - ▪ Observe for signs of heart disease or CHF.
- ❑ Assess the neurologic system.
  - ▪ Observe for abnormal behaviors, such as weak muscle tone or posturing, which could relate to infection or intestinal obstruction.

Nursing Interventions

1. Initiate measures to support the neonate's airway, breathing, and circulation.
   - ▪ Attach the neonate to an apnea monitor.
   - ▪ Observe the infant for apnea spells at rest and while crying.
2. Obtain blood and urine specimens for diagnostic testing to rule out illnesses that may be causing apnea.
   - ▪ Blood:
     - • Complete blood cell count
     - • Blood gas
     - • Serum glucose, electrolytes, calcium
     - • Culture
     - • Toxicology screen
     - • Serum ammonia
   - ▪ Urine:
     - • Culture and sensitivity
     - • Metabolic screen
3. Assist with obtaining a lumbar puncture, if indicated.
   - ▪ Obtain cerebrospinal fluid specimens for:
     - • Culture
     - • Sensitivity
     - • Cell count
     - • Protein
     - • Glucose testing
4. Prepare for diagnostic testing, as indicated.
   - ▪ Echocardiogram or electrocardiogram: May detect

- cardiac abnormality or conduction disorders
  - Electroencephalogram: Evaluate for seizures.
  - Cranial ultrasound/computed tomography: Evaluate for structural abnormalities or hemorrhages; chest radiograph: Evaluate for respiratory or cardiac abnormalities.
5. Prepare for hospitalization, if indicated.

Home Care and Prevention

If the neonate is discharged to home, initiate a referral to home care. Home health care and the primary care provider can provide the family with further instructions, including use of the home apnea monitor and cardiopulmonary resuscitation training. All families should receive education regarding safe sleep practices:

- ❐ Place supine for sleeping.
- ❐ Place neonate in the crib, not in bed with the family.
- ❐ Use non-soft sleeping surfaces.
- ❐ Use of pacifiers

Preventing the neonate from becoming overheated is another safety measure. Educating families about the effects of environmental tobacco smoke and encouraging family members not to smoke around the neonate will help prevent further respiratory complications.

Fluid and Electrolyte Imbalances

Hypernatremia

Hypernatremia represents a deficit of water in relation to the body's sodium stores, which can result from a net water loss or a hypertonic sodium gain. Net water loss accounts for most cases of hypernatremia. Three mechanisms may lead to hypernatremia, alone or in concert:[21]

- ❐ Pure water depletion (e.g., diabetes insipidus)
- ❐ Water depletion exceeding sodium depletion (e.g., diarrhea)
- ❐ Sodium excess (e.g., salt poisoning)

Hypertonic sodium gain usually results from clinical interventions or accidental sodium loading. As a result of increased extracellular sodium concentration, plasma tonicity increases. This increase in tonicity induces the movement of water across cell membranes, causing cellular dehydration.

Sustained hypernatremia occurs only when thirst or access to water is impaired, which places neonates and infants at high risk for this condition. Furthermore, neonates and infants are predisposed to dehydration because of their large surface area-to-weight ratio and relatively large evaporative water losses. In neonates and infants, hypernatremia usually results from diarrhea and sometimes from improperly prepared infant formula or inadequate mother-infant interaction during breast-feeding. Severe hypernatremic dehydration induces brain shrinkage, which can tear cerebral blood vessels, leading to cerebral hemorrhage, seizures, paralysis, and encephalopathy. In infants with prolonged hypernatremia, rapid rehydration with hypotonic fluids may cause cerebral edema, which can lead to coma, convulsions, and death.[19]

Causes and precipitating factors of hypernatremia include:

- ❐ Acute blood loss/hypovolemia
- ❐ Diarrhea
- ❐ Diabetes insipidus (pure renal water loss from failure to secrete or respond to antidiuretic hormone causing loss of water in excess of loss of sodium)
- ❐ Medications that may cause diuresis: Caffeine and theophylline
- ❐ Breast-feeding malnutrition: Inadequate intake in a breast-fed infant with a cycle of reduced milk production and decreasing demand, resulting in severe malnutrition, dehydration, and hypernatremia
- ❐ High inadvertent sodium intake:[21] Can be caused by improper dilution of infant formula

Focused History

- ❐ Gestational age/postconceptual age
- ❐ Current and previous illnesses
- ❐ Intake and output
- ❐ Current and previous medications
- ❐ History of diarrhea
- ❐ History of fever

Focused Assessment

- ❐ Assess the respiratory system.
  - Rate. Apnea may be present.
- ❐ Assess the cardiovascular system.
  - Auscultate the heart for:
    - Rate. Tachycardia may be present.
  - Assess peripheral perfusion. Decreased peripheral pulses with peripheral vasoconstriction (pale, cool, mottled skin with prolonged capillary refill) may be present.
  - Assess blood pressure. Blood pressure may be either normal or low.
    - Assess skin turgor. Mucous membranes may be dry.

- ❏ Assess temperature. Fever may be present.
- ❏ Assess the neurologic system.
  - ▪ Assess the level of consciousness. In breast-feeding malnutrition, possible excessive sleepiness, disinterest in feeding, or irritability may be present. Lethargy may be noted, with coma as a late sign.
  - ▪ Assess for seizure activity.
  - ▪ Assess muscle tone. Tone may be increased.
  - ▪ Assess the neonate's cry, which may be high-pitched.
- ❏ Assess the genitourinary system.
  - ▪ Urine output may be low with a high specific gravity.
  - ▪ Excessive diuresis may be noted.
- ❏ Assess overall development.
- ❏ Weight loss may be noted.

Nursing Interventions

1. Assess and maintain airway, breathing, and circulation.
2. Obtain venous access.
   - ▪ Administer intravenous fluids.
   - ▪ Avoid rapidly decreasing the sodium level because a rapid decline in the serum sodium concentration can cause cerebral edema.
   - ▪ Correct dehydration over 48 to 72 hours.
3. Obtain diagnostic studies.
   - ▪ Blood for electrolytes: Expect high serum sodium (> 150 mEq/L) and osmolality (> 300 mOsm/L) levels.
4. Prepare for hospitalization or transfer and transport to a tertiary care facility (Chapter 8).

Home Care and Prevention[21]

Teaching points for families to prevent hypernatremia include:

- ❏ Avoid making oral rehydration solutions at home or adding salt to any commercial infant formula.
- ❏ Observe for signs of neonatal dehydration and perinatal care, especially with breast-feeding infants.
- ❏ Monitor the breast-fed infant during the first weeks of life to assure adequate hydration.
- ❏ For neonates with diabetes insipidus:
  - ▪ Monitor weight and urine output because clinically significant changes in sodium values are associated with changes in weight.
  - ▪ Restrict sodium and protein intake.
  - ▪ Offer liberal amounts of water.
  - ▪ Ensure thirst develops before taking or giving medications.

Hypoglycemia

Glucose is vital for cellular metabolism throughout the body. Blood glucose concentration is determined by the balance between intake/production of glucose and glucose use by the body.[19] Hypoglycemia is defined as a whole blood glucose concentration of less than 40 mg/dL in neonates regardless of age.

Hypoglycemia in an infant is usually transient and secondary to hyperinsulinism or glycogen depletion. More persistent hypoglycemia can be derived from more significant illnesses, including congenital adrenal hyperplasia, growth hormone deficiency, panhypopituitarism, congenital hyperinsulinism, inborn errors of metabolism, hepatic disease, and sepsis.[21]

Causes of hypoglycemia in the neonate are:

- ❏ Decreased glycogen storage:
  - ▪ Prematurity
  - ▪ Small for gestational age
- ❏ Hyperinsulinism:
  - ▪ Diabetic mother
  - ▪ Insulin-secreting tumor
  - ▪ Beckwith-Wiedemann syndrome (congenital overgrowth syndrome that includes macroglossia; unexplained hypoglycemia in the first 4 months of life; ear creases or pits; abdominal wall defect and macrosomia at birth)
  - ▪ Nesidioblastosis or pancreatic adenoma
  - ▪ Erythroblastosis fetalis
  - ▪ Exchange transfusion
  - ▪ Maternal drugs
- ❏ Other conditions that increase glucose utilization:
  - ▪ Sepsis
  - ▪ Asphyxia
  - ▪ Cold stress
  - ▪ Large for gestational age infants who are not infants of diabetic mothers
  - ▪ Polycythemia or hyperviscosity syndrome
  - ▪ Congenital hypopituitarism
- ❏ Metabolic causes:
  - ▪ Inborn errors of metabolism, primarily disorders of energy metabolism or of fatty acid oxidation
    - • Glycogen storage diseases (types I and III are

most likely to be associated with manifestations in the neonatal period)

- Galactosemia
- Medium-chain acyl-coenzyme A dehydrogenase deficiency
- Hereditary fructose intolerance

All conditions associated with the development of hypoglycemia in the neonate result from one or a combination of two basic mechanisms:

☐ Inadequate production; results from a lack of glycogen stores, an inability to synthesize glucose, or both.

☐ Excessive tissue use; results from increased insulin secretion.[21]

Pregnancy creates a "diabetic-like state" in all mothers from the effects of anti-insulin hormones, such as human placental lactogen, progesterone, and estrogen. Glucose crosses the placenta along concentration gradients via carrier-mediated diffusion. Only 40% to 50% of glucose volume delivered to the placenta gets to the fetus. Insulin and glucagon do not cross the placenta, but the fetus can produce significant amounts of insulin in response to hyperglycemia.

At birth, the maternal glucose source is lost. The neonate's stores of glycogen are usually depleted by 12 hours after birth, and the infant must perform gluconeogenesis to prevent hypoglycemia and to survive. The stress of birth, illness, and hypothermia increases the infant's glucose requirements beyond available stores. Illness and hypothermia can increase the metabolic rate and the glucose requirements.[21]

Focused History

☐ Prematurity

☐ Large or small for gestational age

☐ Diabetic mother

☐ Current and previous illnesses

☐ Intake (oral or intravenous) and output

Focused Assessment

The signs and symptoms of hypoglycemia are variable. At the same glucose levels, some neonates may be asymptomatic whereas others may be symptomatic as listed below. For clinical signs and symptoms to be attributed to hypoglycemia, Whipple's triad must be met:[21] (1) a reliable blood glucose; (2) signs and symptoms consistent with hypoglycemia must be evident; and (3) signs and symptoms resolve after euglycemia is achieved.

☐ Assess the respiratory system for:

- Rate. Tachypnea and irregular respirations may be present.
- Signs of respiratory distress, including apnea

☐ Assess the cardiovascular system for:

- Skin color. Cyanosis may be present.
- Temperature. Hypothermia and temperature instability may be measured.

☐ Assess the neurologic system for:

- Level of consciousness. Lethargy and refusal to feed may be present. Irritability may be noted.
- Muscle tone. Hypotonia may be present. Jitteriness can be present.
- Seizure activity
- Abnormal cry. High-pitched or weak cry may be heard.
- Reflexes. An exaggerated Moro reflex may be elicited.

☐ Measure length and weight.

- The neonate may be small or large for gestational age.

Nursing Interventions[19]

1. Assess and maintain airway, breathing, and circulation.
2. Obtain venous access.
   - Obtain a blood specimen for glucose testing.
3. Treat the hypoglycemia.
   - Offer the infant an oral feeding.
   - If hypoglycemia persists despite feeding, initiate an intravenous glucose infusion: A minibolus (dextrose 10% in water, 2 mL/kg), followed by continuous infusion at a rate of 6 to 8 mg/kg per minute.
4. Initiate measures to reduce neonatal stress.
   - Use warming devices.
   - Prevent cold stress.
     - Provide comforting measures such as swaddling and pacifiers.
     - Encourage the parents to hold the neonate.
5. Implement treatment for the underlying cause of the hypoglycemia (e.g., sepsis).
6. Prepare for hospital admission, if indicated.

Home Care and Prevention

Emergency nurses should be alert to neonates at risk for hypoglycemia. Hypoglycemia is prevented in at-risk neonates by providing glucose substrate through early enteral feedings (human milk or formula) or intravenous glucose at 4 to 6 mg/kg per minute. When tolerated, feedings are preferred over parenteral glucose because milk provides more energy than the equivalent volume of intravenous fluid and may contribute more essential nonglucose substrate. Persistent hypoglycemia may require higher concentrations of dextrose infusion and treatment with glucagon, diazoxide, somatostatin, and corticosteroids. Hypoglycemia should be treated as soon as possible to prevent complications of neurologic damage. Thus, it is very important to teach parents about the recognition and prevention of hypoglycemia.

Hypothermia

Thermoregulation is important for physiologic functioning and neonatal survival.[20] Infants have a higher body surface area-to-weight ratio, causing rapid loss of body heat. The largest surface area on an infant's body is the head. Term infants have three times the body surface as an adult, and preterm infants have five times the body surface as an adult.[20] Therefore, it is extremely important to provide a source of heat when performing resuscitation and other care for newborns. Neonates lose heat by four methods:

❑ Conduction: Infant in direct contact with a cold surface; example: radiograph tables and other surfaces.

❑ Convection: Heat loss through air currents; example: cold, ambient air.

❑ Radiation: Heat loss to an object without direct contact with the object; example: neonate left uncovered or unclothed.

❑ Evaporation: Heat loss through evaporation of fluid; example: loss of heat through integumentary and respiratory systems.

Focused History

❑ Poor feedings

❑ Decreased body temperature: Rectal < 98 °F (< 36.5 °C)

❑ Lethargy

Focused Assessment

❑ Assess the respiratory system for:
  ▪ Rate. Apnea may be present.
  ▪ Signs of respiratory distress

❑ Assess the cardiovascular system for:
  ▪ Rate. Bradycardia may be present.
  ▪ Body temperature. Rectal temperature < 98 °F (< 36.5 °C) is found.

❑ Assess the neurologic system.
  ▪ Lethargy may be noted.

Nursing Interventions

1. Assess and maintain airway, breathing, and circulation.

2. Initiate measures to prevent heat loss.
  ▪ Use a heated radiant warming bed or Isolette. If an Isolette or radiant warmer is not available, provide a heat source such as a heat lamp, positioned about 18 inches away from the neonate.
  ▪ Use a heated mattress, such as a gel mattress.
  ▪ Apply warm blankets.
  ▪ Increase the room temperature.

3. Reassess vital signs and temperature frequently.

Home Care and Prevention

Parents should be instructed in the importance of keeping the neonate warm by:

❑ Applying clothing that is appropriate to the weather

❑ Ensuring that formula and pumped breast milk are warmed and not cold

❑ Checking ambient temperature for drafts and sources of cool air

ED staff should anticipate hypothermia in this population and prevent its onset by:

❑ Keeping the room temperature warm during assessments and treatments

❑ Minimizing skin exposure during assessments and treatments

❑ Limiting time on cold surfaces

❑ Limiting time in cold environments

❑ Avoiding drafts in hallways and rooms

❑ Providing external sources of warmth

Hyperbilirubinemia

Jaundice (yellow skin color) is the clinical manifestation of increased serum bilirubin. It is usually visible when serum levels are about 5 to 7 mg/dL.[22] Jaundice appears first on the face and then progresses caudally as serum bilirubin levels increase.[23]

Bilirubin is the primary degradation product of hemoglobin. It is produced after completion of the natural life span of the red blood cell (RBC), but ineffective erythropoiesis or premature destruction of RBCs can increase its production. Normal neonates produce 6 to 10 mg/dL of bilirubin per kilogram per day.[21] Newly synthesized bilirubin is referred to as unconjugated and is measured as indirect bilirubin. It then binds to albumin in the plasma for transport into the liver. Once in the liver, it detaches from albumin and enters the hepatocyte, where it binds with protein Y, protein Z, and glutathione S-transferase for transport to the smooth endoplasmic reticulum for conjugation (direct bilirubin). The major route of elimination is through conjugation with the aid of the hepatic enzyme glucuronyl transferase in the liver. Ninety-five percent of the conjugated bilirubin is then excreted into bile and subsequently into the intestine for final excretion in the stool.[1,23]

As the production of bilirubin exceeds the newborn capacity to conjugate, plasma levels begin to rise rapidly. Term infants peak at 3 to 5 days of life and preterm (< 37 weeks) peak at 5 to 7 days. When all the binding sites of albumin are filled, free bilirubin circulates in the plasma. This free bilirubin (immeasurable) can then migrate into the brain cells via the blood-brain barrier and cause kernicterus. Kernicterus is acute bilirubin encephalopathy. It is the bilirubin staining of neurons and neuronal injury, particularly of the basal ganglia.[24] It usually becomes evident during the first 5 days of life. The clinical symptoms are lethargy or irritability, hypotonia, paralysis of upward gaze, opisthotonic (backward arching) posturing, and spasticity. Characteristics of fully developed encephalopathy may not be clearly evident for several years. These include hearing loss, choreoathetoid cerebral palsy, gaze abnormalities, especially upward, and intellectual deficits but not usually severe.[23] The risk of kernicterus is believed to be 50% if serum bilirubin levels are ≥ 30 mg/dL.[23]

Causes of hyperbilirubinemia include:

❒ Increased RBC breakdown
  ▪ Blood incompatibilities (ABO, Rh)
  ▪ Sepsis
  ▪ Extravascular blood (bruising, cephalhematoma)
  ▪ Hemoglobinopathy (thalassemia)
❒ Interferences with conjugation
  ▪ Breast milk jaundice
  ▪ Drug reaction (aspirin, sulfa drugs compete with albumin-binding sites)
  ▪ Hypoxia, asphyxia (pH alters ability to bind with albumin)
  ▪ Hypothyroidism (decreased glucuronyl transferase synthesis)
  ▪ Metabolic disorders (glucose-6-phosphate dehydrogenase, pyruvate kinase deficiency)
❒ Abnormal bilirubin excretion
  ▪ Bowel obstruction

The early association of jaundice with breast-feeding is divided into two categories: breast-feeding failure jaundice and breast milk jaundice. Both types result in an exaggerated enterohepatic circulation of bilirubin—one through starvation and the other through altered milk chemistry.

❒ Breast-feeding failure jaundice:
  ▪ Early onset, starts 2 to 4 days of life and is typically seen in the emergency department
  ▪ Related to inadequate frequency of breast-feeding during early days of lactation, causing decreased caloric and fluid intake
  ▪ Can be avoided by frequent breast-feeding and avoidance of glucose and water supplementation[1]
❒ Breast milk jaundice:
  ▪ Starts 3 to 5 days of life and up to 3 to 6 weeks
  ▪ Occurs in 10% to 30% of breast-fed infants
  ▪ Bilirubin levels can be elevated up to 12 to 20 mg/dL for 2 to 3 months.
  ▪ Considered prolonged physiologic jaundice
  ▪ Related to ingredients in breast milk
    • ß-Glucuronidase (enzyme that deconjugates bilirubin) is present in breast milk. An enhanced enteric reabsorption and increased hepatic load of bilirubin results.[1]

The American Academy of Pediatrics[12] does not encourage the interruption of breast-feeding in healthy term infants. However, if the jaundice is severe and breast-feeding is interrupted, bilirubin levels should decrease rapidly. If levels do not decrease by 72 hours, breast milk jaundice is not the diagnosis, and further reasons of hyperbilirubinemia should be pursued. The goal in treating hyperbilirubinemia is prevention of kernicterus. Treatment includes the use of phototherapy, adequate hydration, possible infusion of intravenous immunoglobulin (IVIG) (Rh disease), and in severe cases an exchange transfusion.

Focused History

❒ Onset of jaundice
❒ Feeding amount and frequency
❒ Voiding and stooling patterns
❒ Blood types
❒ Familial history of jaundice
❒ Ethnicity (Asian population at higher risk)

Focused Assessment

❒ Assess the respiratory system.
❒ Assess the cardiovascular system.

- Assess skin turgor. Poor skin turgor indicates dehydration may be present.
- ❏ Assess the neurologic system.
  - Irritability may be noted.
- ❏ Assess the abdomen.
  - Palpate the abdomen. Hepatosplenomegaly may be found.
- ❏ Assess the integumentary system.
  - Assess skin color. Skin may be yellow/jaundiced in color.
  - Assess sclera. Sclera may be yellow in color.
  - Assess for bruising.
  - Assess for cephalhematoma.

Nursing Interventions

1. Assess and maintain airway, breathing, and circulation.
2. Obtain vascular access.
   - Initiate intravenous fluid therapy if dehydration is present.
   - Obtain blood samples for diagnostic testing.
     - Total/direct bilirubin
     - Complete blood cell count with reticulocyte count
     - Type and combs
     - Blood cultures
3. Initiate phototherapy if there is a delay in hospital admission in neonates with high levels of bilirubin.

4. Prepare for hospital admission or transfer and transport to a tertiary care facility (Chapter 8). Hospitalization is required for:
   - Intense phototherapy
   - Intravenous hydration
   - IVIG administration (Rh incompatibility)
   - Possible exchange transfusion
5. Arrange for home care with home phototherapy, if indicated.

Home Care and Prevention

- ❏ Expose the neonate to indirect natural sunlight.
- ❏ Feed the infant frequently.
- ❏ Use home phototherapy lights as ordered.
- ❏ Follow up with the primary care practitioner.

Conclusion

Proper assessment and intervention of neonates presenting to the emergency department are necessary to prevent serious complications of illnesses or congenital malformations that may have previously been undetected. Knowledge of physiologic differences and disease processes is necessary for emergency nurses, as they may be the first to recognize the signs and symptoms of these potentially very ill neonates. The rapid recognition and assessment of neonatal emergencies can lead to quick and proper treatment of this fragile patient population.

References

1. Tappero, E. P., & Honeyfield, M. E. (2003). *Physical assessment of the newborn.* Santa Rosa, CA: NICU Ink.

2. Davidson, M., London, M., & Ladewig, P. (2008). *Olds' maternal-newborn nursing & women's health across the lifespan* (8th ed.). Upper Saddle River, NJ: Pearson Prentice Hall.

3. Thilo, E., & Rosenberg, A. (2007). The newborn infant. In W. Hay, Jr., M. Levin, J. Sondheimer, & R. Deterding (Eds.), *Current diagnosis & treatment in pediatrics* (18th ed., pp. 7). New York: McGraw-Hill.

4. Gomella, T. L., Cunningham, M. D., Eyal, F. G., & Zenk, K. E. (2004). Hyperbilirubinemia, indirect (unconjugated hyperbilirubinemia). In T. Gomella (Ed.), *Neonatology: Management, procedures, on call problems, diseases, and drugs* (5th ed., pp. 247–250). New York: McGraw-Hill.

5. Edwards, M. S. (2006). The immune system: Postnatal bacterial infections. In A. Fanaroff & R. Martin (Eds.), *Neonatal-perinatal medicine. Diseases of the fetus and infant* (8th ed., pp. 791–877). St. Louis, MO: Mosby.

6. Short, M. S. (2004). Linking the sepsis triad of inflammation, coagulation and suppressed fibrinolysis to infants. *Advances in Neonatal Care, 4*(5), 258–273.

7. Witt, C. (2002). Management of neonatal infection, sepsis, and complications. In D. Askin (Ed.), *Infection in the neonate. A comprehensive guide to assessment, management, and nursing care* (2nd ed., pp. 143–162). Santa Rosa, CA: NICU Ink.

8. Brodsky, D., & Martin, C. (2003). Infectious disease and immunology. In Brodsky, D., & Martin, C. (Eds.), *Neonatal review* (pp. 182–194). Philadelphia: Hanley and Belfus.

References (continued)

9. Horns, K. M. (2004). Immunology and infectious disease. In T. Verklan & M. Walden (Eds.), *Core curriculum for neonatal intensive care nursing* (3rd ed., pp. 759–773). St Louis, MO: Elsevier.

10. Schrag, S., Gorwitz, R., Fultz-Butts, K., Schuchat, A. (2002). Prevention of perinatal group B streptococcal disease: Revised guidelines from CDC. *Morbidity and Mortality Weekly Report, 51*(RR11), 1–21.

11. Lynam, L., & Verklan, T. (2004). Neurologic disorders. In M. Verklan & M. Walden (Eds.), *Core curriculum for neonatal intensive care nursing* (3rd ed., pp. 821–857). St Louis, MO: Elsevier.

12. American Academy of Pediatrics. (2006). Respiratory syncytial virus. In L. Pickering, C. Baker, S. Long, & J. McMillan (Eds.), *Red book: 2006 report of the Committee on Infectious Disease* (27th ed., pp. 560–566). Elk Grove Village, IL: Author.

13. Bell, S. G. (2004). Neonatal and viral fungal infections. In D. Askin (Ed.), I*nfection in the neonate. A comprehensive guide to assessment, management, and nursing care* (pp. 83–128). Santa Rosa, CA: NICU Ink.

14. Satou, G. M., Herzberg, G. M., & Erikson, L. C. (2006). *Heart failure, congestive.* Retrieved August 26, 2008, http://www.emedicine.com/ped/TOPIC2636.HTM

15. Miller-Hoover, S. R. (2003). Pediatric and neonatal cardiovascular pharmacology. *Pediatric Nursing, 29*(2),105–113.

16. MacDonald, M. G., Seshia, M. M., & Mullett, M. D. (2005). *Averys neonatology: Pathophysiology and management of the newborn* (6th ed., pp. 539, 545). Philadelphia: Lippincott Williams & Wilkins.

17. Polin, R. A., & Spitzer, A. R. (2007). F*etal and neonatal secrets* (p. 438). St. Louis, MO: Mosby.

18. Nimavat, D. J., Sherman, M. P., Santin, R. L., & Porat, R. M. (2007). *Apnea of prematurity.* Retrieved August 22, 2008, from http://www.emedicine.com/ped/TOPIC1157.HTM

19. Verklan, M., & Walden, M. (2004). *Core curriculum for neonatal intensive care nursing* (3rd ed.). St. Louis, MO: Elsevier.

20. Brousseau, T. J., & Sharieff, G. Q. (2007). *Neonatal emergencies.* Retrieved August 15, 2008, from http://www.medscape.com/viewprogram/7232_pnt

21. Elenberg, E., & Vellaichamy, M. F. (2006). *Fluid and electrolytes.* Retrieved September 16, 2008, from http://www.emedicine.com/ped/topic1082/htm

22. Blackburn, S. T. (2003). *Maternal fetal and neonatal physiology—A clinical perspective* (2nd ed.). Philadelphia: Saunders.

23. Watson, R. L. (2004). Gastrointestinal disorders. In M. Verklan & M. Walden (Eds.), *Core curriculum for neonatal intensive care nursing* (3rd ed., pp. 643–702). St. Louis, MO: Elsevier Saunders.

24. Volpe, J. J. (2001). *Neurology of the newborn* (4th ed., pp. 398–411). Philadelphia: Saunders.

TEN

Common Chief Complaints

Kathleen Merkley, RN, MS, FNP

Introduction

Children present to the emergency department (ED) with a variety of vague, puzzling complaints. Some of these complaints may represent a minor illness or a normal variant, whereas others can represent a life-threatening condition. Whatever the cause, these symptoms often worry parents and challenge ED staff because the cause for the symptom(s) may not be readily apparent. Since young children cannot answer questions concerning history, signs, and symptoms they have been experiencing and cannot describe "where it hurts," ED staff must rely on their own assessment skills, as well as the information the parents are providing.

The purpose of this chapter is to discuss common pediatric complaints seen in the emergency department and their possible causes, as well as nursing assessments and care for such conditions. Because many of the conditions represented by these complaints have been discussed elsewhere in this book references to other chapters are noted.

Fever

Sir William Osler (1849–1919), who is considered the father of internal medicine, once said, "Humanity has but three great enemies: fever, famine, and war; of these by far the greatest, by far the most terrible, is fever."[1] Many practitioners would agree.

Fever is one of the most commonly encountered problems in pediatrics and accounts for 20% to 40% of all ED visits. It is frequently associated with other complaints and compels parents to seek outpatient treatment, often in the emergency department.[2] The majority of children who present to the emergency department with fever are younger than 3 years of age.

Pathophysiology

Fever is a complex process involving numerous responses to infectious and noninfectious inflammatory challenges affecting the autonomic and neuroendocrine systems. Fever may be produced by a number of endogenous and exogenous substances called pyrogens. Exogenous pyrogens (toxins and bacterial and viral products) produce fever by inducing endogenous pyrogens (cytokines). These cytokines include, but are not limited to, interleukin-1, interleukin-6, tumor necrosis factor, and interferon. The hypothalamus responds to these endogenous pyrogens by resetting itself to a higher level and sending out a signal that increases heat production and heat conservation to raise body temperature and release more cytokines.[3]

Cytokines cause numerous beneficial responses in the body such as peripheral vasoconstriction, a drop in vasopressin secretion, curtailed glucose metabolism, fever-induced anorexia, and direction of blood flow to deeper tissues. These responses provide a hostile environment for the invading bacteria or virus.[3]

Benefits of fever include altering the growth and replication of microorganisms; decreased serum levels of zinc, iron, and copper, which are favorite substrates for bacteria; lysosomal breakdown and autodestruction of bacterial and viral cell walls; increased lymphocytic transport and motility of polymorphonuclear neutrophils, which increases the immune response; enhanced phagocytosis; and increased interferon, which has antiviral properties.[3] In general, fever modulates the immune system to work more productively. Instead of being feared, fever should be respected and appreciated for the significant part it plays in fighting infection.[4]

Conditions Associated with Fever in Children

Common infectious causes of fever include otitis media, streptococcus infection, pharyngitis, urinary tract infections, pneumonia, cellulitis, and viral upper respiratory tract illness. Noninfectious causes include high external temperature, overbundling of children in winter months, malignancy, rheumatoid diseases, recent immunization administration, and teething. Life-threatening causes of fever are listed below classified by the affected body system:[4]

- ❏ Central nervous system
  - ▪ Bacterial meningitis
  - ▪ Encephalitis
- ❏ Upper airway
  - ▪ Epiglottitis
  - ▪ Retropharyngeal abscess
  - ▪ Croup
- ❏ Pulmonary
  - ▪ Pneumonia
  - ▪ Tuberculosis
- ❏ Cardiac
  - ▪ Myocarditis
  - ▪ Bacterial endocarditis
  - ▪ Suppurative pericarditis
- ❏ Gastrointestinal
  - ▪ Acute gastroenteritis
  - ▪ Appendicitis
  - ▪ Peritonitis
- ❏ Musculoskeletal
  - ▪ Necrotizing fasciitis
- ❏ Collagen-vascular
  - ▪ Acute rheumatic fever
  - ▪ Kawasaki disease
  - ▪ Stevens-Johnson syndrome
- ❏ Systemic
  - ▪ Meningococcemia
  - ▪ Bacterial sepsis
  - ▪ Rocky Mountain spotted fever
  - ▪ Toxic shock syndrome
- ❏ Miscellaneous
  - ▪ Thyrotoxicosis
  - ▪ Heat stroke
  - ▪ Acute malignancy

When is a Temperature Considered Febrile?

What is a normal temperature? Parents would offer numerous responses, but in reality 97 °F (36.2 °C) to 100.4 °F (38 °C) rectally may be considered normal. Peak diurnal variations may occur between 5:00 and 7:00 p.m. Hot weather, bundling, physical activity, ovulation, and digestion elevate temperature slightly as well. A child should be considered febrile when a rectal temperature of 100.4 °F or 38.0 °C is measured. An oral temperature is usually 0.6 °C lower than rectal temperature, and an axillary temperature is usually 1.1 °C lower than a rectal temperature. Rectal temperatures should be obtained in all infants 6 months and younger. After 6 months, tympanic thermometry is considered more accurate than mercurial or electronic axillary temperature measurements. It is also quick and safe, and thus it is recommended in the pediatric emergency setting.[5]

Focused History

Initially an adequate history should be obtained from the child's caregiver and should include the following questions:

- ❏ When was the onset of the fever?
- ❏ What has been the duration of the fever?
- ❏ What has the child's temperature been?
- ❏ How was the fever measured?
- ❏ What type and dosage of antipyretics and/or other treatments have been administered?
- ❏ When was the last dose of an antipyretic given?
- ❏ What was the child's response to the treatment?
- ❏ Is there an underlying medical problem (such as an immunocompromised status)?
- ❏ Has there been contact with any other infectious person?
- ❏ What current medications (especially antibiotics) has the child been taking?
- ❏ What is the child's current immunization status? Have there been any recent immunizations?
- ❏ Have there been associated symptoms such as vomiting, diarrhea, cough, feeding difficulties, change in cry, poor social interactions, or in the case of infants < 3 months of age possible apnea?
- ❏ For infants < 3 months of age, what is the birth history—including prematurity, maternal infections, congenital/chronic disease states, and previous diagnostic studies?

Focused Assessment

In addition to the assessment of airway, breathing and circulation, the physical assessment includes:

❏ Observation of the child's attentiveness, responsiveness to persons and objects

❏ Work of breathing, feeding activities, and age-related social appropriateness of social interactions and gross motor functions [4]

❏ Quality of the child's cry

❏ Skin color and degree of hydration

❏ Specific examination of focal sites of infections should be evaluated including assessment of the ears, nose, throat, neck, respiratory system, abdomen and skin

Fever causes an increase in the basal metabolic rate, boosting the respiratory rate, oxygen consumption, cardiac output, and fluid and caloric requirements.[3]

The increased respiratory rate results in amplified insensible water loss and this, coupled with the child's refusal to eat or drink, can contribute to dehydration. These symptoms are usually transient and treatable in an otherwise healthy child but those already compromised by a pre-existing condition, such as cardiac disease can be placed at an increased risk.

After a thorough assessment of whether there is evidence of any of the high-risk clinical findings below, appropriate diagnostic testing should be done. These high-risk clinical findings include:[4]

❏ Irritability or toxicity

❏ Altered sensorium

❏ Sniffing position—upper airway compromise

❏ Meningismus

❏ Petechiae/purpura

❏ Cyanosis, dyspnea, pallor

❏ Poor pulses, tachycardia, hypotension

Alpern and Henretig[4] suggest that if an infant or child is noted to be playing with toys or smiling at his or her parent, the febrile illness is most likely not an immediately life-threatening condition. However, the febrile infant or child who appears irritable and/or lethargic while being held by a parent before the examination has high probability of having a serious infection such as meningitis or sepsis. Futhermore, "The complaint or observation that a child's crying increases with parental attempts to comfort, is critical because 'paradoxical irritability' (the infant is quiet at rest, but cries when moved or comforted) is an important sign of meningitis in infancy."[4]

Nursing Interventions

If the child is immunocompromised (sickle cell disease, undergoing chemotherapy, or has had a solid organ, bone marrow or stem cell transplant) it should be assumed that the child is potentially septic and he or she should be treated appropriately. This includes initiating appropriate protocols or referring to a tertiary center for a higher level of care. In other cases, management of the child with fever should be determined by the child's age.

The Febrile Infant < 3 Months of Age

Febrile infants do not display obvious clinical symptoms or findings, making it difficult to discriminate between a minor febrile illness and one that is life threatening. Neonates (< 28 days old) and young infants (< 60 days old) are of particular concern and should be considered septic until proved otherwise.

To avoid missing a serious infection, guidelines have been developed to identify infants at high risk. All infants with temperatures of 100.4 °F (38 °C) or higher who are less than 2 months of age should receive full laboratory investigation for a serious infection (sepsis workup), including a complete blood cell count (CBC), blood culture, urinalysis, urine culture, and lumbar puncture with cerebrospinal fluid (CSF) analysis.[6] In addition, hospital admission and antibiotic therapy should be initiated for any infant < 1 month of age. Infants between 1 and 2 months with normal physical examination and laboratory values may be discharged home with careful observation after antibiotic therapy. Infants between 2 and 3 months of age should receive a CBC and urinalysis. If laboratory work and the physical examination results are within normal limits, the infant may be discharged home with antibiotic therapy.

A herpes simplex polymerase chain reaction study of the cerebrospinal fluid with associated antiviral therapy should be obtained if the infant has a history of herpes simplex virus exposure during delivery; skin, eye, or mouth lesions; respiratory distress; or seizures. If diarrhea is present, a stool sample should be sent for leukocytes and culture. If respiratory distress is noted, a chest radiograph should be obtained.

The Febrile Child Between 3 and 36 Months

After 3 months of age, infants have less risk of serious bacterial illness because of a more mature immune system. However, if they present with signs of focal infection (irritability, tachypnea, meningismus, flank tenderness), they should be carefully evaluated.[4] Children with high fevers, otitis media, and/or a febrile seizure should also be considered at risk for occult bacteremia. Evaluation for a urinary tract infection or pneumonia should also be considered.[7]

Treating Fever

Both parents and nurses have a strong desire to treat fever in children with an antipyretic. Ibuprofen and acetaminophen are safe medications to administer to children when given an appropriate dosage (Table 10.1). There is no scientific evidence that alternating these medications is helpful, and, in fact, it might contribute to a risk of antipyretic toxicity.[8] Aspirin should never be given to children because of its' association with Reye's syndrome. Some authors advocate that sponging with tepid water is effective if done in combination with antipyretics. One study did find that sponging offers very little fever reduction compared with antipyretic medication alone. Children who were sponged experienced increased discomfort, including crying, shivering, and goose bumps.[9]

TABLE 10.1 Antipyretic dosing	
Acetaminophen	*Ibuprofen*
10–15 mg/kg/dose	5–10 mg/kg/dose
Give no more than every 4 hours.	Give only to children > 6 months old.
Give no more than five doses in 24 hours.	Give no more often than every 6 hours.
Avoid in children with liver disease.	Give no more than four doses in 24 hours.
	Avoid in children with renal disease.

Home Care and Prevention

The following aspects of fever are important to discuss with family members:[10]

❒ Fever is the body's natural way of fighting infection. It creates a hostile environment in which bacteria and viruses have difficulty surviving.

❒ Fever is a sign of illness, not a disease.

❒ If fever causes discomfort the child may have acetaminophen or ibuprofen during waking hours. Do not alternate acetaminophen and ibuprofen.

❒ Medical care should be obtained if:

  ▪ The child is under 3 months of age and has a rectal temperature of 100.4 °F (38 °C) or higher.

  ▪ The child is irritable or lethargic.

  ▪ The fever has been present for more than 3 days.

  ▪ The child has symptoms of sore throat, ear pain, abdominal pain, or pain with urination.

  ▪ The child shows signs of dehydration.

  ▪ The child is having trouble breathing.

  ▪ The child has decreased activity.

❒ Aspirin or aspirin-containing products should never be given to a child, because of the risk of Reye's syndrome.

The Child with a Limp

A limp is best described as a walk favoring one leg. It can also be defined as an uneven, laborious gait, usually caused by pain, weakness, or deformity.[10] A limp in a child may be the effect of a benign or emergent condition. Management may range from offering parents reassurance to a surgical intervention, depending on the cause. A limp is most often caused by trauma and often resolves spontaneously. However, a life- or limb-threatening condition must be quickly and properly diagnosed. Some of the etiologies of limp are listed below:[11]

❒ Fractures (toddler's fractures, stress fractures, fractures from nonaccidental trauma)

❒ Cartilage diseases (such as Osgood-Schlatter and Legg-Calvé-Perthes disease)

❒ Sickle cell vaso-occlusive crisis

❒ Slipped capital femoral epiphysis

❒ Tumors (such as a spinal cord tumor and osteogenic sarcoma)

❒ Joint disorders (such as transient synovitis of the hip, septic arthritis, juvenile rheumatoid arthritis)

❒ Infection—osteomyelitis

❒ Soft tissue injury or disease (contusions, tendonitis, cellulitis)

❒ Neurologic disorders—spinal cord tumors, cerebral palsy, meningitis, epidural abscess

❒ Abdominal pathology—appendicitis, pelvic abscess, iliac adenitis

❒ The cause of the limp can be determined by obtaining a thorough history and physical examination. It may be necessary to obtain radiographs or perform diagnostic procedures such as an ultrasound scan. Limps of recent inception are more likely related to trauma or an acute infection, whereas a limp that has been present for a longer period may have a neuromuscular or developmental origin.[12]

Focused History

The following historical information should be obtained:

❒ Recent history of trauma

❒ Onset and duration of limp

- Presence and location of pain
- Associated symptoms (fever, rash, weight loss, anorexia, back pain, etc.)
- Recent history of viral or streptococcal illness
- Whether the limp improves or worsens with activity
- Recent history of new or increased sports activity
- Recent history of antibiotic administration (specifically quinolones)
- Family history (specifically of connective tissue disorders)

Focused Assessment

The focused assessment of a child with a limp should begin by observing the child's gait. This observation should be inconspicuous so that the child does not exaggerate the limp or feel ill at ease. Next the child should be asked to run, hop, and walk on his or her toes and heels.[12] The following actions should then be performed:

- Inspect the limbs and feet for swelling or deformity.
- Assess for strength, reflexes, and sensation in both lower extremities.
- Palpate the bones, muscles, and joints for tenderness and signs of inflammation (redness, warmth).
- Perform range of motion of the joints.
- Evaluate the hips for signs of pain.
- Evaluate the spine for pain. Several sources of hip or groin pain and limp originate in the lower spine, sacroiliac joints, pelvis, abdomen, and retroperitoneum.
- Examine the pattern of wear and size of the child's shoes to make sure they fit properly.[13]

Nursing Interventions

1. Prepare the child for radiographs to exclude fractures, avulsions, dislocations, and tumors.
2. Prepare the child for imaging studies if radiographs are inconclusive.
3. If the limp is associated with fever, a CBC, blood cultures, C-reactive protein level, and erythrocyte sedimentation rate should be obtained.

Home Care and Prevention

Aftercare instructions to the parents of a child who is being discharged home with a limp of unknown etiology should include the following:

- The child should be evaluated at his or her primary care provider's (PCP's) office or in the emergency department every 2 to 3 days if the limp persists. After 1 to 2 weeks with a diagnosis, the child should be referred to an orthopedic specialist.
- The child should return to the emergency department immediately for high fever or the inability to walk.

Inconsolable Crying

Crying is the process by which infants communicate with their environment and is how they signal an unmet need. Causes of crying may range from a benign to a life-threatening condition. Emergency department personnel often encounter infants who "won't stop crying"; therefore, an organized approach to this problem is required.[14]

The differential diagnosis for the crying infant is extensive. The etiology may range from a simple cause such as colic or teething to something as serious as an abdominal surgical emergency. Of special concern is the infant who presents with intractable crying of sudden onset and who is inconsolable despite feeding, rocking, or changing.[15] The most common causes associated with inconsolable crying are listed below:

- Infectious—otitis media, meningitis, sepsis, urinary tract infection, septic arthritis, osteomyelitis, pneumonia, Kawasaki disease
- Cardiovascular—supraventricular tachycardia, congestive heart failure, congenital heart disease
- Gastrointestinal—intussusception, volvulus, appendicitis, reflux esophagitis, constipation, incarcerated hernia, milk protein intolerance
- Traumatic—nonaccidental trauma, skeletal trauma, corneal abrasion
- Nutrition—underfeeding
- Metabolic—hyponatremia, hypernatremia, hypoglycemia
- Integument—diaper dermatitis, hair tourniquet
- Other—narcotic withdrawal, colic, teething

Focused History

The nurse should ascertain some basic history from the parents including:

- Baseline feeding, sleeping, and crying patterns
- Infectious symptoms (otitis media)
- Feeding intolerance, recent change in infant formula
- Vomiting, diarrhea, or signs of constipation
- Recent immunizations
- Possibility of a drug reaction, including maternal drugs that may be transferred via breast milk
- History (a suspicious history, including numerous ED

visits, or a high-risk social situation raises the concern for nonaccidental trauma)

❏ History of fever

❏ Response to Pain

Focused Assessment

In a classic study in 1991, Poole[16] reviewed infants who presented to a pediatric emergency department with a chief complaint of excessive, prolonged crying or a cause not apparent to the parents. He found that physical examination revealed a final diagnosis in 41% of cases and provided clues in another 13%.

The ED nurse should perform a thorough assessment. Carefully observing the infant for a short period of time before beginning the hands-on portion of the examination is helpful. Is the child making eye contact, playful, smiling, breathing normally, and moving all extremities? This information is not accessible once the child has been touched.[15]

The child should be totally undressed, and the skin should be carefully examined. Does the child have good tone and a strong suck? Is the anterior fontanelle tense or bulging? Is any trauma noted? Is there any drainage in the ear canals? Do the mouth and gums have any redness or swelling? Is the infant in respiratory distress? Is a heart murmur auscultated? Is the abdomen tender or distended? Is there tenderness on palpation of the arms and legs? Do the joints exhibit any redness, swelling, or limited range of motion? The goal of the physical assessment is to exclude serious illness. Certain findings if identified in the history or physical examination require further assessment. These concerning findings are listed in Table 10.2.[15]

Poole's 1991 study[16] identified two factors that helped predict the seriousness of an infant crying if the physical examination was not diagnostic: (1) Infants who ceased crying before or during the initial evaluation were unlikely to have a serious underlying illness, and (2) if infants persisted with excessive crying after the initial examination, that was predictive of a serious underlying process.

Laboratory Evaluation

After a careful history and assessment, screening laboratory tests tend to add very little to the diagnosis of a crying infant with the exception of a urinalysis and urine culture. Fluorescein staining of the corneas and eversion of the upper eyelids are recommended and also may lead to a diagnosis.[14] Further consideration of laboratory evaluation is made in light of clinical findings (a rigid abdomen—CBC; dehydration—electrolytes). An infant with a temperature equal to or greater than 100.4 °F (38.0 °C) who is younger than 12 weeks deserves a septic

evaluation.

TABLE 10.2 Concerning Findings Associated with Serious Illness
Fever (100.4 °F, 38.0 °C rectally) or hypothermia in infants < 12 wk of age
Receiving antibiotic therapy
Bilious or projectile emesis
Maternal drug abuse
Not feeding or gaining weight
Recent head trauma
Apnea or cyanosis
Heart rate > 220 beats/minute
Lethargy
Paradoxical irritability
Poor perfusion
Poor tone, jittery
Petechiae or bruising
Respiratory distress
Retinal hemorrhages
Full or bulging fontanelle
Not moving an extremity
Abdominal tenderness or rigidity
Bloody stools

Nursing Interventions

1. Nursing care will depend on the cause of the crying but will always include reassurance and support for the parents.

2. Review techniques to comfort the infant (Chapter 3).

3. Provide support to the parents.

4. Refer the family to a home health nursing agency to assist them with some parenting issues, as well as to assess the family situation to determine whether the parents are at risk for abusing their child.

5. Prepare the family for admission to the hospital, if necessary.

Home Care and Prevention

Careful follow-up is important if the infant is discharged home. Arrangements should be made for a repeat examination within 24 hours in the emergency department or PCP's office. Parents should be encouraged to return sooner for resumption of intractable crying or other concerns.

Abdominal Pain

Abdominal pain is a common complaint in the pediatric population, particularly among school-aged children and adolescents. The etiology of abdominal pain in children varies from serious, life-threatening emergencies to less serious disorders such as colic, constipation, or emotional disturbances. Certain conditions are more commonly associated with specific age groups. Table 10.3 lists the most common etiologies of abdominal pain, by age groups.[17]

TABLE 10.3 Common Etiology of Abdominal Pain by Age Group
Infancy (< 2 years of age)—colic, GERD, gastroenteritis, intussusception, incarcerated hernia
Preschool (2–5 years of age)—gastroenteritis, UTI, appendicitis, pneumonia, sickling syndrome, viral syndromes, constipation, Henoch-Schönlein purpura, intussusception
School age (> 5 years of age)—gastroenteritis, appendicitis, UTI, constipation, diabetes mellitus, testicular torsion, sickling syndrome, nonorganic or psychogenic illness
Adolescent—gastroenteritis, gastritis, colitis, trauma, constipation, appendicitis, UTI, pneumonia, pelvic inflammatory disease, epididymitis, nonorganic or psychogenic illness

Notes: GERD = gastroesophageal reflux disease; UTI = urinary tract infection.

Etiologies of Abdominal Pain in Children

Respiratory illnesses are also linked with abdominal pain. Children with asthma exacerbations and associated muscle fatigue (from increased use of chest wall and abdominal muscles) may complain of abdominal pain. Pneumonia with subsequent muscular pain or diaphragmatic irritation resulting from coughing can also cause abdominal pain.[17]

Unexplained pain in the lower abdomen is a common complaint among adolescent girls and creates a challenge. Although the cause is usually benign and self-limited, occasionally a serious underlying disorder exists. It is important to determine whether the pain is gynecologic in nature.

Recurrent abdominal pain with no known cause can also be related to a psychosocial problem, and a thorough history will help to identify stressors in school, family, or other personal circumstances.

The pathophysiology of abdominal pain depends on the underlying disorder or disease. The type and character of the pain can provide important clues to the underlying pathology. Three neural pathways transmit visceral, somatic, and referred pain:[18]

- *Visceral pain* emanates from the intra-abdominal organs with visceral peritoneum. Visceral pain is characterized as deep or diffuse pain that is colicky or crampy and is often difficult to localize.
- *Somatic or parietal pain* emanates from the abdominal wall, base of the mesenteries, or the diaphragm. It is characterized by sharp, localized pain that is often intense.
- *Referred pain* is pain that emanates from a site distant to the involved organ or area of pathosis. It may be sharp and localized or characterized as a distant ache.

Focused History

The history of the child with abdominal pain includes the following:

- Onset: When did the pain begin, and is it associated with anything in particular?
- Characteristics: Sharp, dull, diffuse, localized, or colicky
- Past Medical history: Underlying disorders, such as cystic fibrosis or sickle cell disease; previous abdominal surgery
- Signs and symptoms associated with the pain: Vomiting (bilious or not), diarrhea, constipation, fever, the presence of blood in the stool or emesis, abdominal distention, or the presence of a mass
- Changes in feeding patterns or appetite
- Changes in level of activity
- Treatments attempted at home: Enemas or the administration of an antiemetic, a cathartic, pain medication, herbal remedy, or an antipyretic
- Social history: The adolescent female should be interviewed separately to determine whether any psychosocial stress is present. Also, determine whether any new stressor (such as new school, recent divorce) exists.

Focused Assessment

The following assessment parameters should be performed:

- Evaluate the infant's or child's appearance and level of activity.
- Evaluate the abdomen: Symmetry, signs of abdominal distention, the presence of obvious masses, visible

bowel loops, and the presence of peristaltic waves.

❏ Auscultate bowel sounds in all four quadrants. Ask the child to point to the most painful area of the abdomen before palpation.

❏ Palpate nonpainful areas before palpating the most painful area. Evaluate for pain to palpation and rebound tenderness.

Nursing Interventions

1. Identify and use an appropriate pediatric pain scale.

2. Make the child as comfortable as possible.

3. Advocate for and administer analgesics as needed.

4. Provide distraction to help relieve pain.

5. Monitor vital signs and pain response.

6. Obtain pregnancy test in menarcheal females.

7. Instruct child and family about continuing to receive nothing by mouth.

Home Care and Prevention

❏ Instruct parents to follow up either in the emergency department or with the primary health care provider if the cause of the abdominal pain is not found.

❏ Explain any dietary restrictions or changes.

❏ Describe signs and symptoms that would require the family to return to the emergency department.

❏ Provide a referral to a child psychologist, if appropriate.

Other Common Complaints Specific to Infants

Other complaints specific to infants that are usually not serious, but are of concern to parents, are listed below, along with their common causes and ED nursing considerations.

Hematochezia or Hematemesis

Causes

Intestinal wall breakdown secondary to ischemia or hemorrhagic necrosis caused by emergent conditions, such as volvulus or Meckel's diverticulum, or by a milk protein intolerance.

❏ Viral gastroenteritis (rotavirus)

❏ Maternal blood, swallowed either at birth or from cracked nipples

❏ The causes of unusual bleeding may represent unique neonatal circumstances that, because of early

discharge, were not discovered at birth, including:

- Hemorrhagic disease of the newborn, which is a self-limiting disorder resulting from a deficiency of vitamin K-dependent clotting factors

- Hemophilia

- Thrombocytopenia resulting from maternal anti-platelet antibodies

Nursing Interventions

1. A careful history and assessment will help to determine the cause. Generally these children should be seen urgently to rule out serious causes. Parents are usually very concerned to see blood.

2. The mother's nipples may have to be evaluated for cracks and bleeding.

3. This condition should be triaged emergently. Assessment should include birth history, trauma, illness, and medications. Look for bruising, cephalhematoma, enlarged liver, spleen, presence of petechiae, and jaundice. If the cause is a long-term condition, such as hemophilia, the parents will need follow-up and referral for counseling (Chapter 23).

4. A complete examination is necessary to rule out more serious conditions.

Common Cold

Causes

The common cold is caused by a virus. Immunologically immature neonates are prone to frequent episodes of colds. Prematurity, congenital disorders such as heart disease, and chronic illnesses increase the susceptibility of the neonate to colds.

Nursing Interventions

1. There is no cure for the common cold, and antibiotics are not helpful. Educating parents about why antibiotics are not needed for a respiratory virus may be required.

2. Supportive care with good follow-up is the only treatment for the common cold, which will usually resolve in about 2 weeks. Parents, however, must be told to return to the emergency department or PCP if there is a decrease in their child's intake or if a fever or other symptoms develop.

3. Parents should be reminded that over-the-counter cold medications have been identified as harmful and should not be administered.

4. Infants may have a respiratory syncytial virus, not just a common cold. They may be experiencing significant

respiratory distress, a condition not seen in infants with cold viruses. See Chapter 14 for further information.

Constipation

Causes

Constipation may be caused by dietary changes, motility disorders, viral illnesses, and anal fissures. Congenital disorders may cause chronic constipation.

Nursing Interventions

1. Constipation usually requires minimal interventions unless an obstruction is suspected.

2. Abdominal and rectal examinations are performed, and a stool sample for occult blood is obtained. Digital rectal stimulation may be necessary to relieve an impaction. Enemas are a last resort and are rarely used.

3. A surgical or gastrointestinal consultation may be necessary for chronic constipation.

Home Care and Prevention

Parents and children should be taught about the importance of a diet high in fiber, adequate hydration, and developing set times to use the bathroom.

Gynecomastia (Enlarged Breasts in the Newborn with Secretion of Milky Fluid)

Causes

❐ Influence of maternal estrogen from pregnancy or from maternal ingestion of birth control pills while breast-feeding may persist for several weeks, but usually resolves in 2 weeks. If it does not resolve, further evaluation will be necessary. The mother may have to be instructed to stop using birth control pills.

Usually no treatment is necessary as this condition resolves on its own in 10 days.

Bleeding/Draining from Circumcision

Cause

Active bleeding, excessive swelling, and an odorous purulent discharge are abnormal. If a plastibel™ is used, a small amount of bloody drainage may be observed when it falls off.

Nursing Interventions

1. Provide hygiene instructions to the parents.

2. A complete septic workup may be necessary if signs and symptoms of infection or fever are present.

3. Surgical consultation may be necessary.

Conclusion

A variety of nonspecific complaints may bring infants and young children to the emergency department. Many of these complaints are self-limiting and benign; however, some may represent serious conditions that need immediate attention. Fever is the most common complaint in the pediatric patient and results in many ED visits. It is important to remember that the ED nurse should focus on the history, the assessment, and the parents' perceptions of the child's condition. Parents know their child better than anyone else does and can often provide clues to their illness. An awareness of common causes of frequent complaints will help the nurse to focus his or her assessment and provide proper interventions.

References

1. Bryan, C. S. (1996). Fever, famine and war: William Osler as an infectious disease specialist. *Clinical Infectious Disease, 23*(5), 1139–1149.

2. Blum, F. C. (2002). Fever. In J. Marx., R. Hockberger, & R. Walls (Eds.), *Rosen's emergency medicine* (pp. 116–118). St. Louis, MO: Mosby.

3. Sugerman, R. A. (2006). Structure and function of the neurologic system. In K. McCance & S. Huether (Eds.), *Pathophysiology: The biological basis for disease in adults and children* (pp. 411–454). Philadelphia: Lippincott Williams & Wilkins.

4. Alpern, E. R., & Henretig, F. M. (2006). Fever. In G. Fleisher, S. Ludwig, & F. Henretig (Eds.), *Textbook of pediatric emergency medicine* (pp. 295–306). Philadelphia: Lippincott Williams & Wilkins.

5. El-Radhi, A. S., & Patel, S. (2006). An evaluation of tympanic thermometry in a paediatric emergency department. *Emergency Medicine Journal, 23*(1), 40–41.

6. Corneli, H. M. (2000). Beyond the fear of fever. *Clinical Pediatric Emergency Medicine, 1*, 94–101.

7. Crocetti, M. T., & Serwint, J. R. (2005). Fever, separating fact from fiction. *Contemporary Pediatrics, 22*(1), 34–42.

8. Sharber, J. (1997). The efficacy of tepid sponge bathing to reduce fever in young children. *American Journal of Emergency Medicine, 15,* 188–192.

9. Baraff, L. J., Schriger, D. L., Bass, J. W., Fleisher, G. F., Klein, J. O., McCracken, G. H., et al. (1993). Practice guideline for the management of infants and children 0 to 36 months of age with fever without source. *Pediatrics, 92,* 1–12.

10. Brady, M. (1993). The child with a limp. *Journal of Pediatric Health Care, 7,* 226–230.

11. Chung, S. M. (1979). Identifying the cause of acute limp in childhood. *Clinical Pediatrics, 13,* 769–772.

12. Kost, S. (2006). Limp. In G. Fleisher, S. Ludwig, & F. Henretig (Eds.), *Textbook of pediatric emergency medicine* (pp. 415–420). Philadelphia: Lippincott Williams & Wilkins.

13. Teach, S. J. (1998). Pediatric disorders: Limp. In R. Aghababian, E. Allison, G. Braen, G. Fleisher, & J. McCabe (Eds.), *Emergency medicine: The core curriculum* (pp. 630–634). Philadelphia: Lippincott Williams & Wilkins.

14. Merkley, K. (2006). The crying infant in the emergency department. *Journal of Emergency Nursing, 32*(6), 535–540.

15. Bolte, R. G. (1998). Intractable crying in infancy and early childhood. In R. Aghababian, E. Allison, G. Braen, G. Fleisher, & J. McCabe (Eds.), *Emergency medicine: The core curriculum* (pp. 622–630). Philadelphia: Lippincott Williams & Wilkins.

16. Poole, S. R. (1991). The infant with acute, unexplained, excessive crying. *Pediatrics, 88,* 450–455.

17. Ruddy, R. (2006). Pain—abdomen. In G. Fleisher, S. Ludwig, & F. Henretig, (Eds.), *Textbook of pediatric emergency medicine* (pp. 469–475). Philadelphia: Lippincott.

18. Boenning, D. A., & Klein, B. L. (1997). Gastrointestinal disorders. In R. Barkin (Ed.), *Pediatric emergency medicine, concepts in clinical practice* (pp. 240–264). St. Louis, MO: Mosby-Year Book.

ELEVEN

Pain Assessment and Management

Tracy Ann Pasek, RN, MSN, CCRN, CIMI
Erin K. Wright, RN, BSN
Catherine E. Campese, RN, MSN, CRNP

"When I hear a baby's cry of pain change to a normal cry of hunger, to my ears, that is the most beautiful music"

—*Albert Schweitzer, 1903*

Introduction

Pain is often the chief complaint for children who are admitted to the emergency department (ED).[1-3] Over the past 15 years, substantial attention has been given to pediatric pain.[4] Regulatory bodies, as well as professional societies, are embracing pediatric pain as a care priority as evidenced in standards and consensus documents. National awareness initiatives are helping to set the standard for pain care while empowering health care consumers.[5,6] Numerous pain assessment scales are available, many of which have been translated into various languages. Moreover, procedural sedation guidelines, advanced pharmacologic therapies, and never-before-considered nonpharmacologic modalities have changed the assessment and management of pain. Despite these advancements, children's pain remains inadequately assessed and undertreated in most emergency departments today.[4]

Pain may be a symptom of illness or injury, or it may be the result of a procedure or treatment. Regardless of its etiology, pain must be alleviated and, optimally, eliminated. When children report pain, it is crucial to believe them and initiate prompt pain relief measures, thereby promoting trust among children, families, and emergency nurses. This chapter provides important information to the emergency nurses who are leading efforts to advocate for infants, children, and adolescents who hurt.

Anatomy and Physiology of Pain

Children perceive, interpret, and respond to pain differently from adults. Pain must be considered as more than just a cluster of physiologic mechanisms and responses. Psychological, biologic, and/or sociologic factors are part of the nature of pain. Cognitive, developmental, and environmental factors further contribute to the totality of the pain experience for patients.

The pain response begins with a noxious stimulus—one that causes actual or potential tissue damage—activating a nociceptor or basic pain receptor. Tissue damage may result from laceration, fracture, or compression of cutaneous (e.g., skin), somatic (e.g., bone), or visceral (e.g., spleen) structures. Children with multisystem trauma may experience pain on all of these levels. For example, a child who requires a thoracotomy with chest tube insertion would experience cutaneous pain (skin incision) with somatic pain (manipulation of the pleura). When tissue is damaged, biochemical mediators such as potassium, substance P, prostaglandin, histamine, and serotonin are released and may activate or sensitize the nociceptors.[7]

Nociceptors

Nociceptors are located in the skin, subcutaneous tissues, periosteum, joint surfaces, arterial walls, fascia, muscles, and viscera.[8] Nociceptors are classified according to the relationship of their activity to pain sensation, and there are three basic classifications:[8]

❑ The conduction velocity of their parent axon (e.g., myelinated A-delta afferents versus unmyelinated C-fiber afferents)

❑ The stimulus modalities that evoke a response (e.g., mechanical, thermal, or chemical)

❑ The temporal characteristics of their response to a stimulus (e.g., rapid versus slow)

Mechanoreceptors are stimulated by mechanical pressure forces such as a crush injury, resulting in the release of chemical mediators that stimulate chemoreceptors and intensify the pain response.[8] Thermoreceptors are stimulated by heat or cold.[8] Their activation modulates the pain response as with application of heat or cold to a sports injury (See Gate Control Theory section). Chemoreceptors are stimulated by chemical mediators, which depolarize the nerve endings and decrease the receptor thresholds.[8] For example; the pain associated with inflammation arises because of chemoreceptor stimulation. Polymodal nociceptors are stimulated by mechanical, chemical, and thermal sensations.[8]

Nerve Fibers

After nociceptor stimulation, the pain stimulus is transmitted to the spinal cord via A-delta or C-fiber afferents.[7] A-delta fibers are fine, moderately myelinated fibers that rapidly conduct the pain stimulus.[7] These fibers transmit the sharp, pricking sensations produced by mechanical stimuli and produce the pain associated with acute conditions.[7] Pain arising from the stimulation of A-delta fibers is easily localized. Localized pain may be readily distinguished by a patient. The pain threshold varies by individual.

C fibers are smaller, unmyelinated, and polymodal. These fibers produce pain that is described as dull, aching, or burning.[7] C fibers are found mostly in the skin and deep tissues.[7] Stimulation of the C fibers causes the pain reported with chronic conditions.[7]

Depending on the age of the child, myelination may be incomplete. However, myelin does not need to be present for pain impulse transmission to occur. So, the traditional thinking that children do not experience pain as intensely as their adult counterparts is a myth. Myelin—a protein sheath—enhances the smoothness and rapidity of pain impulse transmission. For example, infants demonstrate a delayed physical pain response with a needle stick procedure. It takes longer for the noxious stimulus to reach the brain because of incomplete myelination, but this is balanced by the shorter distance the pain impulses have to travel in babies and small children. The delayed pain response must not be mistaken for less intense pain perception. Pain is no less significant for babies than it is for older children, adolescents, or adults.

Pain Impulse Transmission

Pain impulses that arise in peripheral structures (e.g., an injured muscle in the leg) travel via a peripheral nerve to the dorsal horn in the spinal cord[9] (Figure 11.1). The fibers bifurcate, synapse, and cross to the opposite side of the spinal cord.[9] At this point they are transferred to a second nerve that travels up the cord to a part of the brain called the thalamus.[9] From the thalamus, projections go to the somatosensory cortex, where pain is perceived and localized and the pain severity is recorded.[9] Other projections go to the limbic system in the area of the anterior cingulated gyrus, where the emotional reaction to pain is produced.[9] Amplified pain happens when there is an enhanced transmission of nerve impulses from peripheral structures (e.g., muscle, skin) to the brain; pain amplification is sometimes referred to as "central sensitization."[8,9]

The synapse is a major site of pain amplification.[9] A synapse is the chemical junction between an incoming nerve from the periphery and an outgoing nerve to the brain.[9] Glutamate and substance P are two chemicals or neurotransmitters released at this junction.[9] Neurotransmitters attach to receptors on the second nerves, thereby stimulating nerve impulses that travel to the brain.[9]

Gate Control Theory

Although the details are still being sorted out, the gate control theory has endured much debate and has stood the "test of time."[11] The theory states that the transmission of pain from the peripheral nerve through a "gate" in the substantia gelatinosa to central cells is subject to modulation by both intrinsic neurons and controls emanating from the brain.[11–13] Pain stimuli can be transmitted only if the gate is open or partially open.[11–13] The gate can be closed by competing stimuli or inhibitory impulses.[11–13] C fibers activate excitatory systems, which excite output cells.[11–13] Output cells have their activity controlled by the balance of A fibers that modulate or inhibit pain.[11–13] Nurses can apply these principles of plasticity—pain signaling and modulating—if they understand that pain may not be the same in all circumstances. Massage, for example, may modulate pain in the spinal cord by decreasing stress hormone levels. Psychological factors may attenuate pain by modulating activity in the descending pain projections from the brain stem.[7]

A new and evolving pain theory is the neuromatrix theory. It posits that pain is a multidimensional experience produced by neurosignature patterns of nerve impulses—a "feeling" state.[12] As an extension of the gate control theory, the focus of the neuromatrix theory is the brain, not just peripheral fibers, and it encompasses cognitive-evaluative, motivational-affective, and sensory-discriminative systems.[12]

The Effects of Pain

Pain has both short- and long-term effects on children. Neonates who undergo procedures with inadequate analgesia may have changes in their responses to and perceptions of painful experiences that extend into later life.[14–19] Substandard pain control during oncology procedures leads to significantly increased pain scores for subsequent painful procedures.[14,20] Posttraumatic stress disorder may be a negative outcome associated with procedures or stressful medical experiences for which pain and sedation are inadequately managed.[14,21] Fear of needles is an example of a negative outcome from poorly managed pain and anxiety with earlier needle-related procedures. Many adults trace their fear and avoidance

Figure 11.1 Pathways of Pain

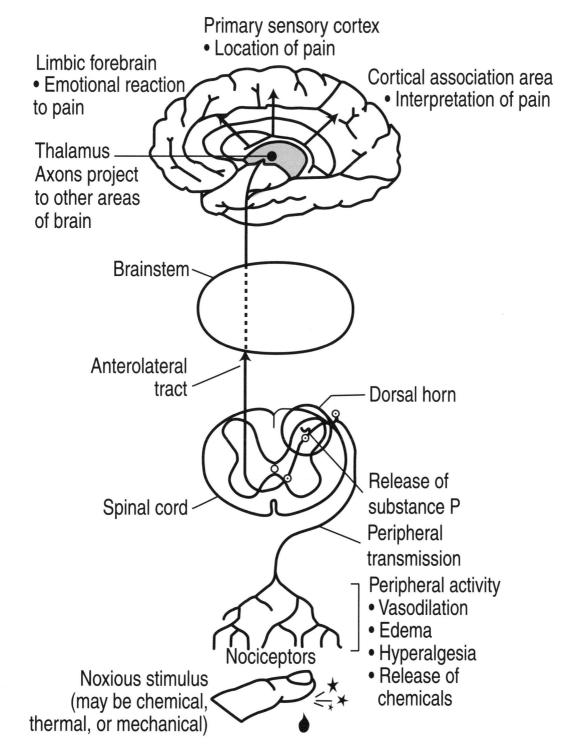

Primary sensory cortex
• Location of pain

Limbic forebrain
• Emotional reaction to pain

Cortical association area
• Interpretation of pain

Thalamus
Axons project to other areas of brain

Brainstem

Anterolateral tract

Dorsal horn

Spinal cord

Release of substance P
Peripheral transmission

Peripheral activity
• Vasodilation
• Edema
• Hyperalgesia
• Release of chemicals

Nociceptors

Noxious stimulus (may be chemical, thermal, or mechanical)

Used with permission from Copstead-Kirkhor, L. C., & Banasik, J. (2005). *Pathophysiology* (3rd ed.). Philadelphia: Saunders.

of necessary medical care to poorly managed painful procedures in their childhood.

The Pain History

The purpose of a pain history (Table 11.1) is twofold. First, the pain history provides information about pain the child is currently experiencing as a presenting symptom to the emergency department. Second, a thorough pain history provides insight about how the child and family cope at home with pain—either related to normal play (e.g., falling) or related to recurrent pain conditions (e.g., intractable headache). The latter enables the emergency nurse to support coping behaviors while the child is in the hospital and understand the meaning of pain for the child and family (e.g., surmountable, catastrophic).[22, 23] Families must provide the history for preverbal or nonverbal children. Verbal children can provide the history with additional information from the family as needed.

TABLE 11.1 Sample Pain History

What to include in a pain history	*Patient/family response*
Location, onset, duration of pain	Right side of head, after football practice, 3 days; "The pain is a killing pain. My head beats when I look at the sun."
Recent/current behavioral changes	Crying, shielding eyes from light, wore sunglasses on the way to the hospital; drowsiness, not finishing dinner, reports nausea
Previous painful experiences	Buckle fracture last year to left thumb
What do you do to help with the pain?	Likes parents nearby; stuffed toys
Home treatments/ remedies before this admission	Rest, acetaminophen, dark room
Effectiveness of treatments, if used	Splashing water on face for drowsiness, partially effective
Effectiveness of coping strategies, if used	Soft pillow for head ineffective
Pain assessment scale used in past, if any	None; "Right now it's a 7/10 when it hurts the most."

The Recognition and Assessment of Pain in Children

Assessment is the first step in recognition and treatment of pain.[14, 24] A self-report should be obtained and should be the primary source of pain intensity estimates whenever possible. Pain assessment scales evolved because of the need to quantify a subjective experience. Several well-validated pain assessment scales exist for children as young as 3 years.[14] Children as young as 3 years and who do not have developmental or communication impairment may be able to quantify pain using simple pain scales.[25–27]

This section provides emergency nurses with an overview of both self-report and observational (behavioral) pediatric pain assessment scales. Included are scales with their respective instructions, validity information, and practical tips specific to clinical application (Table 11.2).

TABLE 11.2 Guidelines for Using Self-Report Pain Assessment Scales with Patients

If a pain assessment scale must be explained to a child more than twice, then it is possible the child is unable to understand how to use it (e.g., stage of development, fear).

When explaining a pain assessment scale to a child for the second time, vary the description only slightly, not drastically.

If a child is unable to use a self-report pain assessment scale, it is important the child does not feel that he or she has failed (e.g., a test).

A pain assessment score is one piece of information. Pain scores do not necessarily reflect patient behaviors (e.g., a child rates sickle cell pain as 9/10, but is not crying or grimacing).

It is acceptable to change pain assessment scales on the basis of changes in a child's clinical condition, for example. Nurses must identify the source of the pain intensity score by means of documentation. Furthermore, there should be no attempt made to equate pain intensity values between scales (e.g., a 2/10 on the FLACC equals a 2/10 on the Wong-Baker FACES Pain Rating Scale. This approach is incorrect.).

A pain assessment scale that exists on a continuum without faces (e.g., a numerical rating scale 0–10) is too abstract for a very young child. Even older children and adolescents prefer a pain assessment scale with faces.

Avoid asking children, "Are you sure?" or "Really?" when they report pain. Children should not feel as though they are being doubted.

A variety of self-report pain assessment scales should be available. Children should be able to see and point to them. Describing a self-report scale (e.g., walking into an examination room and asking, "How is your pain on a scale of 0 to 10?") will not elicit accurate information from younger children.

Anxiety is a component of the pain experience. If a child cries despite the application of a topical local anesthetic for venipuncture, this does not mean pain management has failed. The child may be crying because of fear or sickness.

TABLE 11.2 Guidelines for Using Self-Report Pain Assessment Scales with Patients

Parents may be able to use self-report pain assessment scales with their children. This will free the nurse to do other tasks while fostering parental participation in care. A parent getting the child's self-report is separate from having the parent provide an estimate of the child's pain. It is acceptable for the child's report of pain intensity to be different from the parent's estimate.

Know the primary and secondary demographic of the hospital. Select pain assessment scales that are validated for those populations (e.g., white, African American).

Self-Report Pain Assessment Scales

Visual analog scales consist of a premeasured vertical or horizontal line, where the ends of the line represent the extreme limits of pain intensity.[28] The child is asked to select a point or make a mark along the line to indicate the intensity of his or her pain. Visual analog scales vary according to presence or absence of divisions along the line (e.g., ruler markings), units of measure (e.g., centimeters), and the names of the anchors (e.g., "no pain," "worst pain").[28] Visual analog scales are easy and quick to use. They should be reserved for use with calm patients who are age 8 years and older.[28, 29]

Color Analog Scale

The Color Analog Scale is a visual analog scale employing the creative use of color and width.[28,30] It appears similar to a thermometer and is graded in shades of red (Figure 11.2). Children are able to slide a marker up and down the scale to show how much pain they feel. Corresponding pain ratings are on the reverse side for clinicians to see. The scale is vertical with the anchor "no pain" at the bottom and the anchor "most pain" at the top. It is easy to see how different scale positions would reflect different levels in pain intensity. This scale is useful for children between 5 and 12 years of age who present to the emergency department with acute pain.[30–33] Despite availability and established validity, pain assessment scales employing color are seldom used in emergency departments.

Figure 11.2 Color Analog Scale

Colored Analog Scale staff side (left) and child side (right)

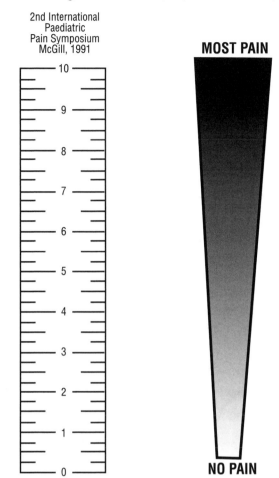

Reprinted with permission from McGrath, P. A., Seifer, C. E., & Speechley, K. N. (1996). A new analogue scale for assessing children's pain: An initial validation study. *Pain, 64,* 435–443.

The Faces Pain Scale—Revised

The Faces Pain Scale—Revised (FPS-R) was adapted from the Faces Pain Scale and has been well validated in many studies[34, 35] (Figure 11.3). The FPS-R may be used with children across the ages 4 through 16 years for the assessment of disease, procedural, and surgical/trauma-related pain.[35] The scale is intended to measure how children feel inside, not how their face looks.[36] Clinicians must remember to show only the faces to children, not the numbers. The absence of smiles and tears may be advantageous in comparison with other scales using faces.[35] Complete instructions are available and the FPS-R is available in 33 translations.[36]

The Wong-Baker FACES Pain Rating Scale

The Wong-Baker FACES Pain Rating Scale (Figure 11.4) is popular and widely used in clinical practice.[28, 37] The Wong-Baker FACES Pain Rating Scale is also available in multiple translations, but there is limited psycho-

Figure 11.3 The Faces Pain Scale—Revised

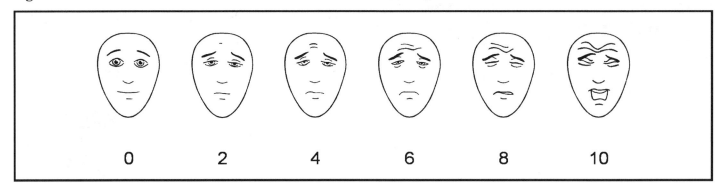

Note: This is a smaller sample of the actual scale. For further instructions and translations on the correct use of the scale in order to get valid responses, please go to http://www.painsourcebook.ca

From Hicks, C. L., von Baeyer, C. L., Spafford, P. A., van Korlaar, I., & Goodenough, B. (2001). The Faces Pain Scale–Revised. Toward a common metric in pediatric pain measurement. *Pain, 93,* 173–183. Reprinted with permission of the International Association for the Study of Pain®.

metric evidence for these translations.[28] Advantages of this scale are that it is simple to use and requires minimal instruction.[38] It can be obtained via the Internet, making it cost-effective.[39] Children have indicated preference for the Wong-Baker FACES Pain Rating Scale relative to other measures (e.g., the Color Analog Scale).[40] One disad-vantage of the Wong-Baker FACES Pain Rating Scale is that children's pain ratings appear to be influenced by the smiling "no pain" anchor. Pain ratings tend to be higher relative to faces scales with neutral "no pain" anchors (e.g., FPS-R).[40, 41] Smiling faces may be more appropriate as measures of pain affect rather than pain intensity.[41]

Figure 11.4 Wong-Baker FACES Pain Rating Scale

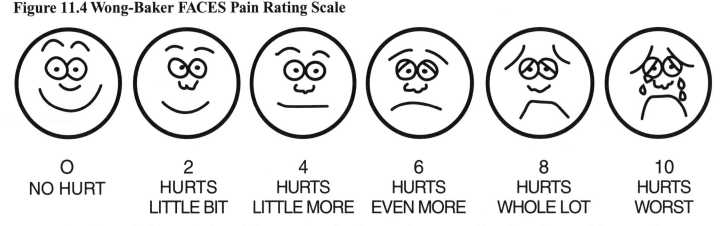

Note: This is a smaller sample of the actual scale. For further instructions and translations on the correct use of the scale in order to get valid responses, please go to http://www.painsourcebook.ca

The FACES Pain Rating Scale is recommended for children 3 years of age and older. To administer, the nurse points to each face stating the words to describe the pain intensity. The nurse asks the child to choose the face that best describes the pain and records the appropriate pain rating number.[37,39]

Used with permission from Hockenberry, M. J., Wilson, D., & Winkelstein, M. L. (2005). *Wong's Essentials of Pediatric Nursing* (7th ed., pp. 1259). St. Louis, MO: Mosby.

Observational (Behavioral) Pain Assessment Scales

Observational or behavioral pain assessment scales should be used for children who are preverbal (e.g., infants) or nonverbal (e.g., cognitively impaired children, patients who have an artificial airway).[42] Nurses should be highly suspicious regarding the presence of pain when caring for children who are developmentally nonverbal (e.g., a child with mental retardation and cerebral palsy). These children may have a higher burden of pain from frequent medical/surgical procedures (e.g., treatment for pancreatitis, orthopedic procedures).[43] Currently, there is no observational pain assessment scale suitable for children with chronic pain (e.g., sickle cell disease) because pain behaviors habituate or dissipate over time despite self-report of pain.[42] When a child who lives with pain reports high pain intensity and that score does not match what most consider to be "typical" pain behavior, pain assessment is quite challenging and complex.

The FLACC Pain Assessment Tool

The FLACC Pain Assessment Scale is an easy-to-use scale that measures pain by quantifying pain behavior with scores ranging from 0 (no pain behaviors) to 10 (most possible pain behaviors).[44] Five categories of behavior are included in the scale: (F) facial expression, (L) leg movement, (A) activity, (C) cry, and (C) consolability.[44,45] The FLACC supplements emergency nurses' clinical judgment by providing a standardized method of interpreting and quantifying pain behaviors in preverbal patients, a vulnerable population.[44] It is useful for assessing pain from surgery, trauma, cancer, or other painful disease processes.[44] It also provides an objective method for evaluating treatments provided to relieve pain regardless of whether a child received opioid or nonopioid analgesics.[44] The FLACC is supported as a standard pain assessment tool for all preverbal children in a health care facility.[44]

Neonatal Pain, Agitation, and Sedation Scale

The Neonatal Pain, Agitation, and Sedation Scale (N-PASS) is a newer scale that is validated for preterm and term babies in the neonatal intensive care unit (Figure 11.5).[46] Many hospitals use the same pain assessment scale for infants across all care settings. There may be applicability of the N-PASS for infants who are acutely ill who are admitted to emergency departments. It is less complex than some other infant pain assessment scales, which may increase the likelihood of it being used by busy nurses in a fast-paced environment. The scale considers endotracheal intubation, neuromuscular blockade, and neurologic depression, which are issues for babies who present with acute illness and progress to critical condition. The diagram of the infant face that demonstrates

Figure 11.5 N-PASS: Neonatal Pain, Agitation, & Sedation Scale

Assessment Criteria	Sedation		Sedation/Pain	Pain/Agitation	
	−2	−1	0	1	2
Crying Irritability	No cry with painful stimuli	Moans or cries minimally with painful stimuli	No sedation/pain signs	Irritable or crying at intervals Consolable	High-pitched or silent-continuous cry Inconsolable
Behavior State	No arousal to any stimuli No spontaneous movement	Arouses minimally to stimuli Little spontaneous movement	No sedation/pain signs	Restless, squirming Awakens frequently	Arching, kicking Constantly awake or Arouses minimally/ no movement (not sedated)
Facial Expression	Mouth is lax No expression	Minimal expression with stimuli	No sedation/pain signs	Any pain expression intermittent	Any pain expression continual
Extremities Tone	No grasp reflex Flaccid tone	Weak grasp reflex ↓ muscle tone	No sedation/pain signs	Intermittent clenched toes, fists or finger splay Body is not tense	Continual clenched toes, fists, or finger splay Body is tense
Vital Signs HR, RR, BP, SaO_2	No variability with stimuli Hypoventilation or apnea	< 10% variability from baseline with stimuli	No sedation/pain signs	↑ 10–20% from baseline SaO_2 76–85% with stimulation— quick ↑	↑ > 20% from baseline SaO_2 ≤ 75% with stimulation—slow ↑

Figure 11.5 N-PASS: Neonatal Pain, Agitation, & Sedation Scale

Premature pain assessment:

+ 3 if < 28 weeks gestation/corrected age

+ 2 if 28–31 weeks gestation/corrected age

+ 1 if 32–35 weeks gestation/corrected age

© Loyola University Health System, Loyola University Chicago, 2008 (Rev. 3/28/08)

Assessment of Sedation

Sedation is scored in addition to pain for each behavioral and physiological criteria to assess the infant's response to stimuli

Sedation does not need to be assessed/scored with every pain assessment/score

Sedation is scored from $0 \rightarrow -2$ for each behavioral and physiological criterion, then summed and noted as a negative score ($0 \rightarrow -10$)

A score of 0 is given if the infant has no signs of sedation, does not under-react

Desired levels of sedation vary according to the situation

"Deep sedation" $\rightarrow$ goal score of -10 to -5

"Light sedation" $\rightarrow$ goal score of -5 to -2

Deep sedation is not recommended unless an infant is receiving ventilatory support, related to the high potential for hypoventilation and apnea

A negative score without the administration of opioids/sedatives may indicate:

The premature infant's response to prolonged or persistent pain/stress

Neurologic depression, sepsis, or other pathology

Assessment of Pain/Agitation

Pain assessment is the fifth vital sign—assessment for pain should be included in every vital sign assessment

Pain is scored from $0 \rightarrow +2$ for each behavioral and physiological criteria, then summed

Points are added to the premature infant's pain score based on the gestational age to compensate for the limited ability to behaviorally communicate pain

Total pain score is documented as a positive number ($0 \rightarrow +13$)

Treatment/interventions are suggested for scores > 3

Interventions for known pain/painful stimuli are indicated before the score reaches 3

The goal of pain treatment/intervention is a score ≤ 3

More frequent pain assessment indications

Indwelling tubes or lines which may cause pain, especially with movement (e.g., chest tubes) $\rightarrow$ at least every 2–4 hours

Receiving analgesics and/or sedatives $\rightarrow$ at least every 2–4 hours

30–60 minutes after an analgesic is given for pain behaviors to assess response to medication

Post-operative $\rightarrow$ at least every 2 hours for 24–48 hours, then every 4 hours until off medications

Pavulon/Paralysis

It is impossible to behaviorally evaluate a paralyzed infant for pain

Increases in heart rate and blood pressure at rest or with stimulation may be the only indicator of a need for more analgesia

Figure 11.5 N-PASS: Neonatal Pain, Agitation, & Sedation Scale

Analgesics should be administered continuously by drip or around-the-clock dosing

Higher, more frequent doses may be required if the infant is post-op, has a chest tube, or other pathology (such as necrotizing enterocolitis [NEC]) that would normally cause pain

Opioid doses should be increased by 10% every 3–5 days as tolerance will occur without symptoms of inadequate pain relief

Scoring Criteria

Crying/Irritability

− 2 → No response to painful stimuli:

- No cry with needle sticks
- No reaction to endotracheal tube (ETT) or nares suctioning
- No response to care giving

− 1 → Moans, sighs, or cries (audible or silent) minimally to painful stimuli, e.g., needle sticks, ETT or nares suctioning, care giving

0 → No sedation signs or No pain/agitation signs

+ 1 → Infant is irritable/crying at intervals—but can be consoled

- If intubated—intermittent silent cry

+ 2 → Any of the following:

- Cry is high-pitched
- Infant cries inconsolably
- If intubated—silent continuous cry

Behavior/State

− 2 → Does not arouse or react to any stimuli:

- Eyes continually shut or open
- No spontaneous movement

− 1 → Little spontaneous movement, arouses briefly and/or minimally to any stimuli

- Opens eyes briefly
- Reacts to suctioning
- Withdraws to pain

0 → No sedation signs or No pain/agitation sign

+ 1 → Any of the following:

- Restless, squirming
- Awakens frequently/easily with minimal or no stimuli

+ 2 → Any of the following:

- Kicking
- Arching
- Constantly awake
- No movement or minimal arousal with stimulation (not sedated, inappropriate for gestational age or clinical situation)

Figure 11.5 N-PASS: Neonatal Pain, Agitation, & Sedation Scale

Facial Expression

− 2 → Any of the following:

- Mouth is lax
- Drooling
- No facial expression at rest or with stimuli

Brows: lowered, drawn together

Forehead: bulge between brows, vertical furrows

Eyes: tightly closed

Cheeks: raised

Nose: broadened, bulging

Nasolabial fold: deepened

Mouth: open, squarish

Facial expression of physical distress and pain in the infant

Reproduced with permission from Wong DL, Hess CS: Wong and Whaley's Clincial Manual of Pediatric Nursing, Ed. 5, 2000, Mosby, St. Louis

−1 → Minimal facial expression with stimuli

0 → No sedation signs or No pain/agitation signs

+ 1 → Any pain face expression observed intermittently

+ 2→ Any pain face expression is continual

Hummel, P., Puchalski, M., Creech, S., & Weiss, M. (2008). Clinical reliability and validity of the N-PASS: Neonatal pain, agitation, and sedation scale. *Journal of Perinatology, 28*(1), 55–60.

facial expression in response to pain may be helpful to new nurse orientees and nurses without prior pediatric experience.

Pain Management

Pharmacologic Pain Interventions

Analgesics decrease or alleviate pain without causing a loss of consciousness.[47] Analgesics fall into two general classes: opioid and nonopioid. Opioids are classified by their affinity to bind with lipids. Opioids that tend to penetrate and bind with lipids are considered lipophilic. Opioids that have less affinity for lipids are considered hydrophilic. The degree to which an opioid is hydrophilic or lipophilic will influence the rate of absorption through the mucosa and entry into the central nervous system via the bloodstream.[48] Opioids are not a substitute for anxiolytic or amnestic agents.[49]

A simple way to explain opioids to children and families is that these medications alter the child's perception of a painful stimulus rather than affecting the source or site of pain. Avoid using the term "narcotic" with children and families as it conjures notions of "street use" and fears of addiction.

Oral analgesics (e.g., acetaminophen) are often adequate to manage mild pain at triage. Children and families may understand that nonopioid oral analgesics treat pain at the source or site by reducing inflammation.

Analgesics

Ketorolac[50]

Therapeutic category: Analgesic; nonnarcotic; nonsteroidal anti-inflammatory agent (NSAID)

Use: Short-term (≤ 5 days) for management of moderate to severe pain. There is a role for IV ketorolac in the management of postconcussive migraine and sickle cell disease vaso-occlusive crisis in the emergency department; consider individualized management plan for the latter

Contraindications: Hypersensitivity to ketorolac, aspirin, other NSAIDs or any component; history of peptic ulcer disease; recent or history of gastrointestinal bleeding; advanced renal disease or renal failure; third-trimester pregnancy; nursing mothers; before or during major surgery; suspected or confirmed cerebrovascular bleeding

Morphine Sulfate[50]

Therapeutic category: Analgesic; narcotic

Use: Relief of moderate to severe acute and chronic pain; pain of myocardial infarction; relieves dyspnea of acute left ventricular failure and pulmonary edema; preanesthetic medication. There is a role for intravenous morphine (bolus; patient-controlled analgesia) in the management of sickle cell disease vaso-occlusive crisis in the emergency department; consider individualized management plan

Contraindications: Hypersensitivity to morphine sulfate; increased intracranial pressure; severe respiratory depression; severe liver or renal insufficiency; acute or severe asthma; gastrointestinal obstruction, especially suspected or known paralytic ileus

Fentanyl[50] **(Table 11.3)**

Therapeutic category: Analgesic; narcotic; general anesthetic

Use: Sedation; relief of pain; preoperative medication; adjunct to general or regional anesthesia; management of chronic pain (transdermal); oral transmucosal: Breakthrough pain in patients tolerant to opioid therapy and who are currently receiving opiates for persistent pain; usually for cancer patients

Contraindications: Hypersensitivity to fentanyl or any component; increased intracranial pressure; severe respiratory depression; severe liver or renal insufficiency; paralytic ileus; transdermal form is not indicated for acute pain management

Hydromorphone[50]

Therapeutic category: Analgesic; narcotic

Use: Management of moderate to severe pain; antitussive at lower doses

Contraindications: Hypersensitivity to hydromorphone or any component; paralytic ileus. There is a role for intravenous hydromorphone in the management of sickle

TABLE 11.3 Overview of Pharmacologic Agents for Procedural Sedation

Drug	Class	Adverse Events	Pediatric Advanced Life Support (PALS) Recommendations Including Reversal Agent(s)
Etomidate	Hypnotic	Nausea Vomiting Respiratory compromise: Brief oxygen desaturation with rare occurrence of bradycardia, transient apnea Transient hypotension Cortisol depression Myoclonus Procedural failure	Safe for pediatric procedural sedation
Fentanyl	Opioid	Nausea Vomiting Respiratory depression Itching Rare occurrence of chest wall rigidity	Safe for pediatric procedural sedation Reversal agents: Naloxone, naltrexone
Midazolam	Benzodiazepine	Hypotension Paradoxical excitability	Safe for pediatric procedural sedation Reversal agent: Flumazenil
Ketamine	Dissociative	Low incidence of hypoxemia Low incidence of laryngospasm Emergence reaction	Safe for pediatric procedural sedation alone or in combination with a benzodiazepine for brief painful procedure

TABLE 11.3 Overview of Pharmacologic Agents for Procedural Sedation

Drug	Class	Adverse Events	Pediatric Advanced Life Support (PALS) Recommendations Including Reversal Agent(s)
Methohexital	Barbiturate	Hypotension Hypoventilation Apnea	Safe for nonpainful procedures or diagnostic studies
Pentobarbital	Barbiturate/sedative	Vomiting Coughing Prolonged sedation Respiratory compromise: Oxygen desaturation Circumoral cyanosis Irritability Paradoxical reaction Emergence reaction	Safe for pediatric procedural sedation for nonpainful procedures Works best for children <8 years
Propofol	Sedative	Hypoxia Hypoventilation Apnea	Safe for nonpainful or painful procedures if used in combination with an opioid

American College of Emergency Physicians. (2004). Clinical policy: Evidence-based approach to pharmacologic agents used in pediatric sedation and analgesia in the emergency department. *Annals of Emergency Medicine, 44*(4), 342–377.

cell disease vaso-occlusive crisis in the emergency department; consider individualized management plan

Topical Local Anesthetics

A number of topical local anesthetics (TLAs) are available for use with children (Table 11.4). They vary according to:

❐ Active ingredient

❐ Concentration

❐ Onset of action

❐ Duration of action

❐ Indications (e.g., intact skin)

❐ Delivery system (e.g., cream, patch)

❐ Excipients (inert substance)

❐ Cost

Analgesic protocols empower emergency nurses to advocate for their patients in advance of procedures such as the need for intravenous cannulation anticipated at triage.[14,51–53] Despite the availability of TLAs and protocols for their use, pain management for intravenous cannulation remains inadequate.[54]

Procedural Sedation Agents

Pediatric procedural sedation is the process of using medications to induce the infant, child, or adolescent into a state of relaxation and cooperation while experiencing a potentially painful and frightening procedure.[55–57] Formerly referred to as "conscious sedation," procedural sedation is now described as existing on a continuum ranging from minimal sedation to general anesthesia.[55–57] The American Society of Anesthesiology (ASA) levels of sedation/analgesia are defined below.[55–57]

Minimal sedation: Also known as anxiolysis. A drug-induced state during which the patient responds normally to verbal command. Cognitive function and coordination may be impaired. The patient's breathing and cardiovascular function are unaffected.

Moderate sedation/analgesia: A drug-induced depressed consciousness during which the patient responds purposefully to verbal command, either alone or accompanied by light tactile stimulation. The patient maintains a patent airway with adequate spontaneous ventilation. Cardiovascular function is usually maintained.

Deep sedation/analgesia: A drug-induced depression of consciousness during which the patient cannot be

Table 11.4 Guidelines for Topical Anesthesia					
Types of Topical Anesthesia	*Usage Guidelines*	*Onset*	*Effectiveness*	*Contraindications/ Complications*	*Application Method*
TAC	Nonmucosal skin lacerations to the face and scalp	Effective 10 to 30 minutes after application	As effective as lidocaine used for lacerations	Rare severe toxicity Seizures Sudden cardiac death No longer supported for use secondary to toxicity issues	2 to 5 mL (1 mL per cm of laceration) applied to wound with cotton or gauze for 10 to 30 minutes
LET	Nonmucosal skin lacerations up to 5 cm in length	20 to 30 minutes	As effective as lidocaine for scalp and face lacerations, but less effective on extremity lacerations	No severe adverse effects reported Involvement of mucous membranes Grossly contaminated wound Allergy to amide anesthetics	1 to 3 mL directly applied to wound for 15 to 30 minutes
Lidocaine 4% cream (L.M.X.⁴®)	Nonmucosal skin Intravenous (IV) cannulation Venipuncture Implantable central venous device access Subcutaneous catheter insertion Lumbar puncture Abscess drainage Joint aspiration	20 to 30 minutes	May depend on the duration of application	Emergent needle stick procedure (e.g., intravenous cannulation) Allergy/ sensitivity to local anesthetics of the amide type Nonintact skin Remove if skin irritation develops	Cleanse site with soap and water. Apply over a minimum of 2 IV sites or 1 other procedure site. Do not disturb site(s) for a minimum of 20 minutes. Protect with a transparent dressing, if needed. Avoid ingestion by patient.

Notes: TAC = Tetracaine, Adrenaline (epinephrine) and cocaine; LET = Lidocaine, epinephrine, and tetracaine

easily aroused, but responds purposefully following repeated or painful stimulation. Independent ventilatory function may be impaired. The patient may require assistance to maintain a patent airway. Spontaneous ventilation may be inadequate. Cardiovascular function is usually maintained.

General anesthesia: A drug-induced loss of consciousness during which the patient is not able

to be aroused, even to painful stimuli. The ability to maintain independent ventilatory function is often impaired. Assistance is often required in maintaining a patent airway. Positive pressure ventilation may be required because of depressed spontaneous ventilation or drug-induced depression of neuromuscular function. Cardiovascular function may be impaired.

A number of medications used alone or concomitantly

are available for procedural sedation (Table 11.3). Qualified professionals with advanced life support skills must be present to care for patients on all points along the sedation continuum. It is important to remember that outcomes and movement along the sedation continuum are less predictable when more than one drug is administered to a child. Appropriate equipment and reversal agents must be immediately available. Emergency nurses must be cognizant of and adhere to hospital-specific procedural sedation guidelines.

The four classes or therapeutic categories used for procedural sedation include analgesics, benzodiazepines, sedatives, and dissociative agents.[58]

Inhalation Agent

Nitrous oxide has been shown to be safe when used in pediatric procedural sedation as part of an established comprehensive sedation program.[59] Advantages to nitrous oxide include the provision of rapid onset and offset of sedation.[59]

Nitrous oxide is administered via a demand unit or constant flow device that mixes 50% nitrous oxide and 50% oxygen. Both systems require an exhalation valve that empties into the unit. The exhalation valve protects clinicians from exposure to the gas. Hospital-specific procedural sedation guidelines should clearly define necessary equipment and monitoring parameters. There is growing evidence to support using concentrations greater than 50% nitrous oxide and safe use of nitrous oxide in general, for children aged 1 to 3 years.[59]

Nonpharmacologic Pain Interventions

There is a plethora of nonpharmacologic therapies available to reduce pain and anxiety for children. Nonpharmacologic interventions can be effective either alone or in combination with analgesics. Nurses should select nonpharmacologic interventions based on the child's development, preference, and availability. Nonpharmacologic interventions are not time-consuming in the fast-paced emergency department. The success of these interventions is dependent on effective communication and planning among the emergency team, child, and family. The Child Life Specialist is a crucial member of the emergency team relative to pain management.[60] Emergency nurses should partner with Child Life Specialists to prevent and relieve children's pain and fear.

Distraction

Memories of pain and distress can influence subsequent anxiety, distress, and/or coping during medical procedures.[61,62] Cartoon distraction has been found to reduce young children's distress during procedures of relative short duration such as venipuncture.[62,63] Televisions and CDs along with videotapes of cartoons and children's programs are essential resources for the emergency nurse. "Treasure chests" are creative child-friendly storage containers for squeeze balls, windmills, kaleidoscopes, and bubbles. All of these are valuable methods to help a child re-focus in preparation for and during painful procedures.

Holding and Positioning

Parent holding and upright positioning may reduce distress with intravenous cannulation in young children.[64] The traditional physical restraint of horizontally positioned patients by multiple care providers must be abandoned. When parents are guided to hold their children in a less vulnerable upright position, the positive outcomes may include increased intravenous cannulation success, enhanced parental participation in care, improved patient and family satisfaction, and, most important, increased patient comfort.[64]

Massage

Massage has a role in pain management for children.[65] The stress hormone cortisol decreases and serotonin and dopamine levels increase following massage.[66] Positive touch counterbalances negative stimuli. Some parents may know how to massage their children and can employ this technique in the emergency department. Massage is not without risk for injured or hemodynamically unstable children. The nurse should obtain a physician order and parent consent prior to teaching massage to families. Nursing documentation should support patient response to and tolerance of massage.

Breast-feeding

Painful procedures potentially disrupt maternal-child bonding and feeding schedules for babies. The measurement of physiologic pain indicators (e.g., heart rate, respiration rate, blood pressure, and oxygen saturation) along with behavioral pain indicators in infants (e.g., cry duration, proportion of time crying, and facial actions) has demonstrated a decreased response to pain with breast milk or breast-feeding.[67,68] Breast-feeding should be encouraged for term or preterm infants who require short painful procedures in the emergency department (e.g., venipuncture, heel lance).[67,68] Breast milk may be offered orally when breast-feeding is not possible.

Compared with artificial formulas, breast milk contains higher concentrations of tryptophan, a precursor of melatonin.[69] Melatonin is associated with increased concentrations of beta endorphins and could possibly be a mechanism for the nociceptive effects of breast milk.[70] Because breast milk and breast-feeding are natural, they are not associated with oral aversion.[71] Neither breast milk nor breast-feeding completely eliminates pain.[71,72]

Sucrose Analgesia

When breast milk or breast-feeding are not options, 24% oral sucrose solution provides safe, effective nonpharmacologic analgesia to infants before and during painful procedures (e.g., heel lance, venipuncture, and lumbar puncture). When optimally offered 2 minutes before a procedure, oral sucrose solution may decrease crying episodes and cry duration in response to pain.[52,73–77] Sucrose analgesia is an adjunct to analgesics (e.g., opioids) and nondrug interventions, such as nonnutritive sucking (e.g., pacifier) and swaddling, thereby mimicking endogenous opioid and nonopioid systems.[76] Sucrose analgesia may be used for neonates up to 1 month old or an adjusted age of 3 months.[52,73–77] Effectiveness with older infants is possible. Sucrose analgesia may be contraindicated with hyperglycemia. Well-intentioned, compassionate nurses may offer sucrose to babies who are to receive nothing by mouth (NPO), considering hunger as painful. Because sucrose increases salivation, verify with a physician whether or not this is a safe intervention in select circumstances (e.g., anticipated surgical procedure). Oral sucrose solution is a food substance, yet some pharmacy departments control it. Regardless of whether oral sucrose solution is stocked in the emergency department or within a pharmacy department, nurses should work to make it readily accessible for use.

Environmental Modification

Modification of the environment can enhance the success of nonpharmacologic interventions. Encouraging families to remain in the examination room during painful procedures will facilitate child and family coping. Families, however, will need support with how to help their child.[22,23] Measures to promote relaxation (e.g., dimming lights, decreasing noise) may be helpful to reduce anxiety and fear associated with pain.

Music

Music therapy has been shown to be an efficacious and valid treatment option for children experiencing pain related to a variety of diagnoses and procedures (e.g., in combination with analgesics for a patient with burns).[78] Music is a form of sensory stimulation, which provokes responses as a result of the familiarity, predictability, and feelings of security associated with it.[78] Music therapy is associated with decreased anxiety, increased comfort,

patient participation in treatment, and decreased length of stay.[78] The relationship between a patient and music therapist is what makes music therapy unique and special. In the absence of a music therapist, provide developmentally appropriate music choices to patients (e.g., CDs, iPods, audiotapes).

Conclusion

The time is right for emergency nurses to advocate for children with pain. Clinical resources are abounding, and the expectation for pain management excellence will only increase on the part of the health care consumer. Medical pain management is offering increased use of advanced therapies, and nurses must keep pace with this progress. Emergency nurses can extend their clinical expertise to initiatives that will increase nurses' influence over process improvement work, clinical innovation, and patient satisfaction relative to pain (Tables 11.5 and 11.6). Few things are more fulfilling than striving to make a child comfortable and the family knowing you have done your absolute best.

The authors gratefully acknowledge Dr. Carl L. von Baeyer, Professor Emeritus of Psychology & Associate Member in Pediatrics, University of Saskatchewan, Canada, for his expert review.

TABLE 11.5 Ways to Take Action for Improved Pain Care in the Emergency Department

Obtain valid and reliable pain assessment scales for your patient population.

Join or form a hospital pain steering committee.

Designate a pain resource nurse to represent your department.

Integrate pain into education opportunities (e.g., new graduate nurse orientation, newsletters, in-service education sessions).

Identify at least one pain-related process improvement indicator.

Build a pain library for your department.

Participate in collaborative pain projects with physicians, pharmacists, and Child Life Specialist.

Join a local or national nursing pain society.

Write and test nursing pain protocols or guidelines.

Ask your manager to routinely share patient/family satisfaction scores related to pain.

Join an electronic mailing list devoted to pediatric pain.

TABLE 11.6 Pain Resources for Pediatric Emergency Nurses

The recognition and assessment of acute pain in children: Recommendations. Royal College of Nursing Institute, 1999. Retrieved November 28, 2008, from http://painsourcebook.ca/pdfs/pps68.pdf

American Academy of Pediatrics & Canadian Paediatric Society. (2000). Prevention and management of pain and stress in the neonate. Committee on Fetus and Newborn, Committee on Drugs, Section on Anesthesiology, Section on Surgery and Canadian Paediatric Society, Fetus and Newborn Committee. [Policy statement]. *Pediatrics, 105*(2), 454–461.

American Pain Society. (2003). *Principles of analgesic use in the treatment of acute pain and cancer pain* (5th ed). Glenview, IL: Author.

Anand, K. J. S., & International Evidence-Based Group for Neonatal Pain. (2001). Consensus statement for the prevention and management of pain in the newborn. *Archives of Pediatric and Adolescent Medicine, 155,* 173–180. Retrieved November 28, 2008, from http://archpedi.ama-assn.org/cgi/reprint/155/2/173.pdf

American Pain Society & American Academy of Pediatrics. (2001). The assessment and management of acute pain in infants, children, and adolescents. [Position statement]. Retrieved November 28, 2008, from http://ampainsoc.org/advocacy/pediatric2.htm

References

1. Cordell, W. H., Keene, K. K., Giles, B. K., Jones, J. B., Jones, J. H., & Brizendine, E. J. (2002). The high prevalence of pain in emergency medical care. *American Journal of Emergency Medicine, 20,* 165–169.

2. Rupp, T., & Delaney, K. A. (2004). Inadequate analgesia in emergency medicine. *Annals of Emergency Medicine, 43,* 494–503.

3. Drendel, A. L., Brousseau, D. C., & Gorelick, M. H. (2006). Pain assessment for pediatric patients in the emergency department. *Pediatrics, 117*(5), 1511–1518.

4. Khan, A. N., & Sachdeva, S. (2007). Current trends in the management of common painful conditions of preschool children in United States pediatric emergency departments. *Clinical Pediatrics, 46*(7), 626–631.

5. Anesiva, Inc. (2008). *Manageivpain.com.* Retrieved November 28, 2008, from http://www.manageIVpain.com

6. The Joint Commission. (2008). *Speak up initiatives.* Retrieved November 28, 2008, from http://www.jointcommission.org/PatientSafety/SpeakUp

7. Edwards, A. D. (2002). Physiology of pain. In B. St. Marie (Ed.), *American Society of Pain Management Nurses core curriculum for pain management nursing* (pp. 121–145). Philadelphia: Saunders.

8. Caterina, M. J., Gold, M. S., & Meyer, R. A. (2005). Molecular biology of nociceptors. In S. Hunt & M. Klotzenburg (Eds.), *The neurobiology of pain* (pp. 1–34). Oxford, England: Oxford University Press.

9. Bennet, R. (2002). *Understanding pain.* Retrieved November 28, 2008, from http://www.myalgia.com/Pain_amplification/Overview.htm

10. Purves, D., Augustine, G. J., Fitzpatrick, D., Katz, L. C., LaMantia, A. S., McNamara, J. O., et al. (2001). *Central pain pathways: The spinothalamic tract.* Retrieved November 28, 2008, from http://www.ncbi.nlm.nih.gov/books/bv.fcgi?rid=neurosci.section.682

11. Dickenson, A. H. (2002). Gate control theory of pain stands the test of time. *British Journal of Anaesthesia, 88*(6), 755–757.

12. Melzack, R. (2001). Pain the neuromatix in the brain. *Journal of Dental Education, 65*(12), 1378-1382.

13. Charlton, J. E. (2005). Anatomy and physiology. In J. C. Charlton (Ed.), *Core curriculum for professional education in pain* (pp. 1–4). Seattle: IASP Press.

14. Zempsky, W. T., Cravero, J. P., & Committee on Pediatric Emergency Medicine, Section on Anesthesiology and Pain Medicine. (2004). Relief of pain and anxiety in pediatric patients in emergency medical systems. *Pediatrics, 114*(5), 1348–1356.

References (continued)

15. Taddio, A., Goldbach, M., Ipp, M., Stevens, B., & Koren, G. (1995). Effect of neonatal circumcision on pain response during vaccination in boys. *Lancet, 345,* 291–292.

16. Taddio, A., Katz, J., Ilersich, A. L., & Koren, G. (1997). Effect of neonatal circumcision on pain response during subsequent routine vaccination. *Lancet, 349,* 599–603.

17. Grunau, R. E., Whitfield, M. F., & Petrie, J. (1998). Children's judgments about pain at age 8–10 years: Do extremely low birthweight (≤ 1000g) children differ from full birthweight peers? *Journal of Child Psychology and Psychiatry, 39,* 587–594.

18. Johnston, C. C., & Stevens, B. J. (1996). Experience in a neonatal intensive care unit affects pain response. *Pediatrics, 98,* 925–930.

19. Grunau, R. V., Whitfield, M. F., & Petrie, J. H. (1994). Pain sensitivity and temperament in extremely low-birth-weight premature toddlers and preterm and full term controls. *Pain, 58,* 341–346.

20. Weisman, S. J., Bernstein, B., & Schechter, N. L. (1998). Consequences of inadequate analgesics during painful procedures in children. *Archives in Pediatric and Adolescent Medicine, 152,* 147–149.

21. Boileau, B., & Robaey, P. (1997). Posttraumatic stress symptoms and medical procedures in children. *Canadian Journal of Psychiatry, 42,* 611–616.

22. Wintgens, A., Lipani, T. A., & Walker, L. S. (2006). Children's appraisal and coping with pain: Relation to maternal ratings of worry and restriction in family activities. *Journal of Pediatric Psychology, 31*(7), 667–673.

23. Hermann, C., Hohmeister, J., Zohsel, K., Ebinger, F., & Flor, H. (2007). The assessment of pain coping and pain-related cognitions in children and adolescents: Current methods and further development. *Journal of Pain, 10,* 802–813.

24. Ducharme, J. (2000). Acute pain and pain control: State of the art. *Annals of Emergency Medicine, 35,* 592–603.

25. Fanurik, D., Koh, J. L., Harrison, R., Conrad, T. M., & Tomerlin, C. (1998). Pain assessment in children with cognitive impairment: An exploration of self-report skills. *Clinical Nursing Research, 7*(2), 103–119.

26. Spagrud, L. J., Piira, T., & von Baeyer, C. L. (2003). Children's self report of pain intensity. *American Journal of Nursing, 103*(12), 62–64.

27. Herr, K., Coyne, P. J., Key, T., Manworren, R., McCaffery, M., Merkel, S., et al. (2006). Pain assessment in the nonverbal patient: Position statement with clinical practice recommendations. *Pain Management Nursing, 7*(2), 44–52.

28. Stinson, J. N., Kavanagh, T., Yamada, J., Gill, N., & Stevens, B. (2006). Systematic review of the psychometric properties, interpretability and feasibility of self-report pain intensity measures for use in clinical trials in children and adolescents. *Pain, 125,* 143–157.

29. Goodenough, B., Addicoat, L., Champion, G., McInerney, M., Young, B., Juniper, K., et al. (1997). Pain in 4- to 6-year-old children receiving intramuscular injections: A comparison of the Faces Pain Scale with other self-report and behavioral measures. *Clinical Journal of Pain, 13*(1), 60–73.

30. McGrath, P. A., Seifer, C. E., & Speechley, K. N. (1996). A new analogue scale for assessing children's pain: An initial validation study. *Pain, 64,* 435–443.

31. McConahay, T., Bryson, M., & Bulloch, B. (2006). Defining mild, moderate, and severe pain by using the color analog scale with children presenting to a pediatric emergency department. *Academic Emergency Medicine, 13,* 341–344.

32. McConahay, T., Bryson, M., & Bulloch, B. (2007). Clinically significant changes in acute pain in a pediatric ED using the Color Analog Scale. American *Journal of Emergency Medicine, 25,* 739–742.

33. Bulloch, B., & Tenenbein, M. (2002). Validation of 2 pain scales for use in the pediatric emergency department. *Pediatrics, 110*(3), e33.

34. Bieri, D., Reeve, R. A., Champion, G. D., Addicoat, L., & Ziegler, J. (1990). The Faces Pain Scale for the self-assessment of the severity of pain experienced by children: Development, initial validation, and preliminary investigation for the ratio scale properties. *Pain, 41,* 139–150.

35. Hicks, C. L., von Baeyer, C. L., Spafford, P., van Korlaar, I., & Goodenough, B. (2001). The Faces Pain Scale—Revised: Toward a common metric in pediatric pain measurement. *Pain, 93,* 173–183.

36. McGrath, P. J., & Finley, G. A. (1999). *Pediatric pain sourcebook of protocols, policies, and pamphlets.* Retrieved November 28, 2008, from http://www.painsourcebook.ca

References (continued)

37. Wong, D. L., Hockenberry-Eaton, M., Wilson, D., Winkelstein, M. L., & Schwartz, P. (2001). *Wong's essentials of pediatric nursing* (6th ed., pp. 1301). St. Louis, MO: Mosby.

38. McRae, M., Rourke, D., Imperial-Perez, F., Eisenring, C., & Ueda, J. (1997). Development of a research-based standard for assessment, intervention, and evaluation of pain after neonatal and pediatric cardiac surgery. *Pediatric Nursing, 23*(3), 263–271.

39. Elsevier, Inc. (2009). *Wong-Baker FACES Pain Rating Scale permission form.* Retrieved April 8, 2009, from http://www.us.elsevierhealth.com/US-promofiles/d/Wong%20Baker%20FACES%20Permissions%20Form.pdf

40. Chambers, C., Hardial, J., Craig, K., Court, C., & Montgomery, C. (2005). Faces scales for the measurement of postoperative pain intensity in children following minor surgery. *Clinical Journal of Pain, 21*(3), 277–285.

41. Chambers, C., Giesbrecht, K., Craig, K., Bennett, S., & Huntsman, E. (1999). A comparison of faces scales for the measurement of pediatric pain: Children's and parents' ratings. *Pain, 83,* 25–35.

42. von Baeyer, C. L., & Spagrud, L. J. (2007). Systematic review of observational (behavioral) measures of pain for children and adolescents aged 3 to 18 years. *Pain, 27,* 140–150.

43. Stevens, B., McGrath, P., Gibbins, S., Beyene, J., Breau, L., Camfield, C., et al. (2003). Procedural pain in newborns at risk for neurologic impairment. *Pain, 105,* 27–35.

44. Manworren, R. C., & Hynan, L. S. (2003). Clinical validation of FLACC: Preverbal patient pain scale. *Pediatric Nursing, 29*(2), 140–146.

45. Merkel, S. I., Voepel-Lewis, T., Shayevitz, J. R., & Malviya, S. (1997). The FLACC: A behavioral scale for scoring postoperative pain in young children. *Pediatric Nursing, 23*(3), 293–297.

46. Hummel, P., Puchalski, M., Creech, S., & Weiss, M. (2008). Clinical reliability and validity of the N-PASS: Neonatal Pain, Agitation, and Sedation Scale. *Journal of Perinatology, 28*(1), 55–60.

47. Ching, J. M., & Burns, S. M. (2006). Pain, sedation and neuromuscular blockade management. In M. Chulay & S. M. Burns (Eds.), *AACN essentials of critical care nursing* (pp. 145–165). New York: McGraw-Hill.

48. Pavan, B., Dalpiaz, A., Ciliberti, N., Biondi, C., Manfredini, S. & Vertuani, S. (2008). Progress in drug delivery to the central nervous system by the prodrug approach. *Molecules, 13,* 1035–1065.

49. Grant, M. J. C., & Webster, H. F. (2006). Pulmonary system. In M. C. Slota (Ed.), *Core curriculum for pediatric critical care nursing* (pp. 40–152). St. Louis, MO: Elsevier.

50. McGhee, B., Howrie, D., Schmitt, C., Nguyen, P., Berry, D., Sandy, J., et al. (2007). *Pediatric drug therapy handbook & formulary* (5th ed.). Hudson, OH: Lexi-Comp.

51. Fein, J. A., Callahan, J. M., Boardman, C. R., & Gorelick, M. H. (1999). Predicting the need for topical anesthetic in the pediatric emergency department. *Pediatrics, 104*(2), e19.

52. Anand, K. J., & International Evidence-Based Group for Neonatal Pain. (2001). Consensus statement for the prevention and management of pain in the newborn. *Archives of Pediatric and Adolescent Medicine, 155,* 173–180.

53. Pasek, T., Thomas, D., Khimji, I., Schmitt, C., Spence, A., & Hanni, R. (2007). Implementation of a nurse-driven topical analgesic protocol: Two steps forward, one step back. *Pediatric Pain Letter, 9*(3), 25–31.

54. Bhargava, R., & Young, K. D. (2007). Procedural pain management patterns in academic pediatric emergency departments. *Academic Emergency Medicine, 14*(5), 479–482.

55. American Society of Anesthesiologists. (n.d.). *Continuum of depth of sedation: Definition of general anesthesia and levels of sedation/analgesia.* Retrieved April 23, 2009, from http://www.asahq.org/publicationsAndServices/standards/20.pdf

56. Sedationfacts.org. (n.d.). *Sedation levels & definitions.* Retrieved November 28, 2008, from http://www.sedationfacts.org/physiology/sedation-levels

57. Cohen, L. B., DeLegge, M. H., Alsenberg, J., Brill, J. V., Inadomi, J. M., Kochman, M. L., et al. (2007). AGA Institute review of endoscopic sedation. *Gastroenterology, 133*(2), 675–701.

58. American College of Emergency Physicians. (2004). Clinical policy: Evidence-based approach to pharmacologic agents used in pediatric sedation and analgesia in the emergency department. *Annals of Emergency Medicine, 44*(4), 342–377.

References (continued)

59. Babl, F. E., Oakley, E., Seaman, C., Barnett, P., & Sharwood, L. N. (2008). High concentration nitrous oxide for procedural sedation in children: Adverse events and depth of sedation. *Pediatrics, 121,* e528–e532.

60. Bandstra, N. F., Skinner, L., LeBlanc, C., Chambers, C. T., Hollon, E. C., Brennan, D., et al. (2008). Role of child life in pediatric pain management: A survey of child life specialists. *Journal of Pain, 9*(4), 320–329.

61. von Baeyer, C. L., Marche, T. A., Rocha, E. M., & Salmon, K. (2004). Children's memory for pain: Overview and implications for practice. *Journal of Pain, 5,* 241–249.

62. Salmon, K., McGuigan, F., & Pereira, J. K. (2006). Brief report: Optimizing children's memory and management of an invasive medical procedure: The influence of procedural narration and distraction. *Journal of Pediatric Psychology, 31*(5), 522–527.

63. McLaren, J., & Cohen, L. L. (2005). A comparison of distraction strategies for venipuncture distress in children. *Journal of Pediatric Psychology, 30,* 387–396.

64. Sparks, L. A, Setlik, J., & Luhman, J. (2007). Parental holding and positioning to decrease IV distress in young children: A randomized controlled trial. *Journal of Pediatric Nursing, 22*(6), 440–447.

65. Field, T. (2001). Massage therapy for children, adolescents and adults. In T. Field (Ed.), *Touch* (pp. 131–153). Cambridge, MA: The MIT Press.

66. Field, T., Hernandez-Reif, M., Diego, M., Schanberg, S., & Khun, C. (2005). Cortisol decreases and serotonin and dopamine increase following massage therapy. *International Journal of Neuroscience, 155*(10), 1397–1413.

67. Blass, E. M., & Shide, D. J. (1995). Mother as a shield: Differential effects of contact and nursing on pain responsivity in infant rats—evidence for non-opioid medication. *Behavioral Neuroscience, 109,* 342–353.

68. Blass, E. M. (1997). Milk-induced hyperalgesia in human newborns. *Pediatrics, 99,* 825–829.

69. Heine, W. E. (1999). The significance of tryptophan in infant nutrition. *Advances in Experimental Medicine and Biology, 467,* 705–710.

70. Barrett, T., Kent, S., & Coudoris, N. (2000). Does melatonin modulate beta-endorphin, corticosterone, and pain threshold? *Life Sciences, 66,* 467–476.

71. Schollin, J. (2004). Analgesic effect of expressed breast milk in procedural pain in neonates. *Acta Pediatrica, 93,* 453–455.

72. Shah, P. S., Aliwalas, L. L., & Shah, V. (2006). *Breastfeeding or breast milk for procedural pain in neonates.* Retrieved November 28, 2008, from http://www.nichd.nih.gov/cochrane/shahprak/shahprak.htm

73. Anseloni, V. C., Weng, H. R., Terayama, R., Letizia, D., Davis, B. J., Ren, K., et al. (2002). Age-dependency of analgesia elicited by intraoral sucrose in acute and persistent pain models. *Pain, 97,* 93–103.

74. Greenburg, C. S. (2002). A sugar-coated pacifier reduces procedural pain in newborns. *Pediatric Nursing, 22*(3), 217–277.

75. American Academy of Pediatrics. (2000). Prevention and management of pain and stress in the neonate. Committee on Fetus and Newborn. Committee on Drugs. Section on Anesthesiology. Section on Surgery and Canadian Paediatric Society. Fetus and Newborn Committee. [Policy Statement]. *Pediatrics, 105*(2), 454–461.

76. Stevens, B., Yamada, J., & Ohlsson, A. (2004). Sucrose for analgesia in newborn infants undergoing painful procedures. *Cochrane Database of Systematic Reviews, 3,* CD0001069.

77. Thompson, D. G. (2005). Utilizing an oral sucrose solution to minimize neonatal pain. *Journal for Specialists in Pediatric Nursing, 10*(1), 3–10.

78. American Music Therapy Association, Inc. (n.d.). *Music therapy in the treatment and management of pain.* Retrieved November 28, 2008, from http://www.musictherapy.org/factsheets/MT%20Pain%202006.pdf

SECTION FOUR
Resuscitation

TWELVE

Neonatal Resuscitation

Regina O'Leary, RN, MSN, CRNP
Kathleen Campbell, RN, CRNP, NNP-BC
Merry Kruger, BA Nursing, NNP-BC
Susan Barbarossa, CRNP

Introduction

The unanticipated delivery of a newborn in the emergency department (ED) is rare in the United States and other countries[1]; rarer still is the resuscitation of a neonate in the emergency department.[1] Approximately 10% of all neonates in the United States require some assistance to begin breathing, and about 1% require extensive resuscitative measures to survive.[2] Although the optimal setting for neonatal resuscitation is in the delivery room with trained personnel and state-of-the-art neonatal-specific equipment, the emergency department or nonhospital area often must serve as a delivery area to attend to an unanticipated birth. Emergency nurses and staff need to be prepared and have the necessary equipment to deliver and resuscitate the newborn. Chances for optimal outcomes for a neonate requiring resuscitation are increased with advanced preparation and necessary equipment (Table 12.1).

The Neonatal Resuscitation Program (NRP)[3] offered by the American Academy of Pediatrics/American Heart Association provides in-depth knowledge and skills in the resuscitation of a newborn. Emergency nurses can attend an NRP course to obtain this specialized knowledge and practice to gain confidence in neonatal resuscitation. This chapter will provide an overview of the factors that necessitate neonatal resuscitation and outline the basic steps for resuscitating the neonate.

Etiology of Unanticipated Birth

The stimulus for early or unanticipated labor is not always known, nor is the length of the labor and delivery stages. For the average nulliparous woman, the total time from active labor to delivery is about 11 hours; for a multiparous woman, the total time from active labor to delivery is about 6 hours.[4]

Contributions to early labor include:[3,4]

- ❏ Obstetric
  - Trauma
  - Premature rupture of membranes (PROM)
  - Vaginal bleeding due to placenta previa or placental abruption
  - Infection
  - Drug use (cocaine or amphetamines)
- ❏ Fetal distress
  - Placental insufficiency
  - Abnormal presentations (breech, transverse lie, shoulder dystocia)
  - Anemia
  - Multiple gestations
  - Asphyxia neonatorum
- ❏ Antepartum factors
  - Maternal diabetes
  - Pregnancy-induced hypertension
  - Chronic hypertension
  - Fetal anemia
  - Maternal infection
  - Polyhydramnios
  - Oligohydramnios
  - Premature Rupture of Membranes (PROM)
  - Fetal hydrops
  - Postterm gestation
  - Multiple gestations
  - Size-dates discrepancy
  - Drug therapy (such as magnesium sulfate)
  - Maternal substance use
  - No prenatal care
  - Age < 16 or > 35 years

TABLE 12.1 Equipment for Neonatal Resuscitation
Suction equipment
Bulb syringe
Mechanical suction
Suction catheters 5–12 French
Meconium aspirator
Bag and mask equipment
Infant Ambu bag with manometer
Facemasks: both newborn and preterm size
Oxygen source with flowmeter
Intubation equipment
Endotracheal tubes size 2.0 to 4.0 internal diameter
Laryngoscope blades size 0 and 1
Stylette
Cloth adhesive tape
Scissors
Skin prep
CO_2 detector
Medications
Epinephrine 1:10,000
Normal saline solution for volume expansion
Sodium bicarbonate 4.2%
Naloxone hydrochloride 0.4 mg/mL
10% dextrose
Normal saline flushes
Umbilical catheterization supplies
Sterile drapes and gloves
Scalpel or scissors
Antiseptic prep solution
Umbilical cord tie
Umbilical catheters sizes 3.5 and 5 French
Three-way stopcock
4.0 silk suture
Syringes 1, 3, 5, 10, 20, 50 mL
Needles 18, 21, and 25 gauge
Warming Supplies
Chemically activated warming pad
Pulse oximeter and oximeter probe
Re-sealable food-grade plastic bag (1 gallon size) or plastic wrap to wrap low birth weight babies in transport incubator or overhead warming bed

❐ Intrapartum factors
  - Emergency Cesarean delivery
  - Forceps or vacuum-assisted delivery
  - Abnormal birth presentation
  - Premature labor
  - Precipitous labor
  - Chorioamnionitis
  - Prolonged rupture of membranes > 18 hours
  - Prolonged labor > 24 hours
  - Macrosomia
  - Fetal bradycardia
  - Nonreassuring fetal heart sounds/fetal distress
  - Use of general anesthesia
  - Narcotic administration to mother within 4 hours of delivery
  - Prolapsed cord
  - Abruptio placentae
  - Significant intrapartum bleeding

Focused History for the Mother

  - Prenatal care. Lack of such care may result in a high-risk delivery.
  - Gravidity
  - Parity
  - Number of live preterm and term births
  - Current pregnancy complications
  - Previous pregnancy complications
  - History of chronic conditions

❐ Labor history
  - Number of babies anticipated
  - Date of last menstrual period. Needed to estimate the gestational age to determine whether the unborn neonate is premature (< 37 weeks gestation).
  - Color of amniotic fluid. Meconium-stained fluid suggests potential risk of meconium aspiration and the need for specialized respiratory care.
  - Time of membranes rupture. Prolonged rupture of membranes can be associated with infectious complications.
  - Signs of infection
  - Duration of labor and contractions
  - Presence of abnormal vaginal bleeding or discharge
  - Maternal drug or alcohol activity, to anticipate possible narcotic withdrawal
  - Fetal activity

Nursing Assessment and Interventions for the Mother

Assessment

☐ Assess maternal heart rate, respiratory rate, and blood pressure.

  ▪ Initiate measures to support airway, breathing, circulation, oxygen saturation, and blood pressure.

☐ Assess maternal cervical dilatation and contraction intensity and duration.

☐ Assess fetal heart sounds using a Doppler; attach a fetal heart monitor to measure fetal heart rate and tolerance to contractions.

Interventions

1. Administer analgesics as indicated and ordered.

2. Provide reassurance and support to the mother.

3. Assist in the delivery of the infant.

4. Prepare for delivery of the placenta.

5. Observe and record amount of bleeding.

6. Perform fundal massage.

7. Prepare mother for transfer to medical facility with maternity services (Chapter 8).

8. Contact family members.

Focused History for the Neonate

☐ Gestational age

☐ Presence of amniotic fluid

☐ Color of amniotic fluid

  ▪ Clear

  ▪ Meconium

☐ Odor of meconium fluid

☐ Respiratory effort

  ▪ Breathing

  ▪ Crying

☐ Muscle tone

☐ Apgar score

Nursing Assessment and Interventions for the Neonate

Prepare to perform in sequence the four categories of neonatal resuscitation.[2] Moving from one category to the next is determined by assessment of respirations, heart rate, and skin color.[2] Approximately 30 seconds of time is used to complete each category, evaluate the neonate's status and decide to continue in the process.[2]

☐ Initiate steps in stabilization (provide warmth, position, clear airway, dry, stimulate, reposition).

☐ Ventilation, including bag-mask or bag-tube ventilation.

☐ Chest compressions.

☐ Administration of epinephrine and/or volume expansion.

1. Perform a rapid assessment and initial steps in stabilization.

  ▪ Place the neonate supine with the head in a neutral position for optimal airway patency.

  ▪ Dry and place the infant on a radiant warmer to avoid hyperthermia and hypothermia. Maintain a normal rectal temperature of 98 °F to 100 °F (36.5 °C to 37.5 °C).

  ▪ In the neonate with meconium present, suction the hypopharynx immediately on delivery of the head and before the delivery of the trunk and shoulders. Perform direct tracheal suctioning to remove the meconium from the airway if the infant is not breathing, has a heart rate < 100 beats per minute, or has poor muscle tone.

  ▪ In the neonate without meconium present, suction the neonate's mouth and then the nose.

2. Perform ventilation, including bag-mask or bag-tube ventilation.

  ▪ Evaluate the adequacy of respiratory effort.

    • Auscultate breath sounds for:

      · Rate

      · Presence and equality

      · Adventitious breath sounds

    • Inspect the chest for:

      · Equal movement

      · Use of accessory muscles

    • Observe for signs of respiratory distress or insufficiency (Chapter 14).

      · Respiratory insufficiency may yield an inadequate heart rate; therefore, the heart rate should be evaluated immediately after the initial respiratory assessment.

    • Stimulate, by drying, warming, or suctioning, the neonate to promote spontaneous respiratory effort.

    • Administer supplemental oxygen if the neonate is

      · Cyanotic

- Breathing with a heart rate > 100 beats per minute
- Perform positive pressure ventilation (PPV) using the bag-mask or bag- tube technique with 100% forced inspiratory oxygen if there is:
  - Inadequate respiratory effort
  - Heart rate < 100 beats per minute
- Continue PPV if there is:
  - Apnea or gasping respirations
  - Heart rate < 100 beats per minute
  - Persistent central cyanosis
- If the heart rate remains at < 60 beats per minute, prepare for endotracheal intubation with the appropriate-sized endotracheal tube by an experienced individual. If that person is not available, continue to use bag-mask ventilation.
- Apply an appropriate-sized pulse oximeter on the neonate's upper extremity.

3. Perform chest compressions.
   - Assess the circulatory status.
     - Palpate the base of the umbilical cord for pulsations:
       - Rate
       - Quality
     - Palpate the brachial and/or femoral arteries for:
       - Rate
       - Quality
       - Comparison with the umbilical cord
   - Auscultate the heart rate.
     - If the apical rate is > 100 beats per minute, continue ongoing assessment of respiratory effort.
     - If the apical rate is < 60 beats per minute despite adequate PPV for 30 seconds, initiate chest compressions.
       - Use the two-finger or two-thumb technique and compress sternum one third the depth of the anterior posterior.
       - Compress at a 3:1 ratio (3 compressions to 1 ventilation) with 90 compressions and 30 breaths to achieve rate of 120 per minute (2 per second).[2]

4. Administer medications and fluids (Table 12.2).
   - Establish intravenous access, with the umbilical vein (UV) as the preferred route.
     - Do not exceed 5- to 6-cm depth of the catheter placement to avoid cannulation of the portal vein.

- Flush the UV catheter with normal saline solution before insertion to avoid the introduction of air into the central circulation.
- Administer epinephrine if the heart rate continues to be < 60 beats per minute despite 30 seconds of adequate ventilation and compression.
- Prepare to administer additional resuscitation medications (Table 12.2).
  - Evaluate peripheral perfusion.
    - Palpate pulses in all four extremities for rate, quality, and equality.
    - Measure capillary refill.
    - Measure skin temperature by touching the skin.
    - Inspect skin color.

5. Provide ongoing nursing care.
   - Calculate an Apgar score (Table 12.3).
     - The Apgar score is never used to determine the need for resuscitation.
   - Obtain laboratory tests, such as:
     - Arterial blood gases
     - Electrolytes
     - Glucose
     - Complete blood cell count
   - Measure urinary output.
   - Monitor the volume of intravenous fluid administered.
   - Perform a rapid general assessment to identify obvious congenital anomalies (Table 12.4).
   - Perform postresuscitation care.
     - Continue to monitor cardiorespiratory function and oxygen saturation levels.
     - Continue to provide supplemental oxygen and mechanical ventilation.
     - Secure venous access sites.
     - Perform serial neurologic examinations.
     - Provide gastric decompression with the insertion of a nasogastric tube.
     - Maintain normothermia with the application of external heat sources.
     - Provide the mother and other family members with frequent updates of the infant's condition.
     - Prepare for transfer or transport to the newborn nursery or level 3 nursery (Chapter 8). Ensure that the neonate is STABLE:
       - Blood **S**ugar is normal.
       - **T**emperature is normal.

- **A**irway and breathing are adequate.
- **B**lood pressure is normal.
- Appropriate **L**aboratory tests are obtained to rule out infection, including complete blood cell count and blood cultures. Antibiotics should be started for any neonate needing resuscitation.
- **E**motional support is provided for the family.
- Ensure that any congenital anomalies are appropriately protected.
- Provide spiritual and social support to the family of the neonate who dies in the emergency department (Chapter 26).

Prevention

The prevention of neonatal resuscitation begins with adequate prenatal care. The reduction of maternal risk factors associated with increased perinatal morbidity should be initiated early in pregnancy. Emergency departments should have in place protocols for attending to unanticipated deliveries and performing neonatal resuscitation. Neonatal nurses, neonatologists, obstetricians, and social services should be involved in developing the protocols and provide their services in the unlikely event of neonatal delivery and resuscitation.

TABLE 12.2 Medications for Neonatal Resuscitation

Medication	Dose/Route	Indications	Considerations	Nursing Implications
Epinephrine 1:10,000 (0.1 mg/mL)	0.01–0.03 mg/kg (0.1–0.3 mL/kg) intravenously through the UV	Cardiac arrest Bradycardia unresponsive to oxygen administration, ventilation, and chest compressions	Venous route is preferred. While obtaining venous access, administer a higher dose (up to 0.1 mg/kg) through the endotracheal tube.	Administer quickly and follow with 0.5 mL to 1 mL of normal saline solution.
Volume expander (isotonic crystalloid, such as normal saline solution)	10 mL/kg intravenously through the UV	Suspected blood loss Shock Lack of response to other resuscitative measures	Repeat as needed. Other acceptable volume expanders include Ringer's lactate, O Rh-negative packed red blood cells.	Administer over a 5- to 10-minute period by syringe or infusion pump. Do not give rapidly, as rapid administration is associated with intraventricular hemorrhage in premature infants.
Naloxone	0.1 mg/kg intravenously or intramuscularly	Not generally recommended for newborns with respiratory depression	Assure adequate heart rate and color through ventilation.	Do not use in infants born to opioid-addicted mothers. Monitor closely for recurring apnea or hypoventilation. Additional doses may be needed.

American Pediatric Association & American Heart Association. (2006). *Textbook of neonatal resuscitation* (5th ed.). Chicago, IL: Author.

TABLE 12.3 Apgar Score

Signs/Score	0	1	2
Heartbeat per minute	Absent	Slow < 100	Over 100
Respiratory effort	Absent	Slow and irregular	Good, crying
Muscle tone	Flaccid	Some flexion	Active motion
Reflex irritability	None	Grimace	Cry or cough
Color	Blue, pale	Body pink, extremities Blue	Completely pink

Notes: The Apgar score was introduced by Virginia Apgar in 1952 to enable quantitative evaluation of the infant's condition shortly after birth. The score reflects the cardiovascular and neuromuscular condition at both 1 minute and 5 minutes of life. The scores do not provide a predicative value for outcome; however, the change in a 1-minute score to a 5-minute score is a meaningful indicator of the effectiveness of the resuscitative efforts. It is important to know that intrapartum events, prematurity, medication, and congenital disease can greatly affect the Apgar score.

Apgar, V. (1953). A proposal for a new method of evaluation of the newborn infant. *Anesthesia Analogues, 32,* 260–267.

TABLE 12.4 Rapid Newborn Assessment and Findings

Airway	Examine the airway for patency. Assure airway patency. ▪ Pass a catheter into each naris to remove secretions; observe for bradycardia, trauma, or edema. ▪ Use a bulb syringe as an alternative to the catheter.
Breathing	Evaluate respiratory effort. ▪ Assess chest wall movement, rate, and pattern to detect signs of distress. ▪ Audible crackles initially should clear in a short period of time, as the fetal lung fluid should absorb as the lungs inflate with air. ▪ Decreased breath sounds may indicate pneumothorax, atelectasis, or consolidation. ▪ Unequal breath sounds may indicate a unilateral pneumothorax or the presence of a mass.
Circulation	Auscultate the heart for: ▪ Regular rhythm ▪ Murmurs Assess the peripheral circulation for: ▪ Color. Most infants are pink at birth with some acrocyanosis of hands and feet. ▪ Acrocyanosis does not respond to oxygen therapy. ▪ Cyanosis and pallor may indicate sepsis, anemia, hyaline membrane disease, or a cardiac anomaly. ▪ Central cyanosis is seen in the mucous membranes. It may occur at delivery if the infant is hypoxic and usually will respond to oxygen therapy. ▪ If cyanosis remains after 100% oxygen therapy initiate a trial of PPV. ▪ If cyanosis persists despite adequate ventilation and oxygen therapy, consider an acyanotic heart lesion or severe lung disease. ▪ Turgor. Elasticity and capillary refill (< 3 seconds). ▪ Temperature. A normal temperature is 98 °F to 100 °F (36.5 °C to 37.5 °C) and should be obtained rectally for an accurate reading. Assess the rectum for both patency and position.

TABLE 12.4 Rapid Newborn Assessment and Findings

Neurologic	Assess the neonate's:
	<ul><li>Activity</li><li>Muscle tone</li><li>Response to stimuli</li><li>Movement of the extremities. Unilateral facial or extremity movement may indicate nerve palsy.</li><li>Examine the feet and hands to determine the presence of all digits in their correct anatomic position.</li><li>Assess for pain (Chapter 11).</li></ul>
Abdomen	<ul><li>Palpate the abdomen for distention; the abdomen should be soft.</li><li>If the abdomen is firm and distended, there may be an intra-abdominal mass. A concave abdomen may indicate a diaphragmatic hernia.</li><li>Inspect the umbilical cord for the presence of two arteries and one vein.</li></ul>
Genitalia	Evaluate the genitalia before announcing the newborn's gender. If there is a question of the infant's gender, a more complete examination should be done before gender assignment.
Vital signs	A normal range for vital signs in the neonate is:<ul><li>Respiratory rate between 40 and 60 breaths per minute.</li><li>Heart rate 100 to 160 beats per minute.</li><li>Pulse oximetry of > 95 % in the term baby.</li><li>Blood pressure with a systolic range of 70 to 50 mm Hg and a diastolic range of 45 to 30 mm Hg.[6]</li><li>Blood pressures should be measured in all four extremities.</li></ul>

References

1. Goh, S. H., Tiah, L., & Lai, S. M. (2005). When the stork arrives unannounced—seven years of emergency deliveries in a non-obstetric general hospital. *Annals of the Academy of Medicine, Singapore, 34*(7), 432–436.

2. American Heart Association, American Academy of Pediatrics. (2006). 2005 American Heart Association (AHA) guidelines for cardiopulmonary resuscitation (CPR) and emergency cardiovascular care (ECC) of pediatric and neonatal patients: Neonatal resuscitation guidelines. *Pediatrics, 117,* e1029–e1038.

3. American Pediatric Association & American Heart Association. (2006). *Textbook of neonatal resuscitation* (5th ed.). Chicago, IL: Author.

4. Cunningham, F. G., Leveno, K. J., Bloom, S. L., Hauth, J. C., Gilstrap, L. C., & Wenstrom, K. D. (2005). *Williams obstetrics* (22nd ed.). New York: McGraw-Hill.

5. Apgar, V. (1953). A proposal for a new method of evaluation of the newborn infant. *Anesthesia Analogues, 32,* 260–267.

6. Davidson, M., London, M., & Ladewig, P. (2008). *Olds' maternal-newborn nursing & women's health across the lifespan* (8th ed.). Upper Saddle River, NJ: Pearson Prentice Hall.

THIRTEEN

Pediatric Resuscitation

Sarah A. Martin, RN, MS, CPNP-PC/AC, CCRN

Introduction

Cardiopulmonary arrest is rarely a sudden event in the pediatric population. Unlike adults, the usual etiologic factor of cardiopulmonary arrest in children is respiratory failure or shock.[1] Therefore, it is of the utmost importance that emergency nurses recognize the child in respiratory distress and intervene accordingly. Early recognition and intervention may prevent respiratory and cardiac failure, thus minimizing subsequent multiple-system organ dysfunction and associated morbidity and mortality.

Although etiology from respiratory failure is the usual scenario in children, sudden cardiac arrest (SCA) can result from unexpected arrhythmias. With the increased awareness of SCA, particularly in athletes, the most recent American Heart Association (AHA) guidelines emphasize the treatment of cardiac arrest from SCA.

The successful resuscitation of infants and children requires knowledge of the etiology, assessment, and interventions, along with advanced life support. The purpose of this chapter is to outline the nursing assessment and interventions for pediatric resuscitation. In-depth knowledge of the care as outlined in algorithms can be obtained by attending a standardized course on pediatric advanced life support (PALS).

The most recent changes in basic life support (BLS) and PALS occurred in 2005.[2] In an attempt to simplify resuscitation care and support the practice of evidence-based care, major changes were made to both the layperson and health care provider care as summarized in Table 13.1.[3,4] These changes include a new emphasis on high-quality BLS, as this intervention provides the foundation for successful resuscitation.

Despite prompt emergency interventions, survival outcomes for the pediatric victim of cardiac arrest are poor at best. A recent meta-analysis describing outcomes of 5,363 children experiencing an out-of-hospital cardiac arrest found that only 12.1% survived to hospital discharge, with only 4% neurologically intact at discharge.[5]

Etiology

Cardiopulmonary arrest occurs most commonly in infants (younger than one year of age) and in adolescents. In most instances, the cause of cardiac arrest is respiratory failure. The etiologies of cardiopulmonary arrest in the infant and child are diverse (Table 13.2). While respiratory compromise is the leading cause of cardiac arrest in infants and young children, trauma remains the leading cause of preventable death in the pediatric population.[6] Children with congenital heart disease may present with cardiac arrest unrelated to respiratory failure. SCA in athletes is most likely related to ventricular fibrillation or ventricular tachycardia.[1] The leading cause of SCA in athletes is hypertrophic cardiomyopathy.

Focused History and Assessment

In the emergency department (ED), caregivers may be asked to care for a cardiac arrest patient for whom resuscitation measures have been initiated in the field or may have a child with pending cardiopulmonary failure present to triage. Regardless of the condition on presentation of the child, the basic sequence of assessing the airway, breathing, circulation, disability, and exposure (A, B, C, D, E) should be done in all situations as presented in the PALS course.[2] Cardiac, respiratory, and oxygen saturation monitoring should be started for the child in cardiopulmonary arrest and the child in pending cardiopulmonary arrest.

The focused history and assessment will be quite different for the child presenting with active resuscitation from the field versus resuscitation in the emergency department. Often for the child in an arrest situation assessment supersedes obtaining a detailed history, and assessment and intervention are the team members' immediate actions.

The Initial Assessment

Airway

Assess the airway for patency, presence of secretions or foreign bodies (chewing gum, teeth, tongue obstruction,

Table 13.1 Changes to Pediatric BLS and PALS

Change	Rationale
Emphasis on effective CPR • Push hard and fast 100 compressions per minute, limit interruption of compressions, allow full recoil of the chest between each compression. • Universal ratios: 30:2 (single rescuer) and 15:2 (two rescuers) for infants and children (except neonates). For adolescents ratio is 30:2 even with two rescuers. • If two rescuers are involved they should switch every 2 minutes. • Child CPR for children 1 year to the onset of puberty versus 8 years.	• Without effective BLS, PALS will add little to positive outcomes. • Assures adequate blood flow. • Permits full expansion of the chest following each compression. • Increases fatigue with increased compressions. • Universal ratios to increase rates of bystander CPR and make it uniform for health care providers.
Airway • Rescue breaths should last 1 second with a visible chest rise. • Use of cuffed or uncuffed endotracheal tube (ETT) with measuring exhaled CO_2 if an advanced airway is used. Exhaled CO_2 is used to confirm placement of the ETT in the airway but the device may not change colors in a child receiving CPR. • Once an advanced airway has been placed, continuous ventilation and compressions with breaths interspersed, suggested ventilation rate of 8 to 10/minute.	• During CPR there is less pulmonary blood flow—fewer breaths with smaller volumes optimize oxygenation and ventilation.[3] • Cuffed ETT may be useful in children with poor lung compliance and increased airway resistance. • Hyperventilation can be harmful as there will be increased intrathoracic pressure and decreased venous return and coronary perfusion pressures.
Medications • Intravenous/intraosseous routes preferred over ETT for administration • Amiodarone preferred drug for pulseless arrest from ventricular fibrillation or ventricular tachycardia	• Unpredictable drug delivery. • Amiodarone known to be a more effective drug.
Defibrillation • Single shock starting with 2 joules/kg then escalating to 4 joules/kg, followed by immediate resumption of CPR. • Chest compressions should be resumed immediately after defibrillation.	• Rapid defibrillation in witnessed arrest has better outcomes. • Primes the heart for the next defibrillation attempt and is the treatment for pulseless electrical activity.
• Automated external defibrillators are recommended for use with children who are at least 1 year of age. Pediatric pads used for children from 1 to 8 years of age. Adult pads used in children over 8 years of age.	• Found to be safe in children over 1 year of age and in a sudden witnessed collapse, should be used.

Notes: CO_2 = carbon dioxide; ETT = endotracheal tube
Doniger, S. J., & Sharieff, G. Q. (2007). Pediatric resuscitation update. *Emergency Medical Clinics of North America, 25,* 947–960.
McDowell, B. M. (2006). Changes in CPR and ECC for pediatric nurses. *Journal for Specialists in Pediatric Nursing, 4,* 251–253.

or small objects), and chest movement, and listen for air movement and breath sounds.

Breathing

Assess respiratory effort.

❏ Respiratory rate (apnea, bradypnea or tachypnea)

❏ Work of breathing: Accessory muscle use and retractions

- Chest expansion and symmetry
- Auscultate for air exchange and adventitious lung sounds.
- Obtain pulse oximetry readings. Note: In a full cardiopulmonary arrest, the blood oxygen saturation will not be measurable with pulse oximetry. A patient can be in shock with a low hemoglobin value and the oxygen saturation reading 100% as the child's existing hemoglobin is fully saturated.

TABLE 13.2 Etiologies of Cardiac and Respiratory Arrest in Infants and Children

Etiology	*Younger than 1 Year*	*1 to 12 Years*	*Adolescence*
Respiratory			
	Pneumonia	Asthma	Asthma
	Bronchiolitis	Upper airway obstruction (e.g., foreign body)	
	Upper airway obstruction (e.g., foreign body and croup)	Bronchiolitis	
	SIDS		
	ALTE		
Cardiac Disease			
	CHD	CHD	CHD
	Dysrhythmias	Dysrhythmias	Dysrhythmias
	Cardiomyopathy	Cardiomyopathy	
Central Nervous System			
	Seizures	Seizures	
	Meningitis	Coma	
	Hydrocephalus		
Infectious Disease			
	Sepsis	Meningitis	
	Pneumonia	Pneumonia	
	Meningitis	Sepsis	
Trauma			
	Child maltreatment	Child maltreatment	Pedestrian, motor vehicle, and bike collisions
	Burns/smoke inhalation	Pedestrian, motor vehicle, and bike collisions	Homicide
	Falls	Burns/smoke inhalation	
		Intracranial hemorrhage (subdural, epidural, and intraventricular hematoma)	
Congenital Anomalies			
	Chromosomal abnormalities		
	Inborn errors of metabolism		

ALTE = apparent life-threatening event; CHD = congenital heart disease; SIDS = sudden infant death syndrome.

Circulation

Assess circulatory status

❑ Skin color and temperature

❑ Heart rate

❑ Heart rhythm

❑ Blood pressure

❑ Central and peripheral pulses. Palpate peripheral pulses for:

  ▪ Quality

  ▪ Equality

  ▪ Rate

❑ Capillary refill time

Disability

Assess neurologic status

❑ AVPU Pediatric Response Scale—*A*lert, Responds to *V*oice, Responds to *P*ain, *U*nresponsive. Evaluate whether the child is alert, responds to verbal stimuli, responds to painful stimuli, or is unresponsive.

❑ Glasgow Coma Scale

❑ Pupillary response to light. Inspect pupils for:

  ▪ Equality

  ▪ Response to light

  ▪ Size

Exposure

❑ Undress the child and assess for trauma (bleeding, burns, or markings suggestive of abuse); palpate extremities.

❑ Institute warming measures to prevent hypothermia.

Focused History for the Child Presenting in Cardiopulmonary Arrest

Events Leading to the Cardiopulmonary Arrest

❑ Trauma related

❑ Suspected child maltreatment (Chapter 44)

❑ Illness related

  ▪ Symptoms

  ▪ Length of illness

  ▪ Current treatment

Length of Time the Child had no Cardiac or Respiratory Function

Initiation of Cardiopulmonary Resuscitation

❑ When cardiopulmonary resuscitation (CPR) was initiated.

❑ Who initiated CPR.

❑ Length of time CPR was administered before ED arrival.

❑ Child's response to CPR (pulses regained or pulses absent).

Initiation of Advanced Life-Support Measures

❑ Airway maintenance with endotracheal intubation or laryngeal mask airway.

❑ Defibrillation or use of an automated external defibrillator.

❑ Initiation of an intravenous or intraosseous infusion.

❑ Administration of intravenous, intraosseous, or endotracheal medications.

Focused History for the Child Presenting in Stabilized Cardiopulmonary Arrest

Previous Health History

❑ Any prodromal signs and symptoms that the child exhibited

❑ Chronic health conditions (e.g., asthma, congenital heart disease, other congenital anomalies, asplenia, central nervous system condition, epilepsy, and HIV)

❑ Allergies

❑ Current medications: prescription, over-the-counter medications, herbal and dietary supplements

❑ Immunization status

❑ Medications prescribed for other persons in the home (To rule out suspected poisoning, Chapter 42)

❑ Presence of existing advanced directive

Additional Assessment Considerations for the Child Presenting in Pending Cardiopulmonary Arrest and Stabilized Cardiopulmonary Arrest

Airway/Breathing

❑ If an endotracheal tube is in place, verify placement with a carbon dioxide detector, and start end-tidal carbon dioxide monitoring if available.

❑ Obtain a chest radiograph.

❑ Although central cyanosis is a sign of respiratory failure and reflects hypoxemia, central cyanosis can also be from congenital heart disease. Patients in decompensated shock will also have central cyanosis/mottling.

  ▪ Peripheral cyanosis reflects poor peripheral perfusion and compensatory vasoconstriction resulting from shock or hypothermia.

Circulation

❑ Auscultate the heart for:

- Rate
  - As a compensatory response to a decreased cardiac output, children's heart rate may initially increase.
  - A decreased heart rate is generally an ominous sign and may occur in the presence of significant hypoxemia.
  - Quality and murmurs.

❑ Measure blood pressure.

❑ Assess systemic perfusion.

❑ Measure urinary output (should be 1 mL/kg/hr) by placing urinary catheter.

Potential Reversible Causes[2]

❑ *Hs*

- Hypovolemia
- Hypoxia
- Hydrogen ion (acidosis)
- Hyperkalemia/hypokalemia
- Hypoglycemia
- Hypothermia

❑ T*s*

- Toxins
- Tamponade
- Tension pneumothorax
- Thrombosis (coronary or pulmonary)
- Trauma

Nursing Assessment and Interventions

1. Initiate BLS maneuvers (Table 13.3).
2. Obtain a complete set of vital signs including temperature measurement.
3. Initiate advanced life support maneuvers.
   - Provide ventilatory assistance.
   - Prepare for tracheal intubation.
   - Prepare for mechanical ventilation.
   - Attempt peripheral venous access.
     - If venous access cannot be established quickly, obtain intraosseous access.
   - Secure central venous access if attempts at peripheral venous and intraosseous access are unsuccessful and a practitioner skilled in the procedure is present.
   - Administer resuscitative medications (Table 13.4).
   - Obtain blood for laboratory testing, such as:
     - Arterial blood gases
     - Electrolytes
     - Glucose
     - Complete blood cell count
     - Toxicology testing (in suspected poisoning)
4. Offer parents frequent updates on their child's condition.
   - The unexpected cardiac or respiratory arrest is a time of crisis (Chapter 26).
   - Facilitate having the family present during resuscitation as requested by the family.[7,8]
   - Consult pastoral care staff and social services to assist with crisis intervention.
5. Perform postresuscitation care.
   - Continue frequent assessment of cardiopulmonary function.
   - Administer humidified oxygen at the highest possible concentration unless objective assessment by blood gas or noninvasive monitoring reflects adequate arterial saturation.
   - Obtain serial neurologic evaluation.
   - Insert a nasogastric tube for gastric decompression if not contraindicated.
   - Insert an indwelling bladder catheter for urine output measurement and bladder decompression if not contraindicated.
   - Maintain normothermia with warming lights, warm blankets, or warm intravenous fluids; current evidence does not support the use of hypothermia; avoid hyperthermia.
   - Prepare for transfer or transport to a pediatric intensive care unit (Chapter 8).

Prevention

The prevention of pediatric cardiopulmonary arrest is early recognition of respiratory distress. The initiation of measures to relieve respiratory distress prevents further cardiopulmonary compromise. Other general preventive measures include anticipatory guidance, injury and illness reduction (Chapter 4), and poison prevention (Chapter 42). Shock can also cause cardiopulmonary arrest, and potential cause and treatment should be instituted (Chapter 38).

TABLE 13.3 BLS for the Infant, Child, and Adult for Health Care Providers

Maneuver	Infant (< 1 Year)	Child (1 Year to Adolescent/ Puberty)	Adolescent
Airway	Head tilt—chin lift Evidence of head/neck trauma; jaw thrust.	Head tilt—chin lift Evidence of head/neck trauma; jaw thrust.	Head tilt—chin lift Evidence of head/neck trauma; jaw thrust without head extension
Breathing	15 to 20 breaths/minute	15 to 20 breaths/minute	10 to 12 breaths/minute
Breathing with advanced airway	8 to 10 breaths/minute	8 to 10 breaths/minute	8 to 10 breaths/minute
Circulation			
Pulse check	Brachial or femoral	Carotid or femoral	Carotid or femoral
Compression area	Center of chest, in between the nipples	Lower half of the sternum	Lower half of the sternum, between the nipples
Compression width	1 Rescuer: Two fingers 2 Rescuers: Two thumbs—encircling hands	2 Hands: Heel of one hand with second on top 1 Hand: Heel of one hand	2 Hands: Heel of one hand with second on top
Compression depth	$\frac{1}{3}$ to $\frac{1}{2}$ the anterior-posterior depth of the chest	$\frac{1}{3}$ to $\frac{1}{2}$ the anterior-posterior depth of the chest	1½ to 2 inches
Compression rate	Approximately 100/minute 1 Rescuer: 30:2 2 Rescuers: 15:2	Approximately 100/minute 1 Rescuer: 30:2 2 Rescuers: 15:2	Approximately 100/minute 1 Rescuer: 30:2
AED	No recommendation for or against use in infants.	Use pediatric pads from 1 to 8 years of age. Use as soon as available for sudden witnessed collapse.	Use adult pads. Use as soon as available for sudden witnessed collapse.
Foreign body airway obstruction— Conscious	Back slaps and chest thrusts	Abdominal thrusts	Abdominal thrusts
Foreign body airway obstruction— Unconscious	CPR	CPR	CPR

Notes: AED = automated external defibrillator.
Tabulated from: American Heart Association. (2006). *Pediatric advanced life support. Professional provider manual.* Dallas, TX: Author.

TABLE 13.4 Commonly Used Resuscitation Medications

Medication	Route/Dose	Indications for Use	Action	Side Effects	Nursing Implications
Epinephrine (Adrenalin)	IV, IO: 0.01 mg/kg (0.1 mL/kg) of 1:10,000 IV/IO every 3 to 5 minutes ETT 0.1 mg/kg (0.1 mL/kg) of 1:1,000 ETT every 3 to 5 minutes	❐ Cardiac arrest ❐ Symptomatic bradycardia unresponsive to ventilation with 100% oxygen ❐ Hypotension related to distributive shock	α-Adrenergic action (vasoconstriction) increases systemic vascular resistance and increases systolic and diastolic BP. ß-Adrenergic actions increases myocardial contractility, increases heart rate, relaxes smooth muscle in the skeletal muscle vascular bed and in the bronchi.	Tachycardia, hypertension, peripheral vasoconstriction, increased myocardial oxygen consumption, cardiac dysrhythmias, anxiety, headache, weakness, tremor, decreased renal and splanchnic blood flow	Incompatible with alkaline solutions. Tissue irritant: extravasation may be treated with phentolamine. High dose not recommended and should only be used for ETT dosing.
Amiodarone	VT (with pulses)/ SVT: IV/IO: 5 mg/kg up to a maximum dose of 300 mg Pulseless VT or ventricular fibrillation: IV/IO: 5 mg/kg (maximum dose of 300 mg), can repeat to a maximum daily dose of 15 mg/kg)	❐ VT—with pulses ❐ SVT ❐ Pulseless VT ❐ Ventricular fibrillation	Prolongs action potential and effective refractory period, slows sinus rate Causes vasodilatation and AV nodal suppression, prolongs Q-T interval	Headache, tremors, pulmonary fibrosis, hypotension, bradycardia, SA node dysfunction, torsades de pointes, coagulation abnormalities	For the patient with pulses (VT or SVT) administer over a 20- to 60-minute period. Do not administer simultaneously with procainamide as can prolong QT interval and can cause hypotension. For pulseless VT and VF, give IV push.

TABLE 13.4 Commonly Used Resuscitation Medications (continued)

Medication	Route/Dose	Indications for Use	Action	Side Effects	Nursing Implications
Adenosine (Adenocard)	IV: 0.1 mg/kg (up to 6 mg) Second dose 0.2 mg/kg (up to 12 mg)	❑ SVT	Causes temporary block of AV node conduction. Stimulates adenosine receptors in the heart and vascular smooth muscle.	Transient, because of its short half-life: Dizziness, throat tightness, hyperventilation, bronchospasm, facial flushing, and sweating	Administer rapid IV push via central venous access if present, at the injection site closest to the patient using the two-syringe technique with both syringes inserted into the injection port simultaneously (administer the medication, then a 5-mL flush of normal saline solution). Provide continuous electrocardiogram monitoring and frequent BP monitoring during administration. A defibrillator should be set up on standby.
Atropine	IV, IO: 0.02 mg/kg ETT: 0.04 to 0.06 mg/kg	❑ Vagally mediated symptomatic bradycardia ❑ Prevent vagally mediated bradycardia ❑ Toxins/ overdose	Parasympathetic drug accelerates the sinus or atrial pacemakers and atrioventricular conduction.	Tachycardia, palpitations, fatigue, headache, restlessness, impaired GI motility, urinary retention, and blurred vision	Dose must be sufficient to produce vagolytic effects. Minimum dose in a child is 0.1 mg. A maximum dose is 0.5 mg in a child and 1 mg in an adolescent. Drug blocks bradycardia associated with hypoxia; monitor the child's oxygen saturation values.

TABLE 13.4 Commonly Used Resuscitation Medications (continued)

Medication	Route/Dose	Indications for Use	Action	Side Effects	Nursing Implications
Lidocaine	IV, IO: 1 mg/kg	❏ Wide-complex VT ❏ Ventricular fibrillation/ pulseless VT ❏ Ventricular ectopy	Decreases automaticity. Suppresses ventricular dysrhythmias.	Seizures (high levels), hypotension, dyspnea, respiratory depression or arrest, nausea, vomiting	Follow initial administration with a lidocaine infusion. The infusion rate should be 20–50 µg/kg/minute. Start the infusion within 15 minutes of the initial bolus dose or repeat half of the initial dose every 15 minutes until a drip is started.
Dextrose	Child—IV, IO: 0.5 to 1 g/kg	❏ Hypoglycemia	Glucose provides a significant energy source during episodes of stress.	Hyperglycemia	Hypertonic glucose ($D_{25}W$ or $D_{50}W$) is hyperosmolar and may sclerose peripheral veins. The concentration of glucose administered to neonates should not exceed $D_{10}W$. Five to 10 mL/kg of $D_{10}W$ will deliver 0.5 to 1 g/kg of glucose and is a fast, easy, and safe way to administer dextrose.

TABLE 13.4 Commonly Used Resuscitation Medications (continued)

Medication	Route/Dose	Indications for Use	Action	Side Effects	Nursing Implications
Calcium chloride 10%	IV, IO: 20 mg/kg, may repeat if clinical indication persists	☐ Emergency treatment of hypocalcemic tetany ☐ Treatment of hypermagnesemia ☐ Cardiac disturbances related to hyperkalemia, hypocalcemia, or calcium channel blocking agent toxicity	Mediates nerve and muscle performance via action potential excitation threshold regulation.	Vasodilatation, hypotension, bradycardia, cardiac arrhythmias, ventricular fibrillation, lethargy, coma, erythema, tissue necrosis, muscle weakness	Give slow IV push in cardiac arrest. Infuse over a 30- to 60-minute period for other indications. Monitor electrocardiogram and BP. Flush IV tubing well if giving calcium and sodium bicarbonate as the two will form an insoluble precipitate in the tubing if allowed to mix.
Sodium bicarbonate	IV: 1 mEq/kg as a single dose	☐ Documented metabolic acidosis ☐ Hypercalcemia ☐ Sodium channel blocker overdose (tricyclic antidepressant)	Elevates the plasma pH	Edema, cerebral hemorrhage (especially with rapid injection), hypernatremia, gastric distention	Tissue necrosis can occur with extravasation. Do not mix with calcium salts, catecholamines, or atropine. The 4.2% solution should be used with infants because of the hyperosmolar nature of the drug. Only give after ensuring adequate ventilation. Flush IV tubing with normal saline afterward.

Notes: BP = blood pressure; $D_{10}W$ = 10% dextrose in water; $D_{25}W$ = 25% dextrose in water; $D_{50}W$ = 50% dextrose in water; ETT = endotracheal tube; IM = intramuscular; IO = intraosseous; IV = intravenous; SA = sinoatrial; AV=atrioventricular node; SVT = supraventricular tachycardia; VT = ventricular tachycardia.

American Heart Association. (2006). Pediatric advanced life support. Professional provider manual. Dallas, TX: Author.

Taketomo, C. K., Hodding, J. H., & Kraus, D. M. (2007). *Pediatric dosage handbook* (14th ed.) Hudson, OH: Lexi-Company.

References

1. Zideman, D. A., & Hazinski, M. F. (2008). Background and epidemiology of pediatric cardiac arrest. *Pediatric Clinics of North America, 55,* 847–859.

2. American Heart Association. (2006). *Pediatric advanced life support (provider manual).* Dallas, TX: Author.

3. Doniger, S. J., & Sharieff, G. Q. (2007). Pediatric resuscitation update. *Emergency Medical Clinics of North America, 25,* 947–960.

4. McDowell, B. M. (2006). Changes in CPR and ECC for pediatric nurses. *Journal for Specialists in Pediatric Nursing, 4,* 251–253.

5. Donoghue, A. J., Nadkarni, V., Berg, R. A., Osmond, M. H., Wells, G., Nesbitt, L., et al. (2005). Out-of-hospital pediatric cardiac arrest: An epidemiologic review and assessment of current knowledge. *Annals of Emergency Medicine, 46*(6), 512–522.

6. McCormack, J. G. & Oglesby, A. (2008). Trauma and burns in children. *Anesthesia and Intensive Care Medicine, 10,* 81–86.

7. Dingeman, R. S., Mitchell, E. A., Meyer, E. C., & Curley, M. A. Q. (2007). Parent presence during complex invasive procedures and cardiopulmonary resuscitation: A systematic review of the literature. *Pediatrics, 120,* 842–854.

8. Henderson, D. P. & Knapp, J. F. (2006). Report of the national consensus conference on family presence during pediatric cardiopulmonary resuscitation and procedures. *Journal of Emergency Nursing, 32,* 23–29.

SECTION FIVE
Clinical Emergencies

FOURTEEN

Respiratory Emergencies

Ramona Randolph, RN, BSN

Introduction

Respiratory illnesses account for almost 10% of pediatric emergency department (ED) visits. Approximately 20% of all pediatric hospital admissions are due to respiratory illness.[1] The anatomy and immaturity of the respiratory system make children more prone to complications and significant morbidity. Presenting symptoms and illnesses can range in severity from minor to life threatening. Emergency nurses must know the implications of these symptoms to be able to recognize the need for immediate intervention. An accurate assessment is essential in reducing the risk of progression of respiratory distress to respiratory failure and cardiac arrest. The purpose of this chapter is to review the common respiratory conditions in the pediatric patient, their signs and symptoms, and the nursing interventions for these conditions.

Respiratory function depends on the following:

❑ Adequate oxygenation to maintain perfusion

❑ Effective elimination of carbon dioxide

Gas exchange occurs between the lung capillaries and the walls of the alveoli. The pressure gradient of the gases between alveolar air and pulmonary blood causes oxygen to diffuse from the alveoli to the blood, and carbon dioxide to diffuse from the blood to the alveoli.[2] Ventilation occurs through inspiration and expiration, as intrathoracic pressures changes and air moves into and out of the lungs.

Respiratory distress is a state characterized by an increased respiratory rate and increased respiratory effort. Respiratory distress may be associated with changes in airway sounds, color, and mental status. These indicators may vary in severity. As the child tires or as the respiratory function cannot be maintained to provide adequate gas exchange, signs of respiratory failure will occur. Respiratory failure is a state of inadequate oxygenation, ventilation, or both and inability to excrete CO_2 produced by the body.

Respiratory distress or failure can be classified into one or more of the following groups:

❑ Upper airway obstruction

❑ Lower airway obstruction

❑ Lung tissue (parenchymal) disease

❑ Disordered control of breathing

Respiratory failure requires immediate interventions to prevent respiratory arrest, which can then ultimately lead to cardiac arrest.[3]

Embryologic Development of the Respiratory System

The development of the respiratory system begins as early as the 16th week of gestation. The following briefly describes the development of the lungs, upper airway, and the pulmonary circulation.

Lungs

The lungs develop in four different stages.[4]

1. Pseudoglandular stage (6–16 weeks). The developing lungs resemble exocrine glands at this stage. By 16 weeks, all major elements of the lung have formed except those involved with gas exchange, and respiration is not possible.

2. Canalicular stage (16–26 weeks). The lumina of the bronchi and terminal bronchioles become larger, and the lung tissue becomes highly vascular. Respiration is possible at the end of this stage because some thin-walled terminal sacs have developed at the ends of the respiratory bronchioles and the lung tissue is well vascularized.

3. Terminal Sac stage (26 weeks to birth). During this stage many more terminal sacs or saccules develop and their epithelium becomes very thin. Capillaries begin to bulge into these sacs. The blood-air barrier is established which permits adequate gas exchange for survival of the fetus if it is born prematurely. Surfactant is formed in amounts sufficient to allow survival of the fetus.

4. Alveolar stage (32 weeks to 8 years). At this stage the lungs are well developed so that they are capable of functioning as soon as the baby is born. This stage in-

cludes the transition from dependence on the placenta for gas exchange to autonomous gas exchange. Mature alveoli do not form until after birth; approximately 95% develop postnatally. Between ages 3 and 8, the adult complement of 300 million alveoli is achieved.

Upper Airway[5]

1. Nose. Nasal cavities begin in the embryo at 4 weeks as widely separated pits on the face. The maxillary sinuses are largest at birth. The ethmoid sinuses are present and increase in size throughout life; frontal and nasal sinuses do not begin to invade the frontal or sphenoid bones until several years after birth.

2. Pharynx. In the 4-week embryo, the oropharyngeal membrane between the foregut and the stomodeum begins to disintegrate to establish continuity between the oral cavity and the pharynx .

3. Larynx. The laryngotracheal groove begins as a ridge on the ventral portion of the pharynx during the fourth week of embryologic life. By the eighth week, vocal cords begin to appear.

4. Trachea. The trachea begins to develop in the 24-day-old embryo and at 26 to 28 days the the bronchial tree begins to develop.

Pulmonary Circulation

Development of the pulmonary circulation closely follows development of the airway and alveoli:

1. Preacinar arteries develop in utero and branch along the airways.

2. Muscular arteries end at the level of the terminal bronchiole in the fetus and newborn but gradually extend to the alveolar level during childhood.

Pediatric Considerations

Infants and young children have anatomic and physiologic characteristics that predispose them to respiratory distress.[2]

❑ Infants are obligatory nose breathers until the age of 6 months, because the elongated epiglottis, positioned high in the pharynx, almost meets the soft palate. Blocked nares do not lead to complete upper airway obstruction. By the sixth month, growth and descent of the larynx reduces the amount of obstruction. Nasal breathing doubles the resistance to airflow and proportionately increases the work of breathing.

❑ The child's epiglottis is longer and more flaccid than that of an adult. The more anterior and cephalad epiglottis in a newborn may make intubation more

difficult.

❑ A small upper airway makes infants more susceptible to obstruction from edema, foreign bodies, or congenital anomalies. In the infant and small child, the narrowest portion of the airway is the cricoid cartilage ring. This is the only point within the larynx at which the walls are completely enclosed in cartilage. Swelling from trauma or infection can lead to additional narrowing in this area, producing large increases in airway resistance.

❑ Smaller lower airways predispose the infant to mucus plugs and ventilation-perfusion mismatch. In addition, because of their limited alveolar space they have a smaller area for gas exchange.[2]

❑ Infants have a more compliant chest wall and poorly developed intercostal muscles. Therefore, the lungs are not well supported. If the airway is obstructed, active inspiration may result in paradoxical chest movement with sternal and intercostal retractions.[2]

❑ The tidal volume of infants and toddlers is largely dependent on the movement of the diaphragm. High intrathoracic pressure or abdominal distention compromises respiration because the intercostal muscles are unable to lift the chest wall.[2]

Focused History

The following history should be obtained for all children who present to the emergency department with a respiratory complaint or signs and symptoms of respiratory distress:

❑ Past medical history, including preexisting medical conditions that may contribute to the respiratory distress (cardiac disease, chronic conditions such as cystic fibrosis, and bronchopulmonary dysplasia)

❑ Immunization status

❑ Onset of symptoms

❑ Associated symptoms

❑ Medications that the child is taking (including over-the-counter medications)

❑ Diet

❑ Diapers and urine output

❑ Trauma

Other history depends on the signs and symptoms. These are discussed later in more detail, for each individual disease or condition.

Physical Assessment

The standard assessment (Chapter 5), focusing on the signs and symptoms of respiratory distress, is done for all children presenting with a respiratory complaint. The initial recognition of respiratory distress is more important than determining the cause. When the assessment is performed:

❏ The child should be allowed to remain with the caregiver and maintain a position in which he or she is most comfortable and able to breathe with the least amount of effort. Often, the child in moderate to severe distress will sit upright with the head, neck, and jaw extended (tripod position).

❏ The child should be approached as gently as possible; anxiety increases the need for oxygen. Observing the child without touching (the "across-the-room assessment") can reveal many signs and symptoms of distress.

❏ The assessment should begin with the least intrusive procedures.

Physical assessment of the child in respiratory distress includes:

❏ Assess the airway.
  ▪ Patency
❏ Assess breathing.
  ▪ Respiratory rate. Normal respiratory rates in children are:[3]
    • Infants = 30 – 60 breaths per minute
    • Toddlers = 24 – 40 breaths per minute
    • Preschoolers = 22 – 34 breaths per minute
    • School-age children = 18 – 30 breaths per minute
    • Adolescents = 12 – 16 breaths per minute
❏ A respiratory rate consistently greater than 60 breaths per minute for any age is abnormal and is a red flag.
❏ Respiratory effort
  ▪ Location and depth of chest retractions
  ▪ Nasal flaring
  ▪ Use of accessory muscles
❏ Presence of abnormal breath sounds
  ▪ Inspiratory or expiratory wheezes
  ▪ Inspiratory stridor
  ▪ Grunting
  ▪ Gurgling
❏ Quality of breath sounds
  ▪ Diminished or absent

❏ Assess circulation.
  ▪ Changes in skin color: Pallor, mottling, or cyanosis
  ▪ Tachycardia or bradycardia
  ▪ Capillary refill time
❏ Assess neurologic status.
  ▪ Restlessness or fatigue
  ▪ Changes in mental status: Confusion or inability to recognize caregiver

Psychosocial Assessment

Respiratory distress causes anxiety to both the child and the caregiver. The goal of the ED nurse is to reduce anxiety by providing a calm environment, individualizing interventions, and considering the child's needs. These needs may include:

❏ Allowing the parent to remain with the child as much as possible.

❏ Providing information about the illness and the child's condition. Often the parent has to be told what the findings are and what they mean. For example, "Your child is breathing very noisily, but I can hear good air movement and her color is good. We will continue to observe her."

❏ Providing privacy.

❏ Allowing the child to make choices when possible.

❏ Providing age-appropriate toys and distraction.

Nursing Interventions

The following interventions are generally performed for the child in respiratory distress. Additional interventions are included under specific conditions:

1. Assess and maintain airway, breathing and circulation.
   ▪ Administer oxygen by a method best tolerated by the child and one that will deliver the highest concentration, such as a pediatric nonrebreather mask for severe respiratory distress.
   ▪ Allow the child to maintain a position of comfort.
   ▪ Ensure that pediatric emergency airway and ventilation equipment is available.
2. Assist ventilations with a pediatric-sized bag-mask either self-inflating or flow inflating.
3. Be prepared to assist with endotracheal intubation:
   ▪ Rapid-sequence induction should be performed.
   ▪ Rapid-sequence induction may be used to induce anesthesia and neuromuscular blockade in a fully or partially conscious child before intubation and is indicated for children requiring emergency intuba-

TABLE 14.1 Steps in Rapid-Sequence Induction

Steps	Comments
1. Preoxygenate	Preoxygenation by spontaneously breathing or bag-mask-ventilating with 100% oxygen for 2 to 5 minutes results in an oxygen reserve. The child should already have cardiac and oximetry monitors and an intravenous line.
2. Premedicate	Medications for premedication may include: Atropine—Used to prevent bradycardia due to vagal response during procedure Lidocaine—Used to prevent increased ICP response to intubation and suppress cough reflex
3. Administer sedatives	Sedatives include: Thiopental—depresses the CNS; does not provide analgesia. Used in children with head injury because it reduces cerebral blood flow and oxygen consumption. Ketamine—produces analgesia, amnesia, and dissociation from the environment with protection of respiratory drive. Drug of choice for children with asthma, respiratory failure, or shock. Diazepam—produces sedation but no analgesia. Can cause respiratory depression. Midazolam—a benzodiazepine but is faster acting and has shorter duration.
4. Administer muscle relaxant	Muscle relaxants include: Succinylcholine Vecuronium Rocuronium
5. Monitor child throughout procedure	Observe for bradycardia, which most always indicates hypoxia. Observe skin color, perfusion, and capillary refill. If signs of hypoxia occur, the procedure should be stopped and the patient should be ventilated.
6. Secure ET tube and confirm placement	The child should be restrained to prevent him or her from pulling tube. Tube placement is confirmed by auscultation, chest radiograph, end-tidal CO_2 monitoring, or improvement in the child's condition.

Notes: CNS = central nervous system; ICP = intracranial pressure.
Ralston, M., & Hazinski, M. F. (2006). *Pediatric advanced life support manual* (pp. 34–43). Dallas, TX: American Heart Association.

anesthesia and neuromuscular blockade in a fully or partially conscious child before intubation and is indicated for children requiring emergency intubation in the emergency department.[3] Table 14.1 lists the steps in rapid-sequence induction.

- Confirm placement of the endotracheal tube (ET) by at least two methods and secure the ET tube.

4. Prepare for mechanical ventilation if the intubated child will be in the emergency department for extended periods of time. Generally, if a patient is being mechanically ventilated in the emergency department, it is desirable to have a respiratory therapist present at all times.

5. Maintain normal temperature to minimize oxygen and fluid requirements.

6. Monitor vital signs.

7. Monitor pulse oximetry.
- Pulse oximetry measures oxygen saturation but does not measure effectiveness of ventilation.
- Failure to detect a pulse signal may be a mechanical error or an indication that the child is in a low-perfusion state and requires urgent treatment.[3]
- Use data in conjunction with assessment and appearance of the child. Do not rely on the monitor to be the only reflection of the child's condition.

8. Encourage oral fluids if the child's respiratory rate is not too rapid, and provide intravenous fluids as ordered for children in severe respiratory distress or respiratory failure.

9. Administer medication as needed (e.g., albuterol, epinephrine).

10. Perform frequent reassessments for the following:

   - Vital signs
   - Airway
   - Breathing
   - Circulation

11. Keep parents informed of the progress in the child's condition, assessment findings, and reason for interventions.

12. Prepare the child and parents for admission or transfer to a pediatric facility (Chapter 8).

Selected Respiratory Emergencies

Croup (Laryngotracheobronchitis)

Croup is a viral infection that causes inflammation of the upper respiratory tract, initially in the pharynx, spreading down to the larynx and occasionally further along the respiratory tract.[6] Croup is usually seen in the late fall and winter and is caused predominantly by the parainfluenza virus. Other viral agents include rhinovirus, influenza A, and respiratory syncytial virus (RSV). Children between the ages of 6 months and 3 years are primarily affected. Croup is the most common cause for stridor in the febrile child.[6]

Pathophysiology

Infection causes endothelial damage, mucus production, loss of ciliary function, and edema along the upper respiratory tract.[6] The characteristic stridor occurs as the child inspires air through a small, edematous airway.

Focused History

- ❏ Gradual onset of symptoms; may be over 1 to 2 days
- ❏ Cold symptoms
- ❏ Cough, worse at night, generally described as a barking, seal-like cough
- ❏ Low-grade fever—temperature less than 101.3 °F (38.5 °C)
- ❏ Hoarse voice

Focused Assessment

The airway assessment described earlier in this chapter is performed. Assessment findings should include the use of a scoring system that will help to decide on the severity of the illness. Individual hospitals may have a specific scoring system. The symptoms used to score the severity of the illness usually are:

- ❏ Tachypnea and tachycardia
- ❏ Inspiratory stridor
- ❏ Expiratory wheezing
- ❏ Suprasternal and subcostal retractions, indicating increased work of breathing
- ❏ Cough
- ❏ Skin color
- ❏ Oxygen saturation
- ❏ Signs and symptoms of dehydration because of an inability to take oral fluids.
- ❏ Fever with a temperature ranging from 100.4 °F to 102.2 °F (38 °C to 39 °C).

Although presenting symptoms may be minor, children with croup are at risk for upper airway obstruction and respiratory failure.

Nursing Interventions

1. Administer oxygen as tolerated by the child and if the oxygen saturation is less than 90% to 95% depending on locale.

2. Provide cool mist with oxygen using a nebulizer.

3. Monitor oxygen saturation.

4. Perform frequent reassessment, including vital signs, location and degree of retractions, frequency and type of cough, breath sounds, and behavior, to detect any deterioration in the child's condition.

5. Encourage fluids.

6. Administer medications as ordered.

   - Racemic epinephrine, administered by nebulizer, may be prescribed for moderate-to-severe croup:
     - The dose is 0.25 mL of 2.25%, diluted with 3 to 5 mL of normal saline solution.[6]
     - Symptoms may be relieved for up to 2 hours after the aerosol treatment.
     - Children are commonly observed in the emergency department for 2 to 3 hours because of the rebound effect of racemic epinephrine, which may cause the condition to worsen.
   - The efficacy of steroid therapy is still being questioned.
     - Oral or intramuscular dexamethasone, 0.6 mg/kg, may be ordered.[6]
     - Oral steroids may be given if the child can tolerate oral intake.

7. Prepare the child for admission or transfer.

Home Care and Prevention

❑ Provide clear oral and written instructions to the parents.

❑ Review the signs of increasing distress and when to return to the hospital.

❑ Provide discharge instructions that include measures that may help if symptoms develop in the child at home:

- Use a vaporizer to provide a cool mist.
- Sit with the child in a bathroom filled with steam.
- Take the child out into the cool night air or sit by an open window.
- Encourage the child to drink cool fluids.
- Manage fever—antipyretics.
- Hand washing.

Epiglottitis (Supraglottitis)

Epiglottitis is a life-threatening bacterial infection causing inflammation and swelling of the epiglottis and surrounding tissue. The incidence of epiglottitis has decreased greatly since the introduction of the Haemophilus influenzae type b (HIB) vaccine.[6] Recent studies show a 95% decrease in the incidence of invasive HIB disease since 1988; it now occurs primarily in undervaccinated children or in infants too young to have completed the primary series of vaccination. Occasionally it may be caused by group A Streptococcus pneumoniae and staphylococcus.[6] Children between the ages of 3 to 7 years are commonly affected.

Pathophysiology

Infection of the epiglottis occurs when organisms pass through the mucosal barrier, resulting in bacteremia. The infection causes inflammation and edema of the epiglottis and rapidly spreads to the entire supraglottic area, resulting in increased secretions and a narrowed upper airway.

Focused History

The history is key to differentiating croup and epiglottitis.

❑ Sudden onset of symptoms; may be within 2 to 4 hours of presenting to the emergency department

❑ High fever

❑ Severe sore throat or difficulty swallowing

❑ Drooling (not always present)

❑ Absence of cough or minimal cough (Severe sore throat makes coughing painful, and the child will resist coughing.)

Focused Assessment

Children with epiglottitis look sick and anxious. However, symptoms of respiratory distress may be absent, and a well-appearing child with minimal symptoms may progress to complete airway obstruction in less than 4 hours. Adolescents may present only with complaints of fever, sore throat, and difficulty swallowing. The assessment should be limited to determining the degree of respiratory distress.

Interventions to support the airway must be started. Avoid upsetting the child, because this may lead to laryngospasm and subsequent airway obstruction.[6] The following areas should be assessed:

❑ Assess airway and breathing.

- Patency
- Drooling or inability to swallow
- Respiratory rate
- Nasal flaring
- The location and depth of retractions
- The presence of stridor

❑ Assess circulation.

- Skin color, for pallor or cyanosis
- Tachycardia

❑ Assess general appearance of the child; may look "sick" and anxious.

Nursing Interventions

Interventions are directed at maintaining a patent airway. If possible, allow the child to remain with the caregiver:[6]

1. Administer oxygen as tolerated by the child.

2. Prepare equipment for bag-mask ventilation and intubation.

   - Direct visualization of the epiglottis and intubation will usually take place in the operating room, but the emergency department should be prepared to intubate.

3. After the airway is secure, place a peripheral intravenous line for fluid resuscitation and for antibiotics (usually Ampicillin and a Cephalosporin to cover *H. influenzae* and *Staphylococcus aureus*).

4. Explain all procedures and treatment to the child and family.

5. A radiograph may be ordered if the airway is stable and there is a question about the diagnosis.

   - Radiographic anteroposterior and lateral views of the neck will show the degree of airway narrowing. This assists in determining the immediate management of the patient but is rarely needed.

- In most cases of severe respiratory distress, radiographs should not be performed before intubation. The nurse and physician should accompany the patient to radiology, equipped with emergency airway equipment.

6. Prepare for admission procedures and/or transfer to the operating room for elective endotracheal intubation.

Home Care and Prevention

Children with epiglottitis will be admitted to the hospital for elective intubation and intravenous antibiotic administration. Because the HIB vaccine appears to be helping to reduce the incidence of epiglottitis, question caregivers about the immunization status of all children presenting to the emergency department. Educate parents on the need to keep immunizations current.

Bronchiolitis

Bronchiolitis is an acute, distressing, potentially life-threatening respiratory condition that affects infants and young children. Children can present with coryza (nasal drainage) and sometimes low-grade fever progressing over a few days to cough, tachypnea, hyperinflation, chest retraction, and widespread crackles, wheezes, or both. Bronchiolitis occurs primarily in children younger than 2 years of age, but the infection is most severe in infants under 6 months.[7] This condition is mainly seen in the winter and spring. RSV is the most common pathogen and is responsible for at least 70% of the children admitted with bronchiolitis. This virus is considered a dangerous pathogen in infancy and early childhood.[2]

Outbreaks of illness caused by RSV are commonly seen during the winter months. High-risk groups for severe infections are infants younger than 6 weeks; premature infants; and those with chronic lung disease of prematurity, congenital heart disease, neurologic disease, or immunodeficiency. Bronchiolitis-associated deaths are fortunately very rare.[7]

Pathophysiology

The infection process results in inflammation and necrosis of the epithelial cells lining the bronchioles and bronchi, which in turn causes the sloughing of these cells leading to the narrowing of the lumen. In addition, edema and the increased mucus production further obstruct the narrowed airways and result in tachypnea and wheezing. Hyperinflation and atelectasis may occur distal to the obstruction.

Focused History

Symptoms of respiratory distress may occur over a few days but also have been noted to occur within hours. Tachypnea is often the first sign and may be accompanied by audible wheezing. Apnea may be the only initial symptom in high-risk infants. Other historical findings include:

- ❏ Cold for 1 to 2 days
- ❏ Low-grade fever, runny nose, and decreased appetite
- ❏ Cough, sometimes with vomiting
- ❏ Difficulty breathing
- ❏ Apnea spells, described by parents

Focused Assessment

The appearance of the child with bronchiolitis will depend on the stage of the illness and the degree of respiratory distress. The rate and work of breathing should be observed before any intrusive procedures are performed. Assessment includes:

- ❏ Assess the airway and breathing.
  - Respiratory rate: Often 50 to 80 breaths per minute or higher. Respirations may be shallow.
  - Retractions: Signs of respiratory fatigue include a reduction in respiratory rate and a concurrent increase in retractions.
  - Wheezing and a prolonged expiratory phase. Breath sounds may be unequal because of the irregular pattern of obstruction.
- ❏ Assess the circulation.
  - Tachycardia
  - Signs of dehydration because of the inability to take oral fluids resulting from increased work of breathing. Skin turgor, fontanelles, urinary output, and the presence or absence of tears should be evaluated.
- ❏ Assess neurologic status.
  - The child may be alert or appear restless or fatigued. Apnea spells may indicate the need for intubation.

The child may have a low-grade fever.

Nursing Interventions

1. Administer oxygen.
2. Ensure the availability of equipment to provide respiratory support.
3. Monitor respiratory rate, heart rate, and oxygen saturation.
4. Allow the caregiver to stay with and hold the infant or child.

5. Suction (nasopharyngeal) frequently (every 2 hours) to remove secretions from the child's airways. This often alleviates respiratory distress and improves oxygen saturation levels.

6. Give oral fluids. Administer intravenous fluids as ordered.

7. Assess the child frequently. Document and report changes in work of breathing, breath sounds, or neurologic and hydration status.

8. Administer medications, as ordered.

    ▪ Currently controversy exists about the efficacy of albuterol in treating bronchiolitis, even though it is widely used.[7]

    ▪ A bronchodilator, delivered via nebulizer, is the initial treatment.

    ▪ Albuterol, 0.1 to 0.3 mL of a 0.5% solution, may be repeated every 20 minutes.[6]

    ▪ Tremors, tachycardia, and vomiting are possible side effects of albuterol.

9. Keep the caregiver informed about procedures and any changes in the child's condition.

10. Children with underlying cardiac or pulmonary disease usually require admission.

Home Care and Prevention

Discharge instructions should include:

❐ Signs that may indicate that the child should be returned to the hospital, such as increased work of breathing, inability or refusal to take fluids, and signs and symptoms of dehydration.

❐ Information on medications.

❐ Instructions to keep infants at home and away from crowds.

❐ Instructions for home use of oxygen if prescribed.

❐ In a high-risk group of children under 1 year of age, palivizumab (Synagis) has been shown to be effective in preventing severe bronchiolitis when given prophylactically.[8]

Asthma

Asthma is defined as a chronic inflammatory disorder of the airways in which many cells or cell elements play a role. The paradigm of asthma has been expanded from bronchospasm and airway inflammation to include airway remodeling in some patients. This means that in some persons who have asthma, airflow limitation may be only partially reversible because of permanent structural changes that occur and are associated with a progressive loss of lung function.[9]

Asthma is the most common chronic disease of childhood and the third leading cause of hospitalizations in children under the age of 15 years. Although the onset of asthma may occur at any age, 80% to 90% of children have their first symptoms before 4 or 5 years of age.[2]

The National Asthma Education and Prevention Program (NAEPP) focuses on achieving and maintaining control for patients with asthma. The classifications under this program are mild intermittent, mild persistent, moderate persistent, and severe persistent. These four categories are listed as steps because they also provide a stepwise approach to pharmacologic therapy and management.[9]

The airway of the asthmatic child is more reactive and sensitive than in a child who does not have asthma because some degree of inflammation of the airway is always present. The degree of airway reactivity determines the severity of chronic asthma. When the child is exposed to certain triggers, the airway becomes hyperresponsive, resulting in bronchospasm, increased inflammation, and mucus production.

These triggers may include:

❐ Allergens

❐ Upper respiratory tract infection

❐ Exercise

❐ Weather

❐ Environmental irritants, such as cigarette smoke and pollution

❐ Emotional stress

❐ Animals

❐ Food allergens or additives

Pathophysiology

Asthma results from complex interactions among inflammatory cells, mediators, and the cells and tissues present in the airways. The recognition of the importance of inflammation has made the use of anti-inflammatory agents a key component of asthma therapy. The airway smooth muscle has an increased responsiveness, which then results in several physiologic manifestations, such as wheezing and dyspnea, with eventual obstruction. Another component of asthma is bronchospasm and obstruction. Exacerbations are episodes of progressively worsening shortness of breath, cough, wheezing, or chest tightness or some combination of these changes. They also are characterized by decreases in expiratory airflow. Hypoxemia can occur during episodes because of mismatching of ventilation and perfusion.[2] Metabolic changes also take place as the increased work of breathing increases the oxygen and energy requirements. Young children are more susceptible to status asthmaticus. Children who continue to display respiratory distress despite vigorous therapeutic measures, especially the use of sympathomimetics, are considered to have status asthmaticus. Status asthmaticus is a medical emergency that can result in respiratory failure and death if untreated.[2] In the child younger than 5 years of age, peripheral airways result in disproportionate increases in resistance to air flow. Respiratory reserve is limited and increases with age as the size of the conducting airways become larger.[6]

Focused History

☐ Tightness in the chest, shortness of breath, coughing, and wheezing

☐ Fatigue, inability to exercise, or chest pain with exercise

☐ Allergy or cold symptoms, runny nose, itchy eyes, or sneezing

☐ Family history

☐ Number and severity of previous episodes

☐ Previous hospitalizations and intubations

☐ Previous steroid use

☐ Current medications and those given before arrival at the emergency department

☐ Recent upper respiratory tract infection or known exposure to other triggers

☐ Duration of current symptoms

☐ Check peak expiratory flow meter reading for personal best and compare with peak expiratory flow rate (PEFR) before child came to the emergency department.[9]

Focused Assessment

The child should be quickly assessed for the degree of respiratory distress.

☐ Assess the airway and breathing. Assessment findings may include:

 - Tachypnea. A decrease in respiratory rate may not be a sign of improvement but may signal fatigue and impending respiratory failure.

 - Wheezing on expiration (may progress to inspiratory and expiratory wheezing) with a prolonged expiratory phase. Absence of wheezing may indicate a severe obstruction with little airflow.

 - Unequal breath sounds that may vary from loud and coarse to quiet and high pitched.

 - Inability to speak, which has been correlated with

hypoxia and a decreased peak flow rate.

 - Nasal flaring

 - Intercostal retractions

 - Use of accessory muscles

 - Cough

☐ Assess circulation and skin color. Findings may include:

 - Pallor or cyanosis

 - Deteriorating mental status and increased tachycardia, which indicate increasing hypoxemia

Nursing Interventions

In addition to the standard interventions performed for the child in respiratory distress, the following should be done as appropriate:

1. Obtain a baseline PEFR using a peak flow meter.

 - This measures the speed at which air is forced out of the lungs.

 - Children older than 4 to 5 years of age can usually perform this test, and children with chronic asthma often use it at home.

 - It is helpful to compare the child's PEFR with the predicted rate for age or the child's normal rate.

 - Normal PEFR varies based on sex and height, as well as characteristics of each meter model. A rate of less than 80% of predicted or personal best is considered abnormal; a rate of less than 50% indicates moderate to severe obstruction.[2]

 - The PEFR also measures the efficacy of medication when the initial measurement is compared with the rate after treatment.

 - The NAEPP recommends that peak flow monitoring be used in children with moderate to severe persistent asthma to determine the severity of exacerbation and to guide therapeutic decisions in the home, school, or emergency department.[9]

2. Administer medications, as ordered.

 - Oxygen is recommended for most patients. Administer supplemental oxygen to maintain an SaO_2 greater than 90%.[9]

 - An inhaled short-acting β-adrenergic bronchodilator is delivered by nebulizer or metered-dose inhaler (MDI) and may be combined with an anticholinergic.[9]

 - Systemic corticosteroids suppress and reverse airway inflammation and are recommended for moderate to severe exacerbations or for patients who fail to respond promptly and completely to an

TABLE 14.2 Recommended Drug Dosages for Asthma Exacerbations

Medication	Dosage
Inhaled short-acting β$_2$-agonists	
Albuterol nebulizer solution (5 mg/mL)	0.15 mg/kg (minimum dose 2.50 mg) every 20 minutes for three doses, then 0.15 to 0.30 mg/kg (up to 10.00 mg) every 1 to 4 hour(s), as needed; or 0.50 mg/kg/hour by continuous nebulization
MDI (90 µg/puff)	Four to eight puffs every 20 minutes for three doses, then every 1 to 4 hour(s) as needed
Systemic (injected) β$_2$-antagonists	
Epinephrine 1:1,000 (1 mg/mL)	0.01 mg/kg (up to 0.30 to 0.50 mg) every 20 minutes for three doses, subcutaneously
	0.01 mg/kg every 20 minutes for three doses, then every 2 to 6 hours, as needed, subcutaneously
Terbutaline (1 mg/mL)	0.25 mg every 20 minutes for three doses, then every 2 to 4 hours
Anticholinergics	
Ipratropium bromide (Atrovent) nebulizer solution (0.25 mg/mL)	0.25 mg every 20 minutes for three doses, then every 2 to 4 hours
Ipratropium bromide (Atrovent) MDI (18 µg/mL)	Four to eight puffs, as needed
Corticosteroids (Dosing applies to all three corticosteroids)	
Prednisone	1 mg/kg every 6 hours for 48 hours, then 1 to 2 mg/kg/day (maximum = 60 mg/day) in two divided doses, until PEFR is 70% of predicted or personal best
Methylprednisolone	
Prednisolone	

National Asthma Education and Prevention Panel. (2007). *Expert panel report 3: Guidelines for the diagnosis and management of asthma* (Publication No. 08-4051). Bethesda, MD: National Institutes of Health, National Heart, Lung, and Blood Institute.

inhaled β2-antagonist.[9] Table 14.2 lists medications for asthma management and recommended dosages.

- Monitor the child for tremors, tachycardia, and vomiting, possible side effects of the medication.

For severe exacerbations unresponsive to initial treatments, whether given before arrival at the acute care setting or in the emergency department, adjunct treatments may be considered to decrease the likelihood of intubation: intravenous magnesium sulfate or heliox may be useful. Consider intravenous magnesium sulfate in patients who have life-threatening exacerbations and in those whose exacerbations remain in the severe category after 1 hour of intensive conventional therapy.[9] Heliox-driven albuterol nebulization for patients can be considered for severe exacerbations after one hour of intensive conventional therapy.[9]

3. Prepare the child and family for admission or transfer (Chapter 8).

Home Care and Prevention

Asthma is disruptive for the child and family, as well as potentially life threatening. The goal of allowing children to lead active, healthy lives can be accomplished by educating not only the child and family, but also teachers, friends, and anyone else involved in the child's care. Ensure that they are well informed about possible triggers and how to avoid those triggers, able to recognize early warning signs, and know how to intervene. Discharge instructions should include recognition of early warning signs, information on medications to be administered at home, and possible asthma triggers. The importance of good follow-up and compliance in taking medications, both bronchodilator and anti-inflammatory, must be emphasized. The NAEPP recommends continuing to assess control on an ongoing basis every 1 to 6 months with the primary care physician. This recommendation will lower recurrent exacerbations and admissions to the hospital.[9]

Patient education should include a written asthma action plan to guide patient self-management of exacerbations at home, especially for patients who have moderate or severe persistent asthma and any patient who has a history of severe exacerbations. A peak flow–based plan may be particularly useful for patients who have difficulty perceiving airflow obstruction and worsening asthma.[9]

Pneumonia

Pneumonia is an inflammation of the lung tissue, usually caused by a viral or bacterial infection. Approximately one in 50 children in the United States has pneumonia annually.[1] The organism causing pneumonia varies according to age and may be bacterial or viral in origin; however, the majority of cases are viral. Some of the causal agents include RSV, parainfluenza virus, adenovirus, rhinovirus, measles, rubella, varicella, and enteroviruses. According to age, the most common bacterial agents are:

- ❏ Newborn: Predominantly group B *streptococci*, the majority caused by aspiration of the organism during delivery

- ❏ Under 3 years: *S. pneumoniae, S. aureus,* and *H. influenzae*

- ❏ Over 3 years: *Mycoplasma pneumoniae, S. pneumoniae*

Children with chronic and acute conditions are at increased risk for development of pneumonia. Pneumonias are generally classified either by site (lobar, bronchial, or interstitial) or by etiologic agent (viral, bacterial, mycoplasmal, or associated with foreign bodies).[2]

Pathophysiology

Infection causes an inflammation in the lung tissue, leading to exudation of fluid and fibrin deposits. Accumulation of this exudate causes the lobar consolidation visible on a radiograph.

Focused History

The history is influenced by the causative agent (viral or bacterial).[6]

- ❏ Viral pneumonia:
  - Development over several days
  - Upper respiratory tract infection for several days
  - Cough
  - Low-grade fever

- ❏ Bacterial pneumonia:
  - Abrupt onset
  - Contact with other children who are sick

  - High fever with chills
  - Increased respiratory rate
  - Wet-sounding cough
  - Tired, less active, decreased appetite
  - Chest or abdominal pain
  - Cough

Focused Assessment

The overall appearance of the child is one who looks sick and is lethargic, especially for those children with a bacterial infection. Assessment findings may include:

- ❏ Tachypnea; grunting respirations
- ❏ Decreased breath sounds; diffuse wheezing
- ❏ Retractions
- ❏ Circumoral pallor or cyanosis
- ❏ Cough
- ❏ Fever; hot and dry skin
- ❏ Chest or abdominal pain

Nursing Interventions

In addition to interventions for the child in respiratory distress, the following should be done:

1. Administer supplemental oxygen as needed.
2. Provide fever management.
3. Encourage oral fluids. It may be necessary to insert a peripheral intravenous line for fluids when drinking is not possible.
4. Administer medications as ordered. Oral, intravenous, or intramuscular antibiotics may be given, depending on the suspected organism.
5. Prepare the child for a chest radiograph.
6. Prepare for admission for indications of the following:
   - Age < 1 year
   - Respiratory compromise
   - Pleural effusion
   - Dehydration
   - Failure to respond to antibiotic therapy within 24 to 48 hours[6]

Home Care and Prevention

- ❏ Educate the caregiver about the importance of continuing antibiotic therapy and returning for recheck to primary doctor if requested.

- ❏ Discuss signs and symptoms of respiratory distress that require the family to return to the emergency department.

❏ Consider immunization with pneumococcal vaccine polyvalent (Pneumovax) (to prevent pneumococcal pneumonia) in children with preexisting conditions, such as cardiac or respiratory disease.

Foreign-Body Aspiration

An aspirated foreign body may cause complete or partial obstruction of the upper or lower airway. Diagnosis is complicated by the similarity of the presenting symptoms to those of other respiratory illnesses.

Aspiration of a foreign body occurs most commonly in children younger than 4 years of age, and 65% of aspirations occur in children younger than 2 years old. Part of a child's normal development is to experiment and explore. Therefore placing objects in their mouth is a contributing factor to the risk of aspiration. This includes the child's being given food and toys that are, by shape and size, inappropriate for the child's age. Ingestion of objects, especially coins, which lodge in the esophagus, may also cause respiratory distress.

Pathophysiology

The effect of the aspirated material depends on the size, shape, and composition of the object, where it becomes lodged, and the local tissue reaction to the foreign body. Aspiration that causes an immediate and complete obstruction of the airway is a life-threatening event and is more likely to occur if the foreign body is lodged in the upper airway. If the foreign body lodges in the bronchi, the symptoms may develop over several days. Symptoms will begin to present as the air becomes trapped, leading to emphysema, atelectasis, pneumonia, and/or tissue erosion.

Focused History

The history may include:

❏ Coughing or a choking, gagging spell

❏ Wheezing or episodes of stridor

❏ Recurrent respiratory tract infections

❏ A history of ingestion

Focused Assessment

Findings will depend on the location and degree of obstruction. In addition to the standard respiratory assessment, the following should be evaluated:

❏ Breath sounds: wheezing or decreased or unequal air movement

❏ Other signs and symptoms of respiratory distress, including color, mental status, and retractions

Nursing Interventions

Acute obstruction:

1. Initiate measures to relieve the airway obstruction in accordance with American Heart Association guidelines (Chapter 13).

2. If a laryngoscopy, bronchoscopy, cricothyroidotomy, or tracheotomy is required, prepare for transfer to the operating room. Have tracheotomy tray and Magill forceps immediately available in the emergency department.

Chronic obstruction:

1. Establish an intravenous line, and administer antibiotics as prescribed. A complete blood cell count and blood culture may be ordered.

2. Obtain a chest radiograph.

Home Care and Prevention

❏ Provide education regarding age-appropriate foods and toys.

❏ Encourage caretakers to attend cardiopulmonary resuscitation classes.

Preexisting Respiratory Conditions

There are several preexisting conditions that may contribute to or cause respiratory distress in children. These include structural defects, such as kyphoscoliosis, tracheomalacia, and congenital defects, as well as cardiopulmonary conditions such as congenital heart defects and cystic fibrosis (CF). The most important aspect of caring for a child with a preexisting condition is to determine what the child's normal respiratory status is. The caregiver knows the child better than anyone and should be asked, "How do you think your child looks today?"

Cystic Fibrosis (CF) is a condition characterized by exocrine gland dysfunction that produces multisystem involvement. It is the most common lethal genetic illness among white children, adolescents, and young adults and is inherited as an autosomal recessive trait located on chromosome.[9]

Patients with CF have, among other interrelated abnormalities, an increase in viscosity of mucus secretions and an increased susceptibility to chronic colonization of the respiratory tract by certain bacteria, especially *Pseudomonas aeruginosa* and *Burkholderia cepacia*.

Goals of CF therapy are to:[2]

1. Prevent or minimize pulmonary complications.

2. Ensure adequate nutrition for growth.

3. Encourage appropriate physical activity.

These children are often brought to the emergency department for complaints related to respiratory or gastrointestinal tract infections. The goal should be to recognize and treat these infections promptly to prevent further complications. The child is treated as any other child with respiratory distress, but it is extremely important to involve the caregiver because he or she will be familiar with usual treatment and the child's baseline condition. Prior records will have to be obtained, and the child's physician should be consulted. Chest physiotherapy may be needed in the emergency department as well.

Conclusion

Children with respiratory problems are at risk for progression to severe respiratory distress and respiratory failure. If cardiopulmonary arrest occurs, the chance for survival is poor. Children will come to the emergency department with symptoms ranging from mild to severe distress. Rapid observation of the child's general appearance, accurate assessment of signs and symptoms, effective intervention, and frequent reassessment are vital to the successful management of respiratory emergencies. Caregivers are a very important resource in determining the severity of illness in children with chronic respiratory conditions.

References

1. Baker, M. D., & Ruddy, R. (2006). Pulmonary emergencies. In G. Fleisher & S. Ludwig (Eds.), *Textbook of pediatric emergency medicine* (5th ed., pp. 1067–1086). Philadelphia: Lippincott Williams & Wilkins.

2. Wilson, D., & Huekel, R. (2007). The child with respiratory dysfunction. In D. Wong (Ed.), *Nursing care of infants and children* (8th ed., pp. 1315–1385). St. Louis, MO: Mosby.

3. Ralston, M., & Hazinski, M. F. (2006). *Pediatric advanced life support manual* (pp. 34–43). Dallas, TX: American Heart Association.

4. Moore, K. L., & Persaud, T. V. N. (2008). *The developing human: Clinically oriented embryology* (8th ed., pp. 197–209). Philadelphia: Saunders.

5. Grant, M. J. C., & Webster, H. (2006). Pulmonary system. In M. C. Slota (Ed.), *Core curriculum for pediatric critical care nursing* (2nd ed., pp.40–157). St. Louis, MO: Elsevier.

6. Fleisher, G. (2006). Infectious disease emergencies. In G. Fleisher & S. Ludwig (Eds.), *Textbook of pediatric emergency medicine* (5th ed., pp. 725–793). Philadelphia: Lippincott Williams & Wilkins.

7. Smyth, R., & Openshaw, P. (2006). Bronchiolitis. *Lancet, 368,* 312–322.

8. Shah, S., & Sharieff, G. (2007). Pediatric respiratory infections. *Emergency Medicine Clinics of North America, 25,* 961–979.

9. National Asthma Education and Prevention Panel. (2007). *Expert panel report 3: Guidelines for the diagnosis and management of asthma* (Publication No. 08-4051). Bethesda, MD: National Institutes of Health, National Heart, Lung, and Blood Institute.

FIFTEEN

Cardiovascular Emergencies

Sue M. Cadwell, RN, MSN, CNA-BC

Introduction

Cardiovascular emergencies in children arise from congenital or acquired heart conditions. Although most congenital cardiac lesions are diagnosed during the antenatal period or early in infancy, cardiac lesions may be detected during emergency department (ED) treatment. Children with congenital heart disease (CHD) may present to the emergency department with congestive heart failure (CHF) or other conditions related to their disease, prompting rapid intervention. Newborns with undiagnosed CHD may present to the emergency department with symptoms that mimic other problems such as sepsis with hypotension. Children with acquired cardiac disease (e.g., dysrhythmias, endocarditis, myocarditis, and pericarditis) are more likely to have their condition diagnosed in the emergency department. The priorities of cardiopulmonary support remain the same for either group. Furthermore, children with heart transplants may also present to the emergency department with signs of heart failure or organ rejection. The purposes of this chapter are to compare and contrast selected congenital and acquired cardiac conditions and to describe the emergency nursing care of children with cardiovascular emergencies.

Embryologic Development of the Cardiovascular System

Cardiac embryologic development is essentially complete by 8 weeks gestation in humans, with the critical period being between 20 and 50 days. The origin of cardiac tissue is the mesoderm. A crescent of mesoderm is formed from a pair of endothelial tubes. These endothelial tubes grow, fuse, and establish a single, straight cardiac tube at approximately 20 days gestation. Cellular development around the cardiac tube results in the formation of a distinct myocardium and endocardium. The contractile activity of the heart with the forward flow of blood is initiated at 22 days gestation.[1] The regulation of heart rate, vascular tone, and cardiac output through sympathetic innervation and circulating catecholamines is present in the fetus as early as 24 to 26 days gestation.

At approximately 23 days gestation, continued growth of the cardiac tube in the confined chest wall causes twisting or looping of the heart. Normally, the bulboventricular mass (as it is now referred to) loops to the right (D-dextro looped), and becomes the right ventricle. If the bulboventricular mass loops to the left (L-levo looped), the right ventricle forms on the left side, resulting in ventricular inversion. Growth of the proximal bulboventricular mass results in the right ventricular mass, while the growth of the midportion results in the ventricular outflow tracts. Growth of the distal portion results in the truncus arteriosus, which eventually divides and becomes the pulmonary artery and aortic root.

Septation of the ventricles occurs after looping. The primitive ventricles are connected through an interventricular foramen, which is the only means by which the right ventricle has access to the circulating blood flow necessary for growth. As the ventricles enlarge, the muscular septum arises from the ventricular floor and grows toward the atrioventricular canal, or endocardial cushion, which is the central portion of endocardial tissue that gives rise to the tricuspid and mitral valves. Until the sixth week of gestation, a communication persists between the ventricles; this is eventually closed by tissue from growth of the muscular septum, endocardial cushion, and conal truncal tissue.

Atrial septation occurs much in the same way ventricular septation does, except that the atrial septum is multilayered. The septum primum forms first and grows toward the endocardial cushion. A communication persists through the ostium primum. As the septum primum joins the atrioventricular canal, small perforations in the septum primum join, to give rise to the septum secundum. The foramen ovale is a flaplike valve that is left open between the growth of the septa primum and secundum, which allows for right-to-left blood flow throughout the remainder of gestational life. As atrial septation occurs, the common pulmonary vein is being formed from the posterior atrial wall. The conal-truncal tissue gives rise to the truncus arteriosus, the common pathway for blood flow exiting the fetal heart. It is ultimately separated into a pulmonary artery and aorta under the influence of blood flow and conal-truncal separation around the 34th day of gestation. As the truncus arteriosus grows, it spirals so that the pulmonary artery arises from the right ventricle and the aorta arises from the left ventricle. Interruptions in any of these processes can result in a ventricular septal defect (VSD), transposition of the great vessels, persistent truncus arteriosus, or unequal-sized great arteries.[2]

Pediatric Considerations

The unique anatomy and physiology of the child contribute to altered physiologic responses to disease states and therapeutic modalities. An immature sympathetic nervous system contributes to a decreased response to sympathetic output and increased sensitivity to parasympathetic output (i.e., vagal input). Thus, there is an inability to alter vascular tone to environmental and external stressors. In newborns and infants, immaturity of the cardiac conduction system and autonomic innervation, as well as numerous metabolic and functional alterations in the developing conduction system, contributes to cardiac dysrhythmias.

Cardiac output per kilogram of body weight is higher in the child than in the adult. The stroke volume in children is fixed because cardiac muscle fibers are less compliant, which means that cardiac output is altered through heart-rate variability. The higher the heart rate, the lower the stroke volume, because there is less filling time. The response of children to the exogenous administration of catecholamines is under investigation; therefore, effective dosing of vasoactive drugs is determined at the bedside with titration to patient response.

Etiology

The etiology of cardiovascular conditions arises from congenital or acquired processes, as described in this chapter.

Family History

❑ Congenital heart defects

❑ Valvular heart disease and/or murmurs

❑ Cardiovascular surgery

❑ Sudden infant deaths

Patient History

❑ Heart defects
  ▪ Type of defect
  ▪ Repair completed or scheduled
  ▪ History of transplantation
  ▪ Current medications
❑ Heart disease
❑ Cardiovascular surgery

Symptoms of the Presenting Illness

❑ Fever (presence and duration)
❑ Fatigue
❑ Chest pain
❑ Dyspnea
❑ Cyanosis
❑ Exercise intolerance
❑ Edema
❑ Diaphoresis

Focused Assessment

Physical Assessment

❑ Assess the respiratory system.
  ▪ Auscultate the chest for:
    • Adventitious sounds, especially crackles.
    • Respiratory rate. In the child with impending cardiac failure, the respiratory rate may be slow, fast, or labored.
❑ Assess the cardiovascular system.
  ▪ Auscultate for:
    • Rate. Broad categories of arrhythmias are bradyarrhythmias, tachyarrhythmias, and pulseless arrest.[3]
    • Rhythm.
    • Clarity. Rubs and faint or muffled heart tones may be indicative of tamponade or pericardial effusion.
    • Benign murmurs:
      · Low-grade (I/VI to III/VI)
      · Occur early in systole
    • Pathologic murmurs:
      · Louder

- Longer (II–IV)
- Timing in the cardiac cycle (diastole) and location suggest their representative pathology.
- Rubs may be indicative of pericardial effusions.

- Evaluate cardiac rhythm by initiating cardiorespiratory monitoring.
- Measure the blood pressure.
  - Blood pressure for the child with suspected congenital cardiac disease should be obtained in both the upper, especially right arm (preductal), and lower extremities for comparison.
- Assess peripheral perfusion.
  - Palpate peripheral pulses for:
    - Equality.
    - Rate.
    - Quality. Although pulse quality is a subjective assessment finding, pulse intensity is often ranked on a 0 to 4+ scale (Chapter 5).
  - Measure core and skin temperature.
    - An elevated core body temperature in the presence of peripherally cool, mottled skin temperature reflects a compensatory vasoconstriction with a resultant shunting of blood flow centrally to preserve vital organ perfusion.
    - Diaphoresis reflects sympathetic response to intrinsic catecholamine release.
  - Inspect the skin, nail beds, and oral mucosa for:
    - Color
    - Lesions
    - Clubbing (results from long-standing cyanotic heart disease)
    - Turgor
  - Measure capillary refill. Prolonged capillary refill (greater than 3 seconds) despite warm ambient temperature reflects compensated cardiac output.[3]
- ❐ Assess level of consciousness: AVPU scale (*A*lert, responds to *V*erbal stimuli, responds to *P*ainful stimuli, *U*nresponsive) or Glasgow Coma Scale (GCS) methods (Chapter 5).
  - With a significant decrease in cardiac output, cerebral perfusion can become impaired, resulting in irritability, agitation, or lethargy.
  - Seizures may be indicative of embolic events, especially in children with unrepaired septal defects.

Psychosocial Assessment

- ❐ Assess the child's previous experience with health care providers.
- ❐ Assess the parent's knowledge of their child's condition; assess their coping strategies.

Nursing Interventions

1. Assess and maintain airway, breathing, and circulation.
   - Initiate maneuvers to maintain airway patency, such as positioning, suctioning, and insertion of an airway adjunct.
   - Prepare for endotracheal intubation in the child who cannot maintain airway patency.
   - Administer 100% oxygen through a nonrebreather mask; initiate assisted ventilation in the child who is not maintaining adequate respiratory effort.
   - Initiate cardiorespiratory monitoring; measure continuous oxygen saturation.
     - Analyze the electrocardiogram (ECG) rhythm on the cardiac monitor.
     - Obtain a 12-lead ECG, if indicated.
     - Obtain blood pressure in the upper and lower extremities.
   - Obtain venous access and initiate an intravenous infusion at the ordered rate.
     - Obtain blood for laboratory studies, such as:
       - Complete blood cell count
       - Electrolytes
     - Administer medications, as ordered.
2. Prepare for diagnostic studies, as needed:
   - Chest radiograph
   - Echocardiogram
3. Reassess the child's neurologic and cardiovascular status.
4. Insert an indwelling bladder catheter to measure urinary output. Urinary output less than 1 mL/kg/hr can reflect inadequate renal perfusion.
5. Inform the family frequently about the child's condition; provide emotional support to the child and family.
6. Prepare for transfer and transport to a tertiary care facility, as indicated (Chapter 8).

Congenital Heart Disease

Etiology

The incidence of congenital heart disease (CHD) in the general population is 8 to 12 per 1000 live births.[4] Maternal infection (e.g., rubella), medication usage, excessive smoking or alcohol intake, maternal age over 40 years, insulin-dependent diabetes, and genetics may contribute to the development of CHD. Many infants born to high-risk mothers have CHD diagnosed in utero because of advances in fetal echocardiography.

Early hospital discharges coupled with physiologic changes in circulation may mask symptoms of cardiac defects in the first few days of life. With the closure of the patent ductus arteriosus (PDA) within the first 7 days of life, ductal-dependent lesions may become apparent, as shocklike signs and symptoms develop in the infant. Often, CHD is associated with other congenital anomalies or syndromes, such as Down syndrome (trisomy 21). Abnormal development of the heart may be coupled with abnormal development of other structures that develop simultaneously during gestation such as tracheal esophageal fistula, renal agenesis, and diaphragmatic hernias.

Table 15.1 summarizes common cardiac lesions and their incidence, pathophysiology, assessment findings, and interventions.

Prevention

Early and thorough prenatal care may prevent the development of cardiac defects, although their true etiology remains unknown. Minimizing identified maternal risk factors also may lessen the incidence of CHD.

TABLE 15.1 Common Cardiac Lesions Seen in the Emergency Department

Lesion	Brief Description	ED Considerations
Atrial Septal Defect	Abnormal opening between the atria	▪ Patients usually asymptomatic ▪ Grade II/IV or III/VI systolic murmur (upper left sternal border) ▪ CHF and pulmonary hypertension can occur
Ventricular Septal Defects	Abnormal opening between the ventricles	▪ May see signs of CHF, including fatigue, shortness of breath ▪ Pulmonary hypertension may be present ▪ Grade II/VI to V/VI systolic murmur may be audible (left lower sternal border)
Patent Ductus Arteriosus	Patency of fetal connection between pulmonary artery and aorta	▪ Continuous "machinery murmur" heard ▪ Usually heard in neonatal period, and closes early in the first week of life ▪ May see signs and symptoms of CHF (lethargy, poor feeding) if the ductus remains patent without underlying CHD or if it closes with an underlying ductal-dependent lesion ▪ Needs aggressive intervention if it closes with a ductal-dependent lesion, including intravenous access and infusion of PGE[1]
Coarctation of the Aorta	Narrowing or kinking of the aorta	▪ Hallmark is discordant blood pressures between upper and lower extremities. ▪ Severe lesions may present with sudden signs of CHF (often after PDA closes naturally) ▪ Needs aggressive intervention, including intravenous access and PGE[1] infusion ▪ Patient may need emergent surgery
Truncus Arteriosus	Failure of normal septation of the embryonic bulbar trunk into the pulmonary artery and aorta, resulting in a single vessel overriding both ventricles[5]	▪ Cyanosis with signs of CHF ▪ May hear systolic/diastolic murmur ▪ May have bounding peripheral pulses with wide pulse pressure ▪ Congestive heart failure starts when pulmonary vascular resistance begins to fall (4–6 weeks of life)[5]

Selected Cardiovascular Emergencies

Ductal-dependent Lesions

A special caution needs to be made regarding ductal-dependent cardiac lesions. Infants presenting with nonspecific symptoms such as tachypnea, lethargy, or poor perfusion (especially without a fever) during the first 3 weeks of life need to be evaluated immediately by a physician for life-saving intervention. Indeed, these patients may present in shock and may even resemble a patient with septic shock.[3]

Ductal-dependent lesions are those that are dependent on a PDA to supply adequate systemic (left-sided lesions) or pulmonary (right-sided lesions) blood flow.

Patients with ductal-dependent lesions may initially appear well for several hours or days. The onset of symptoms occurs as the PDA begins to close and may be abrupt or life threatening as the ductus closes completely.[5] Examples of left-sided ductal-dependent lesions are:

❏ Hypoplastic left heart syndrome

❏ Severe aortic stenosis

❏ Coarctation of the aorta

❏ Interrupted aortic arch

Examples of right-sided ductal-dependent lesions are:

❏ Severe pulmonary stenosis

❏ Tetralogy of Fallot

❏ Pulmonary atresia

The history and physical examination for these patients needs to be focused on the onset of symptoms and will often reveal that the patient was initially well appearing at birth. Initial targeted assessment should include:

❏ Respiratory effort/work of breathing

❏ Cardiovascular assessment to include:

▪ Skin color

▪ Capillary refill

▪ Cardiac rate, presence of murmurs

▪ Upper and lower extremity blood pressures

❏ Body temperature

Nursing interventions should be aimed at getting the patient to life-saving interventions quickly. Key to this is obtaining intravenous access for administration of prostaglandin (PGE[1]), to reestablish patency of the ductus arteriosus.[3] In addition, the nurse will need to be sure the family is kept well informed and educated during the care and treatment of the patient. The patient may need to be prepared for a balloon septostomy or other surgical procedure as well.

Congestive Heart Failure

Congestive heart failure (CHF) is a clinical syndrome manifested by inadequate cardiac output to meet ongoing metabolic demands. Although the primary cause of CHF in children is CHD, a panoply of conditions can be associated with the presentation of CHF in the presence of normal underlying cardiac structure.[6] These lesions result in increased pulmonary blood flow and decreased systemic flow, yielding impaired cardiac performance as the heart is unable to keep up with the body's metabolic demands. Other causes of CHF in children are endocrine/metabolic (electrolyte disturbances, lipid disorders), ingestions, toxins, and chemotherapy agents.

Etiology

Volume and/or pressure overload lesions are the most common etiologies of CHF. Volume overload lesions are the most common cause of CHF in the first 6 months of life and include:

❏ Ventricular-septal defects (VSDs)

❏ Patient ductus arterious (PDA)

❏ Truncus arteriosus

❏ Endocardial cushion defects

Pressure overload lesions often present later in childhood with symptoms such as a murmur, shortness of breath, or poor weight gain, and include:

❏ Critical aortic stenosis

❏ Coarctation of the aorta

❏ Pulmonary stenosis

Acquired heart disease is the second most common etiology of CHF in children. The age of onset for acquired heart disease is nonspecific. Acquired heart diseases include:

❏ Myocarditis

▪ Myocarditis is more common in children older than 1 year of age, although fulminant cases have occurred in the newborn period.

❏ Dilated cardiomyopathy

▪ Dilated cardiomyopathy can occur at any age.

❏ Valvular heart disease

❏ Acute rheumatic fever

❏ Endocarditis

Other etiologies of CHF include:

❏ Dysrhythmias

❏ Supraventricular tachycardia (SVT)

❒ Complete heart block

❒ Pulmonary diseases

❒ Chronic lung disease

❒ Cystic fibrosis

❒ Primary pulmonary hypertension

❒ Cor pulmonale, which is a change in structure or function of the right ventricle (usually right ventricular hypertrophy) from obstructive pulmonary disease

❒ Muscular dystrophy (in adolescents)

❒ Metabolic derangements

❒ Anemia

❒ Acidosis

❒ Hypoglycemia

As described earlier, CHF is the result of a number of pathologic phenomena of cardiac performance and resultant compensatory mechanisms. The endpoint of CHF is the inability of the heart to pump an adequate amount of blood to meet the metabolic needs of the body. Heart failure in children is generally characterized by four hemodynamic states:[5]

❒ Volume overload

 ▪ Usually related to congenital heart lesions with increased pulmonary blood flow from left-to-right shunting.

 ▪ Commonly associated with findings of right ventricular hypertrophy.

❒ Pressure overload

 ▪ Results in impaired systolic myocardial performance.

 ▪ Decreased systemic perfusion and increased afterload from obstructive congenital heart lesions.

❒ High cardiac output demands

 ▪ In high-output failure, myocardial systolic function is preserved, and diastolic dysfunction is present.

 ▪ Conditions that lead to high-output failure include sepsis and severe anemia, in which there is a normal volume status but cardiac output is inadequate for tissue metabolic needs.

❒ Decreased myocardial contractility from

 ▪ Acquired heart disease (e.g., cardiomyopathy, pericarditis).

 ▪ Acidosis.

 ▪ Ventricular dilation: Overstretching of cardiac myofibrils.

In failure states, there is decreased cardiac output with a compensatory ventricular dilation, hypertrophy, and neurohormonal stimulation. Ventricular dilation and hypertrophy occur in response to the demand for increased cardiac output.

❒ Dilation of the cardiac muscle increases the stretch of the fibers, initially increasing the force of contraction. Over time, dilation causes a decreased contractile force.

❒ Hypertrophy of the cardiac muscle results in greater tension and increased pressure in the ventricle, with a resultant compensatory increased systolic ejection force.

❒ Dilation and hypertrophy can have potentially negative effects over time, because there is decreased muscle compliance as a higher filling pressure is required to produce the same stroke volume.

❒ Neurohormonal stimulation includes the renin-angiotensin system and sympathetic-adrenergic discharge.

❒ Stimulation of the renin-angiotensin and aldosterone system promotes reabsorption of salt and water, with a resultant increase in circulating blood volume to increase preload.

❒ Baroreceptors stimulate the sympathetic nervous system, releasing catecholamines, when there is a decrease in cardiac output.

❒ Catecholamines increase the force and rate of myocardial contraction and cause peripheral vasoconstriction.

❒ Atrial natriuretic hormone, produced directly by the right atrial myocytes, is an endogenous diuretic released in response to changes in right atrial pressures.

Focused History

Maternal history (factors associated with an increased incidence of CHD)

❒ Infection

❒ Illnesses

❒ Medication usage

❒ Maternal CHD

Patient History

❒ Failure to thrive or inappropriate growth and development in infants with CHF. There is an increased compensatory sympathetic discharge as a result of increased stress on the child's physiologic state.

❒ Feeding history (infant)

 ▪ Protracted feeding time

 ▪ Diaphoresis or tachypnea during feeding

 ▪ Falling asleep quickly after or during feeding

❒ Energy level and exercise tolerance (older child)

- Shortness of breath
- Puffy eyelids/exercise intolerance
- Swollen feet

Focused Assessment

Physical Assessment

Specific cardiovascular assessment parameters are evaluated.

❑ Assess the respiratory system.
  - Auscultate the chest for:
    - Adventitious sounds. Pulmonary congestion is evidenced by tachypnea, dyspnea, orthopnea (older children), wheezing, crackles, and cough, which may reflect left- or right-sided heart failure.
    - Respiratory rate.
❑ Assess the cardiovascular system.
  - Auscultate the heart for:
    - Rate. Tachycardia, loud murmurs, and gallop rhythm are auscultated in the child with impaired cardiac performance.
  - Palpate peripheral pulses for:
    - Equality.
    - Rate.
    - Quality. Weak pulses may be detected.
    - Rhythm
❑ Inspect the skin for:
  - Capillary refill (delayed).
  - Color (mottling).
  - Temperature (diaphoresis).
  - Edema:
    - Periorbital edema (infants)
    - Peripheral edema (children)
    - Neck vein distention (older children)
    - Hepatomegaly > 2 cm below the right costal margin (infants)
❑ Assess the neurologic system.
  - Assess level of consciousness: AVPU scale (*A*lert, responds to *V*erbal stimuli, responds to *P*ainful stimuli, *U*nresponsive) or Glasgow Coma Scale (GCS) methods.
❑ Obtain other assessment parameters:
  - Measure urinary output.
  - Plot height and weight on a growth chart to determine growth failure.

Psychosocial Assessment

❑ Assess the parents' knowledge of the child's condition.
❑ Assess the family's support systems.
❑ Assess the child's understanding of the current health condition.

Nursing Interventions

1. Place the patient in a position of comfort.
2. Administer supplemental oxygen therapy as needed.
3. Initiate cardiorespiratory and oxygen saturation monitoring.
4. Obtain venous access and initiate an intravenous infusion.
   - Administer medications as needed to relieve pulmonary and systemic venous congestion, improve myocardial performance, and, if possible, reverse the underlying disease process through:
     - Diuretic therapy. Diuretic therapy treats the relative volume overload by decreasing the workload of the heart, and reducing pulmonary and systemic congestion.
     - Inotropic agents. Digoxin (Lanoxin®), the most commonly administered inotropic agent for treatment of CHF, delays atrioventricular conduction, decreases the heart rate, and subsequently increases cardiac filling and output.
     - Afterload-reducing agents. Counteract the compensatory response of increased sympathetic tone in the presence of decreased cardiac output. With afterload reduction, the stroke volume is augmented without a change in the cardiac contractile state.
   - Obtain blood specimens for:
     - Arterial or venous blood gas
     - Complete blood cell count with differential
     - Electrolytes
5. Obtain accurate measurements of intake and output.
6. Weigh the child or estimate the child's weight.
7. Prepare for diagnostic procedures.
   - Obtain a 12-lead ECG.
   - Obtain anteroposterior and lateral chest radiographs.
   - Echocardiogram
8. Prepare for transfer and transport to a tertiary care facility, as needed (Chapter 8).

Home Care and Prevention

Early diagnosis of cardiac conditions and close medical follow-up may help to prevent occurrences of CHF. Monitoring of the child's health allows for adjustments in medication doses to assist in management of CHF. Palliative or corrective cardiovascular surgery may be indicated to prevent or treat CHF. Parents should be taught how to administer medications at home and should be taught the signs of impending CHF, such as activity intolerance and poor feeding.

Dysrhythmias

Dysrhythmias are a relatively infrequent finding in the pediatric patient; however, early recognition of abnormal cardiac rates and rhythms in children is essential to prompt intervention. Common pediatric dysrhythmias include sinus tachycardia, sinus bradycardia, supraventricular tachycardia (SVT), and premature ventricular contractions (PVCs). Regardless of the underlying etiology, treatment of pediatric dysrhythmias is always guided by the principle that rhythm disturbances in children are usually more benign and are generally better tolerated than are their counterparts in adults.

Etiology

Rhythm disturbances occur for different reasons in children than they do in adults. Certain forms of CHD may predispose a child to dysrhythmias, but dysrhythmias may occur in the absence of any such disease. Disorders of rate and rhythm are relatively uncommon in infants and children. When they occur, hypoxia secondary to respira-

TABLE 15.2 Common Pediatric Dysrhythmias

Rhythm	ECG Characteristics	Causes
Sinus tachycardia	Regular rhythm Normal P, QRS, T sequence	Fever, anemia, CHF, anxiety, hypovolemia (resulting from dehydration or fluid loss), and circulatory shock
Sinus bradycardia	P waves usually observed QRS usually normal	Vagal stimulation, increased intracranial pressure, hypothermia, hypoxia, sedation, hyperkalemia, and digitalis toxicity
PVCs	Widened QRS complexes fall early in cardiac cycle	Acquired heart disease, drug toxicities, electrolyte imbalances, increased intracranial pressure, ingestion of toxic substances, acidosis
SVT	Regular rhythm P waves may not be observed QRS usually very narrow	Reentry mechanism involving either an accessory pathway (e.g., Wolff-Parkinson-White syndrome) or the atrioventricular node. Idiopathic SVT without underlying heart disease is found more commonly in infants than in older children. Congenital heart lesions are more prone to SVT (e.g., Ebstein's anomaly, single ventricle disease, and levo-transposition of great arteries).

TABLE 15.3 Sinus Tachycardia Versus Supraventricular Tachycardia

	Sinus Tachycardia	Supraventricular Tachycardia
Rate	Heart rate greater than normal for age, that is, usually < 220 beats/minute in an infant	Heart rate > 230 beats/minute in an infant
History	Fever; volume loss as a result of hemorrhage; vomiting; diarrhea; pain; sepsis; shock	Usually paroxysmal onset with nonspecific findings: irritability, lethargy, and poor feeding
ECG findings	Rate is greater than normal for age. Rhythm is regular. P-wave axis is normal. P-QRS-T wave sequence. QRS duration is normal.	Rhythm is usually regular, but may lack beat-to-beat variability. P waves may not be identifiable. QRS duration is normal (< 0.08 seconds) in most children (> 90%). With persistent tachycardia, ST- and T-wave changes consistent with myocardial ischemia may be present.

tory arrest or asphyxia is the most common precursor.[7] Drug exposures and toxicities must also be considered. Table 15.2 outlines common pediatric dysrhythmias and their characteristics. Because SVT and sinus tachycardia are difficult to differentiate, their specific characteristics are highlighted in Table 15.3.

Dysrhythmias can be precipitated or can occur idiopathically. They are generally well tolerated in children for some time; however, eventually, dysrhythmias can compromise cardiac output if left untreated. This is especially true if the dysrhythmia is a compensatory mechanism for an abnormal state (e.g., tachycardia for hypovolemic states). Such compensatory mechanisms can stress the myocardium and should be evaluated fully before being deemed benign. In some instances, a dysrhythmia is a symptom of an underlying disease process that needs further medical evaluation (e.g., cardiomyopathy, myocarditis, hyperthyroidism, or cardiac tumors). Toxicities can cause a variety of rhythm disturbances by virtue of the drug's chemical composition; exerting effects on the myocardium, as well as the conduction system (Chapter 42).

Focused History

Family History

❏ Abnormal heart rhythms

❏ Mitral valve prolapses

❏ Wolff-Parkinson-White syndrome (an electrical abnormality caused by an extra conduction pathway)

❏ Other conduction disturbances (e.g., long Q-T syndrome)

Patient History

❏ Repaired or unrepaired CHD

❏ History of Wolff-Parkinson-White syndrome

❏ Signs and symptoms of cardiopulmonary distress:
   ▪ Tachypnea
   ▪ Diaphoresis
   ▪ Dyspnea
   ▪ Palpitations or chest pain (older child). Elicit from the older child a description of what the child's chest feels like (e.g., pounding, fluttering, skipping, racing, or jumping).

❏ Precipitating events (activity, fever, or anxiety)

❏ Possible ingestions of medications or other poisons

❏ Previous experience with similar symptoms

❏ Previous consultation with a pediatric cardiologist

Focused Assessment

Physical Assessment

Overall, the assessment for rhythm disturbances is very similar to that of CHF.

❏ Assess the respiratory system.
   ▪ Auscultate the chest for:
      • Respiratory rate
      • Rhythm
      • Adventitious sounds
   ▪ Inspect the chest for accessory muscle use.

❏ Evaluate the cardiovascular system.
   ▪ Auscultate the heart for:
      • Rate
      • Rhythm
      • Clarity
      • Murmurs
   ▪ Evaluate cardiac rhythm by initiating cardiorespiratory monitoring.
   ▪ Measure the blood pressure.
   ▪ Assess peripheral perfusion.
      • Palpate peripheral pulses for equality, quality, and regularity.
      • Measure core and skin temperatures.

Psychosocial Assessment

❏ Assess the parents' knowledge of the child's condition.

❏ Assess the family's support systems.

❏ Assess the child's understanding of the current health condition.

Nursing Interventions

1. Maintain airway patency.

2. Administer supplemental oxygen, if indicated.

3. Initiate cardiorespiratory and oxygen saturation monitoring.
   ▪ Increase the volume of the QRS to detect dysrhythmias and to determine rhythm regularity.

4. Obtain venous access and initiate an intravenous infusion.
   ▪ Obtain blood for laboratory studies.
      • Arterial blood gas
      • Complete blood cell count with differential
      • Electrolytes
      • Toxicology screening, in cases of suspected poisoning

5. Obtain diagnostic tests.
   - 12-lead ECG
   - Chest radiograph
6. Initiate dysrhythmia-specific interventions.
   - Bradycardia
     - Provide supplemental oxygenation.
     - Initiate oxygen saturation monitoring.
     - Initiate chest compressions, if needed.
     - Initiate external cardiac pacing in patients whose condition is unstable.
     - Treat the underlying cause, if known.
   - Sinus tachycardia
     - Determine and treat the underlying cause. Antiarrhythmic therapy is inappropriate for sinus tachycardia that is symptomatic of an underlying condition such as fever, hypovolemia, pain, or anxiety.
   - SVT
     - Cardiology consultation
     - Consider vagal maneuvers if stable:
       · Ice bag applied to an infant's face and eyes without obstructing the airway
       · Asking an older child to perform Valsalva maneuver by blowing through an obstructed straw, blowing on his or her thumb as if it were a trumpet without letting air out while blowing, etc.
     - Administer adenosine 0.1 mg/kg (maximum first dose 6 mg). May double first dose and give once (maximum 12 mg) intravenously.[3]
     - Prepare for synchronized cardioversion if unstable—sedate patient if possible, but do not delay cardioversion.
     - Prepare to administer amiodarone (5 mg/kg intravenously over a 20- to 60-minute period) or procainamide (15 mg/kg intravenously over a 30- to 60-minute period). Do not routinely administer amiodarone or procainamide together,[3] as amiodarone may prohibit the clearing of procainamide.
   - PVCs
     - Determine and eliminate the etiology if known (e.g., electrolyte disturbance or hypoxemia).
     - Benign PVCs (patient asymptomatic). No therapy is indicated.
     - Unifocal PVCs. Can be pathologic, or may be benign, even if they occur as bigeminy.
     - Multifocal PVCs. May signify greater pathology.
     - Initiate lidocaine therapy for symptomatic PVCs or PVCs with increasing frequency (e.g., couplets or triplets).
7. Provide the family with frequent updates on their child's condition; provide psychosocial support as needed.
8. Prepare for transfer and transport to a tertiary care facility, as needed (Chapter 8).

Home Care and Prevention

Close medical follow-up of children predisposed to cardiac dysrhythmias should be assured. The therapeutic benefit of prescribed pharmacologic agents on hospital discharge should be evaluated and monitored. Parents should be encouraged to practice home safety measures with medication and poison storage. Parents and older children can be taught to recognize signs of and predisposing factors for dysrhythmia and to initiate measures to prevent or ameliorate their effects.

Acquired Heart Disease

Recognition of acquired heart disease in infants and children is often difficult because patients may have vague presenting signs and symptoms. The spectrum of presentation ranges from fever, tachypnea, congestion, and respiratory distress to fulminant CHF and cardiovascular compromise, with shock and life-threatening dysrhythmias. Prompt recognition of infants and children in the emergency department who present with acquired heart disease is essential not only to save the lives of these patients but also to protect them from the potential sequelae of untreated acquired heart disease.

Endocarditis

Etiology

Infective endocarditis is a relatively rare, but potentially very serious, infection of the heart's inner lining or heart valves. Although endocarditis can affect children of all ages, it is most commonly seen in children older than 10 years of age and is rarely seen in infants.[8] Patients at risk for endocarditis include those with structural heart defects and bacteremia. All children with CHD are at risk for acquiring infective endocarditis, especially those with turbulent, high-flow lesions, including tetralogy of Fallot, VSD, and PDA.[5] Other patients at risk include those with mitral and aortic valve abnormalities and those undergoing congenital heart surgeries with prosthetic shunts, baffles, homografts, or conduits.

In the emergency department, endocarditis in a patient with undiagnosed CHD may present with vague symptoms that may be overlooked and result in a delay in diagnosis and treatment. Any delay in treatment can result in damage to the heart structure itself. Infective endocarditis is a microbial infection of the endothelium, or the inner lining of the heart, which may include the semilunar or atrioventricular valves. Prosthetic valves are also frequently involved. The most common causative bacteria are Gram-positive cocci; *Streptococcus viridans* and *Staphylococcus aureus* are the most common, with fungi such as *Candida albicans* also responsible for infective endocarditis with a greater virility and poorer prognostic clinical course.[5]

For endocarditis to occur, bacteria must enter the bloodstream via a secondary event (e.g., a dental procedure). Turbulent blood flow from the CHD slowly erodes the endothelial lining in the area of the defect. Platelets and fibrin are deposited in the endothelium as a normal protective mechanism, allowing thrombus formation. Bacteria already in the bloodstream become entrapped in the fibrin network of the thrombus, bacterial multiplication occurs, and vegetative growth ensues, including invasion of the valves and possibly the conduction system. Destruction of the vegetation by phagocytosis cannot occur because of the encasement of bacterial colonies in the fibrin network. These vegetative lesions are very friable and may break off, causing embolic events. Finally, valve closure is impaired because of vegetative growth, causing regurgitation and CHF.

Focused History

Family History

❏ Abnormal heart rhythms

❏ Mitral valve prolapses

❏ Wolff-Parkinson-White syndrome

❏ Other conduction disturbances (e.g., long Q-T syndrome)

Patient History

❏ Underlying cardiac disease

❏ Prior surgeries or procedures (e.g., cardiac catheterization)

❏ History of recent illness or exposures

❏ Recent dental cleanings or procedures or complaints of toothache

❏ Lack of prophylactic antibiotics before dental procedures

❏ Presence of any prosthetic devices, such as pacemakers, central lines, cardiac graft, or artificial valve

❏ Signs and symptoms the child has experienced:
  - Fatigue
  - Anorexia
  - Fever

Focused Assessment

Physical Assessment

❏ Assess the respiratory system.
  - Auscultate the chest for:
    - Respiratory rate
    - Equality of breath sounds
    - Adventitious sounds

❏ Assess the cardiovascular system.
  - Auscultate the heart for:
    - Rate
    - Rhythm
    - Clarity
    - Murmurs. Extracardiac sounds may be auscultated.

❏ Inspect the skin for:
  - Color. Pale skin may result from decreased perfusion. Petechiae in the extremities, nail beds, and mucous membranes may be evidence of embolic events.
  - Temperature. Cool extremities may indicate poor peripheral perfusion.

❏ Measure capillary refill.
  - Delayed capillary refill (> 3 seconds) may indicate early shock (Chapter 38).

❏ Assess the neurologic system.
  - Assess level of consciousness: AVPU scale (*A*lert, responds to *V*erbal stimuli, responds to *P*ainful stimuli, *U*nresponsive) or Glasgow Coma Scale (GCS) methods.

❏ Assess the abdomen.
  - Palpate the abdomen for organ enlargement resulting from right-sided heart failure
    - Hepatomegaly
    - Splenomegaly
    - Lymphadenopathy

❏ Assess the oral cavity for:
  - Caries
  - Lesions
  - Gingival disease

Psychosocial Assessment

❏ Assess the parents' knowledge of the child's condition.

❏ Assess the family's support systems.

❏ Assess the child's understanding of the current health condition.

Nursing Interventions

1. Maintain airway patency.

2. Administer supplemental oxygen, as needed.

3. Initiate cardiorespiratory and oxygen saturation monitoring.

4. Obtain venous access and initiate intravenous therapy.

   ▪ Obtain blood for laboratory studies.

     • Complete blood cell count with differential

     • Blood cultures

     • Erythrocyte sedimentation rate

   ▪ Obtain urine for urinalysis.

5. Administer medications as ordered.

   ▪ Antibiotics

   ▪ Antipyretics

   ▪ Intravenous hydration

6. Provide anticipatory guidance for child and family for lengthy treatment regimen (2 to 6 weeks) and possible surgical intervention.

Home Care and Prevention

Children with CHD who present to the emergency department for treatment may require antibiotic prophylaxis before invasive procedures such as:[5]

❏ Dental procedures with probable bleeding

❏ Biopsies

❏ Wound debridement

❏ Incision and drainage of an infected site

❏ Bronchoscopy

Current American Heart Association recommendations include antibiotic prophylaxis as a reasonable step for patients meeting the following conditions:[9]

❏ Prosthetic cardiac valve or prosthetic material used for cardiac valve repair

❏ Previous infective endocarditis

❏ Congenital heart disease as follows:

   ▪ Unrepaired cyanotic CHD, including palliative shunts and conduits

   ▪ Completely repaired congenital heart defect with prosthetic material or device, whether placed by surgery or by catheter intervention, during the first 6 months after the procedure

   ▪ Repaired CHD with residual defects at the site or adjacent to the site of a prosthetic patch or prosthetic device

❏ Cardiac transplantation recipients in whom cardiac valvulopathy develops

Myocarditis and Pericarditis

Myocarditis is an inflammation of the myocardium, or the heart muscle. Often there is an associated myocellular necrosis.[10] Presentation can range from mild symptoms that go undiagnosed to severe decompensation and sudden death in children. Myocarditis is more common in children older than 1 year of age.

Pericarditis is an inflammation of the pericardium, or the outer lining of the heart. Although similar in etiology to myocarditis, pericarditis follows a more benign clinical course, usually with fewer long-term sequelae.

Focused History

❏ Recent upper respiratory tract infection

❏ Signs of cardiac decompensation

Focused Assessment

Physical Assessment

❏ Assess the respiratory system.

   ▪ Auscultate the chest for:

     • Respiratory rate

     • Equality of breath sounds

     • Adventitious sounds

❏ Assess the cardiovascular system.

   ▪ Auscultate the heart for:

     • Rate

     • Rhythm

     • Clarity

     • Murmurs. Extracardiac sounds, such as a pleural friction rub, may be auscultated.

   ▪ Inspect the skin for:

     • Color. Pale skin may indicate decreased perfusion.

     • Temperature. Cool extremities may indicate poor peripheral perfusion.

     • Measure capillary refill.

   ▪ Delayed capillary refill (> 3 seconds) may indicate early shock.

❏ Assess the neurologic system.

- Assess level of consciousness: AVPU scale (*A*lert, responds to *V*erbal stimuli, responds to *P*ainful stimuli, *U*nresponsive) or Glasgow Coma Scale (GCS) methods.

❏ Assess the abdomen.

- Palpate the abdomen for organ enlargement resulting from right-sided heart failure
  - Hepatomegaly
  - Splenomegaly
  - Lymphadenopathy

Psychosocial Assessment

❏ Assess the parents' knowledge of the child's condition.

❏ Assess the family's support systems.

❏ Assess the child's understanding of the current health condition.

Nursing Interventions

1. Maintain airway patency.

2. Administer supplemental oxygen, as needed.

3. Initiate cardiorespiratory and oxygen saturation monitoring.

4. Place the child in a position of comfort or in a semi-Fowler's position.

5. Obtain venous access and initiate intravenous therapy.
   - Obtain specimens for myocarditis laboratory testing.
     - Complete blood cell count with differential
     - Electrolytes
     - Blood culture
     - Stool culture
     - Throat viral culture
   - Obtain specimens for pericarditis laboratory testing.
     - Blood culture
     - Electrolytes
     - Viral culture

6. Prepare for a possible pericardiocentesis for both therapeutic and diagnostic value in symptomatic patients.[11]
   - Send a sample of pericardial fluid for culture.
   - Prepare for intravascular volume replacement following pericardiocentesis (pericarditis).

7. Prepare the child and parents for procedures and offer emotional support and information.

8. Monitor vital signs and cardiovascular and respiratory status closely.

9. Administer medications, as prescribed.
   - Antipyretics
   - Analgesics
   - Diuretics
   - Inotropic agents
   - Corticosteroids
   - Nonsteroidal anti-inflammatory drugs
   - Intravenous gamma globulin

10. Prepare for transfer and transport to a tertiary care facility, as needed.

Home Care and Prevention

Although prevention of myocarditis is difficult, aggressive initial treatment may prevent recurrence. Routine primary pediatric care should be provided to detect illness and prevent complications. Thorough post-cardiothoracic surgical care and follow-up are imperative.

Prompt recognition of hemodynamic compromise and subtle signs and symptoms of CHF will prevent further decompensation.

Heart Transplantation

Pediatric heart transplantation has been performed for more than 20 years. Emergency departments treating pediatric patients may see transplant recipients presenting for a variety of reasons, and ED personnel should be vigilant for signs and symptoms of transplant rejection in addition to the presence of infection caused by the need for these patients to take immunosuppressants for life.[5]

Signs and symptoms of rejection include:

❏ Fever, with temperature above 100.4 °F (38 °C)

❏ Flulike symptoms such as chills, aches, headaches, nausea, and/or vomiting

❏ Shortness of breath

❏ New chest pain or tenderness

❏ Fatigue or generally feeling "lousy"

❏ Elevation in blood pressure

Although infection is always a risk, pediatric transplant patients may also present with other signs and symptoms that may be chronic and may limit their survival. These conditions include (but are not limited to):

❏ Renal dysfunction

❏ Hypertension

❏ Coronary artery disease caused by chronic rejection

❏ Anemia

Families of transplant patients, as well as the patients

themselves, are invaluable historians, and need to be consulted continually during the ED encounter.

Conclusion

Infants and children may present for ED treatment related to acquired or congenital heart disease. Children with chronic cardiac problems are faced with numerous issues related to their normal growth and development. The child with a heart or heart-lung transplant has unique needs related to an immunocompromised state, as well as infection and rejection. Astute emergency nursing assessments, coupled with emotional support and timely interventions, lend themselves to improved outcomes for these patients and families.

References

1. Bezold, I. (2006). Cardiovascular embryology. In J. A. McMillan, R. D. Feigin, F. A. Oski, & M. D. Jones (Eds.), *Oski's pediatrics: Principles & practice* (3rd ed., pp. 325–338). Philadelphia: Lippincott Williams & Wilkins.

2. Srivastava, D., & Baldwin, H. S. (2001). Molecular determinants of cardiac development. In H. B. Allen, E. B. Clark, H. P. Gutgesell, & D. J. Driscoll (Eds.), *Moss and Adams' heart disease in infants, children, and adolescents: Including the fetus and young adult* (6th ed., Vol. 1, pp. 3–23). Philadelphia: Lippincott Williams & Wilkins.

3. American Heart Association. (2006). *Pediatric advanced life support provider manual* (pp. 115). Dallas, TX: Author.

4. Hoffman, J. I. E., & Kaplan, S. (2002). The incidence of congenital heart disease. *Journal of the American College of Cardiology, 39*(12), 1890–1900.

5. O'Brien, P. A. (2005). The child with cardiovascular dysfunction. In M. J. Hockenberry, D. Wilson, & M. L. Winkelstein (Eds.), *Wong's essentials of pediatric nursing* (7th ed., pp. 890–937). St. Louis, MO: Mosby.

6. Gewitz, M.H., & Woolfe, P. K. (2006). Cardiac Emergencies. In G. Fleisher & S. Ludwig (Eds.), *Textbook of pediatric emergency care* (5th ed., pp. 717-758). Philadelphia, PA: Lippincott, Williams & Wilkins.

7. Aehlert, B. (2006). *Mosby's comprehensive pediatric emergency care* (Rev. ed., pp. 218–325). St. Louis, MO: Mosby.

8. Dajani, A. S., & Taubert, K. S. (2001). Infective endocarditis. In H. D. Allen, E. B. Clark, H. P. Gutgesell, & D. J. Driscoll (Eds.), *Moss and Adams' heart disease in infants, children, and adolescents: Including the fetus and young adult* (6th ed., Vol. 2, pp. 1297–1310). Philadelphia: Lippincott Williams & Wilkins.

9. American Heart Association. (2007). Prevention of infective endocarditis: A guideline from the American Heart Association Rheumatic Fever, Endocarditis and Cardiac Disease Committee; Council on Cardiovascular Disease in the Young and Council on Clinical Cardiology, Council on Cardiovascular Surgery and Anesthesia, and the Quality of Care and Outcomes Research Interdisciplinary Working Group. *Circulation, 116,* 1736–1754.

10. Towbin, J. A. (2001). Myocarditis. In H. D. Allen, E. B. Clark, H. P. Gutgesell, & D. J. Driscoll (Eds.), *Moss and Adams' heart disease in infants, children, and adolescents: Including the fetus and young adult* (6th ed., Vol. 2, pp. 1197–1215). Philadelphia: Lippincott Williams & Wilkins.

11. Rheuban, K. S. (2001). Pericardial diseases. In H. D. Allen, E. B. Clark, H. P. Gutgesell, & D. J. Driscoll (Eds.), Moss and Adams' heart disease in infants, children*, and adolescents: Including the fetus and young adult* (6th ed., Vol. 2, pp. 1287–1296). Philadelphia: Lippincott Williams & Wilkins.

12. American Heart Association. (2005). *Guidelines 2005 for cardiopulmonary resuscitation and emergency cardiovascular care* (pp. IV58–IV77). Dallas, TX: Author.

SIXTEEN

Neurologic Emergencies

Lynn Coletta Simko, PhD, RN, CCRN

Introduction

Neurologic emergencies are relatively common in the pediatric population. Neurologic dysfunction may result from congenital malformations, tumors, infection, brain injuries, genetic defects in metabolism, and other disorders that affect neurologic function. Evaluation of the neurologic status of the pediatric patient is a vital component in the emergency nurse's assessment of injury and illness.

When evaluating pediatric neurologic function, emergency nurses must be aware of the patient's corresponding developmental stages and milestones, as well as age-appropriate levels of neurologic functioning. The purpose of this chapter is to describe common neurologic emergencies and to outline emergency nursing interventions for their recognition and treatment.

Embryologic Development of the Neurologic System

Neurologic (central nervous system [CNS]) malformations cause 75% of fetal deaths and 40% of deaths during infancy; CNS malformations account for 33% of all apparent congenital malformations, and 90% of CNS malformations are defects in neural tube closure.[1] Because many of these neonates receive early surgical intervention, children with congenital neurologic malformations have an increased survival rate; therefore the emergency nurse is more likely to see these children, whether for reasons related or unrelated to their neurologic condition. Therefore, it is important to understand the embryologic development of the nervous system.

The embryologic development of the nervous system is a complex process. Derived from the ectoderm of the embryo, the neural groove develops in the midline of the embryo. The neural groove is bordered by neural folds, which close in the fourth week of embryonic life to form the hollow neural tube.[2,3] The neural tube and surrounding tissues are composed of several different types of cells. Through continued cellular differentiation and cellular migration, the structures of the CNS and peripheral nervous system develop.[2,3]

The CNS comprises the brain and spinal cord, which arise from the neural tube. Before closure of the neural tube is completed, the development of the brain begins. At the cranial end of the neural tube, three vesicles emerge. These vesicles further differentiate to ultimately form the cerebral hemispheres, cerebellum, pons, medulla, and internal structure of the brain.[1–3]

The peripheral nervous system originates from a ridge of ectodermal cells along the neural folds. As the neural tube closes, the neural crests are formed. The neural crest cells migrate through the embryo and differentiate to form the peripheral nervous system, chromaffin cells (found in the adrenal medulla and carotid bodies), and other nonneural structures.[3] The embryonic growth of the nervous system includes the differentiation of neuroepithelial cells, which results in the formation of mature neurons. Cellular migration and differentiation also result in the development of the glial cells, dendrites, axonal pathways, membrane excitability, neurotransmitters, and myelination.[4]

Neurologic disorders are believed to be multifactorial, a combination of genes and environment. Folic acid deficiency during the early stages of pregnancy increases the risk of neural tube defects. Other risk factors include heredity, use of anticonvulsant drugs (especially valproic acid), maternal blood glucose concentrations, and maternal hyperthermia.[5] Table 16.1 compares developmental errors and their outcomes.

Pediatric Considerations

Neurologic development is sequential, and, over time, neurologic responses change to become those seen in adults. Developmental milestones in motor function (Table 16.2), reflexes (Table 16.3), and head growth (Table 16.4) are highlighted.

TABLE 16.1 Neurologic Developmental Errors and Their Description

Developmental Error	Description
Defective closure at the cranial end of the neural tube	
Posterior defects (more common)	*Anencephaly*—soft, bony part of the skull and part of the brain are missing
	Encephalocele—herniation of brain and meninges into a saclike structure through a skull defect
	Meningocele—meninges and spinal fluid in a sac through a vertebral defect that does not involve the spinal cord; occurs in the cervical, thoracic, and lumbar spine
Anterior midline defects	*Cyclopia*—single midline orbit and eye with a protruding noselike appendage above the orbit
Defective closure of the caudal end of the neural tube	*Myelomeningocele (spina bifida cystica)*—herniation of a sac with meninges, spinal fluid, and a segment of the spinal cord with its nerves through an opening in a vertebra. Eighty percent are located in the lumbar and lumbar sacral regions (a final area that closes). The level of the myelomeningocele indicates the level of neurologic involvement; higher levels are associated with extensive levels of neurologic involvement. For example, a thoracic-level lesion involves flaccid paralysis of the lower extremities, abdominal muscle weakness, and absence of bowel and bladder control; and a sacral-level lesion involves normal neurologic function of the lower extremities and bowel and bladder control.
	Two associated conditions are:
	Arnold-Chiari II malformation—downward displacement of the cerebellum, cerebral tonsils, brain stem, and fourth ventricle through the foramen magnum; this can be life threatening
	Tethered cord—the spinal cord is trapped (tethered) from scar tissues that form after the initial surgery to close the open defect and, as the child grows, causes scoliosis, altered gait, loss of muscle strength, changes in bowel and bladder function, and back pain
Failure of the posterior laminae to fuse/ malformation of the axial skeleton	*Spina bifida occulta*—abnormal hair growth along the spine; midline dimple cutaneous angioma; lipoma or dermoid cyst. Most (80%) are located in the lumbar-sacral regions.
Malformations of the axial skeleton	*Craniosynostosis*—premature closure of the cranial sutures during the first 18 to 20 months of life, causing abnormal skull expansion and growth
	Microcephaly—cranial size is below average for the infant's age, gender, gestation, and race
	Congenital hydrocephalus—increased volume of CSF because of blockage within the ventricles, overproduction of cerebrospinal fluid, or a reduced reabsorption of CSF

Gleeson, J. G., Dobyns, W. B., Plawner, L., & Ashwal, S. (2006). Congenital structural defects. In K. F. Swaiman, S. Ashwal, & D. M. Ferriero (Eds.), *Pediatric neurology: Principles and practice* (4th ed., pp. 363–490). St. Louis, MO: Elsevier.

McCormick, B. M., Mackey, W. L., & Wilson, D. (2007). Conditions caused by defects in physical development. In M. J. Hockenberry & D. Wilson (Eds.), *Wong's nursing care of infants and children* (8th ed., pp. 422–498). St. Louis, MO: Elsevier.

Wilkerson, R. R., & Boss, B. J. (2008). Alterations of neurologic function in children. In S. E. Huether & K. L. McCance (Eds.), *Understanding pathophysiology* (4th ed., pp. 405–423). St. Louis, MO: Elsevier.

TABLE 16.2 Major Motor Milestones During the First 24 Months of Life

Age	Motor Development
Newborn/ young infant	The newborn has clenched fists.[42,43] The young infant's normal posture is flexion of the upper and lower extremities with somewhat jerky but vigorous movements.
3–4 Months	The extremities are more supple, and movements become smoother. Hands are open, and the infant will grasp for objects.[42,43]
6 Months	The infant should grasp object with one hand, roll from prone to supine, and sit with support.[30,42]
8 Months	The infant should be able to roll supine to prone and transfer objects between hands.[42,43]
10 Months	The infant sits well, stands while holding on, and grasps and picks up smaller objects; finger-thumb opposition is present.[42,43]
12 Months	The infant stands while holding on and walks with support.
24 Months	The toddler gains independent walking skills and the ability to climb and descend stairs.[42,43]

TABLE 16.3 Primitive Reflexes

Reflex	Age	Description
Moro reflex (startle reflex)	Present until 4 months of age	A sudden release of support that allows the infant's head to drop (in relation to the body) to a pillow or the examiner's hand will elicit the reflex. The infant will open his or her hands, extend and abduct the upper extremity, and then flex the arms, as in an embrace or form a "C."[42,44]
Tonic neck reflex	Present until 4 months of age	Turning the infant's head to one side results in extension of the arm and leg of the side the head is rotated toward and flexion of the arm on the opposite side.[42,44]
Palmar reflex (grasping reflex)	Present until 4–6 months of age	Placement of the examiner's finger in the infant's palm results in the infant's grasping the finger. The infant's grasp will tighten with attempts to remove the finger.[42,44]
Babinski's reflex	Present until about 1 year of age	Stroking the lateral sole of the infant's foot from the heel to the toes will elicit the response, fanning of the toes and hyperextension of the toes.[42,44]

TABLE 16.4 Cranial Development

Characteristic of Cranial Development	Implications
The head accounts for one fourth of the infant's total body height (compared with one eighth of the adult's total body height).	The infant's head represents a larger body surface area from which to lose heat. The head presents a larger area for injury to be sustained.
The infant's skull bones are separated by suture lines that form two fontanelles (anterior and posterior) and allow room for expansion with increased ICP. The adult skull is fixed and cannot expand.	The posterior fontanelle typically closes by 8 weeks of age. The anterior fontanelle closes by 18 months of age. The softer skull affords less protection from injury. Open fontanelles allow for brain expansion with increased ICP, thus delaying brain stem herniation.
The infant's head is the fastest-growing body part.	Head circumference should be measured regularly through the first 5 years of life to detect increased or decreased growth.

Kyle, T. (2008). *Essentials of pediatric nursing* (pp. 466–516). Philadelphia: Lippincott Williams & Wilkins.

Padget, K. (2006). Alteration of neurologic function in children. In K. L. McCance & S. E. Huether (Eds.), *Pathophysiology: The biologic basis for disease in adults and children* (5th ed., pp. 623–654). St. Louis, MO: Elsevier.

Etiology

Neurologic conditions arise from a variety of causes, including alterations in:

❑ Cerebral blood flow

❑ Intracranial pressure (ICP)

❑ Level of consciousness

❑ Motor function

❑ Sensory function

They also may be precipitated by:

❑ Metabolic disturbances (e.g., diabetic ketoacidosis or hypoglycemia)

❑ Infection

❑ Toxic exposures

❑ Alcohol or substance abuse

❑ Hypoxia or anoxia

❑ Intracranial hemorrhage or central venous thrombosis

❑ Shock

❑ Direct and secondary trauma to the central and peripheral nervous system

❑ Stroke

❑ Seizures

Focused History

❑ Onset of the patient's present illness.

- Sequence and development of neurologic symptoms suggestive of ICP

- Changes in level of consciousness, activity level, mentation, communication, sensation, vision, and/or motor abilities. Consciousness is a state of full awareness; alterations in the level of consciousness encompass a range of conditions described by a variety of terms. Definitions of the familiar terms (such as confusion, lethargy, and obtunded) are often obscure and vary among parents and health care providers.

❑ Child's behaviors

- In infants, changes in social behaviors and interaction should be evaluated, including changes in feeding, sleeping, and waking patterns; response to comforting; delays in developmental milestone attainment or regression.[6]

❑ Symptoms

- Headache: location, quality, and duration; changes in vision or visual disturbances

- Vomiting

- Fever

❑ Medications (over-the-counter and prescribed; dietary and herbal supplements)

- Dose

- Time of last dose

- Compliance with dosing regimen

❑ Past health history

- History of congenital or chronic illness or condition and course of treatment

- Presence of a persistent neurologic deficit and normal baseline neurologic function, including usual level of activity, usual and current interactions with others and the environment, baseline cognitive level, usual movement patterns, and muscle tone

❑ Recent falls or injury

- Time of occurrence

- Mechanism of injury

- Changes in behavior since injury

❑ Seizures

- Onset, duration, and description of seizure activity

- Postictal state

❑ Immunization status

❑ Developmental milestones achieved (Chapter 3)

Focused Assessment

Physical Assessment

1. Assess the neurologic system (primary assessment).

- Assess the level of consciousness: A rapid method for evaluating the child's level of consciousness is the AVPU system:[7]

    A = Alert

    V = Responds to verbal commands

    P = Responds only to pain

    U = Unresponsive

- Assess the pupillary size and response.

    • Pupils should be equal in size.

    • Pupils should be round.

    • Pupils should react to light.

    • Reactions should be equal and brisk.

2. Perform a detailed neurologic assessment (secondary assessment).

- Inspect the head for shape and symmetry.

    • Examine the fontanelles: The anterior fontanelle (closes between 6 and 20 months) should be examined when the infant is quiet and positioned at a 45-degree angle.

- The anterior fontanelle may appear sunken in infants who are dehydrated.
- The anterior fontanelle may be bulging in an infant with increased ICP.

▪ Measure the infant's head circumference and compare it with the age-defined diameter.

- An enlarged head may be indicative of hydro-cephalus.
- A small head may be indicative of microcephaly.

▪ Palpate the head for:

- Overriding sutures
- Hematomas
- Step offs
- Bruits over the skull

- Observe the face and head for:
  - Bruises (indicative of child abuse, Chapter 44)
  - Lacerations
  - Other signs of trauma
- Assess the level of consciousness.
  - Use an objective scale to describe the level of consciousness to facilitate trending of the patient's responses and improve communication among health care providers. The scale must be used in conjunction with a prudent neurologic assessment.
  - Measure the level of consciousness with the Glasgow Coma Scale (GCS) (Table 16.5).

3. Assess orientation and mentation.
   ▪ The GCS verbal response is used to evaluate mentation and orientation.

TABLE 16.5 Glasgow Coma Scale

Parameter	Description	Score			
Eye opening	Observe eye-opening activity in relation to stimulus required to elicit the response.	> 2 Years old		< 2 Years old	
		4 Spontaneously		4 Spontaneously	
		3 To speech		3 To speech	
		2 To pain		2 To pain	
		1 No response		1 No response	
Best verbal response	When assessing level of consciousness in children consider that the child or infant may not respond to unfamiliar voices in an unfamiliar environment. Therefore it is helpful to have a parent present to elicit the responses.[8,9,52] Observe the response to questions. In preverbal children, spontaneous vocalization and vocal responses to pain are observed to score this parameter.[8,9,52]	> 2 Years old		< 2 Years old	
		5 Oriented/uses appropriate words and phrases		5 Coos, babbles	
		4 Confused conversation		4 Irritable, cries	
		3 Inappropriate words/screams/cries		3 Cries to pain	
		2 Incomprehensible sounds/garbled sounds		2 Moans to pain	
		1 No response		1 No response	
Best motor response	Observe the response to verbal commands or painful stimuli. In children younger than 2 years of age, this parameter is scored by observing for spontaneous movements, response to touch, or response to painful stimulus.[8,9,52]	> 2 Years old		< 2 Years old	
		6 Obeys command		6 Normal spontaneous movement	
		5 Localizes pain		5 Withdraws to touch	
		4 Withdraws to pain		4 Withdraws to pain	
		3 Abnormal flexion to pain (decorticate rigidity)		3 Abnormal flexion (decorticate rigidity)	
		2 Abnormal extension to pain (decerebrate rigidity)		2 Abnormal extension (decerebrate rigidity)	
		1 No response		1 No response	

- In children, orientation is evaluated through age-appropriate questions.
- In infants or preverbal children, orientation is evaluated through observation of their:
  - Social behaviors
  - Interaction with the environment
  - Recognition of parents and/or familiar objects
- Evaluate the cranial nerves. A gross evaluation of cranial nerve function can be completed relatively quickly. However, the child's condition and developmental level may preclude evaluation of all cranial nerves. Basic cranial nerve evaluation involves eye movement and function (cranial nerves II, III, IV, and VI):[8]
  - Equal rise of eyelids
  - Equality of pupil size; reactivity to light and accommodation
  - Infants younger than 3 months of age should blink at bright light.
  - Infants older than 3 months of age should follow a dangling object, moving the head to follow the object.[6]
  - Evaluation of extraocular movements through the six fields of gaze, visual acuity, visual tracking, and color identification in the conscious child. Complete evaluation of all extraocular movements may not be possible in children younger than 2 to 3 years of age.
  - The position of eyes at rest and the presence of abnormal spontaneous eye movement are noted in the unconscious child or child with an altered level of consciousness.[9] Note the presence of eye deviation, disconjugate gaze, nystagmus, doll's eyes.
- Evaluate the remaining cranial nerves and reflex responses (Table 16.6).
- Evaluate motor function; compare with the major motor milestones attained up to age 24 months: GCS motor response, symmetry of movement, posture.
- Evaluate muscle tone.
  - Muscle tone is the muscle tension or resistance of the muscle to passive movement.[10,11] Abnormalities in muscle tone are related to the location of the neurologic lesion. In the infant, extension and/or scissoring of the legs when lifted vertically denotes increased muscle tone and corticospinal disorder.[10] Table 16.7 highlights the types of abnormal muscle tone.
  - Muscle tone and power are assessed in upper and lower extremities.
  - Child: Ask the child to execute movements such as pushing against the examiner's hands with his or her hands and then feet, grasping the examiner's hands and fingers, and moving extremities against resistance.
- Evaluate muscle power.
  - Muscle power is graded on the basis of the movement with gravity and resistance. Normal power is the ability to move or contract the muscle against gravity and maximal resistance:[12]

    5 = Normal power and strength

    4 = Movement against gravity and variable resistance

    3 = Movement against gravity

    2 = Movement with gravity eliminated

    1 = Muscular contraction without movement

    0 = No muscular contraction

  - Infant: Pull the infant to a sitting position and evaluate the infant's strength and control of the body.[13] Observe the infant's strength, such as withdrawal from touch, to assess motor power.
- Evaluate mobility.
- Evaluate reflexes.
  - Tendon reflexes are elicited in the upper and lower extremities. If the child is unable to relax the extremity being examined, the reflex may not be elicited.
  - Reflexes (including the primitive reflexes) should be evaluated in terms of strength and symmetry. Continued presence of primitive reflexes beyond the expected age, or early cessation, may indicate neurologic dysfunction. Asymmetric reflex responses may indicate injury.
  - Clonus is a rhythmic contraction and relaxation of the muscle when the wrist, ankle, or great toe is flexed. Clonus may be present with motor neuron lesion, cerebral cortex injury, or in metabolic disease.[14]
- Evaluate cerebellar function.
  - The cerebellum regulates motor function and coordination of movement and balance and maintains muscle tone. Observe the child's gait (crawling or walking), balance while standing and/or sitting, performance of repetitive motions.
  - Disturbances of balance and/or involuntary movements are indicative of neurologic dysfunction.

TABLE 16.6 Cranial Nerve and Reflex Responses

Cranial Nerve and Reflex	Responses
Cranial nerves IX (Glossopharyngeal) and X (Vagus)	Ability to swallow Ability to cough Presence of the gag reflex Clarity of speech
Cranial nerves V (Trigeminal), VII (Facial) (corneal reflex)	Ability to blink

Cranial nerves III (Oculomotor), IV (Trochlear), VI (Abducens) (oculocephalic and oculovestibular responses)	Only tested for severe brain stem dysfunction
	Doll's eyes:
	Absence of doll's eyes (abnormal):
	    Eyes move in the same direction as the head is turned.
	Presence of doll's eyes (normal):
	    Eyes move in the opposite direction as the head is turned.
	Ice water caloric test:
	    Lateral nystagmus (normal response)
	    No eye movement or asymmetric eye movement (abnormal response)

Cranial nerves V and VII (facial crying and sucking movement and expression)	Facial symmetry with movement; in infants, facial symmetry during crying and sucking Ability to raise eyebrows, smile, clench teeth, chew Presence of tears with crying Presence and strength of suck reflex
Cranial nerves XI (Spinal Accessory) and XII (Hypoglossal) (motor and muscular function)	Ability to shrug shoulders Ability to turn head and move upper extremities Ability to stick out the tongue In infants, midline tongue position when crying
Cranial nerve VIII (Acoustic) (hearing)	Response to verbal commands and ability to answer questions Ability to repeat words Ability of the infant < 3 months to stop spontaneous movements or sucking in response to voice or sound and then resume the activity Ability of the infant > 3 months to turn head or toward sound, and vocalize in response to sounds or voice

Haymore, J., & Sakallaris, B. R. (2006). Mental status and neurological techniques. In M. E. Z. Estes, *Health assessment & physical examination* (3rd ed., pp. 641–696). Clifton Park, NY: Thomson Delmar Learning.

Kyle, T. (2008). *Essentials of pediatric nursing* (pp. 466–516). Philadelphia: Lippincott Williams & Wilkins.

Taylor, D. A., & Ashwal, S. (2006). Impairment of consciousness and coma. In K. F. Swaiman, S. Ashwal, & D. M. Ferriero (Eds.), *Pediatric neurology: Principles and practice* (4th ed., pp. 1377–1400). St. Louis, MO: Elsevier.

Psychosocial Assessment

❐ Assess the family's understanding of the child's underlying neurologic-related health condition, as needed.

❐ Assess the child's and family's understanding of the child's current neurologic-related health condition.

❐ Assess the child's and family's usual coping strategies.

TABLE 16.7 Types of Muscle Tone Abnormality

Type of Abnormality	Characteristics
Hypertonia or spasticity	Persistent increased muscle tension. With passive stretch of the muscle, there is increased muscle tone or resistance to the movement, which then suddenly gives way or relaxes.[8,11,53]
Hypotonia	Decreased muscle tension and decreased resistance to passive movement. Infants may also exhibit a weak cry, weak suck, and decreased spontaneous movements. In the hypotonic infant, movement of the infant's arm across the chest and neck will result in the elbow crossing the midline (positive scarf sign).[8,10,46]
Abnormal posture or asymmetry of function or strength	Indicative of significant neurologic dysfunction *Decorticate rigidity:* Flexion of elbows, wrist, and fingers, and extension of legs and ankles, indicating ischemia or damage to cerebral hemispheres[11] *Decerebrate posturing:* Extension of arms and legs with rigidity, indicating diffuse cerebral injury or ischemia or damage to brain stem structures[11] *Flaccidity:* Absence of muscle tone

Nursing Interventions

1. Assess and maintain airway, breathing, and circulation.
   - Initiate maneuvers to maintain airway patency; such as positioning, suctioning and insertion of an airway adjunct.
   - Prepare for endotracheal intubation for the child in whom airway patency cannot be maintained.
   - Administer 100% oxygen through a nonrebreather mask; initiate assisted ventilation in the child who is not maintaining adequate respiratory effort and/or if the GCS score is less than 9.
   - Initiate cardiorespiratory monitoring; measure continuous oxygen saturation.
2. Initiate spinal immobilization if trauma is suspected.
3. Obtain venous access and initiate an intravenous infusion at maintenance rate.
   - Obtain blood for laboratory studies: serum medication levels (e.g., valproic acid), toxicology screen, glucose, and electrolytes.
   - Administer analgesics for pain control, as needed (Chapter 11). Closely monitor patients receiving narcotic analgesics that may alter the level of consciousness.
4. Monitor neurologic status.
   - Observe for changes in level of consciousness.
   - Observe for seizures.
5. Protect from injury.
6. Provide psychosocial support to the patient and family.
7. Prevent complications.
8. Prepare for transfer and transport to a tertiary care facility (Chapter 8) or prepare for hospitalization, as needed.

Home Care and Prevention

Patients and families may need time to understand the home care process involved with a neurologic disorder that suddenly presents in their child. Learning about seizures, headaches, or other neurologic conditions helps patients and parents to feel a sense of control. It is important to teach the older child and parents the importance of diligence with prescribed medications to prevent future seizures or other neurologic problems. Finally, older children and families require knowledge of first aid and cardiopulmonary resuscitation and how to access their local emergency medical services (EMS) agency.

Emergency nurses may want to learn more about specific neurologic conditions to prepare teaching materials for parents and other caregivers. Several helpful organizations are:

❐ Spina Bifida Association of America (202/944-3285), http://www.spinabifidaassociation.org.

❐ United Cerebral Palsy Association, Inc. (800/872-5827), http://www.ucp.org.

❐ Epilepsy Foundation of America (800/EFA-1000), http://www.epilepsyfoundation.org.

Selected Neurologic Emergencies

Seizures

Etiology

Seizures are among the more common events that trig-

TABLE 16.8 Comparison of Simple and Complex Febrile Seizures

Simple Febrile Seizures	Complex Febrile Seizures
Associated with a febrile illness with no CNS infection or acute electrolyte imbalance[15]	Associated with a febrile illness with no CNS infection with additional characteristics[16]
Have generalized clonic-tonic motor activity	Have prolonged generalized seizure activity
Last less than 10 to 15 minutes	Last greater than 15 minutes
Have no focal onset	Have focal characteristics
Usually occur in the first 24 hours of the febrile illness	Have recurrent seizures with the same illness and do not recur; more than one seizure in 24 hours

ger an ED visit. A seizure occurs when there is a sudden, abnormal, excessive cerebral electrical discharge. The rate and progression of the electrical discharge, the child's age, and the specific area of the brain involved influence the clinical presentation, which may vary.[8,15] The incidence of seizures during childhood is high. Febrile seizure is the most common seizure occurring in childhood; the typical age of onset is in children younger than 5 years of age with the peak incidence occurring in children between 18 and 24 months old.[8] In the United States, 2% to 5% of children will have a febrile seizure before the age of 5 years.[16] Febrile seizures are categorized as simple and complex (Table 16.8). Seizures are caused by a number of factors that interrupt normal brain function (Table 16.9).

TABLE 16.9 Etiologies of Seizure in Children

Nonrecurrent (acute) seizures[15]

- ❑ Infection (meningitis, encephalitis, brain abscess, shigellosis)
- ❑ Trauma
- ❑ Intracranial bleeding
- ❑ Toxic exposures
- ❑ Metabolic disturbances, including electrolyte imbalances and hypoglycemia
- ❑ Anoxia
- ❑ Brain tumors
- ❑ Fever

Recurrent (chronic) seizures or seizure disorders

- ❑ Idiopathic
- ❑ Injury to the CNS caused by trauma, anoxia, hemorrhage, toxin exposure, or infectious disease
- ❑ Congenital defects
- ❑ Degenerative phenomena

Epilepsy is defined as two or more unprovoked seizures.[15] The average incidence of epilepsy from birth to 16 years is approximately 40 cases in 100,000 children per year. The incidence in the first year of life is about 120 in 100,000. Between 1 and 10 years, the incidence plateaus at 40 to 50 cases in 100,000 children, and in teen years it drops further to about 20 in 100,000.[17] Seizures brought on by acute events such as fever or infection of the CNS or after head trauma are not considered epilepsy.[18] Epileptic seizures are classified into three major categories: partial, generalized, and unclassified (Table 16.10).

Nonepileptic paroxysmal events, such as breath-holding spells, may be mistaken for seizures because the child exhibits twitching or clonic-tonic movements at the end of the episode. Differentiation between these episodes and seizures may be difficult and require electroencephalographic evaluation. Syncope is also considered a nonepileptic paroxysmal event.[19,20]

Status epilepticus is a medical emergency. Generalized seizure activity results in increased tissue oxygen demand arising from muscle contractions, increased cerebral metabolic requirements, increased cerebral blood flow, and potentially increased ICP. Brain damage may occur if insufficient oxygen is delivered to the brain to meet metabolic needs.[8,15,16,21-24] Characteristics of status epilepticus are:

- ❑ Continuous generalized seizure lasting longer than 30 minutes.
- ❑ Recurrent seizures that occur without full recovery of consciousness between seizures.
- ❑ Risk for respiratory depression and hypoxia.

Focused History

- ❑ History of patient's present illness.
  - ▪ Onset of the present illness
  - ▪ Events before seizure onset: changes in expression, repetitive gestures, facial expression, or crying; any

potential ingestion of toxic substance; recent trauma

- Description of body movements or seizure activity
- Duration of movements or seizure; number of seizures
- Level of awareness during seizure
- Color change during seizure; presence of respiratory compromise
- Postictal behaviors
- Associated symptoms (such as fever, vomiting, headache, stiff neck, and back pain)
- Dietary intake and output
- Parent's or caretaker's impressions. If the child has a known seizure disorder, ask whether this seizure was typical of the child's usual seizure activity.
- Current medications (dose, time of last dose, and compliance with dosing regimen)

❐ Past health history.

- Neurologic, metabolic, or bleeding disorders
- Previous seizures, febrile seizures, and last seizure episode
- Family history of febrile seizures, seizure disorder, or epilepsy
- History of cerebrospinal fluid (CSF) shunt device (ventriculoperitoneal shunt), last revision date
- Presence of a persistent neurologic deficit

Focused Assessment

Physical Assessment

1. Assess the respiratory system.
   - Auscultate the chest for:
     - Respiratory rate
     - Respiratory effort. Respiratory depth, and effort may be decreased during a seizure and in the postictal phase. Increased secretions and an altered level of consciousness increase the patient's risk for aspiration and respiratory compromise.
2. Assess the cardiovascular system.
   - Auscultate the heart for:
     - Rate. Tachycardia is typically present during a seizure and may be related to fever, dehydration, or shock and sepsis. Bradycardia may be present in patients with elevated ICP or in those who are having airway obstruction, respiratory depression, hypoventilation, or apnea.
     - Measure blood pressure, including pulse pressure.
     - Alterations in blood pressure (hypotension or hypertension) may arise from a variety of causes. It is critical to evaluate blood pressure readings in relation to the child's age to determine the presence of hypertension, hypotension, and abnormal pulse pressures. Rising systolic readings and widening pulse pressures are associated with increased ICP and/or early septic shock.
   - Measure skin and core temperature.

TABLE 16.10 Categories of Epileptic Seizures

Category of Seizure	Description
Partial seizures	Motor, sensory, autonomic, or psychic manifestation without a loss of consciousness
Simple partial seizures[8,15,17]	Focal motor activity
	Somatosensory symptoms (headache, pins-and-needles sensation, metallic taste)
	Autonomic symptoms (flushing, sweating, salivation)
	Usually persists for 10–20 seconds without postictal symptoms
Complex partial seizures[8,15,17]	Arise from any region of the brain (temporal, frontal, parietal, occipital)
	Observed more often in children 3 years through adolescence
	Involve an impairment of consciousness
	Repetitive automatic behavior—purposeful but inappropriate motor movement, such as facial grimacing, fumbling movements, or running
	Last 30 seconds to several minutes
	Postictal symptoms may include fear, anxiety, sleepiness, lethargy, confusion, sadness.

TABLE 16.10 Categories of Epileptic Seizures (continued)	
Generalized seizures	Brief lapse of consciousness (5 to 15 seconds)
Absence (formerly petit mal)[8,15]	Staring Minor motor movement: Blinking or nystagmus Slight loss of muscle tone Amnesia for episodes Onset usually between 4 and 12 years of age
Tonic-clonic[8,15]	Loss of consciousness, may be preceded by an aura Strained muscle contraction and rigidity of extremities and trunk (tonic); alternates with rhythmic jerking and flexor spasm of the muscles (clonic) Incontinence of urine and/or stool Postictal state may last hours; deep postictal sleep is typical Apneic, may become cyanotic, increased salivation, child may bite tongue
Myoclonic[8,15]	Brief, sudden massive muscle contraction that may involve the whole body or one body part Child may or may not lose consciousness Patient may fall to the ground
Atonic[8,15]	Sudden loss of muscle tone Begin without warning, onset usually between 2 and 5 years Patient will fall to the ground violently if standing Consciousness impaired for a few seconds to a minute Seen in children with Lennox-Gastaut syndrome
Tonic[15]	Brief; average duration of 10 seconds Tonic contraction of muscles; sudden increase extensor muscle tone; impaired consciousness Contraction of respiratory and abdominal muscles may result in periods of apnea or high-pitched cry Occur more frequently at night Patient typically will fall to the ground if standing Postictal state may include confusion, lethargy, and headache
Unclassified epileptic seizures	Seizures that lack sufficient information to classify Several types of epileptic syndromes display a group of signs and symptoms that collectively characterize a particular condition Several syndromes associated with epilepsy occur in infants and children. Two of these are Lennox-Gastaut syndrome and West syndrome.

- Body temperature may be elevated after a prolonged seizure.
- The presence or absence of fever is dependent on the etiology of the seizure (e.g., CNS infection or febrile seizure).

3. Assess the neurologic status.
   - Assess the child's level of consciousness, orientation, mentation.
   - Calculate the GCS score.
   - Evaluate the cranial nerves for:
     - Pupil reaction
     - Extraocular eye movement
     - Blinking

- Gag reflex
- Facial symmetry
- Evaluate eye position and movement.
  - Deviation may be present
  - Nystagmus may be present
- Evaluate motor function.
  - Spontaneous motor response and/or response to stimulus
  - Posture and muscle tone
  - Muscle power
  - Reflexes
- Observe the child's balance while sitting or standing.
  - Ataxia may be present
- Describe seizure activity if present or recurs.
  - Focal versus generalized motor activity
  - Progression of motor activity
  - Type of motor activity (clonic-tonic, clonic, myoclonic, etc.)
  - Duration of seizure: Spontaneous resolution; resolution with medication administration
  - Incontinence of urine and/or stool
- Assess for signs of meningeal irritation.
  - Nuchal rigidity (neck pain and stiffness)
  - Kernig's sign (inability to completely extend leg when patient lies on back with thigh flexed to 90 degrees)
  - Brudzinski's sign (flexion of the hip and knee in response to forward flexion of the neck)
  - Opisthotonos (severe arching of the neck and back caused by extensor muscle spasm)
  - Photophobia (increased sensitivity to light)
- Assess the head for:
  - Injury or surface trauma
  - Bulging anterior fontanelle in infants with open anterior fontanelle
4. Assess the integumentary system.
   - Inspect the skin for:
     - Presence of petechial or purpuric rash. Such rashes may indicate sepsis or meningitis.
     - Surface trauma. Suspicious bruises and bruises in varying stages of healing may be indicative of child maltreatment (Chapter 44).

Psychosocial Assessment

❏ Assess the family's coping strategies. Observing their child having a seizure, especially a first-time seizure, can be very distressing to the parents.

❏ Assess and observe the child's and family's interaction patterns. A lack of concern about the seriousness of the child's condition or unhealthy family interaction patterns may indicate child maltreatment or neglect and warrant further investigation (Chapter 44).

Nursing Interventions

1. Assess and maintain airway, breathing, and circulation.
   - Initiate measures to protect the airway.
     - Initiate the jaw thrust–chin lift maneuver to maintain the airway, as needed.
     - Suction the oropharynx, as needed, to remove secretions.
     - Prepare for endotracheal intubation if prolonged airway patency is needed.
     - Initiate spinal immobilization if trauma is suspected.
     - Prepare to turn the patient in a side-lying position if vomiting occurs.
     - Loosen restrictive clothing.
   - Assure adequate breathing and ventilation.
     - Administer 100% oxygen via nonrebreather mask during active seizure, deep postictal state, or respiratory distress.
     - Initiate bag-mask ventilation with 100% oxygen for hypoventilation and apnea.
   - Initiate cardiorespiratory and oxygen saturation monitoring.
2. Obtain venous access and initiate intravenous infusion at a maintenance rate.
   - Obtain blood for laboratory studies.
     - Electrolytes
     - Glucose
     - Calcium
     - Magnesium
     - Toxicology screen
     - Blood cultures (for both bacterial and viral organisms)
     - Arterial blood gases
     - Complete blood cell count
     - Anticonvulsant levels, if the child routinely takes an anticonvulsant medication

TABLE 16.11 Medications for Acute Seizures

Medications for Acute Seizures	*Medications Used after Benzodiazepine Administration*
Lorazepam, IV: Lorazepam is the drug of first choice because of rapid onset and duration and because it causes less respiratory depression in children over 2 years of age.	Phenytoin, IV, at a rate no greater than 1 mg/kg/minute (maximum 50 mg/minute)
Diazepam, IV, or rectally if there is no IV access	Fosphenytoin. Fosphenytoin dosage is expressed in phenytoin sodium equivalents (PE). Fosphenytoin may be given IV at a rate no greater than 150 mg phenytoin equivalent/minute
Midazolam, IM, or intranasal route, if no IV access	Phenobarbital, IV, at a rate no greater than 1 mg/kg/minute
Consider pyridoxine (neonatal seizure that is refractory to other therapies).	

Notes: IV = intravenously; IM = intramuscularly.

Abend, N. S., & Bonnemann, C. G. (2007). Status epilepticus secondary to hypertensive encephalopathy as the presenting manifestation of Guillain-Barré syndrome. *Pediatric Emergency Care, 23*(9), 659–661.

Bryant, R., & Schultz, R. J. (2007). The child with cerebral dysfunction. In M. J. Hockenberry & D. Wilson (Eds.), *Wong's nursing care of infants and children* (8th ed., pp. 1612–1675). St. Louis, MO: Elsevier.

Kyle, T. (2008). *Essentials of pediatric nursing* (pp. 466–516). Philadelphia: Lippincott Williams & Wilkins.

Morton, L. D., & Pellock, J. M. (2006). Status epilepticus. In K. F. Swaiman, S. Ashwal, & D. M. Ferriero (Eds.), *Pediatric neurology: Principles and practice* (4th ed., pp. 1091–1104). St. Louis, MO: Elsevier.

- Consider prothrombin time/international normalized ratio (INR) and partial thromboplastin time in the neonate or infant.
- Administer medications, as prescribed.
  - Pharmacologic intervention should be initiated as soon as possible for seizures lasting 10 to 15 minutes or longer to stop the seizure because of the risk of brain injury[8,15,16,21] (Table 16.11).
  - Treat documented hypoglycemia. Administer 10% dextrose, intravenously, for neonates. Administer 25% dextrose, intravenously, for infants and older.
- Administer additional medications as prescribed.
  - Antibiotics for a CNS infection
  - Calcium chloride for hypocalcemia
  - Normal or hypertonic saline solution for hyponatremia
  - Gastric decontamination and/or specific antidote for a toxin
  - Osmotic diuretic for increased ICP
3. Monitor the neurologic status.
   - Observe duration and characteristics of seizure activity and signs of improvement.
4. Reassess the child's cardiopulmonary and neurologic status.
5. Prepare for and assist with diagnostic procedures.
   - Neuroimaging (computed tomographic [CT] scan,

magnetic resonance imaging [MRI]): Focal seizure, suspected intracranial bleeding, suspected intracranial lesion, or signs of increased ICP
   - Lumbar puncture and CSF analysis: Suspected CNS infection
6. Inform the family frequently about their child's condition; provide psychosocial and emotional support to the patient and family.
7. Protect the patient from injury.
   - Put side rails up; pad rails as needed. Have oxygen and suction equipment in the room; ensure intravenous access.
   - Place the patient in a side-lying position after the seizure to protect from aspiration of secretions and/or emesis.
8. Prepare for transfer and transport to a tertiary care facility (Chapter 8), hospital admission, or discharge to home.

Home Care and Prevention

The patient and family should be educated about the child's disease process and subsequent plan of care, including follow-up with the child's primary care physician. Although additional teaching and follow-up will be necessary, basic instructions on seizure management and appropriate first-aid measures can be taught on ED discharge.[8,15]

❑ Seizure prevention:

- Supervise the child's baths and swimming; ensure that someone is at home when an adolescent is bathing or swimming.

- Purchase and have the child wear a safety helmet when bicycling, tree-climbing, skateboarding, snowboarding, skiing, rollerblading, or doing other activities that place the child at risk for a head injury.

- Keep bathroom and bedroom doors unlocked to allow quick access in case of an emergency.

- Obtain a medical identification bracelet for the child who may be eventually or potentially diagnosed with a seizure disorder.

- Administer antiseizure and antipyretic medications as prescribed.

❑ First aid for a seizure:

- Remain calm and remain with the child.

- Protect the child from injury by removing dangerous objects and placing the child on the floor in a side-lying position.

- Place a folded jacket, blanket, or towel under the child's head to prevent injury if the child is lying on a hard surface, such as an uncarpeted floor.

- Avoid placing fingers, any objects, fluids, or food in the child's mouth during or after the seizure.

- Talk calmly to the child after the seizure; explain what happened; reassure the child.

❑ Contact EMS when the:

- child's seizure continues for more than 5 minutes.

- child develops respiratory distress.

- seizure activity continues without a postictal phase.

CSF Shunt Dysfunction

Etiology

The placement of a CSF shunt is the current treatment of choice for hydrocephalus. Hydrocephalus may be acquired (e.g., posttrauma or brain tumor) or congenital. In both types of hydrocephalus, excess CSF accumulates in the ventricular system because of:[8,32–34]

❑ Excessive production of CSF

❑ Obstruction of CSF flow in either the ventricles or subarachnoid space

❑ Abnormal absorption of CSF

The most common type of CSF shunt is the ventriculoperitoneal shunt. The proximal end of the ventriculoperitoneal shunt is placed in the lateral ventricle, and the distal end terminates in the peritoneal cavity. CSF shunts may also terminate in the jugular vein (ventriculojugular shunt) or the right atrium (ventriculoatrial shunt). The shunt device drains excess CSF from the ventricles via a pressure gradient. A one-way valve in the shunt tubing prevents retrograde flow of CSF.

Shunt function can be impaired by:[8,25–30]

❑ Obstruction

❑ Infection

- Most shunt infections occur within 2 months of surgery.[8,27]

- Signs of meningeal irritation (e.g., nuchal rigidity) have been reported in only 33% of patients.[27]

- Signs suggestive of shunt infection may include:[27]

  - Fever (42% of patients)

  - Irritability

  - Swelling

  - Erythema

  - Tenderness around the shunt

  - Ventriculoperitoneal shunt—abdominal pain with guarding and rebound tenderness due to pus drainage into the peritoneal cavity

  - Signs of increased ICP

- Catheter migration

- Disruption of shunt integrity

Signs and symptoms of shunt dysfunction are related to increasing ICP. When the shunt device is not functional, excess CSF accumulates and ICP increases. Initial symptoms may be vague or intermittent; symptoms of shunt malfunction are listed in Table 16.12.

Focused History

❑ Onset of the patient's present illness and development of neurologic symptoms

❑ Associated symptoms

- Morning headache with vomiting

- Signs of increased ICP (e.g., vomiting, headache, and changes in level of consciousness or activity)

❑ Dietary intake and output

- Changes from normal feeding habits

- Anorexia

❑ Parent or caretaker's impressions

- Changes in school performance or achieved developmental milestones

❑ Current medications (dose, time of last dose, and compliance with dosing regimen)

TABLE 16.12 Signs of Shunt Malfunction

Initial Symptoms	Additional Symptoms
Vomiting	Vision Changes
Decreased Activity	Seizures
Nausea	Tense or bulging anterior fontanelle (in infants)
Headache	Gait or balance abnormalities
Irritability/behavior change	Altered mental status
"Sunset eyes" (downward gaze)	Fever (if infection is present)
Lethargy	Increased head circumference

McCormick, B. M., Mackey, W. L., & Wilson, D. (2007). Conditions caused by defects in physical development. In M. J. Hockenberry & D. Wilson (Eds.), *Wong's nursing care of infants and children* (8th ed., pp. 422-498). St. Louis, MO: Elsevier.

Steele, D. W. (2006). Neurosurgical emergencies, nontraumatic. In G.R. Fleisher, S. Ludwig, & F.M. Henretig (Eds.), *Textbook of pediatric emergency medicine* (5th ed., pp. 1717-1725). Philadelphia: Lippincott Williams & Wilkins.

❏ Shunt-related history
  - Type of shunt
  - Reason for shunt placement
  - Previous or last episode of shunt dysfunction
  - Date of last shunt revision
❏ History of seizure disorder
❏ History of spina bifida or myelomeningocele
❏ Presence of a persistent neurologic deficit. Determine baseline function.

Focused Assessment

Physical Assessment

1. Assess the respiratory system.
   - Auscultate the chest for respiratory rate. Tachypnea often is present.
   - Auscultate the respiratory pattern. Changes in respiratory pattern and apnea may develop if ICP remains high or continues to increase.
2. Assess the cardiovascular system.
   - Auscultate the heart for rate. Tachycardia may be present in young children. Bradycardia may be present in adolescents.
   - Measure the blood pressure and pulse pressure. Blood pressure fluctuations are seen initially and then rising systolic blood pressure and widening

pulse pressure as ICP increases. Young children may exhibit the triad of wide pulse pressure, increased systolic blood pressure, and tachycardia. Adolescents may exhibit the more classic triad of wide pulse pressure, rising systolic blood pressure, and bradycardia.[11]

3. Assess core and skin temperature. Fever may be present with CNS or shunt infection.
4. Assess the neurologic system.
   - Assess level of consciousness with AVPU or GCS. Alterations in level of consciousness may be subtle initially, including irritability, lethargy, or decreased eye contact.
   - Evaluate the cranial nerves. Sluggish pupil response may be noted. Palsies of cranial nerves IV and VI may also be present, affecting the patient's eye movements and tracking of objects. Upward eye movement may be difficult. Papilledema may be present and result in blurred vision and headache.[8,15,27]
   - Evaluate motor function. Increased tone of lower extremities and positive Babinski's reflex may be present in child who is walking.[26,27] Patients with myelomeningocele may have a baseline alteration in lower extremity motor function or paralysis.
   - Assess balance. Uncoordinated movement, inability to sit unassisted, ataxia, or abnormal gait may be present.
   - Inspect the head. Infants may have an increased head circumference and tense, bulging anterior fontanelle; widened or separated sutures; dilated scalp veins; downturned or "sunset eyes."[8,15]
5. Assess for other neurologic-related findings.
   - Incontinence
   - High-pitched cry

Psychosocial Assessment

❏ Assess the child's and family's understanding of the child's underlying health condition.
❏ Assess the child's and family's prior experience with the health care system.
❏ Assess the child's and family's coping strategies.
  - Children with ongoing health conditions develop a repertoire of coping skills for hospitalizations and procedures. Early evaluation of these skills helps the emergency nurse to plan approaches to care and treatment.

Nursing Interventions

1. Assess and maintain airway, breathing, and circulation.
   - Assure adequate breathing and ventilation.
     - Administer 100% oxygen via nonrebreather mask, as needed.
     - Initiate bag-mask ventilation with 100% oxygen for hypoventilation and apnea.
   - Initiate cardiorespiratory and oxygen saturation monitoring, as needed.
   - Assess patient for signs of shock/septic shock when shunt or CNS infection is suspected.

2. Obtain venous access and initiate intravenous infusion at prescribed rates.
   - Obtain blood for laboratory studies.
     - Electrolytes
     - Glucose
     - Complete blood cell count
     - Cultures as indicated
   - Administer medications, as prescribed.
     - Administer antipyretics to decrease fever and maintain normothermia to decrease metabolic demand. Acetaminophen may be administered rectally if the patient is vomiting or shunt malfunction is suspected.
     - Administer nonnarcotic analgesics for headache.
     - Administer antibiotics for suspected infection as prescribed for preoperative care.
     - Administer other medications as indicated to treat increased ICP:
       - Osmotic diuretics (e.g., mannitol)
       - Corticosteroids (e.g., dexamethasone)

3. Monitor neurologic status for signs of increased ICP.

4. Reassess cardiopulmonary and neurologic status.

5. Position the patient to promote venous outflow.
   - Place the patient in a position of comfort
   - Elevate the head of the bed 30 degrees
   - Maintain the head and neck in midline

6. Prepare for and assist with diagnostic procedures.
   - CT scan to evaluate shunt function
   - Shunt-series radiographs to assess shunt continuity
   - Lumbar puncture and CSF analysis if meningitis is suspected
   - Shunt tap to evaluate for shunt infection
   - Bladder catheterization or assisting the child to void to obtain a urine culture and urine specimen

7. Inform the family frequently about their child's condition; provide psychosocial and emotional support to the patient and family.

8. Prepare for transfer and transport to a tertiary care center (Chapter 8), hospitalization and possible surgical procedure, or discharge to home.

Home Care and Prevention

Children who have CSF shunts and their families are taught to assess the shunt's integrity on a regularly scheduled basis by inspecting the shunt and observing the child's behavior. In general, parents are taught to:[25]

- ❏ Inspect the child's head for CSF, an indication of shunt leakage.
- ❏ Palpate and observe the shunt, which is generally looped subcutaneously behind an ear. The shunt should feel and look round and full, not flat.
- ❏ Observe the shunt for redness, edema, or tenderness.
- ❏ Observe the child for fever or irritability, early indications of shunt infection.
- ❏ Observe for signs of shunt blockage:
  - Fatigue
  - Stiff neck
  - Nausea
  - Seizures
  - Visual disturbances
  - Fever
  - Vomiting

Children and parents know that during a "growth spurt" the shunt may have to be revised. The child is taught to avoid contact sports, but other activities are generally not limited. Emergency nurses should incorporate the family's knowledge into the plan of care during ED treatment and should help to clear up any misconceptions on discharge. Regular follow-up with the child's primary care physician should be encouraged.

Headaches

Etiology

Headaches are common complaints in children and adolescents, occurring in approximately 75% of children by the age of 15 years.[31] Headaches tend to be more common in females after puberty than in males.[32] Headaches in children and adolescents are often mild and of minimal consequence. Although a commonly associated symptom of the febrile response in systemic illnesses, headache can be a symptom of life-threatening conditions. A child presenting with a complaint of headache must be carefully evaluated for signs and symptoms associated with emergent conditions.

Headache pain generally results from vascular effects, muscle contraction, inflammation, and traction/compression.[31] Common causes of headache in children include: [15,31]

- ❐ Febrile illness
- ❐ Sinus and dental infections
- ❐ Trauma
- ❐ Migraine

These causes of headache affect the pain-sensitive structures of the intracranial vascular structures and cranium. Pain-sensitive intracranial vascular structures include:

- ❐ The venous sinuses
- ❐ Portions of the large cerebral arteries
- ❐ The dura mater at the base of the skull

The pain-sensitive structures of the cranium include the:

- ❐ Sinus cavities
- ❐ Teeth
- ❐ Muscles of the head and neck
- ❐ Scalp
- ❐ Orbits

Headache pain results from inflammation, traction on intracranial structures, muscle contraction, or vasodilation that affects the pain-sensitive structures.[31] Severity and associated characteristics are important factors in identifying the etiology of headaches. Table 16.13 compares headaches and their causes and assessment findings.

Focused History

Patient history

- ❐ Headache-specific history.
  - Quality of pain: Throbbing; pressure; squeezing
  - Location of pain: Unilateral or bilateral; frontal, temporal, occipital, or above or behind the eye
  - Duration of pain: Episodic or constant
  - Precipitating events
- ❐ Headache-relief measures and their success.
  - Position change exacerbates pain (may be present with traction headache).
  - Pain awakens from sleep (may be present with traction headache or increased ICP).
  - Pain is relieved by sleep (may get some relief with sleep during migraines).

- ❐ Associated symptoms:
  - Rhinitis
  - Fever
  - Nausea
  - Vomiting
  - Sore throat
  - Stiff neck
  - Visual changes
  - Toothache
- ❐ Changes in dietary intake and output
- ❐ Parent's or caretaker's impressions
- ❐ Current medications
  - Over-the-counter and prescribed
  - Dietary and herbal supplements
  - Dose, time of last dose, and dosing regimen
- ❐ Recent head trauma
- ❐ Recent emotional stress
- ❐ Past medical history
  - Blood and bleeding disorders. Children with blood and bleeding disorders are at greater risk for bleeding from relatively minor head trauma (e.g., hemophilia). Children with sickle cell disease are at higher risk for cerebral infarction and intracranial hemorrhage.
  - Previous similar headache episodes; history of migraine
  - History of neurologic (arterial venous malformations), metabolic, renal, cardiac, or blood disorders
  - History of hypertension
  - Use of birth control pills
  - Allergies
  - Previous sinus infections or dental problems

Family Health History

- ❐ Family history of migraine or headaches

Focused Assessment

Physical Assessment

- ❐ Assess the respiratory system.
  - Auscultate the chest for respiratory rate.
- ❐ Assess the cardiovascular system.
  - Auscultate the heart for rate.
  - Measure the blood pressure.
    - Headache and hypertension may be present in

children with renal disease.

- Children with congenital heart disease (e.g., coarctation of the aorta) may also present with an associated hypertension (Chapter 15).

  - Measure core and skin temperature.
    - Fever may be present, with flushed cheeks and pale skin.

❐ Assess the neurologic system.

  - Assess level of consciousness with the GCS or the AVPU method.
    - Alterations in level of consciousness may be associated with life-threatening infection of the CNS, increased ICP, intra-cranial mass, or intracranial hemorrhage.
  - Evaluate cranial nerves, including an ocular examination.
    - Transient difficulties with speech may be present during migraines.
    - Intracranial tumor and/or increased ICP may cause altered cranial nerve function.
    - Visual acuity disturbances and papilledema may be present.
  - Evaluate motor function.
    - Transient motor deficits may be present with

migraine; however, a complete evaluation is needed to rule out other causes, such as brain lesion or increased ICP.

  - Assess balance.
    - Ataxia while sitting or standing may be evident.
  - Assess for signs of meningeal irritation.
    - Nuchal rigidity
    - Kernig's sign
    - Brudzinski's sign
    - Photophobia
  - Assess for sinus pain by:
    - Palpating the sinuses
    - Observing for edema over the sinuses
  - Listen for bruits over skull and neck.
  - Assess the pain with an age-appropriate pain scale and assessment techniques (Chapter 11).

Psychosocial Assessment

❐ Assess the child's previous experience with headaches.

❐ Assess the child's and the family's coping strategies.

❐ Assess the child's previous pain experience and strategies to cope with pain.

TABLE 16.13 Description, Causes, and Assessment Findings of Different Headache Types

Headache Type	Description	Possible Causes	Associated Symptoms, Characteristics, and Clinical Findings
Inflammatory			
	Infections cause inflammation of pain-sensitive intracranial or extracranial structures and lead to meningeal irritation and increased ICP.	Meningitis Encephalitis Intracranial abscess	Neck stiffness Fever Vomiting Altered level of consciousness
	Infection and inflammation of a sinus causes headache as a primary symptom.	Sinusitis	Rhinitis, nasal congestion, morning cough Facial pain (maxillary) Occipital pain (sphenoid) Frontal pain (frontal sinus in older children) Fever
	Dental infections can cause headaches.	Abscesses	Localized symptoms of tooth pain and sensitivity Fever

TABLE 16.13 Description, Causes, and Assessment Findings of Different Headache Types

Headache Type	Description	Possible Causes	Associated Symptoms, Characteristics, and Clinical Findings
Vascular			
	Increased intracranial vasodilation or arterial dilation causes vascular headaches. Migraine is the most common recurrent headache in children.	Fever related to a viral or systemic illness	Pain in frontal and/or bitemporal area Throbbing Often unilateral pain, but may become generalized Aura may be present (pain begins as the aura wanes) Visual disturbances Transient motor deficits Nausea Vomiting Abdominal pain Photophobia
	Headaches may occur before a seizure or in the postictal phase or may be the only manifestation of the seizure.	Varying causes of seizures	No specific characteristics
	Hypoxia associated with decreased cerebral perfusion results in arterial dilation.	Congestive heart failure Hypertension Vaso-occlusive event, such as sickle cell disease or severe anemia	Throbbing quality Frontal bitemporal headache
Traction/Compression			
	Traction headaches are caused by conditions that shift intracranial structures and place traction on, or cause stretching of, the pain-sensitive dura and/or blood vessels at the base of the brain.	Intracranial hemorrhage Intracranial hematoma Cerebral edema Hydrocephalus Tumors Brain abscess	Symptoms of increased ICP Focal neurologic deficits Drowsiness Vomiting Diplopia Headaches associated with increased ICP; morning headaches with generalized pain, nausea, and vomiting; the child may be awakened from sleep Signs of brain abscess: fever, altered level of consciousness, focal motor weakness, and/or other neurologic deficits

TABLE 16.13 Description, Causes, and Assessment Findings of Different Headache Types

Headache Type	Description	Possible Causes	Associated Symptoms, Characteristics, and Clinical Findings
Tension/muscle contraction			
	Tension headaches are caused by a sustained contraction of the head and neck muscles. These are more common in adolescents than in younger children.	Tension Fatigue	Feeling of tightness or pressure in the back of head and neck; occasionally generalized

Bryant, R., & Schultz, R. J. (2007). The child with cerebral dysfunction. In M. J. Hockenberry & D. Wilson (Eds.), *Wong's nursing care of infants and children* (8th ed., pp. 1612–1675). St. Louis, MO: Elsevier.

King, J. (2007). Neurologic anatomy, physiology, and assessment. In R. Kaplow & S. R. Hardin (Eds.), *Critical care nursing: Synergy for optimal outcomes* (pp. 349–358). Boston: Jones and Bartlett.

Lewis, D. W. (2006). Headaches in infants and children. In K. F. Swaiman, S. Ashwal, & D. M. Ferriero (Eds.), *Pediatric neurology: Principles and practice* (4th ed., pp. 1183–1202). St. Louis, MO: Elsevier.

Nursing Interventions

1. Assess and maintain airway, breathing, and circulation.

2. Reassess the child's neurologic status.

3. Apply pain-relief measures:
   - Darken the room if the child is photophobic.
   - Apply a cool compress for a vascular headache.
   - Administer analgesic medications, as prescribed.
     - Mild analgesics, such as acetaminophen, coupled with rest and/or sleep, will relieve the pain of most headaches.
     - Other medications may be administered for more severe headaches or migraine headaches not responsive to acetaminophen.
   - Administer medications to treat an underlying condition (e.g., hypertension or sinusitis) that is causing the headache.
   - Administer antipyretic therapy for fever; maintain normothermia to decrease metabolic demand.

4. Employ complementary and alternative treatments to relieve pain.
   - Guided imagery
   - Hypnosis
   - Biofeedback
   - Stress management
   - Exercise
   - Dietary modifications
   - Sleep hygiene
   - Acupuncture
   - Massage therapy
   - Aroma therapy

5. Allow the child to rest and/or sleep.

6. Reassess the child's cardiovascular and neurologic status to detect improvement or worsening of condition.

7. Reassess for pain using the same age-appropriate pain scale and assessment techniques (Chapter 11).

8. Prepare for and assist with diagnostic procedures:
   - Neuroimaging: CT scan or MRI for suspected intracranial lesion, intracranial bleeding, or abscess.
   - Lumbar puncture and CSF analysis if CNS infection is suspected (meningitis or encephalitis).
   - Laboratory studies, as indicated, dependent on the patient's presenting symptoms and examination results.

9. Inform the family frequently of the child's condition; provide psychosocial and emotional support to the patient and family.

10. Prepare for transfer and transport to a tertiary care facility (Chapter 8), hospitalization, or discharge to home.

Home Care and Prevention

Headaches can be devastating to the child and family. The patient and family will need education concerning procedures, medications, and pain-relief measures. Home care measures are taught according to the type of headache diagnosed in the patient. Selected home care measures include:[31]

❏ Having the child lie in a dark, quiet room.

❏ Alternating the placement of hot and cold packs on the child's forehead.

❏ Administering over-the-counter or prescribed analgesics or anti-inflammatories.

❏ Teaching the child special relaxation techniques

and recognition of specific triggers that bring on the headache.

Neurotrauma—Traumatic Brain Injury

Etiology

Traumatic brain injury is a leading cause of death and disability in children and has been identified as a significant public health problem worldwide, as well as in the United States.[33] Traumatic brain injury is a common complaint/diagnosis in the pediatric population with more than 100,000 children every year having a traumatic brain injury.[34] Many characteristics make children more susceptible to head trauma than adults. Their head is larger in relation to the body, coupled with a higher center of gravity, causing children to hit their head more readily when involved in motor vehicle injuries, bicycle accidents, and falls.[8] Table 16.14 describes the various head injuries. Chapter 29 discusses head injuries in greater detail.

Focused History

Patient History

❑ Description of the events of the injury

❑ Events surrounding the injury

❑ Mental status at the time of the injury

❑ Primary head injuries
  - Skull fractures
  - Contusions
  - Intracranial hematomas
  - Diffuse injury

❑ Secondary head injuries
  - Hypoxic brain damage
  - Increased ICP
  - Infection
  - Cerebral edema

❑ Associated symptoms
  - Any loss of consciousness
  - Irritability
  - Abnormal behavior
  - Lethargy
  - Vomiting (if so, how many times)
  - Chief complaint of headache
  - Neck pain
  - Visual changes
  - Seizure activity
  - CSF rhinorrhea and otorrhea
  - Bleeding from the ear
  - Orbital or postauricular ecchymosis (Battle's sign)
  - Difficulty with gait
  - Difficulty with articulation
  - Any paralysis (hemiparesis or quadriplegia)
  - Retinal hemorrhage
  - Change in level of consciousness
  - Failure to thrive
  - Transient period of confusion
  - Somnolence
  - Listlessness
  - Pallor
  - Altered mental status (difficulty rousing child)
  - Mounting agitation
  - Marked changes in vital signs
  - Bulging fontanelle (infant)
  - Elevated temperature
  - Papilledema

❑ Parent's or caregiver's impression

❑ Current medications
  - Over-the-counter and prescribed medications
  - Dose, time of last dose, and dosing regimen

❑ Past medical history
  - Any previous head injuries
  - Blood and bleeding disorders. The child with bleeding disorders can present with a large hematoma that will need surgical intervention.
  - History of neurologic, metabolic, renal, cardiac, or blood disorders
  - History of any neurologic deficits
  - History of drug allergies, hemophilia, diabetes mellitus, or epilepsy, which may produce similar symptoms of head injury
  - Use of helmets with bike riding, sport activity
  - Use of car seats and passenger restraint system
  - Any previous admissions for traumatic brain injury[35]

Focused Assessment

Physical Assessment

Follow the ABCs (airway, breathing, circulation).

❑ Assess the respiratory system.

TABLE 16.14 Head Injuries and Common Manifestations

Head Injury	*Manifestations*
Concussion	The most common head injury. A transient and reversible neuronal dysfunction with instantaneous loss of awareness and responsiveness from trauma to the head. Posttraumatic amnesia is characteristic and reflects the extent and severity of injury to the brain after blunt trauma.
Contusion/ laceration	The term laceration and contusion are used to describe actual bruising and tearing of cerebral tissue. Contusions represent petechial hemorrhages or localized bruising along the superficial aspect of the brain at the site of injury (coup injury) or a lesion remote from the site of direct trauma (contrecoup injury). Cerebral lacerations are generally associated with penetrating or depressed skull fractures; however, they may occur without fractures in small children. When lacerations lead to bleeding into and around the tear, more severe and prolonged unconsciousness and paralysis may occur, leaving permanent scarring and some degree of disability. Close neurologic observation is required.
Fractures	A great deal of force is needed to produce a skull fracture in infants and children younger than 2 years of age. The flexibility of the immature skull is able to withstand a greater degree of deformation before a fracture will occur. Skull fractures can result in little or no brain damage but could have serious consequences if the underlying brain tissue is injured.
Linear skull fractures	Consists of a simple break in the skull and is the most common skull fracture. Can be caused by minor head injuries, that is, being struck by a rock, stick, or other object; falls or motor vehicle injuries. Not usually serious unless there is underlying damage to the brain.
Depressed skull fractures	The bone is locally broken and pushing inward causing pressure on the brain. This pressure constitutes a neurosurgical emergency in which the pieces of bone are lifted off of the brain and the brain is inspected for evidence of injury. This type of injury can be caused by impact from a blunt object, that is, hammer or another heavy but fairly small object.
Diastatic skull fracture	Traumatic separation of cranial sutures, commonly affecting the lambdoid sutures, rarely seen beyond the first 4 years of age. Usually treatment is not required, but neurologic observation will be necessary.
Compound skull fracture	A break in the skin and splintering of the bone. The fracture may be linear or depressed. Can be a result of blunt force. The patient usually requires medical interventions, and surgery may be necessary.
Basilar skull fractures	This is a fracture of the bones that form the base of the skull. Can result from a significant force and blunt head trauma. Because of the proximity to the brain stem, this is a serious head injury. Manifestations may include CSF rhinorrhea and otorrhea, bleeding from the ear, and orbital or postauricular ecchymosis (Battle's sign). These children are at increased risk for CNS infection because the fracture may allow a portal of entry into the CNS.
Subdural hematoma	A collection of blood between the dura and cerebrum, usually venous in origin resulting from the rupture of the cortical veins that bridge the subdural space. Ten times more common than epidural bleeds and occurs most often in infancy, with a peak at 6 months until 2 years of age. Common in infants, often as a result of birth trauma, falls, assaults, or abusive head trauma. Symptoms include vomiting, failure to thrive, changes in level of consciousness, retinal hemorrhage, and seizures. Treatment depends on size of clot, clinical symptoms, and area of the brain involved. In some cases, just closely monitoring for resolution is necessary; however, in some cases treatment may include subdural taps in infants and surgical evacuation of the clot in older children. Close monitoring for the signs and symptoms of increased ICP and neurologic status may be indicated.
Epidural hematoma	Collection of blood located outside the dura but within the skull and forms a hematoma. Rarely occurs in children 2 years of age or less. Seen when head trauma is severe and results in a skull fracture. Usually caused by an arterial bleed of the middle meningeal artery. Brain stem impairment, respiratory and cardiovascular function may be compromised. Symptoms include headache, vomiting, and lethargy. Treatment includes prompt surgical evacuation and cauterization of the arterial bleeding. The earlier the bleeding is recognized and treated, the more favorable the clinical outcome. Close monitoring of neurologic function is indicated.

Bryant, R., & Schultz, R. J. (2007). The child with cerebral dysfunction. In M. J. Hockenberry & D. Wilson (Eds.), *Wong's nursing care of infants and children* (8th ed., pp. 1612–1675). St. Louis, MO: Elsevier.

Kyle, T. (2008). *Essentials of pediatric nursing* (pp. 466–516). Philadelphia: Lippincott Williams & Wilkins.

- Auscultate the chest for respiratory rate.
- Deep, rapid, periodic, intermittent or gasping respirations are signs of brain stem involvement.
❑ Assess the cardiovascular system.
- Auscultate the heart rate.
- Measure the blood pressure.
  - Wide fluctuation or noticeable slowing of the pulse and widening pulse pressure or extreme fluctuations in blood pressure are signs of brain stem involvement.
- Measure the core and skin temperature.
  - Fever may be present with flushed cheeks and pale skin.
❑ Assess for spinal cord injury.
- Stabilize neck and spine immediately.
- Use jaw thrust to open airway, not chin lift.
- Five percent to 20% of patients with head injuries have cervical spine injuries.
❑ Assess the neurologic system.
- Assess level of consciousness with the GCS or the AVPU method.
- Alterations in level of consciousness may be associated with life-threatening infection of the CNS, increased ICP, intracranial hematoma, or cerebral edema.
- Evaluate the cranial nerves, including an ocular examination.
  - Difficulties with speech may be present with intracranial hematomas, CNS infection, cerebral edema, or increased ICP.
  - Intracranial hematomas and/or increased ICP may cause altered cranial nerve function.
  - Assess pupillary response: fixed and dilated pupils, fixed and constricted pupils, or sluggish papillary reaction to light will warrant prompt intervention.
- Evaluate motor and sensory function.
  - A complete motor function evaluation as well as sensory function neurologic examination must be done to rule out any further increase in ICP, cerebral edema, intracranial hematomas.
  - Assess for hand grasps and pedal pushes that are equal and strong.
  - Assess for any seizure activity that can be prompted by a head injury.
- Assess for signs of meningeal irritation.
  - Nuchal rigidity

- Kernig's sign
- Brudzinski's sign
- Photophobia
- Clean any abrasions with soap and water.
  - Apply clean dressing.
  - If bleeding, apply ice to relieve pain and swelling.

Psychosocial Assessment

❑ Child's activity level, if he or she is overly inquisitive, has incomplete motor development and lack of judgment and knowledge skills, may place the child at higher risk for a traumatic brain injury.
❑ Children's dependence on others to care for them places them at a high risk for injuries caused by child abuse (abusive head trauma). Assess the family dynamics for possible child abuse.
❑ Assess the family's use of helmets, sport protective gear, auto restraint devices, and car seats for the children. Helmets, protective sporting goods gear, and the use of passive seat restraints, air bags, and car seats have decreased the number of traumatic brain injuries in children.

Nursing Interventions

1. Assess and maintain airway, breathing, and circulation.
2. Reassess the child's neurologic status.
3. Assess for changes in level of consciousness.
4. Assess for signs and symptoms of increased ICP.
5. Keep child on nothing-by-mouth status (NPO) until ordered otherwise.
6. Initiate seizure precautions as ordered.
7. Maintain a quiet environment to help reduce restlessness and irritability.
8. Turn off bright lights in the room.
9. Manage pain and reassess for pain using the same age-appropriate pain scale and assessment techniques (Chapter 11), and administer sedation as ordered. Sedation is controversial in the management of traumatic brain injury, in that most sedation prevents an accurate assessment of level of consciousness of the child, but the administration of acetaminophen will control pain and does not affect the level of consciousness assessment.
10. Observe the level of sedation closely to ensure that level of consciousness will not become altered, which would hinder the ability to assess adequately for neurologic changes.
11. Monitor for the development of complications, which

include hemorrhage, infection, cerebral edema, and herniation.[36]

12. Prepare for and assist with diagnostic procedures:
    - Neuroimaging: CT scan or MRI for suspected intracranial bleeding or edema
    - Laboratory studies, as indicated, dependent on the patient's presenting symptoms and examination results
    - Lumbar punctures are rarely done in suspected traumatic brain injuries and are contraindicated when a risk for increased ICP exists

13. Inform the family frequently of the child's condition; provide psychosocial and emotional support to the patient and family.

14. Encourage family involvement in the child's care.

15. Provide family education on the prevention of childhood traumatic head injuries.

16. Prepare for transfer and transport to a tertiary care facility (Chapter 8), hospitalization, or discharge to home.

Home Care and Prevention

Provide parents and caregivers with clear instructions regarding the care of the child at home. Explain that they must seek medical attention if the child's condition worsens at any time during the first several days after injury.

Children with mild closed head injuries may exhibit some behavioral and cognitive symptoms, such as difficulty paying attention, forgetting things, and problems making sense of what has been seen or heard in the early days of the injury. The majority of children make a full recovery; however, some may experience ongoing cognitive and behavioral difficulties, including attention difficulties and slow information processing. Children who have a moderate to severe traumatic brain injury may remain in a comatose state for a prolonged time. The extent of residual neurologic damage and recovery may be unclear for the child who has a traumatic brain injury. This can be frustrating and stressful for the family and parents. Encourage verbalization of their concerns and feelings. Rehabilitation of the child with permanent brain damage is an essential component of his or her care after a traumatic brain injury. Rehabilitation should begin as soon as possible in the hospital setting and may continue for months to years. This can place a strain on the finances and on the family. Families need to be involved in this rehabilitation process.[8,15,34,37]

Stroke

Etiology

Stroke is defined as a sudden rupture or occlusion of cerebral arteries or veins resulting in focal cerebral damage and clinical neurologic deficits. There has been an increase in the incidence of stroke in the pediatric population. DeVeber[4,38]has identified two reasons for this increase in incidence: one is the widespread availability of CT scans and MRI, which has increased the detection rate for pediatric stroke, and the other is that more effective treatments have increased survival of patients with certain previously lethal primary pediatric diseases that predispose to stroke (i.e., prematurity, congenital heart disease, sickle cell disease). A recent estimate of stroke in the pediatric population is 10.7 per 100,000, with hemorrhagic stroke accounting for 7.8%.[39] A more recent study by Zahuranec et al.[40] reports an incidence of stroke in the pediatric population in a town in southeast Texas as 4.3 per 100,000. All of these findings show the need for a large multicenter collaborative study that could ascertain a more accurate incidence of pediatric stroke.

Strokes are classified as (1) ischemic strokes, which result from occlusion of a cerebral artery or vein from a thrombus or embolus, and (2) hemorrhagic strokes, which result from vascular rupture. There are different causes of ischemic and hemorrhagic strokes (Table 16.15). The diagnostic tool most commonly used to differentiate ischemic from hemorrhagic stroke is a noncontrast head CT scan. Table 16.16 lists the diagnostic studies to be considered when evaluating a child with an acute stroke. The clinical manifestations of stroke in children are highly variable, influenced by the portion of the cerebral vasculature affected and the child's age. Hemiparesis is most often observed with facial weakness. Children younger than 4 years of age are more likely to have associated seizures, whereas older children complain of a headache. The child with a stroke may also present with a diminished level of consciousness.[41] Clinical management of pediatric strokes is highly variable depending on the type of stroke. With hemorrhagic stroke the patient may need emergency surgical intervention to decrease ICP, whereas a patient with an ischemic stroke may need only supportive care.

Focused History

☐ History of patient's present illness
  - Onset of symptoms
  - Progression of symptoms
  - Description of body parts affected
  - Change in level of consciousness

Table 16.15 Causes of Hemorrhagic and Ischemic Strokes

Causes of Hemorrhagic Stroke	Causes of Ischemic Stroke
Secondary hemorrhage into ischemic brain tissue	Vascular disease • Sickle cell disease • Arterial dissection • Homocystinuria • Vasculitis • Moyamoya • Migraine
Arteriovenous malformations	Thrombotic (arterial and sinovenous) • Hypercoagulable state, congenital or acquired • Hyperviscosity (polycythemia, dehydration)
Hemorrhage into intracranial tumor	Cardioembolic • Left atrial myxoma • Cyanotic congenital heart disease • Right-to-left shunts (i.e. patent foramen ovale) • Congenital or acquired valvular defects • Contractile dysfunction • Rhythm disturbance
Vascular malformations • Sickle cell disease • Saccular (berry) aneurysms	
Coagulopathy • Hemmorrhagic disease of the newborn (vitamin K deficiency) • Clotting factor deficiency (VIII, IX, XI) • Thrombocytopenia	
Arterial hypertension • Coarctation of the aorta • Renal vascular or parenchymal disease • Pheochromocytoma • Illicit drugs with sympathomimetic effect • Amphetamines, cocaine	

Steele, D. W. (2006). Neurosurgical emergencies, nontraumatic. In G. R. Fleisher, S. Ludwig, & F. M. Henretig (Eds.), *Textbook of pediatric emergency medicine* (5th ed., pp. 1717–1725). Philadelphia: Lippincott Williams & Wilkins.

- Difficulty walking
- Change in vision
- Difficulty with speech
- Any dizziness, seizures, headache, or nystagmus
- Weakness or paralysis of any extremity
- Current fever

- Current medications (dose, time of last dose, and compliance with dosing regimen)
- ❑ Past health history
- Neurologic, metabolic, or bleeding disorders
- Congenital heart disease
- Sickle cell disease
- Hypertension

Table 16.16 Studies to be Considered in the Evaluation of a Child with an Acute Strokes	
Brain Imaging	**Cardiac**
▪ Non-contrast CT	▪ Electrocardiogram
▪ MRI	▪ Echocardiogram
▪ Angiography (standard or magnetic resonance)	
Chemistry	**Hematologic**
▪ Lactate	▪ Complete blood count
▪ Toxicology screen	▪ Prothormbin and partial thromboplastin times
▪ Urine organic acids	▪ Fibrinogen
▪ Serum amino acids	▪ Hemoglobin electrophoresis
▪ Hepatic transaminases	▪ Erythrocyte sedimentation rate
▪ Blood urea nitrogen	▪ Protein C and S quantification
▪ Cholesterol and triglycerides	▪ Antithrombin III level
Lumbar Puncture	

Gorelick, M. H., & Blackwell, C. D. (2006). Neurologic emergencies. In Fleisher, G. R., Ludwig, S., & Henretig, F. M. (Eds.), *Textbook of Pediatric Emergency Medicine* (5th ed., pp. 759–781). Philadelphia: Lippincott Williams & Wilkins.

▪ Hyperlipidemias

▪ Substance abuse

Focused Assessment

Physical Assessment

❑ Assess the respiratory system.

▪ Auscultate the chest for:

• Respiratory rate

• Respiratory effort. The depth and effort may be decreased if the patient is having a seizure or in the postictal phase. Increased secretions and an altered level of consciousness increase the patient's risk for aspiration and respiratory compromise.

❑ Assess the cardiovascular system.

▪ Auscultate the heart for:

• Rate. Tachycardia can be related to a seizure, fever, or dehydration. Bradycardia may be present in patients with elevated ICP or in those who are having airway obstruction, respiratory depression, hypoventilation, or apnea.

▪ Measure blood pressure. It is critical to evaluate blood pressure readings in relation to the child's age to determine the presence of hypertension or hypotension. Rising systolic reading and widening pulse pressures are associated with increasing ICP.

▪ Temperature. May be elevated after a prolonged seizure. May be elevated with infectious endocarditis.

❑ Assess the neurologic status.

▪ Assess the child's level of consciousness, orientation, mentation.

▪ Bulging anterior fontanelle in infants with open anterior fontanelle

▪ Calculate the GCS score.

▪ Evaluate the cranial nerves for:

• Pupil reaction

• Extraocular eye movements

• Gag reflex

• Facial symmetry

• Tongue deviation

• Presence of nystagmus

▪ Symmetry of motor and sensory function

▪ Presence of ataxia

▪ Both receptive and expressive aphasia

Psychosocial Assessment

❑ Assess the family's coping strategies. Observing the child's neurologic deficits can be very distressing to the parents.

❑ Assess and observe the child's and family's interaction patterns. A lack of concern about the seriousness of the child's condition or unhealthy family interaction patterns may indicate child maltreatment or neglect and warrant further investigation (Chapter 44).

Nursing Interventions

1. Assess and maintain airway, breathing, and circulation.

   - Initiate measures to protect the airway:
     - Suction the oropharynx, as needed, to remove secretions.
     - Prepare for endotracheal intubation if prolonged airway patency is needed.
     - Prepare to turn the patient in a side-lying position if vomiting occurs.
     - Administer 100% oxygen via nonrebreather mask during active seizure or deep postictal state.
     - Assess arterial oxygen saturation, important in cyanotic heart disease, with polycythemia.
     - Elevate head of bed to 30 to 45 degrees to lower diaphragm and to decrease ICP, keep head in a midline neutral position, avoid flexion of the hips.

2. Obtain venous access and initiate intravenous infusion at a maintenance rate.

   - Obtain blood for laboratory studies; note glucose level (hypoglycemia and hyperglycemia can exacerbate ischemic stroke), hemoglobin and hematocrit, toxicology screen, blood cultures, INR, and partial thromboplastin time.

3. Prepare patient for diagnostic studies.

   - A noncontrast CT scan is done to assess for acute bleeding and should be done emergently. CT may be normal in the first 12 to 24 hours after an ischemic stroke.
   - An MRI may show changes as early as 6 hours after infarction.
   - Magnetic resonance angiography may be ordered. It yields further information about blood flow, as well as the structure of cervical and intracranial vessels.
   - Cardiac lesions may require a transthoracic echocardiogram or transesophageal echocardiogram.
   - The usual diagnostic workup for an ischemic stroke is a noncontrast CT scan followed by an MRI.

4. Administer medications, as prescribed, for:

   - seizure activity.
   - hypoglycemia.
   - hypotension. Initiate intravenous fluid administration.
   - hypertension. Administer anti-hypertensive medications as ordered, but lower blood pressure gradually.
   - fever. Administer antipyretics. Fever can occur in children with stroke and may also contribute to ischemic damage. Fever may also be present with infective endocarditis.
   - increased ICP. Administer osmotic diuretic or hypertonic saline solution
   - arterial ischemic stroke. Administer anticoagulants (heparin, low molecular weight heparin, aspirin, warfarin [Coumadin], or thrombolytic therapy). However, ED staff must balance the likelihood of either extension of infarction or a second embolus with the risk of inducing hemorrhage. There have not been large pediatric clinical trials with the use of thrombolytic therapy, so the success of this therapy has been noted anecdotally.

5. Administer blood products as ordered.

   - Acute transfusion is necessary with children with sickle cell disease and stroke to decrease the level of hemoglobin S to less than 30%.

6. Reassess the child's cardiopulmonary and neurologic status.

   - Recheck child's blood pressure; hypertension is a common cause of hemorrhagic stroke.
   - Check child's equality of strength and reflexes in both extremities for evidence of paralysis.
   - Check pupil size, equality, and reaction to light and accommodation.
   - Check the child's level of consciousness.
   - Assess child for focal or generalized seizure activity.
   - Prepare for ICP monitoring.

7. Prepare patient for emergent surgical treatment.

   - Keep child nothing by mouth (NPO).
   - Prepare for ICP monitoring.
   - Continue to assess for increased ICP. Emergency surgical evacuation of the hematoma may be indicated to reverse cerebral herniation and lower ICP.

8. Inform the family frequently about their child's condition; provide psychosocial and emotional support to the child and family.

9. Prepare for transfer and transport to a tertiary care facility or hospital admission.

Home Care and Prevention

The child and family should be educated about the child's disease process and subsequent plan of care, including follow-up with the child's primary care physician, hematologist, and neurologist.

Rehabilitation Therapy

Constraint-induced therapy (which does not focus on impairment) has been shown in a randomized, controlled trial[45] to be effective in children with congenital hemiplegia, thus the deduction of this therapy being valuable for the child after a stroke.

Given the frequency of potentially modifiable neurologic impairments and the known risk of increasing clinical deficits as the child matures, early and aggressive rehabilitation therapy initiated during acute hospitalization for children with persistent deficits is encouraged.[38]

Infants and young children have additional rehabilitation considerations as compared with adults. This includes greater complexity of feeding dysfunction and speech therapy, ongoing modification of rehabilitation as the child grows and develops age-related skills, and the potential for ongoing recovery over longer periods of time. Orthopedic problems such as leg length discrepancy and scoliosis from hemiatrophy of affected limbs are unique to the pediatric population. In addition, specialized pediatric rehabilitation and education teams must be developed because of learning and behavioral deficits unique to this population.

Parents may need encouragement to treat the affected child as normally as possible and to avoid "overprotection."[38]

Conclusion

Neurologic emergencies pose a unique situation for emergency nurses because of the neurologic differences among infants, children, and adolescents. These emergencies can range from life threatening to urgent conditions. Recognition of signs of increased ICP and rapid initiation of measures to prevent complications are the foundation for the emergency nursing care of children with neurologic conditions.

References

1. Padget, K. (2006). Alteration of neurologic function in children. In S. E. Huether & K. L. McCance (Eds.), *Pathophysiology: The biologic basis for disease in adults and children* (5th ed., pp. 623–654). St. Louis, MO: Elsevier.

2. Collins, P. (2009). *Gray's anatomy, the anatomical basis of clinical practice* (40th ed.). St. Louis, MO: Elsevier.

3. Gilman, S., Manter, J. T., Gatz, A. J., & Newman, S. W. (2002). *Manter and Gatz's essentials of clinical neuroanatomy and neurophysiology* (10th ed.). Philadelphia: Davis.

4. Carroll, E. W., & Curtis, R. L. (2005). Organization and control of neural function. In C. M. Porth, *Pathophysiology: Concepts of altered health states* (7th ed., pp. 1113–1157). Philadelphia: Lippincott Williams & Wilkins.

5. Wilkerson, R. R., & Boss, B. J. (2008). Alterations of neurologic function in children. In S. E. Huether & K. L. McCance (Eds.), *Understanding pathophysiology* (4th ed., pp. 405–423). St. Louis, MO: Elsevier.

6. Taylor, D. A., & Ashwal, S. (2006). Impairment of consciousness and coma. In K. F. Swaiman, S. Ashwal, & D. M. Ferriero (Eds.), *Pediatric neurology: Principles and practice* (4th ed., pp. 1377–1400). St. Louis, MO: Elsevier.

7. Wilson, D., Curry, M. R., & DeBoer, S. L. (2007). The child with musculoskeletal or articular dysfunction. In M. J. Hockenberry & D. Wilson (Eds.), *Wong's nursing care of infants and children* (8th ed., pp. 1730–1803). St. Louis, MO: Elsevier.

8. Kyle, T. (2008). *Essentials of pediatric nursing* (pp. 466–516). Philadelphia: Lippincott Williams & Wilkins.

9. Schutzman, S. A. (2006). Injury—head. In G. R. Fleisher, S. Ludwig, & F. M. Henretig (Eds.), *Textbook of pediatric emergency medicine* (5th ed., pp. 373–381). Philadelphia: Lippincott Williams & Wilkins.

10. Boss, B. J., & Wilkerson, R. R. (2006). Concepts of neurologic dysfunction. In S. E. Huether & K. L. McCance (Eds.), *Pathophysiology: the biologic basis for disease in adults and children* (5th ed., pp. 491–546). St. Louis, MO: Elsevier.

11. Boss, B. J. (2008). Concepts of neurologic dysfunction. In S. E. Huether & K. L. McCance (Eds.), *Understanding pathophysiology* (4th ed, pp. 331–368). St. Louis, MO: Elsevier.

12. Estes, M. E. Z. (2006). *Health assessment & physical examination* (3rd ed., pp. 577–640). Clifton Park, NY: Thomson Delmar Learning.

References (continued)

13. Murphy, K. (2006). Pediatric patient. In M. E. Z. Estes, *Health assessment & physical examination* (3rd ed., pp. 829–889). Clifton Park, NY: Thomson Delmar Learning.

14. Haymore, J., & Sakallaris, B. R. (2006). Mental status and neurological techniques. In M. E. Z. Estes, *Health assessment & physical examination* (3rd ed., pp. 641–696). Clifton Park, NY: Thomson Delmar Learning.

15. Bryant, R., & Schultz, R. J. (2007). The child with cerebral dysfunction. In M. J. Hockenberry & D. Wilson (Eds.), *Wong's nursing care of infants and children* (8th ed., pp. 1612–1675). St. Louis, MO: Elsevier.

16. Chiang, V. W. (2006). Seizures. In G. R. Fleisher, S. Ludwig, & F. M. Henretig (Eds.), *Textbook of pediatric emergency medicine* (5th ed., pp. 629–636). Philadelphia: Lippincott Williams & Wilkins.

17. Camfield, P. R., & Camfield, C. S. (2006). Pediatric epilepsy: An overview. In K. F. Swaiman, S. Ashwal, & D. M. Ferriero (Eds.), *Pediatric neurology: Principles and practice* (4th ed., pp. 981–989). St. Louis, MO: Elsevier.

18. Pappano, D., & Osborne, M. (2007). Febrile myoclonus. *Pediatric Emergency Care, 23*(9), 649–650.

19. Roddy, S. M. (2006). Breath-holding spells and reflex anoxic seizures. In K. F. Swaiman, S. Ashwal, & D. M. Ferriero (Eds.), *Pediatric neurology: Principles and practice* (4th ed., pp. 1203–1208). St. Louis, MO: Elsevier.

20. Chaves-Carballo, E. (2006). Syncope and paroxysmal disorders other than epilepsy. In K. F. Swaiman, S. Ashwal, & D. M. Ferriero (Eds.), *Pediatric neurology: Principles and practice* (4th ed., pp. 1209–1223). St. Louis, MO: Elsevier.

21. Morton, L. D., & Pellock, J. M. (2006). Status epilepticus. In K. F. Swaiman, S. Ashwal, & D. M. Ferriero (Eds.), *Pediatric neurology: Principles and practice* (4th ed., pp. 1091–1104). St. Louis, MO: Elsevier.

22. Holsti, M., Sill, B. L., Firth, S. D., Filloux, F. M, Joyce, S. M., & Furnival, R. A. (2007). Prehospital intranasal midazolam for the treatment of pediatric seizures. *Pediatric Emergency Care, 23*(3), 148–153.

23. Abend, N. S., & Bonnemann, C. G. (2007). Status epilepticus secondary to hypertensive encephalopathy as the presenting manifestation of Guillain-Barré syndrome. *Pediatric Emergency Care, 23*(9), 659–661.

24. Strony, R. J., & Dula, D. (2007). Pott puffy tumor in a 4-year-old boy presenting in status epilepticus. P*ediatric Emergency Care, 23*(11), 820–822.

25. McCormick, B. M., Mackey, W. L., & Wilson, D. (2007). Conditions caused by defects in physical development. In M. J. Hockenberry & D. Wilson (Eds.), *Wong's nursing care of infants and children* (8th ed., pp. 422–498). St. Louis, MO: Elsevier.

26. Gleeson, J. G., Dobyns, W. B., Plawner, L., & Ashwal, S. (2006). Congenital structural defects. In K. F. Swaiman, S. Ashwal, & D. M. Ferriero (Eds.), *Pediatric neurology: Principles and practice* (4th ed., pp. 363–490). St. Louis, MO: Elsevier.

27. Steele, D. W. (2006). Neurosurgical emergencies, nontraumatic. In G. R. Fleisher, S. Ludwig, & F. M. Henretig (Eds.), *Textbook of pediatric emergency medicine* (5th ed., pp. 1717–1725). Philadelphia: Lippincott Williams & Wilkins.

28. Pitetti, R. (2007). Emergency department evaluation of ventricular shunt malfunction: Is the shunt series really necessary? *Pediatric Emergency Care, 23*(3), 137–141.

29. Kim, T. Y., Brown, L., & Stewart, G. M. (2007). Test characteristics of parent's visual analog scale score in predicting ventriculoperitoneal shunt malfunction in the pediatric emergency department. *Pediatric Emergency Care, 23*(8), 549–552.

30. Piatt, J. H., & Garon, H. J. L. (2008). Clinical diagnosis of ventriculoperitoneal shunt failure among children with hydrocephalus. *Pediatric Emergency Care, 24*(4), 201–210.

31. King, C. (2006). Headache. In G. R. Fleisher, S. Ludwig, & F. M. Henretig (Eds.), *Textbook of pediatric emergency medicine* (5th ed., pp. 511–518). Philadelphia: Lippincott Williams & Wilkins.

32. Lewis, D. W. (2006). Headaches in infants and children. In K. F. Swaiman, S. Ashwal, & D. M. Ferriero (Eds.), *Pediatric neurology: Principles and practice* (4th ed., pp. 1183–1202). St. Louis, MO: Elsevier.

33. Giza, C. C. (2006). Traumatic brain injury in children. In K. F. Swaiman, S. Ashwal, & D. M. Ferriero (Eds.), *Pediatric neurology: Principles and practice* (4th ed., pp. 1401–1443). St. Louis, MO: Elsevier.

34. Lee, L. K. (2007). Controversies in the sequelae of pediatric mild traumatic brain injury. *Pediatric Emergency Care, 23*(8), 580–583.

References (continued)

35. Thackeray, J. D. (2007). Frena tears and abusive head injury: A cautionary tale. *Pediatric Emergency Care, 23*(10), 735–737.

36. Nilles, E. J., & Spiro, D. M. (2007). Delayed intracerebral hemorrhage from an extracranial ball bullet pellet. *Pediatric Emergency Care, 23*(6), 409–411.

37. Lin, J. J., Chou, M. L., Lin, K. L, Wong, M. C., & Wang, H. S. (2007). Cerebral infarct secondary to traumatic carotid artery dissection. *Pediatric Emergency Care, 23*(3), 166–168.

38. DeVeber, G. A. (2006). Cerebrovascular disease. In Swaiman, K. F., Ashwal, S., & Ferriero, D. M. (Eds.), *Pediatric neurology: Principles and practice* (4th ed., pp. 1759–1801). St. Louis, MO: Elsevier.

39. Lynch, J. K., Hirtz, D. G., deVeber, G., & Nelson, K. B. (2002). Report of the National Institute of Neurologic Disorders and Stroke workshop on perinatal and childhood stroke. *Pediatrics, 109,* 116.

40. Zahuranec, D. B., Brown, D. L., Lisabeth, L. D., & Morgenstern, L. B. (2005). Is it time for a large, collaborative study of pediatric stroke? *Stroke, 36*(9), 1825–1829.

41. Gorelick, M. H., & Blackwell, C. D. (2006). Neurologic emergencies. In G. R. Fleisher, S. Ludwig, & F. M. Henretig, (Eds.), *Textbook of pediatric emergency medicine* (5th ed., pp. 759–781). Philadelphia: Lippincott Williams & Wilkins.

42. Kyle, T. (2008). *Essentials of pediatric nursing* (pp. 71–105). Philadelphia: Lippincott Williams & Wilkins.

43. Wilson, D. (2007). Health promotion of the infant and family. In M. J. Hockenberry & D. Wilson (Eds.), *Wong's nursing care of infants and children* (8th ed., pp. 499–565). St. Louis, MO: Elsevier.

44. Wheeler, B., & Wilson, D. (2007). Health promotion of the newborn and family. In M. J. Hockenberry & D. Wilson (Eds.), *Wong's nursing care of infants and children* (8th ed., pp. 257–309). St. Louis, MO: Elsevier.

45. King, J. (2007). Neurologic anatomy, physiology, and assessment. In R. Kaplow & S. R. Hardin (Eds.), *Critical care nursing: Synergy for optimal outcomes* (pp. 349–358). Boston: Jones and Bartlett.

46. Wheeler, B., & Wilson, D. (2007). Nursing care of the child with a neuromuscular disorder. In M. J. Hockenberry & D. Wilson (Eds.), *Wong's nursing care of infants and children* (8th ed., pp. 257–309). St. Louis, MO: Elsevier.

SEVENTEEN

Gastrointestinal Emergencies

Margaret S. Hannan, PhD, RN, CPNP-BC

Introduction

Gastrointestinal (GI) complaints are common among the pediatric population; the most common complaints are diarrhea, vomiting, and abdominal pain (Chapter 10). For most infants and children, these symptoms represent a relatively minor illness (such as gastroenteritis) that can be easily treated. However, these symptoms may also be indicative of a life-threatening illness such as volvulus, intussusception, or appendicitis. The purposes of this chapter are to review common GI complaints of the infant and child, to describe signs and symptoms of serious GI illnesses, and to discuss nursing care and management of the child with a GI complaint.

Embryologic Development of the GI System

The formation of the GI system is dependent on embryologic folding by the fourth week of gestation. Development of the gut is nearly complete by the 20th week of gestation, and functional maturity occurs by the 33rd to 34th week of gestation, providing nutrition to support fetal growth.[1,2] By week 34, coordinated sucking and swallowing[2,3] and nutritive sucking occur in preparation for extrauterine tasks.[1,2] Birth heralds a neonatal phase of GI adaptation to the demands of enteral nutrition.

Some congenital anomalies occur early in the development of the fetus. These conditions can result in life-threatening emergencies if they are not detected and treated. The etiology and treatment of some of these conditions are discussed later in this chapter.

Pediatric Considerations

❐ The abdominal wall is less muscular in the infant and toddler, making the abdominal organs easier to palpate. In the infant, the liver can be palpated 1 to 2 cm below the right costal margin.[3]

❐ The contour of the abdomen is protuberant in young children because of their relatively large abdominal organs and immature abdominal muscles.[3]

❐ Gastric motility is decreased and somewhat irregular in comparison with that of the adult. Gastric emptying is more frequent.

❐ Gastroesophageal reflux is common during the first 6 months of life because of relaxation of the lower esophageal sphincter.

❐ The neonatal liver is immature but develops during the first year of life. Toxic substances are inefficiently detoxified.

❐ Caloric requirements per kilogram of weight are higher in children than in adults. The basal metabolic rate is highest during the first 2 years of life. The basal metabolic rate increases 12% with each degree centigrade of temperature greater than 98.6 °F (37 °C).[4]

❐ Losses from vomiting and diarrhea as a result of GI infections or disease can cause dehydration and shock in the neonate and child, because the percentage of extracellular fluid volume is higher than that of an adult.

Focused History

The history includes information related to the chief complaint and the symptoms. The following information should be obtained:

- ❏ Events surrounding the illness.
- ❏ Associated symptoms.
- ❏ Changes in feeding or elimination patterns.
- ❏ Character and location of pain associated with the illness: Sharp, dull, diffuse, localized, or colicky (Chapter 11).
- ❏ Changes in the child's activity level.
- ❏ Significant medical history, such as cystic fibrosis, sickle cell disease, or previous abdominal surgery.
- ❏ Family history of GI problems or congenital conditions.

Focused Assessment

Physical Assessment

The physical examination includes the standard pediatric assessment; special attention is paid to the following when the abdomen is examined:

- ❏ Observe the child's movements and nonverbal communication (e.g., facial expressions, hands clenching).[5]
- ❏ Inspect the abdomen for symmetry, abdominal distention, obvious masses, visible bowel loops, and peristaltic waves.
- ❏ Inspect the umbilicus of all children for a hernia and of young infants for ulceration, discharge, or granulation tissue.
- ❏ After auscultating breath sounds to rule out the possibility of pneumonia or reactive airway disease (abdominal pain may be a presenting symptom in young children with respiratory disorders),[3,6] auscultate the abdomen for bowel sounds in all four quadrants.
  - ▪ Bowel sounds are normally heard every 10 to 13 seconds.
- ❏ Palpate the abdomen.
  - ▪ First ask the child to point with one finger to the most painful area of the abdomen; palpate nonpainful areas before palpating the most painful area.
  - ▪ Observe for pain in response to palpation.
  - ▪ Observe for rebound tenderness (pain is increased with the quick release of pressure from palpation).
- ❏ Percuss the abdomen.
  - ▪ Percussion is not routinely done by the registered nurse but can be performed by lightly tapping the abdomen to emit a sound.
  - ▪ Percussion is used to assess the amount and distribution of gas, assess the size and density of organs, and detect the presence of fluid and fluid-filled or solid masses.[7]
- ❏ Rectal examination.
  - ▪ Prepare the child for a rectal examination, which is usually performed by the physician, at the time of exam, not before as this may cause distress to the patient and family.
  - ▪ Tell the child what will happen and instruct him or her to take deep breaths throughout the examination.

Psychosocial Assessment

The abdominal assessment can be difficult to perform in the young child because pain and fear can cause the child to cry throughout the examination. The result is abdominal wall rigidity and no overt clues to the intensity or location of the pain. Additionally, young children cannot verbalize their fears or describe the location or characteristics of their pain. Approaching the child in a calm manner and using distraction, such as talking about the child's favorite activity or cartoon character, may assist in gaining cooperation.

Communicating the need for therapeutic intervention is important for both the child and family. Each intervention should be described to the child in age-appropriate terminology. Fear and pain can overwhelm the child. A consistent, caring nurse can help to allay anxiety. Parents should be allowed to remain with the child as much as possible.

The emergent nature of an illness means the parents have had little time to prepare. Anxiety and guilt are common and normal reactions. The parents should be allowed to express their concerns, and their questions should be answered honestly. They should be kept informed regarding the plan of care and offered frequent updates.

Nursing Interventions

Specific diagnostic testing, treatment, and nursing interventions associated with abdominal pain are reviewed with each diagnostic category within this chapter. As with all emergency department patients, stabilization of the airway, breathing, and circulation has priority. Anticipate any or all of the following interventions for the child with an abdominal complaint:

1. Assure nothing by mouth (NPO) after arrival in the

emergency department.

2. Initiate intravenous fluids to replace losses and correct shock.

3. Insert a nasogastric tube to decompress the stomach.

4. Administer antibiotics and other medications (such as pain medications).

5. Obtain laboratory work and radiographs, as ordered.

6. Prepare the child for surgery and/or admission to the hospital.

7. Provide the family with support and information.

Specific GI Medical Emergencies

Gastroenteritis

Gastroenteritis, or acute, infectious diarrhea, is one of the most common complaints encountered within the pediatric population. In the United States it is estimated that there are 1.5 billion outpatient visits for gastroenteritis.[8]

Gastroenteritis may be caused by a bacterial, viral, or parasitic invasion that produces inflammation of the GI tract:[8,9]

❑ *Viral* etiologies account for approximately 80% of all infectious diarrheas. These include:

- Rotavirus (the most common etiology)
- Norwalk virus
- Adenovirus
- Coxsackie virus
- Echovirus; astrovirus
- Caliciviruses
- Hepatitis A

❑ *Bacterial* etiologies account for 10% to 15% of cases of gastroenteritis in the pediatric population. These include:

- *Campylobacter* (the most common etiology)
- *Escherichia coli*
- *Salmonella*
- *Shigella*
- *Yersinia enterocolitica*

❑ *Parasites* that can produce diarrhea include:

- *Giardia lamblia* (the most common etiology)
- *Cryptosporidium*

Pathophysiology

When the GI tract is invaded by a viral agent, destruction of the mucosal cells of the villi begins. Injury to the intestinal epithelial cells decreases the surface area available for absorption and impairs water and electrolyte transport. Bacterial invasion of the GI tract also produces direct damage to the villi and can produce toxins stimulating an inflammatory response. The formation of mucosal ulcerations, which erode the blood vessels, will lead to bleeding.

Focused History

❑ Onset of the diarrhea

❑ Frequency and volume of stooling

❑ Consistency and color of the stool

❑ Presence or absence of blood or mucus in the stool

❑ Fluid intake including types of fluid, amount, and how tolerated

❑ Urinary output

❑ Weight loss

❑ Associated findings, such as the presence of fever, vomiting, abdominal pain, rash, runny nose, or cough

Focused Assessment

The standard assessment is performed, beginning with an evaluation of the child's overall appearance and age-appropriate activity level.

❑ Assess the airway for patency.

❑ Evaluate breathing for rate and rhythm. Tachypnea or deep breathing may indicate fever and/or metabolic acidosis associated with tissue hypoxia from fluid losses.

❑ Evaluate the circulatory status for signs of decreased peripheral perfusion, which may indicate dehydration or shock.

- Assess the skin color and temperature.
- Assess the strength of peripheral pulses.
- Assess skin turgor.
- Evaluate capillary refill.
- Examine the condition of the fontanelle in infants.
- Inspect mucous membranes for moistness and the eyes for the presence of tearing and/or a sunken appearance.

❑ Obtain the infant's weight with diaper only or minimal clothing; obtain the child's weight with minimal clothing. Clinical findings, correlated with weight loss, are then used to determine the degree of dehydration. These findings are described in Table 17.1

TABLE 17.1 Clinical Manifestations Associated with Degree of Dehydration[9]

	Degree of Dehydration		
Assessment	Mild	Moderate	Severe
Loss of body weight	< 5%	5%–10%	> 10%
Skin color	Pale, cool	Dusky, grayish	Mottled*
Skin turgor	Decreased elasticity	Decreased	Markedly Decreased
Anterior fontanelle (infants)	Flat	Depressed	Very sunken
Thirst	Slight	Moderate	Intense
Tears	Present	Decreased	Absent
Mucous membranes	Normal to dry	Dry	Parched, cracked
Pulse	Normal	Increased, weak	Rapid, thready*
Blood pressure	Normal	Normal to low	Low*
Urine output	Decreased	Oliguria	Azotemia*

*Classic symptoms of impending shock.

Nursing Interventions

1. Stabilize the airway and breathing, as required by the child's condition.
2. Assess the cardiovascular system, including heart rate. If dehydration is present, the method of rehydration will depend on the child's clinical presentation and the degree of dehydration.

- Severe dehydration
  - Obtain immediate venous access and administer a 20 mL/kg bolus of normal saline or lactated Ringer's solution. This may be repeated two more times or until perfusion and mental status improve (maximum total to be given is 60 mL/kg). Once normal perfusion has been restored, one or more of the following approaches may be followed to maintain hydration:[8]
    - Administer 100 mL/kg of oral rehydrating solution (ORS), such as Pedialyte® over a 4-hour period.
    - Administer 5% dextrose half normal saline intravenously at two times maintenance fluid rates.

- Calculate fluid and electrolyte deficits in milliliters, based on the child's weight loss and the suspected degree of dehydration. Each kilogram of weight loss is equal to 1000 mL of fluid loss.
- Calculate daily maintenance fluid requirements (Table 17.2).

TABLE 17.2 Calculations for Maintenance Fluid

1–10 kg	100 mL/kg/day
11–20 kg	1000 + (50 mL/kg for each kg > 10 kg)
> 20 kg	1500 + (20 mL/kg for each kg > 20 kg)
Example 1: 8 kg	6-month-old weighing 8 kg 100 mL * 8 kg = 800 mL 800 mL ÷ 24 hr = 33.3 mL/hr
Example 2: 20 kg + 24 kg 44 kg	12-year-old weighing 44 kg 1500 mL + 1480 mL (24 kg * 20 mL) 2980 mL ÷ 24 hr = 124 mL/hr

- Replace abnormal ongoing losses, such as vomiting and diarrhea at 10 mL/kg.[10]
- Calculate other sources of abnormal losses, such as fever, which increases the metabolic rate by 10% to 12% per degree centigrade greater than 98.6 °F. (37 °C).
- Treat for isotonic (equal proportions of sodium and water have been lost through vomiting and diarrhea) dehydration. Fluid therapy begins with the administration of one half of the fluid deficit and one third of the maintenance requirements, given over the first 8 hours of treatment, using 5% dextrose in half normal saline. Because potassium losses are common, even if serum potassium levels remain normal, add 20 mEq/L of potassium to the solution once renal function has been established (when the child voids). Replace the remaining fluids (half of the deficit and two thirds of the maintenance) over the next 16 hours of therapy.
- During fluid therapy, record all intake and output; monitor perfusion and neurologic status.
- The child with moderate to severe dehydration usually requires hospitalization.

- Mild to moderate dehydration
  - Treat with parenteral fluid therapy or oral replacement fluid (enteral) therapy (ORT).
  - Replace fluid losses with an ORS, such as Pedialyte® if the child is able to tolerate oral fluid:

· Give 20 mL/kg/hr of ORS for 2 to 4 hours via a syringe or continuously via a nasogastric feeding tube.[10] Give an additional 10 mL/kg for each diarrhea stool. If the child tolerates 2 hours of ORT and is clinically improving, the next 2 hours of ORT may be continued at home. Resume an age-appropriate diet in 4 to 6 hours.

· Vomiting alone is not a contraindication to the administration of an ORS; offer children with a history of vomiting frequent, small amounts of the solution rather than large amounts.

· Infants require early reintroduction of normal nutrients into their diet. Allow infants who are breast-feeding to continue to do so and use the ORS to replace ongoing losses.

3. Perform diagnostic testing. Infants and children with gastroenteritis and mild dehydration rarely require specific diagnostic testing unless a coexisting illness is suspected (e.g., in the presence of fever and a toxic appearance).

- A stool culture or other specific testing (e.g., for rotavirus or parasites) may be ordered, depending on the suspected underlying etiology. Stool may also be evaluated for the presence of blood. If blood is present, a stool culture is performed.

- Children with moderate to severe dehydration may require testing, such as:

  • Serum electrolytes to assist in generating a differential diagnosis. Potassium stores are usually depleted in the dehydrated child. In the presence of metabolic acidosis (which occurs with moderate to severe dehydration), intracellular potassium is exchanged for the circulating hydrogen ion, resulting in normal serum potassium level.

  • Blood glucose. The blood glucose level may be low because of decreased intake and increased losses.

  • Hematocrit and hemoglobin. In a dehydrated child, the hematocrit will be higher than normal because of hemoconcentration.

  • Blood urea nitrogen, creatinine, and a urinalysis. The blood urea nitrogen level will be elevated. (It may not be elevated if the child has had decreased protein intake.) The creatinine level will be higher than normal. (Normal values in children are much lower than those in adults.) Urinary specific gravity will be elevated.

Home Care and Prevention

If the infant or child is to be discharged home, the following instructions must be given:

❑ Explain signs and symptoms of dehydration and shock.
  ▪ Decreased or absent urination
  ▪ Dry mucous membranes
  ▪ Sunken fontanelle (in infants)
  ▪ Sunken eyes
  ▪ Lack of tears
  ▪ Excessive sleepiness or lethargy

❑ Provide instructions for use of ORS.
  ▪ Give the infant a full-strength ORS and then progress to breast-feeding or formula.
  ▪ For older children with both vomiting and diarrhea, give an ORS for at least 24 hours.
  ▪ For children of any age, wait at least 2 hours following emesis before offering small, frequent amounts of liquid (10 to 15 mL every 15 to 20 minutes). Many physicians recommend early introduction of bland foods, such as rice cereal. With the initiation of formula or solid foods, the diarrhea may recur but should resolve quickly.

❑ Provide information on the need for adequate hand washing and proper disposal of diapers to prevent the spread of infection to other family members.

❑ Explain that the diapered child must remain out of daycare until the diarrhea has subsided.

Specific GI Surgical Emergencies

Appendicitis

Although appendicitis is the most common acute surgical condition of the abdomen, it is also the most commonly misdiagnosed condition in children. In the United States, appendicitis is diagnosed annually in 70,000 children. The peak incidence is in 11- to 12-year-old children.[11] Appendicitis in children younger than 3 years of age is almost always missed and may lead to death because of this misdiagnosis.[12]

Pathophysiology

Appendicitis is caused by an obstruction of the appendiceal lumen, which can result from inspissated and sometimes calcified fecal matter (fecalith) or from edema of the lymphoid tissue caused by a viral or bacterial infection. Other causes include parasites (e.g., pinworms), carcinoid tumors, and foreign-body obstruction.

When the lumen of the appendix is obstructed, the accumulation of mucoid material causes an increase in intraluminal pressure. Aerobic and anaerobic bacteria within the appendix begin to proliferate. As intraluminal pressure rises, infection and edema impede blood flow, causing ischemia and necrosis. With continued pressure, ischemia and infarction can cause the appendix to become gangrenous. The gangrenous appendix may perforate, releasing bacteria into the abdominal cavity. Young children with appendicitis are more susceptible to early perforation of the appendix because the wall of the appendix is very thin. In this age group, diffuse peritonitis results, because the immature omentum is incapable of "walling off" the infection.

Focused History

The presentation of appendicitis is highly variable in the child, and classic findings are not always present. A high index of suspicion is maintained for any child with a history of abdominal pain. The history should include the onset, location, and character of the abdominal pain.

☐ Early signs of appendicitis:
- Diffuse periumbilical or midabdominal pain
- Abdominal pain with coughing and walking

☐ Progressive appendicitis:
- Anorexia, nausea, and vomiting
- Low-grade fever
- Normal bowel habits, constipation, or diarrhea
- Pain localized to the right lower quadrant

☐ Perforated appendix:
- Increasing fever
- Rapid, shallow respirations
- Diffuse abdominal pain
- Irritability or lethargy

Focused Assessment

The standard pediatric assessment is done. The child's initial clinical appearance depends on the degree of progression of the disease. Early in the course of the illness, the child may complain of diffuse abdominal pain. As the illness progresses, the child may walk bent forward while splinting the abdomen, may refuse to jump during the examination, or may refuse to walk. An additional finding may be refusal or inability to get onto the examination table without assistance. Children with appendicitis prefer to lie very still in bed with the head of the bed elevated and the knees flexed. Assessment findings include:

☐ An altered respiratory pattern, such as rapid, shallow respirations or grunting, either of which can indicate pneumonia or shock, or may be the result of severe abdominal pain. Auscultation of the lung fields and a chest radiograph is required to rule out the presence of pneumonia.

☐ Tachycardia. The child's skin may be flushed or excessively pale.

☐ Continuous but poorly defined or localized abdominal pain (early):
- The pain characteristically localizes in the right lower quadrant of the abdomen at McBurney's point (two-thirds the distance from the pubis to the anterosuperior iliac spine) with progression of the disease.
- Because the location of the appendix can vary, pain may localize in other areas, such as the pelvis, in the right upper quadrant under the gallbladder, over the bladder, or in a retrocecal site, such as over the right flank.[11]

☐ Hypoactive or hyperactive bowel sounds, making auscultation of the abdomen of little benefit in determining the presence of appendicitis.

☐ Rebound tenderness in older children, if peritoneal irritation is present.

☐ Localized right vault tenderness, a mass (abscess), or a retrocecal appendix, as revealed by a rectal examination, performed by the pediatric surgery or emergency care practitioner.[11,13]

☐ Signs and symptoms of perforation:
- Diffuse abdominal tenderness (younger children)
- Immediate, but temporary relief of pain
- Signs and symptoms of toxicity, such as pale skin and marked tachypnea and tachycardia
- Local muscular rigidity with progression from involuntary guarding to a rigid and extremely tender abdomen
- Markedly decreased or absent bowel sounds

Nursing Interventions

1. Assess and stabilize the airway, breathing, and circulation as required.

2. Keep the child NPO.

3. Give a 20 mL/kg bolus of Ringer's lactate solution or normal saline solution if the child is hypovolemic.

4. Monitor for signs of progression of the illness.
- Obtain vital signs frequently.
- Monitor intake and output.
- Observe peripheral perfusion for signs of toxicity or

shock.

- Assess the intensity, location, and character of the abdominal pain to evaluate the progression of the illness.
  - Severe pain requires the administration of an analgesic.

5. Prepare to administer broad-spectrum antibiotics if appendicitis is suspected.

6. Prepare the child for surgery, although surgery may be delayed if peritonitis is present or suspected.

7. Prepare to insert a nasogastric tube if a perforated appendix is suspected.

8. Perform diagnostic testing.

- Complete blood cell count and differential.
  - Early in the course of illness, the white blood cell count is usually between 10,000 and 15,000/mm^3.
  - The differential may reveal increasing numbers of bands and polymorphonuclear leukocytes.
  - With perforation of the appendix, the white blood cell count markedly increases.
- Urinalysis
  - An excessive number of white blood cells in the urine may indicate the presence of a urinary tract infection or may indicate that the inflamed appendix lies over a ureter or adjacent to the bladder.
- Abdominal radiographs
  - The appearance is usually normal early in the course of the illness.
  - As the illness progresses, the abdominal radiograph often reveals diminished air in the GI tract, the result of anorexia and/or vomiting; however, this finding is not diagnostic.
  - A diagnostic finding is the presence of a calcified fecalith in the right lower quadrant.
  - Radiographic findings that may indicate a perforated appendix include the presence of free air in the abdomen or evidence of peritonitis, an emergent condition.
- Serum electrolyte levels, to determine the degree of dehydration and identify fluid shifts.
- Ultrasound examination, to determine the diameter of the appendiceal lumen and to observe for an abdominal mass or free fluid within the abdominal cavity.
- Chest radiograph, to rule out pulmonary problems, such as right lower lobe pneumonia, as a cause of the abdominal pain.

- Computed tomographic scan may be ordered to determine the patency of the appendix and/or to identify any abscesses.

Home Care and Prevention

If signs and symptoms are nonspecific for appendicitis and the family appears to be compliant, the parents may be instructed to return with the child in a specified amount of time, usually 6 to 8 hours, for reevaluation. The parents must be given specific information about signs and symptoms that require immediate return to the emergency department, and they must understand the importance of follow-up. The child should be placed NPO or should be put on a clear liquid diet until the return visit takes place.

Meckel's Diverticulum

Meckel's diverticulum is a congenital anomaly in which there is an outpouching (evagination) of the small intestine. It occurs early in gestation when the vitelline duct, which is located at the umbilicus, fails to close completely. Although Meckel's diverticulum may be an isolated abnormality, it may occur in association with other congenital disorders, such as esophageal atresia, imperforate anus, Down syndrome, and cardiac defects.[14] Meckel's diverticulum affects approximately 2% of the population and is usually painless.[14]

Pathophysiology

Early during embryonic development, the vitelline (omphalomesenteric) duct connects the gut to the yolk sac at the umbilicus. After about 7 weeks of gestation, this duct regresses and eventually is completely reabsorbed. In some children, a fibrous cord or band of tissue may persist between the umbilicus and the bowel, serving as a lead point for later complications. In some cases, the vitelline duct fails to obliterate, leading to several types of deformities, such as a vitelline duct cyst, a patent vitelline duct (allowing passage of gas or bilious drainage), or prolapse of the proximal and distal bowel through a patent duct.[15]

Meckel's diverticulum is the most common of the vitelline duct disorders and is represented by an outpouching of the gut that contains all layers of the intestinal wall and may also contain ectopic tissues, such as ectopic gastric mucosa or ectopic pancreatic tissue.[14]

The most common signs and symptoms include:[14]

❑ Bloody stools, which can be caused by ulceration and hemorrhage of ectopic gastric mucosa within the diverticulum.

❑ Intestinal obstruction, which can be caused by intussusception in which the diverticulum acts as a lead point, prolapse of the bowel through the duct, or volvulus around or herniation through a still-attached fibrous band of tissue.[13,14]

❏ Inflammation of a Meckel's diverticulum, which can present at a later age and is often mistaken for appendicitis.[14]

Focused History

The initial history for the infant or child with Meckel's diverticulum can vary significantly, depending on the severity of the disorder.

❏ A history of vomiting, abdominal distention, and abdominal pain may be associated with intestinal obstruction.

❏ The history associated with rectal bleeding may reveal intermittent bouts of significant bleeding. During these bouts, stools are characteristically brick red or maroon in appearance. Tarry stools are uncommon.

Focused Assessment

❏ Assess general appearance.

❏ Assess airway and breathing.

❏ Assess circulatory status for signs and symptoms of shock (weak or absent peripheral pulses, delayed capillary refill, hypotension, and altered mental status) that may be the result of significant rectal bleeding, intestinal obstruction, or sepsis.

❏ Perform an abdominal assessment.

  ▪ Auscultate for bowel sounds.

  ▪ Palpate for the presence of abdominal pain, tenderness, or distention, which can represent an obstruction or perforation. These findings can easily be misinterpreted as appendicitis. If intussusception is present (discussed later in this chapter), a palpable mass may be present.

❏ Evaluate the stool for the presence of overt and occult blood.

Nursing Interventions

1. Place on supplemental oxygen and administer a fluid bolus if signs of shock are present (Chapter 38).

2. Prepare the child for surgery once the presumptive diagnosis of Meckel's diverticulum is made.

3. Evaluate the child frequently while awaiting surgery

  ▪ Monitor vital signs.

  ▪ Evaluate for signs of shock.

  ▪ Record each stool with description of amount, color, and presence or absence of blood.

▪ Communicate the expected treatment to the family. When possible, the parents should be allowed to remain with the child.

4. Perform diagnostic testing.

  ▪ Diagnostic testing is based on the child's presenting symptoms and the suspected underlying etiology; for example, a history of rectal bleeding requires the evaluation of the stool for occult blood.

  ▪ Other diagnostic testing that may be ordered, depending on symptoms, includes:

    • Complete blood cell count

    • Blood urea nitrogen

    • Electrolytes

    • Blood glucose

    • Blood type and crossmatch if significant blood loss is suspected

    • Abdominal radiographs to rule out an intestinal obstruction or a perforation

    • Meckel's scan (nuclear medicine scan)

Pyloric Stenosis

Pyloric stenosis is an obstruction at the pyloric sphincter resulting from a hypertrophied pyloric muscle. The condition, which is usually manifested in the third to fifth week of life, is one of the most common disorders to require surgery during infancy. Although many theories have been suggested regarding the cause of pyloric stenosis, the etiology remains unknown.

The overall incidence of pyloric stenosis is approximately 1.5 to 4.0 in 1000 births. The disorder affects white infants more commonly than it does African-American or Asian infants.[16] There is a 3:1 to 5:1 male-to-female incidence of pyloric stenosis. Children of parents who had the condition are more likely to have pyloric stenosis; the children of mothers who had the disease are significantly more likely to have the condition.[16]

Pathophysiology

During the first few weeks of life, the pylorus appears to function normally. Within several weeks, however, hypertrophy and hyperplasia of the circular pyloric muscle develops, partially obstructing the pyloric channel. With continued irritation and inflammation of the mucosa, a complete obstruction can occur. Blood-streaked emesis may result from the persistent vomiting, which can produce a mucosal tear or gastritis.

Metabolic derangements and dehydration result from the continued vomiting. With prolonged vomiting, shock can occur. Losses of hydrogen ion and chloride with gastric contents can lead to metabolic alkalosis. Compensatory mechanisms cause sodium to move into the cells and potassium to move out of the cells and be excreted in the urine. The results are hypokalemia, hypochloremia, and occasionally hyponatremia.

Focused History

The typical history is that of an infant who eats well in the first few weeks of life. Within a 2- to 5-week period, the following symptoms occur:

- ❏ The infant vomits after some feedings. Following vomiting, the infant eats vigorously but may vomit again.
- ❏ As the obstruction progresses, the infant vomits with every feeding and the vomiting becomes projectile or "forceful."
- ❏ The vomitus in infants with pyloric stenosis typically includes formula or breast milk from the last feeding and does not contain bile.
- ❏ The vomitus may have a brownish discoloration or bloody streaks, caused by gastritis or mucosal tears resulting from prolonged vomiting.
- ❏ There may be a positive family history of pyloric stenosis.

Focused Assessment

The standard assessment is done. If the vomiting has been excessive and prolonged, the infant will show signs of growth retardation and nutritional deprivation, such as weight loss and loss of subcutaneous tissue. Other findings include:

- ❏ Signs of dehydration (e.g., sunken eyes, absence of tears, dry mucous membranes of the mouth, tenting skin, and decreased urination)
- ❏ Gastric peristaltic waves from left to right following feeding
- ❏ Diminished or absent bowel sounds
- ❏ An enlarged pylorus, or "olive," palpated in the upper abdominal quadrant, to the right of the midline.
  - ▪ To facilitate palpation of the olive, gentle elevation of the infant's lower extremities while the infant is sucking may be required.
  - ▪ Occasionally, gastric emptying with a nasogastric tube is necessary to allow palpation of the olive.

Nursing Interventions

1. Assess airway and breathing and stabilize, as required by the infant's condition.
2. Assess circulatory status.
3. Obtain intravenous access to replace fluids and electrolytes to correct dehydration and metabolic abnormalities.
4. Treat severe dehydration by restoring circulating volume with one or more boluses of 20 mL/kg of normal saline or lactated Ringer's solution.
   - ▪ Follow the same replacement therapy protocol described in the section on gastroenteritis.
   - ▪ Prepare to administer 5% dextrose in 0.45 normal saline with 20 to 40 mEq/L of potassium chloride for optimal fluid and electrolyte replacement.
   - ▪ Administer potassium only after renal function has been established (when the infant voids).
   - ▪ Place infants receiving high doses of potassium chloride on a cardiac monitor and place intravenous fluid on a pump.
   - ▪ Assess the infusion site frequently for signs of infiltration.
5. Insert a nasogastric tube if ordered.
6. Maintain NPO status.
7. Prepare for admission to the hospital.
   - ▪ Give parents information regarding the plan of care, including the anticipated time of surgery and the reason for delaying immediate surgery:
     - • Definitive treatment for pyloric stenosis is surgical intervention after fluid and electrolyte imbalances have been corrected.
     - • Because this correction can take from 24 to 36 hours, the infant generally does not go directly to the operating room from the emergency department but instead is admitted to a general surgical unit for stabilization.
8. Perform diagnostic testing.
   - ▪ Definitive diagnosis of pyloric stenosis can be made by palpation of an olive coupled with classic clinical findings. However, many children are being sent directly for an ultrasound scan of the abdomen by the primary providers.[16]
   - ▪ In the cases where an olive may not be palpable, the following testing may be performed:
     - • Ultrasonography
     - • Upper GI series. Confirmatory findings include a positive "string sign," which represents the narrowed pyloric opening.
     - • Serum electrolytes. The most common diagnosis findings associated with pyloric stenosis include hypochloremia and hypokalemia, which produce metabolic alkalosis.

Malrotation with Volvulus

Malrotation of the bowel is a congenital condition resulting from an abnormal rotation of the intestine during embryonic development. This anomaly can result in torsion or twisting of the intestines and obstruction of the blood supply to the bowel, known as volvulus. Patients with malrotation with volvulus usually present in the early neonatal period. On the other hand, malrotation without volvulus can go unrecognized until childhood, or even adulthood.[16]

Pathophysiology

With abnormal fetal development of the bowel, varying degrees of volvulus can occur at the points of abnormal fixation. Volvulus, or twisting of the small intestine, may produce a partial or complete obstruction of the intestine. In addition, twisting of the mesentery, which contains the blood supply to the intestines, can compromise arterial and venous blood flow and produce bowel ischemia and necrosis within 1 to 2 hours. Without emergent surgical intervention, necrosis of the bowel can lead to perforation and peritonitis, which may ultimately produce septic shock and death. This is a true surgical emergency.

Focused History

Prodromal symptoms vary, depending on the degree of intestinal obstruction.

❑ Several days or weeks of feeding problems, vomiting, and weight loss.

❑ Sudden onset of abdominal pain coupled with bilious vomiting.

Focused Assessment

The standard assessment is done. Signs and symptoms can vary, depending on the degree of obstruction and the length of time elapsed before arrival in the emergency department. The infant with a history of acute-onset abdominal pain and vomiting may initially appear well hydrated and may be actively crying. However, these infants can rapidly become ill, appearing with grunting respirations, an altered mental status, signs of dehydration, and/or signs of shock.

The most remarkable findings in the infant or child with volvulus are:

❑ Bilious emesis

❑ The presence of severe, constant abdominal pain

❑ Abdominal distention

  ▪ Distention may be mild or absent, depending on the location of the obstruction.

  ▪ Palpation of the abdomen will reveal diffuse tenderness; however, this finding may be difficult to identify in the small, already crying infant.

❑ Rectal bleeding

  ▪ This signals bowel ischemia and probable necrosis, which can also be associated with bloody emesis.

Nursing Interventions[17]

Assess and stabilize the airway and breathing, as dictated by the patient's clinical condition.

1. Monitor pulse oximetry, heart rate, and vital signs.

2. Obtain intravenous access to correct fluid deficits.

  ▪ Initiate fluid replacement therapy (see section on gastroenteritis).

  ▪ Treat for shock (Chapter 38).

  ▪ Because of the need for rapid surgical intervention, fluid stabilization may not be completed before surgery.

3. Insert a nasogastric or orogastric tube to decompress the GI tract.

4. Administer broad-spectrum antibiotics.

5. Obtain blood for typing and crossmatching.

6. Continuously monitor vital signs, respiratory status, circulatory status, neurologic status, and intake and output, because infants with volvulus can rapidly decompensate.

7. Accompany the child for all diagnostic testing.

Intussusception

Intussusception is a bowel obstruction caused by the telescoping of one section of bowel into the more distal segment. The majority of children with intussusception are between the ages of 3 months and 5 years. Seventy-five percent present with the first 2 years of life, and > 40% are between 3 and 9 months of age.[18] Intussusception occurs more frequently in males than in females.

In most cases, intussusception occurs in otherwise healthy infants and children, and there is no known etiology. There is higher incidence of cases in the spring and winter corresponding to the peak incidence of viral illnesses (both GI and respiratory). Other cases have been associated with constipation, parasites, or the ingestion of a foreign body. Pathologic conditions, such as Meckel's diverticulum or a GI tumor or cyst, can precipitate an intussusception. Children with cystic fibrosis and children with Henoch-Schönlein purpura are also more prone to the development of intussusception.

Pathophysiology

Intussusception results when one portion of the intestine telescopes into the distal portion. This causes a complete or partial bowel obstruction involving constriction of the mesentery and venous stasis. When blood flow to the intestines is compromised, the bowel becomes edematous, further impairing blood flow. Increased production of mucus from cellular damage, mixed with bloody fluid leaking from the engorged bowel, forms the classic currant-jelly stool.[18] If the intussusception is untreated, arterial blood flow will cease and bowel necrosis will result. Eventually, perforation and peritonitis may occur.

Focused History

❐ Classic history
  ▪ Otherwise healthy infant or child who suddenly cries with colicky, abdominal pain
    • The parent may say the pain seemed to go away and the infant went to sleep or was comfortable, only to later cry out with the same symptoms.
    • The parents may relate a history of lethargy between episodes as the episodic pain progresses.
❐ Atypical findings
  ▪ Lethargy and poor feeding
  ▪ Vomiting

Focused Assessment

The standard pediatric assessment is done. Physical findings can reveal classic findings or may be nonspecific. The following assessment findings may be present:

❐ Irritability
❐ Pale skin
❐ Lethargy
❐ A toxic-appearing, shocklike state that may mimic a postictal state or sepsis
❐ A soft abdomen (early in the illness) and sometimes a sausage-shaped mass, usually in the right upper quadrant
❐ A distended and rigid abdomen as the obstruction progresses
❐ Blood in the stool
  ▪ The classic current-jelly stool is often a late finding of intussusception.

Nursing Interventions

1. Assess and stabilize the airway, breathing, and circulation as required by the infant's or child's condition.
2. Obtain venous access to address fluid and electrolyte needs.
3. Anticipate a barium or air enema if perforation is not suspected.
4. Prepare for surgical intervention if perforation has occurred.
   ▪ Obtain laboratory specimens.
   ▪ Administer broad-spectrum antibiotics.
   ▪ Insert a nasogastric tube to relieve gastric distention and prevent emesis.
5. Continuously monitor the child for signs and symptoms of sepsis.
   ▪ Monitor vital signs.
   ▪ Monitor circulatory status, including skin color and peripheral pulses.
   ▪ Monitor neurologic status.
6. Administer appropriate analgesic for pain management as ordered (Chapter 11).
7. Perform diagnostic testing.
   ▪ The degree of diagnostic testing depends on the initial presentation, but usually consists of:
     • Complete blood cell count, white blood cell count, and differential
     • Serum electrolytes
     • Blood urea nitrogen
     • Blood type and crossmatch (if perforation is suspected)
     • Plain film abdominal radiographs. Findings are often inconclusive and depend on the location, severity, and duration of the symptoms.
     • Ultrasonography. A highly reliable method of identifying intussusception, it is particularly useful in children with an atypical presentation or in whom perforation is suspected.
     • Air enema. The definitive diagnosis and treatment for most cases of intussusception (unless perforation is suspected) is an air enema, which in most cases reduces the intussusception.[18] This procedure is contraindicated if a perforation is suspected. When reduction with an enema is unsuccessful, emergent surgical intervention is required.

Incarcerated Inguinal Hernias

Inguinal hernias in children are indirect hernias. Indirect inguinal hernias are the result of a persistent patent processus vaginalis, an extension of the peritoneal lining, that extends down through the inguinal canal in boys and the round ligament in girls.[2] This is not a result of muscular weakness as seen with an adult hernia.[19] The patent processus vaginalis permits intra-abdominal contents to enter the inguinal region. In boys it is most often the intestine and in girls the ovary. Inguinal hernias occur more often in boys and in preterm infants.

Pathophysiology

When an organ such as the bowel or an ovary protrudes through the patent processus vaginalis it can become incarcerated or trapped. Progressive edema of the incarcerated organ leads to venous obstruction and decreased arterial blood supply, resulting in necrosis and gangrene. If the obstruction is in the bowel, perforation can occur. In boys, pressure on the spermatic cord from the incarceration can cause the testicle to infarct. Incarceration is most commonly seen within the first 6 months of life and is rare after 5 years of age.

Focused History

❏   A bulge in the umbilical area, groin, or scrotal area

❏   A bulge that tends to worsen with crying or straining

If the hernia is incarcerated, the following history may also be present:

- Uncontrolled crying and irritability
- Abdominal pain
- Vomiting

Focused Assessment

The standard assessment is performed. Findings include:

❏   Crying, irritable infant

❏   A firm, discrete mass felt in the abdomen or groin

Additional findings depend on the location and degree of obstruction, and the duration of the incarceration. These symptoms may include:

❏   Local tenderness and swelling over the mass

❏   Abdominal distention

❏   Erythematous or discolored skin over the mass

Nursing Interventions

1. Assess and stabilize the airway, breathing, and circulation as required by the infant's condition. Continuously evaluate the infant or child or with an incarcerated hernia to monitor for changes in circulatory status and level of consciousness.

2. Treatment for an incarcerated hernia in a stable infant with no signs of toxicity or peritonitis is manual reduction of the hernia.

   - Place the infant in the Trendelenburg position.

- Apply a cold pack to the area.
- Administer sedatives as necessary to facilitate manual reduction (Chapter 11).
- Monitor the heart rate and pulse oximetry according to hospital sedation policy.
- Prepare for admission to the hospital for observation and possible elective surgical repair if manual reduction is successful.
- When the infant is quiet and the abdomen is relaxed, apply gentle manual pressure to the mass.
- Elective hernia repair is usually performed within the next few days.

3. When manual reduction is unsuccessful, emergent surgical reduction is required.

   - Maintain NPO status.
   - Record color, consistency, and frequency of emesis.
   - Observe the child for signs of intestinal obstruction (e.g., vomiting or abdominal distention).
   - Prepare for emergency surgical intervention.

4. Perform diagnostic testing.

   - The diagnosis of an incarcerated hernia is based on clinical findings.
   - Diagnostic testing may include abdominal radiograph, ultrasound scan, and/or color-flow Doppler to verify blood flow to the organ.

Hirschsprung's Disease (Congenital Aganglionic Megacolon)

Hirschsprung's disease is a disorder of the large intestine that causes inadequate motility of the affected part of the intestine. The result is a functional obstruction of the large intestine and interference with the normal mechanism of defecation. Hirschsprung's disease is a congenital disorder, and evidence suggests that the affected population has a genetic predisposition to the disease.

Hirschsprung's disease is the leading cause of intestinal obstructions in neonates. The disease is most prevalent in males, and the incidence of Hirschsprung's disease is higher in children with Down syndrome.

Pathophysiology

Hirschsprung's disease is caused by the absence of ganglion cells in the colon. The affected segment may involve a very small portion of the bowel or the entire colon. The obstruction is most commonly located in the rectum and the portion of the large intestine proximal to the rectum. The result of the obstruction is spasm, abnormal motility, and enlargement of the colon proximal to the aganglionic segment. The aganglionic section will be narrow and nonfunctional. Intestinal obstruction or chronic constipation will result. Erosion and eventual ulceration of the colon above the aganglionic section of bowel can lead to acute enterocolitis, perforation, and peritonitis.

Focused History

- ❑ Neonates and infants
  - ▪ Failure to pass meconium within the first 24 to 48 hours following birth
  - ▪ Constipation alternating with diarrhea, if the condition is not diagnosed in the first 48 hours after birth
- ❑ Older children
  - ▪ Chronic constipation, abdominal distention, and bloating or gas
  - ▪ Frequent use of enemas, suppositories, or rectal stimulation to assist the child with defecation
  - ▪ Vomiting uncommon
- ❑ Infants or children
  - ▪ Acute enterocolitis
    - • Fever
    - • Explosive diarrhea
    - • Abdominal tenderness
    - • Vomiting

Focused Assessment

The standard assessment is done. Table 17.3 lists the clinical manifestations of children with Hirschsprung's disease. Most children who present to the emergency department with undiagnosed Hirschsprung's disease appear to be well, although some may appear poorly nourished and anemic. On rare occasions, an infant or child will have a toxic appearance as a result of acute enterocolitis and peritonitis. Other assessment findings may include:

- ❑ Abdominal distention and visible peristalsis
- ❑ A palpable fecal mass
- ❑ Ribbonlike and foul-smelling stools
- ❑ A narrow rectum with little or no feces

Nursing Interventions

The infant or child with signs of peritonitis or sepsis requires emergent management.

1. Maintain the airway, breathing, and circulation.
2. Stabilize fluid and electrolyte levels.
3. Perform a full sepsis workup.
4. Administer broad-spectrum antibiotics.

TABLE 17.3 Clinical Manifestations of Hirschsprung's Disease
Newborn period
Failure to pass meconium within 24 to 48 hours after birth
Poor feeding
Emesis
Abdominal distention
Infancy
Failure to thrive
Constipation, may alternate with diarrhea
Abdominal distention
Episodic vomiting
Ominous signs (often signify the presence of enterocolitis):
Explosive, watery diarrhea
Fever
Childhood*
Constipation
Ribbonlike, foul-smelling stools
Abdominal distention
Visible peristalsis
Easily palpable fecal masses
Poorly nourished

*Symptoms are more chronic.
Wyllie, R. (2007). Motility disorders and Hirschsprung's disease. In R. M. Kliegman, R. E. Behrman, H. B. Jenson, & B. F. Stanton (Eds.), *Nelson textbook of pediatrics* (pp. 1565–1567). Philadelphia: Saunders.

Most infants and children suspected to have Hirschsprung's disease are stable and require only supportive nursing care until diagnostic testing is complete.[20]

1. Obtain vital signs, weight, and abdominal circumference.
2. Place nasogastric tube for gastric decompression.
   - ▪ Rectal irrigations via rectal tube are usually administered by a member of the surgical team.
3. Prepare for admission to a surgical floor and/or surgery.
   - ▪ The urgency of treatment depends on the child's age and clinical presentation.
   - ▪ Usually the infant or child will require a temporary colostomy to allow the proximal bowel to resume normal size and tonicity. This is done only when enterocolitis is under control.

- Definitive repair can then be performed electively as a second stage.
- In newborns, primary repair may be done laparoscopically.

4. Perform diagnostic testing.
   - Abdominal radiograph: The abdominal radiograph will reveal large, dilated loops of intestine and the absence of gas.
   - Barium enema: The barium enema will identify the "transition zone," which is where the dilated bowel proximal meets the narrowed aganglionic section of bowel.
   - Confirmation of the diagnosis is made by rectal biopsy.
   - Anorectal manometric examination may be performed.

Gastrointestinal Foreign Body

Ingestion of foreign bodies is common in young children, particularly in infants, toddlers, and preschoolers. Increasing mobility, natural curiosity, and an affinity for mouthing objects, coupled with decreased supervision, make children in these age groups particularly prone to ingestions. The foreign bodies most commonly ingested by children are:

- Coins
- Buttons
- Marbles
- Small toy parts
- Screws and tacks
- Button batteries
- Chicken or fish bones
- Straight pins

Pathophysiology

The majority of foreign bodies ingested by infants and children pass to the stomach and through the GI tract without incident. In some children, however, ingested foreign bodies become lodged in one of these physiologically narrow areas in the esophagus: the cricopharyngeal muscle, the aortic arch, or the gastroesophageal junction.[21] The cricopharyngeal area is the most common site of lodged foreign bodies in children. The gastroesophageal junction is the least common site.[21]

The danger from foreign-body ingestion is that an irregular or pointed object may puncture or tear the esophagus, the object may compress the trachea and cause respiratory distress, or the object may become lodged in a portion of the esophagus. A lodged object, particularly one that is undetected, can lead to tissue erosion and eventual perforation. Ingestion of button batteries is of particular concern because a button battery lodged in the esophagus can rapidly produce liquefaction necrosis and electrochemical burns.[21,22]

Focused History

Medical care is not sought for the majority of children with GI foreign-body ingestions because the ingestion was not observed and the child exhibited no symptoms. Parents who do bring their child to the emergency department usually observed the ingestion or suspect an ingestion and report the following history:

- Observation of the infant or child mouthing an object that disappeared.
- Observation of the child coughing and gagging after playing with a small object.

The following history would be suggestive of an ingested object when the parents did not observe the incident:

- Coughing and gagging
- Increased salivation
- Refusal to eat or drink
- Pain or discomfort with feeding
- Vomiting

Focused Assessment

The majority of children who have ingested a foreign body appear to be well and have no overt signs and symptoms of an ingestion. Assessment findings may include:

- Coughing, gagging, and/or salivation
- Signs and symptoms of respiratory distress, including tachypnea and retractions (if the object is compressing the trachea)

Nursing Interventions

1. Assess and stabilize the airway, breathing, and circulation as required by the infant's or child's condition.

2. Treatment depends on the type of foreign body ingested and its location. Because the majority of foreign bodies pass through the GI tract without incident, most children are sent home and the parents are told to observe for the presence of the object in the stool. Objects lodged in the esophagus may be treated by:
   - Removal through endoscopy

- Observation for up to 12 hours (if they are located in the lower third of the esophagus and are smooth and round)
- Removal with the indwelling urinary catheter method (if smooth and round)
  - Button batteries lodged anywhere in the esophagus are removed emergently by endoscopy because esophageal burns can occur within hours of the ingestion.

The child with signs and symptoms of respiratory distress requires the following nursing interventions:

1. Prepare for airway support as preparations are made for a portable radiograph examination and emergent removal of the foreign body.
2. Provide supplemental oxygen.
3. Allow the child to maintain a position of comfort.
4. Prepare for surgical intervention if the child has signs or symptoms of esophageal perforation.
   - Accompany the unstable child for all diagnostic testing and/or to the operating room.
   - Prepare the child for esophagoscopy or balloon catheter removal if the object is lodged in the esophagus.
     - Administer sedation as ordered.
     - Accompany the child to the radiology department.
     - Prepare for ventilatory support.
5. Perform diagnostic testing.
   - Anteroposterior and lateral radiographs include the neck, chest, and abdomen.

- Computed tomographic scan or barium swallow may be necessary if the object is radiolucent and is suspected to be lodged in the esophagus.

Home Care and Prevention

When children are discharged after removal of an esophageal foreign body, parents are given the following instructions:

- ❑ Provide a clear liquid diet for 12 to 24 hours and then progress to a regular diet.
- ❑ Seek immediate care if the child begins to have severe abdominal pain, bloody stools, bloody emesis, or repeated emesis, or if a fever develops, whether the object was removed or not.
- ❑ Prevent future episodes of ingestion.
  - Lock cabinets.
  - Remove small objects from the child's environment.

In addition, parents should be given information concerning cardiopulmonary resuscitation classes.

Conclusion

Abdominal complaints are common, and most are benign. The life-threatening emergencies that affect the GI tract are commonly surgical emergencies that can result in shock and sepsis; however, medical conditions, such as gastroenteritis, can cause dehydration, electrolyte imbalances, and shock. Nurses must understand the pathology behind these conditions and accurately assess and treat children who present to the emergency department with complications resulting from these conditions.

References

1. de Santa Barbara, P. (2008). The intestine: Anatomy and physiology. In W. A. Walker, R. E. Kleinman, P. M. Sherman, B. L. Shneider, & I. R. Sanderson (Eds.), *Walker's pediatric gastrointestinal disease* (pp. 207–215). Hamilton, Ontario, Canada: BC Decker.

2. Lloyd, D. A. & Kenny, S. E. (2008). Congenital anomalies including hernias. In W. A. Walker, R. E. Kleinman, P. M. Sherman, B. L. Shneider, & I. R. Sanderson (Eds.), *Walker's pediatric gastrointestinal disease* (pp. 217–231). Hamilton, Ontario, Canada: BC Decker.

3. Wyllie, R. (2007). Normal digestive tract phenomena. In R. M. Kliegman, R. E. Behrman, H. B. Jenson, & B. F. Stanton (Eds.), *Nelson textbook of pediatrics* (pp. 1521–1522). Philadelphia: Saunders.

4. Adam, H. M. (2001). Management of fever. In R. A. Hoekelman, S. B. Friedman, N. M. Nelson, H. M. Siedel, & M. L. Weitzman (Eds.), *Primary pediatric care* (pp. 337–341). St. Louis, MO: Mosby.

5. Murphy, K. (2007). Pediatric assessment. In N. L. Potts & B. L. Mandleco (Eds.), *Pediatric nursing: Caring for children and their families* (pp. 381–413). Clifton Park, NY: Thomson Delmar Learning.

6. Sectish, T. C., & Prober, C. G. (2007). Pneumonia. In R. M. Kliegman, R. E. Behrman, H. B. Jenson, & B. F. Stanton (Eds.), *Nelson textbook of pediatrics* (pp. 1795–1800). Philadelphia: Saunders.

7. Seidel, H. M., Ball, J. W., Dains, J. E., & Benedict, G. W. (2006). *Mosby's guide to physical examination* (6th ed.). St. Louis, MO: Mosby.

References (continued)

8. Bhutta, Z. A. (2007). Acute gastroenteritis in children. In R. M. Kliegman, R. E. Behrman, H. B. Jenson, & B. F. Stanton (Eds.), *Nelson textbook of pediatrics* (pp. 1605–1617). Philadelphia: Saunders.

9. Graf, E. R. (2007). Fluid and electrolyte alterations. In N. L. Potts & B. L. Mandleco (Eds.), *Pediatric nursing: Caring for children and their families* (pp. 587–622). Clifton Park, NY: Thomson Delmar Learning.

10. Mann, C. H. (2008). Vomiting and diarrhea. In J. M. Baren, S. G. Rothrock, J. Brennan & L. Brown (Eds.), *Pediatric emergency medicine* (pp. 567–575). Philadelphia: Saunders.

11. Dunn, J. C. Y. (2006). Appendicitis. In J. L. Grosfeld, J. A. O'Neill, A. G. Coran, E. W. Fonkalsrud (Eds.), *Pediatric surgery* (pp. 1501–1513). St. Louis, MO: Mosby-Year Book.

12. Aiken, J. J., & Oldham, K. T. (2007). Acute appendicitis. In R. M. Kliegman, R. E. Behrman, H. B. Jenson, & B. F. Stanton (Eds.), *Nelson textbook of pediatrics* (pp. 1628–1635). Philadelphia: Saunders.

13. Sawin, R. S. (2005). Appendix and Meckel's diverticulum. In K. T. Oldham, P. M. Colombani, R. P. Foglia, & M. A. Skinner (Eds.), *Principles and practice of pediatric surgery* (pp. 1669–1282). Philadelphia: Lippincott Williams & Wilkins.

14. Snyder, C. L. (2006). Meckel's diverticulum. In J. L. Grosfeld, et al. (Eds.), *Pediatric surgery* (pp. 1304–1312). St. Louis, MO: Mosby-Year Book .

15. Rowe, M. I. (1995). Essentials of pediatric surgery. St. Louis: Mosby.

16. Schwartz, M. Z. (2006). Hypertrophic pyloric stenosis. In J. L. Grosfeld, J. A. O'Neill, A. G. Coran, E. W. Fonkalsrud (Eds.), *Pediatric surgery* (pp. 1215–1224). St. Louis, MO: Mosby-Year Book.

17. Diana-Zerpa, J., & Shapiro-Stolar, T. J. (2007). Malrotation and volvulus. In N. T. Browne (Ed.), *Nursing care of the pediatric surgery patient* (pp. 333–342). Sudbury, MA: Jones and Bartlett Publishers.

18. Ein, S. H., & Daneman, A. (2006). Intussusception. In J. L. Grosfeld, J. A. O'Neill, A. G. Coran, E. W. Fonkalsrud (Eds.), *Pediatric surgery* (pp. 1313–1341). St. Louis, MO: Mosby-Year Book.

19. Aiken, J. J., & Oldham, K. T. (2007). Inguinal hernias. In R. M. Kliegman, R. E. Behrman, H. B. Jenson, & B. F. Stanton (Eds.), *Nelson textbook of pediatrics* (pp. 1644–1650). Philadelphia: Saunders.

20. Klar, M. (2007). Hirschsprung's disease. In N. T. Browne (Eds.), *Nursing care of the pediatric surgery patient* (pp. 289–300). Sudbury, MA: Jones and Bartlett Publishers.

21. Orenstein, S. (2007). Foreign bodies in the esophagus. In R. M. Kliegman, R. E. Behrman, H. B. Jenson, & B. F. Stanton (Eds.), *Nelson textbook of pediatrics* (pp. 1552–1553). Philadelphia: Saunders.

22. Silverberg, M., & Tillotson, R. (2006). Case report: Esophageal foreign body mistaken for impacted button battery. *Pediatric Emergency Care, 22*(4), 262–265.

23. Wyllie, R. (2007). Motility disorders and Hirschsprung's disease. In R. M. Kliegman, R. E. Behrman, H. B. Jenson, & B. F. Stanton (Eds.), *Nelson textbook of pediatrics* (pp. 1565–1567). Philadelphia: Saunders.

EIGHTEEN

Genitourinary Emergencies

Christine Nelson-Tuttle, DNS, RNC, PNP
Rebecca Roloff, RN, MSN, SANE-A, SANE-P
Steven J. Dasta, RN, BSN

Introduction

The genitourinary (GU) system includes organs of the urinary system and the reproductive system. The urinary system maintains the optimal environment for metabolism by excreting waste products from the body and consists of the kidneys, ureters, bladder, and urethra. The reproductive system supplies hormones, as well as eggs and sperm, for sexual growth and fertility. The male reproductive system consists of the scrotum, testicles, and penis, and the female reproductive system consists of the vagina, labia minora and majora, ovaries, and uterus. Because the urologic and reproductive systems are in close anatomic proximity, they are discussed together.

GU conditions range from common, simply treated illnesses to emergent health conditions. Children may present to the emergency department (ED) with congenital GU conditions or acquired conditions that are diagnosed in the emergency department. Emergency nurses must be able to recognize the presence of these conditions and initiate appropriate treatment measures. The purpose of this chapter is to discuss common congenital and acquired GU conditions and to outline emergency nursing treatment of GU concerns.

Embryologic Development of the GU System

Urinary System

The urinary system separates from the rectum at about 6 weeks of gestational age. Protein codes on the Y chromosome initiate development of male genitalia at 7 to 8 weeks' gestation. The embryonic kidneys develop as three distinct, sequentially replaced organs. The collecting ducts form by the fifth fetal month, and any errors in the development of the collecting ducts may result in polycystic kidneys. Fetal urine is produced by 10 to 11 weeks' gestation. In utero, the placenta functions as the major filtering system. As the kidneys mature in utero, the cloaca becomes the urogenital sinus and differentiates into the vesicourethral canal, forming the bladder and upper urethra; the urogenital sinus becomes the main part of the urethra.[1]

Embryologic variations in urinary system development can lead to structural abnormalities, ranging from minor, surgically correctable conditions to those that are incompatible with life. Structural abnormalities of the urinary system cause approximately 45% of the cases of renal failure in children.[1] Table 18.1 outlines common urinary system abnormalities.

Genitalia

For a brief period of development, the embryo has a common genital structure before differentiating into male or female structures. Slight abnormalities during the development of the reproductive structures can cause significant malformations. For example, a hermaphrodite is an individual who has gonads and internal and external reproductive structures of both genders. Genital abnormalities may result from congenital or acquired conditions. Table 18.2 describes common male and female genital abnormalities.

Male Development

The inner portion of the medulla joins with the mesonephric duct; further differentiation forms the seminiferous tubules, efferent ductules, epididymis, and ductus diferens. The genital tubercle elongates and forms the penis. The urethral folds fuse, leaving an opening in the distal end. The labioscrotal swellings form the scrotum.

TABLE 18.1 Common Urinary System Abnormalities

Condition	Description
Ectopic kidneys	Failure of the kidneys to ascend from the pelvis to the abdomen. Kidney function is usually normal.
Horseshoe kidney	Fusion of the kidneys as they ascend, creating a single, U-shaped kidney. Although these children are usually asymptomatic, they may have hematuria following trauma to the pelvic region, a midline abdominal mass, or ureteropelvic junction obstruction.
Renal aplasia	Failure of the uterine duct to differentiate into kidney-forming tissues in utero, resulting in the absence of one or both kidneys.
Hypoplastic or dysplastic kidneys	Development of small, normal kidneys. This may affect one or both kidneys. Bilateral hypoplastic kidneys are a common cause of pediatric renal failure.
Renal dysplasia	Abnormal differentiation of renal tissues. This can be associated with obstruction of the urinary collection system.
Renal agenesis	Failure of one or both of the kidneys to grow. This condition can be hereditary or random. Unilateral renal agenesis occurs in 1 of 1,000 live births, usually in males. Usually the left kidney is absent. The remaining kidney compensates in size, and the child usually leads a healthy life.
Duplication of the urinary collection system	Duplication arising from embryologic maldevelopment. It is usually more common in females and can be familial. The duplication can be bilateral. Vesicoureteral reflux or ureteral obstruction may be present.
Vesicoureteral reflux	Impaired valvular function at the ureterovesical junction that leads to the reflux of bladder urine into the ureter or kidneys. In the presence of a UTI, such reflux of infected urine can lead to pyelonephritis, renal scarring, and chronic renal damage.
Prune-belly syndrome	Absence of abdominal musculature, as well as renal and urinary tract abnormalities and cryptochordism. Males are affected more frequently and severely than are females. Other congenital malformations may be present.

Female Development

The outer portion of the undifferentiated gonads undergoes greater development for later reproduction purposes. The gonads differentiate to form ovaries. The müllerian ducts between the ovaries form the uterus and vagina. There is less elongation of the genital tubercle as it forms the clitoris. The urethral folds, which do not fuse as they do in males, form the labia that surround the vagina.

Pediatric Considerations

Although all of the kidneys' nephrons are present at birth, they are not fully developed. The tubules and glomeruli are variable in size, accounting for the limited ability of the newborn to conserve sodium and excrete sodium loads. This variability resolves around 12 to 14 months of age.

Renal blood flow and the glomerular filtration rate are low at birth and gradually increase as the child develops. The glomerular filtration rate is at approximately 30% to 50% of adult levels by age 1 year because of higher vascular resistance in infants.[1] This is an important consideration when drugs excreted by the renal system are prescribed and when fluid requirements are calculated.

The total extracellular fluid volume is significantly greater in infants than adults. Infants are less able to concentrate urine, making it much more diluted than it is in adults. Mature renal function is usually reached at 1 to 2 years of age.[1]

The infant's bladder is a cylindrical abdominal organ that descends into the pelvis over time. Bladder capacity increases with age from 20 to 50 mL at birth to 700 mL in adulthood. As bladder volume increases, the ability to retain urine improves; with the maturation of the neurogenic pathways by 2 to 3 years of age, bladder sphincter control occurs.[2] Myelination of the spinal cord is necessary for the child to obtain voluntary bladder control.

Etiology

The etiology of GU health conditions arises from congenital or acquired processes as described in this chapter.

TABLE 18.2 Selected Genital Abnormalities		
Finding	*Description*	*Implication*
Hypospadias	Urethral opening on the ventral (underside) of penis	Urinary stream aims downward.
Chordee	Ventral bowing of the penis caused by tight band of fibrous tissue	May make catheterization difficult
Microphallus	Abnormal smallness of the penis	May make catheterization difficult
Cryptochordism	Absence of one or both testes from the scrotal sac	Should be referred to a specialist if finding persists after 6 months of age
Hydrocele	Collection of serous fluid in the scrotal sac; scrotal size may increase with activity and decrease with rest	Referral for management is necessary if the problem persists after 1 year of age or if there is discomfort.
Labial adhesions	Fusion of tissue between the labia minora that covers vaginal opening	Treatment in prepubescent females is necessary only if urinary or vaginal drainage is impaired. May make catheterization difficult.

Focused History

❑ Patient history
- Activity level. A decrease in activity or performance of developmentally appropriate skills may be related to renal disease.
- Onset and duration of symptoms
- Interventions that relieve or worsen the symptoms
- Fever
- Abdominal or back pain
- Recent injuries or illness
- Urination patterns: changes in the urine force or stream; dribbling enuresis; incontinence
- Change in urine color or hematuria
- Urine odor
- Urinary frequency and volume

- Dysuria or urgency
- Sexual history (if applicable)
- Congenital or acquired GU conditions

❑ Family history
- Renal disease
- Renal abnormalities
- Hypertension
- Congenital defects

Focused Assessment

Physical Assessment

❑ Assess the cardiovascular system.
- Measure blood pressure.
  - Hypertension in infants without aortic coarctation can result from a renovascular disorder, such as renal vascular thrombosis, arterial thrombosis, or renal artery stenosis.[3]
  - Hypertension in children may be associated with renal disorders,[3] such as nephritis and chronic renal failure. Severe blunt renal trauma without appropriate follow-up may result in renal scarring that can cause hypertension.
- Observe the skin for color, turgor, and markings.
  - Generalized edema may be present in renal failure.
  - Pallor may be a sign of renal dysfunction.
  - Poor skin turgor may be associated with dehydration.
  - Café au lait spots, neurofibromas, and other skin lesions may suggest renal disorders.[4]

❑ Assess the abdomen.
- Observe the size and shape of the abdomen.
  - Ascites, distention, rigidity, or tenderness may be associated with renal problems.
- Auscultate the great vessels.
  - Bruits auscultated over great vessels may indicate arteriopathy.
  - Bruits noted in the epigastric area may indicate renovascular disease.
- Palpate the abdomen.
  - Palpate the bladder for distention. A distended bladder may be palpable above the symphysis pubis. Persistent bladder distention may indicate a blockage or other emptying abnormality. An enlarged bladder or gynecologic lesion may be palpated as a midline mass in the pelvis.[5]

- Palpate the kidneys (rarely palpable except in neonates or very thin children). Enlarged kidneys may be palpated as upper abdominal or flank masses,[5] indicating a tumor or hydronephrosis.
  - Percuss the back for costovertebral angle tenderness.
    - Fist percussion at the costovertebral angle may elicit tenderness as the kidneys are jarred, indicating possible infection or injury.

☐ Assess the genitalia.
  - Inspect the external genitalia for abnormalities:
    - Note abnormalities in appearance, open or closed wounds, visible foreign bodies, discharge or bleeding, rashes, lesions, and scars.
  - Inspect the external male genitalia for:[5]
    - Scrotal size and character
    - Location and size of the testes
    - Swelling or nodules
    - Penis size. The foreskin is examined for adhesions to the glans, and the meatus is noted for its size and location.[5]
  - Inspect the female external genitalia for:
    - Size and location of the clitoris if there are abnormalities or injuries
    - Presence of labial adhesions or labial fusion
    - Urethral meatus, vaginal introitus,
    - Hymenal ring[5]

☐ Assess the child's height and weight for age and overall appearance.
  - Frequent or chronic urinary tract infections or chronic renal disease are associated with failure to thrive.
  - Congenital scoliosis, facial or external ear deformities, and multiple congenital anomalies may be associated with urologic conditions.[5]

Psychosocial Assessment

☐ Assess the child's understanding of sexual function; determine the significance of this understanding.

☐ Assess the child's terminology for urination.

☐ Assess the family's understanding of their child's preexisting GU condition.
  - Assess the family's understanding of their child's sexual activity.

☐ Assess the child's prior experience with health care professionals and with a GU examination or treatment.

- Injuries and illnesses of the GU system can be difficult for a young patient concerned about modesty, body image, and body integrity.
- Children, especially those of school age, find it difficult to have their genitalia examined by a stranger after so much emphasis is placed on stranger avoidance. There is also anxiety because very little can be visualized, as the majority of the GU system is not easily accessed. Children who have been sexually assaulted may find it even more traumatic to have their genitalia examined (Chapter 45).

Nursing Interventions

1. Assess and maintain airway, breathing, and circulation.

2. Obtain venous access and initiate an intravenous infusion.
   - Obtain blood for laboratory studies, as needed.
   - Administer medications, as needed.

3. Prepare for diagnostic studies, as needed.

4. Assess for pain, as needed (Chapter 11).

5. Reassess the child's neurologic and cardiopulmonary statuses.

6. Insert an indwelling bladder catheter to measure urinary output, or perform a bladder catheterization, as needed.
   - A clean-catch urine specimen is adequate for toilet-trained children with adequate cleaning before specimen collection.
   - Obtain a urine specimen for urinalysis, culture, and sensitivity.

7. Prepare the child for a genital or gynecologic examination.
   - Be prepared to collect culture specimens for *Neisseria gonorrhoeae,* Chlamydia, and possibly streptococcus.
   - Provide psychosocial support to the child and family; inform the family frequently about their child's condition.

8. Prepare for transfer and transport to a tertiary care facility (Chapter 8), hospitalization, or discharge and follow-up to the primary care physician.

Specific Genitourinary Conditions

Urinary Tract Infections

Etiology

Urinary tract infection (UTI) is the presence of a significant amount of bacteria anywhere in the urinary tract. The bacterium that most commonly causes UTI is *Escherichia coli*,[6] which causes 50% of UTIs. Other organisms include *Klebsiella pneumoniae, Citrobacter, Pseudomonas,* and *Staphylococcus saprophyticus. Pseudomonas* or *Proteus* species are found infrequently and often are associated with abnormal GU anatomy or urinary tract instrumentation, such as indwelling catheters and stents.[7]

UTIs are a major concern in children. About 3% to 5% of all girls and 1% of boys will experience a symptomatic UTI before puberty. Females have more recurrences than do males, and 7- to 11-year-old girls are most susceptible because of bacterial ascension of the urethra, which is shorter in length.[8]

Risk factors contributing to UTIs include poor hygiene, lack of fluid intake, sexual activity, and infrequent bladder emptying. Disease severity is affected by bacterial virulence and existing anatomic abnormalities (reflux or obstruction).[6]

Neonatal UTIs usually arise from bacteremic spread, whereas UTIs in infants and children tend to arise from bacteria that travel up the urethra to the bladder.[9] The location of the UTI is often difficult to detect. *Cystitis,* or bladder infection, leads to mucosal inflammation, detrusor muscle hyperactivity, and a decrease in bladder capacity.[8] Characteristics of cystitis include acute onset of fever, vomiting, dysuria, suprapubic pain, and urinary sediment.[4] Urinary reflux into the ureters can propel bacteria to the kidneys, leading to pyelonephritis.

Pyelonephritis, or kidney infection, results in renal edema and an enlarged kidney; renal scarring and abnormal kidney function can result. Repeated infections can lead to chronic renal failure. Signs of pyelonephritis include fever, chills, abdominal and flank pain, and an enlarged kidney.[1,10]

The presence of UTIs should be considered in all febrile infants, especially in the first 2 weeks of age, even when meningitis, sepsis, or other infections are found. (Chapter 9) Neonatal UTIs may be associated with bacteremia.[9]

Focused History

- ❒ Patient history
  - ▪ Foul-smelling urine
  - ▪ Hematuria
  - ▪ Prior episodes of UTIs or other urinary-related problems
  - ▪ Signs and symptoms are variable (Table 18.3)

TABLE 18.3 Symptoms of UTI in Infants and Children		
Young Infants	Older Infants/ Toddlers	Children
Lethargy	Irritability	Complaints of dysuria
Poor appetite	Abdominal pain	Urinary frequency
Irritability	Vomiting	Urinary urgency
Presence or absence of fever	Fever	Abdominal or back pain
	Incontinence in the toilet-trained toddler	

Focused Assessment

Physical Assessment

- ❒ Assess the respiratory system.
  - ▪ Auscultate the chest for:
    - • Respiratory rate. Tachypnea may be present with fever and infection.
- ❒ Assess the cardiovascular system.
  - ▪ Auscultate the heart for:
    - • Rate. Tachycardia may be present with fever and infection.
  - ▪ Assess skin and core temperature.
    - • Fever may be present with infection and sepsis.
  - ▪ Assess the abdomen.
    - • Palpate the abdomen and bladder for pain or tenderness.
  - ▪ Percuss the back.
    - • Tenderness during costovertebral angle percussion may be elicited.
- ❒ Assess the external genitalia.
  - ▪ Observe for mucopurulent vaginal discharge in young females.
  - ▪ Observe for mucopurulent penile discharge in males.
  - ▪ Assess for pain (Chapter 11).

Psychosocial Assessment

- ❒ Assess the child's and family's understanding of UTIs.
- ❒ Assess for coping strategies if the UTI is recurrent.

❑ Assess the child's preparatory and coping strategies for invasive procedures, such as bladder catheterization.

Nursing Interventions

1. Assess and maintain airway, breathing, and circulation.
2. Obtain urine for diagnostic testing.
   - Urine for analysis and culture and sensitivity testing may be obtained through a clean-catch method, urinary bladder catheterization, or suprapubic bladder aspiration:
     - The clean-catch method (or bag method for infants) is not recommended for non-toilet-trained children because contamination from the surrounding tissues can affect the obtained specimen. However, in older children and adolescents, the clean-catch method may result in a reliable urine specimen.
     - Urinary bladder catheterization is the introduction of a catheter into the urinary bladder to obtain a sterile urine specimen.
     - Urine also may be obtained from an existing suprapubic catheter or indwelling urinary bladder catheter.
3. Perform diagnostic testing on the obtained specimen.
   - Urine dipstick tests detect nitrite and leukocyte esterase; when both are positive, the presence of a UTI is almost certain.[11] The urine dipstick test is an important screening test, but it is also crucial that all patients who have a positive urine dipstick (for nitrites and leukocyte esterase), as well as those who are symptomatic, have a urine sample sent for culture.[12]
   - Another method for diagnostic testing is enhanced urinalysis, which consists of counting white blood cells in a Neubauer hemocytometer and counting bacteria in a Gram-stained smear.[4]
   - Although a urinalysis does not detect the presence of bacteria, it does give information about other urinary components, such as the presence of white blood cells.
   - Urine culture analysis is based on the colony counts.[11] Culture results generally are reported in 24 and 48 hours.
4. Administer prescribed antibiotics.
   - The antibiotics most commonly used for simple, uncomplicated UTIs are amoxicillin, ampicillin, trimethoprim-sulfamethoxazole, co-trimoxazole, or a sulfonamide.
   - Cephalosporins and amoxicillin/clavulanate are expensive and rarely necessary unless sensitivities indicate their need.
5. Prepare for transfer or transport to a tertiary care center (Chapter 8) or for hospital admission.
   - Hospitalization may be required for infants and children with high fevers and suspected sepsis.
     - Intravenous antibiotics are administered.
     - Blood specimens are obtained for complete blood cell count and differential, cultures, and electrolytes are obtained.

Home Care and Prevention

The patient and family should receive directions for follow-up, as well as discharge teaching. A urinalysis and culture may be recommended after 48 hours of treatment to determine whether the infection is resolving. This specimen may be tested by the child's primary care provider or at the emergency department.

The patient and family must have resources to obtain the prescribed antibiotic and to receive the follow-up urine cultures. Recurrent or partially treated UTIs can lead to health problems such as hypertension, renal calculi, and chronic renal failure.[13]

Young children may have undetected or undiagnosed congenital abnormalities that predispose them to UTIs. The suspicion of such abnormalities indicates a need for future radiographic evaluations. Renal scanning with dimercaptosuccinic acid is finding popularity because it is more sensitive than the intravenous pyelogram for detecting renal lesions.[14]

The patient and family should be taught strategies to prevent future UTIs:[15]

❑ Drink at least six to eight glasses of water or noncarbonated, caffeine-free fluids daily.

❑ Urinate whenever the "urge" is felt; do not wait.

❑ Wipe from front to back after defecating; change the infant's diaper frequently.

❑ Use cotton underwear to absorb moisture.

❑ Avoid tight-fitting pants.

❑ Avoid bubble baths, scented and colored toilet paper, perfumed soaps, and nonprescription vaginal suppositories, sprays, and douches.

❑ Urinate before and after sexual intercourse.

❑ Change sanitary pads frequently during menstruation.

❑ Use condoms during sexual intercourse.

Glomerulonephritis

Etiology

Glomerulonephritis is an alteration of the glomeruli resulting from an immune response that causes a decrease in glomerular filtration. In glomerulonephritis, the capillary loops in the glomeruli become inflamed and infiltrated with leukocytes, resulting in a decreased blood supply to the glomeruli. Cellular proliferation and edema occlude the lumen of the affected glomeruli, causing a decrease in the glomerular filtration rate. This decreased ability to filter plasma results in excessive accumulation of water and retention of sodium, leading to expanded plasma volumes and clinical findings of circulatory congestion and edema.[16]

Although forms of acute glomerulonephritis are associated with Henoch-Schönlein purpura and disseminated lupus erythematosus, the most common form follows infections from strains of group A β-hemolytic streptococci infecting the pharynx or skin; other causes of glomerulonephritis include postpneumococcal glomerulonephritis, immunoglobulin A nephritis, and hemolytic-uremic syndrome.[16] Poststreptococcal glomerulonephritis follows a latent period of 10 to 14 days after the streptococcal infection before the onset of symptoms.

Glomerulonephritis is diagnosed in children between the ages of 3 and 12 years; the peak incidence is at 7 years of age. (Children with hemolytic-uremic syndrome can be younger.) Males are affected more often than females. Chronic glomerulonephritis is responsible for 53% of cases of renal failure in children and is the most common reason for renal dialysis and kidney transplantation in the school-aged and adolescent populations.[1]

Focused History

❑ Patient history[4]
  ▪ Recent febrile illness (2 to 4 weeks prior) with painful pharyngitis for which treatment was not obtained
  ▪ Fever, malaise, and decreased appetite
  ▪ Sudden onset of oliguria with the production of dark brown, smoky, or tea-colored urine
  ▪ Headache
  ▪ Edema

Focused Assessment

Physical Assessment

❑ Assess the respiratory system.
  ▪ Auscultate the chest for:

  • Respiratory rate
  • Adventitious sounds. Pulmonary congestion may be present.

❑ Assess the cardiovascular system.
  ▪ Auscultate the heart for:
    • Rate

❑ Measure the blood pressure.
  ▪ Hypertension may be present.

❑ Assess the renal system.
  ▪ Observe for signs of renal failure:
    • Note the presence of periorbital edema; pitting edema in the sacrum.
  ▪ Percuss the kidneys for tenderness.
  ▪ Measure the urinary output.

Psychosocial Assessment

❑ Assess the child's and family's coping strategies.

Nursing Interventions

1. Assess and maintain airway, breathing, and circulation.
2. Initiate blood pressure monitoring to observe for hypertension.
3. Obtain venous access and initiate an intravenous infusion at maintenance rate.
   ▪ Restrict salt and fluids to maintain a normal intravascular volume.
   ▪ Administer diuretics to control hypertension and fluid overload, as ordered.
   ▪ Prepare to administer furosemide at 0.5 to 1.0 mg/kg.
   ▪ Prepare to administer sublingual nifedipine (0.25 to 0.5 mg/kg), intravenous diazoxide (2.5 to 5.0 mg/kg), or intravenous hydralazine (0.5 mg/kg) if hypertension is noted.
   ▪ Obtain blood for laboratory studies:
     • Complete blood cell count
     • Electrolytes. Hyperkalemia or dilutional hyponatremia may be noted.
     • Blood urea nitrogen and creatinine. (Both will be elevated.)
     • Antistreptolysin titer (may be elevated)
     • Antideoxyribonuclease B
     • Immunoglobulin G (will be elevated)
     • C3 complement
     • Total protein, albumin, and globulin
     • Antinuclear antibody

- Administer antibiotics
  - Penicillin will be prescribed if the streptococcal infection is still apparent.

4. Obtain urine for urinalysis and culture.
   - A urinalysis may show red blood cells and casts, polymorphonuclear neutrophil leukocytes, and proteinuria.[17]

5. Obtain additional diagnostic information, as ordered.
   - Throat culture
   - Skin culture (if pyoderma is present)
   - Chest radiograph

6. Provide psychosocial support to the child and family.

7. Prepare for transfer or transport to a tertiary care center (Chapter 8) or hospitalization if the child is oliguric or hypertensive.

Home Care and Prevention

Adequate follow-up and discharge teaching includes teaching the parents how to:

❐ Restrict fluid intake.

❐ Administer antihypertensive medications and be aware of their side effects.

❐ Measure their child's blood pressure. Parents may need a stethoscope and sphygmomanometer.

❐ Weigh the child each day.

❐ Recognize the signs of acute renal failure, such as a change in level of consciousness, seizures, difficulty breathing, increase in weight, edema, and decreased urinary output.

Acute Renal Failure

Etiology

Acute renal failure (ARF), the sudden loss of renal function, occurs when bodily fluid homeostasis is disrupted and there is a sudden decrease in the glomerular filtration rate. Circulation to the kidneys may be impaired by arterial or venous obstruction, renal trauma, or obstructive processes, thus decreasing blood flow, which may lead to tubular necrosis. Once this occurs, the kidney may not be able to filter plasma, which may cause a massive loss of salt and water. The glomerular filtration rate will decrease to prevent this water loss from continuing.

Causes of Acute Renal Failure

❐ Shock
   - Hypovolemic
   - Septic
   - Anaphylactic

❐ Dehydration

❐ Diabetic ketoacidosis

❐ Severe burns

❐ Nephrotic syndrome

❐ Renal vessel injury

❐ Diseases that contribute to ARF:
   - Henoch-Schönlein purpura (rare)
   - Hemolytic-uremic syndrome
   - Systemic lupus erythematosus
   - Neoplasms

Focused History

❐ Patient history[18]
   - Dehydration from vomiting or diarrhea; burns
   - Shock
   - Diabetic ketoacidosis
   - Nephrotic syndrome

Focused Assessment

Physical Assessment

❐ Assess the respiratory system.
   - Auscultate the chest for:
     - Adventitious sounds. Pulmonary congestion may be present with fluid overload, leading to pulmonary edema.
     - Respiratory rate. Tachypnea, and then bradypnea, may be present.

❐ Assess the cardiovascular system.
   - Auscultate the heart for:
     - Rate. Tachycardia may be present with early shock and dehydration.
     - Rhythm.
   - Evaluate cardiac rhythm by initiating cardiorespiratory monitoring.
     - Dysrhythmias may be present with congestive heart failure or fluid overload.
   - Measure the blood pressure.
     - Blood pressure may be elevated with early shock.
     - Hypotension will be present with late shock.
   - Assess peripheral perfusion.
     - Palpate the peripheral pulses for quality; equality.
   - Measure core and skin temperature.
   - Inspect the skin for color (pallor present with poor perfusion); edema (may be present with fluid

overload); turgor.

- Measure capillary refill (> 3 seconds in shock states).

❑ Assess the neurologic system.

- Assess the child's level of consciousness with the AVPU (Alert, responds to Voice, responds to Pain, or Unresponsive) method or Glasgow Coma Scale.
  - Lethargy may be present
  - Seizures may be present

❑ Assess the gastrointestinal system.

- Palpate the abdomen for a mass
- Observe for vomiting

❑ Assess the GU system.

- Measure the urinary output.
  - Urinary output will be decreased (less than 0.5 mL/kg/hr) or there will be no urinary output.

❑ Measure or estimate the child's weight.

- An increase in weight may be observed with fluid overload.
- A decrease in weight may be noted with weight loss from vomiting and dehydration.

Nursing Interventions

1. Assess and maintain airway, breathing, and circulation.
   - Administer supplemental oxygen, as needed.
   - Initiate cardiorespiratory monitoring.
   - Measure continuous oxygen saturation.
   - Observe for dysrhythmias
     - Monitor for T-wave changes. Severe hyperkalemia causes dysrhythmias.

2. Obtain venous access and initiate an intravenous infusion at maintenance rate.
   - Obtain blood specimens for:
     - Hemoglobin and hematocrit
     - Blood urea nitrogen and creatinine
     - Electrolytes (sodium, potassium, chloride, phosphorus, calcium, and magnesium). Hyponatremia (less often, hypernatremia), hyperkalemia, hyperphosphatemia, and hypocalcemia may be found.
     - Venous blood gas
     - Uric acid
   - Consider fluid restriction if fluid overload is present.
   - Administer medications, as prescribed.
     - Diuretics may be needed if fluid overload is present.

❑ Prepare for additional diagnostic tests.

- Chest radiograph
- Electrocardiogram
- Echocardiogram

❑ Measure urinary output.

- Insert an indwelling bladder catheter, as needed.

❑ Prepare the patient for possible hemodialysis.

❑ Continuously evaluate the patient for signs of fluid overload, such as congestive heart failure or pulmonary edema, and signs of septic shock.

❑ Provide psychosocial support to the child and family.

❑ Prepare for transfer and transport to a tertiary care facility, if indicated (Chapter 8), or hospitalization.

Home Care and Prevention

Emergency nurses can prevent or ameliorate ARF by anticipating it as a potential complication and by providing early treatment for signs of shock. On hospital discharge, the child may require frequent follow-up related to renal function, as well as the predisposing health condition (e.g., burns) that resulted in the ARF.

Specific Genitourinary Emergencies

Sexually Transmitted Diseases

Etiology

The incidence of sexually transmitted diseases (STDs) is highest in adolescents. Adolescents are considered an at-risk population related to their inexperience and lack of knowledge about STDs. Research has determined that adolescents possess minimal knowledge about non-human immunodeficiency virus STDs, their treatments, and curability.[19] Each year, 2.5 million teenagers are infected with an STD. This represents one of every six sexually active teens and one fifth of all STD cases reported nationally. Adolescents who have sexual intercourse at younger ages are more likely to have multiple partners, increasing their chances of contracting an STD. Adolescents frequently deny that they could be infected with an STD. Other factors that increase the risk are the inconsistent use of protective and contraceptive devices and decreased health care options. Table 18.4 summarizes common STDs and their treatments.

Gardasil®, manufactured by Merck, is the first vaccine developed to prevent cervical cancer, precancerous genital lesions, and genital warts due to human papillomavirus (HPV). The vaccine is effective for four of the more than 100 strains of HPV, two of these strains causing 70% of

TABLE 18.4 Overview of STDs

Disease	Description	Incubation Period	Symptoms	Treatment: Older Children	Treatment: Younger Children
Chlamydia	Caused by *Chlamydia trachomatis,* the most common bacterial STD, present in 5% to 15% of sexually active teenage females and 9% of teenage males	Variable; at least 1 week	Males: Dysuria; urinary frequency; purulent urethral discharge Females: Dysuria; mucopurulent discharge	Doxycycline or Azithromycin	Erythromycin or Azithromycin
Gonorrhea	Caused by *Neisseria gonorrhoeae,* a Gram-negative diplococcus	1 week	Usually occurs 2 to 7 days after exposure ▪ Males: Dysuria; urinary frequency; and purulent urethral discharge ▪ Females: Abnormal vaginal discharge; abnormal menses, dysuria; can be asymptomatic	Ceftriaxone or Cefotaxime	Ceftriaxone or Cefotaxime
Condylomata acyminata (genital warts)	Caused by HPV	Unknown: 3 months to 2 years	Single or multiple soft, fleshy painless growths on genital and/or anal areas	Podophyllum or Podofilox	Tretinoin
Herpes simplex	Caused by herpes simplex virus 1 and 2; present in approximately 20% of adolescents	Neonates: Birth to age 4–6 weeks Others: 2 days to 2 weeks	Single or multiple vesicles that spontaneously rupture to shallow, painful ulcers Subsequent occurrences usually milder	Acyclovir	Acyclovir
Syphilis	Caused by *Treponema pallidum,* a spirochete; this disease is most common in adolescents	10–90 days	Three stages with overlapping symptoms: ▪ Primary stage—painless, indurated chancre at the site of infection ▪ Secondary stage—variable skin rash, lymphadenopathy, low-grade fever, and arthralgia ▪ Tertiary stage—no symptoms and not infectious, but cardiac, neurologic, ophthalmic, and auditory lesions present	Penicillin G	Penicillin G or Benzathine Penicillin

Pickering, L., Baker, C., Long, S., & McClellan, J. (Eds.). (2006). *Red book: Report of the committee on infectious diseases* (27th ed.). Elk Grove Village, IL: American Academy of Pediatrics.

cervical cancer. The Advisory Committee on Immunization Practices recommends that the vaccine be routinely given to girls when they are 11 to 12 years of age.[20]

Focused History

The patient history is obtained from the adolescent patient; if STDs are suspected in a younger child, a history is obtained from the child and the parent. If possible, the child and parent should be interviewed separately.

❏ Male and female patient history

- Frequency and type of sexual activity (oral, vaginal, anal)
- Contraceptive use: Type of contraceptive; frequency and regularity of use
- Number of prior sexual contacts
- Previous STD history and treatment: Skin rashes, lesions, ulcers, and warts
- Fever, malaise, general illness

❏ Female-specific history

- Vaginal discharge (amount, color, and odor)
- Irregular or painful bleeding (dysmenorrhea)
- Urinary complaints (dysuria, frequency, or urgency)
- Abdominal or pelvic pain

❏ Male-specific history

- Penile discharge (amount, color, and odor)

Focused Assessment

Physical Assessment

❏ Assess the abdomen.

- Palpate the spleen. Hepatosplenomegaly may be present.

❏ Assess the skin.

- Inspect the skin. Open and healing lesions or warts may be present.
- Inspect the mucous membranes. Open and healing lesions may be present.

❏ Assess the immune system.

- Palpate the cervical and femoral lymph nodes. Lymphadenopathy may be present.

❏ Assess the genitals.

- Observe for lesions; open wounds; drainage.
- Observe for injuries/abnormalities in a non-sexually active child

Psychosocial Assessment

❏ Assess the adolescent's understanding of sexual activity and STDs.

❏ Assess interactions between the young child and the family.

- Assess for psychosocial factors related to child sexual abuse (Chapter 45).

Nursing Interventions

1. Assist with a pelvic examination and rectal examina-tion.

   - Obtain specimens from the vagina, cervix, and rectum for culture and sensitivity.

2. Assist with the male genital and rectal examination.

   - Obtain specimens from the meatus and rectum for culture and sensitivity.

3. Obtain blood specimens to test for syphilis.

4. Administer medications, as prescribed.

   - Antibiotics
   - Antiviral agents

5. Arrange for an outpatient colposcopy if HPV is suspected.

   - The colposcope is a speculum with magnification for examination of the vagina and cervix.

6. Report STDs to the health department.

Selected Sexual Health Issues

Pelvic Inflammatory Disease

The highest rate of pelvic inflammatory disease is found in adolescents 15 to 19 years old, and many of these patients present to the emergency department for care. Pelvic inflammatory disease needs to be considered with all adolescents who present to the emergency department with abdominal pain.

Psychosocial Assessment

Assess the patient for the following risk factors:

❏ Young age

❏ Multiple sexual partners

❏ History of sexually transmitted infection (gonorrhea, Chlamydia)

❏ Noncompliance with barrier methods

❏ History of pelvic inflammatory disease

The clinical presentation may be varied with minimal to severe symptoms. History of symptoms may include complaints of foul-smelling discharge, irregular vaginal bleeding, difficult and painful urination, nausea, vomiting, and fever. Physical examination will elicit lower abdominal tenderness with possible peritoneal signs. Findings on pelvic examinations will include cervical and vaginal discharge, uterine tenderness, adnexal tenderness, and cervical motion tenderness. Additional diagnostic findings would include temperature greater than 101.3 °F (38.5 °C), white blood cells noted on saline microscopy inspection of vaginal secretions, increased erythrocyte sedimentation rate or C-reactive protein, and a positive Chlamydia or gonococcus culture. Obtain a urine pregnancy test to rule out pregnancy (may be found concurrently with pelvic inflammatory disease[21]).

Inpatient admission should be considered for severe illness, pregnancy, or inability to tolerate outpatient therapy or if there is a concern about noncompliance. All patients should be reassessed within 48 to 72 hours.

Treatment regimen should be intravenous cefoxitin and doxycycline orally or clindamycin and intravenous gentamicin or levofloxacin and intravenous metronidazole. If clinical improvement is noted in 24 hours, the patient may be changed to oral therapy.[7]

Emergency Contraception

Emergency contraception (EC) may be considered in cases of adolescent contraceptive failure or offered for pediatric sexual assault victims to prevent an unwanted pregnancy. Timely use of EC could reduce the risk of pregnancy by as much as 89% to 95% depending on the type of EC used. Three types of EC are available: progestin-only pills and combined oral contraceptive pills and a copper-releasing intrauterine device. Obtain confirmation of negative pregnancy status before administering EC.

Oral EC taken before ovulation disrupts normal follicular development and egg maturation so that ovulation is delayed or prevented. Additionally the luteal phase is altered and the cervical mucus is thickened.

EC taken after ovulation may interfere with any of the processes that occur during the approximately 7-day interval from sperm migration to implementation. Ideally, the treatment should be initiated within 72 hours of the sexual contact.[22]

Home Care and Prevention

Emergency nurses should take every opportunity to teach adolescents abstinence, as well as safe sexual practices. Having literature available may help to engage adolescents in meaningful discussions. Making available family counseling and family practice clinic telephone numbers, as well as local hotlines, may encourage adolescents to seek further knowledge in preventing STD transmission.

Specific Male Genitourinary Emergencies

Acute Scrotum

Testicular torsion and epididymitis are common causes of acute scrotal conditions in young males. Testicular tor-

sion is an emergency situation in which the blood supply to the testis is interrupted; epididymitis is an acute inflammation of the epididymis and is usually diagnosed in the adult male. Table 18.5 compares the clinical presentations of both entities.

Nursing Interventions

1. Prepare the patient for possible operative management or outpatient treatment, as needed.
   - Advise the patient not to eat or drink until it is determined that operative management will not be necessary.
2. Provide privacy during examinations.
   - Obtain a clean-catch urine specimen and prepare patient for diagnostic studies (i.e., ultrasonography).
   - Provide continuity with physicians and nurses.
   - Provide male nurses, if possible and preferred by patient.
3. Provide psychosocial support to the patient and family.
   - There may be uncertainty about long-term ramifications and questions of fertility with testicular torsion.

Other Male Genitourinary Emergencies

Medical and minor traumatic conditions related to the penis may cause parents to seek emergency treatment. Although not life threatening, these conditions are frightening and painful to the child. Table 18.6 summarizes the medical conditions.[23]

Minor traumatic injuries, such as zipper injuries, toilet-seat injuries, or tourniquet-type injuries, may result in an ED visit. In zipper and toilet-seat circumstances, the penis sustains a crush injury, resulting in edema and pain. Bleeding and hematuria may be present. In tourniquet-type injuries, magnifying lenses reveal a long hair or piece of string that is wrapped around the penis, resulting in edema and pain. Local anesthesia or analgesics may be required for the child to tolerate the procedures for removal of the zipper or tourniquet.

Patients and families should be taught prevention of zipper injuries by proper wearing of undergarments and careful closure of zippers. Toilet-seat covers should not be used with young children in the home because they can cause the toilet seat to fall forward onto the child's penis during urination. Parents and caregivers should keep their long hair secured away from their face during diaper changes and other infant/toddler care to avoid tourniquet-type injuries.

TABLE 18.5 Comparison of Testicular Torsion and Epididymitis

Characteristic	Testicular Torsion	Epididymitis
Etiology	Under normal circumstances, the epididymis is posteriorly fixed with close approximation to the testes. The incomplete fixation by the tunica vaginalis allows mobility while providing stability of the testes. In cases of testicular torsion, there is no normal fixation of the testis to prevent rotation. Twisting of the testis results in occlusion of the blood supply, causing venous and arterial occlusion that lead to thrombosis and testicular infarction. The left testicle is affected twice as often as the right, probably because the left spermatic cord is usually longer. Although the exact etiology is unknown, it is believed that congenital anatomic variations and a history of blunt trauma to the lower abdomen may predispose a male to the condition.	Epididymitis is an acute bacterial infection. The most common causative agent is *Chlamydia trachomatis,* followed by *Neisseria gonorrhoeae.* Other causative agents include viruses and trauma.
Age group affected	Testicular torsion may occur at any age but is most common in adolescence. Unfortunately, this age group is least likely to present early for medical care because of concerns about modesty. About one in 160 males are affected. The prevalence is greater in teens with undescended testes.	Epididymitis is uncommon in prepubertal and non-sexually active males. When diagnosed in young males, it is usually a complication of congenital variations in anatomy.
History and physical assessment	Pain is almost always the presenting symptom and may be sudden or gradual in onset. Edema and swelling may be present in one or both sides of the scrotum. The scrotum is swollen and red. There is often a bluish hue to the affected side. Other symptoms include nausea, vomiting, and fever. Doppler examination reveals decreased pulsatile flow to the affected side. Technetium nuclear scanning is very reliable and also confirms decreased perfusion.	Symptoms include gradual onset of scrotal and groin pain with edema; epididymal swelling and tenderness; and urethral discharge. Findings may also include positive cultures for gonorrhea and/or chlamydia.
Treatment	Testicular torsion requires manual detorsion in early stages or, more commonly, surgical management to stop progressive necrosis. Although the chance of salvage may be remote after 6 to 8 hours, even patients with symptoms lasting greater than 12 hours should be explored surgically. There is great variability among patients in their arterial supply to the testicle and in the degree of torsion.	Treatment includes bed rest, scrotal support, and analgesics. Antibiotics such as ceftriaxone and doxycycline or tetracycline are indicated for treatment against gonorrhea and chlamydia.

Starr, N. (2004). Genitourinary diseases, gynecological conditions. In C. Burns, A. Dunn, M. Brady, N. Starr, & C. Blosser (Eds.), *Pediatric primary care* (3rd ed.). Philadelphia: Saunders.

Specific Female Genitourinary Emergencies

Complications of Circumcision

Etiology

Female genital mutilation (FGM), also known as female circumcision, is practiced in at least 26 African countries. It is also practiced in some ethnic groups in Oman, the United Arab Emirates, and Yemen, as well as in parts of India, Indonesia, and Malaysia. The World Health Organization[24] estimates that between 100 and 140 million female adults and children have undergone this complex and controversial procedure. Although illegal in the United States, the practice may still occur in ethnic groups intent to carry out this tradition. As the number of immigrants from these areas or groups increases, emergency nurses must be aware of the practice and the physical and emotional effects on patients.[24] The cultural meaning is part of the socialization of girls into womanhood. It is the marking of marriageability of women, and it symbolizes social control of sexual pleasure. The procedure is gener-

TABLE 18.6 Medical Conditions of the Penis

Characteristic	Paraphimosis	Balanitis	Circumcision Complications
Etiology	Occurs when the retracted foreskin of the uncircumcised male cannot be moved to its regular position. This results in venous congestion, swelling, inflammation, and engorgement. Vascular compromise may occur to the glans. Paraphimosis can be caused by any action that results in manipulation of the penis-including masturbation, intercourse, and irritation by clothing or other objects. Bacteria can also cause an inflamed penis. Occasionally a foreign body, such as hair, can act as a tourniquet.	Inflammation of the foreskin, usually caused by poor hygiene. Debris accumulates under the foreskin, leading to infection.	Although there is no absolute indication for routine male newborn circumcision, it is the most commonly performed surgical procedure in the United States. Hemorrhage is the most common problem. The second most common complication is infection. Although most infections are localized, any generalized infections in a newborn are dangerous. Poor surgical technique can result in severe complications such as necrosis or amputation during the procedure. Poor hygiene at home.
History/ physical assessment	Penile pain and swelling; discoloration	Inflamed and edematous foreskin with a collection of smegma. Older children may report pain and dysuria.	Recent circumcision; bleeding at the site; edema; signs of infection.
Treatment	The patient is given a sedative or a local penile dorsal block. Ice is then briefly applied in attempts to reduce the edema. This is followed by gentle manual traction.	Warm soaks and local care are usually sufficient treatment	Bleeding is usually controlled by direct pressure. For bleeding not controlled by direct pressure, other methods, such as silver nitrate application, epinephrine, fibrin, and suture placement, may be used. Infection may be treated with antibiotics.
Prevention	Although hair and clothing can accidentally restrict blood flow, some foreign bodies are placed purposefully; therefore, experimentation and abuse must always be considered. Although paraphimosis is frequently unpreventable, young uncircumcised males and their parents should be instructed in proper foreskin care.	A review of hygiene with the child and family is necessary.	Hygiene and signs and symptoms of infection should be reviewed. Parents may be concerned about the appearance of the penis. Surgical follow-up may be warranted.

ally performed in girls between the ages of 4 and 10 years. Table 18.7 classifies the circumcision procedures.[26]

Female circumcision or genital mutilation involves cutting off the clitoris and sometimes the labia minora or labia majora. The sides may then be stitched together, leaving only a tiny opening. Besides the obvious risks of infection and severe pain, there are long-lasting physical and emotional ramifications:

❑ Acute physical complications of FGM
- Severe hemorrhage from the clitoral artery
- Shock due to blood loss
- Pain
- Urinary retention resulting from pain and swelling
- Injuries to surrounding organs during the procedure
- Infection, including tetanus, septicemia, and gangrene

TABLE 18.7 Classification of Female Circumcision

Type	Description
Type I clitoridectomy	Removal of part or all of the clitoris.
Type II clitoridectomy	Excision of the clitoris and part of the labia minora. After healing, the clitoris is absent. The urethra and vaginal introitus are not covered.
Type III infibulations	Removal of the clitoris and labia minora. The labia majora are cut to allow raw surfaces that are stitched together. There is a large posterior opening for the passage of urine and menstrual blood.
Type IV infibulation	As above, but only a small opening remains for the passage of urine and menstrual blood.

Toubia, N. (1994). Female circumcision as a public health issue. *New England Journal of Medicine, 331,* 712–716.

- Injuries to the joints or limbs as a result of restraint used during the procedure
- Death resulting from hemorrhage, shock, or septicemia[25]

❏ Long-term effects of FGM

- Dysmenorrhea
- Painful intercourse
- Fistula formation between the vagina, bladder, or rectum
- Pelvic inflammatory disease
- Recurrent pain
- Infertility
- Psychological effects such as absence of sexual desire, feelings of betrayal, bitterness, and anger at being female

Focused History

❏ Patient history

- Recent immigration to the United States
- Cultural beliefs and practices
- GU complaints related to the length of time from the circumcision to ED presentation
- Early complications:
  - Hemorrhage
  - Severe pain
  - Continued bleeding with anemia
- Late complications:
  - Local and systemic infections
  - Abscesses
  - Ulcers
  - Delayed healing
  - Chronic pelvic infections

- Chronic UTIs
- Scarring

Focused Assessment

Physical Assessment

❏ Assess the genitalia. Observe for age-related genital development.

- Obliteration of normal genital landmarks may be present.

❏ Observe for signs of infection or trauma.

- Bloody or purulent vaginal discharge
- Difficulty with urethral catheterization
- Scarring of the external genitalia

❏ Perform or assist with a pelvic examination, as needed.

- Pelvic examinations may be difficult or impossible to perform.

Psychosocial Assessment

❏ Assess the child's and family's cultural beliefs.

- It may be difficult to obtain a history of the female circumcision procedure unless the child is in severe distress because of complications.
- Some cultures view this practice as normal; others may fear retribution or legal investigation if the practice is documented.

Nursing Interventions

1. Assess and maintain airway, breathing, and circulation in the child with sepsis or shock.
2. Communicate a caring attitude to the patient.
   - Avoid forcing procedures, such as bladder catheterization or pelvic examination, if pain and/or fear are elicited.

- Prepare for a possible examination with the patient under anesthesia if necessary.

3. Report the recent female circumcision to the local child protective agency.

- This practice may constitute child maltreatment (Chapter 44).

Home Care and Prevention

Emergency nurses should know whether female circumcisions are being performed in their ED's service area. Becoming involved in local or state efforts to end this practice is one strategy that emergency nurses can employ to prevent future episodes of female circumcision and genital mutilation.

Vaginal Bleeding

Vaginal bleeding may occur in prepubertal or adolescent females. It can have very different etiologies and treatments (Table 18.8).

Nursing Interventions

1. Prepare the patient for a gynecologic examination.

- The gynecologic examination can produce great anxiety in the patient. Positioning of the patient should take into consideration the patient's age and developmental level.
- Sedation or general anesthesia may be necessary for internal examinations, suturing of lacerations, or removal of foreign bodies. The child should not be forced to participate in the examination.

TABLE 18.8 Vaginal Bleeding in Prepubertal Versus Pubertal Females		
Characteristic	**Prepubertal Females**	**Pubertal Females**
Etiology	Vaginitis Trauma—straddle injuries Sexual abuse—masturbation; foreign bodies Tumors Blood dyscrasias Precocious puberty Infection	Normal menstrual bleeding occurs in cycles varying from 21 to 45 days, lasting 2 to 8 days. Blood loss averages 35 to 40 mL. Blood loss greater than 80 mL is considered excessive. Although dysfunctional bleeding may occur during an ovulatory cycle, it usually occurs as abnormal bleeding during an anovulatory cycle. Anovulation may be brought on by stress, illness, extreme athletic activity, and conditions of significantly decreased body fat, such as found in dancers.

History/physical assessment	General physical assessment
	Pelvic examination for:
	
	• Differentiation of vaginal, cervical, or uterine bleeding
	• Diagnosis of cervicitis, trauma, foreign bodies, and malignancies. Bimanual and rectal exam to differentiate tumors and cysts and verify that the source of bleeding is the vagina. Blood from the uterus, urethra, or rectum may initially be diagnosed as vaginal in origin.
		General physical assessment
		Pelvic examination for:
		
		• Differentiation of vaginal, cervical, or uterine bleeding
		• Diagnosis of endometriosis, cervicitis, trauma, foreign bodies, and malignancies. Bimanual and rectal exam to differentiate tumors and cysts and pregnancy-related complications such as:
		  • Ectopic pregnancy
		  • Threatened or incomplete abortions, hydatidiform mole, menstrual history, including tampon/pad usage
		Sexual activity and form of contraception
		Previous infections
		Endocrine disorders
		Hematologic disorders
		Recent stressors
		Medications
		Family history
		Skin inspection for petechiae or bruising

Characteristic	Prepubertal Females	Pubertal Females
TABLE 18.8 Vaginal Bleeding in Prepubertal Versus Pubertal Females (continued)		
ED treatment	Laboratory studies such as: • CBC with differential and platelet count • Sedimentation rate • Thyroid function tests • Blood glucose • PT/PTT • Cervical cultures • Pap smear (may be deferred to follow-up appointment) Radiographic tests may include pelvic ultrasound to rule out masses or anatomic abnormalities.	Laboratory studies such as: • CBC with differential and platelet count • Sedimentation rate • Thyroid function tests • Blood glucose • PT/PTT • Cervical cultures • Pap smear (may be deferred to follow-up appointment) • Pregnancy test Radiographic tests may include pelvic ultrasound to rule out masses or anatomic abnormalities.
Other treatment	Determine underlying cause of bleeding and follow up accordingly.	Management of dysfunctional uterine bleeding is dependent on the source and severity of bleeding: Mild dysfunctional bleeding in patients with a stable hemoglobin level higher than 12 g/dL usually is monitored. Iron supplements are frequently prescribed to prevent anemia. Oral contraceptives may be considered. Patient education is crucial. The patient should start and maintain a menstrual calendar. Moderate dysfunctional bleeding in patients with a hemoglobin level between 10 and 12 g/dL may be treated with all of the aforementioned interventions. Prescribed oral contraceptives will have higher amounts of progestin and estrogen. Folic acid is usually added to iron supplementation. Severe dysfunctional bleeding in patients with a hemoglobin level of less than 10 g/dL usually requires hospital admission, blood transfusion, hormonal therapy, and, if medical therapy is not successful, surgical intervention (dilation and curettage).

Notes: CBC = complete blood cell count; Pap = Papanicolaou; PT = prothrombin time; PTT = partial thromboplastin time.

Home Care and Prevention

Adolescents and their parents should be encouraged to investigate any irregular vaginal bleeding. To alleviate menstrual cramping, adolescents may try:[27]

❒ Placing a heating pad or hot water bottle on the abdomen to relax tight muscles

❒ Taking over-the-counter medications, such as ibuprofen or acetaminophen, as directed

❒ Walking for short distances and/or engaging in light exercises

❒ Eating a well-balanced meal and avoiding caffeinated foods and beverages

❒ Drinking six to eight glasses of water daily

Vulvovaginitis and Vaginal Discharge

Vulvovaginitis and vaginal discharges are common female complaints. Etiologies differ with age (Table 18.9). Other etiologies include leukorrhea, foreign bodies, poor hygiene, chemical irritation, tumors, dermatologic disorders, and STDs.

Home Care and Prevention

Patients should be taught proper personal hygiene. Teaching adolescents about abstinence, as well as safe sexual practices, may prevent future occurrences of these conditions.

Conclusion

GU conditions are fraught with anxiety for parents, children, and adolescents. Emergency nurses must temper the need for thorough treatment with consideration of the child's and adolescent's sexual issues and development. Understanding GU development and its effects on bodily fluid regulation, as well as sexual identity, assists emergency nurses in the provision of expert care to this patient population.

TABLE 18.9 Etiologies of Vulvovaginitis and Vaginal Discharges

Characteristic	*Vulvovaginitis*	*Vaginal Discharge*
Etiology	Allergies; poor hygiene; irritation	Multiple causes
Age	Prepubescent	Postpubescent
History and physical assessment	Presence of: • Genital irritation, itching, pain, and inflammation • Vaginal discharge Onset, duration, quantity, color, consistency, and odor Urinary complaints Recent medication (especially contraceptives and antibiotics) Hygiene measures (soaps, bubble bath, deodorant sprays, and douches) Underlying medical problems	Presence of: • Genital irritation, itching, pain, and inflammation • Vaginal discharge Onset, duration, quantity, color, consistency, and odor Urinary complaints Recent medication (especially contraceptives and antibiotics) Hygiene measures (soaps, bubble bath, deodorant sprays, and douches) Underlying medical problems Any symptoms in sexual partners
Description of discharge	Thin, mucoid Clear, sticky (physiologic leukorrhea at onset of puberty)	Yellow, green, purulent (gonorrhea, chlamydia) Thick, white, pruritic (*Candida albicans*) Thin, frothy, malodorous, yellow-green (*Trichomonas vaginalis*) Gray, clear, fishy odor (*Gardnerella vaginalis*)
Treatment	Symptomatic care with attention to hygiene, removal of foreign bodies, and use of antibiotics specific for a bacterial infection	Symptomatic care with attention to hygiene, removal of foreign bodies, and use of antibiotics specific for a bacterial infection

References

1. McCance, K., & Huether, S. (Eds.). (2005). *Pathophysiology: The biologic basis for disease in adults and children* (5th ed.). St. Louis, MO: Mosby.

2. Ball, J., & Bindler, R. (Eds). (2005). *Child health nursing: Partnering with children & families.* Upper Saddle River, NJ: Pearson Prentice Hall.

3. Palmieri, P. (2002). Obstructive nephropathy: Pathophysiology, diagnosis, and collaborative management. *Nephrology Nursing Journal, 29*(1), 15–23.

4. Ellis, D. (2007). Nephrology. In B. Zitelli & H. Davis (Eds.), *Atlas of pediatric physical diagnosis* (5th ed., pp. 397–420). St. Louis, MO: Mosby.

5. Seidel, H. M., Ball, J. W., Dains, J., & Benedict, G. W. (2003). *Mosby's guide to physical examination* (5th ed.). St. Louis, MO: Mosby.

6. Chon, C. H., Lai, F. C., & Shortcliffe, L. M. (2001). Pediatric urinary tract infections. *Pediatric Clinics of North America, 48*(6), 1441–1459.

7. Pickering, L., Baker, C., Long, S., & McClellan, J. (Eds.). (2006). *Red book: Report of the committee on infectious diseases* (27th ed.). Elk Grove Village, IL: American Academy of Pediatrics.

8. Santen, S. A., & Altieri, M. F. (2001). Pediatric urinary tract infection. *Emergency Medicine Clinics of North America, 19*(3), 675–690.

9. Ishimine, P. (2006). Fever without source in children 0 to 36 months of age. *Pediatric Clinics of North America, 53*(2), 167–194.

10. Hellerstein, S. (2006). Acute urinary tract infection—evaluation and treatment. *Current Opinion in Pediatrics, 18*(2), 134–138.

11. Liao, J. C., & Churchill, B. M. (2001). Pediatric urine testing. *Pediatric Clinics of North America, 48*(6), 1425–1440.

12. Deville, W., Yzermans, J., van Duijn, N., Bezemer, P., van der Windt, D., & Bouter, L. (2004). The urine dipstick test useful to rule out infections. A meta-analysis of the accuracy. *BMC Urology, 4,* 4.

13. Williams, G., Lee, A., & Craig, J. (2001). Antibiotics for the prevention of urinary tract infection in children: A systematic review of randomized controlled trials. *Journal of Pediatrics, 138*(6), 868–874.

14. Lee, J. H., Son, C. H., Lee, M. S., & Park, Y. S. (2006). Vesicoureteral reflux increases the risk of renal scars: A study of unilateral reflux. *Pediatric Nephrology, 21*(9), 1281–1284.

15. Sowden, L., & Betz, C. (Eds.). (2007). *Mosby's pediatric nursing reference.* (6th ed.) St. Louis, MO: Mosby.

16. Kher, K., Schnaper, H., & Makker, S. (2007). *Clinical pediatric nephrology.* New York: McGraw-Hill.

17. Ahn, S., & Ingulli, E. (2008). Acute poststreptococcal glomerulonephritis: An update. *Current Opinion in Pediatrics, 20*(2), 157–162.

18. Barkin, R., & Rosen, P. (2003). *Emergency pediatrics: A guide to ambulatory care* (6th ed). St. Louis, MO: Mosby.

19. Clark, L. R., Jackson, M., & Allen-Taylor, L. (2002). Adolescent knowledge about sexually transmitted diseases. *Sexually Transmitted Diseases, 29*(8), 436–443.

20. Centers for Disease Control and Prevention. (2008). *HPV vaccine—Questions & answers for the public about the safety and effectiveness of the human papillomavirus (HPV) vaccine.* Retrieved October 6, 2008, from http://www.cdc.gov/vaccines/vpd-vac/hpv/hpv-vacsafe-effic.htm

21. Beigi, R. H., & Wiesenfeld, H. C. (2003). Pelvic inflammatory disease: New diagnostic criteria. *Obstetric and Gynecologic Clinics of North America, 30*(4), 777–793.

22. Conard, L., & Gold, M. (2006). What you need to know about providing emergency contraception. *Contemporary Pediatrics, 23*(2), 49–69.

23. Choe, J. M. (2000). Paraphimosis: Current treatment options. *American Family Physician, 62*(12), 2623–2628.

24. Ball, T. (2008). Female genital mutilation. *Nursing Standard, 23*(5), 43–47.

25. Bikoo, M. (2007). Female genital mutilation: Classification and management. *Nursing Standard, 22*(7), 43–49.

26. Toubia, N. (1994). Female circumcision as a public health issue. *New England Journal of Medicine, 331,* 712–716.

27. Starr, N. (2004). Genitourinary diseases, gynecological conditions. In C. Burns, A. Dunn, M. Brady, N. Starr, & C. Blosser (Eds.), *Pediatric primary care* (3rd ed.). Philadelphia: Saunders.

NINETEEN

Musculoskeletal Emergencies

Kathleen Merkley, RN, MS, FNP

Introduction

Musculoskeletal system injury and illness are common occurrences in children presenting to the emergency department (ED) for treatment. These conditions include musculoskeletal trauma (Chapter 36), medical problems, and congenital disorders. Emergency nurses must have the ability to recognize and treat musculoskeletal conditions, as well as understand normal growth and development of the child to prevent future musculoskeletal disability. The purpose of this chapter is to discuss pediatric musculoskeletal conditions and the appropriate nursing interventions.

Embryologic Development of the Musculoskeletal System[1,2]

Development of Bone and Cartilage

❐ Mesodermal cells give rise to mesenchyme—a meshwork of loosely organized embryonic connective tissue.

❐ Bones first appear as condensations of mesenchymal cells that form bone models.

❐ Most flat bones develop in mesenchyme within premembranous sheaths— intramembranous bone formation.

❐ Mesenchymal models of most limb bones are transformed into cartilage bone models, which later become ossified by endochondral bone formation.

❐ Cartilage develops from mesenchyme and first appears in embryos during the fifth week. Three types of cartilage are distinguished: hyaline cartilage, the most widely distributed type; fibrocartilage, found in intervertebral disks; and elastic cartilage, found in the auricle of the ear.

❐ During fetal and postnatal life, there is continuous remodeling of bone by the coordinated action of osteoclasts (cells that reabsorb bone) and osteoblasts (bone-forming cells).

❐ Ossification (cartilaginous bone formation) of limb bones begins at the end of the embryonic period and thereafter makes demands on the maternal supply of calcium and phosphorus.

❐ At birth, the diaphyses are largely ossified, but most of the epiphyses are still cartilaginous. Secondary ossification centers appear in the epiphyses in most bones during the first few years after birth. In most bones, the epiphyses have fused with the diaphysis by 20 years of age.

Development of Joints

❐ During the sixth week, joints begin to develop with the appearance of the interzonal mesenchyme, and by the end of the eighth week, they resemble adult joints.

❐ Joints are classified as fibrous, cartilaginous, or synovial.

▪ Sutures of the cranium are fibrous joints.

▪ Pubic symphysis and the costochondral joints are cartilaginous joints.

- The knee joint is a synovial joint.

Development of Muscle

- ❑ The first indication of myogenesis (muscle formation) is the elongation of the nuclei and cell bodies of mesenchymal cells as they differentiate into myoblasts.

- ❑ These cells fuse to form elongated, multinucleated, cylindrical structures called myotubes.

- ❑ Most skeletal muscles develop before birth, and almost all remaining ones are formed by the end of the first year.

- ❑ Increase in the size of the muscle after the first year results from an increase in the diameter of the fibers because of the formation of more myofilaments.

- ❑ Muscles increase in length and width to grow with the skeleton.

- ❑ Ultimate size depends on the amount of exercise that is performed.

Pediatric Considerations

An understanding of basic pediatric anatomy and physiology, which is involved in bone growth, is essential for a better understanding of appropriate interventions for patients with musculoskeletal emergencies. Following is a review of this information.[3]

- ❑ Bony architecture in children includes a thick and active periosteum, a growth plate (the physis), the metaphysis or shaft of the bone, and an epiphysis (the secondary ossification center where bone growth occurs).

- ❑ Bone in children is more porous and pliable than adult bone. This greater porosity results in bones that bow, bend, or buckle without a complete fracture.

- ❑ Sprains, ligamentous injuries, and dislocations are rare because ligaments attaching one bone to another have greater strength than the associated epiphyseal plates and perichondrial rings.

- ❑ Abnormal patterns of bone growth associated with diseases such as osteogenesis imperfecta and osteoporosis can result in pathologic fractures.

- ❑ Damage to epiphyseal (growth) centers may lead to acute or chronic disruptions in growth of the affected extremity.

- ❑ At certain ages children are susceptible to different type of orthopedic emergencies and trauma.

- ❑ The bones of children exhibit rapid healing because of an active periosteum and abundant blood supply to developing bone; they show extensive remodeling,

accept more angular deformity than do adults', rarely have nonunion, and tolerate prolonged immobilization better.

- ❑ Pathogenic defects are the result of malformation (improper formation of a structure resulting from defective embryologic development), disruption (retarded development resulting from in utero destruction of a normally formed part or deformation), or an antepartum or postpartum alteration of a part that originally developed normally.

- ❑ Disruption of the complex blood supply within the bone can result in avascular necrosis.

Focused History

- ❑ Date of onset of complaint or illness
- ❑ Severity
- ❑ Extent of disability
- ❑ Precipitating factors
- ❑ Associated signs and symptoms
- ❑ Previous treatment and resulting effects
- ❑ Recent trauma
- ❑ New, increased, or repetitive activities that may have contributed to the condition
- ❑ Current prescribed and over-the-counter medications and herbal and dietary supplements
- ❑ Recent exposure to infections
- ❑ History, including:
  - Prenatal and birth history, growth, and development
  - Similar signs and symptoms
  - Previous orthopedic injuries or chronic conditions
  - Recent immunizations
  - Congenital problems

Focused Assessment

Physical Assessment

In addition to the standard assessment described in Chapter 5, the following assessment should be completed:

- ❑ Posture, position, gait
- ❑ Symmetry of motion
- ❑ Range of motion in joints
- ❑ Muscle tone
- ❑ Deformities in limbs or trunk; abnormal prominences or indentations
- ❑ Joint swelling and erythema

- ❏ Use of orthopedic devices, such as braces
- ❏ Pain or tenderness
- ❏ Distal pulses/capillary refill in extremities

Psychosocial Assessment

Many musculoskeletal complaints are painful, and some are life altering and can cause disfigurement. The parents and child will be anxious about the long-term prognosis. The goal of the emergency nurse is to reduce anxiety by providing a calm environment, individualizing interventions, and considering the child's needs. These needs may include:

- ❏ Allowing the parent to remain with the child as much as possible.
- ❏ Providing information about the illness and the child's condition and procedures necessary.
- ❏ Preparing the child and family for necessary procedures.
- ❏ Providing pain management (Chapter 11).
- ❏ Providing privacy.
- ❏ Allowing the child to make choices when possible.
- ❏ Providing age-appropriate toys and distraction.

Nursing Interventions

1. Assess and maintain airway, breathing, and circulation.
2. Establish intravenous access.
   - Obtain blood specimens.
   - Administer intravenous antibiotics as ordered.
3. Administer analgesics (Chapter 11).
4. Prepare child and family for diagnostic procedures.
5. Monitor and reassess vital signs.
6. Prepare for hospitalization, operative management, or discharge to home.

Specific Orthopedic Emergencies

Osteomyelitis

Osteomyelitis is an infection of the bone that is most often bacterial in origin. Bacteria are introduced to the bone in three ways:[3]

- ❏ Through the bloodstream (hematogenous delivery)
- ❏ Direct inoculation (usually resulting from trauma but may be introduced through surgery)
- ❏ Local invasion from an infection in proximity to the infected bone

Although occurring infrequently in children, osteomyelitis is more common in boys, and the highest incidence occurs among infants and preschool children. Osteomyelitis may also occur in neonates who have risk factors of prematurity and complicated deliveries. Adolescents are at a higher risk if they participate in intravenous drug abuse.[4]

The most common infective agents that cause osteomyelitis include:[3]

- ❏ *Staphylococcus aureus* (accounts for most cases)
- ❏ *Pseudomonas aeruginosa* (seen after puncture wounds)
- ❏ Fungal infections (seen in immunocompromised patients)
- ❏ Salmonella (in patients with sickle cell disease)
- ❏ Group B *β-hemolytic streptococcus* (in neonates)

Pathophysiology

In most children the bacteria reach the bone through the bloodstream. Organisms lodge in the end arteries of the bone metaphysis (which contain the growth plate), where there is a rich blood supply. Bacterial proliferation evokes an inflammatory exudate. The periosteum may be damaged or may rupture from the accumulation of purulent material in the confined space. This can also lead to necrosis of the bone cortex. If the metaphysis is contained within a joint capsule, septic arthritis may also result.[3] The long bones of the humerus, tibia, and femur are most often involved.[5]

Focused History

Onset is usually gradual and may occur over several days. Other history often includes:

- ❏ Recent orthopedic surgery, open reduction, and internal fixation of a fracture.
- ❏ Puncture wound, open wound, or open fracture.
- ❏ Recent infection in another location that results in hematogenous spread to the bone via the circulatory system.

Focused Assessment

During a standard physical assessment, the following signs and symptoms may be identified:

- ❏ Fever, with a temperature exceeding 101 °F (38.5 °C)
- ❏ Chills
- ❏ Malaise
- ❏ Limp, inability or refusal to bear weight
- ❏ Pseudoparalysis: In infants, pain with movement; in older children, with upper extremity involvement
- ❏ Tenderness, warmth, and swelling at the site of infection

❏ Pain in the affected area

❏ Failure to thrive, poor feeding, or irritability in infants

❏ Fulminant sepsis in infants

Nursing Interventions

1. Assess and maintain airway, breathing, and circulation.
    - Establish intravenous access.
    - If shock is present, fluid boluses may be necessary.
2. Obtain blood samples for analysis and culture.
    - Laboratory screening of the erythrocyte sedimentation rate (ESR) and C-reactive protein (CRP) provides useful information because bony infection almost always leads to elevation.
    - The white count may also be elevated. Blood cultures are positive 50% of the time. Isolation of a pathogen from the bone confirms the diagnosis.[3]
3. Obtain radiographic and imaging studies.
    - Radiologic findings are often inconclusive early in the course of the disease but later may indicate chronic infection and new bone formation.
    - Radionuclide scanning provides a useful tool for the diagnosis of osteomyelitis. Uptake of compounds such as technetium is seen at sites of increased metabolic activity, which occurs in this type of infection.
    - Magnetic resonance imaging may also be needed to identify the location and extent of bone involvement.[3]
4. Administer pain medications.
5. Administer intravenous antibiotics.
6. Monitor vital signs.
7. Prepare for possible surgical débridement of necrotic bone.
8. Prepare for hospitalization.

Septic Arthritis

Sepsis of the joint occurs when bacteria infiltrates the synovial space. Signs and symptoms of septic joints are similar to those of osteomyelitis. The diagnosis may be especially difficult to identify when both conditions are present simultaneously.

The etiology of septic joints usually occurs from a secondary source of blood-borne bacteria. Septic arthritis is a diagnosis that cannot be missed, given the prospect of rapid joint destruction and permanent disability.[6] Residual sequelae are rare if septic arthritis is diagnosed and treated within 2 days of onset. Outcomes are usually not as favorable if the joint is infected secondary to osteomyelitis. The knee and hip joints are most often involved. The child will often present with a limp or refusing to bear weight on the affected extremity.[7]

Children in whom septic arthritis develops are generally healthy. Boys are affected twice as often as girls. Bacterial causes vary with age and health conditions as follows:[3]

❏ Neonate—group B streptococcus, *Staphylococcus aureus*

❏ 3 months to 3 years— *Staphylococcus aureus, Haemophilus influenzae* in nonimmunized children

❏ Teens—*Neisseria gonorrhoeae*

❏ Sickle cell anemia—Salmonella species

Pathophysiology

Blood-borne bacteria deposit in the joint synovium resulting in an inflammatory reaction. This reaction causes an infiltration of neutrophils (white blood cells) into the synovial fluid. A buildup of purulent material causes swelling in the joint capsule. This leads to physical and radiologic findings, as well as destruction of the articular cartilage.[3]

Focused History

❏ Rapid onset of severe joint pain

❏ Irritability

❏ Refusal to bear weight or use the extremity

❏ Fever

❏ Malaise

❏ Poor feeding in an infant

Focused Assessment

Symptoms may be more dramatic than those of osteomyelitis or traumatic injury. The following signs and symptoms may be present:

❏ Fever, with a temperature of 101 °F (38.5 °C) or higher, and ill-appearing

❏ Child will be resistant to any movement of affected area.[8]

❏ Swollen, erythematous joint

❏ Severe pain with joint range of motion

❏ Pain may radiate to other structures in proximity with infections of deeper joints.

❏ Pain may mimic appendicitis, a pelvic neoplasm, or a urinary tract infection.

❏ Decreased mobility if upper joints are involved

❏ Child abducts and externally rotates the hip for comfort.

❏ Neonates may present with paradoxical irritability and pseudoparalysis of the affected limb.[3]

Nursing Interventions

1. Assess and monitor airway, breathing, and circulation.

2. Provide pain control measures (Chapter 11).

3. Obtain blood samples:

   - ESR and CRP level are consistently elevated.

   - Complete blood cell count—white count will typically be elevated.

   - Blood cultures

4. Obtain radiologic studies: Initially plain radiographs may show a widening of the joint space and soft tissue swelling.

5. Obtain imaging studies: Ultrasound scan may show joint effusions.

6. Assist with joint aspiration (under fluoroscopy), and send specimen for laboratory evaluation: Examination of the synovial fluid indicates a definitive diagnosis.

7. Begin administration of parenteral antibiotics.

8. Monitor and reassess vital signs.

9. Prepare child and family for admission to the hospital and possible surgical intervention.

Juvenile Rheumatoid Arthritis

Juvenile rheumatoid arthritis (JRA) is now the most common rheumatic disease of children in the pediatric population. Pauciarticular onset JRA is the subset of JRA that includes patients with involvement of fewer than five joints and is most prevalent (50%) in the pediatric population. Other types of JRA include polyarticular arthritis with involvement of five or more joints and systemic onset or Still's disease. Still's disease is the least common subset of JRA and manifests with a fever of unknown origin for several weeks or months and associated joint stiffness.[9]

The cause of JRA is unknown, even though it has been reported to occur after traumatic injury or systemic infections. These events are thought to trigger an autoimmune response, which initiates the disease. There may also be a genetic predilection. Pauciarticular JRA affects females more often than males, as does polyarticular disease. Peak incidence occurs between 2 and 3 years of age. It is less common over 5 years of age and rarely begins after 10 years of age.[10]

Pathophysiology

An unknown event triggers inflammation within the synovial membrane of the joint. This inflammation causes fibrin deposits, hyperplasia, and hypertrophy of synovial cells. This leads to an overgrowth of the articular cartilage, causing its destruction and eventually destruction of the underlying bone as well.[9] Immobility of the joint may also result from adhesions between the joint surfaces.

Cardiac involvement (pericarditis, myocarditis, or cardiac tamponade) may be a complication of systemic or Still's disease. Generally, children with JRA do not have the condition diagnosed in the emergency department. Symptomatic complaints such as those listed in the following section may prompt a visit to the emergency department.

Focused History

❏ Fever

❏ Joint pain and swelling

   - Pauciarticular JRA affects the large joints (the elbows, wrists, knees, and elbows).

   - The joints are typically swollen and tender to palpation.

   - They may be warm to the touch but not erythematous.[11]

❏ Polyarticular arthritis is characterized by insidious onset of symmetric synovitis in both large and small joints, accompanied by low-grade fever, morning stiffness, and malaise.[11]

   - Cervical spine involvement is seen in children with severe polyarticular JRA.

   - Neck stiffness that is worst in the morning is the most common symptom noted.

❏ Iridocyclitis (inflammation of the iris and ciliary body) occurs in 10% to 20% of children with JRA.[11]

❏ Pericarditis

❏ Neurologic complaints

❏ Injury to an involved joint

Focused Assessment

A standard physical assessment is performed, focusing on the chief complaint. Children with a previous diagnosis of JRA may come to the emergency department with signs and symptoms of complications mentioned above. The following signs and symptoms may be present and indicative in children who have not previously had a diagnosis of JRA:

❏ Prolonged fevers

❏ Rash

❏ Iridocyclitis

❏ Pain and swelling in joints lasting more than 6 weeks

❏ Signs and symptoms of complications

❏ Signs and symptoms of concurrent illness such as a respiratory infection

Nursing Interventions

1. Assess and maintain airway, breathing, and circulation.
   - Provide supplemental oxygen.
   - Monitor heart rate and rhythm.
   - Observe for signs of pericarditis or pleural effusion.
   - Begin intravenous infusion.
2. Provide pain control through both pharmacologic and nonpharmacologic means (Chapter 11).
3. Early identification and intervention for complications and underlying illness
4. Preserve joint function.
   - Use positioning, splints, rest as ordered to decrease inflammation and prevent further joint damage.
5. Diagnostic testing: No laboratory test is diagnostic of JRA. The diagnosis is made on the basis of history and physical examination results. In polyarticular JRA, the rheumatoid factor (RF) may be elevated. The white blood cell count and levels of acute-phase reactants in the serum are also elevated, often in proportion to the number of joints involved. Radiographs of involved joints may indicate soft-tissue swelling.[11]
6. Provide psychosocial support: JRA is a lifetime disease often resulting in deformity and immobility.
7. Prepare for admission.

Home Care and Prevention

❏ Warm baths, warm packs, electric blankets may help control morning stiffness.

❏ Regular daily exercise—swimming is recommended.

❏ Splinting of actively inflamed, painful joints.

❏ Nonsteroidal anti-inflammatory drug (NSAID) therapy.

❏ Return to the emergency department for persistent fever, chest pain or respiratory distress, visual disturbance.

Other Musculoskeletal Conditions

Several other orthopedic conditions, acquired and congenital, may be found in the pediatric ED patient. These conditions are summarized below, along with the nursing considerations needed to care for these children.

Toxic or Transient Synovitis

Toxic or transient synovitis is a comparatively frequent complaint seen in children between the ages of 18 months and 12 years. This inflammation of the hip causes pain and limited range of motion. The child presents with acute onset of a painful limp or inability to bear weight. Fever is rare. The etiology is unknown, but an infectious cause is suspected. An infection of the hip should be ruled out by evaluating a white blood cell count, ESR, and CRP. Children with an elevated white count or inflammatory markers should have plain radiographs, which exclude pathologic osseous conditions. They should also have a hip ultrasound examination, which identifies joint effusions. Arthrocentesis is performed if the effusion is thought to be bacterial in origin.

ED Considerations

Diagnosis consists of ruling out other serious conditions such as septic arthritis and JRA. The symptoms of toxic synovitis usually improve within several days.[10] Nursing care consist of providing pain management with NSAIDs and encouraging the patient to limit activity. Exacerbations can occur if activity is resumed too soon.

Legg-Calvé-Perthes Disease

Legg-Calvé-Perthes disease (LCPD) is a disorder of the hip that generally affects children between the ages of 4 and 9 years, primarily males. Most children with LCPD are below average height and above average weight. The etiology is unknown. Repeated episodes of ischemia of the femoral head lead to infection and necrosis.[12] Some children remain asymptomatic whereas others present with mild hip pain, a limp, and referred pain to the knee, thigh, or groin.

ED Considerations

Behavioral disorders, such as hyperactivity, are common in children with this condition. Hip radiographs confirm diagnosis. A bone scan may be done to determine the degree of avascularity of the femoral head. Septic arthritis and osteomyelitis must be ruled out. Management of LCPD necessitates a pediatric orthopedist to follow the child through the various stages of the disease.

Slipped Capital Femoral Epiphysis

Slipped capital femoral epiphysis (SCFE) is the most common hip disorder in adolescents. This occurs when there is displacement (slippage) of the proximal femoral epiphysis on the femoral neck. It occurs twice as often in adolescent males (aged 13–15 years) as in adolescent females (aged 11–13 years). African Americans are at greater risk. The etiology is unknown, but obesity and inactivity tend to play a role.

ED Considerations

Hip and knee pain and/or limp are the most frequent chief complaints. Often the child is unable to bear weight. The diagnosis is made on physical examination (range of motion is usually decreased in the affected hip) and radiography. Radiographs of the hip should include two views because SCFE may be missed on an anteroposterior view alone. A frog leg or lateral view can best identify the slippage.[12]

Orthopedic referral is emergent to prevent permanent damage. The treatment is primarily surgical. Nursing care includes restricting weight bearing and preparing the child for admission for surgical repair.

Osgood-Schlatter Disease

Osgood-Schlatter disease is an inflammation of the tibial tubercle. It results from an overuse syndrome that occurs in active adolescents. Repetitive stress on the patellar tendon is thought to cause detachment of cartilage fragments from the tibial tuberosity. The disease typically resolves in late adolescence when the bone becomes stronger than the inserted ligament.

ED Considerations

The child presents with pain in the anterior aspect of the knee. This is aggravated by activity or direct pressure. Symptoms may be initially noted when the child is kneeling or after minor trauma. Examination reveals localized tenderness, and often a prominence of the tibial tuberosity with associated soft tissue swelling is seen.[13] Diagnosis is made solely on physical examination findings. Nursing care consists of education regarding the disease, application of ice, administration of NSAIDs for pain, and instruction on exercises to stretch and strengthen the quadriceps and hamstrings.

Osteogenesis Imperfecta

Osteogenesis imperfecta is a connective tissue disorder that causes osteoporosis in children. It is characterized by recurrent fractures and skeletal deformities. This is an inherited condition characterized by immature collagen formation affecting all connective tissue but primarily the bones. The signs and symptoms depend on the classification of osteogenesis imperfecta (there are four types) and range from frequent long-bone fractures to stillbirth or perinatal death.

ED Considerations

The patient presents to the emergency department for signs and symptoms of fractures resulting from minor trauma or unknown etiology. It is important to distinguish osteogenesis imperfecta from intentional trauma.

Emergency department management includes cervical spine precautions and fracture care. The nurse should be careful when positioning the patient to prevent further injury. The parent and child need support because of frequent ED visits. Pain management is also imperative.

Muscular Dystrophy

Muscular dystrophy is an inherited disorder that results in progressive muscle weakness (myopathy) and loss of muscle mass (atrophy) related to defects in genes, which dictate normal muscle function. The forms that present in childhood are primarily X-linked and are seen in boys 3 to 15 years of age. Duchenne-type muscular dystrophy is the most common and severe form of muscular dystrophy. These patients present first with gait disturbances, including toe walking, waddling, or frequent falling. They also exhibit difficulty getting up from the floor and develop a compensatory lumbar lordosis. Muscle groups are generally nontender. Deep tendon reflexes are initially present but disappear later. Sensory examination result is normal. With increasing impairment, the patient requires braces and crutches to aid in standing. Later a wheelchair is required for continued mobility.

ED Considerations

Common health problems in children with this condition include fall-related injuries, pain, anxiety, and decreased pulmonary function. Weakness of respiratory muscles results in hypoventilation. Some children may require ventilatory support. Nursing care is dependent on the specific illness or injury that brings the patient to the emergency department. Management of pain and acute symptoms is all that can be offered, because there is no effective treatment or cure for muscular dystrophy. It is vital to listen to parents, because they know what usually helps their child. Braces should be removed during assessment and treatment. Family support is essential as this is a progressive and terminal disease.

Conclusion

Musculoskeletal conditions can be caused by trauma, infections, and congenital and acquired conditions. The goals in treatment are to preserve function, control pain, and prevent damage to joints or other musculoskeletal structures. Knowledge of common musculoskeletal conditions and normal pediatric growth and development will assist the nurse in caring for pediatric patients with musculoskeletal complaints.

References

1. Moore, K. L., & Persaud, T. V. N. (2008). *The developing human: Clinically oriented embryology* (8th ed., pp. 339–356). Philadelphia: Saunders.

2. Moore, K. L., & Persaud, T. V. N. (2008). *The developing human: Clinically oriented embryology* (8th ed., pp. 358–363). Philadelphia: Saunders.

3. Fleisher, G. R. (2006). Infectious disease emergencies. In G. Fleisher, S. Ludwig, & F. Henretig (Eds.), *Textbook of pediatric emergency medicine* (pp. 783–851). Philadelphia: Lippincott Willams & Wilkins.

4. Dich, P. Q., Nelson, J. D., & Haltallin, K. C. (1975). Osteomyelitis in infants and children: A review of 163 cases. A*merican Journal of Diseases of Children, 129,* 1273–1278.

5. Nelson, J. D. (1990). Acute osteomyelitis in children. *Infectious Disease Clinics of North America, 4,* 513–521.

6. Shaw, B. A., & Kasser, J. R. (1990). Acute septic arthritis in infancy and childhood. *Clinical Orthopedics, 1,* 212–225.

7. Singer, J. I. (1985). The cause of gait disturbance in 425 pediatric patients. *Pediatric Emergency Care, 1,* 7–10.

8. Lawrence, L. L. (1998). The limping child. *Emergency Medicine Clinics of North America, 16,* 911–922.

9. Sundel, R. P. (2006). Rheumatologic emergencies. In G. Fleisher, S. Ludwig, & F. Henretig (Eds.), *Textbook of pediatric emergency medicine* (pp. 1275–1317). Philadelphia: Lippincott Williams & Wilkins.

10. Cassidy, J. F., & Petty, R. E. (2006). Juvenile rheumatoid arthritis. In J. Cassidy & R. Petty (Eds.). *Textbook of pediatric rheumatology* (pp. 218–240). Philadelphia: Saunders.

11. Joffe, M. D., & Loisell, J. (2006). Orthopedic emergencies. In G. Fleisher, S. Ludwig, & F. Henretig (Eds.), *Textbook of pediatric emergency medicine* (pp. 1689–1716). Philadelphia: Lippincott Williams & Wilkins.

12. Gholve, P. A., Scher, D. M., & Khakharia, S. (2007). Osgood Schlatter syndrome. *Current Opinion in Pediatrics, 19,* 44–50.

13. Decker, J. M. (2006). Weakness/flaccid paralysis. In G. Fleisher, S. Ludwig, & F. Henretig (Eds.), *Textbook of pediatric emergency medicine* (pp. 1691–1700). Philadelphia: Lippincott Williams and Wilkins.

TWENTY

Dermatologic Emergencies

Sue M. Cadwell, RN, MSN, CNA-BC

Introduction

Rashes and skin disorders are frequent complaints of parents and children presenting to the emergency department (ED) and can be cause for concern. Petechial rashes are the most serious dermatologic problem seen in the emergency department, because they may signify the presence of a significant life-threatening illness, which may require rapid intervention.[1] Treatment is generally focused on eliminating the underlying cause of the skin condition and related discomfort or symptoms rather than treating the actual skin condition. Many skin conditions are self-limiting and require only symptomatic relief. However, in the immunosuppressed or chronically ill child they can have a more serious consequence.

A thorough assessment of the skin condition and other related symptoms are necessary to determine the urgency of the problem. The purpose of this chapter is to review common dermatologic conditions and outline their ED treatment.

Embryologic Development of the Integumentary System

The integumentary system consists of the skin and its appendages, which includes hair, nails, glands, mammary glands, and teeth. The skin itself is essentially composed of two layers. The superficial outer layer, the epidermis, is the thinner of the two. The inner layer, the dermis, is thicker connective tissue. These layers develop from two different germ cells: the ectoderm and the mesoderm.[2]

The skin is the largest organ of the body, covering all of the body's external surfaces. Its primary functions are to protect against environmental forces, but it is also the home of the sense of touch. The outer layer of skin begins as a single layer of ectodermal cells. In the beginning developmental stages, these cells form a multilayered ectoderm, and regional differences in structure and function begin to appear. Through the first and second trimesters, this growth continues in stages, contributing to the increase in epidermal thickness. By approximately 21 weeks gestation, the periderm disappears, and the more durable stratum cornium forms.

The epidermis develops into four basic layers. Where the skin is exposed to great friction, a fifth layer is also present. These layers are:

❑ *Stratum basale:* Deepest layer of the epidermis composed of cuboidal or columnar keratinocytes.

❑ *Stratum spinosum:* Eight to 10 layers of many-sided keratinocytes that fit closely together.

❑ *Stratum granulosum:* Middle of the epidermis consisting of three to five layers of flattened keratinocytes.

❑ *Stratum lucidum:* Present only in the skin of the fingertips, the palms of the hands, and soles of the feet.

❑ *Stratum corneum:* The outer 25 to 30 layers of flattened dead keratinocytes, which are continuously shed and replaced by cells from the deeper layers.

The dermis is the deepest part of the skin, composed mostly of connective tissue. The dermis is divided into two regions, which are:

❑ *The papillary region:* The superficial section of the dermis consisting of areolar connective tissue with elastic fibers. This section has papillae, which contain capillaries, corpuscles of touch, and free nerve endings.

❑ *The reticular region:* The deeper section of dermis, which consists of dense irregular connective tissue with bundles of collagen and coarse elastic fibers.[2]

Pediatric Considerations

Skin thickness is variable, depending on the child's age, gender, and the body location. At birth, all the structures within the skin are present, but many of the functions are immature. For example, the epidermis and dermis are loosely bound to each other and are very thin. Slight friction across the epidermis can cause separation of these layers and blister formation.[3] The skin's normal pH is acidic, presumably to ward off bacterial invasion, but the pH of the infant's skin is higher. This high skin pH, coupled with their thinner skin and minimal secretion of sweat and sebum, predisposes infants to dermatologic infections and conditions.

Etiology

Some of the most common dermatologic conditions presenting to the emergency department are caused by:

- Infections
  - Viral
  - Bacterial
  - Fungal
- Infestations (i.e., lice or mites)
- Insect bites (Chapter 41)

The following history, assessment and interventions are standard for most rashes seen in the emergency department.

Focused History

Patient history

- Exposure to potential allergen (drugs; poison oak, ivy, sumac; foods; soaps; perfumes; clothing not washed before use)
- Participation in organized sports activities (potential exposure to community-acquired methicillin-resistant Staphylococcus aureus)
- Recent exposure to persons with an infectious illness and rash
- Appearance of the skin lesions
  - Description
  - Manner of progression
  - Distribution
- Associated symptoms
  - Pain, itching, numbness
  - Fever or chills

- Difficulty breathing, chest tightness, or swelling of the back of throat and/or tongue
- Headache
- Neck pain
- Change in level of consciousness
- Change in appetite or fluid intake
- Noisy respirations or tachypnea
- Sore throat or cough
- Joint pain
- Vomiting or diarrhea

- Pertinent health history
  - Medications (prescribed, over-the-counter, herbal or dietary supplements)
  - Allergies (food, medication, and environmental)
  - Immunization status
  - Home treatments and their effectiveness (e.g., application of calamine lotion)

Family history

- Other family members or close contacts with similar illness and rash.
  - History of anaphylaxis, hypersensitivity reaction, or skin disorders

Focused Assessment

Physical Assessment

- Respiratory system.
  - Inspect the mouth and throat for:
    - Lesions. Note color and distribution.
    - Edema
    - Color of the mucosa
  - Auscultate the chest for:
    - Respiratory rate. Tachypnea may be present with fever.
    - Any abnormal lung sounds
- Cardiovascular system.
  - Auscultate the heart for:
    - Rate. Tachycardia may be present with fever or pain.
    - Murmurs
  - Measure the blood pressure.
  - Assess peripheral perfusion.
    - Palpate peripheral pulses.
    - Measure capillary refill.

- Inspect skin color and temperature.
❏ Neurologic system.
  ▪ AVPU (*A*lert, responds to *V*erbal commands, responds to *P*ainful stimulus, or *U*nresponsive) or Glasgow Coma Scale.
❏ Integumentary system.
  ▪ Inspect and describe the lesions (Table 20.1) or skin condition:
    • Size
    • Location
    • Color
    • Blisters, whiteheads, or pimples
    • Hard or soft centers or borders
    • Fluid or drainage
    • Crusting or healing
    • Configuration and distribution of lesions
    • Flat, raised, or rough
    • Circles with clear centers
    • Diffuse or blotchy
    • Bleeding or bruising under the skin
  ▪ Inspect the condition and color of surrounding skin and appendages.
    • Red streaks
    • Edema
    • Discoloration
    • Turgor
    • Nails
    • Hair
  ▪ Note any skin odor.
  ▪ Note the presence of scars, wounds, or bruises in varying stages of healing.
    • Unexplained surface trauma or bruises in varying stages of healing may be indicative of child maltreatment (Chapter 44).
    • Note the presence of keloids or surgical scars.

Psychosocial Assessment

❏ Assess the child and parents' understanding of the child's health condition.
❏ Assess the child's and parents' coping strategies.
  ▪ Parents are usually concerned about the cause and the contagiousness of the condition, and the potential seriousness of the problem. They may be concerned about the child's appearance and want relief from the uncomfortable or disfiguring symptoms.

TABLE 20.1 Primary Skin Lesions Encountered in Children

Lesion	Description	Example
Macule	Flat, nonpalpable, circumscribed. Discolored.	Freckles, flat moles, purpura
Patch	Flat, nonpalpable; irregular in shape	Vitiligo, port wine mark
Plaque	Raised, scaly lesion > 1 cm in diameter	Eczema, psoriasis
Wheal	Elevated area of irregularly shaped cutaneous edema	Urticaria, insect bites
Papule	Elevated, palpable, firm, circumscribed	Warts, pigmented nevi
Nodule	Similar to papule, but deeper in dermis	Lipomas, erythema nodosum
Vesicle	Elevated, circumscribed, superficial; < 1 cm in diameter	Blister, varicella
Bulla	Vesicle > 1 cm in diameter	Blister, pemphigus vulgaris
Pustule	Similar to vesicle, but filled with purulent fluid	Impetigo, acne
Cyst	Elevated, circumscribed, encapsulated. Filled with liquid or semisolid material	Sebaceous cyst

Notes: From Wilson.[3]

Children may have concerns about how others will react to their physical appearance.

  ▪ Because of the contagious nature of some dermatologic conditions or underlying systemic illness, children may have to cope with feelings of isolation and rejection.
❏ Assess for pain with age-appropriate pain scales and techniques (Chapter 11).

Triage Considerations

❏ Patients with suspected contagious rashes should be placed in a private room as soon as possible.
❏ Conditions that should be seen immediately (highest level of acuity).
  ▪ Children with signs of respiratory failure and shock or altered level of consciousness
  ▪ Neonates with petechial rashes
❏ Conditions that should be seen as soon as possible.

- Patients with lesions that are:
  - Red, blue, or purple
  - Purpuric
  - Petechial
  - Burn-like (scalded skin)
  - Tender to touch (cellulitis)
  - Red streaked
  - Pustular
- Patients with lesions and rashes that are suspected to be infectious
- Nonurgent conditions.
  - Patients with lesions that are not suspected to be infectious or are not associated with a life-threatening illness and have no other signs and symptoms of serious illness.

Nursing Interventions

1. Assess and maintain airway, breathing, and circulation.
   - Administer supplemental oxygen, as needed.
   - Initiate cardiorespiratory and oxygen saturation monitoring, as needed.
2. Obtain venous access and initiate an intravenous infusion, as needed.
   - Obtain blood for laboratory studies as needed, such as complete blood cell count and differential; cultures; sedimentation rate.
3. Administer medications, as prescribed.
   - Administer topical agents for relief of pain, itching, or discomfort.
   - Administer oral analgesics for relief of pain and discomfort (Chapter 11).
   - Administer oral or intramuscular antihistamines, as needed.
4. Obtain other laboratory studies, as needed.
   - Skin culture
   - Mucous membranes culture
5. Inform the family frequently of their child's condition; provide emotional and psychosocial support.
6. Prepare for hospitalization or discharge to home.
7. Observe universal precautions.

Home Care and Prevention

- The child and family should be taught the proper home management of the skin lesions, including the application of topical agents.
- Proper hand washing to prevent the spread of infection

should be demonstrated and discussed.
- Other methods for preventing the spread of infectious or contagious infestations, such as proper hygiene, should be reviewed.
- Education should include keeping vaccination status current.

Specific Dermatologic Conditions

Viral Infections of the Skin

Etiology

Viruses are intracellular parasites that are unable to sustain themselves or reproduce. Therefore, they are dependent on host cells to meet their metabolic needs. After they penetrate a host cell wall, the host is able to create additional virus material. The epidermal cells react to the viral infection through inflammation and vesiculation or may reproduce and form growths.

Viral skin conditions treated in the emergency department may include herpes simplex virus, varicella, rubeola, rubella, and roseola infantum. The incidence of chickenpox, measles, and rubella is low, though outbreaks can occur in undervaccinated populations.

Herpes Simplex Virus

There are two types of herpes simplex virus: type 1— a cold sore or fever blister, and type 2— a genital lesion. These classifications are not mutually exclusive. For example, a type 2 lesion can appear on the mouth, and a type 1 lesion can appear on the genitals. The virus affects children, adolescents, and adults and remains in the body after the first infection. Repeated outbreaks can occur after a cold, fever, or exposure to the sun, or during stressful times or menstruation. Sometimes lesions appear for no apparent reason. The virus may be fatal in immunocompromised children.

Symptoms of herpes simplex may include a stinging or prickling sensation at the site 1 to 2 days before the lesion appears. The lesions occur 2 to 30 days after contact with an infected person and appear as vesicular clusters first, which seep clear fluid, progressing to scab formation. The lesions heal in 1 to 2 weeks. Lesions can be treated with Burrow's solution during weeping stages. Topical therapy may also include penciclovir for cold sores to shorten their duration. Oral antiviral therapy (Acyclovir) may also be used in the initial infection or to reduce severity in recurrence.[4]

Varicella (Chickenpox)

Varicella, one of the most highly contagious infectious

diseases, is transmitted through the respiratory route. Varicella is caused by the herpes zoster virus and affects the skin and mucous membranes. It is believed that the virus resides in the roots of nerves near the spinal cord and may cause shingles later in life. Although the virus is most common in childhood, it affects all age groups. Children who are immunosuppressed as a result of chemotherapy, steroid therapy, or human immunodeficiency virus infection are at high risk for complications and fatality.

General malaise, fever, cough, abdominal pain, or cold symptoms may occur 3 days before an outbreak of lesions. The symptoms include a progressive rash, pruritus, and low-grade fever; these symptoms are less severe in children, are more problematic in adolescents, and can result in pneumonitis. Lesions appear mainly on the trunk, face, and extremities but can occur anywhere on the body. The lesions progress through several stages of raised red areas progressing to blisters and then scabs. Symptoms may persist for 1 to 3 weeks. The infected child is considered contagious 1 to 2 days before the onset of the rash and until all lesions are scabbed over (usually 10 days to 2 weeks) and no new lesions appear.

Treatment may include an antiviral agent (Acyclovir), with supportive diphenhydramine or antihistamines to relieve itching. Varicella-zoster immune globulin (VZIG) may be given to high-risk children after exposure.

Rubeola (Red Measles)

Rubeola is a serious and highly contagious illness caused by a paramyxovirus affecting the skin, eyes, and upper respiratory tract. The virus is most common in children, but all age groups are affected. Preexisting conditions that increase the risk of infection include crowded or unsanitary living conditions, unimmunized population groups, and measles epidemics.

A cough, congestion, conjunctivitis, fever, and Koplik's spots (tiny bluish-white spots) on the buccal mucosa occur 1 to 4 days before the rash appears. The rash appears as a generalized red rash on the forehead and ears, spreading to the trunk and extremities. The rash may be blotchy or irregular, flat or raised. Symptoms may last 3 to 4 days. Rubeola is no longer contagious after the rash is resolved, so the child should be isolated from other children for 4 days after the rash appears. Treatment may include antipyretics to control fever.

Rubella (German Measles; 3-day Measles)

Rubella is a mild, contagious viral illness involving the skin on the face, trunk, and extremities and the lymph glands behind the ears and in the neck. It is most common in springtime. This virus can cause serious birth defects if a pregnant woman is infected with the virus during the first 3 to 4 months of pregnancy.

Enlarged lymph nodes, fever, sore throat, headache, and malaise occur 1 to 3 days before the onset of the rash. The rash is a flat reddish rash, appearing first on the face and spreading to the trunk and extremities. The rash lasts 2 to 3 days, and the infected child is contagious 1 week before the onset of the rash and 1 week after the rash fades. Rubella is typically treated with antipyretics to control fever and analgesics to control discomfort.

Bacterial Infections of the Skin

Etiology

The skin normally harbors bacterial flora, including staphylococci and streptococci. The ability for these organisms to cause infection is related to the specific portal of entry, the number of microorganisms, the virulence of the organism, and host resistance. Children who are immunosuppressed or who have debilitating conditions or a generalized malignancy are at risk for bacterial infections. Infections affecting the skin range from a localized and self-limiting lesion to a generalized systemic illness that manifests skin lesions or problems. Common bacterial dermatologic conditions among children presenting to the emergency department are outlined below.

Abscess

An abscess is a localized collection of pus under the skin that causes fluctuant soft tissue swelling surrounded by erythema. The abscess may be accompanied by local cellulitis, lymphangitis, and fever. Cutaneous abscesses most commonly occur when *Staphylococcus aureus (S. aureus)*, Staphylococcus epidermidis, or Streptococcus (group A) enters the skin through a hair follicle or break in the skin. The causative organism is determined by the location of the abscess and is reflective of the type of microflora of the skin and mucous membranes. Predisposing factors to abscess formation include diminished host defense mechanisms; trauma; foreign bodies; tissue ischemia or breakdown; hematoma or excessive fluid accumulation in the tissue; and sharing of needles, licking of needles, and use of poor injection technique by intravenous drug users.

Recent literature has identified an increase in community-acquired *S. aureus* (CA-MRSA [Chapter 24]) in cultures of soft tissue infections in emergency departments.[5] This increase in the incidence of CA-MRSA is concerning, as some atypical systemic infections requiring hospitalization that may include intensive care have also been attributed to these bacteria.[6]

Abscesses are located most often in the axillary, vulvovaginal, perirectal, head and neck, and buttock areas. A widespread abscess involving several pus-draining ports is usually located in the axilla or groin and involves the sweat glands. Such abscesses respond well to antibiotic therapy.

Boils (Furuncles)

Boils are common, contagious inflammatory nodules that arise from hair follicles. They occur only in hair-bearing parts of the body but are most prevalent on the head, neck, axillae, buttocks, and groin. The red, hard lesion becomes tender and fluctuant over a couple of days. Pain subsides after the lesion discharges pus and a central plug of necrotic material. The infection is usually caused by *S. aureus* that begins in the hair follicle and spreads to the skin's deeper layers. Predisposing factors include friction, moisture, obesity, immunosuppression, colonization by *S. aureus,* poor nutrition, diabetes mellitus, and diminished host defense mechanisms.

Without treatment, the boil may heal in 10 to 20 days. If the boil opens spontaneously, the draining pus may contaminate surrounding skin and cause new boils. Incision and drainage of the boil and administration of antibiotics is the recommended treatment. Symptoms should resolve within 3 to 4 days after treatment.

Cellulitis

Cellulitis is a noncontagious acute infection of the skin and subcutaneous tissues that may occur spontaneously or may secondarily complicate a preexisting wound or other inflammatory process. It generally appears as a diffuse area (5–20 cm) of erythema and warmth, which may be accompanied by red streaks from the area toward the heart. Cellulitis occurs most commonly on the face and lower legs. The infecting organisms are usually staphylococcal and streptococcal organisms or oral-based organisms, such as anaerobic streptococci or *Pasteurella multocida*. Predisposing factors for cellulitis include the use of immunosuppressive or cortisone medications, chronic infection, diminished host defense mechanisms, or any injury or condition that breaks the skin barrier. Symptoms resolve within 7 to 10 days after antibiotic treatment.

Impetigo

Impetigo is a common, highly contagious bacterial infection almost always due to S. aureus but sometimes also due to group B *ß-hemolytic streptococcus* that affects the superficial layers of the skin.[7] It is most prevalent in infants and young children, and it primarily affects the face, arms, leg, or areas of trauma. Predisposing factors for impetigo include a fair complexion, skin sensitive to sun and irritants, poor nutrition, unsanitary living conditions, warm and moist weather, poor hygiene, and diminished host defense mechanisms. The rash appears as a red rash with many small blisters, which form honey-colored crusts after they break.

The symptoms resolve in 10 days after oral or topical treatment; however, scarring may result. Lesions are considered contagious until 24 hours from completion of antibiotic treatment.

Scarlatina (Scarlet Fever)

Scarlatina is a contagious bacterial infection caused by group A *ß-hemolytic streptococci*. This condition is preceded by a streptococcal throat infection and is characterized by a bright red rash, which blanches on pressure and may resemble a sunburn with small bumps. The infection is spread through respiratory secretions. Scarlatina is most prevalent in children between the ages of 2 and 10 years. Predisposing factors include a family history of recurrent streptococcal infections or impetigo, unsanitary living conditions, and exposure to others with sore throats. Treatment consists of antibiotic therapy and treatment to relieve itching.

Staphylococcal Scalded Skin Syndrome

Staphylococcal scalded skin syndrome is an acute bacterial infection that causes the skin to separate and peel off in sheets when touched. A widespread erythematous process that results in the loss of the protective skin barrier, it is caused by group II coagulase-positive staphylococci. The organism produces an exotoxin and colonizes without overt infection. It appears as crusted lesions on the face, neck, axilla, or groin, which progress into large flaccid blisters that break easily, producing skin erosions.

The colonized person can spread the organism through direct contact, so contact precautions need to be observed. In this disease, the upper layer of the skin splits, allowing the toxin to enter the circulation and affect the skin systemically. Staphylococcal scalded skin syndrome is most prevalent among infants, small children younger than 6 years of age, and immunosuppressed adults. The staphylococcus organism can pass from infant to infant in nurseries and usually affects the umbilical stump or the area under the diaper during the first few days of life. In young children, crusted lesions appear initially around the nose or ear. Healing occurs 5 to 7 days after treatment with antibiotics.

Fungal Infections of the Skin

Etiology

Superficial fungal infections are classified as dermatophyte infections and yeast infections. Candidiasis and tinea (ringworm) are two of the most common fungal infections. Both conditions require a suitable environment for infection to occur. Decreased resistance, immunosuppression, diabetes, antineoplastic agents, corticosteroids, and use of potent antibiotics all contribute to the incidence of infection. A moist, warm environment and skin irritation lead to increased susceptibility to infection.

Candidiasis (Moniliasis)

Candidiasis is a contagious yeast infection caused by *Candida albicans,* which is found in the intestinal tract and vagina. Candidiasis affects folds of contiguous skin or adjacent areas of skin that come in contact with each other. The yeast changes from its spore form to the mycelial phase when the skin is damaged and the environment is moist and warm. Its incidence is greatest among infants wearing wet and soiled diapers for prolonged periods of time. However, candidiasis affects older children and adolescents in folds of skin. Oral lesions (thrush), which appear as white plaque on the tongue, esophagus, or trachea, are common in infants.

Common locations for candidiasis are the diaper area; the groin; under the breasts; the folds of skin in scrotal, vaginal, and axillary areas; the inner thighs; the base of the spine; and webs between fingers and toes. In most instances, the lesions appear as red moist papules. A thick, white, cheesy discharge may be present with vaginal lesions.

Candidiasis easily spreads to other areas of the body and from person to person with direct contact. Predisposing factors include thumb sucking, obesity, an uncircumcised penis, antibiotic and steroid use, diabetes, poor nutrition, excessive sweating, and crowded and unsanitary conditions. Treatment consists of application of topical antifungals.

Tinea (Ringworm)

Tinea is a contagious infection that varies in presentation, depending on anatomic location. In general, tinea infections are red and scaly, with well-defined margins and a clear center. The name, tinea, followed by the anatomic location, is used to identify the type of infection:

- Tinea corporis—chest, back, neck, and shoulders
- Tinea capitis—scalp
- Tinea pedis—foot (athlete's foot)
- Tinea cruris—groin (jock itch)
- Tinea unguium—nails
- Tinea barbae—skin and beard

Tinea infections are caused by a group of closely related, filamentous fungi (*Microsporum, Trichophyton,* and *Epidermophyton*) that are transmitted from person to person or animal to person through direct contact. They live in the outer layers of the skin and must multiply rapidly for infection to occur before the dead cells are removed through the normal sloughing process. The infection may also spread from one area of the body to another. Transmission may occur through contact with infected surfaces, such as towels, shoes, hats, or shower stalls. Predisposing factors include prolonged exposure to dark, moist, and warm conditions; overcrowded and unsanitary conditions; obesity; excessive sweating; and friction of the skin against skin with constant movement. Treatment consists of oral or topical antifungals.

Infestations of the Skin

Etiology

Lice and scabies are two of the most common contagious infestations. They cause severe itching and are at times difficult to eradicate. Treatment of the infected person, other family members with symptoms, and clothing and linens is essential to prevent reinfection after treatment.

Pediculosis

Pediculosis includes head lice and body lice (crabs), which are most prevalent in children 4 to 12 years of age. Lice are tiny (3 to 4 mm), blood-sucking parasites; while feeding, they discharge their products of digestion into the skin, causing a severe pruritic response. Lice are difficult to see, except in the groin, where hair distribution is lighter. The presence of eggs (nits) on the hair shaft and complaints of itching are clues to infestation and may be accompanied by red bite marks and hives. The severity of itching correlates to the number of lice and their bites. Matted hair and scalp inflammation indicate a severe infection that may require the hair to be cut if the hair shafts cannot be separated for proper treatment. Lice can live up to 3 days without human contact and are transmitted person to person through direct contact or sharing of clothing, hats, brushes, and combs. Predisposing factors include crowded and unsanitary conditions, exposure to other household members with lice, and sexual contact with an infected person.

Symptoms should resolve within 5 days after treatment; however, lice frequently recur. Treatment includes applying a pediculicide shampoo, taking care not to splash it into the eyes. In addition, all washable clothing, towels, and bed linens must be washed in hot water and dried in a hot dryer for at least 20 minutes. Nonwashable items should be sealed in plastic bags for 14 days if they cannot be washed or vacuumed. All combs, brushes, and hair accessories must be soaked in lice-killing products for 1 hour or in boiling water for 10 minutes. Children should be taught to avoid sharing hair care items, hats, and scarves.[4]

Scabies

Scabies is a contagious skin infection caused by the mite *Sarcoptes scabiei.* Scabies is transmitted through close personal contact and causes severe pruritus because of acquired sensitivity to the organism. The scabies mite can live up to 3 days without human contact. The female mite burrows deep into the skin layers to deposit eggs. The eggs mature into mites in 15 to 60 days and can only be seen through a microscope. Scratching collects the mites and eggs under the nails and spreads the mites to other areas of the body. The skin of the finger webs, wrists, and skin folds under the arms, breasts, elbows, genitals, and buttocks often is involved. The lesions appear as small, itchy blisters that easily break, leaving a characteristic S-shaped distribution pattern or scratch marks and thickened skin. Predisposing factors include crowded and unsanitary conditions, infection with the human immunodeficiency virus, and Down syndrome.

Symptoms usually resolve within 1 to 2 weeks after treatment. Treatment includes application of a scabicide cream or lotion according to directions. On occasion, an oral medication (ivermectin) is administered in cases of severe or refractory scabies, or in children who cannot tolerate a scabicide.[4] Re-treatment may be necessary in 20 days if skin irritation persists.

Conclusion

The treatment of dermatologic conditions almost always requires the support and assistance of family members. In today's emergency department, nurses must be extremely vigilant in observing universal precautions. MRSA can easily be spread by physical contact, as well as contact with items that have not been appropriately cleaned. Except for a few urgent conditions or complications, most dermatologic conditions are safely managed at home. The nurse plays a vital role in educating the child and parent about the condition, management of the treatment regimen at home, expected outcomes, and when to seek medical attention (if the condition worsens, complications occur, or the condition fails to improve with treatment).

Additionally, emergency nurses can teach self-care to older children and involve them in planning treatment schedules. Finally, children and families should be taught simple methods, such as hand washing, for preventing the spread of infection to other body parts or to other people.

References

1. Rosenkrans, J. A. (2002). Petechiae and purpura. In G. R. Strange, W. R. Ahrens, S. Lelyveld, & R. W. Schafermeyer (Eds.), *Pediatric emergency medicine: A comprehensive study guide* (2nd ed., pp. 439–443). New York: McGraw-Hill.

2. Chamley, C. A. (2005). Development of the integumentary system. In C. A. Chamley, P. Carson, & D. Randall (Eds.), *Developmental anatomy and physiology of children: A practical approach* (pp. 37–57). New York: Elsevier Churchill Livingstone.

3. Wilson, D. (2005). Health promotion of the newborn and family. In M. J. Hockenberry (Ed.), *Wong's essentials of pediatric nursing* (7th ed., pp. 175–221). St. Louis, MO: Mosby.

4. Winkelstein, M. L. (2005). The child with integumentary dysfunction. In M. J. Hockenberry (Ed.), *Wong's essentials of pediatric nursing* (7th ed., pp. 1095–1146). St. Louis, MO: Mosby.

5. Olsevich, M., & Kennedy, A. (2007). Emergence of community-acquired methicillin-resistant staphylococcus aureus soft tissue infections. *Journal of Pediatric Surgery, 42,* 765–768.

6. Stankovic, C., & Mahajan, P. V. (2006). Healthy children with invasive community-acquired methicillin-resistant staphylococcus aureus infections. *Pediatric Emergency Care, 22*(5), 361–363.

7. Brennan, P. O. (2003). Dermatological emergencies. In P. O. Brennan, K. Berry, & C. Powell (Eds.), *Handbook of pediatric emergency medicine* (pp. 173–181). London: Informa Healthcare.

TWENTY-ONE

Eye, Ear, Nose, and Throat Emergencies

Donna Ojanen Thomas, RN, MSN

Introduction

Children are brought to emergency departments (EDs) with a variety of eye, ear, nose, and throat (EENT) complaints. These conditions can be the result of:

- ❑ Trauma
- ❑ Exposure to a chemical
- ❑ Infectious organisms
- ❑ Congenital problems
- ❑ Foreign bodies

Traumatic and infectious conditions are the most common EENT complaints treated in the emergency department. Acute otitis media is the most common infection for which antibiotics are prescribed in children, resulting in more than 20 million antibiotic prescriptions annually.[1]

Depending on the presentation and diagnosis, children may be evaluated and treated in the emergency department, require examination and evaluation by an EENT specialist, and/or require surgical intervention and admission. The purpose of this chapter is to discuss specific EENT conditions seen in the emergency department and their assessment and treatment.

Embryologic Development

Eyes

Eye formation is first evident at the beginning of the fourth week of development.[2] The eyelids meet and adhere by about the 10th week and remain adherent until the 26th week. Myelination of the optic nerve fibers, incomplete at birth, is completed after the eyes have been exposed to light for about 10 weeks. The normal newborn can see but not well; he or she is able to fixate points of contrast.

Because of the complexity of eye development, many anomalies may occur, but most of them are uncommon. The eyes and ears are sensitive to the teratogenic effects of infectious agents; the most serious defects result from disturbances of development during the fourth to sixth weeks. Most common anomalies of the eye are related to defects in closure of the retinal fissure, which normally closes during the sixth week. Congenital ptosis (drooping) of the eyelid is a fairly common anomaly.

Ears

The ear consists of three anatomic parts: external, middle, and internal. The development of the ear begins in the fourth week of gestation. The internal (middle) ear is the first to develop and reaches its adult size and shape by the middle of the fetal period (20 to 22 weeks). Parts of the external and middle ear are not fully developed until puberty.

There are many minor abnormalities of the auricle of the ear, but they may be indicative of associated major anomalies (heart or kidneys). Low-set, severely malformed ears are often associated with chromosomal abnormalities, particularly trisomy 18, and in infants affected by maternal ingestions of certain drugs.[2] Congenital deafness can result from abnormal development of the membranous labyrinth and/or bony labyrinth, as well as from abnormalities of the auditory ossicle.[2] Recessive inheritance is the most common cause, but a rubella virus infection near the end of the embryonic period is also known to cause defective hearing.

Structures of the Nose and Throat

Major structures of the face and palate develop between the fourth and eighth weeks of embryonic development. Because of the complicated development, congenital anomalies of the face and palate are common and result from an arrest of development and/or a failure of fusion of the prominences and processes involved. The ethmoid and maxillary sinuses are the first to develop and are present at birth.

Pediatric Considerations

Eyes

The newborn cannot see very well but can fixate points of contrast. Visual acuity has been estimated to be in the range of 20/400. Because the oculomotor system is immature in the newborn and vision and fixation are poor, strabismus is common and usually resolves by 4 to 5 months of age.[2] The lacrimal glands are small and do not function at birth; therefore, for about 1 to 3 months the newborn does not produce tears with crying.[2]

Ears

The external auditory meatus is short at birth, and care must be taken not to injure the tympanic membrane during examination of the ear. The shortness of this meatus also results in a greater likelihood of ear infections because bacteria can easily reach the inner ear and secretions cannot efficiently drain from the middle ear. The external acoustic meatus attains its adult length around the ninth year.

Structures of the Nose and Throat

Most of the paranasal sinuses are rudimentary or absent in newborn infants. The maxillary sinuses are small at birth; they grow slowly until puberty and are not developed until all the permanent teeth have erupted in early adulthood.[3] The frontal and sphenoidal sinuses are not present at birth. The ethmoidal cells are small before the age of 2 years, and they do not begin to grow rapidly until 6 to 8 years of age. Around 2 years of age, the frontal sinuses are formed. They are visible in radiographs by the seventh year. Growth of the paranasal sinuses is important in altering the size and shape of the face during infancy and childhood and in adding resonance to the voice during adolescence. Adenoidal tissue is present in infants and young children and can obstruct the eustachian tubes when inflamed. This tissue usually atrophies by puberty.

Focused History

For all EENT complaints, the following history should be obtained:

- ❐ Onset and duration of symptoms
- ❐ History including current infections, previous surgeries
- ❐ Discharge from eyes, ears, nose
- ❐ Possibility of foreign body insertion
- ❐ Recent exposure to infectious conditions
- ❐ Preexisting conditions (Congenital or Acquired)
- ❐ Fever

Focused Assessment

Physical Assessment

Assessment findings will vary with the condition, and specific assessment findings will be discussed in the sections under individual conditions. All children should receive the following assessment.

- ❐ Assess the airway.
  - Patency—some eent complaints may cause airway obstruction (epistaxis, abscesses)
- ❐ Assess breathing.
  - Respiratory rate
  - Effort
  - Adventitious sounds
  - Quality of breath sounds
- ❐ Assess circulation. Signs and symptoms of shock may be present with prolonged epistaxis or in conditions where the child has had poor oral intake related to pain.
  - Skin color (pallor, mottling, or cyanosis)
  - Heart rate (tachycardia or bradycardia)
  - Capillary refill time
- ❐ Assess neurologic status.
  - Level of consciousness
    - Restlessness or fatigue
    - Changes in mental status: confusion or inability to recognize caregiver

Psychosocial Assessment

Children with eent problems may be difficult to assess and treat because of their anxiety and fear. Parents may be concerned about loss of function and permanent damage to the affected area. Treatment should be explained to the child, as age appropriate, and to the parent or caregiver. The child may be very self-conscious about his or her appearance because some eent conditions, especially those affecting the eye, can be disfiguring.

Nursing Interventions

The following interventions may be necessary. Additional interventions are included under specific conditions.

1. Assess and maintain airway, breathing, and circulation.

   - Administer oxygen by a method best tolerated by the child and one that will deliver the highest concentration, such as a pediatric nonrebreather mask for severe respiratory distress.

   - Allow the child to maintain a position of comfort.

   - Ensure that pediatric emergency airway and ventilation equipment is available.

2. Monitor vital signs.

3. Monitor pulse oximetry.

4. Encourage oral fluids or provide intravenous fluids as ordered for children with signs and symptoms of shock or dehydration.

5. Administer medication as needed (antibiotics, pain medication, fever management).

6. Perform frequent reassessments of the following:

   - Airway

   - Breathing

   - Circulation

   - Vital signs

7. Keep parents informed of the child's condition, assessment findings, and reasons for interventions.

8. Prepare the child and parents for admission, surgical intervention, and/or transfer to a pediatric facility (Chapter 8).

Triage Considerations

- ❒ Triaged as needing to be seen immediately:

   - Conjunctivitis in the neonate. Neonates with conjunctivitis should be presumed to have gonorrhea conjunctivitis until proved otherwise and are at risk for spontaneous corneal perforation.[4]

   - Loss of vision or abrupt changes in visual acuity

   - Periorbital swelling with signs and symptoms of sepsis or restricted eye movement; suspected or confirmed orbital cellulitis

   - Severe pain

   - Severe and prolonged epistaxis

   - Signs and symptoms of shock or respiratory distress with any EENT complaint

   - Foreign body in the throat or airway that is causing or has the potential of causing airway compromise

- ❒ Triaged as needing to be seen as soon as possible:

   - Acute pain

   - Patients with disk batteries lodged in the esophagus or inserted into the ear or nose should be seen as soon as possible because of the risk of erosion and leakage of the battery acid and immediately if causing respiratory compromise.

   - Periorbital swelling without signs and symptoms of sepsis

- ❒ Triaged as not urgent:

   - Minor symptoms in a child who is awake, alert, and afebrile and without sensory deficits

   - Ear checks

Specific Conditions of the Eye

Conjunctivitis

Conjunctivitis is inflammation of the normally clear conjunctiva. There are a number of causes requiring different treatments.

- ❒ Bacterial infections-cause of a large number of cases in children beyond the neonatal period. Table 21.1 lists common bacterial causes of conjunctivitis, and Table 21.2 lists causes and signs and symptoms of nonbacterial causes.

- ❒ Viral infections-more common in older children. The course is usually self-limited and resolves in 10 days. Common pathogens include adenovirus, enterovirus, and herpes simplex virus.

- ❒ Allergies-noninfectious and seasonal conjunctivitis are caused by an allergy to an unknown allergen.

- ❒ Other-causes of conjunctivitis include:

   - Trauma

   - Foreign body

   - Chemical irritants

   - Systemic infections such as rubella and Kawasaki syndrome

The patient's age is often useful in determining a diagnosis. Neonates presenting in the first 3 days of life can have a chemical conjunctivitis caused by silver nitrate used for prophylaxis against gonorrhea, but most hospitals currently use erythromycin ointment.[4]

The time of onset of symptoms after birth can help identify the causative agent.[5] Bacterial conjunctivitis caused by Chlamydia (most common) can occur in 5 to 14 days, whereas that caused by *Neisseria gonorrhoeae* occurs in 2 to 5 days. Gonococcal conjunctivitis is considered a medical emergency because the infection can

TABLE 21.1 Causes and Clinical Features of Bacterial Conjunctivitis

Type of Bacteria	Comments/Clinical Features
Streptococcus pneumoniae *Haemophilus influenzae*	Both of these are common pathogens in children. Symptoms include mild redness and irritation, gritty sensation with tearing in one or both eyes. Since the Haemophilus vaccine (HIB), *H. influenzae* conjunctivitis is not as common.
Neisseria gonorrhoeae	Common cause of conjunctivitis in newborns. Occurs within 2 to 5 days of birth if it is contracted during the birth process. This infection can also develop in adolescents who are sexually active. Signs and symptoms include mucopurulent discharge, unilateral or bilateral.
Pseudomonas	Common cause of conjunctivitis in contact lens wearers.
Chlamydia	Commonly seen in neonates and infants and is usually acquired during the birth process. Conjunctivitis will develop in 50% of infants born to women with vaginal Chlamydia, which may lead to infections in the nasopharynx and lungs. Usually occurs on day 5 to 14 of the child's life. Signs and symptoms include mild to moderate pain, purulent discharge that can be unilateral or bilateral.

TABLE 21.2 Causes, Signs and Symptoms of Nonbacterial Conjunctivitis

Type	Common Pathogens/Cause	Signs and Symptoms
Viral	Adenovirus	Mild to moderate pain, itching eyes, excessive tearing Bilateral symptoms Watery discharge
	Herpes simplex virus	Fever blisters on lips or face Vesicles on eyelids and herpetic lesions on the cornea
Allergic	Known or unknown allergens	Redness of eyes, without pain Bilateral, stringy white discharge Clear watery nasal discharge Chemosis (edema of conjunctiva) Intense pruritus No change in vision
Chemical	Eye irritation such as smoke, silver nitrate instillation in newborns	Eyelid swelling, red conjunctiva, mild purulent drainage

spread to the cornea, producing corneal ulceration and perforation.[6] Herpes simplex virus is a less common cause in the neonatal period.

In children beyond the neonatal period, conjunctivitis is the most common eye disorder and bacterial infections are the most common causes.[5] Bacteria most commonly responsible are *Haemophilus influenzae* (*H. influenzae*), *Streptococcus pneumoniae* (*S. pneumoniae*), and *Staphylococcus aureus* (*S. aureus*). The most common viruses are adenovirus and herpes simplex virus type 1.

Pathophysiology

Conjunctivitis is an inflammatory condition of the membrane that lines the eyelids and covers the exposed surface of the sclera.[7] It is often referred to as "pinkeye" and is one of the most common causes of inflammatory red eye. Conjunctivitis causes vasodilation, migration of inflammatory cells to the affected eye, pain, and tearing. Complications can be severe if the cornea is infected. These complications can include corneal scarring, perforation, or necrosis, leading to permanent blindness or loss of the eye itself. Conjunctivitis may be unilateral or bilateral.

Focused History

❑ Onset and duration of symptoms, such as tearing, itching, burning, and/or red eyes

❑ Recent upper respiratory tract infection or ear infection

❑ Discharge from the eyes (varies with different causes)

❑ Recent exposure to pinkeye

❑ Recurrent symptoms

Focused Assessment

❑ Assess the eye for the following signs and symptoms:

  ▪ Irritated, red eye or infected conjunctiva

  ▪ Tearing, discharge, and pain

  ▪ Severe pain is often associated with herpetic conjunctivitis

  ▪ Tearing, blisterlike swelling of the conjunctiva with itching—usually allergic conjunctivitis

  ▪ Involvement of one or both eyes

  ▪ Photophobia—may be present with infections involving the cornea

  ▪ Assess visual acuity, if necessary. (Vision is not generally affected.)

Nursing Interventions

1. Administer medications as ordered, such as antibiotics (usually eye drops) and pain medications.

2. Because conjunctivitis is so contagious, antibiotics should be instilled in both eyes, even if only one eye is involved, to prevent the transfer of the infection from one eye to the other. To instill eye drops, the following process is helpful:[4]

  ▪ Pull down the lower eyelid and place the drop in the inferior fornix.

  ▪ In resistant children, gently force the eyelid open to expose a small strip of the palpebral conjunctiva, and place a drop in the exposed area.

  ▪ Alternatively, place the eye drop in the sulcus between the medial canthus and the side of the bridge of the nose while the patient is in the supine position.

  ▪ Some of the drop is often expelled on blinking after instillation but the procedure does not need to be repeated, as only approximately 20% of an eye drop is actually absorbed for use.

3. Allergic conjunctivitis may also be treated with antihistamines and topical decongestants.

4. Viral conjunctivitis antibiotics are not needed.

5. Offer comfort measures, to include a darkened room or environment.

6. Newborns-ophthalmic consultation should be done.

7. Some guidelines in the use of medications for treating conjunctivitis include:[4]

  ▪ No topical drugs should be used in patients with contact lenses without consultation of an ophthalmologist.

  ▪ Topical anesthetics should not be prescribed for outpatient use because prolonged use can result in corneal ulcerations.

  ▪ Steroids should never be prescribed by the ED physician. Inappropriate use may lead to glaucoma, cataracts, and increased severity of a corneal viral infection or rebound symptoms when the drug is discontinued.

  ▪ Solutions should be instilled before ointments, if both are used.

Home Care and Prevention

❑ Instruct the parent on the following:

  ▪ Symptomatic treatment measures, such as warm compresses.

  ▪ The extremely contagious nature of the condition: Eye secretions are contagious for 24 to 48 hours after the patient begins taking antibiotics.

  ▪ How to cleanse matted eyelids by wiping from the inner corner to outer corner of eye with a wet cotton ball and warm water.

  ▪ The proper method of instilling ophthalmic medications, to the inner aspect of lower lid.

  ▪ Proper hand-washing techniques and the importance of hand washing to prevent further spread of infection.

Cellulitis

Cellulitis is an acute inflammatory process of the skin and subcutaneous structures. Generally, there is some type of trauma to the skin that provides a portal of entry for invading organisms, but cellulitis may develop in normal skin. There are two types of cellulitis that affect the face:

❑ Orbital (postseptal). Orbital cellulitis is an acute inflammation of the orbital contents posterior to the orbital septum.[8]

  ▪ Deeper and more serious infection behind the septum, involving posterior eye structures

  ▪ May form an abscess and need to be surgically drained

  ▪ Generally seen more often in older children; the

average age is 12 years

❑ Periorbital (preseptal). Periorbital cellulitis is an acute infection and inflammation involving the eyelid and the surrounding tissue anterior to the orbital septum without involvement of the eye or orbital contents:[8]

- More common than orbital cellulitis
- Soft tissue infection of anterior eye structures usually localized to the eyelids and conjunctiva
- Seen more commonly in younger children; the average age is 21 months

Periorbital and orbital cellulitis are serious conditions because of the proximity of the infection to the brain. The most common etiologic agents of cellulitis are *S. aureus, S. pneumoniae,* and *H. influenzae.* The risk of cellulitis caused by an anaerobic organism is increased if there is a history of a human bite. *H. influenzae* type B is less common since the HIB vaccine. In infants, group B streptococcal infection should be considered.

Pathophysiology

Orbital cellulitis results from an extension of an infection in the paranasal or ethmoid sinuses. A pathogen is isolated in only about 30% of cases.[8] Common pathogens include:[5]

❑ *S. pneumoniae*

❑ Nontypeable *H. influenzae*

❑ Group *A streptococcus*

❑ *S. aureus*

In periorbital cellulitis, bacteria invade the periorbital tissues, resulting in the accumulation of inflammatory cells and fluid. Infections in the periorbital area are usually secondary to skin pathogens (often related to trauma) and are often associated with soft tissue injuries such as insect bites or the spread of local infection caused by impetigo, hordeolum, or chalazion. Primary bacteremia can also be a cause of periorbital cellulitis but is rare because of effective vaccination against *S. pneumoniae* and *H. influenzae.* Special consideration should be given to immunosuppressed children and those with diabetes, because they may have a fungal infection that may require surgical débridement.[7]

Focused History

❑ Onset and duration of symptoms

❑ History of sinus, dental, or upper respiratory tract infections

❑ Trauma or a preexisting wound to the affected area, such as a puncture wound or a bug bite

❑ History of systemic symptoms, such as fever, chills, and/or malaise

❑ Preexisting conditions

Focused Assessment

It can be difficult to clinically distinguish between orbital and periorbital cellulitis in children. Because of the seriousness of orbital cellulitis, it must be confirmed or ruled out. General signs and symptoms may include:

❑ Orbital cellulitis

- Erythema, warmth, tenderness
- Swollen eyelids that usually do not extend beyond the superior orbital rim onto the brow
- Pain
- Decreased eye movement
- Proptosis (bulging eye)
- Decreased vision
- Papilledema
- May have signs and symptoms of systemic illness

❑ Periorbital cellulitis

- Erythema, warmth, tenderness
- Pain
- Fever may be present.
- Swollen eyelids
- Bilateral swelling with allergic reaction
- No restriction of eye movement
- May have signs of skin trauma or bug bite

Nursing Interventions

1. Test visual acuity.

2. Prepare patient for laboratory studies and possible computed tomographic (CT) scan (to help differentiate between orbital and periorbital cellulitis).

3. Obtain intravenous access or saline lock to administer antibiotics as ordered.

4. Explain any procedures such as laboratory tests or radiographs to the child in understandable terms.

5. Children less than 2 years of age who have signs of systemic illness should be admitted for parenteral antibiotics and close observations.

6. A full septic workup should be considered before antibiotics are given in the toxic-appearing child.[5]

7. Anticipate surgical or ophthalmologic consultation for orbital cellulitis. All children with orbital cellulitis must be given treatment with intravenous antibiotics.[4]

8. Children with periorbital antibiotics may be given treatment with oral antibiotics and, if no improvement,

will be admitted for intravenous antibiotics.

9. If close follow-up cannot be assured, admission may be necessary.

10. Explain all treatments to the patient and family.

Home Care and Prevention

❏ Provide the following home care instructions:

  ▪ Maintain good general hygiene and carefully cleanse cuts and abrasions that occur near the orbit to prevent orbital cellulitis.

  ▪ Apply cool compresses every 3 to 4 hours to relieve discomfort and inflammation.

  ▪ Continue medication until gone.

  ▪ Discuss symptoms that would require the child to return to the emergency department:

    • Increased fever

    • Increased area of involvement

    • Vision changes

    • No improvement in symptoms

Chalazia and Styes

Chalazia (internal hordeola) and styes (external hordeola) represent blocked glands within the eyelid.[4] More than one lesion may occur at the same time and more than one lid may be involved.

Pathophysiology

A chalazion usually results from obstruction of a meibomian gland of the upper and lower eyelid. The inflammation causes secretions from glands to form a subcutaneous nodule or lipogranuloma. The surrounding tissues may become secondarily infected. Small chalazia may improve and resolve without any treatment. If the chalazion is not treated and continues to increase in size, it may cause pressure on the eye globe, causing astigmatism.

A stye is an acute, localized inflammation of one or more sebaceous glands of the eyelids or eyelashes. Usually there is a tender lump that forms a furuncle. The furuncle often ruptures spontaneously. The cause is often staphylococcus.[8]

Focused History

❏ Previous episodes and treatment-patients have often had recurrent lesions in the same or both eyes

❏ Presence of pain and tenderness of the eyelid

❏ Vision changes

❏ Feeling of pressure on the eye globe because of the nodule

Focused Assessment

Assessment findings include:

❏ Both styes and chalazia may present with localized lid swelling, erythema, and tenderness.

❏ Styes are associated with swelling and purulent drainage at or near the lid margin.

Nursing Interventions

If chalazia are small, chronic, and asymptomatic, they generally do not require treatment and spontaneously disappear within a few months.

Home Care and Prevention[4]

The treatment for both chalazia and styes is the same.

❏ Eyelash scrubs once or twice daily with baby shampoo will help to establish drainage. Baby shampoo should be applied to a washcloth and then used to scrub the base of the eyelashes.

❏ Warm compresses are useful but rarely tolerated by young children.

❏ Antibiotics usually are not helpful, but a topical antibiotic ointment may be prescribed.

❏ If the lesion has not improved in 4 weeks, an ophthalmic consultation may be necessary.

Specific Conditions of the Ear

Otitis Externa

Otitis externa is an inflammation of the external auditory canal and external surface of the tympanic membrane, which can be caused by a variety of conditions that compromise the lining of the canal.[1] It usually follows swimming and is often called swimmer's ear.[9] Ear canal trauma and foreign bodies may also contribute to the development.

Pathophysiology

Otitis externa is caused by frequent exposure of the ear canal to water (swimming), vigorous cleaning of the canal, and trauma. Repeated entry of water in the ear or vigorous cleaning alters the normal protective wax found in the ear and the acidic pH that usually protects the ear from bacteria. Otitis externa can be localized or diffuse. Localized external otitis is the result of an abscessed hair follicle in the outer two thirds of the ear canal, caused by *S. aureus*. Diffuse external otitis is caused by *Pseudomonas aeruginosa,* staphylococci, fungi, or a mixture of Gram-negative and Gram-positive organisms. Viral external otitis is usually caused by herpes simplex or herpes zoster.[9]

Focused History

- ❏ Gradual onset of pain
- ❏ Itching
- ❏ Sensation of obstruction or fullness of the ear
- ❏ History of frequent swimming or vigorous cleaning of the ear canal
- ❏ Otorrhea or discharge from the ear
- ❏ Pulling on the ear

Focused Assessment

- ❏ Increased pain with manipulation of the auricle or tragus
- ❏ Erythema and swelling of the affected ear canal
- ❏ Foul-smelling and purulent drainage from the affected ear
- ❏ Preauricular and postauricular lymphadenopathy

Nursing Interventions

1. Clean the ear to remove exudate and wax and to improve visualization of the ear canal and tympanic membrane.
2. Instill topical medications, as ordered, such as acetic acid otic solution.
3. Severe infections may require topical antibiotics, such as polymyxin B and neomycin.
4. If drops cannot be instilled because of swelling, a wick or gauze sponge may be advanced into the ear canal with forceps and left in place for 24 to 48 hours.
5. If cellulitis is present, broad-spectrum systemic antibiotics should be used.
6. If an abscess is present (localized external otitis) it may be drained and systemic antibiotics may be prescribed.

Home Care and Prevention

Provide the following home care instructions:

- ❏ Apply warm, moist compresses to the affected ear.
- ❏ Keep the ear canal dry with the use of earplugs while showering or swimming.
- ❏ Adhere to follow-up instructions and proper use of medications.
- ❏ Avoid vigorous cleaning of the ear canal.

Acute Otitis Media

Acute otitis media (AOM) is defined as inflammation of the middle ear. AOM is the most common head and neck infection in children and is the second most common diagnosis made in the emergency department.[9] The incidence of AOM peaks at 6 to 20 months and can become chronic and recurrent. AOM can occur as an isolated infection or as a complication of an upper respiratory tract infection (URI).

Risk factors that make children more susceptible to recurrent AOM include:[9,10]

- ❏ The presence of otitis media with effusion, which is noninfected fluid in the middle ear
- ❏ Day care attendance
- ❏ Exposure to secondhand smoke
- ❏ Immune deficiency states
- ❏ Craniofacial anomalies and Down syndrome

The most common organisms causing acute otitis media in all ages are:[9]

- ❏ *S. pneumoniae*
- ❏ *H. influenzae*
- ❏ *Moraxella catarrhalis (M. catarrhalis)*
- ❏ Group A *ß-hemolytic streptococcus* (less common)
- ❏ Various upper respiratory tract viruses

Pathophysiology

Otitis media is common in small children and infants because of the straight position of the eustachian tube. The middle ear drains poorly, and fluid can collect. The fluid provides a medium for bacterial growth. Children with a upper respiratory tract infection (URI) that causes congestion are at risk for infections caused by the collection of bacteria. As the child matures, the eustachian tube becomes more curved, and the child becomes better able to equilibrate negative pressures in the middle ear by swallowing.

Focused History

- ❏ Rapid onset of symptoms
- ❏ Pulling on the ear (infants)
- ❏ Irritability in an infant or toddler
- ❏ Otorrhea
- ❏ Drainage from one or both ears
- ❏ Prior ear infections and response to treatment
- ❏ Symptoms of a viral URI

Focused Assessment

- ❏ Fever
- ❏ Possible decrease in hearing
- ❏ Full or bulging tympanic membrane, distorted light reflex, or absence of landmarks

❒ Decreased tympanic membrane mobility with insufflation and possible erythema of the tympanic membrane (an erythematous tympanic membrane is an inconclusive finding and may result from vascular engorgement, caused by fever or crying)

❒ Lymphadenopathy in the preauricular, postauricular, and cervical areas

❒ Purulent drainage, indicative of a ruptured tympanic membrane

❒ If the child appears ill, further evaluation may be necessary to rule out other infectious conditions, such as sepsis and meningitis

The American Academy of Pediatrics and the American Academy of Family Physicians Clinical Practice Guidelines state that the diagnosis of AOM requires:[11]

❒ A history of acute onset of signs and symptoms

❒ The presence of a middle ear effusion

❒ Signs and symptoms of middle ear inflammation

The guidelines also suggest using antibiotics judiciously in children with uncomplicated AOM because of the increasing antibiotic resistance and the unclear necessity of the use of antibiotics in children with uncomplicated AOM. The guidelines suggest a period of observation without the use of antibiotics for 48 to 72 hours in some children who have uncomplicated AOM.

Nursing Interventions

1. Administer analgesics for pain, such as analgesic ear drops.

2. Administer antipyretics for fever.

3. Administer antibiotics if ordered. Amoxicillin is still the drug of choice, but others may be necessary if the child is allergic to penicillin and if the infection does not improve. Antibiotics should only be used if the infection is confirmed by visualization.

Home Care and Prevention

Provide the following home care instructions:

❒ Elevate the infant's head when feeding and do not prop the bottle.

❒ Do not allow smoking in the house.

❒ Use medications until gone and make a follow-up appointment to recheck the ears.

❒ Return to the emergency department if the child's condition worsens or does not improve.

Mastoiditis

Mastoiditis is an inflammation or infection of any part of the mastoid process. It is classified as acute or chronic. Often, a middle ear infection is the inciting event, which progresses through temporal osteitis to involve the mastoid air cells.[12] Complications can include bacteremia, sepsis, meningitis, abscesses, or empyemas.

Pathophysiology

The most common causative organisms are:

❒ *S. pneumoniae*

❒ *Streptococcus pyogenes*

❒ *S. aureus*

Focused History

❒ Tenderness and dull ache in the area of the mastoid process (irritability in a young infant)

❒ History of low-grade fever

❒ History of otitis media

Focused Assessment

Assessment findings include:

❒ Swelling and erythema behind the mastoid process of the ear.

❒ The pinna may be displaced inferiorly and anteriorly (outward).

❒ Fluctuant, erythematous, and tender mass overlying the mastoid bone (accumulation of subperiosteal pus).[12]

❒ The child may look acutely ill with signs and symptoms of shock or meningitis (Chapters 24 and 38).

Nursing Interventions

1. Administer intravenous antibiotics as prescribed.[12]

   ▪ Cefuroxime or Ampicillin-Sulbactam

   ▪ Clindamycin in patients allergic to Penicillin

   ▪ Intravenous antibiotics are usually given for 7 to 10 days.

2. Assist with obtaining specimens for culture and sensitivity.

3. Prepare the child for a CT scan to determine the extent of the disease.

4. Administer antipyretics and analgesics, as prescribed.

5. Prepare the patient for possible admission or transfer and surgical intervention to remove diseased bone and irrigate the affected area. A myringotomy with or without insertion of a tympanostomy tube is usually

performed for drainage.

Foreign Body in the Ear

The ear is the most common site for insertion of a foreign body (FB) in children between 3 and 8 years of age.[12] Local tissue irritation occurs when small items, such as beads or stones, are inserted in the ear canal. Sometimes small insects may crawl or fly into the ear canal, become trapped, and, if they are still alive, cause discomfort. If a child introduces a vegetable foreign body, such as a pea or dried bean, it generally absorbs moisture, enlarges, and begins to obstruct the ear canal. If the foreign body remains for a period of time, an offensive odor may be noticed. Inorganic objects in the ear may go undetected if they do not cause pain or discharge or interfere with hearing.

Pathophysiology

Objects inserted in the ear canal can cause bleeding as a result of tissue trauma. Tissue irritation and inflammation can occur if the object is retained for an extended period of time. Eventually, the mucosa may erode and an infection may occur.

Focused History

❏ Ear pain

❏ Decreased hearing

❏ Discharge from ear (bloody or purulent)

❏ Swelling or foul odor if the object has been retained for an extended period of time

❏ Complaints of buzzing in the ear (usually indicative of an insect)

Focused Assessment

❏ Erythema and edema of canal

❏ Visualization of the object

❏ Foul odor, discharge, and bleeding

Nursing Interventions

1. Assist with removal of the foreign body. Analgesia and sedation may be necessary to prevent tympanic membrane perforation or bleeding in the uncooperative child.[12] Removal should only be attempted if there is reasonable expectation for removal because repeated, failed attempts may result in increased swelling and trauma and possibly repositioning of the object in a less favorable position.[1] Removal techniques used include:

   ▪ Direct instrumentation with alligator forceps, a curette, or a wire loop.

   ▪ When the FB is a live insect, lidocaine instillation into the ear may quickly calm a frantic patient. A live insect can be drowned with mineral oil before its removal.

   ▪ Irrigation and suction may be used if the object is not vegetable matter.

2. Administer medications, antibiotics, or analgesics, as ordered. Topical antibiotics may be necessary when infection has complicated prolonged exposure to a FB.

3. Prepare for removal of the FB with the patient under anesthesia if necessary.

4. Treat for otitis externa.

5. Referral to an otolaryngologist may be necessary if the FB cannot be removed in the emergency department.

Specific Conditions of the Nose

Sinusitis

Sinusitis is an inflammation or infection of the lining of any sinus. Sinuses include maxillary, ethmoid, frontal, and sphenoid.[12] The infection may be caused by or may lead to a collection of fluid within the sinuses. Sinusitis is categorized by duration of symptoms as:[12]

❏ Acute sinusitis: Symptoms lasting 10 to 30 days

❏ Subacute sinusitis: Symptoms lasting 30 to 90 days

❏ Chronic sinusitis: Symptoms lasting over 3 months

Pathophysiology

Drainage from the paranasal sinuses into the meatus facilitates the movement of secretions and particulate matter. Any condition that obstructs drainage from the sinuses can cause secretions to stagnate, causing an environment for bacteria to grow. Sinusitis can be viral (adenovirus, rhinovirus, or parainfluenza virus), bacterial, or allergic in origin. Most episodes begin with a viral URI, but bacterial superinfection may occur. *S. pneumoniae, nontypeable H. influenzae, M. catarrhalis,* group A *streptococci,* and anaerobes are the usual bacterial causes.

Complications of sinusitis can include:[12]

❏ Cerebral abscess

❏ Cavernous sinus thrombosis

❏ Periorbital cellulitis

❏ Orbital cellulitis (most common)

❏ Bacteremia, sepsis, and meningitis

Focused History

- Fever, headache, and sinus pain that worsens when coughing or leaning forward (in teenage patients)
- Nasal discharge of any consistency
- Prior episodes of same symptoms
- Recent URI or recurrent otitis media
- Daytime cough (dry, wet, may be worse at night)
- Symptoms of more than 10 days duration or high fever lasting more than 3 days

Focused Assessment

The classic presenting symptoms for acute sinusitis in adults and teenage patients with mature sinuses are rarely present in the preadolescent patient.[1] The complaints of children with sinusitis are generally nonspecific and sometimes indistinguishable from those of a common cold. Children may present with the following signs and symptoms:

- "Puffy eyes" or periorbital swelling that is most obvious in early morning after awakening and may decrease and actually disappear during the day
- Purulent (yellow or green) nasal drainage with inflamed, swollen nasal mucosa— drainage may also be thin and clear

Assessment findings in older children:

- Fever—temperature usually greater than 102.2 °F (39 °C)
- Tenderness to percussion over affected sinuses or facial swelling over maxillary, ethmoid, or frontal sinus
- Halitosis

Nursing Interventions

1. Administer antibiotics as ordered. Sinusitis does have a high spontaneous cure rate, but antibiotics remain the mainstay of treatment. The first-line therapy for uncomplicated bacterial sinusitis is high-dose Amoxicillin.[1]
2. CT scan may be ordered.
3. Hospitalization may be necessary for patients with suppurative or intracranial complications such as orbital cellulitis or intracranial abscess.[12]

Home Care and Prevention

For patients who are discharged home, the following instructions should be given:

- Promote sinus drainage by keeping the head of the bed elevated.
- Use heat and warm compresses on the face to help relieve pressure.
- Use a room vaporizer, which may help relieve nasal congestion by liquefying secretions.
- Increase the child's fluid intake.
- Eliminate cigarette smoking in the house.
- Use saline nose drops as directed.
- Avoid swimming or diving during the acute phase of sinusitis.
- Follow up in 24 to 48 hours if there is no improvement; otherwise, follow up in 10 to 14 days.

Foreign Body

Children aged 4 years or younger are commonly seen in the emergency department with a foreign object in the nasal cavity. The nose is the most common site for insertion of a foreign body (FB) in children < 3 years old. Generally, there is no pain; therefore, parents and caregivers may not be aware of the foreign object. Vegetable or organic substances may germinate and swell in the warm, moist environment of the nasal cavity. Inorganic objects, such as small stones, crayons, or beads, may be aspirated if they become dislodged and progress to the pharynx.

Pathophysiology

The pathophysiology is the same as that of a FB in the ear. The FB causes trauma, inflammation, and infection. Most often children place objects in their noses intentionally, because of boredom or curiosity. However, accidental placement of FBs can occur when a child is attempting to smell or sniff an object.

If the object is a small battery from an electronic device, it should be removed as soon as possible, no matter where it is inserted. Button batteries may release small amounts of chemicals and voltage that may lead to alkaline chemical burns, necrosis, or septal-tympanic perforation.[1]

Focused History

- Chronic runny nose, often unilateral
- Most cases will present with a complaint of FB in the nose
- History of pain in the nose, foul smell, and breath
- Unilateral foul-smelling, purulent nasal discharge when the object has been in the nose over a period of time
- Frequent sneezing
- Recurrent epistaxis

Focused Assessment

❐ Purulent nasal drainage, usually unilateral and foul smelling, depending on the length of time the FB has been retained

❐ Edema of the nasal mucosa

❐ Examine both sides of the nose and both ears as children presenting with one FB are at greater risk for FBs at other sites[12]

❐ Visualized FB

❐ Unilateral bleeding from the nose

Nursing Interventions

1. Assist with attempts to remove object with gentle suction or alligator forceps.

2. Have the older child forcibly exhale through the affected nostril while occluding the nonaffected nostril.

3. Refer to an ear, nose, and throat specialist if the object cannot be removed.

Home Care and Prevention

❐ Caution the parent and patient about placing objects in the nose.

Epistaxis

Epistaxis is common in children and can cause significant anxiety in both the child and parents. Although bleeding occasionally occurs secondary to mucosal maceration caused by URIs, nose picking accounts for most cases of recurrent epistaxis. Other causes include facial trauma, foreign bodies, cocaine or heroin sniffing, or sinusitis.[1] Less common causes include hepatic disease, leukemia, idiopathic thrombocytopenia, or coagulopathies.

Pathophysiology

The nose has a rich vascular supply, making it vulnerable to episodes of bleeding, either spontaneously or as a result of localized trauma.[1] Epistaxis can be classified according to location of bleeding in the nasal cavity as either anterior or posterior. Most cases are caused by anterior bleeding and usually arise from a venous vascular plexus on the anterior nasal septum known as Kiesselbach's plexus.[1] This area is fragile and firmly adhered to the cartilage of the septum, making it prone to trauma. Anterior bleeding tends to be characterized with slow, persistent oozing, whereas posterior bleeding tends to bleed more profusely. Posterior bleeding carries a higher risk of airway compromise, aspiration of blood, and life-threatening hemorrhage.

Focused History

❐ Frequency and duration of nosebleeds; amount of bleeding

❐ Recent nasal surgery

❐ Recent trauma or FB

❐ Other signs and symptoms

Focused Assessment

The standard pediatric assessment is done, especially focusing on signs and symptoms of shock, which require immediate treatment. The following signs and symptoms may be present:

❐ Obvious bleeding from one or both nostrils

❐ Fresh blood in the oropharynx; hematemesis

❐ Active bleeding points on the nasal mucosa

❐ Visualized FB

Nursing Interventions

Rarely do children with nosebleeds require emergent treatment. However, if signs and symptoms of shock are present, they must be given treatment immediately. The following interventions may be performed:

1. Assess and maintain airway, breathing, and circulation. Excessive bleeding may put a child at risk of aspiration and airway compromise.

2. Stop bleeding.
   - Stop bleeding by applying pressure to the soft part of the nose for 10 to 15 minutes. Have the child sit upright with his or her head tilted forward.
   - Assist with cauterization or nasal packing if indicated.
   - Monitor airway and be prepared for vomiting of swallowed blood.

3. Administer medications, as ordered, for vasoconstriction or pain.

4. Obtain laboratory analysis if a bleeding disorder is suspected or if the child may have lost enough blood to become hypovolemic (complete blood cell count, coagulation studies, and bleeding times).

5. Insert intravenous catheter if fluid replacement is necessary.

6. Otolaryngologic consultation may be necessary in cases of suspected posterior epistaxis.

Home Care and Prevention

Give the parents the following information:

❐ How to control and stop bleeding.

❏ How to use a humidifier, especially during the winter months.

❏ How to use a lubricant in nostrils to prevent drying and promote hydration.

❏ Reassurance that nosebleeds seldom indicate an underlying disease.

Specific Conditions of the Throat and Pharynx

Pharyngitis

Pharyngitis, an inflammation of the pharynx, is a common URI. The surrounding lymph tissues (tonsils) are commonly infected. Often the chief complaint is "sore throat." Most children with sore throats have self-limiting or easily treated pharyngeal infections, but a few have serious disorders, such as retropharyngeal or lateral pharyngeal abscesses.[13]

Pathophysiology

Pharyngitis is most often caused by respiratory viral infections (adenovirus, parainfluenza virus, or coxsackievirus A).[13] Viral infections are closely followed in frequency by bacterial infections caused by group A *streptococcus (S. pyogenes)*. Another common infectious agent in pharyngitis is the Epstein-Barr virus, which causes infectious mononucleosis (Chapter 24). A potential complication of pharyngitis is peritonsillar abscess, which requires aggressive treatment to prevent airway compromise. This usually occurs in an adolescent who has not been given treatment with antibiotics, but it can occur even if antibiotics have been used. Irritative pharyngitis can lead to a sore throat caused by drying of the pharynx. This condition occurs more commonly during winter. Occasionally a foreign object may be embedded in the pharynx.

Herpetic stomatitis, caused by the herpes simplex virus, is usually confined to the anterior buccal mucosa but may extend to the anterior tonsillar pillars, causing complaints of sore throat.

Focused History

❏ Sore throat

❏ Fever

❏ Signs and symptoms of URI

❏ Headache

❏ Anorexia, fatigue, malaise, and dysphagia

❏ Reduced fluid intake

❏ Exposure to another child or family member with strep throat

❏ Rash

❏ Abdominal pain

Focused Assessment

The physical signs of pharyngitis can mimic those of other disorders. Areas of assessment to evaluate during the standard examination include:

❏ Auscultate heart sounds for possible murmur.

❏ Palpate the abdomen for possible splenic enlargement.

❏ Assess for signs and symptoms of meningitis.

❏ Thoroughly inspect the skin for rashes.

Any child who has obvious stridor, drooling, or trouble breathing may have epiglottitis and should be treated emergently without attempts to examine the pharynx (Chapter 14). The following signs and symptoms may be present in the child with pharyngitis:

❏ Enlarged and tender cervical lymph nodes

❏ Labored respirations

❏ Flushed skin

❏ Enlarged tonsils, with erythema and/or exudate

❏ If an abscess has formed, unilateral bulging and swelling of the affected tonsil with displacement of the uvula along with voice changes may be noted.

The child with streptococcal pharyngitis (strep throat) may present with the same complaints and symptoms as pharyngitis but with the following symptoms:

❏ Fever, with temperature greater than 101 °F (38.3 °C)

❏ Dysphagia

❏ Abdominal pain, headache, and vomiting

❏ Sandpaper rash

❏ Yellow or white exudate on tonsils and pharynx

Nursing Interventions

1. Obtain throat cultures and a streptococcal screen.

2. Administer antipyretics and antibiotics, as ordered.

3. Referral to an otolaryngologist may be considered for patients with repeated streptococcal infections.

4. Prepare the child for hospitalization.

Home Care and Prevention

❏ Provide warm saline gargles, hard candy, and lozenges for pain as appropriate based on child's age.

❏ Ensure adequate bed rest and fluid intake.

❏ Do not allow the child to return to school until antibiotics have been given for 24 hours.

❑ Continue giving the child all antibiotics prescribed until they are gone. If antibiotics are not given until the culture results are obtained, call for results.

Retropharyngeal and Peritonsillar Abscess

❑ A retropharyngeal abscess (RPA) is the accumulation of pus in the retropharyngeal space, which is located in the prevertebral soft tissue of the upper airway. This is uncommon and usually occurs in children less than 4 years of age.[13]

❑ A peritonsillar abscess (PTA) is a localized accumulation of pus between the faucial pillars and the tonsillar capsule. Inflammation progresses from peritonsillar cellulitis to the phlegmon stage and abscess formation.[12] PTA occurs most often in school-aged children and older children.

Pathophysiology

The retropharyngeal space contains lymph nodes that drain the nasopharynx, adenoids, and posterior paranasal sinuses. Bacterial infections of these areas can lead to suppuration of lymph nodes resulting in abscess formation. These lymph nodes usually begin to atrophy during the third to fourth years of life and usually regress completely by 6 years of age.[12]

RPA is usually a result of a complication of nasopharyngitis, tonsillitis, otitis, sinusitis, adenitis, or dental infections. It can also be caused from penetrating trauma such as that occurring when a child is running and falls down with an object in his or her mouth. Bacterial pathogens include *S. pyogenes* and *S. aureus*. Complications of RPA include:

❑ Airway compromise

❑ Rupture of abscess with asphyxiation or aspiration of pus

❑ Vascular complications of the internal jugular vein

The cause of PTA is usually polymicrobial with group A *ß-hemolytic streptococci* being the most common anaerobic pathogen.[12] If untreated, the abscess becomes fluctuant and may spontaneously rupture. Other complications include:[12]

❑ Airway obstruction

❑ Aspiration pneumonia

❑ Mediastinitis

❑ Sepsis

❑ Meningitis

❑ Cerebral abscess

Focused History

❑ Dysphagia and unilateral throat and ear pain

❑ Unilateral tonsillar swelling and deviation of the uvula (PTA)

❑ A feeling of throat swelling

❑ Decreased fluid intake

❑ Fever

❑ History of cough, headache, and malaise

Focused Assessment

❑ Dysphonic—speech quality is often referred to a "hot potato" voice

❑ Dysphagia

❑ Drooling

❑ Trismus (inability to open the mouth)—trismus is a cardinal sign of PTA and results from spasm of the pterygoid muscle[13]

❑ Extremely medially swollen and erythematous tonsil (in PTAs)

❑ Swelling that displaces the soft palate and uvula to the opposite side (in PTAs)

❑ Swelling and erythema of the soft palate

❑ Tender and enlarged cervical lymph nodes

❑ Foul odor of breath

❑ Resistance to neck movement (in RPA)

Nursing Interventions

1. Assess and maintain airway, breathing, and circulation.
   - Severe respiratory distress may be present.
   - Allow the child to maintain a position of comfort.
   - Have emergency airway equipment readily available.

2. Begin intravenous infusion and administer intravenous antibiotics, only after airway is secure.

3. Assist with CT scan or radiograph.

4. Obtain a referral to an ear, nose, and throat specialist.

5. Prepare the patient for admission and possible incision and drainage of the abscess.

6. Keep family informed of plan of care and child's condition.

Conclusion

Eye, ear, nose, and throat conditions are usually relatively minor. However, some conditions can be emergent and, if left untreated, can result in serious complications such as loss of function. Some seemingly minor complaints may cause respiratory distress. Emergency department nurses must be aware of common EENT conditions and know how to recognize and treat them in the emergency department.

References

1. Bernius, M., & Perlin, D. (2006). Pediatric ear, nose, and throat emergencies. *Pediatric Clinics of North America, 53,* 195–214.

2. Moore, K. L., & Persaud, T. V. N. (2008). Eye and ear. In K. L. Moore & T. V. N. Persaud, *The developing human: Clinically oriented embryology* (8th ed., pp. 419–438). Philadelphia: Saunders.

3. Moore, K. L., & Persaud, T. V. N. (2008). Pharyngeal apparatus: In K. L. Moore & T. V. N. Persaud, *The developing human. Clinically oriented embryology* (8th ed., pp. 159–195). Philadelphia: Saunders.

4. Levin, A. V. (2006). Ophthalmic emergencies. In G. Fleisher & S. Ludwig (Eds.), *Textbook of pediatric emergency care* (5th ed., pp. 1653–1661). Philadelphia: Lippincott Williams & Wilkins.

5. Prentis, K., & Dorfman, D. (2008). Pediatric ophthalmology in the emergency department. *Emergency Medicine Clinics of North America, 26,* 181–198.

6. Grover, G., & Silverman, K. (2006). Problems in the early neonatal period. In G. Fleisher & S. Ludwig (Eds.), *Textbook of pediatric emergency care* (5th ed., pp. 1327–1329). Philadelphia: Lippincott Williams & Wilkins.

7. Hoyt, K., & Haley, R. (2005). Assessment and management of eye emergencies. *Topics in Emergency Medicine, 27,* 101–117.

8. Lee, J. E. (2007). Common illness of the head, eyes, ears, nose and throat. In N. Ryan-Wenger (Ed.), *Core curriculum for primary care pediatric nurse practitioners* (pp. 373–413). St. Louis, MO: Mosby.

9. Eldin, L. M., & Potsic, W. (2006). Otolaryngologic emergencies. In G. Fleisher & S. Ludwig (Eds.), *Textbook of pediatric emergency care* (5th ed., pp. 1663–1678). Philadelphia: Lippincott Williams & Wilkins.

10. Paradise, J. L. (2004). Otitis media. In R. E. Behman (Ed.), *Nelson textbook of pediatrics* (17th ed., pp. 2138–2149). Philadelphia: Saunders.

11. American Academy of Pediatrics and American Academy of Family Physicians. (2004). Clinical practice guideline: Diagnosis and management of acute otitis media. *Pediatrics, 113,* 1451–1465.

12. Peacock, P., Spektor, M., & Shah, B. R. (2006). Otolaryngology. In B. R. Shaw & M. Lucchesi (Eds.), *Atlas of pediatric emergency medicine* (pp. 405–426). New York: McGraw-Hill.

13. Fleisher, G. (2006). Sore throat. In G. Fleisher & S. Ludwig (Eds.), *Textbook of pediatric emergency care* (5th ed., pp. 637–640). Philadelphia: Lippincott Williams & Wilkins.

TWENTY-TWO

Endocrine Emergencies

Christine Nelson-Tuttle, DNS, RNC, PNP
Rebecca Roloff, RN, MSN, SANE-A, SANE-P
Steven J. Dasta, RN, BSN

Introduction

Aside from diabetic emergencies, endocrine emergencies are uncommon occurrences in the pediatric population. However, emergency nurses must be aware of the underlying developmental and physiologic processes associated with endocrine imbalances and their emergency department (ED) treatment. Many of these children have endocrine conditions requiring complex chronic management. Emergency nurses should include the parents or primary care providers and, if possible, the primary health care providers for important health care information specific for each patient. The purpose of this chapter is to present a basic overview of the endocrine system and highlight the emergency nursing care of children with endocrine-related imbalances.

Embryologic Development of the Endocrine System

The pituitary, thyroid, parathyroid, and adrenal glands are important endocrine organs in pediatric development. The nervous system and endocrine system are closely related in the development of the pituitary gland. The pituitary gland, located beneath the brain, is surrounded by the sphenoid bone. Embryologically, the pituitary gland develops from both the floor of the brain and the roof of the mouth.[1]

The thyroid gland is the first endocrine gland to appear in the embryo and is noted about 24 days after conception.[2] It originates as an epithelial thickening in the floor of the pharynx. The thyroid forms during the seventh week of fetal development. Cellular differentiation occurs over the next seven weeks, and hormone synthesis begins at 14 weeks.[2] The parathyroid glands develop from the dorsal halves of the pharyngeal pouches.

The adrenal medulla arises embryologically from the neural crest cells and is closely related to the function of the sympathetic nervous system. The adrenal cortex is derived from the same mesoderm that gives rise to the gonads.

Pediatric Considerations

The endocrine system is a feedback system that plays a key role in the body's response to external stimuli. The endocrine system uses hormones to respond to changes in temperature, stress, and traumatic injury. Hormones facilitate the communication network between the cells of the organs of the endocrine system. Alterations in hormone balances cause children to become too fat or too thin, or too short or too tall; distinctive physical features also result.[3] The endocrine system also responds to internal stimuli, such as electrolyte imbalance or changes in osmolality.

The endocrine system consists of endocrine and exocrine glands. Endocrine glands are ductless; they secrete hormones directly into the bloodstream. Exocrine glands secrete through a duct system.

Hormones circulate throughout the body and initiate responses after focusing on target cells. These hormones are responsible for:

❐ Maintenance of internal environment, such as extracellular fluid status, electrolyte regulation, and maintenance of bone, muscle, and body fat storage

❑ Regulation of energy conversion and availability

❑ Reproduction

❑ Growth and development

The organs and tissues are affected by the hormones that circulate throughout the body in a feedback system. Any alteration in the ability of the endocrine system to regulate these multiple functions may lead to a life-threatening emergency. Table 22.1 highlights selected endocrine imbalances in children.

Etiology

The etiology of endocrine imbalances is variable, depending on the involved endocrine glands and hormones. Endocrine gland dysfunction may result from the gland's failure to produce adequate amounts of hormones, synthesis or release of excessive amounts of hormones, or inappropriate response to a hormone.[4]

The hormones themselves may be involved in endocrine imbalances, from causes such as degradation of the hormone at an altered rate, inactivation by antibodies, or ectopic hormone release (hormones produced by nonendocrine tissues).[4]

In other situations, the target cells may fail to respond to the hormones because of receptor-associated disorders associated with water-soluble hormones (e.g., insulin) or intracellular disorders such as inadequate synthesis of a "second messenger" that transduces the hormone signal within the cell.[4]

Focused History

❑ Patient history

  ▪ Changes in activity levels

TABLE 22.1 Selected Endocrine Imbalances in Children

Disease	Description
Panhypopituitarism	Absence of growth hormones, leading to short stature (dwarfism) and loss of secondary sex characteristics.
Hyperpituitarism	Hypersecretion of growth hormone.
	Exposure to continuously excessive levels of growth hormone in children whose epiphyseal plates have not closed, causing gigantism.
Growth hormone deficiency	Normal body proportions with increased adipose tissue in the trunk and extremities; delay in height and bone age.
Thyroid gland disorders	Hyperthyroidism; hypothyroidism.
Turner's syndrome	Genetic in origin; suspect Turner's syndrome in short females with pubic or axillary hair and absence of breast development or menses onset.
Parathyroid gland imbalance	Hypocalcemia; Chvostek's sign (distortion of the face with stimulation of cranial nerve VII); Trousseau's sign (hand cramping with blood pressure measurement).
Adrenal gland imbalance	Cushing's syndrome and increased glucocorticoid action from endogenous or exogenous glucocorticoid exposure, causing a round face, central obesity, excessive fat on the lower cervical and upper thoracic spine, muscle weakness, and wasting in the extremities.
Congenital adrenal hyperplasia	Caused by decreased enzymes necessary for cortisol production in the adrenal cortex and overproduction of the adrenal androgens. Most common cause for ambiguous genitalia in newborn females. Management includes administration of cortisone with dosages increased in times of stress. Children with the salt-losing type of congenital adrenal hyperplasia require aldosterone replacement.
Pheochromocytoma	Rare tumor characterized by secretion of catecholamines. Produces hypertension, tachycardia, headache, weight loss, hyperglycemia, polyuria, polydipsia, and nervousness.
Syndrome of inappropriate antidiuretic hormone secretion (SIADH)	Most common cause of hyponatremia in children, caused by the inappropriate continued secretion and/or action of ADH.

White, P. C. (2007). Disorders of the adrenal glands. In R. E. Behrman, H. Jenson, B. Stanton, & R. M. Kliegman (Eds.), *Nelson textbook of pediatrics* (18th ed.). St. Louis, MO: Elsevier.

- Changes in dietary patterns
- Lack of or excessive physical growth
- Precocious or delayed puberty
- Genetic conditions
- Polyuria
- Polydipsia
❑ Family history
- Endocrine disorders
- Genetic conditions

Focused Assessment

Physical Assessment

❑ Assess the child's growth patterns.

- Measure the child's height and weight; plot them on a growth chart. A change in growth patterns may be related to an endocrine imbalance.
- Observe for secondary sexual characteristics. Observe for breast development and for axillary and pubic hair development. Inquire about the onset of menses.
- Measure vital signs. Increased blood pressure and heart rate may be noted.

Psychosocial Assessment

❑ Assess the child's and family's coping strategies.

❑ Assess the child's and family's knowledge of the child's current health condition.

Nursing Interventions

1. Assess and maintain airway, breathing, and circulation in the child with hemodynamic compromise.

2. Obtain venous access and initiate an intravenous infusion.

   - Obtain blood for laboratory studies, such as; complete blood cell count, electrolytes, glucose, calcium, phosphorus, and magnesium.
   - Administer medications, as needed.

3. Prepare for diagnostic studies, as needed.

4. Reassess the child's neurologic and cardiopulmonary status, as needed.

5. Provide psychosocial support to the child and family.

   - Inform the family members frequently about their child's condition.

6. Initiate referrals as appropriate (e.g., endocrinologist).

7. Prepare for transfer and transport to a tertiary care center (Chapter 8) as needed, hospitalization, or discharge and subsequent referral.

Home Care and Prevention

The onset of an endocrine imbalance may be difficult for the child and family to accept. The child may feel different or have emotional difficulties if puberty is delayed or is precocious.[5] The family should be encouraged to support the child throughout ongoing treatment.

For other endocrine imbalances, proper diet and exercise are needed to promote hormonal balances. Parents and children can be taught healthy food choices and appropriate exercises. Various Web sites and voluntary organizations devoted to specific endocrine disorders are available and are listed throughout this chapter.

Specific Endocrine Emergencies

Diabetic Emergencies

Diabetes mellitus (type I, juvenile onset) is the most common endocrine disorder of childhood and adolescence.[6] In 5% of all people with diabetes this disease was diagnosed during their childhood.[7] Seventy-five percent of patients with newly diagnosed diabetes are children and adolescents.[6]

The two conditions arising from diabetes mellitus are hyperglycemia, or diabetic ketoacidosis (DKA), in which the blood glucose level is higher than the norm for age, and hypoglycemia, in which the blood glucose level is lower than the norm for age.

Although diabetes mellitus type 1 has been more common in patients 8 to 19 years of age, diabetes type 2 now accounts for 8% to 45% of new childhood diabetes.[8] The prevalence of childhood type 2 diabetes has increased by 33% in the past 15 years, following the increasing rates of obesity in the childhood population.[9] Other risk factors include low physical exercise, a diet high in fat, minority race, polycystic ovary syndrome, and type 2 diabetes in a first-degree relative.[7]

Etiology

Diabetes mellitus is caused by insufficient insulin. This lack of insulin causes alterations in the metabolism of carbohydrates, lipids, and proteins. Without adequate insulin, glucose and amino acids cannot be adequately transported to the muscle and adipose tissue. Without sufficient glucose and amino acids, the tissue does not have adequate substances for energy production and protein synthesis.

Metabolic alterations allow for glucose production to occur in the liver. This increase in glucose production by the liver and the inability of the body to utilize energy in the normal method results in hyperglycemia, increased breakdown of fat and proteins, and metabolic acidosis.

Glycosuria occurs when the renal threshold for glucose is surpassed, causing osmotic diuresis and polyuria. The body attempts to compensate with polydipsia. When intake does not compensate for the significant losses, the result is dehydration. As ketones accumulate secondary to the increased breakdown of fats and proteins, vomiting occurs and leads to volume depletion and dehydration. Notable losses of sodium and potassium result from polyuria.[6]

Although hyperglycemia usually is related to diabetes mellitus, hypoglycemia may arise from other causes. Generally, hypoglycemia may be the result of hormone deficiencies, hereditary metabolic errors, or neurologic disorders. Causes of persistent or frequent episodes of hypoglycemia in early infancy include inborn errors of metabolism involving the glyconeogenic enzymes and a defect in amino acid or fat metabolism. Causes of persistent or frequent episodes of hypoglycemia in older children include:[10]

❑ Drug-induced hypoglycemia, caused by ingestion of ethanol, salicylates, or oral hypoglycemic agents

❑ Reye's syndrome

❑ Hepatitis

❑ Insulin overdose

❑ Extrapancreatic tumors, specifically fibrosarcoma, Wilms' tumor, hepatoma, or neuroblastoma

Pediatric Considerations

Several factors influence management of diabetes in the pediatric population:[11]

❑ Greater susceptibility to infection than adults

❑ Numerous emotional and environmental stressors

❑ Additional caloric requirements because of ongoing physical maturation, growth, and greater physical activity

❑ Unpredictable dietary patterns, especially in adolescence

❑ Decreased adherence to prescribed medical management, most often among adolescents,[12] making this population especially at risk for complications from their illness

Focused History

The patient history differs for new-onset diabetes, hypoglycemia, and hyperglycemia (Table 22.2).

Focused Assessment

Physical Assessment

The comparison of physical assessment findings for hypoglycemia and DKA are outlined in Table 22.3.

Psychosocial Assessment

❑ Assess the child's and family's understanding of the disease process.

❑ For the child with a previous diagnosis of diabetes, ascertain the child's and family's coping strategies.

Nursing Interventions

1. Initiate measures to maintain airway, breathing, and circulation.

2. Obtain venous access and initiate intravenous fluids.

3. Obtain a quick-screen blood glucose level.

4. Obtain blood specimens for:
   - Complete blood cell count
   - Glucose
   - Electrolytes
   - Blood urea nitrogen; creatinine
   - pH
   - Phosphorus
   - Magnesium

5. Interpret the screening results.

6. Table 22.4 compares the laboratory data for hypoglycemia and hyperglycemia.

7. Initiate treatment for hypoglycemia (Table 22.5) or DKA (Table 22.6).

8. Reassess the patient's respiratory, cardiovascular, and neurologic systems frequently.[13]

9. Initiate consultations with other health care professionals, such as the child's primary care provider, endocrinologist, and social worker:
   - Education for the patient and family is essential for management of this condition.
   - The initial diagnosis of new-onset diabetes may cause feelings of shock, denial, anger, fear, and guilt in parents and patients.
   - Health care providers must encourage positive coping behaviors and facilitate use of appropriate resources to assure compliance with treatment regimens.

10. Prepare for transfer or transport to a tertiary care center, if needed (Chapter 8).

TABLE 22.2 Historical Findings in New-Onset Diabetes, Hypoglycemia, and Hyperglycemia		
New-Onset Diabetes	*Hypoglycemia* [18]	*Hyperglycemia* [18]
All of these findings may have been present for weeks: ■ Polyuria (more common in patients whose disease was previously undiagnosed or has been poorly managed for a considerable amount of time) ■ Polydipsia (more common in those whose disease was previously undiagnosed or has been poorly managed for a considerable amount of time) ■ Polyphagia ■ Weight loss ■ Abdominal pain ■ Flu-like symptoms (e.g., malaise, vomiting)	■ Infections: Viral or bacterial ■ Poor compliance with insulin ■ Use of steroids or birth control pills ■ Change in diet ■ Emotional stressors ■ Major trauma or surgery ■ Pregnancy, puberty, or thyroid problems ■ Usual insulin regimen and last dose *Infants:* ■ Tremors ■ Seizures ■ Cyanosis or apnea ■ Episodes of limpness or unresponsiveness *Older children:* ■ Anxiety ■ Tremors ■ Fatigue ■ Vomiting	■ Infections: Viral or bacterial ■ Poor compliance with insulin ■ Use of steroids or birth control pills ■ Change in diet ■ Emotional stressors ■ Major trauma or surgery ■ Pregnancy, puberty, or thyroid problems ■ Usual insulin regimen and last dose *Young children:* In very young children, signs and symptoms can be very vague and resemble those of sepsis: ■ Irritability ■ Lethargy ■ Dehydration ■ Enuresis ■ Fatigue ■ Weight loss ■ Abdominal pain

Home Care and Prevention

Management of diabetes is a lifelong process that includes careful consideration of diet, exercise, stress management, and use of insulin. The patient and family are taught to monitor blood glucose and urinary ketone levels and administer the insulin. As the child grows older, the child's responsibility for his or her own management increases. Daily or weekly written records of the child's blood glucose levels, the dose and time of insulin injections, and possible reasons for high and low blood glucose levels are helpful.[14]

The parents and child must learn the signs of hypoglycemia and hyperglycemia and know what to do if these situations occur. Even with minor illnesses, parents should still contact the child's primary care physician for directions or changes in the routine treatment regimen. Noncompliance with prescribed treatment regimens and risk-taking behaviors can lead to many ED visits for the child and family.

Support groups, counseling, and other venues may help children and adolescents to cope with their disease. The American Diabetes Association (800-DIABETES) and the Juvenile Diabetes Research Foundation (800-JDF-CURE) have Web sites (http://www.diabetes.org and http://www.jdrf.org/index.cfm) where additional information can be obtained.

Diabetes Insipidus

Maintenance of the body's water balance is a complex process involving hormonal interaction among the pituitary gland, hypothalamus, and kidneys. The volume of urine is controlled by antidiuretic hormone (ADH), which is produced by the hypothalamus and transported by axons for storage in the posterior pituitary gland.[15] Antidiuretic hormone functions to conserve body water by reducing the amount of water excreted in the urine.

Etiology

Diabetes insipidus is characterized by the impaired ability of the kidneys to conserve urine. There are two types of diabetes insipidus:

1. Central (neurogenic) diabetes insipidus:

   ■ Is caused by an absence or insufficient amount of circulating ADH

TABLE 22.3 Comparison of Physical Assessment Findings in Hypoglycemia and DKA

Assessment Parameter	Hypoglycemia	DKA
Respiratory system	Tachypnea	Deep, rapid respirations (Kussmaul breathing), tachypnea
		Acetone or fruity-smelling breath
Cardiovascular system	Tachycardia	Tachycardia
		Signs of dehydration (increased capillary refill time, doughy skin, dry mucous membranes)
		Increased or decreased blood pressure
Neurologic system	Coma may be noted in severe cases. In infants: generalized symptoms, such as:[19] • Apnea • Breathing difficulties • Tremors • Lethargy • Seizures	Altered mental status that may progress to coma, seizures
Gastrointestinal and genitourinary systems	Hunger	Complaints of increased thirst
Integumentary system	Pallor Diaphoresis	Dry, brittle hair Alopecia Hot, dry skin

TABLE 22.4 Comparison of Laboratory Findings in Hypoglycemia and Hyperglycemia

Laboratory Test	Hypoglycemia	Hyperglycemia
Serum glucose	Lower limit for children is 45 mg/dL of plasma glucose; premature and small-for-age infants and infants younger than 72 hours of age may have lower values[19]	Glucose may range from 300–1,200 mg/dL.[19]
pH	Normal	Blood pH is frequently below 7.3, as extreme diuresis leads to poor tissue perfusion and an increase in lactic acid production.
Sodium	Normal	Mild to moderate hyponatremia results from urinary sodium losses and osmotic dilution.
Potassium	Normal	Potassium may vary widely, from slightly low to mildly elevated, depending on the serum pH (i.e., decreased pH results in increased potassium levels).
Phosphate/bicarbonate	Normal	Phosphate and bicarbonate may be depleted because of the extreme diuresis.
Blood urea nitrogen; creatinine	Not applicable	Levels are increased because of dehydration.

TABLE 22.5 Treatment for Hypoglycemia	
Intervention	*Specific Treatment*
Administer intravenous fluid therapy and medications, as prescribed.	Administer oral high dextrose solution if tolerated and if able to take orally. Administer aqueous glucagon (0.03 mg/kg with a maximum dose of 1.00 mg) if intravenous access is not attainable.[10]
Administer intravenous glucose therapy for patients with an altered level of consciousness.	Administer 1 to 2 mL/kg of 25% glucose over a 2- to 4-minute period in children. Follow with an infusion of 10% dextrose in 0.25% normal saline at a rate sufficient to keep the blood glucose level between 50 and 120 mg/dL.
Monitor serum glucose.	Obtain serum glucose measurements on a regular basis to measure improvement.

- May be caused by a disruption of three processes involving ADH:
  - Disruption in production
  - Disruption in the process of neural pathway transport
  - Disruption in the release of ADH
- May be caused by the following health conditions:[16]
  - Hypothalamic injury, surgery, or ischemia
  - Pituitary injury, surgery, or ischemia
  - Traumatic brain injury
  - Central nervous system infection
  - Cerebral edema
  - Cranial neoplasms
  - Intracranial hemorrhage
2. Nephrogenic (or renal) diabetes insipidus:
   - Is less common
   - Occurs when appropriate levels of ADH are synthesized, but the kidneys' collecting ducts and distal tubules are resistant to the effects of ADH[10]
   - Can be a congenital condition that may present symptomatically the first few weeks of life but not become apparent to health care providers until there are difficulties with toilet training
   - Can also be caused by:
     - Chronic renal disease

- Pregnancy
- Sickle cell disease
- Multiple myeloma

Focused History

❏ Patient history
  - Irritability
  - Fever of unknown origin
  - Dehydration
  - Complaints of extreme thirst

Focused Assessment

Physical Assessment

❏ Assess the respiratory system.
  - Auscultate the chest for:
    - Respiratory rate. Tachypnea may be present with fever.
❏ Assess the cardiovascular system.
  - Auscultate the heart for:
    - Rate. Tachycardia may be present with fever.
  - Assess the peripheral vascular system.
    - Palpate the peripheral pulses for equality and quality. Pulses may be weak with dehydration.
    - Measure capillary refill. Capillary refill may be greater than 3 seconds with dehydration and early shock.
    - Assess core and skin temperature. Fever may be present.
    - Assess skin turgor. Turgor may be poor with dehydration.
    - Measure the blood pressure. Blood pressure may be elevated in early dehydration; hypotension may be evident in late shock or severe dehydration.
❏ Assess the neurologic system.
  - Evaluate the child's level of consciousness with the AVPU (*A*lert, responds to *V*erbal stimuli, responds to *P*ainful stimuli, *U*nresponsive) method or Glasgow Coma Scale.
❏ Assess the genitourinary system.
  - Measure the child's urinary output:
    - Polyuria is the hallmark symptom of diabetes insipidus, with urinary excretion of greater than 30 mL/kg/day. The urine is diluted (< 250 mOsm/kg).

TABLE 22.6 Treatment for DKA

Intervention	Specific Treatment
Administer intravenous fluid therapy and medications, as prescribed.[20]	Initiate replacement of water and electrolytes: • Calculate volume deficit and replace (typically the child has 10%–20% dehydration). • Give 20 mL/kg bolus of normal saline solution over a 20- to 30-minute period.[15] After consultation with the ED physician, repeat a bolus of 10 to 20 mL/kg of normal saline solution if signs of shock are present.[15] • After the bolus, start an infusion of 0.45% normal saline with 20 mEq potassium acetate and 20 mEq potassium phosphate per liter at 1 & 1/2 times maintenance.[21]
Administer insulin. Monitor serum glucose and electrolyte levels. Monitor the patient for complications, such as:[10,13] • Hypokalemia/hyperkalemia • Dysrhythmias • Hypernatremia • Cardiac arrest • Water intoxication • Cerebral edema (abrupt change in the level of consciousness). If increasing cerebral edema is undetected, herniation of the brain stem may occur, resulting in respiratory arrest. • Hypoglycemia	Begin an insulin drip after the first fluid bolus, if the child is hemodynamically stable. Measure the glucose level hourly. The rate of decrease in glucose level should not exceed 80 to 100 mg/dL/hour.

Psychosocial Assessment

❏ Assess the child's and family's knowledge of the child's current health condition.

❏ Assess the child's and family's coping strategies.

Nursing Interventions

1. Assess and maintain airway, breathing, and circulation in the child with dehydration.

2. Obtain venous access and initiate an intravenous infusion.

   • Obtain blood specimens for diagnostic testing of:

      • Glucose. Monitor patients with anterior pituitary deficiency closely for hypoglycemia.

      • Blood urea nitrogen

      • Creatinine

   • Monitor the patient's fluid status to avoid fluid overload.

3. Reassess the child's neurologic and cardiopulmonary status.

4. Administer medications, as prescribed.

   • Prepare for the administration of a diagnostic trial of aqueous vasopressin.

   • Prepare to administer desmopressin acetate intranasally.

5. Prepare for transfer and transport to a tertiary care facility (Chapter 8), hospitalization, or referral and follow-up with the primary care physician.

Home Care and Prevention

The parents should be encouraged to follow up with the prescribed treatment for this condition. Both parents and the child must be taught how to administer the intranasal medication. Consultation with the appropriate health care specialists is warranted.

Thyroid and Adrenal Disorders

Thyroid and adrenal disorders are relatively rare in the pediatric population. Three conditions that may be present in children presenting to the emergency department are hypothyroidism, hyperthyroidism (Graves' disease), and acute adrenal insufficiency. Table 22.7 compares the characteristics of thyroid and adrenal diseases in children.

Home Care and Prevention

Parents and children may require education regarding these endocrine disorders. In hyperthyroidism, for example, parents and children must learn about eating a well-balanced diet to promote growth and to limit calories to prevent excessive weight gain after the disease is under control.[17]

Various agencies are available for additional information about these and other endocrine imbalances. The MAGIC Foundation (800-362-4423), http://www.magicfoundation.org, provides information on hypothyroidism and hyperthyroidism. The National Graves' Disease Foundation (877-NGDF123), http://www.ngdf.org/, also has information about hyperthyroidism. The Human Growth Foundation (800-451-6434), http://www.hgfound.org, has information regarding short stature.

Conclusion

The endocrine system is very complex and is frequently not studied in the depth afforded other body systems because of the relatively few pediatric endocrine emergencies that present to the emergency department. Because of the subtleties of many of the signs and symptoms of endocrine disturbances, it is crucial that emergency nurses have a basic knowledge of the anatomy, physiology, and diseases of the endocrine system. Such knowledge provides the nurse with greater confidence regarding the initiation of specific treatment modalities.

TABLE 22.7 Comparison of Thyroid and Adrenal Diseases

Characteristic	Hypothyroidism	Hyperthyroidism (Graves' Disease)	Acute Adrenal Insufficiency
Definition	Clinical state of thyroid hormone insufficiency	Excessive levels of circulating thyroid hormone; thought to be autoimmune in basis	Insufficient production of corticosteroids by the adrenal cortex[11]; has three forms: • Primary • Secondary • Tertiary
Incidence/ prevalence	One in 3,500 to 4,500 births[10]	Five to seven times more common in females[6]	Rare in children, but life threatening
Causes	*Congenital:* • Inborn errors of metabolism • Autoimmune diseases • Maternal ingestion of drugs or toxins while pregnant *Acquired:* • Iodine or radiation exposure • Trauma to the neck • Neck surgery • Viral or (rarely) bacterial infections or neoplasms[7]	*Congenital:* • Autoimmune disorder • Transient congenital hyperthyroidism *Acquired:* • Acute, subacute or chronic thyroiditis • Thyroid tumors • Other tumors	*Congenital:* • Enzymatic defects • Hypoplasia • Birth defects *Acquired:* • Infections, such as • *Neisseria meningitidis; Streptococcus pneumoniae;* tuberculosis; histoplasmosis • Waterhouse-Friderichsen syndrome (adrenal hemorrhage) • Rapid withdrawal of steroid therapy • Unusual stress, such as surgery or infection, in a patient taking pharmacologic dosages of glucocorticosteroids[11]

TABLE 22.7 Comparison of Thyroid and Adrenal Diseases (continued)

Characteristic	Hypothyroidism	Hyperthyroidism (Graves' Disease)	Acute Adrenal Insufficiency
History	*Congenital:* ■ Prolonged gestation ■ Feeding or sucking difficulties ■ Constipation ■ Lethargy ■ Respiratory problems *Acquired:* ■ Decreased appetite ■ Cold intolerance	May be abrupt but is usually slow in developing. The average duration of symptoms before treatment is 1 year.[10] Symptoms are usually noted in children between the ages of 10 and 14 years: ■ Emotional lability ■ Increased sweating with heat intolerance ■ Increased appetite with or without weight loss ■ Insomnia ■ Tremors	■ Weakness ■ Nausea ■ Vomiting ■ Diarrhea ■ Other historical findings may be consistent with hypoglycemia, hyponatremia, and hypokalemia
Physical assessment	*Congenital:* ■ Respiratory distress ■ Abdominal distention ■ Hypotonia ■ Poor peripheral circulation ■ Hypothermia *Acquired:* ■ Goiter ■ Tenderness of the anterior neck ■ Weakness ■ Cool, dry skin	■ Persistent tachycardia ■ Systolic hypertension with markedly widened pulse pressure ■ Mild exophthalmos ■ Eyelid retraction and stare ■ Tremors ■ Warm, moist skin ■ Thyroid "storm": rare occurrence in children. Sudden onset of hyperthermia, severe tachycardia, and restlessness. ■ Neurologic status may deteriorate to coma ■ Death is rare	■ Nausea, vomiting, diarrhea, and abdominal pain ■ Dehydration leading to circulatory collapse ■ Fever initially, followed by hypothermia ■ Deteriorating level of consciousness progressing to coma

Table 22.7 Comparison of Thyroid and Adrenal Diseases   299

TABLE 22.7 Comparison of Thyroid and Adrenal Diseases (continued)

Characteristic	Hypothyroidism	Hyperthyroidism (Graves' Disease)	Acute Adrenal Insufficiency

Emergency treatment	Perform serum analysis:
	• Thyroxine (T4)
	• Free T4
	• Thyroid-stimulating hormone levels
		Serum analysis:
		• Thyroid function tests
		• Initiate oral antithyroid medication.
		• Administer propranolol intravenously, then orally
			• Maintain airway, breathing, and circulation.
			• Initiate fluid resuscitation with normal saline solution; administer a bolus of 10 to 20 mL/kg over a 20-minute period.
			• Administer 25% dextrose at 2 mL/kg if hypoglycemia is present.
			• Monitor cardiac rhythm and vital signs.
			• Obtain blood specimens and monitor for:
			  • Hypoglycemia
			  • Hyponatremia
			  • Hyperkalemia
			  • Decreased serum cortisol levels
			  • Acidosis

Management	Administration of levothyroxine (Synthroid)	• Activity restrictions
		• Medications such as propranolol and propylthiouracil
		• Radiation (controversial)
		• Surgery if medical management is not successful
			• Adrenal corticosteroid replacement therapy:
			  • Hydrocortisone, 2 mg/kg per dose, every 4 to 6 hours intravenously
			  • Cortisone 1 to 5 mg/kg per 24 hours, divided every 12 to 24 hours to allow tapering of intravenous medications[22]

References

1. Spence, A. (1990). *Basic human anatomy* (3rd ed., pp. 479). Menlo Park, CA: Benjamin Cummings.

2. Baxter, J. D., & Ribeiro, R. C. (2001). Introduction to endocrinology. In F. S. Greenspan & D. C. Gardner (Eds.), *Basic and clinical endocrinology* (6th ed.). New York: McGraw-Hill.

3. Witchel, S. F., & LynShue, K. (2007). Endocrinology. In B. Zitelli & H. Davis (Eds.), *Atlas of pediatric physical diagnosis* (5th ed.). St. Louis, MO: Mosby-Year Book.

4. Huether, S., & Tomky, D. (2005). Alterations of hormonal regulation. In K. McCance & S. Huether (Eds.), *Pathophysiology: The biologic basis for disease in adults and children* (5th ed.). St. Louis, MO: Mosby-Year Book.

5. Miller, B. S., & Zimmerman, D. (2004). Idiopathic short stature in children. *Pediatric Annals, 33*(3), 177–181.

6. Betschart, J. (2004). Endocrine and metabolic diseases. In C. Burns, A. Dunn, M. Brady, N. Starr, & C. Blosser (Eds.), *Pediatric primary care* (3rd ed.). Philadelphia: Saunders.

7. Alemzadeh, R., & Wyatt, D. T. (2004). Diabetes mellitus in children. In R. E. Berhman, R. M. Kliegman, & H. R. Jenson (Eds.), *Nelson textbook of pediatrics* (17th ed., pp. 1947–1972). Philadelphia: Saunders.

8. Peterson, K., Silverstein, J., Kaufman, F., & Warren-Boulton, E. (2007). Management of type 2 diabetes in youth: An update. *American Family Physician, 76*(3), 658–664.

9. Kaufman, F. R. (2002). Type 2 diabetes mellitus in children and youth: A new epidemic. *Journal of Pediatric Endocrinology and Metabolism, 15*(Suppl 2), 737–744.

10. Bacon, G., Spencer, M., Hopwood, N., & Kelch, R. (1990). *A practical approach to pediatric endocrinology.* Chicago: Year Book Medical Publishers.

11. Eisenbrath, G. S., Polonsky, K. S., & Buse, J. B. (2003). In P. R. Larsen, H. Kroneberg, S. Melmed, & K. Polonsky (Eds.), *Williams textbook of endocrinology* (10th ed., pp. 1485–1504). Philadelphia: Saunders.

12. Faulkner, M. S. (2003). Quality of life for adolescents with type 1 diabetes: Parental and youth perspectives. *Pediatric Nursing, 29*(5), 362–368.

13. Glaser, N. (2005). Pediatric diabetic ketoacidosis and hyperglycemic hyperosmolar state. *Pediatric Clinics of North America, 52*(6), 1611–1635.

14. McConnell, E. M. (2001). Achieving optimal diabetic control in adolescence: The continuing enigma. Diabetes and Metabolic Syndrome: *Clinical Research and Review, 17*(10), 67–74.

15. Trimarchi, T. (2006). Endocrine problems in critically ill children: An overview. *AACN Clinical Issues, 17*(1), 66–78.

16. Parks, J. S. (2004). Disorders of the hypothalamus and pituitary gland. In R. E. Behrman, R. M. Kliegman, & H. B. Jenson (Eds.), *Nelson textbook of pediatrics* (17th ed., pp. 1845–1853). Philadelphia: Saunders.

17. Ball, J. (1998). Endocrine. In J. Ball (Ed.), *Mosby's pediatric patient teaching guides* (pp. E1–E18). St. Louis, MO: Mosby-Year Book.

18. Daneman, D. (2006). Type 1 diabetes. *Lancet, 367*, 847–858.

19. Conte, F., & Grumbach, M. (1991). Endocrine disorders. In M. Grossman & R. Dieckmann (Eds.), *Pediatric emergency medicine: A clinician's reference* (pp. 467–473). Philadelphia: Lippincott.

20. Ballal, S. A., & McIntosh, P. (2008). Endocrinology. In J. Robertson & N. Shikofski (Eds.), *The Harriet Lane handbook* (18th ed.) St. Louis, MO: Elsevier.

21. Primary Children's Medical Center. (2000). *DKA protocol: Emergency department.* Salt Lake City, UT: Author.

22. Hoe, F. (2008). Endocrine. In W. Hay, M. Levin, J. Sondheimer, & R. Deterding (Eds.), *Current pediatric diagnosis & treatment* (19th ed.). New York: McGraw-Hill.

TWENTY-THREE

Hematologic and Oncologic Emergencies

Amy M. Pasmann, RN, BSN

Introduction

The blood system can be viewed as life's superhighway. It is a transporter of gases and electrolytes and provides defense mechanisms against microorganisms and injury. One small alteration in any hematologic component can lead to a life-altering, if not life-threatening, condition.

In pediatrics, hematologic disorders can arise in previously healthy children, as well as those with pre-existing conditions. The conditions can be congenital (sickle cell disease, hemophilia) or acquired (idiopathic thrombocytopenia, blood malignancies), and all require immediate recognition by the emergency nurse.

The purpose of this chapter is to address, recognize, and manage selected hematologic conditions and complications, as well as oncologic emergencies resulting from malignancies and their treatment in children who present to the emergency department (ED).

Embryologic Development of the Hematopoietic System

The hematologic system is multifaceted with many functions and "parts." Blood is primarily made up of plasma (circulating volume) and the cellular components: red blood cells (RBCs), white blood cells (WBCs), and platelets.[1] Table 23.1 describes these components and their purposes.

In the early few weeks of embryonic life, primitive nucleated RBCs are produced in the yolk sac. During the middle trimester of gestation, the liver is the main organ for production of RBCs, although RBCs are also produced by the spleen and lymph nodes. By the time of delivery, the bone marrow is the only significant site of hematopoiesis.[2]

Production of RBCs is stimulated primarily by the hormone erythropoietin. During periods of hypoxia, erythropoietin stimulates an increase in RBC production. Before birth, erythropoiesis increases because of the relative hypoxia that is present in utero.[2] At birth the lungs replace the placenta as the source of oxygenation, partial pressure of oxygen (PO_2) increases, and erythropoiesis declines. In children with chronic hypoxia secondary to congenital heart disease, increased erythropoiesis continues.

The production of blood cells, hematopoiesis, occurs secondary to the proliferation and differentiation of hematopoietic stem cells of the bone marrow. Stem cells are pluripotent, meaning they may have the potential to develop into many types of blood cells but are not necessarily committed to a specific cell line.[3] Eventually they develop a commitment to a specific cell line (unipotential stem cells) and are capable of forming only a particular type of cell in the myeloid or lymphoid line.

Pediatric Considerations

Red Blood Cells

Red blood cells (RBCs) in infants survive only 60 to 80 days, as compared with 80 to 100 days in a child and 120 to 150 days in an adult.[4] Under conditions of disease that create hemolysis, RBC production can also occur in extramedullary locations such as the spleen and liver. Typically, blood cell production tends to occur in the "red" (hematopoietic) marrow of the bones. However, because the majority of children's bones consist of mainly hematopoietic marrow, children have more splenic and liver involvement when RBC production is increasing.

TABLE 23.1 Comparison of RBCs, WBCs, and Platelets

Component	Function	Comments
RBCs (erythrocytes)	Transport hemoglobin, which carries oxygen to the lungs and tissues Acid-base buffer responsible for most of the buffering power of whole blood	RBCs have a shorter life span than in the older child and adult: 60–80 days in the neonate, 80–100 days in the child, and 120–150 days in the adult.
WBCs: Neutrophils Eosinophils Basophils Monocytes Lymphocytes Plasma cells	Mobile units of the body's protective system. They are transported in the blood to areas of serious infection and inflammation, providing a rapid and potent defense against infectious agents. Neutrophils, eosinophils, and basophils are called granulocytes, or "polys," because of multiple nuclei. Granulocytes and monocytes protect the body against invading organisms by phagocytosis. Lymphocytes and plasma cells function in connection with the immune system.	Each type of WBC has a specific function. WBCs have a short life span that is decreased when inflammation or infection is present.
Platelets (thrombocytes)	Platelets are fragments of megakaryocytes found in the bone marrow and function to activate the blood-clotting mechanism.	Platelets survive 7–10 days. About 30,000 platelets are formed each day for each microliter of blood. Normal platelet count is 150,000 to 400,000/mm³.

McCance, K. L. (2006) Structure and function of the hematologic system. In K. L. McCance, & S. E. Huether (Eds.), *Pathophysiology: The biologic basis for disease in adults and children* (5th ed, pp. 893–925). St. Louis, MO: Mosby.

This would explain why children with a hemolytic disease process might present with both splenic and liver enlargement.[2]

White Blood Cells

White blood cells (WBCs) are larger than RBCs and less flexible. The half-life of WBCs is the same for all ages (except the elderly): 6 to 8 hours in circulating blood and 4 to 9 days in tissues. Infants have a particularly immature immune system. The infant has fewer circulating phagocytes, and, because the phagocytes that are present are not well developed, infants have a poorer ability to fight infection.

As compared with adults, the average WBC count is higher in infants, as well as in children up to approximately 6 years of age. The WBC count will then continue to decline until adolescence when the lower adult values are reached. The average WBC count is between 5000 and 10,000 for an adult, but may be as high as 6000 to 15,000 for a 1-year-old.[2]

Platelets

Platelets develop from megakaryocytes by a process of proliferation.[3] The average platelet life span is 7 to 10 days. Platelet survival time is decreased in the presence of viral or bacterial infection. The normal platelet count is 150,000 to 400,000/mm³. A low platelet count (thrombocytopenia) results from either an inadequate production or an increased destruction or consumption of platelets.[5] Causes of thrombocytopenia in children include:

❒ Bone marrow failure or suppression

❒ Idiopathic thrombocytopenic purpura (ITP)

❒ Disseminated intravascular coagulation (DIC)

❒ Leukemia

❒ Acute infectious processes

Focused History

The following history should be obtained for any child with a suspected or known hematologic disorder:

❒ Recent illnesses, especially history of fever

❒ Exposures to infectious diseases or other illnesses

❒ History, including family history

❒ Recent immunizations

❒ Events surrounding the current illnesses: onset, duration, and treatment

❒ All current medications, including chemotherapy and over-the-counter medications

Focused Assessment

Physical Assessment

The standard pediatric assessment is done (Chapter 5). A hematologic or oncologic disorder can affect many different body systems, so a thorough assessment is necessary. If the child has a known coagulation problem or has undergone chemotherapy, a rectal temperature should not be taken because of the risk of causing rectal trauma, which can lead to bleeding and infection. Assessment findings that might indicate a hematologic or oncologic disorder include:

❐ Pallor

❐ Weight loss or poor nutritional status

❐ Generalized lymphadenopathy

❐ Lack of energy, lethargy

❐ Frequent infections

❐ Easy bruising

❐ Bleeding that is difficult to control

❐ Petechiae or purpura

❐ Unexplained fever

A child with a known hematologic or oncologic disorder may also present with pain and anxiety. Because these children are at risk for encephalopathy or intracranial hemorrhage, a thorough neurologic examination should be performed. The child should be assessed for either a totally or partially implanted venous access device, which could be a source of infection.

Psychosocial Assessment

The child and family are often fearful of anticipated procedures, treatment, and hospitalization because of unfamiliarity with or previous experiences in the emergency department. The following interventions may be helpful:

❐ Provide emotional support, because hematologic disease may be a chronic illness with the potential for frequent exacerbations.

❐ Anticipate expressions of concern, anger, and frustration if the child or family is frequently seeking treatment at the emergency department or primary care provider.

❐ Provide age-appropriate explanations for all procedures and treatments to both the child and family.

❐ Approach the child in a calm and reassuring manner and allow family members to be with the child.

❐ Offer age-appropriate distractions (e.g., toys or books) to the child.

❐ Offer adolescents an opportunity to discuss issues of concern (e.g., social isolation, loss of independence, "difference" from unaffected peers) in a nonjudgmental atmosphere.

❐ Address complaints of pain promptly and without judgment. Discussion of dependence or addiction to analgesics is not appropriate in the midst of pain.

❐ The family may come to the hospital frequently and appear demanding because they are familiar with the routine. Allowing them to participate and asking for their suggestions during treatment will be helpful. Consulting with a nurse from an inpatient unit who knows the child might also be helpful.

Triage Considerations

❐ Conditions that require immediate care (highest level of triage):

  ▪ Fever (in a child with a known hematologic or oncologic disorder)

  ▪ Severe pain

  ▪ Hypotension

  ▪ Tachycardia

  ▪ Hemorrhage

  ▪ Altered mental status

❐ Conditions that need to be seen as soon as possible:

  ▪ Mild to moderate pain

  ▪ Persistent but mild bleeding (no signs of hypovolemia)

  ▪ Bleeding into a joint

❐ Conditions that are nonurgent:

  ▪ No signs of active bleeding

  ▪ No complaints of pain

  ▪ Stable vital signs

Nursing Interventions

Nursing interventions in a child with a suspected or known hematologic or oncologic condition focus on the airway, breathing, and circulation.

1. Maintain the airway.

2. Provide oxygen and assist breathing, if necessary.

3. Support the circulation. Stop any bleeding. Administer intravenous fluids as needed.

4. Initiate protective isolation: Prevent the immunocompromised child from exposure to others who may be infectious.

5. Support the family and provide information as needed.

Specific interventions for Home Care and Prevention are discussed under each condition.

Specific Hematologic Emergencies

Sickle Cell Disease

Sickle cell disease (SCD) is a generic term used to describe an entire group of symptomatic disorders, the clinical, hematologic, and pathologic features of which are related to the presence of hemoglobin S (HbS). Although SCD is sometimes used to refer to sickle cell anemia (SCA), the terms are not interchangeable. SCA is one of a group of disease states collectively referred to as hemoglobinopathies. SCA is a disorder involving a predominance of HbS, when normal hemoglobin (hemoglobin A [HbA]) is partially or completely replaced by HbS. Other terms for SCA are HbSS and homozygous sickle cell disease.[3]

SCD is an inherited disorder primarily affecting African Americans; however, it is also seen in individuals of Mediterranean, Indian, and Middle Eastern descent. In the United States, SCD is most commonly observed in African Americans and Hispanics from the Caribbean, Central America, and parts of South America.[3]

There appears to be a geographic variable in the incidence of SCD. Among African Americans the incidence of sickle cell trait is 7% to 13%, whereas among East Africans, the incidence is as high as 45%.[3] It is thought that the sickle trait is a protective mechanism against the lethal forms of malaria in the endemic zones of the Mediterranean and Africa.

Pathophysiology

SCD is an inherited, autosomal-recessive disorder. Depending on the mode of inheritance, the disease may be manifested in the following patterns:

❑ *Sickle cell anemia:* The homozygous form of the disease, HbSS. This is the most severe form of SCD.

❑ *Sickle cell trait:* The heterozygous form of the disease, HbA and either HbS or HbAS. It is referred to as the carrier state of SCA. This form rarely exhibits clinical manifestations of SCD except when a child is extremely hypoxic.

❑ *Sickle cell–hemoglobin C disease:* A heterozygous variant of SCD, including both HbS and HbC or HbD.

❑ *Sickle cell–thalassemia disease:* A combination of sickle cell trait and β-thalassemia trait.

When both parents possess the sickle cell trait (HbAS), there is a 25% chance of their producing an offspring with SCA. In the United States, it is estimated that the frequency of SCA is one per 400 to 500 in newborn African Americans.[3]

SCD is several disorders characterized by the abnormal hemoglobin, HbS. Hemoglobin S is formed secondary to a defect in the globin fraction of hemoglobin, which is composed of more than 500 amino acids. The substitution of the amino acid, valine, for glutamic acid in the beta chains of the hemoglobin molecule is the basic defect of SCD.[3]

In deoxygenated, dehydrated, hypoxic, and/or acidotic conditions, the HbS molecule assumes an irregular, "sickled" (crescent moon–shaped) appearance. This sickled shape is associated with increased blood viscosity. Increased blood viscosity impedes flow and further contributes to deoxygenation. Tissue deoxygenation continues and spreads, eventually leading to obstruction within the microcirculation, precipitating tissue ischemia, infarcts, and necrosis, if left untreated.[3]

The clinical features of SCD are the results of obstruction caused by the sickled RBCs and increased destruction of sickled and normal RBCs caught in microcirculation obstructions. Chronic hemolytic anemia is present, subject to periods of acute exacerbation precipitated by dehydration, hypoxia, infection, and/or stress. The sickling, known as sickle cell crisis, may manifest in one or a combination of the following scenarios:[3,6]

Vaso-occlusive crises:

The dominant and most debilitating clinical complications associated with SCD may lead to permanent damage to any organ. Vaso-occlusive crisis may be triggered by infection, exposure to cold, low pH, or localized hypoxemia. There is marked variation in clinical presentation and course.

❑ Cerebral stroke: Cerebral infarction causes a varied presentation of neurologic compromise.

❑ Dactylitis (hand-foot syndrome): Characterized by pain and swelling of the soft tissue of the hands and feet of young children (6 months to 2 years of age). Seen less frequently in older children after the bone marrow of the small bones of the hands and feet loses hematopoietic activity.

❑ Priapism (prolonged, painful, unrelieved penile erection): Penile erection that may persist for hours and cause severe discomfort.

Pain crisis:

❑ The pathophysiology of SCD precipitates moderate to severe pain secondary to the ischemia and compromised microcirculation and, at times, general circulation.

❑ It is not uncommon for a child to present in the emergency department with generalized complaints of pain and localization of specifically painful areas.

❑ Children old enough to understand the pathophysiology and treatment of their condition may also be able to verbalize a request for a specific analgesic and analgesic dose that has worked for them in previous visits or admissions to the hospital.

Acute chest syndrome:

❑ Identified as the leading cause of death and hospitalization among patients with SCD,[7] the cause is largely unknown and treatment is supportive. Pulmonary emboli develop, with or without concomitant infection.

❑ May present with respiratory distress and pain and rapidly progress to respiratory failure.

Aplastic crisis:

Aplastic crisis results when there is an acute, but transient, decrease in the rate of red cell production in the bone marrow. This crisis may be precipitated by infection with human parvovirus-19 (fifth disease).[8] Typically the bone marrow is able to compensate for the shortened life span of the RBCs, and the body maintains a functioning hemoglobin level. In aplastic crisis, the balance is disturbed, typically by infection, and the hemoglobin slowly drops. If oxygen delivery is compromised, a red blood cell transfusion may be indicated; otherwise, if stable, the patient may be able to wait for bone marrow recovery and increased red cell production.[6]

Acute splenic sequestration crisis:

This is seen only in the young child and occurs as the spleen acutely pools large quantities of blood. The spleen can hold as much as one fifth of the body's blood supply at one time.[3] Up to 50% mortality has been reported because of precipitous hypotension, poor perfusion, and ultimate cardiovascular collapse. Sequestration crisis is rapid, and children have been known to die before arriving at the emergency department.[8]

❑ May be characterized with a sudden, rapid, massive enlargement of the spleen.

❑ Patients may suddenly become weak and dyspneic, with a distended abdomen, left-sided abdominal pain, and vomiting, which may progress to shock.

Infection:

❑ Children with SCD are at high risk for infections with *Streptococcus pneumoniae (S. pneumoniae), Haemophilus influenzae (H. influenzae),* and, less commonly, *Staphylococcus aureus (S. aureus)* and *Mycoplasma pneumoniae (M. pneumoniae).*

❑ Defective splenic function appears to be a major factor in susceptibility to infection. After splenic engorgement occurs, the spleen becomes incapable of normal reticuloendothelial function and may become small, fibrotic, and ineffective.

❑ The period of greatest risk is between the ages of 6 months and 3 years, when development of protective antibodies is limited and splenic function is compromised or absent.[6]

❑ Infection can be one of the most common causes of death resulting from SCD. Sepsis and meningitis may develop in 10% of children with SCA during their first 5 years of life, with a mortality rate of 25%.[2]

Focused History

Children with SCD may experience various complications of their illness that may result in a visit to the emergency department. The following history should be obtained:

❑ History
  - Family history of SCD
  - Past hospitalizations
  - Infections
  - Failure to thrive
  - Jaundice
  - Anemia
  - Previous sickling crisis
  - Painful joints
  - Use of penicillin. (Children with SCA often receive penicillin prophylaxis.)

❑ Present illness
  - Dactylitis: Painful swelling of hands and feet present for up to 2 weeks before spontaneously resolving
  - Joint swelling and pain
  - Chest pain
  - Infection: Fever, pain, malaise, and compromised activity
  - Abdominal pain
  - Headache
  - Nausea or vomiting

Focused Assessment

❑ Airway and breathing: Frequent assessment is essential to identify signs and symptoms of respiratory insufficiency because of the patient's increased susceptibility to infection and potential for acute chest crisis.

- Increased respiratory rate (per age-appropriate baseline)
- Increased respiratory effort (retractions, flaring)
- Decreased oxygen saturation (< 90% or normal for geographic location)
- Compromised chest expansion and complaints of chest pain (or abdominal pain—referred chest pain)

❑ Circulation: Findings of septic and/or hypovolemic shock can be present in forms of vaso-occlusive crisis and overwhelming infection.

- Increased heart rate
- Hypotension or normal blood pressure
- Decreased peripheral pulses
- Prolonged capillary refill time
- Pallor
- Cool extremities
- Increased respiratory rate or effort
- Poor urinary output and/or altered level of consciousness

❑ Disability: Altered level of consciousness

❑ Presence of pain: Investigate location, type, and intensity of pain (general and localized).

- Evaluate joints for signs and symptoms of sickling: Swollen, erythematous and painful; decreased range of motion; limping, changes in gait, and/or paresis.
- Evaluate for abdominal tenderness (guarding and rebound pain), hepatosplenomegaly, and vomiting, because these findings may be indicative of sickling in mesenteric or abdominal organ microcirculation. Pain in the left upper quadrant may also be indicative of sequestration crisis secondary to splenic congestion.
- Evaluate for priapism, which is reflective of obstructed microcirculation within the groin.

❑ Hydration status: Monitor for signs of inadequate perfusion.

- Altered level of consciousness
- Increased heart and respiratory rate (per baseline)
- Hypotensive or normal blood pressure
- Decreased peripheral pulses
- Prolonged capillary refill time
- Cool extremities
- "Tacky" mucous membranes in infants
- Pallor
- Decreased urinary output

❑ Eyes

- Evaluate for the presence of increased scleral icterus (jaundice).
- Ask the parent or caregiver to describe how the eyes normally look, because these children may typically exhibit some jaundice.

Nursing Interventions

1. Ensure airway patency.
2. Provide supplemental oxygen in a manner acceptable to the child.
3. Initiate intravenous access for administration of crystalloid and/or colloid intravenous fluids.
   - Crystalloid fluid resuscitation is followed by administration of one and one half to two times maintenance rate.
   - Replacement with 10 to 15 mL/kg of RBCs may be indicated during aplastic or hemolytic crises.
4. Administer analgesics and evaluate effectiveness.
   - Acetaminophen may be effective for mild pain.
   - Opiates will be necessary for moderate to severe pain.
   - The use of aspirin is contraindicated in children with sickle cell.
5. Administer antibiotics after obtaining blood and/or urinary cultures if infection is suspected.
6. Immobilize and support painful joints.

Home Care and Prevention

❑ Discuss preventive strategies with family.

- Ensure adequate fluid intake.
- Avoid high altitude or an abrupt change to high altitude.
- Avoid stressful situations.
- Avoid cold stress.
- Observe for signs and symptoms of infection and promptly initiate medical treatment.

❑ Encourage compliance with prophylactic antibiotic regimens.

❑ Promote compliance with all immunizations, including *H. influenzae.*

❑ Encourage age-appropriate behavior to avoid unnecessary trauma.

❑ Ensure that the child has a primary care provider for follow-up and routine care.

❑ Encourage the child and family to carry a medical information card.

Hemophilia

Until 1952 the term hemophilia was used exclusively to describe the bleeding disorder resulting from lack of factor VIII. Hemophilia is the term now used to collectively describe 90% to 95% of three distinct bleeding disorders resulting from deficiencies of factors VIII, IX, and XI. In this chapter, hemophilia will refer to hemophilia A and hemophilia B. Clinically, hemophilia A and B appear identical. Diagnostic differentiation is dependent on laboratory testing, however; the treatment of these disorders is different.

Hemophilia is the most common inherited coagulation bleeding disorder.[6] The incidence of hemophilia is about 1 in 5000 males, 85% having hemophilia A and 15% hemophilia B. In about two thirds of cases, a positive family history is present.[9]

Pathophysiology

Table 23.2 compares the pathophysiology of the different types of hemophilia and the symptoms associated with each type.

Patients with hemophilia (A and B) are categorized by their potential to experience bleeding based on the amount of factor deficiency. Table 23.3 lists the descriptions of these classifications.

Partial thromboplastin time is prolonged in hemophilia. Results of all other coagulation tests, prothrombin time, bleeding, and platelet count should be normal.

Patients with hemophilia often present during the newborn period at the time of circumcision, when prolonged bleeding is noted.[10] Associated manifestations may include prolonged cord bleeding or the presence of cephalhematoma. As the child gets older, tooth eruption may cause submucosal hematomas to develop. With increasing mobility, the toddler may develop more than the usual amount of bruising. The presence of bruising on the buttocks is unusual, and child abuse should be suspected if present (Chapter 44).

Hemarthrosis, or bleeding into the joints, is the most common complication of hemophilia. Most commonly seen in the knees, elbows, and ankles, hemarthrosis causes pain and limitation of mobility and predisposes the child to degenerative joint changes.[2] Intracranial bleeding or hemorrhage into the neck or abdomen can be life threatening.

Focused History

- ☐ History
    - Bleeding
    - Trauma
    - Pain
    - Family history of bleeding disorders
    - Coagulopathy
    - Thrombocytopenia
    - Previous diagnosis of hemophilia

TABLE 23.2 Characteristics of Hemophilia

Characteristic	Hemophilia A	Hemophilia B	Hemophilia C	von Willebrand's Disease
Factor deficiency	Factor VIII	Factor IX	Factor XI	vWF Factor VIII*
Inheritance	X-linked recessive: Carried by mother and expressed in son	X-linked recessive: Carried by mother and expressed in son	Autosomal recessive: Expressed equally in males and females	Numerous types Types I and II: Autosomal dominant Type III: Autosomal recessive Occurs in both males and females
Symptoms	Symptoms may be mild, moderate, or severe, depending on factor levels	Same as hemophilia A	Bleeding is less severe than in hemophilia A or hemophilia B	Symptoms may be mild, moderate, or severe depending on subgroup: Type I is associated with mild symptoms

*von Willebrand factor (vWF) is a specific clotting protein that normally helps platelets adhere to the wall of a disrupted blood vessel.

- Present illness
  - Manifested by hemarthroses and hematoma formation with minimal or no trauma
  - Prolonged bleeding
  - Spontaneous bleeding
  - Easy bruising
  - Hematuria
  - Pain and swelling in joints

TABLE 23.3 Hemophilia Factor Level and Bleeding Severity

Classification	Active Factor VIII	Potential for Bleeding
Severe	< 1%	May bleed spontaneously
Moderate	1%–5%	Bleed with mild trauma
Mild	6%–50%	Bleed with severe trauma or surgery

Focused Assessment

- Airway and breathing
  - The airway of a child experiencing bleeding as a result of hemophilia is intact unless the airway, oral cavity, chest, or neck is involved.
  - Tachypnea may be observed if the child is hypovolemic.
  - Spontaneous epistaxis is a relatively common finding.
- Circulation: Findings of hypovolemic shock (Chapter 38) can be present during overwhelming bleeding episodes.
- Neurologic system: Neurologic findings may indicate a variety of neurologic insults.
  - Altered level of consciousness, seizures, and headache may be observed in a patient with intracranial bleeding.
  - Paralysis, weakness, back pain, and asymmetric responses to a neurologic examination may be observed in a patient with a spinal cord hematoma.
- Gastrointestinal system
  - In young children with hemophilia, bleeding in the oral cavity is relatively common, secondary to tooth eruption and injury from the bumps or falls from learning to crawl and walk. By the age of 3 to 4 years, 90% of children with hemophilia have experienced bleeding from relatively minor traumatic lacerations to the lip or tongue.[2]

- Frank hemorrhage from the gastrointestinal tract is rarely severe.[6] A child who has swallowed blood from an oral bleeding episode may demonstrate hematemesis, melena, and nausea.
- Genitourinary system
  - Nontraumatic painless hematuria is the most common manifestation of renal bleeding. If a child has experienced trauma, renal damage may present as frank hematuria.
  - Prolonged bleeding from circumcision may be the defining event for the diagnosis of hemophilia in an infant.
- Skin
  - Subcutaneous bleeding, evidenced by ecchymosis and hematomas, is a common finding. Observe these lesions for changes in size and tenderness because an increase in either parameter may be indicative of continued bleeding.
  - Subcutaneous bleeding in the neck may be indicative of bleeding that could compromise the child's airway.
- Musculoskeletal system
  - Hemarthrosis commonly occurs in moderate to severe hemophilia.
  - Signs of hemarthrosis in the affected joints range from tenderness to severe pain, fullness to marked edema, decreased range of motion to refusal to move joint, gait changes in the lower extremities to a limp.

Nursing Interventions

1. Ensure airway patency.
   - Gently clear airway to prevent further trauma.
   - Assist with insertion of an artificial airway, if necessary, in life-threatening airway-bleeding episodes.
   - Provide supplemental oxygen in a manner acceptable to the child.
   - Replace fluid volume deficits with crystalloid and/or colloid fluids.
2. Administer missing coagulation factors and monitor for side effects and efficacy of factor replacement therapy.
   - Hemophilia A: Factor VIII via factor VIII concentrate, cryoprecipitate (factor VIII and fibrinogen), or fresh frozen plasma.
   - Hemophilia B: Factor IX via factor IX concentrate or fresh frozen plasma.
3. Promote comfort via administration of analgesics and evaluate their effectiveness.

4. Treat hemarthrosis
   - Provide rest, cold, immobilization, and elevation of affected joints.
   - Provide analgesia.
   - Avoid aspirin and salicylate-containing medications.

Home Care and Prevention

❑ Encourage child to wear medical alert identification.

❑ Ensure that parents are capable of understanding and executing instructions.
   - Parents should understand the risk for bleeding.
   - Parents can modify activities based on bleeding potential.
   - Parents can promptly recognize bleeding episodes and ensure access to interventions to control or arrest them.

❑ Develop a plan of home treatment of minor bleeding episodes in conjunction with primary care provider and supporting agencies.

Idiopathic Thrombocytopenia

Idiopathic thrombocytopenia (ITP) is a relatively common pediatric disorder characterized by a sudden onset of profound thrombocytopenia in an otherwise healthy child. ITP is a disorder of platelet consumption, in which antiplatelet antibodies bind to the plasma membranes of platelets. This leads to platelet sequestration and destruction by phagocytes at a rate that exceeds the ability of the bone marrow to produce them.[2] Why the autoantibody formation occurs is not clear. The classic presentation of ITP occurs in children 1 to 4 weeks after a viral infection,[5] with acute onset of petechial rash and bruising. Mucocutaneous bleeding, epistaxis, and hematuria can also be presenting symptoms. The child will otherwise appear well.

ITP can be acute or chronic; this discussion will refer to the acute form. Fortunately, spontaneous remission of ITP occurs. In general, about 75% of children recover within 3 months, and more than 90% recover within 3 to 6 months of onset of symptoms.[2]

Focused History

❑ History: Treatment for ITP

❑ Present illness: Abrupt onset of mucocutaneous bleeding in a previously healthy child, with or without epistaxis

❑ Recent viral infection

❑ Current medication usage

Focused Assessment

❑ Airway and breathing: The airway of a child experiencing bleeding from ITP is intact unless the airway or oral cavity is bleeding profusely.
   - Mucocutaneous lesions in the oral cavity rarely compromise the airway.
   - Tachypnea may be observed if circulation is compromised as a result of hypovolemia in large bleeding episodes.
   - Spontaneous epistaxis is also a relatively common finding.

❑ Circulation: Findings of hypovolemic shock (Chapter 38) can be present during serious hemorrhage.

❑ Neurologic system: Headaches, seizures, or altered level of consciousness may be indicative of intracranial bleeding (rare).

❑ Gastrointestinal system: Hemorrhagic bullae of the gums, lips, and other mucous membranes may be present, leading to melena.

❑ Genitourinary system: Hematuria is an occasional finding.

❑ Skin: Asymmetric bleeding is typical, with petechiae, purpura, and ecchymoses found over the trunk and bony prominences in the absence of trauma.

Nursing Interventions

1. Ensure airway patency and provide supplemental oxygen in a manner acceptable to the child.

2. Provide fluid for volume deficit.
   - Administer crystalloid to restore fluid volume.
   - Administer platelets only in life-threatening bleeding situations (intracranial hemorrhage).
   - Administer packed RBCs only if fluid crystalloid resuscitation is unsuccessful in restoring fluid volume or if hemorrhage is severe.

3. Apply ice and gentle pressure to the bleeding site, as appropriate.

4. Provide comfort measures and information to the child and family to decrease anxiety.

5. Administer medications, as ordered.
   - Considerable controversy exists on the most appropriate intervention for non–life-threatening bleeding.
   - A range of therapies may be offered, including administration of oral or intravenous steroids; administration of intravenous immunoglobulin; administration of anti-D for Rh-positive patients; observation without intervention.[5]

Home Care and Prevention

❑ Address knowledge deficits and clarify misconceptions.

- Injury prevention for patients with low platelet levels: Restrict activities to avoid trauma, particularly head injury (e.g., avoid bicycle riding, roller blading, and contact sports, and/or wear a protective helmet during activity). Avoid administering intramuscular injections. Reinforce use of soft toothbrush or sponge Toothettes for oral hygiene to minimize oral bleeding.

- Avoid aspirin and aspirin-containing products, as well as nonsteroidal anti-inflammatory medications.

❑ Explain follow-up care. Refer to primary care physician.

Disseminated Intravascular Coagulation

Disseminated Intravascular Coagulation (DIC) is an acquired hemorrhagic syndrome, characterized by uncontrolled formation and deposition of fibrin thrombi and resulting in consumption of clotting factors, which leads to uncontrolled bleeding.

In the oncology population, DIC can result from:

❑ Acute nonlymphocytic leukemia (also known as ANLL/AML)

❑ Acute promyelocytic leukemia (APML)

❑ Intravascular lysis: Acute tumor lysis syndrome

In oncology patients and in the general pediatric population, DIC can also result from:

❑ Infection or sepsis (Gram-positive and/or Gram-negative organisms)

❑ Hypoxemia or hypoperfusion (e.g., cardiac arrest)

Pathophysiology

DIC is a "consumptive disorder" caused by abnormal activation of the clotting mechanism, resulting in rapid depletion of platelets, prothrombin, and fibrinogen. This hypercoagulable state leads to microthrombi within the vascular system, which, in turn, lead to a situation of simultaneous thrombosis and hemorrhage.[11] DIC may be a result of numerous causes, but, in children, it is commonly attributed to shock.[6]

Focused History

❑ Present illness

- Bleeding from single or multiple sites

- Dizziness, weakness

- Rash: Petechiae, ecchymosis

❑ Past and current medical history

- Neoplasm

- Repeated blood transfusions

- Myelosuppression secondary to chemotherapy

- Medications, including anticoagulants and aspirin

Focused Assessment

❑ Airway and breathing

- The airway may be subject to compromise from compression of soft tissue secondary to bleeding of the neck, oral cavity, and chest.

  • Increased respiratory rate and effort (retractions or flaring)

  • Cyanosis

  • Hemoptysis, nasopharyngeal bleeding, or epistaxis

  • Pulmonary hemorrhage

❑ Circulation: Signs and symptoms consistent with cardiovascular compromise secondary to hypovolemic and/or septic shock may be present.

- Increased heart rate

- Hypotension or normal blood pressure

- ST segment changes on the electrocardiogram

- Cool, mottled extremities

- Decreased peripheral pulses

- Prolonged capillary refill time

- Acrocyanosis

❑ Neurologic system: Signs and symptoms consistent with altered perfusion and/or cerebral bleeding may be present.

- Restlessness or change in mood or affect, lethargy

- Confusion or disorientation

- Alteration in level of consciousness, headache, and/or seizures

❑ Gastrointestinal/genitourinary system

- Melena or frank GI bleeding

- Oliguria or anuria

- Hematuria; urethral bleeding

- Flank pain (secondary to deposition of renal microvascular fibrin)

❑ Skin

- Petechiae

- Purpura

- Ecchymosis

- Oozing from venipuncture sites; wound hematoma
- Pallor

❏ Musculoskeletal system

- Severe muscle pain secondary to ischemia
- Decreased range of motion in areas with active bleeding

Nursing Interventions

1. Monitor vital signs and assess for shock.

2. Maintain airway patency and provide supplemental oxygen in a manner tolerable to the child.

3. Establish intravenous access for administration of crystalloid and/or colloid fluids.

4. Maintain adequate hydration to prevent renal failure (secondary to hemoglobinuria).

5. Monitor:

- Tissue perfusion, including color, temperature, capillary refill, and peripheral pulses.
- Overt or covert bleeding: Urine, stool, emesis, and needle puncture sites.
- Laboratory values: Fibrinogen, prothrombin time, partial thromboplastic time, d-dimer assay, hemoglobin, hematocrit, and platelet count.
- Urinary output.

6. Administer blood products as ordered. Intravenous heparin infusion may be indicated.

7. Protect the child from further injury: Handle gently, avoid repeated venipunctures or invasive measures, decrease environmental stimuli, and promote rest.

8. Monitor therapeutic response of precipitating conditions.

Specific Oncologic Emergencies

Pediatric cancer outcomes and incidence vary by sex, age, and race of the child. Annually, a malignancy is diagnosed in 150 individuals per million (approximately 12,400) in the population younger than 20 years of age.[12] Of that, approximately 1 in 7000 children under the age of 14 years will receive this diagnosis in the United States. The most common pediatric malignancy of children 0 to 14 years is acute lymphoblastic leukemia, followed by tumors of the central nervous system. For children aged 15 to 19 years, Hodgkin's disease and germ cell tumor are the most common. Pediatric cancer remains the leading cause of disease-related death among children 0 to 14 years of age.[13] Overall, 75% of these children will enjoy a long-term, disease-free survival after effective treatment.

The majority of children with cancer are treated by a tertiary care center with a pediatric department dedicated to their care. When complications arise, they do not always present to the center providing their therapy. This presents emergency departments around the country with the challenge of caring for children whose current treatment is unknown. The anticancer therapy selected depends on the disease process. Most therapies include a combination of multiagent chemotherapy, radiation, and surgery. Each of these treatments carries known toxicities and morbidity. Chemotherapeutic agents are known to cause cytopenias, metabolic imbalances, nausea, and vomiting, and these are the primary reasons for the child's frequent visits to the emergency department.

Patients who are unaware of an underlying malignancy or who have progressive disease may present with compression or obstruction of vital organ structures. These instances represent emergent situations for patients.

The purpose of this section is to describe the effects of malignancies (mechanical, systemic, hematopoietic, renal, metabolic) and specific conditions that are side effects of chemotherapy and discuss ED considerations. The pertinent history and assessment findings are summarized under each condition.

Mechanical Effects of Malignancy

Superior Vena Cava Syndrome and Superior Mediastinal Syndrome

Superior vena cava syndrome (SVCS) and superior mediastinal syndrome (SMS) may be used synonymously. SVCS refers to the signs and symptoms of compression or obstruction of the superior vena cava. The term SMS is used when tracheal compression also occurs, therefore referring to the compression on the trachea resulting from the presence of a mediastinal mass.[14] The trachea and bronchus in children are relatively rigid, compared with the superior vena cava, but may be compressed by a mediastinal mass. The relatively small intraluminal diameter of the child's trachea does not tolerate much compromise before the child begins to exhibit symptoms of respiratory distress.

SVCS has a relatively low incidence in pediatrics, accounting for approximately 12% of all thoracic tumors. A more common cause is thrombosis secondary to central venous catheters, and most children with cancer have central lines.[11]

Malignant tumors are the most common primary cause of SVCS and SMS in children. Tumors that may present in the mediastinum, causing SMS, include:

❏ Leukemia

❏ Non-Hodgkin's lymphoma

❏ Neuroblastoma

❏ Hodgkin's disease

ED Considerations

Symptoms arising from malignancy often have a rapid, insidious course because of the doubling time of tumors responsible for SMS. Patients will often present with a brief history of increasing respiratory compromise, including cough, hoarseness, dyspnea, orthopnea, confusion, and chest pain.

Assessment findings may include swelling and cyanosis of the face, neck, and upper extremities; engorged vessels of the chest wall; erythema and edema of the conjunctiva; diaphoresis; coughing and wheezing; chest pain; headache; and visual changes. Symptoms may be exacerbated in the supine position and noted during the physical assessment or during a radiologic examination.[14]

Care is focused on supporting the airway, breathing, and circulation. Patients with new or progressive mediastinal neoplasms will be admitted for observation, diagnosis, supportive care, and initiation of therapy.

Spinal Cord Compression

Spinal cord compression occurs as a result of rapid tumor growth within or surrounding the spinal column. Spinal cord compression develops in approximately 5% of patients with malignancies or at recurrence. Spinal cord compression, while uncommon in children, is usually associated with a space-occupying lesion. Prompt recognition and treatment are required in the hope of preserving neurologic function.[11]

Of children presenting with true cord compression, the primary diagnosis is most commonly Ewing's sarcoma, neuroblastoma, lymphoma, and leukemia. Pediatric solid tumors that may result in cord compression include Wilms' tumor, osteosarcoma, and rhabdomyosarcoma.[11]

ED Considerations

Rapid recognition, evaluation, and treatment of spinal cord compression may prevent permanent neurologic complications. Pain is the most common complaint (80%) in children experiencing cord compression. Progression may be rapid or variable, depending on the underlying disease process. Cord compression should be a high consideration for any child with back pain until proved otherwise.[14]

Assessment findings include:

❏ Localized tenderness to percussion in affected area

❏ Unilateral or bilateral muscle weakness

❏ Increased or decreased tendon reflexes

❏ Loss of sensation, numbness, or paresthesia

❏ Later symptoms may include loss of bowel function or bladder control

Treatment must be immediate and aggressive to prevent further impairment or permanent loss of function. Nursing measures are mainly supportive in maintaining airway, breathing, and circulation and observing for progression of symptoms. Intravenous access for the administration of high-dose corticosteroids, as well as pain control, should be initiated.

Systemic Effects of Malignancy

Acute Tumor Lysis Syndrome

Tumor lysis syndrome (TLS) is an oncologic emergency resulting from the massive necrosis of rapidly dividing tumor cells, usually a result of administration of combination chemotherapy. TLS may occur before the diagnosis of cancer but occurs most frequently during the initial phase of treatment while the child is hospitalized. Laboratory findings include hypocalcemia, hyperuricemia, hyperkalemia, hyperphosphatemia, azotemia, and metabolic acidosis. Acute renal failure can result from the precipitation of uric acid, xanthine, and phosphate in the renal tubules. Severe renal dysfunction may further develop if the patient is experiencing dehydration and oliguria.[15]

Tumor types that commonly result in TLS include Burkitt's lymphoma and T-cell leukemia lymphoma. Either of these malignancies can present with an intra-abdominal component, representing a large tumor "burden."

Rapid cellular death is characterized by the release of intracellular contents. Intracellular components (uric acid, phosphorus, and potassium) are normally excreted by the kidney. Patients with inadequate renal function are unable to excrete ample amounts of these salts. Formation of uric acid crystals in the renal collecting duct or calcium phosphate precipitates in the microvasculature of the kidney may result in renal failure. Hypocalcemia may cause seizures. The sudden release and rise of potassium may result in ventricular arrhythmia and death.[14]

ED Considerations

The child may present to the emergency department with complaints of abdominal pain or fullness, back pain, change in the amount of urine production, vomiting, generalized weakness or fatigue, numbness, and/or tingling. Particular attention should be paid to the child's blood pressure, heart rate and rhythm, and signs of altered levels of consciousness related to hypocalcemia.

Assessment findings include abdominal fullness, decreased urinary output, hypoxia, adenopathy, and petechiae; laboratory results reveal hyperkalemia, uremia, hyperphosphatemia, and hypocalcemia.[11]

Treatment

❏ Hyperhydration with intravenous fluids containing sodium bicarbonate to provide urinary alkalinization.

❏ Monitoring of urine for crystal deposits and pH. (An indwelling bladder catheter is therefore suggested.)

❏ Electrocardiogram monitoring for potential cardiac arrhythmias.

❏ Analysis of blood for uric acid, potassium, calcium, and phosphorus.

❏ Administration of oral allopurinol to decrease uric acid production.

Admission for ongoing management and diagnosis of the underlying disease should be anticipated, including transfer to a pediatric facility equipped to provide critical pediatric care if needed (Chapter 8).

Hyperleukocytosis

Hyperleukocytosis occurs when a peripheral WBC count is greater than 100,000 cells/mm[3].[14,15] Hyperleukocytosis can cause death secondary to central nervous system hemorrhage or thrombosis, pulmonary leukostasis with respiratory failure, or metabolic changes secondary to TLS.

Hyperleukocytosis occurs in previously well children with a short duration of nonspecific complaints. Hyperleukocytosis is seen in 10% of patients with acute lymphocytic leukemia, 20% of patients with ANLL, and 100% of patients with chronic myelogenous leukemia in the acute phase.[15] Cytopenias frequently accompany these diagnoses of leukemia, further contributing to metabolic abnormalities and blood coagulopathies.

The viscosity of the blood is increased in patients with hyperleukocytosis because of the presence of WBC aggregates and thrombin in the microcirculation. Myeloblasts, responsible for acute myelogenous leukemia, are relatively large. The blast cells are not easily deformable and do not pass readily through the microvasculature, resulting in thrombi. Their anaerobic metabolism contributes to lactic acidosis. The blasts, trapped in the microvasculature of the brain or pulmonary parenchyma, may degenerate and release intracellular contents, resulting in tissue damage. TLS, described in the previous section, occurs when the cells release their intracellular contents.

ED Considerations

Clinical signs can include dyspnea, tachypnea, blurred vision, agitation, confusion, or stupor. Assessment find-

ings include hypoxia, cyanosis, papilledema, ataxia, and a WBC count greater than 100,000 cells/mm[3].[11]

Nursing Interventions

1. Initiation of venous access.

2. Assessment of urine output and pH.

3. Blood product support (exchange transfusions, platelets), as well as leukapheresis and chemotherapy administration.

4. Monitoring of blood gases and chemistries.

5. Ongoing neurologic assessment.

6. Admission for further diagnostic evaluation and treatment.

Hematopoietic Effects of Malignancy

Infections are the leading cause of morbidity related to treatment in the pediatric oncology population.[6] A number of coexisting conditions contribute to the increased risk of infection:

❏ Treatment-related alterations in taste, nausea, vomiting, and food aversion contribute to compromised nutritional status and depleted protein stores.

❏ Impaired chemotaxis, a defective macrophage-monocyte system, and immunologic dysfunction result from chemotherapy and steroid administration, as well as from the disease.

❏ The presence of an indwelling venous catheter further compromises the patient's status by providing an additional portal of entry for bacteria.

❏ Neutropenia (discussed in the next section).

Neutropenia

The greatest risk factor for development of infection is treatment-related neutropenia—an absolute neutrophil count less than 500. Treatment-related myelosuppression develops in patients receiving marrow-suppressive chemotherapy approximately 7 to 10 days after administration. The duration and degree of neutropenia are known risk factors for the development of infection. Neutropenia lasting greater than 10 to 14 days and/or an absolute neutrophil count of less than 500 cells/mm[3] greatly increases the risk of infection. The greatest source of bacterial infection is the patient's own microbial flora.

Radiation therapy may have an impact on the production of WBCs, RBCs, and platelets. In young children, marrow production occurs primarily in the bones of the extremities. As children mature, marrow production becomes more central. Lymphocytes are exquisitely sensitive to radiation. Irradiation directly to an area of marrow production has the greatest effect. Cells that pass through the area of radiation during treatment are also affected.

ED Considerations

Fever is often the only sign of infection in the patient who has neutropenia; however, patients may also present acutely ill and in septic shock (Chapter 38) and require immediate attention. The majority of patients are febrile at home and are sent by their oncologist for a physical examination, blood cultures, and evaluation of blood counts. Children who are known to have neutropenia and who present with a history of fever, even though they appear well, should be evaluated immediately. Their status can change quickly, and delay in evaluation and administration of broad-spectrum intravenous antibiotics can have a detrimental effect on their condition.

Prompt management is indicated to prevent the development of a life-threatening infection in the patient with neutropenia presenting with fever.

The history should include:

❒ Dates of last chemotherapy and /or radiation treatments

❒ Presence of a central line

❒ Duration and height of fever

❒ Any associated symptoms (vomiting, diarrhea, associated pain)[16]

Knowing that changes in vital signs may lag behind change in the child's physical status, and because of the risk of development of septic shock, the child's vital signs should be monitored frequently. The child with neutropenia may not demonstrate symptoms of shock until after the administration of antibiotics.[11] Emergency department staff and the oncology department should develop the following protocols:

❒ Triage guidelines for a known oncologic patient with fever that stipulate these patients should be placed in a private room and evaluated immediately.

❒ Prompt administration of antibiotics (after cultures are obtained).

❒ Isolation to protect from infectious patients or rapid admission to the oncology unit.

❒ Restriction of invasive procedures (avoidance of rectal temperatures, medications, and examinations).

Thrombocytopenia and Bleeding

Thrombocytopenia is defined as a quantitative decrease in the number of circulating platelets, often interpreted as a platelet count of fewer than 100,000 cells/mm³. Treatment-related marrow suppression develops in

patients receiving marrow-suppressive chemotherapy approximately 7 to 10 days after administration of chemotherapy. The life span of platelets is approximately 7 to 10 days. When bone marrow production is interrupted by marrow-toxic chemotherapy, a brief period of thrombocytopenia develops.

Children rarely experience severe bleeding at platelet counts greater than 20,000 cells/mm³. The incidence of serious intracranial bleeding increases with platelet counts fewer than 20,000 cells/mm³.[5] The administration of prophylactic platelet transfusion for children who are actively bleeding remains controversial. Frequent transfusion of blood products increases the potential for development of sensitization to foreign antigens found on the surfaces of random-donor platelets (alloimmunization).[6] Each institution or practitioner must weigh the risks and benefits of prophylactic platelet administration.

ED Considerations

A child may present to the emergency department with sites of frank bleeding, dark stool, hematuria, bruising, petechiae, headache, vomiting, dizziness, weakness, or neurologic changes. The history may include recent chemotherapy, previous transfusions, the presence of an implanted venous access device, and fever.

Nursing Interventions

1. Observe for signs and symptoms of covert or overt bleeding.

2. Apply local pressure after venipuncture or invasive procedures.

3. Apply local pressure for epistaxis.

4. Administer platelets as ordered.

   ▪ Obtain a post infusion platelet count.

   ▪ The use of leukocyte-depleted, irradiated, cytomegalovirus-negative blood products is preferred.

Home Care and Prevention

❒ Implement "bleeding precautions" in patients with thrombocytopenia.

❒ Restrict activities that could result in head trauma (e.g., skateboarding, trampolines, or bicycling).

❒ Keep room air humidified to decrease the likelihood that epistaxis will result from dried mucous membranes.

❒ Do not use medications that may interfere with platelet function (aspirin, ibuprofen).

❒ Use an extra-soft toothbrush or oral care sponge.

❒ Notify physician if new bleeding or oozing is noted.

Anemia

Anemia can be defined as a deficiency of RBCs, or hemoglobin leading to a decreased ability to transport oxygen. For the oncologic pediatric patient, anemia is multifactorial and can be a result of marrow infiltration (secondary to malignancy), chemically induced suppression (marrow-toxic chemotherapy), infection, or even hemorrhage.[17] At the time of diagnosis, most children with leukemia are anemic.[16,17]

ED Considerations

The number and severity of symptoms caused by anemia depends on the body's ability to compensate for the reduced oxygen-carrying capacity of the erythrocytes. Depending on the severity of the anemia, and the child's symptoms in the emergency department, a blood transfusion may not be necessary. If the child's hemoglobin range is between 1 and 5 g/dL, in the absence of hemorrhage, a transfusion may be required. The rate at which the blood is transfused should be at a slower rate than usual; anything faster than 3 to 5 mL/kg over a 4-hour period may precipitate heart failure.[16] Recommended blood bank practice for ordering blood for an oncology patient should include irradiated and leukocyte-reduced blood products.[18]

The child may present to the emergency department with complaints of dyspnea, a rapid, pounding heartbeat, dizziness, and fatigue, even at rest. Low-grade fever (temperature of less than 100.4 °F or 38.0 °C) occurs in some anemic individuals and may be the result of leukocyte pyrogens being released from ischemic tissues.

The history obtained should include primary diagnosis, recent chemotherapy, type of chemotherapy administered, previous transfusion reactions, necessary transfusion premedications, and all concurrent medications. The physical assessment may reveal:

- ❑ Gallop arrhythmia
- ❑ Pallor
- ❑ Cyanosis
- ❑ Tachycardia

Nursing Interventions

1. Administer 100% oxygen.
2. Obtain type and crossmatch for transfusion of blood products.
3. Initiate intravenous access.
4. Administer appropriate blood product, per hospital protocol.
5. Monitor for side effects related to blood administration.

Renal and Metabolic Effects of Malignancy

Hemorrhagic Cystitis

Hemorrhagic cystitis is a complication of chemotherapy that can manifest itself as painful urination with the presence of either gross or microscopic blood. The use of cyclophosphamide and ifosfamide as chemotherapeutic agents is a principal cause of this condition. The metabolism of each of these medications creates a metabolite, acrolein that causes mucosal inflammation and bleeding when in contact with the bladder wall. Main features of hemorrhagic cystitis include mucosal edema, necrosis, ulceration, hemorrhage, and leukocyte infiltration of the bladder wall.[18]

Hemorrhagic cystitis may occur hours or years after administration of chemotherapy. Radiation therapy to the pelvis may cause chronic hematuria, requiring long-term urology follow-up.[18]

ED Considerations

The child may present to the emergency department with complaints of lower abdominal pain secondary to bladder spasms, painful urination, and frank blood in the urine and may or may not have fever. A recent history of cyclophosphamide or ifosfamide administration should be assessed.

Nursing Interventions

1. Obtain intravenous access.
2. Administer antispasmodics, as prescribed.
3. Initiate oral or intravenous hydration.
4. Place a double-lumen urinary catheter for bladder irrigation to remove clots.
5. Administer blood products to replace blood loss.

Hypomagnesemia

Nephrotoxicity may develop secondary to a number of chemotherapeutic agents, including cisplatin. Cisplatin, specifically, is associated with both proximal and distal renal tubular damage. Tubular damage can lead to excessive wasting of electrolytes, including magnesium, potassium, bicarbonate, and phosphorus.

ED Considerations

The child with hypomagnesemia may present to the emergency department with malaise, leg and foot cramps, "racing" heart, recent administration of cisplatin, and renal disease. Assessment findings include:

- ❑ Hyperactive deep tendon reflexes
- ❑ Tachycardia

❐ Disorientation

❐ Visual or auditory hallucinations

❐ Seizures

❐ Decreased serum magnesium level

Nursing Interventions

1. Monitor heart rate and rhythm.

2. Obtain 12-lead electrocardiogram.

3. Administer magnesium supplements, and monitor for side effects.

4. Monitor serum magnesium levels.

Home Care and Prevention

❐ Oral magnesium supplementation regimen

❐ Follow-up with the primary physician for repeat serum magnesium levels

Hypercalcemia

Hypercalcemia is defined as a serum calcium level of greater than 12 mg/dL. Organ damage may occur with levels greater than 12, and levels greater than 15 mg/dL can be fatal.[19] Hypercalcemia is less likely to develop in children than in adults. Calcium levels may rise in children with cancer for several reasons, but most commonly it is related to bony destruction secondary to malignancy and/or the tumor itself that may actually secrete an ectopic hormone with parathyroid-like effects. Children with acute lymphoblastic leukemia are more likely to have hypercalcemia but are also more likely to respond to therapy. Patients with solid tumors may present with hypercalcemia further on in therapy and are more resistant to correction.[14]

ED Considerations

Patients with moderately elevated calcium levels may be asymptomatic. Early symptoms of escalating serum calcium levels are nonspecific and commonly associated with cancer. Patients may complain of anorexia, nausea, vomiting, and diarrhea. These symptoms contribute to dehydration and further elevation of calcium. The kidney attempts to reduce the excess calcium, resulting in polyuria, which further exacerbates the situation. Treatment is directed at improving renal excretion of calcium and reducing bone reabsorption.[14] The child may also have symptoms of fatigue, lethargy, confusion, weakness, bradycardia, arrhythmia, thirst, and polyuria.[16]

Nursing Interventions

1. Administer fluids and calcium excreting "loop diuretics," as prescribed.

2. Monitor for side effects.

3. Monitor serum calcium levels.

4. Monitor cardiac rhythm.

5. Obtain 12-lead electrocardiogram.

Other Complications of Chemotherapy

Cardiomyopathy

Cardiomyopathy, a defect of the heart muscle resulting from damage to cardiac myocytes, may present as a late effect of cancer treatment.[15] Chemotherapy, specifically anthracyclines, may cause rhythm disturbances, cardiomyopathy, and cardiac failure. The total dosing, as well as frequency of the chemotherapy given, may increase the risk of cardiac dysfunction. Risk factors for the development of cardiomyopathy related to cancer treatment include:

❐ Age 5 years or younger at time of exposure

❐ Radiation therapy to the mediastinum

❐ Combination of chemotherapy and radiation to the chest area

❐ Underlying cardiac disease

ED Considerations

The child may present to the emergency department with shortness of breath, exercise limitations, fatigue, irregular heart rate, and cough. The history may include a neoplasm treated with anthracycline or radiation, or previous cardiac problems. Assessment findings may include dyspnea, arrhythmia, rales, and cyanosis.

Nursing Interventions

1. Monitor airway, breathing, and circulation.

2. Monitor for signs and symptoms of cardiogenic shock (Chapter 38).

3. Administer diuretics, as prescribed.

4. Limit fluid intake, as directed.

5. Obtain cardiology consultation.

6. Anticipate admission for monitoring and further therapy.

Seizures

Seizures are transient involuntary changes in mentation, behavior, sensation, and motor or autonomic function. In the pediatric cancer patient, increased intracranial pressure as a result of a primary brain neoplasm with a mass effect, or the presence of diffuse metastatic disease to the central nervous system, can cause seizures. Additionally, seizures may be caused by certain metabolic crises inducted by therapy, including hypoglycemia and hyponatremia. Other factors leading to seizures in this population may also include cranial irradiation and side effects of specific chemotherapy drugs.[14]

ED Consideration

Seizures are treated in the same manner as with any other patient (Chapter 16). The cause of the seizures must be determined (and not necessarily assumed to be the result of chemotherapy). Acute management focuses on maintenance of airway, prevention of aspiration, and avoidance of injury.[16] Treatment considerations include:

❑ Evaluation and management of electrolytes

❑ Detailed chemotherapy and/or radiation history, including any medications given intrathecally

❑ Presence or absence of a Ventro-peritoneal shunt

❑ Preparation for radiologic examinations

❑ Medication to prevent prolonged seizures

❑ Neurology consultation

Stroke

A stroke is an acute hemorrhage and formation of thrombosis within the brain, secondary to a coagulation abnormality (Chapter 16). Cerebrovascular accidents that occur during cancer treatment most frequently may be attributed to specific chemotherapy agents and/or infection.[14] Cerebrovascular accidents that occur at presentation of a malignant disease process may be secondary to disease-related coagulation abnormalities. Hyperleukocytosis, discussed earlier, may also be a contributing factor.

ED Considerations

The child may come to the emergency department with complaints of dyspnea, blurred vision, irritability, confusion, stupor, and a history of treatment with L-asparaginase, cranial irradiation, or underlying acute myelogenous leukemia. The nursing assessment may reveal the following signs and symptoms:

❑ Motor function impairment

❑ Speech impairment

❑ Asymmetric pupils

❑ Sensory changes

❑ Ataxia

❑ Altered level of consciousness

❑ Neurology consultation

Nursing Interventions

1. Manage airway, breathing, and circulation.

2. Obtain intravenous access.

3. Perform frequent neurologic assessments.

4. Collect blood for coagulation studies.

5. Administer corticosteroid or hyperosmolar agents, as prescribed.

Typhlitis

The pediatric cancer patient who arrives at the emergency department with complaints of abdominal pain needs a thorough history and assessment. Many cancer patients may present with the typical childhood disorders that are characterized by abdominal pain (i.e., gastroenteritis, appendicitis, constipation). However, the cancer patient with neutropenia is at risk for typhlitis, a form of necrotizing colitis. Typhlitis will affect approximately 6% of patients with leukemia, typically in their first month of therapy.[14]

ED Considerations

The child with typhlitis will present to the emergency department in a very similar fashion as a child with appendicitis. Chief complaints of persistent right lower quadrant pain and fever are often described. The child will have neutropenia and may have a distended abdomen, and, over time, the pain will become more generalized to the entire abdomen. Nausea and vomiting are common, as well as bloody diarrhea.[11]

Nursing Interventions

1. Evaluate bowel sounds and pain level.

2. Obtain intravenous access.

3. Administer bolus and maintenance fluids as needed.

4. Administer pain medication, as directed.

5. Administer broad-spectrum antibiotics.

6. Provide continual nursing assessment and monitoring for signs and symptoms of septic shock.

7. Prepare for possible surgery and/or admission.

Conclusion

The emergency nurse must be astute to the changes that can occur within a patient's hematologic system and must be aware that these changes can quickly compromise the child's life. Recognition and management of a sickle cell patient in crisis can reverse a painful and possibly deadly situation. Understanding the immediate need to infuse factor in a patient with hemophilia with bleeding may save a joint.

In the oncology patient, an accurate history, including recent medications, will direct the emergency nurse in how to proceed with quick and accurate patient care management. Any child with neutropenia presenting with fever requires a rapid assessment and prompt interventions to prevent the child from progressing into septic shock and possibly death.

Life's superhighway can have many roadblocks. Whether hematologic or oncologic, each disorder requires accurate assessment and history taking to understand the mechanisms that are failing. The essentials of clearing the roadblocks are the responsibility of a fast-moving, quick-thinking ED team that has the ability to recognize both the acute and chronic complications of these conditions.

References

1. Swartz, M. K. (2004). Hematologic diseases. In C. E. Burns, M. Brady, C. Blosser, N. Barber Starr, & A. Dunn (Eds.), *Pediatric primary care: A handbook for nurse practitioners* (3rd ed., pp. 649–671). Philadelphia: Saunders.

2. Kline, N. E. (2006). Alterations of hematologic function in children. In K. L. McCance & S. E. Huether (Eds.), *Pathophysiology: The biologic basis for disease in adults and children* (5th ed, pp. 999–1026). St. Louis, MO: Mosby.

3. McCance, K. L. (2006) Structure and function of the hematologic system. In K. L. McCance & S. E. Huether (Eds.), *Pathophysiology: The biologic basis for disease in adults and children* (5th ed, pp. 893–925). St. Louis, MO: Mosby.

4. Brugnara, C., & Platt, O. S. (2009). Neonatal hematology: The neonatal erythrocyte and its disorders. In D. G. Nathan, S. H. Orkin, A. T. Look, & D. Ginsburg (Eds.), *Nathan and Oski's hematology of infancy and childhood* (7th ed, pp. 21–66). Philadelphia: Saunders.

5. Wilson, D. B. (2009). Acquired platelet defects. In D. G. Nathan, S. H. Orkin, A. T. Look, & D. Ginsburg (Eds.), *Nathan and Oski's hematology of infancy and childhood* (6th ed, pp. 1553–1590). Philadelphia: Saunders.

6. Cohen, A. R., & Manno, C. S. (2006). Hematologic emergencies. In G. R. Fleisher, S. Ludwig, F. M. Henretig, R. M Ruddy, & B. K. Silverman (Eds.), *Textbook of pediatric emergency medicine* (5th ed, pp. 921–945). Philadelphia: Lippincott Williams & Wilkins.

7. Vinchinsky, E. P., Neumayr, L. D., Earles, A. N., Williams, R., Lennette, E. T., Dean, D., et al. (2000). Causes and outcomes of the acute chest syndrome in sickle cell disease. *New England Journal of Medicine, 342*(25), 1855–1865.

8. Heeney, M., & Dover, G. J. (2009). Disorders of hemoglobin: Sickle cell disease. In D. G. Nathan, S. H. Orkin, A. T. Look, & D. Ginsburg (Eds.), *Nathan and Oski's hematology of infancy and childhood* (7th ed., pp. 949–1014). Philadelphia: Saunders.

9. Obrien-Shea, J. (2008). Hematology. In N. E. Kline (Ed.), *Essentials of pediatric hematology/oncology nursing: A core curriculum* (pp. 320–323). Glenview, IL: Association of Pediatric Hematology/Oncology Nursing.

10. Malatack, J. B., & Pechansky, L. (2007). Hematology and oncology. In B. Zitelli & H. Davis (Eds.), *Atlas of pediatric physical diagnosis* (5th ed., pp. 403–441). St. Louis, MO: Mosby.

11. Wilson, K. D. (2002). Oncologic emergencies. In G. Foley, D. Fochtman, C. R. Baggott, & K. Patterson Kelly (Eds.), *Nursing care of children and adolescents with cancer* (3rd ed., pp. 334–346). Philadelphia: Saunders.

12. Ruccione, K. (2002). Biologic basis of cancer in children and adolescents. In G. Foley, D. Fochtman, C. R. Baggott, & K. Patterson Kelly (Eds.), *Nursing care of children and adolescents with cancer* (3rd ed, pp. 24–63). Philadelphia: Saunders.

13. Gurney, J. G., & Bondy, M. L. (2006). Epidemiology of childhood cancer. In P. A. Pizzo & D. G. Poplack (Eds.), *Principles and practices of pediatric oncology* (5th ed., pp. 1–13). Philadelphia: Lippincott Williams & Wilkins.

14. Rheingold, S. R., & Lange, B. J. (2006). Oncologic emergencies. In P. A. Pizzo & D. G. Poplack (Eds.), *Principles and practices of pediatric oncology* (5th ed., pp. 1202–1227). Philadelphia: Lippincott Williams & Wilkins.

15. Schaefers, V. (2008). Side effects of treatment. In N. E. Kline (Ed.), *Essentials of pediatric hematology/ oncology nursing: A core curriculum* (pp. 153–155). Glenview, IL: Association of Pediatric Hematology/ Oncology Nursing.

References (continued)

16. Rheingold, S. R., & Lange, B. J. (2006). Oncologic emergencies. In G. R. Fleisher, S. Ludwig, F. M. Henretig, R. M Ruddy, & B. K. Silverman (Eds.), *Textbook of pediatric emergency medicine* (5th ed., pp. 1239–1274). Philadelphia: Lippincott Williams & Wilkins.

17. Hastings, C. A., Lubin, B. H., & Feusner, J. (2006). Hematologic supportive care for children with cancer. In P. A. Pizzo & D. G. Poplack (Eds.), *Principles and practices of pediatric oncology* (5th ed., pp. 1231–1268). Philadelphia: Lippincott Williams & Wilkins.

18. Panzarella, C., et al. (2002). Management of disease and treatment of related complications. In G. Foley, D. Fochtman, C. R. Baggott, & K. Patterson Kelly (Eds.), *Nursing care of children and adolescents with cancer* (3rd ed., pp. 279–318). Philadelphia: Saunders.

19. Allen, D. B., Hagen, S. A., & Carrel, A. L. (2006). Disorders of the endocrine system relevant to pediatric critical illness. In B. P. Fuhrman & J. Zimmerman (Eds.), *Pediatric critical care* (3rd ed., pp. 1105–1124). Philadelphia: Lippincott Williams & Wilkins.

TWENTY-FOUR

Communicable and Infectious Diseases

Phyllis Maria Flavin, RN, BSN

Introduction

Communicable and infectious diseases are frequently encountered in the pediatric population seeking emergency care. Emergency nurses should be familiar with the basic functions of the immune system and should be knowledgeable about the common communicable and infectious diseases affecting infants, children, and adolescents. The purpose of this chapter is to discuss common communicable and infectious diseases and describe their associated care and prevention.

Embryologic Development of the Immune System

The function of the immune system is to recognize self from nonself and to initiate responses to eliminate the foreign substance or antigen. The functions of the immune system are basically of two types: nonspecific and specific. *Nonspecific immune defenses* are activated on exposure to any foreign substance but react similarly, regardless of the type of antigen. The principal activity of this system is phagocytosis. Phagocytic cells include neutrophils and monocytes. *Specific (adaptive) defenses* are those that have the ability to recognize the antigen and respond selectively. The cells responsible for this form of immunity are the lymphocytes, specifically B cells and T cells.

The immune system provides immunity, an inherited or acquired state in which an individual is resistant to the occurrences or the effects of a specific disease. There are two types of immunity.

❑ Passive:

- Temporary immunity is achieved by transfusing plasma proteins either artificially, from another human or an animal that has been actively immunized against an antigen, or naturally, from the mother to the fetus via the placenta.

❑ Active:

- Immune bodies are actively formed against specific antigens, either naturally, by experiencing the disease clinically or subclinically, or artificially, by introducing the antigen (vaccine) into the individual.

- Inappropriate immune responses are categorized as hypersensitivity and immunodeficiency. Hypersensitivity results in autoimmunity, isoimmunity, or allergy. Hypersensitivity reactions can be immediate or delayed; anaphylaxis is an example of the most immediate reaction to antigen reexposure.

Disorders resulting from immune deficiency are the clinical findings of impaired function of one or more components of the immune or inflammatory response (e.g., B cells, T cells, phagocytes, and complement). An immune deficiency is the failure of these mechanisms of self-defense to function normally, thus resulting in an increased susceptibility to infections. Primary (congenital) immune deficiency is caused by a genetic anomaly, whereas secondary (acquired) immune deficiency is caused by another illness, such as cancer or viral infection, or by normal physiologic changes, such as aging.[1]

The neonate is immunologically immature at birth. Although cell-mediated immunologic capabilities begin developing early in gestation and probably are completely functional at birth, antibody production is clearly deficient.[2]

The predominant transfer of antibodies occurs by way of passage of immunoglobulin (Ig)G immunoglobulins from the maternal circulation to that of the fetus. At birth, the fetal circulation may contain nearly adult levels of IgG.[1] After delivery, maternal IgG is rapidly catabolized, and neonatal IgG production increases.[1] The fetal immune system has the capacity to produce IgM and small amounts of IgA before birth,[1] Although some IgA can be detected, the capacity to produce IgA is underdeveloped. Early in gestation, maternal IgG begins crossing the placenta and enters the fetal circulation. At birth, the fetal immature B lymphocytes with surface IgM receptors are found by 10 to 11 weeks in the fetal liver. By 12 weeks, B lymphocytes are found in the peripheral blood and bone marrow. Synthesis of IgG, IgM, and IgE begins around 12 to 15 weeks.

Over time, the immune system matures through passive and active immune activities. The IgA immunoglobulins found in breast milk provide local protection of the mucous membranes in the gastrointestinal tract.[3] Because the IgG immunoglobulins are passively transferred, they have a finite half-life, between 20 and 30 days, and their concentration in serum falls rapidly within the first few months of life, reaching its lowest level between the second and fourth months. During the course of the first few years, the levels of globulin increase because of exposure to environmental antigens.[3] The immunoglobulin levels reach a minimum at 5 to 6 months, occasionally causing transient hypogammaglobulinemia (insufficient quantities of circulating immunoglobulins).[2]

Etiology

Etiologies of communicable and infectious diseases are discussed in this chapter.

Focused History

Patient History

☐ Recent exposure to a person with a suspected communicable or infectious disease

☐ Illness-specific symptoms that may include:[4]

- Neurologic
  - Confusion
  - Restlessness
  - Syncope
  - Irritability
- Skin
  - Prolonged bleeding
  - Bruising easily
  - Petechiae
  - Jaundice
- Eyes
  - Visual disturbances
  - Retinal hemorrhages
  - Pallor
  - Erythema of conjunctivae
- Nose and mouth
  - Epistaxis
  - Gingival bleeding
  - Sore or ulcerated tongue
  - Mucositis
- Lymph nodes
  - Adenopathy
- Respiratory
  - Tachypnea
  - Respiratory tract infection
  - Respiratory distress
  - Dyspnea
  - Hemoptysis
- Cardiovascular
  - Hemodynamic instability
  - Oozing from a venipuncture site
  - Pale skin and mucous membranes
- Gastrointestinal tract
  - Frank or occult bleeding in gastrointestinal fluids
  - Anorexia
  - Altered bowel sounds
  - Diarrhea
  - Constipation
- Genitourinary tract
  - Hematuria
  - Menorrhagia
  - Urinary tract infection
- Mobility
  - Ataxia
  - Altered level of activity
  - Muscle weakness

- Pain in joints, back, shoulders, bones
  - Hemarthrosis
- Recent travel outside of the United States
- Sexual activity, (including nonconsensual sex)[4]
  - Sexual preference
  - Safe-sex practices
  - Multiple partners
- Current medication usage
  - Immunosuppressive agents
  - Chemotherapeutic agents (Chapter 23)
  - Prescription and over-the-counter medications
  - Dietary and herbal supplements

Past Health History

☐ Solid organ or tissue transplantation

☐ Splenectomy

☐ Autoimmune disorders

☐ Allergies

☐ Immunization history

☐ Placement of an implantable venous access device

Family History

☐ Recent exposure to a person with the suspected communicable or infectious disease

☐ Recent travel outside of the United States

☐ Autoimmune diseases

Focused Assessment

Physical Assessment

☐ Assess the airway for patency.

☐ Assess the respiratory system.
  - Auscultate the chest for:
    - Respiratory rate
    - Adventitious sounds

☐ Assess the cardiovascular system.
  - Auscultate the heart for:
    - Rate
    - Rhythm
  - Interpret electrocardiogram readings, as needed.
  - Palpate the peripheral pulses for:
    - Rate
    - Equality

- Measure capillary refill.
- Measure the blood pressure.
- Measure core and skin temperature.
- Palpate the sternum and ribs for tenderness.

☐ Assess the neurologic system.
  - Assess the child's level of consciousness with the AVPU method (*A*lert, responds to *V*erbal stimuli, responds to *P*ain, *U*nresponsive) or Glasgow Coma Scale (GCS).
  - Assess the pupillary responses.
  - Assess for signs of meningeal irritation, as indicated (e.g., Kernig's sign, Brudzinski's sign).
  - Assess for signs of muscle weakness.
  - Assess for pain (Chapter 11).
  - Assess for fatigue.
  - Assess the infant for primitive reflexes.[5] Sucking reflex: responds to a nipple or the examiner's finger in the mouth.

☐ Assess the abdomen.
  - Palpate the abdomen for:
    - Organ enlargement
    - Pain and tenderness

☐ Assess the integumentary system.
  - Observe the skin for:
    - Rashes
    - Petechiae
    - Color
  - Observe the oral mucosa for disease-specific changes.

☐ Assess the lymphatic system.
  - Palpate the cervical, axillary, and femoral lymph nodes for:
    - Size
    - Tenderness
    - Location
    - Texture
    - Fixation

Psychosocial Assessment

☐ Assess the child and family's understanding of communicable or infectious diseases.

☐ Assess the child and family's coping strategies.

☐ Assess for the presence of family support systems.

Nursing Interventions

1. Assess and maintain airway, breathing, and circulation.
   - Initiate maneuvers to maintain airway patency, such as positioning and suctioning, and prepare for insertion of an airway adjunct.
   - Prepare for endotracheal intubation in the child who cannot maintain airway patency.
   - Administer 100% oxygen through a nonrebreather mask.
   - Initiate assisted ventilation in the child in whom adequate respiratory effort is not being maintained.

2. Initiate cardiorespiratory and continuous oxygen saturation monitoring.

3. Obtain venous access and initiate an intravenous infusion at the prescribed rate.
   - Obtain blood specimens for laboratory analysis.
   - Prepare to administer medications, as prescribed:
     - Vasopressors
     - Antibiotics

4. Reassess neurologic status and cardiopulmonary status; assess for pain (Chapter 11).

5. Measure intake and output.

6. Administer oral medications, such as:
   - Acetaminophen
   - Ibuprofen
   - Corticosteroids

7. Prepare for diagnostic tests, as needed.

8. Obtain additional specimens for laboratory analysis, such as:
   - Throat cultures
   - Urine cultures
   - Cerebrospinal fluid cultures

9. Inform the family frequently about the child's condition; provide emotional support to the child and family.

10. Initiate consultations with specialists (e.g., infectious disease specialists), as needed.

11. Inform the local health department of children with communicable and infectious diseases.

12. Prepare for transfer and transport to a tertiary care facility as needed (Chapter 8); prepare for hospitalization as indicated.

Home Care and Prevention

General home care instructions for children with communicable or infectious diseases include:

❑ Use good hand-washing techniques to avoid spreading the illness to other family members.

❑ Avoid using the same eating utensils, cups, and toothbrushes of an infected child to avoid family contamination.

❑ Avoid sharing towels, washcloths, and personal clothing.

❑ Administer medications for their prescribed duration.

❑ Follow up with the child's primary care physician to detect potential disease-associated complications.

❑ Provide adequate rest for the child to recuperate completely.

General guidelines for staff to protect themselves from communicable and infectious diseases include:

❑ Using proper hand washing.

❑ Initiating universal precautions and other protective measures to prevent contamination of themselves or others.

❑ Wearing personal protective equipment appropriate to the level of exposure.

General guidelines for staff who have been exposed to a communicable or infectious disease while caring for patients include:

❑ Knowing the proper steps to take in the event of an exposure.

❑ Reporting the exposure promptly to the designated hospital department (e.g., employee health services, infection control coordinator).

❑ Completing the required treatment and follow-up procedures.

Specific Immunologic Emergencies

Communicable Diseases: Vaccine Preventable

Etiology

Communicable diseases are those diseases that are spread from infected to noninfected individuals. Many deadly pediatric communicable diseases are now prevented through immunizations; however, with international travel into and out of the country, children may be exposed to such diseases, or unvaccinated children may present to the emergency department (ED) for treatment. Table 24.1 lists common vaccine-preventable communicable diseases

TABLE 24.1 Vaccine-Preventable Communicable Diseases: Communicability

Disease/Agent	Route of Transmission	Incubation Period	Communicability Period
Diphtheria/ Corynebacterium diphtheriae	Person to person; spread from the respiratory tract	2 to 7 days but occasionally is longer	The organisms are spread by respiratory droplets and/or by contact with discharges from skin lesions. In untreated people, organisms can be present in discharges from the nose and throat and from eye and skin lesions for 2 to 6 weeks after infection. Patients treated with an appropriate antimicrobial agent usually are communicable for fewer than 4 days. Severe disease occurs more often in people who are not immunized or are immunized inadequately. The incidence of respiratory diphtheria is greatest during autumn and winter, but summer epidemics can occur in warm climates in which skin infections are prevalent.[10]
Measles/viral	Usually direct contact with droplets of infected person	Generally 8 to 12 days with a range from 7 to 18 days	Measles is transmitted by direct contact with infectious droplets or, less commonly, by airborne spread. Patients are contagious from 1 to 2 days before onset of symptoms (3–5 days before rash) to 4 days after appearance of the rash.[10]
Mumps/ paramyxovirus	Saliva contact with or droplet spread from an infected person	Usually 16 to 18 days, but cases may occur from 12 to 25 days after exposure	The period of maximum communicability is from 1 to 2 days before onset of parotid swelling to 5 days after onset of parotid swelling. Virus has been isolated from saliva from 7 days before through 9 days after onset of swelling.[10]
Rubella/rubella virus	Person to person; spread via bodily fluids	Postnatally acquired rubella ranges from 14 to 23 days, usually 16 to 18	Postnatal rubella is transmitted primarily through direct or droplet contact from nasopharyngeal secretions. The peak incidence of infection is during late winter or early spring. The period of maximal communicability extends from a few days after the onset of rash.[10]
Pertussis/ Bordetalla pertussis and Bordetella parapertussis	Person to person; spread via respiratory secretions	7 to 10 days with a range of 5 to 21 days	Transmission occurs by close contact with cases via aerosolized droplets. Neither infection nor immunization provides lifelong immunity. Disease in infants younger than 6 months of age can be atypical with a short catarrhal stage, gagging, gasping, or apnea as prominent early manifestations. Sudden unexpected death can be caused by pertussis.[10]
Polio/enterovirus	Person to person; feces and oropharyngeal secretions	Asymptomatic nonparalytic poliomyelitis is 3 to 6 days. Onset of paralysis in paralytic poliomyelitis 7 to 21 days	Spread is by the fecal-oral and respiratory routes. Infection is more common in infants and young children and occurs at an earlier age among children living in poor hygienic conditions. The risk of paralytic disease after infection increases with age.[10]

TABLE 24.2 Vaccine-Preventable Communicable Diseases: Treatment

Disease/ Agent	Signs/Symptoms/Complications	ED Interventions	Home Care and Prevention

Diphtheria	Pharyngeal, including laryngeal and nasopharyngeal (most common):
	
	• Fever; sore throat; cervical lymphadenopathy; thick gray-white membranes; tachycardia
	
	Cutaneous (common in the tropics)
	
	• Sharply demarcated ulcers
		Confirmed diphtheria:
		
		• Rapid administration of intravenous antitoxin is recommended after the patient is tested for sensitivity.[10] Antitoxin will not neutralize any toxins that have already fixed to tissues but will neutralize the unbound toxin and will prevent further progression of the disease.
		
		Suspected diphtheria:
		
		• Initiate parenteral Erythromycin.
		
		• Initiate parenteral penicillin G.
		
		• Identify and treat close contacts, such as family members, regardless of their immunization status:
		
		  • Obtain a diphtheria culture.
		
		  • Administer either oral erythromycin or intramuscular penicillin G.
		
		  • Administer a booster dose of diphtheria vaccine in previously immunized contacts if they have not received one in more than 5 years.
		
		• Prepare for hospitalization and respiratory isolation.
			Suspected diphtheria:
			
			• Continue parenteral erythromycin for 2 weeks.
			
			• Antimicrobial prophylaxis with oral erythromycin (40–50 mg/kg per day for 10 days, maximum 2 g/day) or a single intramuscular injection of penicillin G benzathine (600,000 Units for children weighing < 30 kg and 1.2 million Units for children ≥ 30 kg and adults). If cultures are positive, an additional 10-day course of erythromycin should be given, and follow-up specimens for cultures should be performed.[10]
			
			• Contact precautions are recommended for patients with cutaneous diphtheria until two cultures of skin lesions taken at least 24 hours apart and 24 hours after cessation of antimicrobial therapy are negative.[10]
			
			• Asymptomatic, previously immunized close contacts should receive a booster dose of an age-appropriate diphtheria toxoid–containing vaccine (DTaP [or DT], Tdap, or Td) if they have not received a booster dose of diphtheria toxoid within 5 years. Asymptomatic close contacts who are not immunized fully (defined as having had fewer than three doses of diphtheria toxoid) or whose immunization status is not known should be immunized with age-appropriate diphtheria toxoid–containing vaccine.[10]
			
			• Maintain strict isolation in hospital. Administer complete care to maintain bed rest. Administer humidified oxygen if prescribed.

TABLE 24.2 Vaccine-Preventable Communicable Diseases: Treatment (continued)

Disease/ Agent	Signs/Symptoms/Complications	ED Interventions	Home Care and Prevention

Measles	■ Fever and malaise, followed in 24 hours by coryza, cough, conjunctivitis, Koplik's spots (small, irregular red spots with a minute, bluish white center)
	■ Cutaneous:
	   ■ Rash appears 3 to 4 days after onset of symptoms; begins as a maculopapular eruption on face and gradually spreads downward
	■ Other signs and symptoms:
	   ■ Anorexia; malaise; generalized lymphadenopathy
	■ Complications:
	   ■ Myocarditis (second week) and neuritis[25]
		■ Institute respiratory isolation.
		■ Provide antibiotics to prevent secondary bacterial infection in high-risk children.
			Maintain isolation until fifth day of rash.
			
			Maintain bed rest and provide quiet activity.
			
			Provide antipyretics; avoid chilling.
			
			Dim lights if photophobia is present; clean eyelids with warm saline solution to remove secretions or crusts; keep child from rubbing eyes.
			
			Use cool-mist vaporizer.
			
			Encourage fluids and soft, bland foods.

Mumps	Fever, headache, malaise, and anorexia for 24 hours, followed by "earache" that is aggravated by chewing
	
	Parotitis:
	   By third day, parotid glands enlarge, accompanied by pain and tenderness
	
	Other signs and symptoms:
	   Submaxillary and sublingual infection
	
	Complications:
	   Sensorineural deafness; postinfectious encephalitis; myocarditis; arthritis; hepatitis; epididymoorchitis; sterility (extremely rare in men); meningitis[25]
		Maintain isolation during period of communicability; institute respiratory precautions during hospitalization.
		
		Provide analgesics for pain and antipyretics for fever.
		
		Intravenous fluids may be necessary for the child who refuses to drink or vomits.
			Maintain bed rest until swelling subsides.
			
			Give analgesics for pain.
			
			Encourage fluids and soft, bland foods; avoid foods that require chewing.
			
			Apply hot or cold compresses to neck, whichever is more comforting.[26]

Rubella	Low-grade fever; headache; malaise; anorexia; mild conjunctivitis; sore throat; cough; lymphadenopathy Cutaneous: Rash first appears on face and rapidly spreads downward; by the end of the first day the body is covered with a discrete, pinkish-red maculopapular exanthem	Maintain respiratory and bodily fluid isolation. Provide analgesics for pain and antipyretics for fever. Isolate child from pregnant women (greatest danger is teratogenic effect on fetus).	Isolate child from pregnant women (greatest danger is teratogenic effect on fetus).

TABLE 24.2 Vaccine-Preventable Communicable Diseases: Treatment (continued)

Disease/ Agent	Signs/Symptoms/Complications	ED Interventions	Home Care and Prevention
Pertussis	Catarrhal phase: • Early symptoms include nasal congestion, tearing, mild conjunctival injection, malaise, and low-grade fever • An initially mild and nonproductive cough develops • These symptoms may last up to 2 weeks Paroxysmal phase: • Cough increases in severity • Severe coughing paroxysms may cause respiratory distress, cyanosis, or posttussive vomiting • This may last for up to 2 months Convalescent phase: • Decreased intensity of the paroxysms and increased time between spasms Complications: • Pneumonia, atelectasis; otitis media; convulsions; hemorrhage (subarachnoid, subconjunctival, epistaxis); weight loss and dehydration; hernia; prolapsed rectum	Institute respiratory and seizure precautions. Provide high humidity and oxygen. Suction gently but often. Encourage fluids; intravenous hydration may be necessary be necessary. Erythromycin, clarithromycin, or azithromycin are appropriate first-line agents for prophylaxis or treatment of pertussis in people 6 months of age or older. Household and other close contacts should receive medical evaluation for possible antibiotic prophylaxis to limit spread of disease.	Maintain isolation during catarrhal stage. Provide restful environment and reduce factors that promote paroxysms (dust, smoke, sudden change in temperature, activity, excitement). Encourage fluids. Provide humidified air; suction gently. Observe for signs of airway obstruction (increased restlessness, apprehension, retractions, cyanosis).[26]
Polio	Abortive or inapparent: Fever; uneasiness; sore throat; headache; anorexia; vomiting; abdominal pain; lasts a few hours to a few days Nonparalytic: Same manifestations as abortive, but more severe, with pain and stiffness in neck, back, and legs Paralytic: Initial course similar to nonparalytic type, followed by recovery and then signs of central nervous system paralysis Complications: Permanent paralysis; respiratory arrest; hypertension	Provide bed rest. Assist ventilation, if necessary. Provide analgesics. Provide sedatives, as necessary, to relieve anxiety and promote rest.	Maintain bed rest. Administer analgesics and sedatives. Participate in physiotherapy procedures (moist hot packs and range-of-motion exercises). Encourage child to move. Observe for respiratory paralysis (difficulty in talking; ineffective cough; inability to hold breath, shallow and rapid respirations); report such signs and symptoms to practitioner; have tracheostomy tray at bedside.[26]

Ball, J., & Bindler, R. (2008). In *Pediatric nursing: 9. Caring for children* (4th ed., pp. 708–709, 560–597, 607–622, 781–782, 832, 963). Upper Saddle River, NJ: Pearson Prentice Hall.

and their disease processes; Table 24.2 lists each disease's signs and symptoms, ED treatment, and home care and prevention. Chapter 20 provides further detailed information related to rubella and rubeola.

Home Care and Prevention

Because of the rising incidence of communicable and infectious diseases, universal precautions should be practiced for all patients presenting for ED treatment. Exposure to bodily fluids is common in the ED, and patients' immunologic status (e.g., human immunodeficiency virus [HIV], hepatitis B [Table 24.3]) may not be known. Appropriate barriers must be used for any patient contact. Hands and other skin surfaces should be washed thoroughly and immediately after exposure to any bodily fluids. EDs should have policies and procedures in place in case a staff member experiences accidental exposure.

After the ED treatment of infectious children and families, ED staff must consider treatment for themselves. For example, rubella titers and booster immunizations may be necessary for staff exposed to a child with rubella. Varicella vaccine may be needed for a staff member who never had varicella as a child. Parents should be encouraged to have their children immunized against the common communicable diseases of childhood (Chapter 4).

Emergency staff must report communicable and infectious diseases to the local health department, as required (Chapter 4). Policies should be in place and enacted should children and families be exposed to a patient with a communicable disease (e.g., rubella) while they are receiving ED treatment.

TABLE 24.3 Hepatitis Types

Type	Immunization Available	Prophylaxis	Primary Transmission	Incubation Period
Hepatitis A	Yes	Immune globulin Hepatitis A vaccine	Fecal-oral	1 month
Hepatitis B	Yes	Hepatitis B immune globulin Hepatitis B vaccine	Needle sticks or sharps exposure Intravenous drug use during pregnancy Sexual activity	100–120 days
Hepatitis C	No	None	Needle sticks or sharps exposure Intravenous drug use During birth	7–9 weeks
Hepatitis D	No	Hepatitis B vaccine	Needle sticks or sharps exposure Intravenous drug use During birth Sexual activity	2–4 months
Hepatitis E	No	None	Fecal-oral	40 days

Ball, J., & Bindler, R. (2008). In *Pediatric nursing: Caring for children* (4th ed., pp. 708–709, 560–597, 607–622, 781–782, 832, 963). Upper Saddle River, NJ: Pearson Prentice Hall.

Communicable Diseases: Non-Vaccine Preventable

Tuberculosis

Etiology

Tuberculosis (TB) has afflicted humans for thousands of years and still remains a major public health concern throughout the world. The majority of children (< 15 years of age) with TB are asymptomatic and are identified by routine tuberculin skin testing or after a TB infection investigation.

In 2006, 13,779 TB cases were reported among all age groups, and 807 (5.9%) were pediatric.[6] The TB rate declined 4.2% from 2006 to 4.4 cases per 100,000 population. Foreign-born persons and racial/ethnic minorities continued to bear a disproportionate burden of TB disease in the United States. *Mycobacterium tuberculosis,* the etiologic agent, is spread by inhalation of droplets produced by the disease. The period from exposure to a positive tuberculin skin test is usually 2 to 10 weeks. Most tuberculous infections resolve without clinical evidence of disease. Often the disease will appear within the first 6 months, although it can be latent for a year or more. While the vast majority of TB cases are classified as pulmonary, the remaining are classified as more serious diseases, known as tuberculous meningitis and miliary TB. Tuberculous meningitis results from infiltration of disease into the central nervous system, and miliary TB results from infiltration of disease into the systemic circulation.

Focused History

Patient history

- Exposure to a person infected with TB
- Cough (mild or absent) or cold symptoms that linger
- Low-grade fever
- Irritability
- Poor appetite
- Weight loss or poor weight gain

Family history

- Presence of a TB-infected person in the home
- Crowded home environment or homelessness

Focused Assessment

Physical Assessment

❏ Assess the respiratory system.
  - Auscultate the chest for:
    - Respiratory rate
    - Adventitious sounds. Cough or shortness of breath may be present
  - Assess for chest pain.
    - Children with pleural involvement present more acutely, exhibiting fever, chest pain, shortness of breath, and evidence of pleural effusion
❏ Assess the cardiovascular system.
  - Auscultate the heart for rate.
  - Measure the blood pressure.
  - Inspect the skin for:
    - Capillary refill
    - Color
    - Temperature
  - Measure core and skin temperatures.
    - Fever may be present

❏ Assess the neurologic system.
  - Assess the level of consciousness with the GCS or AVPU method
  - Assess for signs of meningeal irritation or increased intracranial pressure
    - Children with tuberculous meningitis usually present with a gradual onset of symptoms, including irritability and lethargy, over a 2- to 3-week period
❏ Assess the child's overall appearance.
  - Observe the child's hygiene
  - Measure the child's weight and height
    - Weight loss may have occurred

Psychosocial Assessment

❏ Assess the child's and family's understanding of the disease process.
❏ Assess the child's and family's living conditions and exposure to potential TB sources.

Nursing Interventions

1. Isolate symptomatic children in negative-flow examination rooms.
   - Utilize personal protective equipment, such as N95 masks.
   - Use universal precautions to avoid spread of infection via droplets.
   - Administer supplemental oxygen, as needed.
2. Initiate monitoring of oxygen saturation levels.
3. Prepare for diagnostic testing:[7]
   - Obtain chest radiograph (anteroposterior and lateral views), which are used to supplement other diagnostic methods.[8]
   - Obtain computed tomography (may be used if chest radiograph is not diagnostic).
   - Diagnostic findings for pulmonary TB include enlargement of hilar, mediastinal, and subcarinal lymph nodes; atelectasis; alveolar consolidation, pleural effusion; focal mass.[7,9]
   - Obtain sputum specimens (ideally, three should be obtained) for microscopic examination and mycobacterial culture. Susceptibility testing for isoniazid (INH), rifampin (RIF), and ethambutol (EMB) should be performed on a positive initial culture.[7]
   - Perform tuberculin skin testing and arrange for the skin test to be read in 2 days.
4. Prepare to begin recommended treatment.

Treatment for Children with Active TB

❑ Initiate treatment as soon as the diagnosis of TB is suspected, because of the high risk of disseminated TB in infants and children younger than 4 years of age.

❑ In general, the regimens recommended for adults are also the regimens of choice for infants, children, and adolescents with TB, with the exception that EMB is not used routinely in children.[7]

❑ Administer INH in patients with a positive skin test who are asymptomatic.

❑ Administer antitubercular drugs, including INH, RIF, pyrazinamide (PZA), EMB, and streptomycin. This therapy usually involves a 6-month regimen of two or more of these drugs (daily for 2 months and twice weekly for 4 months).

Treatment for Children with Latent TB

❑ Administer either a single daily dose or two to three times weekly dose of INH for 9 months. Daily RIF may be used if the organism is INH-resistant.[9]

❑ Report cases of TB to the local health department. Health departments may have nurses dedicated to TB cases and follow-up; these nurses can provide guidance in drug dosing and long-term treatment.

❑ Prepare for hospital admission, if needed.

Home Care and Prevention

Prevention involves a high level of suspicion; therefore, early identification and treatment of children with TB are critical. Parents must be told of the importance of having the TB test read within 2 days. Remind the parents that this disease will be reported to the local health department and that other family members may need to receive TB testing. Teach parents about the disease process, medications, possible side effects, and the importance of long-term therapy (e.g., that drug therapy may last for 6 to 12 months). Emphasize the importance of taking the medication on an empty stomach.[9] Because the treatment regimen is complicated, social support services and health department nurse should be contacted to help the family be compliant with the medications.

Asymptomatic children can lead an essentially unrestricted life. They can and should attend school (or daycare), but older children are restricted from vigorous activities such as competitive games and contact sports during the active stage of primary TB.[8]

Other teaching points include:[8]

❑ Promote optimum general health with adequate nutrition and rest.

❑ Emphasize the importance of administering prescribed

medications for their duration.

❑ Reduce parental anxieties to help them deal with the illness more constructively.

❑ Protect children from stresses and infections.

❑ Instruct children in proper hand-washing techniques to prevent the spread of infection.

❑ Follow up with regularly scheduled visits with the primary care practitioner.

Case finding and follow-up of known contacts are important nursing responsibilities. Once a TB diagnosis is made, children and families can be referred to the health department nurses. Every case of TB identified in the community involves nurses in follow-up of known contacts. Early diagnosis affords a means for early protection or treatment and prevents further spread of the disease.[8]

Infectious Mononucleosis

Etiology

Infectious mononucleosis is an acute viral syndrome. The infectious agent is most often the Epstein-Barr virus (EBV). Infectious mononucleosis occurs worldwide and is widespread among young children in developing countries and in socioeconomically depressed groups, where it is usually mild or asymptomatic. In young children, the disease is generally mild and more difficult to recognize, whereas it is recognized most often in high school and college students. In about 50% of those infected, clinical infectious mononucleosis will develop, whereas the others are mostly asymptomatic.

Infectious mononucleosis transmission can be direct contact with infected oropharyngeal and genital tract secretions. The Epstein-Barr virus can survive in saliva for several hours outside the body and can also be transmitted by blood transfusion.[9] Recovery usually occurs in a few weeks, but a very small proportion of individuals may need months to regain their former level of energy. After recovery, the virus remains latent in the lymphoid systems and can be reactivated during periods of immunosuppression.[9]

Focused History

❑ Headache

❑ Anorexia

❑ Abdominal pain

❑ Fever

❑ Sore throat (may be severe)

❑ Fatigue

❑ Exposure to someone with infectious mononucleosis

- ❏ Rash
- ❏ Enlarged, nonpainful cervical lymph nodes
- ❏ Myalgia

Focused Assessment

Physical Assessment

- ❏ Assess the respiratory system.
  - Auscultate the chest for:
    - Respiratory rate. Respiratory rate may be increased with fever.
- ❏ Assess the cardiovascular system.
  - Auscultate the heart for:
    - Rate. Heart rate may be increased in the presence of fever.
  - Measure the blood pressure.
  - Measure core and skin temperature.
    - Fever may be present
- ❏ Assess the neurologic system.
  - Assess the child's level of consciousness with the GCS or AVPU methods
  - Assess the child's motor strength.
    - Fatigue and weakness may be present
- ❏ Assess the lymphatic system.
  - Palpate the posterior cervical lymph nodes
    - Enlarged nodes may be palpated
- ❏ Assess the abdomen.
  - Palpate the abdomen
    - Splenomegaly may be present, occurring in 50% of patients.
- ❏ Assess the integumentary system.
  - Observe the skin color
    - Jaundice may be present

Psychosocial Assessment

- ❏ Assess the child and family's understanding of the disease process.
- ❏ Assess the child's coping strategies as it may be necessary to curtail activities.

Nursing Interventions

1. Administer medications, as prescribed.
   - Administer antipyretics and analgesics for fever and pain control.
   - Prepare to administer nonsteroidal anti-inflammatory drugs or steroids in small doses and

in decreasing amounts over about a week in patients who have symptoms of toxicity or who have severe oropharyngeal involvement.

2. Obtain blood specimens for laboratory testing.
   - Heterophile antibodies
   - Epstein-Barr antibodies
   - Liver function tests

Home Care and Prevention

Patients and families should be instructed on care in the home with infectious mononucleosis.[8]

- ❏ Serve small, frequent meals of soft foods to patients with severe sore throats.
- ❏ Encourage bed rest during the acute phase.
- ❏ Offer frequent fluids, such as water and fruit juices.
- ❏ Avoid medications that contain alcohol, as well as alcoholic beverages.
- ❏ Avoid contact sports, heavy lifting, and strenuous activities to prevent splenic or liver injury.
- ❏ Limit exposure to persons outside the family, especially during the acute phase, to prevent a secondary infection.[8]

Acquired Immunodeficiency Syndrome

Etiology

HIV infection in children and adolescents causes a broad spectrum of disease manifestations and a varied clinical course. Acquired immunodeficiency syndrome (AIDS) represents the most severe end of the clinical spectrum.[10] AIDS is a persistent and progressively debilitating viral infection that affects multiple systems. The AIDS virus commonly attacks the immune and nervous systems.

The estimated number of U.S. children with AIDS diagnosed each year increased from 1984 to 1992, then declined by almost 95% by 2003 to < 100 cases annually. It is estimated that as of 2004, 12,000 to 15,000 HIV-infected children were living in the United States.[11]

HIV is dependent on the cells it infects to reproduce. The AIDS virus attacks and infects the helper T cell (CD4 cell). A depletion in the number of CD4 T cells results in widespread immune dysfunction. The nervous system and other tissues have receptors similar to that on CD4 T cells and thus become targets for primary infections. Because the pathology of AIDS involves the immune system, children are extremely vulnerable to opportunistic infections such as pneumocystic pneumonias.

Modes of HIV transmission in the United States include:[10]

☐ Sexual contact (vaginal, anal, or orogenital).

☐ Percutaneous (from contaminated needles or other sharp instruments) or mucous membrane exposure to contaminated blood or other body fluids.

☐ Mother-to-child transmission during pregnancy, around the time of labor and delivery, and postnatally through breast-feeding.[10]

Focused History

Patient history for the child who is HIV positive:[10, 12]

☐ Lymphedema

☐ Hepatosplenomegaly

☐ Oral candidiasis

☐ Developmental delays

☐ Chronic or recurrent diarrhea

☐ Parotitis

☐ Failure to thrive

☐ Current medications and treatments

☐ Risk factors:[13]
- Maternal blood transfusions
- Intravenous drug use
- Sexual contact or sexual abuse
- Sexual contact with intravenous drug users or bisexual men
- Blood or blood product transfusion

Focused Assessment

Physical Assessment

☐ Assess the respiratory system.
- Breath sounds
- Respiratory status
- Arterial blood gases

☐ Assess the neurologic system.
- Level of consciousness
- Mental status
  - Encephalopathy, the most frequent presentation for HIV-infected children, is characterized by developmental delays, deterioration in motor and intellectual skills, muscle weakness, ataxia, or seizures.

☐ Observe the child's overall size and stature.
- Observe for signs of failure to thrive. Low percentile for height and weight may be found.

☐ Assess the integumentary system.
- Inspect the oral cavity
  - Lesions may be observed
- Inspect the skin
  - Nonhealing wounds may be noted
  - Signs of anemia may be noted [9] (pale conjunctiva, pale mucous membranes)

☐ Assess the lymphatic system.
- Palpate the cervical and femoral lymph nodes
  - Lymphadenopathy may be noted

☐ Assess the abdomen.
- Palpate the abdomen
  - Assess for hepatomegaly and splenomegaly[12]

Psychosocial Assessment

☐ Assess the HIV-positive child's and family's coping strategies.
- For those who are newly diagnosed, assess the child and family's understanding of the meaning of being HIV positive.
- Support services may be needed to help the child and family cope with this new diagnosis.

☐ Assess the child's and family's coping strategies for the child with AIDS.
  - Children with AIDS may have feelings of fear, anxiety, anger, or denial, similar to other children with chronic or life-threatening illnesses.
  - Children and families may present frequently to the emergency department for treatment and may become well known to the staff, so they may be more likely to share their feelings and experiences.
  - Support services may be needed, to help the child and family with a new or ongoing diagnosis of AIDS. Hospice services may need to be consulted for the child in the final stages of AIDS.

Nursing Interventions

1. Administer supplemental oxygen and provide proper positioning for the child in respiratory distress.

2. Initiate cardiorespiratory and oxygen saturation monitoring.

3. Administer medications, as prescribed.
   - Administer antibiotics in the presence of infection.

4. Prepare the child for diagnostic testing.
   - Obtain informed consent for HIV blood testing in accordance with state law. Consent should be

obtained from the parent or legal guardian and recorded in the patient's medical record.[10]

- A positive HIV antibody test result (enzyme immunoassay followed by Western blot analysis) in a child 18 months of age or older indicates infection.[10]

5. Prepare the child and family for hospitalization, if needed.

- Evaluate febrile children who appear toxic for bacterial or opportunistic infections.

6. Provide psychosocial support for the child and family coping with a chronic illness.

Home Care and Prevention

Education concerning the transmission and control of infectious diseases, including HIV infection, is essential for children with HIV infection and anyone involved in their care.[12]

❏ Avoid exposing the HIV-positive child to people with infections, such as varicella, colds, or influenza.

❏ The scope of nursing care will change with new symptoms, changes in treatment, and disease progression. Psychological interventions will vary with unique circumstances of each child and family.[12]

❏ Continue with the regular immunization schedule, including the influenza vaccine.

Emergency nurses also can remind the child and family that HIV cannot be spread through common touch or play. All families, regardless of their HIV status, should teach their children to tell an adult if someone is bleeding and to avoid direct contact with other people's blood and bodily fluids. Emergency nurses can teach methods for prevention of HIV infection to school-aged children and adolescents:

❏ Do not have unprotected sexual intercourse. Condoms plus contraceptive foam or jelly containing nonoxynol-9 should be used. Condoms should be worn during sexual contact with other body orifices, such as the mouth or anus.

❏ Do not inject drugs and do not share needles and syringes. If drugs are injected, the person should use his or her own needles and syringes.

Meningitis and Meningococcemia

Etiology

Infection of the central nervous system (CNS) is the most common cause of fever associated with signs and symptoms of CNS disease in children. Bacterial meningitis is one of the most potentially serious infections occurring in infants and older children. This infection is associated with a high rate of acute complications and risks of long-term morbidity. The causes of bacterial meningitis in the neonatal period (0–28 days) are generally distinct from those in older infants and children[14] (Chapter 9). Meningitis is caused by a bacterial or viral infection that results in inflammation of the meninges. Group B streptococcus, followed by *Escherichia coli*, is the most common cause of neonatal meningitis. The most common cause of bacterial meningitis in children 2 months to 12 years of age in the United States is *Neisseria meningitidis*. Bacterial meningitis caused by *Streptococcus pneumoniae* and *Haemophilus influenzae* type B has become much less common in developed countries since the introduction of universal immunizations against these pathogens beginning at age 2 months.[14] Viral meningoencephalitis is an acute inflammatory process involving the meninges and, to a variable degree, brain tissue. These infections are relatively common and may be caused by a number of different agents.[14]

The bacteria are transmitted by droplets, gaining entry into the cerebrospinal fluid via the vascular system. The incubation period is 1 to 7 days. Long-term effects of meningitis include seizure disorders; speech, hearing, and visual impairments; mental retardation; and behavior changes.

Meningococcemia is a potentially life-threatening disorder in which *N. meningitidis* gains access to the bloodstream. Septic shock is often associated with meningococcemia, and more than one third of patients in whom septic shock develops die. Children with meningococcemia may have meningitis, pericarditis, hypotension, and disseminated intravascular coagulation. Both meningitis and meningococcemia are true emergencies and can be fatal within a few hours, therefore making rapid assessment and immediate action critical.

Focused History

Patient history

❏ Recent illness: rapid onset of fever, chills, malaise, and a rash

❏ Decreased intake

❏ Vomiting and diarrhea

❏ Seizures

❏ Respiratory distress

Family history

❏ Family member or close acquaintance in whom meningitis or meningococcemia has been recently diagnosed.

Focused Assessment

Physical Assessment

Signs and symptoms of meningitis vary by age and may be difficult to diagnose in the neonate (Chapter 9) or infant. Table 24.4 compares physical findings in infants and children.

Psychosocial Assessment

❐ Assess the child and family's understanding of the disease process.

❐ Assess the child and family's exposure to potential infectious sources.

Nursing Interventions

1. Assess and maintain airway, breathing, and circulation.
   - Initiate maneuvers to maintain airway patency.
     • Administer 100% oxygen through a nonre-breather mask; initiate assisted ventilation in the child who is not maintaining adequate respiratory effort.
   - Prepare for endotracheal intubation.
     • Prepare for mechanical ventilation if endotracheal intubation is required (Chapter 14).
   - Initiate cardiorespiratory and continuous oxygen saturation monitoring.

2. Obtain intravenous access and initiate an intravenous infusion.
   - Administer a rapid fluid bolus of 20 mL/kg of a crystalloid fluid (normal saline solution or lactated Ringer's solution) in the child with signs of septic shock (Chapter 38) or poor perfusion.
   - Administer second and third boluses of 20 mL/kg of a crystalloid fluid (normal saline solution or lactated Ringer's solution) if improvement is not observed.
   - Prepare to administer vasopressor agents.
   - Administer antibiotics, as prescribed.
   - Obtain blood specimens for:
     • Complete blood cell count and differential
     • Platelets
     • Electrolytes, blood urea nitrogen, creatinine, and glucose
     • Cultures
     • Prothrombin time and partial thromboplastin time

3. Reassess the child's neurologic status and cardiopulmonary status.
   - Observe and monitor for signs of increased intracranial pressure, including changes in level of consciousness, irritability, sluggish pupillary responses, and decreased movements of extremities.

TABLE 24.4 Comparison of Neurologic Assessment Findings in Infants and Children with Meningitis

Body System	*Infants*	*Children*
Central nervous system	Irritability	Headache
	High-pitched cry	Altered level of consciousness
	Bulging anterior fontanelle	Nuchal rigidity
	Seizure activity	Photophobia
	Nuchal rigidity	Positive Kernig's sign
	Lethargy	Seizure activity
	Altered sleep pattern	Coma
		Positive Brudzinski's sign
Thermoregulation	Fever	Fever
Integumentary status	Petechiae below the nipple line	Petechiae
	Purpura	Purpura
Gastrointestinal status	Poor feeding	Vomiting
	Vomiting	
Respiratory status	Apnea	Tachypnea
Overall appearance	"Looks septic"	"Looks sick"

4. Assist with a lumbar puncture if there are no signs of increased intracranial pressure.
   - Obtain cerebrospinal fluid specimens for laboratory analysis.
     - Culture and sensitivity
     - Glucose
     - Protein
     - Cell count and differential
     - Gram stain
   - Note the color of cerebrospinal fluid.
   - Record the opening and closing pressures in older children.
5. Prepare for the insertion of an indwelling gastric tube and/or bladder catheter.
   - Obtain a urine specimen for laboratory analysis.
     - Urinalysis
     - Culture and sensitivity
6. Monitor fluid and electrolytes for evidence of syndrome of inappropriate antidiuretic hormone, in which decreased serum sodium and serum osmolarity are found.
7. Inform the family frequently about the child's condition; provide emotional support to the child and family.
   - Initiate referrals to social services and hospital spiritual services.
8. Prepare for transfer and transport to a tertiary care facility, as indicated (Chapter 8), or prepare the child and family for admission to the intensive care unit.

Home Care and Prevention

Precautions must be taken by ED staff and family to avoid possible exposure to meningitis. Children suspected of having meningococcemia should be isolated from other patients, and universal precautions should be used by anyone having direct contact with the child. Parents should be taught the proper procedure for applying personal protective equipment and supervised in their application.[15]

Of greatest concern is cross-infection of siblings younger than 6 years old and those attending the same daycare facility. Adults and children who have close contact with the patient should receive Rifampin. Prophylaxis of hospital personnel is usually not necessary. Nurses should take the necessary precautions to protect themselves and others from possible infection.

Encephalitis

Etiology

Encephalitis is an inflammatory process of the CNS that is caused by a variety of organisms, including bacteria, spirochetes, fungi, protozoa, helminthes, and viruses. Most infections are associated with viruses.[15] Encephalitis produces altered function of various portions of the brain and spinal cord. The arthropod-borne (arbovirus) viral encephalitides are a group of clinically similar severe neurologic infections caused by several different viruses. They are transmitted by mosquitoes during outdoor exposure in warmer weather in overlapping regions across most of the United States and much of southern Canada. The principal causes of the arthropod-borne encephalitides of North America include:[16]

- West Nile encephalitis (WNE)
- St. Louis encephalitides (SLE)
- The complex viruses included in the California encephalitis (CE) group of viruses and, less frequently, western equine encephalitis (WEE), eastern equine encephalitis (EEE), and Colorado tick fever
- Venezuelan equine encephalitis (VEE)
- Japanese encephalitis (JE)[16]

Long-term sequelae from encephalitis include:

- Developmental delays
- Neurologic sequelae (variable frequency, depending on age and infecting agent)
- Seizure disorders
- Hemiplegia
- Hemiparesis
- Hearing loss

Focused History

Patient history in mild cases of encephalitis

- Asymptomatic
- Afebrile headache
- Aseptic meningitis

Patient history in severe cases of encephalitis with a rapid onset

- Headache
- High fever
- Meningeal signs
- Stupor
- Disorientation
- Coma

❒   Tremors

❒   Seizures (especially in infants)

Focused Assessment

Physical Assessment

❒   Assess the neurologic system.

  ▪ Assess level of consciousness: AVPU scale (*A*lert, responds to *V*erbal stimuli, responds to *P*ainful stimuli, *U*nresponsive) or Glasgow Coma Scale (GCS) methods.

    • Irritability or a decreased level of consciousness may be noted.

❒   Observe for meningeal signs.

  ▪ Headache

  ▪ Difficulty in moving or refusal to move head and neck

  ▪ Fever

  ▪ Seizure activity

Psychosocial Assessment

❒   Assess the child and family's understanding of the disease process.

❒   Assess the child and family's coping strategies.

❒   Assess the availability of emotional support systems, such as family or neighbors.

Nursing Interventions

1. Assess and maintain airway, breathing, and circulation.

2. Initiate cardiorespiratory and oxygen saturation monitoring.

3. Obtain venous access and initiate an intravenous infusion at maintenance rate.

  ▪ Prepare to administer osmotic diuretics, as needed, to control increased intracranial pressure.

  ▪ Obtain blood specimens for laboratory analysis.

    • Viral studies

4. Perform initial and serial neurologic assessments to detect increases in intracranial pressure, including:

  ▪ Cranial nerve assessments

  ▪ Level of consciousness

  ▪ Pupillary response

  ▪ Fontanelle assessments (infants)

5. Assist with a lumbar puncture if there are no signs of increased intracranial pressure.

  ▪ Obtain cerebrospinal fluid specimens for laboratory analysis.

    • Culture and sensitivity

    • Viral studies

    • Glucose

    • Protein

    • Cell count and differential

    • Gram stains

  ▪ Note the color of the cerebrospinal fluid.

  ▪ Record the opening and closing pressures.

6. Obtain pharyngeal and stool samples for viral cultures to identify the infecting organism.

7. Administer antipyretics to the febrile patient.

8. Antibiotics are not administered, because they are of no value in viral infections. However, the infecting organism may not be diagnosed initially in the ED. Antiviral agents may be ordered.

9. Reassess the child's neurologic status and cardiopulmonary status.

10. Inform the family frequently about the child's condition; provide emotional support to the child and family.

11. Prepare for transfer and transport to a tertiary care facility (Chapter 8) or hospital admission.

Home Care and Prevention

  Prevention of encephalitis begins with the community education regarding the mode of spread and control. Mosquito larvae must be destroyed, and breeding grounds (such as standing pools of water) must be eliminated. Children should avoid exposure to mosquitoes by avoiding outdoor play during hours of biting or by judicious use of repellents. Sleeping and living quarters should be screened. In endemic areas, domestic animals should be immunized or housed away from living quarters.

Methicillin-Resistant Staphylococcus Aureus

Etiology

  Health care-associated methicillin-resistant Staphylococcus aureus (MRSA) accounts for 50% of health care-associated S. aureus infections in large hospitals (> 500 beds).[10] Health care-associated MRSA strains are resistant to multiple drugs, including all β-lactamase-resistant, β-lactam, and cephalosporin antimicrobial agents.[10] There are two types of MRSA.

❒   Community-associated MRSA

  ▪ Isolated from people without risk factors from many cities in the United States, child-care centers, and elsewhere.[10]

- Responsible for community-associated infections in healthy children and adults without typical risk factors.
- Often includes infections of the skin and soft tissue; however, invasive disease and pneumonia can occur.

❑ Community-acquired MRSA (C-MRSA)

- Emerging as a serious skin and soft tissue infection that includes abscesses, cellulites, and necrotizing fasciitis.
- Preventative measures include good hand washing, applying antiseptics and covering cuts and abrasions, use of antibacterial soaps for showers after contact sports, avoidance of sharing towels and razors, and frequent towel washing.[17]

Focused History

❑ Inflammation of skin and subcutaneous tissues with intense redness, swelling, and firm infiltration

❑ Larger lesion with more redness and swelling at a single follicle

❑ Location of wound

❑ Cleansing or treatment measures before ED presentation

❑ Fatigue

❑ Exposure to someone with MRSA

❑ Fever

Focused Assessment

Physical Assessment

❑ Assess the respiratory system.

- Auscultate the chest for:
  - Rate. Respiratory rate may be increased with fever.
  - Adventitious sounds

❑ Assess the cardiovascular system.

- Auscultate the heart for:
  - Rate. Heart rate may be increased in the presence of fever.
- Measure the blood pressure.
- Measure core and skin temperature.
  - Fever may be present

❑ Assess the neurologic system.

- Fatigue and weakness may be present

❑ Assess the integumentary system.

- Observe the skin color for redness
- Assess for lesions or boils

Psychosocial Assessment

❑ Assess the child's and family's understanding of the infectious process.

❑ Assess the child's coping strategies.

Nursing Interventions

1. Assess and maintain airway, breathing, and circulation.

2. Initiate cardiorespiratory and oxygen saturation monitoring, as needed.

3. Obtain venous access for:
   - Intravenous fluid administration
   - Intravenous antibiotic administration

4. Initiate appropriate universal precautions.
   - Ensure hand washing before and after contact with an affected child.
   - Keep skin clean to prevent the spread of infection and to prevent complications.

5. Administer antipyretics for febrile patients.

6. Promote pain relief.
   - Administer analgesics
   - Apply warm, moist compresses to localized lesions

7. Initiate wound therapy, as needed.
   - Apply topical antibiotic agents
   - Assist with incision and drainage of severe lesions, followed by wound irrigation with antibiotics or suitable drain implantation.

8. Prepare for hospital admission or transfer to an appropriate facility (Chapter 8).

Home Care and Prevention

Home care for children with MRSA includes:[18]

❑ Bathing with 1 teaspoon chlorine bleach added to each gallon of bath water twice weekly.

❑ Applying mupirocin (bactroban) to the child's nares twice a day for 2 to 4 weeks.

❑ Avoiding sharing towels or washcloths.

❑ Changing of clothes and underwear daily.

❑ Laundering clothes in hot water.

❑ Disposing of razors after one use.

Home treatment of MRSA-infected wounds includes:[18]

❑ Warning the child and family that squeezing follicular lesions will not hasten the resolution of the infection and that there is a risk of making the lesion worse or spreading the infection.

❑ Teaching hand washing before and after contact with an affected child.

❑ Cautioning the child against touching the infected area.

❑ Instructing the child and family to use warm compresses for pain relief.

❑ Administering the entire medication regimen.

Prevention and management of community-acquired MRSA among athletes includes:[9]

❑ Showering with soap and water after competitions.

❑ Avoiding the practice of sharing towels and personal items.

❑ Covering all wounds.

❑ Encouraging athletes to care for wounds.

❑ Reporting to the coach or trainer those athletes that are potentially infected.

❑ Regularly cleaning shared athletic equipment.

Infectious Diseases

Rabies

Etiology

The frequency of animal bites and the rising incidence of rabies in wild animals make evaluation for treatment a major consideration. Although the incidence of rabies varies greatly among geographic areas, rabies invariably is fatal.[10]

Transmission of the rabies virus occurs after a bite or scratch or after contamination of the mucous membranes or an open wound by an animal infected with the rabies virus. Sources of rabies in the United States include wild and domestic animals. Rabies is rare in vaccinated animals.[19] Wild animals represent the most significant source of rabies in the United States. The highest incidence is among skunks, raccoons, foxes, and bats. Rodents are rarely infected. Infection in animals can be diagnosed by demonstration of virus-specific fluorescent antigen in brain tissue. Suspected rabid animals should be killed in a manner that preserves brain tissue for appropriate examination.[10]

Focused History

❑ Animal involved in the exposure:
  ▪ Type (domestic or wild)
  ▪ Whereabouts (stray, pet, or wild)
  ▪ Animal's rabies status
  ▪ Animal's owner
  ▪ Animal's present location (i.e., caught and detained or unknown)

  ▪ Where the bite occurred (indoors, street, or forest)
❑ Type of wound:
  ▪ Bite (puncture, laceration, or avulsion)
  ▪ Scratch
❑ Location of the wound
❑ Time of occurrence
❑ Provoked or unprovoked attack or contact
❑ Cleansing or treatment measures before ED presentation

Focused Assessment

Physical Assessment

❑ Assess the neurologic system.
  ▪ Assess level of consciousness: AVPU scale (Alert, responds to Verbal stimuli, responds to Painful stimuli, Unresponsive) or Glasgow Coma Scale (GCS) methods.
  ▪ Assess for clinical manifestations of rabies.[10, 15]
    • Initial signs:
      · General malaise
      · Fever
      · Sore throat
    • Excitement phase:
      · Hypersensitivity
      · Increased reaction to external stimuli
      · Seizures
      · Maniacal behavior
      · Choking
    • Severe spasms of respiratory muscles (hydrophobia)
      · Apnea
      · Cyanosis
      · Anoxia
❑ Assess the wound.
  ▪ Observe the type of wound (puncture, scratch, or bite).
  ▪ Note the location of the wound.
  ▪ Observe the depth of the wound.
  ▪ Determine whether underlying structures are involved.

Psychosocial Assessment

❑ Assess the child for fear or apprehension.
  ▪ The child may have been warned about avoiding the particular animal, or the child may have been

teasing the animal.

- In unprovoked attacks, the child may become fearful of animals in the future.

❒ Assess the child's and family's coping strategies.

Nursing Interventions

1. Initiate thorough wound cleansing.

- Irrigate punctures and lacerations thoroughly with normal saline solution.
- Wash the area with povidone-iodine or antimicrobial soap.
- Wash scratches with povidone-iodine or antimicrobial soap and normal saline solution.
- Prepare for suturing, if needed.
  - Prepare for conscious sedation (Chapter 11) in the child with facial or extensive lacerations.
- Apply an antibacterial ointment and bandage the wound.

2. Administer medications, as prescribed.

- The need for tetanus propylaxis and measures to control bacterial infection should be considered.
- Concurrent use of passive and active immunoprophylaxis is required for optimal therapy as soon as possible after exposure, within 24 hours.[10]
  - Three rabies vaccines are licensed for prophylaxis in the United States: human diploid cell vaccine (HDCV) (Imovax), rabies vaccine adsorbed (RVA), and purified chicken embryo cell (PCEC) (RabAvert), but only HDCV and PCEC are being produced.[10]
- Administer the human rabies vaccine.
  - Administer a 1.0 ml dose of vaccine given intramuscularly in the deltoid area or anterolateral aspect of the thigh on the first day of postexposure prophlaxis (day 0), and repeated doses are given on days 3,7,14, and 28 after the first dose, for a total of 5 doses. Care should be taken to ensure that the vaccine is administered intramuscularly.[10]
  - Passive immunization- Human Rabies Immune Globulin (RIG) should be used concomitantly with the first dose of vaccine for postexposure prophylaxis to bridge time between possible rabies exposure and active antibody production induced by the vaccine.[10]
  - The recommended dose of RIG is 20 IU/kg. As much of the dose as possible should be used to infiltrate the wound(s), if present. The remainder is given intramuscularly.[10]

- Because antibody responses in adults who received vaccine in the gluteal area sometimes have been less than those who were injected in the deltoid muscle, the deltoid site always should be used except in infants and young children, in whom the anterolateral thigh is the appropriate site.[10]

3. Prepare the child with severe wounds for operative management and hospitalization.

4. Report the animal bite and suspected rabies cases to the local health department.

5. Report the animal bite to the animal control authorities if the animal is a stray or cannot be located, or if the owners are unknown.

- Unprovoked attacks or behavioral changes in the animal should be interpreted as possible signs of rabies.
- Other considerations should include the type of exposure (bite or nonbite) and the prevalence of rabies in the specified region.
- All carnivores, bats, and woodchucks should be initially regarded as having the rabies virus, and prophylaxis should begin.
- Although wounds inflicted by dogs and cats that appear healthy represent the lowest rabies risk, the animal should be observed for 10 days for any unprovoked attacks or behavioral changes.
- If the animal appears rabid or becomes ill during the period of observation, the child should begin rabies prophylaxis immediately.
- Arrange for the child and family to return to the emergency department or to their health care provider on days 3, 7, 14, and 28 for injections of the human rabies vaccine.

Home Care and Prevention

Prevention of animal bites is both an individual and a community responsibility. Local governments should initiate and maintain effective programs to ensure vaccinations of all dogs, cats, and ferrets and to remove strays and unwanted animals. Further, the community should require that all domestic pets be licensed and leashed, under verbal control, or confined. Regular vaccination and immunization programs should be mandated for all domestic pets. Shelters that put homeless animals up for adoption should require that pets received through them be sterilized to decrease the number of unwanted animals. Emergency department staff should explore patterns of rabies susceptibility in their local areas.

Children should be taught to avoid reservoirs of rabies, particularly live or dead skunks, foxes, and bats. Parents should be advised about bite-prevention measures and animal safety (Chapter 4), provided with instructions for reporting bites, and instructed in proper guidelines for pet selection and care. Parents and children may be concerned about the cosmetic outcomes of facial wounds; they also may fear undergoing rabies vaccination. Parents will have to work with the animal's owner and local health authorities regarding quarantine, rabies status, or euthanasia.

Kawasaki Disease

Etiology

Kawasaki disease (KD) is an acute febrile vasculitis condition of children first described by Dr. Tomisaku Kawasaki in Japan in 1967.[21] The cause of KD is unknown. Coronary artery abnormalities will develop in approximately 20% of untreated children.[21] Most cases of KD occur in children between 1 and 8 years of age. Incomplete KD is more common in infants younger than 12 months of age than in older children.[10] Epidemics generally occur during winter and spring.[10]

Cardiac involvement is the most important manifestation of KD. Myocarditis, manifested as tachycardia out of proportion to fever, occurs in 50% of patients, and a decreased ventricular function occurs in a smaller number of patients.[21] Giant coronary artery aneurysms pose the greatest risk for rupture, thrombosis or stenosis, and myocardial infarction.[21]

Because there is no definitive diagnostic test for KD, its diagnosis is based on the presence of characteristic clinical signs.

❒ Classic KD: Presence of fever for at least 5 days and at least four of five of the other characteristic clinical features of this illness:[21]
  ▪ Rash
  ▪ Irritability
  ▪ Poor appetite and oral intake
  ▪ Decreased urinary output
  ▪ Decreased activity level

❒ Atypical or incomplete KD: Persistent fever but with fewer than four other features of the illness. Incomplete cases are most frequent in infants, who, unfortunately, also have the highest likelihood of the development of coronary artery disease.[21] Accurate identification of incomplete cases is a major clinical challenge.

Focused History

❒ Fever persisting at least 5 days
❒ Rash
❒ Irritability
❒ Poor appetite and oral intake
❒ Decreased urinary output
❒ Decreased activity level

Focused Assessment

Physical Assessment

❒ Assess the respiratory system.
  ▪ Auscultate the chest for:
    • Respiratory rate
    • Adventitious sounds
      · Cough may be present
      · Pulmonary infiltrates may be detected on radiograph
  ▪ Inspect the nose for rhinorrhea
❒ Assess the cardiovascular system.
  ▪ Auscultate the heart for:
    • Rate. Gallop rhythm may be present.
    • Rhythm. Pericardial effusion and valvular insufficiency may be present. The child should be assessed frequently for signs of congestive heart failure, including decreased urinary output, gallop rhythm, tachycardia, and respiratory distress.[22]
  ▪ Cardiac monitoring is suggested:[22]
    • Before the initial electrocardiogram and echocardiogram are recorded and shown to be normal.
    • During infusion of intravenous γ-globulin.
    • In children younger than 1 year of age.
    • In any child with cardiac symptoms.
❒ Assess the central nervous system.
  ▪ Assess level of consciousness: AVPU scale (Alert, responds to Verbal stimuli, responds to Painful stimuli, Unresponsive) or Glasgow Coma Scale (GCS) methods.
❒ Assess for neurologic changes.
  ▪ Irritability
  ▪ Signs of meningeal irritation
  ▪ Photophobia
❒ Assess the gastrointestinal system.
  ▪ Observe for:
    • Diarrhea

- Nausea and vomiting
  - Palpate the abdomen for pain
- ❐ Assess the integumentary system.
  - Observe the skin color:
    - Color may be pale as a result of anemia
    - May be jaundiced
  - Observe for a rash.
  - Observe for induration of hands and feet and desquamation of fingers or toes.
- ❐ Assess for changes in the oral cavity.
  - Erythema and cracking of lips
  - Strawberry tongue
  - Diffuse injection of oral and pharyngeal mucosae
- ❐ Assess the lymphatic system.
  - Palpate the cervical lymph nodes for adenopathy (usually unilateral)

Psychosocial Assessment

- ❐ Assess the child and family's knowledge of the disease process.
- ❐ Assess the child and family's coping strategies.

Nursing Interventions

1. Assess and maintain airway, breathing, and circulation.
   - Initiate cardiorespiratory and oxygen saturation monitoring.
2. Obtain vascular access and initiate an intravenous infusion at a maintenance rate.
   - Administer intravenous fluids cautiously to prevent congestive heart failure.
3. Obtain blood specimens for laboratory analysis.
   - Complete blood cell count (elevated) and differential
   - Platelets (elevated)
   - Erythrocyte sedimentation rate (elevated)
   - Alanine aminotransferase (elevated)
4. Administer medications, as prescribed.[23]
   - During the acute phase of the illness, initiate aspirin therapy. Aspirin therapy inhibits platelet function and may decrease the associated coronary artery disease.
     - Begin aspirin therapy with 80-100 mg/kg/day orally, divided into four doses daily, and continue until the child is afebrile for 48 to 72 hours.
     - Once high dose aspirin is stopped, continue with low-dose aspirin at 3 to 5 mg/kg/day, orally, until

no signs of coronary changes are found by 6 to 8 weeks after the onset of illness.
   - Monitor salicylate levels during high-dose aspirin therapy.
   - Administer intravenous γ-globulin as a single dose of 2 g/kg, together with aspirin. Observe for reactions such as flushing, chills, headache, nausea, and vomiting.
5. Reassess the child's neurologic status and cardiopulmonary status.
6. Monitor intake and output carefully.
   - Obtain a urine specimen; observe for white cells with no bacteria.
7. Prepare for diagnostic testing.
   - An echocardiogram should be obtained early in the acute phase of illness and 6 to 8 weeks after onset.[10]
8. Initiate a cardiology consultation.
9. Inform the family frequently of the child's condition; provide emotional support to the child and family.
10. Prepare for transfer and transport to a tertiary care facility, as needed (Chapter 8), or hospitalization.
    - Hospitalization and cardiorespiratory monitoring are required to detect cardiac complications such as congestive heart failure, pericardial effusions, and dysrhythmias.

Home Care and Prevention

The prognosis for patients receiving treatment within the first 10 days of illness is good. However, long-term morbidity is profound in patients in whom the disease is not diagnosed and treated early in its course. Children with a diagnosis of KD require follow-up for several years, with special attention to the development of coronary artery disease. Children and parents must be taught about the complications of KD.

These children need to be placed in a quiet environment that promotes adequate rest. The parents need to be supported in their efforts to comfort an often inconsolable child. Remind parents that irritability is likely to persist for up to 2 months after the onset of symptoms. Peeling of the hands and feet is painless and occurs primarily in the second and third weeks.[22] Arthritis, especially of the larger weight-bearing joints, may persist for several weeks. Although the arthritis in KD is always temporary, it can be severe enough that some children require treatment with antiarthritic agents once they are no longer taking high-dose aspirin.[22]

Lyme Disease

Etiology

With approximately 20,000 new cases reported each year, Lyme disease (LD) is the most common vector-borne disease in the United States. Cases occur most commonly in northeastern, mid-Atlantic, and north-central states among persons aged 5 to 9 years and 45 to 54 years.[10] Cases peak during summer months, reflecting transmission by nymphal vector ticks during May and June.

Lyme disease is caused by the spirochete Borrelia burgdorferi and is transmitted to humans by the bite of infected ticks. Borrelia burgdorferi enters the skin and bloodstream through the saliva and feces of ticks, especially black-legged and deer ticks.[18] If the disease is left untreated, there is presently no vaccine available for protecting humans against LD.

The clinical manifestations of Lyme disease are divided into three stages:

❑ Early localized

Early localized disease is characterized by a distinctive rash, erythema migrans, at the site of a recent tick bite. Erythema migrans begins as a red macule or papule that usually expands over days to weeks to form a large, annular, erythematous lesion that may increase in size to 5 cm or more in diameter, sometimes with partial central clearing.[10]

❑ Early disseminated

Manifests most commonly as multiple erythema migrans in approximately 15% of the patients. This rash usually occurs several weeks after an infective tick bite. Other common manifestations are arthralgia, headache, and fatigue. Carditis occurs rarely in children and 50% develop arthritis.[10]

❑ Late disease

Late manifestations involve the joints, heart, and nervous system.[24] Some of these patients may have persistent or recurrent symptoms.

Focused History

Patient history

❑ Flu-like symptoms appearing 2 to 21 days after a tick bite:

- Fever
- Headache
- Lethargy
- General aches and pains
- Rash at the tick-bite site
- Outdoor activity, such as camping or hiking

- Tick exposure

Family history

❑ Outdoor activity, such as camping or hiking

❑ Tick exposure

Focused Assessment

Physical Assessment

❑ Assess the cardiovascular system.

- Auscultate the heart for:
  - Rate

❑ Interpret electrocardiogram recordings for dysrhythmias.

- Cardiac manifestations may be present
- Cardiac abnormalities clear over time

❑ Assess the neurologic system.

- Assess level of consciousness: AVPU scale (*A*lert, responds to *V*erbal stimuli, responds to *P*ainful stimuli, *U*nresponsive) or Glasgow Coma Scale (GCS) methods.
- Assess for signs of meningeal irritation or infection.
  - Headache
  - Stiff neck
  - Irritability
  - Photophobia
  - Nausea and vomiting

❑ Assess for limb weakness.

- Progression of LD leads to nerve inflammation, resulting in seventh cranial nerve palsy and weakness of the limbs. These findings generally appear within 4 weeks of the tick bite and occur in 15% to 20% of patients. Infections of the nervous system can progress to meningitis.

❑ Assess the integumentary system.

- Inspect the skin for a rash.[10]
  - The most common feature of LD is a large, red skin rash called erythema migrans, affecting up to 80% of patients.
  - The rash expands outward from the site of the tick bite, beginning 3 to 30 days after the bite.
  - The LD rash is flat, circular, and generally at least 2 inches in diameter.
  - As the rash progresses, it may appear to have a "bull's-eye" appearance, as the central portion partially clears and the outer margins redden.
  - The single rash can become quite large.
  - One or more rashes may be present on other

areas of the skin.

❑ Assess the musculoskeletal system.

▪ Inspect the joints for redness and edema; palpate for fluid.

• Arthritis may be diagnosed in untreated Lyme disease.

Psychosocial Assessment

❑ Assess the child and family's understanding of the disease.

❑ Assess the child and family's coping strategies.

Nursing Interventions

Patients with a tick bite and no evidence of disease are not routinely treated because of the low risk of infection, even in endemic regions.

For patients with a tick bite and evidence of disease.

1. Administer oral antibiotics, as prescribed.[10]

▪ Amoxicillin is the drug of choice for children younger than 8 years of age. For patients who are allergic to penicillin, the alternative drug is cefuroxime. Erythromycin and azithromycin are less effective.[10]

▪ Doxycycline or erythromycin is the drug of choice for children older than 8 years of age.

2. Obtain blood specimens, as needed, to isolate the bacteria or detect antibodies that have developed against the bacteria in the blood.

3. Diagnosis in patients who possibly have early disseminated or late LD should be based on clinical findings and serologic test results.[10]

Home Care and Prevention

Children and families should be educated on protecting themselves from exposure to ticks. In endemic areas tick habitats can include yards and parks, as well as wooded areas. To prevent tick bites, children and families should:[18]

❑ Dress appropriately for the outdoors.

▪ Wear light-colored clothing so that ticks can be spotted easily.

▪ Wear long pants and long-sleeved shirts.

▪ Tuck pant legs into socks and tuck the shirt into the pants when in weeded areas.

❑ Avoid grass and shrubbery where ticks may be lurking; avoid tick-infested areas.

❑ Apply a repellent containing the compound N,N-diethyltoluamide (DEET) to exposed skin areas (except the face).

▪ Follow label directions carefully, and be especially cautious when using any form of DEET on children.

▪ Do not apply DEET to infants, because it may cause seizures.

❑ Wash children's clothes immediately on entering the house to prevent entry of ticks into the home.

❑ Inspect children carefully for ticks twice a day, including close inspection of the neck, scalp, axillae, and groin, after all outdoor activities. A fine-toothed comb may be used to comb the hair for ticks.

❑ Be alert for signs of the skin lesion, especially if children are known to have been exposed to the tick vector.[18]

❑ Inspect pets for ticks.

▪ Contact the veterinarian for the appropriate pet insect repellent.

▪ Use tweezers to remove ticks found on the pet.

▪ Mow the lawn frequently.

❑ Remove attached ticks from skin immediately with fine-tipped tweezers by grasping the tick's head as closely as possible to the exposed skin.

▪ Apply slow and steady pressure to remove the entire tick.

▪ Do not use petroleum jelly, a hot match, nail polish, or other products to remove a tick.[25]

▪ Cleanse the skin afterward with isopropyl alcohol.

▪ Place the tick into a plastic bag with a blade of grass for inspection by the primary care physician.

Conclusion

Although there are many types of communicable and infectious disease emergencies, the initial emergency nursing care generally remains the same. Emergency nurses should work closely with local health departments to determine endemic diseases in their hospital's geographic area. Prevention of transmission to other staff and family members is essential.

References

1. Rote, N. (2006). Alterations in immunity and inflammation. In K. McCance & S. Huether (Eds.), *Pathophysiology: The biologic basis for disease in adults and children* (5th ed.). St. Louis, MO: Mosby.

2. Rote, N., & Trask, B. (2006). Adaptive immunity. In K. McCance & S. Huether (Eds.), *Pathophysiology: The biologic basis for disease in adults and children* (5th ed.). St. Louis, MO: Mosby.

3. Bellanti, J., Zeligs, B., & Pung, Y. (2005). Immunology of the fetus and newborn. In M. MacDonald, M. Mullett, & M. Seshia (Eds.), *Avery's neonatology pathophysiology & management of the newborn* (6th ed., pp. 1153–1155). Philadelphia: Lippincott Williams & Wilkins.

4. Roberts, K., Brinker, D., & Murante, B. (2006). Hematology and immunology. In M. Slota (Ed.), *Core curriculum for pediatric critical care nursing* (2nd ed., pp. 545–619). Philadelphia: Saunders.

5. Thilo, E., & Rosenberg, A. (2007). The newborn infant. In W. Hay, Jr., M. Levin, J. Sondheimer, & R. Deterding (Eds.), *Current diagnosis & treatment in pediatrics* (18th ed., pp. 7). New York: McGraw-Hill.

6. Centers for Disease Control and Prevention. (2008). *Slide Set—Epidemiology of pediatric tuberculosis in the United States, 1993–2006.* Atlanta, GA: Author.

7. American Thoracic Society, Centers for Disease Control and Prevention, & Infectious Diseases Society of America. (2003). Treatment of tuberculosis. *Morbidity and Mortality Weekly Report, 52*(RR11), 1–77.

8. Hueckel, R., & Wilson, D. (2007). The child with respiratory dysfunction. In M. Hockenberry & D. Wilson (Eds.), *Wong's nursing care of infants and children* (8th ed, pp. 1321–1322, 1334–1345). St. Louis, MO: Mosby.

9. Ball, J., & Bindler, R. (2008). In Pediatric nursing: *Caring for children* (4th ed., pp. 708–709, 560–597, 607–622, 781–782, 832, 963). Upper Saddle River, NJ: Pearson Prentice Hall.

10. American Academy of Pediatrics. (2006). *Red book 2006: Report of the Committee of Infectious Diseases* (27th ed.) Elk Grove Village, IL: Author.

11. Yogev, R., & Chadwick, E. (2007). Acquired immunodeficiency syndrome (human immunodeficiency virus). In R. Kliegman, R. Behrman, H. Jenson, & B. Stanton (Eds.), *Nelson textbook of pediatrics* (18th ed.). Philadelphia: Saunders.

12. Bryant, R. (2007). The child with hematologic or immunologic dysfunction. In M. J. Hockenberry, D. Wilson, M. L. Winkelstein, N. E. Klein, & D. Wong, *Wong's nursing care of infants and children* (8th ed., pp. 1545–1552). St. Louis, MO: Mosby.

13. Maldonado, Y. (2006). Acquired immunodeficiency syndrome in the infant. In J. Reminton & J. Klein (Eds.). *Infectious diseases of the fetus and newborn infant* (6th ed., Chapter 21). Philadelphia: Saunders.

14. Prober, C. (2007). Central nervous systems infections. In R. Kliegman, R. Behrman, H. Jenson, & B. Stanton (Eds.), *Nelson textbook of pediatrics* (18th ed.). Philadelphia: Elsevier.

15. Bryant, R. & Schultz, R. (2007). The child with cerebral dysfunction. In M. J. Hockenberry, D. Wilson, M. L. Winkelstein, N. E. Klein, & D. Wong, *Wong's nursing care of infants and children* (8th ed.). St. Louis, MO: Mosby.

16. Halstead, S. B. (2007). Arboviral encephalitis in North America. In R. Kliegman, R. Behrman, H. Jenson, & B. Stanton (Eds.), *Nelson textbook of pediatrics* (18th ed., Chapter 264). Philadelphia: Saunders.

17. Nicol, N.H., Huether, S.E., and Weber, R. (2006). Structure, function, and disorders of the integument. In K. McCance & S. Huether (Eds.), *Pathophysiology: The biologic basis for disease in adults and children* (5th ed.). St. Louis, MO: Mosby.

18. McCord, S. S. (2007). Health problems of middle childhood. In M. J. Hockenberry, D. Wilson, M. L. Winkelstein, N. E. Klein, & D. Wong, *Wong's nursing care of infants and children* (8th ed, pp. 767–769). St. Louis, MO: Mosby.

19. Centers for Disease Control and Prevention. (2006). Compendium of animal rabies prevention and control, 2006. United States, 2006. Recommendations and Reports. *Morbidity and Mortality Weekly Report, 55*(RR-5), 1–8.

20. Manning, S., Rupprecht, C., Fishbein, D., Hanlon, C., Lumlertdacha, B. et al (2008). Human rabies prevention, United States, 2008. Recommendations of the advisory committee on immunizations practices. *Morbidity and Mortality Weekly Report, 57*, 1–26, 28.

21. Rowley, A., & Shulman, S. (2007). Kawasaki disease. In R. Kliegman, R. Behrman, H. Jenson, & B. Stanton (Eds.), *Nelson textbook of pediatrics* (18th ed., Chapter 165). Philadelphia: Saunders.

References (continued)

22. O'Brien, P., & Baker, A. (2007). The child with cardiovascular dysfunction. Childhood. In M. J. Hockenberry, D. Wilson, M. L. Winkelstein, N. E. Klein, & D. Wong, *Wong's nursing care of infants and children* (8th ed., pp. 1481–1485). St. Louis, MO: Mosby.

23. Newburger, J., Takahashi, M., Gerber, M., Gerwitz, M., Tani, L., Burns, J. et al. (2004). Diagnosis, treatment, and long-term management of Kawasaki Disease: A statement for health professionals from the committee on rheumatic fever, endocarditis, and Kawasaki disease, council on cardiovascular disease in the young, American Heart Association. *Pediatrics, 114*(6), 1708–1733.

24. Centers for Disease Control and Prevention. (2007). Lyme disease—United States, 2003–2005. *Morbidity and Mortality Weekly Report, 56*(23), 573–576.

25. Centers for Disease Control and Prevention. (2009). Learn about lyme disease. Retrieved April 14, 2009, from http://www.cdc.gov/ncidod/dvbid/lyme/index.htm

26. Hockenberry, M., & Barrera, P. (2007). Health problems of early childhood. In M. J. Hockenberry, D. Wilson, M. L. Winkelstein, N. E. Klein, & D. Wong, (Eds). *Wong's nursing care of infants and children* (8th ed., pp. 666–675). St. Louis, MO: Mosby.

TWENTY-FIVE

Psychiatric Emergencies

Christine B. Cassesse, MSN, FNP-BC, FPMHNP-BC
Kathryn Puskar, RN, DrPH, FAAN
Kathleen A. Sullivan, RN, PhD

Introduction

Psychiatric emergencies have increased in both frequency and severity in the child and adolescent population.[1] Psychiatric emergencies in children and adolescents are defined as acute disturbance in thought, behavior, mood, or social relationships that require immediate intervention.[2] Early recognition of and intervention in psychiatric emergencies may reduce harm related to violence, aggression, and suicide.[3]

Emergency psychiatric care is very limited and is worsening.[4] With respect to child and adolescent psychiatric emergencies in particular, these limitations are very pronounced. Among a nationwide survey of emergency physicians, less than one-third reported access to pediatric psychiatric services, while 43% reported access to geriatric psychiatric services.[4] Furthermore, the lack of pediatric and adolescent psychiatric beds was cited as a major reason for extended emergency department (ED) stays ("boarding").[4]

Psychiatric emergency visits are among the least comfortable for the ED staff.[5] Emergency department nurses must be comfortable with and confident in providing safe and effective emergency psychiatric care for children, adolescents, and their families. In assessing and intervening with children or adolescents admitted to the emergency department with psychiatric emergencies the emergency nurse needs a basic knowledge of developmental stages and age appropriate behavior (Chapter 3); principles of crisis intervention (Chapter 26); and a basic understanding of the symptoms which might result in psychiatric emergencies. Further understanding of psychiatric diagnoses[2] for emergent, acute and chronic psychiatric conditions is beneficial when caring for this population.

Children with developmental vulnerabilities that affect ED care are discussed at the end of the chapter.

The purpose of this chapter is to describe the etiology and treatment of selected psychiatric emergencies and chronic conditions.

Pediatric Conditions

Etiology

The etiology of psychiatric conditions arises from developmental issues, traumatic events, and other situations.

Focused History

The emergency nurse obtains the history from the parent and pediatric patient separately, then together. The focus of the physical and mental health histories is on health conditions that would affect the use of seclusion or restraint, as outlined below. Table 25.1 compares approaches that can be useful with preadolescents and adolescents.

Physical Health History

❒ Asthma

❒ Obesity

❒ Cardiovascular concerns, particularly a history of arrhythmia

❒ Current medications, including dietary and herbal supplements. Note medications that could prolong the QT interval such as tricyclic antidepressants, SSRIs, typical and atypical antipsychotic agents, stimulants, non stimulant ADHD medication, bronchodilators, antihistamines, antibiotics, anti-emetics, antihypertensive agents, mood stabilizers, anti-cancer drugs, anti-malarial agents, antifungal agents, and immunosuppressant agents

❒ Last meal

Mental Health History

❒ Panic attacks or panic disorders

❒ Current diagnosis (es)

❒ Current medications and adherence with those medications

❒ Past hospitalizations

❒ Past suicide attempts and lethality

❒ Past violence and lethality

❒ Past incidents of seclusion and/or restraint

TABLE 25.1 History Taking Approaches with Preadolescent and Adolescent Patients with Psychiatric Disturbances

Preadolescents	Adolescents
Obtain a history from the parents first; then obtain a history from the child, usually alone, unless the child has separation anxiety.	Obtain a history from the adolescent first and alone; then talk with the parents, if present.
Ascertain the child's understanding of the evaluation and reason for being in the emergency department.	Be honest and objective with the adolescent to build trust. Avoid projecting one's own values onto the adolescent.
Reserve the use of drawings and toys for the end of the interview.	Not needed with adolescents.
Observe the child's interaction with the parents and the evaluator as well as the child's activity level.	Note the adolescent's interaction with the evaluator and the parents, if present.
Ask the child and family, "How do you get along with your friends?" This is probably the most effective screening question to identify major psychopathology. If the child has difficulty with peer relationships or is isolated from them, psychological problems can be expected.	Focus on concerns related to family emancipation, peer pressure, and heterosexual and homosexual exposure; these issues usually are an underlying reason for the adolescent's psychiatric disturbance.

Focused Assessment

There are occasions when the appearance of psychiatric symptoms is secondary to other primary causes (e.g., hypoglycemia, fever, seizure, substance abuse).[6,7] Therefore, the physical health assessment should precede the psychiatric assessment to rule out a physical or neurological etiology for the current psychiatric symptoms.[5,8]

Physical Assessment

☐ Assess the child's height and weight.
- The child's weight is necessary to determine appropriate dosing of medications administered in the ED. The height and weight are necessary to measure the body mass index (BMI) which is relevant when assessing a child for disordered eating.

☐ Assess the respiratory system.
- Rate
- Rhythm
- Effort

☐ Assess the cardiovascular system.
- Rate
- Rhythm
- Measure the blood pressure

☐ Assess peripheral perfusion.
- Measure core and skin temperature
- Inspect the skin color
- Measure capillary refill time

☐ Assess the neurological system.
- Assess the level of consciousness with the AVPU method (*A*lert, responds to *V*erbal stimuli, responds to *P*ain, *U*nresponsive) or the Glasgow Coma Scale (GCS).
- Eye contact
  - Good, partial, or none
- Motor control
  - Note the presence of abnormal gait, movements, tremor, or tics
- Speech
  - Rate, rhythm, volume, and tone of speech
  - Peculiarities of speech, including
    · Pressured speech
    · Slow speech
  - Abnormal speech patterns such as:
    · Derailment (getting 'off track' while speaking on a subject)
    · Circumstantiality (delay in getting to the point by including extraneous details)
    · Tangentiality (responses do not answer the question)
    · Incoherence

☐ Assess thought content for presence or absence of hallucinations, delusions, or illusions.

☐ Compare the patient's developmental level against his or her chronological age (Chapter 3).

- Assess the integumentary system.
  - Lesions
  - Rashes
  - Lacerations
  - Burns
  - Brandings
  - Piercings
  - Tattoos
  - Superficial cutting. Note the stage of healing (acute or scars), number and location of cuts.
- Assess the remaining body systems as needed.

Psychosocial Assessment

Emergency nurses need to be familiar with state laws concerning the age at which an adolescent is able to consent to psychiatric treatment independently; child abuse reporting laws; and rules regarding reporting of suicidal and homicidal behavior. The effect of these laws on the ED treatment must be communicated to the adolescent and parent before proceeding with the psychosocial assessment.

Triage Considerations

The triage nurse is responsible for the conducting and documenting the initial evaluation of the pediatric patient presenting for evaluation of mental health/behavioral concerns, and for those pediatric patients who are exhibiting or have a history of exhibiting violent, self destructive, or suicidal behaviors. The pediatric patient who presents without urgent medical needs, with low risk of suicidality or violence, or with subacute symptoms (may be there for secondary gains) would be triaged as nonurgent.

Pediatric patients who do not appear to be medically stable should be treated for their medical condition prior to any psychiatric assessment. Signs of medical instability include:

- Vital signs out of normal range
- Altered mental status
- Abnormal triage assessment
- Signs and symptoms of drug overdose or acute alcohol intoxication

A personal care attendant (PCA)—a hospital employee with personal injury protection and restraint skills—should provide continuous observation of a patient who has a history of elopement or is currently verbalizing thoughts of elopement. The PCA should be summoned at the time of triage assessment if the child is at high risk for elopement.

- See immediately

Findings that qualify a pediatric patient being triaged as emergent:

- Threatening violence or who has been violent in the past
- Making a suicidal or homicidal threat or gesture, or exhibiting self injurious behaviors consistent with a suicide attempt, after medical stabilization
- At risk for elopement

- See as soon as possible

Findings that qualify a pediatric patient being triaged as urgent:

- Exhibiting symptoms consistent with psychosis (alterations of appearance or inability to perform activities of daily living [ADLs]), inability to respond in an expected way (responding to internal stimuli, acutely paranoid or grandiose), inability to converse rationally
- Performed self-injurious acts not meant to be suicidal, but of an urgent medical nature (deep lacerations, severe burns), after medical stabilization
- Agitated or aggressive
- Suffering from acute trauma or crisis

Nursing Interventions

1. Monitor and maintain airway, breathing and circulation.

2. Monitor mental status and inform the provider/supervisor for evidence of deterioration of mental status or for pediatric patients who are now suggesting thoughts of suicide, violence, or elopement.

3. Remove potential weapons, medications and unsafe objects, including lighters/matches, medications, guns, pocket knives, pens, pencils, belt, tie, and glasses. The presence of such implements may lead to suicidal or homicidal gestures. The patient should be placed in a hospital gown and the personal items removed from the room.

4. Facilitate the pediatric patient's use of appropriate coping skills. Encouraging appropriate coping skills allows the child a greater sense of control and mastery of the current symptoms. Additionally, this facilitation assists ED personnel in designing and implementing an aggression prevention plan. If possible, methods of preventing aggression in the past that have been successful should be utilized. Patient and family preferences should also be considered.

5. Initiate seclusion for any pediatric patient who is agitated, aggressive, or who threatens a violent act. Seclusion can be considered only if the emergency department is equipped with a seclusion room. During seclusion, the pediatric patient must be protected and observed continuously, and the family members are restricted from visitation. Hospital policy dictates the specific occasions during which seclusion may be used, and the procedure for seclusion specific to that institution. Documentation of the events leading to consideration of seclusion and of observation of the pediatric patient during seclusion, including the patient's reaction to seclusion, is essential.

6. Initiate confinement and restraint for any pediatric patient whose behaviors or outbursts are severely aggressive, destructive, violent, or pose imminent danger to self or others. Restraint maneuvers must be performed as a group by personnel trained in safe restraint. Hospital policy will specify the conditions for safe restraint and the procedure for restraint for that specific institution. Physical restraints must be used only as a "last resort," and must be applied and monitored in accordance with hospital policy. Documentation of the events that lead to restraint, and observation of the child in restraints, including their reaction to restraint, is essential.

7. Prepare to administer medications to abate or relieve psychiatric symptoms. Medications to be considered include intramuscular benzodiazepines and typical or atypical antipsychotic agents to provide chemical restraint of an acutely violent, disorganized, or psychotic patient.

8. Obtain serum and urine specimens for toxicology studies, as indicated.

9. Initiate a referral for psychiatric treatment.

   - Outpatient treatment is usually obtained for the pediatric patient who is stable and is not a threat to self or others.

   - Inpatient treatment is usually obtained for the pediatric patient who is unstable or a threat to self or others.

     - Inpatient psychiatric treatment may not be an option that is welcomed by the patient (or family) experiencing acute psychiatric illness. However, inpatient treatment may be necessary to protect the pediatric patient, the family, and the community. Under those circumstances every effort is made to assist the patient (and parent) in understanding the need for inpatient treatment, and eliciting their cooperation. The pediatric patient and parents should be informed of treatments being considered throughout the process of evaluation, including inpatient hospitalization, to eliminate the effect of surprise and gain the cooperation and support of the family. If that is possible, a voluntary commitment can be sought; otherwise, an involuntary commitment may be necessary.

10. Voluntary and involuntary commitment procedures vary by state. Statutes applicable to each state can be accessed at http://www.treatmentadvocacycenter.org. Inform the family frequently of the pediatric patient's condition. Provide emotional support to the patient and family.

11. Prepare for transfer and transport to a psychiatric inpatient facility (Chapter 8), tertiary care facility, hospitalization with a psychiatric referral, or discharge from the emergency department with a psychiatric referral. A smooth transition from the emergency department to hospitalization or home reduces the incidence of violence and crisis. It is helpful if the emergency nurse has knowledge of the institutions to which children and adolescents are commonly referred. Assisting the child and family to understand the reason for transfer, and the policies and procedures at the transfer institution, may prevent behavioral escalation at the time of transfer. If the transfer is to an outside facility, the child should not be sent alone with the family member. Ambulance transfer is the best option to protect the patient who may harm himself or others.

Home Care and Prevention

Emergency nurses should be familiar with the local community agencies that support mental health interventions for children and adolescents. Advocating for youth mental health services in their communities and becoming involved with programs that promote youth mental health are worthy activities in which emergency nurses can participate. Attending continuing education programs that focus on the needs of children and adolescents with psychiatric disorders help emergency nurses keep abreast of current medications and therapies. Emergency nurses should acknowledge their own values and beliefs while empathizing with children and families.

Selected Psychiatric Emergencies

Violence

Violence may occur in the context of a child or adolescent with a psychiatric illness, but a history of a psychiatric illness does not necessarily confer a predilection to violence. Nor does the lack of a psychiatric history preclude that the individual child or adolescent may become violent. Persons with delirium or who are mentally handicapped may become violent more rapidly than those who do not suffer from these disorders.[6,9] Violence may be underreported and better tolerated in families in which violence is an acceptable response to frustration.[6] Corroborating evidence should be sought from other sources such as the school, friends, or the police, if time permits.

Focused History

☐ Diagnoses for which the threat of violence is more acute include:[6,9]

- Conduct Disorder
- Oppositional Defiant Disorder (ODD)
- Attention Deficit/Hyperactivity Disorder (ADHD)
- Bipolar Disorder—manic phase
- Alcohol intoxication. Alcohol is likely to be associated with violence due to its disinhibiting effects, as well as the conceptual and cognitive decline seen with acute alcohol intoxication.[9]
- Illicit drug use. Amphetamines, hallucinogens (PCP, LSD), cocaine and its derivatives, methamphetamine, and sedative-hypnotics[9] can precipitate violent behavior.
- Schizophrenia

☐ "Red flags" from the psychosocial history indicating higher risk of violent behavior include:[6]

- History of past violent behavior
- Impulsivity
- Cruelty to animals
- Past trauma
- Low socioeconomic status. Children and adults with low socioeconomic status are more likely to be both the perpetrators and victims of violence, possibly secondary to being teased or bullied, discriminated against, having a higher incidence of family breakdown and dysfunction, and lack of access to preventative care.[9]

Focused Assessment

If the child's and/or family's behavior begins to escalate during the assessment, safety for oneself and others must be the primary concern. Restraint or seclusion in accordance with established ED guidelines must be enacted.[6]

☐ Assess the child's and family's recollection of previous episodes of violence and their lethality.

- The most violent act the pediatric patient has ever committed.
- Any history of the pediatric patient causing serious physical harm to an individual or pet.
- Expression of thoughts or intent to use violence.

☐ Assess the violent episode.

- Degree to which this is an impulsive act versus premeditation.
- Degree to which this behavior is congruent with the pediatric patient's past behaviors and behavioral style, and mood state.
- Past use of violence, extraordinary rage, access to weapons.
- Risk of self injury during violent behavior.
- Justification of the use of violence by the pediatric patient, and validity of this justification.
- Degree to which the pediatric patient remembers the incident, owns the behavior, expresses remorse.
- Bizarre or delusionary thought content or behavior.
- Command hallucinations (voices ordering acts which are usually violent or destructive).

Nursing Interventions

1. Maintain safety for oneself and others by activating established ED protocols for violent episodes (e.g., seclusion and restraint protocols).

2. Frequently assess the risk for violence during the patient's stay in the emergency department. Such an assessment is accurate only for short periods.

3. Promote safety and non-violence.

- Plan an escape route prior to beginning the assessment and nursing care
- Speak softly and calmly
- Ask questions in a nonjudgmental manner, and to avoid confrontation with the pediatric patient or family
- Use I statements, such as: "I sense that you are upset, can you tell me what is upsetting you?"
- Maintain a neutral position and distance (talk with the pediatric patient and family while seated if possible, and allow the patient personal space)
- Do not attempt to make eye contact unless the patient seeks it
- Project a sense of empathy for the pediatric patient

4. Prepare for transfer to a psychiatric facility, as needed (Chapter 8).

Home Care and Prevention

Concerns over childhood violence do not cease with discharge. Discharge planning must be specific and focused on the safety of the pediatric patient, family, and community. Outpatient follow-up of the pediatric patient must be arranged prior to discharge. The family must be informed of appropriate emergency procedures and crisis services. Suicidal behavior may be prevented by acute attention to its warning signs and risk factors.

Suicidal and Self-Injurious Behavior

Suicide has increased eight percent in adolescents over the past four years, the highest increase in suicide rates in the history of record keeping by the Centers for Disease Control and Prevention (CDC).[10] Approximately 4,900 U.S. adolescents committed suicide in 2004.[11] High risk groups include both males and females from 15 years of age through early adulthood.[11] While females attempt suicide more frequently, males complete suicide more often.[11] Also, as opposed to earlier years where lethal weapons were the most frequent means of committing suicide, suffocation and hanging now have that distinction, particularly among females, followed by firearms and poisoning.[11] Suicide completers have a higher incidence of substance use and abuse than their counterparts.[5]

The risk for suicide is 90% higher in children and adolescents with a major psychiatric disorder than their age matched counterparts.[10] Strong correlates of suicidal behavior include hopelessness and social isolation. Chronic medical illness is also a predisposing risk for suicide. Suicides attempts and completions have a familial tendency.[6] Suicide is often preceded by a feeling of desperation, and this distress is often conveyed to others.[9] Substance use and/or intoxication often precede a suicide attempt.[9] Suicide in the context of acute crisis or substance abuse is not fully correlated with the presence of a mood disorder, and may be better correlated with impulsivity.

The reduction of adequate treatment of depression in children and adolescents following the Food and Drug Administration (FDA) black box warning for antidepressants is postulated to be one reason for the rising rates of suicide in adolescents.[12,13] Careful monitoring of the child/ adolescent started on an antidepressant includes the use of the ED for evaluating suicidal risk. Suicide is more likely early in the treatment of depression, when medication therapy may have improved the patient's energy, but has not yet improved their mood.[10] Most suicides in adolescents being treated for depression occur just prior to or just after starting medication treatment.[10]

Adolescents are more likely to contemplate suicide when faced with academic failure, problems with their family, the law or disruption of relationships.[6] Adolescents with a mental illness may be less able to cope with random traumatic events causing distress, such as the death of a family member.[6] Adolescents are more susceptible to peer pressure, as evidenced by the occurrence of suicide clusters in this vulnerable group.[6] Media portrayals of suicide such as movies or documentaries may precede a suicide attempt in an adolescent.[6]

Self-injurious behaviors can occur in the context of a suicidal act or gesture or can be engaged in for a number of other reasons. Reasons for self-injurious behaviors not associated with suicide can include; mood and/or anxiety disorders, overwhelming stress, adjustment to acute trauma, crisis, or for secondary gain in children with maladaptive personality traits. Self-injurious behaviors may include; cutting, branding, piercing, tattooing and/or burning, restriction of food intake, or binging with purging behaviors have been posited to be self-injurious as well.

The child or adolescent who is actively self injurious or suicidal at the time of assessment may be hospitalized, unless the pediatric patient and family are able and willing to contract for safety, and have the ability to carry out the plan. Careful assessment of suicide risk and impulsivity, as well as careful physical assessment with attention to signs of self-injurious behaviors, personal and family history of suicide attempts or completions, mental status assessment, and family mental status assessment are essential to appropriate discharge of the child from the emergency department.

Focused History

❑   Chronic physical health conditions

❑   Chronic mental health conditions, such as depression

❑   Current medications

❑   Recent traumatic event or life event

❑   Substance use

Focused Assessment

Assessment of suicidal behavior in all children needs to be conducted in the context of an ED visit prompted by suicidal ideation, aggression, or symptoms of a mental health disorder. Discussing suicide does not put the child at increased risk of attempting or completing suicide.[10]

❑   Assessment for children and adolescents who are actively suicidal includes:

   ▪ History of all past suicide attempts including:

      • When the attempt(s) occurred

      • What actually happened (intent vs. attempt)

      • Method used

- How the episode was treated (hospitalization, outpatient evaluation, diagnosis, therapy, medication)
  - Effectiveness of past treatments
- Degree of planning involved with current suicide ideation/attempt
- Availability of firearms, medication, or other methods of lethality (car, garage, poisons, etc.)
- Past and current impulsive behaviors
- Rapidly changing mood and irritability
- Presence or absence of psychotic symptoms

❒ Assessment for children and adolescents at risk for suicide includes:
- Cultural factors. The highest risk for suicide is in Native American, Alaskan Native, and Hispanic populations. African Americans have lowest suicide rates.
- Presence of a previous mental health disorder. The risk for suicide is highest with disruptive disorders, substance use disorders, bipolar disorder in the manic phase, depression, separation anxiety, panic attacks and psychosis.
- Past history of aggressive and/or impulsive behavior.
- Runaway behavior. This behavior is independently associated with high suicide risk.
- Sexual orientation. Gay, lesbian, or bisexual youth are at higher risk for suicide.
- History of childhood sexual or physical abuse.

❒ Assessment of the pediatric patient with a mental illness, but who has not been assessed in the emergency department for current suicidality includes:
- Past or present feelings of suicidality
  - Dangerous behaviors
  - Triggers
  - Attempts
  - Ideation
  - Passive death wish (the family would be better off, no one would miss, etc.)
- Motivating feelings
  - Attempts to gain attention
  - Effect a change in an interpersonal relationship
  - Rejoin a dead family member
  - Get revenge
  - Avoid an intolerable situation
- Current mood symptoms/mood lability

Nursing Interventions

Children and adolescents with acute suicidal behavior.

1. Assess and maintain airway, breathing, and circulation.
2. Obtain serum and urine specimens for toxicology testing, as indicated.
3. Administer antidotes or medications to stabilize the pediatric patient's condition, as indicated (Chapter 42).
4. Initiate referrals to psychiatric services.
   - Obtain collateral information from persons/agencies familiar with this patient and family to assess adequacy of support and supervision available over the coming days/weeks.
5. Maintain safety for oneself and others in accordance with ED policies.
   - Dispose of lethal medications or weapons, or lock securely away from the child/adolescent. Keep keys with the responsible party, such as hospital security, at all times.
6. Establish rapport with the pediatric patient and the family and stress the urgency and importance of treatment.
   - Frankly discuss with the adolescent, in the presence of their parent, the disinhibiting and dangerous effects of alcohol and other drugs.
   - Obtain a "no suicide contract" from the child or adolescent, but warn parents not to decrease their vigilance because a contract is in place.
7. Prepare for hospitalization, transfer to a psychiatric facility (Chapter 8) or discharge to home. An appointment for outpatient psychiatric evaluation should be made, and sources for crisis intervention and support should be identified.
8. Prepare to initiate suicide postvention measures.
   - Unfortunately, all suicide attempts cannot be stopped. The completion of a suicide can be extremely traumatic for the pediatric patient, the family, and the community. Within the family, the completion of a suicide puts the prepubertal child at high risk for development of anxiety and/or depression.[14] A family history of mood disorders, suicide attempts or behaviors, increases a child's vulnerability to suicidal behavior following a peer's suicide.[15] Witnessing a suicide, or viewing the scene of a suicide afterwards increases the child's vulnerability to both post-traumatic stress disorder (PTSD) and anxiety disorders.[15] After a suicide, peers often feel that they had knowledge of the impending suicide and failed to prevent it. Crisis intervention (Chapter 26) and inpatient or outpatient referral for children

and adolescents experiencing a suicide in their lives is essential.

Home Care and Prevention

Families, schools, and communities must be educated about early signs of depression and subsequent suicide acts. Families and friends must take seriously any suicide-related comments, threats, and jokes before these ideas escalate into suicide attempts. Families and friends should maintain an open dialogue about the child or adolescent's suicide-related thoughts. Family members should remove medications, toxic substances, and weapons from the home on the pediatric patient's discharge from the emergency department. The legal ramifications of emergency department discharge followed by another suicide attempt should be considered.

Substance Intoxication

Hallmarks of adolescent substance abuse include impairment of psychosocial and academic functioning.[6] Chronic substance use can be associated with significant family dysfunction and conflict, academic failure, deviant or high risk behaviors, and significant mood, anxiety, and conduct problems.[6]

Focused History

❏ Changes in dietary patterns
❏ Changes in school or employment patterns
❏ Changes in cognition
❏ Impaired attention
❏ Decreased concentration
❏ Chronic fatigue
❏ Changes in peer group, friends and recreational activities
❏ Admitted usage of drugs or alcohol
❏ Changes in sexual activity
❏ Suicide attempts
❏ Depression:
  ▪ Low self-esteem
  ▪ Guilt
  ▪ Feelings of worthlessness
  ▪ Family history of alcohol/drug abuse
  ▪ High levels of family conflict

Focused Assessment

Physical Assessment

❏ Assess the respiratory system.

  ▪ Auscultate the chest for:
    • Respiratory rate. Respiratory depression or rapid, shallow respirations may be present. Chronic cough may be present.
  ▪ Assess for chronic respiratory problems.
    • Chronic nasal congestion, frequent colds, allergies, or epistaxis (from prolonged cocaine inhalation) may be observed.
  ▪ Assess the breath for alcohol odor.
❏ Assess the cardiovascular system.
  ▪ Auscultate the heart for:
    • Heart rate. Tachycardia or bradycardia may be present.
    • Measure the blood pressure.
      · Hypertension may be noted
❏ Assess skin color and temperature.
  ▪ Skin may be cool and clammy
❏ Assess the neurological system.
  ▪ Assess the level of consciousness with the AVPU method (Alert, responds to Verbal stimuli, responds to Pain, Unresponsive) or the Glasgow Coma Scale (GCS).
  ▪ Assess for changes level of consciousness.
    • Confusion
    • Delirium
    • Sleepiness
    • Restlessness
❏ Assess for neurologic alterations.
  ▪ Slurred speech
  ▪ Irritability
  ▪ General apathy
  ▪ Unstable gait
  ▪ Assess pupillary responses.
    • Pupils may be sluggish, pinpoint, or dilated
    • Conjunctiva may be red
  ▪ Assess the abdomen.
    • Nausea, vomiting, and diarrhea may be present
❏ Assess the integumentary system.
  ▪ Observe for needle or track marks, abscesses, or cellulitis
❏ Assess the overall appearance.
  ▪ Note symptoms of malnutrition.
  ▪ Weight loss, dry skin, brittle hair, emaciated appearance.

Psychosocial Assessment

☐ Assess the patient's social support systems.

☐ Observe the interactions between the patient and peers and/or family.

☐ Assess the patient's coping strategies.

☐ Children and adolescents who are unable to effectively cope with the stresses of childhood and adolescence may be at risk for substance abuse.

Nursing Interventions for Acute Drug or Alcohol Overdose

1. Assess and maintain airway, breathing, and circulation.

2. Initiate cardiac, respiratory and oxygen saturation monitoring.

3. Obtain venous access and initiate an intravenous infusion.

   - Obtain blood specimens for toxicology screening.

   - Administer medications to control seizures, as needed (Chapter 16).

   - Prepare to administer 50% dextrose to decrease encephalopathy and alcohol-induced hypoglycemia.

   - Prepare to administer naloxone hydrochloride (Narcan) to reverse the effects of narcotics.

4. Initiate interventions to eliminate the substance from the body (Chapter 42).

5. Obtain urine and gastric samples, as needed for toxicology screening (Chapter 42).

   - Initiate screening if the patient identifies the substance.

   - Test for inhalants as indicated by history.

6. Reassess neurological and cardiopulmonary status.

   - Observe for clinical findings indicative of alcohol intoxication versus alcohol withdrawal.

7. Inform the family frequently of the patient's condition; provide emotional support to the patient and family.

8. Maintain measures to promote patient safety.

9. Initiate psychiatric and social service consultations.

10. Prepare for transfer and transport to a tertiary care center or hospitalization.

Nursing Interventions for Substance Abuse

1. Initiate psychiatric and social service consult.

2. Encourage the patient to initiate contact with a rehabilitation unit for detoxification.

Home Care and Prevention

Emergency nurses should be familiar with community-based programs to which children and families can be referred for help with substance misuse and abuse. Emergency nurses can participate in community outreach programs to help youth avoid drug and alcohol use and abuse. Programs that provide positive reinforcement to children and adolescents who avoid drug and alcohol use should be supported. Education programs designed to assist the child and adolescent in making decisions about drug and alcohol use, to build self-esteem, and to improve communication skills are available through community agencies. The Emergency Nurses Association also offers a program for screening patients for alcohol use. The program is SBIRT—Alcohol screening, brief intervention and referral to treatment.

Other Psychiatric Conditions

Psychosis

Psychosis is an impairment of reality testing. Few behaviors can be more distressing for parents and clinicians alike as the presence of delusions or hallucinations in a child or adolescent. Fortunately these symptoms are rare, and are associated with nonpsychiatric etiologies such as fever, infection, medication/substance use, or epilepsy.[6] The incidence of schizophrenia prior to the age of 7 years old is extremely rare.[6]

The limbic system in the brain serves as the central integrating system or the gateway through which most incoming stimuli must pass. Impairment of this system affects the unifying functions by which all experiences are made congruent with reality. A breakdown in this system results in disorganized perceptual and behavioral responses. Problems in the integrating function of the brain are the inability to factor out minor or irrelevant stimuli, the inability to deal with complexity, and the inability to integrate perceptual activities. When the system is impaired, the result is sensory flooding and excessive attention to minor environmental details, distortion in thinking and perception, and altered sense of self and withdrawal.

A psychotic disorder may be related to a health condition such as a brain tumor or a substance-induced psychosis. Computerized tomograms of the brains of patients with psychoses have shown an increased size of the lateral ventricles and a decrease in brain volume of the frontal lobe. Dopamine, a major neurotransmitter in the brain, has been postulated to be a factor in development of schizophrenia, resulting in a hyperactivity of the dopamine system. Therefore, an organic cause for the psychosis, such as infections, metabolic disturbances, or brain injury, should be entertained.

❏ Assessment of the child or adolescent with confusion or psychosis should begin with a thorough medical assessment including:

- Cardiovascular status
- Neurological status
- Skin assessment
- Other organ assessment as necessary/indicated
- History of present symptoms
- Past medical history
- Medication/substance use history
- Family history
- Social history including abuse history
- Toxicology screen, blood alcohol concentration screen, and other laboratory tests as necessary

❏ Assessment of psychotic symptoms can give important information regarding their origins. Important documentation would include:

- Onset of symptoms: abrupt or gradual
- Associated changes in mood, family or social functioning, academic progress
- Symptoms persist or wax and wane
- Difficulty with organization of speech, problems with monitoring incoming or outgoing communications
- New onset of difficulties with focus, attention, information processing
- Abrupt changes in the topic of conversation; starting another conversation without apparent relationship to the ongoing conversation
- Unclear or obscure reference to people, objects, or events
- Rate, rhythm, and volume of speech that is rapid and loud
- Thought content that is bizarre or relatively normal
- Presence of developmental delays

Treatment of children and adolescents with psychotic symptoms is focused on diagnosis of the underlying cause for these symptoms. Children and adolescents with psychotic symptoms regardless of the cause are at higher risk for aggression, violence, and suicide.[6] Unfortunately, there are no preventive measures for psychoses; however, observance of early warning signs is necessary to provide early treatment and referral. Education of the adolescent and family regarding importance of adherence to medication for prevention of future emergency department visits and hospitalizations is essential.

Comorbid Psychiatric Disorders

Coincidental Cormorbidity

Coincidental comorbidity refers to development of a psychiatric illness in a child with a comorbid physical illness. Causal comorbidity refers to development of psychiatric symptoms or illness specifically within the context of a physical condition.

Most children and families are resilient in adapting to the challenges of a physical illness, and most children with a physical illness do not have identifiable problems with their emotions or behavior.[16] Children with long term or chronic physical illness are at higher risk for comorbid psychiatric disorders.[16] Also, the stress of a chronic illness or an exacerbation of that illness may result in acute decompensation of the child and family in the emergency department.[1] Children and families with psychiatric illness may have more difficulty in coping with a child's physical illness, and are at risk for treatment non-adherence and frequent hospitalization.[17]

When treating the pediatric patient with a chronic physical illness, careful attention should be paid to the following parameters to avoid escalation and decompensation:

❏ Coping style. These are strategies the child uses to cope, favored methods of coping, how can these methods be adapted to the current situation.

❏ Developmental level. The pediatric patient's developmental level can severely impact the ability to cope and cooperate with treatment. Physical disabilities can be important to the adolescent developing independence, individualization, autonomy, and sexual orientation.

❏ History of illness and medical expectations. Difficult, painful, or unsuccessful medical procedures can fuel anxiety in pediatric patients and their families. This distress can lead to more frequent ED visits as routine care and treatment is avoided.

❏ Temperament. The pediatric patient's temperament can lead to differences in adjustment and in coping styles.

❏ High parental anxiety and distress. These emotions can independently interfere with the parent's ability to respond to the pediatric patient's emotional needs and to assist their child with healthy coping.

Procedural preparation such as informing the pediatric patient, modeling and giving permission for negative affective responses, providing distraction and coping strategies (deep breathing, deep muscle relaxation, behavioral rehearsal, positive reinforcement, modeling, visual imagery, and hypnosis) reduce stress and improve cooperation.[18]

The emergency nurse is in a unique position to recognize difficulties with adjustment or true psychiatric illness in pediatric patients and the parents of children presenting with chronic physical illness. Risk evaluation for aggression, violence, and suicidality should be included in the treatment plan for pediatric patients and families with signs of poor coping or adjustment. Appropriate referral of the pediatric patient and/or family member to their primary care provider or mental health specialist should be considered.

A thorough psychiatric evaluation focused on the presence or absence of a comorbid psychiatric illness should be conducted in the emergency department if possible, or scheduled as an outpatient as soon as possible. Pediatric patients who present with frequent substance use often have acute changes in mood, cognitive abilities, and behavior. All children/adolescents assessed for substance use or intoxication should also be assessed for suicide risk. A nonjudgmental approach is essential to engage the child/adolescent/family in considering rehabilitative efforts.

The pediatric patient/family should receive information on sources of support and referral. Family therapy and/ or significant family involvement should be an integral component of treatment. Assessment of the family regarding continuing supervision and support for the child should occur before their release.

Autism

Autism is a spectrum of disorders ranging from Autistic Disorder to Pervasive Developmental Disorder (PDD) to Asperger's Syndrome. There is strong evidence that there is a genetic component, an organic cause, or both. Approximately 30 – 60 in 10,000 children are diagnosed with autism, with males outnumbering females 4:1.[19]

Autism consists of three distinct characteristics:[20–22]

1. Verbal and non-verbal communication deficits.
   - Delay in speaking
   - Difficulty maintaining a conversation in those who do speak
   - Echolalia (involuntary parrot-like repetition of a word/sentence spoken by another person.)
   - Lack of eye contact
   - Diminished facial expression
   - Poor body posture
2. Impaired social interactions.
   - Failure to develop peer relations
   - Lack of sharing experiences or ideas with others
   - Lack of social/emotional reciprocity
   - Lack of empathy
3. Behaviors that are repetitive in nature and narrow in focus. Since children with autism are brought to the emergency department for an illness, injury or other health-related condition, the history focuses on the reason for the ED visit.[22,23]

Assessment specific to autism includes:

- Obtaining information about language development.[21]
- Pediatric patient's response to other people—adults and children.
- Pediatric patient's hearing acuity.
- Information about any alternative and complementary therapies used for the patient.
- Reactions to sedatives or tranquilizers, as autistic children can have the opposite effects from these drugs.

Interventions are initiated that are appropriate for the pediatric patient's medical diagnosis. Additional interventions that promote coping and safety include providing a quiet, calm environment; providing supportive care to the patient and parents; and communicating frequently and consistently with the patient and family.

Attention Deficit Hyperactivity Disorder (ADHD)

Children with Attention Deficit/Hyperactivity Disorder (ADHD) could be seen in the emergency department more as a result of an accidental injury, poisoning, or from side effects of medication used to treat their basic illness. Table 25.2 lists common medications used for treating ADHD. ADHD consists of behaviors of inattention, impulsiveness and hyperactivity.[24] ADHD is more common in boys than girls, occurring in approximately 3–5% of children.[25] There are several theories for the causes of ADHD, although the exact etiology is unknown.

Assessment should focus on a history for the specific reason the pediatric patient is brought to the emergency department.[26,27] Further assessment questions focus on the pediatric patient's activity level and impulsive behavior, a history of hurting or abusing animals or other children, and the pediatric patient's attention span.

Interventions are commensurate with the presenting illness or injury. The pediatric patient and family should be removed from the ED waiting room environment to decrease stimuli, if at all possible. Ongoing emotional support to the patient and family is essential throughout the treatment process. Upon discharge, emergency nurses can offer the following home care recommendations:[28]

- ❑ Reinforce the need to take medication consistently as scheduled
- ❑ Observe for medication side effects
- ❑ Emphasize the need for a stable home environment
- ❑ Direct the parent to community support services
- ❑ Stress the need to limit patient's computer/TV time to no more than 2 hours per day
- ❑ Decrease environmental distractions as much as possible

Conclusion

Caring for children and adolescents with psychiatric emergencies and comorbid conditions is challenging. Updating emergency department policies and procedures for using restraints, initiating referrals, and staffing for suicidal observation are imperative for the delivery of safe and effective care. Collaboration with community agencies helps emergency nurses to provide additional resources to these patients and families as needed. Table 25.3 lists selected national resources that emergency nurses can contact to obtain more information.

Table 25.2 Medications Used in the Treatment of ADHD

Medication	Possible Side Effects
Rapid Onset, Short Duration	
Methylphenidate (Ritalin)	Appetite loss, insomnia, depression, headaches, nervousness, palpitations, angina, arrhythmias, increased tics, seizures
Dextroamphetamine (Dexodrine)	Appetite loss, insomnia, depression, headaches, nervousness, palpitations, angina, arrhythmias, increased tics, seizures, hyperactivity, tremors, dizziness, increased blood pressure, tachycardia
Slower Onset, Longer Duration	
Methyphenidate (Ritalin S-R) (Metadate-ER)	Nervousness, insomnia, loss of appetite, nausea, dizziness, headache, drowsiness, abdominal pain, weight loss
Dextroamphetamine (Dexedrine Spansules)	Appetite loss, insomnia, depression
Pemoline (Cylert)	Headache, nervousness
Rapid Onset, Longer Duration	
Amphetamine Dextroamphetamine (Adderall)	Loss of appetite, insomnia, depression, headaches, nervousness
Methylphenidate (Concerta)	Palpations, angina, arrhythmias, increased tics, seizures, angina, tachycardia
Strattera	Abdominal pain, vomiting, drowsiness or insomnia, anorexia and weight loss, headache, suicidal thoughts

Wilson, B. Shannon, M., Shuldi, K., & Story, C. (2008). *Nurses' drug guide*. Upper Saddle River, NJ: Pearson.
U.S. Food and Drug Administration. (2008). *Medication guide: Strattera®*. Retrieved June 1, 2009, from http://www.fda.gov/downloads/Drugs/DrugSafety/ucm089138.pdf

Table 25.3 Community Resources
Governmental Agencies
National Clearinghouse for Alcohol and Drug Information Center for Substance Abuse Prevention: http://www.ncadi.samhsa.gov
National Institute on Chemical Dependency: http://www.nicd.us
National Institute of Mental Health, National Institutes of Health: http://www.nimh.nih.gov
National Institute on Drug Abuse: http://www.nida.nih.gov/
National Institute of Child Health and Human Development: http://www.nichd.nih.gov
Non-Profit Agencies
Al-Anon Family Group Headquarters: http://www.al-anon.alateen.org
Alcoholics Anonymous: http://www.aa.org
Cocaine Anonymous: http://www.ca.org
Nar-Anon Family Group: http://www.nar-anon.org
Narcotics Anonymous: http://www.na.org
National Council on Alcoholism and Drug Dependence: http://www.ncadd.org
National Runaway Switchboard: (800) RUNAWAY; http://www.1800runaway.org
SADD—Students Against Destructive Decisions: http://www.SADD.org
Autism Society of America: http://www.autismsociety.org
Cure Autism Now: http://www.canfoundation.org
Professional Organizations
EN CARE: http://www.ena.org/ipinstitute
National Council on Drug Abuse: http://www.drugfree.org.sg

References

1. Goldstein, A. B., Silverman, M. A. C., Phillips, S., & Lichenstein, R. (2005). Mental health visits in a pediatric emergency department and their relationship to the school calendar. *Pediatric Emergency Care, 21*(10), 653–657.

2. American Psychiatric Association. (2006). *Diagnostic and statistical manual of mental disorders (DSMIV-TR)* (4th ed.), Arlington, VA: American Psychiatric Publishing, Inc.

3. Andreasen, N. C., & Black,D. W. (2006). *Introductory textbook of psychiatry.* (9th ed., pp. 365–378). Arlington, VA: American Psychiatric Publishing, Inc.

4. American College of Emergency Physicians. (2008). *ACEP psychiatric and substance abuse survey 2008.* Retrieved April 13, 2009, from http://www.acep.org/uploadedFiles/ACEP/Advocacy/federal_issues/PsychiatricBoardingSummary.pdf

5. Christodulu, K. V., Lichenstein, R., Weist, M. D., Shafer, M. E., & Simone, M. (2002). Psychiatric emergencies in children. *Pediatric Emergency Care, 18*(4), 268–270.

6. Thomas, L. E., & King, R. A. (2002). Child and adolescent psychiatric emergencies. In M. Lewis (Ed.), *Child and adolescent psychiatry, a comprehensive textbook* (3rd ed., pp. 1104–1110). Philadelphia: Lippincott Williams & Wilkins.

7. Slater, N., & Constintino, J. N., (1998). Pediatric emergencies in children with psychiatric conditions. *Pediatric Emergency Care, 14*(1), 42–50.

8. Bickley, L. S., & Szilagyi, P. G. (2007). *Bates' guide to physical examination and history taking* (9th ed., pp. 68–69). Philadelphia: Lippincott Williams & Wilkins.

References (continued)

9. Andreasen, N. C., & Black, D. W. (2006). *Introductory textbook of psychiatry* (9th ed., pp. 379–421). Arlington, VA: American Psychiatric Publishing, Inc..

10. Hughes, C., Emslie, G., Crismon, M., Posner, K., Birmaher, B., Ryan, N., et al. (2007). Journal of the American Academy of Child and Adolescent Psychiatry Texas Children's Medication Algorithm Project: Update from the Texas consensus conference panel on medication treatment of childhood major depressive disorder. *Journal of the American Academy of Child and Adolescent Psychiatry, 46*(6), 667–686.

11. Centers for Disease Control and Prevention. (2008). *Suicide prevention.* Retrieved April 13, 2009, from http://www.cdc.gov/ViolencePrevention/suicide/index.html

12. Libby, A., Brent, D., Morrato, E., Orton, H. D., Allen, R., & Valuck, R.J. (2007). Decline in treatment of pediatric depression after FDA advisory on risk of suicidality. *American Journal of Psychiatry, 164,* 884–891.

13. Gibbons, R., Hendricks Brown, C., Hur, K., Marcus, S. M., Bhaumik, D. K., Erkens, J. A., et al. (2007). Early evidence on the effects of regulator's suicidality warnings on SSRI prescriptions and suicide in children and adolescents. *American Journal of Psychiatry, 164,* 1356–1363.

14. Pfeffer, C. R., Martins, P., Mann, J., Sunkenberg, M., Ice, A., Damore, J. P., et al. (1997). Child survivors of suicide: psychosocial characteristics. *Journal of the American Academy of Child and Adolescent Psychiatry, 36,* 65–74.

15. Brent, D. A., Moritz, G., Bridge, J., Perper, J., & Canobbio, R., (1996). Long term impact of exposure to suicide: A three-year controlled follow-up. Journal of the *American Academy of Child and Adolescent Psychiatry, 35*(5), 646–653.

16. Wallander, J. L., Thompson, R. J., & Alriksson-Schmidt, A. (2003). Psychosocial adjustment of children with chronic physical conditions. In M. C. Roberts (Ed.), *Handbook of pediatric psychology* (3rd ed., pp.141–158). New York: Guilford.

17. Garrison, M. M., Katon, W. J., & Richard, L.P. (2005). The impact of psychiatric comorbidities on readmissions for diabetes in youth. *Diabetes Care, 28,* 2150–2154.

18. Blout, R. L., Plira, T., & Cohen, L. L. (2003). Management of pediatric pain and distress due to medical procedures. In M. C. Roberts (Ed.), *Handbook of pediatric psychology* (3rd ed., pp. 216–233). New York: Guilford.

19. National Institute of Neurological Disorders and Stroke. (2009). *NINDS autism information page.* Retrieved April 13, 2009, from http://www.ninds.nih.gov/disorders/autism/autism.htm

20. American Psychiatric Association (APA). (2006). *Diagnostic and statistical manual of mental disorders* (4th ed.). Arlington, VA: American Psychiatric Publishing, Inc.

21. Paul, R., Orlovski, S. M., Marcinko, H. C., & Volkmer, F. (2009). Conversational behaviors in youth with high-functioning ASD and asperger syndrome. *Journal of Autism and Developmental Disorders, 39*(1), 115–125.

22. Inglese, M. D. (2009). Caring for children with autism Goldstein, A. B., Silverman, M. A. C., Phillips, S., & Lichenstein, R. (2005). Mental health visits in a pediatric emergency department and their relationship to the school calendar. *Pediatric Emergency Care, 21*(10), 653–657.

23. American Psychiatric Association. (2006). *Diagnostic and statistical manual of mental disorders (DSMIV-TR)* (4th ed.), Arlington, VA: American Psychiatric Publishing, Inc.

24. Andreasen, N. C., & Black,D. W. (2006). *Introductory textbook of psychiatry.* (9th ed., pp. 365–378). Arlington, VA: American Psychiatric Publishing, Inc.

25. American College of Emergency Physicians. (2008). *ACEP psychiatric and substance abuse survey 2008.* Retrieved April 13, 2009, from http://www.acep.org/uploadedFiles/ACEP/Advocacy/federal_issues/PsychiatricBoardingSummary.pdf

26. Christodulu, K. V., Lichenstein, R., Weist, M. D., Shafer, M. E., & Simone, M. (2002). Psychiatric emergencies in children. *Pediatric Emergency Care, 18*(4), 268–270.

27. Thomas, L. E., & King, R. A. (2002). Child and adolescent psychiatric emergencies. In M. Lewis (Ed.), *Child and adolescent psychiatry, a comprehensive textbook* (3rd ed., pp. 1104–1110). Philadelphia: Lippincott Williams & Wilkins.

28. Slater, N., & Constintino, J. N., (1998). Pediatric emergencies in children with psychiatric conditions. *Pediatric Emergency Care, 14*(1), 42–50.

TWENTY-SIX

Crisis Intervention and Management

Gail Pisarcik Lenehan, RN, MSN, EdD, FAEN, FAAN
Anne Cassels Turner, RN, CEN

Introduction

Caring for a critically ill or injured child in the emergency department (ED) is difficult, especially if death is the end result. The death of a child seems unfair. People tend to view children as innocent and not having had a chance to live their lives. Often nurses are unprepared to deal with the family's anguish and their own emotion. No amount of training can prepare nurses for the indescribable sound of a parent's cry of disbelief at being told that his or her child has died or help nurses "get used to it." However, information on how to better deal with the family and cope with their own emotions will help emergency nurses face these situations in a way that is helpful to families and to themselves.

The purpose of this chapter is to describe interventions to help families cope with crisis situations, such as sudden critical injury, illness, or death of a child; specific situations in the emergency department that may result in the need for crisis intervention; and methods of helping staff to cope with crisis situations.

Pediatric Considerations

There are several challenges in dealing with the critical illness, injury, or death of a child in the emergency department:

❏ Staff and families may have differing philosophies and beliefs concerning illness and death, based on past experiences and cultural influences. While such beliefs cannot be fully explored during the brief ED interactions, they need to be considered.

❏ Emotional situations are not straightforward, and it is not possible to write care process models or standards of care that will work in every situation.

❏ The fast pace of the emergency department allows nurses little time to care for families, let alone take care of their own needs.

Definitions

Many situations that families and staff experience in the emergency department can lead to stress, which can progress to a crisis. Although the terms stress and crisis refer to differing conditions, increasing stress with no relief can lead to a crisis for families as well as staff.

❏ *Stress* is tension, strain, or pressure, such as the feelings that occur after a family has waited for extended periods of time in the emergency department or when the ED staff is overwhelmed by conflicting demands and stimuli.

❏ *Crisis* refers to an acute emotional upset arising from situational, developmental, or social sources resulting in a temporary inability to cope using one's usual problem-solving devices.[1] Examples include sudden illness, injury, or death. Although it is well recognized that many situations in the emergency department can cause a crisis for the family, the involved staff may also experience a crisis.

Crisis management refers to the entire process of working through the crisis to its end point of resolution. Crisis intervention is a short-term helping process that focuses on the resolution of the immediate problem through the use of personal, social, and environmental resources. The positive or negative resolution of the crisis often depends on crisis intervention.[1] Whether a stressful event precipitates a crisis depends on the family's or staff members:

❏ Interpretation of the events.

❏ Coping abilities and previous experience.

❏ Social and personal resources.

Several characteristics of an event may increase the level of stress experienced by a child's family or the staff member:

❏ Sudden onset of the event.

❏ Unanticipated event, especially one that has never been experienced.

❏ Lack of control over the event.

❏ Other stressful events occurring in the family dynamic or in the emergency department.

❏ The meaning that the family attaches to the event. Families may feel responsible for causing or not preventing the event.

Emergency department staff members' ability to respond to a crisis and lend empathy and support depend on their own beliefs, experiences, and support systems.

Focused History

Parents know their child best and can provide invaluable information regarding their child's medical history, normal behavior, and past reactions to stressful situations. The following are important components in the history:[2]

❏ The family's perception of the event or situation.

❏ Availability of support systems.

❏ Previous illness or injury of the child.

❏ Concurrent maturational crisis within the family.

❏ Family's current level of functioning, past experiences, and usual coping mechanisms.

❏ Drug and/or alcohol use by the family, especially if associated with the child's injury.

❏ The family's religious preference.

Focused Assessment

When interacting with members of the family, the nurse should assess for and note family behavior, looking particularly for evidence of behavioral or physical signs of crisis. Signs and symptoms demonstrated by family members in a crisis situation may include:

❏ Behavioral
- Withdrawal or isolation
- Demanding behavior
- Loud crying or shouting
- Self-destructive behavior
- Violence against other family members or the healthcare team
- Anger. Anger is a coping mechanism and can be

allowed as long as it does not cause fear or result in violent behavior that may cause injury to staff or others.

❏ Physical
- Tachycardia
- Hyperventilation
- Chest pain
- Fainting

Nursing Interventions

The ED staff have the potential to provoke or escalate a potentially angry family member who is in tenuous control. How the nurse approaches the family in the emergency department can positively influence their ability to cope with the crisis. In sudden, unexpected situations, families will take their cues from the demeanor and behavior of the staff. The family needs to receive information on what is happening, to participate, as they desire in the care of their child, to receive compassionate support, and to maintain realistic hope. The following are ways to meet these needs of the family:

1. Create a supportive environment.
   - Take the family to a private area to talk with them.
   - Assign one staff member (an emergency nurse, a nursing supervisor, crisis worker) to communicate information about the pediatric patient's condition.
   - Explain that the emergency physician will talk with them as soon as he or she is able to leave the care of the pediatric patient to do so.
   - Allow the family to ask questions and expect expressions of such emotions as guilt, anger, and remorse, depending on the situation.

2. Communicate with the family. Talking with a family whose child is seriously ill or injured is very difficult, but family members will appreciate the contact of someone who is involved or knowledgeable about the care of their child. The following are suggestions for talking with the family:
   - Introduce yourself; use "Mr." or "Mrs." and the name of the child (ask if the child has a nickname that can be used during their ED treatment).
   - Give accurate, honest information, but not more than the family seems to be asking for.
   - Meet the family's physical needs (bathroom, water, tissues). Extras like a warm blanket are often greatly appreciated.
   - Offer realistic hope while resuscitation is still under way, but do not offer false hope.

- Ask about the desire for clergy or religious rights. Many hospitals have a chaplain or spiritual counselor available to offer support.
- Give brief, frequent updates on the child's condition (e.g., "We are doing everything we know how to do to help her.").

3. Communicate with the pediatric patient.
   - Assume that the child can hear what is being said.
   - Assign a staff member to talk to the child during the resuscitation, touching and holding the hand, and letting him or her know what is being done. If family is present, give them permission to talk softly to the child.

Family Presence

Emergency nurses were early champions of family presence.[3] Currently, the Emergency Nurses Association[4], and the American Heart Association support family presence during cardiopulmonary resuscitation[5], and the American Academy of Pediatrics and the American College of Emergency Physicians have acknowledged the benefits of family presence.[6] Experience has shown that this approach is feasible for staff and helpful to families.[7,8] One study of resuscitation interventions and invasive procedures in the emergency department with family present found no interruptions in patient care, with 95% of families reporting that their presence helped them; no parent reported any traumatic memories three months after the event.[9] In another study, 64% of families felt that their presence was beneficial to the patient.[3] The most important needs identified by family members were to:[10]

- ❐ be with the patient.
- ❐ be helpful to the patient.
- ❐ be informed of the patient's condition.
- ❐ be comforted and supported by other family members.
- ❐ be accepted, comforted, and supported by the health care professionals.
- ❐ feel that the patient was receiving the best possible care.

It is well recognized by emergency nurses[11] that family-centered approaches to care are crucial for children. Family presence during resuscitation efforts allows the patient and family to support each other and facilitates the grieving process by bringing a sense of reality to the treatment efforts and the patient's clinical status.[4] Protocols for family presence should be developed and should include the following concepts:

- ❐ Give the family the choice of being present.
- ❐ Prepare the family for what they will see and how the child will look.
- ❐ Assign a support person for the family. This support person will need to:
  - Be prepared to handle emotions (both the family's and their own).
  - Watch for signs from the family that indicate their need to leave the room.
  - Be aware as to when a particularly invasive procedure, such as a thoracotomy, is about to take place to gauge the family's preference to momentarily step out of the room. Some authors have suggested that certain invasive procedures may be too much for families to observe.[12]
  - Be prepared to deal with family emotions, including anger toward staff or other family members. Have a plan to summon help (this should be part of a departmental security plan).
  - Remain confident and nonjudgmental.
  - Listen initially without interrupting the family member.
- ❐ Support cultural differences. The ED staff should have an understanding of the cultural diversity in their geographic location and be aware of cultural practices that may be important, particularly if a child dies. In respecting cultural differences the staff should:
  - Provide an interpreter to translate.
  - Ask the family what would be helpful.
  - Watch family members, especially parents, for cues as to what is acceptable (body space, the use of touch).
  - Help family identify community-based resources reflective of culture.

Specific Crisis Situations

Death of a Child in the Emergency Department

The majority of pediatric deaths occur in the hospital or emergency department. Although the cause may be congenital conditions, chronic illness, and acts of violence, more than half of all childhood deaths are caused by injury. Each year, more than 20,000 children under 19 years of age die from trauma, and 80% of all trauma deaths occur either at the accident scene or in the emergency department.[13] The leading cause of death in children aged 1 to 4 years is unintentional injuries and 42% of deaths in this age group are the result of unintentional injuries and homicides.[14]

The sudden death of a child does not allow the family to

evolve through the stages of accepting death and throws them into an acute grief reaction. It denies family members the opportunity for the anticipatory grief that usually prepares survivors for death following a long illness. The sudden death of a child puts survivors at a much higher risk for prolonged or complicated grief. When the death of a child occurs by homicide or suicide, or when a family member has unintentionally caused the death of the child, extra support understanding, and resources will be needed. Expressions of grief vary from person to person, but are often influenced by the person's cultural background. Studies of the perspectives of the families of trauma victims, including children, who have died reveal a number of insights:[15]

❑   The most important features of delivering bad news were the attitude of the news-giver (ranked most important by 72%), the clarity of the message (70%), privacy of the conversation (65%), and adequate knowledge/ability to answer questions (57%).

❑   The importance of rank or seniority of the news-giver was mixed, with only 24% thinking it of high importance, and 54% ranking it of low or no importance.

■   Touching in the form of handholding, a hug, etc., was unwanted by 30% of the respondents, but acceptable in 24%. The strongest opposition to physical contact during or immediately after bad news came from men.

Nursing Interventions

1.   *Informing the family*

■   Bring the family to a private area, preferably one that is quiet and as close as possible to the child. If possible, all family members should be told at the same time, while together. In this way, if some family members are so engulfed in grief that they can't concentrate, others can remember the information given.

■   If all are not present, give other family members the name of the nurse to ask for when they arrive, and caution them to have someone else drive them if they are distraught. Assign a staff member to watch for arriving family members so that they do not have to wander through the emergency department looking for someone to help them. Table 26.1 lists some "dos and don'ts" for informing a family of a child's death.

2.   *Communicating with siblings*

■   Siblings should be told of the death sensitively and promptly. They may hear of the death along with the rest of the family, or the family can tell them. It is best to work with the family, coaching them on how to approach the child with honesty and reassurance, explaining, for example, that though older family members will be crying because they are sad, they aren't mad at the sibling and they don't mean to ignore the sibling.

■   While the emergency nurse can be supportive toward siblings, it may be better to have the family members tell them.

The approach to siblings should be matched to the child's developmental level.

■   Children younger than 3 years of age may be affected by the loss of a sibling, but have little or no understanding of the meaning of death.

■   Children aged 3 to 5 years may believe that death is reversible or analogous to someone's going away.

■   Children aged 5 to 9 understand that death is permanent but believe that it will not happen to them or affect them, and they are unprepared to encounter it in their own families.

■   Children 9 years or older do understand that death is permanent and can happen to them and their family members.

The following suggestions may be helpful in communicating with siblings:

■   Help parents understand what siblings of different ages understand about death.

■   Give anticipatory guidance to parents regarding what to say to siblings.

•   Reassure them that they were not to blame.

•   Avoid euphemisms such as "your sister has gone to sleep"—the sibling might become afraid of going to sleep.

■   Children should be offered a chance to see their sibling in the emergency department, and the emergency nurse can show that it is all right to touch the child's hand or face, but the sibling should not be forced to see or touch the body after death.

■   If the child who has died is not disfigured, it may help the sibling to see the child, rather than imagining what they look like. What they imagine may be much worse than what is real.

■   Parents should be encouraged to involve siblings in the funeral and burial. To be able to let go and reinvest in life, the children need a clear understanding of what has happened and some closure.

■   Parents should not attempt to protect siblings from sadness. Children will know something is wrong by the way the parents are acting. If they are excluded from the grief, they may believe that they somehow

Table 26.1 Informing the Family of a Child's Death

Do

Tell the family immediately.

Sit down with family—physically join them, with hospital security personnel if the situation seems unsafe.

Be kind, but direct. Speak directly to the person closest to the child (mother or father).

Consider eliciting information about those closest to the child from more distant relatives initially.

Give a brief explanation of what was done in the emergency department and the suspected cause of the death, if known.

Make sure that a physician explains what happened to the child at some point or they may think that no doctor took care of their child.

Allow the family to express grief in their own way.

Stay long enough to answer questions.

Say that you are sorry.

Don't

Tell the family by telephone that a child has died. Tell them that the child is critically ill or injured and that they should have someone drive them to the emergency department immediately.

Say, "I know how you feel."

Imply guilt (of parents, medical care, or others).

Use euphemisms "your child has passed away, or is "gone."

Offer meaningless comfort such as, "It was God's will" or "He is in a better place."

Tell them they can always have another child. This may not be true, and another child will not replace the one who has died.

Tell the family how they should or should not feel. Grief is individual.

Routinely offer sedatives, because this may delay some of the grieving process for later, but be open to the need for a small amount of sleeping medication, or other medication depending on the history of the grieving family member.

are at fault and/or are being punished or ostracized. Normal responses to the loss of a loved one should be explained to children, and they should be told that it is permissible for them to also be sad and to cry.

- Questions should be answered with honesty. Children have a need to talk to someone and to be reassured.

- Prepare the family for how the child will look and feel. Explain any tubes or supplies that remain in or on the body.

3. *Preparing the body*

    - Evidence should be preserved as necessary by leaving tubes in place and following the hospital's guidelines for evidence preservation.

    - Wrapping the baby or young child in a warm blanket or quilt; place a warm blanket over an older child or adolescent.

- Encourage the parents to sit and hold their baby or young child in a rocking chair, as this action can bring comfort. Encourage the family to sit in a chair next to the stretcher with the older child or adolescent.

- Keep the child in the emergency department until they have a chance to see the body, even if keeping the child in the emergency department may tie up a needed treatment room. If there is an urgent need for the treatment room, move the child to a different room and explain to the child's family the need for the relocation.

4. *Viewing the body*

    - Provide privacy.

    - Ask the family if they would like you to stay with them, or return to talk with them at intervals.

    - Ask the family if they would like a chaplain or spiritual counselor present.

- Allow the family ample time to be with the child.
- Give the family permission to leave.
  - Have one nurse remain with the child as the family is leaving.

5. *Concluding the viewing*
   - Provide information regarding the cessation of breast-feeding following an infant's death. (The mother may need to use a breast pump or obtain information from her obstetrician, a lactation specialist, or from the LaLeche League).
   - Provide mementos. Even if the parents do not want mementos, it is often wise to obtain them because the family may call back later and ask for them.
     - Handprints and/or footprints and a lock of hair. Commercially-available kits contain plaster to make a hand or foot imprint.
     - A photograph of the child, as desired by the family. A Polaroid photograph of the baby wrapped in a blanket may be helpful to the family later, especially if the infant is very young and the parents have not had much time to take photographs.
     - The blanket or quilt that the baby was wrapped in when the family viewed and held the baby.

6. *Provide follow-up*
   - Give the family the name of the emergency nurse or crisis worker involved in the care of the child, the names of local support groups, and the hospital Social Services department, as well as the number for the medical examiner in case they have questions for any of these providers.
   - Conduct a follow-up telephone call to answer any questions or provide additional resources. Such calls are made by an emergency nurse or social worker after a certain time (e.g., 2 weeks), or even intervals (e.g., 2 weeks, 6 months, and 1 year). When more than one call is planned, ask the family if they want to be contacted more than once.
   - Give written material concerning the grieving process, support groups, and their contact information. Parents may not be able to process information that has been discussed or given to them at the time, and written information will be useful to them later. Having a prepared "grief packet" with information and resources is helpful.
   - Answer the family's questions about what will happen to their child. The emergency nurse assures the family that he or she will care for their child until the staff from the medical examiner or funeral home arrives.
   - Arrange transportation home for family members, if needed, so they will not have to drive.

7. *Complete all necessary documentation*
   - Complete all required documentation for unanticipated death in the emergency department.
   - Consider maintaining a "death packet" that consists of a prepared envelope with all the necessary forms will make documentation easier and prevent omission of a needed form.

8. *Requesting Organ Donation and Autopsy*
   - *Organ donation.* Requesting organ donation is the law in all states. Every hospital should have policies concerning when and how this request is initiated. A nurse working with the family can alert them beforehand that they will be asked about the donation of organs. This notification, affords them time to think before being confronted with the decision. The donation of organs to another child may be of some comfort for the family.[16] Information about organ donation is provided to the family (Chapter 2).
   - *Autopsy.* An autopsy may be required by law or by request from the family. Explain that the family can ask for a postmortem examination and how they can ask for limited examinations, if an autopsy is not required (e.g., when the child has a history of a terminal illness). If an autopsy is optional, describe common reasons why families might ask for one (e.g., wanting more information for the sake of the siblings" health care), or not have one done (the desire to avoid the impression that the child is being caused more distress, for example). Barriers to asking the family about an autopsy include: fear of offending the family during their acute grief, fear of legal retribution for care that resulted in death, and avoidance of contact with the family after they have been notified of the death.[17] Instruct the family that all they need to do initially is to contact a funeral home. If an autopsy is performed, tell the family who to contact for the results. The emergency nurse can explain that an autospy:[17]
     - is required in all cases of sudden and unattended death and explain any additional state laws that may apply.
     - is not disfiguring.
     - will not preclude funeral arrangements, as the autopsy is conducted within 2–48 hours after death.
     - is not disallowed by most major religions.
     - incurs no cost to the family.

- can help with the family's closure.
- knowledge gained from autopsies adds to medical knowledge.[17]

Sudden Infant Death Syndrome

Sudden Infant Death Syndrome (SIDS) is defined as the sudden death of an infant under 1 year of age that is unexplained by history and remains unexplained after a thorough postmortem examination, including a complete autopsy, investigation of the scene of death and a review of the medical history.[18] It occurs most frequently in infants aged 2–3 months. Sudden Infant Death Syndrome is the third leading cause of death during infancy.[19] The program recommended by the American Academy of Pediatrics Task Force on Infant Positioning[20] seems to have made a significant difference in reducing SIDS deaths.[21] Since 1992, there has been a 44% decline in the SIDS rate, often credited to the "Back to Sleep" campaign, which recommends placing infants on their backs to sleep instead of their stomachs.[22] Autopsy does not point to any pathognomonic routine findings of SIDS and no findings are required for diagnosis.

Some common observations include:

- Petechial hemorrhages
- Pulmonary congestion
- Pulmonary edema
- In autopsies performed on infants who died of SIDS, two-thirds had structural evidence of preexisting, chronic low-grade asphyxia.

Theories that have been or are being researched include:

- Abnormal respiratory control
- Small airway occlusion
- Cardiovascular abnormalities
- Defects of metabolism
- Infection
- Delayed neural development
- Abnormal sleep and arousal states

Maternal and Antenatal Risk Factors[23]

Maternal Social/Behavior Risk Factors

- Smoking and alcohol use (especially periconceptionally and in the first trimester)
- Illegal drug use (especially opiates)
- Inadequate prenatal care
- Low socioeconomic status
- Young maternal age
- Low level of education
- Mother's marital status
- Increased parity
- Short interval between pregnancies

Maternal Antenatal Risk Factors

- Intrauterine hypoxia
- Fetal growth retardation
- Genetic risk factors

Infant Risk Factors

- Age (peak 2–4 months, but peak may be decreasing)
- Male sex
- Race/ethnic background
- No pacifier used at bedtime
- Prematurity
- Prone or side sleeping position
- Recent febrile illness
- Exposure to tobacco smoke
- Soft sleeping surface, soft bedding
- Thermal stress/overheating
- Face covered by bedding
- Shared bed with parents or siblings
- Sleeping in own room rather than parents' room
- Colder season, no central heating

Focused History

When an apneic and pulseless baby is brought to the emergency department, the following history may be indicative of SIDS:

- A healthy baby who was put to sleep for a nap or for the night.
- A child who had a slight cold and may have recently seen a physician for a minor illness.

Focused Assessment

Generally, the child will be lifeless but still may be warm, depending on the length of time since the arrest occurred. The assessment is the same for any child who presents to the emergency department in cardiopulmonary arrest (Chapter 13). The emergency nurse assesses for signs and symptoms of other injuries that may be indicative of child abuse (Chapter 44).

Nursing Interventions

Nursing interventions for the child who is suspected to have died of SIDS are the same as for any death in the emergency department. One SIDS-specific intervention is to refer the family to a local SIDS support group.

Prevention

Although SIDS cannot be prevented entirely, the emergency nurse can give families of neonates literature on the American Academy of Pediatrics' recommendations concerning placement of healthy infants in the supine position. The emergency nurse can also inform parents of risk factors related to SIDS and can be available to answer questions they may have.

Death of a Child by Homicide

Focused Assessment

For the survivors of a young victim of homicide, grief is overwhelming. Parents often feel guilty that they could not protect the child and the situation is compounded if family members, friends, or acquaintances committed the murder. The urge for revenge may be a central issue.

Nursing Interventions

Nursing interventions for the family of a homicide victim are the same as for other victims who die in the emergency department. Evidence preservation and collection become crucial, and the emergency nurse must be familiar with procedures for preserving and collecting evidence for the medical examiner. The brutal or suspicious death of a child will have a particularly intense and lasting impact on emergency staff, as well as families, and support and debriefing should be considered. If the death is thought to be the result of gang violence or acts of terrorism, the following precautions should be taken to protect the staff, family, and other patients:[24]

1. Notify hospital security personnel to provide surveillance.
2. Check for weapons.
3. Observe for any indications of imminent violence by or against family members or visitors.
4. Limit access to the patient, family, and the entire emergency department.
5. Develop media reporting policies to avoid publicizing information that could endanger the family and others.

Nursing Interventions in Situations with Potential for Violence

The potential for violence exists in the emergency departments around the country. The Emergency Nurses Association position statement on Violence in the Emergency Care Setting states: "The risk of workplace violence is a significant occupational hazard facing emergency nurses. Health care organizations must take preventive measures to circumvent workplace violence and ensure the safety of all health care workers, their patients, and visitors."[29] The following are suggestions to help deal with potentially violent situations:

1. If there is the concern about potential violence, contact hospital security personnel, notify them of the situation, and have them remain in the area and help to diffuse the situation, if necessary.
2. Remain confident and nonjudgmental.
3. Speak in a calm, quiet voice.
4. Listen without talking initially.
5. Set realistic limits (e.g., "I would like to help you, but I can't when you raise your voice.").
6. Maintain a path of easy escape.
7. Do not attempt to restrain a family member yourself, follow your institution's policy regarding de-escalation procedures.
8. Review protocols yearly so that all staff members are familiar with actions to take to recognize and prevent violent behavior.

Staff Support and Debriefing After a Critical Incident

Situations such as death of a child, overwhelming numbers of critically ill patients in the department, or act of violence against staff and families are referred to as critical incidents. Critical incidents are defined as any significant emotional event that has the power, because of its own nature or because of the circumstances in which it occurs, to cause unusual psychological distress in normal healthy people.[25] All staff are affected by the emotional aspects of working in an emergency department. Emergency department staff are exposed to critical incidents on a fairly routine basis, and emergency departments should have written policies and procedures concerning support of staff members and coping with critical incidents in the emergency department. The consequences of untreated stress related to crucial incidents can lead to absenteeism, sleep disorders, burnout, health problems, addiction problems and emotional difficulties. Repeated exposure to critical incidents can, over time, contribute to the phenomenon of vicarious traumatization.[26] The Emergency Nurses Association acknowledges the effect of vicarious dramatization of the health care team and encourages support for staff members.[2]

The effectiveness of psychological debriefing in general, and critical incident stress debriefing in particular, has received closer scrutiny over the last decade.[27,28] While debriefing does not necessarily prevent psychiatric disorders or mitigate the effects of traumatic stress[27], it may help defuse and resolve feelings of grief, without pathologizing the reactions. Staff may be given the opportunity to describe their part in the event, what they saw and heard, what was most difficult for them, and importantly, what happened that is of some comfort in reviewing the incident (e.g., good team work, better appreciation of the work of a particular staff member, good care of the child's family, etc.). A debriefing can be a conversation among colleagues that begins with a simple question from a leader to all participants, such as, "What stands out for you when you look back at [the incident]?"

Other suggestions for helping staff cope with death or other critical incidents in the emergency department include:

- ❐ Protocols that describe the treatment of patients or families following death.
- ❐ Education on the grieving process.
- ❐ Evaluation of one's feelings concerning death and available support systems.
- ❐ Support from the hospital chaplain.
- ❐ Recovery time after a death, or an especially traumatic incident, even if only for a short time.
- ❐ Support of each other from ED staff and from the ED Nurse Manager or ED Nursing Director.
- ❐ A sympathy card signed by the staff that directly cared for the child, and sent to family members.
- ❐ Encouragement of ED staff to take care of themselves physically, mentally, and spiritually.
- ❐ Focusing on the positive—most children do get better and go home.

All ED staff, in addition to nurses and physicians, may be affected by a child's death in the emergency department. Therefore, clerical staff, security officers, pre-hospital personnel, transportation workers, and others should be included in a supportive debriefings or offerings of support. Coping with death and critical incidents must be included in orientation programs for new employees. Such inclusion covers the technical aspects of caring for the deceased and the emotional aspects, as well.

Conclusion

Caring for a critically ill or injured children and their families in the emergency department is a difficult challenge physically and emotionally. How nurses treat the family is critical and may affect the family's lasting memories of the trauma or death of their child. Realizing that the grief response is different for every family can help nurses be more accepting and to provide support, which may involve simply saying, "I am sorry."

Although the feelings of the staff are often addressed last, they should not be neglected. Staff members often provide the best support for each other. Giving staff members a break and time to regroup, and importantly, recognizing difficult situations and jobs well done, promotes a healthy work environment.

References

1. Hoff, L. A. (1995). *People in crisis: Understanding and helping* (4th ed.). San Francisco: Josey-Bass.

2. Emergency Nurses Association. (2004). *Emergency nursing pediatric course (ENPC) provider manual.* Des Plaines, IL: Author.

3. Hanson, C., & Strawser, D. (1992) Family presence during cardiopulmonary resuscitation: Foote Hospital emergency department's nine-year perspective. *Journal of Emergency Nursing, 18,* 104.

4. Emergency Nurses Association. (2005). *Position statement: Family presence at the bedside during invasive procedures and/or resuscitation.* Des Plaines, IL: Author.

5. Plantz, D. M. (2008). The death of children in the emergency department: The psychosocial and administrative response. *Pediatric Emergency Care 24,* 632–636.

6. O'Malley, P. J., Brown, K., & Krug, S. E. (2008). Patient- and family-centered care of children in the emergency department. *Pediatrics, 122,* e511–21.

7. Meyers T., Eichhorn D. J., & Guzzetta, D. E. (1998). Do families want to be present during CPR? A retrospective survey. *Journal of Emergency Nursing, 24,* 400–405.

References (continued)

8. Boudreauz, E. D., Francis J. L., & Loyacano T. (2002). Family presence during invasive procedures and resuscitations in the emergency department: A critical review and suggestions for further research. *Annals of Emergency Nursing, 40,* 193–205.

9. Manguren, J., Scott, S. H., & Guzzetta, C. E. (2006). Effects of family presence during resuscitations and invasive procedures in a pediatric emergency department. *Journal of Emergency Nursing, 32,* 225–223.

10. Molter, N. (1979). Needs of relatives of critically ill patients: A descriptive study. *Heart and Lung, 8,* 332–339.

11. Emergency Nurses Association. (2007). *Position paper: Care of the pediatric patient in the emergency setting.* Des Plaines, IL: Author.

12. Williams, J. (2002). Family presence during resuscitation. To see or not to see? *Nursing Clinics of North America. 37,* 211–220.

13. Ziegler, M., & Gonzalez, Del Rey (2000). Major trauma. In G. R. Fleisher & S. Ludwig (Eds.), *Textbook of pediatric emergency medicine* (4th ed., pp. 1259–1269). Philadelphia: Lippincott Williams & Wilkins.

14. Centers for Disease Control and Prevention. (2007). *Deaths: Final Data for 2004.* Retrieved May 8, 2009, from http://www.cdc.gov/nchs/data/nvsr/nvsr55/nvsr55_19.pdf

15. Jurkovich, G. J., Pierce B, Pananen L., & Rivara F. P. (2000). Giving bad news: The family perspective. *The Journal of Trauma: Injury, Infection, and Critical Care, 48,* 865–872.

16. Bellali T., & Papadatou D. (2006). Parental grief following the brain death of a child: Does consent or refusal to organ donation affect their grief ? *Death Studies, 30,* 883–917.

17. Baren, J. M. (2008). End-of-life issues. In J. M. Baren, S. G. Rothrock, J. A. Brennan, & L. Brown, *Pediatric emergency medicine* (pp. 1046). St. Louis, MO: Elsevier.

18. Willinger, M., James, L. S., & Catz, C. (1991). Defining the sudden infant death syndrome (SIDS): Deliberations of an expert panel convened by the National Institute of Child Health and Human Development. *Pediatric Pathology, 11,* 677–684.

19. Mathews, T. J., MacDorman, M. F., & Nenacker, F. (2002). Infant mortality statistics from the 1999 period linked birth/infant deaths data set. *National Vital Statistics Reports, 50,* 1–28.

20. American Academy of Pediatrics. (1992). *To lessen SIDS risk, AAP recommends infants sleep on side or back [news release].* Elk Grove Village, IL: Author.

21. Willinger, M., Ko, C. W., Hoffman, H. J., Kessler, R. C., Corwin, M. J. (2000). Factors associated with caregivers' choice of infant sleep position, 1994–1998. *Journal of the American Medical Association, 283,* 2135–2142.

22. Malloy, M. H., & Freeman, D. H. (2004). Age at death, season, and day of death as indicators of the effect of the back to sleep program on sudden infant death syndrome in the United States, 1992–1999. *Archives of Pediatric & Adolescent Medicine, 158,* 359–365.

23. Hunt C. E., & Hauck F. R. (2004). Sudden infant syndrome. In R. E. Behrman, R. M. Kliegman, H. B. Jenson (Eds), *Nelson Textbook of Pediatrics* (17th ed., pp. 1380–1385). Philadelphia: Saunders.

24. Rollins, J. (1993). Nurses as gangbusters: A response to gang violence in America. *Pediatric Nursing, 19,* 559–567.

25. Mitchell, J. T. (1983). When disaster strikes. The critical incident stress debriefing process. *Journal of the Emergency Medical Services, 1, 36.*

26. McCann, I., & Pearlman, L. (1990) Vicarious traumatization: A framework for understanding the psychological effects of working with victims. *Journal of Traumatic Stress, 3,* 131–149.

27. Arendt, M., & Elklit A. (2001). Effectiveness of psychological debriefing. *Acta Psychiatrica Scandinavica, 104,* 423–437.

28. Boschert, S. (2007). Debriefing patients soon after trauma may stifle recovery. *Clinical Psychiatry News, 35,* 18.

29. Emergency Nurses Association. (2008). *Position Paper: Violence in the Emergency Care Setting.* Des Plaines, IL: Author.

SECTION SIX
Trauma Emergencies

TWENTY-SEVEN

Mechanisms of Injury

Kathryn J. Haley, RN, BSN

Introduction

Injuries are the leading threat to the health and well-being of young people in our society today.[1,2] Death caused by intentional and unintentional injury account for more years of potential life lost for children under the age of 18 years than do deaths caused by sudden infant death syndrome, cancer, and infectious diseases combined.[3] Injury is defined as "any intentional or unintentional damage to the body resulting from acute exposure to thermal, mechanical, electrical, or chemical energy or from the absence of such essentials as heat or oxygen."[4] The injury may be primary, occurring immediately on the transfer of energy (e.g., contusion of fracture), or secondary, occurring in response to the primary injury (e.g., cerebral edema or hypoxia). Most injury events are preventable; therefore they are rarely accidental, and as such the term "accident" is no longer being used in the trauma literature or by health care professionals (i.e., the term motor vehicle crash [MVC] has replaced motor vehicle accident [MVA]).[5] Injuries can be prevented by changing the environment, individual behavior, products, social norms, legislation, and governmental and institutional policy.

Nurses are caring for injured children in trauma center and non-trauma center emergency departments (EDs) across the nation daily. Although it is difficult to accurately describe how many children are treated in emergency departments for injuries, the number is thought to be staggering. Nationally, 5.4% of children had an injury-related ED visit, and approximately $2.3 billion was spent on outpatient injury-related ED visits in 2003.[6] A recent study reported great variability among states in injury-related ED visits for children, ranging from 63.3 to 164.4 per 1,000 children.[6] In 2002, nearly 3,100 children aged 3 years and under, 2,300 children aged 4 to 11 years, and 12,200 aged 12 to 19 years died of injuries.[7] Leading causes of injury-related death vary by age and include:[7,8]

❑ Children under 1 year of age—unintentional suffocation due to choking or strangulation.

❑ Children 1 to 3 years of age—motor vehicle crashes. In 2003, one third of children aged 4 years and younger that died were unrestrained at the time of the crash.

❑ Children 4 to 11 years of age—motor vehicle crashes. Drowning is the second leading cause, and homicide is the fourth cause.

❑ Children 12 to 19 years of age—motor vehicle crashes. The risk for motor vehicle crashes is greater in this group than for any other age category. Homicide is the second cause, followed by suicide as the third leading mechanism.

Pediatric trauma care requires the integration of knowledge related to mechanisms of injury, initial resuscitation, treatment of specific injuries, and injury prevention. The purposes of this chapter are to describe the incidence of pediatric trauma and to discuss common mechanisms of kinetic force injury.

Mechanisms of Injury

Mechanism of injury refers to the method by which energy is transferred from the environment to the child. The term "cause" is often used interchangeably with the term "mechanism." Energy sources are:

- Mechanical or kinetic
- Thermal
- Chemical
- Electrical
- Radiant
- Lack of oxygen
- Lack of thermoregulation

Mechanisms of injury related to kinetic energy are discussed in this chapter. Mechanisms of injury related to thermal, electrical, and radiant energy sources are discussed in Chapter 37; mechanisms of injury related to chemical sources are presented in Chapters 42 and 43; and mechanisms of injury related to a lack of oxygen and a lack of thermoregulation are discussed in Chapters 35, 39, and 40, respectively.

Kinetic Energy Sources and Injuries

The transfer of kinetic energy to the body structures arises from several sources: blunt (injury to internal organs), penetrating (disruption to skin and organ integrity), acceleration-deceleration (abrupt, forceful, forward-and-backward movement), and crushing (direct compression onto body structures).

Blunt Force Trauma

Blunt force trauma constitutes approximately 80% of childhood trauma.[9] In blunt trauma, external evidence of injury may be minimal, and energy is often absorbed by underlying structures; therefore, a high index of suspicion for potential injuries is required.

Falls

Falls are the most common cause of injury for children ages 0 to 14 years requiring hospital admission.[9] Falls from beds, stairs, windows, and playground equipment are common scenarios for childhood fall-related injuries.[10,11] Injuries sustained during falls result from blunt forces and most often involve the extremities, head, and abdomen. The orientation of the body at the time of impact correlates with the pattern of injuries:

- ❑ Feet first impact leads to injury of the ankles and lower extremities, as well as to the lumbar-sacral spine.

- ❑ Buttocks-first impact is associated with pelvic and vertebral injuries.

- ❑ Headfirst impact results in brain, head, face, and cervical spine injuries from axial loading. Young children have a large head in proportion to the body, placing them at greater risk for the head-to-feet orientation on impact and thereby explaining the higher incidence of skull fractures and head injury associated with falls in children.[12]

As with all mechanisms of injury, child maltreatment must be suspected when the history of the fall event is inconsistent and disproportionate with the injury.

Motor Vehicle Crashes

Motor vehicle crashes are the leading cause of death among children.[13] In 2005, there was a daily average of four deaths and 504 injuries in children 14 years and younger.[14] In a recent study, approximately 80% of restraint systems for children were used incorrectly, and in a manner that may increase a child's risk of injury during a crash.[15] The National Highway Traffic Safety Administra-

tion recommends booster seats for children until they are at least 8 years of age or 4 feet 9 inches tall, and that all children aged 12 years and younger should ride in the back seat.[16] Adults should avoid placing children in front of airbags, which if deployed and the child is in path of release can cause significant, if not lethal, injury.[17,18]

Passenger seating arrangements and the use of child restraint devices are key to the prevention of occupant deaths in children. Chapter 4 details car seat usage and safety.

Motor Vehicle–Pedestrian Crashes

Motor vehicle–pedestrian crashes are a lethal cause of pediatric trauma. Child pedestrians are at higher risk for injuries than adults for several reasons:

- ❑ Children are smaller, which makes them difficult for drivers to see, especially if they are between cars or at the side of a parked car.

- ❑ Children are unable to consistently and reliably judge distances and speeds.

- ❑ The child's developmental stage can make it hard to apply traffic rules outside of a mock setting.

The biomechanics associated with motor vehicle–pedestrian crashes are related to the speed and size of the vehicle and the height of the child. The most frequent injuries occur to the head, chest, abdomen, and lower extremities. Depending on the height of the child, contact with the vehicle is first made at the bumper and then the hood of the car. The point of impact with these car parts is at the child's lower extremity and the chest and abdomen, respectively. The child is then thrown onto the hood or windshield and is now moving with the vehicle. The driver usually responds by braking, and the car stops; however, the child slides and rolls, usually head first, to the street. A recent study showed that rarely is the child injured in all three regions; however, an understanding of the biomechanics identifies body regions that are more commonly injured.[19] Prevention strategies for motor vehicle-pedestrian injuries are discussed in Chapter 4.

Bicycle Crashes

Approximately half of the estimated 85 million bicycle riders in the United States are younger than 21 years of age.[20] In 2003, more than 10,000 bicycle-related hospitalizations occurred in children younger than 20 years, which resulted in more than $200 million in inpatient charges.[21] Although a common pastime for children, tragically, bicycles are connected to more childhood injuries than any other consumer product, except for cars.[21,22] Both boys and girls in the 10- to 13-year age group had the highest rate of bicycle-related hospitalization, and nearly 30% of all admissions involved a motor vehicle.[21]

Across all age groups, fractures are the leading injuries[21]; however, head injury is the most frequent cause of admission associated with bicycle crashes. Frequently, when struck, the child becomes airborne and lands headfirst on a hard surface. Anatomically, the young child has a larger head in proportion to the torso, placing him or her at greater risk for head injury during a transfer of kinetic energy. One out of every three children admitted for injuries related to a bicycle crash has a traumatic brain injury.[21] Most traumatic brain injuries were skull fractures and concussions. A recent study showed that helmets reduce the risk of head injury by 88%; unfortunately, compliance with helmet use is generally poor.[23] Other bicycle-related injuries included fractures, lacerations, abdominal injuries (such as those caused by handlebars) and contusion. Use of helmets to prevent head injures is detailed in Chapter 4.

Skates and Non-Powered Scooters

Skateboards and scooters have many of the same physical characteristics. Skateboarding has surged in popularity among the nation's youth, resulting in 50,000 visits to the emergency department and 1,500 hospitalizations each year. During the first nine months in 2000, non-powered scooter-related injuries accounted for nearly 10,000 visits to the emergency department, and 90% of these patients were children younger than 15 years.[24]

Skateboarding falls among older children more commonly result in extremity fractures. Serious head injury is possible and related to collision with a motor vehicle or falling while moving at higher speeds. The American Academy of Pediatrics advises that children younger than 5 years of age not use skateboards and children younger than 10 years should not use skateboards without close supervision by an adult or responsible adolescent.[24]

Scooter falls commonly occur in children younger than 8 years of age. Frequent types of injury include fractures or dislocations. Head and face injuries account for 29% of injuries, whereas upper extremity and knee injuries account for about 35%.[24]

Young children may be at high risk for injury from skateboards and scooters because they have a higher center of gravity, their neuromuscular system is not well developed, their judgment is poor, and they are not sufficiently able to protect themselves from injury.

Appropriately aged children who use skateboards should wear protective clothing, including a helmet, kneepads, and elbow pads, and should skate in designated, safe areas.

Infant Walker-Related Injuries

Infant walkers are a common cause of nonfatal injury to younger children. From 1990 through 2001, there were an estimated 197,000 infant walker-related injuries in children who were younger than 15 months.[25] Parents generally believe that walkers keep their infants and young toddlers safe, but data to support this theory are nonexistent. Recent data suggest that walkers either do not stimulate walking or that they may actually impede crawling and delay walking by several weeks.[26]

Injuries are more frequently caused by falls, either from the walker or while the infant is seated in the walker. Types of injuries include skull fractures, closed head injuries, burns, and poisonings.[26]

The American Academy of Pediatrics recommends a ban on the manufacture and the sale of mobile infant walkers.[26] Safety strategies are outlined in Chapter 4.

Sledding Injuries

Sledding injuries are common during the winter months when icy conditions entice children to sled in potentially dangerous areas. In one study, 181 children were seen in the emergency department of a Midwest pediatric level 1 trauma center or its affiliated urgent care center for injuries sustained from sledding. Of these children, 142 (78%) were between 5 and 14 years of age. The majority of injured sledders were males, and most of the sledders were injured from a fall from the sled, collision with a stationary object, or collision with sledding persons.[27] Head injuries, extremity fractures, and soft tissue injuries were common. In another study, children stuck by motor vehicles while on a sled had higher proportions of head injuries than did those who hit stationary objects or trees. Seven children died because of sledding injuries; all were school-aged children struck by motor vehicles who had low Glasgow Coma Scale scores on ED arrival.[28]

Prevention of sledding injuries includes selecting a designated safe sledding area that is free of trees and obstacles and clear of moving vehicles, a sledding surface that is not icy, a limited number of other sledders in the designated area, and a sledding slope of less than 30 degrees that ends with a flat runoff.[29] The sled should be well maintained, and children should be supervised while sledding. The sledder should dress warmly to prevent cold injuries and avoid wearing loose clothes to prevent strangulation, and parents should consider having the child wear a helmet to prevent a head injury. Sledding in the feet first or sitting-up position may decrease the risk of head injury compared with sledding in a prone, headfirst position. However, suspect lumbosacral spine injuries when the child is injured sledding feet first. Safer sled types are steerable, not snow disks or inner tubes.[29]

Penetrating Forces

Penetrating trauma includes gunshot wounds, stabbing injuries, and injuries from sharp objects, such as toys and glass. Factors that are important when caring for a child with a penetrating injury include the child's age, the environment in which the injury occurred, the wounding agent, the trajectory, the force and velocity, the immediacy of definitive care, and the presence or absence of intent.

Firearm Injuries

Safe Kids reports that Americans possess nearly 200 million firearms.[30] Between 2002 and 2006, 17,322 children, aged 0 to 19 years and injured by firearms, were included in the National Trauma Data Bank Pediatric Report 2007.[9] Children aged 0 to 14 years accounted for 2,347 cases, and aged 15 to 19 years accounted for 14,975 hospital admissions. Death was a result in 12% of the cases. A 2003 Centers for Disease Control and Prevention study reported that 6.1% of children included in a violence survey had carried a gun in the 30 days preceding the survey.[31]

Firearms associated with injuries are handguns, rifles, and shotguns. Nearly 20% of all firearm-related fatalities among children younger than 15 years are unintentional. In 2002, more than 800 children were treated in emergency departments in the United States for unintentional firearm-related injuries.[31] Often the shootings occur when the young child is at home and unsupervised, and a loaded gun is accessible.[31] In adolescents, however, firearm injuries more commonly occur out of the home and usually are associated with violent acts.

Stabbing and Other Penetrating Injuries

Stabbing injuries occur infrequently in the pediatric population. The severity of a stab wound depends on the body system involved, the length of the knife blade, and the angle of penetration.

Toys or other objects also serve as sources of penetrating trauma. Air guns, toy musical instruments, wrought iron fencing, and other innocuous items, such as pencils, can cause serious injury to the affected body areas. Children should be taught to avoid running with objects in their mouths and to avoid climbing pointed fencing. Dangerous toys should be kept away from young children to prevent the occurrence of these penetrating injuries.

Acceleration-Deceleration Forces

Acceleration-deceleration forces cause bodily injury from excessive forces applied during the injury event. For example, in a motor vehicle crash, the child passenger is thrown forward and is stopped by the restraining device. The internal organs, however, may continue to move forward and then abruptly return to their normal position after sustaining damage. Acceleration-deceleration forces occur not only during motor vehicle crashes but also during other injury episodes, such as shaken impact syndrome and sledding, farming, or other occupational injuries. Prevention of acceleration-deceleration injuries is similar to the prevention of blunt force trauma.

Crush Injuries

Crush injuries occur when direct pressure is applied to a body area. Animal bites, entrapment in farm equipment, lawn mower injuries, and compression under a motor vehicle or other heavy object are examples of situations that result in crushing injuries. Degloving injuries occur when the skin, fascia, and perhaps the muscle and bone are torn from the body, usually from shearing forces, such as being struck and run over by a motor vehicle.

Farm-Related Injuries

Comprehensive data are not available on the incidence of farm-related injury among children who live or work on farms; however, a recent study from a Midwest pediatric level 1 trauma center reported 96 children were admitted during a nine-year period for treatment of farm-related injuries, including five deaths.[32]

Farming is the only occupation in which, under specific conditions, children are permitted to operate complicated industrial-type equipment. Additional risk factors include long working hours, lack of developmental and intellectual maturity to operate machinery, and the general isolation associated with the occupation.

Injuries are often caused by being run over by a tractor, entrapment in harvesting equipment, silo entanglements, and animal kicks. The severity of injury varies and includes traumatic asphyxia, major lacerations or amputations, and multisystemic injuries.

Prevention strategies for farm-related injuries include a "no extra seat, no rider" policy for tractor riding; using developmental guidelines for age-appropriate work tasks; and wearing appropriate clothing. Separate young children from farm hazards by fencing in a play area and limiting access to large animals.[33] Recommend enforcement of safety devices such as machine guards and the employment of safe animal-handling practices. Parents should be encouraged to create safe barriers on farms to prevent children from entering hazardous areas.

Lawn Mower Injuries

Injuries related to lawn mowers are devastating and an important cause of pediatric morbidity. Lawn mower injuries can be life threatening, as well as limb threatening. School-aged children and adolescents who operate power mowers may slip under the blade and sustain amputation of the foot or toes. Young children who are held on an adult's lap while positioned on a riding mower can fall from the vehicle and be run over by the moving blade. Adults who operate riding mowers cannot see small children as they are backing up and can run over a child. Approximately 9,500 children are injured annually from lawn mower injuries.[34] In one series of 85 children treated for lawn mower–related injuries at a Midwest pediatric level 1 trauma center, the mean age was 7.6 years, and 65% were boys. Thirty children required surgical intervention; 21.2% of the children had amputations. The most common body region injured was the lower extremity, including injuries to the foot, toe, and leg. The leading mechanism of injury was being run over or backed over, followed by blade contact, thrown object, burn, and fall off the mower.[35]

Prevention of lawn mower injuries includes keeping young children indoors during mower operation, forbidding passengers on riding mowers, and using protective equipment for adolescents who operate lawn mowers. The American Academy of Pediatrics recommends that most children will not be ready to operate a walk-behind mower until at least 12 years of age, or a ride-on mower until at least 16 years of age.[36]

Conclusion

Knowledge of mechanisms of injury allows emergency and trauma nurses to have a high index of suspicion for the resultant injuries in the child who presents to the emergency department for treatment. Efforts to reduce and prevent trauma-related morbidity and mortality are within the purview of emergency and trauma nursing.

References

1. Wesson, E. (2006). Epidemiology of pediatric trauma. In D. Wesson (Ed.), *Pediatric trauma* (pp. 1–5). New York: Taylor & Francis.

2. Aris, E., MacDorman, M. F., Strobino, D. M., & Guyer, B. (2003). Annual summary of vital statistics. *Pediatrics, 112,* 1215–1230.

3. American Academy of Pediatrics. (2008). Policy Statement: Management of pediatric trauma. *Pediatrics, 121,* 849–854.

4. Centers for Disease Control and Prevention. (2008). *Injury and violence (including suicide).* Retrieved April 6, 2009, from http://www.cdc.gov/HealthyYouth/injury/facts.htm

5. Emergency Nurses Association. (2007). *Trauma nursing core course provider manual* (6th ed., pp. 7–18). Des Plaines, IL: Author.

6. Owen, P. L., Zodet, M. W., Berdahl, T., Dougherty, D., McCormick, M. C., & Simpson, L. A. (2008). Annual report on health care for children and youth in the United States: Focus on injury-related emergency department utilization and expenditures. *Ambulatory Pediatrics, 8,* 219–240.

7. Centers for Disease Control and Prevention. (2008). *Welcome to WISQARS™.* Retrieved April 6, 2009, from http://www.cdc.gov/injury/wisqars/

8. Centers for Disease Control and Prevention. (2006). *CDC injury fact book.* Atlanta, GA: Author.

9. American College of Surgeons. (2007). *National Trauma Data Bank pediatric report 2007.* Chicago: Author.

10. Vish, N. L., Powell, E. C., Wiltsek, D., & Sheehan, K. M. (2005). Pediatric window falls: Not just a problem for children in high rises. *Injury Prevention, 11*(5), 300–303.

11. Murray, J. A., Chen, D., Velmahos, G. C., Alo, K., Belzberg, H., Asensio, J. A., et al. (2000). Pediatric fall: Is height a predictor of injury and outcome? *The American Surgeon, 66,* 863–865.

12. Kottmeier, P. (1995). Falls from heights. In W. Buntain (Ed.), *Pediatric trauma* (pp. 450–454). Philadelphia: Saunders.

13. Centers for Disease Control and Prevention. (2008). *Child passenger safety: Fact sheet.* Retrieved April 6, 2009, from http://www.cdc.gov/ncipc/factsheets/childpas.htm

14. National Highway Traffic Safety Administration. (2008). *Traffic safety facts 2006: Children.* Washington, DC: Author.

References (continued)

15. National Highway Traffic Safety Administration. (2006). *Traffic safety facts research note 2005: Misuse of child restraints: Results of a workshop to review field data results.* Washington, DC: Author.

16. National Highway Traffic Safety Administration (2006). *Child Passenger Safety—Studies and Reports.* Retrieved April 6, 2009, from http://www.nhtsa.dot.gov/portal/site/nhtsa/menuitem.9f8c7d6359e0e9bbbf30811060008a0c/

17. Quinones-Hinojosa, A., Jun, P., Manley, G. T., Knudson, M. M., & Gupta, N. (2005). Airbag deployment and improperly restrained children: A lethal combination. *The Journal of Trauma, 59,* 729–733.

18. Grisoni, E. R., Pillai, S. B., Volsko, T. A., Mutabagani, K., Garcia, V., Haley, K., et al. (2000). Pediatric airbag injuries: The Ohio experience. *Journal of Pediatric Surgery, 35*(2), 160–162.

19. Orsborn, R., Haley, K., Hammond, S., & Falcone, R. E. (1999). Pediatric pedestrian versus motor vehicle patterns of injury: Debunking the myth. *Air Medical Journal, 18*(3), 107–110.

20. Rodgers, G. B. (2000) Bicycle and bicycle helmet use patterns in the United States in 1998. *Journal of Safety Research, 31,* 149–158.

21. Summit, S., Sinclair, S., Smith, G., & Huiyun, X. (2007). Pediatric hospitalizations for bicycle-related injuries. *Injury Prevention, 13,* 316–321.

22. National Safe Kids Campaign. (2004). *Bicycle injury fact sheet.* Washington, DC: Author.

23. American Academy of Pediatrics. (2001). Bicycle helmets. *Pediatrics, 108*(4), 103.

24. American Academy of Pediatrics. (2002). Skateboard and scooter injuries. *Pediatrics, 109*(3), 542–543.

25. Shields, B., & Smith, G. (2006). Success in the prevention of infant walker–related injuries: An analysis of national data, 1990–2001. *Pediatrics, 117*(3), e452–e459.

26. American Academy of Pediatrics. (2008). Injuries associated with infant walkers. Reaffirmed August 1, 2008. *Pediatrics, 108*(3), 790–792.

27. Noffsinger, D., Nuss, K., Haley, K., & Ford, N. (2008). Pediatric sledding trauma: Avoiding the collision. *Journal of Trauma Nursing, 14*(4), 58–61.

28. Bernardo, L. M., Gardner, M. J., & Rogers, K. (1998). Pediatric sledding injuries in Pennsylvania. *Journal of Trauma Nursing, 5,* 34–40.

29. American Academy of Pediatrics. (2008). *Winter safety tips.* Retrieved April 6, 2009, from http://www.aap.org/advocacy/releases/decwintertips.cfm

30. Safe Kids USA. (2004). *Injury facts: Firearm injury (unintentional).* Retrieved April 6, 2009, from http://www.usa.safekids.org/tier3_cd.cfm?folder_id=540&content_item_id=1131

31. Grunbaum, J., Kann, L., Kinchen, S., Ross, J. G., Lowry, R., & Harris, W. A. (2004). Youth risk behavior surveillance—United States, 2003. *Morbidity and Mortality Weekly Report, 53*(SS-2), 1–100.

32. Smith, G. A., Scherzer, D. J., Buckley, J. W., Haley, K., & Shields, B. J. (2004). Pediatric farm-related injuries: A series of 96 hospitalized patients. *Clinical Pediatrics, 43,* 335–342.

33. American Academy of Pediatrics. (2001). Prevention of agricultural injuries among children and adolescents. *Pediatrics, 108*(4), 1016–1019.

34. Vollman, D., & Smith, G. A. (2006). Epidemiology of lawn mower–related injuries to children in the United States, 1990–2004. *Pediatrics, 118*(2), e273–e277.

35. Vollman, D., Khosla, K., Shields, K., Beeghly, C., Bonsu, B., & Smith, G. (2005). Lawn mower–related injuries to children. *Journal of Trauma, 59,* 724–728.

36. American Academy of Pediatrics. (2001). Lawn mower–related injuries to children. *Pediatrics, 107,* 1480–1481.

TWENTY-EIGHT

Initial Trauma Assessment and Intervention

Kathryn J. Haley, RN, BSN

Introduction

Pediatric trauma resuscitation requires the skill and expertise of a trauma team dedicated to the care of injured children. The team uses a systematic and prioritized assessment style that includes a primary and secondary focus. The primary assessment identifies life-threatening injuries to the airway, respiratory, circulatory, and neurologic systems, whereas the secondary assessment identifies injuries to the remaining body systems. The purpose of this chapter is to discuss the initial assessment and interventions for the injured child with multiple injuries. The trauma team performs the assessment and interventions simultaneously; however, they are discussed separately for clarification.

Pediatric Trauma-Related Considerations

Although adults' responses to injury are often obvious, children's responses to serious injury are usually subtle. Children have tremendous physiologic reserve and may rapidly decompensate when their compensatory threshold is exhausted. Normal pediatric anatomy and physiology related to injury must be understood to detect abnormalities and implement resuscitation measures in a timely manner.

Airway and Cervical Spine

❒ The airway comprises soft tissues that are pliable and susceptible to edema when traumatized after an injury or during insertion of an oral or nasopharyngeal airway, suctioning, or placement of an endotracheal tube. Even minimal airway edema and/or secretions result in disproportionately higher resistance to airflow.

❒ The tongue is relatively large in comparison to the oral cavity and can easily obstruct the airway of an unconscious child. The large tongue and hypertrophied tonsils of young children make visualization of the vocal cords difficult.

❒ When the young child or infant is in a supine position, the mouth, pharynx, and trachea form a more acute angle; for this reason, the neutral or sniffing position provides ideal alignment for optimal airflow.

❒ The glottis lies in a more superior and anterior position relative to the pharynx. making orotracheal intubation easier than the nasotracheal approach.

❒ The trachea is pliable and easily obstructed when the head and neck are hyperextended or hyperflexed. When the young child is supine during spinal immobilization or diagnostic procedures, the relatively large occiput can cause neck flexion resulting in subsequent airway obstruction and may potentially contribute to injury if the head is allowed to tilt forward.

❒ Children have short, fleshy necks, making inspection for jugular venous distention and tracheal deviation difficult. Rarely are the jugular veins and the trachea visible.

❒ The cervical spine assumes similarity to that of the adult when the child is about 8 years of age. Infants and small children have proportionally larger heads and underdeveloped neck musculature that make them particularly susceptible to flexion and extension injuries of the cervical spine.

Breathing (Respiratory)

❑ Infants and children usually breathe with minimal effort. Respiratory rates and primary muscles used for respiration vary with age. Until children reach the age of 7 or 8 years they will use the diaphragm and abdominal muscles to breathe. Therefore, it is important to observe abdominal excursion in addition to chest movement in this age group.

❑ Children commonly cry before, during, and after injury. The crying child swallows air, resulting in gastric distention. The stomach distends and restricts diaphragm movement and respiratory excursion.

❑ The chest wall in younger children is cartilaginous. Rib fractures rarely are observed in young children and, when present, reflect a powerful force and transfer of energy. Significant injury to the soft tissues of the thorax, heart, and mediastinal structures can occur even without evidence of bony injury.[1] Flail segments are uncommon in children and are usually associated with pulmonary contusion.[2,3]

❑ Breath sounds are easily transmitted through the thin chest wall, despite the presence of a pneumothorax or tracheal malpositioning. Therefore, it is dangerous to rely solely on breath sounds to determine the adequacy of ventilation in injured children.

Circulation

❑ The average circulating blood volume in children is about 80 mL/kg. Small volumes of external or internal hemorrhage may result in shock; thus, rapid stabilization of any ongoing sources of blood loss is vital to successful resuscitation.

❑ Children can compensate for blood losses in excess of 15% to 20% with tachycardia and vasoconstriction. When blood losses are greater than 15%, signs of circulatory failure (tachycardia, decrease in intensity of peripheral pulses, delayed capillary refill, and cool extremities) will be observed. Blood pressure will be normal until an acute loss of 25% to 30% of circulating blood volume occurs.[4,5] Hypotension is a late, ominous sign of shock when the child is no longer able to compensate for worsening condition. Signs of shock may initially be subtle, and it may be difficult to discern whether the tachycardia is related to fear, pain, or shock.

❑ Children generally have a healthy cardiovascular system. The initial response to hypovolemia is vasoconstriction and tachycardia. In early hemorrhage,

tachycardia and tachypnea become more readily apparent, and the rise in diastolic blood pressure results in a narrowed pulse pressure. By increasing their heart rate, children can increase their cardiac output with minimal, if any change, in the stroke volume.[4,6] When compensatory mechanisms fail, tissue hypoxia and hypercapnia occur, leading to bradycardia and hypotension.[7]

Disability (Neurologic)

❑ The cranial cavity is thin and more pliable in younger children. Limited increases in intracranial mass are tolerated better by younger children than by adults because of open fontanelles and the ability to reopen unfused sutures. For these children, signs of an expanding mass may be delayed until rapid decompensation occurs.[5] Also, because of the vascular supply to the scalp, any laceration can result in a significant source of blood loss.[4]

❑ Children are more susceptible to head injury because the head of the child represents a relatively greater proportion of mass and body surface area. Therefore, the head is usually first to crash into a stationary object.

❑ The incomplete myelinization of the brain in children younger than 2 years of age enhances the susceptibility of neural tissue to traumatic injury.[4]

Exposure (Thermoregulation)

❑ Children lose body heat rapidly. Infants younger than 2 years of age have a decreased ability for mature thermoregulatory control. They have a greater body surface area-to-mass ratio than adults, leading to greater transfer of body heat to the environment.

❑ Other developmental factors that influence thermoregulatory balance in children include their lesser quantity of subcutaneous fat, their thin skin with increased permeability, and their delayed shivering and inefficient ability to generate heat.

Etiology

The mechanisms of pediatric injury are discussed in Chapter 27.

Focused History

Children may be unable or unwilling to provide a history of injury. Witnesses, such as family members, neighbors, prehospital medical personnel, and police personnel, should be queried.

Injury History

A useful method for obtaining injury event information from prehospital personnel is the MIVT mnemonic: M = mechanism of injury, I = injuries that are suspected by previous assessment, V = vital sign assessment, and T = treatment initiated and patient responses before arrival. Eliciting information in this format is useful when assessing for types and severity of injury.[4,8]

❑ Mechanism of injury (Table 28.1)

■ Description of the incident including any death(s) of involved persons

■ Time required for extrication and transport

❑ Injuries suspected

■ Prehospital assessment of the child including apparent injuries

■ Description of the injury

❑ Full set of vital signs including any trending changes

❑ Treatment initiated and patient's response to treatment

■ Level of prehospital care received (bystander first aid; advanced trauma life support). This level of support is variable, relative to bystander preparedness, access to 911, level of EMS system response, and time to EMS arrival:

• Airway support

• Breathing assistance

• Application of pressure dressings or splints

• Preservation of amputated body parts

• Performance of cardiopulmonary resuscitation

■ Child's response to the interventions:

• Compare the injury circumstances, the prehospital interventions, and the child's current status.

• Vomiting and choking episode

• Apnea or difficulty breathing

• Length of time the response occurred

• Estimated blood loss

• Loss of consciousness, the length of time the child was unconscious, the presence of amnesia, seizure, and the child's level of consciousness after the injury event (e.g., crying, awake)

• Ambulation after the injury

Additional History

❑ Time of the incident.

■ Comparison of emergency department (ED) presentation time with time of injury (delays in seeking treatment may be an indicator of child

maltreatment) (Chapter 44).

❑ Child's age and developmental capabilities in relation to the injury (Chapter 3).

■ Children's developmental ability to sustain the injury on the basis of the reported history

❑ Credibility of witnesses.

■ Changes in the injury history to match the injuries as they are identified should raise suspicion.

Patient's Health History

The SAMPLE mnemonic is helpful in recalling key information for a quick health history.

❑ *S*igns and symptoms currently experiencing

❑ *A*llergies to medications or environmental agents, including latex

❑ Current *M*edications (over-the-counter, prescribed, or illicit)

❑ *P*resence of chronic illness, immunization status, and presence of hearing or visual aids

❑ Time of the *L*ast meal; consumption of food or alcohol

❑ *E*vents surrounding the injury, as described above

Family History

❑ Involvement of other family members in the injury event

❑ Previous history of injury (e.g., child maltreatment)

Focused Assessment

Physical Assessment

❑ Assess the airway and cervical spine.

❑ Inspect the airway while maintaining cervical spine stabilization for:

■ Patency

• The presence of foreign bodies (chewing gum, loose teeth, vomitus, secretions, and blood). Perform the jaw thrust maneuver and suction the oropharynx while maintaining and protecting cervical spine alignment to avoid airway compromise and compromising spinal stabilization. Prepare for endotracheal intubation if the child is unable to maintain a spontaneous airway. Ventilate the patient with bag-mask device before endotracheal intubation. Suction as needed.

• Listen for the child's ability to speak or make age-appropriate sounds. Ask an age-appropriate

TABLE 28.1 Mechanism of Injury and Pertinent Historical Findings

Mechanism of Injury	Historical Findings
Blunt forces	
Motor vehicle crash	*Point of impact:* Rollover; front; side; rear; T-bone impact *Use of restraints/car safety seat:* Car or booster seat properly affixed to car; two-point or three-point restraints; lower anchors and tether (LATCH) use; airbag deployment *Occupant position in car:* Front- or back-seat passenger; driver; pickup truck passenger Ejection from vehicle *Other vehicle information:* Vehicle speed (if unknown, posted speed for area of crash); object of collision (stationary or moving; object or vehicle) *Other occupant information:* Scene fatalities; entrapment and extrication required; unusual noises, odors, or sights occupants may have endured
Bicycle crash	*Bicycle information:* Object of collision (stationary or moving; object or vehicle); run over; speed of vehicle (if unknown, posted speed for area of crash); vehicle damage (spidered windshield, indentations) *Cyclist information:* Location of cyclist on impact (distance thrown from bicycle); use of bicycle helmet; condition of helmet; condition of bicycle
Pedestrian vs. motor vehicle crash	*Vehicle information:* Speed of vehicle; location of crash (intersection, midblock, road, driveway); vehicle damage (spidered windshield, indentations) *Pedestrian information:* Run over by or pinned under vehicle: type of surface; witness account of point of impact; location of pedestrian on impact (distance thrown from vehicle)
Farm machinery	*Machinery information:* Type of surface (soil, road, gravel, fertilized area); length of blade: machine use at time of injury; potential chemical exposure (pesticide, gasoline) *Patient information:* Duration of entrapment before rescue; body areas involved (hands vs. legs)
Falls	*Fall information:* Height of fall; location of fall (tree vs. second-story window); type of landing surface *Patient information:* Body areas that first hit the ground

TABLE 28.1 Mechanism of Injury and Pertinent Historical Findings (continued)

Mechanism of Injury	Historical Findings
Penetrating forces	
Gunshot wound	*Penetrating object:*
	Type of firearm; caliber of bullets; number of shots fired
	Patient information:
	Distance of child from shooter; number of wounds; location of wounds
Stab wound	*Penetrating object:*
	Type of object (such as wrought iron fence, fork, or javelin); type of knife and length of blade
	Patient information:
	Number of wounds; location of wounds; object impaled in child
Crushing forces	
	Crushing object:
	Animal (type of animal, domesticated vs. wild; rabies status); machinery (type of machinery, entrapment, duration of entrapment); furniture
	Patient information:
	Number of wounds; location of wounds: preservation of amputated body parts

question, such as, "What is your name?" An appropriate verbal response indicates the level of consciousness, airway patency, and ability to ventilate.

- Note breath odor for alcohol and other substances of abuse (alcohol, marijuana, or fruity odor). Follow institutional guidelines for screening for substances of abuse.

❏ Inspect the anterior neck for:

- Jugular vein distention.
- Tracheal deviation. Inspect for these abnormalities before cervical collar placement. If the collar is in place a trauma team member should be assigned to maintain the child's head and neck in a neutral position, while the neck is inspected for injuries. Once the assessment is complete the collar is secured.

❏ Maintain cervical and spinal stabilization.

- Protect the cervical spine. Cervical spine protection is a concept that includes in-line manual stabilization and complete spinal immobilization to prohibit movement that may cause new injury.[8]
- Apply a correctly sized and fitted cervical collar to prevent flexion and extension of the cervical spine. Do not hyperextend, flex, or rotate the neck during collar placement.
- Apply towel rolls or commercially available age-

and size-appropriate blocks to prevent lateral head movement.

- Apply a commercially available spinal immobilization board to prevent spinal movement. Tape or straps used with head blocks or towels must extend to the rigid surface beneath the child. Limit the duration of spinal immobilization to 30 minutes or less or follow institution guidelines.
- Assess occipital alignment. It may be necessary to place towel rolls under the shoulders to maintain normoflexion.

❏ Assess the respiratory system (breathing).

- Observe the chest for:
  - Deformity
    - Surface trauma
    - Soft tissue and bony chest wall integrity
    - Penetrating wounds
  - Spontaneous chest rise and fall
  - Rate and depth of respirations
  - Skin color
  - Presence and quality of bilateral breath sounds
  - Presence of indicators of increased work of breathing
    - Nasal flaring

- Substernal, subcostal, intercostal, supra-clavicular, suprasternal retractions
- Expiratory grunting
- Accessory muscle use
- Quality and equality of chest expansion
- Signs of respiratory distress
■ Auscultate the chest high in the axillae and anterior chest for:
  - Presence of breath sounds
  - Respiratory rate
■ Palpate the rib cage for:
  - Tenderness
  - Crepitus
  - Flail segments
■ Palpate the sternum for:
  - Tenderness
  - Deformity
■ Administer supplemental oxygen by a nonrebreather mask (100% oxygen).
■ Provide assisted or complete ventilation.
■ Measure oxygen saturation by a pulse oximeter, if readily available.
❑ Assess the cardiovascular system.
■ Inspect quickly for areas of open hemorrhage or amputation:
  - Control open hemorrhage with pressure dressings
■ Auscultate heart sounds for:
  - Rate. Initiate chest compressions if the pulse is absent or if a nonperfusing rate is present (Chapter 13).
  - Rhythm
  - Quality. Observe for Beck's triad (muffled heart tones, distended neck veins, and general signs of shock), which may indicate cardiac tamponade.[8]
■ Palpate central and peripheral pulses for:
  - Presence
    - Palpate a radial or brachial pulse
  - Assess the adequacy of peripheral circulation.
    - Compare both the central and peripheral pulses. Central pulses are typically stronger than peripheral pulses. Significant variation between peripheral and central pulses occurs with vasoconstriction associated with hypovolemic shock.
    - Central pulses are palpated at the femoral,

carotid (in older children), and axillary vessel.
  - Peripheral pulses are palpated in the pediatric shock victim at the brachial or radial site.[4,6]
- Assess skin color (pale, mottled, dusky, cyanotic), temperature, and moisture
- Measure capillary refill.
■ Establish one or two large-bore intravenous lines or intraosseous access based on assessment findings.
❑ Assess the neurologic system (disability).
■ After the assessment of airway, breathing, and circulation, perform a brief neurologic evaluation to determine the extent of disability. Consider the child's age and development level and incorporate the parent when indicated.[9]
■ Quickly assess the level of consciousness using the mnemonic AVPU: *A*lert, responds to *V*erbal stimulus, responds to *P*ainful stimulus, *U*nresponsive.[10]
  - Responsiveness may be difficult to evaluate in the nonverbal child
  - Observe for alterations in developmentally expected behaviors, such as inability to focus and follow objects in a 6-month-old infant
■ Assess the pupils for:
  - Size
  - Shape
  - Reactivity to light
  - Equality
❑ Expose the patient to continue the assessment. Provide environmental control. To prevent hypothermia:
■ Undress the child to further identify other potential injuries:
  - Scissors and the cutting of clothes can be frightening to the child and adolescent. Provide emotional support using appropriate developmental phrases.
  - Cutting of clothing may damage or destroy physical evidence in cases with legal implications such as child maltreatment, homicide, or other acts of violence. Consider clothing evidence and package accordingly (i.e., place in paper bag, seal, label, chain of evidence documentation).
■ Initiate warming measures to prevent radiant heat loss.
  - Warm the ambient air by increasing the room temperature
  - Apply overhead warming lights
  - Apply warmed blankets to prevent convective heat loss, provide comfort, and assure modesty

- Provide warmed intravenous fluids via commercial fluid warmer

❑ Consider the need for transfer. Matching patient needs with resources is complex. Not all hospitals have resources that an injured patient requires. During the primary assessment enough information may be collected that enables prompt initiation of transfer needs for higher-level trauma care.[8]

❑ Provide opportunity for family presence.
  ▪ Assign a member of the resuscitation team to provide emotional support to the parents. Facilitate the process for the parent or child to be together during the initial resuscitation.[11]

❑ Obtain a full set of vital signs (heart rate, blood pressure, respiratory rate, temperature, estimated weight in kilograms).
  ▪ Trend vital signs

❑ Give comfort measures.

❑ Obtain a head-to-toe assessment.
  ▪ Inspect the head for:
    • Lacerations
    • Abrasions
    • Contusions
    • Puncture wounds
    • Foreign bodies, such as glass and metal
  ▪ Palpate the head for:
    • Depressions
    • Step-off defects
    • Pain
    • Hematomas
    • The condition of the anterior and posterior fontanelles in children younger than 2 years of age. A tense, raised fontanelle in the calm or comatose young child may indicate increased intracranial pressure.
  ▪ Assess the neurologic system.
    • A more in-depth assessment of the neurologic system is performed here. The patient will be assessed by using either the Glasgow Coma Scale (GCS) score or Pediatric GCS score. Changes of two points in the GCS score are significant clues of hypovolemia, hypoxia, or increased intracranial pressure. Sudden changes in GCS score may demand immediate interventions.
  ▪ Inspect the face and oral cavity for:
    • Deformity. Midfacial fractures, which are described with use of the Le Fort classification

system, are rare in children younger than 12 years of age.[12]
    • Lacerations
    • Symmetry. Ask the child to smile and grimace and open and close the mouth; note any deviations. Irregular mouth and tooth positioning or inability to close the mouth may be indicative of a fractured mandible.
    • Impaled objects
    • Ecchymosis around the eyes (raccoon's eyes)
  ▪ Palpate the forehead, orbits, maxilla, and mandible for:
    • Tenderness
    • Pain
    • Step-off deformities
    • Crepitus
    • Stability
  ▪ Inspect the oral cavity for:
    • Lacerations
    • Loose, chipped, or missing teeth. In children, missing teeth may be a normal finding unrelated to the trauma. Parents can usually give a reliable dental history.
    • Orthodontia apparatus. Observe for damage, including loose or penetrating wires.
  ▪ Inspect the pupils of the eyes for:
    • Size. An irregular pupil or blood in the anterior chamber (hyphema) should be reported immediately.
    • Equality. Unequal pupils may be indicative of increased intracranial pressure on the cranial nerves and may be an early indication of brain stem herniation.
    • Reaction to light. Nonreactive or sluggish pupils may be associated with head injury, drug use, alcohol intoxication, or other pathology.
  ▪ Inspect the eyes for:
    • Extraocular movements. Entrapment of ocular muscles from a blowout fracture may inhibit upward eye movement. "Sundowning" may indicate increased intracranial pressure.
    • Visual acuity. Request the younger child to point to a familiar object. Ask the older child about the quality of vision.
    • Scleral deformity and hemorrhages. Scleral hemorrhages may indicate compression injury, such as traumatic asphyxia.

- Remove the child's contact lenses, if present.
- Secure penetrating objects and lightly patch both eyes, avoiding direct pressure on the eyes.
  - Assess the ears.
    - Inspect for unusual drainage, such as blood or clear fluid from the external ear canal, which may be cerebrospinal fluid.
    - Inspect the tympanic membrane for hematotympanum.
    - Inspect the mastoid process for ecchymosis (Battle's sign). Although usually not evident until hours after an injury, Battle's sign usually indicates a basilar skull fracture.
  - Inspect the nose for:
    - Deformity
    - Septal deviation or septal hematoma
    - Rhinorrhea. Clear rhinorrhea may indicate a cerebrospinal fluid leak. If cerebrospinal fluid or drainage is present, notify the physician and do not insert a gastric tube through the nose.[8]
  - Assess the neck.
    - Open the cervical collar, always maintaining neutral positioning and alignment; secure the cervical collar once the neck is assessed.
  - Inspect the anterior neck for:
    - Edema
    - Lacerations
    - Abrasions
    - Avulsions
    - Puncture wounds
    - Jugular vein distention
  - Palpate the anterior neck for:
    - Pain
    - Subcutaneous emphysema or crepitus (indicates disruption of the trachea or bronchial tree)
    - Tracheal deviation. Normal tracheal position is midline. In the young child with a thick, short neck, tracheal deviation is assessed at the sternal notch. If trachea deviation is observed it may be a sign of potential life-threatening injury or complications (tension pneumothorax).
  - Palpate the cervical spine (posterior neck) for:
    - Tenderness. Children with cervical spine injury commonly complain of tenderness when the cervical vertebrae are palpated. Remind the verbal child to answer "yes" about tenderness rather than to nod or shake the head for confirma-

tion. For the nonverbal child, palpate while using distraction methods; observe for facial grimace or crying.
- Pain
- Posterior neck deformity. Maintain cervical spine stabilization by using an appropriately sized cervical collar and a rigid spinal stabilization board with additional devices to prevent head-spine movement. Successful cervical immobilization includes restriction of lateral, flexion, and extension movements of the head and cervical spine and restraint of the head, shoulders, hips, and legs. The efficacy of common immobilization techniques was examined, and it was found that no single immobilization device or technique is ideal in consistently protecting the cervical spine from angulation.[13] Secure the collar and maintain cervical stabilization once assessment of the neck is completed.
  - Assess the child's voice for:
    - Quality
    - Phonation. A hoarse, muffled voice may indicate laryngeal injury; anticipate potential airway compromise.
- Inspect the chest for:
    - Abrasions. Linear ecchymosis may indicate seat belt and shoulder belt injury.
    - Lacerations and contusions
    - Symmetry during inspiration and expiration
    - Open wounds
    - Scars
    - Paradoxical movements during inspiration and expiration
    - Use of accessory muscles
    - Respiratory rate and depth
    - Scars from healed chest tube sites, central lines, surgical incisions, or penetrating wounds
  - Auscultate the entire chest for:
    - Equality, quality, and characteristics of breath sounds
    - Respiratory rate, depth, pattern, and effort
  - Palpate the anterior rib cage and clavicles for:
    - Tenderness
    - Crepitus
    - Deformity. Children are particularly ticklish in these areas, so anticipate and prepare for additional movement.

- Percuss the chest for:
  - Tympany
  - Resonancy
- Auscultate heart sounds for:
  - Rate
  - Rhythm
  - Quality
- Inspect the abdomen for:
  - Surface trauma (lacerations, abrasions, ecchymoses, and contusions)
  - Impaled objects
  - Exposed abdominal contents
  - Scars
  - Distention
- Auscultate the abdomen for the presence of bowel sounds.
  - Suspect a paralytic ileus in the absence of bowel sounds. Bowel sounds may be difficult to assess in a busy, noisy trauma room.
- Palpate the abdomen gently in all four quadrants for:
  - Tenderness
  - Rigidity
- Palpate the lower abdomen gently for:
  - Bladder distention
  - Tenderness. Ask the verbal child to point with one finger to the painful area to localize symptoms.
- Inspect the pelvis for:
  - Surface trauma (contusions, lacerations, and abrasions)
- Palpate the pelvis for:
  - Stability
  - Tenderness. Any pain or displacement on palpation is indicative of a pelvic fracture.
  - Femoral pulses
- Inspect the external genitalia, urinary meatus, perineum, and rectum for:
  - Surface trauma (contusions, lacerations, and abrasions)
  - Bleeding. Blood at the urinary meatus may signify a urethral injury; therefore, an indwelling bladder catheter is not inserted.
  - Bruising
  - Foreign objects

- Priapism, indicating spinal cord injury
- Assist with testing of rectal sphincter tone (usually completed by the trauma surgeon) by preparing the child for the examination.
- Inspect the musculoskeletal extremities for:
  - Surface trauma (abrasions and contusions)
  - Deformities
  - Edema
  - Open wounds
  - Bleeding
  - Impaled objects
- Assess the neurovascular status.
  - Skin temperature
  - Color
  - Capillary refill
  - Equality and amplitude of peripheral pulses compared with central pulses
  - Sensation. Ask the verbal child to describe if the toes and fingers are being touched. Observe the nonverbal child for withdrawal on touch to the toes and fingers to validate neuromotor integrity.
- Assess neuromotor integrity and strength.
  - Ask the verbal child to wiggle the fingers and toes.
  - Perform hand grips and foot flexion and extension with the verbal child.
- ❑ Inspect posterior surfaces.
  - Cautiously logroll the child to the side as a single unit. If possible, rolling should be done away from the side of obvious injury.
    - One member of the trauma team should be assigned to maintain neutral cervical stabilization and should function as the lead communicator during logrolling.
    - Assess motor and neurovascular status before and after the back inspection.
  - Inspect the posterior surface of the body for:
    - Deformity
    - Surface trauma (abrasions, lacerations, contusions, and ecchymoses). Bruising in the flank area may indicate renal trauma.
    - Impaled objects
    - Open wounds
    - Penetrating wounds
  - Palpate each vertebra for:
    - Stability

- Tenderness
  - Palpate the entire surface of the back for:
    - Deformity
    - Tenderness
  - Inspect the posterior aspect of each extremity for:
    - Surface trauma (abrasions, lacerations, contusions, and ecchymoses)
    - Impaled objects

Psychosocial Assessment

❑ Assess the child and family's coping strategies.

❑ Assess the child and family's understanding of the injury and treatment.

Triage of the Pediatric Trauma Patient

The injured child may be triaged several times and by several different methods, guidelines, or scoring tools immediately after the injury. Fundamental to trauma care is a triage process to ensure that the right patient goes to the right place at the right time. Matching trauma resources with patient need is essential and potentially lifesaving.

Optimal triage for appropriate pediatric trauma care requires established guidelines, which vary among hospitals, regions, and states. Established triage guidelines are required for:

❑ Prehospital transport decisions (Chapter 8)

❑ Interfacility transfer (Chapter 8)

❑ Trauma team activation

❑ Emergency department triage

❑ Disaster management (Chapter 43)

Trauma scoring is an objective method for determining injury severity. On the basis of the trauma score and according to established guidelines, the injured child may be admitted to a trauma center. The two most common trauma scores used in pediatrics are the Revised Trauma Score (RTS) and the Pediatric Trauma Score (PTS).

❑ The RTS is an adult score that can be used in children. It is comprised of the respiratory rate, systolic blood pressure, and GCS score.

❑ The PTS is exclusive to pediatrics.
  - It combines physiologic and anatomic measures to assess the severity of injury (airway, systolic blood pressure, central nervous system status, skeletal fractures, and cutaneous injuries).
  - The PTS values range from -6 to 12; PTS of 8 or

less in injured children may suggest that care should be provided in a pediatric trauma center.[14,15]

Nursing Interventions

1. Assess and maintain airway and cervical spine stabilization.
   - Open and maintain the airway while the cervical spine is manually stabilized in a neutral position:
     - Ask the conscious child to open the mouth.
     - Open the unconscious child's mouth with the jaw thrust maneuver while maintaining cervical spine stabilization.
     - Place a small pad under the upper back and shoulders of the younger child to balance the flexion created by the child's large occiput.
     - Avoid movement of the neck, because spinal cord injury may occur.
   - Suction the mouth and upper airway with a large rigid tonsil suction in the presence of debris, blood, or secretions.
     - Avoid deep oral suctioning, because stimulation of the posterior pharynx, larynx, or trachea may cause vagal stimulation with resultant bradycardia.
   - Insert an airway adjunct in conjunction with the jaw thrust maneuver in the unconscious child who is unable to maintain a patent airway.
     - Insert an oropharyngeal airway.
     - Insert a nasopharyngeal airway in the absence of head injury. A nasopharyngeal airway is better tolerated in the conscious patient but generally is not used in the pediatric trauma patient when a basilar or cribriform plate fracture is suspected because of the risk of entry in the cranial vault.
   - Prepare for oral endotracheal intubation while maintaining cervical spine stabilization. The nasotracheal route is contraindicated because:
     - It is difficult to insert an endotracheal tube blindly through the pediatric vocal cords.
     - It is associated with adenoid tissue trauma.
     - There is a risk of insertion into the cranial vault through a cribriform fracture.
   - Endotracheal intubation is indicated in the pediatric trauma patient when:[7]
     - A functional or anatomic airway obstruction is present.
     - The GCS or modified GCS score is 8 or less.
     - There is a need for prolonged ventilatory support.

- Respiratory arrest occurs.
- Hypoxemia occurs despite administration of supplemental oxygen.
- Prepare for rapid-sequence induction; when indicated, it is a useful adjunct for the skilled, trained clinician.
- Insert an orogastric tube or a nasogastric tube (in the absence of basilar skull fracture) to prevent gastric distention and restricted ventilation.
- Prepare for needle cricothyrotomy or tracheostomy for children in whom airway control is not possible because of craniofacial injuries.
- Maintain cervical and spinal stabilization until evaluation of the cervical spine is completed.
  - Because of the young child's large head-to-torso ratio, either elevation of the back from a commercially available pediatric spinal stabilization board or placement of a towel under the shoulders will enhance the optimal head and neck position for cervical neutrality.[4]
  - Maintain immobilization of the infant or child arriving restrained in an infant car seat. Carefully remove the infant or child, maintaining spinal protection.[4]
  - Maintain complete spinal immobilization.
  - Apply commercially available cervical collar using manufacturer's instructions.
  - Towel rolls or commercially available immobilization devices are used to prevent lateral cervical movement.
  - Commercially available immobilization devices for pediatrics provide complete spinal immobilization in young children; long backboards or short backboards also can be used to complete the immobilization process.
- Follow institutional guidelines for need for radiographs or ultrasound examination: Emergency and trauma centers vary in use of radiography to evaluate trauma victims.[3] Avoiding unnecessary radiography is important, especially for children, because of risks associated with their lifetime exposure to radiographs.
  - Lateral radiographs are taken to assess for gross malalignment or distraction; C1 through C7 should be included, as well as the C7-T1 junction.
  - Obtain anterior-posterior and lateral views of the thoracic and lumbar spine, as ordered.

2. Initiate measures to assess and maintain breathing.
   - Administer supplemental 100% oxygen through a nonrebreather mask to the patient who has a patent airway and effective respiratory effort (adequate bilateral, symmetric chest rise, and air entry without central cyanosis).
   - Obtain and monitor oxygen saturation measurements to determine the adequacy of oxygenation. Detect percentage of oxygen saturation in the blood and then trend to assess breathing effectiveness.
   - Initiate artificial ventilation with a bag-mask and 100% supplemental oxygen in the presence of apnea or ineffective respiratory effort. Maintain oxygen saturation levels at better than 95%.
   - Prepare for endotracheal intubation in the patient whose respiratory effectiveness has not improved with administration of supplemental oxygen.
   - Prepare for mechanical ventilation when a prolonged need for control of airway and breathing is anticipated.
   - Prepare for thoracostomy and chest tube insertion in the presence of hemothorax, pneumothorax, or hemopneumothorax.

3. Initiate measures to maintain circulation.
   - Perform continuous cardiorespiratory, oxygen saturation, and blood pressure monitoring.
   - Apply direct pressure to control external hemorrhage.
   - Obtain vascular access with one or two short, large-bore intravenous catheters, preferably in the upper extremities, in the child with suspected moderate to major trauma:
     - Prepare for intraosseous infusion if vascular access is not rapidly achievable.
     - Obtain blood specimens for laboratory analysis. Individualize the tests to match patient assessment.
     - When shock is suspected, a warmed fluid bolus of 20 mL/kg of crystalloid is given.
   - Provide rapid volume replacement in the child with signs of compensated or uncompensated shock.
     - Reassess the child for signs of improvement (heart rate, mentation, capillary refill, and blood pressure).
     - Administer a second bolus of 20 mL/kg of a crystalloid solution if symptoms of shock persist. Reassess the child for signs of improvement.
     - After two to three boluses, anticipate administration of a bolus of warmed O-negative packed red

blood cells (10 mL/kg). Blood transfusion is a lifesaving measure in the presence of significant blood loss. Results of compatibility studies for blood should not delay transfusion of blood. Rapidly administered, warmed, O-negative packed red blood cells will suffice until type-specific blood is available.[7] Anticipate that other blood products may be required after multiple units of administration of packed red cells. Follow institutional massive transfusion policy as indicated.

- Begin cardiopulmonary resuscitation in the child whose pulse is absent or inadequate.
  - Thoracotomy and open cardiac massage are rarely indicated in the pediatric victim of blunt trauma arrest; prognosis is poor.[16]
- Control external hemorrhage with pressure dressings.
- Insert an indwelling urinary bladder catheter in the absence of genitourinary trauma.
  - Measure urinary output
  - Prepare sample for urinalysis

4. Assess and maintain neurologic functioning.
  - Perform ongoing neurologic assessments to identify signs of increasing intracranial pressure in head-injured children.
    - Changes in level of consciousness
    - Vomiting and irritability
    - Disorientation
    - Seizures
  - Prepare to follow institutional guidelines regarding severe pediatric head injury (Chapter 29).[17,18]

5. Promote thermoregulation.
  - Obtain ongoing core temperature measurements (oral, rectal, or bladder).
  - Initiative passive warming measures.
    - Apply warming blankets
    - Increase ambient room temperature
    - Apply overhead heating lights
  - Initiate active warming measures.
    - Administer warmed intravenous fluid

6. Provide ongoing psychosocial support to the injured child and family (Chapter 26).
  - Offer the family the opportunity to accompany their child to other hospital areas, such as the computed tomography scan or radiology department. Even a few moments together provides much-needed reassurance to the child and family.
  - Prepare the child and family for transfer to a trauma center, as needed (Chapter 8).

7. Perform additional interventions as needed.
  - Prepare to splint or cast deformed and fractured extremities.
    - Monitor motor and neurovascular status before and after splinting and casting.
  - Prepare for suturing and wound care.
  - Begin treatment of the amputated wound and part.
    - Amputations are either partial (limb or digit attached) or complete (limb or digit removed). Complete amputations are either the guillotine type (clean, well-defined edges that enhance reattachment) or the crush-avulsion type (irregular separation with additional soft tissue, bone, nerve, and vascular trauma that may contraindicate reattachment). The amputated part is wrapped in sterile gauze moistened with normal saline solution, placed in a labeled container, and then placed in an ice water bath. The window of time for reimplantation varies by amputated part and is optimized by appropriate cooling measures.[19]
    - Assess the stump for neurovascular integrity and bleeding.
  - Prepare for diagnostic testing.
    - Radiographs
    - Focused assessment sonography in trauma (FAST) may be useful for intra-abdominal fluid or pericardial tamponade. FAST usage in pediatric trauma is controversial. Few studies on the efficacy of ultrasound examination have been reported.[5]
    - Computed tomography scan
    - Other tests (i.e., angiography, xenon studies)

8. Provide age-appropriate distraction measures and administer medications, as prescribed.
  - Tetanus immunization
  - Antibiotics
  - Analgesics (Chapter 11)

9. Initiate consultations with other health care professionals.
  - Social services
  - Chaplain services
  - Child life specialists
  - Medical subspecialists

10. Prepare for transfer and transport to a trauma center (Chapter 8) or hospital admission.

11. Initiate support measures for the family whose child dies in the emergency department (Chapter 26).

Conclusion

Timely assessment of and interventions for the injured child may mean the difference between a functional or devastating outcome. Nurses function in many different roles in trauma teams, including those of leadership, documenter, and bedside caregivers. Trauma and emergency nurses must be prepared to care for injured children and their families. Participation in ongoing educational activities, such as mock trauma codes and simulation exercises, may help enhance assessment and intervention skills.

References

1. Moulton, S. (2000). Early management of the child with multiple injuries. *Clinical Orthopaedics and Related Research, 376,* 6–14.

2. Dilley, A. (2006). Pediatric thoracic trauma. In D. Wesson (Ed.), *Pediatric trauma* (pp. 245–246). New York: Taylor & Francis.

3. Letton, R. (2006). The ABCs of pediatric trauma. In D. Wesson (Ed.), *Pediatric trauma* (pp. 43–58). New York: Taylor & Francis.

4. Emergency Nurses Association. (2004). *Emergency nursing pediatric course (provider manual)* (3rd ed., pp. 82, 117–140). Des Plaines, IL: Author.

5. Advanced Trauma Life Support. (2004). *Advanced trauma life support (provider manual)* (pp. 250–251). Chicago: Author.

6. American Heart Association. (2006). *Pediatric advanced life support (provider manual)* (pp. 61–71). Dallas, TX: Author.

7. American Heart Association (1997). *Textbook of pediatric advanced life support.* Dallas, TX: Author

8. Emergency Nurses Association. (2007). *Trauma nursing core course (provider manual)* (pp. 33–49). Des Plaines, IL: Author.

9. Emergency Nurses Association. (2004). *Emergency nursing pediatric course (provider manual)* (3rd ed., pp. 41–53). Des Plaines, IL: Author.

10. Waltzman, M., & Mooney, D. (2006). Major trauma. In G. Fleisher, S. Ludwig, & F. Henretig (Eds.), *Textbook of pediatric emergency medicine* (5th ed., pp. 1349–1355). Philadelphia: Lippincott Williams & Wilkins.

11. Emergency Nurses Association. (2001). *Position Statement: Family presence at the bedside during invasive procedures and resuscitation.* Des Plaines, IL: Author.

12. Neuman, M., & Eirkson, E. (2006). Facial trauma. In G. Fleisher, S. Ludwig, & F. Henretig (Eds.), *Textbook of pediatric emergency medicine* (5th ed., pp. 1480). Philadelphia: Lippincott Williams & Wilkins.

13. Curan, C., Dietrich, A., Bowman, M., Ginn-Pease, M., & King, D. (1995). Pediatric cervical-spine immobilization: Achieving neutral position? *Journal of Trauma, 39,* 729–732.

14. Eichelberger, M., Gotschall, C., Sacco, W, Bowman, L., Mangubat, E., & Lowenstein, A. (1989). A comparison of the Trauma Score, the Revised Trauma Score, and the Pediatric Trauma Score. *Annals of Emergency Medicine, 18,* 939–942.

15. Furnival, R., & Schunk, J. (1999). ABCs of scoring systems for pediatric trauma. *Pediatric Emergency Care, 15*(3), 215–223.

16. Clemence, B. (2000). Emergency department thoracotomy: Nursing implications for pediatric cases. *International Journal of Trauma Nursing, 6,* 123–127.

17. Adelson, P., Bratton, S. L., Carney, N. A., Chesnut, R. M., du Coudray, H., Goldstein B., et al., American Association for Surgery for Surgery of Trauma; Child Neurology Society; International Society for Pediatric Neurosurgery; International Trauma Anesthesia and Critical Care Society; Society of Critical Care Medicine; World Federation of Pediatric Intensive and Critical Care Societies. (2003). Guidelines for the acute medical management of severe traumatic brain injury in infants, children, and adolescents. *Pediatric Critical Care Medicine, 4*(3), S1–S71.

18. Xing, W., Jin, H., Liangfu, Z., Chaowei, F., Guozhen, H., Yehan, W., et al. (2008). Epidemiology of traumatic brain injury in Eastern China, 2004: A prospective large case study. *Journal of Trauma, 64,* 1313–1319.

19. Gray, A. (2006). Pediatric orthopedic trauma. In D. Wesson (Ed.), *Pediatric trauma* (pp. 332–334). New York: Taylor & Francis.

TWENTY-NINE

Head Trauma/ Traumatic Brain Injury

Christine Nelson-Tuttle, DNS, RNC, PNP
Rebecca Roloff, RN, MSN, SANE-A, SANE-P
Steven J. Dasta, RN, BSN

Introduction

Traumatic brain injuries are the most common injuries in childhood. Traumatic brain injury is the leading cause of death among injured children. Most deaths occur within the first 4 hours after injury. It has been reported that 60% to 80% of children with multiple injuries sustain head injuries. Children are at greatest risk when they are under 5 years of age or during adolescence. In children and adolescents who have a moderate or severe head injury, a permanent disability injury may develop such as seizure disorders, cognitive impairment, learning disorders, and behavioral and emotional problems.[1] Thorough assessment with prompt nursing interventions is crucial in decreasing the potential permanent adverse outcomes. Table 29.1 outlines common pediatric head injuries.

Phases of Injury

There are two phases of brain injury:

❒ Primary injury occurs at impact when traumatic forces are applied to the brain, and the brain comes into contact with the interior skull.[2] Resulting injuries include contusions, skull fractures, and diffuse axonal injury.[2]

❒ Secondary injury occurs as the sequela of the injured brain and includes injuries such as cerebral edema, hypoxia, or increased intracranial pressure.[2]

Guidelines for treating children with head injury are controversial and are evolving. The decisions made during the initial minutes of management often influence the child's outcome.

Pediatric Considerations

Selected anatomic and physiologic features affect injuries to the brain.

❒ Children up to approximately 3 years of age have skulls that are pliable and thinner and have nonfused cranial sutures. Therefore, blunt forces applied to the skull cause more local brain injury[2] because energy is absorbed by the brain and not the skull.

■ The nonfused sutures allow intracranial expansions in the presence of increased intracranial pressure (ICP).

■ Management of increased ICP (ICP greater than 15 to 20 mm Hg) should not be delayed because of this anatomic difference.

❒ The intact and open ventricles and cisterns are essential to cerebral integrity. If they are compressed or invisible on a computed tomography (CT) scan, the prognosis is poor.

❒ The central nervous system has a limited ability for regeneration. Children, though, tend to have better outcomes than adults after severe head injury, although the exact reason for this difference is unclear.[3]

❒ Children have relatively large heads and weak neck musculature; therefore, the head is more likely to sustain impact injuries. Children, unlike adults, may have hemorrhagic shock from head trauma and subsequent blood loss. Because of the large head size in proportion to the body, it is possible for the child to have hypovolemia from an isolated skull fracture.[4]

TABLE 29.1 Common Types of Head Injury

Injury	Description	Signs and Symptoms
Linear skull fracture	Nondepressed fracture of the skull along or perpendicular to a suture line; can be diastatic (separation of sutures), resulting in a "growing" fracture	Fracture site pain and tenderness; swelling; cephalhematoma at fracture site
Basilar skull fracture	Fracture of the bones at the skull base	Headache; altered GCS score; otorrhea (blood or cerebrospinal fluid); hemotympanum; Battle's sign (suggests a mastoid fracture); raccoon's eyes (due to intraorbital bleeding from fracture); agitation; irritability
Depressed skull fracture	Fracture of the skull from a direct blow; can be "ping pong" (indentation in the infant skull)	Altered GCS score (may not always be present); palpable depression at the fracture site; laceration or abrasion of scalp
Concussion	Closed head injury from direct blow or deceleration	Usually no localizing signs; occasionally nausea, vomiting, headache, brief alteration in level of consciousness, amnesia, dizziness
Diffuse axonal injuries	Diffuse white matter damage resulting typically from acceleration-deceleration injuries	Altered level of consciousness
Intracranial bleeding	Vascular injuries resulting in hematoma (intracerebral, subdural, or epidural) or subarachnoid hemorrhage, caused by direct blows to head or violent shaking	Altered level of consciousness, unilateral dilated pupil (sometimes a late sign indicative of herniation); headache; seizures; changes in vital signs; vomiting; irritability. Intracranial bleeding may progress slowly; symptoms may develop hours to days after the injury.

Etiology

- ❑ Blunt forces—energy is transmitted to the brain.
  - Bicycle crashes
  - Motor vehicle crashes
  - Motorcycle crashes
  - Sports (e.g., football, helmet to helmet)
  - Falls from heights to non-yielding surfaces
  - Auto-pedestrian collisions
  - Intentional acts (e.g., abusive head trauma)
  - Acts of violence (e.g., blunt forces to the head)
  - Play activities (e.g., sledding)
- ❑ Penetrating forces—energy is applied directly to the brain.
  - Impalement or other penetrating objects (e.g., lawn darts)
  - Gunshot wounds
  - Knife wounds

- ❑ Acceleration-deceleration forces
  - Motor vehicle crashes
  - Sports activities
  - Falls
  - Intentional acts (e.g., abusive head trauma)
- ❑ Crushing forces
  - Pedestrian-motor vehicle crashes
  - Farm equipment or machinery
  - Animal bites

Focused History

Mechanism of Injury

- ❑ Bicycle crash
  - Presence of helmet; condition of helmet after injury (e.g., intact or broken)
  - Speed and type of oncoming vehicle
  - Speed of bicycle
  - Stationary object struck (e.g., tree or car)

❏ Motorcycle crash
- Presence of helmet
- Speed and type of oncoming vehicle
- Speed of motorcycle
- Stationary object struck (e.g., tree or car)

❏ Sports-related injury
- Use of protective equipment, including helmet
- Type of sport

❏ Fall from height to non-yielding surface
- Height from which the child fell
- Surface on which the child fell

❏ Pedestrian incident
- Speed of vehicle

❏ Child maltreatment (Chapter 44)

❏ Play activities:
- Type of activity

❏ Gunshot wound
- Type of weapon
- Caliber of bullet
- Distance or range from which bullet was fired

❏ Penetrating wound
- Type of penetrating object
- Impaled or removed before EMS arrival

❏ Crushing force
- Type of farm equipment or machinery
- Type of animal (e.g., horse)

Neurologic Symptoms Following the Injury

❏ Loss of consciousness after the injury event
❏ Continued loss of consciousness or altered Glasgow Coma Scale (GCS) score (mental status changes)
❏ Pupillary changes
❏ Visual disturbances
❏ Vomiting
❏ Seizure activity
❏ Headache
❏ Decreased activity level
❏ Amnesia to the event or ongoing amnesia (short term)
❏ Weakness
❏ Neck pain

Injury-Related Information

❏ Witnesses
❏ Prehospital treatment

Focused Assessment

Physical Assessment

❏ Assess the airway, respiratory, and cardiovascular systems (Chapter 28).
❏ Assess the neurologic system.
- Assess the level of consciousness with the GCS, pediatric GCS, or AVPU method (*A*lert; responds to *V*erbal stimuli; responds to *P*ain; *U*nresponsive).
  - Changes of 2 points in the GCS score indicate potential hypovolemia, hypoxia, or increased ICP. Sudden changes may demand immediate intervention.
  - Score values indicate the following severity of head injury.[5]

TABLE 29.2 Severity Classification for Head Injuries	
Mild	No loss of consciousness
	Normal physical examination results
	Initial GCS score 15
	Minor soft-tissue injuries
Moderate	Loss of consciousness < 5 minutes
	Normal physical examination results
	Initial GCS score 13–15
Severe	Loss of consciousness > 5 minutes
	One or more high-risk criteria
	GCS score < 13

Notes: From Jarvis.[6]

- Serial documentation of the GCS score and pupillary responses provide ongoing assessment for intracranial hemorrhage, increased ICP, and brain stem herniation.
- Each assessment, especially the GCS score, will be useful for the neurosurgeon to determine appropriate treatment guidelines for ICP management.
- Assess the pupils for:
  - Equality
  - Size
  - Reactivity to light and accommodation

- Assess neuromuscular activity.
  - Gait
  - Upper and lower extremity strength
  - Movement or posturing
- Assess the child's activity level and response to the emergency department (ED) environment.
- Assess for signs of increased ICP, which can occur very quickly in head trauma.
  - Hypotension and hypoxia related to inadequate airway and breathing or brain stem injury contribute to hypercapnia, hyperemia, and increased ICP.
  - Elevation in ICP from hypoxia can be delayed.
  - Cushing response: A triad of hypertension, bradycardia, and irregular respirations.
  - Decerebrate or decorticate posturing.
  - Seizures (may or may not be related to increased ICP).
- Observe for signs of cerebrospinal fluid leakage (suggestive of a basilar skull fracture).
  - Otorrhea
  - Rhinorrhea
- Inspect the face and head for:
  - Surface trauma (lacerations, contusions, and ecchymoses)
  - Battle's sign (ecchymoses in the mastoid area)
  - Raccoon's eyes (periorbital ecchymoses)
- Palpate the head for:
  - Step-offs
  - Depressions
  - Elevations
- Perform (or assist with) an otoscopic evaluation to detect hemotympanum.

❑ Assess the remaining body systems (Chapter 5).

Psychosocial Assessment

❑ Assess the child's and family's coping strategies.

❑ Assess the child's and family's understanding of the child's head injury.

Nursing Interventions for the Child with a Severe Head Injury

1. Assess and maintain the airway with the jaw thrust maneuver or through insertion of an oral airway while maintaining cervical spine immobilization and stabilization.
   - Prepare for orotracheal intubation with rapid-sequence induction to minimize coughing, agitation, and movement that could increase the ICP. The orotracheal route is preferred because of the possibility of a cribriform plate fracture.[6]
   - Perform a brief neurologic assessment before the induction as a guide to future treatment.

2. Administer 100% oxygen by bag-mask ventilation.
   - Although hyperventilation with 100% oxygen has become controversial, it may be initiated in the child with severe head injury. Hyperventilation decreases ICP by cerebral vasoconstriction and a decrease in cerebral blood volume. The potential adverse consideration is the possibility of ischemia to brain tissue from the decreased cerebral blood flow.[7]
     - The $PaCO_2$ is maintained at approximately 30–35 mmHg.[2] A lower $PaCO_2$ results in an increased pH and decreased cerebral tissue acidosis; arterioles constrict, decreasing cerebral blood flow, cerebral blood volume, and ICP.[8] SaO_2 should be maintained at greater than 90%.
     - Caution must be used with hyperventilation, because excessive arteriolar constriction may result, which limits not only cerebral blood flow but also cerebral perfusion, causing hypoxic injury to an already compromised brain.
   - Prepare for mechanical ventilation.

3. Obtain venous access and initiate an intravenous infusion.
   - Administer isotonic intravenous fluids in the child with head injury and signs of hypovolemic shock.
     - Never administer 5% dextrose or 10% dextrose in water.
   - The higher priority in management is maintaining adequate circulation and perfusion. More damage can be done if the patient has a decreased vascular volume and hypotension.
   - Osmotic agents such as mannitol may be ordered for patients with severe head injuries resulting in cerebral edema and intracranial hypertension.[9]
     - These agents remove free water from brain cells within an intact blood-brain barrier.[8]
     - Intravenous mannitol may be administered once an indwelling bladder catheter is placed, blood pressure and perfusion are adequate, and there is evidence of increased ICP.
   - Obtain blood specimens for laboratory analysis, such as an ethanol level or toxicology screening, as needed.

4. Measure the child's level of consciousness and neurologic responses.

5. Maintain normothermia during the ED treatment.

6. Perform ongoing assessments of the child's cardiopulmonary, oxygen saturation, and neurologic statuses.

   ▪ These assessments allow early detection of intracranial hemorrhage, increased ICP, and brain stem herniation.

   ▪ A deteriorating neurologic state in any child with an acute brain insult should be considered a life-threatening condition.

7. Insert an orogastric tube to prevent gastric distention.

8. Insert an indwelling bladder catheter to measure urinary output.

9. Prepare for diagnostic testing, such as CT scanning without contrast.

   ▪ CT scanning is widely used to identify acute intracranial injury. If the ventricles and cisterns are compressed or invisible on the CT scan, morbidity and mortality are expected.

10. Prepare for operative management.

    ▪ Pediatric patients with severe traumatic brain injury are more likely to have diffuse severe cerebral edema than adults. Only 15% to 20% of children with head injury require surgical intervention.[10]

11. Inform the family frequently about the child's condition and results of diagnostic tests.

    ▪ Present the option for family presence (Chapter 26).

12. Provide emotional support to the child and family.

13. Initiate consultations with social services, neurosurgery, and other specialists, as needed.

14. Prepare for transfer or transport to a trauma center (Chapter 8) or admission to the hospital.

Nursing Interventions for the Child with a Mild Head Injury

1. Perform ongoing neurologic assessments. Observe for signs of increased ICP, such as vomiting and changes in level of consciousness.

2. Prepare for diagnostic procedures, such as radiographs and CT scan.

3. Inform the family frequently about the child's condition.

4. Administer an analgesic (e.g., acetaminophen), as prescribed.

5. Provide emotional support to the child and family.

6. Prepare for hospitalization for observation or discharge to home.

Home Care and Prevention

Many head injuries can be prevented through the proper use of protective equipment during play and sports activities. Reinforcement with coaches and adults who supervise sports activities is essential.

Parents should be prepared for changes in their child's usual behavior after a head injury, such as changes in sleep patterns, bad dreams, emotional lability, difficulty staying on task, learning problems, and short-term memory loss.[11] Parents of a child with a mild head injury should be instructed to observe their child every 2 hours for the first 24 hours after injury for changes in the level of consciousness, the child's ability to talk, and movement.[12] Parents can be encouraged to provide quiet activities for the child, such as board games, reading, videos, or puzzles. Acetaminophen may be prescribed for headache.

Parents should contact the emergency department or their primary care physician if the child exhibits any of these symptoms in the first few days after a mild head injury:[12]

❒ Severe headaches not relieved with analgesics

❒ Persistent vomiting (more than three times in 24 hours)

❒ Projectile vomiting

❒ Confusion, restless, excessive sleepiness, or a change in personality

❒ Seizure activity

❒ Uncoordinated gait or balance; weakness

❒ Difficulty eating

❒ Rhinorrhea or otorrhea

Nurses should give careful care directions for parents of young athletes having a second concussion soon after a first concussion (second impact syndrome) because of the cumulative effect of these injuries. This type of injury can result in acute brain swelling, significant neurologic or cognitive deficits, or sometimes death. The child should be removed from sports participation (including physical education class) for a minimum of 7 days to the entire sports season, depending on the severity of the concussion and the extent and duration of the neurologic symptoms.[13]

Parents should be taught about postconcussive syndrome, which usually lasts 4 to 6 weeks and includes symptoms such as memory loss, headaches, fatigue, mood changes, sleep changes, and difficulty in remembering directions and activities.[14] The child needs supervision for safe behaviors.[14] Parents can help their child to recover by being patient, taking extra time with the child, giving the child extra help, and providing quiet times for work and school. Follow-up visits with the child's primary care physician should be scheduled, and discussions with the child's school nurse and teacher about the child's learning needs should occur before the child reenters school.[14]

Parents whose children sustain a severe head injury may expect a longer rehabilitation process or permanent cognitive and emotional changes. However, the permanent level of function after a head injury is not determined in the ED setting.

Conclusion

Head injuries are a common phenomenon requiring ED treatment. Ongoing assessments and interventions are crucial to detecting early changes in ICP. Home care after a mild head injury is augmented with instructions for the parents and caregivers.

References

1. Adekoya, N., Thurman, D. L., White, D. D., & Webb, K. W. (2002). Surveillance for traumatic brain injury deaths—United States, 1989–1998. *Morbidity and Mortality Weekly Report, 51*(SS-10), 1–14.

2. Greenes, D., & Madsen, J. (2000). Neurotrauma. In G. Fleisher & S. Ludwig (Eds.), *Textbook of pediatric emergency medicine* (4th ed., pp. 1271–1296). Philadelphia: Lippincott Williams & Wilkins.

3. Anderson, V., Catroppa, C., Morse, S., Haritou, F., & Rosenfeld, J. (2000). Recovery of intellectual ability following traumatic brain injury in childhood: Impact of injury severity and age at injury. *Pediatric Neurosurgery, 32*(6), 282–290.

4. Sacchetti, A., Belfer, R., & Doolin, E. (2001). Pediatric trauma. In P. Ferrera, S. Colucciello, J. Marx, V. Verdile, & M. Gibbs (Eds.), *Trauma management* (pp. 504–532). St. Louis, MO: Mosby-Year Book.

5. Schutzman, S. A., & Greenes, D. S. (2001). Pediatric minor head injury. *Annals of Emergency Medicine, 27*(1), 65–74.

6. Jarvis, D. A. (2008). Head injury. In A. Lalani & S. Schneeweiss (Eds.), *Handbook of pediatric emergency medicine* (pp. 43–49). Boston: Jones and Bartlett.

7. Stochetti, N., Maas, A., Chleregato, A., & van der Plas, A. (2005). Hyperventilation in head injury. *Chest, 127,* 1812–1827.

8. Adelson, P. D., Bratton, S. L., Carney, N. A., Chesnut, R. M., du Coudray, H. E., Goldstein, B., et al. (2003). Guidelines for the acute medical management of severe traumatic brain injury in infants, children, and adolescents. Chapter 6. Threshold for treatment of intracranial hypertension. *Pediatric Critical Care Medicine, 4*(3 Suppl), S25–S27.

9. Knapp, J. (2005). Hyperosmolar therapy in the treatment of severe head injury in children: Mannitol and hypertonic saline. *AACN Clinical Issues, 16*(2), 199–211.

10. Giza, C., Mink, R., & Madikians, A. (2007). Pediatric traumatic brain injury: Not just little adults. *Current Opinions in Critical Care, 13,* 143–152.

11. Michaud, L. J., Semes-Concepcion, J., Duhaime, A. C., & Lazar, M. F. (2002). Traumatic brain injury. In M. L. Batshaw (Ed.), *Children with disabilities* (5th ed., pp. 525–545). Baltimore: Brookes.

12. Cook, R., Schweer, L., Shebesta, K., Hartjes, K., & Falcone, R. (2006). Mild traumatic brain injury in children: Just another bump on the head? *Journal of Trauma Nursing, 13*(2), 58–65.

13. Guskiewicz, K. M., Weaver, N. L., Padua, D. A., & Garrett, W. E. (2000). Epidemiology of concussion in collegiate and high school football players. *American Journal of Sports Medicine, 28*(5), 643–650.

14. Bishop, N. B. (2006). Traumatic brain injury: A primer for primary care physicians. *Current Problems in Pediatrics and Adolescent Healthcare, 36,* 318–331.

Spinal Cord Trauma

Christine Nelson-Tuttle, DNS, RNC, PNP
Rebecca Roloff, RN, MSN, SANE-A, SANE-P
Steven J. Dasta, RN, BSN

Introduction

Spinal column and spinal cord injuries are uncommon in the pediatric population. Children are more likely to sustain head trauma than cervical spine injury. Unfortunately, there are significant morbidity and mortality associated with spinal cord injuries in children, and immediate care is crucial to decrease sequelae.[1]

Spinal injury can occur in the cervical, thoracic, lumbar, or sacral spine regions (Table 30.1) and can include concussions, contusions, lacerations, transections, and hemorrhage. Blood vessel injury can result in a direct injury to the cord itself.[2] Selected injuries are listed in Table 30.2. These injuries result from:[3]

❏ Hyperextension (fracture and dislocation of the posterior elements)

❏ Hyperflexion (fracture or dislocation of the vertebral bodies, disks, or ligaments)

❏ Vertical compression (shattering fractures)

❏ Rotational forces (fractures and rupture of supporting ligaments)

Younger children tend to have fractures of the upper cervical region, whereas older children and adolescents more often have fractures involving the lower cervical spine area.

Pediatric Considerations

Spinal injuries in children are related to the following anatomic differences:

❏ The infant's spine is composed mostly of cartilage, and the intervertebral disk spaces appear wide in relation to the vertebral bodies.[8] As the child grows, the vertebral bodies ossify, and the amount of cartilage decreases.[8] Children younger than 9 years of age are susceptible to cervical spine injuries because of the large head size in proportion to the body, weak neck musculature, and horizontal facets.[9]

❏ The spine is more elastic and mobile, causing dislocation and spontaneous realignment without bony or ligamental disruption.[6] The wedge-shaped vertebrae are prone to forward slipping between adjacent vertebrae.[10]

❏ The level of maximum flexion in the cervical spine descends as the child grows older. Maximum flexion occurs at C2–C3 in infants and young children, at C3–C4 in children 5 to 6 years of age, and at C5–C6 in adolescents.[12,13]

❏ Spinal cord injuries always are suspected in children with multiple injuries.

Etiology

❏ Blunt forces
- Pedestrian incidents
- Sports activities (more common in adolescents)
- Diving. Axial loading occurs when the weight of the body is compressed on the cervical spine.
- Child maltreatment
- Falls
- Motor vehicle crashes
- Acts of violence

❏ Penetrating forces
- Gunshot wounds
- Penetrating wounds

❏ Acceleration-deceleration forces
- Motor vehicle crashes
- Sports activities

TABLE 30.1 Spinal Cord Injury Characteristics

Region of Spine	Characteristics of Injuries
Cervical	Larger head and weaker neck musculature in children cause 60%–70% of cervical spine fractures in the C1–C2 range compared with 16% in adults.
	Injuries in C1–C2 segment cause respiratory arrest and death without ventilator support.
	Diaphragm function is present when injury is at or below C5 level.
	Some function of upper extremities may be possible when injury is at C6–C7 level.
	Sensory level is lost below sternum resulting in loss of sphincter function.
Thoracic	20% of spinal injuries in children 8–14 years of age.
	Functional capacity may likely include full use of upper extremities including intrinsic muscles of hands.
	Poor trunk balance.
Thoracolumbar	Good trunk balance.
	Good respiratory function.
	Full control of muscles in abdomen.
Lumbar	Most injuries occur at the L2–L4 level.
	Second most common area of injury in children.
	Frequent site of injuries sustained in motor vehicle crash when child is wearing lap belt.
	Loss of foot and ankle function.

Vogel, L., Hickey, K., Klass, S., & Anderson, C. (2004). Unique issues in pediatric spinal cord injury. *Orthopaedic Nursing, 23*(5), 300–308.
Calpin, C. (2008). Cervical spine injuries. In A. Lalani & S. Schneeweiss (Eds.), *Handbook of pediatric emergency medicine* (pp. 50–57). Boston: Jones and Bartlett.
Ball, J., & Binder, R. (2006). *Child health nursing: Partnering with children and families* (pp. 1297–1366). Upper Saddle River, NJ: Pearson Prentice Hall

TABLE 30.2 Selected Spinal Injuries

Spinal Injury	Description
Craniocervical dislocation	Diagnosed in younger children after acceleration-deceleration mechanism of injury. It is usually lethal, because it involves the high spinal cord and brain stem.
"Hangman fracture" (fracture of the posterior arch of the axis)	Occurs in older children; requires immobilization.
Thoracolumbar fractures	Compression fractures—occur with hyperflexion injuries, causing pain with sitting and on palpation. Treatment includes bed rest.
	Burst fractures—result from axial loading

Scully, T., & Luerssen, T. (1995). Spinal cord injuries. In W. Buntain (Ed.), *Management of pediatric trauma* (pp. 189–199). Philadelphia: Saunders.

❏ Crushing forces
- Animal bites
- Machinery
- Hangings

Focused History

Mechanism of Injury

❏ Pedestrian incidents
- Speed of vehicle

❏ Sports activity (more common in adolescents)
- Type of sport

❏ Diving
- Depth of water
- Type of surface struck (e.g., cement)

❏ Child maltreatment (Chapter 44)

❏ Fall
- Height from which child fell
- Yielding or unyielding surface

- ❐ Motor vehicle crash
  - ▪ Passenger or driver
  - ▪ Type of collision (head-on, T-bone, rear-end, or lateral)
  - ▪ Type of safety restraint used
  - ▪ Child's position in the car
  - ▪ Air bag deployment
- ❐ Act of violence
  - ▪ Perpetrator
  - ▪ Type of force used
- ❐ Gunshot wound
  - ▪ Type of weapon
  - ▪ Caliber of bullet
  - ▪ Distance from which bullets were fired
- ❐ Penetrating wound
  - ▪ Type of penetrating object
  - ▪ Impaled or removed
- ❐ Crushing wound
  - ▪ Hanging versus autoeroticism
  - ▪ Type of biting animal
  - ▪ Type of machinery

Neurologic Symptoms Following the Injury

- ❐ Loss of consciousness after the injury event
- ❐ Numbness or tingling in the fingers or toes
- ❐ Weakness or paralysis of the upper and/or lower extremities
- ❐ Priapism
- ❐ Loss of bowel or bladder control
- ❐ Loss of sphincter tone

Injury-Related Information

- ❐ Witnesses
- ❐ Prehospital treatment
- ❐ Report of hearing a "crack" or "snap" at the time of injury

Focused Assessment

Physical Assessment

- ❐ Assess the airway and respiratory system.
  - ▪ Assess the airway for:
    - • Patency

- ▪ Auscultate the chest for:
  - • Respiratory rate. Apnea or bradypnea indicates a high-level spinal cord or brain stem injury.
- ❐ Assess the circulatory system.
  - ▪ Auscultate the heart for:
    - • Rate. Tachycardia may be present with hypovolemic shock or anxiety; bradycardia may be present in spinal shock.
- ❐ Assess the neurologic system.
- ❐ Assess the level of consciousness with the Glasgow Coma Scale, pediatric Glasgow Coma Scale, or AVPU (*A*lert, responds to *V*erbal stimuli, responds to *P*ainful stimuli, *U*nresponsive) methods.
  - • Assess movement and strength of the extremities.
  - • Assess tendon reflexes.
  - ▪ Observe for signs of spinal cord injury. The symptoms of spinal cord injury are not easily discerned in young children and are variable depending on the child's age, the injury location, the spinal fracture stability, and other systemic injuries. Generally, signs of spinal cord injury include:
    - • Flaccid extremities
    - • Paralysis
    - • Numbness, tingling, and paresthesia
    - • Paresis
    - • Priapism
- ❐ Assess the abdomen.
  - ▪ Inspect the abdomen for ecchymosis or abrasions caused by use of a lap belt in a motor vehicle crash. Chance fracture (posterior transverse fracture through the lumbar vertebral bodies) should be suspected.
  - ▪ Assess the rectal tone (May alternately be done with back assessment.).
- ❐ Assess the back (performed during the secondary assessment [Chapter 28]).
  - ▪ Palpate the spinal column for tenderness, leaving the cervical collar intact.
  - ▪ Vertebral fractures may be detected.
  - ▪ Inspect the back for:
    - • Surface trauma
    - • Edema
    - • Deformities

Psychosocial Assessment

- ❐ Assess the child's and family's coping strategies.

❏ Assess the child's and family's understanding of the spinal cord injury.

- During emergency department (ED) treatment, the level of function may improve or worsen, and the prognosis usually is not known, causing stress and anxiety for the child and family.

Nursing Interventions

1. Assess and maintain the airway using the jaw thrust maneuver while maintaining cervical spinal immobilization.

   - Do not hyperextend, flex, or rotate the neck during these maneuvers. Infants and young children have a large occiput.
     - Positioning them supine on a backboard may cause their cervical vertebrae to flex and move anteriorly.
     - It may be necessary to place padding under the child's shoulders to bring the shoulders into horizontal alignment with the auditory meatus.[12]
     - All children should be assessed to assure that the head and neck are in proper alignment as no equipment can accommodate all individual needs.[13]
   - Prepare for endotracheal intubation in the child with a high cervical spinal cord injury.
   - Maintain spinal immobilization to prevent the worsening of an existing spinal cord injury.
     - Assume that any child with a head injury, who is unconscious, or who sustained multiple injuries has a spinal cord injury until proved otherwise.
   - Spinal immobilization must remain intact until diagnostic tests and patient assessment findings determine the absence of spinal cord injury. Nurses should be knowledgeable on the policies and procedures on spinal immobilization and removal of immobilization devices used in their specific institution.

2. Initiate measures to support respiratory effort.
   - Administer 100% oxygen via face mask or other means, as tolerated by the child.
   - Initiate bag-mask ventilation in the child with apnea or bradypnea.
   - Prepare for mechanical ventilation.
   - Initiate cardiorespiratory and oxygen saturation monitoring.

3. Obtain venous access and initiate an intravenous infusion.
   - Administer medications as prescribed.
   - Administer high-dose methylprednisolone (dosages used vary among institutions) within 6 to 8 hours after injury.

4. Perform serial cardiopulmonary and neurologic assessments to detect improvement or worsening in the child's condition. Assessment timing should be determined on the basis of patient condition and the policies of the individual institution.
   - Assess children with lower spinal cord injury for worsening of their respiratory and circulatory statuses, and perform serial neurologic assessments.
   - Neurogenic shock may accompany spinal cord injury (Chapter 38).
   - Perform careful and ongoing assessments for the nonverbal, unconscious, or multiply injured child, to exclude the possibility of spinal cord injury and to measure progression of cord edema.

5. Prepare for diagnostic tests including:
   - Radiographs of the lateral, anterior-posterior, and odontoid views of the cervical spine. In one study in eight children aged 9 to 68 months who fell fewer than 5 feet and sustained cervical spine fractures or cervical spinal cord injury, all had limited range of motion of the neck or neck pain. Therefore, young children who are asymptomatic after sustaining short falls may not require radiographic tests of the cervical spine.[14]
   - Radiographs of the anterior-posterior and lateral views of the thoracic and lumbar spine.
   - Flexion-extension radiographs of the cervical spine. These may be obtained by an experienced physician for the child who does not have vertebral or ligamentous disruption; the child should never move the neck past the range of comfort.[15]
   - Computed tomography scan
   - MRI

6. Insert a nasogastric or orogastric tube for gastric decompression.

7. Insert an indwelling bladder catheter for bladder decompression and measurement of urinary output.

8. Provide emotional support to the child and family.
   - The awake child may be very frightened by the ensuing neurologic symptoms and immobilization; continuous consolation by parents and assigned staff is indicated.
   - Use diversion techniques to console the distraught child while observing for facial grimace indicating

pain during vertebral palpation.

9. Inform the family frequently of the child's condition.

10. Initiate consultations with social services, neurosurgery, and other specialties, as needed.

11. Prepare for transfer and transport to a trauma center (Chapter 8); prepare for hospitalization.

Home Care and Prevention

Spinal cord injuries can be prevented by teaching children safety measures during sporting and diving activities. It is important to teach parents, coaches, and adults who supervise sports activities how to prevent injuries, including the player's use of proper equipment and the adult's removal of players from action when they complain of numbness, tingling, or electric shock sensations. The recent changes in rules prohibiting head-first contact of spearheading involving student football players has led to a dramatic decrease in the number of spinal cord injuries in these young athletes.[12]

Spinal Cord Injury Without Radiographic Abnormality

Unique to the pediatric age group is the phenomenon of spinal cord injury without radiographic abnormality (SCIWORA). A potential explanation for SCIWORA is related to the difference in elasticity between the spinal column and the spinal cord of children. The less elastic spinal cord is more prone to injury.[4] The distinctive anatomic and physiologic characteristics of younger children make them more likely to exhibit SCIWORA when compared with older children. Two thirds of SCIWORA cases occur in children aged 8 years and younger, including infants.[5]

The phenomenon is more common in the cervical and thoracic spine region and is rarely found in the lumbar spine. The injury is associated with the increased elasticity of the child's immature spine and the greater flexibility from ligamentous laxity.

❐ During hyperflexion or hyperextension, the spine can elongate without injury.

❐ The spinal cord stretches beyond its normal range, leading to tears, contusion, or transection.

❐ The spinal cord and vertebrae return to normal length and alignment, respectively.

❐ Reversible disk protrusion and transient subluxation are other mechanisms of SCIWORA.

❐ Symptoms of spinal cord injury may occur immediately or be delayed, in some cases as long as 4 days after injury, and radiographs and computed tomography studies reveal no bony abnormalities.

Treatment of SCIWORA includes hospitalization and diagnostic tests, such as somatosensory-evoked potentials, spinal radiographs, computed tomography scans, and magnetic resonance imaging (MRI).[6] The increased use of MRI has given evidence to the extent of injury of nonbony supporting tissues in the vertebral column. The findings provide the structural basis for the occult instability in the spine after SCIWORA.[7]

Although children with SCIWORA are usually fitted with a Guilford brace or posterior resting splint, recent research indicates that there may be benefits of patients being immobilized for shorter periods of time.[7] Home care of the child includes careful skin care, bathing with assistance, refraining from organized contact sports, and keeping follow-up appointments with the neurosurgeon.[6]

When spinal cord injuries occur, the outcome can be permanent and devastating for the child and family. Recovery can be maximized by prompt and meticulous assessment, recognition, spinal immobilization, and treatment. The outcome is varied and directly related to the severity of cord injury.

Conclusion

Although relatively rare, spinal cord injuries in children evoke feelings of distress in the child, family, and ED staff. Debriefing of the ED staff after the care of such a patient may be needed (Chapter 26). Awareness of the potential for spinal cord injury is imperative, especially in the multiply injured, nonverbal, or unconscious child.

References

1. Martin, B. (2005). Paediatric cervical spine injuries. *Injury, 36*(1), 14–20.

2. Massagli, T. (2000). Medical and rehabilitation issues in the care of children with spinal cord injury. *Physical Medicine and Rehabilitation Clinics of North America, 11*(1), 169–182.

3. Vernon-Levett, P. (1998). Neurologic system. In P. Slota (Ed.), *Core curriculum for pediatric critical care nursing* (pp. 274–359). Philadelphia: Saunders.

4. Buhs, C., Cullen, M., & Klein, M. (2000). The pediatric trauma C-spine: Is the "odontoid" view necessary? *Journal of Pediatric Surgery, 35,* 994–997.

5. Vogel, L., Hickey, K., Klass, S., & Anderson, C. (2004). Unique issues in pediatric spinal cord injury. *Orthopaedic Nursing, 23*(5), 300–308.

6. Lang, S., & Bernardo, L. (1993). SCIWORA syndrome: Nursing assessment. *Dimensions of Critical Care Nursing, 12,* 247–254.

7. Pang, D. (2004). Spinal cord injury without radiographic abnormality in children, 2 decades later. *Neurosurgery, 55*(6), 1325–1343.

8. Scully, T., & Luerssen, T. (1995). Spinal cord injuries. In W. Buntain (Ed.), *Management of pediatric trauma* (pp. 189–199). Philadelphia: Saunders.

9. Eleraky, M., Theodore, N., Adams, M., Rekate, H., & Sonntrag, V. (2000). Pediatric cervical spine injuries. Report of 102 cases and review of the literature. *Journal of Neurosurgery, 92,* 12–17.

10. Wong, D., & Hockenberry, M. (2003). *Nursing care of infants and children* (pp. 1832–1870). St. Louis, MO: Mosby.

11. Loder, R. (2001). The cervical spine. In R. Morrissy & S. Weinstein (Eds.), *Lovell and Winter pediatric orthopedics.* Philadelphia: Lippincott Williams & Wilkins.

12. Nypaver, M., & Treloar, D. (1994). Neutral cervical spine positioning in children. *Annals of Emergency Medicine, 23*(2), 208–211.

13. DeBoer, S., & Seaver, M. (2004). Pediatric spinal immobilization: C-spines, car seats, and color-coded collars. *Journal of Emergency Nursing, 30*(5), 481–484.

14. Schwartz, G., Wright, S., Fein, J., Sugarman, J., Pasternack, J., & Salhanick, S. (1997). Pediatric cervical spine injury sustained in falls from low heights. *Annals of Emergency Medicine, 30,* 249–252.

15. McCall, T., Fassett, D., & Brockmeyer, D. (2006). Cervical spine trauma in children: A review. *Neurosurgery Focus, 20*(2), 1–8.

16. Calpin, C. (2008). Cervical spine injuries. In A. Lalani & S. Schneeweiss (Eds.), *Handbook of pediatric emergency medicine* (pp. 50–57). Boston: Jones and Bartlett.

17. Ball, J., & Binder, R. (2006). *Child health nursing: Partnering with children and families* (pp. 1297–1366). Upper Saddle River, NJ: Pearson Prentice Hall.

18. Vanore, M. & Perks, D. (2005). Transient spinal cord injuries in the young athlete. *Journal of Trauma Nursing, 12*(4), 127–1301.

THIRTY-ONE

Oral and Maxillofacial Trauma

Dana L. Noffsinger, RN, CPNP

Introduction

Children are uniquely susceptible to facial trauma because of their greater head-to-body mass ratio.[1] The management of pediatric patients with facial injuries requires attention to morphologic and physiologic nuances specific to the growing child.[2] Minor injuries such as corneal abrasions and avulsed teeth are associated with a rapid recovery and good outcome. Major injuries such as mandibular and midfacial fractures may require operative management. Specialized care is required to properly evaluate and treat these injuries.[2]

Pediatric Considerations

Selected anatomic features are associated with differences in pediatric oral and maxillofacial trauma care.

❐ Smaller airway diameter increases the risk of compromise due to swelling, obstruction or blood.

❐ Presence of secondary and primary dentition has an impact on decisions in treating dental injuries.

❐ Early treatment (within 2–4 days) of fractures is preferred because of rapid bone healing in children.[3]

Etiology

❐ Blunt forces
- Motor vehicle crashes
- Pedestrian–motor vehicle crashes
- Falls
- Sports activities
- Bicycle crashes
- Child maltreatment (Chapter 44)
- Acts of violence

❐ Penetrating forces
- Gunshot wounds
- Penetrating wounds
- Machinery

❐ Acceleration/deceleration forces
- Motor vehicle crashes
- Falls
- Collisions (sledding, skating, etc.)

❐ Crushing forces
- Human bites
- Animal bites
- Machinery

Focused History

Mechanism of Injury

❐ Motor vehicle crash
- Child's position in the vehicle
- Safety restraint usage
- Type of motor vehicles
- Speed of vehicle

- Ejection from vehicle
- ❒ Pedestrian–motor vehicle crash
  - Speed of car
  - Details of impact (did car roll over child, was child pinned by the vehicle)
- ❒ Fall
  - Height of fall
  - Surface on which the child fell (yielding or non-yielding)
- ❒ Sports activity
  - Use of protective equipment
  - Type of sport
- ❒ Bicycle crash
  - Helmet use
  - Speed of bicycle
  - Type of crash (moving vehicle, stationary object, or fall from a bike)
  - Child maltreatment (Chapter 44)
- ❒ Act of violence
  - Perpetrator
  - Use of weapons
- ❒ Gunshot wound
  - Caliber of bullet
  - Distance from gun
- ❒ Penetrating wound
  - Type of object
  - Object left in and secured or removed before emergency department (ED) arrival
- ❒ Human bite
  - Person involved (family member or other)
- ❒ Animal bite
  - Type of animal
  - Domestic versus wild
  - Rabies status

Symptoms Following the Injury

- ❒ Ability to maintain a patent airway
- ❒ Amount of blood loss
- ❒ Loss of consciousness

Injury-Related Information

- ❒ Witnesses
- ❒ Prehospital treatment
- ❒ Preservation of avulsed tissue or tooth

Focused Assessment

In the injured patient, facial injuries need to be prioritized accordingly, taking into account life- or limb-threatening injuries first. The American College of Surgeons Advanced Trauma Life Support system of care should be used to prioritize care of the injured patient. Although facial injuries may sometimes be shocking in appearance, they are not always life threatening. Their care can often be delayed while assessing and treating potential life-threatening injuries. Facial injuries resulting in potential life-threatening conditions include:[4]

- ❒ Facial injuries resulting in airway compromise due to bleeding, foreign bodies, swelling, or facial mobility.
- ❒ Anterior neck injuries resulting in airway compromise.
- ❒ Injuries resulting in profuse blood loss.

Physical Assessment

- ❒ Assess the airway and cervical spine.
  - Inspect the airway for:
    - Patency
    - Presence of foreign bodies
  - Listen for the child's ability to speak or make age-appropriate sounds
  - Maintain cervical and spinal alignment
    - Severe maxillofacial trauma suggests cervical spine involvement
- ❒ Assess the respiratory system.
  - Inspect the chest for bilateral chest rise and fall.
  - Auscultate the chest for:
    - Respiratory rate
    - Adventitious sounds
- ❒ Assess the cardiovascular system.
  - Auscultate the heart for:
    - Rate
    - Rhythm
  - Measure the blood pressure
  - Palpate central and peripheral pulses for:
    - Presence
    - Quality
    - Equality
  - Assess peripheral perfusion.
    - Observe skin color
    - Measure capillary refill
    - Measure core and skin temperature

□ Assess the neurologic system.

- Assess the level of consciousness with the Glasgow Coma Scale or AVPU (*A*lert, responds to *V*erbal stimuli, responds to *P*ainful stimuli, *U*nresponsive) method.

- Assess the pupils for:
  - Size
  - Shape
  - Reactivity to light
  - Accommodation
  - Associated ocular findings must be noted to identify vision-threatening injuries.[4] Table 31.1 lists common eye injuries and their treatment.

- Inspect the head for:
  - Surface trauma
  - Puncture wounds

TABLE 31.1 Ocular Injuries

Injury	*Description*	*Etiology*	*Physical Examination Findings*	*Interventions*
Vision-threatening injuries				
Retrobulbar hemorrhage[6]	Orbital hemorrhage in the space surrounding the globe. Results in a rise of intraorbital pressure—may compress the optic nerve or central retinal artery.	Blunt trauma causing injury to orbital blood vessels.	Proptosis— downward displacement of the globe Limited ocular movement Vision disturbance/loss Increased intraocular pressure	Obtain immediate ophthalmology consultation for decompression.
Traumatic optic neuropathy[6]	Avulsion, transection, compression, or contusion of the optic nerve.	Direct blunt trauma or fracture extending into the orbital canal.	Decreased visual acuity or blindness Visual field cuts Afferent pupillary defect Pallor of the optic disk	Obtain ophthalmology consultation. Treatment is controversial. Administer high-dose methyprednisolone. Prepare for the surgical decompression.
Globe injuries[4]				
	Open globe injury: Full-thickness wound to the corneoscleral wall of the eye.	Blunt trauma: Globe rupture Penetrating trauma: Lacerations, puncture wounds	Blood-stained tears Globe may appear collapsed. Prolapse of intraocular contents Fluid leaking from the wound Decreased visual acuity Presence of hyphema	Obtain ophthalmology consultation. Place an eye shield to prevent rubbing of the eye (especially in young children). Position upright. Avoid Valsalva-type maneuvers.

TABLE 31.1 Ocular Injuries (continued)

Injury	Description	Etiology	Physical Examination Findings	Interventions
	Closed globe injury: Contusions, superficial foreign bodies, or lacerations.	Blunt trauma Penetrating trauma: Lacerations	Decreased visual acuity Presence of hyphema	Obtain ophthalmology consultation. Position upright. Avoid Valsalva-type maneuvers.
Loss of eyelid integrity[4]	Laceration or avulsion of the eyelid.	Inability to effectively close the eyelids rapidly results in desiccation of the cornea, ulceration, and potentially loss of sight.	Unable to close eyelid completely Complains of eye dryness	Instill eye drops for lubrication. Place an eye shield to protect cornea from abrasion.
Chemical injury[6]	Alkaline chemicals: Typically more severe because of liquefactive necrosis of tissues. Acidic chemicals: Coagulation necrosis limits the depth of injury of tissues.	Alkaline chemicals: Drain cleaners, detergents, industrial solvents, and lime Acidic chemicals : battery acid; glass cleaners; lime, calcium and rust removal products	Tearing Pain/burning Corneal cloudiness Scleral whitening	Irrigate immediate using copious amounts of water for 30 minutes. Remove particles with a cotton swab. Apply a topical anesthetic. Obtain ophthalmology consultation.
Other eye injuries				
Corneal abrasion[7,8]	Traumatic defect in the corneal epithelium, which leaves the corneal nerve endings exposed and causes severe pain.	Introduction of dirt or other abrasive material into the eye Exposure to ultraviolet light Foreign objects (e.g., fingers, tree branches) Chemical exposure	Complaints of pain and a gritty feeling like sand in the eye Excessive tearing Pain that worsens with blinking (indicates that the foreign body remains in the eye) Redness, edema, and erythema Photophobia Normal or decreased visual acuity	Remove contact lenses, if present. Assist with fluorescein staining and ultra-violet light or slit-lamp examination. Administer ocular antibiotic drops or ointment. Administer ocular or oral analgesics. Assist with foreign-body removal. Patching of the eye is no longer recommended.[8] Bandage contact lenses reduce repeated irritation of blinking.[7] Teach the child and parents methods for eye drop or ointment instillation.

TABLE 31.1 Ocular Injuries (continued)

Injury	Description	Etiology	Physical Examination Findings	Interventions
Hyphema	Blood in the anterior chamber of the eye.	Blunt force trauma to the eye or head. May be seen with globe injuries.	Impaired or normal visual acuity Description of vision as being "blood-tinged" Half-moon appearance of blood at the bottom of the iris	Perform visual acuity test. Assist with slit-lamp examination. Position the patient upright with the head of the bed elevated 30 to 45 degrees. Patch both eyes, placing a metal shield on the affected eye. Avoid aspirin-containing analgesics.
Orbital wall fractures[6]	Blunt force causes an acute rise in intraorbital pressure causing fracture of the thin-walled orbits. Sometimes called "orbital blow-out fractures."	Blunt-force trauma to the eye.	Pain Periorbital edema Ecchymosis Normal or altered vision Subcutaneous emphysema Ipsilateral epistaxis Hyperesthesia of the upper lip and cheek Limited upward gaze with vertical diplopia (entrapped inferior rectus muscle and orbital fat) Enophthalmos	Check for limitation of eye movement. Initiate an ophthalmology consultation. Prepare for facial computed tomographic examination. Prepare for possible operative management.

- Gunshot wounds
- Foreign bodies, such as glass or metal
- Avulsions
  - Palpate the head for:
    - Depressions
    - Step-off defects
    - Pain
    - Hematomas or swelling
    - The integrity of the anterior and posterior fontanelle in children younger than 2 years of age
- ☐ Assess the face and oral cavity.

- Inspect the face for:
  - Deformity
  - Midfacial fractures are rare in children because of the incomplete calcification of the facial bones. Complex fractures may be classified by using the Le Fort system to describe the pattern of fractures. The Le Fort system classifies midfacial fractures from I to III, based on the extent and depth of the fracture.
  - Surface trauma
  - Symmetry
  - Assess for malocclusion by asking the child to smile, grimace, and open and close the mouth.

Malocclusion can also be determined if the child cannot hold a tongue depressor between his or her teeth on both sides.[3] Inability to perform these tasks is indicative of a mandibular fracture.

- Impaled objects
- Raccoon's eyes (indicates possible basilar skull fracture)
- Battle's sign (bruising of the mastoid process)

■ Palpate the forehead, orbits, maxilla, and mandible for:

- Tenderness
- Pain
- Step-off deformities
- Crepitus
- Stability

■ Assess the facial nerves.

- Note numbness of the cheek, lower teeth, or lower lip[3]
- Assess for motor nerve function by having the child wrinkle the forehead, close and open the eyes fully, smile, show the teeth, and close the mouth tightly.[3] Motor nerve injuries are amenable to repair if detected in a timely fashion.[3]

❒ Inspect the oral cavity and structures (gums, lips, and tongue) for:

■ Lacerations

■ Tooth subluxation—loosened within the socket. May require stabilization if markedly mobile.

■ Dental fractures are treated on the basis of the depth of the injury.[5]

- Enamel fractures—chalky white appearance. Sharp edges can be smoothed with an emery board with cosmetic treatment nonurgently.
- Dentin fractures—ivory-yellow appearance. Hot and cold sensitivity. The dentin layer protecting the pulp is thinner in children; therefore coverage of the area may be required.
- Pulp exposure—pink blush or drop of blood after tooth is wiped clean. Excruciating pain due to nerve exposure or no pain due to disruption of neurovascular supply. Dental care is needed within 24 hours because of contamination of the pulp chamber.

■ Tooth avulsion[5]

- If tooth is unaccounted for, aspiration or entrapment in soft tissues must be considered.
- Missing teeth may be a normal finding unrelated to trauma because of loss of primary teeth.

Obtain history from caregivers.

- Avulsed tooth storage:
  - Hanks' solution/Save-A-Tooth® is preferable—can maintain tooth viability for 12 to 24 hours
  - Milk is second-best option because of availability, good osmolarity, and concentration of calcium and magnesium
  - Saliva is a reasonable option
  - Plain water and dry storage are poor options for avulsed tooth transport

- Management of recovered avulsed teeth depends on the age of the patient and time teeth are out of the socket.
  - 6 months to 6 years—primary teeth are not reimplanted
  - Over 6 years—need to determine primary versus permanent teeth

- Reimplant tooth into socket within 30 minutes for best success.
  - Success of reimplantation drops 1% for each minute over 30 minutes tooth is left out of the socket.

- Check tetanus immunization status and treat accordingly.

❒ Assess the eyes, ears, and nose.

■ Inspect the pupils for:

- Size
- Equality
- Reaction to light

■ Inspect the eyes.

- Extraocular movements
- Visual acuity. Request the younger child to point to a familiar object or family member. Ask the older child about the quality of vision. Perform a visual acuity test.
- Scleral deformity and hemorrhages
- Contact lenses or other foreign bodies
- Impaled objects

■ Inspect the external ear canal for otorrhea, which may be cerebrospinal fluid.

■ Inspect the external ear for:

- Lacerations
- Avulsions
- Missing and/or preserved tissue

■ Inspect the mastoid process for ecchymosis (Battle's sign).

- Inspect the nose for:
  - Deformity
  - Septal deviation or septal hematoma
  - Rhinorrhea. Clear rhinorrhea may indicate a cerebrospinal fluid leak.
  - Palpate the bridge and dorsum of the nose to detect fractures or dislocations.
  - Nasal fractures may be difficult to detect clinically because of swelling.
- ❐ Assess the cervical spine while maintaining stabilization.
  - Palpate the cervical spine (posterior neck) for:
    - Tenderness
    - Malaligned vertebrae

Psychosocial Assessment

- ❐ Assess the child's and family's coping strategies.
- ❐ Assess the child's and family's understanding of the injuries.

Nursing Interventions

1. Assess and maintain airway and cervical spine stabilization.
   - Open and maintain the airway while the cervical spine is manually immobilized in a neutral position.
   - Use the jaw thrust method.
   - Prepare for endotracheal intubation.
   - Suction the mouth and upper airway with a large, rigid tonsillar suction in the presence of debris, blood, or secretions. Avoid deep oral suctioning, because stimulation of the posterior pharynx, larynx, or trachea may cause vagal stimulation with resultant bradycardia.

2. Initiate measures to support respiratory function.
   - Administer supplemental 100% oxygen with a nonrebreather mask.
   - Initiate bag-mask ventilation with 100% oxygen in the presence of apnea or ineffective respiratory effort.
   - Prepare for mechanical ventilation.

3. Initiate measures to maintain circulation.
   - Initiate cardiorespiratory and oxygen saturation monitoring.
   - Obtain vascular access and initiate fluid resuscitation.
   - Obtain blood specimens for laboratory analysis.

- Complete blood cell count and differential
- Prothrombin time and partial thromboplastin time
- Type and crossmatch
- Toxicology screening (if alcohol or drug use is suspected)

4. Monitor neurologic status.

5. Prepare for diagnostic testing, as needed.
   - Radiographs of the face
     - Panoramic view (Panorex) of the teeth and dentoalveolar structures
     - Computed tomographic scans

6. Prepare for interventions.
   - Assist with wound repair with or without conscious sedation for external ear laceration or abrasion.
     - Administer local anesthesia
     - Irrigate with normal saline solution
     - Remove devitalized tissue
     - Realign cartilaginous landmarks
     - Suture with nonresorbable sutures
     - Administer oral or intravenous antibiotics as prescribed.
   - Assist with tooth reimplantation.[5]
     - Handle the tooth only by its crown
     - Rinse the avulsed tooth with sterile normal saline solution
     - Do not scrub or scrape
     - Suction or irrigate tooth socket if needed
     - Insert tooth into its socket in the right direction
     - Once the tooth has been placed in socket correctly, have the child apply pressure by biting on a piece of gauze
     - If it is not being reimplanted, place the avulsed permanent tooth in a clean container, fill with Hanks' solution or milk, and label the container with the child's name, the date, and the time
     - Refer the family to a dentist or oral maxillofacial surgeon
   - Assist with septal hematoma drainage or nasal packing, as needed.
   - Administer medications, as prescribed.
     - Tetanus prophylaxis
     - Antibiotics
   - Stabilize impaled objects.
   - Assist with tracheostomy, as needed.

7. Insert an orogastric tube for gastric decompression, as needed. Nasogastric intubation in the setting of facial trauma has an increased risk of insertion into the brain.

8. Assess for pain; administer analgesics, as prescribed.

9. Inform the family frequently of the child's condition.

10. Provide emotional support to the child and family.

11. Initiate consultations with social services and surgical subspecialists, such as oral maxillofacial surgeons or ophthalmologists.

   ▪ Consult child protective services if child maltreatment is suspected.

   ▪ Contact law enforcement if violence was involved.

12. Prepare for transfer and transport to a trauma center (Chapter 8); prepare for operative management and hospitalization, as needed.

Home Care and Prevention

Following a minor maxillofacial injury, the child returns home with the family. The family will require instructions specific to the ED treatment. Sutures can be removed by the child's primary care physician or by the treating ED physician or specialist. Follow-up with an ophthalmologist or dentist may be required.

Major maxillofacial trauma generally requires operative management. The child's facial features may be changed, and reconstructive surgeries may be required. Fractures of the face are managed with the goal of restoring anatomic alignment.[3] Counseling may be necessary for the family and child to cope with changes in body image.

Prevention of oral and maxillofacial injuries includes the use of proper protective equipment during sports- and work-related activities, proper positioning and restraint during motor vehicle travel, conflict resolution measures to prevent violence, and family support to prevent child maltreatment.

Conclusion

Oral and maxillofacial trauma ranges from minor injuries to major trauma with operative management. Wearing protective equipment while engaged in sports or recreational activities (e.g., mouth guard, helmets with a face mask) may prevent or lessen the severity of oral and facial trauma. Children sustaining severe facial trauma may require reconstructive surgeries; psychological interventions and follow-up will be warranted.

References

1. Eggensperger-Wymann, N. M., Holze, A., Zachariou, Z., & Iizuka, T. (2008). Pediatric craniofacial trauma. *Journal of Maxillofacial Surgeons, 66,* 58–64.

2. Costello, B. J., Papadopoulos, H., & Ruiz, R. (2005). Pediatric craniomaxillofacial trauma. *Clinical Pediatric Emergency Medicine, 6,* 32–40.

3. Neuman, M. I., & Eriksson, E. (2006). Facial trauma. In Fleisher, G. R., Ludwig, S., Henretig, F. M., Ruddy, R. M., & Silverman, B. K., *The textbook of pediatric emergency medicine* (5th ed., pp. 1475–1477). Philadelphia: Lippincott Williams & Wilkins.

4. Perry, M., Dancey, A., Mireskandari, K., Oakley, P., Davies, S., & Cameron, M. (2004). Emergency care in facial trauma—a maxillofacial and ophthalmic perspective. *Injury, 36,* 875–896.

5. Amsterdam, J. T. (2006). Oral medicine. In Marx, J., Hockberger, R., & Walls, R. (Eds.), *Rosen's emergency medicine: Concepts and clinical practice* (6th ed., pp. 1044–1052). Philadelphia: Saunders.

6. Brunette, D. D. (2006). Ophthalmology. In Marx, J., Hockberger, R., & Walls, R. (Eds.), *Rosen's emergency medicine: Concepts and clinical practice* (6th ed., pp. 1044–1052). Philadelphia: Saunders.

7. Dargin, J. M., & Lowenstein, R. A. (2008). The painful eye. *Emergency Medicine Clinics of North America, 26,* 199–216.

8. Aslam, S. A., Sheth, H. G., & Vaughan, A. J. (2007). Emergency management of corneal injuries. *Injury, 38,* 594–597.

THIRTY-TWO

Thoracic Trauma

Kathleen Schenkel, RN, BSN, MSN, CEN

Introduction

Thoracic trauma, with blunt injury being the most common, is considered a multisystem injury. These injuries include trauma to the chest wall, trachea, bronchi, lungs, heart, thoracic aorta and great vessels, esophagus, and diaphragm[1] (Tables 32.1 and 32.2). Most thoracic injuries that children sustain are frequently managed without surgery. The presence of rib fractures in children may indicate significant underlying injury. Most children do not have the comorbidities found in the adults, and they usually recover faster than adults. If the child arrives at the emergency department (ED) in cardiopulmonary arrest after chest injury, the chances of survival are dismal. ED thoracotomy is rarely performed. However, pediatric patients presenting with cardiac arrest or tamponade caused by penetrating trauma, with vital signs present in the field or emergency department, have the best chance of survival, although small, if ED thoracotomy is performed.[1]

Pediatric Considerations

Several pediatric anatomic features affect thoracic injury patterns.

❒ The child's ribs are cartilaginous, making rib fractures uncommon.

❒ When rib fractures are present, a significant force of energy has been sustained.

❒ Rib fractures can occur with or without flail segments. Although flail chest segments are obvious in adults, they are often less striking in the pediatric patient.

❒ Children with rib fractures usually present with chest pain and varying degrees of respiratory distress in response to potential intrapleural injury.

❒ Children are anatomically protected against blunt thoracic trauma because of the compliance of the rib cage. Compressibility of the rib cage will dissipate the force of impact, which lessens the likelihood of bony injury.[2]

❒ The child's chest cavity easily can contain a significant volume of blood. Therefore, hypovolemic shock can occur quickly with a hemopneumothorax.

❒ The mediastinum is mobile, contributing to the low incidence of major vessel and airway injury in the pediatric population.[3]

Etiology

❒ Blunt forces
- Pedestrian–motor vehicle crashes
- Motor vehicle crashes
- Child maltreatment
- Acts of violence
- Falls from a height
- Bicycle crashes

❒ Penetrating forces
- Gunshot wounds
- Penetrating wounds

❒ Acceleration-deceleration forces
- Motor vehicle crashes
- Sports activities

❒ Crushing forces
- Animal bites
- Machinery

TABLE 32.1 Selected Pulmonary Injuries

Injury	Description
Pulmonary contusion	Although pulmonary contusion is present on admission, it may not be apparent on radiographs until 24 to 48 hours after injury. Pulmonary contusion results from blunt force trauma after a motor vehicle crash, bicycle crash, or abusive episode. Signs and symptoms include tachypnea, dyspnea, decreased breath sounds, and general worsening pulmonary status. Specific treatment includes administering high-flow oxygen and initiating cardiorespiratory monitoring. Mechanical ventilation is usually required.
Traumatic asphyxia	An almost exclusively pediatric injury with its own unique pattern. At time of injury, the glottis is closed and the thoracoabdominal muscles are tense. The superficial capillaries of the face, upper chest, and neck are disrupted by the significant, rapid, forceful, backflow up the valveless venous system of the inferior and superior vena cava into the head and neck, resulting in petechiae. Below the injury, no abnormality will be noted. This injury results from blunt force trauma following vehicular and farm equipment runovers. This injury is diagnosed in the unrestrained driver involved in a high-velocity motor vehicle crash, in the unrestrained front-seat passenger held on the lap of a restrained or unrestrained passenger, or in the driver when the child is crushed between the dashboard and the passenger or the steering wheel and the driver. Specific treatment includes high-flow oxygen delivery and cardiorespiratory monitoring.
Tracheobronchial rupture	Tracheobronchial ruptures from blunt thoracic trauma are rare in the pediatric population.[1] Death usually occurs within the first hour after tracheobronchial rupture, which is most often the result of blunt force trauma to the neck.[3] Signs and symptoms include subcutaneous emphysema, dyspnea, sternal tenderness, and hemoptysis.[3] Specific treatment includes endotracheal intubation, chest tube insertion, and operative management.

TABLE 32.2 Selected Cardiac and Great-Vessel Injuries

Injury	Description
Cardiac contusion	Less common in children than in adults, it is caused by blunt force trauma to the chest, resulting in myocardial bruising. Presenting signs and symptoms include tachycardia and normal skin color, temperature, and capillary refill. Specific interventions include obtaining a 12-lead electrocardiogram, observation for ectopy, administration of antiarrhythmic therapy or inotropic support, and serial monitoring of creatinine kinase levels.
Cardiac tamponade	This injury is rare in pediatric trauma and is associated with penetrating forces. Once injury occurs, there is an accumulation of blood in the pericardial sac, compressing the heart and causing eventual circulatory collapse. Children may initially appear alert and anxious and rapidly progress to vascular compromise. Signs and symptoms include tachycardia, tachypnea, decreased capillary refill, Beck's triad (distended neck veins [usually not visible in the younger child], muffled heart tones, and a widened pulse pressure). Specific interventions include preparation for a rapid pericardiocentesis and operative management.
Great-vessel injury	Traumatic aortic disruption occurs in the older adolescent population and is the result of acceleration-deceleration or penetrating forces. Signs and symptoms include midscapular back pain, unexplained hypotension, upper extremity hypertension, bilateral femoral pulse deficits, large amounts of initial chest tube drainage, sternal fracture, and widened mediastinum on a chest radiograph.[3] Specific treatment is operative management.

Focused History

Mechanism of Injury

- ❐ Motor vehicle crash
  - Passenger or driver
  - Seating position in vehicle
  - Type of vehicle
  - Type of crash
  - Use of safety restraints, including child car safety seats, booster seats, restraints, and air bags (for drivers and older front seat passengers)
- ❐ Bicycle crash
  - Presence of helmet
  - Speed and type of oncoming vehicle
  - Speed of bicycle
  - Stationary object struck (e.g., tree or car)
- ❐ Sports-related injury
  - Use of protective equipment, including helmet
  - Type of sport
- ❐ Fall from height to non-yielding surface
  - Height from which the child fell
  - Surface on which the child fell
- ❐ Pedestrian incident
  - Speed of vehicle
  - Child maltreatment (Chapter 44)
- ❐ Act of violence
  - Description of the incident
- ❐ Gunshot wound
  - Type of weapon
  - Caliber of bullet
  - Distance or range from which bullet was fired
- ❐ Penetrating wound
  - Type of penetrating object
  - Impaled or removed
- ❐ Crushing injury
  - Type of machinery
  - Type of biting animal

Cardiopulmonary Symptoms After the Injury

- ❐ Tachypnea
- ❐ Dyspnea
- ❐ Hoarse voice
- ❐ Facial or truncal petechiae
- ❐ Surface trauma to the chest
- ❐ Pain

Injury-Related Information

- ❐ Witnesses
- ❐ Prehospital treatment

Focused Assessment

Physical Assessment

1. Assess the airway and respiratory system while maintaining cervical spine precautions.
   - Assess the airway for:
     - Patency
     - Position of the trachea (midline or deviated)
   - Auscultate the chest for:
     - Respiratory rate
     - Breath sounds, which may be decreased or absent in a child with a pneumothorax or hemothorax (Table 32.3)
   - Palpate the chest for:
     - Crepitus
     - Pain/tenderness
     - Subcutaneous emphysema
   - Inspect the chest for:
     - Surface trauma
     - Petechiae (also to the face and neck)
     - Paradoxical movements or flail segments
2. Assess the cardiovascular system.
   - Auscultate the heart for:
     - Rate. Tachycardia may be present.
     - Rhythm
     - Heart sounds
   - Measure the blood pressure.
   - Measure capillary refill.
   - Measure skin color and temperature.
3. Assess the face and neck for:
   - Edema
   - Subcutaneous emphysema
   - Tracheal deviation
   - Jugular venous distention
   - Petechiae
     - Subconjunctival hemorrhages
     - Face

TABLE 32.3 Comparisons of Pneumothoraces

Injury	Incidence/Mechanism of Injury	Signs/Symptoms	Treatment
Open pneumothorax (sucking chest wound)	Rare/penetrating trauma	Respiratory distress Decreased/absent breath sounds on the affected side "Sucking" sound on inspiration Tracheal deviation toward the affected hemithorax	Initiate positive-pressure ventilation. Cover the wound with an occlusive dressing. Tape three of the four sides, allowing the fourth to release entrapped air during exhalation. Prepare for chest tube insertion or operative management.

Simple pneumothorax	Common/blunt-force trauma	Pneumothorax < 15% and no other injury:
		
		    Commonly asymptomatic
		
		Pneumothorax > 15% with other injuries:
		
		    Respiratory distress
		
		    Absent breath sounds on the affected side
		
		    Pain
			Prepare for chest tube insertion for lung reexpansion and prevention of tension pneumothorax.

Hemothorax	Rare/blunt-force or penetrating trauma. The source of bleeding is often an intercostal artery lacerated by a fractured rib. Bleeding may also be due to a major vascular injury or pulmonary parenchymal injury.	Signs of hypovolemic shock Respiratory distress Absent breath sounds on the affected side Dullness with percussion	Prepare for chest tube insertion; prepare for autotransfuser. Initiate fluid resuscitation.
Tension pneumothorax (accumulation of air under pressure in the pleural space)	Rare/blunt or penetrating forces that disrupt the tracheobronchial structures or lung parenchyma. Air enters the pleural space and becomes entrapped. The entrapped air displaces the mediastinum, creating a shift that can interfere with central venous return and lead to decreased cardiac output.	Respiratory distress Dyspnea Tachypnea Decreased breath sounds on the affected side Tracheal deviation away from the affected side (difficult to see in the younger child with a short neck) Distended neck veins (difficult to assess in the younger child) Profound respiratory distress and failure with eventual circulatory collapse, if unrecognized, shock	Prepare for immediate placement of a needle thoracostomy in the second intercostal space below the second rib at the midclavicular line. Prepare for chest tube insertion.

Psychosocial Assessment

❑ Assess the child's and family's understanding of the injury.

❑ Assess the child's and family's coping strategies.

Nursing Interventions

1. Assess and maintain the airway using the jaw thrust maneuver.
   - Prepare for endotracheal intubation.
2. Administer continuous high-flow oxygen.
   - Initiate bag-mask ventilations for the child with apnea or bradypnea.
   - Prepare for mechanical ventilation.
   - Initiate cardiorespiratory and oxygen saturation monitoring.
   - Prepare for needle decompression, thoracostomy, and chest tube insertion, as needed.
3. Obtain venous access and initiate an intravenous infusion.
   - Obtain blood specimens for laboratory analysis:
     - Creatinine kinase
     - Complete blood cell count and differential
4. Administer analgesics, as prescribed (Chapter 11).
5. Assess the child's neurologic status.
6. Prepare for diagnostic tests.
   - 12-lead electrocardiogram
   - Anterior-posterior and lateral radiographs of the chest
7. Inform the family frequently about the child's condition.
8. Provide emotional support to the child and family.
9. Initiate consultations with social services, surgery, and other subspecialties, as needed.
10. Prepare for transfer and transport to a trauma center (Chapter 8) or hospitalization.

Home Care and Prevention

Prevention of chest trauma includes routine usage of child safety restraints and other safety measures (Chapter 4). It is not uncommon for children to be admitted for observation after thoracic trauma because of the possibility of underlying injuries. Therefore, parents should be informed as soon as possible that their child may need to stay in the hospital.

Conclusion

Cardiopulmonary trauma is a potential source of life-threatening injuries in the pediatric population. Although such injuries are rare, emergency nurses must maintain a high index of suspicion for their presence. Continuous monitoring of the child's clinical condition will elicit key indicators of deterioration and decompensation, which warrant further interventions.

References

1. Kadish, H. (2006). Thoracic trauma. In G. Fleischer, S. Ludwig, & F. Henretig (Eds.), *Textbook of pediatric emergency medicine* (5th ed., pp. 1433–1452). Philadelphia: Lippincott Williams & Wilkins.

2. Avarello, J., & Cantor, R. (2007). Pediatric major trauma: An approach to evaluation and management. *Emergency Medicine Clinics of North America, 25,* 803–836.

3. Webster, H., & Grant, M. (2006). Pulmonary system. In M. Slota (Ed.), *Core curriculum for pediatric critical care nursing* (pp. 40–160). Philadelphia: Saunders.

THIRTY-THREE

Abdominal Trauma

Nancy Mecham, APRN, FNP-BC, CEN

Introduction

Potentially life-threatening abdominal injuries are common in the pediatric population (Table 33.1). About 10% of trauma-related injuries in children have documented abdominal injuries; however, abdominal injury is the most commonly unrecognized cause of fatal injuries.[1] Although trauma is considered a surgical disease, nonoperative management of traumatic abdominal injuries is now becoming the standard of care in pediatric trauma management.[1] Successful outcome after abdominal trauma is dependent on its prompt recognition, adequate resuscitation, rapid surgical repair when indicated, and severity of additional injuries.

Pediatric Considerations

Anatomic differences place children at greater risk for abdominal trauma than adults because the child's abdomen is less protected from kinetic forces.[1,2]

❑ The abdominal wall is thin and protuberant, with less muscle and subcutaneous tissue.

❑ The abdominal organs are in close proximity, and multiple abdominal organ injuries are possible.

❑ The liver and spleen, located below the rib cage, are in a more anterior position than in the adult.

❑ The liver and spleen are proportionately larger in children than in adults.

❑ When compressed during a trauma event, the compliant ribs do not afford protection to the abdominal organs, leading to liver and spleen damage.

❑ Children have compact torsos with smaller anterior-posterior diameters, which provide a smaller area to dissipate the force of the injury.

❑ Large amounts of blood can be lost into the abdominal cavity, masking signs of shock.

❑ Children have a remarkable ability to compensate for significant blood losses into the abdominal cavity.

❑ Hemorrhagic shock caused by solid-organ injury is a major cause of morbidity and mortality in the injured child.

Etiology

❑ Blunt forces
- Bicycle crashes
- Child maltreatment (Chapter 44)
- Pedestrian incidents
- Falls
- Sports activities
- Motor vehicle crashes
- Acts of violence

❑ Penetrating forces
- Gunshot wounds
- Penetrating wounds, including impaled objects, such as iron fence posts

TABLE 33.1 Specific Abdominal Injuries

Abdominal Organ	Frequency of Injury	Signs and Symptoms	Results of Diagnostic Tests	Additional ED Management
Spleen	Most commonly injured abdominal organ[5]	External left upper quadrant trauma Generalized or localized left upper quadrant pain Kehr's sign Nausea and vomiting Signs of hypovolemic shock	Decreased hematocrit Increased white blood cell count CT scan may reveal free fluid or air in the abdomen	Prepare for hospitalization. Splenectomy is rarely indicated.
Liver Grade I: subcapsular hematoma; capsular tears Grade II: minor parenchymal lacerations Grade III: deep parenchymal lacerations Grade IV: burst liver injuries[6,7]	Second most commonly injured abdominal organ[6] Most common source of lethal hemorrhage[1]	External right upper quadrant trauma Generalized or localized right upper quadrant pain Diffuse abdominal tenderness or rebound tenderness Abdominal distention Rigidity Kehr's sign Nausea and vomiting Signs of hypovolemic shock	Elevated liver enzymes Decreased hematocrit	Prepare for hospitalization and observation. Subcapsular hematoma and organ failure result in hemorrhage, but bleeding often stops spontaneously allowing for nonoperative approach in most cases.
Duodenum	Duodenal hematoma occurs more often in children, most likely because of lack of rib protection Can result from lap belt injury	Centralized abdominal pain with periumbilical bruising	Intraperitoneal air on abdominal radiograph (if hollow viscus is present) Upper gastrointestinal series (CT and ultrasound scans) to locate the injury[1]	Prepare for operative management. Many injuries are found later during laparotomy because of periotonitis or fever.[1]
Stomach	Infrequently injured	External trauma to the upper abdomen Bloody gastric drainage Board-like abdomen and severe pain indicate perforation	Free air on abdominal radiograph Upper gastrointestinal series locates injured area.	Prepare for operative management.

TABLE 33.1 Specific Abdominal Injuries (continued)				
Abdominal Organ	*Frequency of Injury*	*Signs and Symptoms*	*Results of Diagnostic Tests*	*Additional ED Management*
Pancreas	Infrequently injured	Diffuse abdominal tenderness Deep epigastric pain radiating to the back Bilious vomiting	Elevated amylase and lipase Ultrasound or CT scan with contrast[1]	Severe injury is rare but when it occurs hypovolemia and peritonitis may result.[1] Pseudocysts can develop; most often from bicycle handle-bar injuries.[1]

- ❐ Acceleration-deceleration forces
  - Motor vehicle crashes
  - Falls
  - Sports activities
- ❐ Crushing forces
  - Animal bites
  - Machinery

Focused History

Mechanism of Injury

- ❐ Motor vehicle crash
  - Passenger or driver
  - Seating position in vehicle
  - Speed of vehicle
  - Type of vehicle
  - Type of crash
  - Use of safety restraints
  - Vehicular ejection
- ❐ Bicycle crash
  - Use of helmet
  - Speed and type of oncoming vehicle
  - Speed of bicycle
  - Stationary object struck (e.g., tree, car, or bicycle handlebar)
- ❐ Sports-related injury
  - Use of protective equipment, including helmet
  - Type of sport
- ❐ Fall from height onto a yeilding or non-yielding surface
  - Height from which the child fell
  - Surface onto which the child fell

- ❐ Pedestrian incidents
  - Speed of vehicle
- ❐ Child maltreatment (Chapter 44)
- ❐ Act of violence
  - Description of the incident
- ❐ Gunshot wound
  - Type of weapon
  - Caliber of bullet
  - Distance or range from which bullet was fired
- ❐ Penetrating wound
  - Type of penetrating object
  - Object impaled or removed
- ❐ Crushing wound
  - Type and size of biting animal
  - Type of machinery

Injury-Related Information

- ❐ Witnesses
- ❐ Prehospital treatment

Focused Assessment

Physical Assessment

- ❐ Assess the airway, breathing, circulation, and neuro-logic systems (Chapter 28).
- ❐ Inspect the abdomen for:
  - Surface trauma, such as abrasions, ecchymosis, tire tracks, or penetrating objects
  - A distinctive pattern resulting from a seat belt injury
    - Children tend to be at greater risk for seat belt injuries because they frequently ride in the back seat, where the protective restraint devices are

commonly lap seat belts that are designed to fit and restrain an adult passenger.

- When the seat belt does not fit properly, small children are likely to maneuver themselves into unsafe traveling positions—placing the shoulder belt behind their back or slouching down, which positions the seat belt on their abdomen instead of being correctly positioned across their hip bones.

- During a motor vehicle crash, deceleration forces pull the child forward against the lap belt. The resulting triad of injuries is external belt marks (abdominal ecchymosis or actual belt embedment in subcutaneous tissue); hollow viscus injury (duodenal perforation, mesenteric disruption, small bowel transection, or bladder rupture); and compression or flexion-distraction fractures of the lumbar spine (Chance fracture).[1,3]

❏ Observe the pediatric patient for:

- Kehr's sign (left shoulder pain). Free blood in the abdomen irritates the diaphragm and the phrenic nerve, referring pain to the left shoulder.

- Nausea and vomiting

- Abdominal distention
  - Rupture of intra-abdominal contents

❏ Auscultate the abdomen for bowel sounds.

- The absence of bowel sounds, although nonspecific, is suggestive of an ileus, which typically results after abdominal injury.

❏ Palpate the abdomen gently for:

- Rebound tenderness, pain, and guarding

- Peritoneal signs, which can be obscured by an altered mental status, and abdominal tenderness, which may be obscured by pain elsewhere

- Distention, rigidity, and masses
  - Presence of blood on rectal examination may indicate bowel perforation.

❏ Assess the remaining body systems.

❏ Assess for pain using an age-appropriate pain scale (Chapter 11).

Psychosocial Assessment

❏ Assess the pediatric patient and family for their coping strategies.

❏ Assess the pediatric patient and family for understanding of the injury.

Nursing Interventions

1. Provide necessary interventions to maintain airway.

   - Perform the jaw thrust maneuver, if needed.

   - Suction airway, if needed.

   - Maintain cervical spine precautions.

2. Provide necessary interventions to maintain breathing.

   - Administer continuous high-flow oxygen via a nonrebreather mask.

   - Assist ventilations, as needed, with bag-mask ventilation.

   - Prepare for endotracheal intubation, as needed, while maintaining cervical spine precautions.

   - Initiate cardiorespiratory and oxygen saturation monitoring.

3. Provide necessary interventions to maintain circulation.

   - Obtain venous access.
     - Consider intraosseous access early for the child with signs of shock.

   - Prepare to initiate fluid therapy, if needed.
     - Warmed intravenous fluids are recommended to prevent hypothermia.
     - Initiate fluid boluses of 20 mL/kg of normal saline or lactated Ringer's solution administered rapidly (over a 5- to 10-minute period) with the goal of attaining normal circulatory status.[4]
     - Reassess circulatory status after each bolus.
     - Assess lung sounds after each bolus.
     - In patients with hypovolemic shock secondary to hemorrhage, the 20 mL/kg bolus may need to be repeated three times for a total of 60 mL/kg, and then consider transfusion of 10 mL/kg packed red blood cells.[4]

4. Obtain blood specimens for laboratory analysis.

   - Complete blood cell count and differential

   - Liver enzymes

   - Amylase

   - Lipase

   - Prothrombin time/partial thromboplastin time

   - Type and crossmatch

   - Stool Hemoccult test

5. Assess the child's neurologic status.

   - Assess the level of consciousness with the GCS, pediatric GCS, or AVPU method (Alert; responds to Verbal stimuli; responds to Pain; Unresponsive).

- Observe the child's response to the environment and procedures.

6. Insert a nasogastric or orogastric tube. Placement of the tube before the abdominal examination will cause gastric decompression and thus facilitate the abdominal examination and prevent aspiration of gastric contents if vomiting occurs.
   - Aspirate a sample of stomach contents and evaluate for blood or bile.
   - Reassess the abdomen for distention; if the abdomen remains distended after decompression, suspect intra-abdominal bleeding.
   - Measure the gastric output.

7. Place a bladder catheter for monitoring urine output, unless there is blood at the urinary meatus.

8. Reassess the child's cardiopulmonary, neurologic, and abdominal status frequently.

9. Prepare for diagnostic procedures such as:
   - Ultrasound examination
   - Focused abdominal sonography for trauma (FAST)
     - May be helpful to assess for presence of intra-abdominal fluid
   - Diagnostic peritoneal lavage. Is not commonly used but may be used when FAST ultrasound is not available.[2]
     - The presence of blood in the peritoneal cavity, as determined by ultrasound or diagnostic peritoneal lavage, provides little value other than confirmation of its presence. The child's overall appearance is evidence of ongoing bleeding and is the basis for determining management pathways.
   - Computed tomography (CT) studies with and without contrast

10. Inform the family frequently of the child's condition.

11. Provide ongoing emotional support to the child and family.

12. Initiate consultations to social services, surgery, and other subspecialties.

13. Prepare for transfer and transport to a trauma center (Chapter 8), or prepare for hospitalization.

Home Care and Prevention

Abdominal injuries can be prevented through the use of safety devices during work and play.

❑ Car safety seats, booster seats, and vehicle seat belts for all ages, regardless of position in the vehicle.

❑ Helmets and protective pads for all wheeled sports activities (bicycling, skateboarding, rollerblading, and using a scooter).

❑ Appropriate safety equipment during sports activity.

❑ Gun safety courses for school-aged children and adolescents.

❑ Helmets during motorized vehicle use (all-terrain vehicle [ATV] use, snowmobiling, or motorcycle riding).

Parents should be prepared for at least a 24-hour hospitalization for observation of the child after an abdominal injury. Analgesics may be withheld to detect changes in the child's condition; therefore, nonpharmacologic measures to relieve pain should be attempted (Chapter 11).

Conclusion

Because of its frequency, emergency nurses should be prepared for abdominal trauma and its sequelae. Being prepared to do a rapid focused assessment, obtaining necessary screening laboratory studies, and administering fluid or blood products rapidly are all part of the challenge of caring for the child with abdominal trauma. The emotional support and comfort provided by the nurse, for both the child and the family, during invasive procedures, diagnostic testing, and frequent abdominal assessments can help to assist the family through this stressful situation.

References

1. Saldino, R., & Lund, D. (2006). Abdominal trauma. In G. Fleisher & S. Ludwig (Eds.), *Textbook of pediatric emergency medicine* (pp. 1453–1462). Philadelphia: Lippincott Williams & Wilkins.

2. Emergency Nurses Association. (2007). *Trauma nursing core course (TNCC) provider manual.* (6th ed., pp. 230–233). Des Plaines, IL: Author.

3. Durbin, D. R., Arbogast, K. B., & Moll, E. K. (2001). Seat belt syndrome in children: A case report and review of the literature. *Pediatric Emergency Care, 17*(17), 474–478.

4. Ralston, M., Hazinski, M., Zaritsky, A., Schexnayder, S., & Kleinman, M. (2006). *Textbook of pediatric advanced life support.* Chicago: American Academy of Pediatrics and American Heart Association.

5. Wise, B., Mudd, S., & Wilson, M. (2002). Management of blunt abdominal trauma in children. *Journal of Trauma Nursing, 9*(1), 6–13.

6. Schafermeyer, R. (1993). Pediatric trauma. *Emergency Medicine Clinics of North America, 11,* 187–205.

7. Emergency Nurses Association. (2007). *Trauma nursing core course (TNCC) provider manual* (6th ed, pp. 149–163). Des Plaines, IL: Author.

THIRTY-FOUR

Genitourinary Trauma

Christine Nelson-Tuttle, DNS, RNC, PNP
Rebecca Roloff, RN, MSN, SANE-A, SANE-P
Steven J. Dasta, RN, BSN

Introduction

Genitourinary (GU) injury is common in children. GU injuries occur to the kidneys, ureter, bladder, and urethra (Table 34.1). In males, the scrotum, testicles, and penis may be injured, whereas females may sustain injury to the perineal area. Death from GU injury is rare. Treatment is specific for the location and extent of injury and may include bed rest, observation, placement of diverting catheters, or surgical exploration.[1]

Pediatric Considerations

The following anatomic differences place children at risk for GU injuries.

❏ The child's kidney, one of the most frequently injured organs, is larger in relation to abdominal size and is less protected by the lower ribs than is the adult's kidney.[2]

- The kidney lacks perinephric fat and has more fetal renal lobulation (remains of the fusion lines between reniculi). These lobulations usually disappear as the kidney matures, but can persist in later childhood and adulthood.

- The kidney is relatively mobile and can be easily pushed against the ribs or vertebrae, causing crushing or tearing.

- Rapid deceleration may cause excessive movement of the kidneys and stretching or tearing of the renal vessels.

- Preexisting known or unknown renal conditions (e.g., Wilms' tumor, ectopic kidneys, or enlarged kidneys) may be present.

❏ Although ureteral trauma is rare,[1] ureteral elasticity and torso flexibility allow ureteral injuries to occur.

❏ In small children, the bladder essentially is an abdominal organ, which makes it vulnerable to blunt force injuries.

- Full bladders are common in children, as they may not take the time to empty their bladders; while rare, the distended bladder is more likely to rupture in children compared with adults.[2]

❏ Injury to the anterior (distal) urethra is uncommon in boys because of the urethra's mobility; therefore, any injury to this area is most likely iatrogenic. Injury to the urethra in females is rare; contusion may result from foreign bodies or self-inflicted trauma.[3]

❏ Although pelvic fractures are often associated with GU injuries in adults, such fractures are less common in children because of the flexible pelvis.

TABLE 34.1 Specific GU Injuries and Their Treatment

Organ	Mechanism of Injury	Physical Assessment Findings	Additional ED Management
Kidney	Penetrating trauma (gunshot wound, stabbing) Blunt trauma Rapid deceleration in falls and motor vehicle collision	Flank tenderness, pain and bruising, hematuria Types of injury: Type 1: Renal contusion Type 2: Cortical laceration Type 3: Calyx tear Type 4: Complete tear or rupture Type 5: Vascular pedicle injury Type 6: Ureteropelvic disruption	Prepare for radiographic tests. Prepare for operative management.
Ureter	Acceleration Deceleration	Flank mass Leakage of urine from a wound Oliguria Enlarging flank mass Hematuria	Prepare for diagnostic testing, such as ultrasonography, computed tomography scan, and retrograde pyelography. Prepare for operative management.
Bladder	Blunt trauma Penetrating trauma Self-inflicted trauma (placement of objects into the urethra) Iatrogenic trauma (e.g., vigorous performance of the Credé maneuver, placement of an abdominal paracentesis catheter, or suprapubic tap)	Four classes: Contusion: Hematuria without renal injury Extraperitoneal rupture: Concomitant pelvic fracture or penetrating injury; extravasation of contrast media Intraperitoneal rupture: Transmission of blunt forces or penetrating forces; assessment findings similar to abdominal trauma Combined extraperitoneal and intraperitoneal rupture: Pelvic fracture	Prepare for diagnostic testing (retrograde urethrogram). Prepare for operative management.
Urethra (partial or complete tear)	Blunt trauma	Associated pelvic fracture Associated straddle injuries	Prepare for retrograde urethrogram to visualize the entire urethra. Avoid placement of an indwelling bladder catheter with the presence of meatal blood.

Lobe, T., Gore., D., & Swischuk, L. (1995). Urinary tract injuries. In W. Buntain (Ed.), *Management of pediatric trauma* (pp. 371–382). Philadelphia: Saunders.

Etiology

❑ Blunt forces

- Motor vehicle crashes or passenger-side air bag deployment[1]
- Falls
- Sports activities (usually associated with a blow to the flank)
- Kicks to the flank by large animals
- Child maltreatment (Chapter 44)
- Straddle mishaps onto the bar of a bicycle or playground equipment
- Industrial mishaps (mill work, farming)
- Sexual stimulation activities

❏ Penetrating forces
- Gunshot wounds
- Penetrating injuries
- Impaled or inserted foreign bodies

❏ Acceleration-deceleration forces
- Motor vehicle crashes
- Sports activities

❏ Crushing forces
- Animal bites
- Machinery

Focused History

Mechanism of Injury

❏ Motor vehicle crash
- Passenger or driver
- Seating position in vehicle
- Type of vehicle
- Type of crash
- Use of safety restraints

❏ Sports-related injury
- Use of protective equipment, including helmet
- Type of sport

❏ Kick to the flank by a large animal
- Type of animal
- Size of animal

❏ Child maltreatment (Chapter 44)

❏ Act of violence or sexual assault (Chapter 45)

❏ Gunshot wound
- Type of weapon
- Caliber of bullet
- Distance or range from which bullet was fired

❏ Penetrating wound
- Type of penetrating object
- Impaled, inserted, or removed

❏ Crushing wound
- Type of biting animal
- Type of machinery

❏ Falls
- Height
- Surface

GU Symptoms Following the Injury

❏ Abdominal pain or tenderness

❏ Flank pain or tenderness

❏ Back pain

❏ Surface trauma to the abdomen, flank, or genital area

❏ Hematuria

❏ Painful urination or inability to urinate

❏ Pain with defecation or inability to defecate

❏ Vaginal bleeding

❏ Edematous/ecchymotic scrotum

Injury-Related Information

❏ Witnesses

❏ Prehospital treatment

Focused Assessment

Physical Assessment

❏ Assess the airway, respiratory, cardiovascular, and neurologic systems.

❏ Assess the abdomen.
- Inspect the abdomen for:
  - Surface trauma, such as abrasions, ecchymosis, and penetrating objects
- Observe the child for nausea and vomiting.
- Auscultate the abdomen for bowel sounds.
- Palpate the abdomen gently for:
  - Rebound tenderness, pain, and guarding. Peritoneal signs can be obscured by an altered mental status, and abdominal tenderness may be obscured by pain elsewhere.
  - Distention
  - Rigidity
- Inspect the back for surface trauma or penetrating injury.
- Palpate the back for costovertebral angle tenderness.

❏ Assess the GU system.
- Inspect the genital area for bruising, lacerations, and the presence of a foreign body.
- Assess for premenarchal or postmenarchal bleeding. Assess for vaginal bleeding; if present, assess the volume of bleeding and the length of time the bleeding has occurred.
- Assess the female genitalia (Chapter 45). Hymenal injuries were reported as rarely caused

by unintentional trauma. Hymenal injury should be investigated as potential sexual abuse.[4]

- When abuse or assault is suspected, preserve any evidence (e.g., clothing) and proceed with a victim assault assessment (Chapter 45).
- Assess the male genitalia for open wounds, loss of skin, patterns of ecchymosis, and constricting objects.
- Penile circumference is assessed for edema, and scrotum is assessed for edema and ecchymoses.[4]
- Inspect the urinary meatus for the presence of blood. Blood at the urinary meatus is indicative of a urethral tear.
- Inspect the anus for bruising, tears, and the presence of a foreign body.

❑ Assess the remaining systems.

❑ Assess for pain using an age-appropriate pain scale (Chapter 11).

Psychosocial Assessment

❑ Assess the child's and family's understanding of the injury.

- Use words that are familiar to the child for describing the genital area.
- Assure the child's and family's privacy to obtain an accurate history and to protect them from further emotional duress.[5]

❑ Assess the child's and family's coping strategies.

- GU injuries resulting from assault or abuse can have devastating effects on the child and family.
- Early assessment with qualified individuals, such as a victim advocate or child abuse team, is beneficial to the child and family (Chapter 45).

Nursing Interventions

1. Initiate measures to maintain airway, breathing, and circulation.
   - Obtain serial assessments to detect signs of hypovolemic shock.
2. Obtain a urine specimen (clean catch specimen) to evaluate for hematuria from an awake, cooperative child who is medically stable.
3. Obtain a urine specimen through urinary bladder catheterization in the child who is medically unstable. Do not attempt urinary bladder catheterization in children with blood at the urinary meatus, blood in the scrotum, or an abnormally positioned or abnormally mobile prostate[6] to avoid further traumatic injury.

- There appears to be no direct correlation between degree of hematuria and severity of injury; therefore, any child who has significant hematuria is suspected of having injury to the kidney or to any other part of the urinary system until proved otherwise.[7]

4. Measure urinary output.
5. Administer analgesics to decrease pain and to promote cooperation, if other injuries do not preclude their use.[3]
6. Prepare for wound cleaning and repair.
   - If the child is uncomfortable with or refuses to participate in the assessment and intervention, examination under anesthesia should be performed, especially in cases of sexual assault or abuse.
7. Prepare for diagnostic testing.[3]
   - Computed tomography scan
   - Radiographs of the kidneys, ureters, and bladder
   - Ultrasonography
   - Intravenous pyelogram
   - Urethrogram
   - Retrograde urethrography
8. Inform the family frequently of the child's condition.
9. Provide emotional support to the child and family; maintain the child's modesty and privacy during assessments and treatments.
10. Initiate consultations to social services and medical subspecialties, as needed.
    - Contact child protective services and the police if assault or abuse is suspected.
11. Prepare for transfer and transport to a trauma center if needed (Chapter 8), or prepare for hospitalization and possible operative management.
    - Injuries may be much more severe than those demonstrated in the initial ED evaluation.[3]

Home Care and Prevention

Prevention of GU injuries involves the normal safety measures taken for motor vehicles, sports, and other play activities. Preventive measures for child sexual abuse are discussed in Chapter 45. Parents should be prepared for at least a 24-hour hospitalization of the child for observation of worsening symptoms of GU injury.

Conclusion

Emergency nurses should have a high index of suspicion for GU injuries in children with multiple trauma. The nurse must promote the child's modesty and comfort to gain the child's cooperation during a urogenital assessment and treatment.

References

1. Gausche-Hill, M. (2002). Genitourinary trauma. In G. Strange, W. Ahrens, S. Lelyveld, & R. Schafermeyer (Eds.), *Pediatric emergency medicine* (pp. 415–424). New York: McGraw-Hill.

2. Ellis, D. (2007). Nephrology. In B. Zitelli & H. Davis (Eds.), *Atlas of pediatric physical diagnosis* (5th ed., pp. 397–420). St. Louis, MO: Mosby.

3. Shan, B., & Lucches, M. (2006). *Atlas of pediatric emergency medicine* (pp. 848–876). New York: McGraw-Hill.

4. Starr, N. (2008) Genitourinary diseases. In C. Burns, M. Brady, A. Dunn, N. Starr, & C. Blosser (Eds.), *Pediatric primary care* (4th ed.). St. Louis, MO: Elsevier.

5. Ball, J., & Bindler, R. (Eds.). (2005). *Child health nursing: Partnering with children & families.* Upper Saddle River, NJ: Pearson Prentice Hall.

6. Lobe, T., Gore., D., & Swischuk, L. (1995). Urinary tract injuries. In W. Buntain (Ed.), *Management of pediatric trauma* (pp. 371–382). Philadelphia: Saunders.

7. Nguyen, M., & Das, S. (2002). Pediatric renal trauma. *Urology, 59*(5), 762–766.

THIRTY-FIVE

Submersion Injuries

Shauna Hansen, RN, APRN, BSN

Introduction

Historically, drowning has been defined as death occurring within 24 hours of submersion; near drowning has been defined as survival for at least 24 hours after submersion. More recent literature has urged for international consensus defining drowning as the process of experiencing respiratory impairment from submersion/immersion in liquid.[1] Despite multiple definitions, drowning and near drowning are a major cause of childhood morbidity and mortality worldwide. In children 12 to 23 months of age, drowning was the leading cause of accidental death and the second leading cause of death overall.[2] School-aged children and adolescents may overestimate their swimming abilities, become fatigued, and then drown.[3] Teenagers are also high risk because adult supervision decreases and impulsive behavior increases. However, coexisting trauma, drug or alcohol use, and suicidal intent must be considered in each case.

The physiologic consequences of drowning are primarily due to hypoxic-ischemic and reperfusion injuries. The devastating long-term neurologic consequences of drowning occur almost exclusively among patients who have drowning-associated asphyxia cardiac arrests.[2] Because of improved preventive efforts, drowning rates have declined over the past 20 years. However, it is estimated that 80% of drowning incidents remain preventable.[2]

Pediatric Considerations

Children drown in either fresh or salt water.

❏ Contrary to earlier beliefs, pulmonary injuries from freshwater and saltwater drowning typically do not differ substantially.[2] Ingestion, rather than aspiration, is more likely to cause clinically significant electrolyte imbalances including hyponatremia from ingestion of large volumes of fresh water or hypernatremia with ingestion of large volumes of salt water.

❏ The "mammalian diving" response is believed to protect human beings during submersion episodes. Bradycardia and peripheral vasoconstriction occur, primarily shunting blood to the brain and heart, and afford several minutes of additional perfusion.[3]

Etiology

Younger Children

❏ *Bathtubs:* Parents and caregivers need to be advised that they should never leave children alone or in the care of another young child while in bathtubs.[4] Adults should not be involved in any other distracting activity while supervising children. Bathtub drowning in children older than 1 year should arouse suspicion of intentional injury (Chapter 44).

❏ *Hot tubs or spas:* Hot tubs, as well as swimming pools or spas, may have uncovered suction devices that trap the child's hair or other body parts, thus forcibly submerging the child.

❏ *Swimming pools:* Children tend to overestimate their swimming ability, and this, combined with lack of appropriate supervision, increases the risk of drowning.[4]

❏ *Buckets or pails:* Young toddlers who are learning to walk pull themselves to a standing position, peer into the bucket filled with liquid, and submerge themselves into the bucket. They are not strong enough to right themselves or to extricate themselves from the bucket, thus leading to a drowning injury. If chemically treated water is in the bucket, there is an associated high mortality rate due to pulmonary injury.

Older Children and Adolescents

❏ Swimming pools

❏ Large bodies of water, such as lakes, rivers, and oceans

❏ Irrigation ditches

Focused History

- ❏ Body of water in which the child was submerged:
  - Bathtub or hot tub
  - Swimming pool
  - Bucket or pail
  - Toilet
  - Large body of water, such as a lake, river, or ocean
- ❏ Composition of the water:
  - Fresh
  - Salt
  - Chemically treated (e.g., cleaning chemicals in a bucket or toilet)
- ❏ Temperature of the water:
  - Warm
  - Cold
- ❏ Events surrounding the submersion:
  - Length of time the child was left unattended or believed to be submerged; presence of witnesses
  - Diving from a height
  - Operating watercraft (e.g., Jet Skis or motorboat)
  - Consumption of alcohol or other substances
- ❏ Symptoms following the submersion:
  - Coughing, sputtering
  - Loss of consciousness
  - Loss of cardiopulmonary function
  - Vomiting
- ❏ Prehospital treatment:
  - Cardiopulmonary resuscitation
  - Airway management
  - Application of spinal immobilization
  - Intravenous access

Focused Assessment

Physical Assessment

- ❏ Assess the airway and cervical spine.
  - Listen for signs of airway obstruction.
  - Observe for foreign material, such as vomitus or water.
  - Assess for signs of spinal cord injury (Chapter 30). The near drowning may have resulted from a spinal cord injury sustained when the patient dove into shallow water. Maintain spinal immobilization during assessment and management.
- ❏ Assess the respiratory system.
- ❏ Auscultate the chest for:
  - Respiratory rate. Apnea, bradypnea, or tachypnea may be present.
  - Adventitious sounds. Rales, rhonchi, grunting, or wheezing may be present.
  - Observe the chest for accessory muscle use, such as retractions.
- ❏ Assess the cardiovascular system.
  - Auscultate the heart for:
    - Rate. Asystole or bradycardia may be present.
    - Rhythm
    - Blood pressure
    - Peripheral perfusion
      - · Measure capillary refill. Capillary refill should be less than 3 seconds.
      - · Measure core and skin temperature. Hypothermia may be present.
      - · Observe skin color and texture. Cyanosis and mottling may be noted.
- ❏ Assess the neurologic system.
  - Measure the level of consciousness with the AVPU (Alert, responds to Verbal stimuli, responds to Painful stimuli, Unresponsive) method or Glasgow Coma Scale.
  - Measure pupillary response. Pupils may be unresponsive, fixed, and dilated if submersion was prolonged.
  - Observe for posturing.
- ❏ Assess the gastrointestinal and genitourinary systems.
  - Auscultate bowel sounds
  - Observe for abdominal rigidity
  - Observe for urinary output
- ❏ Assess the integumentary system. Observe for surface trauma, especially on the head and face.
- ❏ Assess the musculoskeletal system. Observe for muscle tone and strength in all four extremities. Muscle flaccidity may indicate spinal cord injury.

Psychosocial Assessment

- ❏ Assess the family's coping strategies. Finding a submerged sibling or child is devastating for the involved family members. Guilt and fear may be experienced. Early intervention with social services is essential.
- ❏ Assess the family's understanding of the injury. Family members may not appreciate the severity of

the child's injury. Reports in the popular press about children who survive cold-water submersions may give the family false hope.

❏ Present the facts, as they are available. This helps the family to make realistic decisions about their child's course of hospitalization and treatment.

Nursing Interventions

1. Assess and maintain the airway and cervical spine.
   - Prepare for endotracheal intubation.
   - Maintain cervical spine precautions until it is determined that a spinal cord injury is not present.

2. Initiate measures to support cardiorespiratory function.
   - Administer 100% oxygen.
   - Prepare for mechanical ventilation.
   - Initiate cardiopulmonary resuscitation as needed.
   - Initiate cardiorespiratory and oxygen saturation monitoring. Capnography monitoring will be beneficial.
   - Evaluate electrocardiogram readings. Nonspecific ST- and T-wave changes may be noted.

3. Obtain venous access and administer intravenous fluids.
   - Administer medications, such as vasopressor agents, as prescribed.
   - Obtain blood specimens for laboratory analysis, including:
     - Electrolytes. Fresh and salt water rarely have an effect on serum electrolyte levels. This is due to the massive amounts of water that must be aspirated before achieving any clinical significance.[3]
     - Blood urea nitrogen and creatinine
     - Creatinine kinase
     - Complete blood cell count
     - Alcohol and toxicology screening as appropriate
     - Anticonvulsant therapy drug levels if indicated by history

4. Monitor the child's cardiopulmonary and neurologic status. Observe for signs of increased intracranial pressure, and titrate the intravenous fluids accordingly.

5. Remove the child's wet clothing, and measure the child's temperature.
   - Prepare for active rewarming measures (Chapter 40), such as:
     - Gastric lavage

- Peritoneal lavage
- Pleural lavage via chest tubes
- Warm intravenous fluids
- Cardiopulmonary bypass

6. Observe for electrocardiographic changes, dysrhythmias, and ventricular fibrillation during rewarming.

7. Insert a nasogastric tube to reduce gastric dilation; measure the output.

8. Insert an indwelling bladder catheter to measure urinary output.

9. Prepare for diagnostic tests including:
   - Chest radiographs
   - Cervical spine radiographs
   - Arterial blood gases

10. Inform the family frequently of the child's condition.

11. Provide emotional support to the child and family.

12. Initiate consultations with staff from social services, medical subspecialties, and child protective services, as needed.

13. Prepare for transfer and transport to a tertiary care center (Chapter 8) or hospital admission.

Home Care and Prevention

The ultimate outcome of serious immersion accidents depends on the duration of submersion, the degree of pulmonary damage by aspiration, and the initial resuscitative measures.[3] Poor outcomes are due largely to drowning-associated cardiac arrest with resultant neurologic injury.[2] Children who sustained a witnessed, short submersion and do not lose consciousness or require cardiopulmonary resuscitation generally require 24-hour observation for any complications. Parents should be prepared for this admission.

Pool fencing is an important prevention strategy to decrease the risk of drowning in swimming pools.[4] Fences should be:

❏ Unclimbable

❏ Self-closing

❏ Self-locking

❏ At least 5 feet in height

❏ Built to surround the pool on all sides

❏ Constructed so that slats or bars are less than 4 inches apart

Adults who own pools, as well as adolescents, should be trained in cardiopulmonary resuscitation. Water safety training should begin at an early age. As children grow older, these safety rules should be reinforced, and the use of drugs and alcohol during water-related activities should be discouraged. Use of pool covers with motion alarms should be considered.

To further prevent drownings in the home, children should be supervised at all times while in the bathtub. Buckets of water should never be left unattended. Backyard ponds should be properly secured, and children should be educated regarding the dangers thereof.

Conclusion

Drowning and near drowning may be infrequent occurrences among the pediatric population presenting to the emergency department, depending on the emergency department's geographic location. Rapid assessment of the child's condition and prompt interventions may save the child's life. Emergency nurses should be aware of the possible role of child maltreatment or neglect in submersion injuries involving young children. Emergency nurses can become involved in water safety activities in their community to prevent these tragedies from occurring.

References

1. Idris, A., Berg, R., Bierens, J., Bossaert, L., Branche, C. M., Gabrielli, A., et al. (2003). Recommended guidelines for uniform reporting of data from drowning: The "Utstein style." *Resuscitation, 59,* 45–57.

2. Meyer, R., Theodorou, A., & Berg, R. (2006). Childhood drowning. *Pediatrics in Review, 27,* 163–169.

3. Fleisher G., Ludwig, S., & Henretig, F. (2006). *Textbook of pediatric emergency medicine* (5th ed., pp. 1009–1012). Philadelphia: Lippincott Williams & Wilkins.

4. Brenner, R. (2003). Prevention of drowning in infants, children, and adolescents. *Pediatrics, 112,* 437–439.

THIRTY-SIX

Musculoskeletal Trauma

Kathleen Merkley, RN, MS, NP

Introduction

Musculoskeletal trauma accounts for 10% to 15% of pediatric emergency department visits. As the society as a whole grows more sedentary, it is interesting to note that orthopedic injuries sustained by children and adolescents appear to be on the rise in recent years, in part because of the rapid growth of organized sports.[1]

Musculoskeletal trauma differs greatly in the pediatric population because of a number of anatomic and physiologic differences from those of the adult population. Injury in small children usually results from falls. As children grow older, injury is most often related to sports injuries or motor vehicle crashes and auto-pedestrian incidents. During adolescence, injury can also be caused by violent acts. Emergency care of the patient with musculoskeletal trauma is intended to prevent loss of function and prevent abnormal growth and deformity.

Pediatric Considerations

The musculoskeletal structure of children is very different from that of adults. These differences are outlined below:[2]

❒ Bony architecture includes a thick, active periosteum (high bone-forming potential); a growth plate called a physis; an epiphysis, which is a secondary ossification center; and the metaphysis or shaft of the bone.

❒ The bones are in a dynamic state of growth and repair that predisposes them to patterns of injury.

❒ Bones are more porous and pliable resulting in bones that bow, bend, or buckle without complete fractures.

❒ Damage to the physeal centers (often called growth plates) may lead to acute or chronic disruptions in growth of the affected extremity.

❒ Joint and ligamentous injuries are rare; traumatic forces are more likely to result in physeal injury.

❒ An active periosteum results in rapidly healing bones. Nonunion of a fracture is extremely rare. The younger the child, the faster the rate of bone healing because of the abundant supply of blood.

Mechanisms of Injury

❒ High-speed/high-impact activities contributing to injury
  ▪ Skiing
  ▪ Snowboarding
  ▪ Inline skating
  ▪ Skateboarding
  ▪ Climbing
  ▪ Bicycling
  ▪ All-terrain vehicle or motocross

❒ Traditional sports activities
  ▪ Soccer
  ▪ Football
  ▪ Basketball
  ▪ Trampolines
  ▪ Gymnastics
  ▪ Falls

❒ Other
  ▪ Motor vehicle crashes

- Pedestrian-motor vehicle crashes
- Intentional trauma
- Gunshot wounds

Injury Prevention

A number of the following strategies may be helpful in preventing pediatric musculoskeletal trauma, especially during sports-related activities:

- ❐ Provide safety equipment.
- ❐ Encourage children and adolescents to wear helmets, elbow and kneepads, and wrist guards when participating in sports that involve physical contact or risk of fall at moderate or high speeds.
- ❐ Promote adult supervision during contact sports.
- ❐ Ensure that parents and coaches are trained in basic first aid that includes recognizing an injury and removing the player from the game.
- ❐ Provide discharge instructions that emphasize that young athletes require an adequate recovery time to allow injuries to heal properly.
- ❐ Parents, athletes, and coaches should respect the body's need to heal and should identify alternative strategies for keeping the athlete a part of the team until the injury heals.
- ❐ Encourage young athletes to employ proper training, strengthening, and stretching exercises particular to their sport.
- ❐ Ensure that team players are of the same physical maturation, weight, size, and skill.

Focused History

The following information should be obtained:

- ❐ Mechanism of injury
  - Type of activity
  - Use of protective equipment
  - Height of fall if applicable
- ❐ Inability to use affected extremity
- ❐ Presence or absence of motor strength
- ❐ Loss of neurovascular function
- ❐ Open wounds or deformities
- ❐ Pain above, below, or at the injury site
- ❐ Current medications including over the counter and herbal supplements

Focused Assessment

Specific attention should be paid to the child's neurologic exam by observing cognition and behavior. All uninjured extremities and joints should be examined while trying to distract the child from the examination itself. This also allows detection of unsuspected areas of injury.[1]

- ❐ Observe the child's motor patterns and behavior.
  - Guarding
  - Not moving an extremity
- ❐ Assess the musculoskeletal system.
  - Inspect the extremity for:
    - Edema
    - Bruising
    - Deformity
    - Open wounds
    - Puncture injuries
- ❐ Palpate the extremity below and above the injury for:
  - Pain
  - Deformity
- ❐ Measure motor strength and movement in the injured and non-injured extremities.
- ❐ Measure the neurovascular status in the injured and non-injured extremities.
- ❐ Assess for pain (Chapter 11).

Nursing Interventions

1. Maintain airway, breathing, and circulation (Chapter 28).
2. Initiate measures to promote musculoskeletal function.
   - Immobilization of injury
   - Frequent reassessment of sensory, motor, and neurovascular status
3. Implement comfort measures (ice, elevation).
4. Administer pain medication.
5. Prepare for diagnostic tests.
6. Provide emotional support to patient and family members.
7. Prepare for transfer and transport to a trauma center (Chapter 8); prepare for hospitalization or discharge to home.

Fractures Unique to Children

The anatomic and physiologic differences in children account for a number of injuries that are unique to the pediatric population. These injuries include torus fractures, greenstick fractures, bowing deformities, avulsion fractures, growth plate or physeal injuries, and ligamentous injuries.

Torus (Buckle) Fracture

❑ Occurs in the metaphyseal region of the bone
❑ Results from a compressive load-type injury
❑ Cortex of the bone buckles
❑ Stable fracture pattern

Greenstick Fracture

❑ Most common fracture in children: 50% of fractures[2]
❑ Incomplete fracture
❑ Cortex remains intact on one side
❑ Angulation and rotation common

Bowing Deformities

❑ Force is longitudinal
❑ Stops short of creating a fracture
❑ May cause deformity of the bony structure

Avulsion Fracture

❑ Strong muscular attachments adhere to secondary centers of ossification
❑ Occurs during intense muscle contraction
❑ Most often occurs in the pelvis

Physeal (Growth Plate) Fractures

These fractures occur at the physis (growth plate). They are most commonly seen in adolescents and occur most often in the upper limbs. They are classified as follows:[1]

Salter-Harris Type I

❑ Separation of the metaphysis from the epiphysis through the zone of provisional calcification
❑ Diagnosis is difficult
❑ Displacement is minimal
❑ Usually benign

Salter-Harris Type II

❑ Most common pediatric physeal fracture
❑ Like a type I, except that a portion of the metaphyseal bone is displaced with the epiphyseal fragment
❑ Fracture through the physis and metaphysis; the epiphysis is not involved

❑ Good prognosis

Salter-Harris Type III and IV

❑ Intra-articular injuries that involve the growth plate
❑ Must restore anatomic position to restore normal joint mechanics and prevent growth arrest
❑ Needs orthopedic consultation because of an increased risk of functional disability

Salter-Harris Type V

❑ Results from axial compression of the growth plate
❑ Difficult to diagnose
❑ Radiograph may appear normal
❑ Diagnosis often made after growth arrest becomes evident

Ligamentous Injuries

❑ Ligaments exert greater mechanical strength than epiphysis, physis, or perichondrial rings
❑ Epiphyseal separation requires less force than tearing of the ligament
❑ True sprains unusual before adolescence
❑ More likely an occult or Salter-Harris fracture if radiographs are normal

Open Fractures

❑ Complications increase, specifically the incidence of infection.
❑ A thorough neurovascular examination should be done on admission and frequently thereafter.
❑ Intravenous access and intravenous antibiotics should be administered.
❑ Surgical intervention is required so the patient should be put on nothing-by-mouth (NPO) status immediately.

Multiple Trauma

❑ Pediatric fractures are rarely life threatening even though they appear noticeable.
❑ A thorough evaluation of the ABCs is critical.
❑ Blood loss may be significant from pelvic and femur fractures.
❑ Early immobilization is important.

Compartment Syndrome

Compartment syndrome results from decreased vascular perfusion due to increased tissue pressures in a closed fascial compartment of an extremity. If left untreated, muscle necrosis and nerve palsies may result.[1] It occurs after fractures, crush injuries and cast placement.

❑ May affect any limb, but most commonly occurs in the anterior compartment of the leg.

❑ Pain is out of proportion to the magnitude of injury.

❑ The muscular compartment is hard, tense, and swollen.

❑ The patient experiences:
- Decreased sensation
- Pallor
- Pulselessness
- Paresthesias
- Paralysis

❑ Pain on passive stretch is the most reliable clinical finding.

❑ Measures to promote peripheral perfusion should be immediately initiated.
- Position the extremity at or below the level of the heart.
- Remove any constrictive dressings or elastic bandages.
- Split an existing cast.

❑ Requires immediate orthopedic evaluation.

❑ A fasciotomy may be performed if compartment pressure measurements are elevated.

❑ Parents should be taught the signs and symptoms of compartment syndrome before discharge if their child is wearing a cast or circumferential dressing. It should be stressed that a delay in seeking treatment after the onset of symptoms may result in muscle weakness, contractures, and delayed fracture healing.

Intentional Trauma

❑ Up to 20% of children who are victims of intentional trauma sustain fractures with a large percentage of these seen in infants younger than 1 year of age.[3]

❑ A limited number of fracture types are specific for child maltreatment (e.g., spiral fractures, epiphyseal-metaphyseal rib fractures).

❑ Injury or fracture may be out of proportion for the history given.

❑ Fractures may be inconsistent with the developmental stage of the child.

❑ Fractures may be seen with associated injuries.

❑ Multiple fractures may be seen in various stages of healing.

Common Injuries of the Upper Extremities and Treatment

Clavicle Fractures

❑ Most commonly fractured bone in children.[1]

❑ Half of these fractures occur in children under 10 years of age.[1]

❑ Etiology
- Direct force
- Indirect force from landing on an outstretched hand

❑ Eighty percent of fractures occur in the midshaft of the clavicle.

❑ Fracture type is usually greenstick or bowing.

❑ Asymmetry of the clavicles is noted.

❑ Treatment includes a sling, sling and swath, or figure-of-eight dressing.

❑ Healing occurs within 3 to 6 weeks.

❑ Surgical repair is necessary if:
- Subclavian compromise
- Unstable
- Open fracture

Proximal Humeral Fractures

❑ Etiology—from falling backward onto shoulder.

❑ May involve the growth plate of the proximal humerus.[4]

❑ Simple immobilization with a sling and swath for several weeks.

❑ Surgery repair is rarely required.

❑ Observe for possible radial nerve injury.
- Loss of strength in extension of wrist and fingers.
- Loss of sensation in the web space between thumb and index finger.

Humeral Shaft Fractures

❑ Etiology—direct blow or twisting type injury.

❑ If spiral fracture in patient < 3 years of age consider intentional trauma.[4]

❑ Fractures heal well in displaced position.

❑ Treatment includes a sugar-tong splint and sling.

❑ Observe for possible radial nerve injury.

- Loss of strength in extension of wrist and fingers.
- Loss of sensation in the web space between thumb and index finger.

Elbow Fractures

❐ Priorities for care if an elbow fracture is suspected:
  - Neurovascular assessment
  - Fracture stabilization
  - Splint limb in deformed position
  - Nothing by mouth (NPO)
  - Frequent neurovascular examinations
❐ Most common—supracondylar fractures 50%, followed by lateral condylar fractures, medial epicondylar fractures, and radial neck fractures.[1]
❐ Occur in children aged 3 to 10 years.
❐ Etiology—fall on outstretched arm with hyperextension of the elbow.
❐ Neurovascular injury seen in 8% of injuries.[1]
❐ Posterior displacement normal.
❐ Child will often hold elbow in flexion.
❐ May have referred pain to wrist.
❐ Nondisplaced fractures require a posterior splint.
❐ Displaced fractures require surgical repair.
❐ Orthopedic referral is necessary.

Radial Head Subluxation (Nursemaid's Elbow)

❐ Annular ligament partially detaches, slips into radiohumeral joint, and becomes entrapped.
❐ Mechanism of injury caused by axial traction (yanking or pulling on the child's arm) is a classic historical finding.
❐ Injury of children from a few months to 5 years of age.[4]
❐ Child holds arm in pronation with the elbow flexed.
❐ Minimal pain.
❐ Obtaining radiographs is controversial; most often diagnosis can be made from history and presentation. Radiographs should be obtained if there is a history of trauma.
❐ Reduction most often achieved with supination and flexion.

Distal Radius and Ulna Fractures

❐ Occur more often than all other bones except the clavicle.[4]

❐ Incidence of neurovascular compromise is low.
❐ Etiology—fall on outstretched hand.
❐ Greenstick injuries are common.
❐ Capacity to remodel is excellent.
❐ Volar splint then short arm cast for 3 to 4 weeks.
❐ Orthopedic referral for injuries with angulation > 10 degrees.

Common Injuries of the Lower Extremities and Treatment

Slipped Capital Femoral Epiphysis

Slipped capital femoral epiphysis is the most common hip disorder of adolescence. It results from a structural weakness of the proximal femoral epiphysis.

Femoral Fractures

❐ Usually result from high-energy mechanisms, such as motor vehicle crashes or auto-pedestrian incidents.
❐ Children with femur fractures often have other significant injuries of the head, chest, or abdomen and require a full trauma evaluation.
❐ Seventy percent of femur fractures occur along the femoral shaft.[1]
❐ Intentional trauma should be ruled out in children younger than 2 years of age.
❐ Definitive treatment depends on the age of the patient and the severity of the fracture:
  - Birth to 10 years of age—Buck's traction and spica cast.
  - Adolescents—open reduction and intramedullary rodding.

Knee Injuries

❐ In children, ligaments are stronger than the physeal cartilage; thus fractures of a physis are more common.[1]
❐ Common fractures of the knee include:
  - Fracture of the distal femoral physis
  - Tibial spine avulsion
  - Tibial tuberosity avulsion
  - Patellar fractures
  - Patellar dislocations
❐ Rare but most serious: long bone fracture.[4]
❐ Ligamentous injuries uncommon.

❑ Knee injuries should always be evaluated radiographically.

Tibia and Fibula Fractures

❑ Most common lower extremity fractures in children.

❑ Most fractures are stable, can be placed in a posterior splint and sent for orthopedic referral within a week.

❑ Healing time is rapid—usually 6 to 8 weeks.[1]

❑ Also a common site for stress fractures.

Toddler's Fractures

❑ Occur in children 9 to 36 months of age.

❑ The child limps or refuses to walk.

❑ Usually no history of injury can be recollected.

❑ Caused by an oblique nondisplaced fracture of the distal tibia.

❑ If radiographs negative, splint and repeat films in 8 to 10 days.

Home Care and Prevention

❑ Provide instructions on crutch walking. An example of crutch walking instructions for patients can be found at http://www.chw.org/display/PPF/DocID/22584/nav/1/router.asp

❑ Instruct on the importance of activity modification.

❑ Provide information about narcotic and over-the-counter analgesics.

❑ Demonstrate application of immobilization devices such as; splints, elastic bandages, slings, etc., with return demonstration given by parent/guardian.

❑ Instruct parents about the signs of neurovascular compromise and to return immediately to the emergency department if they occur:

- Severe pain not relieved by analgesics
- Increased or decreased skin temperature
- Tingling with decreased sensation
- Pallor, delayed capillary refill
- Inability to move fingers or toes

❑ Discuss importance of elevation and icing the injury.

❑ Educate about the significance of keeping splints and casts clean and dry.

Conclusion

Although rarely life threatening, musculoskeletal trauma can affect the child's mobility and growth as the child develops. Early recognition of neurovascular compromise may save a child's limb function and improve the functional outcome. Emergency nurses can become involved in teaching coaches, trainers, adults, and adolescents how to recognize and prevent sports injuries.

References

1. Bachman, D., & Santora, S. (2006). Orthopedic trauma. In G. Fleisher, S. Ludwig, & F. Henretig (Eds.), *Textbook of pediatric emergency medicine* (pp. 1525–1569). Philadelphia: Lippincott Williams & Wilkins.

2. Huurmann, W. W., & Ginsburg, G. M. (1997). Musculoskeletal injury in children. *Pediatrics in Review, 18,* 429–440.

3. Kocher, M. S., Kasser, J. R. (2000). Orthopaedic aspects of child abuse. *Journal of the American Academy of Orthopedic Surgery, 8*(1), 10–20.

4. Overly, F., & Steele, D. W. (2003). Orthopedic emergencies. *Clinical Pediatric Emergency Medicine, 2,* 106–117.

THIRTY-SEVEN

Burn Trauma

Mary Jo Cerepani, RN, MSN, CRNP, CEN

Introduction

Burns are the second leading cause of death among children 0 to 4 years of age and the third leading cause of death in children aged 4 to 9 years.[1] Each year, 2,500 children in the United States die from burns, and nearly 10,000 suffer permanent disability.[2] Although most burns are not fatal, they can be disfiguring and disabling.

Children are at greater risk for burn injury because of their inability to recognize a dangerous situation; they also are less likely to respond appropriately when an injury occurs. Table 37.1 outlines risk factors associated with burn injuries in the pediatric population. The purpose of this chapter is to describe the mechanisms of burn trauma and to outline the nursing assessment and intervention for the child who has sustained a burn injury.

Pediatric Considerations

Children are more likely to sustain a serious burn and more likely to die from it than are adults. This increased likelihood of morbidity and mortality is related to the unique physiologic and pathophysiologic changes in children following a burn injury.

❒ The child's small airway diameter is easily obstructed by edema and mucus.

■ Inhalation injuries are devastating, because they lead to rapid edema and airway obstruction.

■ Young children rely on the diaphragm for breathing; chest eschar can restrict diaphragmatic movement and impede respiratory effort.

■ Oxygen consumption is high (6–8 mL/kg) in children, and this demand is increased following a burn injury.

❒ Decreased cardiac output occurs after a burn injury because of decreased preload due to third spacing into the interstitial space. Inadequate fluid resuscitation results if this physiologic factor is not recognized early.

❒ Children have a larger body surface-area-to-weight ratio than do adults, placing them at increased risk for hypothermia due to convective and evaporative heat loss following a thermal injury.

❒ Young children have thin, delicate skin and shallow dermal appendages; therefore, a deeper thickness of burn injury occurs at lower temperatures and shorter exposure times and increases children's susceptibility to the effects of thermal injury.

❒ Children have greater metabolic needs because they have less glycogen stored in the liver, resulting in hypoglycemia.

❒ The ability to concentrate urine increases with age; inadequate fluid resuscitation can impair renal function.

■ Fluid resuscitation following major burns must be carefully calculated. In pediatric patients, fluid resuscitation requirements are not only calculated on the amount of surface burned, but on the types of burns sustained and the volume of urine produced hourly.

TABLE 37.1 Risk Factors Associated with Burn Injuries

Age Group	Developmental Factors and Activities	Burn Injury Risk
Infants	Young infants: Splashing and spilling of hot liquids while held by adults during meal	Scald burn
	Crawling infants: pulling tablecloths and hot items onto themselves	Scald burn
	Older infants in baby walkers; pulling hot items onto themselves	Scald burn
Toddlers	Exploring environment; learning to walk and run; learning to feed self	Scald burn
	Biting on electrical cords; placing fingers into electrical outlets	Electrical burn
	Exploring chemicals kept in kitchen and bathroom	Chemical burn
Preschoolers	Learning to turn on the water for a bath	Scald burn
	Imitating parents by grabbing and pulling on pots and pans; striking matches	Flame burn
School-aged Children	Participating in household cleaning and mixing cleaning agents	Chemical inhalation injury
	Experiencing peer pressure and dares to perform potentially dangerous activities	Electrical injury; flame burn
	Learning to use matches to light barbecue grills, campfires, candles and fireworks	Flame burn
	Playing with chemistry sets	Chemical and flame injury
Adolescents	Working in restaurants	Scald burn
	Using gasoline-powered equipment, such as lawnmowers and cars	Flame burn
	Using hair dryers or electric radios while standing on a wet bathroom floor	Flame or electrical burn
	Being exposed to electricity during home repairs or in the outdoors	Electrical burn
	Playing sport outdoors during an electrical storm	Lighting injury
	Smoking cigarettes in enclosed spaces where gasoline or flammable agents are stored	Flame or flash burn
	Sniffing gasoline or natural gas	Flame or chemical burn
	Returning to a burning building to rescue people or pets	Flame burn; inhalation injury

Bernardo, L., & Sullivan, K. (1990). Care of the pediatric patient with burns. In R. Trofiono (Ed.), *Care of the burn-injuried patient* (pp. 249–276). Philadelphia: Davis.

Thermal Burns

Thermal burns result from exposure to hot temperatures. The skin of infants and children can only tolerate exposure to temperatures at or below 111 °F (43.8 °C).

Scald

❒ Scald burns are the most common thermal injuries in children younger than 3 years of age.

■ The greatest number of scald burns occurs in the bathroom and kitchen.

■ Contact with hot liquids such as tea, coffee, or water

may cause a full-thickness burn in only 1 second.

❒ Prolonged exposure to tap water heated to 125 °F (52 °C) or higher may cause a full-thickness burn.

❒ Immersion in scalding water results in wound demarcation which can be indicative of child maltreatment; further assessment is required (Chapter 44).

Flame

❒ Flame injuries are more common in older children; however, children from birth to 5 years of age are at the greatest risk for fire-related deaths in the home.

❑ Flame burns are the second most common burns in children 3 years of age and older.

❑ Flame injuries may be caused by matches or lighters, house fires, faulty electrical wiring, cooking incidents, fireworks, wood stoves, or kerosene heaters.

❑ The flame burn is often associated with an inhalation injury from the hot air and toxic fumes emanating from the burning substances.

- The combustible material of the surrounding environment may produce toxic fumes (e.g., carbon monoxide), which can significantly compromise the respiratory system. A patient burned outdoors has a lower risk of inhalation injury; however, the absence of a history of entrapment (confinement in a closed space) does not exclude inhalation injury.

Flash Burns

❑ Flash burns are caused by an explosion or ignition of gasoline fumes, or an electrical flash.

❑ These burns may cause severe facial edema and inhalation injury from increased heat production.

Contact Burns

❑ Contact burns are caused from exposure to hot objects (e.g., radiator, iron, hot tar, or hot grease). Many of these burns result in a full-thickness burn.

Chemical Burns

Chemical burns may be caused by common household cleaners, gasoline, paint removers, disc batteries, and other toxic chemicals stored in the home or garage (Chapter 42).

Electrical Injuries

Electrical injuries are uncommon in the pediatric population, due to the increased awareness of how to protect pediatric patients from injury. Nonfatal electrical injuries still occur, typically in infants and toddlers who bite on electrical cords or place their fingers, tongues, or small objects into electrical outlets. Adolescents have an increased risk of electrical injury, but only due to their risk taking behaviors (e.g., may climb on transmission towers, sustaining a fatal high-voltage electrical injury). Adolescents may be exposed to electrical risks in employment opportunities, such as industrial settings.

Radiation Injuries

These injuries are rare in the pediatric patient but may result from radiation therapy or from prolonged exposure to ultraviolet light from the sun.

Unintentional Versus Intentional Injuries

Burn injuries can occur at the workplace, home, and in association with motor vehicle crashes and recreational activity. Most often, these burn injuries are unintentional. Intentional burns most often occur to young children. Thorough investigation of any burn injuries to a child requires additional assessment to detect possible child maltreatment (Chapter 44) and to prevent future injuries or death.

Pathophysiology of Burn Injuries

Integumentary System

❑ The skin is composed of three layers of tissue (Chapter 20).

❑ Burn injuries cause significant changes in local tissue morphology and systemic physiology.

- Tissue destruction following thermal contact is a function of both intensity and duration of exposure. On the microscopic level, tissue destruction is characterized by a zone effect:
  - The inner zone of coagulation is where irreversible cellular death occurs.
  - The zone of stasis surrounds the zone of coagulation and has the potential for healing if perfusion and moisturization are preserved.
  - The outer zone of hyperemia is characterized by redness and the ability for rapid healing.

❑ Increased capillary permeability results in fluid shifts from the intravascular space to the interstitial space (third spacing). This fluid and protein shift results in edema, decreased cardiac output, and hemoconcentration.

❑ The maximum amount of edema will occur 8 to 12 hours post injury in small burns and up to 24 hours post injury in large burns. Capillary integrity may be restored 18 to 24 hours post injury in small burns and up to 30 hours post injury in large burns.[3]

Respiratory System

Direct injury to the respiratory tract can occur with the inhalation of smoke and products of combustion.

Pulmonary edema results from fluid shifts following the burn injury.

Neurologic System

Alteration in mental status may result from hypoxia and fluid shifts within the brain tissue.

Gastrointestinal System

Ileus may occur from peripheral circulatory collapse and is usually found in patients with burns involving 20% of the total body surface area (TBSA).

Genitourinary System

A decreased circulating fluid volume results in a decrease in the renal plasma flow and in the glomerular filtration rate and a subsequent decrease in urinary output. Fluid shifts may cause renal damage, such as tubular necrosis, if intravenous fluid resuscitation is inadequate.

Metabolic Changes

A hypermetabolic state occurs as a result of a major burn. This hypermetabolic state increases caloric and nitrogen demands of the body to achieve proper wound healing. Burn wounds are unlike any other disease state in that the injury produces such a great demand for glucose, protein, and fat.

Focused History

Mechanism of Burn Injury

Historical findings for each mechanism of injury are outlined in their respective sections.

Injury History

❑ Time of burn injury
- Delays in seeking emergency department (ED) treatment may be indicative of child maltreatment (Chapter 44) and require additional investigation by the emergency department staff.
- Duration of contact with the burn agent.

❑ Location at the time of injury
- Establishes an index of suspicion for inhalation injury if the burn occurred in an enclosed space.

❑ Circumstances surrounding the injury
- Presence or absence of adult supervision may be indicative of child maltreatment (Chapter 44).

❑ Association with another mechanism of injury

- Injuries sustained in a motor vehicle crash may be far more significant than that of the thermal burn.
- Being thrown from an open window or jumping from a significant height during a house fire may result in fractures or internal injuries in addition to thermal and inhalation injuries.

Prehospital Treatment

❑ Efforts employed to stop the burning process.

❑ Initial aid to treat the burn wound, including home treatments or remedies (e.g., application of butter, ointments, and dressings).

Focused Assessment

Physical Assessment

The burn wound has the lowest priority; airway, breathing, and circulation are the most important systems to support.

❑ Assess the airway.
- Assess for sounds of airway compromise.
  - Stridor
  - Hoarseness

❑ Inspect the mouth for burn wounds from chemicals, electricity, or thermal sources.

❑ Note the presence of carbonaceous sputum, singed nasal hairs, and lip edema.

❑ Assess the respiratory system.
- Auscultate the chest for:
  - Respiratory rate
  - Adventitious breath sounds. Adventitious sounds in a patient with a history of entrapment in an enclosed space may indicate an inhalation injury.

❑ Inspect the chest for equal expansion and symmetry.

❑ Assess the cardiovascular system.
- Auscultate the heart for:
  - Rate
  - Rhythm
  - Quality
  - Measure the blood pressure
- Assess the peripheral perfusion.
  - Palpate peripheral pulses for equality and quality. Circumferential eschar may restrict peripheral perfusion.
  - Measure core and skin temperature.
  - Measure capillary refill.

- Inspect the skin color.
  - Assess the neurologic system.
    - Assess the level of consciousness with AVPU (*A*lert, responds to *V*erbal stimuli, responds to *P*ainful stimuli, *U*nresponsive) method or the Glasgow coma scale (GCS).
  - Assess for pain (Chapter 11).
  - Assess the gastrointestinal and genitourinary systems.
    - Inspect the abdomen for distention or rigidity.
    - Auscultate the abdomen for bowel sounds.
    - Gently palpate the abdomen for pain and tenderness.
    - Observe for vomiting.
    - Note the presence of urinary output.
- Assess the integumentary system to determine the TBSA burned.
  - Assess the burn wound for:
    - Location.
    - Depth. Burns are categorized as superficial, partial-thickness, and full-thickness injury on the basis of depth and the ability for regeneration. The differentiation between deep partial-thickness and full-thickness burn injury is often difficult to make at the time of the initial assessment. Table 37.2 summarizes the characteristics of burn wounds.[4]
    - Percentage. Use the Modified Lund and Browder chart to calculate the percentage of total body surface area (TBSA) burned (Figure 37.1).
  - Classify the burn injury (Table 37.3).
- Assess the musculoskeletal system.
  - Observe for circumferential burns of the extremities or digits.
  - Observe for deformities or open fractures.
  - Assess the fingers and toes for color, sensitivity, and motion.

Psychosocial Assessment

- Assess the child's and family's coping strategies.
  - A burn injury is extremely stressful for both the family and the patient.
  - More than one family member may have been involved in the burning episode, including the parents.
  - Other family members may be involved in the emergency department treatment.

- Assess the child's prior hospital experiences, especially with painful procedures.
  - The pain of burn injuries causes both fear and anxiety in pediatric patients of all ages.
  - Patients and families alike are concerned about the cosmetic appearance following a burn injury; early referral to burn surgeons or plastic surgeons is essential to optimize the patient's cosmetic and functional outcomes.
- Assess the family dynamics.
  - The child's and family's statements and reactions should be documented precisely as witnessed.
  - In the case of child maltreatment, often stories are changed and children may have a flat affect as a result of the abuse (Chapter 44).
  - Assess for signs of prior abuse by inspecting the child for cigarette burns, burns on the back, signs of demarcation from immersion into hot liquids or bath water, or other scars (Chapter 44).

Nursing Interventions for Moderate and Major Burns[5]

1. Stop the burning process if this has not occurred in the prehospital setting.
   - Extinguish flames by having the child stop, drop, and roll. Alternatively, wrap the patient in a blanket to smother the flames.
   - Apply room temperature water to thermal burns; however, major burn injuries should not be cooled for more than a few minutes because of the child's temperature liability and the risk of hypothermia.
     - Assess for heat dissipation from the skin by holding a hand over the burned area. If heat is felt, the burning process is still in progress.
   - Remove burned clothing. If clothing has stuck to the tissue, cut around the clothing.
   - Remove any watches, rings, or other objects from injured extremities. Because of fluid shifts, a tourniquet-like effect will result in the loss of arterial circulation.
2. Maintain airway patency.
   - Open the airway with the chin lift-jaw thrust technique.
   - Prepare for endotracheal intubation in the patient with a suspected inhalation injury, airway injury, or altered level of consciousness.
3. Initiate measures to support respiratory effort.
   - Administer high-flow oxygen.

Table 37.2 Summary of Burn Characteristics

Category	Depth	Appearance	Pain Level	Healing Time
Superficial	Involves entire epidermis	Red, dry, flaky skin Similar to a sunburn Blisters are not present	Painful	3–5 days without scarring
Superficial partial-thickness	Involves only the epidermis and the upper dermal layers	Wet "weeping" areas with or without blister formation Blanching with pressure Mild to moderate edema	Very painful	10–21 days, usually without scarring
Deep partial-thickness	Involves the entire epidermis; includes destruction of the dermal papillae but spares sweat glands and hair follicles	Cherry pink or mottled red appearance May have lost pin-prick sensation but retains pressure sensation Considered a full-thickness burn in children	Very painful	May require excision and grafting
Full-thickness	Involves the epidermis, including destruction of all dermal appendages and epithelial elements	White, charred, and leathery Firm eschar with thrombosed vessels	No pain	Excision and grafting required, because no spontaneous regeneration is possible

- Initiate assisted ventilations with bag-valve-mask ventilation.
- Prepare for mechanical ventilation in the patient with suspected inhalation or airway injury.

4. Initiate interventions to support the circulation.
   - Initiate cardiorespiratory and oxygen saturation monitoring.
   - Measure blood pressure, preferably in an unburned extremity. If the extremity is burned, an open gauze pad can be placed over the burn before the cuff is applied. Do not obtain the blood pressure in a circumferentially burned extremity.
   - Obtain venous access with large-bore intravenous catheters, preferably in unburned extremities (burned extremities can be cannulated if the burns are not circumferential).
   - Initiate an intraosseous infusion in an unburned extremity if venous access is not attained within 90 seconds or three attempts. Prepare for a venous cutdown or central line placement, if needed.
     - Initiate intravenous fluid resuscitation in patients with burns involving greater than 10% of TBSA. Then calculate and infuse the lactated Ringer's solution for fluid resuscitation based on the calculated TBSA burned (Table 37.4). There are

numerous calculations to determine the amount of fluid to infuse (e.g., Parkland, Carvajal). This calculation is a recommendation only; fluid resuscitation requirements are dictated by the physiologic status of the patient, with urine output being the most important indicator of this status.[10]

- Obtain blood specimens for laboratory analysis.
  - Complete blood count and differential
  - Electrolytes
  - Blood urea nitrogen, creatinine, and glucose
  - Prothrombin time and partial thromboplastin time
  - Alcohol and toxicology screening, if indicated

5. Assess the child's neurologic status and assess for pain.

6. Insert a nasogastric tube for gastric decompression if the burns involve more than 25% TBSA.
   - Measure gastric output. Paralytic ileus can be an early complication of a severe burn injury.

7. Insert an indwelling bladder catheter to measure urinary volume and specific gravity.
   - Urinary output is the best indicator of the adequacy of resuscitation. While the formula for calculating

Figure 37.1 Modified Lund and Browder Chart

	Age (years)					
Burned Area	1	1 to 4	5 to 9	10 to 14	15	Adult
	Total Body Surface (%)					
Head	19	17	13	11	9	7
Neck	2	2	2	2	2	3
Anterior Trunk	13	13	13	13	13	13
Posterior Trunk	13	13	13	13	13	13
Right Buttock	2.5	2.5	2.5	2.5	2.5	2.5
Left Buttock	2.5	2.5	2.5	2.5	2.5	2.5
Genitalia	1	1	1	1	1	1
Right Upper Arm	4	4	4	4	4	4
Left Upper Arm	4	4	4	4	4	4
Right Lower Arm	3	3	3	3	3	3
Left Lower Arm	3	3	3	3	3	3
Right Hand	2.5	2.5	2.5	2.5	2.5	2.5
Left Hand	2.5	2.5	2.5	2.5	2.5	2.5
Right Thigh	5.5	6.5	8	8.5	9	9.5
Left Thigh	5.5	6.5	8	8.5	9	9.5
Right Leg	5	5	5.5	6	6.5	7
Left Leg	5	5	5.5	6	6.5	7
Right Foot	3.5	3.5	3.5	3.5	3.5	3.5
Left Foot	3.5	3.5	3.5	3.5	3.5	3.5

Emergency Nurses Association. (2007). *Trauma nursing core course (provider manual).* (6th ed., pp. 197–224). Des Plaines, IL: Author.

urinary output is in Table 37.5, generally urine output should be at least 1 mL per kg of body weight per hour of urine.[10]

- Obtain a urine specimen for:
  - Urinalysis
  - Urinary chorionic gonadotropin (in menarcheal age females)
  - Toxicology screening, if indicated

8. Initiate measures to maintain normothermia.
- Increase the room temperature.
- Cover the patient with warm blankets or sheets.
- For wounds covering a large percentage of TBSA, no antimicrobial dressings are needed, because the burn treatment center staff will cleanse and treat the wound on the child's arrival.
- Administer warmed intravenous fluids.

9. Administer medication, as prescribed.
- Administer tetanus prophylaxis if the child's immunizations are not current. A burn wound is considered contaminated tissue that requires tetanus prophylaxis.
- Administer intravenous narcotic analgesics for pain management (Chapter 11). The intravenous route is used because fluid shifts following the burn injury and during fluid resuscitation cause sporadic uptake

TABLE 37.3 Classification of Burn Injuries

Classification	Description
Minor	< 10% total body surface area affected by superficial or superficial partial-thickness burns
	No burns involving the face, hands, feet, joints, or perineum
	No respiratory involvement
	No pre-existing diseases
Moderate	> 10% total body surface area affected by any deep partial thickness or full-thickness burns
	No burns involving the face, hands, feet, joints, or perineum
	No respiratory involvement
	No electrical burn injury
	No circumferential burn
Major	> 5% total body surface area affected by full-thickness burns
	> 10% total body surface area affected by deep partial-thickness burns involving the face, hands, feet, joints, or perineum
	Any chemical burn
	Any suspicion of inhalation injury
	Any electrical injury
	Any preexisting medical condition

TABLE 37.4 Calculations for Intravenous Fluid Resuscitation

Parkland Formula: Percent of the total body surface area burned × child's weight in kilograms × 4 mL = number of mL to be infused in 24 hours, in addition to maintenance fluids in children ≤ 5 years of age.

Administer one half of this amount in the first 8 hours.

Administer one quarter of the original amount in the next 8 hours.

Administer the final one quarter of the solution in the last 8 hours.

Example

25% TBSA burned × 40 kgs × 4 mL = 4,000 mL of lactated Ringer's solution to be infused in 24 hours.

Administer 2,000 mL (1/2 of 4,000 mL) in the first 8 hours (a rate of 250 mL/hour).

Administer 1000 mL (1/4 of 4,000 mL) in the next 8 hours (a rate of 125 mL/hour).

Administer 1000 mL (1/4 of 4,000 mL) in the final 8 hours (a rate of 125 mL/hour).

of medications, leading to inadequate dosing. Suggested intravenous analgesics are:

- Morphine sulfate, 0.1–0.2 mg/kg/dose, every 2–4 hours, as needed, maximum = 15.0 mg/dose.
- Fentanyl, 1–2 μg/kg/dose, every 30–60 minutes, as needed.

10. Prepare for additional procedures.
   - Prepare for tissue pressure measurements in extremities with circumferential burns.
   - Prepare for escharotomies if tissue pressures are high.
   - Prepare for radiographs, such as chest, extremity, or abdomen, depending on associated injuries.

11. Inform the family frequently of the child's condition; support their presence during emergency department treatment.

12. Provide emotional support to the child and family.
   - Explain all procedures and treatments.

Table 37.5 Formula for Calculating Urinary Output

Formula	Example
Child's weight < 30 kg: Urinary output is 1.0–2.0 mL per kg per hour.	1.0–2.0 mL x 25 kg per hour = 25–50 mL per hour minimum urinary output should be maintained.
Child's weight > 30 kg: Urinary output is 0.5 mL per kg per hour.	0.5 mL x 40 kg per hour = 20 mL per hour minimum urinary output should be maintained.

- Encourage the family to touch or hold the child in unburned areas.
- Be honest about expected outcomes.
- If child maltreatment is suspected, complete the required reporting forms and photograph the burns; contact social services and child protective services. Explain to the family why this action has been taken.

13. Initiate consultations with social services personnel, medical subspecialists, and community agencies, as needed.

14. Prepare for transfer and transport to a burn center.
    - Transfer is initiated for all children with severe burn injuries and, as needed, children with moderate burn injuries.
    - Explain to the patient and family the importance of and need for specialized burn care.

15. Initiate interventions to assist the family whose child has died from burn injuries, consider a debriefing for the involved staff members (Chapter 26).

Nursing Interventions for Minor Burns[6]

1. Stop the burning process.
   - Pour room temperature water over the thermal burn. Never apply ice to the burn because additional tissue damage may result.

2. Assess the child's level of pain, and initiate pharmacologic and nonpharmacologic interventions prior to performing wound care (Chapter 11).
   - Prepare to administer oral narcotic and nonnarcotic analgesics.
     - Acetaminophen with codeine
     - Morphine sulfate concentrated oral solution, 0.2 to 0.5 mg/kg/dose, every 4 to 6 hours
     - Acetaminophen, 10 to 15 mg/kg/dose, not to exceed 2.6 grams over 24 hours

3. Perform wound care.

- Wash the burn wound with a mild soap.
- Leave blisters intact to promote wound healing; debride broken blisters and any necrotic tissue that is present around the wound.
- Apply an antimicrobial agent to the burn wound.
  - Apply silver sulfadiazine cream if the patient is not allergic to sulfa medications and the burn wound is not on the face (silver sulfadiazine may cause skin discoloration when applied to the face).
  - Apply Bacitracin if the child is allergic to sulfa medications or if the burn is on the face.
- Encourage the patient to participate in the wound care, if the patient desires to do so. Patients who participate in their wound care may feel a sense of control.
- Dress the burn wound.
  - Facial burns are generally left open to air when ointment is applied.
  - Chest burns can be covered with sterile gauze pads; a cotton t-shirt or stockinette (Hyginette™) dressing can be applied to keep the gauze pads in place.
  - Extremity burns can be covered with gauze pads and a stockinette (Hyginette™).
  - Burned fingers and toes should be separated with small gauze pads to prevent webbing on healing.
  - Perineal burns can be covered with gauze and a diaper; they must be cleaned after each urination or defecation.

Home Care and Prevention

Children with moderate and major burn wounds are hospitalized in burn trauma centers until their wounds are healed. For families whose children have minor burn wounds, home care instructions are reviewed prior to emergency department discharge. Parents should be reminded that approximately 10 to 20 days are needed for complete wound healing.[7]

❑ Demonstrate the wound care the family will perform at home; usually, wound care is performed twice a day.[8]

  ▪ The parents should wash their hands before changing the burn wound dressing.

  ▪ The child's burn wound should be soaked in warm water for about 10 minutes. The child should be encouraged to play with water toys.

❑ The wound should be gently washed with a clean washcloth and a mild soap to remove all of the antimicrobial agent.[8]

  ▪ The wound should be dried with a clean towel.

  ▪ A thin layer of the prescribed antimicrobial ointment should be applied directly onto the gauze pad, and then the pad should be anchored with tape or stockinette (Hyginette™).

  ▪ Provide opportunities for return demonstrations to allay the family's anxieties about performing these procedures at home and to increase their confidence in their ability to comply with the treatment process.

  ▪ Give burn wound supplies to the family on discharge or give the family a prescription for the purchase of the necessary supplies.

❑ Teach the patient and family the signs and symptoms of burn wound infection (fever, redness, swelling, purulent drainage, cloudy fluid, decreased appetite, and decreased activity).

❑ Assure adequate analgesia with a written prescription or with access to over-the-counter medication.

  ▪ Consider providing an antihistamine, such as diphenhydramine, to allay itching as the wound heals.

  ▪ Review with the family strategies for incorporating pharmacologic and nonpharmacologic pain management techniques into their home care.

  ▪ Parents may become very distressed at the wound's appearance as well as their child's crying. Discuss ways for parents to cope with their feelings.

❑ Have the patient and family return to the emergency department within 24 hours for a wound check and to review the wound care regimen. If an ED return is not possible, make a referral for home care or an appointment with the primary care provider.

❑ Contact social services and child protective services in cases of suspected child maltreatment; initiate the proper reporting mechanism (Chapter 44).

Specific Burn Injuries

Smoke Inhalation

Pulmonary pathology frequently accompanies major thermal trauma. The presence of an inhalation injury significantly increases the morbidity and mortality associated with a given size of total body surface burn. Aggressive diagnostic and therapeutic maneuvers are essential to overall management.[7] There are three types of inhalation injury (Table 37.6):

❑ Supraglottic

❑ Tracheobronchial

❑ Alveolar

Etiology

❑ Flame

❑ Chemical

Focused History

❑ Flame. Entrapment in an enclosed space or motor vehicle.

❑ Chemical. Ingestion or inhalation of a chemical (Chapter 42).

Inhalation Injury-Specific Symptoms

❑ Respiratory-related symptoms:

  ▪ Drooling, choking

  ▪ Carbonaceous sputum

  ▪ Singed hair

  ▪ Upper airway obstruction

Other Historical Findings

❑ Prehospital treatment

❑ Witnesses

❑ Involvement of other family members

❑ Removed from an enclosed space

❑ Chemical bottle found near the patient

Focused Assessment

Physical Assessment

❑ Assess for signs of potential inhalation injury.[1]

❑ Listen for sounds of airway compromise or obstruction.

  ▪ Stridor

  ▪ Hoarseness

  ▪ Harsh cough

Table 37.6 Comparison of Inhalation Injuries and Their Treatment

Injury	Cause	Description	Treatment
Supraglottic injury	Direct heat injury leads to upper airway edema severe enough to cause an obstructive phenomenon. Heat injury below the vocal cords is uncommon because the child is unable to inhale a large enough volume of air with enough heat-carrying capacity to cause damage.	Obvious edema and associated stridor. Significant lip and oral edema; the amount of lip edema generally correlates with the amount of vocal cord edema.	Patients with severe lip and vocal cord edema require endotracheal intubation to avert an occlusive phenomenon. Patients may develop upper airway obstruction secondary to edema during the resuscitative process.
Tracheobronchial injury	Incomplete products of combustion (nitrates, polyvinyls, polyurethane gases) act as toxic agents, damaging the tracheobronchial mucosa and causing a "chemical" injury.	Airway edema; alveolar membrane damage. Mucosal sloughing and associated tracheobronchitis occur and ultimately lead to a pneumonic process.	Prepare for endotracheal intubation. Administer intravenous antibiotics, as prescribed.
Alveolar injury	Occurs in a small number of patients (5% of all patients who survive to the emergency department).[11]	Severe alveolar damage leading to a respiratory distress-type syndrome. Irreversible hypoxia immediately following extrication from a fire.	These patients generally die rapidly, despite aggressive clinical intervention.

❏ Inspect the face.
- Singed facial or nasal hair
- Facial burns
- Blisters to the lips and face
- Soot in the nose and mouth
- Carbonaceous sputum

❏ Auscultate the chest for:
- Adventitious sounds
- Respiratory rate

❏ Observe the chest for:
- Retractions
- Use of accessory muscles
- Restricted chest expansion

❏ Assess the child's neurologic status.
- Agitation
- Stupor

Psychosocial Assessment

❏ Assess the child's and family's coping strategies.

❏ Assess the child's and family's understanding of the injury process.
- Other family members may be affected.
- The family may not have adequate social or financial resources following a home fire; social services intervention may be needed.

Nursing Interventions

1. Assess and maintain the airway.
   - Prepare for endotracheal intubation.
   - Prepare for mechanical ventilation.
   - Perform endotracheal lavage and suctioning, as needed.
2. Administer high-flow humidified supplemental oxygen by mask or bag mask ventilation.
3. Initiate cardiorespiratory and oxygen saturation monitoring.
4. Obtain venous access and initiate fluid resuscitation.
   - Obtain arterial blood gases and carboxyhemoglobin (CO) levels.
   - CO level > 10% indicates potential inhalation

injury.[9]

5. Monitor the child's neurologic status.

6. Prepare for diagnostic procedures.

   - Chest radiograph

   - Direct visualization of the airway with laryngoscopy or bronchoscopy[9]

7. Continue with burn wound treatment, as needed.

8. Inform the family frequently of the child's condition.

9. Provide emotional support to the child and family.

10. Prepare for transfer and transport to a burn center.

Carbon Monoxide Poisoning

Carbon monoxide is a colorless, odorless gas. It affects the brain because carboxyhemoglobin formation hinders systemic oxygen delivery. Metabolic acidosis and elevation in serum enzymes indicate muscle and liver damage in severe cases. Carboxyhemoglobin levels higher than 25% in children may cause symptoms of lethargy and syncope.[7]

Etiology

❒ Poorly ventilated fireplaces

❒ Space heaters

❒ Automobile exhaust that leaks into a house from the garage

❒ Poorly ventilated, malfunctioning furnaces

❒ House fires

Focused History

❒ Rescued from an enclosed space

❒ Activation of a carbon monoxide detector

❒ Loss of consciousness

Focused Assessment

Physical Assessment

❒ Assess the respiratory system.

   - Auscultate the chest for:

     • Adventitious sounds

     • Respiratory rate. Tachypnea may be present.

   - Inspect for signs related to inhalation injury in the event of a house fire.

❒ Assess the cardiovascular system.

   - Auscultate the heart for:

     • Rate. Tachycardia may be present.

     • Rhythm

   - Measure the blood pressure.

   - Assess the peripheral circulation.

   - Measure capillary refill time.

❒ Assess the neurologic system.

   - Assess the level of consciousness with the GCS, pediatric GCS, or AVPU method (*A*lert; responds to *V*erbal stimuli; responds to *P*ain; *U*nresponsive).

   - Observe for signs of hypoxia:

     • Agitation

     • Anxiety

     • Irritability

     • Stupor

Psychosocial Assessment

❒ Assess the child's and family's coping strategies.

❒ Assess the child's and family's understanding of the injury process.

   - Other family members may be affected.

   - The family may not have adequate social or financial resources to make changes in their home environment; social services intervention may be needed.

Nursing Interventions

1. Assess and maintain the airway.

   - Prepare for endotracheal intubation

   - Prepare for mechanical ventilation

2. Administer high-flow humidified supplemental oxygen.

3. Initiate cardiorespiratory monitoring.

   - Avoid oxygen saturation monitoring, because it will read a combination of carboxyhemoglobin plus oxygen-saturated hemoglobin. The monitoring does not differentiate between the two types of hemoglobin, making the readings falsely high.

4. Obtain venous access and initiate fluid resuscitation, as needed.

5. Obtain arterial, venous, or capillary blood gases and carboxyhemoglobin levels. Prepare to treat based on the carboxyhemoglobin level and symptoms (Table 37.7).

6. Prepare for a chest radiograph.

7. Continue with burn care treatment, as needed.

8. Inform the family frequently of the child's condition.

9. Provide emotional support to the child and family.

10. Prepare for transfer and transport to a burn center, as

Table 37.7 Carboxyhemoglobin Levels, Symptoms, and Treatment

Carboxyhemoglobin level	Symptoms	Treatment
15–40%	Headache, nausea, vomiting, or dizziness	Administer 100% oxygen.
		Obtain arterial blood gas levels and a carboxyhemoglobin level.
40–60%	Confusion, disorientation, or loss of consciousness	Administer 100% oxygen.
		Prepare for endotracheal intubation.
		Prepare for hyperbaric oxygen therapy.
		Obtain arterial blood gas levels and a carboxyhemoglobin level.
50–70%	Asphyxiation	Administer 100% oxygen.
		Prepare for endotracheal intubation.

needed.

Chemical Burns[3]

Chemical injuries generally result from the young child's normal curiosity while exploring the kitchen or bathroom and playing with home cleaning agents. The body areas most frequently involved are the head, neck, and/or extremities because these are most often exposed. The chemical agents ultimately destroy protein integrity by either a coagulation or denaturation process. This degradation of protein may continue to a depth well below the superficial skin changes that characterize the initial injury presentation. Chemical injuries may be accompanied by significant deep pathology with only minimal cutaneous effect, an important consideration in the resuscitation of children with large chemical injuries. Chemical agents have a prolonged effect after contact with the skin and go on to cause progressive damage if immediate intervention is not accomplished (Chapter 42).

Electrical Injuries

Electrical injuries occur from contact with high or low electrical voltage (Table 37.8). Each year approximately 4,000 emergency department visits result from electrical injuries, with the majority of these injuries occurring in children.[10] Tissue injury results as the electrical current's energy is converted to heat. Cutaneous injury generally results from the relationship that exists between the passage of current and body resistance. Electric current has a propensity to cause necrosis of tissue as a result of thrombosis of major vascular systems. The electrical current injures the endothelial cells of small and medium blood vessels, resulting in the deposition of fibrin and platelets, which may ultimately occlude the vessel. Unlike

thermal injury, an electrical injury may be a progressive and dynamic lesion that evolves over many days. Children who sustain high-voltage electrical injuries may present with a multitude of problems that are significantly different from those exhibited by children who present with thermal cutaneous injuries. Aggressive intervention is essential to manage the many facets of pathology that might occur in high-voltage electrical injuries.

Etiology

❏ Alternating current sources:
  ▪ Fuse boxes in the home
  ▪ Electrical outlets in the home
  ▪ Home appliances
❏ Direct current sources:
  ▪ Power lines
  ▪ Defibrillators

Focused History

❏ Source of the electrical current
❏ Voltage of the electrical current
❏ Amount of time the child was in contact with the electrical source
❏ Path of the electricity

Focused Assessment

Physical Assessment[8]

1. Assess the respiratory system.
  ▪ Auscultate the chest for:
    • Respiratory rate
    • Adventitious sounds

TABLE 37.8 Comparison of Electrical Burn Injuries

Characteristic	Low-Voltage Injuries	High-Voltage Injuries
Voltage	120–1000 volts	> 1000 volts
Current	Alternating (household electrical outlets, fuse boxes)	Direct (power lines)
Where injuries occur	Home	Outdoors Workplace
Effect on body systems: neurologic, cardiovascular, musculoskeletal, skin	Loss of consciousness Ventricular fibrillation Possible compartment syndrome Full thickness burns	Coexisting injuries from falls Renal failure from myoglobinuria Muscle necrosis Full thickness burns

2. Assess the cardiovascular system.
   - Auscultate the heart for:
     - Rate
     - Rhythm
     - Quality
   - Measure the blood pressure.
   - Assess the peripheral circulation.
     - Palpate the peripheral pulses for quality/equality
   - Assess core and peripheral temperature.
   - Measure capillary refill.
   - Assess skin color and texture.
3. Assess the neurologic system.
   - Assess the level of consciousness with the GCS, pediatric GCS, or AVPU method (*A*lert; responds to *V*erbal stimuli; responds to *P*ain; *U*nresponsive).
4. Assess the integumentary system.
   - Inspect the skin for thermal wounds, entrance and exit wounds
5. Assess the musculoskeletal system.
   - Observe for deformities or dislocations
   - Observe for impaired mobility
   - Assess for the presence of the six Ps:
     - Assess for *pain*
     - Test for *paresthesia*
     - Palpate for *pulselessness*
     - Observe for *pallor*
     - Test for *paralysis*
     - Palpate for *polar* (skin temperature)

Nursing Interventions for Major Electrical Injuries

1. Assess and maintain the airway and cervical spine.
   - Prepare for endotracheal intubation
   - Initiate spinal immobilization as needed
2. Maintain respiratory function.
   - Administer 100% oxygen
   - Prepare for mechanical ventilation
   - Initiate cardiorespiratory and oxygen saturation monitoring.
     - Monitor the child for electrocardiogram changes
3. Support the cardiovascular system.
   - Obtain venous access and initiate fluid resuscitation
   - Fluid administration flushes myoglobin and hemoglobin from the kidneys. These proteins precipitate in the renal tubules and can result in acute tubular necrosis if urinary output is not maintained.
   - Obtain blood specimens for laboratory analysis.
     - Creatine kinase
     - Creatine kinase MB
4. Monitor the neurologic status.
   - Observe for seizure activity.
     - Administer medications, as prescribed, for seizure activity
   - Assess for pain (Chapter 11).
     - Administer analgesics, as prescribed
5. Insert a nasogastric tube and indwelling bladder catheter.
   - Obtain a urine specimen for:
     - Urinalysis
     - Myoglobin

- Measure urinary output.
  - Note the color of urine (tea-colored or black urine indicates the presence of myoglobin)

6. Inspect the electrical injury for its location; calculate the TBSA affected and the severity.
   - Remove any jewelry from the injured extremity to decrease the tourniquet-like effect, which may cause vascular ischemia.

7. Assess the injured extremities for fascial compartment compression, because of the propensity for vessel thrombosis and associated muscle nonviability.
   - Prepare for tissue pressure measurement and subsequent fasciotomy in the operating room.
   - Monitor peripheral pulses and peripheral perfusion continuously so that impaired circulation may be recognized and appropriate decompression procedures may be instituted quickly.

8. Inform the family frequently of the child's condition.

9. Provide emotional support to the child and family.

10. Initiate consultations with social services personnel and medical subspecialists.

11. Prepare for transfer and transport to a burn center.

Nursing Interventions for Minor (Localized) Electrical Injuries

1. Inspect the electrical injury for its location; calculate the TBSA affected and the severity.

2. Obtain an electrocardiogram.

3. Obtain blood specimens for laboratory analysis:
   - Creatine kinase
   - Creatine kinase MB

4. Obtain a urine specimen for myoglobin.

5. Initiate consultation with a burn center, plastic surgeon, or pediatric surgeon.

6. Provide follow-up for subsequent treatment:
   - Patients must be examined regularly (e.g., daily) to detect the presence of underlying nonviable tissue in the areas of entrance and exit wounds and over the intervening areas. This inspection detects evolving nonviable tissue and allows for the initiation of appropriate interventions, such as debridement.

7. Prepare for hospitalization, because patients with electrical injuries should be observed for a minimum of 24 hours.

Lightning Injuries

Lightning kills between 80 and 100 people a year in the United States alone. Lightning is direct current of 100,000,000 volts, and up to 200,000 amps.[2] Multiple strikes can occur on the same location.

Etiology[2]

- Direct strike:
  - The lightning directly contacts the patient.
- Side flash:
  - Current flows between a person and a nearby object struck by lightning.
  - Current travels on the surface of the body and not through it, resulting in superficial cutaneous burns (splashed on spidery and arborescent pattern).

Focused History

- Nature of the injury:
  - How and where the injury occurred.
  - Witnesses to the event.
- Symptoms following the lightning strike:
  - Loss of consciousness; seizure
  - Cardiopulmonary arrest
  - Amnesia
  - Additional systemic injuries (e.g., if the child was thrown into the air)
- Treatment initiated:
  - Cardiopulmonary resuscitation

Focused Assessment

Physical Assessment

- Assess the respiratory system.
  - Auscultate the chest for:
    - Respiratory rate
    - Adventitious sounds
- Assess the cardiovascular system.
  - Auscultate the heart for:
    - Rate
    - Rhythm
    - Quality
  - Measure the blood pressure
  - Assess peripheral perfusion
  - Measure capillary refill time
- Assess the neurologic system.
  - Assess the level of consciousness with the GCS, pediatric GCS, or AVPU method (*A*lert; responds to *V*erbal stimuli; responds to *P*ain; *U*nresponsive).
  - Observe for seizure activity

- Assess for signs of a spinal cord injury (Chapter 30)
☐ Assess the integumentary system.
  - Inspect the skin for thermal wounds
  - Inspect the skin for lightning spots
☐ Assess the musculoskeletal system.
  - Observe for deformities or dislocations
  - Palpate the peripheral pulses for intensity and equality
  - Observe for impaired mobility

Psychosocial Assessment

☐ Assess the child's and family's coping strategies.
  - Additional family members or friends may have been involved in the lightning strike.
  - Parents may blame each other or may blame coaches or other adults if outdoor sports activities were in progress during the lightning strike.
☐ Assess the child's and family's understanding of the lightning injury.

Nursing Interventions

1. Assess and maintain airway and cervical spine immobilization.
   - Prepare for endotracheal intubation, as needed
   - Maintain spinal precautions
2. Initiate measures to promote respiratory function.
   - Administer supplemental oxygen
   - Prepare for mechanical ventilation
   - If necessary, administer cardiopulmonary resuscitation
   - Initiate cardiorespiratory and oxygen saturation monitoring:
     - Monitor the child for electrocardiogram changes
3. Initiate measures to support the cardiovascular system.
   - Obtain venous access and initiate fluid resuscitation to flush myoglobin and hemoglobin from the kidneys.
     - Myoglobin and hemoglobin precipitate in the renal tubules and can result in acute tubular necrosis if urinary output is not maintained.
   - Obtain blood specimens for laboratory analysis.
     - Creatine kinase
     - Creatine kinase MB
   - Assess peripheral pulses for vascular compromise, which may necessitate escharotomy.
4. Monitor the neurologic system.

- Observe for seizure activity.
  - Administer anticonvulsant therapy, as prescribed
- Assess for pain (Chapter 11).
  - Administer analgesics, as prescribed
5. Remove any watches, rings, belts, clothing, or anything that may cause a tourniquet-like effect.
6. Insert an indwelling bladder catheter.
   - Monitor urinary output
   - Obtain urine for myoglobin
7. Inform the family frequently of the child's condition.
8. Provide emotional support to the child and family.
9. Initiate consultations with social services personnel and medical subspecialists as needed.
10. Prepare for transfer and transport to a burn center or trauma center.

Radiation Therapy Injuries

Radiation therapy may cause skin reactions in the treated area (Table 37.9). Patients and caregivers should be given the following instructions:

☐ Wash the treated area with tepid water and soft washcloth.
☐ Do not use any soaps, lotions, deodorants, medicines, cosmetics, talcum powder, or other substances in the treated area.
☐ Protect the area from the sun. If possible, cover treated skin with light clothing before going out of doors. Apply a PABA-free sunscreen or a sunblocking product with a sun protection factor of a least 15.

TABLE 37.9 Acute Radiation Morbidity Scoring Criteria	
Score	*Criteria*
0	No change over baseline
1	Follicular, faint or dull erythema; epilation; dry desquamation; decreased sweating
2	Tender or bright erythema; patchy, moist desquamation; moderate edema
3	Confluent, moist desquamation other than skin folds; pitting edema
4	Ulceration; hemorrhage necrosis

Burn Prevention

Children of all ages are at risk for burn injuries, especially in the home setting. Simple everyday acts of bathing, cooking, using gasoline or kerosene-powered equipment, storing paint and household chemicals, using a fireplace, having a gas or electric furnace, and even using electricity place everyone at risk for a burn injury. Because of the severity of the injuries that can result, fire and burn prevention should be an ongoing concern for every individual and family.

Kitchen Safety

The kitchen is the single most dangerous room in the home for burns. Extra care must be taken when food is being cooked, especially if there are children in the house. A fire extinguisher and box of baking soda should be kept readily available to quell a fire. Guidelines for kitchen safety are given in Table 37.10.

Bathroom Safety

The bathroom is the second most dangerous room for thermal and electrical burns. Guidelines for bathroom safety are listed in Table 37.11.

General Home Fire Prevention

House fires are a leading cause of death in infants and children. Guidelines to prevent fires in the home include those listed in Table 37.12.

Burn Safety Outdoors

See Table 37.13 for a list of burn safety measures during outdoor activities.

Teaching Children Burn Safety

Children as young as preschoolers can be taught the basic principles of burn safety. They can also be taught how to respond to a fire or other emergencies that could occur in the home setting. Emergency nurses can teach basic burn prevention strategies to children and families.

TABLE 37.10 Guidelines for Kitchen Safety

Safety Measure	Rationale
Turn pot handles inward while cooking.	Avoids unintentional contact with a curious child's hand or an adult's hand or body.
Avoid lifting and carrying boiling or hot liquids.	Decreases risk of spilling or splashing.
Avoid wearing loose-fitting clothes, especially loose housedresses or full sleeves; keep potholders, dish towels, and curtains away from the stove.	Prevents the fabric from hanging too close to hot burners and igniting.
Keep electrical cords away from crawling infants and young children; avoid overloading electrical circuits with small kitchen appliances; consider unplugging small appliances after each use.	Deters children from biting on them and helps family members avoid tripping over them; avoids electrical fires.
Store detergents, cleaning fluids, drain cleaners, and other dangerous substances where curious children cannot get to them.	Prevents burn and poisoning injuries.
Contain grease fires with a lid and turn off the burner. Do not throw water on the fire.	Water may cause the grease to splash out of the pan, spreading the flames.
Set a timer while cooking.	Serves as a reminder to turn off the oven or any burners after use.
Remove any metal or aluminum foil before heating foods in a microwave oven.	Avoids a potential fire or spark.
Carefully test the temperature of foods and beverages heated in a microwave before feeding them to infants and young children.	Microwaves can heat liquids very quickly, without necessarily warming the container.

Table 37.11 Guidelines for Bathroom Safety

Safety Measure	Rationale
Always test the temperature of bath water before placing an infant or child into the tub.	Avoids scald burns.
Keep electrical appliances and cords away from the tub.	Avoids electrical injuries.
Set the water heater temperature at or below 125 °F (52 °C).	Prevents scald injuries.
Never leave children alone while they are in the bathtub.	Children may slip or bump the hot water faucet, causing a scald injury; drowning may occur.
Teach children to turn on the cold water first, and then the hot water.	Avoids scalding injuries.

Before a Fire Occurs

- ☐ Identify two escape routes from every room in the house, in the event that a room is blocked by flames or smoke.
- ☐ Obtain escape ladders to provide a safe exit from second or third floor bedrooms and ensure that they are easily accessible and in good condition.
- ☐ Establish a meeting place outside the house so family members will know immediately if anyone is left inside. Teach children never to return to the burning home to retrieve pets, toys, or other family members.
- ☐ Practice family fire drills so that all family members are familiar with what they should do and where they should go.
- ☐ Teach children how to call for help (911 or other emergency numbers). Consider placing the emergency number on a speed dial or having the number posted on the telephone.

TABLE 37.12 General Home Fire Prevention

Safety Measure	Rationale
Always make sure matches and lighters are out of children's reach.	Avoids flame burns; the most frequent cause of fatal home fires is carelessly discarded cigarettes.
Install smoke detectors outside of each bedroom and on every floor.	Alerts family members to the presence of fire regardless of their location in the home.
Check smoke detectors and carbon monoxide regularly; a recognized time for checking them is at the end of daylight savings time. Extinguish all cigarettes and ashes completely prior to their disposal.	Ensures that the batteries are functioning.
Unplug any appliance when the electrical cord begins smoking or gives off a strange odor.	Prevents fires.
Check the plugs and cords on all lights and appliances regularly to make sure that they are not damaged or frayed. Replace them when damage appears.	Prevents electrical fires.
Do not overload outlets or extension cords.	Prevents electrical fires.
Do not run extension cords under rugs.	Prevents electrical fires.
Replace blown fuses with ones of the correct amperage.	Cord damage or breakage may go undetected. Avoids overloading the electrical circuit.
If an odor of gas is noted, go to a neighbor's to call for help; do not turn on electrical lights or strike a match to see where the gas fumes are originating.	Electrical sparks created inside the telephone could be enough to ignite the gas.
Have furnaces checked each fall before using them; have chimneys cleaned periodically.	Prevents carbon monoxide poisoning; prevents flame injuries.
Close bedroom doors at night.	The barrier between the family member and the smoke may provide critical, lifesaving minutes.
Place "tot finders" stickers in bedroom windows.	May alert firefighters to the presence of children in the home.

TABLE 37.13 Burn Safety Measures for Outdoor Activities	
Safety Measure	*Rationale*
Avoid smoking cigarettes while filling the lawn mower or other tools with gasoline.	Prevents a possible spark that would ignite the gasoline.
Turn gas- or kerosene-powered tools off before adding more fuel.	A spill could be ignited by a spark from the engine.
Store gasoline and other flammable liquids in metal safety containers outside of the house.	Prevents ignition and fire.
When starting a charcoal grill, use an electric starter, solid fuel, or specialized charcoal starter fuel. Never add more liquid fuel once the fire has started.	Prevents a flash-type burn.
When starting a propane gas grill, always have the match lit before turning on the gas. Keep the grill and propane tank stored outside, away from the house.	Prevents an explosion and burn injury.
Keep children away from outdoor grills; keep starter fuels, matches, and lighters out of their reach.	Prevents flame and chemical burns.
Leave fireworks to the professionals; attend community-sponsored fireworks events.	Fireworks cause thousands of burns and fires each year.
When camping, clear the campfire area of leaves and brush; soak the campfire with water and ensure that it is completely out before going to bed or leaving the campsite. Never build a fire inside a tent.	Prevents an uncontrolled fire; prevents inhalation and flame burns. Prevents surface burns and inhalation injuries.
Seek shelter in a lightning storm	Prevents lightning injuries.

When a Fire Occurs

❒ Teach children to get out of the house or building as quickly as possible and stay out.

❒ Call 911 or other emergency numbers immediately.

❒ Teach children that if they have to go through smoke to crawl on their hands and knees out of the house; smoke rises toward the ceiling, so traveling low to the floor prevents inhalation of smoke.

❒ If trapped in a room, close the door and try to keep as much smoke from entering as possible. Cover all of the cracks around the door and air vents. Hold a cloth, wet, if possible, over the mouth and nose and try to signal from a window for help. If there is a telephone in the room, call 911 or another emergency number immediately and advise them about the entrapment and their location.

When Clothing Catches Fire

❒ Teach children to stop, drop, and roll if their clothes catch fire. Running fans the flames and worsens the situation.

- Stop what you are doing.
- Drop to the floor and cover your face with your hands.
- Roll until the flames are smothered.

❒ Teach young children to get an adult right away if someone else's clothes catch on fire; teach school-aged children and adolescents to smother the flames by wrapping the person in a blanket, sheet, or rug.

Conclusion

Burn injuries cause needless death and disability in the pediatric population. Emergency nurses need to understand the unique challenges and differences that put children at risk for burn injuries. Becoming involved in seasonal educational efforts and campaigns to mitigate burn injuries (e.g., camp fires in the summer, electric heater injuries in the winter) is a venue for emergency nurses to explore. Be mindful of the importance of rapid emergency treatment for burn injuries. This includes the importance of proper fluid resuscitation, including the need for normothermia, and proper wound care. Practicing burn safety with children not only identifies adults as role models for safe behavior, but reinforces the demonstrated burn safety behaviors.

References

1. Herndon, D. N., & Lee, J. O. (2007). *Total burn care* (3rd ed.). Philadelphia: Saunders.

2. American Burn Association. (2005). *American Burn Life Support Course.* Chicago: Author.

3. Edlich, R., Martin, M., & Long, W. (2006). Thermal burns. In J. A. Marx, J. A. Rosen, R. S. Hockberger, & R. M. Walls (Eds.), *Rosen's emergency medicine, concepts and clinical practice* (6th ed.). St. Louis, MO: Mosby.

4. Emergency Nurses Association. (2005). *Sheehy's manual of emergency care* (6th ed.). St. Louis, MO: Mosby.

5. National Fire Prevention Association. (2006). *Learn not to burn® program.* Quincy, MA: Author.

6. King, C., Henretig, F. M., King, B. R., Loiselle, J. M., Ruddy, R. M., & Wiley, J. F. (2008). *Textbook of pediatric emergency procedures* (2nd ed.). Philadelphia: Lippincott Williams & Wilkins.

7. Barkin, R. M. (2003). *Emergency pediatrics: A guide to ambulatory care* (6th ed.). St. Louis, MO: Elsevier.

8. Sharieff, G. Q., Joseph, M. M., & Wylie, T. W. (2005). *Pediatric emergency medicine* (1st ed.). New York: McGraw-Hill.

9. Herndon, D. N. (2007). *Total burn care* (3rd ed.). Philadelphia: Saunders.

10. Joffe, M. (2006). Burns. In G. R. Fleisher, S. Ludwig, F. M. Henretig, R. Ruddy, & B. K. Silverman (Eds.), *Textbook of pediatric emergency medicine* (5th ed., pp. 1517–1524). Philadelphia: Lippincott Williams & Wilkins.

11. Gaisford, J., Slater, H., & Goldfarb, I. (1983). *The management of burn trauma: A unified approach.* Pittsburgh, PA: Synapse Publications.

THIRTY-EIGHT

Shock

Nancy Mecham, APRN, FNP-BC, CEN

Introduction

The common pathway for all types of shock is inadequate tissue perfusion and oxygen supply to meet the metabolic needs of the tissues. Inadequate tissue perfusion results in anaerobic metabolism, the accumulation of lactic acid, and a resulting metabolic acidosis. As the shock state progresses, microvascular perfusion is impaired, resulting in cellular damage, the release of vasoactive substances, and eventual individual organ dysfunction. Death results if treatment is not initiated in a timely manner to stop this cascade of events.

The purpose of this chapter is to discuss the different types and causes of shock, clinical presentations, and treatments, and to stress the importance of early recognition and management of shock in the pediatric patient.

Pediatric Considerations

Specific differences in the cardiovascular system of the pediatric patient have clinical significance that relate to the child's ability to compensate for the fluid loss or fluid shifts that occur in the shock state.[1-4] *Cardiac output* is the most important factor to consider in relation to circulation, for it is the cardiac output that is responsible for the transport of substances to and from the tissues of the body. Infants and children have a higher cardiac output than adults (200 mL/kg/minute versus 100 mL/kg/minute).[2] The higher cardiac output is necessary because the pediatric patient has a higher oxygen demand due to a higher metabolic rate. The higher cardiac output also provides for a child's higher oxygen consumption (6 to 8 mL/kg/minute compared with 3 to 4 mL/kg/minute in adults).[2]

Cardiac output is equal to heart rate multiplied by stroke volume. Stroke volume represents the pumping function of the ventricle and is derived from the preload, contractility, and afterload. In pediatric patients the myocardial fibers are shorter and less elastic, which means the myocardium has poorer compliance and less ability to adjust stroke volume in an altered cardiac output state.[1,2] Because the child is not able to adjust stroke volume to alter cardiac output, the heart rate increases. This explains why tachycardia is such an important and early indicator of decreased perfusion in pediatric patients.[1,2]

Children have a greater percent of total body water than adults (80 mL/kg versus 70 mL/kg in adults), and because of the higher metabolic rate and higher cardiac output, children are more susceptible to even small losses that are not replaced and at a greater risk for dehydration. Part of the challenge in recognizing shock in children is that they are able to maintain an adequate cardiac output for long periods of time because of the compensatory mechanism of peripheral vasoconstriction. In a child, 25% to 30% of intravascular fluids can be displaced before a decrease in blood pressure will be noted and the child will move to the hypotensive shock state.[1] Often by the time the hypotensive shock state is recognized the child may be in critical condition.

Etiology

Shock can be categorized by four basic types: hypovolemic, distributive (septic, anaphylactic, and neurogenic), cardiogenic, and obstructive.[1,3]

Hypovolemic shock is the most common cause of shock in the pediatric patient. It is characterized by an inadequate circulating intravascular volume usually as a result of dehydration or hemorrhage.[1–3]

Distributive shock is characterized by inadequate distribution of fluid volume. This is caused by a systemic vasodilatation and capillary fluid leak that leads to a relative hypovolemia. Septic shock, anaphylactic shock, and neurogenic shock are types of distributive shock that lead to this fluid shifting.[1–3]

❏ *Septic* shock is the most common form of distributive shock. It is caused by an infectious organism that stimulates the immune system and a systemic inflammatory response.

❏ *Anaphylactic* shock is an acute multisystem allergic response to a food, drug, or other allergen. Along with the systemic vasodilatation that occurs there is also a pulmonary vasoconstriction. This response can occur in seconds to minutes after exposure. Death can be immediate.[5]

❏ *Neurogenic* shock is caused by massive vasodilatation from a loss of sympathetic nervous system tone as a result of spinal cord injury or high-level spinal anesthesia. The triad of hypotension, bradycardia, and hypothermia manifests neurogenic shock. Table 38.1 compares the types of distributive shock.

Cardiogenic shock is characterized by myocardial dysfunction. Fluid volume is generally normal or slightly increased, but the dysfunction of the myocardium affects cardiac output. This can be caused by a dysfunction that leads to pump failure such as a rhythm abnormality, drug toxicity, or congenital heart disease.[1–3] Another example of a child in cardiogenic shock may be the child who presents with viral myocarditis or a previously undiagnosed cardiomyopathy.[6]

Obstructive shock occurs when there is impaired cardiac output caused by a physical obstruction to blood flow.[1,3] An example of obstructive shock may be a result of closure of the ductal-dependent lesion in a neonate. Cardiac tamponade, tension pneumothorax, or pulmonary embolisms are also conditions that can lead to obstructive shock.[1,3]

Signs and Symptoms of Shock

The clinical presentation of the shock state in the pediatric patient can vary depending on the specific cause and can be subtle in the early stages. However, early recognition and initiation of treatment have been shown to provide the child with the best chance of survival regardless of the type of shock.[1,7–9]

General signs of shock may be seen as a result of the body's cardiovascular compensatory response to inadequate perfusion.[1,3,4] The heart rate increases to increase cardiac output, and the child begins to exhibit tachycardia. There is an increase in the systemic vascular resistance (vasoconstriction) as the body attempts to shunt the blood volume from the periphery (skin) to the central circulation. This causes changes in pulses, skin, and mental status. Extremities become cool, pale, and mottled. The capillary refill time is greater than 3 seconds, pulses become weak and thready, and the mental status becomes altered. This clinical presentation is sometimes referred to as a *cold shock*.[1,3,4,7]

In distributive shock there is a maldistribution of fluid volume and not an actual loss of fluid volume from the body. This fluid shift from the intravascular space to the extravascular space results in a relative hypovolemic state. The cardiovascular compensatory response to this shock state may be the clinical presentation of a cold shock state or, more commonly, may be a decrease in the systemic vascular resistance (vasodilatation) and cardiac output may be increased, decreased, or normal. This clinical presentation is sometimes referred to as a *warm shock*.[1,3,4,7] In this case, there is an increased blood flow to the skin that creates warm/hot extremities, bounding peripheral pulses, a flushed, ruddy appearance to the skin, a flash capillary refill time (< 1 second), tachycardia, and altered mental status.[1,7]

Blood pressure is not useful as a presenting symptom of shock; however, the presence of hypotension along with other clinical signs of shock confirms the severity of the shock state. The child with clinical symptoms of shock and a normal blood pressure is said to be in a compensated shock state. A child may remain in the compensated state for hours. However, when a child with clinical signs of shock becomes hypotensive, he or she moves to what is referred to as a hypotensive shock state.[1] This move from compensated shock to hypotensive shock may take only a few minutes. Thus, if the hypotensive shock state is not recognized and treated the child will progress to an irreversible shock state that will result in end organ damage, cardiac arrest, and death.[1]

Focused History

Patient History

Secondary Assessment[1,2]

Recent illness or significant past history may be suggestive that the patient is at risk for a shock state.

❏ Fever

   ▪ History of immunosuppression

- History of recent viral illness
- Presence of petechial or purpuric lesions

❏ Respiratory illness

❏ Gastroenteritis

❏ Burn injury

❏ Trauma

Exposure to allergens with or without past history of allergic reaction (e.g., tree nuts, insect bites and stings, eggs, shellfish, antibiotics) may be suggestive that the patient is at risk for anaphylactic shock.[4]

❏ Presence of respiratory symptoms

- Dyspnea
- Wheeze
- Stridor
- Hypoxemia

❏ Presence of cardiovascular symptoms

- Hypotension
- Syncope

❏ Presence of skin and/or mucosal symptoms

- Hives
- Itching or flushing
- Angioedema
- Swollen lips or tongue

❏ Presence of gastrointestinal symptoms

- Diarrhea
- Vomiting

History of cardiac disease may be suggestive that the patient is at risk for cardiogenic or obstructive shock. Previous spinal cord injury may be suggestive that the patient is at risk for a neurogenic shock state.

Focused Physical Assessment

Primary Assessment[1,2]

❏ Assess the airway for patency.

- Edema
- Swollen lips, tongue, or uvula
- Vomitus or other secretions
- Drooling
- Occlusion from the tongue

❏ Assess breathing.

- Observe the work of breathing.
  - Retractions
  - Nasal flaring

- Respiratory rate. May be increased or decreased depending on the type of shock and stage of illness.
- Dyspnea

- Auscultate lungs for breath sounds.
  - Wheezing
  - Rales
  - Rhonchi
  - Absent

❏ Assess the integumentary system.

- Color
- Pale
- Gray
- Cyanotic
- Temperature
- Cool
- Hot, flushed

❏ Assess the cardiovascular system.

- Heart rate
  - Increased heart rates may reflect a compensatory measure to increase cardiac output.
  - Decreased heart rates may be an ominous late sign of cardiovascular decompensation.

- Mental status
  - Decreased perfusion to the brain can cause mental status changes that can range from subtle to profound lethargy.
  - Listening to the parents' concerns for changes in normal activity, feeding, or sleeping patterns is important when assessing mental status of a child.

- Skin perfusion
  - Color
    - Pale, gray, cyanotic
    - Mottled (cold shock)
    - Flushed, ruddy appearance (warm shock)
  - Capillary refill
    - Greater than 3 seconds (cold shock)
    - Less than 1 second (flash) (warm shock)
  - Peripheral pulses
    - Weak (cold shock)
    - Bounding (warm shock)
  - Temperature
    - Cool (cold shock)

· Hot (warm shock)

- Blood pressure
  - Normal systolic blood pressure may be a reflection of compensatory mechanisms (tachycardia and vasoconstriction).
  - Declining systolic blood pressure is a sign of a hypotensive shock; immediate intervention is required to prevent cardiopulmonary arrest.

❒ Assess the neurologic system.
  - Assess the level of consciousness with AVPU (*A*lert, responds to *V*erbal stimuli, responds to *P*ainful stimuli, *U*nresponsive) method or the Glasgow coma scale (GCS).
  - Observe the child's response to the environment and procedures.

❒ Assess skin for other key signs.
  - Presence of rash, lesions, or swelling
  - Petechial or purpuric lesions
  - Hives

Psychosocial Assessment

❒ Assess the child's and family's understanding of the current health condition.

❒ Children in hypotensive shock can be near death on presentation to the emergency department (ED).

❒ Assess the child's and family's coping strategies and social support system.

❒ Consider the family members' emotional needs.

❒ Facilitate family presence during any of the resuscitative efforts in the emergency department (Chapter 26).

Nursing Interventions for Shock

1. Maintain airway patency.
   - Suction the airway.
   - Provide airway adjuncts, if needed to maintain an open airway.

2. Administer supplemental oxygen.
   - Provide 100% oxygen through a nonrebreather mask.
   - Provide bag-mask ventilation to the child requiring assisted ventilation.
   - Prepare for possible endotracheal intubation.

3. Initiate continuous cardiopulmonary and oxygen saturation monitoring.
   - Administer supplemental oxygen regardless of saturation level.

- An alteration in perfusion may hinder oxygen saturation monitoring.

4. Obtain venous access.
   - Prepare to place intraosseous access, if a peripheral IV line cannot be obtained quickly, particularly in the patient with hypotensive shock.

5. Initiate fluid resuscitation.
   - Hypovolemic shock
     - Initiate fluid boluses of 20 mL/kg of normal saline (NS) or lactated Ringer's (LR) solution administered rapidly with the goal of attaining normal perfusion.[1,3,4]
     - Reassess perfusion status after each bolus.
     - Assess lung sounds after each bolus.
     - In patients with hypovolemic shock secondary to dehydration, repeat the 20 mL/kg boluses three times up to a total of 60 mL/kg. If no response in perfusion status after fluid boluses, consider an ongoing fluid loss, underestimated fluid loss, or different cause of shock state.[1,3]
     - In patients with hypovolemic shock secondary to hemorrhage, repeat the 20 mL/kg fluid boluses three times for a total of 60 mL/kg and then consider transfusion of 10 mL/kg packed red blood cells.[1]
   - Distributive shock
     - Septic shock
       · Rapidly repeat fluid boluses to drastically increase the child's chance of survival.[1,7–9]
       · Reasses perfusion status after each bolus.
       · Reassess lungs after each bolus for potential fluid overload.
       · If there is not an improvement in perfusion status after 60 mL/kg in the first hour after recognition of shock, a fluid refractory shock state should be recognized and vasoactive medications considered.
     - Anaphylactic shock
       · Initiate fluid bolus of 20 mL/kg of NS or LR administered with the goal of attaining normal perfusion[1,5]; repeat as needed.
       · Reassess perfusion status after each bolus.
     - Neurogenic shock
       · Children with neurogenic shock who have hypotension and either hypothermia or hyperthermia often need warming and cooling measures along with intravenous fluids.[1]

- Initiate a fluid bolus of 20 mL/kg of NS or LR solution administered rapidly with the goal of attaining an improved perfusion status; repeat as needed.
  - Reassess perfusion status after each bolus.
- Cardiogenic shock
  - Initiate a fluid bolus of 5–10 mL/kg of NS or LR solution administered slowly over a 10- to 20-minute period with the goal of attaining an improved perfusion status[1]; repeat as needed.
  - Perfusion status should be reassessed after each bolus.
  - Lungs should be assessed after each bolus for potential fluid overload.
- Obstructive shock
  - Shock state may resemble hypovolemic shock early in the clinical presentation. A fluid bolus of 10 to 20 mL/kg NS or LR solution administered over a 10- to 20-minute period is reasonable.[1]

6. Administer medications as prescribed.
- Distributive shock
  - Septic shock
    - Initiate vasoactive therapy for shock that is refractory to fluid resuscitation.
      - Dopamine—in compensated shock state
      - Norepinephrine—in hypotensive warm shock
      - Epinephrine—in hypotensive cold shock
    - Antibiotic therapy
  - Anaphylactic shock
    - First line:
      - Administer epinephrine 1:1,000 intramuscularly (0.01 mL/kg, maximum dose of 0.5 mL)[5,10,11]
    - Second line:[5]
      - H1 antihistamines—diphenhydramine
      - H2 antihistamines—ranitidine
      - Corticosteroids—methylprednisolone succinate
  - Neurogenic shock
    - Initiate vasoactive therapy for shock that is refractory to fluid resuscitation and warming or cooling measures.[1,3]
      - Norepinephrine infusion or epinephrine infusion
- Cardiogenic shock[1–3]

- Prepare to administer:
  - Diuretics, if pulmonary edema is present
  - Vasodilators—milrinone infusion
  - Analgesics and sedatives, used cautiously, may be of use to reduce the stress response
- Obstructive shock
  - Other medications or treatments should be directed to the cause of the obstruction.[1,3]
    - Cardiac tamponade: Possible pericardiocentesis
    - Tension pneumothorax: Needle decompression and chest tube placement
    - Ductal dependent lesion: Prostaglandin E infusion
    - Pulmonary embolism: Possible anticoagulants

7. Obtain blood for laboratory studies.
- Blood gas analysis (venous, capillary, or arterial)
- Electrolytes, including an ionized calcium (iCA) level
- Glucose should be obtained early, and hypoglycemia corrected early
- Lactate level
- Complete blood cell count with differential and platelet count
- Consider prothrombin time/partial thromboplastin time for patients with suspected coagulopathies such as hemorrhage or sepsis
- Cultures
  - Blood and urine
  - Cerebrospinal fluid
- Trauma patients also require
  - Type and crossmatch
  - Liver function tests

8. Insert a nasogastric tube, as needed for gastric decompression.
9. Insert an indwelling bladder catheter, as needed.
10. Measure intake and output.
11. Prepare for transfer and transport to a pediatric intensive care unit or tertiary care facility (Chapter 8).
12. Provide frequent updates on the child's condition to the family; consider having the family present during procedures and treatment.
13. Initiate social support through social services, clergy, or other consultation.
14. Initiate debriefing for the staff if the child dies in the emergency department, if available and desired.

Home Care and Prevention

❐ Teach families to watch for signs and symptoms of hydration status early when they have a child with gastroenteritis that is being treated at home.

❐ Teach families about the importance of medical alert bracelets for children who are allergic to foods, bee stings, and other allergens and also about carrying an epinephrine autoinjector with them at all times.

❐ Families of children with multiple or complex medical conditions should be told their child's baseline vital signs and assessment parameters so that they can assist health care providers to recognize abnormalities early. These families should also be taught when to take their child for medical evaluation.

❐ Families of children with immunosuppression need to be taught when to take their child's temperature and have parameters for when to take their child for evaluation.

Conclusion

Assessing a child for shock is part of the routine history and primary assessment that should be performed by every nurse on every pediatric patient. The key to early recognition of shock is to connect suspicious history and assessment findings to an assumption that the child may be in a shock state. The failure to notice or to put the history and assessment pieces together quickly and intervene promptly may be a fatal mistake. One approach is to have a high index of suspicion and consider the possibility of shock on every pediatric patient.

TABLE 38.1 Comparisons of Distributive Shock States

	Anaphylactic	*Neurogenic*	*Septic*
Etiology	Allergen exposure	Spinal cord injury High levels of spinal anesthesia Nervous system damage Ganglionic and adrenergic blocking agents	Infectious organisms
Pathophysiology: Vasodilatation that precedes a maldistribution of blood flow (functional hypovolemic state)	Hypersensitivity reaction, causing vasodilatation and capillary leakage.	Vasodilatation caused by loss of sympathetic nervous system tone.	Following an insult with an infectious agent, a series of events is produced by chemical mediators and cascades, resulting in endothelial cell destruction, massive vasodilatation, increased capillary permeability

Physical assessment	Respiratory symptoms:
	  Dyspnea
	  Wheezing
	  Stridor
	  Chest tightness
	Cardiovascular symptoms:
	  Hypotension
	  Syncope
	Skin/mucosal symptoms:
	  Hives
	  Swelling of lips, tongue, or uvula
	  Angioedema
	Gastrointestinal symptoms:
	  Diarrhea
	  Vomiting
		Cardiovascular symptoms:
		  Bradycardia
		  Hypotension
		  Initially, warm extremities, low diastolic blood pressure, and a wide pulse pressure are found, which are related to the interruption of sympathetic outflow.
		  Vasomotor tone vanishes, resulting in pooling of blood in the extremities and inadequate venous return
		  Altered mental status
			Decreased systemic perfusion:
			  Tachycardia
			  Altered mental status
			Pulses:
			  Decreased (cold shock)
			  Bounding (warm shock)
			Capillary refill:
			  Delayed > 3 seconds (cold shock)
			  Flash < 2 seconds (warm shock)
			Skin color/temperature:
			  Cool/mottled (cold shock)
			  Hot/flushed (warm shock)
			Blood pressure:
			  Normal blood pressure (compensated)
			  Hypotension (hypotensive)

TABLE 38.1 Comparisons of Distributive Shock States (continued)

	Anaphylactic	*Neurogenic*	*Septic*
Treatment	Assess and maintain airway patency and cardiopulmonary function. Administer epinephrine 1:1,000 intramuscularly (0.01 mL/kg, maximum dose of 0.5 mL) Apply oxygen Place on cardiac monitor Obtain intravenous access 　Administer 20 mL/kg NS or LR bolus Possible second-line treatment: H1 antihistamines—diphenhydramine H2 antihistamines— ranitidine Corticosteroids—methylprednisolone succinate	Assess and maintain airway patency and cardiopulmonary function. Obtain venous access and initiate intravenous fluids at normal maintenance infusion rates. Administer vasopressor therapy as prescribed.	Assess and maintain airway patency and cardiopulmonary function. Obtain intravenous access. Administer 20 mL/kg NS bolus; reassess perfusion status after the bolus. Reassess lung sounds after each bolus. Prepare to repeat 20 mL/kg NS bolus, up to 60 mL/kg in first hour of recognition of symptoms. If patient is unresponsive to fluid resuscitation: 　Administer vasopressors, as prescribed. Obtain laboratory tests as ordered: 　Blood/urine/cerebrospinal fluid cultures 　Lactate 　Complete blood cell count 　Electrolytes 　Prothrombin time/partial thromboplastin time Antibiotic therapy, as prescribed

Anchor, J., & Settipane, R. (2004). Appropriate use of epinephrine in anaphylaxis. *American Journal of Emergency Medicine, 22,* 488–490.

Ralston, M., Hazinski, M., Zaritsky, A., Schexnayder, S., & Kleinman, M. (2006). *Textbook of pediatric advanced life support.* Chicago: American Academy of Pediatrics and American Heart Association.

Sampson, H. A., Muñoz-Furlong, A., Campbell, R. L., Adkinson, N. F., Jr., Bock, S. A., Branum, A., et al. (2006). Second symposium on the definition and management of anaphylaxis: Summary report—Second National Institute of Allergy and Infectious Disease/Food Allergy and Anaphylaxis network symposium. *Journal of Allergy and Clinical Immunology, 17,* 391–397.

References

1. Ralston, M., Hazinski, M., Zaritsky, A., Schexnayder, S., & Kleinman, M. (2006). *Textbook of pediatric advanced life support.* Chicago: American Academy of Pediatrics and American Heart Association.

2. Emergency Nurses Association. (2004). *Emergency nursing pediatric course.* Des Plaines, IL: Author.

3. Bell, L. (2006). Shock. In G. Fleisher, S. Ludwig, & F. Henretig (Eds.), *Textbook of pediatric emergency medicine* (pp. 51–62). Philadelphia: Lippincott Williams & Wilkins.

4. Hazinski, M., Mondozzi, M., & Urdiales Baker, R. (2006). Shock, multiple organ dysfunction syndrome, and burns in children. In K. McCance & S. Huether (Eds.), *Pathophysiology: The biologic basics for disease in adults and children* (pp. 1655–1680). St. Louis, MO: Mosby.

5. Sampson, H. A., Muñoz-Furlong, A., Campbell, R. L., Adkinson, N. F., Jr., Bock, S. A., Branum, A., et al. (2006). Second symposium on the definition and management of anaphylaxis: Summary report—Second National Institute of Allergy and Infectious Disease/Food Allergy and Anaphylaxis network symposium. *Journal of Allergy and Clinical Immunology, 17,* 391–397.

6. Mecham, N. (2004). Acute viral myocarditis in the ED pediatric patient: Three case presentations. *Journal of Emergency Nursing, 30*(2), 179–182.

7. Carcillo, J., & Fields, A. (2002). Task Force Committee Members. Clinical practice guidelines for hemodynamic support of pediatric and neonatal patients in septic shock. *Critical Care Medicine, 30,* 1365–1378.

8. Goldstein, B., Giroir, B., Randolph A., & International Consensus Conference on Pediatric Sepsis. (2005). International pediatric sepsis consensus conference: Definitions for sepsis and organ dysfunction in pediatrics. *Pediatric Critical Care Medicine, 6*(1), 2–8.

9. Dellinger, R. P., Levy, M. M., Carlet, J. M., Bion, J., Parker, M. M., Jaeschke, R., et al. (2008). Surviving Sepsis Campaign: International guidelines for management of severe sepsis and septic shock: 2008. *Intensive Care Medicine, 34,* 17–60.

10. Anchor, J., & Settipane, R. (2004). Appropriate use of epinephrine in anaphylaxis. *American Journal of Emergency Medicine, 22,* 488–490.

11. Simons, F. E., Roberts, J. R., Gu, X., & Simons, K. J. (1998). Epinephrine absorption in children with a history of anaphylaxis. *Journal of Allergy and Clinical Immunology, 101,* 33–37.

SECTION SEVEN
Environmental-Related Emergencies

THIRTY-NINE

Heat-Related Emergencies

Nancy J. Denke, RN, MSN, FNP-C, CCRN

Introduction

Heat-related emergencies are a common occurrence during the summer months. They can be mild events that respond readily to simple management techniques or life-threatening events that require immediate intervention. To provide appropriate care, the emergency nurse must understand normal and abnormal thermoregulation and be able to identify children at risk for heat injuries.

Heat-related illnesses occur when the systems used by the body to regulate heat become overwhelmed and cannot compensate. Heat-related deaths occur most commonly in adults, particularly the elderly, but children are also vulnerable to serious injury or death. These injuries can result from being left in a small unventilated area such as a car, excessive physical activities, or underlying illness. Substance abuse (alcohol or drugs) in conjunction with environmental factors can place a child at higher risk for hyperthermic injuries.[1]

McLaren et al. demonstrated that on sunny days, even when the ambient temperature is mild or relatively cool, there is rapid and significant heating of the interior of vehicles. They found that in general, after 60 minutes, one can expect a 40 °F (4.4 °C) increase in internal temperatures for ambient temperatures spanning 72 to 96 °F (22.2–35.5 °C), putting children and pets at significant risk.[2,3] In 2008 (as of July 15, 2008), there had been 375 incidents of children left unattended in a parked car, with 92 fatalities.[4] There is currently legislation to prosecute individuals who leave children unattended in hot cars. However, an Associated Press study found that a "wide disparity exists in sentences for leaving kids to die in hot cars" both in the frequency of prosecutions and length of sentences in hyperthermia deaths.[4,5] Car-related heat illness and death are preventable by not leaving young children in vehicles.

The purpose of this chapter is to discuss common heat-related emergencies, their assessment, and nursing interventions.

Pathophysiology

Thermoregulation, the maintenance of normal body temperature, is accomplished by balancing heat load and heat dissipation:

❏ *Heat load* is determined by metabolic, kinetic, and environmental conditions. Metabolism produces about 100 kcal of heat per hour. Muscle activity during exercise produces 300 to 600 kcal or more of heat per hour. The body also absorbs heat from the environment.[6]

❏ *Heat dissipation* occurs primarily through evaporation of sweat. The evaporation of sweat from the skin plays a major role in heat dissipation during exercise and is the primary thermoregulatory mechanism when the ambient temperature is above 68 °F (20 °C).[7]

❏ *Radiation,* the transfer of heat through electromagnetic waves, and *conduction*, the transfer of heat through direct contact, also play a role in heat dissipation.

❏ *Convection* is heat loss by the transfer of heat through air currents. Excess clothing, low wind velocity, and an air temperature that is near body temperature can impede convection.

Children produce more heat for their body size than adults and are less efficient with regulating their temperatures. They exhibit a slower speed of acclimatization, have a lower sweating rate, and produce more metabolic rate per kilogram of body weight, placing a great strain on thermoregulatory mechanisms.[1] Though children have more sweat glands than adults, their sweat glands are smaller and less efficient. They sweat less and have a higher threshold for sweating compared with adults, making it harder for them to lose body heat by evaporation.[8]

The hypothalamus acts as a thermostat to maintain the core body temperature between 98.6–99.5 °F (36–37.5 °C) despite the wide variations that are encountered in ambient temperature.[9] Hyperthermia represents an elevation of the core temperature resulting from an imbalance between absorption of heat from the environment and an inability to dissipate heat. When heat begins to build, the hypothalamus signals the autonomic nervous system to reduce sympathetic vasoconstrictor tone. Cardiac output rises, increasing circulation to the skin. Heat from the core is lost as the blood circulates to the periphery and sweating begins.[9]

When the body reaches the point that dissipation can no longer keep up with heat accumulation, the body temperature begins to rise. Cellular enzyme systems fail above 107.68 °F (42.08 °C). Further heat insult denatures proteins and results in the metabolic process leading to organ and system failure.[9]

Pediatric Considerations

Several physiologic factors increase the risk of heat-related emergencies in children:[9]

❏ Greater surface area to mass ratio, allowing for greater transfer of heat from the environment to the body, via radiation.

❏ Increased production of metabolic heat per kilogram of body weight when moving.

❏ Poor ability to acclimate to hot conditions because of immature thermoregulatory control mechanisms.

❏ Inability to increase cardiac output, with a great ability to alter peripheral blood flow. (Children < 5 years of age do not increase their cardiac output compared with older children.)

❏ Lower blood volume.

❏ Lower amount of sweat produced per gland.

❏ Longer time to acclimatize to heat and a higher core temperature during endurance activities than adults.[8]

❏ Presence of chronic childhood diseases, such as cystic fibrosis, quadriplegia, and congenital anhidrosis, decreasing the ability to sweat or causing excess losses of sodium.[10]

❏ Sickle cell disease/crisis can be precipitated by prolonged exposure to environmental heat and subsequent dehydration.[8,11]

❏ Acute febrile illnesses increase risk for heat injury.

Several developmental, behavioral, environmental, and health risk factors predispose children to heat-related emergencies:

❏ Children lack the instinct to replace fluid losses and are dependent on adults to meet these needs.

❏ Infants are at higher risk because of inability to move independently from one environment to another.[9]

❏ Young, nonambulatory children depend on adults to move them from direct sunlight and from cars.

❏ Lack of air-conditioning or proper ventilation.

❏ Lack of acclimatization—acclimatization can take days to weeks.

❏ Vapor-impermeable uniforms, helmets, and shoulder pads, worn when children participate in organized sports, limit heat dissipation by decreasing evaporation of sweat and convection of heat.

❏ Child may not want to take a break from the sport or activity or may not be permitted to do so. There may be a perception that taking a break will show signs of weakness.

❏ Medications that increase heat production include thyroid hormones and sympathomimetics.[12]

❏ Antihistamines, phenothiazine, anticholinergics, β-blockers, and alcohol, as well as street drugs, including phencyclidine (PCP) and D-lysergic acid diethylamide (LSD), impair normal sweating and increase risk of heat injury.

❏ Amphetamines and cocaine increase muscle activity and heat production and may increase the risk of heat injury.

❏ Alcohol, caffeinated beverages, and diuretics increase fluid loss through urination, which can lead to dehydration and heat-related illness.[8]

❏ A fatal event can occur within 20 minutes if normal heat loss mechanisms are overwhelmed; close observation of an active child is important.

Focused History

❏ Recent exposure to circumstances that may lead to overheating

❏ Length of exposure to heat

❏ Temperature and humidity level during exposure

❏ Activities preceding onset of symptoms

❏ Preexisting illnesses or drug use

❏ Treatment before arrival in the emergency department

Focused Assessment

Physical Assessment

Any child who presents with a core temperature > 104 °F (40 °C) with altered level of consciousness (irritability, confusion, loss of consciousness) should be thought to have a heat-related injury. Other initial assessment findings may be tachypnea, tachycardia, and normotension. Signs and symptoms of heat-related injuries are discussed under specific conditions later in this chapter.

Laboratory Values[13]

❏ Electrocardiogram—will show changes similar to myocardial ischemia.

❏ Glucose level—hypoglycemia may occur because of increased use of glucose or hepatic damage leading to impaired gluconeogenesis.

❏ Serum lactate—elevated because of circulatory shock and hepatic dysfunction.

- ❏ Creatine phosphokinase (CPK)/myoglobinuria—elevated because of rhabdomyolysis due to tissue destruction.
- ❏ Liver enzymes—can be elevated in the "thousands" because of hepatic injury.
- ❏ Hyponatremia/hyperkalemia.
- ❏ Prothrombin time, activated partial thromboplastin time, fibrinogen, and platelets—prolonged because of hepatic injury (may see hypercoagulopathy initially, but within the first 24 hours disseminated intravascular coagulation [DIC] may develop).
- ❏ Elevated D dimer
- ❏ Blood urea nitrogen (BUN)/creatinine—elevated because of renal insufficiency (BUN > creatinine) and respond well with rehydration.
- ❏ Complete blood cell count (CBC)—hematocrit declines in the first 24 hours but responds well to rehydration.
- ❏ Progressive anemia common because of destruction of red blood cells (RBCs).
- ❏ Neutrophils that look like "a bunch of grapes."
- ❏ Arterial blood gas—metabolic acidosis.
- ❏ Urinalysis—proteinuria, hematuria, myoglobinuria, or granular casts provide evidence of acute renal failure or rhabdomyolysis. Increased specific gravity.
- ❏ Chest radiograph—pulmonary edema due to endothelial damage.
- ❏ Computed tomographic scan of head—to look for cerebral edema.

Psychosocial Assessment

- ❏ Was the child properly supervised before the illness?
- ❏ Is the child's condition the result of caregiver neglect or ignorance of the child's needs?
- ❏ Was housing on upper floors without air conditioning/ventilation a factor?

Initial Treatment of Heat-Related Emergencies

1. Maintain airway and breathing. Obtain venous access. Initate volume replacement with 0.9% normal saline solution (NS) at a 20 mL/kg bolus over a 20-minute period to restore circulating volume.
2. Remove from heat source, and begin aggressive cooling to < 101 °F (38.3 °C).
3. Obtain laboratory values—CBC, BUN/creatinine, liver enzymes, CPK, calcium, and coagulation studies.

May need to transfuse RBCs for anemia in the first 48 hours. If coagulopathy, may need fresh frozen plasma and/or platelets.

4. Prepare to administer:
   - Use of vasopressors—usually for the first 24 to 48 hours.
   - Bicarbonate drip—useful in alkalization of urine to prevent acute myoglobinuric renal failure secondary to rhabdomyolysis (1.9 mEq/kg intravenously every 1 to 2 hours as needed [prn]).
   - Mannitol (Osmitrol)—used to prevent damage to kidneys by myoglobin in rhabdomyolysis and acute renal failure (0.5 to 1 g/kg intravenously followed by 0.25 to 0.5 g/kg intravenously every 4 to 6 hours).
   - Diazepam (Valium)—used for seizure activity (0.05 to 0.3 mg/kg/dose intravenously over a 2- to 3-minute period, not to exceed 5 mg/dose in children < 5 years, and 10 mg/dose in children > 5 years: 0.5 mg/kg per rectum, followed by 0.25 mg/kg in 10 minutes prn).
   - Chlorpromazine (Thorazine)—used to suppress shivering (0.5 to 1 mg/kg/dose intravenously).

Specific Heat-Related Emergencies

There are three common heat-related emergencies: heat cramps, heat exhaustion, and heat stroke. Heat cramps, heat exhaustion, and heat stroke represent the spectrum of heat-stress-induced illness. Heat stroke is the most serious form of heat-related injury and must be treated aggressively. In heat illness, normal heat transfer mechanisms are overwhelmed, and central thermoregulatory control is ineffective.[13] Table 39.1 compares the signs, symptoms, and interventions for each condition.

Heat Cramps/Stress

Heat cramps are sporadic, painful muscle spasms that result from profuse sweating and loss of electrolytes during prolonged periods of exercise in a warm environment. Sodium depletion can potentiate the effect of calcium on skeletal muscle. Cramping usually affects the large muscle groups being used, and the most common area of cramping is in the large muscles of the legs. Heat cramps may occur during activity or several hours later. Drinking hypotonic fluids (water) to replace fluid losses contributes to the cramping, because it worsens the hyponatremia by diluting the circulating sodium. Core temperature remains within normal range.

TABLE 39.1 Comparison of Heat Cramps, Heat Exhaustion, and Heat Stroke

Condition	Signs and Symptoms	Interventions
Heat cramps	Sporadic, painful cramps, especially in the extremities and abdomen Flushed moist skin Mild fever, usually < 102 °F (38.8 °C)	Move the child to a cool, shaded area Remove excess clothing Fan Replace fluid loss; an (oral) electrolyte solution can be used Manage salt intake
Heat exhaustion	Temperature > 104 °F (40 °C) Pale moist skin Sweating may be absent or present. Muscle cramps/tenderness Headache Weakness Orthostatic changes Tachycardia Increased thirst Nausea, vomiting Piloerection	Move the child to a cool, shaded area Remove clothing Provide intravenous fluids to correct hypovolemia (20 mL/kg bolus) Instruct patient to avoid heat stress for next few days and how to correctly replace fluids and electrolytes
Heat stroke	Temperature > 104 °F (40 °C) CNS dysfunction—seizures, delirium, coma, due to decrease in cerebral perfusion leading to cerebral ischemia Severe headaches, irritability Cerebellar dysfunction—ataxia, confusion Wet/dry hot skin Signs of distributive shock—vasodilation with hypotension, normal cardiac index and central venous pressure Tachycardia Hypotension—late sign Hyperventilation Hypovolemia secondary to sweating Nausea/vomiting/diarrhea Gastrointestinal bleeding—secondary to mucosal swelling and petechiae and endotoxin injury Oliguria Anhidrosis is a late sign. Purpura, conjunctival hemorrhage secondary to coagulopathies (DIC)	Maintain airway and breathing Two large-bore intravenous lines—20 mg/kg NS bolus Check glucose level—then administer 0.5 to 1 mg/kg Dextrose (1 to 2 mL/kg D50 or 2 to 4 mL/kg D25) Obtain laboratory specimens—CBC, electrolytes, CPK Monitor for cardiac dysrhythmias Undress, begin cooling by spraying with room-temperature water, and position fan across the body Monitor for rhabdomyolysis Alcohol baths are contraindicated Antipyretics are not effective and should not be given Prevent shivering—may give lorazepam (0.1 mg/kg)

Bernardo, L. M., Crane, P. A., & Veenema, T. G. (2006). Treatment and prevention of pediatric heat-related illnesses at mass gatherings and special events. *Dimensions in Critical Care Nursing, 25*(4), 165–171.

Hoppe, J., Sinert, R., Kunihiro, A., & Foster, J. (2008). *Heat exhaustion and heatstroke.* Retrieved April 17, 2009, from http://www.emedicine.com/EMERG/topic236.htm

Heat Exhaustion

Heat exhaustion is a condition resulting from exposure to high temperatures, excessive sweating, and insufficient fluid and/or salt replacement. Its symptoms are vague, from general irritability to impending heat stroke, with a core temperature ranging from normal to < 104.8 °F (40 °C).[8,14,15] There are two categories of heat exhaustion:

1. Hyponatremic (salt depletion) heat exhaustion—results from replacement of fluid and electrolyte losses with water only (often seen in children with cystic fibrosis).

2. Hypernatremic (water depletion) heat exhaustion—results from loss of fluid and electrolytes without replacement of any kind.

If not treated promptly, heat exhaustion may progress to heat stroke, which can be fatal.

Heat Stroke

Heat stroke is a life-threatening emergency. Heat stroke can result from direct exposure to the sun's rays or from high environmental temperatures without exposure to the sun. It is characterized by a temperature higher than 104.9 °F (40.5 °C) with central nervous system (CNS) dysfunction (delirium and/or coma).[3] The body's ability to dissipate heat is overwhelmed, and sweating is impaired. The brain is particularly sensitive to heat; therefore, neurologic symptoms occur early. Profound volume depletion occurs. Respiratory alkalosis and metabolic acidosis are common. Without immediate intervention, widespread organ injury and death can occur.[12,14]

Heat stroke can be divided into two categories:[8]

1. *Classic* or *nonexertional heat stroke*—generally affects infants and small children because they are dependent on adults to alter their environment and provide them with fluids. It develops over a period of days.

2. *Exertional heat stroke*—develops rapidly and occurs most commonly in vigorously active individuals (exercising or working) in a hot environment, who may not be acclimated to the hot environment.

Heat Stress Injuries in Sports

Heat stroke in athletes is entirely preventable. Exertional heat illness is generally the result of increased heat production and impaired dissipation of heat. It should be treated aggressively to avoid life-threatening complications.[15,16]

❑ Significant risk factors for heat illness include dehydration, hot and humid climate, obesity, low physical fitness, lack of acclimatization, and previous history of heat stroke, sleep deprivation, medications (especially diuretics or antidepressants), sweat gland dysfunction, and upper respiratory or gastrointestinal illness.

❑ Dehydration, with fluid loss occasionally as high as 6% to 10% of body weight, appears to be one of the most common risk factors for heat illness in patients exercising in the heat.[17]

❑ Children thermoregulate effectively in normal weather conditions with rehydration and proper clothing but have a decreased ability to adapt to temperature extremes.

❑ Children acclimate to heat more slowly and show less heat dissipation than adults in a hot environment because of a lower sweat rate.

❑ Children who are overweight or wear heavy clothing, such as marching band or football uniforms, during exertion are also more susceptible.

❑ Children often do not think to rest when having fun and may not drink enough fluids when playing, exercising, or participating in sports.

❑ Maximize recovery between training sessions by:

- Avoiding stress and trying to relax
- Getting out of the sun as soon as possible
- Moving to a cool environment immediately after practice
- Staying in the shade or air-conditioning when possible
- Lying down and resting for a short period of time between training sessions
- Getting a high quality and quantity of sleep
- Eating balanced meals to replace lost fluids and energy used
- Avoiding excessive clothing

Home Care and Prevention

Instruct parents to:

❑ Never leave a child alone in a car, especially in warm temperatures. Keep car windows open in the driveway at home to prevent children from becoming locked in the car.

❑ Be aware of and educate supervising adults (parents, babysitters, and coaches) of the dangers involved with strenuous exercise in a hot environment.

❑ Schedule athletic practices for early morning or in the evening—more work can be done in cooler and less humid conditions. This allows players to focus on sport techniques and maintain proper mechanics, and reduces the exposure to heat-related injuries.

❏ Never rely on thirst—Drink plenty of fluids before, during, and after practice and competition. Hydration is important in preventing heat-related illnesses and assuring optimal performance.

❏ Prehydrate 30 minutes before any activity—drink until no longer thirsty plus another 8 ounces. Children weighing less than 90 pounds should drink 5 ounces every 20 minutes of activity. Children weighing more than 90 pounds should drink 8 ounces every 20 minutes.

❏ Avoid carbonated and caffeine-containing beverages—carbonation gives a feeling of fullness, and caffeine increases metabolism and produces more heat.

❏ Be especially careful to take precautions if the child has a preexisting health condition that increases the risk of heat illness.

❏ Cognitive ability and the capacity to make a rational decision are compromised with heat related disorders. If a child is suspected of having a problem with the heat, err on the side of caution and insist he or she discontinue strenuous activities, get into shade, and cool down.

❏ Adopt a buddy system when playing or exercising in the heat. The buddy can be the first one to notice cognitive behavior changes and alert an adult.

❏ Dress appropriately—clothing should be loose fitting and allow for effective air circulation. Wicking materials can aid heat loss through evaporation.

❏ Avoid factors that can contribute to dehydration:

- Heat
- Humidity
- Altitude
- Inadequate fluid consumption
- Caffeine and alcohol consumption
- Tight-fitting clothes and clothes that do not allow evaporation

Conclusion

Children, because of various physiologic and developmental factors, are at risk for hyperthermia. Emergency nurses must be aware of the different types of heat-related injury and intervene to prevent a mild case of heat exhaustion from progressing into life-threatening heat stroke. Parents and children must be given information about prevention of these conditions, especially the dangers of leaving children in a closed car.

References

1. Ciorciari, A. J. (2002). Environmental emergencies. In E. F. Crain & J. C. Gershel (Eds.), *Clinical manual of emergency pediatrics* (4th ed., pp. 187–189). New York: McGraw-Hill.

2. McLaren, C., Null, J., & Quinn, J. (2005). Heat stress from enclosed vehicles: Moderate ambient temperatures cause significant temperature rise in enclosed vehicles. *Pediatrics, 116,* e109–e112.

3. Argaud, L., Ferry, T., Le, Q., Marfisi, A., Cioba, D., Cache, P., et al. (2007). Heat waves and heat-related illness: Preparing for the increasing influence of climate on health in temperate areas. *Archives of Internal Medicine, 298* (8), 917–919.

4. Kidsandcars.org. (2009). *Hyperthermia incidents (heat stroke).* Retrieved April 17, 2009, from http://www.kidsandcars.org

5. Null, J. (2008). *Hyperthermia deaths of children in vehicles.* Retrieved April 17, 2009, from http://ggweather.com/heat/

6. Waters, T. A. (2001). Heat illness: Tips for recognition and treatment. *Cleveland Clinic Journal of Medicine , 68* (8), 685–687.

7. Wexler, R. K. (2002). Evaluation and treatment of heat-related illnesses. *American Family Physician, 65,* 2307–2314, 2319–2320.

8. Bernardo, L. M., Crane, P. A., & Veenema, T. G. (2006). Treatment and prevention of pediatric heat-related illnesses at mass gatherings and special events. *Dimensions in Critical Care Nursing, 25* (4), 165–171.

9. Grubenhoff, J. A., du Ford, K., & Roosevelt, G. E. (2007). Heat related illness. *Clinical Pediatric Emergency Medicine, 8*(1), 59–64.

10. Walker, J. (2003). Heat-related emergencies. In D. O. Thomas & L. M. Bernardo (Eds.), *Core curriculum for pediatric emergency nursing* (pp. 503–506). Sudbury, MA: Jones & Bartlett.

11. Pretzlaff, R. K. (2002). Death of an adolescent athlete with sickle cell trait caused by exertional heat stroke. *Pediatric Critical Care Medicine, 3*(3), 308–310.

References (continued)

12. Bytomski, J., & Squire, D. (2003). Heat illness in children. *Current Sports & Medical Reports, 2,* 320–324.

13. Jardine, D. S. (2007). Heat illness and heat stroke. *Pediatrics in Review, 28*(7), 249–256.

14. Hoppe, J., Sinert, R., Kunihiro, A., & Foster, J. (2008). *Heat exhaustion and heatstroke.* Retrieved April 17, 2009, from http://www.emedicine.com/EMERG/topic236.htm

15. Howe, A. S., & Boden, B. P. (2007). Heat-related illness in athletes. *American Journal of Sports Medicine, 35,* 1384–1395.

16. Binkley, H. M., Beckett, J., Casa, D. J., Kleiner, D. M., & Plummer, P. E. (2002). National Athletic Trainers' Association Position Statement: Exertional heat illnesses. *Journal of Athletic Training, 37*(3), 329–343.

17. Coris, E. E., Ramirez, A. M., & Van Durme, D. J. (2004). Heat illness in athletes: The dangerous combination of heat, humidity and exercise. *Sports Medicine, 34*(1), 9–16.

FORTY

Cold-Related Emergencies

Nancy J. Denke, RN, MSN, FNP-C, CCRN

Introduction

Cold injuries in children result from simple to prolonged exposure to a cold environment, such as an immersion in cold water. These injuries occur when the body is unable to produce sufficient heat to balance heat loss, because of the immaturity of the child's adaptive behavioral and physiologic responses to thermal stress. Accidental or recreational hypothermia can also be augmented when the child has an underlying illness/injury that may disrupt his or her thermoregulatory mechanisms. An infant undressed and left uncovered in a cool environment can become hypothermic during examination and therapeutic procedures. It is essential that emergency nurses be aware of the factors that increase the risk and be able to provide immediate, effective treatment. The purpose of this chapter is to discuss selected conditions related to exposure to cold temperatures and nursing interventions to treat and prevent these conditions.

Pathophysiology

Hypothermia exists when the core body temperature falls below 95.08 °F (35.08 °C),[1] usually caused by accidental exposure to cold temperatures. Human core temperature is normally maintained within 1.08 °F (0.68 °C) of normal. This represents a fine balance between heat production and heat loss. When core temperature begins to fall below 98.68 °F (37.08 °C), physiologic mechanisms that produce and conserve heat are activated.[2] These mechanisms include:

❐ Vasoconstriction—occurs as a homeostatic mechanism to prevent heat loss.

❐ Thermoregulation—a complex process mediated by the anterior hypothalamus, which initiates a number of responses aimed at heat production and conservation. Most heat generation occurs through muscle activity. Cold increases preshivering muscle tone, doubling heat production.

❐ Maximum heat production lasts only a few hours because of fatigue and glycogen depletion. When fatigue occurs, muscle activity declines or ceases, and the core temperature falls.

❐ Exposure to cold increases activity in the afferent fibers, which stimulate the anterior hypothalamus; vasoconstriction occurs and reduces blood flow to the cooling skin.

❐ Colder blood reaches temperature-sensitive neurons in the hypothalamus, which initiates various responses in the autonomic nervous system, the endocrine system, extrapyramidal skeletal muscle stimulation, and shivering. These responses aim either to increase heat production or to reduce heat loss.[3]

❐ In the newborn, brown fat is the site of heat production. Blood flows through the brown fat producing heat in what is called nonshivering thermogenesis.

❐ Cold stress increases preshivering muscle tone, and heat production can double. Maximal heat production lasts only a few hours because of fatigue and glycogen depletion.

❐ The hypothalamus has numerous effects on various organ systems:[4,5]

  ▪ Central nervous system (CNS)—cerebral perfusion autoregulation is lost at approximately 77 °F (25 °C): depression of the CNS; poor sucking; ataxia; irritability.

- Respiratory—tachypnea initially, but as the metabolic rate decreases there is a decrease in the respiratory rate.
- Cardiovascular—initially tachycardia; peripheral constriction.
- Gastrointestinal—ileus; gastric dilation (seen in neonates); vomiting; poor rectal tone.
- Renal—renal blood flow is decreased; initially a large diuresis of dilute urine secondary to vasoconstriction (peripherally).

Although surface temperature of the body, especially the extremities, may drop nearly close to environmental temperatures, several mechanisms work to conserve heat and to protect blood and core structures from ambient air temperature, humidity, and wind.[2] Sweating ceases, decreasing heat loss by evaporation, and vasoconstriction of cutaneous and subcutaneous vessels reduces losses further. Table 40.1 describes other responses to decreasing body temperature.

There is a misconception that cold penetrates. However, in reality, heat flows from hot to cold. The speed of the movement depends on the temperature difference. The greater the difference, the faster the heat flows from the warm body to the cold environment.

Children lose heat by different mechanisms. Newborns in particular lose heat by *evaporation* soon after birth (with the evaporation of amniotic fluid from the skin surface) or *conduction* (cold blankets or beds). The major mechanisms of heat loss can affect each pediatric patient differently. Healthy children's compensatory responses to heat loss are through the following mechanisms:

❑ *Radiation*—the transfer of heat through electromagnetic waves. This is the major cause of heat loss (55% to 65% of loss).[6] The greater the surface area to mass ratio, the increased loss by radiation. Therefore, insulation and subcutaneous fat can assist to diminish these losses.

❑ *Conduction*—the direct transfer of heat. Two percent to 3% of the heat loss is through this mechanism, but this may increase up to five times in wet clothing and up to 25 times in cold water.[6]

❑ *Convection*—the transfer of heat through air currents.

❑ *Evaporation and respiration*—most commonly, evaporation of sweat. (Two percent to 9% lost in heating inspired air and 20% to 27% lost to insensible evaporation from the skin and lungs).[7]

TABLE 40.1 Signs and Symptoms of Cold Injury

Body Temperature and Pathophysiology	Signs and Symptoms
89.6–95.08 °F (32.0–35.08 °C)	Sympathetic response causes peripheral vasoconstriction
	Slowing of mental status
	Inappropriate behavior or judgment
	Shivering preserved
82.0–89.68 °F (28.0–32.08 °C)	Body function slows down progressively
	Coma likely at temperature < 86 °F (30 °C)
	Cyanosis
	Edema may develop
	Muscle rigidity replaces shivering
	Respirations and pulses are hard to detect
	The metabolism slows approximately 6% for each degree decrease in body temperature
	At 82.5 °F (28.08 °C) the basal metabolic rate falls by half
	Oxygen consumption and carbon dioxide production decrease
	Compensatory mechanisms fail
77.0–82.08 °F (25.0–28.08 °C)	Coma with dilated nonreactive pupils
	Cardiac conduction decreases and cardiac irritability increases
	Circulatory collapse begins as stroke volume, filling pressure, contractility, and heart rate decrease
< 77.08 °F (25.08 °C)	Dysrhythmias, ranging from bradycardia to ventricular fibrillation, asystole, arrest
	Apnea

Gleeson, J. G., Dobyns, W. B., Plawner, L., & Ashwal, S. (2006). Congenital structural defects. In K. F. Swaiman, S. Ashwal, & D. M. Ferriero (Eds.), Pediatric nBessen, H. A. (2003). Hypothermia. In J. E. Tintinalli, G. D. Kelen, & J. S. Stapczynski (Eds.), *Emergency medicine: A compre¬hensive study guide* (6th ed., pp. 846–849). New York: McGraw-Hill.
Ciorciari, A. J. (2003). Frostbite. In E. F. Crain & J. C. Gerschel (Eds.), *Clinical manual of emergency pediatrics* (4th ed., pp. 185–187). New York: McGraw-Hill.

Pediatric Considerations

The thermoregulatory mechanisms that are actively present in adults are far less efficient in the pediatric population. Infants and young children are at significantly high risk for hypothermia, particularly in cold-water immersions. Physiologic, health, and behavioral factors may increase the risk:[6]

❑ Physiologic factors
  - Large body to surface area ratio/larger body surface area to weight ratio
  - Less adaptive abilities
  - Minimal subcutaneous fat
  - Thin skin with increased permeability
  - Prolonged exposure to moisture (wet skin) cools faster because of heat lost from evaporation
  - Inefficient neuromuscular and cardiovascular responses
  - Delayed shivering and inefficient ability to produce heat

❑ Health and behavioral factors
  - Malnutrition
  - Drug or alcohol intoxication, which can impair the ability to feel the cold and the body's ability to react normally to the cold stimulus
  - Incapacitating illnesses such as severe infection or diabetic ketoacidosis
  - Immobilizing injuries such as paralysis
  - Hypothyroidism and Addison's disease
  - Psychiatric disease
  - Trauma
  - Previous cold injury, which leads to a twofold increase risk of hypothermia
  - Improper behavioral response—"just does not know when to come in from the cold"
  - Altitude, mountain climbing
  - Inadequate or constrictive clothing
  - Cross-country skiing

Focused History

❑ Type of exposure (such as submersion in cold water or exposure to cold outdoor environment).
❑ Temperature of the environment; wind chill and humidity factors.
❑ Length of exposure.
❑ Preexisting medical conditions that might increase the risk for hypothermia.

❑ Drug or alcohol use.
❑ Unacclimated individual
  - Altitude
  - History suggestive of abusive head trauma (AHT, shaken impact syndrome) (Chapter 44).

Focused Assessment

Physical Assessment

Any child with cold skin, altered mental status, and bradycardia should be considered to be hypothermic until proved otherwise.[5]

A low-reading thermometer is essential. Ordinary thermometers do not record less than 93.28 °F (34.08 °C). Rectal or indwelling urinary catheter probes are designed to measure low temperatures. An esophageal probe will most accurately measure core temperature.[5] The focused assessment will include the following points:

❑ Level of consciousness—drowsiness, apathy, irritability, confusion
❑ Heart rate and rhythm, and blood pressure—bradycardia, bradypnea
❑ Assessment for other injuries, lack of mobility, poor diet
❑ Glucose—bedside glucose
❑ Grading of the hypothermia as mild, moderate, or profound/severe:[5,8]
  - *Mild*— 89.6 to 95.0 °F (32 to 35.08 °C)
  - *Moderate*—82.4 to 89.6 °F (28 to 32.0 °C)
  - *Profound/severe*—82.4 °F (< 28 °C)

The signs and symptoms of hypothermia depend on the degree of hypothermia and are listed in Table 40.1.

Psychosocial Assessment

Children are at risk for cold injuries because they are likely to become absorbed in outdoor play and sporting activities, often not realizing that an injury is occurring. Also, they are more likely to wear clothing that restricts circulation or to continue playing in wet clothing.

Homelessness places children at special risk for cold injuries.

❑ The child should always be assessed for evidence that abuse or neglect may have contributed to the injury. For example, was the child improperly clothed for the conditions or left outside for an extended period of time without supervision?

Nursing Interventions

1. Assess and maintain airway, breathing, and circulation.
   - Assist with cardiopulmonary resuscitation as necessary.
   - Handle the child gently, because rough handling may precipitate ventricular fibrillation.
2. Assist with intubation as necessary.
   - Administer warmed, humidified 100% oxygen.
3. Continuously monitor oxygen saturation.
4. Establish intravenous access.
   - Administer intravenous fluid 104 °F (40 °C) using a fluid warmer.
5. Monitor heart rate and rhythm continuously.
   - Be prepared to treat dysrhythmias.
6. Gently remove all wet or cold clothing.
7. Assist with rewarming techniques (Table 40.2).
   - Begin with passive rewarming—Bair Hugger®, warmed blankets, ambient temperature (90 °F/ 32 °C).

TABLE 40.2 Rewarming Techniques	
Passive rewarming	Layered blankets
	Warm room
Active rewarming (external or internal)	Intravenous access before warming in case dysrhythmias occur
	Electric warming blankets or pads; hot water bottles—be careful of thermal injury to hypoperfused tissue
	Radiant warming
	Forced air
	Warm blankets
	Monitor cardiopulmonary status during aggressive rewarming
Core rewarming (effective, safe, and easy)	Warmed intravenous fluids
	Warmed, humidified oxygen—used to decrease the amplitude of shivering, which minimizes the energy expended
	Warmed nasogastric, peritoneal, bladder, or pleural lavage
	Extracorporeal circulation on heart-lung machine

8. Obtain laboratory studies—complete blood cell count, bedside/glucose, basic metabolic panel, ammonia, prothrombin time/partial thromboplastin time, arterial blood gas, fibrinogen, and type and crossmatch for two units packed red blood cells.[1]
9. Insert nasogastric tube; lavage with normal saline solution at 104 °F (40 °C).
10. Insert bladder catheter; lavage with normal saline solution at 104 °F (40 °C).

Specific Cold-Related Emergencies

Frostbite

Frostbite is one of the most common cold-related injuries. It occurs when the individual is unable to adequately protect himself or herself from the environment. Frostbite may occur within minutes or hours after exposure depending on the amount of protection and the severity of exposure. Children who live in colder climates and participate in winter sports are at risk for these injuries.

Frostbite is defined as "the freezing and crystallizing of fluids in the interstitial and cellular spaces when the normal thermal homeostasis is interrupted due to the prolonged exposure to cold."[5] The incidence and severity of frostbite in children is directly influenced by environmental factors, including wind chill, humidity, and contact with high thermal conductors, such as water or metal.[9,10] Cold ambient air alone is not as dangerous as when it is combined with windy conditions, humidity, and skin wetness.[10] Severe injury can occur at temperatures above freezing if these factors are present.[11] Exposed areas of the body most often affected are the hands, feet, cheeks, chin, and nose. Early cold injury is referred to as frost nip. Frost nip will quickly progress to frostbite if treatment is not initiated promptly. Health care workers must be able to recognize and differentiate signs of frostbite and initiate the proper treatment immediately.

The initial body response to prolonged exposure to cold temperatures is peripheral vasoconstriction, which compromises blood flow to the area. The blood becomes more viscous, decreasing capillary perfusion and causing sludging and thrombosis. The surrounding tissue becomes ischemic, with an increase in vascular permeability, resulting in swelling. When the tissue temperature drops below 32.08 °F (0.04 °C), freezing ice crystals begin to form in the extracellular compartment. Intracellular fluid is drawn out by osmosis, resulting in cellular dehydration, denatured proteins, enzyme destruction, and altered cellular membranes. The end result is irreversible tissue damage.[12]

Focused History

The history is the same as was discussed earlier in this chapter.

Focused Assessment

The clinical findings of frostbite depend on the severity of the exposure. Frostbite is classified as superficial or deep (Table 40.3) or by degrees (Table 40.4).

TABLE 40.3 Clinical Findings in Frostbite

Description	Signs and Symptoms
Superficial	Involves the skin and subcutaneous tissue
	Burning, tingling, and numbness may be present
Deep	Involves the muscles, nerves, blood vessels, and bone
	Burning, tingling, and numbness may be present
	Tissue will not reperfuse after blanching
	A grayish cast to the skin may be present while the underlying tissue remains soft
	Skin may become painful and flushed with rewarming
	Fluid-filled blisters may develop over the next 24 hours
	Tissue will appear pale or gray, is hard, and cannot be depressed
	There is a lack of sensation in the involved area
	After warming, the area will become grossly swollen
	Tissue will eventually turn purple-black and dry with small hemorrhagic blebs

- ❏ Airway and breathing—frostbite often occurs simultaneously with hypothermia. Stabilization and prevention of life-threatening events always take priority over the treatment of local cold injury.
- ❏ Circulation and skin integrity of the affected area:
  - Swelling/edema
  - Pliability of subcutaneous tissue
  - Skin color—Erythemic–white–mottled
    - Hard outer layer may be noted.
    - Demarcation between living and nonviable tissue appears approximately 1 month after the injury.
  - Sensation—decreased

- Decrease in flexibility—especially in deep tissue injury
- Peripheral pulse
- Capillary refill
- Presence of clear blisters that can lead to a dark eschar that sloughs off in approximately 4 weeks, necrosis, or gangrene.
- Increased risk of infection due to necrotic or gangrenous tissue.
- Assess for pain using an age appropriate pain scale (Chapter 11).

TABLE 40.4 Classification of Frostbite

Degree	Signs and Symptoms
First	Central, pale area
	Surrounding erythema
Second	Blister formation
	Blister surrounded by erythema and edema
Third	Hemorrhagic blisters
	Eschar formation
Fourth	Necrosis
	Tissue loss

Flarity, K. (2007). Environmental emergencies. In K. S. Hoyt & J. Selfridge-Thomas (Eds.), *Emergency nursing core curriculum* (6th ed., pp. 310–348). St. Louis, MO: Elsevier.

Nursing Interventions

1. Remove wet or constrictive clothing and place in dry loose clothing.
2. Assess and maintain airway, breathing and circulation.
   - Establish patent airway and effective breathing.
   - Establish intravenous access with two large-bore intravenous catheters.
3. Correct any systemic hypothermia to a core temperature of 93.2 °F (34 °C).
4. Avoid mechanical friction to decrease tissue injury.
5. In severe cases, keep the injured area away from sources of heat until rapid rewarming can be done.
6. Give analgesics before rewarming—ibuprofen 10 mg/kg every 8 hours by mouth or morphine (0.1 to 0.2 mg/kg intravenously every 4 hours).
7. Initiate rapid rewarming measures (thawing may take 20 to 40 minutes).[13,14]
   - Passive rewarming involves the use of blankets to cover the body and head; depending on shivering thermogenesis, the warming rate may be 32.9 to

35.6 °F (0.5 to 2 °C) per hour with this technique.

- Apply warm packs to the face and ears.
- Submerge extremities in a warm water bath.
- Use a warm circulating water bath of 104.0 to 107.68 °F (40.0 to 42.08 °C) measured with a thermometer.
- Encourage gentle motion of the injured part during rewarming.
- Carefully suspend the affected part in the bath; do not allow it to touch the sides or bottom.
- Maintain the water temperature. Always remove the body part before adding hot water.
- Continue rewarming until the area is completely thawed. The part will feel pliable, and erythema will be present distal to the injury.

8. Provide postwarming care.

- Elevate the extremity and splint the area.
- Protect the skin from reexposure or further injury.
- Separate the fingers or toes with sterile gauze to prevent tissue-to-tissue contact.
- Reevaluate the injury frequently for changes in color, increased edema, increased or decreased sensation, and formation of blisters.

9. Provide wound care.

- Blister management is controversial. Some practitioners advocate débridement; others believe that all blisters should be left intact.
- Aspiration of clear blisters is thought to prevent thromboxane- and prostaglandin-mediated tissue damage.[14]
- Most agree that hemorrhagic blisters should not be débrided because desiccation of deep dermal layers will worsen the outcome.
- Apply sterile nonadhesive dressings to the affected areas.
- Change dressing two to four times a day.
- Apply topical silver sulfadiazine (Silvadene®, Thermazene™) cream to open wounds.
- Topical aloe vera cream applied every 6 hours has been shown to improve the microcirculation by inhibiting the arachidonic cascade, especially the synthesis of thromboxane.[15]

10. Consider administration of prophylactic systemic antibiotics.[16]

- Frostbite infections tend to involve staphylococci, streptococci, enterococci, and Pseudomonas pathogens.

- Penicillin G intravenously every 6 hours works well for 48 to 72 hours. Dosing is 50,000 U/kg. (Decreases the risk of streptococci infections during the edema period.)

11. Update tetanus immunity, as needed.

12. Gabapentin (Neurontin®)—used in severe frostbite because of the very painful peripheral neuropathy.

13. Surgical care

- Amputation—avoided until complete demarcation occurs, since it is difficult to predict severity of injury. Fingers and toes will autoamputate in 3 to 6 weeks.
- Fasciotomy

14. Investigational therapies

- Limaprost (prostaglandin E1 analogue) as a therapeutic vasodilator to increase peripheral blood flow
- Low molecular weight dextran as an antisludging agent to decrease red blood cell clumping
- Vitamin C
- Hyperbaric oxygen

15. Physical therapy and rehabilitation to increase flexibility.

16. Psychological counseling to assist child and family to cope with disability.

Home Care and Prevention

❑ Prevention is the best treatment—wear a hat and use mittens instead of gloves. (Mittens tend to decrease the surface area exposed to the cold). Cover face.

❑ Avoid reexposure.

❑ Avoid lengthy exposure to cold. Avoid remaining in same position for prolonged periods.

❑ Wear layered, loose-fitting clothing. Avoid wearing tight-fitting footwear that may impair circulation.

❑ Keep dry.

❑ Be aware that wind chill, humidity, or contact with water or metal can increase the risk of sustaining a cold injury.

❑ Seek shelter from wind and cold.

❑ Keep small children away from potential hazards such as frozen lakes or streams.

❑ Increase fluid and caloric intake in cold weather.

Cold Water Immersion

Cold water immersion is a risk of recreational activities in oceans, lakes, streams, and pools during winter months. The definition of cold water varies in the literature. In

Danzi[19] the author describes cold water as follows: "the temperature of thermally natural water, in which heat loss balances heat production for a nude subject at rest, is approximately 91.4 °F (33 °C). Hypothermia eventually results from immersion in water below this temperature." Cold water immersion is associated with hypothermia and near drowning and must be treated in the same way. Drowning is discussed in Chapter 35.

Conclusion

Children are at risk for cold injuries because of physiologic, health, and behavioral factors. Infants can experience hypothermia simply from being examined in a cold room. Nurses must understand the conditions that place infants and children at risk for cold injuries and be familiar with rewarming techniques for any condition, from mild frostbite to severe hypothermia.

References

1. Bernardo, L. M., Henker, R., & O'Connor, J. (2000). Pediatric critical care: Treatment of trauma-associated hypothermia in children: Evidence-based practice. *American Journal of Critical Care, 9,* 227–236.

2. Baum, C. R. (2000). Accidental hypothermia. In G. L. Fleisher & S. Ludwig (Eds.), *Textbook of pediatric emergency medicine* (4th ed., pp. 955–959). Philadelphia: Lippincott Williams & Wilkins.

3. Mallet, M. L. (2002). Pathophysiology of accidental hypothermia. *QMJ Medicine: An International Journal of Medicine, 95,* 775–785.

4. Ishimine, P. (2008). Hypothermia. In J. M. Baren, S. G. Rothrock, J. Brennen, & L. Brown (Eds.), *Emergency pediatrics.* Philadelphia: Saunders.

5. Ciorciari, A. J. (2003). Frostbite. In E. F. Crain & J. C. Gerschel (Eds.), *Clinical manual of emergency pediatrics* (4th ed., pp. 185–187). New York: McGraw-Hill.

6. Tucker, C., & Schauben, J. (1998). Environmental and toxicologic emergencies. In T. E. Soud & J. S. Rogers (Eds.), *Manual of pediatric emergency nursing* (pp. 622–659). St. Louis, MO: Mosby.

7. Danzi, D. F. (2008). Accidental hypothermia. In P. Rosen & R. Barkin (Eds.), *Rosen's emergency medicine: Concepts and clinical practice* (online, pp. 2236–2254). St. Louis, MO: Elsevier.

8. Gausche-Hill, M., Fuchs, S., & Yamamoto, L. (2007). *APLS: Pediatric emergency medicine resource* (4th ed., pp. 220–223). Sudbury, MA: Jones and Bartlett.

9. Baum, C. (2003). Environmental emergencies: weighing the ounce of prevention. *Clinical Pediatric Emergency Medicine, 4*(2), 121–126.

10. Gambrell, R. C. (2002). Environmental conditions and youth sports. In R. B. Birrer, B. Griesemer, & M. B. Cataletto, *Pediatric sports medicine for primary care* (pp. 98–99). Philadelphia: Lippincott Williams & Wilkins.

11. Rabold, M. (2004). Bite and other localized injuries. In J. E. Tintinelli, G. D. Kelen, & J. S. Stapczynski, *Emergency medicine: A comprehensive study guide* (6th ed.). New York: McGraw-Hill.

12. Danzi, D. F. (2008). Frostbite. In P. Rosen & R. Barkin (Eds.), *Rosen's emergency medicine: Concepts and clinical practice* (online, pp. 2228–2236). St. Louis, MO: Elsevier.

13. Cheng, D., Thompson, T. M. & Yakobi, R. (2008). *Frostbite.* Retrieved April 17, 2009, from http://www.emedicine.com/ped/topic803.htm

14. Part 10: First aid. (2005). *Circulation, 112*(Suppl 1), III-115–III-125.

15. Biem, J., Koehncke, N., Classen, J., & Dosman, D. (2003). Out of the cold: Management of hypothermia and frostbite. *Canadian Medical Association Journal, 168,* 305–312.

16. Heggers, J. P., McCauley, R. L., & Phillips, L. G. (2007). Cold-induced injury: Frostbite. In D. N. Herndon (Ed.), *Total burn care.* Philadelphia: Saunders.

17. Bessen, H. A. (2003). Hypothermia. In J. E. Tintinalli, G. D. Kelen, & J. S. Stapczynski (Eds.), *Emergency medicine: A comprehensive study guide* (6th ed., pp. 846–849). New York: McGraw-Hill.

18. Steinman, A. M., & Hayward, J. S. (2007). Cold water immersion. In P. S. Auerbach, *Wilderness medicine: Management of wilderness and environmental emergencies* (5th ed.). St. Louis, MO: Mosby.

19. Danzi, D. F. (2007). Accidental hypothermia. In P. S. Auerbach, *Wilderness medicine: Management of wilderness and environmental emergencies* (5th ed.), St. Louis, MO: Mosby.

FORTY-ONE

Bites and Stings

Nancy J. Denke, RN, MSN, FNP-C, CCRN

Introduction

Animal and human bites account for 1% of all ED visits. While these bites pose a risk for disfigurement rabies and infection, most bites present few problems other than transient swelling and discomfort. Most bites are easily managed with over-the-counter anti-histamines and analgesics. Emergency nurses must be prepared to recognize and treat the child who presents with a toxic envenomation from a number of sources, including spiders, scorpions and snakes. Emergency nurses also must be aware of the types of bites that might occur in their area of practice. The purpose of this chapter is to discuss common bites and stings that may occur in the pediatric patient and specific nursing interventions.

Pediatric Considerations

Bites that may not present a threat to an adult will be much more severe in a child because the child receives a larger dose of venom per kilogram of body weight than does an adult. The smaller the child, the greater the threat to the child's health.

Focused History

❏ Type of bite (spider, snake, scorpion, marine animal, animal, human)

❏ Time the bite occurred

❏ Location of the bite on the child's body

❏ Activities that might have placed the child at risk for getting bitten (e.g., playing outdoors in tall grass, around woodpiles, in sheds, garages, and barns)

❏ Allergies

❏ Medical history

❏ Immunization status

❏ First aid rendered at the scene. Prehospital interventions may include the following:

- Maintenance of airway, breathing, and circulation

- Reassurance of the child and family

- Minimization of systemic venom effects without increasing the risk of local tissue damage

- Transport of the child to a medical facility

- Consultation with the poison control center

Focused Assessment

The standard pediatric assessment is done (Chapter 5). The following information must also be obtained:

❏ Location and number of bite marks, punctures, and scratches

❏ Appearance of the bite (redness, swelling, drainage, discoloration)

Specific Conditions

Snake Bites

Approximately 8000 bites from poisonous snakes occur each year in the United States, resulting in 5 to 15 deaths annually.[2] Venomous snakes can be found in almost every state. Fifty percent of the bite victims are children.[2,3] Most bites occur in adolescents and young adults while they are trying to handle or provoke the snake. Snakes are poikilothermic and are most active during warm weather and in the daylight. Most bites occur between April and October. Males are far more likely to be bitten than females. Younger children are most likely to be bitten on the lower extremities.[2–5]

The majority of venomous snakes in this country are pit vipers from the Crotalidae family, including rattlesnakes, cottonmouths, water moccasins, and copperheads. Venomous snakes can be found in almost every state and are responsible for 90% of snake bites.[3] Coral snakes, of the Elapidae family, found in the Southeast account for 2% to 3% of bites, and "exotic" snakes account for the other 3% to 5%.[3,5] Table 41.1 describes differentiation of venomous, nonvenomous, and coral snakes.

Pathophysiology

The venom is a complex mixture of enzymes, the major function of which is to immobilize, digest, and kill the snake's prey. This venom is made up of proteolytic enzymes, lipids, histamine, leukotrienes, kinins, and thrombin-like enzymes that contribute to the local tissue cytotoxicity, hematotoxicity, and neurotoxic effects seen after an envenomation.[3,6] During a strike the snake's mouth opens about 180 degrees, and the fangs rotate down at right angles to the jaw. A snake can lunge about half of its body length from a coiled position when it strikes. Approximately 20% to 25% of bites are "dry bites," which do not manifest any symptoms of envenomation, but 20% to 75% of stored venom may be discharged in a bite.[6] Extremities are the most common bite sites in children.

TABLE 41.1 Differentiation of Venomous, Nonvenomous, and Coral Snakes

Venomous Pit Viper	Nonvenomous Pit Viper	Coral Snake
Vertical elliptical pupils	Normal pupils	Round pupils
"Cat's eyes"	Double row of subcaudal scales	Black snout
Triangular-shaped head	No fangs, only multiple teeth	Short, fixed maxillary fangs
Two movable recurved fangs		Yellow rings adjacent to red rings
Indentation or pit between eye and nostril		"Red on yellow kills a fellow, red on black venom lack."

Clinical Manifestations

The severity of the bite depends on:

☐ Type of snake

- *Pit viper venom* contains a combination of toxins (primarily hemotoxins). The venom is injected by the snake's fangs and is more dangerous than that of a coral snake because a large amount can be injected. The venom can cause the following signs and symptoms:

  - Local tissue necrosis
  - Excruciating pain and swelling at bite site. (Swelling begins within 3 minutes after the bite and may continue with enough severity to burst the skin).
  - Bleeding gums
  - Severe headache, thirst
  - Nausea, vomiting, weakness, sweating
  - Formation of blood-filled vesicles
  - Hemolysis of red blood cells
  - Defects in coagulation with disseminated intra-vascular clotting (DIC)—increased prothrombin times and decreased platelet counts with active bleeding
  - Tachycardia, hypotension→hypovolemic shock→renal failure
  - Decreased level of consciousness
  - Respiratory paralysis→massive pulmonary edema
  - Renal failure secondary to rhabdomyolysis

- *Coral snake venom* contains mainly neurotoxic components that produce mild local signs even in the case of major envenomations. The coral snake has teeth and must chew the victim to inject the venom. Systemic signs are delayed (slower than the Crotalidae). However, once they begin, they are severe and progress rapidly. They include:

  - Nausea and vomiting
  - Excessive perspiration
  - Chills and often rapid onset of fever
  - Impairment of circulation—irregular heartbeat, hypotension, weakness, and

exhaustion→circulatory system collapse

- Mental status changes—severe headache, confusion, unconsciousness
- Bulbar palsy, the destruction of the nerve centers of the medulla oblongata, characterized by an inability to speak and swallow
- Ptosis, drooping of the upper eyelids resulting from paralysis of the oculomotor nerve
- Visual and hearing changes—blurred vision, difficulty hearing
- Uncoordinated and muscle twitching
- Descending muscle paralysis leading to respiratory distress and respiratory failure

☐ The age, health, and size of the child

☐ The site and number of bites

☐ The time lapse before the child receives definitive treatment

☐ The amount of venom injected

Nursing Interventions

1. Maintain airway, breathing and circulation. Immobilize the injured extremity.

2. Establish two large-bore intravenous catheters: one for crystalloid resuscitation and one for administration of antivenom, if necessary.

3. Obtain laboratory studies to include:
   - Urinalysis
   - Complete blood cell count (CBC)
   - Blood urea nitrogen (BUN), creatinine
   - Prothrombin time (PT)/partial thromboplastin time (PTT)

4. Monitor vital signs. Maintain NPO status.

5. Perform sequential circumferential measurements of the affected area every 15 to 30 minutes to assess the rate of spread and effectiveness of treatment.

6. Consider administration of vasopressors and monitoring of central venous pressure if the patient is exhibiting signs of shock.

7. Grade the envenomation of pit viper bites to determine the need for antivenom (Table 41.2). On the basis of limited data, Crotalidae Polyvalent Immune Fab (ovine) (CroFab®) has been shown to be a safe and efficacious antivenom for use in children, as well as adults.[17]

8. Administer other therapy as necessary, including:
   - Pain medications
   - Broad-spectrum antibiotics (not routinely needed)

- Tetanus toxoid or tetanus immune globulin, depending on the patient's immunization status
- Wound debridement

9. Administer antivenom. Table 41.3 lists information and precautions concerning antivenom.

10. Monitor the patient for adverse reactions.

11. Treat anaphylaxis related to antivenom, as necessary.
    - Secure airway, as necessary.
    - Administer epinephrine
      - 0.01 mL/kg, 1:1,000 subcutaneously/intramuscularly
      - 0.1 mL/kg, 1:10,000 intravenously or endotracheally
    - Administer antihistamines—the child can be premedicated to prevent or minimize allergic reactions.
      - H_2 blockers (cimetidine, ranitidine)
      - H_1 blockers (diphenhydramine)
      - β2 agonists and/or aminophylline to ease bronchospasm
      - Corticosteroids for anti-inflammatory effects and possible prevention of late-phase allergic response[3]

12. Initiate measures to prevent complications and promote healing.
    - Do not cut or incise the bite; do not apply ice or heat to the bite site; don not apply oral (mouth) suction; do not remove dressings/elastic wraps; do not try to kill the snake for identification as this may lead to other people being bitten.

Spider And Scorpion Bites

Fifty species of spiders found in the United States have fangs capable of penetrating human skin. Only two species, the black widow and the brown recluse, can cause fatalities.[1]

Pathophysiology and Nursing Interventions

The *black widow* is found in every state except Alaska. The female is responsible for all human envenomation because the male is not big enough to inflict bites. The adult female black widow spider has a shiny, jet black, spherical abdomen with a characteristic red/orange hourglass marking on the abdomen. The black widow spider is a cobweb builder whose silk is very strong and who builds its web near the ground in a dark, sheltered site. The web serves to trap the spider's food, which includes a variety of insects (cockroaches and beetles). Outdoors, its webs are usually

TABLE 41.2 Grading of Pit Viper Envenomation

Severity	Findings	Laboratory Changes
Minimal	Fang marks	Platelet count > 100,000
	Local pain/swelling/redness	Normal laboratory values
	Normal vital signs	
	No systemic toxicity	
Moderate	Fang marks	Doubling of PT/PTT
	Severe local pain	Decreased fibrinogen
	Swelling > 6–12 inches	Decrease in hematocrit
	Normal vital signs—other than tachycardia	Thrombocytopenia—platelets < 100,000
	Weakness	
	Metallic taste, perioral paresthesia	
	Nausea, vomiting	
Severe	All bites to the head and neck	Thrombocytopenia
	Fang marks	Increased clotting times—DIC
	Generalized petechiae, ecchymosis	Coagulopathy
	Respiratory distress	Metabolic acidosis
	Blood-tinged sputum, spontaneous bleeding	Anemia
	Initial presentation consistent with shock	
	Renal dysfunction	
	Altered mental status→convulsions	
	Poor peripheral perfusion	

built in woodpiles, under stones, and in hollow stumps. It can also be found in outbuildings such as toilets, sheds, and garages. Indoors, the spider prefers undisturbed, cluttered areas in basements and crawl spaces. The bite of a black widow spider initially may go unnoticed, but some people report a short stabbing pain.

The *brown recluse* is most commonly found in the central Midwestern states southward to the Gulf of Mexico.[7] Coloration can range from light tan to dark brown with a dark violin marking on the cephalothorax. It is a reclusive creature that seeks and prefers seclusion. Brown recluse spiders generally occupy dark, undisturbed sites, and they can occur indoors or outdoors. Indoors, they may be found in attics, basements, crawl spaces, cellars, and closets. They may seek shelter in storage boxes, shoes, clothing, and folded linens and behind furniture. They also may be found outdoors in such areas as barns, storage sheds, garages, underneath logs, loose stones in rock piles, and stacks of lumber.

Several species of scorpion are found in the United States. The only medically significant stings occur in the Southwest, by the bark scorpion. The scorpion may be straw-colored, yellow, or light brown and is approximately 5 cm in length.[8] Scorpions usually hide during the day and become active at night when they feed and mate. Scorpions are dry-land creatures and are not normally found in extremely damp areas. However, they do require some moisture and are often attracted to the damp areas around plumbing and the evaporators of air-conditioning units. Inside the home, scorpions are most often found in crawl spaces, attracted to kitchens, bathrooms, and other areas where water is available. Scorpions glow brightly under ultraviolet light (black light). They are basically shy creatures and will not sting humans unless they are handled or stepped on. Very few people die of scorpion stings, but the stings are most dangerous to the very young. The best prevention is to be sure that all clothes and shoes are shaken before putting on and avoid walking barefoot in the home. Table 41.4 lists signs, symptoms, and treatment of various spider and scorpion bites.

TABLE 41.3 Antivenom Information

Antivenom Information and Supply	Precautions/Nursing Implications

Determine need for antivenom (CroFab®—crotaline Fab) and give as promptly as possible.
 	
Initial dose: 4–6 vials (no change in dose for pediatrics).
 	
Reconstitute each vial with 10 mL of sterile water.
 	
Dilution of the antivenom in 250 mL of normal saline with administration over 1 hour. Start infusion at 25–50 mL/hour for the first 10 minutes, observing closely for any adverse reactions.
 	
If initial infusion is tolerated, increase rate to a maximum of 250 mL/hour.
 	
Stop infusion if any problem develops at any time and treat accordingly.
 	
Assess 1 hour after infusion for initial control (arrest of progression of venom-induced effects).
 	
Repeat doses of 4–6 vials until initial control achieved.
 	
Once initial control is achieved, maintenance dosing is recommended.
 	
Maintenance dose—two vials every 6 hours for three doses.
	Obtain antivenom.
	   Contact the local poison control center.
	   Contact the local zoo. Zoos are required to keep adequate antivenom stores for venomous snakes in the possession of the zoo.
	   Administer antivenom early; within 6 hours of snake-bite to prevent clinical deterioration and the occurrence of systemic coagulation abnormalities.
	Obtain patient history.
	   Ask about allergies -- papaya, sheep serum, latex, bromelain (pineapple extract).
	   Ask about medication history, specifically asking about Beta-blocker, which may affect response to allergy treatment.
	Stabilize airway and breathing.
	Initiate intravenous access.
	   Obtain laboratory specimens -- CBC, PT/PTT, fibrinogen, chemistry panel, creatine phosphokinase, type and screen.
	   Provide pain relief with opioid analgesia; avoid nonsteroidal anti-inflammatory drugs. Update tetanus prophylaxis.
	   Monitor for rhabdomyolysis. Aggressive fluid hydration can treat this, but can require alkalinization, diuresis, and even dialysis if renal failure develops.
	   Observe for anaphylactic reaction.
	Treat the wound.
	   Mark leading edge of redness.
	   Elevate snake-bitten extremity after antivenom is started.
	   Recheck wound after last dose dose of antivenom.
	   Recheck all patients every 2 to 3 days for 2 weeks with the following laboratory specimens: CBC, PT/PTT, and fibrinogen. If patient had rhabdomyolysis include: creatine kinase, electrolytes, BUN/creatinine and urinalysis.

Savage Laboratories. (2000). *Crofab®: Crotalidae Polyvalent Immune Fab (Ovine) packet insert.* Melville, NY: Author.

Animal Bites

Children experience bites from a variety of animals or even from other children. They are bitten more often than adults. The majority of animal bites involve dogs and cats. Dog bites cause a crushing-type wound, and cat bites cause puncture wounds due to their sharp pointed teeth that may inoculate bacteria into deep tissue.[9] Most dog bites occur in boys between the ages of 5 and 9 years old, with the head and neck being the most common site of bites in children up to age 10 years. The majority of rodent bites are caused by rats and occur at night on the face or hands of children <5 years old where living conditions are poor.[10]

Although parents are concerned about cosmetics, excessive bleeding, or rabies, the most common complication of animal bites is infection. Infection is a concern because of the variety of organisms found in the human mouth or in dog and cat bites. Dog bites are associated with a lower incidence of infection than human bites, but cat bites or scratches have a higher risk for infection.[11] Rabies is the most serious concern. Rabies is commonly carried by raccoons, foxes, skunks, undomesticated dogs and cats, and bats (Chapter 24).

TABLE 41.4 Spider and Insect Bites		
	Clinical Manifestation	*Treatment*

Black widow (neurotoxic)	Two tiny puncture marks
	
	Mild redness/swelling
	
	Initial prickling fades→radiating pain along extremity within 30 minutes
	
	Tender regional lymphadenopathy, minimal edema
	
	"Target" or "halo" fades within 12 hours
	
	Chest pain and respiratory failure with bites to upper body
	
	Abdominal pain with bites to the lower body
	
	Muscle cramping within 1 hour of bite
	
	Increased heart rate and systolic blood pressure
		Laboratory studies:
		
		  Not helpful
		
		Analgesics
		
		  Morphine intravenously—if severe
		
		  Diazepam intravenously
		
		Hypertension
		
		  May be alleviated with analgesia
		
		  If persistent, consider—
		
		    Nitroprusside
		
		Antivenom—1–2 vials diluted in 50–100 mL normal saline solution; infused over 1 hour
		
		Calcium gluconate
		
		  Questionable

Brown recluse (dermone-crotic)	Often unnoticed painless bite→localized erythema (white ring macule)
	
	Pain 1–8 hour after bite
	
	"Target" or "bull's-eye lesion": central vesicle, with ischemic and erythematous ring
	
	Subcutaneous discoloration, forming of eschar and sloughing of tissue margins→eschar falls off leaving an open ulcer
	
	Regional lymphadenopathy
	
	Fever, chills, malaise
	
	Nausea/vomiting, renal failure
	
	Thrombocytopenia, DIC
	
	Recluse spelled backwards—"ulcer"
		Obtain laboratory studies:
		
		  CBC
		
		  PT/PTT
		
		  BUN, creatinine
		
		  Urinalysis
		
		Apply ice
		
		Topical corticosteroids
		
		Antipruritic agents
		
		  Hydralazine
		
		  Diphenhydramine
		
		Antibiotics for secondary infections
		
		Supportive care
		
		  Surgery—débridement
		
		  Hematologist—coagulopathy

TABLE 41.4 Spider and Insect Bites (continued)

	Clinical Manifestation	Treatment

Scorpion	Extreme localized burning pain
	
	Numbness at the sting, numbness around mouth or face
	
	No local swelling or erythema
	
	Regional lymphadenopathy
	
	Agitation, restlessness, hyperactivity
	
	Slurred speech
	
	Nystagmus, diplopia, roving eyes
	
	Involuntary muscle jerking, fasciculation, twitching, seizures
	
	Increase in heart rate and blood pressure
	
	Salivation and diaphoresis
	
	Children under the age of 10 years are more likely to experience more severe symptoms.
		Laboratory studies:
		  Not helpful
		Ice and immobilization of area
		Local anesthetics
		Analgesia
		  Avoid narcotics, which worsen arrhythmias.
		Supportive care
		  Barbiturates for central nervous system symptoms
		  Propranolol—tachyarrhythmias
		  Hydralazine/nifedipine for increased blood pressure
		  Calcium gluconate 10% for muscle spasms
		Antivenom (Bioclon®) only available in Arizona—to be used in the intensive care unit

Church, J. A. (2008). With antropod envenomations: Immunological and toxic considerations. *Clinical Pediatric Emergency Medicine, 9*(2), 117–122.
Rangan, C. (2007). Emergency department evaluation and treatment for children with arthropod envenomations: Immunologic and toxicologic considerations. *Clinical Pediatric Emergency Medicine, 8*(2), 104–109.

Pathophysiology

Skin and soft tissue injuries are the first concern in evaluating animal or human bites. The two major types of bite wounds are:[1]

❐ Puncture—this small break in the skin carries a significant risk of infection.

❐ Lacerations—controversies exist concerning suturing lacerations, but generally those on the face are sutured because the risk of infection is lower on the face, as a result of the excellent blood supply to the face.

Nursing Interventions

1. Aggressively cleanse the wound.

2. Irrigate under pressure with a commercially purchased device or a 35-mL syringe with an 18-gauge angio-catheter.

3. Anticipate the need for a radiograph to identify underlying fractures.

4. Assist with suturing if indicated (because of the risk of infection, some bite wounds may not be sutured immediately).

   ▪ Immediate suturing is not recommended for wounds at high risk of becoming infected, including crush injuries, puncture wounds, cat or human bites, or bites to the hand).

5. Administer tetanus toxoid.

6. Administer antibiotics, if appropriate. (Cat bites are usually treated with amoxicillin/clavulanate potassium [Augmentin®] because of the high risk of infection).

7. Prepare to administer rabies vaccine.

8. Report bites to animal control department, per protocol.

9. Give follow-up information to family regarding signs and symptoms of infection, the need to return to the emergency department, and wound care.

Marine Animal Bites and Stings

Marine animal (aquatic organism) bites and stings occur in areas of the country near the ocean. These organisms usually do not prey on people but cause injuries when they are disturbed. These bites can result in a secondary infection from contaminated fresh and salt water. The three groups of aquatic organisms include:[12]

❐ Creatures that bite and may transmit neurotoxic venom (sharks, barracudas, octopi, sea snakes).

❐ Creatures that sting by means of nematocysts or stinging capsules and produce an acid wound, such as jellyfish, hydrozoans, sea anemones, and corals.

❐ Creatures that have spines, producing traumatic

puncture wounds, and release toxins from venom sacs, producing cardiovascular, respiratory, or neurologic complications (stingrays, scorpion fish, and sea urchins).

Venomous Fish

There are 250 species of venomous fish, with stingrays being the most common species.[13] They are flat round-bodied fish that burrow underneath the sand in shallow water. When startled, the fish will thrust its spiny tail up and forward, driving its venomous spine into the foot or lower extremity of the intruder. These spines are serrated or barbed and are difficult to remove. The venom is instantly active, causing tissue necrosis and cardiovascular disturbances.

Intense pain (out of proportion to the injury) peaks at 1 hour and lasts 48 hours. Treatment consists of irrigation with saline solution to dilute the venom and to dislodge the barbed sheath. The injured part is then immersed in warm water (not > 113 °F or 45 °C) for 30 to 60 minutes to inactivate the heat-labile components of the venom. Analgesia and débridement of the wound are required. Treatment with a broad-spectrum antibiotic (trimethoprim-sulfamethoxazole, ciprofloxacin) or a third-generation cephalosporin is indicated because of the concern for infection by the Vibrio species.[13]

Pathophysiology and Nursing Interventions

Emergency department staff must be familiar with the types of marine bites and stings that occur in their area of practice and the proper treatment. (Tables 41.5 and 41.6 list signs, symptoms, and treatment of invertebrate and vertebrate stings and bites.)

Home Care and Prevention

❏ Avoid areas inhabited by snakes. **Leave snakes alone!** (This is the best and number one method to prevent snakebites.)

❏ Do not attempt to tease, play with, or capture snakes.

❏ Wear high-top boots and long pants when working, playing, or hiking in areas inhabited by snakes, spiders, or other insects.

  ▪ Wear gloves and a long-sleeved shirt when handling stored cardboard boxes, firewood, lumber, and rocks.

  ▪ Be sure to inspect these clothing items for spiders before putting them on. Shake out clothing and shoes before getting dressed.

❏ Become familiar with the insects and spiders in the area.

TABLE 41.5 Clinical Features and Treatment of Some Common Invertebrate Stings and Bites

Animal	Injury	Treatment
Portuguese man-of-war (Cnidaria)	Contain thousand of stinging cells (nematocysts) Muscle cramps Vomiting Cardiovascular collapse Electric shock-like sensation Multiple linear welts Headache	Use gloves or forceps to remove tentacles to prevent poisoning to emergency staff. Apply baking soda and seawater paste to tentacles, and then scrape off. Apply topical 5% acetic acid (vinegar). Irrigate with seawater not fresh water. Fresh water activates nematocysts. Shave affected area. Observe patient for at least 8 hours if having systemic symptoms. Severe symptoms may require hospitalization and supportive care.
Fire coral (Cnidaria)	Contain thousand of stinging cells (nematocysts) Redness/urticaria Hemorrhage Zosteriform rash Abdominal pain	Apply topical 5% acetic acid (vinegar). Use gloves or forceps to prevent poisoning to caregiver. Irrigate with seawater not fresh water. Fresh water activates nematocysts. Shave affected area.

TABLE 41.5 Clinical Features and Treatment of Some Common Invertebrate Stings and Bites (continued)

Animal	Injury	Treatment
Jellyfish (Cnidaria)	Contain thousand of stinging cells (nematocysts) Mildly toxic Painful welts with characteristic pattern Muscle spasms	Rinse with sea water not fresh water. Fresh water activates nematocysts. Use gloves or forceps to prevent poisoning to caregiver.
Elkhorn coral	Intense stinging Weeping ulcers Sloughing, if untreated	Same as above. Débride wound. Administer antibiotics.
Sea urchin (Echinoderm)	Echinoderms are nonvenomous, but the spines are coated with toxin Long sharp spines made of calcium carbonate easily penetrate skin and wet suits Penetration causes intense pain, redness, swelling, and aching Complications include tattooing of the skin, secondary infection, and granuloma formation	Remove any spines. Soak the wound in warm water. Use antibiotics if secondary infection occurs.
Sea cucumber	Same as above Nonvenomous Skin contact may cause an inflammatory response—contact dermatitis. Corneal injury	Apply topical corticosteroid cream. Apply topical 5% acetic acid (vinegar) to detoxify. Conduct an eye examination.
Coneshell	Local reaction Pain Paresthesia Respiratory paralysis→death	Use hot water (105 °F or 40.5 °C). Apply pressure bandage. Apply a loose tourniquet. Apply direct pressure. Administer naloxone. Administer neostigmine (use with caution).
Octopus	Painless bites—similar to bee sting Suction wound If envenomation occurs, symptoms will occur within 10 minutes Blurred vision Ataxia Muscle paralysis Occasionally neurotoxic symptoms Respiratory failure→cardiac arrest, death	Irrigate the wound. Apply direct compression with gauze and bandage.

Erickson, T. B., & Auerbach, P. (2004). Marine envenomations and seafood poisonings. In T. B. Erickson, W. R. Aherns, S. E. Aks, C. R. Baum, & L. J. Ling, *Pediatric toxicology: Diagnosis and management of the poisoned child* (pp. 524–533). New York: McGraw-Hill.

Erickson, T. B., Herman, B. E., & Bowman, M. (2002). Marine envenomations. In G. R. Strange, W. R. Ahrens, & S. Lelyveld, *Pediatric emergency medicine: A comprehensive study guide* (2nd ed., pp. 686–689). New York: McGraw-Hill.

TABLE 41.6 Clinical Features and Treatment of Some Common Vertebrate Stings and Bites

Animal	Injury	Treatment

Stingray (Chondrichthyes)	Barbed tail—causing puncture wound or laceration that bleeds profusely
	
	Intense pain—beginning within 30 minutes of injury with greatest intensity at 90 minutes
	
	Pain and edema at site of injury
	
	Nausea, vomiting, syncope, weakness, and anxiety
	
	Hypotension
	
	Muscle spasm, seizures
	
	Arrhythmias→death
		Prevent complications of venom.
		
		Alleviate pain.
		
		Administer antihistamines.
		    Hydroxyzine 2 mg/kg/day divided three times a day
		    Diphenhydramine 5 mg/kg/day divided four times a day
		
		Prevent secondary infection—wound care.
		
		Treat shock with intravenous fluids.
		
		Place extremity in hot water (104–113 °F or 40–45 °C) for 30–90 minutes.

Catfish	Spine inflicts a puncture wound/laceration Soft tissue swelling due to embedded spines Localized pain Occasional systemic signs	Irrigate with sterile saline solution. Place extremity in hot water (104–113 °F or 40–45 °C) for 30–60 minutes. Provide analgesia.
Weeverfish	Found in the Mediterranean, eastern Atlantic Ocean, and European coast Lacerations or puncture wounds Pain swelling, ischemia	Same as stingray. Administer intravenous calcium gluconate if pain persists.
Scorpionfish	Intense pain Rash—vesicles Severe gastrointestinal symptoms Respiratory distress→cardiac dysrhythmias	Same as for stingray. Antivenom is used only with severe envenomation.

Erickson, T. B., & Auerbach, P. (2004). Marine envenomations and seafood poisonings. In T. B. Erickson, W. R. Aherns, S. E. Aks, C. R. Baum, & L. J. Ling, *Pediatric toxicology: Diagnosis and management of the poisoned child* (pp. 524–533). New York: McGraw-Hill.

Erickson, T. B., Herman, B. E., & Bowman, M. (2002). Marine envenomations. In G. R. Strange, W. R. Ahrens, & S. Lelyveld, *Pediatric emergency medicine: A comprehensive study guide* (2nd ed., pp. 686–689). New York: McGraw-Hill.

❏ When possible, keep children away from areas where there is an increased risk of encountering insects and spiders.

❏ Shake out clothing, sleeping bags, and shoes when camping.

❏ Do not allow children to play barefoot in the grass.

❏ Avoid wearing brightly colored or flowered clothing, which is more likely to attract stinging insects.

❏ Teach children about pets and how to approach them.

❏ Teach children to avoid unfamiliar animals or pets and what to do if approached by one.

❏ Be aware of types of marine animals capable of inflicting a toxic envenomation.

❏ Avoid contact with marine animals that can be harmful.

Conclusion

A variety of bites and stings may result in ED visits. Nurses should be familiar with the types of bites that are common in their area of practice and how to obtain the necessary antivenom. Bites and stings can be more serious in pediatric patients because of their small size. Prevention is the key to avoiding bites and stings.

References

1. Cirociari, A. J., & Touger, M. (2003). Wound care and minor trauma. In E. F. Crain & J. C. Gershel, *Clinical manual of emergency pediatrics* (4th ed., pp. 669–677). New York: McGraw-Hill.

2. Bowman, M. (2003). From stingers to fangs: Evaluating and managing bites and envenomations. *Trauma Reports, 4*(3), 1–12.

3. Erickson, T. B., Herman, B. E., & Bowman, M. (2002). Snake envenomation. In G. R. Strange, W. R. Ahrens, & S. Lelyveld, *Pediatric emergency medicine: A comprehensive study guide* (2nd ed., pp. 676–680). New York: McGraw-Hill.

4. Calello, D. P., Osterhoudt, K. C., & Bond, G. R. (2008). Envenomation management and tick removal. In C. King, F. M. Henretig, B. R. King, J. Loiselle, & R. M. Ruddy (Eds.), *Textbook of pediatric procedures* (2nd ed., pp. 1185–1198). Philadelphia: Lippincott Williams & Wilkins.

5. Schmidt, J. (2005). Antivenom therapy for snakebites in children: Is there evidence? *Current Opinion in Pediatrics, 17*(2), 234–238.

6. Richardson, W. H., Offerman, S. R., & Clark, R. F. (2004). Snake envenomation. In T. B. Erickson, W. R. Aherns, S. E. Aks, C. R. Baum, & L. J. Ling, *Pediatric toxicology: Diagnosis and management of the poisoned child* (pp. 548–556). New York: McGraw-Hill.

7. Otten, E. J. (2006). Venomous animal injuries. In J. A. Marx, R. S. Hockberger, R. M. Walls, & J. G. Adams (Eds.), *Rosen's emergency medicine: Concepts and clinical practice* (6th ed., pp. 924–940). St. Louis, MO: Mosby.

8. Tong, T. C., Schneir, A. B., & Clark, R. F. (2004). Anthropoid bites and stings. In T. B. Erickson, W. R. Aherns, S. E. Aks, C. R. Baum, & L. J. Ling, *Pediatric toxicology: Diagnosis and management of the poisoned child* (pp. 556–567). New York: McGraw-Hill.

9. Stump, J. L. (2006). *Bites, animal.* February 2, 2006. Retrieved April 17, 2009, from http://www.emedicine.com/emerg/topic60.htm

10. Townes, D. A. (2002). Human and animal bites. In G. R. Strange, W. R. Ahrens, & S. Lelyveld, *Pediatric emergency medicine: A comprehensive study guide* (2nd ed., pp. 673–676). New York: McGraw-Hill.

11. Hodge, D., & Tecklenburg, F. W. (2005). Bites and stings. In G. R. Fleisher, S. Ludwig, F. M. Henretig, R. M. Ruddy, & B. K. Silverman (Eds.), *Textbook of pediatric emergency medicine* (5th ed., pp. 1045–1067). Philadelphia: Lippincott Williams & Wilkins.

12. Semonin-Holleran, R. (2000). Environmental emergencies. In R. Semonin-Holleran, *Emergency nursing core curriculum* (5th ed., pp. 171–205). Philadelphia: Saunders.

13. Erickson, T. B., & Auerbach, P. (2004). Marine envenomations and seafood poisonings. In T. B. Erickson, W. R. Aherns, S. E. Aks, C. R. Baum, & L. J. Ling, *Pediatric toxicology: Diagnosis and management of the poisoned child* (pp. 524–533). New York: McGraw-Hill.

14. Rangan, C. (2007). Emergency department evaluation and treatment for children with arthropod envenomations: Immunologic and toxicologic considerations. *Clinical Pediatric Emergency Medicine, 8*(2), 104–109.

15. Erickson, T. B., Herman, B. E., & Bowman, M. (2002). Marine envenomations. In G. R. Strange, W. R. Ahrens, & S. Lelyveld, *Pediatric emergency medicine: A comprehensive study guide* (2nd ed., pp. 686–689). New York: McGraw-Hill.

16. Behm, M. O., & Kearns, G.L. (2003). Crotaline Fab antivenom for treatment of children with rattlesnake envenomation. *Pediatrics, 112*(6), 1458–1459.

17. Erickson, T. B., Herman, B. E., & Bowman, M. (2002). Spider and Arthropod bites. In G. R. Strange, W. R. Ahrens, & S. Lelyveld, *Pediatric emergency medicine: A comprehensive study guide* (2nd ed., pp. 680–686). New York: McGraw-Hill.

18. Ludwig, S. (2004). Bites and stings. In G. R. Fleisher, S. Ludwig, & M. Baskin (Eds.), *Atlas of pediatric emergency medicine* (pp. 44–59). Philadelphia: Lippincott Williams & Wilkins.

19. Osnaya-Romero, N., Hernández, T. J. M., Basurto, G., Andrade, S., Figueroa, J. M., Carvajal, Y., et al. (2008). Serum electrolyte changes in pediatric patients stung by scorpions. *Journal of Venomous Animals and Toxins including Tropical Diseases, 14*(2), 372–377.

20. Ozgonenel, B. (2001). Envenomations: Spiders and scorpions. In M. W. Lieh-Lai, K. A. Ling-McGeorge, M. C. Asi-Bautista, & C. Reid (Eds.), *Pediatric acute care* (2nd ed., pp. 150–152). Philadelphia: Lippincott Williams & Wilkins.

21. Ozgonenel, B. (2001). Envenomations: Snake bites. In M. W. Lieh-Lai, K. A. Ling-McGeorge, M. C. Asi-Bautista, & C. Reid (Eds). *Pediatric acute care* (2nd ed., pp. 152–154). Philadelphia: Lippincott Williams & Wilkins.

References (continued)

22. Ruha, A. M., Curry, S. C., Beuhler, M., Katz, K., Brooks, D. E., Graeme, K. A., et al. (2002). Initial postmarketing experience with crotalidae polyvalent immune Fab for treatment of rattlesnake envenomation. *Annals of Emergency Medicine, 39,* 609–615.

FORTY-TWO

Toxicologic Emergencies

**Rose Ann Gould Soloway,
RN, BSN, MSEd, DABAT**

Introduction

Perhaps more than any other common pediatric emergency, poisoning elicits multisystem responses in its victims. Proper assessment and treatment of a poisoned child require knowledge of normal growth and development plus astute history-taking and physical assessment skills. The purpose of this chapter is to discuss common and potentially dangerous poison exposures for which accurate and effective emergency department (ED) assessment and treatment can have a significant impact on patient outcome.

There are hundreds of thousands of drugs and chemicals in use, any of which may be involved in a poisoning or poison exposure. A poison exposure is an inappropriate contact with or use of a chemical, drug, or natural toxin, by any route of exposure. Poisoning means that symptoms actually resulted from a drug, toxin, or chemical poison exposure. Most poison exposures are managed at home with the assistance of a poison center, but seriously poisoned children are referred or transported to the emergency department for treatment.

Epidemiology

In 2007, the American Association of Poison Control Centers' National Poison Data System reported 2,482,041 human poison exposures.[1] The majority of exposures in young children are unintentional. Intentional exposures (e.g., suicide and abuse of drugs and chemicals) predominate after the age of 13 years. Therefore, as the age of poisoning victims increases, the number of fatalities increases (Table 42.1).

Pediatric poison exposures reflect the availability of potentially poisonous substances (Table 42.2). More than 90% of all exposures occur in a residence,[1] but the substances most commonly involved are not necessarily the most dangerous. The leading causes of fatalities from poison exposures among all ages are listed in Table 42.3.

In 2007, the U.S. Centers for Disease Control and Prevention reported that, over the 5-year period from 1999 to 2004, the poisoning death rate rose 113.3% in persons aged 15 to 24 years, largely as a result of drug overdoses.[2]

After a poisoning or poison exposure, the patient may be asymptomatic or symptomatic. In the *asymptomatic patient,* no obvious life-threatening effects are observed. The poison center is contacted to determine whether any treatment is required. (The poison center may have been contacted by the family or a prehospital care provider before an asymptomatic patient arrives in the emergency department, to determine whether evaluation is necessary). In the *symptomatic patient,* the obvious effects are observed. The patient's condition is stabilized in the emergency department, and the poison center is contacted to determine whether a specific antidote, treatment, or clinical or laboratory assessment is required.

Pediatric Considerations

Pediatric considerations in poison exposures relate to children's physiologic immaturity and developmental maturation. Infants' small size, immature organ systems, and high metabolic needs place them at great risk of dangerous medical consequences from many poison exposures. Toddlers' immature taste buds allow them to swallow items that seem noxious to adults. Their small size and immature organ systems place them at greater risk than adults of dangerous medical consequences of poison exposures.

Normal curiosity and imitation lead to unintentional poisonings in children of almost any age. Toddlers learn by

TABLE 42.1 Number of Pediatric Poison Exposures and Fatalities, 2007

Age (years)	Number of Exposures	Percent of All Exposures	Number of Fatalities	Percentage of All Fatalities in Database (All Ages)
Under 6	1,271,595	51.23	35	2.8
6–12	155,913	6.28	47	3.8
13–19	170,780	6.88	102	8.2

Bronstein, A. C., Spyker, D. A., Cantilena, L. C., Green, J. L., Rumack, B. H., Heard, S. E., et al. (2008). 2007 Annual report of the American Association of Poison Control Centers' National Poison Data System. *Clinical Toxicology, 46,* 927–1057.

TABLE 42.2 Most Common Pediatric Poison Exposures, 2007

Less than 6 Years of Age	6–19 Years of Age
Cosmetics and personal care products	Household cleaning products
Household cleaning substances	Analgesics
Analgesics	Foreign bodies
Foreign bodies/toys/miscellaneous	Cosmetics and personal care products
Topical preparations	Cough and cold preparations
Cough and cold preparations	Bites and envenomations
Vitamins	Food products and food poisoning
Pesticides	Sedatives/hypnotics/antipsychotics
Plants	Stimulants and street drugs
Antihistamines	Antihistamines

Bronstein, A. C., Spyker, D. A., Cantilena, L. C., Green, J. L., Rumack, B. H., Heard, S. E., et al. (2008). 2007 Annual report of the American Association of Poison Control Centers' National Poison Data System. *Clinical Toxicology, 46,* 927–1057.

imitating adults and climb to reach and ingest a medicine or product used by adults. They are unable to associate cause and effect, making them susceptible to repeated poison exposures. Older children desire self-sufficiency, which may lead to inappropriate medication use. Although school-aged children can read labels, they may not understand them completely. They also may have an imperfect grasp of cause and effect, leading to possible problems with the use of household products and school chemicals. Preadolescents and adolescents experiment with drugs, alcohol, and inhalants. Adolescents may be exposed to poisons in the workplace.

TABLE 42.3 Most Common Causes of Poison-Related Fatalities, All Ages, 2007

Sedatives/hypnotics/antipsychotics
Opioids
Antidepressants
Acetaminophen in combination with other medications
Cardiovascular drugs
Stimulants and street drugs
Alcohols
Acetaminophen only
Anticonvulsants
Fumes/gases/vapors

Bronstein, A. C., Spyker, D. A., Cantilena, L. C., Green, J. L., Rumack, B. H., Heard, S. E., et al. (2008). 2007 Annual report of the American Association of Poison Control Centers' National Poison Data System. *Clinical Toxicology, 46,* 927–1057.

Etiology

Pediatric poison exposures occur unintentionally or intentionally.

❑ Unintentional poison exposures

▪ A change in family routine may precipitate poison exposures, either because routinely locked medications and chemicals are left within reach or because less attention is paid to children and their activities. Environmental factors (e.g., a carbon monoxide leak or chemical spill) may affect all family members.

▪ Infants may be poisoned as a result of therapeutic errors.[1] The wrong drug may be dispensed or administered. Parents may administer a drug intended for older children, mistakenly thinking that a smaller dose will be safe for younger children. They may misread the label or administer extra doses because of confusion about who is administering the medicine. Infants and toddlers may be poisoned by older siblings who want to "help" while parents are not looking, and toddlers may pick up containers left within their reach by family members.

❒ Intentional poison exposures

■ Parents or caregivers may intentionally administer a poison or medication that results in a poison exposure either to harm the child or to create symptoms in the child so that emergency care can be rendered (e.g., factitious disorder by proxy; Chapter 44).

■ Preadolescents and adolescents may deliberately incur a poisoning (e.g., alcohol, illicit drugs, or medications) as a suicide gesture or suicide attempt (Chapter 25).

Focused History

Historical information about both asymptomatic and symptomatic patients after a poison exposure or poisoning is obtained as applicable from the patient, the parents or caregivers, and witnesses.

Family History

❒ Recent visitors at the home

❒ A change in the home environment, including home improvement projects or restoration

❒ Medicines used by family members (prescription, nonprescription, foreign, herbal, botanical, homeopathic, veterinary, and dietary supplements)

❒ Witnesses to the event

❒ Involvement or exposure of other children or adults

❒ History of psychiatric illness in the patient, family members, or others with whom the child spends time

Patient History

❒ Concurrent intentional or unintentional trauma, which may be precipitated by exposure to drugs or chemicals

❒ Time recently spent outside of the home, and the length of time

❒ Agent to which the child was exposed

❒ Time of the exposure

❒ Route of the exposure (Table 42.4)

❒ Symptoms after the exposure, their time of onset, and the sequence of their appearance

❒ First aid measures employed, by whom, and when. The effects of inappropriate first aid treatment may need to be considered before the initiation of appropriate treatment.

TABLE 42.4 Route-specific History Findings

Route	Historical Data
Ingestions	Availability of the medication or product container. Sometimes the actual contents of the product are different from what the parent thinks.
	The number of pills or amount of fluid in the container before and after the exposure.
Inhalations	Availability of the chemical container or product.
	Exposure to a fire while in an enclosed space (risk of carbon monoxide and cyanide poisoning).
Cutaneous or ocular exposures	Availability of the product container. Sometimes the actual contents of the product are different from what the parent thinks (e.g., a lawn care product that seems like fertilizer may also contain an insecticide).
	The amount of the substance in the container before and after the exposure.

Focused Assessment

Physical Assessment

Children with suspected poison exposure require a physical assessment (Tables 42.5 and 42.6).

❒ Assess the respiratory system.

■ Auscultate the chest for:

• Respiratory rate. Tachypnea or bradypnea may be present, depending on the poison exposure.

• Adventitious sounds. Wheezing may be heard with aspirated substances.

❒ Assess the cardiovascular system.

■ Auscultate the heart for:

• Rate. Tachycardia or bradycardia may be present, depending on the poison exposure.

• Rhythm. Irregular heart rhythms may occur with selected poison exposures.

• Measure the blood pressure.

• Assess peripheral perfusion.

■ Palpate peripheral pulses for quality and equality.

■ Measure core and skin temperature.

TABLE 42.5 Symptom Status, Poison Exposure, Assessment, and Interventions

Symptom Status	Poison Exposure	Assessment and Interventions
Symptomatic	No history of poison exposure	<ul><li>Maintain a high index of suspicion that a poisoning may have occurred.</li><li>Consider poisoning in children with:<ul><li>Multiple symptoms</li><li>Abnormal assessment findings (e.g., abnormal ECG)</li><li>Abnormal laboratory findings with no obvious cause</li></ul></li><li>Immediately consult the poison center.</li></ul>
Symptomatic	History of poison exposure	<ul><li>Initiate further evaluation and treatment.</li><li>Clinical and laboratory findings vary among the toxic agents (Table 42.6).</li><li>Consult the poison center.</li></ul>
Asymptomatic	History of poison exposure	<ul><li>Consult the poison center to determine whether any assessment or medical intervention is necessary.</li><li>Initiate psychosocial assessment if indicated.</li></ul>

TABLE 42.6 Clinical and/or Laboratory Findings in Poisoning

Agitation	Anticholinergics,[a] phencyclidine, sympathomimetics,[b] withdrawal from ethanol and sedative-hypnotics
Alopecia	Alkylating agents, radiation, selenium, thallium
Ataxia	Benzodiazepines, carbamazepine, carbon monoxide, ethanol, hypoglycemia, lithium, mercury, nitrous oxide, phenytoin
Blindness or decreased visual acuity	Caustics (direct), cocaine, cisplatin, mercury, methanol, quinine, thallium
Blue skin	Amiodarone, FD&C #1 dye, methemoglobin, silver
Constipation	Anticholinergics,[a] botulism, lead, opioids, thallium (severe)
Tinnitus, deafness	Aminoglycosides, cisplatin, metals, loop diuretics, quinine, salicylates
Diaphoresis	Amphetamines, cholinergics,[c] hypoglycemia, opioid withdrawal, salicylates, serotonin syndrome, sympathomimetics,[b] withdrawal from ethanol and sedative-hypnotics
Diarrhea	Arsenic and other metals, boric acid (blue-green), botanical irritants, cathartics, cholinergics,[c] colchicines, iron, lithium, opioid withdrawal, radiation
Dysesthesias, paresthesias	Acrylamide, arsenic, ciguatera, cocaine, colchicines, thallium
Gum discoloration	Arsenic, bismuth, hypervitaminosis A, lead, mercury
Hallucinations	Anticholinergics,[a] dopamine agonists, ergot alkaloids, ethanol, ethanol and sedative-hypnotic withdrawal, LSD, phencyclidine, sympathomimetics,[b] tryptamines (e.g., AMT)
Headache	Carbon monoxide, hypoglycemia, monoamine oxidase inhibitor/food interaction (hypertensive crisis), serotonin syndrome
Metabolic acidosis (elevated anion gap) (MUDPILES)	Methanol, uremia, ketoacidosis (diabetic, starvation, alcoholic), paraldehyde, phenformin, metformin, iron, INH, lactic acidosis, cyanide, protease inhibitors, ethylene glycol, salicylates, toluene
Miosis	Cholinergics,[c] clonidine, opioids, phencyclidine, phenothiazines

TABLE 42.6 Clinical and/or Laboratory Findings in Poisoning (continued)	
Mydriasis	Anticholinergics,[a] botulism, opioid withdrawal, sympathomimetics[b]
Nystagmus	Barbiturates, carbamazepine, carbon monoxide, ethanol, lithium, monoamine oxidase inhibitors, phencyclidine, phenytoin, quinine
Purpura	Anticoagulant rodenticides, clopidogrel, corticosteroids, heparin, pit viper venom, quinine, salicylates, warfarin
Radiopaque ingestions	Arsenic, chloral hydrate, enteric-coated tablets, halogenated hydrocarbons, metals (e.g., iron, lead)
Red skin	Anticholinergics,[a] boric acid, disulfiram, scombroid, vancomycin
Rhabdomyolysis	Carbon monoxide, doxylamine, HMG CoA reductase inhibitors, sympathomimetics,[b] *Tricholoma equestre*
Salivation	Arsenic, caustics, cholinergics,[c] ketamine, mercury, phencyclidine, strychnine
Seizures	Bupropion, carbon monoxide, cyclic antidepressants, *Gyromitra* mushrooms, hypoglycemia, INH, methylxanthines, withdrawal from ethanol and sedative-hypnotics
Tremor	Antipsychotics, arsenic, carbon monoxide, cholinergics,[c] ethanol, lithium, mercury, methyl bromide, sympathomimetics,[b] thyroid replacement
Weakness	Botulism, diuretics, magnesium, paralytic shellfish, steroids, toluene
Yellow skin	Acetaminophen (late), pyrrolizidine alkaloids, ß-carotene, amatoxin mushrooms, dinitrophenol

AMT = amitriptyline; FD&C = Food, Drug, & Cosmetic Act; HMG CoA = 3-hydroxy-3-methylglutaryl coenzyme A; LSD = lysergic acid diethylamide.

[a]*Anticholinergics: e.g., antihistamines, atropine, cyclic antidepressants, scopolamine.*

[b]*Sympathomimetics: e.g., amphetamines, ß-adrenergic agents, cocaine, ephedrine.*

[c]*Cholinergics: e.g., muscarinic mushrooms, organic phosphorous compounds and carbamates including select Alzheimer drugs and physostigmine, pilocarpine, and other direct-acting drugs.*

Flomenbaum, N. E.,, Goldfrank, L. R., Hoffman, R. S., Howland, M. A., Lewin, N. A., & Nelson, L. S. (Eds.). (2006). *Goldfrank's toxicologic emergencies* (8th ed., pp. 39). New York: Appleton & Lange. Used with permission.

- Inspect the skin for:
  - Color
  - Temperature
  - Moisture
- Measure capillary refill.
❏ Assess the neurologic system.
  - Measure the level of consciousness with the AVPU (*A*lert, responds to *V*erbal stimuli, responds to *P*ainful stimuli, *U*nresponsive) method or the Glasgow Coma Scale method.
  - Observe the child's:
    - Gait
    - Motor function
    - Sensory function
    - Reflexes
❏ Assess the gastrointestinal and genitourinary systems.
  - Assess the abdomen for:
    - Distention
    - Bowel sounds
  - Note the presence of vomiting
  - Measure urinary output
❏ Assess the integumentary system.
  - Assess for topical contamination (Chapter 43).
  - Assess for burns, wounds, or other signs of trauma or neglect (Chapter 44).
❏ Assess the child's overall appearance.
  - Note the child's hygiene and level of nourishment.
  - Weigh the child; compare with established norms.

Psychosocial Assessment

❏ Assess the quality of the child's and family's interaction patterns.
❏ Intentional poisoning or unintentional poisoning from neglect in the young child may have occurred (Chapter 44).
❏ Intentional poisoning as a plea for attention may have occurred in the older child (Chapter 25).
❏ Assess the child's and family's coping strategies.

❏ Assess the parents' response to the poison exposure (e.g., extreme guilt versus nonchalance).

❏ Assess parental familiarity with age-specific growth, development, and behavior. Assess whether the poison exposure is typical of the child's age and developmental level.

Triage Considerations

See Immediately

❏ All potential poisonings are triaged as see immediately, including:

- Known or suspected poison exposure with:
  - Inability to maintain a spontaneous patent airway
  - Respiratory distress or insufficiency
  - Cardiovascular compromise
  - Altered level of consciousness

Nursing Interventions

1. Assess and maintain airway, breathing, and circulation (Chapter 28).

   - Initiate maneuvers to maintain airway patency, such as positioning, suctioning, and insertion of an oral airway.

   - Prepare for endotracheal intubation in the child who cannot maintain spontaneous airway patency.

   - Administer 100% oxygen through a nonrebreather mask; initiate assisted ventilations in the child who is not maintaining adequate respiratory effort.

   - Initiate cardiorespiratory, blood pressure, and oxygen saturation monitoring.
     - Observe and analyze cardiac rhythm.
     - Obtain a 12-lead electrocardiogram (ECG), if indicated.

2. Obtain venous access and initiate an intravenous infusion, as needed.

   - Obtain blood and/or urine for toxicology screening.

     - Toxicology screening is initiated to identify the presence or absence of some suspected drugs or chemicals. The terms *drug screen, negative drug screen,* and *comprehensive toxicology screen* are meaningless unless it is known exactly which substances are being screened for. The drugs included in a drug screen vary among institutions.

     - Ask the laboratory what bodily fluid is preferred; depending on the drug and the test to be used,

blood or urine may be required. In some circumstances (e.g., for unknown drugs or mushroom spores), gastric fluid can be tested.

- Provide the laboratory with as much information as possible about the patient's history and condition to help the laboratory narrow down the testing procedures.

- Become familiar with the laboratory's procedures and definitions. For example, serum levels of therapeutic drugs may be performed only on specified days, and stat may be defined in hours, not minutes.

3. Initiate decontamination procedures, if indicated (Tables 42.7 and 42.8).

4. Prepare to administer antidotes, as prescribed.

   - Antidotes are available for relatively few substances, although they can be lifesaving in some poisonings (Table 42.9).

5. Prepare the patient for specific diagnostic tests.

   - Radiographs

     - Radiographs may be useful in some conditions, such as button battery ingestions.

       · If a button battery has been swallowed, it is a medical emergency if the battery is retained in the esophagus. The patient is in no immediate danger if the battery has passed at least to the stomach.[3]

   - Radiopaque drugs and chemicals (Table 42.6) can be visualized on abdominal films, indicating their placement and amount.

   - Some swallowed packets of illegal drugs may also be visualized with radiographs.

6. Prepare for possible enhanced elimination modalities.

   - Forced diuresis

     - It is occasionally indicated for substances that are eliminated renally (e.g., lithium).

     - It is used less often in children than adults because of the risk of fluid and electrolyte disturbances.

   - Ion-trapping

     - This occurs by administration of sodium bicarbonate, which alkalinizes the urine, promoting elimination of salicylates and phenobarbital.

   - Extracorporeal elimination (hemodialysis or hemoperfusion)

     - This is indicated for serious poisoning by ethylene glycol, methanol, salicylates, lithium, and theophylline, among others.

- Dangerously poisoned children who are too young for hemodialysis or hemoperfusion may be candidates for exchange transfusion.

7. Initiate consultations, as needed.
    - Poison center
        - Early consultation with the poison center is the best way of assuring that a child's condition does not worsen unnecessarily and assuring that appropriate treatment options are considered as the child's condition changes. To be connected automatically to the closest poison center call 1-800-222-1222.

- Social services
- Child protective services, if child neglect is suspected (Chapter 44)
- Pediatric medical subspecialists
- Hazardous materials personnel (Chapter 43)

8. Inform the family frequently of their child's condition; provide psychosocial and emotional support to the child and family (Chapter 3).
9. Reassess the child's cardiorespiratory and neurologic status.
10. Prepare for transfer and transport to a tertiary care facility (Chapter 8), hospital admission, or discharge to home.

TABLE 42.7 Route of Exposure and Decontamination Procedures

Route of Exposure	Decontamination Procedure
Ocular	Remove contact lenses if present. Irrigation with tap water or normal saline through tubing and irrigating lens for at least 20 minutes after exposure to an acid and 30 minutes after exposure to an alkaline substance. Irrigation has been sufficient when a pH strip, touched gently to the cul de sac, registers a neutral pH.
Dermal	Irrigation with running water at least 20 minutes after exposure to an acid and 30 minutes after exposure to an alkaline substance. With older children and adolescents, effective irrigation can be achieved in a shower. Emergency nurses may need to initiate hazardous materials decontamination procedures to protect themselves and the patient. Depending on the poison, local and/or systemic effects may be expected.
Inhalation	Removal of the child to fresh air, then other measures as indicated by the nature of the poison, including oxygen administration, respiratory support, observation for pulmonary effects (which are delayed for some poisons), and assessment and treatment of systemic effects.
Ingestion	May require gastrointestinal decontamination (Table 42.9). The use of specific measures depends on the poison, its physical form, the amount, the time between exposure and presentation, and the patient's condition.

Babineau, M. R., & Sanchez, L. D. (2008). Ophthalmologic procedures in the emergency department. *Emergency Clinics of North America, 26,* 17–34.

TABLE 42.8 Methods of Gastrointestinal Decontamination

Gastrointestinal Decontamination Method	Indications	Contraindications	Procedure	Specific Considerations
Ipecac syrup	Not indicated in the ED. Rarely recommended in the home setting.			If a patient has received ipecac syrup before arrival in the ED, expect one or more episodes of vomiting for about 1 hour after administration. Diarrhea is possible within the following 24 hours.
Gastric lavage	Recommended infrequently or never, depending on clinicians' interpretation of current literature. Sometimes recommended for patients who have ingested an extremely toxic amount of drug within 1 hour of ED presentation.	Ingestion of caustic substances Ingestion of hydrocarbons	Secure the airway. Warm normal saline for installation. Insert largest possible orogastric tube (16–32 French) and check placement. Place patient in left lateral Trendelenburg position with head down. Instill 50–100 mL of warm normal saline at a time, allow it to remain in the stomach for a few minutes, then drain by gravity. Repeat until lavage fluid is clear.	Gastric lavage is difficult at best in young children. Efficacy is limited by the respective sizes of the child, tube, and tablets. Activated charcoal and cathartic can be administered before the lavage tube is withdrawn.

TABLE 42.8 Methods of Gastrointestinal Decontamination (continued)

Gastrointestinal Decontamination Method	Indications	Contraindications	Procedure	Specific Considerations
Activated charcoal Mechanism: Specially processed form of charcoal possesses multiple binding sites; adsorbs to most substances, thereby preventing their absorption into the bloodstream. Available suspended in sorbitol, in an aqueous solution, and as a powder to be measured and mixed with water.	Ingestion of potentially dangerous or life-threatening quantities of most drugs and poisons.	Substances not absorbed by activated charcoal (e.g., iron, lithium, ethanol). Ingestions of hydrocarbons.	Single doses are indicated for most serious ingestions. Administer orally or via gastric tube. Dose: ▪ Infants and toddlers: 0.5–1.0 g/kg of body weight, 25g minimum/dose ▪ Older children: 25–50 g/dose ▪ Adolescents and adults: 50–100 g/dose	Multiple doses of activated charcoal, every 2 to 6 hours, will enhance the elimination of some drugs, including carbamazepine, dapsone, phenobarbital, quinine, and theophylline.[37] Patient must be alert or airway must be protected to avoid aspiration of charcoal. If multiple doses of charcoal are indicated, the presence of bowel sounds must be verified before administration of each dose. If multiple doses of charcoal are indicated, a cathartic must not be administered more than once per day, to avoid fluid and electrolyte disturbances. Warn parents of the passage of black stools, which is normal and expected but may be alarming. Commercial suspensions are much easier to administer than charcoal powder, which is difficult to measure and mix properly.

TABLE 42.8 Methods of Gastrointestinal Decontamination (continued)

Gastrointestinal Decontamination Method	Indications	Contraindications	Procedure	Specific Considerations
Cathartics: ■ Sorbitol, alone or in suspension with activated charcoal ■ Magnesium citrate Mechanism: Promotes elimination of charcoal-poison complex.	Ingestions for which activated charcoal is administered.		Administer with or after activated charcoal Dose for sorbitol: Young children: 0.5 g/kg Adolescents: 1 g/kg Dose for magnesium citrate: 4 mg/kg	In children receiving multiple doses of activated charcoal, administer no more than once per day. Do not administer with each charcoal dose.
Whole bowel irrigation	Ingestions in which above methods are insufficient to prevent life-threatening effects, (e.g., from enteric-coated drugs, sustained-release preparations, and substances not absorbed by activated charcoal).	Gastrointestinal bleeding Gastrointestinal tract abnormalities	Dose for polyethylene glycol electrolyte solutions: Administer with or after activated charcoal Young children: 0.5 L/hour orally or by nasogastric tube until rectal effluent is clear or drug removal is documented Adolescents: 1 L/hour orally or by nasogastric tube until rectal effluent is clear or drug removal is documented.	Procedure is similar to preparations used before gastrointestinal procedures and surgery. There is a slight risk of fluid and electrolyte imbalance.[38] Intact pills can be identified in rectal effluent. Observe for vomiting and electrolyte imbalance. An antiemetic may be required.

American Academy of Clinical Toxicology & European Association of Poisons Centres and Clinical Toxicologists. (2005). Position paper: Single-dose activated charcoal. *Clinical Toxicology, 43,* 61–87.

American Academy of Clinical Toxicology & European Association of Poisons Centres and Clinical Toxicologists. (2004). Position paper: Cathartics. *Clinical Toxicology, 42*(3), 243–253.

American Academy of Clinical Toxicology & European Association of Poisons Centres and Clinical Toxicologists. (2004). Position paper: Gastric lavage. *Clinical Toxicology, 42*(7), 933–943.

American Academy of Clinical Toxicology & European Association of Poisons Centres and Clinical Toxicologists. (2004). Position paper: Ipecac syrup. *Clinical Toxicology, 42*(2), 133–143.

American Academy of Clinical Toxicology & European Association of Poisons Centres and Clinical Toxicologists. (2004). Position paper: Whole bowel irrigation. *Clinical Toxicology, 42*(6), 843–854.

American Academy of Clinical Toxicology & European Association of Poisons Centres and Clinical Toxicologists. (1999). Position statement and practice guidelines on the use of multi-dose activated charcoal in the treatment of acute poisoning. *Clinical Toxicology, 37*(6), 731–751.

Kaczorowski, J. M., & Was, P. (1996). Five days of whole-bowel irrigation in a case of pediatric iron ingestion. *Annals of Emergency Medicine, 27*(2), 258–263.

TABLE 42.9 Selected Substances with Specific Antidotes

Substance	Antidote
Acetaminophen	N-acetyl L-cysteine: IV, PO
Carbon monoxide	Oxygen, including hyperbaric oxygen
Cyanide	Cyanokit (hydroxocobalamin), cyanide antidote treatment kit (amyl nitrite, sodium nitrite, sodium thiosulfate)
Digitalis	Digitalis Fab fragments
Envenomations—pit viper (Crotalidae)	Antivenom
Ethylene glycol	Fomepizole, ethanol
Hypoglycemic agents	Octreotide
Iron	Deferoxamine
INH	Pyridoxine
Methanol	Fomepizole, ethanol
Opioids	Naloxone
Organophosphate insecticides	Atropine, 2-PAM

Notes: IV = intravenous; PO = by mouth.

Home Care and Prevention

Discharge to home after an unintentional poisoning requires anticipatory guidance to prevent future poison exposures (Table 42.10). Emergency nurses should provide the parents with the poison center telephone number, 1-800-222-1222, to keep by the telephone. The parents should be reminded that the poison center will call the family to be sure that the child is recovering as expected, to refer the child for additional care if indicated, and to answer any questions about the poisoning episode. The poison center will take this opportunity to send poison prevention information to the home; the local poison center may provide the emergency department with poison prevention materials for distribution at its discretion. Parents may not be receptive to poison prevention education after the emergency treatment. Once their anxiety has diminished somewhat, they may be more receptive.

Parents should receive discharge instructions specific to the poison and the treatment. Parents may need to observe their child for specific effects after the treatment, such as dark stools following charcoal administration.

Selected Toxicologic Emergencies—Poisoning By Pharmaceutical Agents

Acetaminophen

Sources

❏ Hundreds of brand-name and generic prescription and nonprescription medicines, including single- and multiple-ingredient analgesics and combination drugs for allergies, colds, and insomnia.

Routes of Exposure

❏ Oral tablets (regular and sustained release)

❏ Liquids

❏ Rectal suppositories

Mechanism of Toxicity

❏ For children over the age of 10 years, metabolism of acetaminophen results in the production of small amounts of N-acetyl-p-benzoquinone imine (NAPQI), a toxic metabolite that is usually detoxified by the enzyme glutathione.

  ▪ In an overdose, larger amounts of NAPQI are generated; the resulting accumulation depletes glutathione and damages hepatocytes.

  ▪ Renal damage sometimes occurs.[4]

❏ A different metabolic pathway in young children provides some protection from liver damage, but this protection is not complete in all cases.[5]

❏ Because hepatotoxic effects are due to metabolites, the onset of toxicity is delayed.

❏ The earliest symptoms are gastrointestinal, occurring 6 to 14 hours after exposure. Over a period of 24 to 72 hours, liver enzymes rise, gastrointestinal symptoms increase, and right upper quadrant pain may develop.

❏ If antidotal treatment with N-acetyl-L-cysteine (NAC) is begun within 8 hours, recovery is expected without toxic sequelae. If not, progressive liver injury is possible and may be fatal unless a liver transplantation is performed.

Focused History

❏ Exact product ingested (brand name, strength, regular or sustained release)

❏ Time of ingestion

❏ Acute or chronic exposure

❏ Intentional or unintentional exposure

TABLE 42.10 Anticipatory Guidance for Poison Prevention

Identify the most dangerous poisons at home and where they are stored: Medicines, caustic cleaning products, pesticides, antifreeze, windshield washer solution, alcoholic beverages, hydrocarbons.

Purchase medicines and household products in child-resistant packaging. Replace caps securely after use.

Lock dangerous poisons out of sight and reach of children.

Store products in their original containers.

Take medicines where children cannot watch. Children learn by imitation!

Call medicine by its proper name. Do not call medicine "candy."

Before taking or giving a drug, read the label. If necessary, put on your eyeglasses and turn on the light.

Give prescription medicines only to the person for whom they were prescribed. Give over-the-counter medicines only as recommended on the label, unless your pediatrician advises otherwise.

Discard old medicines. Unless the label recommends flushing the drug, fill a metal container or plastic bag that can be sealed with used coffee grounds, kitty litter, or something else unpalatable. Place the drug inside, wrap or tape the container securely, and dispose with household trash.

Call your poison center before a poisoning occurs. The poison center will send you information about poisons specific to your area, information about teaching poison prevention to children, and telephone stickers with the poison center's emergency phone number.

Post the telephone number of the poison center on or near the telephone (1-800-222-1222).

Call the poison center immediately in case of a possible poisoning.

❐ If this information is not available, or if the history may not be reliable, a toxic exposure must be presumed to have occurred unless ruled out by laboratory evaluation. The presence or absence of symptoms and their time and sequence of onset may help confirm or refute the history.

Focused Physical Assessment

❐ Gastrointestinal system
  ▪ Gastrointestinal symptoms (nausea and vomiting)
  ▪ Right upper quadrant pain

Laboratory Tests

❐ A blood sample for acetaminophen levels must be drawn no sooner than 4 hours after exposure, to allow time for peak absorption.

❐ Obtain a repeat level 4 hours after the first if:
  ▪ the history is uncertain.
  ▪ the ingestion is chronic.
  ▪ sustained-release dosage forms are involved.

❐ Toxicity is predicted by plotting the level of acetaminophen in the blood and time of ingestion on the Rumack-Matthew nomogram (Figure 42.1). A level of 140 µg/mL at 4 hours after ingestion is predictive of possible hepatic toxicity if the antidote is not administered.

❐ Other laboratory studies include baseline hepatic and renal function studies.

Nursing Interventions

1. Support airway, breathing, and circulation (Chapter 28).
2. Administer activated charcoal with a cathartic in patients with a toxic dose confirmed by history or laboratory analysis.
3. Administer NAC (Table 42.11) if a toxic level is found at any time after 4 hours after ingestion.[6]
  ▪ Once the need for NAC has been established, additional acetaminophen levels are no longer necessary.
  ▪ The full course of therapy must be completed even if acetaminophen levels subsequently decline, because the antidote is used to treat the effects of the metabolite, which is not being measured.

Figure 42.1 Nomogram for Assessment of Acetaminophen Toxicity

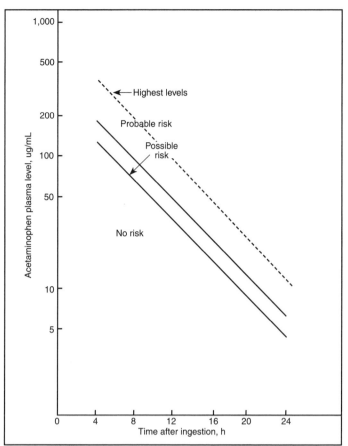

Adapted from Rumack, B. H., Peterson, R. C., Koch, G. G., & Amara, I. A. (1981). Acetaminophen overdose: 662 cases with evaluation of oral acetyl-cysteine treatment. *Archives of Internal Medicine, 141,* 382. Used with permission.

Special Considerations

A child may ingest a fatal dose of acetaminophen, yet experience no symptoms of consequence for a day or more. The ideal time to administer the antidote, which is highly effective in preventing fatalities, is within 8 hours of the overdose, before significant metabolism of the drug and symptoms occur; however, later administration is still useful. Therefore, the emergency nurse must have a high index of suspicion for acetaminophen poisoning.

❒ Consider the possibility of acetaminophen poisoning in virtually any patient who presents with an intentional drug overdose: it is widely available, frequently involved in drug overdoses, causes no early symptoms, is readily treated, yet may cause death if the diagnosis is not made.

❒ Also consider acetaminophen poisoning in children who present with gastrointestinal complaints, as well as those with evidence of hepatic abnormalities.

Tricyclic Antidepressants

Sources

❒ Numerous oral preparations, including amitriptyline, clomipramine, desipramine, doxepin, imipramine, nortriptyline, protriptyline, and trimipramine. None of these drugs is intended for use in very young children.

❒ Imipramine is sometimes prescribed for nocturnal enuresis in children aged 5 years and older.

❒ Preteens and adolescents may receive these drugs for treatment of depression.

Route of Exposure

❒ Oral tablets

Mechanism of Toxicity

❒ Anticholinergic effects, α-adrenergic blocking effects, decreased reuptake of norepinephrine, and cardiac membrane depressant effects occur to a greater or lesser extent, depending on the exact agent involved.[7]

❒ Only one or two ingested tricyclic antidepressant tablets are potentially dangerous to a young child.[8]

Focused History

❒ Time of ingestion

❒ Nature and timing of any symptoms

Focused Physical Assessment

❒ Cardiovascular system
  ▪ Significant dysrhythmias, with ECG changes including sinus tachycardia and prolonged PR, QRS, and QT intervals
  ▪ Hypotension

❒ Neurologic system
  ▪ Seizures. Severe toxicity may present as the sudden onset of seizures and coma within 30 minutes of ingestion, though not all children present so dramatically.
  ▪ Hallucinations
  ▪ Coma

❒ Gastrointestinal system
  ▪ Decreased bowel sounds

Laboratory Tests

❒ Laboratory measures of the drugs themselves correlate generally with expected toxicity, but will not be available to the ED staff and, in any case, do not guide treatment.

TABLE 42.11 Administration of NAC for Acetaminophen Poisoning

Intravenous, for adults and children ≥ 40 kg:
Infuse a loading dose of 150 mg/kg in 200 mL of D5W over a 15-minute period.
Infuse the first maintenance dose of 50 mg/kg in 500 mL D5W over a 4-hour period.
Infuse the second maintenance dose of 100 mg/kg in 1000 mL D5W over a 16-hour period.
Oral:
Administer a loading dose of 140 mg/kg of body weight, diluted three to one in a liquid palatable to the patient.
Pour the mixture over ice and offer it through a straw from a covered container to conceal NAC's objectionable odor.
Administer 17 additional doses of 70 mg/kg every 4 hours until the entire 18-dose treatment is completed.
Repeat any dose vomited within 1 hour of its administration. If vomiting is persistent, an antiemetic may prevent subsequent vomiting episodes. If vomiting continues, a gastric tube may be placed under fluoroscopy into the duodenum for instillation of NAC directly into the small bowel.
If the child is unable to tolerate oral NAC with the above measures, contact the poison center for information about intravenous NAC.
Communicate with the inpatient nursing unit to provide continuity in the dosing regimen, because the patient may not receive the entire course of NAC in the ED.
Activated charcoal, whether in single or multiple doses, can be given to patients receiving NAC by mouth.

Notes: D5W = 5% dextrose in water.
Data from Acetadote® (acetylcysteine) injection package insert.
Rumack, B. H., Peterson, R. C., Koch, G. G., & Amara, I. A. (1981). Acetaminophen overdose: 662 cases with evaluation of oral acetylcysteine treatment. *Archives of Internal Medicine, 141,* 380–385.

Nursing Interventions

1. Support airway, breathing, and circulation (Chapter 28).
2. Obtain a careful history.
3. Perform ongoing physical assessments to determine the required duration of observation and the need for admission.
4. Assess cardiovascular status, with continuous cardio-respiratory monitoring and measurement of arterial blood gases.
5. Perform gastrointestinal decontamination with gastric lavage and administer multiple doses of activated charcoal.
6. Administer medications:[9]
   - Sodium bicarbonate—the first-line drug to treat the many manifestations of this overdose. Titrate to maintain the serum pH between 7.45 and 7.55.
   - Lidocaine or magnesium citrate—used to treat ventricular dysrhythmias
   - Benzodiazepines or propofol—used to treat seizures
   - Norepinephrine—used to treat hypotension not responsive to positioning or intravenous fluids
7. Discharge to home children who present without symptoms and who remain asymptomatic for 6 hours after ingestion.
8. Patients in whom symptoms develop must be admitted to the intensive care unit for at least 24 hours for multiple doses of activated charcoal and continuous ECG monitoring.

Special Considerations

- Amoxapine is an antidepressant without the significant cardiac toxicity of other cyclic antidepressants; in overdose, it causes status epilepticus. Aggressive treatment of seizures is necessary to prevent hypoxic brain injury and significant hyperthermia.

Calcium Channel Blockers

Sources

- Drugs used to treat hypertension, angina, and arrhythmias, including amlodipine, diltiazem, felodipine, isradipine, nicardipine, nifedipine, nimodipine, and verapamil

Routes of Exposure

- Oral
- Intravenous

Mechanism of Toxicity

❏ In overdose, side effects are extensions of therapeutic effects.

❏ By slowing calcium influx into myocardial and nodal cells and vascular tissue, these agents cause conduction delays, decreased peripheral resistance, and decreased myocardial contractility.

❏ Ingestion of any amount of these drugs is dangerous and potentially lethal in children.[10] Because many preparations are sustained release, the onset of toxicity may be delayed and the duration of symptoms may be prolonged.

Focused History

❏ Time of ingestion

❏ Number of pills ingested, regular or sustained release

❏ Onset of symptoms

Physical Assessment

❏ Cardiovascular system
  ▪ Hypotension, decreased cardiac output, conduction delays, heart block and other dysrhythmias

❏ Neurologic system
  ▪ Depressed CNS function, hypoxia, seizures, and metabolic acidosis

❏ Metabolic system
  ▪ Hyperglycemia, because calcium is required for insulin release

Laboratory Tests

❏ None specific to the drug; levels not generally available

Nursing Interventions

1. Support airway, breathing and circulation (Chapter 28).

2. Perform careful ongoing assessments of respiratory, cardiovascular, neurologic, and metabolic status in every child who may have ingested or even sucked on these preparations.

3. Perform gastrointestinal decontamination.
  ▪ Administration of activated charcoal and a cathartic is indicated.
  ▪ Consider whole bowel irrigation if it is possible that pills have moved into the intestinal tract and for sustained-release preparations.

4. Prepare for the administration of intravenous drugs.[11]
  ▪ Administer intravenous calcium supplementation (preferably calcium chloride) in symptomatic children, although this is not always effective in reversing hypotension and other cardiovascular effects.
  ▪ Glucagon may increase heart rate, though this, too, is not always effective.
  ▪ High-dose insulin/euglycemic therapy is promising but also not always effective.

Special Considerations

❏ There is no antidote for overdose, and there are no universally effective treatments for calcium channel blocker ingestions (in children or adults). It is essential that even the possibility of ingestion of these drugs in children be considered a potentially fatal event. Rapid action to decontaminate the gastrointestinal tract and treat early manifestations of toxicity may present the best chance a child has of surviving ingestion of a calcium channel-blocking drug.

Digitalis

Sources

❏ Pills, liquids, and intravenous preparations

❏ Plants including Digitalis purpurea (foxglove) and Nerium oleander (oleander)

❏ Toad toxins (bufotoxins)

Routes of Exposure

❏ Oral
  ▪ Intentional or unintentional overdose of medication
  ▪ Ingestion of plant material or teas brewed from plant material, for example, D. purpura (foxglove), Nerium species (oleander), and Thevetia species (yellow oleander)
  ▪ Compounds containing bufotoxins found in topical aphrodisiacs or nonwestern medicines[12]
  ▪ Chronic toxicity in patients taking digitalis

❏ Intravenous preparations—intentional or unintentional overdose

Mechanism of Toxicity

❏ Digitalis binds to and inhibits the action of Na^+–K^{++}–adenosine triphosphatase at receptors on cardiac and smooth muscle, resulting in increased intracellular sodium and calcium, depleted intracellular potassium, and markedly increased extracellular potassium.

Focused History

☐ Determine whether the overdose is:

- Acute
- Chronic
- Acute in a child undergoing chronic therapy. A child prescribed digitalis will be seriously (acutely) poisoned at a lower serum level than a patient with an acute overdose only, because receptor sites are already saturated.

Focused Physical Assessment

☐ Cardiovascular system

- Bradycardia and numerous other dysrhythmias, including heart block, and hypotension due to a decrease in nodal conduction and cellular contraction

☐ Neurologic system

- Lethargy
- Visual changes, including yellow or greenish "halos" in chronic overdoses

☐ Gastrointestinal system

- Elevated serum potassium levels, unless the patient is receiving concomitant diuretic therapy
- Gastrointestinal effects (nausea and vomiting)
- Signs of dehydration (Chapter 17)

Laboratory Tests

☐ Serum digitalis level

☐ Serum hepatic studies (digitalis is metabolized by the liver)

☐ Serum renal studies (digitalis is excreted by the kidneys)

Nursing Interventions

1. Support airway, breathing, and circulation (Chapter 28).
2. Initiate continuous ECG and blood pressure monitoring.
3. Administer digoxin immune Fab fragments to the child with severe or life-threatening ECG abnormalities (Table 42.12).
4. Administer activated charcoal.
5. Initiate intravenous hydration, if needed.

Special Considerations

☐ Although a therapeutic digitalis level is 0.5 to 2.0 ng/mL, toxicity is possible within that range.

Diphenoxylate/Atropine

Sources

☐ Oral prescription drug used to treat diarrhea, such as Lomotil® or generic preparations

Route of Exposure

☐ Oral

Mechanism of Toxicity

☐ The combination of an opioid and atropine (an anticholinergic) slows peristalsis, the desired therapeutic effect.

☐ Children can experience significant opioid toxicity

TABLE 42.12 Administration of Digoxin Immune (Fab) Fragments

Notify the pharmacy that Digibind is required. It may be necessary to obtain additional supplies from other facilities. A delay in procuring and administering the antidote could cost the child's life.
Dosing depends on the amount of digitalis ingested; each vial of 40-mg digoxin immune (Fab) fragments will bind 0.6 mg of digitalis.
If the ingested amount of digitalis is unknown, contact the local poison center to calculate the dose of digoxin immune (Fab) fragments; the calculation includes the digitalis level, its volume of distribution, and patient characteristics.
Determine whether the laboratory is measuring total or free digitalis levels.
• Free digitalis level (unbound digitalis): This level determines whether the child is at risk for continued toxicity and whether a child who requires therapeutic levels of digitalis remains adequately digitalized.
• Total digitalis level (digitalis already bound to the antidote plus free digitalis): This is not useful for determining management of an overdose.

Bauman, J. L., DiDomenico, R. J., & Galanter, W. L. (2006). Mechanisms, manifestations, and management of digoxin toxicity in the modern era. *American Journal of Cardiovascular Drugs, 6*(2), 77–86.

from diphenoxylate, yet delayed absorption may mean delayed toxicity.

❏ The opioid effects may occur as long as 24 hours after ingestion.[13]

❏ In young children, the ingestion of even one tablet is associated with toxicity, including delayed toxicity.

History

❏ Number of pills ingested

❏ Time of ingestion

❏ Symptoms since ingestion

Focused Physical Assessment

❏ Respiratory system
  ▪ Respiratory depression, bradypnea

❏ Neurologic system
  ▪ Pinpoint pupils
  ▪ Decreased level of consciousness

Laboratory Tests

❏ None

Nursing Interventions

1. Support airway, breathing, and circulation (Chapter 28).

2. Administer activated charcoal and a cathartic, depending on the time of post-ingestion.

3. Administer naloxone to treat symptoms of opioid overdose.

4. Hospitalize and initiate 24-hour cardiorespiratory monitoring for young children with a history of any ingestion of this drug.

Special Considerations

❏ Because the onset of symptoms is delayed, it can be difficult to convince parents and health care professionals that an apparently healthy child is at risk for significant opioid toxicity.

Iron

Sources

❏ Numerous types of vitamin and mineral supplements, both pediatric and adult, in solid and liquid formulations

❏ Prenatal vitamins with iron and adult-strength iron supplements are a significant cause of poisoning death in young children. Serious iron poisoning also occurs in pregnant teens who deliberately take overdoses of their own prenatal vitamins.

Route of Exposure

❏ Oral

Mechanism of Toxicity[14]

❏ Initially, iron has a corrosive effect on the gastrointestinal mucosa, causing significant bleeding, which contributes to cardiovascular shock.

❏ The damaged gastrointestinal mucosa allows increased absorption of iron, which damages hepatocytes and blood vessels.

❏ As iron is metabolized, generation of hydrogen ions contributes to metabolic acidosis.

❏ The ultimate effects of iron poisoning depend on the amount ingested and the rapidity with which the child receives adequate medical care.

❏ Mild toxicity is predicted with ingestions of 20 to 40 mg/kg of elemental iron, and significant toxicity with ingestions of > 60 mg/kg.

❏ As few as 10 adult-strength iron supplements are potentially lethal to a 10-kg child.

❏ Iron poisoning is described in stages, although poisoning events in individual children may occur differently (Table 42.13).

Focused History

❏ Type of iron preparation

❏ Amount of iron preparation

❏ Time of ingestion
  ▪ If a patient with a history of iron ingestion seems asymptomatic, assess for the occurrence of any gastrointestinal symptoms in the last 12 to 24 hours.

Focused Physical Assessment

❏ Cardiovascular system
  ▪ Hypotension may occur.

❏ Gastrointestinal system
  ▪ Dehydration may occur.

Laboratory Tests

❏ Immediate serum iron level

❏ Immediate complete blood cell count

❏ Electrolytes

❏ Hepatic studies

❏ Renal studies

TABLE 42.13 Phases of Iron Poisoning

Phases	Onset of Symptoms after Ingestion	Symptoms
Phase I	30 minutes to 2 hours	Nausea Vomiting Diarrhea (may be bloody) Abdominal discomfort
Phase II	2 to 12 hours	"Latent phase": Children become asymptomatic and appear to have recovered. However, significant toxicity is developing.
Phase III	12 to 48 hours	Sudden cardiovascular collapse Metabolic abnormalities and hepatic injury (acidosis and coagulopathies) Decreased level of consciousness, coma, pulmonary edema, and hepatorenal failure Children who survive this phase may recover fully or may have complications such as intestinal necrosis, causing their death days or weeks later.
Phase IV	2 to 4 days	This phase may occur in seriously poisoned children who survive their poisoning episode; this includes pyloric stenosis, secondary to corrosive injury, which requires corrective surgery.

Tenenbein, M. (2001). Iron. In M. D. Ford, K. A. Kelaney, L. J. Ling, & T. Erickson (Eds.), *Clinical toxicology* (pp. 305–309). Philadelphia: Saunders.

❏   Arterial blood gases

❏   Immediate stool guaiac

❏   Blood for typing and crossmatching if the stool is guaiac-positive

Nursing Interventions

1. Support airway, breathing, and circulation (Chapter 28).

2. Perform gastrointestinal decontamination if the ingestion was recent (about 1 hour for a liquid preparation or a few hours for solid dosage forms). Activated charcoal is not effective and is not indicated, unless other substances that do adsorb to charcoal were also ingested.

3. Obtain an abdominal radiograph if adult-strength tablets were involved, to aid in documenting the position and number of the ingested iron pills. A negative radiograph does not negate the possibility of ingestion of an iron-containing preparation.

    ▪   Liquids and pediatric chewable vitamins with iron will not be visible on a radiograph.

4. If a potentially dangerous number of iron pills have reached the intestinal tract, initiate whole bowel irrigation until all pills have been counted in the rectal effluent or a subsequent radiograph documents their passage.

5. Administer deferoxamine, the antidote for iron poisoning. Deferoxamine complexes with iron, forming ferrioxamine, which is water soluble and excreted renally.[15]

    ▪   The usual intravenous dose of deferoxamine is 15 mg/kg per hour.

    ▪   Deferoxamine is indicated for symptomatic children with a serum iron level of 350 µg/dL and for all children with a level greater than 500 µg/dL.

    ▪   Large doses of deferoxamine can cause significant hypotension, usually when given too quickly or at greater than 15 mg/kg per hour, thereby limiting its use in dangerously poisoned children.

    ▪   Deferoxamine should not be administered intramuscularly to an iron-poisoned child, because there may be insufficient or erratic absorption in hypotensive children.

Special Considerations

❏   The potential dangers of iron overdose are underestimated by parents and health care professionals alike, who recognize that iron is an essential dietary element and may believe it to be innocuous.

    ▪   Early signs of iron toxicity are sometimes not recognized as serious; children progress through the asymptomatic phase and then are brought to the emergency department after becoming seriously ill.

- Health professionals should consider iron poisoning in a child with gastrointestinal bleeding, coagulopathies, and acidosis.[16]

☐ Iron is prescribed regularly for pregnant women, who are likely to have young children at home. If a child has ingested iron, determine whether other siblings may have done the same.

Isoniazid

Sources

☐ Oral drug used to treat tuberculosis

Route of exposure

☐ Oral

Mechanism of Toxicity

☐ An overdose of isoniazid (INH) rapidly depletes the body's stores of pyridoxine (vitamin B6).

- Pyridoxine is necessary for synthesis of gamma-aminobutyric acid (GABA), an inhibitory neurotransmitter.

Focused History

☐ Family or patient treatment for tuberculosis
☐ Refractory seizures before presentation[17]

Focused Physical Assessment

☐ Neurologic system
- Seizures or a postictal state

Laboratory Tests

☐ Arterial blood gases

Nursing Interventions

1. Support airway, breathing, and circulation (Chapter 28).
2. Initiate measures to protect patient if seizure activity occurs (Chapter 16).
3. Administer intravenous pyridoxine.[18]
   - Known dose of ingested INH: Administer an equal amount of pyridoxine.
   - Unknown dose of ingested INH: Administer 5 g of pyridoxine.
4. Administer diazepam.
   - Diazepam enhances the effects of GABA, but it is not a substitute for pyridoxine.

5. Treat acidosis.
6. Administer activated charcoal and a cathartic.

Special Considerations

The incidence of tuberculosis in the United States has risen in recent years. There is increased prevalence among some immigrant groups and patients infected with the human immunodeficiency virus. Consider medical, social, and environmental factors when assessing the likelihood of INH as a cause of recalcitrant seizures.

Oral Hypoglycemic Agents

Sources

Oral agents taken by adults with type 2 diabetes, including chlorpropamide, glipizide, glyburide, and tolbutamide.

Route of Exposure

☐ Oral

Mechanism of Toxicity

☐ Ingestion of hypoglycemic agents by patients without diabetes is expected to cause hypoglycemia.

☐ Delayed onset of persistent hypoglycemia may occur, especially with the second-generation sulfonylureas such as glipizide and glyburide, or sustained-release preparations.

☐ Ingestion of any amount of these drugs is dangerous in children, who may not manifest significant hypoglycemia until nearly 24 hours after ingestion. Any child who ingests any amount of these drugs should be evaluated in the emergency department.

Focused History

☐ Suspected or witnessed ingestion
☐ Neurologic changes indicative of hypoglycemia such as weakness; dizziness; tremulousness; irritability; cool, clammy skin; unconsciousness; and seizures

Focused Physical Assessment

☐ Neurologic system
- Altered level of consciousness
- Signs of hypoglycemia

Laboratory Tests

☐ Immediate serum glucose level
☐ Serum glucose levels repeated at least every 2 hours

Nursing Interventions

1. Support airway, breathing, and circulation (Chapter 28)

2. Initiate measures to protect patient should seizure activity occur (Chapter 16).

3. Obtain an immediate serum glucose level and administer intravenous glucose, if needed.

   ▪ Should hypoglycemia persist or recur, consider administration of glucagon or octreotide.[19]

4. Administer activated charcoal and a cathartic.

5. Monitor serum glucose levels closely.

Special Considerations

❐ After the ingestion of oral hypoglycemic agents, check glucose every 1 to 2 hours. If the level drops below 60 mg/dL, whether or not symptoms occur, admit the child for monitoring and further treatment.[20]

Salicylates

Sources

❐ Aspirin (acetylsalicylic acid), in regular, sustained-release, and enteric-coated formulations, alone or in combination with prescription and nonprescription drugs

❐ Bismuth subsalicylate, in over-the-counter gastrointestinal preparations

❐ Oil of wintergreen (methyl salicylate), sold alone as a liquid, as a flavoring agent, as an ingredient in over-the-counter topical preparations to relieve muscle and joint pains, and with isopropyl alcohol in green rubbing alcohol

Routes of Exposure

❐ Oral

   ▪ Poisonings may occur from acute or chronic ingestion of aspirin and aspirin-containing drugs or from ingestion of oil of wintergreen, which is intended for external use only.

❐ Rectal suppositories

❐ Topical

Mechanism of Toxicity

❐ Salicylate poisoning disrupts metabolism, resulting in a complex cascade of events.

❐ Depending on the time since ingestion, children may present with no metabolic abnormalities, respiratory alkalosis, or metabolic acidosis. If a child is acidotic, salicylate moves more easily into the central nervous system (CNS).

❐ Other manifestations of salicylate toxicity include fever, hypoglycemia, gastrointestinal irritation, tinnitus, and altered platelet function.

❐ Acute, chronic, and acute poisonings in someone taking the drug chronically are all possible. Toxicity occurs at lower blood levels when an acute overdose occurs in someone who takes a salicylate chronically.

❐ Acute ingestion of salicylates can lead to rapid deterioration, even in children who do not appear acutely ill on presentation.

❐ Depending on the time since ingestion, children may present with no metabolic abnormalities, respiratory alkalosis, or metabolic acidosis.

Focused History

❐ Suspected or known salicylate ingestion.

   ▪ Determine the exact preparation, how much is missing, over what period of time the drug was taken, and the nature of the illness for which it was taken.

   ▪ Because aspirin is metabolized hepatically and excreted renally, the child's health history is important to ascertain renal or hepatic abnormalities.

❐ Unknown salicylate ingestion.

   ▪ Ascertain concurrent or recent illnesses in the child and whether aspirin was administered during the illness.

   ▪ Aspirin may be given initially to treat a fever but actually causes a fever if chronic toxicity develops.

   ▪ Chronic salicylate intoxication can mimic a number of viral or flu-like presentations.

   ▪ Ascertain whether salicylate preparations are in the home.

Focused Physical Assessment

❐ Respiratory system

   ▪ Tachypnea, signs of pulmonary edema

❐ Cardiovascular system

   ▪ Tachycardia

❐ Neurologic system

   ▪ Lethargy, seizures, and coma may occur.

   ▪ Tinnitus is common.

   ▪ Hyperthermia

❐ Gastrointestinal system

   ▪ Signs of dehydration (Chapter 17)

   ▪ Gastrointestinal bleeding

- Metabolic system
  - Electrolyte imbalance
- Hematologic system
  - Coagulopathies
- Integumentary system
  - Fever
  - Diaphoresis

Laboratory Tests

- Obtain serum electrolyte levels, glucose levels, renal and hepatic function tests, and arterial blood gases.
- Ingestion of liquid preparation.
  - Obtain a salicylate level 1 to 2 hours after ingestion.
- Ingestion of a solid (tablet) preparation.
  - Obtain a salicylate level 1 to 2 hours after ingestion. Then obtain serial levels to confirm that the level is declining.
- Ingestion of a solid preparation in a chronic ingestion or a large acute ingestion in a chronic user.
  - Obtain a salicylate level immediately and every 2 hours, to confirm that the level is declining.

Nursing Interventions

1. Support airway, breathing, and circulation (Chapter 28).
2. Administer activated charcoal.
   - Should the child remain in the emergency department longer than 3 hours, administer subsequent doses of charcoal without a cathartic every 3 hours.[21]
3. Obtain a serum salicylate level and correct fluid and electrolyte imbalances.
   - Administer intravenous sodium bicarbonate to achieve a urine pH of approximately 8.0, because salicylates are eliminated more quickly in alkaline urine.
4. Hydrate with intravenous fluids containing supplemental potassium.
5. In children, the Done nomogram (Figure 42.2) has been used to predict toxicity by plotting the salicylate level against the time of ingestion. This may be useful in children who present 6 hours or more after the ingestion. However, a child with serious toxicity is likely to be symptomatic at this point.
6. A subsequent serum salicylate level is often necessary to rule out continued absorption from sustained-release or enteric-coated preparations, or from a concretion of aspirin tablets in the stomach.

Figure 42.2 Nomogram Relating Serum Salicylate Concentration and Expected Severity of Intoxication at Varying Intervals After the Ingestion of a Single Dose of Salicylate

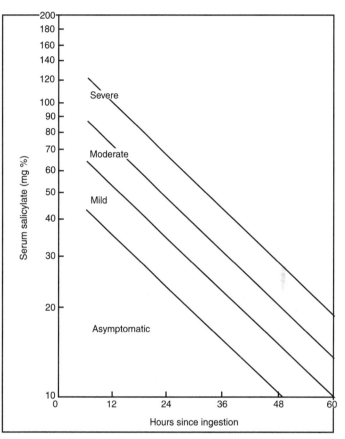

Done, A. K. (1960). Salicylate intoxication: Significance of measurements of salicylate in blood in cases of acute ingestion. *Pediatrics, 26*(5), 805. Used with permission.

7. Prepare for hemodialysis in children with significant symptoms, salicylate levels greater than 100 mg/dL after acute poisoning, or lower salicylate levels after chronic ingestion.
8. Initiate supportive care.
   - Continue ongoing cardiorespiratory monitoring.
   - Obtain serial salicylate levels to assure that serum salicylate levels are decreasing.

Special Considerations

- At one time, aspirin was a leading cause of poisoning death in children. Because of passive measures to prevent salicylate poisoning (child-resistant containers, limited number of baby aspirin tablets per bottle), many health care providers are unfamiliar with its disastrous history. Consequently, emergency professionals may not appreciate the rapidly fatal effects of salicylate poisoning. Many parents do not think of aspirin as particularly dangerous and may not call a poison center until their child is symptomatic. Teenagers may attempt suicide with aspirin simply because it is so widely available.

❑ A high index of suspicion, careful history, vigorous gastrointestinal decontamination, and careful attention to salicylate levels and the child's response to treatment are imperative to prevent unnecessary fatalities from this common drug.

Sympathomimetic Drugs

Sources

❑ Legal drugs

- Decongestants, whether in combination cough/cold and allergy products or as single-ingredient preparations

- Stimulants, including caffeine

- Methylphenidate (Ritalin®), dexmethylphenidate, amphetamine, and dextroamphetamine, prescription drugs used to treat hyperactivity and attention-deficit disorders

- Weight control agents, including amphetamines and related drugs

- "Street speed" (or any number of other rapidly changing names), including legal drugs packaged and sold illegally, often as stimulants

- Herbal drugs and dietary supplements containing ephedrine, derived from the plants of the genus Ephedra (ma huang)

❑ Illegal drugs

- Cocaine: Injection; inhalation ("snorting" by abusers or inhalation of second-hand smoke by children[22]) and smoking of "crack"; ingestion by children who find it in their homes, by breast-fed babies,[23] or by teens and adults attempting to avoid arrest for drug possession

- Illicit amphetamines: Injection, ingestion, and smoking of many types, including methamphetamine, MDMA ("Ecstasy"), and other hallucinogenic amphetamines

Routes of Exposure

❑ Oral

❑ Injection

❑ Inhalation

Mechanism of Toxicity

❑ Uncontrolled stimulation of the sympathetic nervous system ("fight or flight" response) causes tachycardia, tachypnea, hypertension, miosis, hyperthermia, and CNS stimulation.

❑ The half-life of cocaine is about 4 to 6 hours, and of amphetamines about 18 to 24 hours. Clinically, poisonings by these agents cannot be differentiated, and the treatment is the same.

Focused History

❑ Often difficult to obtain when the poisonings involve illicit substances or legal substances diverted for illicit sale.

- Determine whether ingested illegal drugs were contained in some type of vial, condom, balloon, or package. Leakage of the drug from containers can cause continuing effects, and breakage could cause the sudden onset of seizures, hyperthermia, hypertension, dysrhythmias, and death.

❑ CNS effects (seizures, hyperthermia, agitation, tremors, or hallucinations)

❑ Cardiac effects (chest pain, hypertension, or tachycardia)

Focused Physical Assessment

❑ Respiratory system

- Tachypnea

❑ Cardiovascular system

- Chest pain from myocardial ischemia

- Tachydysrhythmias

- Hypertension

- Peripheral vasodilation with central vasoconstriction

❑ Neurologic system

- Headache from extreme hypertension

- Agitation

- Tremors

- Seizures

- Hyperthermia

Laboratory Tests

❑ Laboratory identification of the agent involved can help predict the duration of effects.

❑ Other studies will be dictated by the child's physical condition, such as whether the child has evidence of cardiac or CNS involvement.

Nursing Interventions

1. Support airway, breathing, and circulation (Chapter 28).

    ▪ Initiate measures to control ventricular dysrhythmias and hypertension.

2. Support neurologic function.

    ▪ Initiate measures to control hyperthermia and seizures.

3. Support renal function.

    ▪ Administer intravenous fluids to combat renal failure secondary to hypovolemia.[24]

4. Administer activated charcoal for oral exposures.

5. Consider abdominal radiographs, because ingested packets of drugs may be visible. Whole bowel irrigation may be indicated for ingestion of drug packets.

Special Considerations

❐ Although substance abusers will often smoke or inject drugs to obtain the most rapid effects, these substances also are absorbed from the gastrointestinal tract. This poses a hazard to children who swallow legal or illegal stimulants and to those under arrest who may have swallowed drugs and been released to jail sooner than is medically wise. If the child has used illegal drugs, the presentation and clinical course may be affected by adulterants such as quinine, lidocaine, strychnine, and a host of other substances.

    ▪ Idiosyncratic reactions may occur from usual doses of these drugs; overdose is not necessary for a patient to present with the sudden onset of significant symptoms.

Selected Toxicologic Emergencies—Poisoning by Nonpharmaceutical Agents

Caustic Substances

Sources

❐ Acids (e.g., hydrochloric or sulfuric acid often found in household products):

    ▪ Toilet bowl cleaners, some bathroom cleaning products, swimming pool chemicals, automobile batteries, and products used to clean concrete and bricks

❐ Alkaline chemicals (e.g., sodium hydroxide, potassium hydroxide, calcium hydroxide, or sodium carbonate, often found in household products):

    ▪ Drain openers, laundry detergent, electric dishwasher detergent, oven cleaner, industrial-strength cleaners, concrete, cement, and liquid from damaged dry cell batteries

❐ Children may be exposed to caustic chemicals, either acids or alkaline substances, if people in the home are involved in the illicit manufacture of methamphetamine or cocaine.[25,26]

❐ Hydrofluoric acid has a different toxicity from other caustics and will be considered separately.

Routes of Exposure

❐ Ingestion

❐ Inhalation

❐ Ocular

❐ Dermal

Mechanism of Toxicity

❐ *Acids* dehydrate tissue and precipitate surface proteins, resulting in coagulation necrosis. A hard eschar develops, which inhibits penetration of the acid into deeper tissue.

❐ *Alkalines* cause a liquefaction necrosis; disrupted cell membranes provide no barrier to deeper penetration of the chemical with continuing injury. Saponification, a result of alkaline action on lipids in cell membranes, causes the soapy appearance of the tissue.

❐ For all tissues affected, injury can range from mild irritation to full-thickness chemical burns; the degree of severity can be compared to first-, second-, and third-degree thermal burns (Chapter 37). The extent of injury after ingestion, dermal, or ocular exposure to a caustic substance is determined by:

    ▪ The pH of the product, with the most severe injury expected with products with a pH of < 2 or > 12.

    ▪ The duration of contact with tissue. Even substances that usually are mildly irritating at worst, such as household bleach, can cause more significant injury with prolonged contact.

    ▪ The product formulation. Liquid substances quickly transit the oropharynx and esophagus, so the greatest injury is typically seen in the stomach. Granular substances may adhere to tissues in the mouth and oropharynx, causing a greater likelihood of burns to the lips, tongue, oropharynx, and esophagus.

    ▪ The adequacy of irrigation, for ocular and dermal exposures.

❐ Pulmonary edema may occur after inhalation of caustic substances. It is usually delayed for at least several hours, during which time cellular membrane destruction occurs, with subsequent leakage of capillary fluid into the lungs and disruption of gas exchange across alveolar membranes.

Focused History

❑ Treatment must be initiated before or concurrent with the history and assessment.

❑ Identify the exact product, so that the poison center can advise about the pH, or check the pH of the product itself.

❑ Determine whether the exposure was unintentional or intentional.

■ Suicidal ingestions in teenagers and adults usually involve larger amounts of product and more significant injury (Chapter 25).

Focused Physical Assessment

❑ Ingestion[27]

■ Examine for visible burns.

■ Evaluate respiratory function. Oral edema may compromise the airway. Product may have been aspirated.

■ Ascertain presence or absence of oral, chest, or epigastric pain.

■ Assess for abdominal distention.

❑ Ocular exposure

■ Examine the cornea and surrounding tissue.

❑ Dermal exposure

■ Determine depth, percent, and extent of injury (Chapter 37).

Laboratory Tests

❑ Oral exposures: Serum electrolytes

❑ Assess for skin integrity (Chapter 37)

❑ Inhalation exposures: Arterial blood gases

Nursing Interventions

1. For all exposures, support airway, breathing, and circulation (Chapter 28).

2. Oral exposures:

■ Administer a small amount of water if the child is able to swallow.

■ Assess for visible burns to the lips, face, and oropharynx.

■ Evaluate respiratory function, because oral edema may compromise the airway and some product may have been aspirated. Maintain the airway and

prepare for a tracheostomy, if necessary.

■ Assess for chest or epigastric pain, although absence of such pain does not rule out esophageal or gastric burns.

■ Assess for abdominal distention, which may indicate perforation.

■ Obtain a thorough laboratory evaluation and monitor for acid-base imbalances.

■ Anticipate gastrointestinal bleeding and consult a gastroenterologist. Esophagoscopy may be performed soon after ingestion or may be delayed for 24 or 48 hours.

■ Anticipate the administration of antibiotics if infection develops. The use of steroids is controversial, and steroids are generally not used in the management of these patients.

3. Inhalation exposures:

■ Assess respiratory function.

• The delayed onset of pulmonary edema may be anticipated with such common inhalants as chlorine gas.

• When ignited, a number of products and chemicals generate phosgene gas, a severe respiratory irritant.

· Assess for carbon monoxide and cyanide poisoning if exposure was a result of fire.

4. Ocular exposures:

■ Irrigate the eye immediately if it was not done in the prehospital setting. Prolonged irrigation is needed until the ocular pH returns to neutral, a minimum of 20 minutes for acids and 30 minutes to 1 hour for alkaline chemicals.

■ Check ocular pH by gently touching a pH strip to the cul de sac.

■ Examine the cornea for injury.

■ Treat the corneal injury.

■ Consult an ophthalmologist.

5. Dermal exposures:

■ Irrigate the skin immediately if it was not done in the prehospital setting (Chapter 43).

■ Determine the extent of injury as for a thermal burn of similar degree (Chapter 37). The child with a severe chemical burn is at risk of the same systemic effects as a child with a thermal burn of similar degree. Fluid loss, electrolyte imbalance, and risk of infection must all be considered.

Special Considerations

❒ Caustic burns can be devastating, painful injuries that require long-term treatment. Ocular exposures may lead to permanent blindness. Dermal exposures may cause scarring. Survivors of caustic ingestions may face decades of repeated surgeries to maintain esophageal patency.

❒ Emergency staff must protect themselves from the same consequences by careful handling of the patient, any emesis, any contaminated clothing, and the caustic material itself (Chapter 43).

Hydrogen Fluoride (Hydrofluoric Acid)

Sources

Rust removers for home and commercial use, air conditioning coil cleaners, wire wheel cleaners, and industrial products to etch glass and computer chips.

Routes of Exposure

❒ Oral

❒ Ocular

❒ Dermal (most common, from using the product without gloves or with damaged gloves)

❒ Inhalation

Mechanism of Toxicity

❒ Unlike other acids, hydrofluoric acid can penetrate intact skin. Free fluoride is liberated and can bind with calcium and magnesium.

❒ With hydrofluoric acid concentrations of greater than 50%, tissue burns are immediately evident, as they would be with other acids.

❒ With hydrofluoric acid concentrations of less than 50%, skin effects are delayed and may be minimal.

❒ The absorption of hydrofluoric acid causes the delayed onset of deep pain at the site of exposure and may cause hypomagnesemia and fatal systemic hypocalcemia.

❒ Severe toxicity has been reported with small body surface area exposures,[28] with pediatric ingestions,[29] and with inhalation.[30]

Focused History

❒ Product name, to determine the hydrofluoric acid concentration

❒ Time of exposure

❒ Nature and timing of symptoms

❒ Time and type of decontamination procedures. (Often, decontamination was not done because skin exposures initially may be painless.)

Focused Physical Assessment

❒ Integumentary system

   ▪ Assess for ocular, dermal, and oral burns (Chapter 37).

Laboratory Tests

❒ Serial calcium levels for exposures greater than the most trivial skin contact, inhalation, and ingestion, to determine the risk of hypocalcemia and subsequent ventricular fibrillation.

Nursing Interventions

1. For all exposures:
   ▪ Support airway, breathing, and circulation (Chapter 28).
   ▪ Initiate continuous cardiorespiratory monitoring.
   ▪ Monitor electrolyte, calcium, and magnesium levels.
   ▪ Treat decreased calcium levels with intravenous calcium chloride or calcium gluconate.

2. Decontaminate ocular exposures.
   ▪ Treat by irrigating for at least 20 minutes.
   ▪ Immediate consultation with ophthalmology is essential; opinions differ as to the best therapy, but as is often the case, such disagreement simply highlights the fact that there are no universally effective treatments.

3. Decontaminate dermal exposures.
   ▪ Treat by irrigating for at least 20 minutes.
   ▪ Closely monitor calcium levels.
   ▪ Treat pain:
      • The delayed pain that develops at the site of exposure is deep, severe, and often not controlled by narcotics. Often, fingers are the site of exposure, with intense pain and blanching. Pain may seem disproportionate to the visible injury. The key to treatment is replacement of tissue calcium.
         · This can sometimes be accomplished by application of a calcium gel, which is rubbed in until the pain subsides; application is repeated as pain recurs.
         · Intra-arterial calcium infusion may be the treatment of choice, not only to relieve pain but to prevent destruction of soft tissue and bone.

4. Treatment for inhalation exposures:
   - Initiate treatment as in respiratory injury from other causes.
   - Monitor serial calcium levels.
5. Treatment for ingestion exposures:
   - Perform dilution; then initiate a gastrointestinal consultation. The child is at risk for complications of caustic ingestion, as well as the potentially fatal effects of hypocalcemia.

Special Considerations

Parents are astounded to learn that agents of such extreme toxicity may be in the garage or laundry room. Because toxicity is unexpected and visible effects may be minimal, parents may not seek advice until a child is ill. Health care providers not familiar with this poisoning may underestimate the extreme toxicity of seemingly minimal exposures.

Ethanol

Source

- ❑ Alcoholic beverages
- ❑ Mouthwash
- ❑ Cosmetics (facial toners, astringents, or hair spray)
- ❑ Antidote for ethylene glycol and methanol poisoning

Routes of Exposure

- ❑ Oral
- ❑ Dermal
- ❑ Intravenous (for therapeutic administration)

Mechanism of Toxicity

- ❑ Ethanol is a CNS depressant.
- ❑ In children, ethanol may also cause hypoglycemia because of small hepatic glycogen stores.
- ❑ Acute poisoning causes CNS depression, respiratory depression, and ataxia. Hypoglycemic effects include seizures and coma.
- ❑ Extremely high ethanol levels, coma, and death can result from ingestion of household products containing ethanol and from binge drinking.
- ❑ Preteens and teenagers may be chronic ethanol abusers who develop a tolerance for CNS depressant effects.

Focused History

- ❑ Time of ingestion (determines the usefulness of gastrointestinal decontamination)
- ❑ Ingestion of other drugs (potential for enhanced CNS depressant effects)
- ❑ Type of product ingested
- ❑ Amount of ethanol ingested

Focused Physical Assessment

- ❑ Respiratory system
  - Respiratory depression occurs with acute poisoning.
- ❑ Neurologic system
  - CNS depression and ataxia occur with acute poisoning.
  - Seizures and coma can result from hypoglycemia.

Laboratory Tests

- ❑ Serum ethanol level
- ❑ Serum glucose level
- ❑ Electrolytes
- ❑ Arterial blood gases

Nursing Interventions

1. Support airway, breathing, and circulation (Chapter 28).
2. Obtain blood for laboratory tests.
3. Initiate gastric decontamination with gastric lavage if the ingestion has been within the past hour, because lavage may retrieve some unabsorbed ethanol.
   - Activated charcoal is ineffective.
4. Maintain fluid and electrolyte status.
5. Monitor arterial blood gases and ethanol and glucose levels; monitor acid-base balance.
6. Prepare for hemodialysis in severely symptomatic patients.

Special Considerations

- ❑ Because of their small size, young children are especially susceptible to the CNS depressant effects of ethanol, something that parents may not realize when giving a children "just a taste" of an alcoholic beverage or some beer to "help them sleep."
- ❑ Teenagers who are inexperienced drinkers overestimate their capacity for alcohol or drink on a dare. Some preteens and teenagers will be ethanol dependent, and so must be monitored for withdrawal symptoms when being treated for other conditions[31] (Chapter 25).

Ethylene Glycol

Sources

- ❑ Automobile antifreeze (nearly 100% ethylene glycol)
- ❑ Related chemicals such as diethylene glycol and ethylene glycol monobutyl ether, found in some solvents and cleaning products
  - Although the degree of toxicity may differ from ethylene glycol, effects and treatment are the same.

Routes of Exposure

- ❑ Oral
  - Unintentional ingestions in children. (The chemical has a sweet taste.)
  - Used as an ethanol surrogate or in suicide attempts by adolescents and adults.

Mechanism of Toxicity

- ❑ Toxicity occurs as a result of metabolism by alcohol dehydrogenase.
- ❑ Production of several organic acids causes significant acidosis.
- ❑ One metabolite is oxalic acid, which precipitates with calcium to form calcium oxalate crystals. These crystals are deposited in soft tissue and in the kidneys, where they may cause renal failure.
- ❑ Because toxicity results from the action of metabolites and not that of the ethylene glycol itself, the onset of symptoms is delayed for approximately 12 to 24 hours.
- ❑ Beginning about 8 to 10 hours after ingestion, calcium oxalate crystals may be identified in the urine.
- ❑ Effects similar to those of alcoholic inebriation may occur initially. They are accompanied or followed by lethargy, abdominal pain, ataxia, seizures, coma, and renal failure; death may occur.
- ❑ An anion gap metabolic acidosis will be pronounced, and there will be a widened osmolal gap.
- ❑ Ethylene glycol poisoning should be suspected in any child with CNS depression accompanied by metabolic acidosis.

Focused History

- ❑ Identify potential sources:
  - Child playing near someone working on a car
  - Use of ethylene glycol as an ethanol surrogate, intentionally or otherwise
  - Have someone examine the home or other locations where the patient spent time within the previous 24 hours.
- ❑ Time of symptom onset

Focused Physical Assessment

- ❑ Neurologic system
  - Lethargy
  - Ataxia
  - Seizures
  - Coma
- ❑ Gastrointestinal system
  - Abdominal pain

Laboratory Tests

- ❑ Ethylene glycol levels
- ❑ Ethanol levels
- ❑ Arterial blood gases
- ❑ Baseline renal function studies
- ❑ Examination of urine for oxalate crystals

Nursing Interventions

1. Support airway, breathing, and circulation (Chapter 28).
2. Initiate gastrointestinal decontamination if the ingestion was within the previous hour.
3. Obtain serum laboratory tests to determine whether there are anion and osmolar gaps.
4. Administer an antidote, either fomepizole or ethanol. These drugs are competitive inhibitors of alcohol dehydrogenase, which is necessary for ethylene glycol metabolism.[32]
   - Fomepizole:
     - Loading dose: 15 mg/kg, administered intravenously
     - Subsequent doses: 10 mg/kg every 12 hours for four doses. Then, 15 mg/kg every 12 hours until ethylene glycol level is < 20 mg/dL
   - Ethanol:
     - Titrate an intravenous ethanol drip to achieve and maintain a blood ethanol level of 100 mg/dL
     - Monitor serum glucose levels to prevent ethanol-induced hypoglycemia
   - Administer pyridoxine, which may enhance the conversion of toxic metabolites to carbon dioxide and water.
   - Administer sodium bicarbonate to correct acidosis, which may be refractory.

5. Prepare for hemodialysis.
   - Hemodialysis is required if the ethylene glycol level is greater than 50 mg/dL

Special Considerations

- Small amounts of ethylene glycol can cause significant toxicity and death. Parents and others may underestimate the danger from small ingestions, because the child is typically asymptomatic for many hours.
- The best time to recognize and treat ethylene glycol poisoning is before any symptoms occur. Onset of symptoms indicates the presence of toxic metabolites, with the likelihood of significant CNS and renal consequences, including permanent renal damage and peripheral neuropathies in children who survive.

Methanol

Sources

- Windshield washer fluid (nearly 100% methanol)
- Some gasoline additives
- Chafing dish fuel
- Model airplane fuel

Route of Exposure

- Oral

Mechanism of Toxicity

- Methanol is metabolized briefly to formaldehyde, then to formic acid and other organic acids.
- Formic acid is responsible for optic nerve changes, leading to permanent blindness.
- Significant acidosis also is characteristic of this poisoning.
- Symptoms are caused by metabolites; therefore, no symptoms or vague symptoms occur for 10 to 12 hours or longer after ingestion. Then, the child will complain of such ocular symptoms as dim, blurred, or double vision.
- Symptoms of inebriation, abdominal pain, and lethargy also may occur, followed by seizures and coma.
- Anion gap metabolic acidosis will be pronounced, and there will be a widened osmolar gap.

Focused History

- A high index of suspicion is essential
- Time of symptom onset
- Access to methanol-containing fluids

Focused Physical Assessment

- Neurologic system
  - Ocular symptoms such as dim, blurred, or double vision
- Metabolic system
  - Metabolic acidosis

Laboratory Tests

- Serum methanol levels
- Serum ethanol levels
- Arterial blood gases

Nursing Interventions

1. Support airway, breathing, and circulation (Chapter 28).
2. Obtain blood for laboratory tests; determine whether anion and osmolar gaps are present.
3. Perform gastrointestinal decontamination if the ingestion was within the previous hour.
4. Administer an antidote, either fomepizole or ethanol. These drugs are competitive inhibitors of alcohol dehydrogenase, which is necessary for methanol metabolism.[32]
   - Fomepizole:
     - Loading dose: 15 mg/kg, administered intravenously
     - Subsequent doses: 10 mg/kg every 12 hours for four doses. Then, 15 mg/kg every 12 hours until methanol level is < 20 mg/dL
   - Ethanol:
     - Titrate an intravenous ethanol drip to achieve and maintain a serum ethanol level of 100 mg/dL
     - Monitor serum glucose levels to prevent ethanol-induced hypoglycemia
     - Both ethanol and methanol are metabolized by alcohol dehydrogenase; when both agents are present, alcohol dehydrogenase will preferentially metabolize ethanol. Maintenance of serum ethanol level of 100 mg/dL prevents generation of toxic metabolites of methanol
5. Administer folic acid:
   - It enhances the conversion of toxic metabolites to nontoxic compounds; leucovorin may be given instead if the child is still asymptomatic.
6. Administer sodium bicarbonate to correct acidosis, which may be refractory.
7. Prepare for hemodialysis.

- Hemodialysis is required if the methanol level is greater than 50 mg/dL

8. Continuously assess the child's neurologic status.

9. Obtain ophthalmologic consultation; hyperemic discs are characteristic of early methanol poisoning.

Special Considerations

- Methanol is toxic in small amounts, and symptoms are delayed. Parents may underestimate the danger to children who are playing nearby when someone is working on a car.

- The best time to institute treatment is before symptoms occur. Otherwise, permanent blindness and permanent peripheral neuropathies are possible in patients who survive.

Hydrocarbons

Sources

- Gasoline
- Kerosene
- Turpentine
- Lighter fluid
- Charcoal lighter fluid
- Furniture polish
- Lamp oil
- All hydrocarbons of low or relatively low viscosity

Routes of Exposure

- Oral
- Dermal
- Ocular
- Inhalation

Mechanism of Toxicity

The toxicity of hydrocarbons differs, depending on the route of exposure.

Ingestion Exposure

Sources

- Gasoline
- Kerosene
- Turpentine
- Lighter fluid
- Charcoal lighter fluid
- Furniture polish

- Lamp oil
- All hydrocarbons of low or relatively low viscosity

Mechanism of Toxicity

- Toxicity occurs from aspiration into the lungs, not actual ingestion.
- Aspiration of even small amounts of hydrocarbons may result in disruption of surfactant with alveolar collapse, respiratory irritation, and pneumonitis.
- Hypoxia produces cyanosis and CNS depression.
- Initial respiratory findings include coughing, wheezing, and rales.
- Pneumonitis produces typical systemic effects of infection, including fever.

Focused History

- Ascertain whether the child coughed or choked. If either occurred when the child attempted to swallow the product, the risk of aspiration is great.
- Time of ingestion

Focused Physical Assessment

- Respiratory system. Assess signs of respiratory distress, such as coughing, wheezing, rales.

Laboratory Tests

- Arterial blood gases

Nursing Interventions

1. For all ingestions, support airway, breathing, and circulation (Chapter 28).

2. For ingestion without evidence of aspiration, dilute the hydrocarbon. Observe at home for 24 hours for the development of respiratory effects.

3. If child has a history of coughing or choking while ingesting a hydrocarbon, but currently is asymptomatic, support respiratory function. Obtain a chest radiograph, no sooner than 2 hours after the event, to assess pulmonary changes. If, at 2 hours, the chest radiograph is negative and the child remains asymptomatic with no signs of pulmonary damage, the child may be discharged home. The poison center will follow up for 24 hours for the unlikely development of delayed pulmonary effects. If the child has symptoms and/ or the chest radiography shows signs of pulmonary damage, admit the child for observation.[33]

4. If child presents with respiratory symptoms,

support respiratory function, obtain a chest radiograph immediately, and admit for symptomatic and supportive care.

Special Considerations

❑ Parents are often unaware that tiny amounts of these products can be dangerous or even fatal to their children. Products such as charcoal lighter fluid, lamp oils, and furniture polish are often within children's reach. On the other hand, parents are alarmed by labels advising that "Ingestion can be fatal." In fact, ingestion is not fatal, but aspiration can be.

Ocular and Dermal Exposures

Sources

❑ Gasoline

❑ Kerosene

❑ Turpentine

❑ Lighter fluid

❑ Charcoal lighter fluid

❑ Furniture polish

❑ Lamp oil

❑ All hydrocarbons of low or relatively low viscosity

Routes of Exposure

❑ Eye

❑ Skin

Mechanism of Toxicity

❑ These products have a defatting action on both skin and ocular tissue.

❑ Depending on the duration of exposure, effects may range from mild irritation or corneal abrasion to corneal burns.

❑ Likewise, effects on the skin range from mild irritation to full-thickness burns after lengthy contact, such as might occur if someone is trapped under a vehicle in a pool of spilled gasoline.

Focused History

❑ Time of exposure

❑ Duration of exposure

Focused Physical Assessment

❑ Eye: Ocular pain, tearing, redness

❑ Integumentary system: Partial, deep-partial, and full-thickness burns

Laboratory Tests

❑ Obtain blood for laboratory analysis for significant dermal injury, as with thermal burns (Chapter 37).

Nursing Interventions

1. Support airway, breathing, and circulation (Chapter 28).

2. For ocular exposures, initiate irrigation of the eye. If there is evidence of ocular pain or irritation after irrigation, obtain ophthalmologic consultation for possible corneal injury.

3. For dermal exposure, initiate irrigation. Remove the patient's contaminated clothing.

▪ Initiate burn wound care (Chapter 37).

Inhalation Exposure

Sources

❑ All of the aforementioned sources plus butane, propane, toluene, and other hydrocarbons used as aerosol propellants and solvents; helium; nitrous oxide

Routes of Exposure

❑ Workplace use in areas with insufficient ventilation

❑ Deliberate abuse by "huffing," "bagging," or "sniffing"[34]

Mechanism of Toxicity

❑ In most cases, the mechanism of toxicity is displacement of oxygen and asphyxiation. Hypoxia leads to euphoria (the desired effect for inhalant abusers), sensitization of the myocardium, and an increase in circulating catecholamines, resulting in the sudden onset of ventricular fibrillation and death.

Focused History

❑ Workplace exposure: Determine whether other victims were exposed, as one or more workers along with unprotected rescuers may become unconscious.

❑ Suspected abuse exposure: Determine the product name, because some hydrocarbons are associated with toxicities other than the consequences of hypoxia, especially with long-term use.

Focused Physical Assessment

❑ Respiratory system: Respiratory distress

❑ Cardiovascular system: Dysrhythmias

❑ Neurologic system: Altered level of consciousness

Laboratory Tests

❏ Although many hydrocarbons can be evaluated in the laboratory, these tests are not available and not helpful to ED personnel, and are often used for forensic purposes instead.

Nursing Interventions

1. Support airway, breathing, and circulation (Chapter 28).

2. Initiate measures to control seizures and treat dysrhythmias.

3. Follow up with the involved workplace management; consider reporting to the Occupational Safety and Health Administration (OSHA).

4. Follow up with counseling for intentional abuse.

Special Considerations

❏ *Sudden sniffing death syndrome* describes the outcome of concentrating and inhaling hydrocarbons and some other substances such as nitrous oxide: A sudden shout, running for several yards, then collapsing in ventricular fibrillation. Parents are usually unaware of inhalant abuse by their children, because the products abused are legal and readily available.

Organophosphate Insecticides

Sources

❏ Numerous products intended for indoor and outdoor residential applications, by homeowners and professional pest control applicators, and agricultural pesticides (diazinon, Dursban, fenthion, malathion, and many others)

Routes of Exposure

❏ Ingestion

❏ Inhalation

❏ Dermal

❏ Toxicity is the same by all routes of exposure

Mechanism of Toxicity

❏ Organophosphate insecticides are acetylcholinesterase inhibitors. By binding to acetylcholinesterase, they allow continued action of acetylcholine at receptor sites throughout the nervous system. They also prevent the hydrolysis of acetylcholine and the reuptake of choline into presynaptic nerve cells. If not disrupted, the acetylcholinesterase-organophosphate bond becomes permanent in about 24 hours. The initial result is excessive cholinergic stimulation, eventually followed by depletion of acetylcholine and decreased cholinergic stimulation.

❏ Muscarinic effects can be remembered by the mnemonic "SLUDGE": *S*alivation, *L*acrimation, *U*rination, *D*efecation, *G*astrointestinal (nausea, diarrhea), *E*yes (pinpoint pupils)/*E*mesis.

❏ Nicotinic effects can be remembered by the mnemonic "MTWtHF": *M*ydriasis, muscle twitching, and muscle cramps; *T*achycardia; *W*eakness; *H*ypertension; *F*asciculations. CNS effects include lethargy, seizure, and coma. What the mnemonic does not describe is significant bronchorrhea, which may present the biggest challenge in early ED management.

Focused History

❏ Product name

❏ Amount of product involved in the exposure

❏ Routes of exposure

❏ Time of exposure

Focused Physical Assessment

❏ Respiratory system: Bronchorrhea

❏ Cardiovascular system: Tachycardia and hypertension

❏ Neurologic status: Lethargy, seizures, and coma

Laboratory Tests

❏ Red blood cell cholinesterase level

❏ The more easily obtained plasma cholinesterase level is less useful because it can be affected by many things besides actual acetylcholinesterase inhibition

Nursing Interventions

1. For all exposures:
   ▪ Support airway, breathing, and circulation (Chapter 28).

2. Ingestion exposure:
   ▪ Initiate gastrointestinal decontamination if indicated.[35]
   ▪ Administer an intravenous infusion of atropine.
     • Atropine occupies muscarinic acetylcholine receptor sites and terminates symptoms of cholinergic excess.
     • Titrate atropine to the production of bronchial secretions.
     • Repeat the dose as needed to keep the bronchial tree clear.

- The pediatric dose is 0.05 mg/kg, repeated every 10 to 30 minutes as necessary. The endpoint is not a specific total dose, but drying of pulmonary secretions.
- Auscultate for the disappearance of rales, and observe for lessening of bronchorrhea.
- Monitor for tachycardia. (If administration of atropine results in significant tachycardia, organophosphate poisoning is unlikely to be the cause of the patient's symptoms.)

- Administer an intravenous infusion of pralidoxime (2-PAM).
  - 2-PAM cleaves the organophosphate-acetylcholinesterase bond before it becomes permanent.
  - Administration of 2-PAM can begin concurrently with atropine, but must begin within 24 hours of exposure, before the organophosphate-acetylcholinesterase bond becomes permanent. The dose is 25 to 50 mg/kg. This dose may be repeated in 1 hour and then every 6 to 12 hours as needed. The goal is not a specific amount but relief of muscle weakness, especially diaphragmatic weakness. Both drugs may be needed for days, depending on the half-life of the pesticide and its degree of fat solubility.

3. Dermal exposure:
- Initiate decontamination procedures (Chapter 43).
- Discard any contaminated leather garments, belts, shoes, etc.; leather is skin and absorbs these chemicals.

Special Considerations

❒ The amounts of atropine and 2-PAM needed may seem excessive to the emergency nurse unfamiliar with organophosphate insecticide poisoning. Fearful of tachycardia or other effects of atropine "overdose," the emergency nurse may be reluctant to administer the large amounts needed. In fact, a seriously poisoned child can tolerate the huge amounts needed, up to several grams of atropine over the course of treatment. It cannot be overemphasized that sufficient amounts of these drugs are the mainstays of treatment of this life-threatening poisoning.

❒ ED personnel may be contaminated by patients' clothing and emesis. Personal protective clothing may be necessary.[36]

❒ Other ED patients may be at risk if someone contaminated with significant amounts of organophosphate compounds is admitted before being decontaminated.

Conclusion

Children experiencing poison exposures or poisonings, and their care providers, benefit greatly from the advice rendered by poison centers. Poison centers offer expert advice about recognizing and treating poison exposures 24 hours a day, 7 days a week. Regional poison centers are staffed by board-certified medical toxicologists, board-certified clinical toxicologists, and registered nurses and pharmacists who are nationally certified as specialists in poison information.

Emergency nurses who contact their local poison center gain the obvious immediate benefit of expert, individualized treatment advice. Other benefits of contacting the poison center include:

❒ Follow-up by the poison center, whether the child is discharged home or admitted to an inpatient unit, assuring continuity of care.

❒ Anonymous entry of the child's case into the only national database of human poison exposures, the American Association of Poison Control Centers National Poison Data System. Cases from poison centers nationwide are uploaded to this national database approximately every 5 minutes. In addition to tabulating poison exposures and their associated medical outcomes, this system identifies potential public health emergencies, for example clinical indications of a chemical or biological weapons exposure. It also identifies trends in poisonings and previously unsuspected hazards amenable to regulatory action or educational intervention. These data also guide research to improve the recognition and treatment of poisoning.

Every poison center in the United States may be reached by calling 1-800-222-1222. Callers are automatically connected to the local poison center.

References

1. Bronstein, A. C., Spyker, D. A., Cantilena, L. C., Green, J. L., Rumack, B. H., Heard, S. E., et al. (2008). 2007 Annual report of the American Association of Poison Control Centers' National Poison Data System. *Clinical Toxicology, 46,* 927–1057.

2. Centers for Disease Control and Prevention. (2007). Unintentional poisoning deaths—United States, 1999–2004. *Morbidity and Mortality Weekly Report, 56,* 93–96.

3. Litovitz, T. L., & Schmitz, B. F. (1992). Ingestion of cylindrical and button batteries: An analysis of 2382 cases. *Pediatrics, 89*(4), 747–757.

4. Boutis, K. & Shannon, M. (2001). Nephrotoxicity after acute severe acetaminophen poisoning in adolescents. *Clinical Toxicology, 39*(5), 441–445.

5. Larson, A. M. (2007). Acetaminophen hepatotoxicity. *Clinics in Liver Disease, 11,* 525–548.

6. Marzullo, L. (2005). An update of N-acetylcysteine treatment for acute acetaminophen toxicity in children. *Current Opinion in Pediatrics, 17,* 239–245.

7. Kerr, G. W., McGuffie, A. C., & Wilkie, S. (2001). Tricyclic antidepressant overdose: A review. *Emergency Medicine Journal, 18,* 236–241.

8. Rosenbaum, T. G., & Kou, M. (2005). Are one or two dangerous? Tricyclic antidepressant exposure in toddlers. *Journal of Emergency Medicine, 28*(2), 169–174.

9. Liebelt, E. (2006). Cyclic antidepressants. In N. E. Flomenbaum, L. R. Goldfrank, R. S. Hoffman, M. A. Howland, N. A. Lewin, & L. S. Nelson (Eds.). *Goldfrank's toxicologic emergencies* (8th ed., pp. 1083–1097). New York: Appleton & Lange.

10. Lee, D. C., Green, T., Dougherty, T., & Pearigen, P. (2000). Fatal nifedipine ingestions in children. *Journal of Emergency Medicine, 19*(4), 359–361.

11. Kerns, W. (2007). Management of ß-adrenergic blocker and calcium channel antagonist toxicity. *Emergency Medicine Clinics of North America, 25,* 309–331.

12. Gowda, R. M., Cohen, R. A., & Khan, I. A. (2003). Toad venom poisoning: Resemblance to digoxin toxicity and therapeutic implications. *Heart, 89*(4), e14.

13. McCarron, M. M., Challoner, K. R., & Thompson, G. A. (1991). Diphenoxylate-atropine (Lomotil) overdose in children: An update (report of eight cases and review of the literature). *Pediatrics, 8*(5), 694–700.

14. Tenenbein, M. (2001). Iron. In M. D. Ford, K. A. Kelaney, L. J. Ling, & T. Erickson (Eds.), *Clinical toxicology* (pp. 305–309). Philadelphia: Saunders.

15. Howland, M. A. (2006). Deferoxamine. In N. E. Flomenbaum, L. R. Goldfrank, R. S. Hoffman, M. A. Howland, N. A. Lewin, & L. S. Nelson (Eds.), *Goldfrank's toxicologic emergencies* (8th ed., pp. 638–642). New York: Appleton & Lange.

16. Aldridge, M. D. (2007). Acute iron poisoning: What every pediatric intensive care unit nurse should know. *Dimensions of Critical Care Nursing, 26*(2), 43–48.

17. Caksen, H., Odabas, D., Erol, M., Anlar, O., Tuncer, T., & Atas, B. (2003). Do not overlook acute isoniazid poisoning in children with status epilepticus. *Journal of Child Neurology, 18,* 142–143.

18. Maw, G., & Aitkin, P. (2003). Isoniazid overdose: A case series, literature review and survey of antidote availability. *Clinical Drug Investigation, 23*(7), 479–485.

19. Rowden, A. K., & Fasano, C. J. (2007). Emergency management of oral hypoglycemic drug toxicity. *Emergency Medicine Clinics of North America, 25,* 347–356.

20. Little, G. L., & Boniface, K. S. (2005). Are one or two dangerous? Sulfonylurea exposure in toddlers. *Journal of Emergency Medicine, 28*(30), 305–310.

21. O'Malley, G. F. (2007). Emergency department management of the salicylate-poisoned patient. *Emergency Medicine Clinics of North America, 25,* 333–346.

22. Bateman, D. A., & Heagarty, M. C. (1989). Passive freebase cocaine ("crack") inhalation by infants and toddlers. *American Journal of Diseases of Children, 143,* 25–27.

23. Chaney, N. E., Franke, J., & Wadlington, W. G. (1988). Cocaine convulsions in a breast-feeding baby. *Journal of Pediatrics 112*(1), 134–135.

24. Mokhlesi, B., Garimella, P. S., Joffe, A., & Velho, V. (2004). Street drug abuse leading to critical illness. *Intensive Care Medicine, 30,* 1526–1536.

25. Farst, K., Duncan, J. M, Moss, M., Ray, R. M., Kokoska, E., & James, L. P. (2007). Methamphetamine exposure presenting as caustic ingestions in children. *Annals of Emergency Medicine, 49*(3), 341–343.

26. Massa, N., & Ludemann, J. P. (2004). Pediatric caustic ingestion and parental cocaine abuse. *International Journal of Pediatric Otorhinolaryngology, 68,* 1513–1517.

References (continued)

27. Camp, N. E. (2005). Understanding the assessment and treatment of caustic ingestions and the resulting burns. *Journal of Emergency Nursing, 31*(6), 594–596.

28. Bertolini, J. C. (1992). Hydrofluoric acid: A review of toxicity. *Journal of Emergency Medicine, 10,* 163–166.

29. Klasner, A. E., Scalzo, A. J., Blume, C., Johnson, P., & Thompson, M. W. (1996). Marked hypocalcemia and ventricular fibrillation in two pediatric patients exposed to a fluoride-containing wheel cleaner. *Annals of Emergency Medicine, 28*(6), 713–718.

30. Salzman, M., & O'Malley, R. N. (2007). Updates on the evaluation and management of caustic exposures. *Emergency Medicine Clinics of North America, 25,* 459–476.

31. Haynes, J. F. (2006). Medical management of adolescent drug overdoses. *Adolescent Medicine Clinics, 17,* 353–379.

32. Betten, D. P., Vohra, R. B., Cook, M. D., Matteucci, M. J., & Clark, R. F. (2006). Antidote use in the critically ill poisoned patient. *Journal of Intensive Care Medicine, 22*(5), 255–277.

33. Lewander, W. J., & Aleguas, A. (2007). Petroleum distillates and plant hydrocarbons. In M. W. Shannon, S. W. Borron, & M. J. Burns (Eds.), *Haddad and Winchester's clinical management of poisoning and drug overdoses* (4th ed., pp. 1343–1346). Philadelphia: Saunders.

34. Williams, J. F., Storck, M., & Committee on Substance Abuse and Committee on Native American Child Health. (2007). Inhalant abuse. *Pediatrics, 119*(5), 1009–1017.

35. Roberts, D. M., & Aaron, C. K. (2007). Managing acute organophosphorus pesticide poisoning. *British Medical Journal, 334,* 629–634.

36. Centers for Disease Control and Prevention. (2001). Nosocomial poisoning associated with emergency department treatment of organophosphate toxicity—Georgia, 2000. *Morbidity and Mortality Weekly Report, 49*(51), 1156–1158.

37. American Academy of Clinical Toxicology & European Association of Poisons Centres and Clinical Toxicologists. (1999). Position statement and practice guidelines on the use of multi-dose activated charcoal in the treatment of acute poisoning. *Clinical Toxicology, 37*(6), 731–751.

38. Kaczorowski, J. M., & Was, P. (1996). Five days of whole-bowel irrigation in a case of pediatric iron ingestion. *Annals of Emergency Medicine, 27*(2), 258–263.

FORTY-THREE

Nuclear, Biological, and Chemical Emergencies

Michael Beach DNP, ACNP-BC, PNP

Introduction

Children are at significant risk, as are adults, for exposure to nuclear, biological, and chemical exposure through either unintentional or intentional exposure.[1] Although, as of this writing, no significant intentional incident has occurred in the United States since the September 11, 2001, attacks, the risk for terrorist attack remains real. Hazardous chemicals that may be used for a terrorist attack remain available. These, including nerve agents, vesicants, poisons, and irritants, pose a significant risk for intentional release causing great harm. Also, large amounts of hazardous materials (HAZMAT) are transported daily through rural and metropolitan areas, by truck and rail, creating the potential for significant unintentional exposure. Cities and towns large enough to have water treatment facilities store chlorine, a chemical with the potential to cause significant irritation and respiratory concerns. Other hazardous materials are involved in manufacturing and processing in most of the industries that citizens have come to depend on for normal life.[1] While every step possible is taken to make the storage and shipment of these chemicals the safest possible, the risk of chemical spills remains.

Biological and infectious disease concerns such as pandemic infections from the H1N1 flu or other viral or bacterial agents also remain significant. With today's mobile lifestyle, world travel is common creating a rich environment for the spread of biological agents to which people may have little resistance. Intentional release of a number of potential biological agents is a significant concern. In the past, these attempts may have been limited by the intention of the terrorist to live after the attack. In today's world of suicide bombers, this may not be a limiting factor.

Nuclear material used to manufacture a nuclear fusion or fission device is tightly controlled and may be difficult to obtain, but thousands of devices were manufactured by world powers during and after the cold war and still exist; some of these devices are rumored to be as small as a briefcase. Besides nuclear explosions of devastating effect, conventional explosives packed with radioactive material detonated in a highly populated area or one essential to the economy or environment would cause panic and injury and might create an area uninhabitable for a very long time.

All of these scenarios would affect children and adults; often, however, children have special needs and concerns. Children have a significantly larger body surface area for their size than adults. This may leave them more at risk from contamination. Children are also not fully developed making the potential long-term effects of disease and illness from nuclear, chemical, and biological exposure more significant. Last, children are often quite resilient, but the effects of an unintentional or intentional biological, chemical, or nuclear event on family, friends, and all they know could be significant, creating lasting psychological issues.[1-4] The purpose of this chapter is to apply principles of disaster preparedness to the pediatric population.

Pediatric Considerations

Developmental Factors

Infants

Young families are often very mobile today and may live near transportation routes used by trucking or rail industries. This may increase their infants' risk for unintentional exposure from a hazardous material spill. In the same sense, they are at risk of exposure from an intentional release of nuclear, biological, or chemical agents. They are at risk from both direct exposure and contact or "offgassing" from a caregiver's clothing.[1,4]

Toddlers and Preschoolers

Toddlers and preschoolers have an increased risk of exposure from curiosity and exploration because they are mobile and often choose to taste everything with which they come in contact. As with infants, they are also at risk from exposure of hazardous agents as they travel with their parents and caregivers or if they live near industry or transportation routes.[1,4,5]

School-aged Children and Adolescents

School-aged children have become more and more independent and mobile. School and social activities create a life independent of parents, and traveling about the community may place them outside the supervision of adults. They are intensely curious without significant fear of death or injury. They lack the experiences that instill caution in most adults. Adolescents are even more mobile after they have earned the right to drive, which increases risk of exposure as they travel highways or near rail lines. Violence, an increasing concern in today's society, may also lead to exposure to irritants such as self-defense sprays or tear gas. These agents are preferable to more lethal defensive and offensive weapons.[1,4,5]

Household Factors

Household cleaners, bleaches, toilet and drain cleaners, paints, solvents, and a variety of sprays are common in most homes. Although some may be out of reach of or locked away from curious children, often there may be others left within reach. Toddlers and curious school-aged children and adolescents are often at risk for unintentional or purposeful exposure. Huffing, or breathing in toxic solvents or chemicals, may or may not be in style at any given moment but always seems to be an issue for some children. Curiosity may also be the motivation for ingestion of very toxic and irritating chemicals. Close living quarters and large ethnic families may also contribute to the spread of infectious disease such as tuberculosis or various strains of influenza or from the intentional release of any number of biological agents. The mobility of other families and the increasingly large distances between family members as they spread across the country may also contribute to the spread of biological agents from an intentional or natural outbreak.[1,4]

Environmental Factors

Often chemicals used in industrial and commercial settings are more powerful than those commonly used in the home. Transportation and storage of these agents always pose a threat of spill or leakage. Children may be at risk of exposure to these chemicals through the school environment directly or through proximity to industry or transportation routes.[1,4,6]

Physiologic Factors

Several factors may cause greater effects of hazardous materials on children. These may include a faster metabolic rate, faster respirations than adults, and a greater body surface area to mass ratio, each increasing the absorption or effect of the offending agent. Pediatric physiologic factors that can influence the absorption of the substance and its systemic effects are listed in Table 43.1.[1–4,6]

Etiology

Children are at risk for exposure to many biological, chemical, and nuclear agents from a variety of sources. Although seemingly rare, the potential for unintentional or intentional exposure is high. Because children are in many ways uniquely at risk from the effects of these agents, there should be strong concerns and awareness from parents, caregivers, and authorities.

There are physiologically four main routes of entry into the body: inhalation, absorption, ingestion, and injection. Of these, inhalation, absorption, and ingestion are of greatest concern in the pediatric population:[6]

❐ *Inhalation.* Inhalation involves the breathing in of vapors or dust from a hazardous material. Inhalation may be the route of choice for some gases such as chlorine or phosgene and may also be a significant entry point for radioactive dust from a "dirty bomb." Inhalation allows the agent great contact to the bloodstream through alveolar capillary exchange. Other agents work primarily on the lungs causing significant long-term effects. Children are at increased risk for inhalation-related exposure compared to adults because:

   ▪ They are shorter in height and closer to the ground where many chemicals and toxins are more concentrated.

   ▪ Their respiratory and heart rates are faster, which allows more of the toxin to enter the lungs and bloodstream.

❐ *Chemical agents* are irritants to the airways and mucous membranes, causing the victim to leave the scene immediately. Others pose no such irritation to warn the victims of potentially life-threatening exposures.

❐ *Biological agents* may prefer the lungs as their source of entry into the body or may be spread through droplets from coughs or simple breathing. Although some agents, such as anthrax, pose no communicable threat, others spread through droplet and airborne transmission, such as smallpox. With anthrax, the intentional release of spores is an inhalation threat. Botulism is not an inhalation threat under normal circumstances; however, inhalation botulism remains a potential terrorist threat.

❐ *Absorption.* Although the skin remains an effective barrier against most substances, there are those agents

TABLE 43.1 Physiologic Considerations in Pediatric HAZMAT and Biohazard Exposures

Physiologic Differences in Children	Nursing Considerations
Smaller body mass and larger body surface area affect absorption and severity of effects.	More rapid absorption of hazardous materials and more serious systemic effects can occur. Children have an increased risk of absorption of chemicals and toxicity from skin exposure. Children's larger body surface area makes temperature control difficult, and copious amounts of water used in decontamination may lead to hypothermia.
Smaller airways can easily obstruct with minimal swelling.	Pediatric inhalation exposures of toxic and irritating agents can quickly lead to respiratory distress.
Skin is thinner and more fragile.	Children have an increased risk of absorption of chemicals and toxicity from skin exposure.
Higher respiratory rate contributes to alveolar ventilation that can be as great as that in an adult.	Any respiratory contact with hazardous materials can lead to more significant effects in a child than in an adult in the same situation. Even with low levels of contaminants in the air, a child's high respiratory rate and rapid pulmonary air exchange can lead to a significant exposure over time.
The child's immune system is immature.	Children are more susceptible to infections or illness for which they have not been immunized.
The child's vascular and gastrointestinal system can absorb materials quickly.	Hazardous materials can be transported rapidly into the circulatory system and reach lethal levels.
Heart rate is faster.	Children have a faster heart rate, which causes the toxin to move through the body faster.

that are designed to penetrate the skin. Absorption is the passing of a substance through the skin into the capillary system. As compared to adults, children, especially infants through preschool-age, may be at particular risk for absorption because of their:

- large body surface area in relation to their mass.
- lack of experience or cognitive function to remove themselves from a potentially hazardous situation.
- thinner skin and higher water content.

❏ *Chemical agents.* Nerve agents and their precursor, insecticides, are absorbed through the skin and have significant systemic effects. Some agents are designed to or do have the unintentional effect on the skin itself, inflicting burns or infections that destroy the skin and its function as a barrier. Vesicants such as mustard gas cause significant burns to those exposed. Because they are absorbed by the clothing, skin contact and the effects of the agent are increased. Other chemicals, such as solvents, also cause burns but do so to a lesser degree.

❏ *Ingestion.* Ingestion, in this instance, is the absorption of toxic materials from the gastrointestinal (GI) tract. Materials may be ingested intentionally or unintentionally. The absorption begins with the mucous membranes of the mouth and continues throughout the GI tract. Hazardous materials in contact with portions of the GI tract can cause local and often systemic effects.

- Chemical agents that can be ingested include gasoline, antifreeze, household cleaning products, and both acidic and alkaloid substances. Some substances may saturate the body, releasing hazardous fumes (off-gassing) from the body. Off-gassing occurs when the body becomes so saturated with a chemical that the chemical is released from the body through the skin. It may then be inhaled or absorbed by health care workers caring for the victim. Examples include pesticides and fertilizers. This off-gassing of a hazardous material from a patient can put emergency nurses at risk if they are not adequately prepared.[7]

- Biological agents, such as anthrax and botulism, can be ingested through contaminated foods.

Assessing and Treating a Child Involved in a Biological, Chemical, or Nuclear Incident

Focused History

While it is essential for both the victim and health care providers to gather as much information as possible concerning the exposure event,[6] at no time should the victim be allowed to place health care providers or the emergency department (ED) at risk of contamination or injury.[6] In the case of unknown toxic agents, health care providers need to assume that they are at risk and wear appropriate protective clothing. This includes rubber boots, double rubber gloves, Tyvek® or other impervious overalls, and a powered air purifying respirator (PAPR) hood with an appropriate filtered respirator. Unknown biological agents require full isolation gowns, gloves, mask, and eye protection. Nuclear incidents should be treated as chemical incidents under the control of experts from the radiology department. The following are important components of the history.

Chemical

- ❏ Type or characteristics of the agent. The type of agent may be available from the child's parents or caregivers or EMS. If unknown, as in potential mass exposures, the characteristics may help direct treatment. (Some methods and resources for hazardous material identification are listed in Tables 43.2 and 43.3.)
- ❏ Length of time the victim was exposed to the agent.
- ❏ Length of time from the exposure to ED presentation.
- ❏ Concentration of the substance.
- ❏ Exposure in a confined or open area.
- ❏ Route of exposure: inhalation, ingestion, or absorption.
- ❏ Presence of continued sources of contamination such as caregivers, vehicles, or the home.
- ❏ The history or identification of others who may be exposed.
- ❏ Treatment rendered prior to ED presentation.

Biological

- ❏ Onset of signs and symptoms.
- ❏ Current and recent illnesses. Many biological agents have a prodromal period followed by a partial recovery.
- ❏ Others either in or close to the family who are symptomatic.
- ❏ Common food or gathering source, for example, whether everyone ate the same food or attended the same event.
- ❏ Treatment rendered prior to ED presentation.

Nuclear

- ❏ Type of nuclear incident.
- ❏ Type of nuclear material, if known.
- ❏ Traumatic injuries.
- ❏ Chances of inhalation or ingestion of contaminated material.
- ❏ Length of time the victim was exposed before removal from the site and decontamination.
- ❏ Proximity of the victim to the source of radiation.
- ❏ Onset of signs and symptoms of radiation poisoning beginning after exposure.
- ❏ Treatment rendered prior to ED presentation.

Decontamination and Initial Assessment

For chemical and nuclear incidents, it is essential for the victim, as well as the providers and the emergency department, that the victim be decontaminated at the scene as soon as possible. It should also be assumed that victims will present to the emergency department through family and Good Samaritans without decontamination. Because of this possibility, ED personnel should be prepared to provide decontamination, utilizing proper protective clothing and decontamination equipment and following established protocols. The only assessment that should be done before decontamination is brief initial assessment of the ABCDs: Airway, Breathing, Circulation, and Disability. Although some initial steps may be taken to correct these, the extent of intervention is dependent on the number of victims and the availability of resources. A thorough head-to-toe assessment should be completed after proper decontamination.

Triage Considerations

Triage has different priorities when dealing with mass casualty incidents (MCI) or when the number of victims is limited and does not overwhelm the system. When there are a few victims, all available resources are used to care for the victims no matter how severe their injuries and how slim their chance of survival.[8–10] In a MCI or disaster event, triage decisions center on who can be saved with the available limited resources and who will be allowed to die. This will be extremely difficult when evaluating children.[6,11–14]

TABLE 43.2 Resources for Hazardous Material Identification

Resource	Description/Comments
Federal Emergency Management Agency http://www.fema.gov/index.shtm	This site is a source of educational independent studies and other resources dealing with disaster and mass casualty preparation.
U.S. Department of Health and Human Services, Agency for Healthcare Research and Quality http://www.ahrq.gov/	This site is a source of information of regulations and planning for emergencies.
Center for Disease Control and Prevention http://www.cdc.gov/	This site is a source of information concerning disease diagnosis, treatment, and reporting.
U.S. Department of Transportation Identification Standards	This agency establishes identification standards for transporting hazardous materials. This system has been designed as a national standard to help reduce confusion in chemical transport and can be cross-referenced for more information. Transportation vehicles are required to have several placards visible that list the following: ▪ The hazardous properties of the material. ▪ A four-digit number for identification of the material.
Material Safety Data Sheet (MSDS)	Government regulations require businesses to maintain a MSDS for every chemical used. Each data sheet describes the exposure risks of the material, serious dosage levels, treatment, and chemicals contained in the substance.
Local and national governmental agencies	These agencies provide 24-hour support and up-to-date information. They include the Chemical Transportation Emergency Center, local fire departments, and regional poison control centers (Table 43.3).

Triage in the Field during a Disaster or MCI

Triage is the most difficult and psychologically taxing position because it is vital to move quickly from victim to victim without providing more than a few basic interventions. Victims will be identified in four categories: minor, delayed, immediate, and expectant/deceased. Color-coded triage tags are used to identify the victim and the victim's status.

Minor: Victims classified as minor will wait and be the last to be treated or transported to the hospital or clinic. They have few minor injuries, and their condition is stable. They are often called the walking wounded. Their triage tag color is green.

Delayed: Those victims who are classified as delayed are more seriously wounded but their condition remains stable. They will be treated or transported after the victims marked immediate. The delayed triage tag color is yellow.

Immediate: Those victims classified as immediate are those with life-threatening injuries who probably can be saved. These victims are treated and transported first and their triage tag color is red.

Expectant/deceased: These victims are dead at the scene or are not expected to survive. Their triage tag color is black.

Frequent reassessment of all victims, especially those in the minor and delayed category, is imperative. Victims may move up but never back in the classification system. For example, a victim may move from delayed to immediate but never from delayed to minor. Infants should be reassessed first.[11]

Although several systems exist to triage multiple victims, the JumpSTART Pediatric MCI Triage Tool [15](an adaptation of the Simple Triage and Rapid Treatment [START] system for adults), is specific to the pediatric population. This system uses a rapid assessment of a few basic parameters to judge the victim's status. The JumpSTART system first asks all those who can walk to move to a specific location; these are classified as minor. Next each remaining victim is assessed for airway, breathing, perfusion, and responsiveness. Immediate victims are treated and transported first; those who are judged not able to be saved are provided comfort measures. Victims in the delayed or minor category are treated and transported after the immediate victims.

TABLE 43.3 Hazardous Material Incident Information Resources

Agency	Description	Phone Number and Web Site (If Applicable)
Chemical Transportation Emergency Center (CHEMTREC)	24-Hour information on all hazardous products with an emphasis on transportation emergencies	1-800-262-8200 http://www.chemtrec.com/Chemtrec/
National Response Center and Terrorist Hotline	24-Hour identification of hazardous material and incident control	1-800-424-8802 http://www.nrc.uscg.mil/nrchp.html
Agency for Toxic Substances and Disease Registry	24-Hour assistance for health-related effects	http://www.atsdr.cdc.gov/
National Pesticide Information Center	Information regarding pesticide exposures	1-800-858-7378 http://nptn.orst.edu
Radiation Emergency Assistance Center/Training Site (REACTS)	Emergency consultation for radioactive incidents	1-865-576-1005 http://orise.orau.gov/reacts/
American Association of Poison Control Centers	Lists poison control centers that offer 24-Hour identification of hazardous materials and their treatment	1-800-222-1222 http://www.aapcc.org/DNN/
Centers for Disease Control and Prevention	Information on biohazards and diseases	1-888-232-4636 http://www.cdc.gov/
Federal Emergency Management Agency	Information on all hazards and disasters	1-800-621-FEMA http://www.fema.gov/

Triage in the Hospital Setting [6,16]

See Immediately

Children with any exposure to a hazardous material are triaged immediately to avoid exposure to ED staff and patients. A child exposed to a hazardous material needs to be immediately decontaminated and treated for life-threatening concerns.

☐ Rapidly identify situations where contamination exists and limit the exposure to health care providers and the emergency department. Decontaminate the victim and treat life-threatening conditions. Any areas inadvertently contaminated must be sealed for decontamination. Any personnel contaminated must be immediately decontaminated. If the condition is related to a biohazard, similar steps should be taken to isolate the victim, and staff should wear appropriate protective isolation clothing and masks.

☐ Any area where the child has been should be sealed off until it is clear that no residual contamination is present and the area has been decontaminated. Emergency department staff may need to use protective gear if immediate risks are identified.

☐ It is imperative that hazardous materials do not spread within the hospital system. If there is a risk that hazardous or biohazardous materials have been brought to the emergency department, the ED staff should not only protect themselves but involve the hospital engineers and local health department to ensure that nothing is spread in the ventilation system or to other hospital areas.

Post Triage Disposition

In a disaster or MCI, hospitals and health care systems will be overwhelmed by the number of victims and severity of injuries. Some of the victims will present from the scene with disaster tags classifying them as minor, delayed, immediate, and deceased. Immediate victims should be retriaged first and sent to the appropriate treatment area: the emergency department or directly to the operating room. Delayed and minor victims should be sent to a holding area to be treated later. Nurses will be called upon to monitor and treat these victims as necessary and may need to act without usual supervision.

Those victims presenting directly to the hospital should be triaged similar to those at the scene. The JumpSTART system works well in this initial classification of victims. Again, reassessment is vital for both minor and delayed victims because children may decompensate rapidly.

For chemical and biologic exposures, massive amounts of medications, such as atropine or antibiotics, will be required for timely patient care. Each hospital should have in place its own 'stockpile' of selected medications for this purpose. Also, ED staff should know their protocol for obtaining large volumes of these medications and supportive supplies through the Strategic National Stockpile.

Preparation for Chemical or Nuclear Decontamination

Nursing Interventions

The Joint Commission has stated that each institution must have a plan for the decontamination of patients exposed to chemical and nuclear agents. It is also important that this plan be realistic and practiced regularly. By law, each state is required to establish a state emergency response commission (SERC) and local emergency planning committees (LEPC).[1] The emergency department should work with these agencies, as well as local fire and emergency agencies, to establish a coordinated plan that is practical and useful.[4,18] Not only does this type of plan improve communication, but it can maximize the efficient use of resources and establish important roles in a contamination emergency before it occurs.[1]

Personal protective gear should be provided for staff involved with decontaminating a contaminated child. The U.S. Environmental Protection Agency has identified and defined four levels of protection for working with hazardous materials.[19]

☐ *Level A* provides the highest level of protection with a completely sealed impervious suit with a completely self-contained breathing apparatus. This is used when the substance is unknown or the specific substance requires this level of protection.

☐ *Level B* protection involves disposable chemical-resistant coveralls of a protective material such as Tyvek®; double-gloving with nitrile gloves, rubber over-boots, and duct tape for sealing all seams and openings; and a self-contained breathing apparatus.

☐ *Level C* protection can be achieved with a full-face air-purifying respirator with a multichemical filter cartridge; disposable chemical-resistant coveralls of a protective material such as Tyvek®; and double-gloving with nitrile gloves, rubber over-boots, and duct tape for sealing all seams and openings. Level C was developed specifically for use in the hospital environment where the substance is known.

☐ *Level D* is the standard uniform and precautions normally used on a day-to-day basis.

Prehospital Decontamination

☐ All decontamination should occur at the scene of the exposure in the established hot, warm and cold zones.

   ▪ Hot zone: The hot zone is established where the contamination occurred. Only life-threatening conditions are treated in the hot zone.

   ▪ Warm zone: The warm zone is where decontamination occurs; life-threatening conditions are treated concurrently. Special consideration to wind and movement of the chemical or radiation should be given as the location of decontamination equipment is established.

   ▪ Cold zone: As victims are decontaminated, they move into the cold zone where ideally there is no contamination.

ED Decontamination

Even though all decontamination should occur at the scene of the exposure, many victims will bring themselves and their children directly to the hospital before being triaged and decontaminated at the scene. Therefore, the emergency department must be prepared to decontaminate victims and those who have come in contact with them. Under these circumstances, the hot, warm and cold zones are established. Only life-threatening conditions are treated in the hot and warm zones, concurrent with decontamination. Level C protective clothing is worn for this process. Emergency nurses should be sufficiently trained to identify a potential exposure as quickly as possible and well trained in preparation and response. Resuscitation supplies should be available, and nurses should practice their use under these potentially extreme circumstances. Other considerations for establishing a decontamination area are listed in Table 43.4.

☐ Hot zone: As with decontamination at the scene, a hot zone is created where victims are held until they are decontaminated.

☐ Warm zone: The warm zone is the area where decontamination occurs, with large quantities of water under low pressure possibly with soap. All clothing and jewelry are removed, and the victim is washed thoroughly. Particular attention is paid to the eyes and airway.

☐ Cold zone: After receiving decontamination treatment, the victim is moved to the cold zone for evaluation and treatment.

TABLE 43.4 Setting Up an ED Decontamination Area

Setup Needs	Outdoor Setup	Indoor Setup
Ventilation system	Ventilation is not generally required outdoors. Keep the decontamination area away from hospital air intakes.	A ventilation system is required to provide a negative-pressure flow of air. All air from the area has to be vented to the outside. Charcoal filters are recommended in air systems.
Collection of drainage	Drainage collection can be established with large plastic basins or commercial collection tanks. In some cases it may be possible to allow some hazardous materials to go down the sewer system. Check with your local authorities.	Plastic basins or permanent commercial collection tanks can be used for drainage collection. It must be designed for easy access, cleaning, and HAZMAT disposal.
Water source	Large supply of low-pressure water for decontamination must be available. Temperature control of the water is needed.	Large supply of low-pressure water for decontamination must be available. Temperature control of the water is needed.
Privacy	A curtain system or a commercial decontamination tent is needed to maintain privacy.	Individual rooms and curtains to provide privacy may be easily established.
Environmental	A decontamination tent with heaters and lights may be needed to provide outdoor decontamination during bad weather or cold conditions.	Temperature control and lighting are usually easily designed in an internal decontamination area.
Cost and care	An outside decontamination area can usually be established relatively inexpensively. Time is needed for setup and preparation before patient decontamination can start.	The cost of establishing an area indoors can be expensive. Setup time in preparation for a HAZMAT incident is usually less than for an outdoor system.

Key points to consider when conducting decontamination:

❏ Be aware of toxic odors. Most exposures will not pose a serious risk to ED staff if rapidly identified and properly decontaminated. However, a small percentage of patients may still pose significant risk to health care workers because of off-gassing,[20] as for example in those patients exposed to an organophosphate or pesticides.

❏ If chemical odors from the patient are detected, or if there is a history of an exposure involving a substance that could pose continued risk, the patient should be treated in a negative pressure area where fumes cannot be exposed to others.[1]

❏ Staff should continue to use adequate respiratory protection and appropriate protective clothing until it is clear that there is no further risk.

❏ If indoor resources do not exist to safely care for this patient population, it may be necessary to continue care in an outdoor decontamination area with adequate outdoor ventilation.

Specific Interventions in Decontamination

1. *Care of the child in the hot zone:* Assessment and treatment of the child should focus on only the most basic concerns: airway, breathing, circulation, and disability. All other treatments should be delayed until after decontamination. If respiratory distress is likely or present, oxygen should be administered immediately. Any medical devices applied before the patient is decontaminated should be replaced with clean devices after decontamination so that hazardous materials are not transported from the hot zone to other areas.

2. *Care of the child in the warm zone:* Medical care in the decontamination area is mostly symptomatic and supportive for life-threatening concerns. The major goals of decontamination are to remove the hazardous material from the patient, if possible; to stop the toxic effects of the substance; and to keep the child from contaminating those caring for him or her.[4] Because contact with hazardous materials is probable, respiratory and contact protection using protection level C is recommended.[21] During decontamination, consider the privacy and comfort needs of the child. Infants may need to be brought through the decontamination area in a carrier, which may make thorough decontamina-

tion difficult. Toddlers and schoolchildren may be very afraid and require accompaniment or coaxing. Under extreme weather conditions where decontamination must occur outside, hypothermia is a grave concern. Children will need to be rewarmed quickly to avoid complications. The overriding concern is the decontamination of the child. Recognize that help may be needed to thoroughly decontaminate all areas of the body. The steps in the process of decontaminating pediatric patients include:

- Remove contaminated clothing immediately. This can eliminate 70% to 80% of the contaminant.[19]

- Place contaminated clothing or waste in plastic bags for proper disposal. Place patient information tag on bag as it may be necessary for forensic evidence. It may be necessary to store this waste in the hot zone until those qualified to remove hazardous wastes can arrive.

- Remove large pieces of the contaminant with forceps before the shower. Some contaminants, such as elemental metals (sodium, lithium), may explode on contact with water. These types of contamination should be covered with mineral oil and removed completely before water irrigation.[16]

- Wash the child with copious amounts of water for at least 15 minutes. A mild soap may be helpful in removing contaminants.[16,22] Vigorous scrubbing of the skin should be avoided, especially in children because skin damage can occur easily. If hot water is used, the risk of chemical reactivity is increased. Cool water showers are recommended for decontamination. However, cool water showers can be very uncomfortable and may result in hypothermia in pediatric patients. A warm shower will be better tolerated and will decrease the risk of hypothermia. It is important to control the water temperature for decontamination. The decision to use warm versus cool water should be based on the type and extent of the contamination and the needs of the patient.

- The decontamination process should start with any contaminated wounds, followed by the eyes, mucous membranes, skin, nail beds, and hair. Patients exposed to aerosol contamination should have the mouth, nose, and ears carefully cleaned. Ocular exposures require prompt removal of contact lenses and irrigation of the eyes. The folds of the skin, as well as all body openings, should be carefully cleaned.[22] Irrigation runoff should flow away from cleaned areas and down so that previously washed places are not recontaminated.[16,23]

- After the child is decontaminated, he or she can move through the warm zone, an area where ED staff provide further treatment and verify that the patient has received adequate decontamination. There is less risk to ED staff in the warm zone, and level C or possibly D protection, as the victim moves from the warm zone to the cold zone, should be adequate (Table 43.5). A more thorough assessment can be conducted and attention can be given to wounds or injuries that might require special irrigation and decontamination. When dealing with any type of a hazardous material incident the health care professional should maintain communication with local public health agencies and civil authorities.

3. *Care of the child in the cold zone:* When it is verified that the child is fully decontaminated, the child is moved to the cold zone, where definitive treatment is given. The cold zone can be located in any area of the emergency department. HAZMAT protection is not needed in this area. Each decontamination area should be clearly marked so that people and supplies do not cross over from a contaminated area to a clean area.

4. *Cleanup.* After any decontamination process there should be a plan for decontamination of involved staff, equipment, and rooms. Proper cleanup will include the disposal of any hazardous materials or collected waste.

Specific Hazmat Emergencies

In all cases of HAZMAT or biohazard exposure, the following actions should be included as part of any treatment guidelines:

- ❐ Evacuate the patient from the exposure area.
- ❐ Remove contaminated clothing.
- ❐ Wash contaminated surfaces thoroughly with mild soap (no oils) and water.
- ❐ Provide oxygen therapy for patients with respiratory involvement.

Additionally, attention must be given to the airway, breathing, circulation, disability, and any other injury or specific problem.

Chemical Hazards

Some of the specific types of materials likely to be encountered in the pediatric population are listed. The focus of these specific guidelines is to address the HAZMAT exposure; attention to other medical needs of the patient is assumed.

TABLE 43.5 U.S. Environmental Protection Agency HAZMAT Protection Levels

Level	Indications	Respiratory Protection	Clothing	Gloves
Level A	HAZMAT workers dealing in areas of very high concentration of toxic materials need level A protection.	Self-contained, positive-pressure breathing device	Fully encapsulated chemical-resistant suit	Double layers of attached chemical-resistant gloves
Level B	Full respiratory protection is needed; low concentrations of hazardous materials are expected.	Positive-pressure respiratory protection, self-contained or attached to hose	Chemical-resistant overalls with head and foot protection	Double layers of chemical-resistant gloves and boots, taped to sleeve
Level C	There are low levels of known hazardous material; air contamination is expected to be minimal.	Positive-pressure respiratory protection with canister filter	Chemical-resistant suit	Double layers of chemical-resistant gloves and boots, taped to sleeve
Level D	There is no danger of HAZMAT exposure.	None; simple face mask, if desired	Standard work clothes	Gloves, if desired

Chlorine

Chlorine is used as a disinfectant and for water purification.

Pathophysiology

Commonly, chlorine is used in association with residential swimming pools and spas and is used extensively in water treatment facilities. Chlorine has a strong, pungent odor and may be seen as a greenish-yellow vapor cloud. It is heavier than air and will settle in low-lying areas. In a confined space it will remain concentrated; in the open it will disperse with air movement. It is an irritant and will cause victims to flee. Chlorine can cause sloughing of airway epithelium and intense inflammation of the respiratory system.[24]

Signs and Symptoms

❑ *Mild exposure:* Burning sensation of the nose, mouth, and throat associated with irritation of the eyes.

❑ *Increased exposure:* Paroxysmal cough. In some cases, the cough will be associated with hematemesis. Headache, weakness, wheezing, nausea, nasal drainage, hoarseness, tachypnea, chest pains, and palpitations may also occur.

❑ *Severe exposure:* Productive cough and difficulty breathing, cyanosis, worsening respiratory status, and rales because of pulmonary edema and congestion. Severe hematemesis and death can occur because of

progressive respiratory failure caused by sloughing of the airways.

Nursing Interventions

1. Chlorine usually dissipates quickly, so these patients generally pose little risk for contaminating other health care workers. Unless there is gross chlorine contamination, these patients do not have to be decontaminated before coming to the emergency department.

2. Remove clothing to reduce the risk of off-gassing. Any exposure residue on the clothing or skin can cause trapped gases to be released.

3. Provide 100% oxygen for respiratory exposure.

4. Treat bronchoconstriction with inhaled bronchodilators. Intubation may be necessary in severe cases.

5. Rinse eyes with normal saline solution using a Morgan lens®.

6. Thoroughly wash the mouth and face if chlorine-generating compounds have been ingested.

7. Do not induce vomiting because of the risk of aspiration.

Hydrocarbons

Hydrocarbons include gasoline, kerosene, and their constituents. These products may be found in glues, propellants, lighter fluids, and other products.

Pathophysiology

Hydrocarbons can defat the skin and mucous membranes, causing irritation and chemical burns. They can be absorbed though the lungs, skin, or GI tract. Inhalation injuries are common with exposure to these products. Ingestion and surface exposure may also be seen.[25]

Signs and Symptoms

❒ Respiratory exposure: Nausea, vomiting, light-headedness, and dizziness. Chronic inhalation can lead to irreversible central nervous system injury.

❒ Systemic exposure: Cardiac dysrhythmias and liver and renal abnormalities.

❒ Severe exposure: Unconsciousness and respiratory depression.

Nursing Interventions

1. Wash any solvents from the skin with large amounts of a mild soap and water.

2. Provide oxygen therapy for inhalation exposures.

3. Irrigate eyes with copious amounts of normal saline solution using a Morgan lens® if they have been exposed.

4. Do not induce vomiting in patients with ingestion exposures because of the risk of aspiration. If the substance must be removed from the stomach, it should be done by gastric lavage while there is appropriate airway control with a cuffed endotracheal tube to prevent aspiration.

Methanol (Methyl Alcohol)

Methanol can be found in many household products including paint removers, glass cleaners, brake fluid, antifreeze, and windshield washer and deicer.

Pathophysiology

Methanol ingestion may be identified by the presence of an increased anion and osmolar gap. Treatment focuses on life-support measures. When metabolized by the liver, methanol forms formic acid, which inhibits mitochondrial respiration. This results in tissue hypoxia and metabolic acidosis, which can lead to optic nerve damage and blindness.[26]

Signs and Symptoms

Signs and symptoms can be delayed for many hours, making contamination more difficult to successfully treat. Symptoms include:

❒ Visual disturbances

❒ Nausea, vomiting, and abdominal pain

❒ Headache, weakness, and dizziness

❒ In severe cases, coma and seizures associated with cerebral edema. Death results from myocardial depression, bradycardia, hypotension, shock, and respiratory arrest.

Nursing Interventions

1. Contaminated clothing should be removed, and the child should be washed with water if the skin or eyes are involved. After 30 to 60 minutes of ingestion, the methanol is usually already absorbed into the system, so gastric lavage may not be helpful.

2. Treat inhalation exposures with oxygen.

3. Do not induce vomiting because of the risk of central nervous system depression.

4. Prepare to administer an ethanol infusion and dialysis, depending on the severity of contamination.

Self-Defense Sprays

These products are commonly available in many stores. Various chemicals may be used in self-defense sprays; the most common are oleoresin capsicum (cayenne pepper) and chloroacetophenone (Mace®).[6,27]

Pathophysiology

Self-defense sprays are classified as irritants and cause direct irritation to nerve endings of the eyes, mucous membranes, respiratory system, and skin.

Signs and Symptoms

❒ Most symptoms are self-limiting and will resolve after 20 minutes.

❒ Contact dermatitis, erythema, edema, vesication, purpura, difficulty breathing, pulmonary edema, and lacrimation are among the symptoms.

❒ Conjunctivitis may persist for 1 to 2 days.

❒ Bronchopneumonia may develop if prolonged exposure in an enclosed space has occurred.

❒ Laryngospasm can occur. Asthmatics may be more sensitive to bronchoconstriction and at greater risk for respiratory arrest.[28]

Nursing Interventions

1. Treatment focuses on removal of the agent and irrigation.

2. Provide fresh air or oxygen to alleviate respiratory complaints.

3. Irrigate the eyes for up to 30 minutes.

4. Provide a cool shower for 10 minutes. Avoid scrubbing and soap initially. During the initial part of the shower additional chemicals may be released from the hair, temporarily worsening eye and skin irritation.

5. Add mild soap (no oils in soap) after the first 10 minutes. Oils in the soap decrease the effectiveness of breaking up and removing some of the sprays.

6. Blot dry with a towel. Avoid vigorous scrubbing.

Organophosphates

Organophosphates are found in many insecticides. They are also found in nerve agents (commonly called gases though they are generally not a gas).[4,29,30]

Pathophysiology

Organophosphates interfere with the normal degradation of acetylcholine by the enzyme cholinesterase, which causes a cholinergic crisis. They inhibit nerve fibers from resetting after activation, so that nerves remain in a constant state of excitement. Initially, the interference of organophosphates is reversible if treated; however, after approximately 48 hours (longer and shorter for nerve agents), the blockade of the enzyme is not reversible, and normal nervous function can return only after the synthesis of new enzymes, a process that takes weeks to months.[31]

Signs and Symptoms

❑ Immediately after exposure, headache, nausea, dizziness, anxiety, and restlessness may occur.

❑ With continued exposure, muscle fasciculation, weakness, abdominal cramps, pulmonary edema, and respiratory failure may occur.

❑ Continued interference with acetylcholine also leads to a glandular hypersecretion. The resulting signs and symptoms are known by the acronym SLUDGE: *S*alivation, *L*acrimation, *U*rination, *D*efecation, *G*astrointestinal upset, and *E*mesis.[32]

❑ With continued exposure the victim will develop flaccid paralysis and seizures. Seizures are very difficult to diagnose if the victim has flaccid paralysis. Rhythmic movement of the eyes may be the only physical manifestation.

Nursing Interventions

1. The use of protective clothing and respiratory protection is very important for hospital staff involved in the decontamination. Off-gassing is a risk with these patients.

2. Remove all clothing and wash exposed surfaces several times with soap and water.

3. Initiate life support measures and seizure precautions.

4. Administer medications as ordered. Atropine and pralidoxime may be required for severe cases.

   ▪ Atropine antagonizes the hypersecretion effects of organophosphates and can be given as a dose of 0.02 mg/kg up to a total dose of 1 mg. Organophosphates in insecticides may require larger doses than nerve agents used by terrorists. If this dose shows some positive effect, it should be administered in large enough doses to keep SLUDGE effects reversed. The effects of the agent will probably last longer than the effects of the medication, and frequent dosing may be required. Atropine will not help in reversing respiratory muscle weakness.

   ▪ Pralidoxime can be used in early stages of organophosphate contamination to restore some enzyme function and may help to restore some respiratory function.

5. Administer benzodiazepines to control seizures. Seizures related to organophosphates do not begin from a central focus in the brain, but initiate from the whole brain and can be extremely damaging from both the seizure and the buildup of lactic acid. They do not respond to antiseizure medications such as dilantin.

6. Consider gastric lavage or administration of activated charcoal if the child has ingested organophosphates.

Cyanide

Cyanide is commonly used in many manufacturing processes. It is common in much industrial waste.[6]

Pathophysiology

Cyanide binds with Fe^{3+} at the mitochondrial level and prevents the transport and utilization of oxygen. This leads to anaerobic energy production and the buildup of lactic acid. Cyanide crosses the blood-brain barrier easily and, once across, may interfere with neurotransmitters. It also increases intravascular resistance. Early signs of cyanide poisoning may be evident in as little as a few minutes.[6,33]

Signs and Symptoms

❑ Early signs and symptoms include dizziness, headache, weakness, diaphoresis, and rapid respirations.

❑ The victim may state that he or she detected an odor of bitter almonds or may have a cherry red flush.

❑ Because the effect of cyanide poisoning is to block the use of oxygen at the cellular level, venous blood oxygen levels will approach that of arterial blood.

❐ Ophthalmic examination will reveal that both retinal arteries and veins appear the same.

❐ Hypoxia continues; the victim will exhibit decreasing level of consciousness progressing to unresponsiveness.

❐ The victim will progress through hemodynamic instability, arrhythmias, seizures, apnea, and cardiac arrest.

❐ Throughout all of this, the oxygen saturation of the blood will remain high.

Nursing Interventions

1. Personnel should wear at least level C personal protective equipment to avoid becoming affected by both the cyanide present on the victim's clothing and skin and the victim's breathing.

2. Immediately decontaminate the victim.

3. Flush the victim's eyes with normal saline or lactated Ringer's solution.

4. If ingestion has occurred, do not induce vomiting as this has shown to increase mortality. If the ingestion occurred less than 1 hour prior, the victim may be given activated charcoal.

5. Administer oxygen to allow the functional mitochondria as much opportunity as possible to function normally.

6. Administer the cyanide antidote to create a state of methemoglobinemia. Contact the local poison control center or refer to the Centers for Disease Control and Prevention website for specific dosing instructions.

Phosgene

Phosgene is used in the manufacturing of dyes, pesticides, plastics, polyurethane, and pharmaceuticals. It is also identified by several names including carbonyl chloride, carbon oxychloride, oxychloride, and carbonic acid chloride. CG is the military designation for phosgene. It was used extensively in World War I as a chemical weapon.

Pathophysiology

Phosgene does not react as easily with water compared to chlorine and therefore exhibits its effects with the lower respiratory tract. In the lower respiratory tract it disrupts cellular function as well as the surfactant layer, resulting in impaired lung function and inflammation. If the concentration is high enough, greater than 500 parts per million, the effects become systematic. It causes hemolysis and red blood cell (RBC) hyperaggregation. Pulmonary sludging occurs, leading to cor pulmonale and death. Phosgene exposure also causes hemolysis and RBC hyperaggregation.

Signs and Symptoms

❐ Odor of new-mown hay

❐ Begins with a mild cough, latent period of 2 to 15 hours, followed by rapid progressive pulmonary edema, significant fluid loss

Nursing Interventions

1. Treatment for exposure to both chlorine and phosgene is supportive.

2. Provide airway control.

3. Prepare to administer ß-agonist inhalers.

4. Monitor for changes in oxygen saturation. A normal oxygen saturation may not indicate positive prognosis.

5. Monitor for transient cardiac arrhythmias, which should be limited and resolved with oxygenation.

6. Prepare to treat pulmonary edema.

7. The use of diuretics will have limited positive effect and will only contribute to volume depletion. Patients may lose up to 1 L of fluid per hour to capillary leakage.

Biohazards

Anthrax (Bacillus anthracis)

Pathophysiology

Anthrax is an aerobic, gram-positive bacterium. It is spore forming and nonmotile. It is naturally occurring in soil throughout the world. Spores can be cultured and developed to spread very easily. The anthrax outbreak of October 2001 demonstrated a virulence of this disease that had not been previously appreciated; it is, however, difficult to weaponize for effective distribution. Anthrax is associated with three types of infections:[34]

❐ *Cutaneous* infections are the most common and are associated with some animal-processing industries. Bacteria infect broken or open skin, and an infection develops in about 12 days. Patients present with pruritic macular or papular lesions, which progress into vesicles. After 1 to 2 weeks a painless depressed black eschar dries, loosens, and falls off. The black eschar gives anthrax its name after anthracite coal.

❐ *Gastrointestinal* infections are rare and associated with eating contaminated meat. Patients present with oropharyngeal lesions or are characterized by fever, malaise, nausea, vomiting, and anorexia, much like the flu.

❏ *Inhalation-caused* infections are rare except in terrorist attacks and can be fatal. Spores inhaled into the alveoli are ingested by macrophages and transported to the mediastinal lymphatic system. The bacteria can then germinate and reproduce. The course of the illness is worsened by the toxins the bacteria produce. Initial presentation may include fever, dyspnea, cough, headache, nausea and vomiting, abdominal pain, and chest pain.[34-36]

Signs and Symptoms

❏ Inhalational anthrax initially presents with fever, dyspnea, cough, headache, nausea and vomiting, abdominal pain, and chest pain.

❏ With a worsening inhalational anthrax the patient will have worsening shortness of breath, diaphoresis, shock, hemorrhagic meningitis, delirium, and coma.

❏ Gastrointestinal or oropharyngeal anthrax is characterized by oral lesions or by fever, malaise, nausea, vomiting, and anorexia, again, much like the flu.

❏ Cutaneous anthrax begins as a painless pruritic macular or papular lesion, much like an insect bite.

  ▪ By day 2 the lesion has swollen, vesiculates, and ruptures to form a depressed ulcer. Smaller lesions may form around the primary lesion.

  ▪ The clear serosanguineous fluid in these lesions contains large quantities of the bacilli.

  ▪ The area surrounding the lesion will be swollen.

  ▪ The black eschar forms over the depression, dries, and falls off in 1 to 2 weeks.

Nursing Interventions

1. Remove any contaminated clothing and thoroughly shower with soap.

2. Prevent any material with anthrax spores from coming into the hospital.

  ▪ Anthrax is not contagious from one person to another; however, the spores can move about easily in the air.

3. Prepare to administer antibiotic therapy. Anthrax usually responds well to appropriate antibiotics if started early enough. Ciprofloxacin is the antibiotic of choice. Ciprofloxacin is normally not recommended for children because of a poor side effect profile; however, the risk posed by anthrax and other biological agents outweighs the risks from the antibiotic. Contact the local or state health department for current recommendations for antibiotic choice and dosing.

Botulism

Botulinum toxin occurs from Clostridium botulinum. It is considered to be the most poisonous substance known.

Pathophysiology

Clostridium botulinum is usually found in unprocessed or poorly processed foods. It can also be found in improperly cared for or cooked food. Once ingested, the bacteria produce the toxin that causes botulism. The toxin spreads into the body and binds in the neuromuscular junction, blocking acetylcholine. This leads to a rapid paralysis. Botulism is always associated with a common food source. If no common foods are found, a terrorist incident using inhaled botulinum should be suspected. Botulism affects the victim in one of three ways:

❏ Food borne: The most common route, usually the result of poorly prepared or canned foods.

❏ Wound: Wound botulism comes from an open wound contaminated with the botulinum toxin.

❏ Infantile: Infants are at risk for botulism poisoning if fed raw honey.

Signs and Symptoms

❏ A sudden and rapidly spreading descending flaccid paralysis occurs. This symptom can be confused with Guillain-Barré syndrome or other neuromuscular diseases. The paralysis will be bilateral.

❏ Cranial nerves will be affected; double vision is often the symptom.

❏ Paralysis will affect the neck and respiratory systems and may require ventilator care.

❏ The sensorium is not affected at any point in the progression of the disease.

Nursing Interventions

1. It is essential that the disease be diagnosed early because the only intervention to stop the progression of the disease is administration of the antitoxin.

2. The antitoxin will halt the progression of the disease but not reverse any paralysis present.

3. Prepare for intubation and airway management.

4. Treat symptomatically. The patient may require weeks or months of intubation before neurologic function begins to return.

5. Although the patient may be paralyzed, botulism has no effect on cerebral function, and the patient may be completely aware of his or her surroundings.

Plague

Yersinia pestis bacilli are naturally occurring bacteria that spread from the fleas of rats to humans. Plague can also be mechanically aerosolized for use in a terrorist attack.[34]

Pathophysiology

Usually the bacteria enter the body through a flea bite and migrate to the lymph nodes where the bacteria reside in the lymph. A secondary pneumonic form develops when the bacteria from the bubonic form infect the lungs. Septicemia plague accounts for approximately 15% of the cases. It is manifested by gram-negative sepsis without development of the bubo. Pneumonic plague is caused by the inhalation of the bacteria or, as stated, secondary to primary bubonic plague. It accounts for only 2% of the cases of plague. Plague meningitis has symptoms similar to other forms of meningitis and is often found in children after ineffective treatment of another form of plague.[34]

Signs and Symptoms

- ❑ Headache, fever, chills, malaise, and exhaustion
- ❑ With bubonic form, buboes form down the lymphatic system from the flea bite, most often in the femoral or inguinal areas. The buboes range in size from 1 to 10 cm and are extremely painful. The buboes are not fluctuant but may point, open, and drain spontaneously.
- ❑ If septicemia develops it will mimic meningococcemia. Small artery thrombosis will develop in the nose and digits. Appendages will become necrotic; more proximal purpuric lesions will develop. Gangrene is a late finding of the disease progression.
- ❑ With pneumonic plague, headache, fever, chills, malaise, exhaustion, cough, hemoptysis, chest pain, dyspnea, stridor, and cyanosis occur.
- ❑ Death is the result of respiratory failure, bleeding, and circulatory collapse.

Nursing Interventions

1. Treatment is supportive.
2. Prepare to administer streptomycin, with gentamicin as first alternate choice. Beyond this, doxycycline, ciprofloxacin, or chloramphenicol may be used.
3. Standard universal precautions with droplet protection are employed.

Tularemia

Tularemia is endemic to most parts of the world, including the United States. It is a highly virulent disease requiring only a small number of organisms to cause infection. The disease has a very high morbidity imposing significant illness for a significant period of time. If untreated, there is a 60% mortality rate; this rate declines to 2% with adequate treatment. The natural vector of tularemia is ingestion of contaminated meat or insect bite.

Pathophysiology

Francisella tularensis, the bacterium causing tularemia, is extremely hardy and survives even frigid conditions for years. Aerosolized, it could affect large numbers of victims and contaminate the environment for very long periods of time.

Signs and Symptoms

- ❑ *Ulceroglandular tularemia* is manifested by ulcerative lesions on the skin or mucous membranes with lymphadenopathy.
- ❑ *Oculoglandular tularemia* is similar to Ulcerglandular tularemia except that the lesions appear on the eye with purulent conjunctivitis, chemosis, and significant pain.
- ❑ *Glandular tularemia* has all of the above signs and symptoms without lesions.
  - ▪ Left untreated, the lymph nodes will drain through the skin. These are the most common presentation of the disease.
- ❑ *Oropharyngeal tularemia* presents with pharyngitis, stomatitis, and cervical lymphadenopathy, much like a typical streptococcal pharyngitis. The patient may also complain of abdominal pain, nausea, vomiting, and diarrhea.
- ❑ *Tularemic pneumonia* occurs as a result of inhalation of the pathogens. The initial symptoms are the same as with other forms with a worsening cough and other respiratory symptoms. Dyspnea, chest pain, and hemoptysis worsen, progressing to respiratory failure if untreated.
- ❑ *Typhoidal tularemia* is systemic illness without a known source of infection. Patients are febrile, obtunded, and hypotensive, progressing to shock, multiorgan failure, disseminated intravascular coagulation, renal failure, meningitis, and death.

Nursing Interventions

1. Prepare to treat with antibiotics; Gentamicin is the first choice.
2. Utilize standard precautions when providing patient care. Laboratory specimens are highly contagious.

Hospital protocols should be followed for collecting and delivering such specimens.

3. Be aware that tularemia is a long, debilitating disease that requires supportive care.

Smallpox

Pathophysiology

Smallpox (variola major) was eradicated from the world in 1980. After eradication the vaccination program was stopped. Two reservoirs remained, one in the United States and the other in the former Soviet Union. If there was an unintentional or intentional release of the virus, there would be little or no resistance to this devastating disease. The disease is similar to chickenpox with much more devastating effects and mortality. A supply of the vaccine remains but is limited. The side effects of the vaccine can also be devastating but are always preferable to the disease.[34,37]

Signs and Symptoms

❏ High fever, malaise, severe headache, and backache

❏ Maculopapular rash that starts in the mouth, pharynx, face, and forearms, then spreads to trunk and legs. Rash becomes vesicular and then pustular.

❏ Rash is circumferential, appearing more on the face and extremities than the trunk (chickenpox appears more on the trunk).

❏ Flat and hemorrhagic types of smallpox also occur with a flat rash and bleeding; both are often fatal.

❏ Death is thought to result from the toxemia associated with immune complexes and antigens. Encephalitis can also develop.[37]

Nursing Interventions

1. Any case of smallpox should be considered an extreme emergency. Public health officials and the Centers for Disease Control and Prevention should be contacted immediately.

2. Initiate strict isolation. These patients will be very sick and should be kept in a negative-pressure room.

3. Administer vaccination to all those exposed and those working with the victim. Vaccines may be distributed to anybody in close proximity to the outbreak in an attempt to contain the outbreak.

4. Treat the patient symptomatically. It is unknown whether current antiviral agents will be effective against the disease.

Prevention of Hazmat Exposure

Complete prevention of HAZMAT exposure is difficult because of the large number of chemicals used daily. The potential risk of exposure increases each day. However, some steps can be taken to reduce this risk to children and families in the home.[1]

❏ Assure that all chemical substances are kept out of reach and sight of children, preferably in a cupboard that can be locked.

❏ Lock all substances and keep them in their original containers. Use child-resistant caps.

❏ Dispose of unneeded chemicals rather than keeping products that have little or no use.

❏ Be familiar with the product warnings and the way to use each product properly.

❏ Look for alternatives to hazardous products that may be just as effective but less dangerous, such as "green" household cleaning agents..

The emergency department must be prepared for both small scale and large scale mass contaminations. An education plan should be in place to train ED staff not only about the proper use of equipment and personal protection devices but also about the effects of various hazardous materials and what to expect during a contamination incident.[1,4]

Conclusion

Children exposed to hazardous materials or biohazards are at risk to have rapid and serious complications. Contamination can pose a significant risk to all those who come in contact with affected children, including ED staff and other emergency patients. Proper planning and preparation are essential to providing safe and effective care. This planning must include preparations for individual and mass contaminations. It also must include practice using effective, realistic drills. Every emergency department should have clear protocols and guidelines established to successfully care for the pediatric patient exposed to hazardous materials.

References

1. Committee on Environmental Health & Committee on Infectious Diseases. (2006). Chemical-biological terrorism and its impact on children. *Pediatrics, 118*(3), 1267–1278.

2. American Academy of Pediatrics Committee on Pediatric Emergency Medicine, American Academy of Pediatrics Committee on Medical Liability, & Task Force on Terrorism. (2006). The pediatrician and disaster preparedness. *Pediatrics, 117*(2), 560–565.

3. Markenson, D., Reynolds, S., American Academy of Pediatrics Committee on Pediatric Emergency Medicine, & Task Force on Terrorism. (2006). The pediatrician and disaster preparedness. *Pediatrics, 117*(2), e340–e362.

4. Brandenburg, M. A., & Arneson, W. L. (2007). Pediatric disaster response in developed countries: Ten guiding principles. *American Journal of Disaster Medicine, 2*(3), 151–162.

5. Madrid, P. A., & Schacher, S. J. (2006). A critical concern: Pediatrician self-care after disasters. *Pediatrics, 117*(5 Pt 3), S454–S457.

6. Lynch, E. L., & Thomas, T. L. (2004). Pediatric considerations in chemical exposures: Are we prepared? *Pediatric Emergency Care, 20*(3), 198–208.

7. Merritt, N. L., & Anderson, M. J. (1989). Malathion overdose: When one patient creates a departmental hazard. *Journal of Emergency Nursing, 15*(6), 463–465.

8. Phillips, S., Rond, P. C., Kelly, S. M., & Swartz, P. D. (1996). The need for pediatric-specific triage criteria: Results from the Florida Trauma Triage Study. *Pediatric Emergency Care, 12*(6), 394–399.

9. Nuss, K. E., Dietrich, A. M., & Smith, G. A. (2001). Effectiveness of a pediatric trauma team protocol. *Pediatric Emergency Care, 17*(2), 96–100.

10. Marcin, J. P., & Pollack, M. M. (2002). Triage scoring systems, severity of illness measures, and mortality prediction models in pediatric trauma. *Critical Care Medicine, 30*(11 Suppl), S457–S467.

11. Romig, L. E. (2002). Pediatric triage. A system to JumpSTART your triage of young patients at MCIs. *JEMS: A Journal of Emergency Medical Services, 27*(7), 52–58.

12. Klein, B. L. (1993). Prehospital care of the injured child: An analysis of selected premises. *Critical Care Medicine, 21*(9 Suppl), S393–S394.

13. Bernardo, L. M. (2007). Unique needs of children in disasters and other public health emergencies. In T. Veenema (Ed.) *Disaster nursing and emergency preparedness for chemical, biological, and radiological terrorism and other hazards* (pp. 224–261). New York: Springer Publishing Co.

14. O'Neill, K. A., & Molczan, K. (2003). Pediatric triage: A 2-tier, 5-level system in the United States. *Pediatric Emergency Care, 19*(4), 285–290.

15. Romig, L. (2008). *JumpSTART and MCI triage tool.* Retrieved April 3, 2009, from http://www.jumpstarttriage.com/JumpSTART_and_MCI_Triage.php

16. Brousseau, D. C., Mistry, R. D., & Alessandrini, E. A. (2006). Methods of categorizing emergency department visit urgency: A survey of pediatric emergency medicine physicians. *Pediatric Emergency Care, 22*(9), 635–639.

17. Kirk, M. A., Cisek, J., & Rose, S. R. (1994). Emergency department response to hazardous materials incidents. *Emergency Medicine Clinics of North America, 12*(2), 461–481.

18. American Health Consultants. (2001). JCAHO president calls for bioterror preparedness. *Hospital Peer Review, 26*(12), 165–166.

19. Cox, R. D. (1994). Decontamination and management of hazardous materials exposure victims in the emergency department. *Annals of Emergency Medicine, 23*(4), 761–770.

20. Schultz, M., Cisek, J., & Wabeke, R. (1995). Simulated exposure of hospital emergency personnel to solvent vapors and respirable dust during decontamination of chemically exposed patients. *Annals of Emergency Medicine, 26*(3), 324–329.

21. Levitin, H. W., & Siegelson, H. J. (1996). Hazardous materials, disaster medical planning and response. *Emergency Medicine Clinics of North America, 14*(2), 317–348.

22. Emergency Management Institute. (1992). Hazardous materials workshop for EMS providers. Washington, DC: Federal Emergency Management Agency.

23. Leonard, R. B. (1993, June). Hazardous materials accidents: Initial scene assessment and patient care. *Aviation, Space, and Environmental Medicine,* 546–551.

24. Segal, E., & Lang, E. (2001). Toxicity, chlorine gas. Retrieved April 3, 2009, from http://www.emedicine.com/emerg/topic851.htm

References (continued)

25. Maffeo, R. (1996). Gasoline exposure. *American Journal of Nursing, 96*(8), 47.

26. Korabathina, K., Benbadis, S. & Likosky, D. (2001). Methanol. Retrieved April 3, 2009, from http://www. emedicine.com/neuro/topic217.htm

27. Claman, F. L., & Patterson, D. L. (1995). Personal aerosol protection devices. Caring for the victims of exposure. *Nurse Practitioner, 20*(11), 52–58.

28. Ross, D., & Siddle, B. (1998). Use of force, policies and training recommendations: Based on the medical implications of oleoresin capsicum. Millstadt, IL: PPCT Management Systems, Inc.

29. Henretig, F. M., Cieslak, T. J., Eitzen, E. (2002). Biological and chemical terrorism *Journal of Pediatrics, 141*(3), 311–326.

30. Foltin, G., Tunik, M., Curran, J., Marshall, L., Bove, J., Van Amerongen, R., et al. (2006). Pediatric nerve agent poisoning: Medical and operational considerations for emergency medical services in a large American city. *Pediatric Emergency Care, 22*(4), 239–244.

31. Noeller, T. P. (2001). Biological and chemical terrorism: Recognition and management. *Cleveland Clinic Journal of Medicine, 68*(12), 1001–1013.

32. Rothrock, S. C. (1999). *The pediatric emergency pocketbook* (3rd ed.). Winter Park, FL: Mako Publishing.

33. Lynch, M. (2005). Atropine use in children after nerve gas exposure. *Journal of Pediatric Nursing, 20*(6), 477–484.

34. Stocker, J. T. (2006). Clinical and pathologic differential diagnosis of selected potential bioterrorism agents of interest to pediatric health care providers. *Clinics in Laboratory Medicine, 26*(2), 329–344.

35. Inglesby, T. V, O'Toole, T., Henderson, D. A., Bartlett, J. G., Ascher, M. A., Eitzen, E., et al. (1999). Anthrax as a biological weapon. *Journal of the American Medical Association, 287*(17), 2236–2252.

36. Broussard, L. A. (2001). Biological agents: Weapons of warfare and bioterrorism. *Molecular Diagnosis, 6*(4), 323–333.

37. Woods, R., McCarthy, T., Barry, M. A., & Mahon, B. (2004). Diagnosing smallpox: Would you know it if you saw it? *Biosecurity & Bioterrorism, 2*(3), 157–163.

SECTION EIGHT
Psychosocial Emergencies

FORTY-FOUR

Child Maltreatment

Susan J. Kelley, PhD, RN, FAAN

Introduction

Child maltreatment, a serious social and public health problem, is frequently encountered by emergency nurses. The severity of child maltreatment ranges from emotional neglect to child fatalities. Emergency nurses play a critical role in the identification, treatment, and prevention of child maltreatment.

Child maltreatment generally is grouped into four major categories: neglect, physical abuse, sexual abuse, and psychological maltreatment (Table 44.1). Although the behaviors that characterize these forms of maltreatment are often distinct from each other, it is important to note that these different types of abuse often co-occur. The purpose of this chapter is to discuss the recognition and treatment of children who have experienced one or more forms of neglect and physical abuse. The sexual abuse of children is to be addressed in Chapter 45.

Etiology and Epidemiology

According to the Children's Bureau of the U.S. Department of Health and Human Services, an estimated 905,000 children were victims of child maltreatment in 2006.[1] This represents a victimization rate of 12.1 per 1,000 children. Of these child victims, 64.1% experienced neglect, 16% were physically abused, 8.8% were sexually abused, 6.6% were psychologically abused, and 2.2% experienced medical neglect. In addition, 15.5% of child victims experienced "other" types of maltreatment such as abandonment and prenatal substance abuse exposure. Many of the children were reported to be victims of multiple forms of child maltreatment. Nearly three quarters (74.7%) of children had no known history of prior victimization. Infants under 1 year of age and children aged 1 to 3 years had the highest incidents of maltreatment. The vast majority (83%) were victimized by a parent acting alone or with another person.[1]

In 2006, an estimated 1,530 children died as a result of child maltreatment. Children under 4 years of age accounted for nearly 80% of child fatalities, with children under 1 year accounting for 40% of those deaths. Children under the age of 1 year are at greatest risk of death due to maltreatment.[1]

Focused History

When possible, the child and parent are interviewed separately to determine whether there are any discrepancies between the parents' and the child's accounts of the injury or the living conditions. When interviewed alone, the child is more likely to accurately report the cause of the injury and the identity of the abuser. If more than one caretaker is present, interviewing each separately may reveal discrepancies in offered explanations. In some emergency departments, a social worker will conduct the in-depth history.

❐ Family risk factors and history associated with child maltreatment include:

- Substance abuse
- Social isolation; lack of family support
- Intimate partner violence/domestic violence
- Violent community
- Poverty (major single risk factor for neglect)
- Economic pressures and other stressors
- Crowded or inadequate housing

TABLE 44.1 Categories of Child Maltreatment

Category	Definition	Description
Neglect	Failure to meet a child's basic needs, including food, shelter, clothing, health care, education, and a safe environment.	Includes acts of omission rather than commission, as in the case of physical abuse. May or may not be intentional. Also includes failure-to-thrive syndrome, where an infant or child is inadequately nourished, leading to poor growth and development.
Physical abuse	Physical injury to a child inflicted by a parent or caretaker through excessive and inappropriate physical force.	Typically episodic and often the result of "corporal punishment". Factitious disorder by proxy (Munchausen syndrome by proxy) is an unusual yet very serious form of physical abuse in which a caregiver, a mother, induces illness in her child.
Sexual abuse	Any sexual contact between a child and adult (or considerably older child) whether by physical force, persuasion, or coercion.	Includes noncontact acts, such as exhibitionism, sexually explicit language, showing children sexually explicit materials, and voyeurism (Chapter 45).
Psychological	Parental or caregiver behaviors that are cruel, degrading, terrorizing, isolating or rejecting.	Can occur independently and is almost always embedded within or accompanying other forms of maltreatment. One of the most difficulty types of CM to document and particularly difficult to determine in an emergency department setting where contacts with families are generally brief.

❏ Parental risk factors associated with child maltreatment include:

- Low self-esteem
- Social isolation
- Reliance on physical punishment for discipline
- Unrealistic expectations of children
- Role reversal
- Childhood history of abuse
- Depression or other mental health disorder
- Substance abuse
- History of criminal activity or incarceration

❏ Child risk factors associated with child maltreatment include:

- Premature birth
- Prenatal drug exposure
- Developmental disability
- Physical disability
- Chronic illness

- Product of a multiple birth
- Young age, birth to 3 years of age

Focused Assessment

Physical Assessment

Whenever child maltreatment is suspected, a thorough nursing assessment is indicated after the child has been triaged.

❏ Assess the respiratory system.

- Assess the mouth for signs of trauma and patent airway.
- Auscultate the chest for:
  - Respiratory rate. Tachypnea may be present in the child with respiratory distress; bradypnea may be present in the child with shock.
- Observe the chest for:
  - Bruises
  - Paradoxical movement. Blunt force trauma to the chest may have occurred.

❏ Assess the cardiovascular system.

- Auscultate the heart for:
  - Rate. Tachycardia may be present in early shock or dehydration; bradycardia may be present with late shock.
- Measure the blood pressure.
  - Hypotension may be seen in late shock.
- Palpate peripheral pulses for:
  - Equality
  - Quality

❏ Assess the neurologic system.

- Assess the child's level of consciousness with the AVPU method (*A*lert, responds to *V*erbal stimuli, responds to *P*ainful stimuli, *U*nresponsive) or Glasgow Coma Scale method.
  - Decreased level of consciousness may indicate shock, head injury, or ingestion of toxins.

❏ Assess the integumentary system.[4]

- Assess for alterations in skin integrity.
- Note the presence of:
  - Bruises—location, size, pattern, color. Although the color of a bruise may not accurately determine its age, bruises with multiple colors could indicate repeated incidents of abuse over time.
  - Scars—location, size, pattern. Linear and geometric patterns are often intentional.

❏ Assess the child's overall appearance and behavior.

- Assess for appropriate clothing according to climate.
- Note hygiene, both general and dental.
  - Lack of cleanliness and poor oral hygiene may be an indicator of neglect.

❏ Measure the child's weight and height to determine whether they are appropriate for age and birth history with standardized growth chart.

❏ Measure head circumference and determine whether appropriate for age according to standardized growth chart.

Psychosocial Assessment

❏ Assess the child's and family's interaction patterns.

❏ Assess the family's involvement with child protective services (CPS).

- Parents or child may volunteer this history.
- The local CPS office may be contacted by the designated member of the emergency department

(ED). This is often done by the hospital social worker.

❏ Assess the family's resources.

- Level of resources
- Source of income
- Level of education
- Housing

❏ Assess the family's composition.

- Number of children in home
- Number of adults in home

❏ Have any children in family spent time in foster care?

❏ Assess social support system.

❏ Assess for history of parental/partner substance abuse.

Nursing Interventions

1. Assess and maintain airway, breathing, and circulation as needed in cases of life-threatening trauma (Chapter 28).

2. Initiate measures to diagnose and treat injuries, as outlined in the trauma-specific chapters (Chapters 29–38).

3. Prepare for diagnostic procedures.

4. Provide psychosocial support.
   - Establish a rapport with family.
   - Convey concern and empathy.
   - Use a nonjudgmental, noncritical approach.
     - Judgmental attitudes hinder communication and limit information.
     - Acknowledge demands of parenting.
     - Discuss alternatives to corporal punishment.
     - Focus on the health and well-being of the child.
     - Encourage parents to discuss their feelings about the child's injury; such feelings may include anger, grief, or guilt.

5. Document the history and observed injuries.
   - Document all statements made by the child and parents as direct quotes.
   - Document time of all statements, in case the history changes over time.
   - Document all injuries noting their size, shape, color, and location.
   - Document nonverbal interactions between parent and child.

6. Photo document all injuries.
   - Use a hospital photographer for reliable and profes-

sional photographs.

- If a photographer is not available, use a high-quality digital camera that is kept in the emergency department.

- Document the child's name, birth date, and medical record number; include a ruler in the photo, as well as a standard color chart.

7. Report suspected child abuse and neglect to CPS, hospital child protection team (if available), and law enforcement agency, when indicated.

- Every state has a law requiring the reporting of suspected child maltreatment to designated child protection or law enforcement authorities. Although anyone in any state may report a suspicion of child abuse, reporting laws usually mandate reporting only for professionals who have regular contact with children.[2] In all 50 states, nurses are mandated reporters.

- Reporting requirements provide that a report must be made if the mandated reporter suspects or has reason to believe that a child has been abused or neglected[2]; the nurse does not need to "know for sure" that abuse or neglect occurred. A professional who postpones reporting until all doubt is eliminated probably will have violated the reporting law.[2]

- Reporting laws deliberately leave the ultimate decision about whether abuse or neglect occurred to investigating officials, not to the mandated reporters such as nurses.[2]

- Emergency nurses reporting child maltreatment in good faith are typically immune from civil or criminal liability, whereas nurses who knowingly or intentionally fail to report suspected abuse or neglect are subject to civil or criminal liability. Some states impose criminal liability even if the mandated reporter did not realize the child was abused when a reasonable professional would have suspected abuse.[2] Deliberate failure to report suspected abuse is a crime.[2]

- An emergency nurse, physician, or social worker should inform the parents of this report. Emphasize that the report is a legal requirement and not meant to be punitive toward the parents.

- Parents should be alerted to the possibility they will be contacted by CPS and that a home visit is likely to occur. They should also be informed that this is a referral for services, and not a criminal complaint.

- Arrangements should be made with hospital security or local law enforcement agencies should the ED staff suspect that a parent will remove the child against medical advice.

8. Prepare for the child's transfer and transport to a tertiary care center, hospitalization, or discharge to CPS.

- Immediate removal of the child from the abusive home is necessary when there is imminent danger to the child's safety.

9. Refer the family to other health care and social service professionals, as necessary.

- Primary care provider for follow-up assessment and services.

- Social worker for information on community resources.

- Support groups for parenting and child care.

- Public health or community health nursing services.

- Public assistance programs, such as TANF (temporary assistance to needy families) and WIC (women, infants, and children food program).

Specific Child Maltreatment Emergencies

Child Neglect

Neglect, the most prevalent form of child maltreatment, is a major threat to the health and well-being of children.[3] Neglect tends to be chronic, whereas physical abuse is typically episodic. In addition to physical neglect, a child may be subjected to emotional, medical, or educational neglect. Over one half of fatal child maltreatment cases result from neglect.[3]

Parents suspected of neglect often have inadequate financial resources, lower educational attainment, lack of parenting skills, and poor problem-solving skills. Neglect may also be manifested in failure-to-thrive (FTT) syndrome, a diagnostic term used to describe a lack of growth according to expected norms for age and gender, which typically occurs in the first 2 years of life.[4]

Focused History

Family and Social history

- ❏ Lack of adequate resources
- ❏ Social isolation
- ❏ Unsafe or unsanitary housing conditions
- ❏ Failure to provide for basic needs including food, clothing, education, and health care
- ❏ Lack of supervision of child, resulting in unintentional injuries or poisonings

Patient History

- ☐ Inadequate immunization status
- ☐ Abandonment or inadequate supervision
- ☐ Educational neglect, such as frequent school absences or truancy
- ☐ Unattended medical problems
- ☐ Inadequate dietary intake

Focused Assessment

Physical Assessment

- ☐ Specific growth parameters are evaluated.
  - ▪ Assess the child's anthropometric measures (weight, height, and head circumference).
    - • A child whose weight falls below the fifth percentile on an anthropometric (growth) chart may be at risk for failure to thrive (FTT) syndrome. Underlying medical causes for poor weight gain need to be explored.
  - ▪ Assess the child's nutritional status.
    - • Neglect may include malnourishment.
  - ▪ Assess the child's hygiene.
    - • Inappropriate clothing for the season and poor personal and oral hygiene (such as unattended dental caries) may be observed.
- ☐ Assess for age-appropriate interactions.
  - ▪ Note the infant's and child's attentiveness to the environment.
    - • Children with a dull, inactive, and excessively passive and fatigued appearance may be neglected. Also, children who are detached or excessively fearful may be neglected.
  - ▪ Assess for bald spots on an infant's head.
    - • Bald spots may result if the infant is left in a crib for long periods of time.
  - ▪ Assess for developmental delays (Chapter 3).
    - • A standardized screening tool, such as the Stages and Ages Questionnaire[5], can be used to screen for developmental delays.

Psychosocial Assessment

- ☐ Assess parent's interest in child's well-being.
- ☐ Assess the child's and family's interaction patterns.
- ☐ Assess parent's access to resources.
- ☐ Assess the family's prior involvement with CPS.
- ☐ Assess family composition.

Nursing Interventions

1. Ensure safety of child while in emergency department.
2. Treat injuries or dehydration as appropriate.
3. Prepare for diagnostic procedures.
4. Provide psychosocial support to the child and family.
5. Utilize written and photo documentation of the child's history and observed neglect.
6. Report cases of suspected neglect to CPS and the hospital child protection team (if available).
7. Refer the family to other health care professionals, as necessary.
8. If it is determined that the child is not in immediate harm if discharged home, provide discharge instructions as appropriate and information on available community resources.

Home Care and Prevention

Parents may need guidance in identifying community resources available to them for assistance with housing, food, and other basic necessities. Referrals to such agencies may be initiated in the emergency department or through a referral to the public health department. Educating parents on proper nutritional choices and dental care (Chapter 5) and providing resources to accomplish these recommendations requires the support of other hospital and community resources. Emergency nurses may choose to teach parenting classes to community groups or may choose to be involved in local shelters or homeless clinics to provide counseling to families at risk.

Physical Abuse

Many cases of child physical abuse are identified in the emergency department when a caregiver seeks treatment for the child with an inflicted injury. In some cases, the inflicted injury is identified inadvertently when the child is treated for an unrelated illness or injury. For example, a rib fracture resulting from abuse may be diagnosed when a chest radiograph is obtained to diagnose pneumonia.

The injuries related to physical abuse may range from a cutaneous lesion to death. In addition to physical injury, a body of literature has documented the long-term health consequences associated with physical abuse. Those include:

- ☐ Chronic health issues
- ☐ Depression, posttraumatic stress disorder, or other psychiatric condition
- ☐ Cognitive or perceptual problems
- ☐ Aggressive or violent behavior

❒ Interpersonal problems

Munchausen syndrome by proxy (MSBP), also known as "factitious disorder by proxy" (FDBP), is a somewhat rare form of physical abuse. In cases of MSPB, a parent or other caregiver deliberately falsifies a child's illness through fabrication or creation of symptoms and then seeks medical care[6] (Table 44.2). Less commonly, MSBP may also involve falsification of psychological or developmental symptoms. Younger children are more vulnerable to this type of maltreatment and are at a significant risk for short- and long-term physical and psychological harm, and even death.[6] It is important to note that perpetrators of MSBP often seek care at multiple hospitals, are knowledgeable about disease symptoms, and appear very concerned with their child's health.

Focused History

Family and Social History

❒ Denial of any knowledge of cause or mechanism of injury.
  ▪ Parent is reluctant to give information.
  ▪ Parent blames sibling for injury.
❒ Delay in seeking medical attention.
  ▪ Abusive parents ignore the seriousness of an injury in the hope that the injury will heal without medical attention, thereby avoiding detection and legal action.
❒ Inappropriate emotional response to severity of injury.
❒ Previous placement of a child in foster care.
❒ Previous involvement with CPS.
❒ Presence of "crisis" factors at home.
❒ Substance abuse by caregiver.
❒ Previous history of abuse in the caregiver.
❒ Family history of sudden infant death syndrome or unexplained deaths.
❒ Family history of bleeding or bone disorders.

Patient History

❒ Health history, including a history of repeated injuries or hospitalizations.
  ▪ Abusive parents often seek medical care at many different treatment facilities to avoid being identified.
  ▪ The child's medical record, when available, may provide documentation of previous suspicious injuries.
❒ History inconsistent with existing injury or inconsistencies in the provided history—a cardinal finding.

❒ Child developmentally incapable of specified self-injury.
  ▪ Determine whether the child is developmentally able to have injured himself or herself in such a manner; suspect child abuse if the child's developmental capabilities do not coincide with the mechanism or severity of injury.
❒ Acute change in the child's behavior or activity without any provided history (e.g., sudden limp, irritability, swollen arm).

Focused Assessment

Physical Assessment

❒ Assess the neurologic system.
  ▪ Assess the child's level of consciousness using the AVPU (*A*lert, responds to *V*erbal stimuli, responds to *P*ainful stimuli, *U*nresponsive) method or Glasgow Coma Scale method.
    • Children with an altered level of consciousness may have craniocerebral trauma, including subarachnoid or subdural hematomas.
  ▪ Observe the head for swelling or edema of the scalp, lacerations, and other signs of trauma.
    • Abusive head trauma (AHT) is the leading cause of death in abused children.[7] The majority of deaths from head trauma among children younger than 2 years are the result of maltreatment.[7]
    • AHT may result from direct trauma, vigorous shaking, or a combination of direct trauma and shaking. Resultant injuries are diagnosed as shaken baby syndrome (SBS).
    • SBS is a unique and prevalent form of intracranial injury that may have no external evidence of head trauma.
    • SBS results from acceleration-deceleration injuries due to vigorous shaking, which may or may not involve blunt trauma to the head.
    • SBS victims may present with seizures, sleepiness, vomiting, and irritability.
    • Physical findings in SBS include retinal hemorrhages, hemotympanum, subdural or subarachnoid hemorrhages, cerebral edema, grip marks to chest and upper arms, and fractures of the humeri or ribs.
❒ Assess the abdomen.
  ▪ Observe the abdomen for bruising or other signs of external trauma.
    • Abdominal injuries are the second leading cause of fatalities in abused children.[8]

TABLE 44.2 Characteristics of Munchausen Syndrome by Proxy (MSBP)

Tend to be younger children.

- School-aged children may be abused in this manner.
- Older children may aid in the parents' deceptions to protect them or because of an intense fear of retribution by the MSBP parent.

Often long history of suspicious symptoms

Mothers are the perpetrators in the vast majority of identified cases of MSBP.

- Frequently, the mother has chronic, poorly defined medical problems.
- In many instances the mother has trained in one of the health care professions and is, therefore, adept at making falsified information appear credible.
- The mother often appears genuinely concerned and sometimes overconcerned over her child's illness and, when the child is hospitalized, rarely leaves the child's bedside.
- Perpetrator typically continues victimizing the child in the hospital.

Perpetrator may induce physical findings in their children by:

- Manual suffocation
- Administration of drugs or toxic substances or contaminating central lines
- Placing their own blood in the child's urine, vomitus, or stool specimens

Drugs often used in MSBP include:

- Laxatives to induce severe diarrhea
- Insulin to induce hypoglycemia and seizures
- Ipecac to induce vomiting
- Drugs or alcohol to cause an alteration in level of consciousness
- Salt may be added to an infant's formula to induce hypernatremia

Clinical indicators of MSBP are:

- Recurrent illnesses for which no cause is identified
- Unusual symptoms that do not make clinical sense
- Problems that consistently occur in the presence of a specific person
- Unexplained death or illness in one or more siblings
- Frequent visits to various hospitals that result in normal findings
- The presence of drugs that induced the symptoms in a toxicology screen
- Discrepancies between the history and physical findings
- Numerous hospitalizations at many different hospitals

Clinical presentations often include:

- Seizures
- Apnea
- Diarrhea
- Vomiting
- Bleeding
- Rash
- Fever
- Central nervous system depression

- Blunt abdominal trauma, the most common type of inflicted abdominal trauma in children, is usually the result of a child's being punched or kicked in the abdomen.

- When children sustain inflicted blows to the abdomen, the intestines and solid organs are compressed between the striking object and the vertebral column.[9] It may result in intra-abdominal hemorrhage with few external signs of trauma.

- Unintentionally injured children are usually seen immediately after the injury, whereas care is often delayed in abusive injuries.

- The high mortality resulting from these injuries may be due to intra-abdominal hemorrhage with resulting hypovolemic shock, peritonitis, delay in seeking medical attention, or failure of emergency personnel to make the correct diagnosis when lifesaving surgery is needed.

- Severe internal injuries may not be immediately detected. This is because of the parent's failure to give an accurate history of trauma and because there may be little or no external evidence of abdominal trauma at the time of examination.

❑ Observe for vomiting, guarding, abdominal pain, and signs of cardiovascular failure.

  - Bilious vomiting may be present, suggesting an obstruction.

❑ Assess the integumentary system for signs of trauma.

  - Observe for cutaneous lesions.

    - Cutaneous lesions are the most common manifestation of physical abuse and are the most easily recognized sign of abuse. The buttocks and hips are the most commonly injured areas involving physical abuse. The face is the second most common area for contusions related to abuse.[10]

    - The pattern of a bruise may reflect the method or instrument used to injure a child.

    - A comparison of intentional versus unintentional bruises is described in Table 44.3.

    - Cutaneous lesions resulting from blunt forces and instruments are described in Table 44.4.

  - Observe for burns.

    - Inflicted burns are involved in approximately 10% of severe cases of child abuse and are the third leading cause of death related to child abuse.[10]

    - Ten percent to 25% of burns in hospitalized children involve child maltreatment.[10]

- Burns are divided by source of heat such as scalds by hot liquids, flame, contact with hot objects, electrical, chemical, and radiation.[10]

- Children who repeatedly suffer burns should be carefully evaluated for abuse.

- Suspicion should be raised when treatment for burns is delayed more than 24 hours or when the parent who was not home at the time of the burning seeks health care.

- Table 44.5 compares unintentional and intentional burn patterns from scalds, contact with hot objects, and cigarettes.

❑ Assess the musculoskeletal system.

  - Observe for deformed extremities, indicating long bone fractures.

    - Injuries to bones are more common in abused children younger than 2 years, whereas unintentional fractures occur more commonly among school-aged children.

    - Fractures and dislocations that are inconsistent with the mechanism of injury are highly suspect.

    - Table 44.6 compares fracture types with their probable cause.

  - Observe for pain, tenderness, edema, and inability to use the extremity.

    - In cases of inflicted injury, caretakers often delay seeking medical treatment; therefore, manifestations typically seen in the acute phase of skeletal injury, such as swelling and tenderness, may not be present.

❑ Assess the eyes and ocular ability.

  - Perform simple vision screening by having the verbal child count fingers or objects; have the preverbal child or infant follow/track an object.

  - Inflicted eye injuries may leave no external evidence of trauma. Thus, an ophthalmologic examination by indirect light is essential in suspected cases of child abuse.

  - Eye injuries that can result from physical abuse include:

    - Periorbital ecchymosis, often indicative of a basilar skull fracture

    - Fractures of the orbital bones

    - Subconjunctival hemorrhage

    - Dislocated lens

    - Retinal detachment

    - Retinal hemorrhage

    - Hyphema

TABLE 44.3 Comparison of Intentional and Unintentional Injuries Resulting in Bruising

Characteristic	Unintentional	Intentional
Location	Bony prominences (forehead, elbows, knees, and shins) or anterior surfaces	Abdomen, back, buttocks, genitals, posterior thighs; areas typically protected by clothing; bruises over noncontiguous areas
Color	It is not possible to accurately determine the age of a bruise from its color.	Varying configurations and shapes
Shape	Uniform shape, such as a skinned knee or a scratch on the arm	Varying configurations and shapes

TABLE 44.4 Cutaneous Lesions Typically Resulting from Intentional Injury

Method of Injury	Resulting Cutaneous Lesions
Mechanical forces:	
Doubled-over extension or lamp cord	Characteristic loop-shaped marks are typically found on the back, buttocks, upper arms, and thighs.
Belt, strap, buckle, or stick	Linear marks often found over curved body surfaces.
	An imprint of the belt buckle may be noted.
Spoon, paddle, spatula, or hairbrush	Oval or other shaped marks.
Hand	Characteristic parallel linear marks may be noted, representing the spaces between the fingers.
Coat hanger	Hangers leave a wider loop mark caused by the hanger's flat base.
Cords or ropes	Rope "ligature" marks on the ankles, wrist, or torso indicate that a child has been bound.
	Cords or rope used to bind ankles, wrists, and neck leave thin, circumferential bruises; thicker marks may indicate that the child has been tied with sheets.
Clothes or objects to gag infants and young children to stop their crying	Gag marks leave down-turned lesions at the corners of the mouth.
Human forces:	
Grabbing	Circular or oval marks on the upper arm may be the result of a caregiver forcibly grasping a child and applying pressure to the site.
Hair pulling	Areas of irregular hair loss characterized by broken, uneven hair may result from a child's being pulled by the hair (traction or traumatic alopecia).
	Bleeding under the scalp may also result from hair pulling.
Force-feeding	Injuries to the labial frenulum and lingual frenulum may result from a bottle or spoon being forced into the child's mouth.
Physical forces	Teeth may be loosened or knocked out from blunt trauma to the face.
Blunt	Oral lacerations also may occur from a direct blow to the face.
Human bites	Marks may resemble a double horseshoe or are an irregular doughnut-shaped mark.
	Bite marks are measured to determine if they were inflicted by an adult or child. (Adult bite marks have a 3-cm or greater distance between the canines.)
	Human bites typically do not leave puncture marks.

- Corneal abrasion
- Optic atrophy

❒ Assess the ears.

  ▪ Observe for evidence of inflicted injuries.

    - Contusions about the external ear, including behind the ear.
    - Ecchymosis on the internal surface of the pinna may be the result of boxing the ear and crushing it against the skull or pinching the ear.
    - Battle's sign (the presence of ecchymosis behind the ear), indicative of a basilar skull fracture (Chapter 29).

  ▪ Perform or assist with an otoscopic examination to detect hemotympanum and perforation of the tympanic membrane, resulting from a direct blow to the ear.

Psychosocial Assessment

❒ Assess the child's and family's interaction patterns.

❒ Assess the family's prior involvement with CPS.

❒ Assess the family's composition.

❒ Consult with the child's primary care provider to determine whether there have been prior episodes of suspicious behaviors or injuries.

❒ Evaluate the risk for subsequent injury if the child is discharged home from the emergency department.

❒ Ascertain the availability of social support systems.

TABLE 44.5 Comparisons of Intentional and Unintentional Burn Injuries		
Burn Etiology	*Intentional*	*Unintentional*
Scalds: ▪ Immersion injuries—occur when the child is forcibly held in the hot water for a prolonged period of time, such as a few minutes.	▪ Tend to be full thickness. The presence of clothing tends to cause more severe burns because there is longer contact between the hot water and the skin. Initially the clothing is protective; the extent of the burn depends on the duration of exposure to the hot liquid and temperature of liquid. ▪ Uniform in depth ▪ Symmetrical ▪ Have sharp lines of demarcation ▪ Often involve bilateral burns of the feet, hands, and buttocks ▪ Usually spare flexion creases because the child flexes the extremities in the hot water ▪ Often appear "sock-shaped" on the feet, "glove-shaped" on the hands, and "doughnut-shaped" on the buttocks ▪ Doughnut-shaped burns occur when a child is forcibly held down in water with the buttock flat against the bathtub. The unburned area ("doughnut hole") is the result of the buttocks being forcibly held down against the bottom of the tub and, thus, that area being spared prolonged contact with the hot water. ▪ Typically caused by tap water	▪ Tend to be partial thickness ▪ "Arrowhead" shape, with widest and deepest part of burn at top (or first point of contact)[10] ▪ Uneven in depth ▪ Asymmetrical ▪ Usually not as clearly demarcated on the edges ▪ May be unilateral; if bilateral, burn depth is not deep ▪ May not be deep or extensive ▪ Are not extensive or severe and do not depict the configuration of the hot object ▪ Often caused by boiling water, coffee, soups, and other foodstuffs

TABLE 44.5 Comparisons of Intentional and Unintentional Burn Injuries (continued)

Burn Etiology	Intentional	Unintentional
Oral burns	May occur from excessively hot food or fluids placed in the child's mouth	
Intentional pour burns	Usually on the back; typically does not have splash pattern	
Contact burns	Sharply demarcated edges Depict the patterned configuration of a heating object including: • Steam irons • Electric stove burners • Hot plates • Forks • Knives • Radiators (toddlers being toilet trained may be placed on radiators to dry their wet diapers, resulting in burns to the buttocks) • Furnace grates • Hair dryers • Candles • Curling irons • Car cigarette lighters • Cigarette lighters	Indistinct margins caused by object falling onto child or child's attempt to escape.
Cigarette burns	Occurs from deliberate attempts to burn the child. Multiple in number and healing stage. Found on the soles of the feet, palms of the hands, buttocks, or back. Tend to be circular and 7 to 10 mm in diameter and often third-degree burns.	May occur when sudden movement causes momentary contact with a lighted cigarette. Singular burn Typically occur about the face when a young child walks into a lighted cigarette held by an adult at waist height. Usually shallower, more irregular, and less circumscribed than deliberately inflicted ones.

TABLE 44.6 Comparison of Fracture Type and Probable Cause

Type of Fracture	Probable Cause
Spiral fracture of long bones	Intentional twisting of the extremity; spiral fractures of the humerus are particularly suspicious; femoral fractures in infants and toddlers are often a result of abuse
Rib fractures	Frequently multiple, bilateral, and posterior, often reflecting a squeezing of the chest
Skull, nose, or facial fractures	Frequently the result of abuse
Fractures to the sternum, spinous processes, scapulae; humeral fractures in children less than 3 years of age	Result of intense blunt forces
Femur fractures in children younger than 1 year of age (nonambulatory)	Frequently the result of abuse
Fractures of the epiphyseal-metaphyseal junction; transverse fractures	Result of abuse
Multiple fractures of different ages	Result of abuse

Nursing Interventions

1. Assess and maintain airway, breathing, circulation, and disability (Chapter 28).
2. Obtain specific diagnostic tests to determine the extent of the injuries, identify the cause of the injury or illness, and determine whether prior injuries, such as fractures, have occurred.
   - Obtain radiographs of the injured extremity to identify previous fractures.
     - Multiple fractures, especially bilateral, in various stages of healing indicate repeated abuse.
     - The possibility that multiple fractures are related to an underlying disease, such as osteogenesis imperfecta, scurvy, syphilis, rickets, neoplasia, or osteomyelitis, should be considered. The presence of these rare disorders can be ruled out by appropriate diagnostic procedures.
   - Obtain a skeletal survey in children younger than 2 years of age when indicated for suspected abuse.
   - Obtain coagulation studies to rule out blood dyscrasias for multiple bruises.
   - Obtain skull radiographs and computed tomography scans to determine the presence of bilateral skull fractures, multiple skull fractures, skull fractures with widths greater than 5 mm, subdural hematomas, and separation of sutures arising from chronic subdural hematoma.
   - Obtain cervical spine radiographs to detect subluxation or dislocation; anticipate spinal cord injury without radiographic abnormality (SCIWORA)

(Chapter 30).

3. Provide psychosocial support.
4. Utilize careful written and photo documentation of the child's history and observed injuries.
5. Report cases of suspected abuse to CPS and the hospital child protection team (if available).
6. Refer the family to other health care and social service professionals as necessary.
7. Prepare for transfer or transport to a tertiary care center, hospitalization, or discharge to CPS.

Prevention

The general public views nurses as one of the most trusted groups of professionals. This trust can be parlayed with high-risk families by reaching out to those who are struggling to provide nurturing and safe environments for their children. Emergency nurses should identify opportunities to provide information related to child safety and parenting skills to all families. This can be accomplished by providing families with referrals to resources within their community that help strengthen families and enhance child development. Nurses may also help to prevent abuse and neglect by assisting families in identifying sources of social support and other resources for effective parenting. Families at risk for child maltreatment can benefit from referrals to home visitation programs (e.g., Healthy Families America, an initiative of Prevent Child Abuse America; SafeCare, an evidence-based, parent-training curriculum for at-risk parents; and the Nurse-Family Partnership, a home visitation program for first-time parents). Some communities offer telephone hotlines for parents experiencing high levels of stress. In addition, emergency nurses can routinely provide information to parents on normal child growth and development and effective parenting strategies. Nurses need to pay particular attention to the safety of children when there is a history of domestic violence or substance abuse in the family.

Conclusion

Child maltreatment is an all-too-common phenomenon with serious long-term physical and mental health consequences. Astute observations of child and family dynamics, understanding of the causes of intentional and unintentional injury, and prompt recognition of serious injury help emergency nurses to decrease the morbidity and mortality associated with child maltreatment. Emergency nurses are mandated by law to report suspected abuse and neglect. Collaborating with the hospital's child protection team is essential for facilitating the care of maltreated children. Some states mandate completion of continuing education programs on child maltreatment for renewal of nursing licenses.

Caring for an abused child in the emergency department is often a source of emotional stress for health care professionals. This phenomenon is typically referred to as "vicarious victimization" or "compassion fatigue." Opportunities should be provided to nursing staff to reflect on their experiences and feelings related to caring for victims of abuse. Professionals in psychology, psychiatry, and social work are often available to facilitate such discussions.

References

1. Children's Bureau. (2006). *Child maltreatment 2006.* Washington, DC: Administration for Children and Families, Department of Health and Human Services.

2. Myers, J. E. B. (2005). Legal issues. In A. P. Giardino & R. Alexander (Eds.), *Child maltreatment: A clinical reference* (3rd ed., pp. 707–721). St. Louis, MO: G.W. Medical Publishing.

3. Joffe, M. D., Giardino, A. P., & O'Sullivan, A. L. (2005). Neglect and abandonment. In A. P. Giardino & R. Alexander (Eds.), *Child maltreatment: A clinical reference* (3rd ed., pp. 153–193). St. Louis, MO: G.W. Medical Publishing.

4. Kolagotla, L., Sandel, M., & Frank, D. (2005). Failure to thrive: A reconceptualization. In A. P. Giardino & R. Alexander (Eds.), *Child maltreatment: A clinical reference* (3rd ed., pp. 195–208). St. Louis, MO: G.W. Medical Publishing.

5. Sparling, J., Lewis, I., & Ramey, C. T. (1995). *Partners for learning: Birth to 36 months.* Lewisville, NC: Kaplan Press.

6. Feldman, M. D., & Sheridan, M. S. (2005). Munchausen syndrome by proxy. In A. P. Giardino & R. Alexander (Eds.), *Child maltreatment: A clinical reference* (3rd ed., pp. 395–408). St. Louis, MO: G.W. Medical Publishing.

7. Starling, S. P. (2005). Head injury. In A. P. Giardino & R. Alexander (Eds.), *Child maltreatment: A clinical reference* (3rd ed., pp. 37–62). St. Louis, MO: G.W. Medical Publishing.

8. Giardino, E. R., Brown, K. M., & Giardino, A. P. (2003). The physical examination in the evaluation of child maltreatment: Physical and sexual abuse examinations. In E. R. Giardino & A. P. Giardino (Eds.), *Nursing approach to the evaluation of child maltreatment* (pp. 69–135). St. Louis, MO: G.W. Medical Publishing.

9. Bechtrel, K. (2005). Thoracoabdominal injuries. In A. P. Giardino & R. Alexander (Eds.), *Child maltreatment: A clinical reference* (3rd ed., pp. 103–112). St. Louis, MO: G.W. Medical Publishing.

10. Johnson, C., & French, G. (2005). Bruises and burns in child maltreatment. In A. P. Giardino & R. Alexander (Eds.), *Child maltreatment: A clinical reference* (3rd ed., pp. 63–81). St. Louis, MO: G.W. Medical Publishing.

FORTY-FIVE

Child Sexual Abuse

Julie Ann Melini, RN, MS, FNP-C, SANE-A, SANE-P

Introduction

Dating back to the earliest of recorded time there has been an awareness of incest, referring to sexual intercourse between persons too closely related to marry. This behavior has been recognized and prohibited almost universally across cultures throughout time.[1] However, it was not until the 1970s that child sexual abuse was recognized as a problem occurring with frequent incidence in our society. This new awareness brought about federal legislation in 1974, the Child Abuse Prevention and Treatment Act (CAPTA; P.L. 93-247), along with the establishment of the National Center on Child Abuse and Neglect. The purpose of this chapter is to discuss the recognition and treatment of victims of sexual abuse.

Etiology

Most definitions of sexual abuse are based on work done by CAPTA. Finkel and DeJong[2] define child sexual abuse as the involvement of children or adolescents in sexual activities they do not understand, to which they cannot give informed consent, or that violate social taboos. Christian and Giardino[3] describe sexual abuse as an array of activities including:

❐ Genital exposure by the perpetrator

❐ Observation of the child by the perpetrator when the child is dressing, undressing, bathing, or toileting outside the cultural norms

❐ Kissing

❐ Fondling

❐ Masturbation

- By the perpetrator while the child watches
- Perpetrator observing the child masturbating

❐ Oral sex

- Fellatio: Mouth to the penis
- Cunnilingus: Mouth to the vagina

❐ Genital penetration with:

- Object
- Fingers
- Perpetrator's penis

Child pornography is another form of child sexual abuse. With the wide use of the internet, allowing perpetrators to send and receive images without direct outside contact, child pornography has become much more prevalent. Child pornography encompasses a wide range of activities including arranging and photographing in any media any sexual acts involving children, and the distribution of this material.[4]

The National Child Abuse and Neglect Data System (NCANDS) identified 83,810 children as victims of sexual abuse (substantiated reports) in 2005.[5] This does not represent all of the children sexually abused. Many cases go unreported, and many reported cases cannot be substantiated because of lack of evidence. Retrospective studies indicate that one out of four females and one out of six males are sexually abused before they are 18 years of age.[6]

Recognizing that a child is being sexually abused can be difficult. Children often do not disclose the abuse and sexual acts between themselves and the perpetrator nor is the event often witnessed. Concern that sexual abuse may have occurred is often initiated by the child's behavior. The disparity between substantiated cases and retrospective reports of abuse demonstrates that many children are being sexually abused who do not have any behavior changes or these changes are not recognized.

Likewise, perpetrators are difficult to profile. Many abusers are successfully employed, active in community affairs, and do not have prior criminal records.[2] In the past, convicted perpetrators were subject to only a criminal penalty. In more recent years, in an effort to protect children from repeat offenders there is a sex offender registry, public notification, and post-incarceration civil commitment. Additionally, there has been a development of sex offender treatment programs within the correctional setting.[7]

Sexual abuse of children is a crime in every state in the United States. Stopping the perpetrator can only be accomplished if the abuse is reported. The law requires that professionals, including nurses, report suspected child abuse to authorities. The requirement to report is based on a reasonable suspicion of maltreatment; it does not require that the professional knows that the abuse has occurred.[8] The nurse, or any reporting professional, should not be performing an investigation; this is the role of law enforcement.[8]

Focused History

Getting a history from an adult is standard procedure. It is equally important to obtain a history from any child capable of talking.[2] There is often a misperception that physical evidence will confirm whether or not sexual abuse has occurred. Experience has shown that the most important information is what the child states about his or her experience.[9]

Reports of child sexual abuse are much different from that of an adult rape. Few children present immediately, and they are unlikely to have acute injury.[9] Children can be groomed by a perpetrator for increasing sexual involvement over a period of time. It is often a secret between the perpetrator and the child, accompanied with threats of harm or coercion for a special favor. The child is confused because the activity may "feel good." Children do not know the exact physical act of intercourse unless they have been taught. They may state that "he put it inside" even though only intralabial intercourse may have occurred without any penetration into the vaginal opening. The child, not understanding ejaculation, may report getting "peed on" or that he or she "got wet with sticky stuff." However, children are also easily influenced by parental reactions and by what they hear the parent report.

Talk with the adult accompanying the child, discussing his or her concerns. Do this without the child in the room. The child should not be present when the parent discusses his or her concerns.[10] The child witnessing the parent's disclosure may react in one of two ways. If the child has been sexually abused and sees that this has made the parent upset, the child may recant and deny that anything happened. The other reaction may be a child who has not been abused but hears the parent's concerns over and over and eventually believes that this is what really happened.

Talk with the child without others in the room, asking general questions. Never push the child to disclose. There are trained experts in the area of interviewing a child regarding sexual abuse, and this can occur at a later date. Whether or not the child discloses anything, he or she needs a complete examination, including the genitalia. Just because the child does not disclose at this time does not mean that nothing happened. It must be reported if a suspicion exists.

Frasier[11] gives some general guidelines when speaking to children or adolescents about sexual abuse:

❏ Speak to the parent alone. Get a complete medical, social, and family history, in addition to physical and behavioral symptoms.

❏ Speak to the child alone. Building a rapport with the child and careful explanation to the parent will facilitate this.

❏ When talking to the child, begin with neutral topics to help the child feel more comfortable answering questions about the abuse. Neutral topics may include school, a recent or upcoming holiday, or other area of interest to the child.

❏ Begin with open-ended, non-direct questions such as "Do you know why you are here?" or "Can you tell me what happened to you?"

❏ Younger children may need some direction, such as "Has anyone ever touched your private parts?" Some follow-up questions may be necessary to help the child understand what this means. One way to describe private parts would be those areas covered with a swimming suit.

❏ Avoid leading questions: "Did your Uncle Joey touch your pee pee?"

❏ Use language that is developmentally appropriate and use words the child is familiar with. Clarify with the parent before talking to the child what terms the child uses for the genital and anal areas.

❏ Be honest. Do not make promises that cannot be kept to get information from child.

❏ Do not use bribery such as "You will get a treat if you

tell me what Uncle Joey did to you."

❏ Do not force a child to tell what happened. Information that is forced from a child is not reliable. The child may lie if he or she is forced in a situation.

❏ Document exact wording of the questions and answers given, using the child's terms.

Be attentive and supportive with anything the child states. Do not convey verbally or nonverbally any indication of shock, negative feelings, or judgment. It is also important to reassure the child that what happened is not his or her fault.

Focused Assessment

Physical Assessment

Physical findings in the sexually abused child are uncommon. Frasier[11] attributes this to:

❏ Delayed reporting by the child. Children seen weeks, or even a few days, after the abuse will have had time to heal, leaving no evidence of trauma.

❏ Child perpetrators are careful not to cause pain or injury. The child is less likely to disclose the incident if there is no pain or injury. Children who experience discomfort as a result of the sexual contact are less likely to be deceived into the activity again.

❏ Children are also confused when the perpetrator is someone they trust and have been taught to look up to and obey. They may not be sure it is wrong.

When the examination is done within 72 hours of the abuse, physical findings are present in approximately 13% of the cases; when the examination occurs more than 72 hours after the incident physical findings drop to less than 4%.[13] Palusci et al.[13] describe the findings such as:

❏ Vaginal lacerations

❏ Hymenal tears

❏ Hymenal abrasions

❏ Anal lacerations

❏ Bruising

However, these findings are not conclusive by themselves that sexual abuse has occurred. Straddle injuries, blunt force trauma from a bicycle crossbar, monkey bars, or other objects can provide a reasonable accidental explanation for these injuries. Even though findings are uncommon, the child with possible sexual abuse needs a complete head-to-toe examination, including the anogenital areas. The medical examination when there is a concern of child sexual abuse should not be painful, uncomfortable, or forced.[14]

Children often present to the emergency department (ED) with other complaints that should include sexual abuse as potential cause. Some of these nonspecific findings include:

❏ Abdominal pain

❏ Eating disorders

❏ Dysuria

❏ Enuresis and/or encopresis

❏ Rectal pain

❏ Vaginal or urethral discharge

Psychosocial Assessment

When dealing with a suspected victim of sexual abuse, the nurse needs to convey interest, sincerity, and respect. Forensic investigating agencies (Child Protective Service agency and the law enforcement agency) will do the detailed interview. However, the nurse needs some information to medically care for the child. Inquiring about the family norms and any change in the child's behavior can be helpful in the assessment process. For example:

❏ Sleeping arrangements (e.g., child sleeps with parents)

❏ Exposure to nudity or pornography

❏ Sudden appearance of unusual fears or nightmares

❏ Runaway or suicidal thoughts or gestures

❏ Nonorganic pain or illness

❏ School problems

❏ Sexual acting out behavior

Lippman[15] and Frasier[11] give examples of behaviors that may be related to sexual abuse.

❏ Specific to sexual abuse:
  - Sexual activities or knowledge beyond the developmental level of a child that age
  - Explicit description of sexual contact
  - Compulsive masturbation
  - Excessive sexual curiosity, sexual acting out

❏ Nonspecific symptoms (sexual abuse may be one of many possible causes):
  - Nightmares
  - Developmental regression
  - Undue fear of strangers
  - Other symptoms of posttraumatic stress disorder
  - Aggression or other abrupt behavior changes

Triage Considerations

Triage decisions for the possibly sexually abused child are based on medical condition, as well as preservation of evidence and providing a safe environment for the child.

The following types of injuries related to sexual abuse should be seen immediately (triaged at the highest level of urgency):

❏ Strangulation injuries, affecting airway and causing respiratory compromise

❏ Respiratory depression, possible date rape drug ingestion

❏ Excessive uncontrolled bleeding. This could be from the genital area or rectum or signs of internal bleeding from blunt trauma, causing hypovolemia and its complications.

The following complaints should be seen as soon as possible:

❏ Sexual contact reportedly occurring in the past 72 hours. Prompt evidence collection is vital. As time lapses from the incident evidence decreases.

❏ Current acute medical problems associated with onset of abuse (e.g., vaginal or rectal bleeding or discharge; severe abdominal pain, lacerations; bruising or other anogenital injuries)

❏ Severe emotional distress of child or caregiver (possible threat to self or others)

❏ Any child for whom safety is a concern (e.g., when there is concern that the caregiver will leave with the child or the perpetrator may have access to the child)

The following medical issues can be referred for assessment by an expert in pediatric sexual abuse within 1 week:

❏ Sexual contact beyond 72 hours (too late for evidence collection)

❏ Nonacute symptoms, possibly related to abuse (vaginal or rectal discharge, nonacute genital pain, blisters in genital or rectal area, enuresis, encopresis)

❏ Serious behavioral problems (refusing to attend school, nightmares, extreme fears)

❏ Danger of upcoming contact with alleged perpetrator, such as a weekend visit or during school attendance. The examination needs to be done before an unsupervised contact with the perpetrator.

Referral to a medical care provider with expertise in child sexual abuse and colposcopy evaluations is appropriate under the following circumstances:

❏ There has been no possible contact with alleged perpetrator for the past 2 weeks.

❏ There are no current medical problems relating to the abuse (e.g., no genital bleeding, no vaginal or rectal discharge, no continuing abdominal or genital pain).

❏ The child is adequately protected from ongoing abuse

until the examination can be done.

Nursing Interventions

Nursing interventions may vary depending on state laws and regulations, as well as protocols established by individual communities and hospitals. A pediatric expert trained in both the examination and the collection of evidence ideally performs the pediatric sexual assault examination. This could be a Sexual Assault Nurse Examiner (SANE) or physician with specific training in the area of child sexual abuse. The Office for Victims of Crime (OVC) under the U.S. Department of Justice supports the training and utilization of nurses in the sexual assault examination. A SANE offers patients who have been sexually assaulted prompt, compassionate care and comprehensive forensic evidence collection.[16] In many areas across the country these trained nurses get the history, do a physical assessment, gather evidence, and work with law enforcement agencies in preserving the chain of evidence.

Nursing interventions for the sexually abused child include:

1. Reporting allegations to the proper authorities.
2. Recording a complete medical history.
3. Performing a complete physical examination, focusing on evidence of trauma, pregnancy, sexually transmitted diseases (STDs), and the collection of evidence.
4. Making an assessment of the patient's psychological status.
5. Documenting the evidence of trauma, including photographs of physical findings.

There are many variables in the assessment and diagnosis of pediatric sexual abuse. The pediatric sexual assault examination is different from the adult examination for the following reasons:

❏ Psychosocial development. Children should not be expected to have an adult understanding of sexual activities. Such knowledge beyond what is expected for the child's developmental level is indicative of sexual abuse.[11]

❏ Physical development. Before estrogen stimulation, which begins about menarche, the hymen is thin tissue with translucent edges without the elasticity or fullness of an estrogenized hymen.

❏ The types of abuse perpetrated on children. The perpetrator usually does not have a desire to harm the child physically. This is one aspect that differentiates sexual abuse from classic rape.[9]

❏ The types of forensic evidence to be collected. In the

prepubescent girl only the external genitalia need to be examined. If there is not extensive injury or bleeding noted on the external examination no internal speculum examination is needed. Examinations requiring internal exploration or repair are best done under general anesthesia.[11]

Sexual Assault Examination Goals

The pediatric sexual assault examiner should do the following:

❒ Obtain a history from the adult accompanying the child, as well as from the child.

❒ Identify any trauma or infection and treat or refer for treatment.

❒ Collect and preserve forensic evidence, following protocols developed by the reporting agencies involved.

❒ Involve the appropriate reporting and investigative agencies. Reporting laws differ from state to state; familiarity with state laws is important.[11]

❒ Initiate social and emotional healing.

❒ Prevent further trauma.

❒ Identify other possible causes for symptoms.

Sexual Assault Examination Steps

The child must be completely informed and cooperative with the examination. Coercion, deceit, or force should not be used to perform the examination. The abused child is already a victim of abuse through the use of authority and control, with no control over what he or she has experienced.[9] The examination should not be traumatic or painful to the child.[11] Taking time to prepare the child for the examination, developing trust, and ensuring that there will be no pain and that the child is in control allows for a cooperative examination without need for sedation. The child is given as much control as possible during the examination. Each step is explained beforehand.[14] Table 45.1 describes helpful tips in performing a genital examination in a child.

The examination includes a head-to-toe examination assessment, beginning with noninvasive areas that the child is comfortable and familiar with from previous medical experiences.

1. Begin by listening to the heart and lungs, palpating the abdomen, and looking in the ears and mouth.

2. The anal and genital areas are examined last. The frog leg position with the feet together and knees bent and relaxed to the sides is comfortable for many children and allows for an adequate examination of the vaginal area using gentle traction of the labia majora. Older children with longer legs may do better using stirrups.

▪ Traction should not be painful for the child. Common errors that make the examination painful include pinching the labia majora too tightly or pulling traction laterally (instead of anteriorly) causing stretching and possibly laceration to the posterior fourchette.

TABLE 45.1 Helpful Tips for Performing a Genital Examination in a Child

Explain all aspects of the evaluation appropriate for the child's developmental level and interest.	Talk directly to the child. Use simple terms, and allow the child to see and handle equipment used in the exam. Demonstrate the exam on a stuffed toy. Allow the child to practice positioning before the exam while dressed.
Offer choices, giving the child as much control as possible.	What support person the child wants in the room, if any; whether he or she wears a patient gown or wraps in a sheet; which ear is looked at first are examples of choices the child can make.
Give the child control during the exam.	Explain that the exam will not hurt. Back this up by explaining that if anything does hurt the examiner will stop and do it differently.
Follow through on promises.	If the child indicates the exam is painful the examiner should stop and reposition the traction. Holding the labia gently and pulling anteriorly instead of laterally may be more comfortable for the child.
Use distraction during the exam.	Use of books, songs, talking with parent about a fun experience work well to distract the child during the genital exam.
Reassure the child after the exam.	Explain to the child honestly that the child is healthy and his or her body is normal, or that it is healing and will be healthy and normal soon. This is important in the psychological healing process for a child.

- There is no need for a speculum examination in the prepubescent child. If there is significant vaginal or anal bleeding from trauma the child will need to be evaluated and repaired under general anesthesia.

- If the examination needs to be completed for forensic and/or medical purposes and the child refuses the examination, anesthesia or conscious sedation is a consideration.[12] Sedation is generally not necessary if there is adequate preparation by skilled examiners and assistants.

- A colposcope is ideal for magnification and the identification of injury. Very few emergency departments have access to a colposcope for these examinations. A magnifying glass with a gooseneck lamp or an otoscope is an acceptable alternative.[11]

- Photographs capture what is seen at the time of evaluation, allowing other experts to evaluate the photo documentation rather than having the child examined a second time.[11] Photographs also preserve accurate documentation of what was seen at the time of the examination in much better detail than can be drawn or described in words.

3. Evaluation of the anus.

- The anus can be easily visualized by having the child supine on the bed, knees pulled up to chest with the arms wrapped around the legs. Most children understand if they are told to hold their legs like when doing a cannonball into the swimming pool.

- The external anal tissue generally has symmetric, circumferentially radiating folds called rugae. These rugae must be smoothed so that the tissue may be examined closely for injury.

- There is much disagreement regarding the interpretation of anal findings. Because of several variables, a child may or may not have any physical findings after the insertion of a penis or other object into the anus.[12] Some of these variables include:
  - Presence of force
  - Use of lubrication
  - Degree of cooperation from the child
  - Number of episodes of penetration. Children experiencing multiple episodes learn how to relax their anus to minimize pain and injury from the assault.
  - Time interval since the last contact

- Some normal anal findings are often misidentified as abuse.
  - Venous pooling: Circumferential swelling of the vessels around the anus can occur normally after traction has been applied to the anus during the examination. Have the child stand and walk around for a few minutes, then reexamine. The swelling and discoloration should be gone.
  - Smooth-shaped areas in the midline of the verge, which appear to be a congenital anomaly.[2]

4. Consider other possible causes for the child's symptoms.

- It is not the nurse's role to diagnose, but the nurse should be aware of other possible causes for symptoms that are often mistaken for sexual abuse. Assessment and documentation should help in identifying other causes. Table 45.2 describes other possible causes that could be mistaken for child abuse.

Evidence Collection

Emergency departments have protocols for collection and preservation of evidence reflecting individual hospital circumstances, as well as area laws and regulations. Regardless of differences in protocols there are some standards for evidence collection.

❏ The patient undresses carefully, to keep any debris in the clothing. Each piece of clothing is placed in a separate paper bag.

- Plastic bags are not breathable; clothing placed in plastic bags will mold and be useless for forensic evaluation.

- If there is loose debris in the clothing that may fall off, place two pieces of paper on the floor for the patient to stand on while disrobing. The top paper is carefully folded to maintain any debris that falls from the patient or the clothing. The bottom paper is to prevent contamination from the floor of the top evidence paper and can be discarded.

❏ Samples are collected to identify the patient and to differentiate the patient from the perpetrator, including:

- Hair samples, 15 to 30 pieces of hair including roots (head hair and/or pubic hair)

- Saliva, on a swab for DNA testing

- Blood, collected for DNA testing

- Many crime laboratories would like more than one type of sample for DNA identification (e.g., hair and blood). Pulling hair and drawing blood can be painful and traumatic for the young child. Collecting samples for patient DNA identification can be done at a later time if needed.

TABLE 45.2 Other Causes of Symptoms Resembling Child Sexual Abuse

Possible Cause	*Nursing Actions*
Straddle injury	Obtain a history and document from the child.
	Photograph the injury.
Streptococcal infection, *Haemophilus influenzae*	Culture the rash.
	Photograph and document description of rash.
Yeast infection, lichen sclerosus et atrophicus, diaper dermatitis, contact dermatitis, and phytodermatitis	Photograph and document description of rash.
Hydrometrocolpos	Observe excessive mucus from vagina.
	Culture discharge to rule out infection.
	Photograph and document description of discharge.
Hemangioma, perineural clefts and pits, urethral prolapse	Photograph and document description of lesion.
Foreign body in vagina or rectum	Obtain a history from the child (children often do not acknowledge they put an object into their rectum or vagina).
	Observe for foreign body by external exam.
	Document presence of discharge and any other findings. Photograph any findings.
	Refer the patient to surgery or pediatric gynecologist for an internal exam under anesthesia.

Ludwig, S. (2006). Psychological emergencies. In G. R. Fleisher, S. Ludwig, & F. M. Henretig (Eds.), *Textbook of pediatric emergency medicine* (5th ed., pp. 1780–1794). Philadelphia: Lippincott Williams & Wilkins.

❐ Swab collection
  ▪ Evidence samples are collected before culture samples.
  ▪ Two swabs are collected at the same time whenever possible. (One swab is for the prosecution, and one saved for the defense to evaluate.) The swabs are rotated to ensure uniform distribution of the sample. Swabs must be dry and packaged in cardboard or paper to prevent molding.
  ▪ A slide is made from the swabs when the possibility of sperm exists. Nonmotile sperm have been identified in specimens collected from the cervix over a week after sexual intercourse.[3]
❐ Collection of any debris that may be related to the incident (e.g., loose hair, glass, grass, dirt).
❐ Collection of any object that may contain evidence (e.g., diaper, sanitary pad, blanket).

Sexually Transmitted Disease Testing and Treatment

The identification of a sexually transmitted disease

(STD) is important for the case, as well as for the child's health. The Centers for Disease Control and Prevention (CDC) published recommendations for testing and treatment in child sexual abuse cases. CDC Sexually Transmitted Diseases Treatment Guidelines 2006[17] recommend that the decision to test for STDs be made on an individual basis. The following situations involve a high risk for STD, indicating a need to test:[17]

❐ The child has symptoms of an STD (e.g., vaginal discharge or pain, genital itching or odor, urinary symptoms, and genital ulcers or lesions).
❐ A suspected perpetrator has an STD or is at high risk for one (e.g., multiple sex partners, history of STD).
❐ Someone else in the household has an STD.
❐ Parent or patient requests testing.
❐ There is evidence of genital, oral, or anal penetration or ejaculation.
❐ Only tests with high specificity should be used in these cases because of the legal and psychosocial consequences of false positives.[17]
  ▪ Cultures have always been viewed as the gold

standard.

- Polymerase chain reaction (PCR) testing from the site, as well as urine testing, is highly reliable.

❑ Specimens are collected from any possible source including oral, rectal, vaginal, and cervical. Cervical swabs are not collected from the prepubescent child.

Any time STDs, such as gonorrhea or syphilis, are identified outside of the neonatal period, it can be concluded that the child has been sexually abused. Herpes simplex, Chlamydia trachomatis infection, and trichomoniasis usually occur through sexual contact, indicating the child has probably been sexually abused. Diseases such as condylomata, scabies, pediculosis, and *Gardnerella vaginalis* infection may be the result of sexual abuse, but could be from other causes. Children who present with these diseases are possibly being sexually abused.[10]

Blood tests to consider in the child who has possibly been sexually abused include:

❑ Pregnancy test

❑ Syphilis serology

❑ Hepatitis B and C

❑ HIV testing

❑ Blood and urine toxicology screen

❑ Alcohol level and other date rape drug testing

Urine testing includes:

❑ Toxicology screen

❑ Date rape drugs

❑ STD (gonorrhea and Chlamydia) PCR testing, and sperm

- Have the child urinate a small amount of urine into a cup at the beginning of void before cleaning or wiping. Bacteria are present at the urethral opening, so bacteria and/or sperm will be washed into the cup with a small amount of urine.

❑ Urinalysis and culture: The incidence of urinary tract infection is increased with sexual abuse.

Documentation

The medical record in the child sexual abuse case provides valuable information for a multidisciplinary team review, court proceedings, or as a reference should there be new allegations of abuse.[18] The nurse must do careful documentation of the questions asked or the events surrounding the child's statements in conjunction with the exact words of the child in direct quotations. It is the medical provider's role to state the facts objectively without any judgment as to the validity of the facts.[11]

The medical record needs to be complete, including all aspects of the examination. A checklist may be helpful to ensure that all information is properly documented. Table 45.3 lists elements of documentation to be completed after the sexual assault evaluation.

Medication and Follow-up

CDC recommends:[17]

❑ Prophylactic treatment is not indicated for prepubescent children because there is a very low incidence of STDs in children.

❑ Prophylactic treatment for the adolescent (and adult) includes single doses of the following:[17]

- Ceftriaxone 125 mg intramuscularly (gonorrhea)

- Metronidazole 2 g orally (trichomoniasis)

- Azithromycin 1 g orally (Chlamydia)

- Emergency contraception (e.g., Plan B) (pregnancy prevention)

- Hepatitis B vaccination intramuscularly (if not previously vaccinated)

  - Additional vaccinations are needed in 1 and 6 months.

  - No hepatitis B immunoglobulin (HBIG) is needed; one vaccine after exposure should adequately protect against hepatitis B virus infection.

❑ If the abuse was recent, a follow-up examination should be done at 2 weeks and again at 12 weeks after the most recent sexual exposure.

- Reevaluate for STDs.

- Reevaluate for the healing of injury as needed.

- Some testing (e.g., HIV, syphilis, and hepatitis B) requires additional testing at 6 months after last sexual contact.

❑ Referral to a child abuse specialist for evaluation and counseling should be done within 1 or 2 days after the ED visit.

Home Care and Prevention

Before discharge the nurse must ensure that:

❑ The child is medically and psychologically stable.

❑ The child will be protected from the alleged perpetrator.

❑ The child and family have received verbal and written instructions for follow-up care with:

- A health care practitioner with expertise in child sexual abuse.

TABLE 45.3 Documentation of the Sexual Assault Examination

Medical history	Document child's name and date of birth (age).
	Identify any underlying diseases, surgeries, known anatomic variances that may explain physical findings.
	Note current medications, allergies, and immunization status.
History of event	Include date, time, referral source, person(s) accompanying child to exam.
	Time of event, as well as time of disclosure. Explain event surrounding disclosure.
	Talk with the parent (adult accompanying child) separately; document this conversation.
	Talk with the child alone, asking general open-ended questions (document question asked and child's response). Document child's demeanor during this conversation.
Physical exam	Written description of all findings.
	Diagram drawings of all findings.
	Photographs of findings and genital pictures to document normal exam, as well as any abnormal findings.
Evidence collection	List and describe all evidence collected.
Medical intervention	Document all medical testing, results, and treatment.
Reporting and referrals	Document agencies, names, and any associated case numbers related to the incident.
Discharge instructions	Maintain a copy of the instructions for follow-up care, referrals, and medical instructions given to the family.

- Law enforcement and/or Department of Child and Family Services.
- A patient advocacy program.
- Parent support groups or agencies (e.g., Rape Recovery Center).

❑ Completed reports are submitted as mandated to state reporting agencies.

❑ Discharge instructions also need to include the following:
- Recommendations for follow-up care.
- Telephone numbers for follow-up calls and questions.
- Instructions for taking medications and follow-up testing.
- Community resources for:
  - Crime victim reparations
  - Medical care
  - Health Department for additional immunizations and STD concerns
  - Counseling

Prevention for child sexual abuse is focused on the potential patient, teaching children how to respond to sexual assault or abuse.[19] It is important to take advantage of teaching opportunities with all children in the emergency department. When examining genitalia as part of a medical examination for any medical concern, discuss with the child the appropriateness of the medical examination being done at this time. Explain to the child that they are in the hospital and the parent is there. Ask the parent for permission to do the genital examination in front of the child, acknowledging that it is important for mom or dad to say it is OK. Be careful asking for the child's permission; he or she may say "no." It is better to proceed with the examination as long as the child does not protest. Keep the child's genitalia as private as possible by keeping the area covered with a sheet, and lifting only far enough for the examination. It is also prudent to have another ED staff member as a chaperone during the genital examination.

Child sexual abuse is very underreported. Medical providers often see children multiple times before sexual abuse is identified. Keep child abuse in the differential diagnosis on all children seen in the emergency department.

Conclusion

Child sexual abuse is a common chief complaint in the emergency department. In addition, children who come to the emergency department for other reasons may be identified as being sexually abused during their ED visit. Children need help being protected from anyone who may be sexually abusing them. It is the role of the nurse to recognize and report possible sexual abuse cases.

Nurses play an important role in the process of the sexual abuse case. They are mandated by law to report concerns of sexual abuse to law enforcement or other government agencies such as Department of Child and Family Services. The nurse is also responsible for setting the tone of the evaluation as a healing process rather than another abusive event. Careful assessment, collection of evidence, and documentation are critical in providing information for the legal system to be able to identify the abuse and abuser. However, it is not uncommon for

the sexually abused child to have no physical findings or forensic evidence at the time of the examination.

As with any child presenting to the emergency department, children of suspected sexual abuse need a full head-to-toe assessment and care to ensure physical health. The psychological affects of being sexually abused cannot be forgotten. Reassure the child and the family that the child is (or will be) healthy and able to function normally. Offer information on community resources for both the child and the family. All children and their families deserve to be treated with respect and nonjudgmental care.

Children can heal and live normal healthy lives after a sexual abuse experience. Often the emergency department is the child's first interaction in that healing process.

References

1. Trickett, P. K. (2006). Defining child sexual abuse. In M. M. Feerick, J. F. Knutson, P. K. Trickett, & S. M. Flanzer (Eds.), *Child abuse and neglect: Definitions, classifications, & a framework for research* (pp. 129–145). Baltimore: Brookes.

2. Finkel, M. A., & DeJong, A. R. (2001). Medical findings in child sexual abuse. In R. M. Reece & S. Ludwig (Eds.), *Child abuse: Medical diagnosis and management* (2nd ed., pp. 207–286). Philadelphia: Lippincott Williams & Wilkins.

3. Christian, C.W., & Giardino, A. P. (2002). Forensic evidence collection. In M. A. Finkel & A. P. Giardino (Eds.), *Medical evaluation of child sexual abuse: A practical guide* (2nd ed., pp. 131–145). Thousand Oaks, CA: Sage.

4. Childers, K. (2005). Health problems of toddlers and preschoolers. In M. J. Hockenberry, D. Wilson, & M. L. Winkelstein (Eds.), *Wong's essentials of pediatric nursing* (7th ed., pp. 462–470). St. Louis, MO: Mosby.

5. U.S. Department of Health and Human Services, Administration for Children and Families. (2007). *Maltreatment types of victims, 2005. Child maltreatment 2005.* Retrieved April 17, 2009, from http://www. acf.hhs.gov/programs/cb/pubs/cm05/table3_6.htm

6. Dube, S. R., Anda, R. F., Whitfield, C. L., Brown, D. W., Felitti, V. J., Dong, M., et al. (2005). Long-term consequence of childhood sexual abuse by gender of patient. *American Journal of Preventive Medicine, 28*(5), 430–438.

7. Caffin, M., Letourneau, E., & Silovsky, J. F. (2002). Adults, adolescents and children who sexually abuse children. In J. E. B. Myers, L. Berliner, J. Briere, C. T. Hendrix, C. Jenny, & T. A. Reid, *The APSAC handbook on child maltreatment* (2nd ed., pp. 205–232). Thousand Oaks, CA: Sage.

8. Myers, J. E. B. (2002). Risk management for professionals working with maltreated children and adult survivors. In J. E. B. Myers, L. Berliner, J. Briere, C. T. Hendrix, C. Jenny, & T. A. Reid, *The APSAC handbook on child maltreatment* (2nd ed., pp. 403–427). Thousand Oaks, CA: Sage.

9. Finkel, M. A. (2002). The evaluation. In M. A. Finkel & A. P. Giardino (Eds.), *Medical evaluation of child sexual abuse: A practical guide* (2nd ed., pp. 23–37). Thousand Oaks, CA: Sage.

10. Ludwig, S. (2006). Psychological emergencies. In G. R. Fleisher, S. Ludwig, & F. M. Henretig (Eds.), *Textbook of pediatric emergency medicine* (5th ed., pp. 1780–1794). Philadelphia: Lippincott Williams & Wilkins.

11. Frasier, L. D. (2008). Sexual abuse in children and adolescents. In R. M. Perkin, J. D. Swift, D. A. Newton, & S. G. Anas (Eds.), *Pediatric hospital medicine textbook of inpatient management* (2nd ed., pp. 776–781). Philadelphia: Lippincott Williams & Wilkins.

12. Finkel, M. A. (2002). Physical examination. In M. A. Finkel & A. P. Giardino (Eds.), *Medical evaluation of child sexual abuse: A practical guide* (2nd ed., pp. 39–98). Thousand Oaks, CA: Sage.

References (continued)

13. Palusci, V. J., Cox, E. O., Shatz, E. M., & Schultze, J. M. (2006). Urgent medical assessment after child sexual abuse. *Child Abuse and Neglect, 30,* 367–380.

14. Rosas, A. J. (2005). Medical diagnosis of child abuse and neglect. In P. F. Talley (Ed.), *Handbook for the treatment of abused and neglected children* (pp. 39–62). New York: Haworth Press.

15. Lippman, J. (2002). Psychological issues. In M. A. Finkel & A. P. Giardino (Eds.), *Medical evaluation of child sexual abuse: A practical guide* (2nd ed., pp. 193–213). Thousand Oaks, CA: Sage.

16. U.S. Department of Justice. (2007). *Sexual assault nurse examiner (SANE) programs: Improving the community response to sexual assault victims.* Retrieved April 17, 2009, from http://www.ojp.usdoj.gov/ovc/publications/bulletins/sane_4_2001/welcome.html

17. Centers for Disease Control and Prevention. (2006). *Sexually transmitted diseases treatment guidelines 2006.* Retrieved April 17, 2009, from http://www.cdc.gov/std/treatment/2006/sexual-assault.htm#children

18. Finkel, M. A. (2002). Documentation, report formulation, and conclusions. In M. A. Finkel & A. P. Giardino (Eds.), *Medical evaluation of child sexual abuse: A practical guide* (2nd ed., pp. 251–264). Thousand Oaks, CA: Sage.

19. Daro, D., & Donnelly, A. C. (2002). Child abuse prevention. In J. E. B. Myers, L. Berliner, J. Briere, C. T. Hendrix, C. Jenny, & T. A. Reid, *The APSAC handbook on child maltreatment* (2nd ed., pp. 431–444). Thousand Oaks, CA: Sage.

INDEX

C

D

H

I

W

Y

Z